Popular Music
and the
Underground
Foundations of Jazz, Blues, Country, and Rock, 1900–1950

Chuck Mancuso

Co-Editors: Dave Lampe and Reg Gilbert
Design and Layout: Chuck Mancuso and Christine Szeluga
Cover Design: Dave Meinzer

KENDALL/HUNT PUBLISHING COMPANY
4050 Westmark Drive   Dubuque, Iowa 52002

Cover design and layout by Dave Meinzer. All
of the pictures on the cover, courtesy of the
Frank Driggs Collection—artists on the front
cover, clockwise from top right corner are:
Amos Milburn, Tommy Dorsey, Louise Massey
the Westerners, Charlie Parker and Dizzy
Gillespie, Lil Green, Bing Crosby and guitarist
Eddie Lang.

Library of Congress Catalog Card Number: 93-80479

ISBN 0-8403-9088-2

Printed in the United States of America.
10   9   8   7   6   5   4   3   2   1

DEDICATION

This book is respectfully dedicated to:

William H. Tallmadge
My mentor and friend who opened my eyes and ears to the world of music scholarship;

Mary A. Mancuso and Chuck Mancuso, Sr.
My mother and late father, who provided me with a loving and supportive home environment;

Dr. Edward O. Smith
The professor who believed in me before I believed in myself.

Peter D. Durham
Whose vision and generosity made this dream become a reality.

Contents

Foreword

By: Charles Keil

You are about to read the results of a long and very special tradition of scholarship and teaching that was acquired and is now practiced by Professor Chuck Mancuso. His mentor, William Tallmadge, during a very fruitful career as a teacher, developed a classifying or taxonomic approach to America's music, mapping and naming very carefully and descriptively who was where and when, and doing what. This descriptive and taxonomic system worked very well in survey courses year after year, and has oriented thousands of students to the basic information about our musical creativity as Americans.

Fortunately, William Tallmadge found exactly the right disciple in Chuck Mancuso, who picked up his courses and further refined this descriptive approach by adding more and more images to his slide collection (now numbering over 35,000), more and more taped examples (both audio and video) of every kind of American music, and more and more carefully refined definitions of musical styles that have emerged in America over the years. Now, when students enter a Mancuso classroom, they are treated to three slide projectors popping images on the screens, the best examples from every style and idiom on tape, edited video samples, and very well organized lectures that delineate, in detail, who was where, and when, doing what in American music.

This teaching method has also produced scholarship at its very best. The Mancuso taxonomic system is comprehensive, encyclopedic—I'm tempted to coin the word "omnivalent" because he finds a way to value everything. He has been constantly alert to leave nothing of any significance out of the picture. The system is cumulative. Every year, the description of past periods and phases, the nomenclature, the examples, the charts, are improved and clarified. The system strives for objectivity by attending carefully to both quantitative and qualitative criteria for evaluating the importance of any piece or style of music. Duke Ellington may have been the greater musician, a genius, but Paul Whiteman sold a vastly greater number of records in the decades when their production overlapped. The Mancuso system strives to pay attention to both facts of our musical life, in every time and place. The system, because it is fundamentally descriptive, lets you, the reader, look for the deeper explanations, the possible forces of causality. Is it simply racism that keeps so much of black music underground for so long? Is it class snobbery that slows the development of underground hillbilly music into mainstream country and western? Are the wellsprings of underground music bubbling up and unstoppable; the music of the poor and oppressed having a greater vitality and forcing itself on the mainstream, eventually; or did the small and big record companies combine to exploit the underground by drilling deeper and deeper, packaging, ever more efficiently, the sounds of "rebellion" that young audiences were looking for? You get to be the judge.

Like Charles Hamm's deeply documented text, *Yesterdays*, this book takes "what sold most" in sheet music and records as its center of focal point—popular music. From this point of view, some stars and styles "gain entree" to the center of great sales, consistently; others reach the center, once or twice, but never become steadily central from a sales or quantitative point of view; still other performers or artists whom we now recognize as great, were always marginal or peripheral to the quantitative center in their lifetimes. So, in all of these chapters, there is a judicious balancing going on, an insistence that you get to know who was most popular in each era, even though some of these people are completely forgotten today, and an insistence that you see and hear just how musics from the underground, the wellsprings, managed to surface and be heard and work their way into the mainstream.

Actually, the hearing is also left up to you. Music is music. If words could describe musical feelings and meanings, we wouldn't need music at all. Those of us who have been studying music a long time have come to realize that each bit of it will mean something different or be felt slightly or very differently by each and every person in a specific context. Individual and social tastes in music are constantly shifting with time and place. Any common denominators of meaning or feeling are fleeting and completely defined by context. So listen for yourself. Make your own interpretation. Don't be surprised if your interpretation does or does not match anyone else's. No book can put you inside the music, but this book does a lot of what only a book can do. It gives you facts and many of them. It gives you charts and lists from "Ziegfield Follies highlights" all the way to "honkers" and "doo-woppers," each of which summarizes a range of facts and events very efficiently and provides an overview. This text gives you a rich abundance of images never assembled in one place before, and each image has both obvious and sometimes hidden information. Pay careful attention to those images designed to sell the music, the record covers, the advertisements, the posters, and ask yourself, "who is the audience?" and, "would I have bought in to this image and sound?"

I know that the audience for this particular book is going to be a big one, because such a solid continuity of scholarship and teaching has gone into it. The wisdom and clarity derived from many classes taught is summarized here, and can now be spread far and wide. With this book, carefully digested, you will be ready to spot and name the next new style, the revival of something tried and true, the twisting of something old into something bizarre. It is my hope that some readers will want to join the Tallmadge-Mancuso scholarly tradition, in earnest, by teaching this book and adding to it in time. All it takes is deep love of the music, all of it, and a passion to figure out where each artist and sound fits in that shifting kaleidoscope, "the overall scheme of things."

Introduction and Preface

This book is intended to be a thorough interpretive history of America's pre-rock, popular commercial music spanning 1900-1950, referred to throughout this text as "mainstream" or "popular" music. To tell that story with any completeness, one must also investigate the less popular musical forms that influenced it, called in this book "underground" music. Chapter 1 details the many factors that go into making any given song, or artist, a creature of the mainstream or underground worlds.

The first half of twentieth-century American commercial music can be divided into three parts: (1) pre-WWI preparatory forms (Chapter 2); (2) post-WWI jazz, blues, and country music in their original forms, ending about the middle of the Great Depression (Chapters 3-7); and (3) post-1934 mature versions of those musical styles (Chapters 8-14). The book deals mainly with the two later periods and the styles that were born in them. The second period, 1917-1934, is commonly called the Jazz Age, although it might be better called the Age of Emergent Musical Forms—jazz, blues and country music all have their commercial origin in this time period. The third period, 1935-1950, is commonly called the Swing Era, although it could be more appropriately characterized as the Era of Emergent Musical Modernism; the jazz, blues, and country music of the previous period turned into a panoply of mature musical descendants—bebop and cool jazz, the many varieties of rhythm and blues (including electric blues), bluegrass, western swing, honky tonk, and urban folk music—that are in many cases still widely performed today almost exactly as they were then.

The attribution of specific beginning and ending dates, to inherently amorphous historical movements, is usually both distorting and clarifying. There was a lot more music, great music, being created in both periods than just jazz (in fact, a very specific form of commercially diluted jazz), that gives the Jazz Age and the Swing Era their historically accepted names. However, there is also a historical truth to the rough division of years that is traditionally associated with those periods.

The year 1917 marked the U.S. entrance into World War I, sparking a frenzy of pro-war songwriting by New York City's professional tunesmiths. It would be the last hurrah of the dominant popular music of the time— piano/vocal compositions distributed primarily on sheet music. The year also saw the release of the first jazz record, which was followed, in 1920, by the first blues record, and, in 1923, by the first country music record. 1935 saw the ascendance to dominant popularity of an orchestral variety of dance-oriented music, often but not always jazz-based, that inaugurated the so-called "Swing Era." The rise of jazz in the "Jazz Age" was accompanied by the growth of other musical styles. The "Swing Era" was no different. The rise of big band jazz was accompanied by the emergence of dozens of other styles—swing combos and bebop, to name just two, out of jazz itself; rhythm and blues out of the jazz and blues; the electric guitar combos out of blues, and the singing cowboy, bluegrass, and many other styles out of country.

This book divides history into specific time periods, because doing so makes it easier for both historian and reader to understand broad trends, and to organize what might otherwise be only a mass of indistinguishable facts. By the same logic, the book divides each historical period by style. This approach solves one problem—the impenetrability and distortions of the simple chronological account. However, another problem is then faced—the difficulty of placing those elements (artists or styles) that are transitional, eclectic, or otherwise hard to categorize. History doesn't always comfortably niche into defined time slots or categories. Musical artists do not start and stop making music on given dates, and musical styles are not born (and do not die), they evolve. For instance, blues singer Robert Johnson recorded in 1936 and 1937. But his musical education began much earlier, in the late 1920s, and any good account of his music must place him with his stylistic siblings, the rural blues artists, who have their origins in the 1920s. Accordingly, in this book, Johnson is discussed in Chapter 4, which covers the rise of country blues in the 1917-1934 period.

Placing entire musical styles can face similar problems. The stylistically similar Cajun and zydeco music use some instruments more commonly found in country music, and Cajun music was often played in a barn-dance-like setting, typical of country music performance. However in this book, Cajun and zydeco are categorized with the blues, because they usually used both melodic and lyric structures typical of blues. Sometimes chronological and stylistic problems appear in a single figure. The great Belgian Gypsy guitarist Django Reinhardt had a hugely influential acoustic guitar style that was inspired by the traditional jazz chamber duo of Eddie Lang and Joe Venuti. Reinhardt played into the 1950s, and his material beginning in the 1930s became increasingly swing oriented. However, in this book he has been placed in the chapter on traditional jazz, because in that music lies the origin of his playing style, which was the source of his greatest impact on American popular music. In general, the discussion of an artist is, for the most part, placed according to the time of that artist's greatest impact. Musical styles are placed chronologically according to the time of their emergence as a musical form, and stylistically according to the specifics of their stylistic character. Judgment calls all, but hopefully good ones.

Readers might notice that the chapters dealing with the period 1935-1950 are, in sum, far lengthier than those dealing with the period 1900-1934. In short, there was a synergy in the simultaneous maturation of styles (jazz, blues and country music) and of media technologies (talking movies, radio, and especially the record) that drove both artistic innovation and market penetration. The result was an exponential growth in the number of musical styles and performers that emerged, despite the restraining influence of the Great Depression.

Special Features

This book has a number of special features. Most apparent should be the panoply of pictures. Of course, pictures make a book more enjoyable to read, but they can also be as historically enlightening as any text. Also included are a particularly large number of publicity shots, concert posters, and record advertisements, which reveal the myriad ways that the artists under discussion were marketed. This image-making was often crucial to both the artists' contemporary success and, surprisingly, to their later critical appraisal. Most of the pictures have extensive (sometimes very extensive) captions. These should be treated much as footnotes found at the bottom of pages in other books—interesting information that further illuminates points made in the main text, but are not essential to the book's narrative.

This text also has a very large number of charts that summarize often difficult-to-find information on artists and styles. These charts run the gamut from the historically central (for example, "Early New Orleans Rhythm and Blues Artists"), to the significant but obscure ("Other Southeast Mountaineer Brother Groups"), to the merely amusing (no other book can match the recitation of cowboy film horse names found in the "Singing Cowboys" chart). The reader is invited to view these charts as works in progress. Any corrections, additions, or suggestions for new chart topics are encouraged.

A final aspect of the book, and a particularly significant one when dealing with a historical study of culture, is that of contemporary connections. Music of the past often remains alive in the form of its own existence, in the fact of its parenting various contemporary musical descendants, and sometimes in the efforts of those artists who attempt to recreate it. For every kind of reader, whether the musical history student, the avid fan, or the casual listener, the music of the past can have power in the present. In its most basic form, this power is manifest in simply listening to the historical document. Most of the music discussed in this book is available on compact disc, sometimes sounding better than it did when it was originally released (more and more old-time performances are also coming out on videotape). But the power of past music is also evident in the understanding of how it has shaped the music of the present. Just ask the Rolling Stones or Linda Ronstadt. And, of course, past music projects present power whenever it is performed live.

This publication attempts to utilize all three of these avenues (pictures, charts, and contemporary connections) for "enlivening" past music. The text regularly discusses subsequent impact of artists and styles, and frequently points out contemporary performers of past music. (Chapter 10 is entirely devoted to this effort.) Further provided is a detailed discography and videography, drawn directly from catalogs of currently available material, making it easy for the reader to obtain the music itself.

The scope of this book does not allow the fullest exploration of a number of issues that have had critical roles in shaping American popular music. Three issues in particular deserve books of their own. The first of these is the history of the mainstream popular artists of the first quarter of the century. As noted in a few places in this book, some artists during this period attained a popularity that could only be compared to that of the Beatles in modern times. A number of them released more material than anyone in modern times. Yet most of these artists have virtually nothing written about them. The result is a painfully cursory understanding of the musical milieu from which jazz, country, and blues were born.

A second issue that bears further study is the financial underpinning of the activity detailed here. Many of the choices that musicians make are dictated by the pay they will receive; it was no less true in the 1920s, '30s, '40s, and '50s than it is today. Copyright and royalty arrangements, touring expenses and salaries, record distribution structures, union work rules, club, radio, theater, and film finances—the list of monetary considerations that could influence a musician's artistic decisions is endless, and so far it is not very well understood.

The third, and perhaps most important area of further study, could be called that of the "gatekeepers." These are people who, by virtue of their position in the music industry, have a role in deciding who will make a recording, broadcast over a given radio network, or perform in a specific film. In general gatekeepers decide how musicians will work. Two major categories of gatekeeper; producers and managers, deserve special attention. Producers have the greatest direct artistic impact; they decide what songs get recorded, broadcast, or performed on film. Managers have a more indirect, but just as important, artistic impact—they get musicians to the point of being produced. Producers denied Robert Johnson the opportunity to record Bing Crosby and country and western material; managers gave Louis Armstrong entree to the big time of major record labels and Hollywood. Both groups have long been nearly invisible hands in the making of American music.

Background

Popular music was ever present in my childhood home. By age eight, I liked music enough to independently poke through my father's record collection, and one day, put Pete Johnson on the phonograph. I was thunderstruck by boogie woogie! Thereafter, every Saturday morning became a ritual of investigating my father's albums (in the days when an album meant a series of heavy 78 records enclosed in paper sleeves and bound by a hard cover). My father, Charles, Sr., was a lover of piano jazz, so I became familiar with the recordings of pianists such as Pete Johnson ("Roll "Em Pete"), Freddie Slack ("Cow, Cow Boogie"), Meade Lux Lewis ("Honky Tonk Train"), and my father's absolute favorite, Frankie Carle ("Sunrise Serenade"). By the time I was twelve, I was neatly lettering music lists of my favorite recordings in a notebook entitled "Chuck's Top Ten." Then I would go to Miller's Drugstore on Grant Street in Buffalo, New York, and spend some of my allowance on records (three for a dollar). My favorites were vocal groups with great-sounding names like the Ravens, the Orioles, the Hilltoppers, the Gaylords, the Four Aces, and the Four Lads.   The rest of my allowance was spent at the Saturday movie matinee at the Rialto Theatre . I preferred the Rialto because it cost nine cents versus the fourteen cents required at the Victoria Theatre. At the Rialto I could see Roy Rogers, "King of the Cowboys." As a card-carrying member of his "Saddle Pal Club," could I ask for anything more? On Wednesdays, I looked through the afternoon newspaper, cutting out the ads for movies opening at the major downtown movie houses and pasting them into my movie scrapbook.

All this interest in music and film led my parents to send my younger brother, Rick, and me to tap-dancing school. Twice a week we clicked and clacked, with heel-toe precision to the strains of songs like "Ragtime Cowboy Joe." My brother and I never became star students of the Betty Rogers School of Dance, but Michael DiFiglia, did. Later he would change his name and gain Broadway fame as Michael Bennett. When I reached my teens, my brother and I became members of the Butler Mitchell Boys Club. There, sports took over our lives until a couple of counselors in the game room began playing a radio station that featured jazz. The sounds of Erroll Garner, Stan Kenton, Count Basie, Oscar Peterson, among others, captivated me. Soon I wanted to learn everything I could about jazz music, (for some reason this never grabbed a hold of my brother or any of my buddies). Consumed with jazz, I read nearly every jazz book written, collected *Down Beat*, *Metronome*, and *Jazz Journal* magazines, and began buying jazz record albums (by this time the 78 record had been replaced by the 33 1/3 long-play record). My mother and father were understanding about my record collecting and let me have an extra room, aptly labelled the "Music Room," for all my records, magazines, and books. By the end of high school, I had amassed a couple thousand recordings—mostly jazz and Hollywood musicals. I may not have been much of a dancer, but I loved musicals. Favorites included Gene Kelly, and his athletic leaps to music, and the brilliantly dazzling technicolor films of tall and lanky Dan Dailey, dancing with the cute and curvaceous Betty Grable. Around this time I met someone who shared my enthusiasm for jazz—Paul Gresham. I met Paul at a downtown record store and we started talking about jazz. Soon Paul was visiting my house on the Italian West Side of Buffalo a couple of days a week, and I was visiting his house on the African-American East Side, several times a week. We shared articles and books and traded records. Paul was studying saxophone and as he was a decent piano player, I started taking piano lessons from him. In time I was off to college, and Paul became a professional musician, eventually leading his own, cutting-edge unit called Birthright.

Mentor

Fortunately, I attended Buffalo State College, and it was there that I met Professor William H. Tallmadge. A classical music professor, Tallmadge had an unusual inspiration in the mid-1950s. He introduced a college survey course entitled "Afro-American Music", in 1956. There were no more than a half-dozen such offerings in the United States at the time. The feeling of the contemporary music establishment was that popular music was not worthy of academic stature. I took Tallmadge's course in 1963 and he suggested, on the basis of a weekly column I wrote for the school newspaper ("Chaz With Jazz"), that I teach one week on the subject of jazz of the 1950s and 1960s. It was Pete Johnson all over again. That week crystalized my calling for me. I loved music; I liked learning about music; I liked teaching music. I took all the courses that Professor Tallmadge taught: "Country Music," "Folk Music," and "Urban Blues and Rock." I increased the effort I put into my weekly articles and reviews of jazz and blues artists who came into Buffalo to perform at the Royal Arms, the Bon Ton, the Pine Grill, the Renaissance, and the Revelot. Eventually, my column was retitled "Both Sides Now" (after the Joni Mitchell song) because I began investigating the rock scene.

After graduation, I worked as a teacher of special education at Baker Hall, a home for emotionally disturbed boys in Lackawanna, New York, just south of Buffalo. There I introduced courses on jazz and rock. By 1969 I was completing a masters degree in exceptional education and also working as a teaching assistant with Professor Tallmadge. Between 1970 and 1975, I co-taught the old "Afro-American Music" course, retitled "Jazz Rock Foundations" with Tallmadge. I was honored to take over Professor Tallmadge's courses in 1976. Tallmadge retired to Berea, Kentucky, where he holds a chair at Berea College. He also holds masters world records in the over-seventy race walking competitions, and is an active participant in "Body Recall," a program of health and fitness for elders. In 1994, Tallmadge became a licensed associate thanatologist, specializing in anxiety of the terminally ill.

Academe

The Academe embraced jazz music in the 1950s and 1960s. The origins of this change lie in two developments of the 1930s and 1940s. First, books on the history of jazz began to be written, though rarely were the books written by people of academe. Second, music education schools began building marching bands for their athletic programs. The band leaders they hired, many of them jazz players, in time began to suggest that the schools offer courses in the history of jazz. With this foundation, a number of trailblazers—at first, only rarely members of the academic music establishment—sought legitimacy for jazz music in university curricula. Alan Merriam wrote in *Record Changer* magazine in 1949, "The average legitimate music school has little, if any, interest in jazz, and often is violently opposed to it in any forms, although these barriers are slowly being lifted." Merriam, co-founder of the Society for Ethnomusicology and editor of its music journal, taught in the anthropology and African studies programs of Indiana University in the 1960s and 1970s. Merriam's long-term aim was to convince anthropologists of the importance of the arts in anthropological study. Two of Merriam's disciples, Charles Keil and Steven Feld, were inspired by Merriam to investigate the origins of American popular music. In their co-authored book, *Music Grooves*, Keil and Feld engage in a series of scholarly and personal dialogues asserting, among other things, the obsolescence of "high art" music culture because of its irrelevance to mass participation in music.

The fact that jazz music became the first of the popular music forms to gain academic legitimacy has caused a schism between jazz and other pop forms such as blues, country, and pre-rock top forty. Academe's elevation of jazz may have something to do with the fact that, like classical music, jazz can be seen as primarily an instrumental performance form, rather than a vocal form. It may not be an accident that the beginnings of jazz's academic legitimacy coincides with the rise of the more artistic forms of jazz—bebop, cool, and its descendants.

Jazz as presented in academe is somewhat removed from its social context. Academic jazz histories frequently de-emphasize the fact that jazz was originally an entertainment music performed for dancers. The understanding of jazz as popular music began to disappear. Jazz became high art. Furthermore, academe in the 1950s, and to the present day, tends to present the history of jazz as the history of popular music in America. A majority of university courses, currently taught as introductions to popular music, are in fact, jazz history courses. Jazz may be the most interesting form of American popular music from a technical point of view, but it is far from the only significant form of American popular music and not even the only form to display substantial technical innovations. Jazz is merely a part of the larger American musical picture. Some jazz proselytizers call the music "America's only original contribution to the arts," and assert, to take one of the most common and egregious examples, that the songs of Tin Pan Alley are artless, populist drivel that only became worthwhile when covered and "improved" by the geniuses of jazz. Tin Pan Alley songs would take the same hit during the 1960s and 1970s, when the first serious histories of rock were written. The premise of many of these histories is that pre-rock pop music was moon-june slop played by post-swing has-beens, and that it took the youth-oriented energy of rock'n'roll to finally create a legitimately exciting pop landscape. Such arguments are simplistic and undeniably elitist. They assert, in effect, that jazz and rock, respectively, are "better" than what their champions see as "silly Hollywood musicals," "redneck hillbilly drivel," "pretentious cabaret singing," "repetitious rhythm and blues blaring," and on and on. But the fact is, the musical forms so slighted are merely the victims of personal taste—that of many (though not all) of the intellectuals who teach and write about popular music. Jazz was for a long time, and rock still is, subject to similar derogation. When not abhorred for ideological reasons, popular music of all kinds was long seen as modern folk music, that is, simple music for the simple, common people. For jazz, that all changed in the 1940s. Small-band variants on swing began to be played in New York City after-hours clubs, and these new kinds of jazz eventually became what is now known as the bebop and cool movements. These jazz variants contained stylistic and ideological similarities to the high art model of the serious music establishment—a primarily instrumental form and an emphasis on virtuosity, to name just two. As a result, the new jazz was embraced by a number of young jazz critics of the time on just those terms. In *Serious Music and All That Jazz*, Henry Pleasants summarizes the scene nicely:

"Ironically, and perhaps inevitably, the attitudes of the bop musician with respect to the artist's place in society have been precisely those of the Serious-music elite that refused to let him in. All the familiar and fashionable cultural superstitions were embraced, the relevant taboos observed. The Artist stands above, and must be independent of, the public. Only Artists are qualified to pass judgement on fellow Artists. The public has a solemn obligation to listen, to render homage and to pay. It is not the Artist's business to please the public; and any Artist who tries to do so is Compromising His Integrity, Prostituting His Art, Selling Out and Going Commercial. Entertainment is beneath the true Artist's calling. And so on . . . These young critics were, to be sure, merely aping the attitudes of their colleagues on the Serious side who had been many years ahead of them in subscribing to the Cult of the Artist and in defaulting their proper role as spokesmen for the lay public. To anyone experienced in Serious-music criticism, most jazz criticism was—and still is—a parody of remembered nonsense. All the dreary rituals of Serious-music criticism have been assiduously rehearsed, including the quest for originality, the detection of imitation, the analysis of style and attribution of influences, the romance of the Artist Who Bucks the Tide, and so on, with the critic eager to be identified with the discovery of new genius, and with the musician searching for the new departure that would attract the critic's attention."

The fundamentals were in place; all that was needed was a means to bridge the divide between the modern jazz and classical music cultures. The streetwise, largely black modern jazz progenitors and the largely white, cloistered professors of academe needed to begin to communicate. This was achieved through the medium of the jazz critic, and, perhaps, the rise of the civil rights movement and the beginning of northern white interest—especially pronounced on university campuses—in assisting it. These statements are by no means intended to dismiss the creative efforts of the jazz modernists such as Charlie Parker, Dizzy Gillespie, and Thelonious Monk, the architects of the bebop movement, whose work will undoubtedly be listened to for centuries on its own terms. The point here is the change of attitude engendered by the jazz modernists and the impact this had on popular music history. Jazz and rock music have both had an enormous pull as an alternative to other music forms, and the passionate followers of the forms have created many wonderful histories. There are more history, analysis, and biographies written about jazz and rock than all of the other American forms combined. Serious history and analysis of country music did not begin until Bill C. Malone's groundbreaking *Country Music U.S.A.* was published in 1968. As of 1995, there still were no overviews of two major country genres, western swing and honky tonk. It wasn't until 1966 that a serious look was given to the urbanized form of the blues in Charles Keil's *Urban Blues*, and an overview history of that form wasn't rendered until Arnold Shaw's 1976 *Honkers and Shouters*. The first analysis of the compositions of key Tin Pan Alley composers that placed them as equals with Bach, Beethoven and the rest did not come until Alec Wilder's 1974 *The American Popular Song—The Great Innovators, 1900-1950*. But, I digress.

The distorted picture of American popular music promulgated in the 1950s was the picture I came of age gazing at. My main love was jazz, and I subscribed to a number of fashionable elitist beliefs about it. They are easy to sum up. Like many others, I believed that there was jazz (the great specialized music from the heavens) and all the other dreck. But jazz was not, as so many histories had led me to believe, the center of American popular music. Teaching popular music courses at Buffalo Sate College in the 1970s showed me my error. At Buffalo State, as at most colleges then (and some still), popular music history focused on jazz and rock. My basic course, "Jazz Rock Foundations," oddly did not really look very deeply into foundations. For jazz, I did not discuss the popular (and in some cases stylistically seminal) jazz-inspired dance bands of the 1920s. For rock, I virtually ignored the immense contribution of country music, particularly honky tonk.

The American music scene is very much like America. We are a country of many ethnic groups. The cliche of the American melting pot was never more true than in the world of American music, which is a magnificent smorgasbord of aural delights. No American musical form is "owned" by any race, as many writers have suggested for both jazz and rock'n'roll (for example, the surprisingly common characterization of jazz as "African-American classical music"). As historian/musician Dr. Billy Taylor so prudently observes, "Jazz is American music. It says something about who we are. It is not just black classical music, but American classical music." (This author's intent is not to undervalue the vast contributions of African-Americans in the development of jazz musical forms.) Every one of the score of major American musical forms is the product of a number of American subcultures.

By the early 1980s, as I taught my survey courses and re-read many of the key histories of jazz I came to the realization that simply focusing on jazz and blues and arriving at the end product of rock'n'roll was too narrow. I asked myself, "Where does popular music fit into this mix?" And I wondered about the place of country music, a form as long-lived as jazz and still very popular. After all, jazz music by every accounting made up less than 10 percent of the records sold in the 1970s and 1980s, and a smaller percentage of radio and film time.

I decided to find the answers to these and many other questions about the big picture of American popular music. I read more obscure sources and earned masters degrees in film and popular culture. By 1986, I felt that I had a sense of the larger picture, and resolved to tell the story as I know it in this book. I have developed a credo: No single form of music is superior to any other. The many parts of the big American music picture are very much interconnected.

A few popular music historians share this general perspective. Three in particular have had a significant influence on my thinking: Frank Driggs, Nick Tosches, and Peter Guralnick. Driggs is the only major jazz thinker to give a full measure of respect to country music, and to many of the mainstream popular artists like Paul Whiteman and Ruth Etting. Tosches was one of the first writers to show strong evidence of the impact of country music on rock. Guralnick has interviewed hundreds of musicians in the last twenty years, and he specializes in revealing the often astonishing breadth of cross-influences that lie behind most American music. In order to make their great contributions to American musical history, all three had to transcend the legacy of musical elitism that characterizes much of the American music intelligentsia. In his 1978 book, *Lost Highway: Journeys and Arrivals of American Music*, Guralnick addressed this terrible burden directly:

"Another thing I learned is to distrust critical canons, to suspect the sweeping critical pronouncement. For one thing there is no telling, of course, what the future may bring, and all the endless prognostications and analyses only spoil the fun of surprise anyway. Over twelve or thirteen years I have been writing about music, I have heard one Singing Sensation after another touted as the next something, and no doubt have added to the list myself. None of this is relevant, though, except to racehorse handicappers. All the figures in this book have contributed work of solid worth. So have scores of others, from Van Morrison to Gene Austin, from Bing Crosby to Big Mama Thornton or Elvis Costello. The point that must never be lost sight of is that it's all music, again perhaps a truism, but one that bears repeating amid the absolute dictums that thunder down from Olympus. When I spoke to Son Seals, he expressed an admiration for Kate Smith; Jerry Lee Lewis cited Al Jolson; and Elvis Presley aspired to be the next Dean Martin. Again and again I've had my own preconceptions challenged (both musically and within a broader social framework), over and over I've had my own frame of reference expanded to the point where critical purism now seems an altogether stiff and inappropriate response. Criticism, it seems to me, should expand, not narrow horizons, but it cannot do that if one artist is continually being played off against another, if achievement is measured not on its own terms but against some arbitrary, unreal standard, if the critic does not listen with his or her ears (and emotions) rather than from some abstract ideological commitment. Like E. M. Forster, I like to imagine the various artists that I admire 'seated together in a room,' or in this case perhaps playing, quietly, together in a room, forming a kind of creative continuum in which time and classification become irrelevant in the face of what they so clearly share, the common process of creation."

Acknowledgements

This project began in late 1990, when I began receiving inquiries from a number of book companies about writing a history of popular music. Mark Gridley, author of *Jazz Styles*, the best selling jazz textbook in America, had suggested to each of those companies that on the basis of my courses at Buffalo State, I had a potential book. I had been content to refine my teaching skills, which took most of my time—three screen visuals (of about 250 slides per lecture) with tightly edited audio and video music samples. However, with convincing arguments from Gridley, Charlie Keil, and William Tallmadge, I decided to embark on what I feared would be a long journey.

The Performing Arts Department Chairman at that time, Myron Nadel, and the Dean of Arts and Humanities, Dr. Patricia Cummins, were extremely supportive, and I took a one-semester sabbatical in the Spring of 1991 to begin this work. The book had to be visual, so inquiries were sent and phone calls made to numerous record companies and national picture collections, seeking publicity photos, advertisements, graphics, and so forth. One of my most talented ex-students, John Bobey, helped me during this early period.

After writing part of the book and laying out what I wanted each page to look like, I realized it would be impossible to achieve the end product I desired. If the book couldn't have the "look" I envisioned, there wasn't even remote interest on my part to complete it—so I packed it up and it remained untouched for about a year. People inquired about the project and I replied that it was simply too big to tackle. Then two writer friends of mine came visiting from Boulder, Colorado—Ron and Cheryl Hoover. I showed them my "mock-ups" of the book, and their enthusiasm was heartening and professionally encouraging.

However, it wasn't until a couple of months later when Peter Durham, C.E.O. of the Durham Companies, insisted on seeing the project, that the wheels began to turn. Durham, a very good friend, said he would provide logistical support in the critically-important areas of legal, secretarial and layout.

Nearly three years later the project was completed, camera ready for the publisher. Without Peter Durham this book would still exist as pages of research, bound in manila envelopes—just a dream in "mock ups." Durham Executive Vice-President Christine Szeluga oversaw the entire project, from beginning to end. In addition, she was a creative light in the layout of the book. Joe Hausbeck, the firm's lawyer, worked with the people at Kendall-Hunt Publishers, especially my editor, Bill Kay, on legal issues and permissions. Julie Krueger did the major secretarial work, which included tons of rewrites and copy re-edits. I can't possibly thank the Durham Companies enough!

My writing skills, which had gotten quite rusty over the years, were greatly improved by the editing skills of Professor Dave Lampe (English Department of Buffalo State) and Reg Gilbert (Great Lakes Laboratories). They each, literally, walked me through this project and made many important suggestions and changes that are much appreciated. Gilbert, along with Cathy Carfagna, did the copy editing which was a massive undertaking—especially the constant changes and updating of the charts. After everyone else had their editorial look, Mary Ann Lauricella (Lauricella Public Relations, Inc.) applied her expertise in a final editing proof. Dave Meinzer, an ex-student of William Tallmadge's, designed the cover and completed two charts. I had no other designer in mind, as this completed an organic circle, professionally, for me.

There were so many people who helped along the way—they will be noted in the Further Acknowledgements section. It is to Barbara Goldman Barone I must give special thanks. She assisted as a master of all trades, acting as a critical reader and serving as an Information Consultant/Librarian Resources Specialist. Throughout the entire project she provided encouragement, love, and an unerring sense of support.

Further Acknowledgements

Back in 1991, when I sat down with John Bobey, my ex-student who was graduating at the time, I laid out a plan that called for contacting over one hundred record companies and photo collection organizations. Together we called on the phone and mailed out inquires about the use of album cover graphics, promotional photographs of artists, and general information about archival reproductions. After a couple of months, the mailman was bombarding my home with catalogs, promotional packets, and photo collection price lists. Eventually Johnny Bobey moved on to New York where he worked for "The Charlie Rose Show" and "The Late Show with David Letterman."

This was just the beginning of a long quest to secure as many visual displays as my bank account could sustain. After putting the book on hold for awhile, as noted in the preface, I began back in earnest, with the help of Peter Durham and his company, in 1993. What follows, dear reader, is a reconstruction, of sorts, of the photo permissions, as well as the editing and proof-reading assistance I received along the way to completion of this book project.

My first approvals for record cover permissions came in 1991 from two very gracious record company owners, whose love of music is reflected in the vast catalog of the "underground music" they promote: Chris Strachwitz of Arhoolie Records and George H. Buck of Audiophile and its many off-shoot labels. They both sent me numerous LP and CD covers, and gave me a good deal of encouragement on the phone and in letter form. The first musicians to respond in a like manner were Brian Nalepka of the Manhattan Rhythm Kings, and Ian Whitcomb. In both instances, I had a number of phone conversations and letter entreaties about my book project. Brian shared with me the problems of book publishing and promotion. In 1994 he told me of the time and efforts that his wife had put into the biography of guitarist-legend, Les Paul (*Les Paul: An American Original* by Mary Alice Shaughnessy, 1993). Ian wrote me a number of wonderful letters, signing off on one of them with a postscript that revealed the dog sitting at his feet was given to him by crooner legend, Rudy Vallee. Ian read through a couple of my early chapters and even gave me a number of suggestions for my "Crooner Chart." I would also like to thank: Debra C. Rath and Arnold S. Caplin of Biograph Records; Geary Chansley of MCA Records (Decca); Tim Johnson and Greg Dawson of the Ballroom for the ads of Blossom Dearie and John Wallowitch; Jonas Bernholm of Mr. R&B/Route 66 Records (of Stockholm, Sweden); Jeff Alexson of Kaleidoscope Records; Mardelle Cordero and Michelle Anderson of the Welk Music Group (Vanguard Records); Sally King of Antone Records (I wasn't able to fit in some of their artists this time around, but I would like to be on record as saying that this company has some of the GREAT, swinging sounds of Texas roots music. Also, let it be known that I'm one of the world's biggest Marcia Ball fans!); Jean Luc Young of Charly Records, by way of London, England (thanks especially for your extreme generosity–when I asked for those particular CD covers; I never expected to have discs to go along with them); Production coordinator David Forte and owner Bruce Iglauer of Alligator Records; and thanks, too, to the folks at Kicking Mule Records, Discovery Records, and DRG Records.

My first picture-hunting trips began during the Spring of 1991 when I visited New York City and investigated the holdings at Culver Pictures, Movie Star News, and the various collections of the New York Public Libraries. For my October trip of that year I had contacted my ex-student, Steve Ralbovsky, who was then working as a high-ranking executive for Elektra Records. I have such fond memories of Steve and his group of musically talented friends who took numerous courses from me between 1977-1982–the single most creative bunch of students I've ever been associated with–Scott Schiller, Andrew Elias, Maurice Narcis, Geoffrey Copp, Jeff Pollack, Jamie Lembeck, and one or two others. This amazing circle of students put on cutting-edge concerts, did radio work, wrote and published articles and magazines, and taught me a great deal about the current music industry. Steve Ralbovsky was the leader of all this swirl of activity, and after he graduated I looked forward to his letters and post cards while he was on the road managing the B52s and Mink DeVille, and then as a record producer for Columbia Records before joining

Elektra. Steve set up meetings for me with influential record producer Bob Krasnow, and Atlantic Records founder, Ahmet Ertegun. Now, most people would get their biggest charges out of meeting big stars in popular music, like Madonna, Whitney Houston, Bruce Springsteen or Mick Jagger of the Rolling Stones. For me, meeting a writer like Peter Guralnick, or Frank Driggs, or producers such as Bob Krasnow or Ahmet Ertegun is the absolute wish fulfillment. Krasnow was polite and interested in what I was trying to accomplish, and said anything from the Elektra/Warner/Atlantic Records catalog would have to be approved by Ahmet Ertegun. Next, THE MAN! Ahmet Ertegun. I would like to report that my three hour visit with him was due to my knowledge, wit, and charm. After all, I did spend close to three hours with one of the busiest, though partially retired, moguls in the music industry. With a booming welcome of " Well, Chuck Mancuso, of Buffalo, New York, what can I do to help you?" our meeting began. I sputtered and stammered on about how I respected his total involvement in music from early rhythm and blues to rock super groups of the sixties. About how noble his career support of cabaret has been, and so on. He looked at my project and approved, until half way through chapter four, he saw the subtitle "Sex, Drugs, and Rock'n'Roll." He said, "What's this! Rock'n'Roll didn't occur until the 1950s." I explained that, of course, rock and roll didn't occur back in the 1930s, but I was using the hook to make connections with America's fear of minority music and habits on the middle class culture. And blues artists, such as Bo Carter, and Frankie "Half Pint" Jaxon, were a few of the precursors of rock music. Frankie Jaxon was a favorite of Ertegun's; we discussed his career with relish. All of this and the ensuing dialog about the book, his various producing projects (I listened intently as he played his newly recorded masters of items he produced by zydeco great Rockin' Dopsie, and a spiraling, dramatic duet by Placido Domingo and Linda Ronstadt), and music, in general, did not take up all of that time. What took up much of the time was the Clarence Thomas hearings which were on television just behind his desk. Every couple of minutes, he would apologetically hush me, turn up the sound, and shake his head as he watched, muttering, "This is the damnest thing." It certainly was. My girlfriend, Barbara Goldman Barone and I were staying at the Yale Club, and would watch the final decision with a packed house of "Yalies" that very evening. (Clarence Thomas and his "accuser" Anita Hill were, one time, at Yale.)

1993 was the most productive year for picture accumulation. With Peter Durham donating secretarial, legal, and layout assistance, I now had the support staff that a large project like this needed. I knew I had to set up appointments with some of the major photo collections in America--some of these collections were controlled by individuals, and others were part of libraries and museum archives. They all cost money. I thought that if I paid the money "up front" I could work out a better deal price-wise. By "up front", I mean that the individual and corporate collections wouldn't have to wait for the book to be published before they got paid by the publishing house. My legal counsel, Joe Hausbeck, and my editor, Bill Kay, were able to increase the figure that Kendall-Hunt would provide for photos for my project. (It would still be thousands of dollars less than what it would actually cost with travel and extra pictures, but it was a big help.) However, I knew that with the cost of older photographs and permissions running between $25 and $200 a piece, my dreams of having a book with over 700 photos was looking bleak. I looked at my bank account, took a deep breath, and began making appointments with those in charge of the key collections. In mid-July 1993, I was back in New York, first with John Fernandez and Jill Vetter, of Carnegie Hall, who saw my project and were very supportive. Fernandez spoke on my behalf to those in charge and helped to make the cost affordable--I used 26 photos from their collection and will never forget their genuine enthusiasm and outright kindness. Fernandez even gave me a collection of taped radio shows from past Carnegie Hall tributes. Fernandez and Vetter have moved on to other jobs, and, in June 1995, I had the pleasure of collaborating with Associate Archivist Kathleen Saraceni, who provided me with the Frank Sinatra Celebration advertisement for the three evening concert series in late July of that year. My stops at the various museums were also very beneficial. Marty Jacobs helped me with the collection at the Museum of the City of New York. Diane Powers led me through the myriad of photo possibilities at the New York Public Library. I also spent a profitable afternoon accumulating pictures at the Schomburg Library.
Mark Gridley had suggested that, since I was going to be in New York for a week, I should call on Frank Driggs, because he probably had the most varied and famous collection of photos and ads. After

agreeing on a noon, two hour consultation at his Brooklyn home, I took the subway to the end of the Flatbush line and walked a couple of miles on what was surely the hottest day of the year. Frank brought me down into his basement and wanted to know about the project. I showed him mockups of my layout and read him a couple of items I thought were part of the core of my philosophy: not to denigrate artists, but try to report the facts of history as honestly as possible. He said he was in agreement with me about the unfair treatment of Paul Whiteman and shared with me an enthusiasm for the works of Ruth Etting, Louis Armstrong, Louis Jordan, the Blue Sky Boys, Bob Wills, and so many more. Here, I was in the company of a jazz-oriented historian, who shared a genuine affection for what many considered "non-hip" popular music, rhythm and blues, and, most unusual, coming from a noted jazz writer, country music. That two hour meeting extended nearly six hours and was the beginning of a long distance friendship that remains, today. Driggs has warned me that many of the jazz critics/historians may not like what I have to say, but he has agreed that much of it should be said.

It was during this trip that I also rekindled an old Butler Mitchell Boys Club friendship with Joe Grafasi, who is an established Broadway stage and Hollywood film actor. Dinners with Joe and his wife, Jane Ira Bloom, the celebrated jazz saxophonist, and with Steve Ralbovsky and his wife, Elaine, made this trip especially pleasurable. Also, Barbara's uncle Leslie Goldman, a lawyer-cameraman-turned actor, escorted us from one insider spot to another. Thanks to all.

The next trip to New York, a couple of months later, was primarily to connect with more record companies. I would like to express my gratitude to the following companies for the use of album cover graphics: Jamie Pawliczek (Legal Intern) of BMG Music (RCA Records); Kevin Monahan, Chris Jennings, Susan Mendola, and Lisa Williams of Arista Records; Shirley Ford for the pictures and ads for the 92 Street Y; Michael Lang and Lisa Rothblum of PolyGram Records (Verve); Francois Zalacain of SunnySide Communications Inc.; and Mr. Brightman for his large donation of covers from Stash Records.

The next stop was the Library of Congress in Washington, D.C. I was fortunate to be able to time my visit to coincide with that of my good friend, Ken LoBene, who was at a HUD conference. Ken made certain I didn't get lost around the city, and showed me the fine dining spots at night. For a researcher, being at the Library of Congress is truly a heavenly experience. My contact, Mary Ibach, had all the information I had requested, set and ready to go when I showed up. At the end of each day, she would cover my long table with a large covering and a note attesting to the contents as being mine. I could have spent another week at the Prints and Photo Division of the Library of Congress , but four days was it. I also secured material at the Folk Division, helped by Mr. Jerry Parsons and Ms. Jennifer Cutting. I came away from the Library of Congress with close to 100 pictures.

My final formal visit was to the Southern Folklife Collection at North Carolina University, at Chapel Hill. Before making the trip, I called and set up an appointment for two days over the winter break of 1993. I also called UCLA (the University of California at Los Angeles) to talk with the people at the John Edwards Memorial Foundation (no one answered). I had coveted a number of pictures, especially an ad of Patsy Montana and one of Ken Maynard, from their collection and wanted to know what their costs would be per picture. I found the prices and the service very much to my liking at North Carolina. I made mention to some of the archivists that the same two pictures I had called UCLA about were in their collection. I was then informed that UCLA had sold off their collection to the Southern Folklife Collection a couple of years before—what luck. I also would like to thank the people at the "Grand Ole Opry" for the four photos they sent me for the book (found in Chapter 7).

Also, in 1993, I secured permissions from the following: Paul De Pass for the terrific graphic of *The 1940's Radio Hour*; Scott Fedro, Elektra Records and the Morra, Breener, Steinberg & Tenenbaum Group for the Michael Feinstein advertisement; Ira Koslow, the Peter Asher Management Group, and Elektra Records for the Linda Ronstadt ad; Josephine Maniaracina and Justin D. Walker of Sony Music (Columbia

Records) for their series of letters and calls that finally resulted in a good number of important album covers and early trade ads; Dave Nelson, Editor of *Living Blues*, for his magazine's covers; Bruce Ricker, President of Rhapsody Films, for the use of a number of video covers and the ad for *Last of The Blue Devils*; the late Carl Jefferson and Elizabeth Bell of Concord Records; Barbara McGurn, Public Relations Manager of the Algonquin; Evan Kopelson and Whitney Broussard of Capitol Records, Inc.; Glenn Sabin, Publisher of *Jazz Times*; Robert Koestler (owner), and Promotion Director, Jennifer Dirkes, of Delmark Records; Susan Pontillo, Manager of Media Relations for V.I.E.W. Video/34 East 23rd St., New York, NY 10010, (800) 843-9843; Elaine Rizleris, Controller/Circulation Manager of *Down Beat* magazine– the company was not only supportive of my using past covers, but also allowed me to shoot pictures and articles from the inside text (photography shooting was done by Steve Mangione and Phil Geraci of Buffalo State's Instructional Resources Center; on site, from the archival collection of, the Buffalo & Erie County Public Library); Marie Rothenberg, Customer Service for The Good Time Record Company; Kathy Kim and the Smithsonian Collection of Recordings; Harold Leventhal, the lawyer and curator of Woody Gutherie Publications Inc.; Suzanne and Michael Wallis, of the Wallis Group, for the use of the book cover of *Route 66: The Mother Road*; R. Wayne Martin, Executive Vice President of Shanachie Entertainment Corp; William P. Gottlieb for the use of some of his famous photos of jazz performers of the 1940s–Bill is one of the only photographers, who took pictures of jazz performers, (many of them while he was a staff member at *Down Beat* magazine) who is still around to profit from his work. (In early 1995, Bill called to say that he had consummated an agreement with the Library of Congress to purchase his collection.) Thanks also to the good folks at Reference Records; and to Yves Beauvis and Ahmet Ertegun of Atlantic Records.

In 1994 and 1995, I completed the picture acquisition component of the book by receiving permissions from the following: Galen Gart of Big Nickel Publications; Dave Freeman of County Records; Gary Reid of Rebel Records; Glenn Dicker of Rounder Records; Joe Fields of Muse Records; Paula Klaw of Movie Star News; Frank D. Vigeant, Publicity Manager for Harold Shaw Concerts, Inc. (representing Bolcom and Morris); Jeffrey T. Span and Jim Steinblat of ASCAP (American Society of Composers, Authors and Publishers); Michael Fagin of *Jazziz* magazine; The Buffalo Philharmonic; Michael Mahoney, Assistant Deputy of the Buffalo & Erie County Public Library; Ed Sobala for his photographs of Al Tinney and Mark Murphy and Bobby Militello; Mark Goldman, owner and chief entrepreneur of Buffalo's center for jazz and cabaret, the Calumet Arts Cafe; and my final photo permission grant, secured on June 23, 1995, in the back of the touring bus of Asleep at the Wheel. The great Ray Benson, a walking-talking-singing-guitar playing-historian of monumental proportions, signed on, and after perusing a couple of my chapters, doffed his ten-gallon hat, and said, "Go forth, and spread the word."

Finally, some salutations to a number of people who took the time and effort to read small or large sections of the text and review the layout design. John Phinney, a Buffalo school teacher and good friend, looked at the then-first sentence of the book and said, "The entire world wasn't at peace in 1917!" Right off the bat I knew this book was going to need a lot of editing. I have mentioned Dave Lampe and Reg Gilbert, my co-editors earlier. However, I must reaffirm that they had their hands full with advancing my writing skills. They were, thankfully, very patient with me and mightily improved the final copy. I can't say enough about the extra hours they spent with me, especially at the end of the project, where Reg helped me write and clarify sections of the book. Cathy Carfagna and Mary Ann Lauricella, again, as noted earlier, did much to improve and refine the text. All of them, along with Peter Durham, spent a great deal of time after the 521 pages of text were sent out, plowing through the annotated bibliography and the lengthy discography/videography, and index.

Readers also were used for particular chapters; Michael Wright of the music section of the Buffalo State's Performing Art Department read through the first seven chapters, and had solid editing advice; Al Riess, Associate Librarian of the Butler Library at Buffalo State, gave me much needed assistance in the areas of folk and country music, as well as suggestions on the bibliography and discography/videography; Nick Churchill spent many days making corrections on the first half of the book, and his suggestions to make the book an easier read were helpful; Trish Heart, one of my very best ex-students and friends, read through many chapters, made a number of suggestions and provided the inspiration for the Peekskill incident in Chapter 14 that I had overlooked; Dr. James Patrick of the University of Buffalo music department, spent two days with me after spending a week reading the jazz chapters, and had constructive criticisms as well as suggestions on how to improve certain problems; Jim Gavin read the chapter on "Revival of the 1930s and 40s" and offered illuminating ideas; Mark Gridley spent almost a week at my house going over every word and concept relating to jazz—his help and concern for the project will never be forgotten; Don Metz, one-time head of Hallwalls, and presently the Director of Administration of the Burchfield-Penney Art Center, and for two years professor of additional classes in my Jazz Rock Foundations classes at Buffalo State College—thank you for your suggestions; some five or ten students from my Music 206 class provided comments and suggestions, but, sad to say, at this time your evaluation sheets are in one of the forty or fifty boxes of papers that are stacked throughout my basement and attic; so, I can't list your names at this time—I owe you.

There were also a good number of friends who gave a brief final read once the project was in its completion stages: Charlie Keil, Dr. Edward O. Smith, Paul Donoghue, Bill Baker and Judy Duggan, John Jablonski, Dave Sharpe, Dave Meinzer, Ace Gomez, Mary Mancuso, Blaze and Joan LaDuca, Galen Gart, Jim Dawson, Robert Naples, Sal Macaluso, Al Kozen, Drew Kahn, Dick Crossett, Mark Goldman, Cynthia Olson, Bill Tallmadge, Adame and Joe Mancuso, Marshall Duguay, Horace Mann, Al Wallack, and Sid Ehreneich. My great friends from Toronto, Canada, Peter Scheinders and Londos D'Arrigo, along with Buffalo's Bob Petrick, were particularly helpful in the area of jazz, theater and vocal music. Thanks also to my "artist-in-resident" and keeper of the flame for all things cultural and historic, Toma Yavanovich.

Additionally, I must say thank you to Norma Jean Lamb, Head Music Librarian at the Buffalo and Erie County Public Library—you'll never know how many ways you assisted me over the past few years. And what would Chris Szeluga and I have done without the measuring aid (Ansco Measuring Scaler) supplied by Professor Frank Eckmair. And when extra records/CDs not found in my own collection were needed so I could analyze them, in stepped Dave Meinzer, Cathy Carfagna, and my good friend, the biggest Greek in Buffalo, Lambrose Touris (terrific additions were provided by "Lambie" with the Dorothy Donegan releases and the resplendent *Saturday Night and Sunday Morning* tribute with Ralph Stanley and friends). Additionally, there were the Durham Company typists and final copy-edit readers who completed the task of preparing the changes for finished copy: Amy Judelsohn, Sue Proskey, Mary Donlin, Dawn Gillette, Barbara Judelsohn, Colleen Durham, Caron Dux, Julie Renda, Marydonna Budniewski, David Kawaler, Lorrie Pfentner, Marilynn Newton, Lisa Fix, Mary Grupka, Rosemary Blando, Patricia Butcher, Marcia Dauer, Donna Dunn, Ellen Fechter, Ingrid Graf, Thelma Johnson-Godert, Richard Peck, Monica Washington, and Judy Nagy. Thank you all. And now I will have no more excuses for being SAD and tired when I scrimmage and play league games with my Masters Basketball group.

So, let us now enter into what pianist-singer-songwriter Dave Frishberg calls "The Dear Departed Past." One doesn't need to be hopelessly old fashioned to enjoy the memories of those golden days of dusty sheet music and scratchy records, and "to the echoes of tomorrow, soon to be memories at last. Memories that will someday reappear—loud and clear in the dear departed past."

Note: The author views the charts and discography/videography as "works in progress." Readers who wish to correct, amplify, praise or denounce are encouraged to write to the author. Also, for teachers who would like some guidelines on teaching this massive information in a single semester, there is an audio tape of the author explaining how to go about it. A folder of notes and listening sheets that are used in the Mus 206 (Jazz Rock Foundations) class are included. For more information write to: Chuck Mancuso, P.O. Box 677, Buffalo, NY 14207

List of Charts

POPULAR MUSIC AND THE UNDERGROUND

American music is a stew of styles and influences. Even in their purest form, musical styles were combinations and adaptations of recognizable earlier forms. Popular music was usually distilled from underground styles, further blurring the differences; and when popular music worked its way into underground forms, the cycle would begin again.
The influence of these tiers flows both up and down.

Influence Flows UP

Influence Flows DOWN

1st TIER

Popular Bands & Singers
Broadway Songwriters & Musicals
Hollywood Movies

This is the mainstream of popular music. This music dominated the pop charts and was the most commercially successful. It reached the public through major record labels, nationally syndicated radio, film, theater, and clubs.

2nd TIER UNDERGROUND

Many artists filtered up from the underground and made brief or occasional impacts on the popular music of the day, either with their own performances or by having their songs and/or styles adapted by more popular performers. Some music survived the journey intact; other examples were "cleaned up" for mass appeal.

3rd TIER UNDERGROUND

This is where music existed in its purest, most original form. Underground music was often unique to one ethnic group, one regional area, or even one part of one city.

JAZZ	BLUES	COUNTRY & FOLK
Ragtime	Minstrelsy	Broadsides
Dixieland/Traditional	Classic/Tent Shows	Mountain Music
Stride Piano	Rural/Delta	String Bands
Pre-Swing Bands	Hokum	Solo Singers
Black Show Bands	Archival	Barn Dance Shows
Mainstream Jazz	Cajun/Zydeco	Bluegrass
Bebop	City Blues	Tex-Mex
Cool	(Bluebeat, Electric Blues)	Singing Cowboys
Progressive	Jump and Jive Combos	Western Swing
Cult & Cabaret Vocals	Club Combos	Honky Tonk
Repertory Revivalists	Doo-Wop Vocals	

Chapter 1

MAINSTREAM POP AND THE UNDERGROUND

Aside from Bing Crosby, Frank Sinatra was the foremost vocal influence of the first half of the twentieth century. The 1995, 80th birthday celebration for Sinatra at Carnegie Hall is subtitled "American Song Celebration," and the jazz and cabaret artists listed above are a small portion of the participants. Gary Giddins, one of America's most esteemed jazz critics, wrote of Sinatra's legacy (in the June 20, 1995 *Village Voice*), "The Sinatra achievement is not least a guide to modern orchestration—a how-to concerning the adaptation of old pop to a post bop consciousness. A peerless interpreter of our best lyricists, Sinatra is expected to demonstrate unexpected depths in the work of Larry Hart, Ira Gershwin, Johnny Burke, Cole Porter, Johnny Mercer, and Irving Berlin. But the test of his transformative powers are those songs beyond redemption, an area in which his ability is at one with Armstrong, Crosby, Holiday, and very few others. Who else would sing 'The Curse of an Aching Heart,' previously the subject of burlesques by Fats Waller and Laurel and Hardy (in *Blotto*), but in Sinatra's hands a joyous, straight-faced romp? Sinatra's imperviousness to the song's clumsiness is symptomatic. The generosity he hasn't always been able to summon in life is the very marrow of his gift to music."

All history resonates in the present, but the musical past in particular refuses obsolescence. On the surface, "old time" music from the first half of this century has little in common with today's popular music styles—grunge, rap and hip-hop, heavy metal, and contemporary soul and country.

Yet older music remains all around us. It is there in television commercials (Cindy Crawford selling soda to the strains of Duke Ellington's "I Got it Bad And That Ain't Good," complete with Johnny Hodges's luscious alto solo), in films (older songs dominate the soundtracks from Nora Ephron's *When Harry Met Sally* to Woody Allen's *Bullets Over Broadway*, among many others). It is there in Broadway revivals (*Show Boat*, *Guys and Dolls*, and *Crazy for You*, based on George Gershwin's *Girl Crazy*, to name just three); in original musical revues centered on the lives of musical greats, such as *Jelly's Last Jam* (Jelly Roll Morton), *Ain't Misbehavin'* (Fats Waller), and *Five Guys Named Moe* (Louis Jordan). And, it is there in albums by contemporary musical stars that rework older songs (Eric Clapton's "roots"

1

tribute to older bluesmen, *From the Cradle*, and Linda Ronstadt's trio of Nelson Riddle-orchestrated classics of the 1930s and 1940s, just two of scores of albums in this vein); in the virtual torrent of tribute albums by "various artists," the most well-known of which may be the pulsating Cole Porter compilation, *Red, Hot and Blue*; and in revivals of their own material by the older greats themselves, Frank Sinatra's *Duets* releases foremost among them.

But all this music no longer has the pop character it had when it was created. Old-time music is now produced for lovers of music history, eccentrics, and as mood and period-setting vehicles for material products or other forms of entertainment. These current uses of old-time music obscure its origins. Like Whitney Houston's "I Will Always Love You," Nirvana's "Smells Like Teen Spirit," and Garth Brooks's "Learning to Live Again," old-time songs in their day expressed, embodied, and capitalized on the feelings and needs of the American people of the time. Whatever power we understand popular music to have today, old-time music had in arguably greater degree, given the more limited entertainment options of Americans of decades past.

The graphic on the page preceding Chapter 1, *Popular Music and the Underground*, illustrates the interrelationship of the various forms of commercial music of the first half century. Making historical sense of the melange is the basis for this current review of those interconnections. This book represents a thorough study of music in America. It creates a historical sense of order from among thousands of references of musical people, places and pieces, scattered throughout books, magazines, newspapers, albums, and videos in public and private archives. (Insight, and explanation, is presented in the "Introduction and Preface.")

Courtesy Michael's Pub

Mel Torme is a prime example of a contemporary artist with deep roots in the musical past. Torme's career extends as far back as 1930, when he sang as a five-year old with the Coon-Sanders orchestra on the radio, right through the 1940s with bands during the swing era. During the spring and summer of 1995 Torme was seen in a major soda commercial, free-falling off a building, as a group of grunge rockers gasp in amazement. rockers gasped in amazement.

Courtesy Algonquin Hotel

Creme de la creme cabaret singer, Julie Wilson began performing during the 1940s with the Johnny Long Orchestra. Wilson represents an elegant group of entertainers who appeal to a more sophisticated and urbane cadre of followers compared to the masses that make up the "Hit Parade" crowd. Because of that audience's egalitarian posture the cabaret tradition has seldom been accounted for in the histories of jazz and pop music. The pop-jazz stylings of Torme and his clan, the jazz cabaret cult vocalists, the nostalgia-camp movement, and Julie Wilson and her cabaret tradition, are all featured in Chapter 10 (Revival of '30s and '40s), which investigates contemporary artists that center their musical material on "The Golden Age of Pop."

The American Music Terrain

Any attempt to investigate this older music—American popular music of the first fifty years of this century—encounters a difficult problem. What exactly is "popular" music? Over the years the term has referred to a number of different forms and styles, but certain attributes of popular music remain constant. Popular music of every period is music made for and liked by the average consumer, a mythical person who is relatively musically uneducated and who typically uses music to entertain rather than edify. Music writers have long debated the origin of popular music, whether it dates from early church music of the first millennium, or from the music played by roaming troubadours of the European Renaissance, or classical music, or perhaps only from the songs performed in English "pleasure gardens" of the late eighteenth century.

This debate is one of semantics as much as anything. In this book we are concerned with popular music as a commercial phenomenon—music as a commodity bought and sold in greater or lesser quantities on the open market, particularly in the form of records.

Courtesy Buffalo & Erie County Public Library

Sheet music provided the amateur and professional peano player the musical notation and song lyrics. The notation was generally in a simplified form to accommodate the vocal ranges and limited piano skills of the buyer.

In 1919, the song "Dardanella" was a smash hit. The sheet music sales exceeded one million copies. However, the recording of the song by Ben Selvin's Novelty Orchestra sold millions, foretelling the fate of sheet music as the major translator of pop music. "Dardanella" was the first song to sell more copies on record than on sheet music.

Commercial popular music in America begins with sheet music, which was written and printed for amateur piano players for use on the large number of pianos in homes and taverns all over the United States. Sheet music began to be sold in significant ("popular") numbers after the Civil War, and by the turn of the century was a mass market phenomenon similar in almost all respects to the music market of today. A given song could sell into the millions and was sold in stores and bars and by street vendors. They would play them on horse-drawn carts much as radio and television sample new songs for audiences today. The surprising fact is that the basic structure of the music scene has been the same for more than one hundred years.

The Record

In the 1880s Thomas Edison invented the record player. The first versions of this device played cylinders, not platters, but the technology was the same—a needle running along a groove. By the 1920s the record began to exceed sheet music in sales.

This book concentrates on the forms of popular music sold on records. Performance in hotels and clubs, on stage, in films, and on radio had an important impact on a given song and artist's popularity, and, in fact, could make an artist as wealthy and even wealthier than purely recorded popularity could. This book does not ignore this reality. In fact, the access of certain (usually urban, white) artists to these forums made all the difference in their ability to become well-known, that is, "popular."

But for all that, the evangelical (audience-building) and historical (archivally available) power of hotel, club, stage, film, and radio performance was and remains limited. Hotel, club, and stage performance, which often paid handsomely, played to relatively smaller numbers of people and has been imperfectly historically preserved. The film and radio media, which were both more widely seen and heard, and substantially more lucrative than hotel, club and stage performance, suffered from the age-old weakness of *broad*casting—they had to program material for the largest possible audience, an audience understood in terms of its lowest common denominator. Accordingly, these media were inflexible. If a given radio program or film could not attract, or be thought unable to attract, a relatively large minimum-size audience, that radio program would not be produced.

The 78 record. A series of 78 records (four to eight and sometimes more) placed in sleeves and covered by a hardbound jacket was called a record album—a name which continued to describe the long-play 33 1/3 records introduced by the Columbia Record Company in 1948. After all, the new records could hold on a single platter as many songs as the former "albums."

The record had none of these drawbacks. Evangelically speaking, it could be produced in quantities from a hundred into the millions. It could therefore be played to audiences large and small, rich and poor, rural and urban, black and white. Historically speaking, the record, of course, is a record—of the music it contains. Almost all the hotel and club performances of the period covered by this book, most of the radio performances, and many of the stage performances, have been lost to history.

This book's focus on the record has two additional rationales. First, historical debate over the origins of musical forms and styles is frequently too speculative. We often can know very little of how and why people began to play in the many ways they have in this country in the last hundred years. Records, however, are indisputable evidence of the existence, and often the influence too, of the music they contain.

Much more important, is the incalculable revolutionizing impact that the record had on American music making. This impact was twofold. First, the record was a vastly more versatile medium for distributing music. Sheet music was piano music that could be mass marketed only because a large number of Americans could both play the piano and read piano sheet music. Sheet music could not distribute any other form of music. In rural areas guitar and fiddle playing may have been relatively common, but few who played those instruments were able to read music. Ensemble playing, even of just four musicians, was even more impractical on sheet music. ~~Records were inherently able to distribute a much wider range of music~~ than sheet music could.

The jukebox, introduced around 1928, was a mechanical record machine, activated by coins. By the end of the 1930s jukeboxes were found in most cafes, diners, soda shops, beaneries, honkytonks and roadside booths. Arnold Shaw points out in the *Dictionary of American Pop/Rock*, that, "By 1942, because of the growth of jukebox usage, the president of the American Federation of Musicians labeled the record 'the no. 1 scab' of music and established a ban on recording. While live performances on the radio made hits in the pop field before the rise of the disk jockey in the early fifties, juke-boxes played an enormous role in developing hits in the R&B and C&W fields."

This versatility of distribution came at a price—records were made by professionals, using the term loosely. You or at least your friends might play sheet music, live, in the home or a local tavern. The record was made by people you did not know, usually in some other city. But that is another story.

The second major impact of the record on American music making was its ability to cross-pollinate the many different regional styles of music either already in existence or in the process of being created. As even the most cursory survey of American popular music shows, after the advent of the record there was an exponential growth in the way Americans made music. Partly this was due to the ability of the record to suddenly document the many forms of music that had been played unnoticed for years in the country's byways. But just as importantly, the record brought to each byway the music made in a dozen others. Musicians with almost no contact with anything outside a twenty-five-mile radius of their home could hear records made by people hundreds of miles away. They came to learn how to play their instruments by playing and replaying the records, and they came to think about the possibilities of every aspect of musical style—instrumental combinations, forms of melody, singing technique, tonal, rhythmic, and harmonic variation—the list goes on. The record, like a wind bearing the seeds of foreign vegetation to lonely ocean islands, brought every corner of isolated musical America into the living rooms and taverns of every other similarly isolated corner. The result was a diversity of musical style, instrumental technique, and ensemble invention unknown any time or place before in the world.

Tiers of Commercial Success

The first popular music on phonograph record was of four basic types: marching band music, pop ragtime, vaudeville and Broadway singing, and sentimental ballads sung by barbershop-like harmony groups. After World War I and into the early 1920s came early jazz, jazz-oriented dance band music, female blues singing, and rural country music featuring string instruments. These forms were followed in the late 1920s and 1930s by one-man blues troubadours, black jug bands, male crooners and female torch singers, singing cowboys, Broadway and Hollywood-derived hit songs, big band and western swing music, and honky tonk. The 1940s saw the rise of swing band vocalists and the creation of boogie woogie, rhythm and blues, and the modern jazz forms eventually to be called bebop and cool.

Thousands of musicians produced all this music, each with varying degrees of commercial success. This success could be characterized as being on one of three general levels, called in this book simply first tier, second tier, and bottom tier. Those on the first tier of commercial success made a lot of money and achieved very high recognition among all classes of music con-

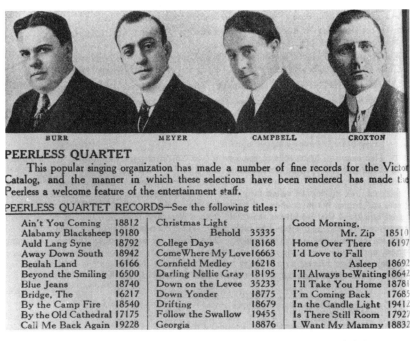

BURR   MEYER   CAMPBELL   CROXTON

PEERLESS QUARTET

This popular singing organization has made a number of fine records for the Victor Catalog, and the manner in which these selections have been rendered has made the Peerless a welcome feature of the entertainment staff.

PEERLESS QUARTET RECORDS—See the following titles:

Ain't You Coming	18812	Christmas Light		Good Morning,	
Alabamy Blacksheep	19180	Behold	35335	Mr. Zip	18510
Auld Lang Syne	18792	College Days	18168	Home Over There	16197
Away Down South	18942	Come Where My Love	16663	I'd Love to Fall	
Beulah Land	16166	Cornfield Medley	16218	Asleep	18692
Beyond the Smiling	16500	Darling Nellie Gray	18195	I'll Always be Waiting	18642
Blue Jeans	18740	Down on the Levee	35233	I'll Take You Home	18781
Bridge, The	16217	Down Yonder	18775	I'm Coming Back	17685
By the Camp Fire	18540	Drifting	18679	In the Candle Light	19412
By the Old Cathedral	17175	Follow the Swallow	19455	Is There Still Room	17927
Call Me Back Again	19228	Georgia	18876	I Want My Mammy	18832

Author's collection

The Peerless Quartet, like the Hayden and American Quartets, sang sentimental songs as well as novelty numbers. These barbershop harmony groups were extremely popular prior to the emergence of the Jazz Age. The recordings of the Peerless Quartet, like most of the superstars of the first quarter of this century, cannot be found in today's music stores.

sumers. Those on the second tier made a very good living and achieved substantial recognition, often because of successful "crossover" hits. Those on the bottom tier barely made a living in music or made a decent living only sporadically, and were virtually unknown outside a small, regionally defined set of music consumers.

Because of their relatively less popular recognition, the second and third tiers of success can be contrasted with the first tier in a number of ways. The second and third tiers form a sort of "underground" of popular music in relation to the first tier, which could be called the "mainstream" of popular music. "Mainstream" and "underground" can be characterized in several ways.

In terms of musical form, mainstream popular music between 1917 and 1950 was almost always show music or dance bands, and the singers who emanated from those bands. Most jazz players as well as blues, and country players were consigned to only underground levels of success.

In terms of players, mainstream popular musicians were always white. Blacks, Hispanics, and other ethnic musicians such as Cajun players never got beyond underground musical success.

In terms of listeners, mainstream popular audiences, which were by no means always larger than underground audiences, were more likely to be urban and contained many more middle- and upper-class people. Underground music was much more likely to appeal to rural audiences, working and lower middle-class people, and, for those interested in more than classical music, the musical intelligentsia.

In terms of regional origins, mainstream popular music almost always hailed from the East or Midwest (and, with the advent of talking movies, Hollywood), which were the centers of theatrical production, music publishing, and music criticism ranging from books to fanzines. Music from the South and West (with the notable exception of Hollywood) was always relegated to second- or third-tier success.

In terms of media, mainstream popular music was the music of stage, film and national radio broadcasts. Underground music was the music of regional and local radio broadcasts.

Curiously, music history is often, perhaps even regularly, unkind to the musicians who achieved mainstream popular success. By contrast, it is often very kind to those who achieved only underground success. Paul Whiteman was easily the biggest-selling dance band leader from 1920 to 1934, and a fine musician and talent scout in the bargain. Despite his achievements, the man is not well known today and almost completely unappreciated. On the other hand, Robert Johnson, easily one of the most obscure blues players of the 1930s, has today become the most celebrated rural bluesman of the pre-rock era. This is principally due to his influence on a few famous English blues players of the 1960s, and on through them the blues critical music establishment.

Mainstream ("Popular") Music

"Popular music" is understood by almost all observers to be the music that "most people" listen to. However, this understanding is invariably inflated, depending on the outlook of the observer.

For the general music consumer of the period covered in this book, popular music was defined largely stylistically—it was jazz-oriented dance music produced by large orchestras. Popular music was the combination of the Western European heritage of melody, harmony, and written score, and the African heritage of syncopation, improvisation, and emotionally hot performance style. The 1920s were called the "Jazz Age," and the period from 1935 through the early 1940s was hailed as the "Swing Era." Both musical movements had been inspired by jazz performers, even if some of the most popular participants in them were not necessarily jazz players.

For the musical critic of newspaper, magazine, and book, popular music has been, and to some degree remains, something reaching for the lowest common denominator in regard to musical taste. If the multitudes enjoy it, how good can it be? The longevity of this critical attitude, which goes back at least

6

to Plato, can be examined by looking at the requirements of the critical effort. To criticize a field of endeavor, the critic must be able to divide it into "good" and "bad." It is only natural that the critic will therefore develop an ever-increasing ability to discern relative technical virtuosity, choice of repertoire and style, and authenticity of feeling. As these critical facilities create a gap between the critic's taste and that of a mass audience with a different agenda—say, the desire to dance for hours, or to play music in a small room at high volume—it is only natural that most critics develop a disdain for "popular" music for the very reason that it is popular.

For the guardians of society—generally politicians, preachers, teachers, and parents—popular music has always been, and remains to this day, a threat to social order. Whether we are talking about the musical tastes of the wildly dancing collegians and flappers of the 1920s, or the jitterbugging teenagers of the 1930s and 1940s, or the rock'n'roll teens of the 1950s, or the Beatlemaniacs of the 1960s, or the disco club patrons and punkers of the 1970s, or the hip-hoppers and mosh pit slam dancers of the 1980s and 1990s, one attitude has remained constant—the condemnation of the musical taste of the young by the guardians of social stability. One thing music history teaches us is that there is nothing entirely new, and that the social guardians of every generation will usually think that our nation is on a downward spiral in part because the popular music of the youth of the day isn't up to the standards of previous generations.

Writing about the baleful influences attributed to the popular music of the late nineteenth century, Nicholas Tawa notes in *The Way to Tin Pan Alley*, "Some critics said the self-satisfied spirit of the bourgeoisie was reflected; others saw an aspect of herd conformity battened on by capitalistic exploiters; still others claimed popular song as a representation of debased culture sinking to the lowest common denominator of aesthetic discernment. Most of these criticisms, on balance, had some truth to them, especially when Tin Pan Alley thinking permeated the popular-song world after the 1890s."

This would not be the case forever. With the advent of Bob Dylan and the Beatles in the mid-1960s, contemporary music journalists gave what had been called rock'n'roll a new name, "rock," and judged it good—aesthetically riveting and intellectually pleasing. For the first time in this century critics of popular music viewed "pop" as something neither kitsch nor declasse. But again, this is another story.

Paul Whiteman led the most important orchestra of the early period of popular music. Edward Jablonski, writing in *The Encyclopedia of American Music*, claims, "Whiteman's was a remarkable band which did indeed employ true jazz musicians from time to time, but it was really one of the first big bands—an industry that would flourish in the '30s and early '40s. Whiteman's activities during the Jazz Age would earn him bad press from the professional jazz critics who surfaced in such books as *Jazzmen* and such little magazines as *Jazz Information* and *The Jazz Record* in the late '30s and '40s. Three types of bands flourished during the '20s: jazz bands in the racier clubs and speakeasies, the dance band in the more respectable clubs and country club dances, and the potted palm orchestras [so named because the band seemed to be hidden behind potted palms; sometimes referred to as salon orchestras] in the more genteel settings of hotels, country clubs, and the homes of the wealthy."

The typical evaluation of popular music during the time period discussed in this book (with the possible exception of a very select half dozen or so jazz big bands), was that the music was "diluted, sweetened, sentimentalized and trivialized . . . the product of white songwriters for predominantly white audiences tending towards wishful thinking, dreams and ineffectual nostalgia, realistic fantasy, self-pity and sentimental cliches masquerading as emotion." So spoke a renowned linguist and later U.S. senator, S.I. Hayakawa, of the music of the rock'n'roll era, but he might as well have been paraphrasing the attitudes of critics ever since the turn of the century, if not before.

Courtesy Buffalo & Erie County Public Library

Bing Crosby is the undisputed number one star of the first half of the twentieth century. Crosby masterfully sang jazz and every kind of pop song. By the late 1920s he was softly singing into the electric microphone, which led observers to label the style "crooning." Crosby may not have been the first "crooner," but he was the style's foremost exponent.

An authoritative, if perhaps overbroad, definition of popular music is offered by Charles Hamm in one of the most respected studies of popular music history, *Yesterdays: Popular Song in America*. Hamm defines "popular song" as a piece of music that is "written for, and most often performed by, a single voice or a small group of singers, accompanied by either a single chord-playing instrument or some sort of band, ensemble, or small orchestra; usually first performed and popularized in some form of secular stage entertainment, and afterward consumed (performed or listened to) in the home; compiled and marketed with the goal of financial gain; designed to be performed by and listened to by persons of limited musical training and ability; and produced and disseminated in physical form—as sheet music in its early history, and in various forms of mechanical reproduction in the twentieth century."

Movie Star News

Hollywood, Broadway and radio superstar Eddie Cantor with Broadway great Ethel Merman in MGM's 1934 opus *Kid Millions*. Cantor and Merman, along with singers Kate Smith and Vaughn DeLeath are examples of star entertainers whose recordings sold just moderately well. Some underground artists such as Bessie Smith, Jimmie Rodgers, and Fats Waller, among others, sold more recordings than many of the stars of the time. But the stars had greater access to the Broadway stage, national radio hookups, and starring roles in motion pictures.

This book uses a somewhat more succinct definition of popular music: the music that the general public favors at a given time. One might think it relatively easy to know what was popular at a given time—look at music sales. This is certainly true today. People listen to music in a variety of forms—on television or VCR, on radio, and in movie theaters—but no music is popular in one of these forms while being unknown or almost so in the primary modes of music distribution—CD and tape sales.

The picture was more complicated during most of the period under study in this book. Millions listened to Kate Smith and Eddie Cantor on radio, and saw them star in a number of major Hollywood films as well, yet not as many bought their records. The inverse was also true. Bessie Smith and Jimmie Rodgers sold millions of records, but had only regional stage presence and virtually no film or radio profile at all.

Ascertaining who was popular in the period covered by this book is complicated by our historical perspective. For almost sixty years historians and critics have looked at the past and decided both which artists and what songs they preferred and which of these artists were of "historical significance." That is, which artists were important influences on selected later musicians and musical styles. Identifying preferred music and sorting through history for figures of particular significance, are, of course, the raison d'etre of the critic and the historian, respectively. But as practiced in the music world since the late 1930s, criticism and history-telling have somewhat neglected the simple, straight story of America's music—who was popular and why. In the process, these professionals have simply ignored a number of both talented and popular artists (and even entire musical styles) while, in some cases, exaggerating the importance of other artists (and musical styles).

Thus, the jazz of this period—though not all the forms of jazz played during this time—is the most historically valorized form of music, while the country and western sector of the same time has been relatively ignored. Ironically, while jazz was the dominant form of popular music before 1950, country music today has emerged from its pre-1950s state of virtual pop orphanage to become a commercial juggernaut—and jazz has sunk to the status of strictly cult music.

Keeping all this in mind, this book sets out to stitch together an accurate picture of who was popular, who was less popular but still somewhat known, and who, although perhaps historically significant, was relatively unknown. With this as a base, the book attempts to discuss the complex interrelationships of the artists and musical styles that occupy these levels of popularity.

Movie Star News

Unlike most of the popular music after the 1950s, this earlier period's musical hits of the first half of the century were usually written by professional, nonperforming tunesmiths who provided songs for plot lines in Broadway musicals or Hollywood films. Irving Berlin, the "Dean of American Song," wrote for scores of musical revues and musical comedies before writing for Hollywood. He was the only songwriter whose name was placed *above* the title of a film on the marquee. Both Fred Astaire and Ginger Rogers, who were to become film's greatest dance couple, had their starts (separately) on Broadway.

The Underground

In contrast to the artists of the popular mainstream, the musical "underground" of performers were primarily those artists who were considered unacceptable for the mass (white) market because they were too "other" —too regional, too raw, too socially dangerous—or simply because they were black or, almost as detrimental, hillbilly. These artists were by no means always the artistically innovative unknowns that one might intuitively think of when asked to name some underground performers. As defined in this book, their underground character is not necessarily a function of the music they played, although certainly their music was a very significant contributing factor in defining their status. Rather, it is a function of how the pop music establishment viewed them, as well as the results of the societal constraints placed upon them and the resulting lack of complete commercial success. Underground artists ran the gamut from the nearly acceptable, for example, Count Basie, to the completely unacceptable, for example, Bo Carter, a veritable king of raunchy songs. These two artists differ in almost every respect—in the sophistication of their work, in their class outlook, in their audience, in their historical reputation—but they shared in the time they worked the virtual guarantee that they would not be granted mainstream popular status.

But it is also a fact that what went for Count Basie went double for Bo Carter. Second-tier artists at least got to *think* about a shot at the big time; third-tier artists did not. Early underground jazz, blues, and country artists were virtually never given an opportunity to perform on national radio hookups, appear in the more prestigious theaters, hotels, or nightclubs, or be seen in Hollywood films. To see a performance of a third-tier traditional jazzman like Bunk Johnson, a rural bluesman like Blind Lemon Jefferson, or a country string band like Charlie Poole's North Carolina Ramblers, one would have had to go to the region where that artist performed. Bunk Johnson would be playing in a rural Louisiana brass marching band or in a small juke joint, (the economically deprived cafes that housed a juke box) the major source of record-listening in poor communities. Blind Lemon Jefferson would be found playing on street corners or outdoor picnics in Dallas. And Charlie Poole would likely be found performing at school houses or tent shows somewhere in the mountains of North Carolina. None of these performers had access to the national spotlight that was available to the better-known artists.

Thankfully, the third-tier performers had access to the 78 record, which saved for posterity much of their "roots" music for future generations of Americans. The records that these performers made were marketed as "race" or "hillbilly" music, and they were distributed in geographic regions that favored them. During the early 1920s, record companies sent field units into the South to find and record the artists who made these kinds of music. They advertised in local newspapers for "original, down home talent," set up in downtown hotel suites, and waited for the performers to arrive from far and wide.

Sitting outside these hotel rooms, awaiting their auditions, white farmers with fiddles and guitars would sit next to blacks clutching guitars and harmonicas. Most of these performers were given a flat fee for each "side" (of a record) they recorded. Most were not informed of songwriting copyright protection and did not receive royalties for records eventually sold. The record company executives acted as gatekeepers who allowed lesser-known artists an opportunity to gain star recognition in their communities, but seldom were these "stars" included in the bigger profits.

Third-tier artists are only half of the underground story. Colorful as they often are, perhaps the most interesting of the artists covered in this book are those of the second tier. These are the artists who achieved a substantial degree of success—regular work, financial security, recognition outside of a narrow geographic area—but did not gain the sustained national attention—nationwide radio hookups, central Hollywood movie roles, prestigious nightclub and theater bookings—of the first tier of popular artists, the mainstream.

The second-tier artists are interesting because, although they gained only limited recognition at the time they were working, today they are often far and away better known than their first-tier counterparts. At the time they were active, second-tier artists like Louis Armstrong, Duke Ellington, and Billie Holiday (in jazz), Bessie Smith, Louis Jordan, and Dinah Washington (blues), and Jimmie Rodgers, Gene Autry,

Ben Selvin's career as a bandleader spanned 1917 to 1934. According to big band authority George T. Simon, Selvin recorded over nine thousand discs, making him "the most prolific recording artist of all time." Selvin began leading his own band in 1917 at the Moulin Rouge on Broadway and by 1934 had recorded under an astounding number of pseudonyms. The dearth of information about this popular mainstream bandleader is not surprising, given the lack of attention to artists of the first quarter of this century. With all of those recordings to draw from there hasn't been an available album of Ben Selvin's music in years.

and Bob Wills (country), ranged from fairly well-known and respected in some circles (Armstrong was one of these), to known but begrudingly respected (Autry). Yet these and many other artists of this tier over time gained stature in the estimation of critics and historians, so that today they are considered greats of their respective genres. At the time they were certainly much more visible and better known than the likes of Bunk Johnson, Blind Lemon Jefferson, and Charlie Poole. But compared to the popular giants of various periods covered in this book—Paul Whiteman, Al Jolson, Ben Selvin, Ruth Etting, Guy Lombardo, Bing Crosby, Benny Goodman, Kay Kyser, Frank Sinatra, and the Andrews Sisters—the second-tier artists were less widely known. The major pop stars all recorded for major record labels, headlined nationally syndicated radio shows, starred in major Hollywood films, and were seen by the world at large.

For music writers and historians, however, the opposite has pretty much been the case. In general, these people have written artistic rather than popular histories of American music, with the result that many less popular artists have been given much more attention and contemporary recognition than the more popular artists of the time. Two cases are particularly instructive. Billy Murray, a sentimental and novelty balladeer most popular from the beginning of the century to the middle of World War I, was easily the best-selling recording artist of his time. Yet, it is difficult to find even passing references to him in most music histories and almost impossible to find a recording of him today. The same is true for bandleader Ben Selvin. He was active in the 1920s and 1930s and has the distinction of recording more songs than any musical artist before or since. Yet, once again, the material available on him adds up to only a few paragraphs—and like Billy Murray, no album package can be found of his work. Most contemporary music historians follow the taste of our times and write about the musicians currently in favor: Louis Armstrong, Fletcher Henderson, Duke Ellington, Robert Johnson, Billie Holiday, Lester Young, Charlie Parker, Miles Davis, and the like, at the expense of what they consider "popular pap" of the time.

Fats Waller, the great pianist-singer-humorist, was the leading hit-maker of the underground during the first half of the twentieth century (sixty-three chart hits and six number ones). Like most second-tier underground stars Waller's career was languishing until he secured astute management. And, like most African-American artists of this period, that meant white management. The prejudicial practices in America made it extremely difficult, if not impossible, for most blacks to get ahead. In the entertainment industry there were those select few like Fats Waller who did achieve "crossover" success into mainstream pop. When Waller hired Phil Ponce, a white music industry veteran, his career changed for the better.

Ben Selvin's Recording Pseudonyms: 1921-1933

Violinist, vocalist, composer and bandleader—later RCA Victor "Artists' Manager," Ben Selvin, is said to have made over nine thousand recordings under many names—over a hundred pseudonyms. This sampler gives two representative examples of Selvin's pseudonyms between 1921 and 1933. The leader usually recorded under the title of Selvin's Novelty Orchestra or Selvin's Dance Orchestra. In 1931 alone, Selvin made an untold number of recordings under his own name and as: the Cavaliers, Johnny Walker and His Orchestra, Mickie Alpert and His Orchestra, Enrique Madriguera's Havana Casino Orchestra, Madriquera Y Sus Notas Magicas, Chester Leighton and His Sophomores, Frank Auburn and His Orchestra, Wally Edwards and His Orchestra, Ray Selley and His Orchestra, Ed Lloyd and His Orchestra, Jack Whitney and His Orchestra, Sam Nash and His Orchestra, Roof Garden Orchestra, Buddy Campbell and His Orchestra, Golden Terrace Orchestra, Roy Carroll and His Sands Point Orchestra, Lloyd Keating and His Music, Phil Hughes and His High Hatters, Jack Whitney and His Orchestra, Ted Raph and His Orchestra, the Knickerbockers, Jerry Fenweyck and His Orchestra, Georgia Moonlight Serenaders, Cloverdale Country Club Orchestra, Ariel Dance Orchestra, Ed Parker and His Orchestra, D'Orsay Dance Orchestra, the Campus Collegiates, Hotel Commodore Dance Orchestra, and the Broadway Bandits.

Pseudonym	Song	Label	Year
Frisco Syncopators	Mr. Gallagher and Mr. Shean	Broadway	1921
Moulin Rouge Orchestra	Three O'Clock in the Morning	Arto	1921
Regal Dance Orchestra	Do It Again	Regal	1922
Majestic Dance Orchestra	Truly	Puritan	1922
Palm Beach Players	Dreamy Melody	Beltona	1923
Cleveland Society Orchestra	A Kiss in the Dark	Ace	1923
Erco Novelty Orchestra	Charley, My Boy	Citizen	1924
The Cavaliers	I Wonder What's Become of Sally	Columbia	1924
Hollywood Dance Orchestra	Paddlin' Madelin' Home	Starr	1925
The Knickerbockers	The Original Charleston	Columbia	1925
Kensington Serenaders	Meet Me in the Moonlight	Vocalion	1926
Denza Dance Band	Too Many Parties and too Many Pals	Columbia	1926
The Rhythmic Troubadours	Up in the Clouds	Regal	1927
The Broadway Nitelites	Bye, Bye, Pretty Baby	Columbia	1927
Musical Comedy Orchestra	Moon of My Delight	Harmony	1928
Stella Dance Band	Ramona	Columbia	1928
Perley Stevans and His Orchestra	I Kiss Your Hand, Madame	Harmony	1929
Roof Garden Orchestra	Why?	Parlophone	1929
Columbia Photo Players	Live and Love Today	Columbia	1930
Johnny Walker and His Orchestra	Personally, I Love You	Columbia	1930
Mickie Alpert and His Orchestra	I Surrender, Dear	Columbia	1931
Georgia Moonlight Serenaders	Many Happy Returns of the Day	Harmony	1931
Cloverdale Country Club Orchestra	Goodnight, Moon	Okeh	1932
Lloyd Keating and His Music	Auf Wiedersehen, My Dear	Harmony	1932
Fran Frey and His Orchestra	Learn to Croon	Columbia	1933
The Broadway Bandits	Dinner at Eight	Regal Zonophone	1933

Source: Brian Rust's The American Dance Band Discography: 1917-1942

Duke Ellington, to use the most prominent second-tier example, had a fair number of hits during his long and distinguished career and has become the most highly regarded band leader in jazz history. However, of the thousands of records he made between the 1920s and the 1970s, Ellington had only two recordings that made number one on the charts (on a third number one hit he provided backing for Bing Crosby). In major Hollywood film releases Ellington and his band performed a number or two, but he wasn't the star or the main focus.

Duke Ellington and other black entertainers of the time, like Lena Horne and Cab Calloway, were usually not part of film storylines, so that when these films were shown in the South, their musical sequences could simply be deleted. (*Stormy Weather* and *Cabin in the Sky,* two major Hollywood all-black cast films of the 1940s, were rare exceptions to the rule.) Ellington did not have his own nationally syndicated radio show like Paul Whiteman or Benny Goodman. Between 1927 and 1930 Ellington did receive national recognition by being heard on over two hundred broadcasts from the Cotton Club in Harlem, which did enhance his reputation, but his "Jungle Band" mainly provided background music for the club's elaborate variety shows. Air checks from those broadcasts provide examples of the white announcers referring to an exotic, noble savage, jungle-type atmosphere, and to the band leader as the "greatest living master of jungle music, the rip-roaring harmony-hound, none other than Duke

Ellington." We are talking here about Duke Ellington, the bandleader in America who has more books written about him than any other bandleader, a man widely recognized even then as a musical genius. As important and recognized as he was, Ellington is a second- tier artist because, relatively speaking, he just wasn't as solidly successful as his first-tier counterparts. The second-tier stars were usually represented by white managers who signed them to major record labels, occasionally were featured on syndicated radio shows, and had walk-on, rather than star roles in Hollywood movies. Their success came from their abilities to "cross over," to capture, albeit momentarily, the attention of the mass audience. Their regional or ethnic identities (hillbilly or black) meant that they could not compete with Bing Crosby, Paul Whiteman or Tommy Dorsey.

But many second-tier artists have been revenged for being short-changed for all those years: they are famous today. Some of their first-tier counterparts are unknowns. Popularity should not be the end-all of pop music history, but neither should it be ignored. Duke Ellington's music has lasted, and not only because contemporary critics like it. But it is also the case that Paul Whiteman's music, for example, has not lasted, largely because it has been ignored by critics both past and present.

Courtesy American Society of Composers, Authors, and Publishers

Duke Ellington emerged as a star at the Cotton Club in Harlem under the management direction of Irving Mills, with whom Ellington had a fourteen-year business relationship, ending in 1939. Very little has been unearthed about the great majority of popular, jazz, blues, and country artists' finances. John Edward Hasse, writing in *Beyond Category: The Life and Genius of Duke Ellington,* gives some information on one of Ellington's more successful years: "A 1944 year-end financial statement prepared by the accounting firm of Frendel, Brown and Company showed Duke Ellington, Inc., had an income of $405,000 (twice the gross reported just two years earlier, confirming that Ellington's marketability was rising) and expenses of $394,000, which yielded a profit of just $11,000." As Hesse notes, "He was doing well, though not getting rich."

Ellington led a band longer than any bandleader in the history of American music—1927 to 1974. During the aftermath of the war years most large orchestras of the swing era suffered economically. Donald Clarke notes in *The Rise and Fall of Popular Music*, that, "The decline in the quality of Ellington's output is only relative. More personnel changes than at any other time in the band's history must have been dispiriting; times were hard for bands and from the late 1940s the band lost money and was kept going by Ellington's royalties."

Duke Ellington's music speaks for itself, but so would Paul Whiteman's, if in somewhat less artistically sophisticated ways, were it only given the chance. Like most American music, both artists' work speaks for their complex musical origins as well as for themselves and the audience they served.

Mainstream Stars: 1900-1950		
Artist	Chart Hits	# 1 Hits
1. Bing Crosby	294	36
2. Paul Whiteman	219	32
3. Guy Lombardo	202	26
4. Tommy Dorsey	185	17
5. Billy Murray	169	18
6. Benny Goodman	162	16
7. Glenn Miller	129	23
8. Henry Burr	116	16
9. Peerless Quartet	108	6
10. Ben Selvin	107	8
11. Ted Lewis	102	6
12. Jimmy Dorsey	100	12
13. Sammy Kaye	98	8
14. Harry MacDonough	97	15
15. Al Jolson	91	23
16. Arthur Collins and Byron Harlan	89	12
17. Andrews Sisters	88	6
18. Frank Sinatra	80	4
19. Freddie Martin	79	6
Leo Reisman	79	5
20. Kay Kyser	78	1

Source: Joel Whitburn's Pop Memories 1890-1954

Underground Stars: 1900-1950		
Artist	Charted Hits	# 1 Hits
Jazz		
1. Duke Ellington	68	3
2. Fats Waller	63	6
3. Louis Armstrong	61	1
4. Cab Calloway	43	1
5. Ella Fitzgerald	42	3
6. Billie Holiday	39	1
Blues (Rhythm and Blues)		
1. Mills Brothers	50	4
2. Ink Spots	45	6
3. Nat King Cole	29	3
4. Louis Jordan	19	1
5. Lionel Hampton	15	1
6. Bessie Smith	12	6
Country (and Western)		
1. Vernon Dalhart	27	1
2. Gene Autry	24	1
3. Jimmy Wakely	11	1
4. Eddy Arnold	11	0
5. Bob Wills	9	0
6. Jimmie Rodgers	8	0

Source: Joel Whitburn's Pop Memories 1890-1954

These charts represent, respectively, the mainstream popular and underground music that Americans listened to from 1900 to 1950. These charts also represent, for the most part, music that is currently held in low regard (much of the mainstream pop). Music that is, in many instances, today considered to be classic (much of the underground). The numbers are not pristine indicators of the total musical picture, however. Consider the following analysis:

1) Kay Kyser's 78 charted hits and Duke Ellington's 68 total are farther apart than the numbers suggest. Kyser's hits were more consistently in the top ten (47 out of 78), which was not the case for Ellington (22 out of 68), and he had 11 number one hits to Ellington's 3 in a chart career that lasted fourteen years versus Ellington's twenty. (The reference here, to the numbers of the top ten recordings, have been calculated by the author, and are not reprinted in this book.)

2) Fats Waller, on the other hand, had a greater hit ratio than any other underground performer—his 63 hits and 6 number ones were amassed in fifteen years before he died prematurely at the age of thirty-nine.

3) Glenn Miller's hit ratio was the greatest of all—from (essentially) 1938 to his death in 1944—in seven years he had over 125 charted hits and 23 number one hits.

4) Both Ben Selvin and Vernon Dalhart are served well by the charts for their respective musical styles, however, there is no indication given to the enormity of their total output, which would have been reflected in their total record sales, if those record sales, if those numbers were available. Both had a penchant for recording under pseudonyms, and are reputed to have used over one hundred different assumed professional names.

5) The overall reliability of the chart information. It is understandable that this timeframe fascination with jazz-oriented dance bands ran high at the expense of country music, therefore Vernon Dalhart and Jimmie Rodgers seem to be cast suspiciously low. Recent changes in the tabulating of national record store sales have resulted in a volcanic upsurge of country's retail numbers today. It simply raises doubts about past measurement practices.

6) The numbers of the pre-jazz era vocalists (Billy Murray, Henry Burr, Harry McDonough, the Peerless Quartet, and the team of Arthur Collins and Byron Harlan, reflect the post-Gay Nineties sentimental parlor-song era which occurred during the infancy years of the phonograph player. This is not to cast doubt on the significance of these artists, especially Billy Murray, who also had three separate charting identities with a duo and two groups—but their record sales numbers in contrast to those artists of the 1930s and 1940s was considerably lower. It is hard to find a recording of any of these pre-jazz age artists today.

7) A number of vocalists are somewhat hindered by the overall tabulation system which places a separate heading which doesn't total in the overall numbers. Bing Crosby's hits with the Andrews Sisters, and vice versa, as well as with others, are counted independently. Hits sung by an artist while a member of an orchestra tabulates for that leader, (e.g., Frank Sinatra's hits while a member of the Harry James and Tommy Dorsey bands, as well as being a member of the Pied Pipers vocal group, do not count toward the singer's overall total numbers.

8) Finally, there is an aspect of illegitimacy in the "Blues (Rhythm and Blues)" category. The Mills Brothers and Ink Spots were not primarily blues singers—they were often closer to the barbershop harmonies of groups like the Peerless Quartet, American Quartet, and Hayden Quartet (the big three of pre-jazz pop vocal groups) than to any other style. However, both groups were regulars on *Billboard* magazine's Harlem Hit Parade charts (now referred to as rhythm and blues). Their smooth vocal harmonies, dapper dress style, occasional jazz and jive novelties, and prestigious guest appearances in film and their radio shows, provided the main models for the doo wop groups like the Ravens, Orioles, and those that followed in the 1950s and '60s. Nat King Cole, Louis Jordan, and Lionel Hampton essentially came from the world of jazz, but in the 1940s, with the advent of the modernists (beboppers), these three, along with many other jazzers, were relegated to the "Harlem Hit Parade" (read, rhythm and blues). Bessie Smith is the only *true* blues artist in this chart, but hardly any blues performers were charted during this time period. During the 1940s much of rhythm and blues was really jazz-with-a-beat.

So what does this all mean? Considering all factors, the pop mainstream reflects the artists that sold records to the most people. The histories that promulgate the underground artists over the mainstream are those that choose to focus on musical aesthetics more than true popularity. The underground, however, did provide examples of genius (Louis Armstrong and Duke Ellington), a wellspring of musical authenticity (Bessie Smith and Jimmie Rodgers, to name just two), and a font of musical descendents (Bob Wills and the Mills Brothers).

Library of Congress

Country music being made in the home. British and Scottish ballads of old as well as religious songs were favorites of practitioners of mountaineer or hillbilly music. Record executives realized that the low cost of recording regional artists, like those above, could mean big profits for the record companies. This underground music was given various names—"Old Southern Tunes," "Folk Music," "Old Southern Favorites," and sometimes "Hillbilly Music."

The picture above is a Library of Congress shot of a string band led by Fields Ward of Virginia (the members are unidentified). Ward was better known to folklorists than to the commercial country audience because of his reluctance to make recordings. His recordings for Okeh Records in 1927, and for the Bennett Record Company in 1929 led to his life-long embitterment toward the commercial world of record-making. The first releases were considered unsatisfactory, and from the second session, which Ward felt was representative of his best work, the recordings were not even released. Ward worked with a number of groups over the years, including: the Grayson County Railsplitters, the Buck Mountain String Band (led by his Uncle Wade), and with a family band called the Bogtrotters. According to Barry McCloud in *Definitive Country*, the Bogtrotters "won numerous prizes at the fiddlers' convention held in Galax in 1935 and were a big hit at the Whitetop Folk Festival that same year. They also came to the attention of northern, urban audiences and between 1937 and 1942, various combinations of the Bogtrotters recorded, in Galax and Washington D.C., a number of tunes for Alan Lomax at the Library of Congress."

Library of Congress

African-Americans who recorded for the record companies from the 1920s to the 1940s, were referred to as "Race Artists." Above, is Reverend Gary Davis, a blind blues singer who began his professional career at the turn of the century as a street singer busking on corners. (Busking was the universal practice of earning money by entertaining on well-traveled street corners.) Broadway's nine-time Tony Award winner, Tommy Tune, opened a musical entitled *Buskers* in the fall of 1995. By 1933, Davis was a Baptist minister who sang gospel, played ragtime guitar, and sang blues. He made his first recordings in 1935. In blues circles, Davis is best known for his song "Candy Man" (not the Sammy Davis, Jr. pop hit).

America's premier assimilationist of underground music: Ray Benson of Asleep at the Wheel. Ray Benson, like a great majority of the underground musicians he admires, is not well known to today's mainstream popular audience. He is a widely respected leader of a country music group which is best known for playing a brand of western swing and honky tonk music. His Asleep at the Wheel unit made its recording debut for United Artists in 1974 (*Comin' Right at Ya*), and the group has been firmly directed by the musical sensibility of its lean 6'7" leader ever since. All styles of underground forms are represented by Benson's charges—jazz, blues, and country (and many of the subgenres within).

Benson, as might be expected, is an avid collector of records. "The record player is my university, I've got 50 years of the greatest teachers in the world that I can sit right there on the record player. And that's how they learned, too, by listening to other musicians, and by developing their ears. I enjoy Wynonie Harris, Roy Brown, Lucky Millinder, Joe Turner, I like a lot of modern jazz, all the bop stuff, love Art Tatum, Benny Goodman, Hank Williams, Merle Haggard, George Jones, Spade Cooley. All the boogie woogie piano players, Fats Waller I love. There are so many, and not all of them are huge selling artists. Most are just good musicians, people who plied the trade, did the craft, and were great at it; they had something to say, emotionally." (*Down Beat* magazine, June 17, 1975.)

In an interview with David Zimmerman in *USA Today* (November 2, 1993), Benson noted that western swing great Bob Wills didn't think of himself as a country musician, "He considered himself a big band leader a la Glenn Miller and Tommy Dorsey, although he had fiddles and steel guitar." Benson has been a leader in the area of trying to break down barriers between musical forms—especially the incompatibility factor between jazz and country. "I hasten to remind people that jazz was born in the South in New Orleans and Mississippi and in Oklahoma and Texas and Kansas. I never saw any incompatibility."

16

Chapter 2

THE BEGINNING

In the beginning there was no jazz, blues, country, or rock. These musical forms were created as the result of an amazing cross-cultural mix found only in the United States. Possibly the most significant development in twentieth century music has been the maturation of African-American musical culture and its integration with several other American musical traditions.

William Tallmadge, in his *Jazz Rock Foundations,* (privately published), points out that African slaves brought to this hemisphere two separate but related musical cultures. The slaves from the rainforest areas along the coast of West Africa brought with them their percussive instruments and polyrhythms, while the Muslim slaves from the savannah areas of West Africa brought their inflected tonal system and their skills on bowed and plucked stringed instruments (their *bania* became the American banjo). In America the two musical systems blended with Western European music to form a completely new musical culture.

The newly arrived slaves possessed a highly developed tradition of music-making characterized by at least ten West African elements that served to differentiate their music from that of Europeans:

1. Syncopation
2. Polymeter
3. Improvisation
4. Dominance of percussion
5. Emotional or "hot" performance
6. Trance
7. Leader-chorus
8. Vocal harmony in parallel intervals
9. Unity of song and dance
10. Neutral third (in Muslim areas)

Library of Congress

A brief description of these elements will outline some of the main differences between the European and African musical traditions. *Syncopation* occurs when an instrument or voice sounds a fraction of a movement in advance or behind the beat. Syncopation was to become an ubiquitous feature of all African-American music. Most music from the Old World Featured music that was on the beat (sometimes called "square" by jazz musicians). Africans performed with a natural inclination not only to syncopate but to include many different rhythms simultaneously—*polymeter*. A number of early missionaries to West Africa reported that Africans had no sense of rhythm. In actuality, the European ear, accustomed to hearing hymn tunes and four-square rhythms, was unable to comprehend the intricate complexities of the more rhythmically advanced Africans.

Library of Congress
Artwork by Miguel Covarrubias.

While the written musical score has been the trademark of Western music, African tradition relied on improvisation—on-the-spot alterations of the basic music. When a written composition is repeated, each repetition is approximately the same. This is rarely true of the repeated African performance.

The African tradition is also dominated by percussive effects. While harmony and melody are the two strongest characteristics of European music, rhythmic propulsion dominates the African heritage. Work songs were sung to the stroke of a hammer or hoe, and spirituals were sung to the accompaniment of clapping or foot-tapping. Later, in America, drums and tambourines would support gospel songs, and drums would be a basic instrument in jazz and rock.

The ritual music of West Africa was highly emotional. This charged (or "hot") performance was transferred to the Americas by the slaves, where it was later heard in blues, gospel, jazz, and rock. As Tallmadge contends, "The hot, emotional character of much African traditional music is directly related to those elements in the music which can induce a state of hypnosis or trance in some listeners or participants." Repetition of drum rhythms, hand claps, bass lines, and short melodic phrases (riffs) creates a hypnotic, trance-like effect. In both African tribal rites where members are "possessed," it is the constant, pulsating rhythms that induces the trance-like state. Most popular dance crazes, be it the flapper era of the twenties, the swing of the thirties, disco of the seventies, the mosh pit of the eighties, or the pulsating throb of the industrial techno-rave of the nineties, feature repetitive, trance-inducing rhythms.

Library of Congress

The Library of Congress lists this picture as "Dahomey man beating drum." The talking drum, an African tradition, is one of the most important aspects of rhythm in the African-American tradition. In *Stomping the Blues*, Albert Murray has noted that the talking drum effect carried over into the riffs of the black swing bands like those of Count Basie in the 1930s and 1940s.

Library of Congress

The dominance of percussion is one of the most important elements of the African-American musical tradition. The beating of drums, the tapping of wooden blocks, the repetitious thumping of string bass, or the striking of a xylophone are all examples of percussion. Above, the African equivalent of the xylophone.

A response style of leader-chorus singing of psalms, called "precenting" or "lining-out," came to America from England. The style was applied to hymns and introduced to slaves in Virginia by 1750. About a hundred years later slaves and freedmen came in contact with another white form of response hymnody called gospel song. In both cases black singers found a similarity with their own musical backgrounds, and appropriated and Africanized elements of the white forms.

Music-making in West Africa was largely functional, that is, it accompanied activities such as praising a deity, paddling a boat, harvesting, traveling from one village to another, puberty ceremonies, and much else. Usually, some form of dancing and singing accompanied these activities. Also, the singing was usually harmonized in parallel intervals, most often parallel thirds.

18

Lastly, in savannah areas of West Africa, particularly among the Muslim tribes, certain tones of the scale are slightly lowered in pitch when compared to European standards. Muslim slaves transferred this tonal system to America, where such pitches, when combined with the European harmonic system, produced a totally new musical effect that has been called "blues tonality" or "blue notes."

A number of these African elements were common in European folk music. However, the strongest legacy of the white European traditions in America was harmony, melody, counterpoint, compositional forms and instrumentation (keyboard, trumpet, saxophone, among others). It was the blending of these elements of African and European music that resulted in an unparalleled musical quiltwork. The forms of jazz, blues, country, and rock were all born in the United States. The off-stated claim by jazz historians, players, and fans that jazz is the only original musical art form created in America is well-intended but wrong-headed. The various forms of blues, country and rock'n'roll were created as part of America's unique musical melange and are just as significant as jazz. These forms all were part of the underground and at various times, as this book will point out, made contributions in large and small ways to the popular music scene.

Minstrelsy: Blackface or Ethiopian Music

EDDIE CANTOR

Movie Star News

Along with Al Jolson, Eddie Cantor was the only star to portray blackface minstrels in Hollywood with any regularity. While black-face (originally called burnt cork) was not common in American popular music after the 1920s, the tradition continued into the late 1940s in the more conservative South. Country musicians of significance like Roy Acuff (in the 1930s) and Bill Monroe (in the 1940s) featured blackface entertainment as part of their show.

The banjo was derived from the African *bania*. This caricature drawing is representative of the Daddy Rice — "Jim Crow" tradition.

Probably the first massive input of black culture into mainstream America was the development of the minstrel show. Formed between 1820 and 1840, minstrelsy became the first original theatrical form created in America. Called "black face," or "Ethiopian music," it featured whites using burnt cork to blacken their faces and take on broad characterizations of black speech, dance, and music. Little of the minstrel show was a true reflection of African-American culture. Sometime between 1829 and 1832 Thomas Dartmouth ("Daddy") Rice became famous for his song and dance, "Jim Crow," which was a caricature of a certain illiterate black stablehand. The act was first presented at the Bowery Theater in New York City to delighted audiences, who found Rice's portrayal of black people amusing. Rice performed with great success in England in 1836. A typical minstrel show was made up of three parts: Introduction (interlocuter with Mr. Tambo and Mr. Bones), Olio (variety acts and burlesque/parody), and ensemble finale (walk around, cakewalk).

In the introduction, "Mr. Interlocutor" would come out on stage and welcome the audience. He would sit or stand in the center of a semicircle of four or five men in blackface who played tambourines and engage the "end men," Mr. Tambo (who played tambourine), and Mr. Bones (who played bone castanets), in jokes and songs. After this humorous opening the interlocutor would move on to the "Olio" section, which featured independent acts such as a singer of a popular song of the day, an animal act, an instrumental group, or a burlesque or parody of a well-known play (perhaps *Uncle Tom's Cabin*, or a well-known opera). This portion of the show became the basis of the vaudeville show of the first three decades of the twentieth century and future television variety shows (such as that hosted by Ed Sullivan). The burlesque, or parody, was the basis of topical humor television shows like "Saturday Night Live." The final section, the "ensemble finale," featured banjo picking, and a full chorus singing and dancing. The dancing was sometimes called a "walk around," which featured high-stepping numbers such as the cakewalk.

Musicologists have referred to the simple beginnings of minstrelsy, 1842 to 1875, as its "Golden Age." The more commercialized period, from 1875 to 1895, was labeled the "Second Age of Minstrelsy." The later period featured much larger casts, and the show also tended to become more overtly racist by placing an emphasis on the "darky" as comic buffoon (a happy-go-lucky, chicken-stealin', foot-shufflin' ignoramus who was lazy but over-sexed). In spite of this, minstrel shows were popular in many black communities (especially in the rural South), and by 1865, blacks themselves (such as the Georgia Minstrels) entered the minstrel field.

Primrose and West's Big Minstrels were one of the more popular troupes during the late 1800s and early 1900s in America. This ad pictures the most famous of all the walk arounds.

Bert Williams: The first Black star on Broadway.

Bert Williams (1874-1922), born in the British West Indies, was one of the few blacks to star on Broadway. He debuted with his partner, George Walker, in 1896, when they were billed "The Two Real Coons." They encapsulated the two main contrasting minstrel show figures, Jim Dandy and Zip Coon. After Walker's death in 1911, Williams went on to greater fame as a solo artist. He introduced his signature song, "Nobody," in 1910, and between 1911 and 1919 (except for 1914) he appeared with the Ziegfeld Follies. He broke from the Follies in 1914 because he was given headline honors on the Keith circuit at $2,000 per week. Williams was a proud, educated man who resented having to work in blackface. But he recognized the circumstance of his life as an entertainer. In 1917 he wrote an article for *American* magazine that noted, in part: "How do I know what I might be if I were a white man? I might be a sandhog, burrowing away and losing my health for $8 a day. I might be a streetcar conductor at $12 or $15 a week. There is many a white man less fortunate and less equipped than I am. In fact, I have never been able to discover that there was anything disgraceful in being a colored man. But I have found it inconvenient—in America."

Minstrel Troupes

Troupe	Key Songs/Information	Began
Virginia Minstrels	Jimmy Crack Corn (Blue Tail Fly)	1843
Virginia Serenaders	Old Dan Tucker; I Wish I Was in Dixie's Land; led by E. P. Christy	1843
Bryant's Minstrels	Dixie; Down in Alabam; Ain't I Glad I Got Out de Wilderness (The Old Grey Mare)	1857
Brooker & Clayton's Georgia Minstrels	First black minstrel troupe of note	1865
Buckley's Serenaders	Regulars on southern circuit	1853
J. W. Rayror & Earl Pierce's version of Christy Minstrels	Nelly Gray; Purloined name and sent to London	1857
Montague's Christy Minstrels/Queen's Minstrels	British troupe of 50 performers	1860s
Mohawk Minstrels	Brothers James & William Francis in England became leading publishers of minstrel and music-hall songs	1870s

America's First Great Songwriter

Stephen Foster did not write only happy minstrel songs. Two of the most enduring ballads in American popular music were his tributes to his wife: "Jeanie With the Light Brown Hair" and the lovely "Beautiful Dreamer." His embarassment at writing minstrel songs led him to sell (cheaply) the rights to a few of his songs to E. P. Christy.

Stephen Foster (1826-1864) was one of the first truly popular tunesmiths in America. He sought fame writing serious ballad compositions and was embarrassed by his association with minstrel songs. As a result, Foster signed over the rights to many of his minstrel songs to others. And while he made a decent living with his drawing-room ballads (it is estimated that he received about $15,000 in royalties between 1849 and 1860), his minstrel songs would eventually be the source of his later fame. Songs such as "Oh! Susanna" (1848), "Camptown Races" (1850), "Old Folks at Home" (or "Swanee River") (1851), "My Old Kentucky Home" (1853), and "Old Black Joe" (1860) were made famous by Christy's Minstrels. As Ian Whitcomb points out in *After the Ball: Pop Music from Rag to Rock*, "Foster is the first pop composer but he lived in prehistoric times, pre-Chas K. Harris, pre-Alley, pre-pleasure."

In *All the Years of American Popular Music* David Ewen contends that **Dan Emmett** (1815-1904) should be considered the founding father of the minstrel show, as well the first major composer to emanate from it. Emmett, a white man, wrote his first "black" song, "Bill Crowder," in the late 1830s. It was based on the melody of Daddy Rice's tune, "Gumbo Chaff." The song was sung in a circus setting in Cincinnati, Ohio; the performer was a blackface equestrian.

According to Ewen, "Emmett made his stage debut as a blackface performer with the Cincinnati Circus company by doing Negro impersonations, playing the banjo and singing. In the early 1840s he also appeared with Spalding's North American Circus. Then, in 1842, Emmett formed an act with Frank Brower, a dancer, singer, and one of the earliest known stage performers on the bones." Emmett made his formal debut with his group, the Virginia Minstrels, at the Bowery Amphitheater on February 6, 1843. The *New York Herald* reported, "First night of the novel, grotesque, original, and surprisingly melodious Ethiopian band, entitled the Virginia Minstrels, being an exclusively musical entertainment combining the banjo, violin, bone castanets, and tambourine, and entirely exempt from the vulgarities and other objectionable features which have hitherto characterized Negro extravaganzas."

The Virginia Minstrels developed as a four-man troupe that wore costumes of black plantation workers, seated on stage in a semicircle. Emmett, on violin, and Billy Whitlock, playing tambourine, placed themselves in the center. At either end were Dick Pelham, who also played tambourine, and Frank Brower, who played bone castanets. Ewen continues, "In blackface, they played their instruments, sang, and indulged in humorous banter or in question-and-answer routines in Negro dialect." Songs such as "De Boatman's Dance" and "Old Dan Tucker" proved very popular with the audience at that performance. In 1846 Emmett introduced "De Blue Tail Fly," which was also known as "Jim Crack Corn" or "Jimmy Crack Corn." Burl Ives would introduce this to his folk music audience over radio during the 1940s. Emmett wrote his classic song, "Dixie," for the Bryant's Minstrels in 1859.

The success of Emmett's Virginia Minstrels led to a rash of imitators. Most important of those imitators was the troupe led by **E. P. Christy** (1815-1862), who called his original group "Christy's Original Band of Virginia Minstrels." He began with a four-man group in Buffalo, New York, in 1843, but it wasn't until he appeared in New York City in 1846, with an enlarged troupe, that he became famous. Ewen asserts, "If the Virginia Minstrels offered the bare skeleton of a minstrel show, Christy's Minstrels endowed it with muscles, sinews and flesh, developing the physiognomy by which the minstrel show would henceforth be identified."

Edwin P. Christy was considered "the greatest minstrel of them all," according to Ewen. He wrote "Goodnight Ladies" and claimed authorship of many of Stephen Foster's classic songs. Christy retired a wealthy man in 1854. His company was taken over by one George N. Harrington, who took Christy's name and image. Less than six months after the 1851 publication of "Old Folks at Home," Stephen Foster wrote Christy a letter. Highlights from that letter include: "As I once intimated to you, I had the intention of omitting my name on my Ethiopian songs, owing to the prejudice against them by some, which might injure my reputation as a writer of another style of music, but I find that by my efforts I have done a great deal to build up a taste for the Ethiopian songs among refined people by making the words suitable to their taste, instead of the trashy and really offensive words which belong to songs of that order. Therefore, I have concluded to reinstate my name on my songs and to pursue the Ethiopian business without fear or shame and lend all my energies to making the business here, at the same time that I will be able to establish my name as the Ethiopian song-writer. But I am not encouraged in undertaking this so long as, 'The Old Folks at Home' stares me in the face with another's name on it."

Library of Congress

A sheet music cover of Christy's Minstrels. The group of six men are the minstrel performers in various poses.

By the twentieth century, Christy followers like George Evans, Eddie Leonard, and Lew Dockstader headed companies of over a hundred minstrels. Evans was known as "Honey Boy," after his popular song "I'll Be True to My Honey Boy," and he wrote the classic "In the Good Old Summertime." Dockstader often combined with the great minstrel George Primrose, and later toured the country with his own show, the Dockstader's Minstrels. A young Al Jolson was a member of Dockstader's Minstrels beginning in 1908.

By the turn of the century the minstrel show was on the decline in America. Not only was it considered somewhat embarrassing, but vaudeville had appropriated many of its best elements. Many popular artists had their start as blackface performers. The most famous, of course, was Al Jolson. Popular music stars Eddie Cantor, Sophie Tucker, and country music great Jimmie Rodgers, all white, and Bert Williams, the most successful black artist of the pre-1917 to 1934 period, all started in blackface.

Ragtime

Out of the banjo songs of minstrelsy developed a syncopated music set against a march-type ("oompah") bass line. To "rag" a musical selection was to syncopate it, and in the late 1800s the word represented a wide variety of music. As we know it today, ragtime refers to the composed piano and band music that reached its pinnacle of success between 1895 and 1917. Ragtime is a merger of African and European traditions. Not all ragtime was composed; there were banjo players and pianists who played rags without following a score ("ear players"). Also, there were vocal rags known as "coon" songs that came out of the minstrel show. The longest lasting rags, however, have been the composed piano pieces that have been defined as "classic rag."

Courtesy William H. Tallmadge
Ben Harney, left, and John Biller, right.

Ben Harney (1871-1938), published "You've Been a Good Old Wagon but You've Done Broke Down," in 1895, establishing himself as the originator of both the ragtime song and piano ragtime. Harney's successful New York debut in 1896 "established his reputation as the first of the ragtime pianists," claims William Tallmadge in *Ben Harney: The Middlesboro Years.* Harney's life has been reported with speculative and fanciful bits of confusing misinformation. It has been reported that he was African-American or mulatto and that he attended military school as a youngster. Tallmadge's findings conclude that he was in fact the scion of two distinguished Kentucky families, the Harneys of Louisville and the Draffens of Anderson County, near Frankfort, Kentucky, the state capital.

Harney was white. He was influenced by black music and may have played the banjo as a young man. Middlesboro, Kentucky, was a boom town due to extensive coal, iron, and virgin timber resources exploited by entrepreneur Alexander Arthur to the tune of $30 million. While in Middlesboro, Harney worked as a clerk at the post office and played piano and composed songs in his spare time.

By the time Harney left Middlesboro for Louisville he had already begun performing "You've Been a Good Old Wagon." The song was taken to John Biller, musical director for Maucauley's Theater, and together they put on paper the first ragtime composition. The song was published in 1895 by the Greenup Music Company in Louisville. Tallmadge notes that, "Harney's stick dance, which he performed during the stop-time portion of the 'Dance' section of 'You've Been a Good Old Wagon But You've Done Broke Down,' was a kind of rhythmic tap dance that Ben did with his feet and a cane. An attenuated version of the stick dance was continued by Scott Joplin in his 1906 version, the 'Ragtime Dance.'"

Ewen contends that, "More than any other single person, Ben Harney was a pioneer in spreading the gospel of ragtime to New York in the 1890s. In 1896 he came to New York, making his debut as a performer of piano rags and as a singer at the Union Square Theater. He went on to star billing at Tony Pastor's Music Hall and to tour vaudeville houses in the East and Midwest." Harney apparently was quite a showman and was the first to "rag" classical music pieces such as Mendelssohn's "Spring Song," Rubinstein's "Melody in F," and the "Intermezzo" from Mascagni's *Cavalleria Rusticana*.

Harney's gains additional stature in the ragtime movement because of his 1897 *Ragtime Instructor*, which became the first primer on how to play ragtime music. Harney's demonstrations of how any piece of music could be played in ragtime did much to popularize the movement.

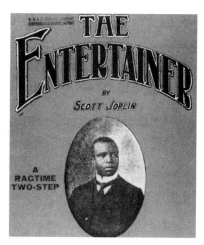

Courtesy Buffalo & Erie County Public Library

"The Entertainer" was used as a main theme in the 1973 film *The Sting*, starring Robert Redford and Paul Newman. Millions of Americans began humming this Joplin song, and albums by Joshua Rifkin and Gunther Schuller topped the classical music charts and placed high on the pop charts.

Classic Ragtime Compositions

Composer	Composition	Date
W. H. Krell	Mississippi Rag	1897
Tom Turpin	Harlem Rag	1897
Scott Joplin	Maple Leaf Rag	1899
Soctt Joplin	The Easy Winners	1901
Scott Joplin	Sunflower Slow Drag	1901
Scott Joplin	The Entertainer	1902
Charles L. Johnson	Dill Pickles	1906
James Scott	Frog Legs Rag	1906
Louis Chauvin-Joplin	Heliotrope Bouquet	1907
George Botsford	Black and White Rag	1908
Joseph Lamb	Sensation Rag	1908
James Scott	Grace and Beauty	1910
Clarence Woods	Slippery Elm Rag	1912
Joseph Lamb	American Beauty Rag	1913
Arthur Mathews	Pastime Rag No. 1	1913

Scott Joplin (1868-1917), the "King of Ragtime Writers," was the son of a railroad worker who had been born a slave. Joplin's parents were both musical; the father had played violin in plantation bands, and the mother sang and played banjo. As a teenager Joplin mastered the piano and began playing professionally in the bars and honky tonks around his hometown area of Texarkana. He organized the Texas Medley Quartet, and by 1885 he was playing piano in St. Louis at the Silver Dollar Saloon.

Joplin established a solid reputation around the Midwest and it is said that in 1893 he played outside the fairgrounds at the World's Colombian Exposition in Chicago. By 1895 he was seriously working toward publication of his music. Settled in Sedalia, Missouri, Joplin found good fortune when he met up with a publisher who was impressed with his compositions. In 1899 John Stark published Joplin's "Maple Leaf Rag" and it proved to be a big success, selling 75,000 copies of sheet music. Joplin wrote other hits, such as "Peacherine Rag," "The Easy Winners," "Elite Syncopations," and "The Entertainer," but he was not satisfied with commercial success; he sought classical status for his music.

Courtesy Biograph Records

Scott Joplin today is the best-known composer-artist of ragtime music. However, during his lifetime he was an underground performer. Because of the success of the film, *The Sting,* there was a general revival of ragtime music during the early 1970s. The film's producer, Roy G. Hill, heard Gunther Schuller's New England Conservatory Ragtime Ensemble recording of Joplin's *Red Back Book* and wanted Schuller to score the film. Because of contract obligations neither Schuller or Joshua Rifkin scored *The Sting.* Instead, Marvin Hamlisch was brought in to score the film for which he won an Academy Award.

Although he continued writing ragtime numbers, by 1911 he had become obsessed with the idea of putting on a full-scale opera. Unfortunately, his attempts to produce *A Guest of Honor,* (1903) *and Treemonisha* (1907) were never realized during his lifetime. After he failed to produce *Treemonisha* in Harlem in 1915, he had an emotional breakdown and was committed to the Manhattan State Hospital, where he died four years later. In 1976 Billy Dee Williams starred in a movie biography entitled *Scott Joplin, King of Ragtime*, with jazz archivist Dick Hyman providing the piano parts.

There were many other great ragtime names besides Ben Harney and Scott Joplin, most significantly James Scott (known as the "Little Professor"), Joseph Lamb (the most successful of the white eastern pianists), Tom Turpin (a saloon owner and composer of "Harlem Rag"), and Eubie Blake (whose career extended from ragtime to black show music and pop). And there were pianists like Felix Arndt ("Menette," "Toots," and "Soup to Nuts"), and Zez Confrey ("Kitten on the Keys," "Dizzy Fingers," and "Stumbling"), who composed ragtime novelty numbers that found large audiences between 1910 and the early 1920s.

Ragtime proved to be something that audiences were craving during the later 1890s, and the music industry made the most of it. Song publishers and dance orchestras provided popular songs for the mass audience and America was caught up in a ragtime frenzy. As far as the audience for popular music was concerned, ragtime was a vocal form of syncopated music rather than a genre of composition.

Philip Furia writes in *The Poets of Tin Pan Alley: A History of America's Great Lyricists*, "The key figure in the outward spread of ragtime syncopation and vernacular lyrics to Broadway was **George M. Cohan** (1878-1942). Although his earliest songs, such as 'When the Girl You Love Is Many Miles Away' (1893), were in the elevated, sentimental

Popular Ragtime Songs

Composer	Title	Year
Ben Harney	You've Been a Good Old Wagon But You've Done Broke Down	1895
Kerry Mills	At the Georgia Camp Meeting	1897
Hughie Cannon	Bill Bailey, Won't You Please Come Home?	1902
Bob Cole and J. Rosamond Johnson	Under the Bamboo Tree	1902
Harry Von Tilzer	What You Goin' to Do When the Rent Comes Round?	1905
Charles L. Johnson	Dill Pickles	1906
Harry Von Tilzer	Under the Yum Yum Tree	1910
Irving Berlin	Alexander's Ragtime Band	1911
Lewis Muir	Ragtime Cowboy Joe	1912
Lewis Muir	Waiting for the Robert E. Lee	1912
Irving Berlin	That International Rag	1913
Chris Smith	Ballin' the Jack	1913
Euday L. Bowman	12th Street Rag	1914
James Reese Europe	The Castle Walk	1914
Eubie Blake	Chevy Chase	1914
Eubie Blake	Charleston Rag	1917

strain, he quickly turned to 'coon' songs. Learning that the 'coon' song code word for sex was 'heat', 'Dar's No Coon Warm Enough for Me,' 'A Hot Coon From Memphis,' 'She's My Warm Baby,' 'A Red Hot Coon,' 'The Warmest Colored Gal in Town,' the teenaged Cohan quickly added his own 'The Warmest Baby in the Bunch' (1896). He then shrewdly reversed the formula with 'You're Growing Cold, Cold, Cold,' advertised as 'the story of a coon with an iceberg heart.' Contributing to the glut of 'coon' technology songs with 'I Guess I'll Have to Telegraph My Baby' (1898), Cohan used slang even more coyly. In Cohan's hands the energetic dialect of the caricatured 'coon' metamorphosed into the vernacular ease of a jaunty, cosmopolite who could even salute the flag in slang ['You're a Grand Old Rag'], though complaints from several patriotic societies forced him to revise his original line, to 'you're a grand old flag.'"

The top dance team of this era, Vernon and Irene Castle, pranced to ragtime. Endless rolls of piano ragtime were produced, and the most famous rag of all, "Alexander's Ragtime Band," made its debut in 1911, resulting in the composer of the piece, Irving Berlin, being hailed as the "King of Ragtime."

1940s-1960s: Ragtime Revival

Performer	Significance	Year
Wally Rose of Yerba Buena Jass Band	"Black & White Rag" created renewed interest in classic ragtime	1941
Paul Lingle	Good Time label sessions	1952
Brun Campbell — "The Ragtime Kid"	Euphonic label — reworks of Joplin	1940s
Pee Wee Hunt	"12th Street Rag" — the most popular rendition sold 3 million	1948
Joe "Fingers" Carr (Lou Busch)	"Ragtime Cowboy Joe" (with Jo Stafford and Paul Weston); "Ivory Rag," and numerous Capitol releases	1950
Crazy Otto (Johnny Maddox)	Dot Records star; he made over 40 LPs	1955
"Big Tiny" Little	Lawrence Welk feature like Carr & Otto, honky-tonkish	1950s
Max Morath	TV shows "The Ragtime Era "and "The Turn of the Century, " and excellent releases on the Vanguard label; authentic stylist	1960
Knuckles O'Toole (Dick Hyman)	Series of popular, though honky tonkish, releases	1960s

Irving Berlin (1888-1989), unlike his hero Cohan, did not write "coon" songs. Berlin was a pragmatist as well as the most versatile and longest-lasting songwriter that ever graced Tin Pan Alley. He understood that audiences wanted lively dance music and he saw ragtime as the form that could provide it. Charles Hamm writes in *Yesterdays*: "Ragtime songs were the craze, and Berlin turned them out by the dozens: 'Yiddle on Your Fiddle, Play Some Ragtime' (1909), 'That Mezmerizing Mendelssohn Tune' (1909), 'Stop That Rag' (1910), 'Dat Draggy Rag' (1910), 'Oh, That Beautiful Rag' (1910), and 'Ragtime Violin' (1911) all enjoyed some degree of success as vaudeville songs and as sheet music. Berlin probably never heard true ragtime as played by the great black ragtime pianists of the day, but he knew, very well, the popular ragtime songs that skimmed off several superficial elements of the ragtime style and transplanted them into otherwise typical popular songs. 'Alexander's Ragtime Band,' written and published in 1911, shot the young songwriter to the top of the struggling heap of aspiring composers."

James Reese Europe (1881-1919) was drawn to New York because of the musical opportunities afforded to trained black musicians there. By 1910 he was president of the most prestigious black musicians union, the Clef Club. Europe led the Clef Club Orchestra in a number of concerts featuring a potpourri of musical styles. On May 2, 1912, Europe made history by presenting a ragtime concert on the finest concert stage in America, Carnegie Hall. This was a first for black musicians. In 1914 Europe left the Clef Club and became the musical director for Vernon and Irene Castle, a married couple who created a dance sensation in America, anticipating the "Jazz Age" by some seven years. The Castles did away with what they considered vulgar animal dances (the Turkey Trot, the Grizzly Bear, the Bunny Hug, and the like) and chose, instead, a step they learned from Europe, who, in turn, had learned it from W.C. Handy. The Castles turned th step into the Fox Trot, which created a nation-wide dance craze. (Apparently the Castles didn't consider the fox a vulgar animal.)

Carnegie Hall Archives

During the early 1900s, the excitement and opportunities of New York City attracted James Reese Europe from his southern roots (he was born in Mobile, Alabama). With a background in classical music (he studied composition with, among others, Enrico Hurlei of the Marine Corps Band) Europe demanded that his musicians play music as it was written. Between 1904 and 1910, Europe was associated with most of the major figures in black musical theater, including Bob Cole, Bert Williams, and George Walker.

Picture Collection, The Branch Libraries, The New York Public Library

The Castles and Social Dancing In America. Vernon and Irene Castle helped create the phenomenon of social dancing in America. The young married couple became a sensation in Paris at the Cafe de Paris and at the elegant Casino de Deauville in 1911. Returning to America they established "the dansant" (afternoon tea and dance) at the Louis Martin restaurant. At Bustanoby's, a salon orchestra conducted by Sigmund Romberg played some ragtime numbers and, lo and behold, the patrons got up from their tables and began to dance. Classy restaurants and hotels began featuring dances and this helped create what would become the American nightclub scene.

Above, the cast of *Watch Your Step*, a musical written for the Castles by Irving Berlin in 1914. The Castle's are third and fourth from the left. By this time the Castles were the darlings of America; they founded the Vernon Castle School of Dancing, an elite dance palace called Castle House, as well as nightclubs and resorts. Both were fashion as well as dance trendsetters, sporting complete custom-made outfits from shirts to shoes and hats. In 1939 Fred Astaire and Ginger Rogers starred in *The Story of Vernon and Irene Castle*. James Reese Europe, with his pianist Ford Dabney, wrote or coarranged the "Castle Walk," "Castle House Rag," "Castle Valse Classique," "Castle Classic Waltz," and "Castle Lame Duck," among many others, for the popular dance team that earned as much as $30,000 a week on the vaudeville circuit.

Photographs and Prints Division, Schomburg Center for Research in Black Culture, The New York Public Library, Astor, Lenox and Tilden Foundation

James Reese Europe's Clef Club Orchestra, 1912.

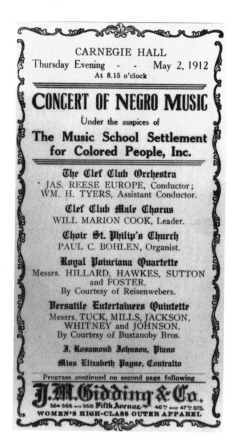

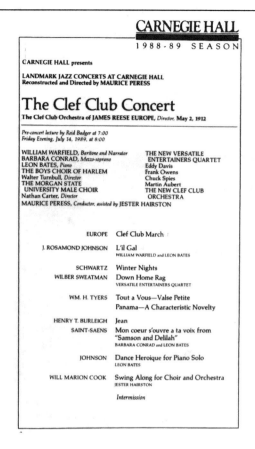

Carnegie Hall Archives   *Carnegie Hall Archives*

James Reese Europe's "Concert of Negro Music," performed entirely by African-American instrumentalists and singers, was the first concert of its kind performed at Carnegie Hall. The 125-member orchestra performed a program that covered the full black music spectrum, from folk music to ragtime and concert music forms. Europe was responsible for organizing the Clef Club Orchestra. The large aggregation was made up of violins, cellos, mandolins, banjos, harp guitars, bass violins, traps, timpani, and pianos (sometimes ten or more). The orchestra gave its first organized concert with 100 members at Harlem's Manhattan Casino on May 26, 1910. Called the "First Monster Musical Melange and Dance Fest," the show was a tremendous success. After a couple more concerts, the ensemble was ready to make its debut at Carnegie Hall.

Left, the original program for the historic May 2, 1912 concert. From the first number, Europe's rousing "Clef Club March," to the finale, the jammed audience applauded its approval. Receipts from the concert netted close to $5,000 for the Music School Settlement for Colored People, Inc., in Harlem. The orchestra returned to Carnegie Hall for similar concerts in 1913 and 1914.
Right, the program for the reconstructed concert given on July 14, 1989, under the direction of Maurice Peress, an American conductor who was the central figure of the highly lauded reconstruction of the 1924 Paul Whiteman Aeolian Hall concert. Over the years Peress has been involved in reproductions the works of Duke Ellington (such as the opera comique *Queenie Pie*, *Harlem*, and *Black, Brown, and Beige*), and a number of other American composers. Peress considers himself a specialist in what he calls "the golden age of America's vernacular-inspired music."

Europe's orchestra become the first black recording unit for the Victor Record Company in late 1914, with "The Castle Walk." At the outbreak of World War I, Europe was commissioned a lieutenant and named bandmaster of the 369th Infantry Band, nicknamed "the Hellfighters." Considered the best band in the entire armed forces, Europe's unit included drum major Bill "Bojangles" Robinson and musical assistant Noble Sissle, both of whom played roles in the Harlem Renaissance. At the peak of his career the prominent bandleader was murdered by one of his own band members, Herbert Wright, a snare drummer, ostensibly enraged by sarcastic remarks Europe made about his performance.

W. C. Handy (1873-1958) was an instrumentalist, conductor, and composer who blended elements of ragtime, jazz, and blues. He was the first to take traditional blues forms and transcribe them into written form (music notation). Handy worked as bandmaster and cornet player with Mahara's Minstrels for nearly fifteen years beginning in 1894. He then served as director of the Black Knights of Pythias band in Clarksdale, Mississippi, where he eventually orchestrated a number of local tunes. Handy's first successful composition was a campaign song written for the prospective mayor of Memphis, Tennessee, E. H. Crump. The song, "Memphis Blues," was published in 1912. Handy gained some fame but made little money on the song because he sold the rights to a New York publisher for $50. In 1914 Handy started his own publishing house and released future classics such as "St. Louis Blues" and "Yellow Dog Blues" (1914), "Joe Turner Blues" (1915), "Beale Street Blues" (1917), and "Harlem Blues" (1923). Handy published numerous books and an autobiography. Hollywood made a biographical movie of Handy in 1958, *St. Louis Blues*, starring Nat King Cole and Eartha Kitt.

Tin Pan Alley

During the latter part of the 1800s, New York's Union Square was the hub of the nation's theatrical and songwriting district. In 1900, theaters and restaurants moved northward to 28th Street between 5th Avenue and Broadway. The leading publishing houses followed. There, according to legend, the name Tin Pan Alley emerged in 1903 from a conversation between composer-journalist Monroe Rosenfeld and composer Harry Von Tilzer ("A Bird in a Gilded Cage" and "Take Me Out to the Ballgame"). Von Tilzer explained that at the request of neighbors he muted his piano by placing newspaper strips behind the strings, producing a tinny sound.

A good number of buildings in this area housed hundreds of small rooms with pianos banging away creating songs for the nation to play and sing. These professional tunesmiths worked for publishing houses that made sheet music promoted by "song pluggers." The song plugger took his company's latest release to demonstrate at music stores, restaurants, and taverns. Some even equipped a flatbed truck with a piano and ventured into crowded areas singing their company's most recent compositions.

Library of Congress

The Father of the Blues. W. C. Handy was not the "inventor" of the blues, but he anticipated the movement just before the vogue of the "classic blues" singers like Bessie Smith and popular singers like Sophie Tucker. Handy was a synthesizer who made the blues palatable for Tin Pan Alley and public consumption. As Arnold Shaw summarizes in *Black Popular Music in America*, "The term 'father' should be understood to mean, not that he generated the form, but that he nurtured, protected, enhanced, and boosted it. The popularity of his pieces contributed greatly to the flood of blues that inundated Tin Pan Alley during the 1920s as an offshoot of the Harlem Renaissance."

Library of Congress

The first songwriting district. Before the turn of the century, small publishing houses were located around Union Square on 14th Street between third and fourth Avenues. This was the home of Tony Pastor's Music Hall, as well, as many theaters, restaurants, dance halls, and penny arcades.

The leading publishing houses of the day, like M. Witmark and Sons, F. A. Mills, Joseph W. Stern and Company, Jerome H. Remick, Shapiro-Bernstein & Co., Leo Feist, Inc. ("You Can't Go Wrong With a Feist Song"), all from Union Square, and Broder and Schlam from San Francisco and Charles K. Harris from Milwaukee, all resided on 28th Street by 1900.

A number of songwriters became publishers because of the profits that could be made as a result of copyright protection laws, which only became easily enforceable with the forwarding of the American Society of Composers, Authors and Publishers in 1914 . ASCAP came into existence following Victor Herbert's lawsuit against a New York City restaurant that was using his music without giving him any monetary compensation. By 1917 ASCAP had developed the machinery to license and collect fees from the thousands of theaters, cabarets, and restaurants that performed music by its writers.

Charles K. Harris (1867-1930) was attracted to music when he first heard minstrel songs as a young boy. He constructed a banjo, began strumming his favorite songs, and soon was entertaining in small theaters in Milwaukee. After seeing a theatrical performance of *The Skating Rink*, Harris was convinced that he could write better songs than he had just heard. He went home and wrote "Since Maggie Learned to Skate" and convinced the star of the show to use his number. Harris was sixteen and on his way to a career as a songwriter.

Harris eventually had a little shop with a sign advertising "Songs Written to Order." In 1892 he published a song "After the Ball," that became the first to sell several million copies of sheet music. The song is a sad tale told by an old man explaining to his young niece why he never married as a young man. He saw his sweetheart kiss a strange man and jealousy convinced him that she was unfaithful. He left her only to find out years later that the stranger was his sweetheart's brother.

New York Public Library

By the 1920s, the Alley men had moved their wares into buildings on Broadway between 42nd and 49th Streets. The T. B. Harms building, above is seen nestled at the corner of Broadway and 42nd Street. As Ian Whitcomb notes, Tin Pan Alley was "not so much an actual place, it was more a way of business life."

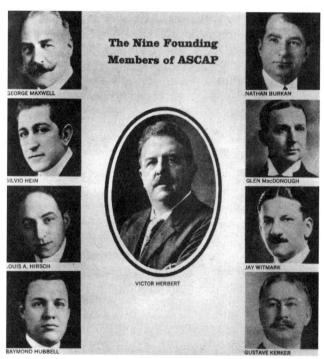

Courtesy American Society of Composers, Authors and Publishers

31

Sigmund Spaeth, the dean of writers on early popular music, calls "After the Ball" the first song to "sweep the country," the first "smashing, sensational success" of popular music.

"After the Ball" was introduced in a vaudeville theater in Milwaukee by a singer who forgot the words. Harris then bribed a prominent performer, J. Aldrich Libbey, to include it in his hit show, *A Trip to Chinatown*. He paid Libby $500 and gave him a percentage of the sheet music sales. This in effect became the first celebrated instance of "payola." The song swept the nation. Legendary bandleader John Philip Sousa ("The March King") played the ballad at the World Exposition in 1893 and vaudevillian Helene Mora made it her signature tune. Harris realized an astounding profit of $25,000 a week from sheet music sales! Songwriting had become big business. Harris noted the importance of appealing to the public: "When writing popular songs always bear in mind that it is the masses, the untrained musical public, that you must look to for support and popularity, therefore, do not offer them anything which in subject and melody does not appeal to their ears." Other songwriters took note of this. Paul Dresser ("My Gal Sal") and Harry Von Tilzer ("A Bird in a Gilded Cage"), to name just two, wrote sentimental songs that were melodious and relatively easy to play on piano, another important element in commercial success.

The Musical Stars

The songs that sold the most sheet music and recordings during the period of 1900 to 1917 were an extension of the vocal tradition of barbershop harmony groups. Barbershop style harks back to the black spirituals in its harmonic texture though not its content. Originally this was a style of unaccompanied singing in harmony by male quartets that developed in the nineteenth century in barbershops. The Peerless Quartet ("Let Me Call You Sweetheart" and "I Didn't Raise My Boy to Be a Soldier"), the American Quartet ("Casey Jones" and "Moonlight Bay"), and the Haydn Quartet ("In the Good Old Summertime," "Sweet Adeline," and "Put on Your Old Gray Bonnet") were the "big three" of the vocal groups during the pioneer age of popular recording.

Sentimental ballads and comedy numbers were the releases that gained the biggest favor with audiences of the time. Arthur Collins and Byron Harlan, a comedy singing duo, and solo singers like Henry Burr, Frank Stanley, Harry MacDonough, and Billy Murray (they all sang in one or two of the "big three" vocal groups as well) were big stars.

Ada Jones (1873-1922) was the biggest-selling female recording star of this time period, but, like the others just mentioned, she is not known to audiences of today. Discovered by singer Billy Murray, she was the first woman to achieve world fame on records. She recorded on more than fifty labels and released more than two thousand recordings. She sang what was considered "low brow" music of all kinds: dialect songs, coon songs, and country songs. She said, "I have come to take delight in interpreting the songs that are born of the people and sung by the people, they express the real sentiments of the times. And I believe that the world is enriched by the melodies that come from the masses."

Author's collection

Billy Murray (1877-1954), according to Joel Whitburn in his *Pop Memories, 1890-1954*, was "the most sensational record seller of the entire pre-1920 pioneer era. His many duets with Ada Jones made them the king and queen of the era's popular recordings; Billy also established himself as the official interpreter of George M. Cohan, since he recorded the definitive hit version of nearly every Cohan song from 1905 on." Murray was raised in Denver, which accounts for his early nickname, the "Denver Nightingale." He sang with a clear, tenor voice and was a quick wit who featured comedy songs ("Big Bad Bill," "It's a Lotta Bologny," and "Charley, My Boy") along with sentimental ballads ("Pretty Baby" and "By the Light of the Silvery Moon").

Author's collection

Author's collection

Murray worked honky tonks and vaudeville stages throughout America before making his first recordings in 1903. According to Whitburn, no other singer sang lead on so many group hits. He sang with the American and Haydn Quartets and the Heidelberg Quintet. Names like Sophie Tucker, Lillian Russell, Nora Bayes, Al Jolson, and Eddie Cantor from this time period are better known than Billy Murray to audiences of today, but none of them sold as many recordings.

Sophie Tucker (1888-1966) was a large woman with a brazen personality. She began her career as a blackface entertainer singing minstrel coon songs (she was billed as a "Coon Shouter" at Tony Pastor's Music Hall). One evening her trunk with costumes and makeup didn't arrive at the Howard Atheneum Theater in Boston and she had to go on stage without blackface. She did well enough to later renounce blackface for good, declaring, "I can hold an audience without it." She turned to ragtime and had success with such songs as "The Cubanola Glide" and "Carrie."

Tucker became a superstar with her rousing rendition of Shelton Brooks's number "Some of These Days" in 1910. The song became her theme: "I've turned it inside out, singing it in every way imaginable, as a dramatic song, as a novelty number, as a sentimental ballad, and always audiences have loved it and asked for it." Tucker then became known as "The Last of the Red Hot Mamas" (based on the 1929 Jack Yellen and Milton Ager song she made famous, "I'm the Last of the Red Hot Mamas," which she sang in her screen debut, *Honky Tonk,* that same year). During her sixty-year career in show business, Tucker mastered every form of entertainment—stage, film, radio, TV, and recording. Tucker's raunchy stories and larger-than-life stage presence delighted audiences throughout the years and had a big impact on a young artist in the 1970s, Bette Midler, who often made reference to the brassy star of yesteryear.

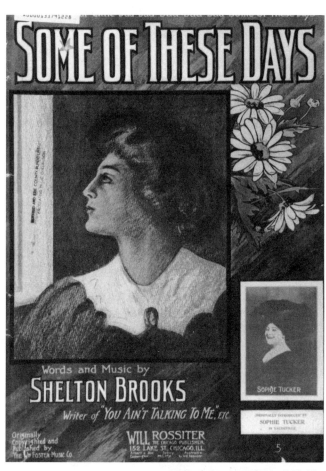

Courtesy Buffalo and Erie County Public Library

The Last of the Red Hot Mamas. Sophie Tucker was a superstar of cabaret, revue, burlesque, and vaudeville. She appeared at Tony Pastor's Music Hall as well as in the Ziegfeld Follies, and introduced such hits as Irving Berlin's "The Grizzly Bear," which initiated the animal dance craze in 1911, "Darktown Strutters' Ball," "Aggravatin' Papa," "You've Got to See Mama Every Night," "Papa, Better Watch Your Step," "Old King Tut," "Mama Goes Where Papa Goes," "Red Hot Mama," "Nobody Knows What a Red-Head Mama Can Do," "I Ain't Got Nobody," "After You've Gone," "There'll Be Some Changes Made," "He's a Good Man to Have Around," and "Real Estate Papa You Ain't Gonna Sub-Divide Me." In 1945 Tucker wrote her autobiography, *Some of These Days.*

The cacophonous sounds of jazz as interpreted by popular bands changed the face of popular music by the 1920s. The dance craze phenomenon initiated by the Castles along with the music hall stars, vocal quartets, and baritone and tenor balladers of the 1900 to 1917 period (see chart) did not become part of the "Jazz Age." Like the "Good Old Days" whence they came, theirs would be nothing more than memories for older listeners who felt threatened by the stirring sounds of the jazz-oriented orchestras and the cooing, crooning singers of the twenties.

In the 1890s, music halls run by impresarios such as Tony Pastor, the Shuberts, and Weber and Fields provided entertainment for the entire family. Vaudeville was home to many female vocalists. Eva Tanguay built her reputation on her ability to put over a song through sheer enthusiasm. She was known as the "I Don't Care Girl," based on her 1905 rendition of that song, as well as her diffident attitude toward coworkers and her audience. Tanguay even parodied her own proclivities with the song, "Egotistical Eva." Blanche Ring's stardom began in 1902, when she introduced "In the Good Old Summertime." Two other Ring classics are "I've Got Rings on My Fingers" (1909) and "Come, Josephine, In My Flying Machine" (1910).

Two of the greatest stars of the music hall tradition were Lillian Russell and Nora Bayes. **Lillian Russell** (1861-1922), a beauty known for her hourglass figure, was first noticed in 1880 singing at Tony Pastor's and then moved on to a series of six rowdy Weber & Fields revues, most importantly *Twirly Whirly* in 1902, in which she introduced her biggest hit, "Come Down, Ma Evenin' Star." Celebrated as the personification of womanly beauty, Russell was called the "Queen of Comic Opera." In 1940, Alice Faye played her in the biopic *Lillian Russell*. **Nora Bayes** (1880-1928), whose flamboyant style on and off stage made her one of the most famous women of her time, had her first hit in 1902 with "Down Where the Wurzburger Flows," resulting in her being titled "The Wurzburger Girl." Married five times, her union with cowriter and husband Jack Norworth led to her most famous song, "Shine on Harvest Moon," which they introduced in the *Ziegfeld Follies of 1908*. Ann Sheridan starred as Bayes and Dennis Morgan as Norworth in the 1944 biopic *Shine on Harvest Moon*.

Curators of Early Pop America

Most entertainers of any era are concerned with writing or performing songs of the here and now. The artists of today understandably concern themselves primarily with creating contemporary songs that their respective audiences can connect with (this can cover everything from Garth Brooks in country music to Ice-T in rap). Very few performers concern themselves with the music from the late 1800s to the 1930s. There is, however, a small cult of artists who have spent much of their careers studying and performing the music of the pre-swing era. Some, like the indefatigable Max Morath, stake their claim as ragtime specialists. John Eaton, jazz pianist and historian, is a wry humorist and observant scholar of the early American popular music scene. Ian Whitcomb and the team of William Bolcom and Joan Morris have established themselves as the premier curators of the entire spectrum of early American popular music, everything from the ragtime forms to early dance band music right up to the crooning men and torch singing women.

Ian Whitcomb is a one-man music industry for the old-time songs of Tin Pan Alley. His recordings are finely tuned evocations of one-time hits. And his dance band, right, as the promo reads, is " ten piece, good old fashioned dance band playing fox-trots, waltzes, tangos and novelties for your dancing and listening pleasure. Ian leads the band singing, talking, strumming his ukulele, and pumping his accordion."

Ian Whitcomb (1941-   ) is a youthful-looking Britisher who collected old sheet music as a youngster. Swept away by the first wave of rock' n 'roll, he performed rock music and was part of the second wave of rock, the British Invasion. Essentially a one-hit wonder, with a chart smash in 1966, "You Turn Me On," Whitcomb settled in America and followed his first love, early Tin Pan Alley music.

Over the years Whitcomb became an important author of books like *After the Ball: Pop Music from Rag to Rock*. He spent three years researching *After the Ball*, which was published in 1972 by Penguin. The *New Yorker* praised the book as a "freewheeling, diverting history," and called Whitcomb a "brash, learned, funny, perspicacious" young man. Whitcomb also wrote *Tin Pan Alley*: *A Pictorial History* (1919-1939), and *Irving Berlin and Ragtime America,* among a number of other books. His writing is not only informative, but also witty and personal. His recordings and videos are among the best re-creations of early American popular music, and his dance band is one of the few performing groups in the 1990s that truly captures the essence of that bygone era. In 1993, Whitcomb presented a musical *LotusLand*, based on his novel about a fictitous "Whispering Singer," Rollo Danks. Buck Henry and Michael Feinstein joined Whitcomb in this tuneful experimental musical comedy, which still awaits a major theatrical production.

William Bolcom (1938-   ) and Joan Morris began performing the American popular song repertoire in 1972 and celebrated the occasion in 1993 with a benefit concert with Max Morath *(Yesterdays: An Afternoon of American Popular Song and Ragtime Piano)* for the Institute for Studies in American Music. Bolcom is a composer-pianist who has managed to carve out a career that combines classical music, ragtime, old Tin Pan Alley songs, and a position in academia (he teaches at the University of Michigan School of Music, as does Morris). In 1988 Bolcom won the Pulitzer Prize for music for his "Twelve New Etudes for Piano." Together the duo has been giving concerts that are lively anthologies of classic American popular songs. Bolcom acts as accompanist and narrator, while Morris, a mezzo-soprano, interprets the lyrics of songs as wide-ranging as Charles Harris's "After the Ball" and the rock'n'roll of Leiber and Stoller's "Love Potion No. 9."

The *New Yorker* once described Morris as "America's finest singer," and her ability to mix classical techniques with popular music sensibilities is rare indeed. An evening concert will find this duet ("they duet right," wrote one newspaper) performing Stephen Foster's "Was My Brother in Battle," Harry Wood's "When the Red, Red Robin," Irving Berlin's "I Love a Piano," and Scott Joplin's "Pineapple Rag" and "Heliotrope Bouquet," among many others that span the wide landscape of American popular music. This is a duo that extracts the feeling of turn-of-the-century parlor intimacy.

Courtesy Shaw Concerts, Inc.

Musical Curators. William Bolcolm (piano) and Joan Morris (vocal).

Top Selling Artists: 1900-17

Artist	Top 10 Hits	#1 Hits	Biggest Hit	Weeks. at #1	Year
Billy Murray	129	17	By the Light of the Silvery Moon	7	1911
Harry MacDonough	97	15	Down By the Old Mill Stream	7	1911
Arthur Collins and Byron Harlan	86	11	Alexander's Ragtime Band	10	1911
Peerless Quartet	76	6	Let Me Call You Sweetheart	7	1909
Henry Burr	68	11	I Wonder Who's Kissing Her Now	8	1909
Ada Jones	62	7	I've Got Rings on My Fingers	4	1909
Haydn Quartet	60	12	Put on Your Old Gray Bonnet	11	1909
American Quartet (Billy Murray lead)	57	12	Casey Jones	11	1910
Prince's Orchestra	57	3	Hello, Hawaii, How Are You?	5	1916
Frank Stanley	54	3	Good Evening, Caroline	5	1909
Byron Harlan	52	12	School Days (When We Were a Couple of Kids)	11	1907
John McCormack	42	7	It's a Long, Long Way to Tipperary	8	1915
Ada Jones and Billy Murray	42	6	Let's Take an Old-Fashioned Walk	6	1906
Walter Van Brunt	40	1	Sympathy	2	1910
Henry Burr and Albert Campbell	29	6	I'm on My Way to Mandelay	6	1914

Source: Joel Whitburn's Pop Memories, 1890-1954

Whose Music?

The success of "Alexander's Ragtime Band" in 1911 underscores the importance of the impact of the underground musical forms on the popular music world. Some critics have a rather disingenuous view of white people ripping off black people , for. example that, Irving Berlin who was white, "stole" musical ideas from blacks like Scott Joplin. This contention asserts that Paul Whiteman and later Benny Goodman, Bill Haley, and Elvis Presley ripped off black artists with inferior copies of their songs and basked in the glory of stardom while the creators of the forms were ignored. This book, if it is anything, is a *celebration* of underground artists of all races and musical styles. However, it does not denigrate the masters of pop (the mainstream) because the great majority of pop artists were simply assimilating the hodge-podge of available multi-ethnic musical forms.

Why, for instance, were Bing Crosby and Elvis Presley two of the biggest record sellers (or icons) of the first and second half of the twentieth century, respectively? Yes, because they were white. But also because they mixed many of the musical forms that existed in America: ballads, blues, jazz, country, Hawaiian, and so on. Returning to Irving Berlin and ragtime, Ian Whitcomb in *Irving Berlin and Ragtime America*, writes, "As to the music that was re-discovered in the 1950s and enshrined as 'Classic Ragtime,' with Scott Joplin as its martyred saint, Berlin had this to say: 'You know, I never did find out what ragtime was.' The trick, unconsciously played, was in capturing a nervous restlessness that was in the air, a dancing virus (of "Alexander's Ragtime Band") 'No-one was more flabbergasted than I was at the smashing hit it made,' he told a reporter in the 1920s. Why America and the world were so obsessed with the spectre of whites as blacks was a matter for historians and not for Alleymen. But one thing was quite clear, the all-dancing, all-laughing, all-excited, chickened-out, watermelon-gorged Negro was actually a marionette whose strings were wound tightly round the fingers of the songsmiths of America. And all Irving was doing was serving the public to the best of his abilities. The sooner this dancing coon could be eliminated the better!"

Irving Berlin was America's leading songwriter of the first half of the twentieth century. His "Alexander's Ragtime Band" became a sensational hit in 1911. Most listeners viewed his up-tempo, raggy, pop hit as the "real thing." In 1938, 20th Century-Fox released *Alexander's Ragtime Band*, starring Alice Faye, Tyrone Power, and Don Ameche. The film featured a compendium of 20 Berlin classics set during the ragtime era.

Whitcomb continues, "It has been the Big Lie that blacks are born with a monopoly on the Big Beat. This injustice, starting in the eighteenth century, lasted well into the Age of Rock: Mick Jagger's strutting and shouting shows that the white nigger-minstrel tradition is still alive. Historians, explaining the popularity of the minstrel show (from the 1850s until the late 1890s it was America's favorite entertainment and its only theatrical contribution), claim that the black mask was an attempt to satisfy a variety of cultural needs within the instant USA (a country founded on theories and rules). These needs included: All-American folk heroes speaking the plain truth in dialect (as opposed to the high-falutin' European culture of the East Coast elite); licensed Fools who, from behind the blackface mask, could satirize the topics of the day whether they be immigration, women's rights, redskin uprisings, or crazes for phrenology and electricity."

What "Alexander's Ragtime Band" did was create unbridled excitement in pop music America. Let's conclude, again with Whitcomb: "The words bore traces of minstrelsy. The excited singer, exhorting his honey to hurry (and, oddly, 'let's meander'), proclaimed that Alexander's was the 'bestest band what am,' noting that, 'the clarinet is a colored pet.' Yet the cover artwork and most performances depicted Alexander's band as white-face. The song, therefore, wasn't shackled but could race free through the new electric world. It was, in fact, a clarion-call summons to everybody to come take part in some twentieth-century fun. A similar summons became the anthem of 1950s youth when rock 'n' roll arrived: Bill Haley, the square-dance caller instructing his hon' to get her glad rags on and 'Rock Around the Clock.'"

Pre-Jazz Age Musicals

The musicals chosen here are those that depict the time of the 1800s to World War I and with storylines centering on "authentic" songs of the period. *Meet Me In St. Louis* (MGM, 1944) is not listed (primarily) because, even though it includes some turn-of-the century songs of the time, the key songs are contemporary numbers written by Ralph Blane and Hugh Martin. On the other hand, *Lillian Russell* (Fox, 1940), a musical not nearly as artistic as *St. Louis,* is listed because all of the musical numbers are actual songs from that time period.

Film	Studio	Story Line	Stars	Released
The Florodora Girl	MGM	One of 1st musicals set in 1800s	Marion Davis	1930
Harmony Lane	Mascot	First of 3 films based on life of Stephen Foster	Douglas Montgomery	1935
Alexander's Ragtime Band	20th Century-Fox	The Irving Berlin extravaganza that helped ignite the nostalgia revival	Alice Faye Tyrone Power	1938
San Francisco	MGM	Nob Hill high society mixed with a love triangle and the earthquake.	Janette MacDonald Clark Gable Spencer Tracy	1939
The Great Victor Herbert	Paramount	Biopic of the great composer with catalogue of sentimental classics	Walter Connolly	1939
The Star Maker	Paramount	Story of kid stars impresario Gus Edwards ("School Days")	Bing Crosby	1939
Swanee River	20th Century-Fox	Fictionalized tale of Stephen Foster	Don Ameche	1939
The Story of Vernon and Irene Castle	RKO	Biopic of 1st dance couple of pop; glorious authentic pre-WWI dances	Fred Astaire Ginger Rogers	1939
Lillian Russell	20th Century-Fox	Biopic of hourglass-figured songstress of the Gay '90s	Alice Faye Don Ameche	1940
Tin Pan Alley	20th Century-Fox	1915 to 1918 story of song pluggers and composers	Alice Faye Betty Grable	1940
Birth of the Blues	Paramount	Early jazz and blues classics in one of Crosby's favorite roles	Bing Crosby	1941
Yankee Doodle Dandy	Warner Brothers	One of the best biopics (an Academy Award winner for Cagney as showman George M. Cohan)	James Cagney	1942
My Gal Sal	20th Century Fox	Story of composer Paul Dresser and gal in his life (fictitious); great songs	Rita Hayworth Victor Mature	1942
Broadway	Universal	The "good old days" told in flashback	George Raft	1942
For Me and My Gal	MGM	WWI showfolks on the boards and in love	Judy Garland Gene Kelly	1942
Hello, Frisco, Hello	20th Century-Fox	Period musical on Barbary Coast; old songs and new classic, "You'll Never Know"	Alice Faye John Payne	1943
Dixie	Paramount	Tale about minstrel composer Dan Emmett of the Virginia Minstrels	Bing Crosby Dorothy Lamour	1943
Coney Island	20th Century-Fox	Turn-of-the century fun; a typical move away from the reality of WWI	Betty Grable George Montgomery	1943
Shine on Harvest Moon	Warner Brothers	Reel-life version of songwriter Jack Norworth and vaudeville queen Nora Bayes	Ann Sheridan Dennis Morgan	1944

Pre-Jazz Age Musicals, continued

Film	Studio	Story Line	Stars	Released
Atlantic City	Republic	Young impresario turns boardwalk town into international playground	Brad Taylor	1944
Irish Eyes Are Smiling	20th Century-Fox	Fictional story about Broadway composer Ernest R. Ball	Dick Haymes, June Harver	1944
The Dolly Sisters	20th Century-Fox	Authentic story of Hungarian music hall sister act	Alice Faye, Betty Grable	1945
I Wonder Who's Kissing Her Now	20th Century-Fox	Composer Joe Howard and his Gay-'90s hits loosely interpreted	Mark Stevens, June Haver	1947
My Wild Irish Rose	Warner Brothers	Life of composer Chauncey Olcott ("When Irish Eyes Are Smiling.")	Dennis Morgan, Arlene Dahl	1947
Easter Parade	MGM	17 Irving Berlin songs in this fictional story about a vaudeville team at the turn of the century	Fred Astaire, Judy Garland	1948
Look for the Silver Lining	Warner Brothers	Flashback tale of vaudeville star Marilyn Miller wih many classics by Jerome Kern	June Haver, Ray Bolger, Gordon MacRae	1949
In the Good Old Summertime	MGM	A quaint musical based on delightful 1940 film *The Shop Around the Corner* (which starred Jimmy Stewart and Margaret O'Sullivan)	Judy Garland, Van Johnson	1949
Oh You Beautiful Doll	20th Century-Fox	Tin Pan Alley hitman Fred Fisher receives Hollywood treatment (lots of old-time classics here)	Mark Stevens, June Haver, S. Z. Sakall	1949
The Daughter of Rosie O'Grady	Warner Brothers	Haver falls in love with entrepreneur Tony Pastor	June Haver, Gordon MacRae	1950
On Moonlight Bay	Warner Brothers	Fictional story with old-time standards	Doris Day, Gordon MacRae	1951
Golden Girl	20th Century-Fox	Loosely based on Civil War-period star Lotte Crabtree and the peak of her career at New York's Niblo Gardens	Mitizi Gaynor, Dale Robertson	1951
I'll See You in My Dreams	Warner Brothers	Story of Gus Kahn (hits from 1915 on); good feeling for early Tin Pan Alley	Danny Thomas, Doris Day	1951
I Dream of Jeanie	Republic	Weakest of Stephen Foster biopics (good for Ray Middleton's turn as E. P. Christy)	Billy Shirley, Eileen Christ	1952
Stars and Stripes Forever	20th Century-Fox	John Philip Sousa ("March King") receives the Hollywood treatment	Clifton Webb, Debra Paget	1952
The I-Don't-Care Girl	20th Century-Fox	Poor storyline, good production numbers, about tempestuous vaudeville vixen Eva Tanguay	Mitzi Gaynor, David Wayne	1953
By the Light of the Silvery Moon	Warner Brothers	Turn-of-the-century tale with authentic songs and dances set in local theater	Doris Day, Gordon MacRae	1953
Scott Joplin, King of Ragtime	Universal	Musically satisfying but downbeat tale about classic ragtime's best known composer	Billy Dee Williams, Art Carney	1976
Pretty Baby	Paramount	Tale of Storyville prostitutes; atmospheric ragtime and jazz sounds	Brooke Shields, Keith Carradine	1978

POPULAR MUSIC: 1917-1934

George M. Cohan's war classic, sung by vaudeville superstar Nora Bayes, was the most popular and lasting of the World War I songs.

By the time the United States entered WWI, there was a pro-war mood sweeping the nation as men marched off to "smash the Hun."

This sheet music from just before the war is considered the first protest song.

The "War to End War" had been going on more than three years when the first American soldiers set foot in Europe in June 1917. Some 4.7 million U.S. citizens entered the military after Congress declared war on Germany. This conflict pitted the Allies (France, Britain, and Russia) against the Central Powers (Germany, Austria-Hungary, Bulgaria, and Turkey). These troops are seen marching down Main St. in Buffalo, New York.

The years 1900 to 1917, dubbed "The Good Old Days," were a time in which America was prosperous and at peace. That peace was shattered on July 28, 1914, when war broke out in Europe, but the United States initially took little interest in "that mess in Europe." In an effort to reach France, Germany had attacked Belgium; thus England declared war on Germany. The United States was sympathetic toward England and Belgium, but tried to keep out of the conflict.

American popular music had its finger on the pulse of the nation. Nora Bayes, the biggest star of vaudeville, emoted the nation's isolationist impulse with "I Didn't Raise My Boy to Be a Soldier" and "Please Don't Take My Darling Boy Away." Woodrow Wilson's second campaign featured the Democratic theme song, "Elect Wilson, He Kept Us Out of War."

However, on April 16, 1917, when America decided to enter what would later be called World War I, the music dramatically changed its tune . "Goodbye Broadway, Hello France," "Pack Up Your Troubles in Your Old Kit Bag", and "Over There" were just a few of the popular songs that reflected support for the doughboys.

The Roaring Twenties: The Jazz Age

Library of Congress

As did the novels of F. Scott Fitzgerald whose *Tales of the Jazz Age* he illustrated, John Held, Jr., cartoonist, captured the flapper better than any other via his numerous works for *Life* magazine. Flappers were young women who tried to appear sophisticated in dress and behavior during the jazz-charged 1920s.

In *The Jazz Age: Popular Music in the 1920s,* Arnold Shaw remarks, "The Collegian or cake-eater, as well as the flapper, two emblematic figures of the 1920s, found an eye-arresting commentator in John Held, Jr., whose cartoons imparted a doll-like innocence to the smart set, with their rolled stockings, short skirts, bobbed hair, and wild parties." This underground music of jazz made a brief visit to mainstream pop during the 1920s. Much of what was considered "jazz" during that period was later disclaimed by "jazz" historians.

President	Years	Party	Motto
Woodrow Wilson	1917-21	Democrat	He kept us out of war"
Warren G. Harding V.P. Calvin Coolidge	1921-23	Republican	"A return to normalcy"
Calvin Coolidge	1923-25	Republican	(Harding dies of apoplectic stroke August 23)
Calvin Coolidge	1925-29	Republican	"Keep cool with Coolidge"
Herbert C. Hoover	1929-33	Republican	"The ideals of the American people"
Franklin D. Roosevelt	1933-37	Democrat	"A New Deal to restore this country to prosperity"

U.S. Presidents

Library of Congress

Women's suffrage: The Nineteenth Amendment to the U.S. Constitution.

On November 11, 1918, World War I was over and some 2 million servicemen returned home. By 1920 two new constitutional amendments had come into force. The Nineteenth Amendment to the Constitution was long overdue: women's suffrage. The Eighteenth Amendment, Prohibition (the Volstead Act, passed over the veto of President Woodrow Wilson) shortly proved to be extremely unpopular. Many Americans simply ignored Prohibition by drinking illegally. Many veterans of the Great War felt they'd been double-crossed, that the bill had been railroaded through while they were fighting the "war to end all wars." They had fought to make the world safe for democracy and now, in the land of the free, no one was legally able to buy beer, wine, or liquor.

What seemed like a financial boom after World War I was, in reality, false hope based on speculation. Nearly 80 percent of America's families had an annual income of less than three thousand dollars—the "Roaring Twenties" didn't roar for the masses. Much of America's finances were based on credit and on paper assets that would lead to the beginning of slow ruination on October 29, 1929, when the New York Stock Exchange experienced its greatest single-day decline in history. The twenties ended with the start of the Great Depression, but the years leading up to the end were filled with madcap antics that hid the grim reality.

The naive romanticism of the Jazz Age was perhaps best recounted in the writings of F. Scott Fitzgerald. After two successful novels, *This Side of Paradise* (1920) and *The Beautiful and the Damned* (1922), Fitzgerald released a collection of short stories about flappers and the nouveau riche entitled *Tales of the Jazz Age* (1923). He envisioned the twenties as a time when "people danced in a champagne haze on the rooftop of the world." Fitzgerald depicted the world as one big party. Life was to be lived to its fullest with drink, dance, and jazzy music. College student J.D. Spalding wrote in his school newspaper *Kollege Kapers*: "It's applesauce to say that football is the bee's knees this season. Every cake-eater knows that the way to land a flapper is to stroke the skins, badger the banjo, squeeze the sax, tease the trumpet. And if you're keen for a neck session in a jalopy, whip out your uke!" (That is, the ukulele, adopted by Hawaiians from Portuguese sailors.)

Indeed the Jazz Age was an era of dance and song. Few decades had been so defined by their music. The publishing houses and songwriters that were part of the long-time music industry known as Tin Pan Alley churned out song after song for the dance bands and vocalists of the time. Stars like Al Jolson, Rudy Vallee, Bing Crosby, and Ruth Etting were dependent upon Tin Pan Alley to supply them with a continuous flow of new material. Unlike contemporary songwriter-performers Chuck Berry, Bob Dylan, Billy Joel, Joni Mitchell, Sting, Prince, Michael Jackson, and Bruce Springsteen, these stars of yesteryear looked to the Alleymen for their material.

Courtesy Smithsonian Collection of Recordings

David Ewen, author of a multitude of books on popular music, crowned the most influential and lasting composers of Tin Pan Alley "The Big Five." He was referring to Irving Berlin and Cole Porter, and, pictured above, Jerome Kern, George Gershwin, and Richard Rodgers.

Post-War Hitmen of Tin Pan Alley

Songwriter	Hit Song	Performer	Year
Edgar Leslie, E. Ray Goetz & George Meyer	For Me and My Gal	Van & Schenck	1917
P. G. Wodehouse & Jerome Kern	Till the Clouds Roll By	Anna Wheaton & James Harrod	1917
George M. Cohan	Over There	American Quartet	1917
Joseph McCarthy & Harry Carroll	I'm Always Chasing Rainbows	Charles Harrison	1918
Otto Harbach & Louis A. Hirsch	The Love Nest	John Steel	1920
Buddy DeSylva & Louis Silvers	April Showers	Al Jolson	1922
Gus Kahn & Walter Donaldson	My Buddy	Henry Burr	1922
Irving Berlin	What'll I Do?	Paul Whiteman	1924
Irving Caesar & Vincent Youmans	Tea for Two	Milton Harris	1925
Lorenz Hart & Richard Rodgers	Manhattan	Ben Selvin	1925
George Whiting & Walter Donaldson	My Blue Heaven	Gene Austin	1927
Mitchell Parish & Hoagy Carmichael	Stardust	Isham Jones	1929
Arthur Freed & Nacio Herb Brown	Singin' in the Rain	Cliff Edwards	1929
Ted Koehler & Harold Arlen	Get Happy	Ruth Etting	1930
Bert Kalmar & Harry Ruby	Three Little Words	Bing Crosby	1930
H. Leo Robin & Ralph Ringer	Please	Bing Crosby	1932
Mack Gordon & Harry Ravel	Did You Ever See a Dream Walking?	Eddy Duchin	1933
Cole Porter	You're the Top	Cole Porter	1934
Al Dubin & Harry Warren	I Only Have Eyes for You	Ben Selvin	1934

As the twenties and thirties wore on, more sophisticated songs would be written primarily for professional entertainers of the stage, records, radio, and film. America would move away from being a nation of performers to becoming a nation of passive listeners. Ian Whitcomb points out in *After the Ball*: "The magic-gadgets *molded* pop music as well. They were both servant and master. Here are a few of the changes they brought about: 1) Rise of the star, who was known by all the world but who knew precious few of the world. 2) Therefore an increase in distance between performer and audience. 3) And much more reliance on professionals. 4) Resulting in a temporary banishment of homemade music. 5) Rise of the bland universal well-made song. 6) Fall of sheet music and piano music and piano empire."

Broadway

By the twenties, the three main forms of musical theater were the operetta, the revue, and the musical comedy. Operetta, which had been the dominant form throughout the late 1800s, was based on the traditions of Viennese, English, and French comic opera. Victor Herbert (*Naughty Marietta*, 1910), Rudolf Friml (*Rosemarie*, 1924), and Sigmund Romberg (*The Student Prince in Heidelberg*, 1924) were the leading composers of American operetta. The musically ambitious scores and romantic locales metamorphosed into Jerome Kern's crowning achievement, *Show Boat*, and eventually into the musical plays of Rodgers and Hammerstein, Lerner and Loewe, and Brock and Harnick. These musical writing teams used aspects of operetta technique for their productions, but the true operetta was pretty much on its way out, except for revivals of past hits. Most Americans preferred the native locales and the jazzy swagger of the revues and musical comedy to operetta by the end of the twenties.

Key Broadway Operettas

Operetta	Composer	Year	Theater	Performances
Maytime	Sigmund Romberg	1917	Shubert	492
Blossom Time	Sigmund Romberg	1921	Ambassador	516
Rose Marie	Rudolf Friml	1924	Imperial	557
The Student Prince	Sigmund Romberg	1924	Jolson's 59th Street	608
The Vagabond King	Rudolf Friml	1925	Casino	511
Countess Maritza	Emmerich Kalman	1926	Shubert	321
The Desert Song	Sigmund Romberg	1926	Casino	471
Rio Rita	Harry Tierney	1927	Ziegfeld	494
The Three Musketeers	Rudolf Friml	1928	Lyric	318
The New Moon	Sigmund Romberg	1928	Imperial	509
The Great Waltz	Johann Strauss Jr.	1934	Center	298

Source: Stanley Green, Broadway Musicals Show By Show

Author's collection

Left, sheet music images from the glorious past of the *Ziegfeld Follies*. Eddie Cantor reached stardom when he joined the *Ziegfeld Follies of 1917*. He also appeared in the *Follies* in 1918, 1919, 1923, and 1927. Cantor later starred in radio, films, and television. Some of his most memorable musical numbers were "You'd Be Surprised, " "Dinah," "Ida," "My Baby Just Cares for Me," "Makin' Whoopie," and his most famous, "If You Knew Susie."

Right, bandleader Art Hickman's composition "Hold Me" was one of the hits from the 1920 *Follies*.

Courtesy Smithsonian Collection of Recordings

The thirteenth edition of the *Ziegfeld Follies* gave the series a theme song in Irving Berlin's "A Pretty Girl Is Like a Melody"; a minstrel show from Eddie Cantor and Bert Williams; showgirls clad as salad ingredients performing "The Follies Salad"; Ben Ali Haggin's tableaux depicting the 13th *Follies;* and a scene showing Lady Godiva astride a white horse. The grand finale was a tribute to the Salvation Army's morale-boosting contributions to the war.

Courtesy Sony Music

Cy Coleman, Betty Comden, and Adolph Green composed the music for Peter Stone's *The Will Rogers Follies: A Life in Revue,* which opened on Broadway in 1991 and toured the country in 1993. Tommy Tune provided the lively choreography and directed. "Never Met a Man I Didn't Like" was the show's most memorable number. Keith Carradine starred in the original and in 1993 headed the touring company. Carradine was replaced on Broadway by country music stars Mac Davis and Larry Gatlin, respectively.

Will Rogers was an Oklahoma cowboy-entertainer whose rope tricks and wry commentary, often read right out of the daily newspapers, graced the *Ziegfeld Follies* beginning in 1917.

The revue emanated from the minstrel "Olio" section and then vaudeville to become a kind of "end of the year review" of noteworthy incidents or individuals performed via a succession of scenes in dialogue and song. One might think of the revue as an end of the year "Saturday Night Live." The revue featured a parade of stars performing their specialties in grand productions by entrepreneurs like Florenz Ziegfeld and the Shubert Brothers.

The most successful and famous of the revues were the annual *Ziegfeld Follies*, which began in 1907. Ziegfeld died in

Ziegfeld Follies Highlights

Edition	Stars	Hit Songs/Highlight
Follies of 1917	Will Rogers, Fanny Brice, Eddie Cantor	War tribute with Star-Spangled Banner
Follies of 1919	Will Rogers, Fanny Brice, Eddie Cantor, W. C. Fields, Marilyn Miller, Bert Williams	A Pretty Girl Is Like a Melody; I Want to See a Minstrel Show; Mandy
Follies of 1921	Fanny Brice, W .C. Fields, Van & Schenck	My Man; Second Hand Rose; I'm an Indian
Follies of 1922	Will Rogers, Olsen & Johnson, Gallagher & Sheen	Mr. Gallagher and Mr. Sheen
Follies of 1927	Eddie Cantor, Ruth Etting, Claire Luce, Cliff Edwards	My Blue Heaven; Shaking the Blues Away
Follies of 1931	Harry Richman, Ruth Etting, Helen Morgan	Half-Caste Woman
Follies of 1934	Fanny Brice, Jane Froman, Willie & Eugene Howard	Rose of Washington Square; Wagon Wheels; The Last Roundup
Follies of 1936	Fanny Brice, Bob Hope, Judy Canova	I Can't Get Started

1931 and the Shubert Brothers organization bought the rights to the title and produced it from 1934 until the final Broadway production of the *Follies* in 1943.

Ziegfeld hired some of the major songwriters of the day, including Jerome Kern, George Gershwin, and Irving Berlin, who composed "A Pretty Girl Is Like a Melody" for the 1919 edition of the revue. The *Follies* showed off beautiful women in glittering and revealing silk and satin costumes created by the best couturiers, against glorious sets by artists such as Joseph Urban. Many of the greatest singers and comedians performed for Ziegfeld, including W. C. Fields, Eddie Cantor, Fanny Brice, Will Rogers, Ed Wynn, and Bert Williams (one of the few blacks to play the "Great White Way").

George White's Scandals of 1931 featured the hit songs "The Thrill Is Gone" and "Life Is Just a Bowl of Cherries." White was coauthor and appeared in most of the shows himself. The *Scandals* appeared from 1919 to 1926, from 1928 to 1929, 1930, and in 1939.

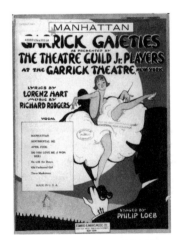

Richard Rodgers and Lorenz Hart created music for the Theatre Guild's revue, which opened at the Garrick Theatre in the spring of 1925. The show was supposed to run for only a few performances, but it played the entire season, no doubt due to the team's first hit success, "Manhattan." The revue also included a song, "Mountain Greenery," that years later became a favorite of jazz musicians.

George White, who once danced in the *Follies*, originated *George White's Scandals* in 1919. Dancer Ann Pennington (who introduced the "Black Bottom", and its associated dance), George Gershwin, Paul Whiteman, Rudy Vallee, Ethel Merman, Bert Lahr, and Harry Richman were *Scandals* luminaries. After the first *Scandals* Ziegfeld wired White that he would pay him $2,000 a week if he and Pennington would come back to the *Follies*. White, feeling confident after his initial success, wired back that he would pay Ziegfeld and actress Billie Burke (Ziegfeld's second wife) $3,000 a week to go into the next *Scandals*.

Today *George White's Scandals* are best known as the springboard from which George Gershwin flexed his Broadway muscles before writing his first musical comedy success, *Lady Be Good!* in 1924. Gershwin wrote six songs for the second *Scandals*, but didn't have a hit for White until 1922, when Winnie Lightner sang "I'll Build a Stairway to Paradise." It was this production that saw Gershwin's ambitious one-act opera, *Blue Monday,* a twenty-five-minute ballet, close after opening night. Paul Whiteman, who led the pit band for that performance, was so impressed with the serious piece that he eventually commissioned Gershwin to write his "Rhapsody in Blue" for his concert at Aeolian Hall a year and a half later. Gershwin last wrote for the *Scandals* in 1924, when Lightner introduced "Somebody Loves Me," which became a standard.

Other revues of note were John Murray Anderson's *Greenwich Village Follies*, Irving Berlin's *Music Box Revues*, Earl Carroll's *Vanities*, the Theatre Guild's *Garrick Gaieties*, and the Howard Dietz and Arthur Schwartz collaboration, *The Little Show.*

By far the most influential and most performed of the theatrical forms was the musical comedy, which told a story, usually featured an attractive couple in love, often aided and abetted by a secondary, comic-relief couple (an influence of French farce), and presented dances and hummable tunes. The majority of musical comedies ended with a resolution of any lovers' conflict and a happy ending.

Let us investigate some musicals comedies from this period. Surprisingly, *No, No, Nanette* (1925) was one of the only musicals to feature a flapper as a central character. The story centered on a young girl's unconventional lifestyle, which collided with the older generation's expectations of proper behavior. Nanette reflected the post-war needs of many young women who had been liberated by women's suffrage and the Jazz Age. As songwriter Hoagy Carmichael noted, the post-war period entered "with a bang of bad booze, players with jangled morals and wild weekends." The musical score was constructed by lyricist Irving Caesar and composer Vincent Youmans.

No, No, Nanette focused on the flapper and became the most successful musical comedy of the 1925 season. The show opened in Detroit in April 1923, but because of the success of its two great numbers, "Tea for Two" and "I Want to Be Happy," it sold out every city it played in and didn't reach New York until 1925. The musical made its producers over $2 million and composer Youmans about $500,000.

Amidst boozy, flaming youth proclamations like "petting parties with the smarties," "flappers," and "fly and free," and "preachers mock us because we're bad," came two classic standards, "Tea for Two" and "I Want to Be Happy." Youmans also provided music for *Hit the Deck* (1927), which produced the standard "Sometimes I'm Happy," and the Hollywood musical *Flying Down to Rio* (1933). He will be remembered best of all, however, for *No, No, Nanette*, which was revived on Broadway in 1971 with Ruby Keeler. Zelda Fitzgerald summed up this musical best when she observed, "Vincent Youmans wrote the music for those twilights just after the war. They were wonderful. They hung above the city like an indigo wash."

Most of the musical comedies were lightweight affairs with predictable tales of young love overcoming obstacles, and music and dance sandwiched in throughout. Jerome Kern led a revolution in musical theater with his Princess Theatre musicals, such as *Very Good Eddie* (1915) and *Oh, Boy!* (1917). Working with P. G. Wodehouse and Guy Bolton, Kern, like Cohan, created distinctly American musicals. They featured songs that evolved from characters and situations that seemed believable. But their musicals were more intimate and subtle than those of Cohan, which had a style that was more exuberant and rah-rah. As Gerald Bordman observed about the team of Wodehouse, Bolton and Kern, "They brought American musical comedy into the twentieth century." Between 1924 and 1925, there were forty-six musicals on Broadway most of them about "gals and gags." Kern loosened up European operetta with graceful tunes, and he advanced the musical comedy beyond an assembly of catchy tunes. He felt that songs must be suited to the "action and mood of the play."

In 1927, *Show Boat*, based on Edna Ferber's novel, resulted in the foremost critical and popular achievement of the musical theater of the 1920s. It could, unlike most other musicals of the time, withstand comparison with "legitimate" play. Brooks Atkinson of the *New York Times* the best known theatrical critic of his era, stated that *Show Boat* was "the greatest American musical ever written." Alan Jay Lerner, a first-rate lyricist (*My Fair Lady, Camelot*, and *Gigi*, among others) writes of Hammerstein and Kern's work forf *Show Boat* in his book *The Musical Theatre,* "The entire score was studded with both brilliance and depth, almost as if each man had suddenly opened a door in his creative soul behind which a greater artist had been waiting to see the sunlight."

Show Boat was a key work in the history of the American musical. Jerome Kern's compositions mated with Oscar Hammerstein's lyrics to produce seven hit songs. When Kern read Edna Ferber's novel in 1926, before he was halfway through he excitedly telephoned Oscar Hammerstein to tell him he was going to make *Show Boat* into a musical. Kern exclaimed, "It's a million-dollar title!" Ferber was reluctant to see her cherished story adapted into a musical with fifty scantily clad showgirls dancing on the deck of the *Cotton Blossom*, the showboat of her story. When Kern played and sang "Ol' Man River" for her, she wrote in her memoirs, "The music mounted, mounted, and I give you my word my hair stood on end, the tears came to my eyes. I breathed like a heroine in a melodrama. That was music that would outlast Jerome Kern's day and mine."

Three film versions have appeared: a primitive release in 1929, Universal's 1936 version with Allan Jones, Irene Dunne, Helen Morgan, Charles Winninger, and Paul Robeson, and the 1951 MGM technicolor spectacular with Howard Keel, Kathryn Grayson, Ava Gardner, Joe E. Brown, and William Warfield. Throughout the years, *Show Boat* has been one of the most beloved musicals in the annals of American stage history.

Cole Porter wrote in the minor mode more extensively than any show composer before or after him, according to Arnold Shaw. This is particularly odd because Porter was a wealthy midwesterner, not Jewish like a majority of the songwriters of his circle. Called by Cecil Smith the "song laureate of the Lost Generation, a man of high society, litterateur and genteel pornographer," Porter was able to poke fun at the rich and powerful. Richard Rodgers noted in his autobiography, *Musical Stages*, "It's surely one of the ironies of the musical theatre that, despite the abundance of Jewish composers, the one who has written the most enduring 'Jewish' music should be an Episcopalian millionaire who was born on a farm in Peru, Indiana."

Show Boat was revolutionary in theater because of its serious content, which included racism, unhappy relationships, miscegenation and operatic songs such as "Can't Help Lovin' Dat Man," "Make Believe," and "Ol' Man River." This serious break from the froth and fun of "Gals & Gags" led critics to refer to this show as a "musical play." The fall 1993 production of *Show Boat* in Toronto, Ontario, proved very successful, and the next year the show moved to New York where it won a number of Tony Awards.

Anything Goes (1934) was another example of a musical with antics that reflected the carefree Jazz Age. Cole Porter's compositions and lyrics for the show have lasted like few others of this period. Ethel Merman starred as Reno Sweeny, a nightclub singer sailing on an oceanliner from New York to Southampton, England. William Gaxton as Billy Crocker (a friend of Reno's) stows aboard the ship to be near Harcourt, the heiress he loves, and Public Enemy No. 13 (the bumbling Victor Moore) masquerades as the Rev. Dr. Moon. By the end of the story Reno snares a titled Englishman, Billy gets his heiress, and Dr. Moon is officially declared harmless.

The classic numbers included "You're the Top," "I Get a Kick Out of You," "Blow, Gabriel, Blow," "All Through the Night," and "Anything Goes." Hollywood cast Bing Crosby in the Gaxton role in 1936 and kept only four of the twelve Porter songs; the movie also cut out the cocaine reference in "I Get a Kick Out of You." In 1956 Paramount again filmed the Porter classic, with Crosby, Donald O'Connor, and Mitzi Gayner.

Other notable musical comedies from the era included *Lady, Be Good* (1924, music by George Gershwin, lyrics by Ira Gershwin, starring Fred Astaire and his sister Adele); *Oh, Kay!* (1926, music by George Gershwin, lyrics by Ira Gershwin, starring Gertrude Lawrence, who introduced "Someone to Watch Over Me"); *Girl Crazy* (1930, music by George Gershwin, lyrics by Ira Gershwin; the show made a star of Ethel Merman and had songs including "I Got Rhythm," "But Not for Me," and "Embraceable You"); *The Gay Divorce* (1932, music and lyrics by Cole Porter, with Fred Astaire and Claire Luce, featuring "Night and Day"); *As Thousands Cheer* (1933, music and lyrics by Irving Berlin, with Marilyn Miller, Clifton Webb, and Ethel Waters, featuring such classic songs as "Easter Parade," "Heat Wave," and "Supper Time"); and *Roberta,* (1933, music by Jerome Kern, lyrics Otto Harbach, starring Lydia Roberti, Bob Hope, and Tamara, and featuring "Smoke Gets in Your Eyes").

Key Broadway Musicals: 1917-34

Musical	Music/Lyrics	Song/ Performer	Peak Position	Year
Sinbad	Jean Schwartz & Sam Lewis	Rock-A-Bye Your Baby (Al Jolson)	1	1918
Ziegfeld Follies of 1919	Irving Berlin	A Pretty Girl Is Like a Melody (John Steel)	1	1919
Irene	Harry Tierney & Joseph McCarthy	Alice Blue Gown (Edith Day)	1	1919
Sally	Jerome Kern & Buddy DeSylva	Looking for the Silver Lining (M. Harris)	1	1920
Ziegfeld Follies of 1921	Maurice Yvain & Channing Pollock	My Man (Fannie Brice)	1	1921
George White's Scandals	George Gershwin & B. DeSylva Ira Gershwin	I'll Build a Stairway to Paradise (Paul Whiteman)	1	1922 / 1923
Lady Be Good	G. Gershwin & Ira Gershwin	Fascinating Rhythm (Cliff Edwards)	6	1925
No, No, Nanette	Vincent Youmans & Irving Caesar	I Want to Be Happy (Vincent Lopez)	2	1925
Sunny	Jerome Kern & Otto Harbach	Who (George Olsen)	1	1926
Oh, Kay!	G. & I. Gershwin	Someone to Watch Over Me (Gertrude Lawrence)	2	1926
Good News!	B. G. DeSylva, Ray Henderson & Lew Brown	The Best Things in Life Are Free (George Olsen)	3	1927
A Connecticut Yankee	Richard Rodgers & Lorenz Hart	My Heart Stood Still (Ben Selvin)	5	1928
Show Boat	J. Kern & O. Hammerstein II	Ol' Man River (Paul Whiteman)	1	1928
Blackbirds of 1928	Jimmy McHugh & Dorothy Fields	I Can't Give You Anything But Love (Cliff Edwards)	1	1928
Follow Thru	DeSylva, Henderson & Brown	Button Up Your Overcoat (Helen Kane)	3	1929
Girl Crazy	G. Gershwin & I. Gershwin	Embraceable You (Red Nichols)	2	1930
Three's a Crowd	Arthur Schwartz & Howard Dietz	Body and Soul (Paul Whiteman) (written Green, Sour, Heyman)	1	1930
The Band Wagon	A. Schwartz & H. Dietz	Dancing in the Dark (Ben Selvin)	3	1931
Gay Divorce	Cole Porter	Night and Day (Fred Astaire/ Leo Reisman)	1	1932
Roberta	J. Kern & O. Harbach	Smoke Gets in Your Eyes (Paul Whiteman)	1	1933
Ziegfeld Follies of 1934	Peter DeRose & Billy Hill	Wagon Wheels (Paul Whiteman)	2	1934
Anything Goes	Cole Porter	You're the Top (Paul Whiteman)	2	1934
		I Get a Kick Out of You (P. Whiteman)	3	1934
		Anything Goes (Paul Whiteman)	5	1934
		All Through the Night (P. Whiteman)	8	1934

Source: Joel Whitburn's Pop Memories, 1890-1954

The Dance Bands

The early 1920s saw fierce competition between records and radio. The phonograph record was selling at an all-time high in 1922, when some 110 million were sold. However, radio, with nine stations in 1920, exploded into six hundred stations by 1922. Radio was a one-time investment, and listeners didn't have to get up to change the record every three minutes. The tunesmiths and entertainers adapted to each form and subsequent technical changes as time went on. Whatever the venue, record, radio, or the eventual talkie film; music would be provided by the songwriters for the professional entertainers.

By the 1920s the dance band was the main source of musical entertainment. The bands were of many types—sweet bands, society bands, hot bands, and novelty bands, all trying to satisfy America's appetite for dancing. The Jazz Age had loosened libidos and corsets and there seemed to be no end to the variety of dances that the flapper could do. From the intimate waltz to the sultry black bottom, the Charleston, and the shimmy, to the endless series of animal dances, experimentation was the order of the day. To audiences of the 1920s, this dance music was "jazz," after all, this period was called the Jazz Age.

The Popular Bands

Band	Hit (or Theme) Song	Year
Irving Aaronson & his Commanders	Let's Misbehave	1928
Gus Arnheim & His Orchestra	Sweet and Lovely	1931
Ben Bernie & His Orchestra	Sweet Georgia Brown	1925
Emil Coleman & His Orchestra	Smoke Gets in Your Eyes	1934
Zez Confrey & His Orchestra	Kitten on the Keys	1921
Eddy Duchin & His Orchestra	Let's Fall in Love	1934
Carl Fenton & His Orchestra	Love Sends a Little Gift of Roses	1923
Jan Garber & His Orchestra	All I Do Is Dream of You	1934
Jean Goldkette & His Orchestra	Tiptoe Through the Tulips	1929
Glen Gray's Casa Loma Orchestra	Blue Moon	1934
Art Hickman Orchestra	Rose Room	1916
Isham Jones & His Orchestra	I'll See You in My Dreams	1925
Wayne King & His Orchestra	The Waltz You Saved for Me	1930
Sam Lanin & His Orchestra	It Had to Be You	1924
Ted Lewis & His Band	When My Baby Smiles at Me	1920
Guy Lombardo's Royal Canadians	Charmaine!	1927
Vincent Lopez & His Orchestra	Nola	1922
Clyde McCoy & His Orchestra	Sugar Blues	1931
Ray Noble & His Orchestra	The Very Thought of You	1934
George Olsen & His Orchestra	The Last Roundup	1933
Leo Reisman & His Orchestra	Night and Day	1932
Ben Selvin & His Orchestra	Darandella	1919
Nat Shilkret & the Victor Orchestra	Dancing With Tears in My Eyes	1930
Paul Sprecht & His Orchestra	Static Strut	1926
Fred Waring's Pennsylvanians	Memory Lane	1924
Ted Weems & His Orchestra	Heartaches	1933
Paul Whiteman & His Orchestra	Whispering	1920

One of the finest dance bands between 1920 and 1934 was Isham Jones's organization, which featured outstanding arrangements and impeccable musicianship.

Large orchestras were the order of the day for dance-conscious America. From left, Guy Lombardo and his Royal Canadians, Fred Waring's Pennsylvanians, and Jan Garber and his Orchestra.

Big modern dance bands were made up of instrumental "sections": the brass section of trumpets and trombones, the reed section of saxophones and clarinets, and the rhythm section of piano, drums, banjo, and sometimes tuba. In later groups the tuba would be replaced by the standup bass and the banjo by rhythm guitar. Some of the "classier" bands even had string sections. All of the successful bands had singers who were musically and socially subservient to the band leader.

The leading bands of the day made regular recordings and were featured on radio broadcasts from ballrooms or hotels: Jean Goldkette at the Greystone Ballroom in Detroit, Gus Arnheim at the Coconut Grove in Los Angeles, Leo Reisman at the Brunswick Hotel in Boston, Guy Lombardo at the Roosevelt Grill in New York. The first to establish the concept of remote broadcasting was pianist-bandleader Vincent Lopez, who began the trend in 1921 at the Pennsylvania Grill in New York.

When it was considered an event for a well-known band to play the New York Paramount Theater for a two-week engagement, Paul Whiteman played the enormous palace for two *years* at $12,500 per week!

America's First Dance Band Leader. According to Leo Walker in *The Wonderful Era of the Great Dance Bands*, in 1913 Art Hickman, a drummer and some-time piano player, was approached by the manager of the San Francisco Seals, a minor league baseball team, with an idea for organizing a series of dances to keep the evenings from dragging during the long training season. The band was well received and eventually booked into the Rose Room of the prestigious St. Francis Hotel for that summer season. The band consisted of six pieces: piano, two banjos, drums, trombone, and trumpet. Soon violin and bass were added.

This was just the beginning. Ferde Grofe, who was well versed in jazz and classical music, was brought in as pianist and arranger. And by 1916, the vaudeville saxophone team of Bert Ralton and Clyde Doerr joined the band, creating a small reed choir. So, by 1916 Art Hickman had initiated the basic format for dance bands in America. The bands of Ben Bernie and Ben Selvin, among many others, became better known to audiences of the 1920s, than Art Hickman—but it was Hickman who initiated the form. In fact, if anyone deserves the title of the "Father of Big Bands," it is Art Hickman.

One of the unheralded early bandleaders was **Art Hickman** (1886-1930). This pioneer helped establish the instrumentation, style, voicing, and rhythm of early dance bands. His first home base was the St. Francis Hotel in San Francisco. Ian Whitcomb exclaims, "The saxophone! During the roaring twenties the curvy saxophone played with a lot of wobble and a cute popping was to become the symbol of the Jazz Age. But here, way back in 1916, was this Art Hickman pioneering a modern-type dance band with a saxophone section even before the appearance of jazz bands!" Hickman enlarged his band and in 1919 moved on to New York, where he composed his theme song, "Rose Room." His band was featured in the *Ziegfeld Follies of 1920*. In 1921, Hickman and his band opened the new Coconut Grove at the Ambassador Hotel in Los Angeles. Pioneer jazz authority Charles Edward Smith proclaimed (*Down Beat*, August 15, 1959), "Contrary to the widespread misconception, inspiration in swing bands was inspired not by jazz, but by popular dance bands, such as that of Art Hickman."

Paul Whiteman, long after his days as the top hit maker had ended, was still a big name in the music business. He even wrote books: *Jazz* (1926), *How to Be a Bandleader* (1941), and *Records for the Millions* (1948).

Of all of the bands of this era, none equalled the reign of **Paul Whiteman** (1890-1967). His was not only the most successful and influential, but also the most creative of the bands of this time. Whiteman, throughout his career and after, was much maligned by the jazz world because he held the title of "The King of Jazz." The jazz community views his title with the same disdain it holds for Irving Berlin being crowned "The King of Ragtime." In both cases the jazz community is correct, as our investigations of the "underground" will show. On the other hand, the venomous attacks upon Whiteman ("White Man" appropriating the black man's music) miss the point in the context of popular music.

Paul Whiteman played violin and viola in the Denver and San Francisco symphony orchestras before forming his first band in 1919 with arranger-pianist Ferde Grofe, whom he hired away from Art Hickman. Whiteman's band managed to incorporate elements of symphony, jazz, and pop. Jazz, which was in its infancy, had a much looser definition than today and was synonymous with dance music. In 1920, while the band was in residency at the Ambassador Hotel in Los Angeles, the Victor Record Company released "Whispering" backed with "Japanese Sandman." It became the best selling record of the year. Whiteman would go on to record over two hundred hits through 1936. According to *Joel Whitburn's Pop Memories*, Whiteman had thirty-two number one records between 1920 and 1934, far outdistancing any other band.

Charles Schwartz's biography, *Gershwin: His Life and Music*, claims, "Thus, for many, the listening experience associated with the *Rhapsody* besides being a decidedly pleasant one, has come to represent a relatively painless way of absorbing 'culture,' a factor that cannot be overlooked in explaining the popularity of the *Rhapsody*. The 'culture' inherent in the *Rhapsody*, of course, is more in keeping with Tin Pan Alley, Broadway, and the Jazz Age of the 1920s than with traditional art music in which the works of acknowledged European masters are emphasized. Simply by virtue of its uniqueness and popularity, the *Rhapsody* has helped to break down some of the stultifying traditions associated with the concert hall and, in doing so, has been responsible for attracting new audiences to concert halls."

Whiteman's early model for a jazz-oriented dance orchestra was that of Art Hickman. Thomas A. DeLong wrote in *Pops: Paul Whiteman, King of Jazz*, "on a visit to the Fairmont Hotel he [Whiteman] took particular note of an innovative young bandleader, Art Hickman. De-emphasizing the prevailing brassy texture, Hickman had added more saxophones to his group, giving a lush but jazzy sound to his music. The dominant tonal effect of the additional two or three saxophones pleased Paul."

Whiteman's arrangers, Grofe and Bill Challis (who joined in 1928), helped to advance popular big band arranging. Whiteman labeled his music "Paul Whiteman's Jazz Classique," and eventually referred to his style as "symphonic jazz." Challis even left "open spaces" in some arrangements to allow for improvised solos. The jazz elements certainly tower above most of the popular bands of the time that dominated the music charts.

Whiteman included in his band some of the best white jazz players of the period. Henry Busse, an original member on trumpet, co-wrote and was featured on the million-selling "Wang Wang Blues" and is said to have started a vogue for "sweet jazz" with his solo on "When Day Is Done" in 1927. Red Nichols, Jimmy and Tommy Dorsey, Frankie Trumbauer, Red McKenzie, Miff Mole, Jack Teagarden, Joe Venuti, Eddie Lang, and Bix Beiderbecke (for whom after Beiderbecke's departure from the band, Whiteman always kept an open chair) were among the better known instrumentalists who played in the band at one time or another. Mildred Bailey, the first featured female band singer, and a trio called the Rhythm Boys (Al Rinker, Harry Barris, Bailey's brother and Bing Crosby) created vocal jazz for the masses that holds up well today.

Whiteman's attempts to fuse the serious, high-minded respectability of classical music with the vitality of dance band music and jazz culminated in a concert he held on February 12, 1924, at New York's Aeolin Hall. Titled an "Experiment in Modern Music," this concert was Whiteman's attempt to demonstrate the ways in which he was making "discordant jazz" palatable to the pop audience. The gray world of light commercial music that lies between true folk and popular music on one hand and classical high art on the other is called *Mesomusica*. The apotheosis of *Mesomusica* in that long concert was the premier performance of George Gershwin's "Rhapsody in Blue."

Frank Driggs Collection

"Hello, everybody, Lopez speaking." Pianist-bandleader **Vincent Lopez** (1898-1975) appropriated a piano composition by Felix Arndt that was a musical portrait of his sweetheart, Nola Locke, and presented the song "Nola" to her as a gift in 1915. Lopez featured it at the Pekin Restaurant on Broadway just prior to the 1920s. In 1921, he pioneered a series of broadcasts on WJX radio in Newark, New Jersey, opening them with the greeting, "Hello, everybody, Lopez speaking," to the strains of "Nola." Lopez was a big favorite of the high society, whose members danced to his romantic sounds at the Hotel Pennsylvania, Hotel St. Regis, and Hotel Taft (for twenty-seven years) in New York City.

The Singers

One of the best ways to reflect on the mindset of popular music is to investigate its lyrics. Generally speaking, most of what becomes popular is that which is inoffensive and pleasing to the mass population. As a result, dance numbers and love songs have held the nation spellbound from the 1920s to the 1990s. Most of the lyrics of these songs are quite sentimental and have only the most remote connection with reality. The key element of pop music, it must be underlined, is that the audience at large must like it and buy it. Irving Berlin, when told of songwriters who wrote for themselves, exclaimed, "The mob is always right. A good song embodies the feeling of the mob and a songwriter is not much more than a mirror which reflects those feelings. I write a song to please the public—and if the public doesn't like it in New Haven, I change it!"

It is the vocalist who sings the words of the pop songs, and from roughly 1910 to 1930 **Al Jolson** (1886-1950) laid legitimate claim to his title as "The World's Greatest Entertainer." Jolson made his mark as a brash, improvisational performer in the Shubert extravaganza *La Belle Paree* in 1911. Two years later in Shubert's *The Honeymoon Express* Jolson sang his first true standard, "You Made Me Love You." He introduced George Gershwin's first hit, "Swanee," now perhaps the song most identified with him, in 1919.

Entering the twenties, Jolson was the best-known entertainer throughout the world. His highly charged vocal style was often delivered in blackface with white gloves, bent down on one knee and pleading for his "Mammy," or pining for those "April Showers," or waving "Toot, Toot, Tootsie, Goodbye." Jolson's electrifying performances were hard to resist. His was the pre-electrical microphone era, 1924, when a performer on stage had to shout to be heard in the back of the auditorium. Jolson was at his best when he could wander around the stage and walk up runways, which were modeled for him to be closer to his audience as they cheered. Jolson was, as the cliche says, larger than life. His big-belting style, with its constant ad-libbing and animated ramblings, was not captured well by tightly scripted radio or talking film.

The acknowledged kiss of death to the silent film era saw a wide-eyed Jolson announcing to the audience, "You ain't heard nothin' yet," in Warner Brothers' *The Jazz Singer* (1927). Jolson was right. A new medium was created, the talking film, and although Jolson had an even bigger success with the follow up, *The Singing Fool* (1928), by the next decade there would be new stars who would be better suited to the nuances of the electrical microphone and the talking film. Enter the crooners.

Courtesy *Good Time Music*

Al Jolson in blackface. The world's most famous post-minstrel blackface performer.

Courtesy *Buffalo & Erie County Public Library*

George Gershwin's first hit, with words by Irving Caesar, was introduced as incidental music by Arthur Pryor's Band at the Capitol Theatre in New York on October 24, 1919. Nothing much happened to the song until Al Jolson introduced it at a Sunday night concert at the Winter Garden Theater and then interpolated it into the musical *Sinbad*. The result was a resounding success.

Entertainer Georgie Jessel wrote of Jolson in *This Way, Miss:* "He was only content while singing and acknowledging applause; the rest of the time he was champing at the bit while getting ready to go and if he was not on, he was disconsolate. He was cruel most times, *but God, what a great artist he was!*"

Little Jakie Rabinowitz declares he will run away

Ten years later, as Jack Robin, he sings in "Coffee Dan's"

Mary Dale promises to get Jack a chance in vaudeville

WARNER BROS. Supreme Triumph

AL JOLSON

"The Jazz Singer"

Based upon the play by Samson Raphaelson
as produced upon the spoken stage by
Lewis & Gordon and Sam H. Harris

A WARNER BROS. EXTENDED RUN PRODUCTION

In her ballet dance Mary was irresistible

Grateful for her help, Jack loved Mary

The art of crooning-singing romantic lyrics of tuneful songs in an intimate manner-occurred with the advent of electrical recording. Crooning is etched in most people's minds as something Bing Crosby developed. Crosby would later become the most famous of the crooners, but at the time of this style's entrance into the world of pop, he was a hot jazz singer with Al Rinker en route from Gonzaga University to join Paul Whiteman as a Rhythm Boy. Crosby did not whisper his songs like most of the singers who have been labelled "crooners." In fact, Crosby's first influence was the highly charged vocal style of Al Jolson, and certainly Crosby's application of vocal interpretation is by far the jazziest of the "whispering" singers who, after 1925, cooed quietly into the newly invented microphones. Be that as it may, Crosby was stuck with the term, and all of those that followed him were labelled, as he was, "crooner." Along with Crosby, Rudy Vallee and Russ Columbo were considered the preeminent popular crooners of the late 1920s and 1930s. Prior to Crosby's shift from jazz to romantic murmurings, the leaders of crooning included: Vaughn DeLeath, renowned as the first woman to sing on radio (15,000 songs performed on 2,000 broadcasts), and credited by some as the first "crooner"; Art Gillham ("The Whispering Pianist"); "Whispering" Billy Day; "Whispering" Bobby Gray; Confidential Charlie; Cliff Edwards ("Ukulele Ike"); and "Whispering" Jack Smith.

"Whispering" Jack Smith.

"Whispering" Jack Smith (1899-1951) had been a successful cabaret singer after World War I and was known as the "Friendly Song Delineator." During the war he had been injured by an exploding gas shell, which forced him to develop his unusual half-singing, half-talking style. He had twelve hits in the top twenty for Victor between 1926 and 1928. Smith's biggest hit, "Gimme a Little Kiss, Will Ya, Huh?" provides us with a good example of the coy, yet innocent manner in which romance was expressed in popular music of this time. Seeking a kiss, Smith asks his partner, "but what's a little kiss between a feller and his girl?" This was considered risque for a popular song.

Rudy Vallee (1901-1986) played saxophone with the Yale Collegians in 1924-1925 and sang in pre-Crosby crooner style, assisted by a megaphone. He graduated from Yale in 1927 and became the first male singing star of radio performing from New York's Heigh-Ho Club in 1928. Vallee's new group was called the Connecticut Yankees and he opened each show with the greeting, "Heigh-ho, everybody." The next year Vallee's new weekly radio show was titled "The Fleishmann Hour" and it ran for ten years, ultimately assisting the careers of George Burns and Gracie Allen, Edgar Bergen and Charlie McCarthy, and Alice Faye.

Frank Driggs Collection

Rudy Vallee and his band in the 1929 film *The Vagabond Lover*. Born Hubert Prior, Vallee taught himself to play the saxophone by listening to the records of Rudy Wiedoeft, from whom he borrowed the name Rudy. Years before Frank Sinatra started riots at the Paramount Theater in 1943, Rudy Vallee caused such a commotion with his three-day stand in February 1929, at Keith's 81st Street Theater, that mounted police were called out to restore order.

Author's collection

Vallee resuscitated a forgotten University of Maine school song when he introduced it on his NBC radio program and at a personal appearance at the Paramount Theatre in New York in 1930. As a result, the "Stein Song" became one of his best known recordings and remains in the collegiate oral tradition today (see right).

Author's collection

Through 1934 Vallee's recordings on Victor and Columbia were constantly in the top twenty. His radio theme was "My Time Is Your Time," and the first film in which he starred, 1929's *The Vagabond Lover,* cemented his image as the post-collegiate heart-throb of the Jazz Age.

Song	Peak Position	Year	Song	Peak Position	Year
Sweetheart of My Dreams	5	1929	When Yuba Plays the Rhumba on the Tuba	2	1931
If I Had You	7	1929	Life is Just a Bowl of Cherries	3	1931
Marie	2	1929	The Thrill is Gone	10	1931
Honey	1	1929	My Song	10	1931
Weary River	2	1929	I Guess I'll Have to Change My Plan (The Blue Pajama Song)	2	1932
Deep Night	2	1929			
Lover Come Back To Me	9	1929	Strange Interlude	6	1932
Croquette	10	1929	Let's Put Out the Lights	2	1932
My Time is Your Time	8	1929	Brother, Can You Spare a Dime?	1	1932
I'm Just a Vagabond Lover	5	1929	How Deep is the Ocean?	7	1932
S'posin'	7	1929	Here It Is Monday	10	1932
Pretending	10	1929	Just an Echo in the Valley	3	1933
Lonely Troubador	2	1929	Whisper Waltz	6	1933
A Little Kiss Each Morning (A Little Kiss Each Night)	3	1930	The Girl in the Little Green Hat	10	1933
			Maybe it's Because I Love You Too Much	6	1933
Stein Song (University of Maine)	1	1930			
If I Had a Girl Like You	3	1930	The Shadow Waltz	6	1933
Betty Co-Ed	4	1930	Everything I Have is Yours	3	1934
Just a Little Longer	8	1930	Orchids in the Moonlight	4	1934
Confessin' (That I Love You)	4	1930	Flying Down to Rio	6	1934
Sweetheart of My Student Days	9	1930	You Oughtta Be in Pictures	5	1934
You're Driving Me Crazy! What Did I Do?	3	1930	Nasty Man	10	1934
			Lost in a Fog	4	1934
Would You Like to Take a Walk?	4	1931	The Drunkard Song (There is a Tavern in the Town)	6	1934

Source: Joel Whitburn's Pop Memories, 1890-1954.

Rudy Vallee's Big Hits

Bing Crosby (1903-1977) was the most popular entertainer of the twentieth century's first fifty years. His easygoing manner and breezy baritone made him a natural for radio, film, and television. It has been estimated that Crosby had over three hundred hits and sold over four hundred million records. Jazz critic Ralph Gleason says, "He has the gift of free melodic articulation and rhythmic feeling that is the essence of jazz." After leaving Paul Whiteman, Crosby and the Rhythm Boys joined Gus Arnheim's Orchestra at the Coconut Grove in 1929. Crosby's first hit as a solo singer, "I Surrender Dear," led to a radio contract at CBS in 1931. In his first year over the airwaves Crosby had a total of twelve top five songs. He commissioned "Where the Blue of the Night (Meets

Courtesy Buffalo & Erie County Public Library

Bing Crosby sang jazz and scat as a member of Paul Whiteman's Rhythm Boys. The "hot" numbers included a great deal of clowning around. Crosby had left his college group, the Musicaladers, formed by Al Rinker, to tour in 1925 with Rinker in a unit they called Two Boys and a Piano. Whiteman signed the duo in 1926 and put them together with Harry Barris as the Rhythm Boys. Among their key recordings were "Side by Side" and "Changes" (1928), which included Bix Beiderbecke's most celebrated cornet solo with the Whiteman band.

Courtesy Buffalo & Erie County Public Library

Courtesy Sony Music

the Gold of the Day)" in 1932 and it became his radio theme song.

After a series of shorts with the comic director Mack Sennett, that undoubtedly helped sharpen his comic flair, Crosby made his first feature film for Paramount Pictures, *The Big Broadcast of 1932.* He would subsequently appear in over sixty feature films. Crosby took the popular song out of the realm of the vaudeville singers and paved the way for the many who copied his relaxed phrasing, impeccable diction, warmth of approach, and rich baritone quality, all of which, taken together, made the most banal song into a work of art. In many ways, Crosby helped invent popular singing. His informal phrasing and husky baritone made the earlier "whispering" crooners, with their high nasal vocals, sound downright "wimpy." The popularity of these "crooning" vocalists even led to a popular ditty of 1931 titled "Crosby, Columbo, and Vallee."

Crosby's unique and innate sense of rhythm qualified him to be called a jazz singer (his thirties recordings with Duke Ellington and Paul Whiteman attest to that). He brought a jazzman's phrasing and sense of improvisation to everything he did. He introduced scat singing to the pop audience and was a talented whistler. Will Friedwald, whose exhaustive vocal study, *Jazz Singing: America's Great Voices from Bessie Smith to Be Bop and Beyond,* is the most thorough and insightful history written on the subject, . He declares, "Crosby's greatest accomplishment, the result of all this alchemy, was the application of jazz to the music of Tin Pan Alley. The significance of 'hot' music to ballads in particular, had been a nut that no one had been able to crack, especially vocally. Certainly Crosby's assimilation of Armstrong's rhythmic advances gave him a major jump on the competition."

Other Crooners

Singer	Biggest Hit/Theme	Year
Gene Austin	My Blue Heaven	1927
Smith Ballew	Time on My Hands (You in My Arms)	1931
Al Bowlly	Isle of Capri	1934
Lew Bray	We Can't Use Each Other Anymore	1929
Sam Browne	Here Lies Love	1932
Chick Bullock	Underneath the Harlem Moon	1932
Russ Columbo	You Call it Madness (But I Call It Love)	1931
Sam Coslow	Learn to Croon	1933
Cliff Edwards (Ukelele Ike)	Singin' in the Rain	1929
Seger Ellis	When You're Smiling	1928
Little Jack Little	I'm in the Mood for Love	1935
Pat O'Mally	Got a Date With an Angel	1931
Will Osborne	Cocktails for Two	1934
Harry Richman	Puttin' on the Ritz	1930
Willard Robinson	Deep Elm	1927
Val Rosing	Please	1932
Lannie Ross	That's My Desire	1932
Arthur Tracy	Marta	1932

Crosby's No. 1 Hits: 1931-1934

Song	Year
Out of Nowhere	1931
Just One More Chance	1931
At Your Command	1931
Dinah	1931
Please	1932
Brother, Can You Spare a Dime?	1932
You're Getting to Be a Habit With Me	1933
Shadow Waltz	1933
Little Dutch Mill	1934
Love in Bloom	1934
June in January	1934

By 1931 Bing Crosby had become the nation's premier vocalist, and he dominated the decades of the thirties and forties. Crosby became such an institution that changing styles did not dim his appeal. A perennial like Frank Sinatra and Elvis Presley, he remained a star even when his form of music was no longer dominant.

Courtesy Buffalo & Erie County Public Library

Harry Richman was a pianist for performers like Nora Bayes and Sophie Tucker before he established himself as a night club and recording star beginning in 1926. He introduced Irving Berlin's "Puttin' on the Ritz" in 1930. Morton Downey sang with Paul Whiteman from 1919 to the mid twenties, making him the first significant big band singer in popular music. He was best known for his work on radio beginning in 1931 with a fifteen minute singing show several times a week. Downey's theme song was "Wabash Moon," which he sang and whistled.

Singing was one of the few areas in which a woman could make her mark on popular music. The earliest of the female stars began in vaudeville or on the Broadway stage. One of the earliest superstars was Marion Harris, who made some of the earliest blues recordings during the pre-1920s period (she was white), and had a great influence on Ruth Etting. Very little can be found about her in any history. One of the greatest stars of the stage and radio was **Fanny Brice** (1891-1951), a Jewish comedic performer best known for her dialect songs and the way in which her "down home" persona contrasted with the rest of the scantily clad females of Florenz Ziegfeld's shows.

Courtesy Good Time Records

The release of the film *Pennies from Heaven* in 1981 led to a comeback for the elderly "Street Singer," Arthur Tracey. He was booked into a New York club on the basis of his version of the song "Pennies from Heaven" being lip-synched and danced to by actor Vernel Bagneris.

Key Torch Song.

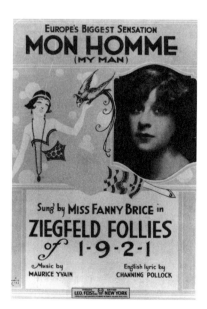

Mon Homme, 1921, sheet music cover. Museum of the City of New York, 51.43.3. The Theater Collection

Frank Driggs Collection

Ruth Etting was one of the first vocalists to master the radio and recording microphone. In their *Discovering Great Singers of Classic Pop,* Roy Hemming and David Hajdu write, "Her intimate, almost cooingly soft-voiced sound (so different from the open-voiced vaudeville and theatrical style of the day) quickly won her the sobriquet 'Chicago's Sweetheart of the Air.' Etting never hesitated to admit that she copied her style at first from Marion Harris. But to distinguish herself from Harris, she began alternating the tempo within parts of a song, singing some phrases in half-time or double-time 'to create and maintain interest' (as she once put it)." Etting starred on Broadway (*Whoopee, Simple Simon, The 9:15 Revue*) and radio (her own shows were sponsored by Oldsmobile in 1934 and Kellogg's College Prom in 1935). She was not as successful in film—however, between her nightclub bookings, recordings, and Broadway, her salary soared to $2,500 a week.

Brice entered show business at the age of thirteen, playing in burlesque and vaudeville. She eventually made the big time when she was featured in the *Ziegfeld Follies.* Her rendition of Irving Berlin's "Sadie Salome, Go Home" in 1909 (she used a Yiddish accent), caught the attention of Ziegfeld, who starred her in the *Follies* of that year. By the 1940s she created a character known as Baby Snooks that kept her in the public eye. Brice's best-known songs included comic selections such as "Second Hand Rose," "Mrs. Cohen at the Beach," and "I'm an Indian." One of the unusual things about Brice was that her signature song was not a comedy number, but a serious, heartbreaking song, "My Man." Barbra Streisand dug deep into the past when she reprised Brice's life in 1964's Broadway show *Funny Girl,* when it was made into a film in 1968. Streisand repeated the tribute in a 1975 film sequel, *Funny Lady.*

The Torch Trio

	Torch Song	Peak Position	Year
Ruth Etting	Lonesome and Sorry	3	1926
	Deed I Do	2	1927
	Shaking the Blues Away	4	1927
	Love Me or Leave Me	2	1929
	I'll Get By as Long as I Have You	3	1929
	Mean to Me	3	1929
	Ten Cents a Dance	5	1930
	Guilty	4	1931
Helen Morgan	A Tree in the Park	9	1927
	Bill	4	1928
	Can't Help Lovin' Dat Man	7	1928
	Mean to Me	11	1929
	Why Was I Born?	8	1930
	Body and Soul	16	1930
Libby Holman	Am I Blue	4	1929
	Moanin' Low	5	1929
	Find Me a Primitive Man	19	1929
	Body and Soul	3	1930
	Something to Remember You By	6	1930
	Love for Sale	5	1931

Movie Star News

Funny Girl starring Barbra Streisand as Fanny Brice. Omar Sharif, right, played the part of Nickie Arnstein. Alice Faye had portrayed a thinly veiled Brice in the 1939 Fox film *Rose of Washington Square*, but to contemporary audiences Fanny Brice will always be Barbra Streisand.

The Torch Trio

Library of Congress   *Frank Driggs Collection*   *Frank Driggs Collection*

Ruth Etting (1907-1978) was Morgan's closest rival, and on record she was to have even greater success. In fact, Etting, who also began her career in Chicago, was the best selling female artist of this time period and was known as the "Sweetheart of Columbia Records." Her first success in New York was as a featured singer in the *Ziegfeld Follies of 1927.* Her life was complicated by a romance with a Chicago gangster successfully depicted in the 1955 film *Love Me or Leave Me*, in which Doris Day played Etting and James Cagney played Moe "the Gimp" Snyder. While Day didn't look or sound like Etting, the film receives high marks for accuracy and the powerful performances by its two stars.

Helen Morgan (1900-1941) was considered the "Queen of Chicago," where she developed the sensual technique of sitting elegantly atop the piano, eyelids drooped, delivering her sad laments. Morgan's great success on radio and records were slight compared to her sensational nightclub appearances. Her style seemed best suited to the intimacy of cafe society. Morgan fronted a series of nightclubs named after her in New York. The singer was often the subject of controversial newspaper headlines. Morgan's biggest success on the Broadway stage was in *Show Boat,* but her last years were spent in poverty. In 1957, Warner Brothers starred Ann Blyth (voice dubbed by Gogi Grant) in a less-than-inspired biopic, *The Helen Morgan Story.*

Libby Holman (1904-1971) was an olive-skinned beauty who hailed from Cincinnati. She was a successful Broadway performer, often appearing with Clifton Webb. In 1929's *The Little Show* Holman introduced two of her signature songs, "Moanin' Low" and "Body and Soul." Holman's brooding vocal style and tempestuous private life led her to be labeled "the dark purple menace." Holman became a "cause celebre" in the 1940s with her duets with a black folk singer, Josh White, at sophisticated New York clubs and concert halls. Holman's amazing life, which is stranger than much fiction, was detailed in Jon Bradshaw's 1985 *Dreams That Money Can Buy: The Tragic Life of Libby Holman.*

While the men established the vocal style of "crooning" in the twenties and thirties, the white female singers created the "torch song." In *The Jazz Age*, Arnold Shaw saw a contrast to the flapper image of women during the twenties. Depicted as light-hearted, fun-filled, jazz-age thrill-seekers, Shaw notes that the musical theater reflected "the visage of the tragic music." Shaw described the kind of songs they sang as "a song of lost love with the singer carrying a torch for one who no longer shares, or perhaps, has never shared, the other person's feelings, also, songs of slavish submissiveness in the face of mistreatment. Sometimes, the torch song is described as a white blues." The leading torch singers of this era were Ruth Etting, Helen Morgan, and Libby Holman. Morgan, who popularized the tradition of leaning (with arched back) or sitting on the piano while singing, was the best known of these torch singers. All three women led lives that mirrored the melancholy tunes and lyrics they sang.

The Depression and the Early 1930s

Library of Congress

Reginald Marsh's 1930s depiction of down-and-out Americans who stood in bread and soup lines during the Great Depression.

By 1930 breadlines were appearing in American cities and by 1932 some twelve million Americans, nearly 25 percent of the workforce, were unemployed. Franklin Roosevelt, the Democratic nominee for president in 1932, declared the need for government intervention as he galvanized audiences with promises of caring for the "forgotten man." Roosevelt easily defeated Herbert Hoover, carrying forty-two states, with 472 electoral votes to Hoover's 59.

In addition to overturning Prohibition, the new president led the way with his New Deal and its three R's: relief, recovery, and reform. Roosevelt introduced fifteen new laws and programs in his first one hundred days in office. Progress was slow, but most importantly, the majority of Americans believed that Roosevelt was doing the best he could.

Through this difficult time America turned to entertainment to help escape the realities of the day. Occasionally a touch of truth would be found in pop songs like "Brother, Can You Spare a Dime?" But, the songs that made people happy, such as "Life Is Just a Bowl of Cherries," "Night and Day," and "I've Got My Love to Keep Me Warm," were preferred over gloom and doom songs. One merely has to look at the top hits on the charts during this time to see this fact.

Moviegoing was essential to Depression-riddled America. In the year just before the beginning of the Depression, 1929, some 500 features were released, 335 of which were talkies. With the advent of talkies came musical film and a need for actors and singers from the Broadway stage. For the first time, American audiences could see people they had been hearing on record and radio. Hollywood moved fast, offering vast amounts of money to Tin Pan Alley songwriters and radio and Broadway musical stars. The songs introduced in talkies became a new source for charted songs. It should be no surprise that the early musicals were reworks of the Broadway ideal: operettas, revues, or musical comedies. The most immediate impact on popular music was made by the revue and the musical comedy.

The revue was the least cinematic of the musicals, but they were conceived as film company showcases. Revues introduced well-known stars in front of curtained stages and offered a potpourri of independent performances. The shows had everything from comics Laurel and Hardy putting on a

62

magic act to Joan Crawford singing and dancing (a painful sight in "Gotta Feelin' for You," in MGM's *The Hollywood Revue of 1929*). In 1930 *Paramount of Parade* featured a dozen directors sending forth artists such as Maurice Chevalier with chorus girls performing "Sweeping the Clouds Away" and the "It" girl, Clara Bow, dancing with sailors and singing "I'm True to the Navy Now." Warner Brothers' 1929 *The Show of Shows* had everything: Ted Lewis doing a "pirate jazz" ditty, a scene from *Richard III* featuring John Barrymore, dog star Rin-Tin-Tin barking an introduction, a broadly enacted operetta piece, an Al Jolson imitation and a bicycle number, among others. The highlight of the film was Winnie Lightner dwarfed amidst a skyscraper-like bathtub vocalizing "Singin' in the Bathtub."

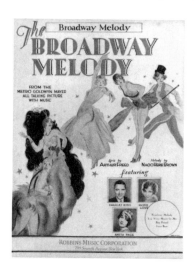

Author's collection

The first of the "all talking all singing all dancing" pictures, as MGM advertised in 1929, was the musical comedy *The Broadway Melody*. Hollywood was recreating in musical comedy, just as it did in the operetta and the revue, everything it knew about the conventions of Broadway. *The Broadway Melody* was the first of many that told the story of the backstage musical. It showed the hard work of auditions, rehearsals, and putting on the show. Not everyone in America could go to a Broadway musical in New York, but now, with the magic of talkies, they could go to their local movie house and see and hear the wonders of Hollywood's version of "good old" Broadway. Songs written by Nacio Herb Brown and Arthur Freed were featured ("You Were Meant For Me"), but Cohan's "Give My Regards to Broadway" and Victor Herbert's "In Old New York" were interpolated to ensure identification with the city. The studio spent $280,000 on the film, which returned a whopping $4 million and won an Oscar as best film of the year. Audiences were so enthralled that backstage musicals became the rage (followups included *Broadway Babies, Broadway Scandals*, and *The Gold Diggers of Broadway*).

Successful Broadway shows were also adapted into Hollywood musicals, among them *Sunny Side Up, Good News, Rio Rita, No, No, Nanette, Hit the Deck, Sally, Little Johnny Jones, Follow Thru, Whoopee*, and *Flying High*. Some of the problems of following the Broadway formula for the silver screen were that Broadway musicals ran close to three hours and included twelve to fourteen songs or more. Hollywood had to compress both the length of the musical and the number of songs. Theater musicals were also established physically with an eye on how the entire stage looked from somewhere in the middle of the auditorium. Early Hollywood musicals took this approach and the films ended up looking static. Finally, most of America's best songwriters lived on the East Coast, and, like many of people in the theater, they had a rather condescending attitude toward the "Philistines" of the West Coast. Filmgoers of 1932 must have begun thinking the same thing, because after the initial explosion there was a precipitous decline in Hollywood musicals. In 1928 Hollywood produced some sixty musicals, and by 1930 more than seventy, but in 1932 there were less than fifteen movie musicals, and only two, director Ernest Lubitsch's *One Hour With You* and *The Kid from Spain*, starring Eddie Cantor, made a profit. The film musical was considered dead. But suddenly, in 1933, came the genre's first geniuses, Busby Berkeley and Fred Astaire.

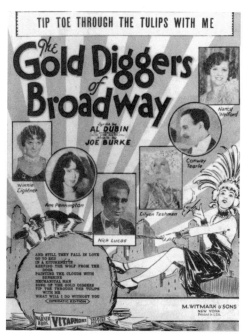

Author's collection

The Gold Diggers of Broadway was a musical revue with an all-star cast that included Ann Pennington, Winnie Lightner, and Nick Lucas, whose "Tiptoe Through the Tulips With Me" would be revived in 1969 by singer Tiny Tim.

Ted Lewis: "Is Everybody Happy?" A master showman, Lewis was a clarinetist, singer, bandleader and songwriter who became a popular entertainer after long years in vaudeville. He was a star on radio and, like Rudy Vallee and Bing Crosby, moved into Hollywood picture making. An early talkie, *Is Everybody Happy?* (1929) was based on his famous spoken interlude. Lewis had more than a hundred hits between 1920 and 1933 on Columbia Records. One of his classic numbers was a shadow dance to "Me and My Shadow," which he performed with "shadow," Eddie Chester, who worked in the background, imitating Lewis's choreographed moves simultaneously. Lewis was known as the "High-Hat Tragedian of Song." As far as the masses were concerned Lewis was a jazz artist. After all, he did perform snappy, jazz-oriented songs, and this was the "Jazz Age." In addition, Lewis was a primary influence on later jazz great Woody Herman. Underground jazz artists of this period, like Louis Armstrong, Bix Beiderbecke, Sidney Bechet, King Oliver, and Jelly Roll Morton were not yet well known to the wide public.

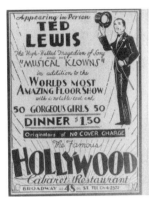 

Frank Driggs Collection

Busby Berkeley (1895-1976) had no formal training in dance but had been a successful New York choreographer for seven years with twenty-one opening nights to his credit during the twenties. He came to Hollywood in 1930 and worked on four films (three of which starred Eddie Cantor) before preparing to return to New York. The head of production for Warner Brothers, Darryl F. Zannuck, convinced him to stay on for one more film, *42nd Street*. This production changed the fortunes of the musical film in Hollywood. It was a typical backstage musical, but its salvation was Berkeley's imaginative choreography and camera eye. Berkeley's genius was that he pushed the decorative possibilities of chorus girls, grand pianos, neon-lit violins, overhead shots,, and optical illusions to the limit. Most importantly, Berkeley showed what could be done with a moving camera, changing the view of the musical from a static, third-row-center theater seat by creating flamboyant, kaleidoscopic patterns from vantage points that only the movable camera could capture. In *42nd Street* the dancers seldom danced; they were moved about with Berkeley's direction, which called for innumerable camera setups.

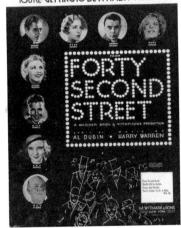

Author's collection

Movie Star News

Left, the opening scene from *Gold Diggers of 1933*. *Right*, Warner Baxter as the hard-driving stage director giving a pep talk to Ruby Keeler, to his left, and the other chorines in *42nd Street*.

Dames (1934) featured Harry Warren and Al Dubin's "I Only Have Eyes for You," sung by Dick Powell to Ruby Keeler in a dream sequence that featured scores of floating Keeler cutout faces.

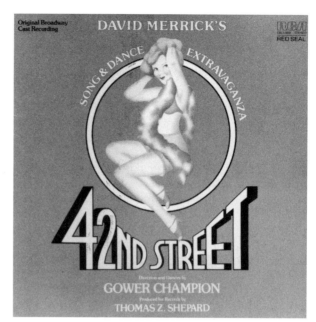

42nd Street Comes to Broadway. The successful reprise of *42nd Street* made its Broadway debut at the Winter Garden Theatre on August 25, 1980, and was seen in London at the Theatre Royal, Drury Lane, in 1984. The theatrical production added classic Warren and Dubin songs from other Warner Brothers films.

Before Berkeley came along, most filmed musicals were singing musicals. Berkeley put the emphasis on extravagant dance numbers. With the ultimate success of *42nd Street*, Berkeley stayed in Hollywood for most of his career. Between 1933 and 1934 he choreographed seven more films for Warner Brothers. The prosperity of Warner's was not that of a one-man show, however. More than any other film genre, the musical is a collaborative endeavor, and script writers, scene designers, orchestrators, songwriters and actors, can make or break any project.

With so many failing with the musical, what made the Warner Brothers' efforts work? The company had an attitude that fit the times. In the midst of the Depression, it gave audiences a taste of the "proletarian musical." These were musicals that were not far removed from the realities of unemployment. They were backstage stories about "putting on a show," but without sufficient production capital. Those putting on the show had to work hard and hope for a break or they'd be walking the streets. The director of the show was not unlike President Roosevelt trying to find a New Deal for the people. In *42nd Street,* the director pleads with youngster Ruby Keeler to go out and give the performance of her life lest the show be a failure. The *Gold Diggers of 1933* opens with chorus girls dressed in coins singing, "We're in the Money," only to have the rehearsal stopped by the sheriff because the producers have run out of same. Later, when the show is put on, Joan Blondell sings "(Remember) My Forgotten Man", a song about what Roosevelt famously called " forgotten men," the soldiers who returned from the WWI. And in 1933's *Footlight Parade*, an American flag is produced and a gigantic picture of Roosevelt shown in the patriotic "Shanghai Lil" number. Though these films touched on the Depression, the numbers were uplifting, and the pace and humor were spirited.

One more thing must be mentioned about the achievements of the Warner Brothers musicals—the songs. Composed by Harry Warren with lyrics by Al Dubin, the songs became immediate hits on the popular music charts. In 1933, for example, "Forty-Second Street" by Don Bestor and both "You're Getting to Be a Habit With Me" and "Shadow Waltz" by Bing Crosby, became number 1 hits.

Fred Astaire and RKO

Fred Astaire (1899-1986) began his career on Broadway performing with his sister Adele. They were the darlings of the smart set in New York, with hit shows like *Lady Be Good* (1924), *Funny Face* (1927), and *The Band Wagon* (1931). When Adele stopped performing to marry a British aristocrat, Fred worked solo and had success in *Gay Divorce* (1932) opposite Claire Luce. Astaire's Hollywood screen test resulted in a famous memo, "Can't act, can't sing, slightly bald. Can dance a little." Astaire was signed to a contract by Radio Keith Orpheum, but he made screen debut on loan to MGM for *Dancing Lady* (1933), playing himself opposite Joan Crawford and Clark Gable.

Astaire's RKO career began in 1933 opposite Ginger Rogers in *Flying Down to Rio*. They played the secondary, comedic couple to the film's top-billed love duo, Dolores Del Rio and Gene Raymond. They stole the film with their south-of-the-border number, "The Carioca." In 1934 they were given top billing in *The Gay Divorcee*. Reviewer Andre Sennwald summed up Astaire's persona: "The audience meets Mr. Astaire and the film at their best when he is adjusting his cravat to an elaborate dance routine or saying delicious things with his flashing feet that a lyricist would have difficulty putting into words." Astaire and Rogers established their screen identities as Hollywood's most famous dancing couple, reuniting for eight more films.

Astaire combined grace and inventiveness in dance, to become the screen's foremost song-and-dance man. He was also a very accomplished vocalist although he strained to make his high notes, (adding a sense of drama to his style) and he always sang in tune. Aside from Bing Crosby, Astaire introduced more certifiable standards in film than any other singer. It should be noted, too, that with

Bandwagon, 1931. Museum of the City of New York. The Theater Collection

The darlings of the New York theater crowd were Fred and sister Adele Astaire, seen here in 1931's *Bandwagon*. They made ten major Broadway musicals between 1917 and 1931. Adele quit show business to marry Charles Cavendish a British aristocrat. In his autobiography, *Steps in Time,* Astaire said his sister's departure put his career in crisis because he had always played the secondary comic relief to his sister's leading lady role (obviously they never played lead romantic roles opposite each other) However, through his engaging persona as a man-about-town entertainer Astaire was able to achieve even greater cinematic popularity.

Movie Star News

Left, film poster from the first Fred Astaire and Ginger Rogers film. Note that Rogers is billed fourth, ahead of Astaire. Future films would bill them as the stars, with Astaire's name first. *Right,* this remake of the 1932 stage hit excluded all but one of Cole Porter's songs ("Night and Day"). The newly appointed film censorship board retitled *Gay Divorce,* making it *The Gay Divorcee.* The thinking seems to have been that while a divorcee could conceivably be gay (as in mirthful), a divorce could not.

Author's collection

"The Continental" was a south-of-the-border follow-up to "The Carioca." This Herb Magidson and Con Conrad tune was an interpolation in a Cole Porter score and in 1934, became the first to win the Academy Award for best song in a motion picture.

Astaire's arrival in Hollywood there was new approval of Tinseltown among Broadway professionals. Irving Berlin came out to California and wrote for Astaire, as did George and Ira Gershwin. Whereas Berkeley made the dance a kaleidoscopic group spectacle, Astaire eventually created the intimate dance of love for two, with the individual solo dance filmed full-frame so that the dancer's moves could be seen completely. The RKO stories were quite different from Warner Brothers' gritty, everyman chronicles. The world of Astaire and Rogers were the never-never land of Art Deco. Designer Van Nest Polglase created what was called the "Big White Set," filled with streamlined chrome and shiny bakelite floors. Money was seldom an issue in these fairy tales. What mattered was Astaire convincing Rogers that, despite complications, he really did love her, which was showcased in their dancing.

So, this is the mainstream overview of the world of popular music between 1917 and 1934. Not one of the top-selling artists of this period had been a force between 1900 and 1917 (see charts). In pop music, styles change quickly. With this knowledge in hand, we are now ready to embark on a journey into the musical underground.

Key Hollywood Musicals: 1927-34

Musical/Studio/Stars	Hit Song	Year
The Jazz Singer /Warner Brothers/Al Jolson	Toot Toot Tootsie Goodbye; April Showers; Mammy	1927
The Singing Fool /Warner Brothers/ Al Jolson	Sonny Boy; It All Depends on You; I'm Sittin' on Top of the World	1928
The Broadway Melody /MGM/Charles King Bessie Love, Anita Page	You Were Meant for Me; The Wedding of the Painted Doll; Broadway Melody	1929
The Hollywood Revue of 1929/MGM/ assorted studio stars	Singin' in the Rain; Nobody but You; You Were Meant for Me	1929
Gold Diggers of Broadway /Warner Brothers/ Winnie Lightner, Nick Lucas	Tiptoe Through the Tulips; Painting the Clouds with Sunshine; Singin' in the Bathtub	1929
The Love Parade /Paramount/Maurice Chevalier, Jeanette MacDonald	(No hits; Ernst Lubitsch's first sound film as director)	1929
King of Jazz/Universal/Paul Whiteman & assorted stars	Rhapsody in Blue; Mississippi Mud; It Happened in Monterey	1930
Palmy Days /MGM/Eddie Cantor, George Raft	My Honey Said Yes Yes	1931
The Big Broadcast/Paramount/Bing Crosby, George Burns, Gracie Allen, Kate Smith, Mills Brothers, Boswell Sisters, Cab Calloway	Marta; Crazy People; Dinah; Minnie the Moocher; When the Moon Comes Over the Mountain; Where the Blue of the Night (Meets the Gold of the Day); Tiger Rag; Here Lies Love	1932
Love Me Tonight /Paramount/Maurice Chevalier, Jeanette MacDonald	Isn't It Romantic?; Mimi; Lover	1932
The Kid From Spain/MGM/Eddie Cantor, Robert Young	What a Perfect Combination	1932
She Done Him Wrong/Paramount/Mae West, Cary Grant	A Guy What Takes His Time; I Wonder Where My Easy Rider's Gone	1933
42nd Street /Warner Brothers/Dick Powell, Ruby Keeler	You're Getting to Be a Habit With Me; Shuffle Off to Buffalo; 42nd Street	1933
Gold Diggers of 1933/Warner Brothers/ Dick Powell, Ruby Keeler	We're in the Money; My Forgotten Man	1933
Flying Down to Rio/RKO/Delores Del Rio, Gene Raymond, Fred Astaire, Ginger Rogers	The Carioca; Music Makes Me; Orchids in the Moonlight	1933
Going Hollywood /MGM/Bing Crosby, Marion Davies	Temptation; After Sundown; Beautiful Girl	1933
Roman Scandals /MGM/Eddie Cantor, Ruth Etting	Build a Little Home; No More Love	1933
Dames/Warner Brothers/Dick Powell, Ruby Keeler	I Only Have Eyes for You; Try to See It My Way; Dames	1934
Here Is My Heart/Paramount/Bing Crosby, Kitty Carlisle	Around the Corner; With Every Breath I Take	1934
The Gay Divorcee/RKO/Fred Astaire, Ginger Rogers	Night and Day; The Continental	1934

Top Selling Artists: 1917-34

Artist	Top 20 Hits	No. 1 Hits	Top Hit (weeks)	Year
Paul Whiteman	204	32	Whispering (11)	1920
Ted Lewis	101	6	In a Shanty in Old Shanty Town (10)	1932
Guy Lombardo	79	11	Charmine! (7)	1927
Al Jolson	71	16	Sonny Boy (12)	1928
Bing Crosby	70	11	June in January (7)	1934
Isham Jones	68	8	I'll See You in My Dreams (7)	1925
Rudy Vallee	61	3	Stein Song (University of Maine) (10)	1930
Ruth Etting	61	1	Life is a Song (12)	1935
Leo Reisman	58	4	Night and Day (vocal, Fred Astaire) (10)	1932
Ben Selvin	57	7	Dardenella (13)	1920
Nat Shilkret	54	1	Dancing With Tears in My Eyes (7)	1930
Fred Waring	50	5	Little White Lies (6)	1930
Marion Harris	43	4	Look for the Silver Lining (10)	1921

Source: Joel Whitburn's Pop Memories 1890-1954

Grammy Hall of Fame: 1900-1934

Song	Year	Performer	Label	Inducted
Nobody	1906	Bert Williams	Columbia	1981
Rhapsody in Blue	1927	Paul Whiteman's Concert Orchestra with George Gershwin	Victor	1947
My Blue Heaven	1928	Gene Austin	Victor	1991
Singin' the Blues	1927	Frankie Trumbauer featuring Bix Beiderbecke	Okeh	1977
In a Mist	1927	Bix Beiderbecke	Okeh	1980
West End Blues	1928	Louis Armstrong & His Hot Five	Okeh	1974
Black And Tan Fantasy	1928	Duke Ellington & His Orchestra	Victor	1981
Empty Bed Blues	1928	Bessie Smith	Columbia	1983
Blue Yodel (#1 For Texas)	1928	Jimmie Rodgers	Victor	1985
Ain't Misbehavin'	1929	Fats Waller	Victor	1984
Pine Top's Boogie Woogie	1929	Clarence "Pine Top" Smith	Vocalion	1983
Mood Indigo	1931	Duke Ellington & His Orchestra	Brunswick	1975
Show Boat	1932	Paul Robeson, Helen Morgan	Brunswick	1991
Crazy Blues	1920	Mamie Smith	Okeh	1993

Source: National Academy of Recording Arts & Sciences

Frank Driggs Collection

Say Goodbye to the crooners. Aside from Bing Crosby, the advent of swing in the mid-thirties was the swan song for America's crooners. **Gene Austin** (1900-1972) was an amiable vocal and piano stylist, who had a career on radio and records, and he was known as "The Voice of the Southland." Austin's most famous recording, "My Blue Heaven," was the second-biggest non-holiday record seller of the entire pre-1950 era. **Russ Columbo** (1908-1934) was Bing Crosby's chief crooning rival. The handsome singer's theme was "You Call It Madness." Columbo's "Prisoner of Love" became a lasting classic later recorded by the Ink Spots and Perry Como. Columbo was killed in a bizarre gun accident.

Chapter 4

THE BLUES

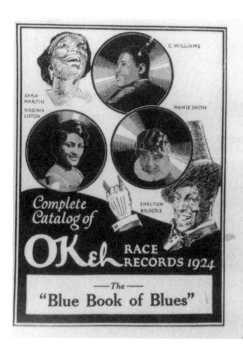

Frank Driggs Collectione

Race record ads. Okeh Records's success with Mamie Smith's "Crazy Blues" created a stir in the record industry. Record companies sought black female singers like Smith to record on their newly established "race series" of recorded releases. Okeh, the first of the companies to issue race records, numbered its releases as its 8000 series. Paramount followed in 1921 with their 12000 series and Columbia was next, in 1922, with its 14000D series. Other key companies and series were Vocalion's, 1000 series (1925), Perfect's 100 series (1925), Brunswick's 7000 series (1926), and Victor's V38500 series (1927).

Blues is a form of music and poetry developed by black people in the United States sometime after the Civil War. Much blues material was played and listened to by the poorest and most uneducated black people. Blues musicians lived somewhat less restricted by social conventions and this resulted in constant attacks from the church and the burgeoning black middle class. Often the blues was referred to as "the Devil's music." The blues form was probably derived from moans (non-lyrical humming), and field hollers (rhythmic vocalizing, sometimes referred to as "arhoolies"). There are many modifications of blues's structure. What has been regarded as the classic form of the blues is known as the A-A-B lyric-stanza form (see mock lyric stanza below). This usually consists of a twelve-measure standardized chordal sequence. A blues chorus usually falls into a twelve-bar pattern, divided into three call-and-response sections. The call, a lyric line, is followed by an instrumental response.

Key of C major:

A	A	B
call 1-2 response 3-4	call 5-6 response 7-8	call 9-10 response 11-12
I	IV I	V I
C chord	F chord C chord	G chord C chord

A) *It's Monday mornin' and I'm feelin' so sad*
A) *Oh, my, it's Monday mornin' and I'm feelin' so sad*
B) *Got to go to school, you know I'm feelin' mighty bad*

The first blues songs were performed by migrant freedmen who put words and storylines to the moans and field hollers. From this tradition, a formalized, though oral and unwritten, blues structure—a folk form—developed. And out of this folk form emerged a commercial entertainment genre. Recordings mediated the music of these black underground troubadours. Although rural bluesmen were the first to perform the blues, it was the recorded female vocalists who first brought the blues national attention.

Classic Blues Singers

The classic blues *style* (as distinct from the classic blues *form*—the A-A-B structure) featured black female vocalists who made race records and toured the vaudeville and tent show circuit between the years of 1920 and 1930. On stage, these singers often danced and performed in dramatic or comedic skits. Musically, they were the first to merge vocal blues with instrumental jazz. The breakthrough for vocal blues on record occurred when **Mamie Smith** (1883-1946) recorded Perry Bradford's "Crazy Blues" for the Okeh label. The record was issued in November 1920 and was advertised widely in black communities. The success of "Crazy Blues" was unprecedented and helped create a demand for other black female singers. Okeh Records supervisor Ralph S. Peer published an ad in the *Chicago Defender* on May 23, 1920, announcing "The World's Greatest Race Artists on the World's Greatest Race Records," and thereafter the term was used to describe an entire specialized field of blacks on record. Smith was billed "Queen of the Blues" and as Derrick Stewart Baxter noted in *Ma Rainey and the Classic Blues Singers*, "It was her pioneering work that paved the way for every other blues artist, regardless of style".

Get this number for your phonograph on Okeh Record No. 4169

Frank Driggs Collection

Mamie Smith's groups were listed as the "Jazz Hounds," or "Her Gang." Performers played to segregated audiences, and when black blues artists played for whites they usually steered away from raunchy material. In advertisements intended for white audiences they often used the tag, "Passed by the Board of Censorship." Pianist Willie "The Lion" Smith, above, claimed in his, autobiography, *Music on My Mind*, that Smith "was a very high-class entertainer, as well as being one of the best-looking women in the business." Smith was one of many black females who played in the classier night clubs and performed on stage with her various touring revues. She made more black films than any of the other Classic Blues Singers.

Other females who were successful recording blues artists in (1921) were Lucille Hegamin ("The Jazz Me Blues," and "I'll Be Good but I'll Be Lonesome" backed with "Arkansas Blues," featuring jazz support of her Blue Flame Syncopators), Alberta Hunter ("How Long Daddy, How Long?"), Ethel Waters ("Down Home Blues"), and Trixie Smith ("Trixie's Blues").

By 1923 race records had come into their own with many companies releasing songs by a plethora of black vaudeville female singers that were categorized as the "Classic Blues Singers"(see chart). Two tower over the others in influence and talent: "Ma" Rainey and Bessie Smith.

Frank Driggs Collection

Courtesy Black Swan Records   Courtesy Yazoo Records

Mother of the Blues: "Ma" Rainey. "Ma" Rainey worked for the three most popular touring tent shows of the period: F. S. Wolcott's Rabbit Foot Minstrels, Pete Werley's Florida Cotton Blossoms, and Silas Green's Company from New Orleans. When Paramount released "Dream Blues," the company designed a blue and yellow picture label, according to Frank Driggs, "probably the first in the history of popular records." This was years before Al Jolson, Ted Lewis, or Paul Whiteman, national stars of the highest order on records, had their own picture labels.

"Ma" Rainey (1886-1939), whose real name was Gertrude Pridgett, was called the "Mother of the Blues." Born into a family of minstrel troupers, she married William "Pa" Rainey. When they were with Tolliver's Circus and Musical Extravaganza, they were billed as "Rainey & Rainey, Assassinators of the Blues" (1914-16). Eventually they performed with the Rabbit Foot Minstrels, which played the South, maintaining close links to the poor black working-class audience.

From 1923 to 1929 "Ma" Rainey's authoritative style was to be the mainstay of the Paramount 12000 series, which promoted itself as the "Popular Race Record." "Ma" Rainey (her first name always appeared in quotes) could boast of having more nicknames than any of the classic blues singers. She was billed the "Gold Necklace Woman of the Blues," the "Paramount Wildcat," the "Songbird of the South," the "Black Nightingale," and the "Mother of the Blues." She recorded with raw, rural jug bands as well as with jazz instrumentation. In all, she made around ninety sides for Paramount Records.

Rainey helped establish the "tough woman" stance that many classic blues singers would uphold over the years. Songs celebrating "antisocial" activities such as prostitution, drugs, and sex with both men and women were part of the thematic fabric that churchgoing folks and other "respectable" people found reprehensible. In *Nothing but the Blues: The Music and the Musicians,* Lawrence Cohn declares that Rainey "dealt frankly with social deviancy, combining humor with an expression of shock when she sang of finding her man with another man ('Sissy Blues') but celebrating lesbianism in her first-person ('Prove It on Me Blues') and bemoaning the life of a prostitute in ('Hustling Blues')." These and other tough-minded songs pull no punches. They are blues at their best, allowing humor to merge with grief, and candor to displace vulgarity. Rainey must have been quite a sight—bejewelled in diamonds, pearls, and gold coins all topped with a glittering beaded headband, and she accessorized the outfit by swishing a large ostrich-feather fan. Rainey featured an enormous eagle backdrop on stage and would appear out of a giant replica of a Victrola. Eventually, she was successfully running her own traveling show, which carried some four trunks of scenery, which including her own with a picture of the Paramount label on it. Rainey's deep, rich, contralto voice majestically moaned and roared. Hers was not the most sophisticated of the classic voices. Her audience was the downtrodden in the deep South who understood when she sang of having "Many days of sorrow, many nights of woe / And a ball and chain, everywhere I go" ("Chain Gang Blues," 1926). During the 1980s, August Wilson's musical play, *"Ma" Rainey's Black Bottom,* resurrected many of the classic blues songs of the past.

The Empress of the Blues. Bessie Smith, at her peak, commanded $2,000 per week for her theater appearances. Chris Albertson writes in *Bessie Smith: Empress of the Blues*: "By 1924 Bessie had became the highest-paid black entertainer in the country and had been proclaimed the Empress of the Blues. The following summer she added real class to her tours by purchasing her own railroad car. Seventy-eight feet long, it could accommodate the whole show with seven staterooms comfortably sleeping twenty-eight of the more privileged performers, and a lower level that housed as many as thirty-five additional troupers. A room in the rear of the car stored the electric generator used to light up Bessie's tent, the huge canvas and cases of soft drinks, Crackerjacks, peanuts and other items sold by Bessie's crew doubling as vendors."

Novelist and photographer Carl Van Vechten exclaimed, "It was the real thing—a woman cutting her heart open with a knife until it was exposed for all of us to see, so that we suffered as she suffered, exposed with a rhythmic ferocity, indeed, which could hardly be borne." In *Shadow and Act* Ralph Ellison praised, "Bessie Smith might have been a 'Blues Queen' to the society at large, but within the tighter Negro community where the blues were a total way of life, and major expression of an attitude towards life, she was a priestess, a celebrant who affirmed the values of the group and man's ability to deal with chaos."

When Smith died, thousands of people attended her funeral in Philadelphia. It wasn't until 1970 that a tombstone was placed on the grave site. Popular rock singer Janis Joplin, along with Juanita Green, provided the gift, which read:

THE GREATEST BLUES SINGER
IN THE WORLD WILL NEVER
STOP SINGING
BESSIE SMITH
1894 - 1937

She recorded 60 of the world's greatest vocal blues records without a microphone.

When Bessie made her early recordings the microphone hadn't even been invented.

Her 5-ft. 9-in. 200-pound body would send a booming voice through a cone-shaped horn which activated a stylus that cut the master.

But even this crude way of recording could not distort the genius of Bessie's voice. Her pitch was considered phenomenal. She could hit a note right in the middle and shade a vowel a thousand different ways.

Sixty songs exist today that Bessie recorded without a microphone. All are included on five two-record albums which contain all 160 recordings (existing) of her voice.

The third album of this series has just been released, called "Empty Bed Blues." It contains 31 songs made by Bessie during the years 1924 (pre-microphone) and 1928.

"Bessie didn't mess with the mike," John Hammond, executive producer of these albums, recently said in a national magazine. "She had to come up before the days of the microphone so she developed a pair of pipes you couldn't believe."

Fortunately, because of these albums, John, we can believe. We can believe.

On Columbia Records

Bessie Smith (1894-1937), considered the greatest of all the female blues singers, worked with Rainey between 1912 and 1915. The legacy of her recorded works (1923-33) survives on Columbia Records-some 160 selections. Columbia's recording director, Frank Walker, had heard Smith sing in a small club in Selma, Alabama, and finally signed her to record a cover record of Alberta Hunter's "Down Hearted Blues" on February 17, 1923. Considering that at the time, the blues was still a very underground form of music, the record amazingly became a huge hit, selling some 780,000 copies in six months. A total of fifteen of Smith's records made the charts, thus making Smith the best-known blues vocalist of the period. Dubbed the "Empress of the Blues," she recorded with some of the finest jazzmen of the era: trumpeters Louis Armstrong and Joe Smith, pianists Fletcher Henderson and James P. Johnson, and, most engaging of all, trombonist Charlie Green ("Trombone Cholly"), with whom Smith made some of her warmest and wittiest recordings. At her peak, Smith was paid an unheard of sum of $250 a side and her success was said to have saved Columbia from bankruptcy. Smith's imperial voice and statuesque figure dominated the stage as she sang hits like "'Taint Nobody's Bizness if I Do," "Nobody Knows You When You're Down and Out," "After You've Gone," "St. Louis Blues," and "Shipwreck Blues." Like most of the better-known classic singers, Smith toured the black vaudeville circuit throughout the South and even played some of the major northern cities. She signed with the prestigious Theater Owners Booking Association (TOBA-known among black artists as Tough on Black Artists or Tough on Black Asses). The Depression severely hampered Smith's career, as it did that of most black artists, because their audience was poor and could no longer afford the luxury of going to costly theatrical spectacles. As a result, black show business was nearly obliterated during the Depression.

Courtesy of V.I.E.W. Video, 34 E. 23rd St., New York, NY 10010 800-843-9843

Certainly the longest-lasting career of the classic blues singers belonged to **Alberta Hunter** (1897-1985). Hunter starred in cabaret and vaudeville. In 1927 she played the role of Queenie opposite Paul Robeson in *Show Boat* at London's Drury Lane Theatre. Hunter was billed as the "Prima Donna of the Blues Singers," the "Idol of Dreamland," "America's Foremost Brown Blues Singer," and "Marian Anderson of the Blues." Hunter began a comeback at Barney Josephson's The Cookery in 1977. Although her "Down Home Blues" brought Hunter fame and some fortune (she collected royalties into the 1980s) her theme song was "My Castle's Rockin'. "

Courtesy DRG Records

Claudie Segovia and Hector Orezzoli's musical revue, *Black and Blue*, played Broadway in the late 1980s. Ruth Brown, Linda Hopkins, and Carrie Smith were the three divas that shared the stage. Classic blues and jazz selections such as "St. Louis Blues," "I Want a Big Butter and Egg Man," "'Taint Nobody's Bizness if I Do," "I Can't Give You Anything but Love," "Black and Tan Fantasy," and "Black and Blue" were among the standout numbers.

Courtesy Alligator Records

Saffire (the "Uppity Blues Women") presented blues from a female perspective. Combining original material ("Middle Aged Blues Boogie," "Even Yuppies Get the Blues", and "Fess Up When You Mess Up") with blues standards ("I Almost Lost My Mind" and "Wild Women Don't Have the Blues") the group gained great acceptance as a spirited performing unit during the late 1980s and 1990s.

Smith's last recordings were made with John Hammond (a beginner who would become legendary as a producer) supervising. In November 1933, she refused to sing blues, claiming that the style was old-fashioned. Smith said that she sensed that audiences wanted something with more of a jazz-swing feel. Although Smith had come upon hard times (she received only $50 per side for the November sessions), the four cuts she made with Hammond showed that her new style could have been compatible with the new music to come ("Gimmie a Pigfoot" is the highlight of that session). Unfortunately, Smith's comeback was cut short when she was mortally injured in a car crash. Edward Albee's *The Death of Bessie Smith* was based on the theory that segregation policies denied her hospital admittance. Further investigation has shown that Smith's injuries were so severe that her life was beyond saving. "To my way of thinking," declared John Hammond, "Bessie Smith was the greatest artist American jazz ever produced; in fact, I'm not sure that her art did not reach beyond the limits of the term jazz. She was one of those rare beings, a completely integrated artist capable of projecting her whole personality into music."

Other Classic Blues Singers

Singer	Nickname	Classic Recording
May Alix	Queen of the Nightclubs	Big Butter and Egg Man
Lottie Beaman	Kansas City Butterball	Mama Can't Lose
Gladys Bentley	Broadway's Queen of Song & Jazz	(Male impersonator/Harlem clubs)
Esther Bigeon	Girl With the Million Dollar Smile	Panama Limited Blues
Bessie Brown	Original Bessie Brown	Lonesome Monday Morning Blues
Alice Leslie Carter	International Blues Singer	Decatur Street Blues
Martha Copeland	Everybody's Mammy	Good Time Mother
Ida Cox	Uncrowned Queen of the Blues/Sepia Mae West	Wild Women Don't Have the Blues
Lucille Hegamin	Harlem's Favorite/Cameo Girl	He May Be Your Man
Maggie Jones (aka Fae Barnes)	Texas Nightingale	Single Woman's Blues
Daisy Martin	Girl With a Smile	If You Don't Believe I Love You
Sara Martin	Colored Sophie Tucker	Mean Tight Mama
Lizzie Miles	Creole Songbird/Black Rose of Paris	I Hate a Man Like You
Monette Moore (aka Susie Smith)	Girl of Smiles	Show Girl Blues
Clara Smith	World's Champion Moaner/Queen of the Moaners	Awful Moaning Blues
Trixie Smith	Southern Nightingale	Freight Train Blues
Victoria Spivey	Texas Moaner/Queen Vee/Queen of the Blues	Black Snake Blues
Eva Taylor	Dixie Nightingale/Queen of the Moaners	May We Meet Again
Sippie Wallace	Texas Nightingale	Mighty Tight Woman
Ethel Waters	Sweet Mama Stringbean/Ebony Nora Bayes	Jazzin' Babies Blues
Edith Wilson	Queen of the Blues/Aunt Jemima	He May Be Your Man

The Rural Blues

If classic blues was part of the world of entertainment, then rural, or country blues, was folklore. It was music in the oral (unwritten) tradition, played by migratory workers singing of their hard times. Those workers usually accompanied themselves with guitar or harmonica. Some of the main features of the rural blues include:

1) Slow tempos that suited the pace of rural life
2) Simple instrumentation (acoustic guitar, banjo, or harmonica)
3) Women problems, boll weevils, mules, tough times as themes
4) Expression of deeply felt emotion
5) Wide circulation and various copied and absorbed styles

Rural blues was a form carried by men roving from town to town seeking work. Most of these bluesmen worked in the fields or in factories during the day, as they were unable to sustain a musical career as their only form of employment. Those with reputations as superior performers would be sought out by field representatives of record companies to record for a flat fee per side. These bluesmen seldom, if ever, received any royalties for songs they composed.

There is very little European influence on rural blues music. Robert Palmer, author of *Deep Blues*, notes that the music of early bluesmen like Charlie Patton has often been referred to as "primitive." In the 1993 Masters of American Music Video series *Bluesland: A Portrait in American Music*, Palmer dispels the long-held notion that the roving country bluesmen were musically uneducated. "The whole idea of primitive blues is really a funny one. My feeling is that if you want to listen to something primitive, you should listen to Mozart, because if you hear Mozart there's almost no rhythmic variation in it. It's a one, two, three, four forever. No cross rhythms or polyrhythms to speak of. That's how all of the tonal qualities of the instruments tend to be very clean and pristine, there's no kind of textural variety like you would get in the blues in terms of roughening the texture out on certain words, playing around with the pitch on certain words. Nothing like that in Mozart."

Albert Murray, (author of *Stompin' the Blues*) is also quoted in the same video. Building on his original thesis that the blues is a ritual of purification, Murray asserts that blues is not performed to whine about problems, but instead is a celebration used to stomp away the blues. Murray argues that blues performers were artists who affirmed life in the face of adversity. Few blues songs dealt with poverty and injustice. Like most poets, blues artists wrote and sang about the one thematic universal love. Murray notes,"If you escape from the problem, you're not dealing with it. But the blues is for confrontation and improvisation. Confrontation of the fact that life's a low-down dirty shame, or a dangerous proposition at best. And then you improvise playfully–playfully, hopefully, playfully. If you do it playfully, in come options which are gonna add up to elegance, which is beautiful. Now you're making art."

The success of the female classic singers, competition from radio, and the low cost of rural performers added up to an appealing profit potential for record companies. The initial sales of Papa Charlie Jackson, acknowledged to be the first of the men who recorded blues, in 1925, and of Blind Blake (noted for his ragtime guitar), encouraged companies to send out field units to find and record male talent. The race market boomed between 1927 and 1930, with gospel and blues records being issued at a rate of ten a week, more than double the figure for 1925. There were five leading companies manufacturing race records, issuing them under seven main labels: Columbia and Okeh, Paramount, Vocalion and Brunswick, and Gennett and Victor.

During the early development of the blues (from the 1890 to the 1930s), there were three main geographic regions from which arose general styles of blues performance. With the advent of the phonograph record, some of these geographic distinctions would begin to break down and intertwine, as recordings could be widely listened to and styles copied.

Southeast Seaboard Bluesmen

Bluesman/Group	Area	Key Recording	Years
Pink Anderson	South Carolina	Meet Me in the Bottom	1928
Kokomo Arnold	Georgia	Milk Cow Blues	1930
DeFord Bailey	Tennessee	Pan American Blues	1927
Barbecue Bob	Georgia	Yo Yo Blues	1927-30
Ed Bell	Alabama	Mamish Blues	1920s
Blind Blake	Georgia	Early Morning Blues	1920
Sleepy John Estes	Tennessee	Brownsville Blues	1928-30
Blind Boy Fuller	North Carolina	Pistol Snapper Blues	1938
Jim Jackson	Tennessee	Kansas City Blues	1927-29
Furry Lewis	Tennessee	Shake 'Em on Down	1927-29
Memphis Jug Band	Tennessee	Stealin' Stealin'	1928
Frank Stokes	Tennessee	Mr. Crumb	1927-29
Roosevelt Sykes	Arkansas	The Honeydripper	1927-41
Cannon's Jug Stompers	Tennessee	Feather Bed	1928
Robert Wilkins	Tennessee	Rolling Stone Blues	1928-35

The three main geographic blues regions were the:

1) Southeast Seaboard (primarily the Carolinas, Alabama, and Georgia)

2) Southwest Territories (primarily Texas and Oklahoma),

3) Mississippi Delta (along the banks of the Mississippi River)

The *Southeast Seaboard* style has the closest connection to the British ballads and fiddle tunes. Many historians refer to this general region as the Piedmont blues area. It includes parts of the Carolinas, Virginia, and Georgia around the Appalachian Mountains. Fiddles, harmonicas, guitars, and banjo were the main instruments featured. Atlanta, Georgia, became a key area for musicians to find work, especially on Decatur Street, where itinerant bluesmen flocked.

The delicate slide work of **Blind Willie McTell** (1901-1959) included twelve-string guitar rags, minstrel songs, religious music, and white hillbilly. Like many of the migratory bluesmen, McTell recorded under many pseudonyms, breaking record company obligations again and again. He recorded as Red Hot Willie, Blind Sammy, Peg and Whistle Red, Barrelhouse Sammy, Georgia Bill, and many others. His "Statesboro Blues" is known today because it was previously covered by the Allman Brothers. McTell sang, "Wake up, mama, turn your lamp down low/Have you got the nerve to drive Papa McTell from your door?"

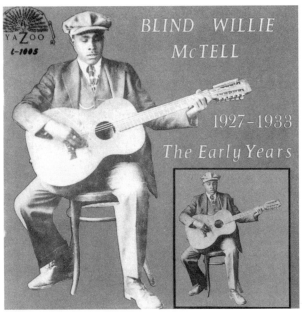

Courtesy Yazoo Records

Blind Willie McTell's recording career stretched from 1927 to 1956 and he made over 120 titles during fourteen separate sessions. He was one of the rare blind bluesmen who seldom used a lead man -- he used to lead other blind bluesmen about. McTell followed the tobacco market in the South, playing for farmers, buyers, and merchants. He also played for vacationers in Miami and the Georgia Sea Islands.

Peg Leg Howell was a country blues singer and guitarist who was the first significant Atlanta bluesman to record in 1926. Howell's first recording was "New Prison Blues" (1926), and his repertoire included hillbilly tunes that the group played for white dances ("Turkey in the Straw" and "Turkey Buzzard Blues"). In keeping with the indictment that the blues was the devil's music, "Low Down Rounder Blues" (1928) claims, "My friends has turned against me, smiling in my face/ Since I been disobedient I must travel in disgrace/ I cannot shun the devil, he stays right by my side." Howell called his musicians his "Gang" and had a fiddler, Eddie Anthony, in his group. Anthony, who was also from Atlanta, Georgia, was one of the few black country fiddlers to make numerous recordings. He recorded under his own name and with Peg Leg Howell's group. His "Warm Wipe Stomp" was a lively piece played at country dances.

The southeastern states had more jug and jook bands than the Southeast Seaboard and the Southwest Territories. The states of Tennessee and Kentucky, further inland than the other seaboard states, provided the bulk of these groups. Louisville-based Whistler and His Jug Band may have been the earliest jug band to record in 1924, with their song "Chicago Flip." Whistler (Buford Threlkeld) played guitar and nose flute as he led his group of harmonica, washboard, kazoo, and jug blowers throughout the South, playing tent and medicine shows. Selections such as "Jailhouse Blues," "I'm a Jazz Baby," and "Foldin' Bed" were standout recordings. The group can be seen on the Shanachie video release *Things Ain't Like They Used to Be* (1993). Len Fowler's Washboard Wonders, Ed Kelly's Washboard Band, the Dixieland Jug Blowers, the Dallas Jamboree Jug Band, the Dallas String Band with Coley Jones, the Birmingham Jug Band, and Washboard Sam and His Washboard Band were just a few of the better-known jug and jook units that recorded during the 1920s through the 1940s. Of all the jug bands the best known were the Memphis Jug Band and Cannon's Jug Stompers.

The Memphis Jug Band recorded some sixty titles between 1927 and 1934. Will Shade, who played guitar and harmonica, led his group through spirited, good-time numbers such as "Stealin' Stealin'," "Cocaine Habit Blues," "He's in the Jailhouse Now," and the band's theme, "K. C. Moan." During the 1960s, the Even Dozen Jug Band and Canned Heat each recorded the Memphis Jug Band's "On the Road Again."

More influential than Shade's Memphis Jug Band was Gus Cannon's Jug Stompers. **Gus Cannon** (1883-1979) was sometimes referred to as "Banjo Joe." He left his native Mississippi for Ripley, Tennessee, where he worked on a farm. In 1916, he met up with harmonica player Noah Lewis and guitarist Ashley Thompson and the trio played for dances and country suppers. Before formalizing his group in 1928, Cannon played in a variety of traveling medicine shows throughout the South. He started with Dr. Stokey, then moved on to Dr. Willie Lewis, Dr. W. B. Milton, Dr. Benson, and Dr. C. Hangerson. In these shows, he provided entertainment by singing and playing his banjo while the doctors pitched their pills and miracle tonics. Cannon noted, "Had all that cork on our face, made us look blacker. Y'know, the doctor would advertise his stuff and I'd run out there in the audience with soap, tonics."

Cannon's Jug Stompers made its recording debut in 1928 and though Cannon was the leader, the real star was Noah Lewis: "Lawd, he used to blow the hell outta that harp. He could play two harps at the same time," recounted Cannon. The group's best-known recordings were "Minglewood Blues" and "Feather Bed." The Jug Stompers were very effective performing before both black and white audiences because they were such versatile entertainers. They even played for dances at country breakdowns, performing waltzes, square dances, and slow drags.

Paul Oliver in *The Story of the Blues* calls Cannon's Jug Stompers the greatest of all the jug bands and notes, "They made the link between the Saturday-night dance, the medicine show pitch and the minstrel troupe, by bringing the blues to all of them." In the 1960s, folksinger Dave Van Ronk modeled his Ragtime Jug Stompers on Cannon's group and in 1963 the Rooftop Singers had a pop hit with one of the old Jug Stompers recordings, "Walk Right In."

© 1991 BMG Music

A compilation of the best groups around Memphis: The Memphis Jug Band ("K. C. Moan," "On the Road Again"), Jim Jackson ("I'm Wild About My Lovin'"), Frank Stokes ("Downtown Blues"), and Cannon's Jug Stompers ("Walk Right In" and "Viola Lee Blues," the latter covered by the Grateful Dead on their first release in 1969).

Courtesy Yazoo Records

77

The *Southwest Territories* (Texas, Oklahoma, and Louisiana) were noted for distinctive single-note guitar runs, a smooth vocal delivery, and an open, rather than dense, accompaniment texture. Foremost among the bluesmen of the area was **Blind Lemon Jefferson** (1897-1929), who worked on street corners before making records for Paramount beginning in 1925. He had a retinue of future-famous bluesmen who started as lead men, among them Leadbelly, Josh White, and T-Bone Walker. During the 1920s in the Deep South, there were very few clubs where rural performers could entertain. Consequently Jefferson, with his guide in tow, would seek out the picnics, barbecues, whiskey houses, and heavily populated street corners near saloons in the red light district of East Dallas. Jefferson's world was populated with "bad liquor," "heavy-hip mamas," "dirty mistreaters," and "easy riders."

Courtesy Yazoo Records

King of the Country Blues. So called by Paramount Records, Blind Lemon Jefferson was the best-known male rural blues artist of his time and one of the most important bluesmen in popular music history. This collection includes his sexually boasting classics "Easy Rider Blues" and "Booger Rooger Blues," as well as "Hot Dogs," "Rabbit Foot Blues," and "Matchbox Blues." David Evans, writing in *Nothing But the Blues*, (edited by Lawrence Cohn), contends, "His success as a recording artist enabled him to live well and indulge his pleasures in women, and drink, but he remained a rambler between his home state of Texas and the recording studio in Chicago, in Memphis and down in the Delta during the cotton harvest season, in the coal camps of West Virginia, wherever there was money and a demand for his music."

During his time, Jefferson was probably the best known of all the rural artists. His sound was raw, almost archaic, yet his guitar playing was very facile. B. B. King claims Jefferson as his first influence. According to an April 1926 ad from the *Chicago Defender*: "Here's a real old-fashioned blues by a real old-fashioned blues singer Blind Lemon Jefferson from Dallas. This 'Booster Blues' and 'Dry Southern Blues' on the reverse side are two of Blind Lemon's old-time tunes. With his singing he plays the guitar in the real southern style."

Jefferson sang every kind of song and his successes included "Prison Cell Blues," "'Lectric Chair Blues," "Low Down Mojo Blues," "Matchbox Blues," "Please See That My Grave Is Kept Clean," and his most famous song, "Black Snake Moan," a very sexual blues. Classic blues singer Victoria Spivey had originally recorded the song for Okeh Records in May 1926, with no sexual overtones intended. The recording was a smash hit for her. Jefferson recorded the tune six months later and altered some of the words. His recording resulted in a song of intense, phallic imagery: "Black snake crawling in my room/ Some pretty mama better get this black snake soon."

Other major recording artists of the Texas region were Henry Thomas, also called "Ragtime Texas," who was also a noted quill, or panpipe player ("Texas Easy Street Blues" and "Cottonfield Blues"), Texas Alexander ("Blue Devil Blues" and "Rolling Mill Blues"), Blind Willie Johnson, Whistlin' Alex Moore, Johnny Head, Little Hat Jones, Mance Lipscomb, and a cousin of Texas Alexander who didn't record during this time period but who would become the last great Texas country blues star, Sam "Lightnin'" Hopkins. Leadbelly, who came from Louisiana, recorded during this time but will be covered in chapter 14 because he was to have his greatest influence in the urban folk movement.

The most influential of the rural styles is that of the *Mississippi Delta*. The delta is associated with the cotton area of the northeast Mississippi and includes towns and counties that are not within the drainage system of the Yazoo River. The delta style used a dark and percussive vocal approach as if the singing were forced. An almost choked-growl manner would alternate with falsetto moans. The guitar technique employed a heavy chordal approach and included the bottleneck style—use of a smoothed neck of a bottle or thimble-like contraption usually placed on a finger of the left hand that the performer slides up and down the strings as notes are struck with the right hand, thus resulting in a sustaining sound or a violin-like glissando. These vocal, musical, and technical elements were the basic form that literally moved up the Mississippi and, when plugged in, became the Chicago bar blues of Muddy Waters, Howlin' Wolf and their followers during the 1950s and 1960s.

The "Founder of the Delta Blues" was **Charlie Patton** (1887-1934). He worked on the Will Dockerey plantation, a five-thousand acre farm on the Sunflower River, until he realized that performing could release him from the tedious and unglamorous life of a farmhand. Patton developed into a great entertainer, tossing the guitar high into the air, catching it and continuing to play. He also instituted a technique of playing the guitar behind his head and did little shuffle dances as he performed. One of Patton's followers, Son House, disapproved of his "clowning," but it proved very popular with Patton's rural audience.

The main body of Patton's recordings were the forty-two sides he made for Paramount between 1929 and 1930 and his last twenty-six sides for Vocalion in 1934 (only ten of which were originally released). Patton's best-known composition, "Pony Blues," was resurrected into a hit as "Stone Pony Blues" in 1968 by the electric blues band Canned Heat, which was led by blues archivists-collectors, Bob "the Bear" Hite and Al "Blind Owl" Wilson. Stephen Galt and Gayle Wardlow note in *King of the Delta Blues*, "He remained most memorable as a personal presence, a symbol of frivolity in an age of morose religion, and as a figure who embodied all that was boisterous and excessive about the culture that supported him."

Son House (1902-1988), **Mississippi John Hurt** (1892-1966) and **Skip James** (1902-1969) were Delta bluesmen who recorded during the early 1930s, and late in their careers, experienced a resurgence of popularity with white audiences. The folk revival of the late 1950s and early 1960s sought all of them out, and they all played the Newport Folk Festival (Hurt, 1963 and 1964; James, 1964; House, 1964 and 1969). All three toured the country, played coffee houses and nightclubs, and were featured on the college circuit.

Courtesy Yazoo Records

The only known picture of the "Founder of the Delta Blues". Patton auditioned for Jackson record store owner H. C. Speir, who recorded a plethora of bluesmen. Speir said simply, "He beat 'em all." Patton played for the rowdy all-night dances and his gritty voice and percussive guitar style was more than up to the challenge. "Screamin' and Hollerin' Blues," " Down the Dirt Road Blues," "Banty Rooster," "High Water Everywhere," "Shake It and Break It," and "Pony Blues" are his classics, all on this CD.

Other Mississippi Delta Bluesmen

Bluesman	Best-Known Song	Years
Ishman Bracey	Suitcase Full of Blues	1928-30
Willie Brown	M&O Blues	1927-32
Sam Collins	Riverside Blues	1930s
Tommy Johnson	Canned Heat Blues	1928-30
Rube Lacy	Mississippi Jail House Moan	1927-32
Furry Lewis	Furry's Blues	1927-28
Tommy McClennan	Bottle It Up and Go	1930s
Mississippi Sheiks	Sitting on Top of the World	1930s
Bukka White	Parchman Farm	1930s
Robert Wilkins	Rolling Stone Blues	1928-35
Big Joe Williams	Baby Please Don't Go	1930s

Skip James recorded for H. C. Speir in 1931 (twenty-six or seventeen songs, depending on the sources) and didn't make another record until he was rediscovered in 1964. His best-known classics are "I'm So Glad" (reworked by Cream) and "Hard Times Killing Floor Blues" (reworked by Michael Bloomfield's Electric Flag).

Mississippi John Hurt was rediscovered in 1963 when a blues collector, Tom Hoskins, listened to Hurt's 1920s recording of "Avalon Blues" and tracked him down living in the town of Avalon, Mississippi. Samuel Charters in *The Country Blues* claims, "He is a brilliant guitarist and a singer with a fine sense of phrasing and emotional communication."

Son House began his career in 1930 on Paramount Records. House is considered by many blues authorities to have been the primary teacher of Robert Johnson and Muddy Waters. His best known song is "Death Letter." In this chilling song, after he learns his loved one is dead, he goes to see her body at the morgue ("lying on the cooling board").

Robert Johnson: King of the Delta Blues.

Of all of the country bluesmen there is none that has received as much acclaim, nor has as deep an influence on today's rock performers, as **Robert Johnson** (1911-1938). Although he recorded his entire body of work during just two series of recording sessions in San Antonio and Dallas, Texas, in 1936 and 1937, outside of this chapter's time span, Johnson is covered here because his work is inextricably bound to this era and style. Johnson has been referred to as the "King of the Delta Blues Singers." Legend tells of a young Johnson failing to impress others with his limited guitar playing then disappearing and returning a short time later to amaze everyone with his fantastic ability, causing one of his mentors, Son House, to declare, "He must have sold his soul to the devil to play like that."

Once he left farming behind him, Johnson made Helena, Arkansas, his home base and played all over the Mississippi and Arkansas Delta areas—Yazoo City, Hollendale, Lamonte, Lobdell, Beulah, Gunnison, Marianna, Clarksdale, Frairs Point, Rosedale, Itta Bena, and many other towns. Like many of the bluesmen, Johnson didn't sing only blues to his audiences. He included popular songs of the day such as "My Blue Heaven," "Yes, Sir, That's My Baby," and "Tumbling Tumbleweeds." However, bluesmen seldom recorded these kinds of numbers because record executives reasoned that race records were supposed to be an alternative to the popular songs of the day.

Some Rock Covers of Robert Johnson

Robert Johnson	Year	Covered By	Year
Come on in My Kitchen	1936	Delaney and Bonnie	1970s
Come on in My Kitchen	1936	Steve Miller	1973
Cross Road Blues	1936	Cream (Eric Clapton)	1968
I Believe I'll Dust My Broom	1936	Rising Sons	1965/1992
I Believe I'll Dust My Broom	1936	Z .Z. Top	1979
I'm a Steady Rollin' Man	1937	Eric Clapton	1973
Last Fair Deal Gone Down	1936	Rising Sons	1965/1992
Love in Vain	1937	Rolling Stones	1970
Rambling on My Mind	1936	John Mayall's Blues Breakers with (Eric Clapton)	1965/1975
Stop Breakin' Down Blues	1937	Rolling Stones	1972
Sweet Home Chicago	1937	The Blues Brothers	1980
Traveling Riverside Blues	1937	Led Zeppelin	1990
Walking Blues	1936	Paul Butterfield	1966
Walking Blues	1936	Taj Mahal	1967
Walking Blues	1936	Bonnie Raitt	1971
Walking Blues	1936	Grateful Dead	1990

Courtesy Yazoo Records

This is an eye-and ear-opening release. It features original blues numbers on which Robert Johnson based some of his classics . For example: Kokomo Arnold's "Milk Cow Blues" (1934) was the basis for Johnson's "Milkcow's Calf Blues", and Scrapper Blackwell's "Kokomo Blues" (1928) was the source for Johnson's "Sweet Home Chicago." There are fourteen examples of blues roots influences on the "King of the Delta" compiled on this collection.

Courtesy Biograph Records

Johnny Shines (1915-1993) noted that "the big guy was Robert (Johnson)." Shines traveled with Johnson from 1935 to 1937, then moved to Chicago. By 1957 he was out of the music scene, but in 1964 a British blues collector encouraged him to return to touring and recording. Shines's "Dynaflow Blues" was based on Johnson's "Terraplane Blues," while his "Milkcow Blues" is a version of Johnson's "Milkcow's Calf Blues." Shines's recording of "Tell Me Mama" is a song he claims to have learned from Johnson but that Johnson never recorded.

Robert Johnson's first session, in November 1936, resulted in a song that would be in the closest he would ever come to having a hit during his lifetime, "Terraplane Blues." This release helped Johnson achieve fame in the Delta, where his appearances were widely attended. Johnson's songs often reflected the broken romances he encountered, the dissatisfaction with his place in society, which led him to ramble, and guilt, which often resulted in connections with the "demonic spirit." Examples of romance, or unrequited love, include "Kindhearted Woman Blues," "Come on in My Kitchen," and "Love in Vain." Examples of rambling include "Rambling on My Mind," "Walking Blues," "I'm a Steady Rollin' Man," "Stones in My Passway" and "Cross Road Blues." Examples of the "demonic spirit" include "Me and the Devil Blues," "Hellhound on My Trail," and "Preaching Blues (Up Jumped the Devil)."

Johnson's stark and poetic lyrics accompanied by his stinging guitar created an eerie, almost existential quality. In 1990, for the first time, all forty-one takes of Johnson's twenty-nine songs could be found on a digitally remastered boxed set. Entitled *Robert Johnson: The Complete Recordings* (Columbia), it has so far been the best-selling double CD set in country blues history. Johnson may have summed up his blues best when he sang, "The stuff I got'll bust your brains out, baby/It'll make you lose your mind" ("Stop Breakin' Down Blues"). This is likely because Johnson has long been the greatest rural blues influence on today's rockers. Keith Richards of the Rolling Stones reminisces, "You'd think you were getting a handle on playing the blues, and then to hear Johnson — whoa! There's a long way to go yet." Eric Clapton, perhaps rock's closest link to Johnson, says that Johnson was "the greatest folk blues guitar player that ever lived– the greatest singer, the greatest writer." Johnson's grisly and mysterious death (he is believed to have been poisoned by a jealous husband) on August 16, 1938, is investigated by bluesman John Hammond in a 1992 video, *The Search for Robert Johnson*. The video includes visits with Johnson's friends and relatives.

As noted earlier, Johnson's followers were legion. Perhaps the closest to him was Johnny Shines, who played many of the same rural towns. Shines and Johnson often faced each other as rivals "cutting heads," a bluesman's term for competing on opposite corners of a street trying to attract the biggest crowd. Shines also traveled and performed with Johnson, and was considered the foremost rural blues interpreter of Johnson's works. Of the citified bluesmen who carried on Johnson's legacy, Elmore James was the prime mover. He created excitement with his slashing amplified bottleneck excursions of raw, throbbing Chicago blues based on the Johnson style. James's signature song was an incendiary 1952 reading of Johnson's "I Believe I'll Dust My Broom". James even named his group The Broomdusters. The connection continues from Elmore James to Hound Dog Taylor and the Houserockers to the contemporary white blues hero, George Thorogood and his band, the Destroyers.

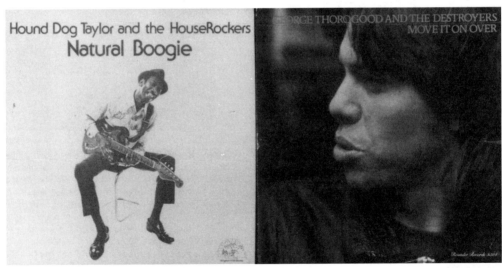

Courtesy Alligator Records   Rounder Records

House Rockin' Guitar.

Barrelhouse Piano and Boogie Woogie

Just as there were roaming rural blues singers, there were also piano players who entertained throughout the South. Most taverns and jook joints (sometimes called barrelhouses because beer barrels were turned upside down and used as tables) had a battered upright piano. These being the days before the jukebox, or the modern sound systems and cable television of the 1980s and 1990s, entertainment had to be homemade. Piano players also served as main entertainers in the lumber, levee, and railroad camps. They hoboed from spot to spot by hitching car rides or hopping freight trains ("riding the rails").

Cow Cow Davenport at the piano with fellow pianist-announcer Art Hodes. Davenport left his native Alabama around the time of World War I to work as a musician, singer, and dancer. Through the early 1920s Davenport teamed with Dora Carr working as "Davenport and Company," touring extensively on TOBA and other circuts. By the mid-1920s he teamed with Ivy Smith in a unit they called "Chicago Steppers," and by the 1930s he was calling his own revue, "Cow Cow's Chicago Steppers."

Two of the earliest pianists to win acclaim via recordings were Clarence "Pinetop" Smith and Cow Cow Davenport. Both used rolling, repeated bass-line figures ("ostinato") that imitated train rhythms. Above these, the pianist's right hand would perform melodic lines or cross-rhythmic riffs. These walking-bass blues lines, which had many variations, were referred to as "boogie woogie." Smith, who had worked with "Ma" Rainey and comic entertainers Butterbeans and Susie, settled in Chicago and released his classic "Pine Top's Boogie" in 1928. Davenport is claimed to have given the form its title when he discovered Smith and told him, "you sure have got a mean boogie woogie." Smith had never heard the term before.

Smith's 1927 Paramount recording of "Jim Crow Blues" is a ringing indictment of the racist policies he endured: "I'm tired of being Jim Crowed, going to leave this Jim Crow town/Doggone my black soul, I'm sweet Chicago bound." Davenport used to pass out business cards that read, "Cow Cow Davenport The man who gave America Boogie-Woogie." Bandleader Tommy Dorsey scored in 1939 with a million-selling version of 'Pine Top's Boogie" that featured a temperate piano solo by Dean Kincaid. Davenport had recorded his original "Cow Cow Blues" as a vocal in 1924. His classic instrumental boogie version was released in 1928, and it was a big hit for Freddie Slack and Ella Mae Morse as "Cow Cow Boogie" in 1942.

Montana Taylor ("Detroit Rocks"), Meade Lux Lewis ("Honky Tonk Train Blues"), Cripple Clarence Lofton ("Streamline Train"), Little Brother Montgomery ("Vicksburg Blues"), Roosevelt Sykes ("The Honeydripper"), Speckled Red ("The Dirty Dozens"), and Jimmy "Papa" Yancy ("Yancy Stomp") were just a few of the many piano players who established the barrelhouse and boogie-woogie piano stylings during the 1920s and early 1930s. In the late thirties a boogie-woogie craze filtered up into the umbrella world of popular music via John Hammond's successful Carnegie Hall concert, "From Spirituals to Swing."

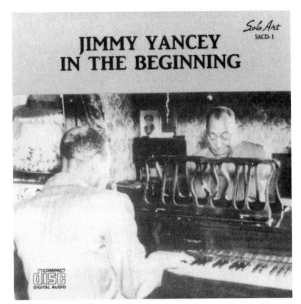

Courtesy Solo Art Records

Courtesy Delmark Records

Speckled Red and "The Dirty Dozens." Like many itinerant piano players, Speckled Red, also known as Detroit Red, worked in a variety of settings throughout his long career, which stretched from the early 1920s to the early 1970s. Red played house rent parties, juke joints, medicine and minstrel shows, as well as serving as an intermission pianist in clubs. He was an albino African American and acquired his moniker, "Speckled Red," because of his pink and speckled skin pigmentation. He was the older brother of Willie "Piano Red" Perryman.

In the biographical dictionary of blues artists, *Blues Who's Who* by Sheldon Harris, writer Tony Standish praises Speckled Red thusly, "His harsh yet humorous voice and his clipped, percussive and powerful piano playing stamped him as one who could take his place among the elite of the barrelhouse and boogie pianists."

Yancey, one of the fathers of boogie woogie, wasn't recorded until 1939, when an enterprising bartender from Brooklyn, Dan Qualey, who also happened to be a record collector, started an independent record company called Solo Art. Qualey loved piano, so he only recorded piano players. He located Yancey and made several historic recordings. Historian William Russell called Yancey "the Buddy Bolden of the Boogie Woogie" (more about Yancey and boogie woogie revival in Chapter 8).

In less than a year Qualey recorded fifty-five ten-inch sides by six piano artists at their peak (the others were Meade Lux Lewis, Albert Ammons, Pete Johnson, Cripple Clarence Lofton, and Art Hodes). Recording halted when Qualey ran out of money. In 1948 he sold his masters to Rudi Blesh and Harriet Janis (authors of *They All Played Ragtime*), who had started their own small record company, Circle, in 1946. In the mid-1960s, the Circle and Solo Art masters were purchased by George Buck, Jr., of Jazzology Records (he also bought the rights to Paramount Records). Buck has been one of the main preservationists of the underground forms of blues and jazz. His Audiophile Record company specializes in jazz cabaret vocalists.

Speckled Red (Rufus G. Perryman) played rent parties and clubs throughout the twenties and thirties and recorded until his death in 1973. He was known for his 1929 "raunch and roll" classic, "The Dirty Dozens." According to Arnold Shaw's *Dictionary of American Pop Rock*. The 'Dirty Dozens' is a gambit of black origin in which insults are traded until one contender is accused of having sex with his mother (mother-f-----), at which point physical violence supersedes verbal abuse. Curiously, the gambit is supposed to have originated in a patter song of a religious nature whose purpose was to teach the young biblical lore. In time, the content was transformed into the erotic and sacriligious "Dirty Dozens." This aggressiveness is one of the mainstays of the "I'm top you're not" attitude of many of today's bad-boy (and girl) gangsta rap groups.

Early Boogie Woogie Pianists

Piano Player	Best Known Song
Cow Cow Davenport	Cow Cow Boogie
Blind Leroy Garnett	Louisiana Glide
Jim Jackson	Jim Jackson's Jamboree
Meade Lux Lewis	Honky Tonk Train
Cripple Clarence Lofton	Brown Skin Gal
Little Brother Montgomery	Vicksburg Blues
Romeo Nelson	Head Rag Hop
Turner Porrish	Trenches
Charlie Spand	Hasting Street
Speckled Red	The Honeydripper
Freddy Shane	Mr. Freddy's Blues
Pine Top Smith	Pine Top's Boogie
Montana Taylor	Detroit Rocks
Hersal Thomas	Suitcase Blues
Sugar Underwood	David Street Blues
Wesley Wallace	No. 20

Citified Blues & Hokum

By the turn of the century, more and more black people were moving to city centers for better job opportunities. Traveling blues performers found themselves playing in small clubs with additional accompaniment which called for a more rehearsed and sophisticated approach than before. The use of piano, bass, and drums, and occasionally trumpet and saxophone, was a format that the rural bluesman seldom used in the country setting of picnics and barbecues, or on street corners. So we can say that the citified blues began a period of more intense rehearsals and collaborative interaction between musicians.

Pianist **Leroy Carr** (1905-1935), accompanied by guitarist Scrapper Blackwell, was one of the precursors of city blues. The duo's influential recordings made between 1928 and 1934, were immensely popular with blues devotees and other musicians. Working primarily in their home town of Indianapolis, Indiana ("Naptown"), along Indiana Avenue (considered the colored "Main Street",) and recording usually in Chicago, they created an intoxicating blend of blues piano, biting guitar, and smooth vocals. Carr and Blackwell were the most successful of all of the blues teams of this early period (Sonny Terry and Brownie McGhee would be the next widely popular blues team, in the 1940s-to-1970s period). According to blues author Giles Oakley *The Devil's Music: A History of the Blues*, Carr and Blackwell "showed an almost telepathic sympathy in their duets."

By the mid-1920s, Carr was singing his famous "How Long Blues," which became his trademark song before it was finally recorded in 1928. Like many blues songs, it is closely based on an already existing song—Ida Cox's "How Long Daddy, How Long." Carr's recording was a hit and eventual followups such as "How Long Blues No. 2," "How Long Blues No. 3," and "New How Long, How Long Blues," extended the initial idea. A careful listening to Carr's falsetto technique at the end of certain choruses, make it apparent that Robert Johnson was very much under Carr's spell. Other important Carr recordings include "Midnight Hour Blues," "Hurry Down Sunshine (See What Tomorrow Bring)," "Hustler's Blues," "Mean Mistreater Mama," and "Blues Before Sunrise."

Leroy Carr died of nephritis, a kidney disease brought on by acute alcoholism. Drink was, unfortunately, a work hazard that plagued many a blues performer. Carr's legacy was profound; his songs were regularly included in the repertoires of numerous urban blues performers of subsequent generations. In his "Blues Before Sunrise," the singer moans, "I had the blues before sunrise, with tears standing in my eyes." After a pause, Carr continues, "It's such a miserable feeling, a feeling I do despise." In 1994 Eric Clapton recorded Carr's "Blues Before Sunrise," and "How Long Blues" on his successful *From the Cradle* release.

The simple pleasures of "Saturday night revelry."

What made Leroy Carr one of the best blues singers of all time, killed him.

It's been said that to sing the blues, you have to live them. Leroy Carr did both.

Carr died on April 29, 1935, one month after his 30th birthday.

But before he died, he had established himself as one of our greatest blues singers.

He and Scrapper Blackwell made these sixteen old 78 sides between 1932 and 1934, when Leroy's voice was at its peak. Some of the sides also feature the guitar playing of Josh White. Although he's not very well known today, many critics regard Leroy Carr as a male counterpart of Bessie Smith.

The only trouble was, Leroy Carr had the worst kind of blues: he drank himself to death.

The work of **Lonnie Johnson** (1899-1970), a blues guitarist with a fine jazz feel (he also played piano, violin, and sang), made a lasting impression on city blues stylists. He recorded with the Louis Armstrong Hot Five ("I'm Not Rough," "Hotter Than That," and "Savoy Blues") in 1927, with Duke Ellington ("The Mooche") in 1928, and with the Chocolate Dandies. Johnson made some remarkable sides with white guitarist Eddie Lang, and he accompanied numerous others in various capacities right up into the 1960s, making his one of the longest and most prolific careers in blues history. Johnson's delicate single-note guitar technique, which included a sophisticated chordal vocabulary and metrical deftness, has been cited as a direct inspiration for electric guitar pioneer Charlie Christian. Lawrence Cohn states outright in *Nothing But the Blues,* "Johnson drew extraordinary music and ironic poetry from his bittersweet life's experiences, and he is remembered as the first influential—and quintessential—urban bluesman." Lonnie Johnson was probably the strongest guitar influence on Robert Johnson, according to Peter Guralnick, writing in *The Story of Robert Johnson.* Lonnie Johnson's billing was, "The World's Greatest Blues Singer."

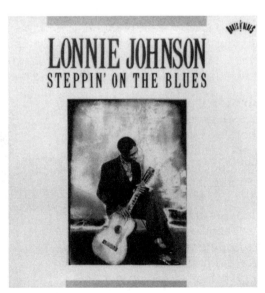

Considered the most influential and celebrated of early blues guitarists, Lonnie Johnson certainly had the most expansive career. He was an in-demand accompanist, a fine blues singer, and a jazz player of note and he also recorded as a pianist and violinist.

A sophisticated and dapper-looking Georgia Tom adorns this album cover. Before moving on to gospel music in 1932, Thomas A. Dorsey recorded as Barrel House Tom, and Georgia Tom. Dorsey, along with Tampa Red, popularized Hokum, a minstrel term for good-natured times with sexual overtones that mixed guitars, piano, and kazoo in imitation of the country string bands, but with an urban sophistication.

Dorsey put the beat into gospel music. He was the subject of the 1982 documentary *Say Amen, Somebody*, and, as James T. Jones IV concluded in Dorsey's obituary in *USA Today* : "Dorsey's creation has spread from choir lofts to the national music charts. It's more popular now than ever, reaching a whole new audience through such artists as the Winans and Hawkins family acts, rapper Hammer and the Sounds of Blackness choir, who've combined feverish testimony with pop/R&B beats. Dorsey not only showed the church that gospel could be *sung*, but taught the world to say hallelujah."

Billed as the "Guitar Wizard," Tampa Red moved to Chicago by the mid 1920s. After working with Georgia Tom he made recordings with his "Chicago Five" with pianist Black Bob and clarinetist Arnett Nelson. Red also worked with pianist Big Maceo Merriweather in Chicago. One of Red's most raunchy and suggestive numbers was recorded by Joe McCoy's Harlem Hamfats: "Let's Get Drunk and Truck." Tampa Red recorded close to two hundred titles between 1934 and 1953 for Bluebird and Victor record companies. He was an important influence on younger bluesmen who transformed urban blues after world War II as he hosted players in his house at Thirty-fifth and State streets in Chicago. Composer-bassist Willie Dixon, one of the future stars of Chicago's Chess Records, noted fondly in his autobiography, *I Am the Blues: The Willie Dixon Story*, "Tampa Red's house was a madhouse with old-time musicians. Lester Melrose [Bluebird's record producer] would be drinking all the time and Tampa Red's wife would be cooking chicken and we'd be having a ball."

The most intriguing and provocative of the citified blues was initiated by **Georgia Tom** (Thomas A. Dorsey, 1899-1993) and **Tampa Red** (Hudson Whittaker, 1900-1981). Georgia Tom was a pianist known as "Barrelhouse Tom" when he was making the rounds of the Atlanta house party circuit. Paramount's esteemed recording director, Mayo Williams, dubbed him "Georgia Tom" shortly before his recording debut in 1928. One of "Ma" Rainey's last recording sessions, in September 1928, was made with Georgia Tom on piano and Tampa Red on guitar.

The story goes that Tampa Red had a song he wanted Georgia Tom to set lyrics to but the latter was determined to devote his energies to religious music. Eventually Red talked him into completing "It's Tight Like That," which they recorded for Vocalion in 1928. Their first royalty check was for $2,400.19. Georgia Tom put religious music on hold and the "hokum" movement was launched.

Because the duo recorded the song as the Hokum Boys, hokum became a term that referred to good-time or party blues featuring double-entendre lyrics that were sometimes sly and witty and other times overt and crude. Dorsey credited Papa Charlie Jackson with launching the hokum concept. Jackson was one of the first bluesmen to record, in 1924, and had a repertoire of raunchy songs such as "Shave 'Em Dry," "You Put It In, I'll Take It Out," and "Shake That Thing" (1925), which was the basis for "It's Tight Like That." To the scatting strains of "beedle um bum," the Hokum boys sang of their girl as being "tall and slim," and when "she gets it, it's too bad Jim," because it's "tight like that." This suggestive number about lovemaking found an appreciative audience.

Dorsey recorded about four records as a featured vocalist and accompanied Tampa Red on most of Red's releases in the late 1920s. Tampa Red brought to the group what Dorsey referred to as a "lively beat" and an outstanding slide guitar style that resulted in his billing as the "Guitar Wizard." Dorsey recorded other hokum tunes with Kansas City Kitty (Mozalle Ardson), "The Doctor's Blues" and "Gym's Too Much for Me" (1930); with Frankie "Half-Pint" Jaxon, the supreme hokum singer, "Jive Man Blues" and "It's Heated" (1929); and with Big Bill Broonzy, "Come on In (Ain't Nobody Here But Me)" (1931). However, it was Dorsey's work with Tampa Red that created the strongest link with the hokum craze. Dorsey brought a sense of wit and sophistication to the art of blues lyrics that was seldom matched during the early era of blues recordings.

Frank Driggs Collection

The Hokum Boys, which often included Bob Robinson on lead vocal, followed their initial hit with "Selling That Stuff" and "Beedle Um Bum" (1928), "Pig Meat Blues" (1929), and "But They Got It Fixed Right On" (1930). Georgia Tom noted that, "Blues, hokum; now they had such a thing they called hokum. It had live beats to it. We didn't want to call ourselves blues singers, and we didn't want to call ourselves popular singers." Many groups were quick to add hokum to their group name as a result of the style's appeal. The Hokum Trio, The Famous Hokum Boys, The Hokum Jug Band, and the Harum Scarums are examples of units that sang comic, ribbing tunes accompanying themselves on guitars, piano, kazoo, string bass, and jugs in imitation of country string bands.

The Depression put an end to Georgia Tom's involvement with secular music. By 1932, he began touring the country with Miss Sallie Martin and they formed the National Convention of Gospel Choirs and Choruses. Dorsey helped create gospel music ("Gospel songs have a beat, and carry a more profound message than the Spirituals, which was a spontaneous outburst of slavery days," Dorsey claimed). Dorsey's compositions are among the revered classics of the idiom: "Take My Hand, Precious Lord," "(There'll Be) Peace in the Valley," "I'm Waiting for Jesus," "If You See My Saviour," "It's a Highway to Heaven," and "Old Ship Zion."

Frankie "Half Pint" Jaxon (1895-c. 1940) was born in Alabama but raised in Kansas City. He began touring with southern traveling shows as a vocalist. Jaxon's high, shrill voice sounded feminine; and he often worked as a female impersonator; Jaxon was said to be a big attraction in Atlantic City (Gladys Bentley, a classic blues singer impersonated men in Harlem around this time.) Jaxon worked with King Oliver, Ollie Powers, and Freddie Keppard in Chicago and Bennie Moten in Kansas City. He was best known for his hokum songs with Cow Cow Davenport and Tampa Red, and was also a member of Tampa Red's Hokum Jug Band and the Harlem Hamfats. Jaxon was recognized as an outrageous performer with his high-pitched, salacious vocals on songs like "How Long," "Hannah Fell in Love With My Piano," "How Can I Get It," "Can't Wait Till You Get Home," and his signature song, "Fan It!"

Frank Driggs Collection

One of the strangest careers in the blues was that of Frankie "Half Pint" Jaxon. Raised in Kansas City, he did not possess the "typical" shouting voice associated with bluesmen in that city. He worked with jazz bands (King Oliver, Freddie Keppard, Ollie Powers, and Carroll Dickerson at the Sunset Cafe and the Plantation) in Chicago throughout the 1920s. After working with Tampa Red (where his female impersonation of "My Daddy Rocks Me" contains what surely must be one of the first imitations of an orgasm on record) Jaxon played with Bennie Moten's band and sang with the Harlem Hamfats. Jaxon was most associated with "Fan It!" but nearly everything he recorded, from "Operation Blues" to a variety of wild blues selections on an album entitled *Saturday Night Scrontch*, is oddly captivating.

NOTICE!

STOP

Help Save The Youth of America

DON'T BUY NEGRO RECORDS

(If you don't want to serve negroes in your place of business, then do not have negro records on your juke box or listen to negro records on the radio.)

The screaming, idiotic words, and savage music of these records are undermining the morals of our white youth in America.

Call the advertisers of the radio stations that play this type of music and complain to them!

Don't Let Your Children Buy, or Listen

To These Negro Records

For additional copies of this circular, write

CITIZENS COUNCIL OF GREATER NEW ORLEANS, INC.
P. O. BOX 51715   N. O., La. 70150

Permission is granted to re-print this circular

Author's collection

Sex, Drugs, and Rock 'n' Roll

Long before Elvis Presley shook his hips in the 1950s and the Parents Music Resource Center sought to persuade record companies to print ratings on records in the mid-1980s, jazz and blues-oriented music was considered lewd and offensive by many people. Law-abiding citizens and church-going folks ascribed to what might be labeled "middle class values," which demanded proper language and respectful deportment. By this standard, many performers in the world of jazz and blues (and certain country artists) were deemed outcasts. For their part, the musicians were concerned with entertaining their audiences, and if those audiences delighted in songs that made them dance wildly or that told raunchy tales of the flesh, then so be it.

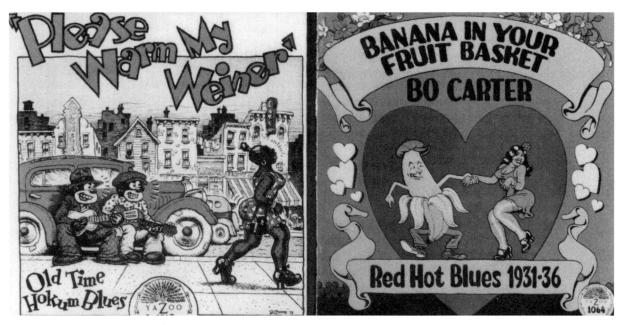

Courtesy Yazoo Records

Bo Carter: "King of Raunch." Born Bo Chatman, Carter, along with brothers Lonnie and Sam, played with the popular Mississippi Sheiks, who played breakdowns, waltzes, and popular jazz tunes. The Sheiks followed the typical course of rural performance venues—playing at country dances, picnics, parties, suppers, and fish fries throughout Mississippi, Tennessee, Georgia, Louisiana, and Illinois. Between 1928 and 1940, Chatman had a distinguished solo career singing bawdy songs under the name Bo Carter. A real "Howling Tom Cat," Carter gained his greatest recognition as a solo artist performing double-entendre selections such as "Ants in My Pants," "Mashing That Thing," "Let Me Roll Your Lemon," "My Pencil Don't Write No More," "Pin in Your Cushion," "Ram Rod Daddy," "Banana in My Fruitbasket," and "Please Warm My Weiner."

Ethnic minorities have always had an ambivalent relationship with the establishment. Most members of minority groups have traditionally tried to assimilate the rules and behavioral norms of majority society, but some inevitably forge an alternative lifestyle at odds with conventional morality.

According to Harry Shapiro in *Waiting for the Man: The Story of Drugs and Popular Music*, America's male-dominated WASP ethos included a feeling of superiority over minorities of all types. He contends that its "twentieth-century enemies have included Jewish and Italian gangsters, communists, student activists, sexually and politically independent women and jazz and rock musicians."

Courtesy Stash Records

The musicians who performed jazz, blues, and country music in the 1920s and 1930s were, for the most part, making recordings called "race" or "hillbilly" music that were not released to the general public. Many of the major labels gave a special numerical designation to separate certain jazz, blues, and country recordings from the general popular music. While the 1920s may have been called the "Jazz Age," the kind of jazz (and blues, for that matter) that the general public heard was quite watered down. "Offensive" material never achieved wide release.

The fact that most jazz and blues was recorded on "race" labels during the 1920s and early 1930s should make it easier to understand why it took so long for the history of these seminal forms to be taught in the schools. Courses in jazz history were not commonplace in college curricula until the 1970s, and courses in blues, country, and rock didn't enter the fold until the 1980s and 1990s, if at all. The low regard accorded these forms is due, in large part, to the open and uncritical references to sex, alcohol, and drugs that they often contain. Rock'n'roll, for instance, is a term that originally meant lovemaking. "My Daddy Rocks Me (With a Steady Roll)" features a singer who exclaims that her man is going to put his hot dog inside her roll and rock her all night long. During the instrumental solo she wails and moans orgasmically. This is a long way from "Give Me a Little Kiss, Will Ya, Huh?"

Courtesy Ray & Judy Balzer

Elvis the Pelvis and "Hound Dog" Lorenz. Elvis Presley at Buffalo's Memorial Auditorium, 1956. He is seen here being introduced by Buffalo's kingpin rock'n'roll disc jockey, George "Hound Dog" Lorenz, who played black rhythm and blues on the radio. Lorenz's jive jargon differed from that of the mainstream jocks who were spinning Perry Como and Doris Day during the early 1950s. Like Alan Freed, Lorenz was an atypical d. j. who preferred the earthy, underground sounds of black artists that were the bedrock of early Presley material. During his pre-Hollywood years Presley was young, wild, and sexy, but however suggestive he might have been, Presley was otherwise pretty tame, especially lyrically, when compared to the adult raunch of hokum and R&B stars of the 1940s like Wynonie Harris.

Many jazz and blues performers sang openly about sex and drugs and seemed unconcerned about offending their audience. Those jazz and blues players who "crossed over" to the popular market did not or could not feature these kinds of lyrics, or, if they did, it was very rarely. Moreover, these songs were usually disguised through metaphor or obscure titles or lyrics. Consider for a moment the tremendous controversy that Elvis Presley created in 1956 when he was seen on television bumping and grinding. Culturally, all hell broke loose. However, Elvis did not sing raunchy songs. Elvis Presley could have become a pop icon in the 1950s while purveying risque lyrics.

Imagine if Presley sang the sexual metaphors that were used in the 1920s and 1930s: references to jelly rolls, bananas, donuts or boasts of being an "easy rider," or being a "kitchen man" or "handy man" who could fix a woman's plumbing or her coffee grinder, or handle her oven. Could we imagine Presley proclaiming, "Now the girl I love is long and slim/When she gets it, it's too bad, Jim" ("It's Tight Like That," 1928) Of course not, because while Presley did test the boundaries of good taste (loud, aggressive, and rhythmic music) as a popular music star, he didn't indulge in offensive lyrics.

Courtesy Stash Records

Some Hokum Raunch: 1920s and 1930s

Performer	Songs
Lucille Bogan	Alley Boogie; Tricks Ain't Walking No More; Shave 'Em Dry, Women Won't Need No Men, B.D. (Bull Dyke) Blues; Sweet Petunia
Butterbeans & Susie	Elevator Papa, Switchboard Mama; I Got Your Bath Water On; When My Man Shimmies
Bo Carter	My Pencil Won't Write No More; All Around Man; Ants in My Pants; Please Warm My Weiner; Banana in Your Fruit Basket; Let Me Roll Your Lemon; Ram Rod Daddy
Georgia Tom & Tampa Red	It's Tight Like That; Gee But It's Hard; But They Get It Fixed Right On; Let Me Play with Your Poodle
Charlie "Papa" Jackson	Shake That Thing; You Put It In, I'll Take It Out
Frankie "Half Pint" Jaxon	Easy Rider; Jive Man Blues; My Daddy Rocks Me (With a Steady Roll); Wet It!; Fan It!
Memphis Minnie	Banana Man Blues; Hustlin' Woman Blues; It's Hard to Please My Man; Me and My Chauffeur
"Ma" Rainey	Walking the Street; Hustlin' Blues; Don't Fish in My Sea; Prove It on Me; Sissy Blues
Bessie Smith	Nobody in Town Can Bake Sweet Jelly Roll Like Mine; Sugar in My Bowl; Empty Bed Blues; I'm Wild About That Thing; Cold in Hand Blues; Do Your Duty; You've Got to Give Me Some
Clara Smith	The Moanin' Blues; Kitchen Mechanic Blues; Hustlin' Blues; It Must Be Good; It's Tight Like That
Sam Theard	New Shave 'Em Dry; She's Givin' It Away
Ethel Waters	You Can't Proposition Me; My Handy Man

Drugs were another taboo topic. Alcohol consumption was illegal from 1920 to 1933, although marijuana wasn't declared illegal until 1937. When thinking of the Jazz Age, speakeasies, cabarets, and booze immediately come to mind. The success of America's "temperance movement" in bringing about Prohibition, perversely encouraged many people to take a "walk on the wild side." In *Really the Blues*, Mezz Mezzrow, a jazz clarinetist of the time, observes, "It struck me funny how the top and bottom crusts in society were always getting together during the Prohibition era. In this swanky club which was run by members of the notorious Purple Gang, Detroit's bluebloods used to congregate—the Grosse Point mob on a slumming kick, rubbing elbows with Louis the Wop's mob." Observes Albert Goldman, "For the cats and kittens of the Jazz Age, marijuana was kicks, climbs, jollies and high times jumpin' to the beat of a hot horn or a mean licorice stick." A songwriter like Cole Porter, who hailed from wealth, didn't worry about the raised eyebrows of the middle class when he wrote of champagne and cocaine in "I Get a Kick Out of You" (1934). His cavalier attitude toward sex in songs such as "Let's Do It" (1934), "Love for Sale" (1929), or "You've Got That Thing" (1929) was indicative of an attitude that was harmonious with the underground world of minorities and musicians.

Those wealthy types who went "slumming" up to Harlem to notorious cabarets like Connie's Inn and the Cotton Club to hear the "jungle music" of black bands such as Duke Ellington and Cab Calloway created an intriguing bond with the outcasts of society—the jazz and blues musicians, who were minorities such as Italians, Jews, and, especially, blacks.

"Among the young whites (often Jewish or Italians) in revolt against traditionalist values, the most rebellious were the jazz musicians," claims Shapiro, who notes that most mobsters were immigrants who had a feeling of sympathy for fellow outlaws—hard-pressed white musicians and displaced black musicians from the South. The wealthy and bohemian types were drawn to this alternative music and lifestyle. The most astute observer of this development was probably writer-photographer Carl Van Vechten. At their mid-Manhattan salon, in which blacks and whites mixed freely, he and his wife played host to an eclectic assortment of literary, theatrical, and musical figures.

Courtesy Stash Records

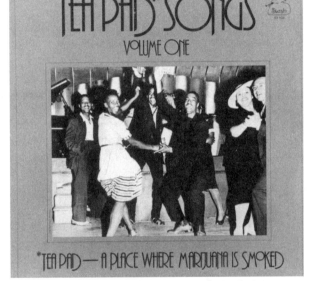

Courtesy Stash Records

Some Early Drug Songs

Name	Title	Year
Victoria Spivey	Dope Head Blues	1927
Luke Gordon	Cocaine Blues	1927
Frankie "Half Pint" Jaxon	Willie the Weeper	1927
Ernest Rodgers	Willie the Chimney Sweeper	1927
Zel Meyer	Pipe Dream Blues	1929
Memphis Jug Band	Cocaine Habit Blues	1930
Cab Calloway	Minnie the Moocher	1931
Cab Calloway	Kicking the Gong Around	1931
Cab Calloway	The Man From Harlem	1932
Cab Calloway	Reefer Man	1932
Benny Goodman (Jack Teagarden, vocal)	Texas Tea Party	1933
Leadbelly	Take a Whiff on Me	1934
Cleo Brown	The Stuff Is Here and It's Mellow	1935
Willie Bryant	A Viper's Moon	1935
Freddy Taylor	Blue Drag	1935
Harlem Hamfats	The Weed Smoker's Dream	1936
Andy Kirk	All the Jive Is Gone	1936
Stuff Smith	You'se a Viper	1936

In the mixed world of blacks and uppercrust or bohemian whites, jazz and blues music mixed freely with liberal attitudes about sex and drugs. So when the Harrison Narcotics Act of 1914 put America in the lead to fight the global war against drugs (cocaine and heroin) and the Marijuana Tax of 1937 outlawed nonmedical possession of the drug (called gage, stash, reefer, muggles, weed, pot, Mary Jane, tea, mezz, or mezzrow), the underground solidified. That laws were enlisted against drug users whose lifestyles posed a threat to the majority of white society is understandable. The concern here is neither to condone nor reject the alternative lifestyles, but, rather, to point out the gap that was created between the two social groups.

Shapiro concludes that, "In consequence, drugs went underground, an appropriate place for satanic pleasures. Equally appropriate was their association with the new voice in the black community-blues ('the devil's music') and jazz. Blacks, jungle rhythms and drugs: an unholy trinity to make the stiff-necked WASP quail, the gutter journalist rub his hands with glee and the thrill-seeker hit the streets." This outlaw underground world is the source of much of the ideology of rock'n'roll.

Louisiana Blues: Cajun and Zydeco

Library of Congress

Weekend "fais do do" held in a large barn with musicians providing music for dancing. Babysitters attended the children in another area of the barn or in a home adjoining it. The males, young and old, were corralled separately (left) and watched over by attendant (man facing camera, with hat). The males were allowed out to dance with the ladies and court them.

One of the more recent phenomenons in the world of blues has been a fascination with Cajun and zydeco music. First, there was an interest in Cajun food—blackened fish and all things associated with the popular chef-supreme Paul Prudhomme. This led to a connection with the music of the bayou region. For years Cajun and zydeco was an insulated musical form known only to the inhabitants of Louisiana and a few diehard aficionados.

The word Cajun comes from Acadia, a former French colony in what is now Nova Scotia, Canada. The Acadians were caught in the middle of territorial conflict between France and Britain when Acadia fell to the British in 1710. The French farmers remained as neutrals under the 1713 Treaty of Utrecht. This uneasy truce came to an end in 1755, when the Acadians were exiled for refusing to swear allegiance to the British crown. Large numbers of them left the area, many settling in southwest Louisiana. (Longfellow writes of this migration in his *Evangeline*.) The Acadians intermingled with other ethnic groups and the resulting cultural blend came to be known as Cajun. Barry Jean Ancelet, writing in *The Makers of Cajun Music,* states: "In south Louisiana today, French-speaking whites generally call themselves Cajuns, though some maintain the traditional distinction by calling themselves French Creoles. French-speaking blacks ordinarily call themselves Creoles. These distinctions are frequently overlooked by outsiders, who lump all groups together as 'Cajuns.' 'Cajun music' in the title of this book is used as a generic term to refer to the music of French South Louisiana, though black musicians often call their music 'Creole.'"

These people created a music that was a mixture of French, Celtic, and Anglo-Saxon folk songs. Waltz numbers, lullabies, and lively two-steps (known as "specials") were performed at home as parlor or front-porch entertainments. The main instruments were the fiddle, guitar, triangle (*petit fer*), which was struck percussively with a metal spike, and the accordion, usually a diatonic, or button accordion. The accordion was probably introduced to the Louisiana area by German immigrants in the 1870s.

Because these people were so isolated and poor, the earliest performances were centered on home and church. The home performances were referred to as *bals de maison*. Front rooms were cleared of furniture and readied for all-night dance sessions. Eventually public dances known as *fais do do* were established in larger halls. Like much of the folk and blues music of the pre-1920s, the earliest innovators are but faded memories.

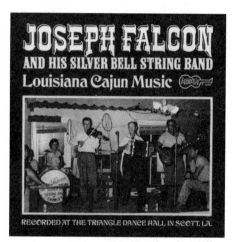

Courtesy Arhoolie Records, 10341 San Pablo Ave., El Cerritto, CA, 94530

Accordionist Joseph Falcon, the man who made the first Cajun record in 1928, "Allons a Lafayette" ("Let's Go to Lafayette"). He was recorded for this album in 1963 at a real fais do do in Crowley, Louisiana. Falcon's second wife, Theresa Meaux Falcon, played drums and vocalized.

The first French Cajun release was made in New Orleans on April 27, 1928, for Columbia Records by Joseph Falcon and his wife Cleoma Breaux. The song, "Allons a Lafayette", backed with "The Waltz That Carried Me to My Grave," was a success and enabled Falcon to leave farming and work exclusively as a musician. The song "Allons a Lafayette" was typical of white Cajun blues themes. The male singer pleads with the lady to travel with him to Lafayette so that they can get married ("in order to change your name"). The singer continues to make his plea of love, tinged with the sadness that he and his intended are far apart and she hasn't agreed to the union yet.

Falcon traveled throughout Louisiana and East Texas recording for Columbia, Decca, Bluebird, and Okeh during the 1930s. His style of aggressive accordion playing allegedly fell out of favor so he refused to record after 1937 (he continued to play for dances in the Crowley area). In 1929, Cleoma, with brothers Amidie and Ophy Breaux, made "Ma Blonde Est Partie," which was the first version of the classic "Jole Blon", a song of dozens of renditions and almost as many variations on its name.

Falcon's "Lafayette" led to a rash of releases of Cajun music by other record companies such as Paramount, Okeh, Brunswick/Vocalion, and Victor. Leo Soileau made the first Cajun fiddle recording, "Mama Where You At?" for Victor in October 1928. Soileau created an interest in hot fiddle music that he adapted to outside music sources such as the western swing style. By 1934, Soileau's unit was called Leo Soileau's Three Aces (drums were added, but accordion was out). Popular Soileau recordings included "La Valse de Gueydan," "Hackberry Hop," and "Le Gran Mamou."

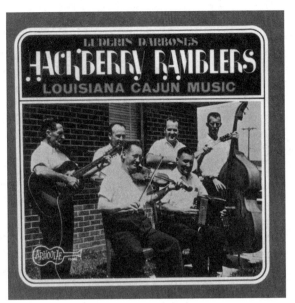

Courtesy Arhoolie Records, 10341 San Pablo, El Ceritto, CA 94530

During the early 1930s, the Hackberry Ramblers popularized Cajun tradition with a series of recordings for the Bluebird label. This Arhoolie release features recreations of those 1930s classics with original members Luderin Darbone (leader and fiddle player), Ed Duhon (accordion) and Lennis Sonnier (guitar). The Hackberry Ramblers and Harry Choates placed an emphasis on the fiddle and guitar, and boasted drum kits and electric steel guitars, making them, in effect, Cajun string bands.

Iry LeJune (1928-1955) is the transitional figure who rekindled interest in the accordion during the post-war years of the 1940s. Considered by many to be the greatest Cajun accordionist of all time, his "La Valse du Port d'amour (The Love Bridge Waltz)" in 1948 placed a re-emphasis on not only the accordion, after years of Americanized western string band sounds, but also on lyrics sung in French language. His son, Eddie LeJune, continues his work to this day. The other great accordionist of this post-war period was Nathan Abshire, a masterful blues player, whose "Pine Grove Blues" became a Cajun classic.

The Hackberry Ramblers, formed in 1933 under the direction of Luderin Darbone, mixed Cajun, hillbilly, and blues, and became the premier organization throughout the thirties and forties. Some of their classics include "Eh Las Bas," "Corinne Corinna," "Te Petite et Te Meon," "You've Got to Hi De Hi," and their biggest success, "Jole Blonde," sung by second guitarist Lennis Sonnier.

Harry Choates was by far the biggest individual star of Cajun music. Choates couldn't speak French but he could sing it; he was a fiddle player extraordinaire and a very dynamic performer. "Eh Ha, Ha!" became his trademark. In 1946 Choates recorded "Jole Blonde" and this came to be revered as the classic rendition of the song. "Jole Blon" (remember, there are many different spellings) is the anthem of Cajun music. It is a simple song of love: "Jole Blon, pretty girl/dear little one, pretty heart/you let me go away." Unfortunately, Choates, the "Fiddle King of Cajun Swing," was a tragic figure whose boozing led to an early death in a Texas jail at the age of twenty-eight in 1951.

Other Cajun Classics

Performer	Key Recording	Year
Joe Werner and the Riverside Ramblers	Wondering	1936
Happy Fats and the Rayne-Bo Ramblers	Les Veuve a Kita La Coulee	1941
Chuck Guillory and His Rhythm Boys	Tolan Waltz	1948
Floyd LeBlanc	Over the Waves	1948
Iry Lejune and the Oklahoma Tornadoes	La Valse du Pont d'Amour	1948
Acadian Stars	War Widow Waltz	1948
Nathan Abshire and the Pine Grove Boys	Pine Grove Blues	1949
Papa Caire	Big Texas	1949
Lawrence Walker and His Wandering Aces	Evangeline Waltz	1951
Vin Bruce	Dans la Louisianne	1952
Link Davis	Big Mamou	1952
Gene Rodrigue	Dans le Coeur de la Ville	1953
Doc Guidry	Chere Cherie	1953
Traveler Playboys	Sha Ba Ba	1955
Austin Pitre and the Evangeline Playboys	Flumes Dans Faires	1959
Rambling Aces	99 Years Waltz	1960
Rusty and Doug Kershaw	Louisiana Man	1961
Belton Richard and His Musical Aces	Just en Reve	1962
Dewey Balfa and His Musical Brothers	Drunkard's Sorrow Waltz	1967
Jimmy C. Newman	Lacke pas la Patate	1974

Recently artists such as Marc Savoy, Zachary Richard and Michael Doucet, have done much to rekindle the spirit of the rich heritage of the Cajun tradition. Savoy, an accordion maker, is a powerful proselytizer for retention of French history and stands strong against any diluting of Cajun music. Richard is best known to the fringe rock audience as the "Mick Jagger of Cajun Music." A one-time militant who refused to sing in English, he presently mixes his Cajun with rock. Doucet has been a relentless researcher and archivist who over the years has led eclectic groups such as the Choteau (referred to as the "Cajun Grateful Dead"), Beausoleil (purist French Cajun) and Cajun Brew (a mix of Cajun, rock, jazz, and zydeco).

Courtesy Arhoolie Records, 10341 San Pablo, El Ceritto, CA, 94530

"Parrian de la Musique Cajun" ("The Godfather of Cajun Music"), Harry Choates. His band played a combination of Cajun and western swing for audiences that loved to dance. Choates played mostly around Port Arthur, San Antonio, and Austin, Texas. His burial marker in Port Arthur reads: "A Tribute To Harry Choates, A Man Who Passed On With His Cajun Music That Will Live In Our Hearts Forever."

Courtesy Arhoolie Records, 10341 San Pablo, El Ceritto, CA. 94530

Led by folklorist and fiddler-vocalist Michael Doucet, Beausoleil is an all-acoustic band that reworks classic Cajun tunes. "Beausoleil" translates to "beautiful sunshine," but the phrase refers to Beausoleil Broussard, an Acadian rebel leader.

Zydeco: L'Haricots Sont pas Sales

Zydeco is the black French Cajun tradition with a stronger rhythmic thrust; in effect it is rhythm and blues Cajun music performed by blacks. The term zydeco is the creolized variant of *les haricots* ("snap beans"), inspired by an old one-step tune, "L'Haricots Sont pas Sales" ("The Snap Beans Aren't Salted"). The predecessor of zydeco was "La La" or "La Musique Creole," which was dance music played at black country dances and house parties.

The father figure of this tradition is accordionist-singer **Amadee Ardoin** (1900-late 1930s). The performer's first name has also been spelled "Amedee" and "Amede." In 1928 Ardoin won an accordion contest in Opelousas, Louisiana, which led to a recording contract in New Orleans. Ardoin and Dennis McGee, the fiddle contest winner, (they had been playing together since 1921), recorded selections such as "Madame Etienne," "Tante Aline," and "Two Step D'Eunice."

It must have been an odd sight in those times seeing a black accordionist and a white fiddler playing and singing for the segregated parties of white and black dancers. Ardoin preferred to play with McGee for white audiences because the pay was better and the jobs more regular than in the black community. Legend has it that Ardoin was badly beaten by a group of whites at some point and never fully recovered. While living in Crowley in the late 1930s, he was committed to the state mental institution in Pineville, where he likely died soon after. The Louisiana State Bureau of Vital Statistics has no record of his birth or death.

McGee, interviewed in *The Makers of Cajun Music*, commented about his musical relationship with Ardoin between 1928 and 1932: "Amedee and I worked together. We worked for the same people. We were both sharecroppers. . . . The boss liked music, so at night he would have us get together and play some. I would play the fiddle and Amede would play the accordion and we would both sing. . . When Oscar [Comeaux] went broke and quit farming, Amede left to come live in Eunice, and I came to live here, too. That's when we really started playing seriously. We started playing all over the area. We would go as far as old Mr. Leleux's dance hall in Bayou Queue de Tortue. And for Dumas Herpin. We brought so many people to Dumas's place that they climbed up on the little fence that they had put to protect musicians from the crowd and they broke it. They came rolling in like balls. It was really funny to see. The people wanted to come to us. We were making good music in those days."

Amadé Ardoin
Louisiana Cajun Music Vol. 6
The First Black Zydeco Recording Artist

His Original Recordings
1928–1938

OLD TIMEY 124

Courtesy Arhoolie Records, 10341 San Pablo, El Cerrito CA, 94530

In 1929 Amadee Ardoin became the first black to establish vocal and accordion classics on record. In later years, this music would be called zydeco.

There are great gaps in the history of zydeco, perhaps because of the small market and the fact that the Depression was especially hard on the rural black market. One artist who kept the flame alive was a cousin of Ardoin's, Alphonse "Bois Sec" Ardoin. He followed his cousin around and emulated his accordion style, playing house parties and weddings, but Alphonse's mother didn't want him to be a musician, and when Amade stopped playing professionally, so did Alphonse. In 1948 he returned to the music scene and joined forces with fiddler Canray Fontenot to play house dances as the Duralde Ramblers.

Nicholas Spitzer's entry on zydeco in the *Encyclopedia of Southern Culture* notes, "Because of the cultural interchange between Cajuns and Creoles in southwest Louisiana, there has been a tendency to overlook the differences between Cajun music and zydeco. Cajun music places more emphasis on developing the melodic line, while zydeco melodies are played much faster and consist of Acadian or Afro-American blues tunes placed in an Afro-Caribbean rhythmic framework. The rhythms are highly syncopated, with accents often shifting to various beats. While Cajun bands make wide use of the violin (an Acadian inheritance), they rarely play the vest *frottoir* (a metal washboard-like gadget worn as a vest and played with spoons, can openers, or thimbles). Played by old-time and rural zydeco groups, the vest frottoir has its antecedents in Africa and the Caribbean as a scraped animal jaw, notched stick, and, later, a washboard. The current model, made in Louisiana by tinsmiths, became popular in the 1930s when sheet metal was introduced to the area for roofing and barn siding." The first important record by a zydeco performer was 1950's "Bon Ton Roula" ("Let the Good Times Roll"), by Clarence Garlow. Boozoo Chavis' classic 1954 recording of "Paper in My Shoe" in 1954 was another big, regional hit, but it wasn't until Clifton Chenier came along that zydeco had a national star.

Courtesy Arhoolie Records, 10341 San Pablo, El Ceritto, CA, 94530

Clifton Chenier: King of Zydeco. Chenier single-handedly revived the form during the late 1950s and after with his compelling accordion playing and his salty French patois delivery. Chenier described his music as "simply the French two-step with new hinges so she can swing."

Courtesy Living Blues

Living Blues, one of America's premier blues magazines, with Rockin' Dopsie on the cover of its feature issue on zydeco music, July-August 1991. The issue covers contemporary zydeco units led by Boozoo Chavis, Chubby Carrier, John Delafose, and C. J. Chenier, as well as thumbnail sketches of Jo Jo Reed, Queen Ida, the Sam Brothers, Rockin' Sidney, Terrance Simien, and others.

Clifton Chenier (1925-1987) was an accordionist and singer whose home was in Opelousas, Louisiana, but his headquarters was in Port Arthur, Texas, which had a large Cajun community, many of whose members worked in the local oil industry. Chenier's father played accordion and took his sons Clifton and Cleveland to local parties where he performed. In time Clifton mastered the accordion and Cleveland the rub board. During the early 1940s they worked with Clarence Garlow and by 1947 they struck out on their own, calling their group the Hot Sizzling Band. Recording and traveling throughout the South in the 1950s and 1960s with his band, by now called the Zodico Ramblers, Clifton was billed the "Black King of the South." Chenier played on touring R&B caravans but it wasn't until he joined Chris Strachwitz's Arhoolie Records label in 1964 that he began to receive the acclaim that led him to be known as the "King of Zydeco."

Throughout the 1970s Chenier toured with his Red Hot Louisiana Band wearing a crown, and it was he, more than anyone, who achieved recognition for zydeco music. Les Blank's *Dry Wood and Hot Peppers* (Flower Films, 1973), captured Chenier in performance and in his off-stage lifestyle. C. J. Chenier, Clifton's son, was born and raised in Port Arthur and joined his father's band as a saxophone replacement for John Hart, who was the premier zydeco saxophonist. By 1984 C. J. picked up an accordion and after his father's death led his own zydeco group.

Today, Chenier's one-time sideman, Stanley Dural, known as Buckwheat Zydeco, is perhaps the most successful of the many zydeco artists. Dural has made inroads similar to that of Michael Doucet in Cajun music, with his ability to incorporate outside forms into his music, as demonstrated on his rendition of Bob Dylan's "On a Night Like This."

Archivists in Action

Courtesy Sony Music

The 1965 release of *Rising Sons*, featuring Taj Mahal and Ry Cooder, was rereleased by Columbia/Legacy in 1992.

Courtesy Sony Music

Taj Mahal has been a staunch archivist on behalf of African-American musical forms, especially those older forms of "archaic blues." In a *Down Beat* article in the early 1990s, Mahal chided the black middle class and churchgoers of the past for suppressing the rich African-American experience of blues music.

A number of contemporary performers have centered much of their professional existence on studying, collecting, writing, performing, teaching, and recording the music of the blues masters covered in this chapter. In a sense, these performers are the popular culture brethren of musicologist/folklorists such as John and Alan Lomax. These are performers who are most definitely a part of the underground; seldom, if ever, have they had a top forty hit. Ry Cooder and Taj Mahal are perhaps the best known of these archivists. They started their careers together in 1964 as members of a duo known as the Rising Sons. Together they played respectful renditions of songs by early bluesmen such as Peg Leg Howell, Blind Reverend Gary Davis, Robert Johnson, and Blind Willie Johnson, among many others. Both Ry Cooder and Taj Mahal have gone on to solo pursuits covering the width of "roots music."

Ry Cooder (1947-) has been one of the most prolific session men in the music business. He has backed Captain Beefheart, Phil Ochs, Randy Newman, George Harrison, and the Rolling Stones among many others, as well as composing several film scores: *The Long Riders* (1980), *Southern Comfort* (1981), *The Border* (1981), *Streets of Fire* (1984), *Paris, Texas* (1984), *Brewster's Millions* (1985), *Alamo Bay* (1985), *Blue City* (1986), *Crossroads* (1986), and *Geronimo (*1993), among others. Cooder is best known, however, as an archivist and curator of American roots music. He has recorded songs about the Great Depression (*Into the Purple Valley*, 1972), Tex-Mex and Hawaiian music (*Chicken Skin Music*, 1976), traditional jazz (*Jazz*, 1977) and rhythm and blues (*Bop Till You Drop*, 1979).

Taj Mahal (1940-) has been a tireless advocate of roots music throughout his career. He is one of the very few African-Americans who has based his work on the rural tradition of blues music. Mahal has noted in interviews that the black church and middle class have often been embarrassed about the blues legacy. Mahal's first album (*Taj Mahal: The Natch'l Blues*, 1968) established his commitment as one of the great curators of early blues forms. Mahal wrote the soundtrack and performed in *Sounder* (1971) and in 1990 he composed the music for *Mulebone*, an African-American play based on the collaborative work of Langston Hughes and Zora Neale Hurston.

Others who should be recognized for full-time commitment to the older blues forms are the Traum brothers, Artie and Happy, and Stefan Grossman (all of whom created "how to" books, cassettes, and videos on ragtime and blues forms); John Hammond (son of the celebrated record producer, who recently performed and hosted a 1992 video—*In Search for Robert Johnson*, which included interviews from Johnson heirs as well as Johnson disciples David "Honeyboy" Edwards and Johnny Shines; in 1992 Hammond also appeared on an "Austin City Limits" television show with Robert Jr. Lockwood, Robert Johnson's nephew, reprising songs associated with Johnson; and Sparkey Rucker, who, along with Taj Mahal, is one of the very few black artists working in the context of the older blues forms. Rucker has stated in interviews that very few blacks have been drawn to rural blues because for many it has a slave, plantation stigma.

Courtesy Shanachie Records

Stefan Grossman became the student and biographer of Reverend Gary Davis, and also studied with rural blues legends Mississippi John Hurt, Fred McDowell, Mance Lipscomb, and Skip James. During the mid-1960s Grossman was a member of the Even Dozen Jug Band, and played with the Fugs and Mitch Ryder. Later he formed his own label, Kicking Mule Records, which specialized in fingerpicking music.

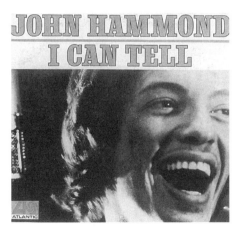

Courtesy of Atlantic Recording Corporation

Courtesy Flying Fish Records

Left, John Paul Hammond was raised in a household that was filled with jazz and blues. His father, John Henry Hammond, Jr., was an avid collector, writer, and record executive who brought many of the black jazz and blues artists he respected into his home. Young John grew up surrounded by the likes of bluesmen Brownie McGhee and Sonny Terry and developed a lifelong love affair with the blues. *Right*, Sparkey and Rhonda Rucker on the cover of one of their collaborations on Flying Fish Records. Along with Taj Mahal, Sparkey Rucker keeps alive the flame of African-American rural blues "roots music."

Chapter 5

ORIGINS OF JAZZ

Photographs and Prints Division, Schomburg Center for Research in Black Culture, The New York Public Library, Astor, Lenox and Tilden Foundation

THE VICTOR PHONOGRAPH CO.
PRESENTS
THE WORLD'S GREATEST ENTERTAINERS
Original Dixieland Jazz Band
Direct from Reisenweber's, Columbus Circle, 58th St., New York

The Most Imitated
Band in the World

The Best Known
Dance Combination

The Creators of Jazz

The Sensation of
Two Continents

The Only and
Unexcelled

You Have Danced

To Their

Records, Now

Dance to

The Original

PLAYING AT
WILLA GARDEN
Wednesday, October 12th, 1921
Dancing from 8:30 to 12:30
Admision, .90 Tax, .09

Positively their first
appearance in this City

SOME OF THEIR LATEST RELEASES

18457	At the Jazz Band Ball / Ostrich Walk	18772	Jazz Me Blues / St. Louis Blues
18483	Bluin the Blues / Sensation Rag	18717	Margie / Palesteena
18255	Dixieland Jazz Band / Livery Stable Blues	18722	Sweet Mamma / Broadway Rose
18472	Skeleton Jangle / Tiger Rag	18564	Lazy Daddy / Fidgety Feet
18729	Crazy Blues / Home Again Blues	18513	Mourning Blues / Clarinet Marmalade Blues

On sale at the J. H. Troup Music House, 15 South Market Square

Frank Driggs Collection

The first jazz record was released on March 7, 1917, by a white New Orleans group called the **Original Dixieland Jazz Band**. The record featured "Livery Stable Blues" on one side and "Dixie Jass Band One-Step" on the other. "Livery Stable Blues," also known as "Barnyard Blues," featured animal sounds such as a crowing rooster, a whinnying horse, and a braying donkey. That first jazz recording listed the group as the Original Dixieland Jass Band ("Jass" was soon changed to "Jazz"). The group, led by cornet player Nick La-Rocca, left the Crescent City for Chicago in 1916 and then went on to New York, where it created a sensation at Reisenweber's, a restaurant and dance palace located in mid-Manhattan. "Darktown Strutter's Ball," released four months later, became very popular, and the group's biggest-selling record, "Tiger Rag," became the first jazz record to make number one on the charts, according to *Joel Whitburn's Pop Memories.* The record stayed there for two weeks, beginning the week of August 17, 1918.

The band traveled to England, where it made the new jazz sounds accepted internationally, and continued recording until the mid-twenties, when the band broke up. Gunther Schuller, writing in *Early Jazz: Its Roots and Musical Development,* contends that the Original Dixieland Jazz Band's use of hokum barnyard sounds has been exaggerated by critics, and that the band's imitators, like Earl Fuller or the Louisiana Five, made a fetish out of those corny effects that stigmatized jazz. Of the Original Dixieland Jazz Band, Schuller claims, "[They] were an infuriating mixture of bad and good, of tasteless vulgarity and good musical intuitions. But beyond the music the ODJB left behind, it held, for better and for worse, a crucial place in the formative period of jazz." Although the Original Dixieland Jazz Band's sound was rather stiff, the group did establish what would be the prototype instrumental makeup for a traditional jazz band: a front line of cornet or trumpet, which usually carried the main melody, clarinet, which played high-pitched counter-melodies, and trombone, which played extended harmony lines, all supported by a rhythm section of drums and piano.

Courtesy Buffalo & Erie County Public Library

The debate over the origins of jazz has raged since the music began. Many claim it was born in New Orleans; others say there were jazz bands in many cities, and that the story that jazz began in New Orleans and traveled up the Mississippi River is merely myth. Without recorded evidence, it is difficult to know for certain. There were brass bands playing an assortment of sounds that mixed syncopated ragtime and spontaneous improvisation in many city centers at the turn of the century. Some, or many, of these units, may have played a music that bears some resemblance to what we know today to be jazz. What we do know is that a majority of the well-known jazz records made before 1925 were released by New Orleans players.

New Orleans was built by the French around 1718. The city had various periods of French and Spanish rule until the United States took it over in 1803. The attitude toward minorities was different in this area compared to that in the other states. The Catholic religion saw all people as one and allowed freedoms, such as Sunday dance and ritual for black people in Congo Square, not permitted in other southern states. New Orleans had free blacks as early as 1722. The city had two black populations: "Creoles of Color" and African Negro. The Creoles of Color, as they were referred to at the time, emerged from the old French colonial culture and were not descendants of slaves. Originally a Creole meant a person—black or white—who spoke French or Spanish and was born in the New World. Our interest is in the black Creoles.

Courtesy Jazzology Records

Cornetist Nick LaRocca, seated.

By 1860 there were 400,000 Creoles listed in the Louisiana census. Many of them were free and listed as F.M.C.—"Free Man of Color." They were mostly well-educated, successful businessmen, landowners, and merchants who attended opera and could play and read classical music. There was a wide separation between the Creoles, who lived downtown, and the African Negroes, who lived uptown and worked as unskilled laborers or house servants. Quotes from well-known Creole jazz musicians reflect the condescending attitude they had toward their darker, less educated brethren. Jelly Roll Morton had very little patience with those who couldn't read music, and spoke of "those black Negroes who couldn't stick to those little black dots." Of the prevailing Creole attitude toward African Negroes, Johnny St. Cyr, who played with Louis Armstrong, told Alan Lomax, "The mulattoes were actually more prejudiced than the white people of that time." Much of this separation would change when a state

Playing a funeral for the Young Men Olympians Benevolent Association, 1951: left to right, Willie Pajeaud, Emanuel Paul, Albert Warner, Robert Lewis, Charles Henry, Joseph Clark (Grand Marshal unkown).

Eureka Brass Band
NEW ORLEANS
FUNERAL & PARADE
The Original 1951 Session

Courtesy Jazzology Records

Brass Bands in New Orleans. The Eureka Brass Band in 1951. William Schafer, in his *Brass Bands in New Orleans Jazz*, asserts, "Brass bands gave jazz its instrumentation, its instrumental techniques, its basic repertoire. Only at the turn of the century, as the music we now call jazz began to be amalgamated by nonreading musicians, did brass bands incorporate much head [unwritten] music into their repertoires. Only slowly did they shift from reading standard printed band arrangements to developing improvisational head arrangements."

"white supremacy" act, "Code No. 111," was passed in 1894. The new law denied the Creoles their one-time favored place in society and cast them into the same status as African Negroes. The meeting point of the Creoles, trained in the European tradition, with the more freewheeling, improvising, rhythm-conscious uptown black musicians, and both with white interpreters as a third force, pretty much led to the beginnings of jazz. Some have contended that jazz is thoroughly an expression of African roots. This ignores the facts. Jazz developed in America, not Africa, and was an acculturative amalgamation of European and African origins arbitrated by American synthesis.

In his history *The Making of Jazz,* James Lincoln Collier sums up the pre-jazz state of affairs: "By 1890 there were three separate and distinct fusions of African and European music: ragtime, and black-American folk music (blues), both created by blacks, and the popularized version of black folk music, made principally by whites." In 1993, Collier more fully elaborated his theoretical challenge to jazz historical orthodoxy in *Jazz: The American Theme Song.* Of the Creoles, Collier asserts that, "Their music was different, and it was different in ways that resembled what jazz would come to be. My central point then, is that jazz did not arise from some generalized 'black culture' or 'black experience.' As I believe, the Creoles were key to the process, and they possessed a culture that was substantially different from that of the Southern black laboring man that produced the spirituals and field hollers. They spoke French rather than English; were Catholic, not Protestant; were artisans and small business people rather than day laborers; and most important, despite the obvious African residuals in their religious practices, language, and folkways, saw themselves as inheritors of a European culture. They were not people of the

One of the Earliest jazz bands, hailing from New Orleans, is this one, called the "Original Creole Orchestra" and including in its personnel, left to right at top, Adie Venson, Freddie Keppard, George Bacquet and Bill Johnson. Below, Charles Johnson, Jimmie Polla and Norwood Williams. Keppard was king of cornetists until Joe Oliver whittled him down. Bacquet was one of the early clarinetists and still plays today. The date? About 1912. They never recorded. *Down Beat* Photo.

Courtesy Down Beat

Fate Marable's Orchestra was the most famous of the Mississippi riverboat bands. This picture, taken in 1919, shows the orchestra aboard the Streckfus Line flagship, the *S.S. Capitol*. Marable was a tough taskmaster who hired Louis Armstrong. The red-headed leader is at the piano with Armstrong (third from right), Boyd Atkins (second from left), Johnny St. Cyr (fourth from left), and Baby Dodds (extreme right).

Frank Driggs Collection

The Carroll Dickerson Band at the Sunset Cafe, Chicago, in 1923. Violinist Dickerson was a well-known Chicago leader (he also directed the Mills Blue Rhythm Band). This floor show featured Bessie Smith rival Mary Stafford (hands raised) and singer-dancer Frankie "Half Pint" Jaxon (doing the split).

Frank Driggs Collection

Armand J. Piron and His Novelty Orchestra at Tranchina's Restaurant, New Orleans, 1922. Piron, a Creole, played violin left-handed and wrote songs such as "Sister Kate," "Day by Day," and "Kiss Me Sweet." He wouldn't hire players who couldn't pass for white.

Frank Driggs Collection

sanctified church with its ring-shouts, but of a voodoo-tinctured Catholicism; not of the work song, but of the Creole love ditty and to some extent the French opera; not of the slow drag, but the schottische and the mazurka; and perhaps most critically, most of them had no recent history of slavery."

There was a great deal of music to be heard in New Orleans and it had many sources. The name of the city's most legendary entertainment district derives from Sidney Story, a crusading politician who initiated an 1897 ordinance that confined prostitution to a thirty-eight-block area along Canal Street. The inhabitants of this most famous "tenderloin" district called it Storyville. Piano players were summoned to provide musical entertainment in its many brothels. Often referred to as "professors," they played in shabby houses of repute as well as elegant mansions bedecked with mirrors and expensive chandeliers. Today the piano seems an inevitable part of the bands of early jazz. However, pianos were not portable and were not used in marching bands. Authors Lewis Porter, Michael Ullman, and Ed Hazell, writing in *Jazz: From its Origins to the Present*, contend, "Nonetheless, pianists did have an impact on early jazz. They were, after all, usually the most carefully trained instrumentalists, and in the groups in which they did appear, they were frequently called upon to be arranger and musical director. But for the most part in New Orleans at the turn of the century, they played as soloists or with small groups in bars and even brothels."

Many social clubs, fraternal orders, and taverns hired musicians. Brass bands also played outdoor events away from Storyville, such as picnics, barbecues, and dances. These events were often advertised atop horse-drawn wagons with bands playing, the trombone over the edge so as not to hit anyone with the slide, thus the term "tailgate trombone." And many funerals provided music to and from the burial grounds.

New Orleans Traditional Bands

Group/Leader	Observations
Ed Allen's Whispering Gold Orchestra	Regulars on the Streckfus boat line
Red Allen's Brass Band	For years top perennial; national acclaim in 1960s
Lee Collins Band	2nd-generation trumpeter; replaced Armstrong in King Oliver's band in 1924
Halfway House Dance Orchestra	Leon Rappolo & Abbie Brunies; "Pussy Cat Rag"
Louisiana Shakers	Debut 1930; featured sax stylist John Handy
Johnny Miller's Frolickers	"Panama," 1929, the "apogee of white New Orleans jazz in the 1920s"
Sam Morgan's Jazz Band	Featured fluid sax of Earl Fouche; "Sing On"
New Orleans Owls	During mid-1920s "Finest band in the South;" "Stomp Off, Let's Go," 1925
Albert Nicholas Band	Reed player co-led with Barney Bigard; modeled on white duo Tony Parenti & Tony Papalia
Original Crescent City Jazzers	Considered Mobile's hottest jazz unit
The Original Tuxedo Orchestra	Leading trumpeter of New Orleans, 1925-50, was Oscar "Papa" Celestin
Buddy Petit	Great hot cornetist according to Jelly Roll Morton
Armand Piron's Novelty Orchestra	Played country club & restaurant circuit, 1916-34; light-skinned blacks only!
Prima-Sharkey Orchestra	Trumpeters Sharkey Bonano & Leon Prima (Louis Prima's older brother)
Henry "Kid" Rena	Worked w/ Kid Ory; taxi dance jobs; 1940s revival
Joe Robichaux's Rhythm Boys	"King Kong Stomp," 1933; vocalist Joan Lunceford the "Ella Fitzgerald of the South"
Southern Syncopators	Creole group featured trumpet of Sidney Desvignes & piano of Fats Picone
Nat Towle's Creole Harmony Kings	Prominent band in Southwest during 1930s
Kid Thomas Valentine	In Eton Theodore Band; re- discovered 1950s-80s (Preservation Jazz Band)
Manuel Perez's Garden of Joy Orchestra	Parade brass band and society boat band

Source: Frank Driggs & Harris Lewine, Black Beauty, White Heat: A Pictorial History

An important ingredient in the early marching bands were colorful cornet-player leaders like Buddy Bolden (the first celebrated "King," who never recorded), Buddy Petit and Chris Kelly (also unrecorded), Lee Collins, Henry "Kid" Rena, Kid Thomas Valentine, and Freddie Keppard. Creoles, blacks, and Italians made up the majority of ethnic groups performing in the early years. A good number of Italians were among the first jazzmen; this was a large ethnic group in New Orleans gainfully employed as merchants, produce store owners, barbers, builders, and the like. Many units are not known to today's audience because they didn't produce a large body of recordings.

The diaspora of New Orleans jazz musicians was greatly invigorated after 1917, when Storyville was closed down by the U.S. Navy. Musicians moved to Los Angeles, San Francisco, New York, and Memphis, but Chicago was the city of choice for many of the most well-known New Orleans players. As a result, Chicago became the next major center for traditional jazz. Of the many greats that made musical history from New Orleans, we will briefly look at four: Jelly Roll Morton, Sidney Bechet, King Oliver, and Louis Armstrong.

Jelly Roll Morton, along with the under-publicized Tony Jackson (author of "Pretty Baby," who was, according to banjoist Johnny St. Cyr, "considered among all who knew him the greatest single handed entertainer in the world"), was the top keyboard player in New Orleans. Jelly Roll was a "name" when he left New Orleans to travel the country playing music and working as a pool hustler, pimp, bellhop, tailor, peddler, night-club manager, minstrel, fight promoter, and card shark.

The highlight of Jelly Roll Morton's career was his meticulously detailed arrangements written for his group the Red Hot Peppers. The group was formed in 1926 to meet a contract commitment with the Victor Recording Company. The group cut fifty-seven sides for Victor, and music publishers Walter and Lester Melrose lent firm assistance as producers of these sessions. Donald D. Megill and Richard S. Demory, in their *Introduction to Jazz History*, note, "The group's instrumentation and personnel were never firmly organized. Jelly Roll recruited musicians he felt could best bring each of his compositions and arrangements to life. The band assembled for the first date [September 15, 1926] did, however, constitute a sort of basic organization. It contained a clarinet, trumpet, and trombone, and a rhythm section consisting of piano, bass, drums, and banjo. In the second session, on September 21, 1926, Jelly Roll added two clarinets, and in the third session two violins."

In the spring of 1938 Morton was living in obscurity in Washington, D.C., and he heard a radio show (NBC's "Believe It or Not") say that W.C. Handy was the originator of jazz and blues. Morton wrote a 4,000 word salvo setting the record straight. He proclaimed, "It is evidently known beyond contradiction that New Orleans is the cradle of jazz, and I, myself, happened to be the creator in the year 1902." *Down Beat* magazine reported the controversy, and soon Morton was a celebrity again. Alan Lomax recorded his reminiscences for the Folk Music Archive in the Coolidge Auditorium of the Library of Congress, which resulted in one of the sparks for the "Revival of New Orleans Music" (noted at the end of this chapter).

Jelly Roll Morton (1890-1941) was an influential pianist and the first important composer and arranger in jazz. He was a light-skinned Creole who grew up hearing the music of the first New Orleans legends, Buddy Bolden and Freddie Keppard. He played solo piano in the brothels and even hustled as a pimp, one of his many occupations outside of music.

Those who knew Morton considered him quite boastful, but he could often back up his claims. One such boast was that he "invented" jazz. No one man could legitimately lay claim to that, but Morton was among the first to make the transition from ragtime piano to the looser, improvised approach of jazz. In his *Jazz: History, Instruments, Musicians, Recordings,* John Fordham presents a sensible overview of Morton's accomplishments: "He upset ragtime's regular meters and expanded the instrumentation of the orthodox New Orleans band to feature groups of instruments playing harmonically, as in the Red Hot Peppers's clarinet sections. Conceiving of the jazz ensemble as a palette of contrasting tone colors, Jelly Roll Morton pioneered techniques that would later contribute to orchestral jazz."

Morton's peak years were in Chicago between 1923 and 1927, when he released a series of well-rehearsed compositions with his famous group, the Red Hot Peppers. In his compositions, Morton often included something he referred to as the "Latin tinge," that is, Spanish elements derived from the habanera (an amalgam of musical elements, among them a rhythm derived from the Spanish habanera dance). Morton's classic recordings include "Jelly Roll Blues," "Grandpa's Spells," "Black Bottom Stomp," "Wild Man Blues," "The Crave," "Chicago Breakdown," "Wolverine Blues," "The Chant," and his most enduring composition, which found favor during the swing era, "King Porter Stomp."

Jelly Roll Morton was the first important jazz composer; he reserved space in his compositions for improvisation, and meticulously rehearsed musicians playing his music. He is the main link between formal classic ragtime and the looser jazz piano style. Morton's colorful life was brought to Broadway in a controversial, but very thought-provoking 1993 musical entitled *Jelly's Last Jam*. Also important were the series of musical plays about Morton created by Vernel Bagneris (see the end of this chapter for more on Bagneris).

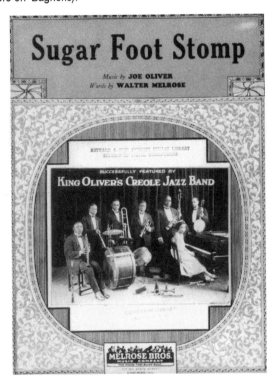

One of the classics of early jazz was "Dippermouth Blues" by King Oliver's Creole Jazz Band (1923). This selection was also released as "Sugar Foot Stomp" and featured the easy two-beat dance rhythm that kept tempo in the moderate range of 140 to 190 beats per minute. King Oliver's instrumental recordings were among the first to feature improvisation by a black band. Left to right, the band consisted of Johnny Dodds, clarinet; Baby Dodds, drums; Honore Dutrey, trombone; Louis Armstrong, cornet; Joe "King" Oliver, cornet; Lil Hardin, piano; and Bill Johnson, banjo.

Joe "King" Oliver (1885-1938) was one of the best known cornet players in New Orleans. He favored "muted" sounds, which he would create by using ash trays, handkerchiefs, tin cups and whatever else came to hand to cast over the bell of his horn. Oliver's bands recorded a wide variety of musical styles: blues, stomps, rags, and pop tunes. The classic New Orleans style employed collective improvisation resulting in polyphonic (Greek for "many voiced"; use of simultaneous melodies) playing. Oliver is said to have instituted the technique known as "breaks," which featured a single instrument playing a brief series of notes. Breaks were the antecedent of the solo.

Oliver and his Creole Jazz Band were playing the Lincoln Gardens in Chicago in 1922 when Oliver summoned young Louis Armstrong from New Orleans to play second cornet. Many authorities feel the recordings with Oliver playing lead and Armstrong playing second cornet are Oliver's crowning achievements. Others point out that Oliver's main achievement was that he provided a main model for young Armstrong, who would soon be a leader. Selections such as "Dippermouth Blues," "Froggie Moore," and "High Society Rag" reflect the double-cornet technique. Oliver's strength was on slow to medium-tempo blues numbers like "Someday Sweetheart" and "St. James' Infirmary," where tightly structured group playing created an infectious momentum.

The third of the early leaders of classic New Orleans traditional jazz was clarinet and soprano saxophonist **Sidney Bechet** (1897-1959). Bechet became the first individual international jazz star. Early in his career Bechet toured Europe with black conductor Will Marion Cook's Southern Syncopated Orchestra (1919), garnering plaudits from the critics. Throughout his career Bechet would return to Europe for extended stays. He became the first significant saxophone player in jazz, and the first to master the soprano sax.

Because Bechet was in Europe between 1919 and 1922, he did not record during that time. His first recording date came in 1923, ("Kansas City Blues" and "Wild Cat Blues") under the leadership of Clarence Williams. Bechet would work with Williams, a prolific composer who used the band names Red Onion Jazz Babies and the Clarence Williams Blue Five. A number of historians believe that Bechet was the first great soloist in jazz. Contemporaries like guitarist Danny Barker claim he was the most advanced soloist in New Orleans. This was years before Louis Armstrong emerged as a star soloist. Duke Ellington, a man not prone to hyperbole, stated simply, "Bechet, the greatest of all originators. Bechet, symbol of jazz."

Bechet's best known recordings are "Shreveport Blues" (1923), "Cake Walkin' Babies" (1924), "Blue Horizon" (1934), and "Summertime" (1938). Bechet's "Texas Moaner" (1941) jumps off the record with passionate playing that unfurls, phrase after meaty phrase. One merely has to listen to his trills and certain repeated phrases on "Summertime" to realize the profound impact this "older" stylist had on the soprano saxophone technique of John Coltrane, who revived htat neglected instrument during the 1960s.

Rosalie & Theodore Cron Collection, Carnegie Hall Archives

Sidney Bechet was the first important saxophone player in jazz. While in London, in 1919, Bechet bought his first straight model soprano sax. He carefully worked out intricate embellishments on the songs in his repertoire that, despite appearances, were set pieces rather than improvisations. Bechet was admired for his ferocious, biting attack on whatever reed instrument he played—clarinet or soprano saxophone. Bechet's use of fast and wide vibrato was instantly recognizable, as was his effective use of slurs. In 1960 Bechet's autobiography, *Treat It Gentle,* was published posthumously. During the revival of Dixieland that began in the late 1930s, Bechet made a series of recordings on Blue Note Records that gained new acclaim for him, especially with "Summertime" and "Wild Man Blues." John Chilton wrote the authoritative biography, *Sidney Bechet: The Wizard of Jazz,* in 1987.

Louis Armstrong (1901-1971) was born in New Orleans. He learned cornet at the Colored Waifs' Home, where he was sent in 1912 after firing a pistol. He played in a series of bands before joining King Oliver in Chicago. Lil Hardin, the band's pianist, convinced Armstrong to leave the band and work under his own name. Lil became his second wife, and by 1925 she was billing him as "The World's Greatest Trumpeter." Armstrong made a slew of recordings between 1924 and 1928, but in just thirty-three sides released on Okeh Records between 1925 and 1927, with an all-star unit known as the Hot Five and Hot Seven, he brought jazz to a new level of excellence.

Armstrong elaborated on two elements of jazz, the stop chorus and the break, to establish the solo as a main ingredient in a jazz performance. The stop chorus performed the function of a standard chorus, but it was broken up into several short, repeated phrases executed by the band as a whole and started and stopped in unison. The break was basically a very short version of today's individual solo, usually inserted at the end of an ensemble passage, but without otherwise interrupting the normal flow of a song. Some traditionalists frowned on the concept of the individual solo, claiming that it encouraged "showboating" and placed the individual star above the group. Listening to early Armstrong in the traditional ensemble style, one gets the feeling of an artist who had been placed in a straightjacket and needed to burst out.

King Oliver's Jazz Band sold many records for Paramount's race series. Oliver is seated to the right of the drummer in this advertisement. Louis Armstrong, who played second cornet to Oliver's lead, is standing, third from right. Fellow trumpeter Mutt Carey stated in (Martin Williams's *Jazz Masters of New Orleans*): "[Oliver] was the greatest freak trumpeter I ever knew. He did most of his playing with cups, glasses, buckets, and mutes. He was the best gut-bucket man I ever heard. I called him freak because the sounds he made were not made by the valves but through these artificial devices. In contrast, Louis played everything through the horn."

The first superstar of jazz:. Louis Armstrong conquered poverty and racism to become the world's best known and loved player of jazz music. He began as an unknown cornet player out of New Orleans and by mid-1925 emerged as a trumpet leader of the all-star aggregation working out of Chicago known as the Hot Five, and later, the Hot Seven. By 1929 Armstrong left the small group format behind to lead larger bands that featured his golden horn and raspy-voiced vocals performing Tin Pan Alley pop songs. This increased the size of Armstrong's audience tremendously. In 1936 Armstrong was featured in *Pennies from Heaven*, the first of many major Hollywood films in which he would appear. In 1947 Armstrong returned to the small combo format with his All-Stars, which at various times featured greats such as Jack Teagarden (trombone), Barney Bigard (clarinet), Billy Kyle (piano), Earl Hines (piano), and Trummy Young (trombone). From the 1950s until his death in 1971 Armstrong was acknowledged worldwide as America's "Ambassador of Jazz."

Contrary to the complaints of the traditionalists, Armstrong liberated the soloist to project individuality not above but rather within the confines of the group experience. One could compare the small jazz unit to a basketball team. Basketball thrives on team unity but it allows for individuals to "create" and dispatch techniques, and to execute highly individual "moves" to achieve a goal. Armstrong didn't solo just to showboat. In fact, on the very first release of the Hot Five ("Cornet Chop Suey")he introduced each member by name and allowed each a solo spot . Armstrong used the solo as a means to an end. The collective improvisations of the earlier era had reached a dead end; Armstrong retained the order of collective playing, but gave it a new spark of life.

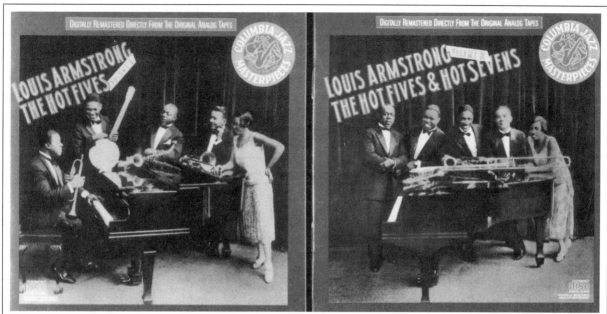

The Hot Five and Hot Seven bands.. Left, Louis Armstrong, trumpet; Johnny St. Cyr, banjo; Johnny Dodds, saxophone and clarinet; Kid Ory, trombone; Lil Hardin, piano. Right, Johnny Dodds, Louis Armstrong, Johnny St. Cyr, Kid Ory, and Lil Hardin. Duke Ellington said of Armstrong, "I loved and respected Louis Armstrong. He was born poor, died rich, and never hurt anyone on the way."

Masterpieces such as "Potato Head Blues" and "West End Blues," to cite just two among many worthy examples, have both great ensemble passages and stunning solos by Armstrong that literally jolt the listener. There is none of the stiffness of ragtime elements evident in many of the earlier New Orleans jazz players. These records are loose and exhilarating. One can almost feel their shouts of freedom. Armstrong also had an ability to take a cold brass instrument and breathe warmth into it—he humanized the trumpet. Armstrong had complete control over the trumpet while playing in the upper register. He could hit high C a hundred times in succession, as well as achieve warm tones in the lower register without wavering. Musicians were astounded not only by his technique but also by his expressive creativity. Armstrong provided a new model, a raised standard, that other players would have to emulate.

Armstrong was a vocal innovator as well. He never would have made it as a "legitimate" singer; his voice was too raspy. But in jazz, a musical form of inclusion rather than exclusion, such limitations have often proved illuminating instead of debilitating. Armstrong showed that the voice could project personality and attitude. His singing was joyful, and executed with an

Earl "Fatha" Hines (1903-1983) created a rough, "bright" piano sound referred to as the "trumpet style" or "horn-like" technique. Before playing piano he trained as a trumpeter, so his musical conception was that of a horn player, not that of a pianist. Hines played the piano with great force because in the days before amplification he had to punch out his solos loudly so that he could be heard over the din of the orchestra he led. In addition to his classic recordings with Louis Armstrong ("West End Blues" and "Weather Bird"), Hines gained fame via radio broadcasts and tours of his band, which he led at the Grand Terrace Ballroom in Chicago from 1928 to 1939.

instrumentalist's flair. Armstrong sang "around" the beat—intentionally ahead or behind it—which gave him tremendous rhythmic versatility. Armstrong proved to be the master of this technique, eventually called "rhythmic displacement." On "Heebie Jeebies" Armstrong introduced the "scat" technique—improvised nonsense sounds similar to an instrumental passage. Scat singing has been an integral part of the jazz vocabulary ever since.

Louis Armstrong's ascendency into the world of popular music was a conscious decision made by two of the great trumpeter's managers. First was Tommy Rockwell, who moved Armstrong into the arena of New York show business by having him sing and play songs familiar to the popular audiences of the day. To the horror of many jazz aficionados, Armstrong stated that he admired the Guy Lombardo Orchestra. So in 1929, Rockwell put together a band that was similar to Lombardo's—proficient but not loaded with great jazz talent. A move from the smaller, independent Okeh Record Company to the Victor Recording Company gave Armstrong not only greater prestige, but wider record distribution. Later, Joe Glaser would ably direct Armstrong's career in a similar vein. Cries of "selling out" followed, but Armstrong, like most entertainers of any kind of music, desired wider exposure and sought to make more money; Rockwell and Glaser made this possible. Most artists in popular culture who attain wide audience support have had much help in the area of management. Duke Ellington, Count Basie, Ella Fitzgerald, Jimmie Rodgers, Bing Crosby, Gene Autry, Louis Jordan, Nat "King" Cole, Benny Goodman, Elvis Presley, the Beatles, and many others all had astute management that launched and maintained their careers.

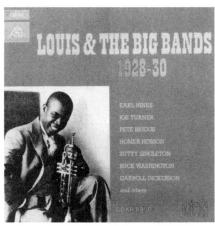

Courtesy DRG Records

By 1928 Louis Armstrong fronted bigger orchestras and began cutting records that featured popular songs. This recording has him in the group of musical director Carroll Dickerson ("Some of These Days," "When You're Smiling," "Exactly Like You," and "Dinah") and featured with pianist-conductor Luis Russell ("I Can't Give You Anything but Love," "St. Louis Blues," "Rockin' Chair," and "Blue, Turning Grey Over You").

After 1928 Armstrong focused on black show music and mainstream music. He would eventually be signed up to make motion pictures, and this new acceptance by the general public would create a much heavier emphasis on Armstrong as "entertainer" over Armstrong as "innovator." Throughout the ensuing decades Armstrong would be the best known and most loved of the jazzmen. Even when new forms of jazz replaced his older style, he was always a top-billed artist. In the 1960s he had a top five

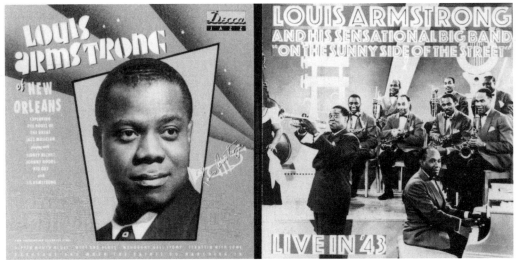

Courtesy MCA Records   *Courtesy Stash Records*

Armstrong goes pop. Throughout the 1930s and 1940s Armstrong's larger units performed in large clubs and ballrooms as well as on radio and in film. Armstrong reworked most of his earlier classics, and along the way introduced new popular music selections to his vast repertoire. By this time Armstrong was one of the biggest draws in jazz.

hit with "Hello Dolly!" and "What a Wonderful World" was revived in the 1988 movie *Good Morning Vietnam.* By the 1990s advertisers were using the sound of Satchmo's voice (often imitated by Chicago singer Ron Hawking) for ads marketing Canada Dry soft drinks ("Young at Heart"), Fisher-Price hair- and skin-care products ("We've Got a Face You Can Trust"), Hershey's Chocolate Bar Flavor puddings ("You're So Good, I Could Eat You With a Spoon"), and Milk-Bone T. C. (tartar control) Dog Biscuits ("When You're Smiling"). Armstrong was also part of a Diet Coke special effects ad that superimposed rock star Elton John over James Cagney, Humprey Bogart, and the trumpet great. A made-for-television biopic starred Ben Vereen.

Significant Early Louis Armstrong Recordings

Leader	Record Company	Song	Year
King Oliver	Gennett	Dippermouth Blues	1923
King Oliver	Gennett	Chimes Blues/Froggie Moore	1923
Erskine Tate	Vocalion	Stomp Off, Let's Go	1924
Fletcher Henderson	Vocalion	Mandy, Make Up Your Mind	1924
Clarence Williams	Okeh	Everybody Loves My Baby	1925
Bessie Smith	Columbia	St. Louis Blues/Cold in Hand Blues	1925
Clara Smith	Columbia	Shipwrecked Blues	1925
Bertha "Chippie" Hill	Okeh	Lonesome Weary Blues/Lovesick Blues	1925
Louis Armstrong	Okeh	Heebie Jeebies/Muskrat Ramble	1925
Louis Armstrong	Okeh	Cornet Chop Suey/My Heart	1926
Lil's Hot Shots	Vocalion	Drop That Sack/Georgia Bo Bo	1926
Louis Armstrong	Okeh	Big Butter & Egg Man (with May Alix)	1926
Louis Armstrong	Okeh	Wild Man Blues	1927
Louis Armstrong	Okeh	Alligator Crawl	1927
Louis Armstrong	Okeh	West End Blues (with Earl Hines)	1928
Louis Armstrong	Okeh	Weather Bird (with Earl Hines)	1928
Louis Armstrong	Okeh	Ain't Misbehavin'/Black and Blue	1929
Louis Armstrong	Okeh/Decca	I Can't Give You Anything But Love	1929
Louis Armstrong	Okeh	When You're Smiling	1929
Louis Armstrong	Columbia	Sweethearts on Parade	1930
Louis Armstrong	Okeh	Star Dust	1931
Louis Armstrong	Okeh	Between the Devil and the Deep Blue Sea	1932
Louis Armstrong	Okeh	I Gotta Right to Sing the Blues	1933

Chicago and the White Influx

The excitement of the new jazz music captivated much of America, and it wasn't long before musicians tried to emulate these sounds. As previously noted, a majority of innovations in jazz have emanated from African Americans. However, it is incorrect to hold that other races did not create new concepts in jazz. White jazzmen in New Orleans, like Jack "Papa" Laine, Johnny Stein, and Tom Brown, with his Ragtime Band, all played a jazz-styled music before jazz was "discovered" by the nation in 1917. Many outstanding white players made significant contributions during the early period of jazz, including Bix Beiderbecke, Joe Venuti, Eddie Lang, Jack Teagarden, Pee Wee Russell, and Django Reinhardt (a European), among many others.

The Original Dixieland Jazz Band did introduce jazz on record. But musically they cannot compare to excellent all-around groups such as the Original Memphis Five and the New Orleans Rhythm Kings. The **New Orleans Rhythm Kings** (1922-1925), a white group from New Orleans, played a more swinging style of collective improvisation. Around 1921 they were playing in Chicago at the Friars Inn and had a tremendous influence on their midwestern listeners. Their recordings were copied note for note by many future players, including Bix Beiderbecke and members of the Austin High Gang. It should be noted here that records often provided the only communication between and professional learning experience for aspiring musicians. In some cases individuals were not able to see live performances because of distance, age, or lack of money. Also, schools did not teach anything about jazz, nor did music companies provide songbooks notating solos, as is the case today. The simple process of listening to a record for four, or eight, or sixteen bars of music, and then picking up the arm of the phonograph and trying to duplicate the sound inspired untold artists over the years. Black jazz greats Benny Carter and Lester Young copied Frankie Trumbauer solos note for note off records. Trumbauer and Beiderbecke laid down the foundations for the eventual "cool" movement in jazz.

Social dancing was the primary recreation of the 1920s and 1930s, and it needed live music. Both black and white bands were hired to accommodate the dancers. Often overlooked by modern jazz audiences is that most of the jazz greats of this early period, including Jelly Roll Morton, Duke Ellington, Louis Armstrong, and Bix Beiderbecke, played for dancers. These jazzmen had to keep their audiences satisfied, or they would not be hired to play for them again.

Frank Driggs Collection

The New Orleans Rhythm Kings, Chicago, 1922. Left to right, George Brunis, trombone; Frank Snyder, drums; Paul Mares, cornet and leader; Arnold Loyocane, bass; Elmer Schoebel, piano; Jack Pettis, C-melody saxophone; Leon Roppollo, clarinet. The New Orleans Rhythm Kings filled the gap left in Chicago by the Original Dixieland Jazz Band when it moved on to New York. The Rhythm Kings featured a high-energy program that included clowning and placed a premium on showmanship, a quality appreciated by the cabaret audience at the mob-controlled Friars Inn. Along with the Original Memphis Five (Phil Napoleon, cornet, and Miff Mole, trombone) the Rhythm Kings were considered the finest of the early white creators of hot jazz.

Bix Beiderbecke (1903-1931) was one of the first great white practitioners of jazz. Beiderbecke was born in Davenport, Iowa, and was considered a musical prodigy, playing piano by the time he was five. To a middle class family, classical music was proper, but young Bix's attraction to the "evil" influence of jazz was so strong that it led him to drop out of high school. By 1923 Beiderbecke had mastered the cornet and joined a midwestern group called the Wolverines. His clear sound dominated the eight-piece band, but Beiderbecke got bored and coached Jimmy McPartland to take his place in 1924.

Bix Beiderbecke. Above, Beiderbecke in center (arrow) with the original Wolverine Orchestra in 1924. Below, Beiderbecke (second from right) and the Rhythm Jugglers with Don Murray, clarinet (third from right), and Tommy Dorsey, trombone (far right).

Wolverine Banner Bright Then

Cincinnati—This rare old picture of Bix and the Wolverines was taken in the early 20s in Cincinnati. The band was organized by Dud Mecum, composer of the old hit *Angry*, to play the Stockton club, near Hamilton, Ohio. Later Mecum pulled out to return to Chicago and Dick Voynow took over on piano. Left to right, holding their Wolverine banner, are Min Leibrock, bass; George Johnson, tenor sax; Bix Beiderbecke, cornet; Jimmy Hartwell, clarinet; Voynow; Bob Gillette, banjo; Vic Moore, drums, and Al Gandee, trombone. Photo courtesy of Bud Bel.

Beiderbecke played a short time with orchestra leader Jean Goldkette, but was released because he was a poor music reader. Beiderbecke then joined Paul Whiteman's orchestra, and shortly achieved a prominence few jazzmen were accorded at that time.

Beiderbecke's most meaningful recordings were made with small units. In one of these he met Frankie Trumbauer, who was probably the outstanding saxophone player of this early period. Trumbauer played the C-melody saxophone, an instrument whose size is somewhere between the tenor and alto saxophones. Trumbauer created a pure, light sound that employed a slow vibrato. His solos were precise and melodic. Lester Young based his cool, light style of tenor saxophone playing on Trumbauer's floating sound. Beiderbecke made many of his most influential recordings with Trumbauer in 1927. Along with Trumbauer, guitarist Eddie Lang, and saxophonists Jimmy Dorsey and Adrian Rollini, Beiderbecke waxed classics such as "Singin' the Blues," "I'm Comin', Virginia" "Way Down Yonder in New Orleans," and "Riverboat Shuffle." He developed a close association with pianist-songwriter Hoagy Carmichael. Two of Carmichael's standards, "Star Dust" (sometimes spelled "Stardust"), and "Skylark," are said to have been based on Beiderbecke improvisations.

Beiderbecke allowed his classical tendencies to shape his playing style. This was particularly noticeable on piano compositions like "In a Mist," "Flashes," "In the Dark," and "Candlelights." Beiderbecke was heavily influenced by classical composers such as Debussy, Ravel, and Stravinsky, and would take musician friends up to his room, put a red or blue light bulb in a lamp for atmosphere, and play records of these composers. Beiderbecke's cornet playing was warm, precise, and lyrical.

As a composer and pianist Beiderbecke's understated and cool elegance shines. He never learned to read music very well (even his own piano compositions had to be written down for him). Five of his compositions were transcribed by Jean Goldkette's fine arranger, Bill Challis. Today Beiderbecke is remembered primarily for his recorded cornet playing, which was featured in an odd assortment of groups including the Wolverine Orchestra, the Sioux City Six, Beiderbecke's own Rhythm Jugglers, and the orchestras of Frankie Trumbauer, Jean Goldkette, and Paul Whiteman.

Many jazz writers have called Beiderbecke the first "jazz impressionist," and the first white player to strongly influence black players. Legend has it that

Comparing Armstrong and Beiderbecke:

Characteristic	Armstrong	Beiderbecke
Command of instrument	Virtuoso	Solid
Tone quality	Full	Bell-like
	Hot	Warm
	Brassy	Dry
Range	Wide	Moderate
Improvisatory character	Outgoing	Reflective
Rhythmic conception	Swinging	Closer to ragtime
Influences	Chris Kelly	Nick LaRocca
	Buddy Petit	Emmett Hardy
	Joe "King" Oliver	Ragtime
Birthplace	New Orleans	Davenport, Iowa

Source: Mark Gridley, Jazz Styles: History and Analysis, 5th Edition

The Jean Goldkette Orchestra at the University of Pennsylvania in 1927. Goldkette's band, along with Ben Pollack's was able to blend a pop sensibility with classical jazz form. Goldkette had nearly twenty bands working at one time and was the big name in the Midwest. Don Murray, clarinet, is seated left, and Bix Beiderbecke, cornet, is seated fifth from the left. The band broke up in late 1927, but not before a recording oustanding sides as "Idolizing," "Proud of a Baby Like You," "My Pretty Girl," and "Clementine."

Rex Stewart, the trumpet star of the Fletcher Henderson orchestra, recalled in *Jazz Masters of the Thirties* a battle of the bands with the Jean Goldkette unit in 1927: "and we were supposed to be the world's greatest dance orchestra. And up pops this Johnny-come-lately white band from out in the sticks, cutting us...we simply could not compete... Their arrangements were top imaginative and their rhythm too strong... We learned that Jean Goldkette's orchestra was, without any question, the greatest in the world."

Louis Armstrong once lent Beiderbecke his horn so that he could sit in with Armstrong's band, something he had never done for anyone else. Armstrong once said of Beiderbecke, "Ain't none of them play like him yet." Most historians agree that Beiderbecke was the most influential white player of his time. Since both he and Armstrong played cornet during the 1920s it has been natural to compare the two. Armstrong had great command of his instrument and took greater risks; Beiderbecke, on the other hand, appeared at times to be cautious, as if he were "aiming" at his notes.

Mark Gridley in his *Jazz Styles: History and Analysis* states that Beiderbecke had less command of his instrument than Armstrong and that his tone was softer and of less weight, resulting in a less brassy sound than Armstrong's. "He was less dramatic and more subtle. In contrast to Armstrong's assured, outgoing style, Beiderbecke was quieter and considerably more restrained. He played more in the instrument's middle register than does Armstrong, who likes high notes. Beiderbecke also paid more attention to stringing together unusual note choices and acknowledging every passing chord in the progression, something he knew well because he was also a good pianist."

Beiderbecke on Columbia. Beiderbecke made many of his classic recordings with Frankie Trumbauer between February and May 1927. With "Singin' the Blues," Richard Hadlock notes, "A legitimate jazz ballad style was announced — a method whereby attractive songs could be played sweetly without losing authentic jazz feeling and without sacrificing virility."

The Austin High Gang was a group of musicians inspired by the recordings of the New Orleans Rhythm Kings and the live performances of Armstrong and Beiderbecke. They were a loose assortment of white Chicago stylists who played together off and on for years, first in Chicago and then in New York. The original core group, Frank Teschemacher, Jimmy and Dick McPartland, and Bud Freeman, attended Austin High School, where they formed a schoolboy band playing the popular music of the day. Then they heard jazz. They were so enamored with the New Orleans Rhythm Kings playing at the Friar's Inn that they named their first jazz unit the Blue Friars. In time, the circle of players enlarged to include Red Mc-Kenzie, Dave Tough, Mezz Mezzrow, Joe Sullivan, Gene Krupa, and Eddie Condon.

Red McKenzie and Eddie Condon literally became team captains and musical entrepreneurs for what would generally be regarded as the "Windy City," "Chicago," or "Austin High" sound. The sound was basically an adaptation of the New Orleans traditional style with a heavier reliance on arrangements, popular songs of the time, and the emergence of the saxophone as a leading voice. During the late 1920s, McKenzie's groups, sometimes called the Mound City Blue Blowers, often featured the leader playing solos on a paper comb.

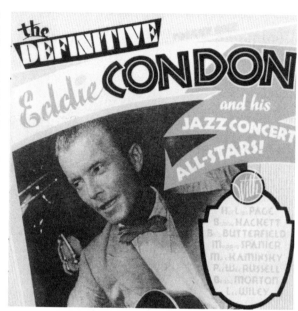

Courtesy Stash Records

Rhythm guitarist Eddie Condon was the leader of the "Chicago Gang" of white players who came to New York in the 1940s. Condon played at his own club, in concerts, and at a Greenwich Village hangout, Nick's. Condon's stalwarts (Bobby Hackett's sweet trumpet, Pee Wee Russell's piquant clarinet, and Bud Freeman's sax styling among many others) mixed Dixie two-beat stomps with, four-four rhythms on pop standards. Although considered strictly Dixie to some, Condon's gangs by the forties were actually closer to what historian Stanley Dance has labeled "mainstream."

Eddie Condon (1905-1973), a banjoist and guitarist, was the most forceful and long-lasting of the Chicago leaders. He was an exuberant lover of jazz and constantly promoted the form, often mixing black and white players in recording sessions as early as 1931. Condon's all-star recordings had a broad scope. For example, as McKenzie and Condon's Chicagoans in 1927, "Sugar" was played by a large ensemble featuring solos by tenorist Bud Freeman, clarinetist Frankie Teschmacher, cornetist Jimmy McPartland, and pianist Joe Sullivan. On the 1933 recording "Stay on the Right Side, Sister," Bing Crosby's vocal is backed by future swing stars Jimmy Dorsey on clarinet, Tommy Dorsey on trombone, and Bunny Berigan on trumpet; "The Eel" (1933) featured a trio of horn men who would often perform together in New York during the 1940s and 1950s as part of the Dixie or Trad revival: Bud Freeman, tenor saxophone, Pee Wee Russell, clarinet, and Max Kaminsky, trumpet.

Outside of the McKenzie-Condon axis was **Red Nichols** (1905-1965), one of the most successful trumpet-bandleaders of the era. His small group recordings, beginning in 1926 as Red and Miff's Stompers, featured Miff Mole on trombone. Mole, one of the first to recognize that the trombone could be more than just a ground bass rhythm instrument, became one of the best trombone soloists. Nichols was a trumpet player in the Beiderbecke mold; he had more hits than any of the other white players. His groups over the years featured many of the great white players of the time, including Glenn Miller, Benny Goodman, Eddie Lang, Joe Venuti, Wingy Manone, and the Boswell Sisters. Because of his great popularity Nichols was consigned to a place of low regard by many jazz historians. But the fact is that Nichols performed with an easy, melodic sound that ranked with the best of his era.

By 1927 the trumpeter usually recorded as Red Nichols and His Five Pennies, and between 1927 and 1932 he had nineteen records that were big sellers (Joel Whitburn defines these as top twenty hits). Nichols's biggest hits included "Ida Sweet as Apple Cider" (1927), "Embraceable You" (1930), and "Peanut Vendor" (1931), which featured trombone great Jack Teagarden. The 1959 film *The Five Pennies*, starring Danny Kaye, was based on Nichols's life.

Not much has been said thus far about the vocalists of white traditional or Dixie jazz. Actually, because of the heavy reliance by white players on the popular songs of the day, vocals were of greater importance in this category of music. The Rhythm Boys (Bing Crosby, Al Rinker, and Barry Harris) made the first impact with a series of hits with the Paul Whiteman Orchestra beginning in 1927. These included "I'm Comin' Virginia," "Changes," "Mississippi Mud," "Out of Town Gal," and "It Happened in Monterey." Mildred Bailey, Jack Teagarden, and Hoagy Carmichael all had hits for Whiteman. Of this trio, Teagarden was primarily an instrumentalist of the highest order, and Bailey was to make her presence felt during the swing era.

Courtesy Jazzology Records

Red Nichols was an in-demand trumpeter who played in many groups (Lanin's Red Heads, Paul Whiteman, Cass Hogan, Don Voorhees, The Hottenots, Louisiana Rhythm Kings, Charleston Chasers, Red and Miff's Stompers, to name just some) before forming His Five Pennies in 1923. In 1932 Nichols began using his famous mourning theme, "Wail of the Winds."

Hoagy Carmichael (1899-1981) is another example of a midwesterner (he was raised in Bloomington, Indiana) embracing urban-oriented jazz music. Best known as a composer, Carmichael is often overooked as a significant figure in the history of jazz. He went to Indiana University, where he played piano at dances to help pay for his education. He then abandoned a law career to play piano in small dives. Carmichael and Bix Beiderbecke, whose cornet mouthpiece Carmichael always carried after Biederbecke died, performed together and for a while were roommates. Carmichael had a marvelous way of reflecting the ambience of small-town America in music he wrote with lyricists such as Mitchell Parrish, Johnny Mercer, and Frank Loesser. Carmichael's tunes were usually not boy-loves-girl songs, but rather allegories about old rocking chairs, lazy rivers, birds in flight, and everyday flowers in bloom.

Courtesy MCA Records

Hoagy Carmichael, composer of one of the greatest standards of all time, "Star Dust." Carmichael wrote in his autobiography, *The Star Dust Road*, "This melody was bigger than I. It didn't seem a part of me. Maybe I hadn't written it at all. It didn't sound familiar even. To lay my claims, I wanted to shout back at it, 'Maybe I didn't write you, but I found you.'"

Courtesy Smithsonian Collection of Recordings

Among his great compositions were were "Star Dust" (according to some reports the most recorded love song of all time) and "Georgia on My Mind".

Hoagy Carmichael's legacy remains that of a songwriter, but he had endearing vocal capabilities, as well. A featured entertainer on radio and film, his tenure as a jazz vocalist was regretably short. Carmichael's singing was always in the spirit of jazz. His easy drawl, and his ability to lag behind the beat were masterfully applied to the rhythm and texture of his compositions. Carmichael's early jazz recordings during the late twenties and early thirties, and his later releases with West Coast jazzmen during the fifties, illustrate his style of singing. Selections such as "Riverboat Shuffle," "New Orleans," "Washboard Blues," "Old Man Harlem," "The Old Music Master," and "Up a Lazy River" have remained in the repertoires of many jazz organizations.

Frank Driggs Collection

The Boswell Sisters: "The greatest of all vocal groups." The Boswell Sisters were raised in New Orleans and before they were singers they had performed with the New Orleans Philharmonic as instrumentalists. In 1931 they signed a record contract with Jack Kapp of Brunswick Records and joined the cast of the "Fleischmann's Yeast Hour" radio show, hosted by Rudy Vallee. Two of their early recordings, "Whadja Do to Me?" (1930) and "Heebie Jeebies" (1931), showcase their mastery of the "blend" and the "beat." The Bozzies, as they were sometimes called, beautifully blended their voices via harmony singing as well through the use of conterpoint and harmonic substitutions. Beat-wise, their rhythm was unparallelled and they sang with a great sense of dynamics. Will Friedwald in *Jazz Singing* laments, "Too bad no group came along to succeed the Boswells as succinctly as the Bozzies took up where the Rhythm Boys left off. Too bad that in the fifty years since then no group has ever replaced them or beat them at what they did best." Too bad also that the late 1980s Broadway revue *Heebie Jeebies* didn't take off. Maybe someday a talented female trio will turn their attentions to the Boswell Sisters. Presently a male trio, the Manhattan Rhythm Kings, does the best job of singing Boswell tunes.

The Boswell Sisters (Martha, 1905-1958; Connie, or Connee, 1907-1976; and Hevetia, or Vet, 1911-1988) played several instruments and Connie wrote the complex vocal arrangements for the group (due to polio she worked in a wheelchair). They played toy instruments and made buzzing, humming, and scatting sounds that were not only playful but ingenious. They recorded with many of the top jazzmen of the thirties and created a harmonized jazz vocal sound that would be diluted and commercialized by the Andrews Sisters in the forties.

"Shout, Sister, Shout," recorded in 1931, was the first of some seventy classic sides cut by this breezy trio that author Will Friedwald in *Jazz Singers* calls "the greatest of all vocal groups." They merrily rambled through readings of "When I Take My Sugar to Tea," "Roll On, Mississippi, Roll On" (both backed by the Dorsey brothers), "I Found a Million Dollar Baby," "Dinah," "Heebie Jeebies," "Rock and Roll" (the first popular song to use the title, in the 1934 film *Transatlantic Merry-Go-Round*), and their only number one hit, "The Object of My Affection," 1935.

Friedwald compares the Boswells to master arranger Gil Evans, who was an integral part of the modern jazz movement (see Chapter 11). Like the Boswells, Evans wrote arrangements that differed so much from the original that they approached recomposition. Friedwald says, "What really makes the Boswells spiritual kin to Gil Evans involves their incorporation of indigenous material into charts of other people's music . . . they add original pieces of music that have absolutely nothing to do with the original composition." With the breakup of the trio in late 1935, Connie, now Connee, became an influential solo act. Ella Fitzgerald always said that Connee Boswell was her chief influence.

Pioneer of the jazz guitar, Eddie Lang (1902-1933). Lang came into prominence with the Mound City Blue Blowers (1924-25) and was a pioneer of the jazz guitar. In addition to his influential duo efforts with Joe Venuti , Lang worked with the Paul Whiteman Orchestra as well as with Bing Crosby when the singer went solo and into movies. Lang recorded guitar duets with bluesman Lonnie Johnson under the pseudonym "Blind Willie Dunn." It was Lang, more than any other jazz player, who was responsible for the guitar replacing the banjo as the rhythm instrument of favor among dance band and "hot" jazz units of the 1920s. He died as a result of complications following a tonsillectomy.

The first jazz violin great: Joe Venuti (1903-1978), whose career stretched from the 1920s to the 1970s, was known as the "Mad Fiddler from Philly." The collaborations between Venuti and guitarist Eddie Lang established the first significant "chamber unit" in jazz history. The duo's "Stringing the Blues" (1926) is one of their most memorable numbers. Venuti's big band 1935-1943, featured his theme "Last Night."

European Connections

Europe's main contribution to early jazz was as the source of a new, enthusiastic audience for the music of many black jazz artists. Louis Armstrong, Sidney Bechet, Bricktop, Alberta Hunter, Josephine Baker and bandleader Sam Wooding were the most celebrated of those who visited during the twenties and early thirties. The first books on jazz were not written by Americans, but by Europeans: Robert Goffin, Charles Delaunay, and Hughes Panassie, whose *Le Jazz Hot* was very influential. There were not many European jazz performers during this early period who could compare with Americans, black or white. The one exception was the team of guitarist **Django Reinhardt** (1910-1953) and violinist **Stephane Grappelli** (1908-).

Courtesy Swing Records and Jazz/Stash Records

Django Reinhardt became one of the greatest influences in jazz guitar history. *Jazz: From its Origins to the Present* states, "His poise, cool tone and inventiveness at fast tempos were suggestive of innovations to come. It is certain that the beboppers were aware of Reinhardt. Reinhardt, and Grappelli for that matter, used double time in a way the boppers echoed, and he used some of the chord substitutions they liked. He experimented with the whole tone scale in pieces such as the strange-sounding, oddly titled 'Diminushing!' Perhaps the boppers even borrowed the idea of '-ology' titles — 'Anthropology,' 'Orinthology,' 'Crazology'— from Reinhardt's 1935 'Djangology,' a straightforward piece until one gets to the four-bar bridge."

Frank Driggs Collection

The Quintette of the Hot Club of France. From left, Stephane Grappelli, violin; Joseph Reinhardt, guitar; Django Reinhardt, guitar; Louis Vola, bass; and Pierre Ferret, guitar.

Reinhardt was a Belgian gypsy whose left hand was partially paralyzed in a caravan fire in 1928, forcing him to develop techniques to work around the impairment. Both Reinhardt and Grappelli were influenced by the duet recordings of guitarist Eddie Lang and violinist Joe Venuti. According to Grappelli, who was French, the first time he heard Eddie Lang with Bix Beiderbecke on piano he was so impressed that he transcribed the solo off the record. The recordings of Lang and Venuti were among the first to establish a chamber music technique in jazz. Later Reinhardt and Grappelli would elaborate on this technique.

In 1933 the two Europeans were in a society orchestra at the Hotel Claridge in Paris on the Champs Elysees. During a break they tried to mimic Lang and Venuti's rendition of "Dinah," and were so taken with the sound that they decided to put together a combo. Author Hughes Panassie was a friend of theirs and Grappelli thought it a good idea to play off of the title of his magazine, *Le Jazz Hot.* So the group, consisting of three guitars, bass, and violin, acquired the name Quintette of the Hot Club of France. Their earliest recordings, in 1934 and 1935, were their own renditions of American jazz releases such as "Tiger Rag," "Dinah," "Lady, Be Good," "Swannee River," and "The Sheik of Araby." Eventually the two leaders coauthored classic compositions such as "Appel Direct," "Daphne," "Souvenirs," "Nocturne," and "Djangology." Reinhardt's "Nuages" was a European favorite during the war years. Reinhardt performed throughout the swing era but his spirit of performance was initiated and formed via the traditional stylists. Violinist Grappelli established one of the longest-lasting careers in jazz history; he was still headlining concerts as late as the mid-1990s.

Django Reinhardt and his guitar style are kept alive by an annual music festival held at Samois-sur-Seine, the French village where Reinhardt spent his last years. The festival hosts contemporary performers like Reinhardt's son, Babik; Garry Potter, Boulou and Elios Ferre, the Gypsy Kids, the Stochelo Rosenberg Trio, Serge Krief, and perhaps the best known of Reinhardt's disciples, Bireili Lagrene. A worthwhile video about Reinhardt is the 1992 Shanachie release, *Gypsy Guitar: The Legacy of Django Reinhardt.*

The Dixieland Revival

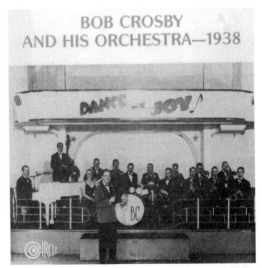

Courtesy Circle Records

© 1968 BMG Music

Bob Crosby's band of 1935 was the first of the swing-era units that played Dixieland on a regular basis. He was in the vanguard of the Dixieland revival with his eight-man small group, the Bobcats. His was also one of the most successful bands recreating boogie woogie during the late 1930s and early 1940s ("Little Rock Getaway," "Honky Tonk Train," and "Boogie Woogie Maxine").

Muggsy Spanier (1906-1967), a cornetist, was a big part of the dixieland revival of the 1940s. He was a member of the Ted Lewis band from 1929 to 1936, and then joined the Ben Pollack band from 1936 to 1938. Spanier was a successful leader of the Ragtimers, a small Dixieland group that played at Chicago's Sherman Hotel and then at Nick's in New York in 1938-39. The sixteen 78 sides from the reissued album above were considered among the best examples of neo-Dixieland. This album is still considered a classic.

The revival of traditional jazz, sometimes termed "the Dixieland revival," began during the late 1930s and expanded through the 1940s and 1950s. There were two key factors that led to a renewed appreciation of the original jazz: John Hammond's two Carnegie Hall concerts, *From Spirituals to Swing* in 1938 and 1939, which featured a number of "old time players" of traditional jazz, and the publication of the book *Jazzmen* in 1939 by Fredrick Ramsey, Jr., and Charles Edward Smith.

A number of other factors led to a re-appreciation of "the real thing." Record companies were reissuing earlier recordings that had been out of circulation for years. Once forgotten greats like Jelly Roll Morton and Sidney Bechet forged "comebacks." In 1938 Morton made a series of new releases for the Library of Congress. Interviewed by Alan Lomax, Morton presented colorful opinions and observations of early jazz history; he also demonstrated various musical styles and played some of his own compositions. By 1939 Morton returned to the commercial recording studio, with releases for Bluebird. Sidney Bechet's 1939 recordings for the fledging Blue Note label included a surprise hit, "Summertime." Milt Gabler's Commodore Records issued traditionalist recordings that helped create an interest by club owners in booking traditional artists into their clubs.

Just before the celebrated revival of traditional jazz, **Bob Crosby**'s big band had created excitement by playing in the style of the old Red Nichols and Miff Mole groups. Crosby (1913-1993), the brother of Bing, was an amiable singer-leader of a group he called the Bobcats, whose sidemen included many of the best Dixieland players of the time: trumpeters Yank Lawson, Muggsy Spanier, and Billy Butterfield, highly regarded clarinetist Irving Fazola, pianists Jess Stacy, Joe Sullivan, and Bob Zurke, bassist Bob Haggard, and drummer Ray Bauduc. The Bobcats had Dixie-oriented hits such as "South Rampart Street Parade," "Fidgety Feet," and the Bauduc-Haggart duo classic "Big Noise From Winnetka." The World's Greatest Jazz Band, formed in 1968, was a successful continuation of Crosby's musical style.

DOWN BEAT

VOL. 16—NO. 14 (Copyright, 1949, Down Beat, Inc.) CHICAGO, JULY 29, 1949

Old Name, New Band, Ensconced In Nick's

New York—New band at Nick's in the Village here is Phil Napoleon's revived Memphis five, with Phil Olivella, clarinet; Frank Signorelli, piano; Napoleon, trumpet; Andy Russo, trombone; Tony Spargo, drums, and Jack Fay, bass. Only Napoleon and Signorelli were with the Original Memphis five. Jimmy Lytell, clarinet; Jack Roth, drums, and Miff Mole or Vincent Grande, trombone, made up the old unit. Since this shot was taken, Signorelli was replaced by Joe Rann.

Courtesy Down Beat

Eddie Condon's revivalist troupe (which included the exuberant, fiery playing of Wild Bill Davison on trumpet and Tony Parenti on clarinet) kept the Dixie flame burning by playing at Nick's in Greenwich Village and by a series of jazz concerts, beginning in 1942, at the Town Hall. In 1945 he opened his own club, Condon's, in Greenwich Village. Condon pointed out in *Eddie Condon's Scrapbook of Jazz* that, "The Saloon on West Third was the first place in the world with a jazz musician's name above the door. Paul Smith designed the sign [a cubistic guitar enshrined below an "Eddie Condon" signature] and it became a symbol associated with me ever since." In 1958, Condon moved his club to the upper east side. Condon's family of players were some of the staunchest followers of Dixieland music. Condon's 1948 autobiography, *We Called It Music,* contains highly entertaining insights from this champion of traditional and mainstream jazz.

JIM ROBINSON, BUNK, BABY DODDS, LAWRENCE MARRERO, GEORGE LEWIS, ALCIDE PAVAGEAU

Courtesy American Music Records

New York—Bunk Johnson's already famous New Orleans band, with (left to right) Jim Robinson, trombone; Alcide Pavageau, bass; Bunk, trumpet; Baby Dodds, drums; George Lewis, clarinet; and pianist Alton Purnell and banjoist Lawrence Marerro not shown, have taken over the Stuyvesant Casino on Second avenue nightly except Mondays. Reception to the band has been terrific, if limited mainly to adherents of N. O. style jazz. But the outfit has nabbed more space in national magazines (*Time, New Yorker* and *The Nation* included) than any other modern band has for ages.

Courtesy Down Beat

On September 28, 1945, the authors of *Jazzmen,* with the help of jazz enthusiast William Russell, brought up an old New Orleans trumpet player, **Bunk Johnson** (1889-1949), who had been working in a rice field outside New Iberia, Louisiana, to play with a band at New York's Stuyvesant Casino. The elderly Johnson became the "cause celebre" of the traditionalists' purist beliefs. According to Samuel B. Charters and Leonard Kunstadt in their *Jazz: A History of the New York Scene,* the traditionalists firmly believed that Johnson's band "was the last pure band, the only one playing true jazz, and that newer styles were somehow a corruption of this older style. The result was a critical battle of increasing virulence that has still not completely died." Johnson and his talented clarinetist, George Lewis (who had played clarinet in the Eureka Brass Band in the 1920s and the Olympia Band in the 1930s), did the most to reawaken the interest in the older jazz form.

Not everything in the Dixieland revival was happening in New York. For instance, in the San Francisco Bay area at the Big Bear Tavern, around 1936 trumpeter Lu Watters and trombonist Turk Murphy led a rehearsal group that emulated ragtime and the early jazz classics of Jelly Roll Morton and King Oliver. By 1941 Watters formed the Yerba Buena Jazz Band at the Dawn Club. The group played stomps, blues, rags, and ensemble jazz interpretations based on the classic King Oliver standards. Pianist Wally Rose, whose "Black and White Rag" was the biggest "hit" of this grouping on the coast, said, "We really pioneered the revival of ragtime, because at that time it was the height of the swing era and everything like ragtime was going backward in time." By 1947 the group moved over to Hambone Kelly's in El Cerrito and stirred a lot of attention by reorganizing to form a two-trumpet front line reminiscent of the King Oliver-Louis Armstrong unit of the early 1920s, with Bob Scobey on second trumpet and Turk Murphy on growling trombone, which he styled after Kid Ory. Murphy and Scobey left to form groups of their own in 1949 and 1950.

The "Whorehouse Five" At Hambone Kelly's 1949
Lu Watters – trumpet; Clancy Hayes – banjo (guest);
Bill Dart – drums; Bob Helm – clarinet;
Dick Lammi – sousaphone; Wally Rose – piano.

Jazz Traditionalists and Revivalists Today

 After the revival clamor died down by the 1960s, except for the Louis Armstrong All Star units and the popularity of clarinetist Pete Fountain and trumpeter Al Hirt, traditional music did not have much of an impact on the modern musical scene. However, there have been wonderful groups during the 1980s and 1990s that have played repertory concerts and made tribute recordings of the older musical traditions. These projects have served as educational and entertaining reminders of the fun and excitement that the older forms brought to their audiences.

Listeners to most jazz radio programming of the past thirty-five years, not counting non-prime time "specialist" hours here and there, would get the idea that not much happened to jazz before the advent of John Coltrane and Miles Davis and their innovations in 1950s and 1960s. The emphasis on the post-Coltrane and Davis music ignores the large number of performers who have chosen to work in the "classic jazz" styles of traditional and swing. This section will take a look at those key performers who are the "traditionalists and revivalists in jazz." Admittedly, there is an overlap with swing-oriented mainstream revivalists. For example, two of the key artists, Bob Wilber and Dick Hyman, have both reworked music of traditionalists like Sidney Bechet and Jelly Roll Morton as well as the later swing stylists such as Benny Goodman and his followers. Wilber, because of his roots, is more closely tied to trad. Hyman, on the other hand, is more closely linked with the mainstream revival and he will be covered in chapter 9.

Courtesy Jazzology Records

A youthful Bob Wilber, left, leader of an enthusiastic group of Scarsdale, New York, highschoolers known as the Wildcats (which included pianist Dick Wellstood), seen in the early 1950s with his mentor, the legendary Sidney Bechet, right.

Courtesy Jazzology Records

Bob Wilber has been in the forefront of the trad revival movement of the past forty years. This release features King Oiver classics performed in the older "New Orleans" style.

Bob Wilber (1928-) is one of the most committed revivalists of traditional jazz on today's music scene although he has included reworkings of swing music. Wilber is nothing if not diverse. He has collaborated on projects with the Widespread Depression Orchestra; he recreated Benny Goodman material and formed the Cotton Club Band, which played music for the film *The Cotton Club*; he recorded popular standards on albums of key composers of Tin Pan Alley, such as Gershwin, Porter, and Rodgers and Hart; in the 1950s he worked in modernist Lennie Tristano's group; and he has interpreted numerous modern jazz numbers of Dizzy Gillespie and Charlie Parker.

However, it is Wilber's indefatigable championing of the traditional repertoire that has made his name. As a young musician during the late 1940s, Wilber established a revivalist group whose members were mostly from Scarsdale, New York, an affluent Westchester County village about forty minutes from Broadway. The group, which included pianist Dick Wellstood, played traditionalist music at a time when most young players were following the modern jazz of Charlie Parker and Dizzy Gillespie. Wilber studied and also recorded with Sidney Bechet. Over the years Wilber became Bechet's best known interpreter.

During the 1960s and 1970s Wilber was part of Dick Gibson's jazz parties in Denver and Gibson's traditionalist collective, known as the World's Greatest Jazz Band. Wilber has reproduced on record and in concert the music of Hoagy Carmichael, Jimmy Noone (the great trad clarinetist), King Oliver, Jelly Roll Morton, and of course, Sidney Bechet. In 1981 he formed Bechet Legacy and also created with fellow reedman Kenny Davern a group called Soprano Summit. Wilber has been commited to the traditional repertoire longer than anyone else on the scene today.

Courtesy of Concord Jazz, Inc.

Courtesy Jazzology Records

Bob Wilber and the trad repertoire.

Mention should also be made of some of the key performers noted in Chip Deffaa's *Traditionalists and Revivalists in Jazz*. Bass saxist, tubaist, bassist, and bandleader Vince Giordano, a tireless interpreter of older orchestral charts, pianist Terry Waldo, who focuses on authentic ragtime, and Eddy Davis, who works with a variety of 1920s-based trad groups, are three individuals who at various times played together and now work independently. Deffaa interviewed a number of other players, and his book is worthwhile for anyone interested in this largely ignored area of early dance band music of the 1920s and traditional or Dixieland music.

Vince Giordano (1960-   ) is of particular interest. A collector of stock and special arrangements played by orchestras during the 1920s and 1930s, Giordano leads tuxedo-clad musicians on a trip to the past that is today finding favor with sophisticated celebrants who want to dance. His Nighthawks have played dinners and dances for some of the most influential society types in New York: black-tie galas at the Metropolitan Museum of Art, the Friends of the Library, the New York City Ballet and the Cafe Carlyle. The band takes its name from the 1920s dance band of Kansas City, the Coon-Sanders Nighthawks. Giordano plays an assortment of instruments, including string bass, bass sax, tuba, and piano. While he is a talented performer, it is his penchant for the dance sounds of the California Ramblers, Jean Goldkette, Isham Jones, Duke Ellington, and the rest of the old-time groups that has made his units particularly distinctive.

Courtesy Circle Records

Vince Giordano and the Nighthawks. Revivalist tribute by the Goldkette Project, as played by Vince Giordano and the Nighthawks (1988). Classics such as "Ostrich Walk," "Clarinet Marmalade," "Riverboat Shuffle," "I've Found a New Baby," and "On the Alamo" are a few of the classic arrangements that Bill Challis wrote for Jean Goldkette in the 1920s. Contemporary all-stars such as Dick Wellstood, Bob, Wilber, and Tom Pletcher are featured.

Giordano's adherence to the older sounds led him to interview as many sidemen and leaders as he could find. He is especially fond of his association with Jean Goldkette's star arranger, Bill Challis. Challis said of Giordano, "Vincent was my star pupil." As archivist, curator, and educator Giordano has become the premier revival orchestrater in the world. Chip Deffaa in *Traditionalists and Revivalists* outlines a small sampling of Giordano's musical pallet: "Night after night, Girodano's men offer the likes of 'Clementine' and 'Pretty Girl,' just the way Jean Goldkette played those numbers, 'Ida,' exactly as Red Nichols and the Five Pennies handled it on their million-selling record of 1927, and 'The Creeper,' as done by the young Duke Ellington. They revel in King Oliver's 'Snag It,' the California Ramblers' 'Zulu Wail,' Ben Pollack's 'Waitin' for Katie,' and Bennie Moten's 'Small Black.' And when Giordano introduces even the most obscure of the pop tunes, he does so with a real respect and affection for the material."

Another important revivalist profiled by Deffaa is **Vernel Bagneris** (1949-   ). Bagneris (pronounced BAH-ne-reese) wasn't the first to investigate the colorful life of Jelly Roll Morton, whose story fascinates even observers who aren't interested in jazz music. Alan Lomax wrote *Mr. Jelly Roll* in 1950, and Laurie Wright improved on the facts in 1980 with *Mr. Jelly Lord*. In the early 1970s pianist Bob Greene used to tour the country telling engaging stories and playing music in a program entitled *Bob Greene's The World of Jelly Roll Morton*. Dick Hyman recreated Morton classics via transcriptions with his 1974 RCA release, *Ferdinand "Jelly Roll" Morton Transcriptions for Orchestra*. More recently Broadway portrayed the colorful musician in 1992's *Jelly's Last Jam,* which starred Gregory Hines. As written and directed by George C. Wolfe, the story of *Jelly's Last Jam* dealt with some of the psychological and social conflicts within the Morton psyche.

Before *Jelly's Last Jam*, however, there was writer-director-actor Vernel Bagneris's vision of the complex artist entitled *Jelly Roll Morton: A Me-Morial.* Bagneris had previous success with a small-scale show about the female classic blues world, *One Mo' Time.* That show opened at a jazz night club, the Village Gate, in 1979, and was followed nearly ten years later by *Further Mo!* Bagneris likes to work on a small scale because he can keep control of his projects. "That's why I've never directed a Broadway musical yet or tried to step out in any large way. I find it more peaceful for me in my life to have controllable elements."

In *Jelly Roll Morton: A Me-Morial*, Bagneris played the part of the great jazzman in a two-man show, ably assisted by pianist Terry Waldo. Deffaa summarizes, "Bagneris was true to the spirit of Morton both as a man and as a musician. Moving about eccentrically but with a sly sense of style as he sang 'Jelly Roll Blues,' Bagneris projected an irresistable self-confidence. Moments later, explaining how he believed his bad luck was due to someone's having put a voodoo spell on him, he captured the pathos that was no less a part of Morton's makeup." The show was performed at Michael's Pub, a jazz and cabaret club in New York in the fall of 1992. It was originally presented in 1991 at the Oslo, Norway, Jazz Festival, with Morten Gunnar Larsen at the piano.

In March 1994, Bagneris returned to Michael's, where he presented another two-man revue based on Morton's life. This time the show was titled *Jelly Roll Morton: Hoo-Dude,* and featured the Larsen arrangements and piano accompaniment. In August 1994, the duo more or less combined the two shows into *Jelly Roll! The Music and the Man*, which opened at the 47th Street Theatre (the show moved to Kaufman Theater during the winter of 1995). Vincent Canby raved in the *New York Times*, "It's one of the most revivifying entertainments to be found on Broadway or off."

Traditionalists and revivalists like Giordano and Bagneris are constantly creating their visions of the past with clever, heart-felt performances that attempt to convey the excitement and creativity of yesterday's music. Who knows where it will lead? It's not likely that these underground archivists will ever reach the pop marketplace; but we are richer because of their passion and devotion to the past. Giordano's continued searching for old music charts has led him to recently put together, of all things,

Courtesy Michael's Pub

Michael's Pub: Home of repertoire revivals. Gil Wiest has been the driving force behind New York's Michael's Pub, which gained preeminence as the top home of repertoire revivals. Over the years he has provided a stage for numerous musical tributes and revues of masters of the past (songwriters, instrumentalists, singers, and the like). Every Monday night since 1974 the club plays host to celebrity-clarinetist Woody Allen and the New Orleans Funeral and Ragtime Orchestra. In 1993, Allen participated in *The Bunk Project*, led by revivalist Eddy Davis, which reworked many of Bunk Johnson's classic selections.

a project based on the music of Leroy Shield, who wrote the music for Hal Roach comedy shorts like the "Young Rascals" and Laurel and Hardy. And Bagneris, who performed the title song to the underrated musical *Pennies From Heaven* (1981), is projected to direct and star in a Broadway musical comedy version of the old "Amos & Andy" radio show, to be called *Fresh Air Taxi*.

Another important curator in the dissemination of traditional music is record company owner George H. Buck, noted already in the chapter on the blues as being a unique record company owner who serves as a historian and preservationist. To recap, he bought the rights to the Circle and Solo Art masters in the mid-1960s and owns the rights to Paramount and Black Swan releases from the 1920s. Along with all of this are his Jazzology, American Music, Progressive, GHB, and Audiophile labels, as well as a regular magazine, *Jazzology Newsletter*, which includes articles and tributes focusing on traditional music, blues and cabaret. In 1994 Buck's Audiophile Records released a tribute to Hoagy Carmichael by pianist singer Bob Dorough, vocalist Barbara Lea, and historian-cornet player Dick Sudhalter. The trio had a press release-cabaret performance in April 1994 at the Ballroom in New York. In September 1994 Dorough brought his Carmichael tribute to Michael's Pub. Of all of the songwriters who sang, Carmichael had the longest and most fertile association with jazz and some of the greatest players of the music accompanying him. He recorded with many other jazz greats of the traditional style, and in 1956 Carmichael recorded with bop-inspired players on *Hoagy Carmichael With the Pacific Jazzmen*.

Carmichael's music is well known today because of the many cover versions of his hits such as Willie Nelson and Aaron Neville singing "Stardust" and Ray Charles and Michael Bolton vocalizing "Georgia on My Mind." Perhaps Carmichael's biggest influence on today's music scene is the enormous sway he has had over some of the singer-songwriter-pianists plying their wares in the jazz nightclubs. Mose Allison, Georgie Fame, Bob Dorough, Dave Frishberg, Ben Sidran, and even rocker (but jazz inspired) Randy Newman all incorporate elements of Carmichael's style. The master, wrote Sidran in his tribute song, "Old Hoagy," was "Sittin' in a corner, a cigarette hanging out of his mouth/There's old Hoagy, singing 'bout our life."

Chapter 6

THE HARLEM RENAISSANCE

Photographs and Prints Division, Schomburg Center for Research in Black Culture, The New York Public Library, Astor, Lenox and Tilden Foundation

A major change occurred in the living patterns of American blacks around the time of World War I. Although there had been small black communities growing in urban centers, it wasn't until the flowering of Harlem, in New York City, the area above 110th Street, that a major movement and identity would be shaped. One Hundred and Tenth Street was regarded as the "Mason-Dixon Line" of Harlem; that is, the streets above 110th Street were referred to as Harlem. During the late 1800s, Harlem had been a white suburb of Manhattan. There were great expectations among whites for Harlem and its beautiful brownstone buildings, because between 1878 and 1881 the railroad lines were elevated and extended to 129th Street. This made it possible for Manhattanites to have easy access to Harlem's outer reaches, and thousands of whites began flocking to the area. This resulted in real estate speculation, but the market bottomed out in 1904 and 1905, and white property owners either fled or rented to incoming blacks. By the twenties, Harlem had become a thriving black middle class neighborhood.

One result was the Harlem Renaissance, the post-World War I growth of black intellectual and artistic achievement. There had never been such a pool of black writers creating prose and poetry for newspaper and literary magazines including the *Messenger*, the *Challenge*, the *Voice*, the *Crusader*, the *Negro World*, and the *Emancipator*. During this time, the National Association for the Advancement of Colored People, the New York Urban League, and the magazines *Opportunity* and *Crisis* provided cash prizes for outstanding literature. Winners of the magazine prizes included Arna Bentemps, Cecil Blue, Waring Cuney, Frank Horne, and Lucy Ariel Williams, among others.

Writers with a black perspective on the minority experience in America were being heard loud and clear. The esteemed author Langston Hughes said of his arrival in Harlem for the first time that when he emerged from the subway at 135th Street and Lenox Avenue, he was so excited at the sight of so many fellow black people that he wanted to shake everyone's hand.

Connie's Inn, located on the corner of 131st Street and Seventh Avenue, opened in 1921 as the Shuffle Inn to play off of the hit musical *Shuffle Along*. Harlem's famous Tree of Hope stood in front of the building, which was ideally located on a busy corner. The owners, George and Connie Immerman, were in the delicatessen business before they started their nightclub, which they soon renamed Connie's Inn. The club, like its competitors, featured elaborate floor shows. The club's peak came when Louis Armstrong appeared in the 1929 production of *Hot Chocolates,* written by Andy Rasaf and Fats Waller, and featuring such hits as "Ain't Misbehavin'," "Black and Blue," and "Can't We Get Together."

Ed Small's club, Small's Paradise opened in 1925. It became, along with Connie's Inn and the Cotton Club, known as one of the most powerful and influential nightclubs in Harlem during the Depression. Located at 2294 Seventh Avenue at West 135th Street. Small's club was a cellar dance spot that could accommodate over 1,000 people. Small's Paradise was referred to as a Black and Tan club because of the mixing of black and white folks (unlike the Cotton Club which was strictly black entertainment for white patrons). The club featured waiters who danced the "Charleston" while twirling full trays of bootleg booze, and the waiters also sang. Pianist Charlie Johnson led the house band for ten years, beginning in 1925.

Museum of the City of New York (top)

Photographs and Prints Division, Schomburg Center for Research in Black Culture, The New York Public Library, Astor, Lenox and Tilden Foundation (bottom)

Some Harlem Renaissance Writers

Author	Book Title	Year
W. E. B. DuBois	Dark Water	1920
Benjamin Brawley	A Social History of the American Negro	1921
Georgia Douglass Johnson	Bronze	1922
James Weldon Johnson	Book of American Poetry	1922
Claude McKay	Harlem Shadows	1922
Jean Toomer	Cane	1923
Jessie Fauset	The Gift of Black Folk	1924
Walter White	The Fire in Flint	1924
Countee Cullen	Color	1925
Alain Locke	The New Negro: An Interpretation	1925
Langston Hughes	The Weary Blues	1926
Carl Van Vechten	Nigger Heaven	1926
Eric Waldron	Tropic Death	1926
Walter White	Flight	1926
Rudolph Fisher	Walls of Jericho	1928
Nella Larson	Quicksand	1928
Claude McKay	Home to Harlem	1928
Jessie Fauset	Plum Bun	1929
Countee Cullen	The Black Christ	1929
Taylor Gordon	Born to Be	1929
Georgia Douglass Johnson	An Autumn Love Cycle	1929
Claude McKay	Banjo	1929
Wallace Thurman	A Judge Lynch	1929
James Weldon Johnson	Black Manhattan	1930
Zora Neale Hurston	Mules and Men	1935

The main leaders of the Harlem Renaissance were Jessie Redmond Fauset, Charles S. Johnson, Casper Holstein, Alain Locke, Walter White, and James Weldon Johnson. Known as "The Six," they attempted to become arbiters of taste and culture by celebrating the black cultural heritage and furthering black artistic creation. The Harlem Renaissance leaders aspired to create, in the words and title of Alain Locke's 1925 book, *The New Negro*, black people who were the equal of the white man. There would be no more bowing or crawling in subservience.

However, the movement's greatest expression and its biggest boost came from its musical and theatrical output.

The leaders of the Harlem Renaissance shunned "musical dens of iniquity." They reasoned that jazz-oriented music in the cabarets was viewed by whites as a form of "primitive indulgence," as indicated by the whites who were eagerly "slumming" up to Harlem. As a result, the early years of the Harlem Renaissance were marked by conflicts between the black intelligensia and black entertainers. The jazzmen and show business types referred to the high brows as the "dicty" set—Fletcher Henderson's "Dicty's Blues" in 1923 and Duke Ellington's "Dicty Glide" in 1929 were arrows pointed at what musicians viewed as snobbery on the part of the Six and their followers.

In time the "upper class" intellectuals and the "lower class" entertainers managed to patch up their differences and intermingle in the cabarets. James Weldon Johnson wrote of the importance of the music world and of the cultured comportment of artists like Henderson and Ellington, which eased the hostility between the two groups. The Harlem Renaissance notwithstanding, a number of black artists during this period sought asylum from racial prejudice by moving to Europe. France became a particularly safe haven for black entertainers, as Will Marion Cook and James Reese Europe had discovered during the war years. Ada "Bricktop" Smith, who was the first black woman of note to open her own cabaret (in 1924) and Josephine Baker, who in 1925 made her celebrated debut in sensational fashion at the Champs Elysees bedecked in feathers and little else, whetted the appetites of the French for African-American musical and cultural talents. Sam Wooding went to Europe during this time and became the most famous jazz bandleader outside America. His account of the international jazz connection has added greatly to its heretofore uncharted history.

During this time musicians in New Orleans and Chicago etched out styles of jazz that were influential and that impacted on New York. While New York had Tin Pan and Shubert Alleys plugging popular music, the city hadn't really developed a consistent mode of jazz. In fact, in 1921, the president of the highly regarded Clef Club, a black musical organization, warned its members of the dangers of not following written arrangements more closely. Jazz music, especially to the aspiring African-American middle class, was viewed as disreputable.

Rosalie and Theodore Cron Collection, Carnegie Hall Archives

Father of Stride Piano. The stride pianists were always trying to improve their technique. James P. Johnson told interviewer Tom Davin, "In practicing technique, I would play in the dark to get familiar with the keyboard. To develop clear touch and the feel of the piano, I'd put a bedsheet over the keyboard and play difficult pieces through it. I had gotten power and was building a serious orchestral piano. I did rag variations of *William Tell Overture*, Greig's *Peer Gynt Suite*, and even a Russian rag based on Rachmaninoff's *Prelude in C# Minor*, which was just getting popular then."

Harlem Stride Piano

Certain East Coast players began to transform ragtime piano into something looser, faster, more improvised into "stride" piano. Stride has its roots in ragtime but features a percussive accent on the bass afterbeat by the left hand, while the right hand embroiders melodically on the treble portion of the piano. Acccording to Mark Gridley in *Jazz Styles*, "Stride piano playing uses percussive, striding, left-hand figures in which low bass notes alternate with mid-range chords, while the right hand plays melodies and embellishments in a very energetic fashion." The stride players were literally one-man bands; they often didn't use bass players or drummers. Instead they created all of the rhythm and time-keeping functions themselves. Many of them began as ragtime performers or had had a great deal of classical music training.

The stride pianists not only played in the nightclubs, but also led society bands, performed in theatrical pit bands, accompanied silent films, and made piano rolls. They also played at New York rent-house parties (gatherings in tenement dwellings that collected money for rent), where they played for food and drink long into the early hours of the morning.

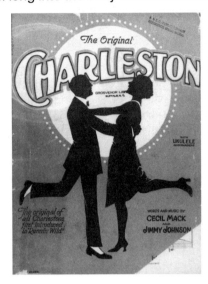

The "Charleston" first appeared in the black musical *Runnin' Wild*, which opened on October 29, 1923, at the Colonial Theatre. The show's star, Elisabeth Welch, introduced the dance which, in Gerald Bordman's observation, "ultimately expressed and symbolized the whole gaudy era about to explode. It pronounced the best for the 'lost generation' and liberated the whole jazz movement."

In 1916, James P. Johnson became the first black composer to make piano rolls for the Aeolian Company. Later he cut piano rolls for the QRS Company and was instrumental in getting his protege, Fats Waller, a contract with QRS.

James P. Johnson (1894-1955) was called the "Father of Stride Piano." He has been referred to as the East Coast equivalent to Jelly Roll Morton. Johnson incorporated elements of ragtime as well as the cakewalks and ring shouts of the Deep South in his new style.

Johnson was greatly influenced by Luckey Roberts, who created difficult pianistic tricks such as unusual chord voicings (harmonies) and extremely rapid tempos, techniques that had allowed him to win many piano "cutting contests." The ticklers, as piano players were called at that time, had to develop certain gambits to distinguish their playing styles from that of their peers. Johnson was considered to be the foremost of these players because he elaborated on Roberts's techniques. He brought a harmonic sophistication to the piano that was the result of classical music training and a close study of Roberts's style.

Duke Ellington noted that musicians would stop player pianos in order to copy James P. Johnson's classic "Carolina Shout" note for note. Johnson used unusual practice techniques to expand his dexterity. He would include passages from Beethoven and Liszt in his stomps and ballads that would startle fellow pianists and please listeners. His stride showpieces, in addition to "Carolina Shout," included "Keep Off the Grass" and "Mule Walk." In addition to playing solo, Johnson was a fine accompanist backing Bessie Smith and Ethel Waters. He also wrote and played for theatrical productions such as *Plantation Days*, 1922, *Runnin' Wild*, 1923, and *Keep Shufflin'*, 1928. He even wrote a number of popular songs, such as "Old Fashioned Love," "Charleston," "If I Could Be With You (One Hour Tonight)," introduced by Ruth Etting, and "Way Down Yonder in New Orleans." Like most northeastern pianists, Johnson was deeply in touch with European concert music. He wrote *Yamekraw: A Negro Rhapsody* for orchestra, chorus, jazz band, and solo piano (performed in Carnegie Hall in 1928), as well as "Symphony Harlem" in 1932 and a short opera with poet Langston Hughes, *De Organiser*.

Certainly one of the most colorful and beguiling of the stride greats was **Willie "The Lion" Smith** (1897-1973). One of the most subtle of the stride players despite his humorous persona, Smith was the pianist and leader of Mamie Smith's 1920 classic blues recording, "Crazy Blues," and played piano in numerous New York clubs throughout his long career. During the Harlem Renaissance, Smith held long residencies at Harlem clubs such as Leroy's, Small's Paradise, Barron's Exclusive Club, and Pod's and Jerry's. Smith's best known compositions include "Echoes of Spring," inspired by the music of Schubert, "Morning Air," "Rippling Waters," and "Portrait of the Duke." Ellington revered Smith and would often follow him, in his younger years, when the master played at the Capitol Club on 140th Street and Lenox Avenue. Duke paid tribute to Smith with a composition entitled "Portrait of the Lion." *The New Grove Dictionary of Jazz* states, "as an entertainer, Smith's flamboyant behavior and dashing appearance with derby hat and fat cigar, became almost legendary. As a pianist and composer, his blending of ragtime, impressionism, and counterpoint, coupled with an ability to contrast delicate and subtle melodic lines with passages of intense swing, constituted a unique contribution to the jazz tradition."

Picture Collection, The Branch Libraries, The New York Public Library

Of all of the black jazz performers of the first half of the twentieth century, Fats Waller had the most hit recordings. Waller performed some of the most humorous songs of his era: "Your Feet's Too Big," "Your Socks Don't Match," "The Joint Is Jumpin'" and "Hold Tight (I Want Some Sea Food Mama)," to list just a few. Waller filmed four musical shorts in 1940: "Your Feet's Too Big," "The Joint Is Jumpin'," "Honeysuckle Rose", and "Ain't Misbehavin'." They can be found on a number of video releases today.

Fats Waller (1904-1943) was one of the best piano players in jazz history. He began playing the instrument at an early age. As a teenager, Waller won a talent contest by playing "Carolina Shout." Waller was a protege of James P. Johnson and received lessons from him. He developed a reputation playing in the Harlem cabarets and at rent parties, then worked as an organist at one of Harlem's best venues, the Lincoln Theatre. Waller's piano style was basically ragtime jazz played with a light, precise bounce that can be heard on his best-known instrumental piece, "Handful of Keys." Jazz pianists of the era played with an excellent swinging feel. Waller's composition of "Jitterbug Waltz" is an excellent example of his light, bouncy style.

Waller was a happy-go-lucky person who paid little attention to mundane matters like balancing a check-book. He often sold songs for immediate payment, losing all future royalties. Waller was better known to audiences for his comic antics at the piano than as an artist. His music has been labeled "Happy Jazz," and there is no doubt that he was the crown prince of jazz humor. Waller recorded novelty songs and sappy love songs often punctuated by humorous, muttered asides such as, "I wonder what the poor people are doing tonight," or "One never knows, do one," or "No, Lady, we can't haul your ashes out for twenty-five cents. That'd be bad business."

Frank Driggs Collection

Willie "The Lion" Smith.

Waller's most celebrated compositions were collaborations with poet-lyricist Andy Razaf (born Andrea Menentania Razafinkeriefo). Together they wrote such endearing classics as "Honeysuckle Rose," "Ain't Misbehavin'," "Black and Blue," and "Keepin' Out of Mischief Now." These songs, and others, were written for theatrical productions on the black stage such as *Land of Coal*, and *Hot Chocolates* (both 1929). The connection between black dance and black theater and jazz was significant during the 1920s and 1930s. Many revisionist historians have ranted over the "Uncle Tom" elements of jazz entertainers such as Armstrong or Waller, as if their parading and mugging was an embarrassment. The question might be asked, an embarrassment for whom? No doubt there are those who prefer their jazz in the context of a serious performance. However, these two masters of "Happy Jazz" were giving audiences humor with a high level of technical accomplishment. Waller was popular with jazz as well as popular audiences, as his sixty-three top twenty hits attest. In relation to the pop mainstream, Waller, like Armstrong, was a second tier underground artist.

© 1987 BMG Music (top)

Courtesy Biograph Records (bottom)

Fats Waller began his amazing recording career as a leader in 1926 with "St. Louis Blues" and his own composition, "Lenox Avenue Blues." His long association with RCA Victor resulted in many classic hits that have been repackaged on CDs for today's audience. This Biograph release features eleven of the nineteen piano rolls that Waller cut for QRS between 1923 and 1927. Waller was paid $100 for each piano roll, his first being "Got to Cool My Doggies Now."

© 1978 BMG Music

Ain't Misbehavin', a lively celebration associated with Fats Waller's music, was one of the most bouyantly successful modern black revues in Broadway history. The show opened in 1978 at the tiny Manhattan Theatre Club, but its startling success resulted in a move to Broadway's Longacre Theatre. *Ain't Misbehavin'* won three Tony awards in 1978, one of them for best musical.

Big Band Jazz

Bands played for a variety of functions including theatrical productions and dances in New York during the twenties. Band leaders were expected to feature popular music of the day. The New Orleans styles that were making the rounds at this time featured groups playing wild, cacophonous sounds that featured collective improvisation. This music was too wild and uncivilized for high society ballrooms. Nevertheless the freedom and excitement of the New Orleans tradition slowly found its way into New

York in the form of bands led by Duke El-lington, Fletcher Henderson, Horace Henderson (Fletcher's brother), Luis Russell, Claude Hopkins, Don Redman, and others.

These band leaders did not begin as jazz performers. They came from upper-middle class black families. The music they were reared on was classical music, not blues or jazz. As been noted on a number of occasions Upper and Middle class black families look down on blues and jazz. These college-trained, future band leaders helped elevate the stature of jazz music during the Harlem Renaissance. All of them except El-lington had university degrees, and Duke could have gone to college on a scholarship to the Pratt Institute of Art if he had wanted. When they were leading bands early in their careers, they played polite, popular music for a refined audience.

Courtesy the Smithsonian Collection

The Fletcher Henderson-led big bands stressed improvised jazz of the pre-swing era. Henderson helped the early bands gravitate toward the steady four-four rhythm and created a model for many of the swing bands. Henderson's band had a ten year stay at the Roseland Ballroom—the band replaced the Creole orchestra of Armand J. Piron, which was essentially a society dance band. After all, Henderson was now playing in a mid-Manhattan white dance hall opposite Sam Lanin's Orhcestra. Lanin's Orchestra was white and disapproved of playing opposite a black band, so they left the Roseland and as a result, Fletcher Henderson gained great prominence during this period as the featured star of the famous dance emporium.

Fletcher Henderson (1897-1952) typified the changes that most of these leaders underwent. He was born in Cuthbert, Georgia. His parents were college graduates, his father a school principal and his mother a music teacher. As a young boy, Henderson played classical piano. After graduating from college with a chemistry degree, he went to New York. In college, Henderson earned money leading a band, so he had experience playing for dancers. After working for a publishing company, Henderson accompanied female blues artists on record. He also headed a dance band at the Club Alabam near Times Square in 1923 and at the Roseland Ballroom in 1924. Henderson's earliest recordings were quite ragged. For example, the 1924 release of "Linger Awhile" features tenor saxophonist Coleman Hawkins playing a stilted, "slap tongue" solo, and a brass duo concocting a "doo-waka, doo-waka" racket.

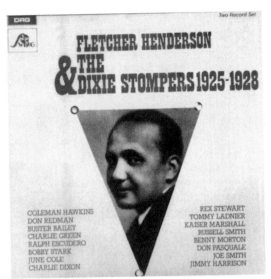

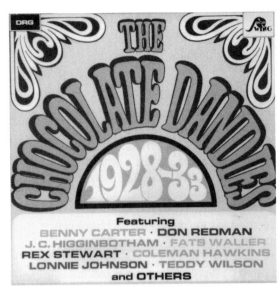

Fletcher Henderson was nicknamed "Smack" because of the smacking sounds he made with his lips. Henderson hired the greatest string of tenor saxmen in pre-war jazz: Coleman Hawkins, Lester Young, Ben Webster, and Chu Berry. He often used compositions and arrangements by his brother Horace ("Down South Camp Meetin'," "Wrappin' It Up," and "Big John's Special").

After McKinney's Cotton Pickers made their first records in 1928, they recorded as the Chocolate Dandies. The new name was taken from the title of the successful 1924 musical by Sissle and Blake. Gunther Schuller in *Early Jazz* calls Benny Carter's Chocolate Dandies of 1930, "One of the first 'all-star' bands ever assembled."

Don Redman & McKinney's Cotton Pickers, Greystone Ballroom, Detroit, 1930 Leader Don Redman alto sax/vocals, 6th from right. In 1927 Redman was signed by Jean Goldkette to become musical director of McKinney's Cotton Pickers. Redman had just left Fletcher Henderson's band and found himself rehearsing some of Goldkette's white bands, as well as the Cotton Pickers. Redman released some of his earliest sides as the Chocolate Dandies even though the group was essentially the Cotton Pickers. Some hits included "Milenberg Joys," "If I Could Be With You One Hour Tonight," "Four or Five Times," "Nobody's Sweetheart," and "My Blue Heaven."

When Louis Armstrong joined the band in 1924, his was one of three trumpets (for simplicity's sake, trumpet will henceforth be routinely noted instead of cornet because most brass players were switching to this instrument for its versatility—Bix Beiderbecke being a major exception). There was one trombone, three reedmen, and a rhythm section of piano, banjo, tuba, and drums. By 1927, the size of the band and the intricacies of the arrangements helped establish what would become the prototype of the big bands:

1) the brass section (trumpets and trombones),
2) the reed section (saxophones and occasional clainet and flute) and
3) the rhythm section (piano, bass, drums, and guitar)

Such a large ensemble depended upon an arranger to write out a musical score. Unlike the smaller New Orleans combos, collective improvisation would not operate smoothly in large aggregations. Many of the dance orchestras had been flourishing with the concept of three sections, but Henderson put a stronger emphasis on jazz. First and foremost was the fact that Henderson had at his disposal most of the top black soloists of the day. He also had **Don Redman** (1900-1964) as his first arranger. It must be underscored here that the earlier dance bands of Art Hickman, and Paul Specht had been playing arranged jazz *prior* to 1920. Don Redman had worked under the now-forgotten Paul Specht. Also, Bill Challis had already been using the trumpet-trombone-saxophone choirs in 1920. Along with Paul Whiteman and Ferde Grofe, these early trend-setters paved the way for Fletcher Henderson and Don Redman to place a greater emphasis on jazz soloing *after* 1923. Redman was a thoroughly schooled musician who was one of the best early jazz arrangers. He gained respect for his ability to write separate parts for reed and brass "choirs," leaving room for hot jazz solos; he also placed sections in opposition; that is, he played the sections off against one another. This call-and-response pattern of repeated harmonic and rhythmic motifs was referred to as "riffs." Riffs became one of the most exciting additions to the big band repertoire. Redman left the band in 1927 to become the leader of McKinney's Cotton Pickers.

Henderson is considered to have been a poor organizer of men and apparently a lackadaisical and hapless businessman, but he was a tremendously talented arranger. By 1934 Henderson's band had established the sound on which swing would be based, with sterling renditions such as "Sugar Foot Stomp," "Down South Camp Meetin'," "Big John's Special," "Wrappin' It Up," and "King Porter Stomp." Henderson never reaped the rewards of his innovations. Because of his weakness as a leader and businessman, Henderson's band broke up and he went into a decline. Columbia Records re-released his works years later under the title *A Study in Frustration*. During the swing era Henderson wrote arrangements for a band leader who emulated his innovations, Benny Goodman.

New York Pre-Swing Big Bands

Group	Comments, Stars, Recordings
California Ramblers	Adrian Rollini (sax, xylophone) played Rambler Inn in Bronx; "Vo-Do-Do Do-De-O Blues"
Benny Carter's Savoy Playboys	Centered on Carter's smooth and precise sax work and arrangements; folded 1930
Jean Goldkette Orchestra	Out of Detroit; Bill Challis arrangements; Beiderbecke & Trumbauer
Claude Hopkins Orchestra	Handsome pianist leader at Roseland Ballroom; theme ; "I Would Do Anything for You"
Sam Lanin Orchestra	Roseland Ballroom job paid high wages; Dorsey brothers & Red Nichols
Mills Blue Rhythm Band	5 leaders in 7 years; Irving Mills's backup band at Cotton Club for Ellington and Calloway
Ben Pollack Orchestra	1928-29 at Park Central Grill with Goodman Teagarden; "My Kind of Love"
Adrian Rollini Band	With Eddie Lang & Joe Venuti, Beiderbecke and Trumbauer at Club New Yorker; "Krazy Kat" and Beiderbecke's "At the Jazz Band Ball"
Royal Flush Orchestra	Leader Fess Williams opened Savoy Ballroom in 1926; great showmanship
Luis Russell Orchestra	Pianist-leader worked for numbers king Casper Holstein at Saratoga Club 1929-31; "Louisiana Swing," "Jersey Lightning," and "Saratoga Shout"
Paul Specht's Orchestra	Violinist-leader with recording "I Wish I Could Shimmy Like My Sister Kate"
Rex Stewart Band	Great trumpeter left Fletcher Henderson in 1933 and formed unit at Empire Ballroom

Source: Frank Driggs and Harris Lewine, Black Beauty, White Heat: A Pictorial History of Classic Jazz, 1920-1950.

Chicago's Windy City Band Scene: 1917-34.

Chicago's Pre-Swing Big Bands

Group	Comments, Stars, Recordings
Louis Armstrong's Stompers	1927 Armstrong replaced Carroll Dickerson at Sunset Cafe; "Chicago Breakdown"
Walter Barnes's Royal Creolians	Opened extravagant and lush Al Capone-owned Cotton Club in 1928
Doc Cook's Dreamland Orchestra	In 1921 featured Jimmy Noone, clarinet, and Freddie Keppard, cornet
Carroll Dickerson Band	Violinist-leader led groups at Sunset Cafe throughout 1920s; Mary Stafford, vocals
Elgar's Dreamland Orchestra	Leader Charlie Elgar played violin and led groups from 1914 to 1930
Jean Goldkette Orchestra	White jazz to perfection by combining popular music and jazz; "My Pretty Girl"
Earl Hines Band	1928 opened mob-run Grand Terrace Cafe, 1928; network broadcasts
Jelly Roll's Red Hot Peppers	1926 recordings "Black Bottom Stomp," "Doctor Jazz," and "The Chant"
Ray Miller Orchestra	1927-29 band ranked with Pollack; College Inn in Hotel Sherman his home base
Husk O'Hare's Wolverines	1926 unit filled by Austin High Gang's Teschemacher, Lannigan, Freeman, Tough, Jimmy and Dick McPartland
King Oliver's Dixie Stompers	1926 band featured Bob Shoffner on trumpet; "Snag It," "Sugarfoot Stomp," "Wa Wa Wa"
Cassino Simpson Band	Pianist-leader took over Jabbo Smith's group in 1931; a hot band
Eddie South's Alabamians	Violinist-leader of group 1927 South, Windy City super star called "The Black Angel"
Sammy Stewart Band	Pianist-organist Stewart brought some of the first arrangements to Chicago in 1923
Jesse Stone's Cyclones	Arranger-composer in 1933 at the newly formed El Morocco
Erskine Tate's Orchestra	Violinist Tate directed pit orchestras at Chicago's best theaters; "Little Symphony"
Albert Wynn's Paradise Orchestra	Jazz and show tunes featuring the leader-trombonist, and trumpeter Doc Cheatham

Source: Frank Driggs and Harris Lewine, Black Beauty, White Heat: A Pictorial History of Classic Jazz, 1920-1950.

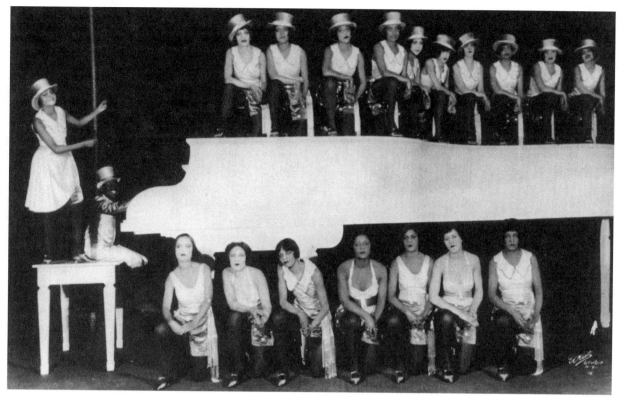

Florence Mills (standing on piano bench) and troupe of musical cohorts in *Dixie to Broadway,* 1924. The *New York World* newspaper caption to this photo read, "Dream Realized As Race Plays Broadway: The long-cherished dream of Williams and Walker, Cole and Johnson and Ernest Hogan to see a colored musical comedy successfully playing in the very heart of Broadway is at last a reality. For years these Negro stars labored and sacrificed to gratify an ambition now being realized by Florence Mills, who is scoring a pronounced hit in *Dixie to Broadway* at the Broadhurst."

Black Show Music

Just as mid-Manhattan had its musical theatrical traditions, so too would Harlem. Black productions in and around Broadway were not that common a sight, but there had been a few, such as *A Trip to Coon Town* in 1898, *In Dahomey* in 1902, *Abyssinia* in 1906, and *Bandana Land* in 1907. After that, most of the black shows were produced in Harlem at the Lincoln and Lafayette theaters. What many people saw as the landmark event in the beginning of the commercial Harlem Renaissance was the tremendous success of the musical comedy *Shuffle Along*, which opened at the 63rd Street Music Hall on May 22, 1921. This show became the catalyst for downtown interest in Harlem. The lively dance numbers and jazzy songs were performed as a daring synthesis of ragtime and operetta, and had a tremendous impact on the development of the Broadway musical. Broadway show music after *Shuffle Along,* except

Noble Sissle and Eubie Blake. Museum of the City of New York. The Theater Collection

"The Dixie Duo," Noble Sissle, left, and Eubie Blake, right. Sissle and Blake were partners from 1915 until Sissle's death in 1975 (occasionally they split, only to reunite). Sissle was a sophisticated singer from a proper background while Blake, an ebullient piano-player-composer and lyricist, plied his early trade in the taverns.

for operetta, became faster-paced and more syncopated. Dancing on Broadway also showed the influence of this show, as many from the chorus were immediately hired to teach jazz dance to white people (Florenz Ziegfeld and George White opened special studios for this purpose).

Composer-ragtime pianist **Eubie Blake** (1883-1983) and lyricist **Noble Sissle** (1899-1975) had been members of James Reese Europe's Society Orchestra in New York just before World War I. After the war, Sissle and Blake worked as the "Dixie Duo" in vaudeville. They had hoped to work together with Europe to put together his dream of restoring blacks to the American stage, but Europe's death ended that possibility. Instead they combined forces with writer-performers Flournoy Miller and Aubrey Lyles to put on their own show, *Shuffle Along.* The plot was based on a Miller and Lyles vaudeville sketch known as both "The Mayor of Dixie" and "The Mayor of Jimtown." The show opened to enthusiastic reviews and even added a midnight show on Wednesdays so that fellow theater people could view it.

The musicians in the pit band were all well trained. In his biography, Blake pointed out that the musicians were instructed to memorize the score because audiences didn't believe that blacks could read music—they thought it was all just natural ability. Quite the contrary. As conductor,

Blake had before him a number of concert virtuosos, including violist Hall Johnson, who went on to write large-scale choral works and head the Hall Johnson Chorale and oboist William Grant Still, who would go on to be considered the dean of black American composers.

One of the musical highlights of *Shuffle Along* occurred late in the second act of the show. The dramatic action stopped and Blake left the pit to join Sissle on stage to perform what they called "A Few Minutes With Sissle and Blake." They rendered a quartet of songs, the most rousing being their interpretations of "How Ya' Gonna Keep 'Em Down on the Farm," and "Mirindy," both associated with their mentor, James Reese Europe. The finale of the show, "Baltimore Buzz," created the biggest stir. Other songs of note were the memorable ballad, "Love Will Find a Way," "Bandana Days," "In Honeysuckle Time," "Gypsy Blues," recorded by Paul Whiteman, and "I'm Just Wild About Harry," which would become even more famous in 1948 when it was used as Harry S Truman's presidential campaign song.

After years of being out of the public eye Blake made a resounding comeback in the late 1960s. John Hammond recorded the redoubtable entertainer in 1968 and 1969 for Columbia Records, and Robert Kimball and William Bolcom's 1973 biography, *Reminiscing With*

I'm Just Wild About Harry, sheet music cover. Museum of the City of New York. The Theater Collection

Sissle and Blake, resulted in a triumphant return to concert halls and nightclubs. In 1979 a musical revue, *Eubie!*, headlined by Gregory and Maurice Hines, graced the Broadway stage with a revival of black Broadway's syncopated tunes and dance routines.

Florence Mills (1895-1927) became the biggest black theatrical star of the Harlem Renaissance. Mills replaced Gertrude Saunders as the star of *Shuffle Along*.

Allen Woll says in *Black Musical Theatre: From Coontown to Dreamgirls*, "Mills's rendition of 'I'm Craving for That Kind of Love' stopped the show every night, easing all memory of Saunders' performance. Her rise was meteoric, and Lew Leslie gave her *Plantation Revue* (1922) as a starring vehicle. She toured European capitals in a new Leslie show (*From Dover to Dixie*) and returned to New York city for *Dixie to Broadway* in 1924."

James Weildon Johnson says of Mills in *Black Manhattan*, "One might best string out a list of words such as: pixy, elf, radiant, exotic, Peter Pan, wood-nymph, wistful, piquant, magnetism, witchery, madness, flame; and then despairingly exclaim: 'Oh, you know what I mean.' She could be whimsical, she could be almost grotesque, but she had good taste that never allowed her to be coarse. She could be risque, she could be seductive; but it was impossible for her to be vulgar, for she possessed a naivete that was alchemic. As a pantomimist and a singing and dancing comedienne she had no superior in any place or in any race."

Florence Mills. Museum of the City of New York. The Theater Collection

Florence Mills the "Little Black Bird of Black Broadway." Noble Sissle observed that, "She was Dresden china, and she turned into a stick of dynamite." Bricktop claims that on her opening night Mills received an amazing seventeen encores. However, Mills was fragile and died of appendicitis on November 2, 1927. Her funeral was the occasion of the greatest outpouring of love and respect and grief that Harlem had ever experienced. Over 250,000 people lined the streets to see the passing of the cortege that held the most famous and beloved black star of the twenties. No Mills recordings exist. Mills also performed in the *Plantation Revue* and in *Dixie to Broadway* in which she sang the torchy "I'm a Little Blackbird Looking for a Bluebird," which Lena Horne said was the source of Mills's moniker. "Mandy, Make Up Your Mind" was another Mills classic from this show. Duke Ellington wrote a musical tribute to Florence Mills in 1928, titled "Black Beauty."

Josephine Baker (1906-1975), was a teenage chorus girl in *Shuffle Along* making thirty dollars a week in the early 1920s. Baker eventually moved to Paris, France, and on October 2, 1925, she made her debut in a show called *La Revue Negre*. The finale of the evening was a "Charleston Cabaret," whose featured number has come to be known as "La Danse de Sauvage." Baker sauntered onto the stage wearing a handful of feathers. At mid-stage she met a nearly nude male. She slid herself down her partner's legs and proceeded to offer him every soft spot of her body. She pranced about to the music and made wild movements that roused the crowd. That night Baker established her fame.

Ain't Misbehavin', sheet music cover. Museum of the City of New York, 72.76.47. The Theater Collection

Photographs and Prints Division, Schomburg Center for Research in Black Culture, The New York Public Library, Astor, Lenox and Tilden Foundation

Josephine Baker, the most famous international black star, as depicted by artist Paul Colin in 1925's *La Revue Negre* poster. Baker went on to become an international star performing at the Folies-Bergere and making motion pictures in Paris. Baker helped define the Jazz Age in Europe.

Hot Chocolates started as a musical revue and floor show at Connie's Inn. It moved to the Hudson Theatre in June 1929. The all-black revue featured Louis Armstrong rising from the orchestra pit each evening to perform "Ain't Misbehavin'," Fats Waller's eventual theme song. Waller wrote the classic tune with lyricist Andy Razaf, who penned the words to many of the composer's melodies, including "Black and Blue," introduced by Edith Wilson, "Honeysuckle Rose," "Blue Turning Grey Over You," and "Keepin' Out of Mischief Now."

Photographs and Prints Division, Schomburg Center for Research in Black Culture, The New York Public Library, Astor, Lenox and Tilden Foundation

Macbeth comes to the Lafayette Theatre. At 2,000 seats the Lafayette Theatre was the largest and most prestigious showcase for legitimate theatrical events in Harlem. The Lafayette was located at 131st Street and Seventh Avenue.

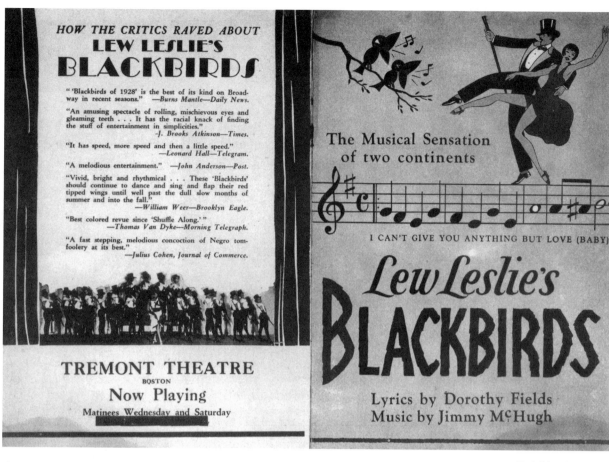

Key Black Shows of the Harlem Renaissance

Year	Shows	Comments
1921	Shuffle Along	The musical that launched the black musical theater onslaught of the 1920s.
1922	Liza	Produced by Maceo Pinkard; its 169-performance run was a big success
1922	Strut Miss Lizzie	Billed as "Glorifying the Creole Beauty"; Creamer and Layton interpolated their hits into the play
1922	Plantation Revue	Cast included composer Sheldon Brooks, Florence Mills, and Will Vodery
1923	Runnin' Wild	Miller and Lyles, billed as "America's Foremost Colored Comedians"; music of James P. Johnson; in the finale of act one, Elizabeth Welch danced with chorus to the "Charleston"; a big success
1924	Chocolate Dandies	Score by Sissle and Blake; ran 96 performances; attempted to break *Shuffle Along* formula
1924	Dixie to Broadway	Showcase for Florence Mills, billed by Fields as "world's greatest colored entertainer"
1928	Keep Shufflin'	Miller and Lyles tried to recapture the success of *Shuffle Along*; music by Fats Waller and James P. Johnson; 104 performances
1928	Blackbirds of 1928	Bill Robinson danced to "Doin' the New Low Down," Aida Ward sang "I Can't Give You Anything But Love, Baby"; Dorothy Fields and Jimmy McHugh wrote the musical score for Lew Leslie's "all-white-creation for an all-black cast"; 518 performances
1929	Pansy	Maceo Pinkard's black collegiate musical; Bessie Smith sang "If the Blues Don't Get You"
1929	Hot Chocolates	Opened at Connie's Inn then moved to Broadway for a six-month run; music by Fats Waller, lyrics by Andy Razaf; Louis Armstrong sang and played "Ain't Misbehavin'"
1930	Lew Leslie's Blackbirds	Black composers Razaf and Blake used for this version of *Blackbirds* with Ethel Waters, Flournoy Miller; "Memories of You" became one of Blake's all-time standards

Shuffle Along had many imitators, but none matched its success. Lew Leslie put *Blackbirds of 1928* into the Liberty Theatre on May 7, 1928, where it ran for 518 performances. In 1926, Leslie had exhibited a successful *Blackbirds* revue in London starring Florence Mills, and he had hoped to build the 1928 Broadway show around her. Unfortunately, Mills died unexpectedly. Leslie hired Adelaide Hall and Aida Ward, along with Bill "Bojangles" Robinson and billed the production, "A distinctive and unique entertainment with an all-star cast of 100 colored artists." Dorothy Fields and Jimmy McHugh, two white songwriters, wrote rhythm numbers "Doin' the New Low Down" and "Diga Diga Doo," as well as ballads such as "I Must Have That Man" and "Porgy" (a capsule version of Gershwin's opera *Porgy and Bess* eight years before the fact). The biggest success was the song that became an all-time standard, "I Can't Give You Anything but Love (Baby)," first introduced by Patsy Kelly in the 1927 revue *Delmar's Revels*. It was then interpreted by Aida Ward, who sang it in collaboration with Willard MacLean and Bill Robinson. During the run of the show, the song was taken over by Adelaide Hall. Louis Armstrong made the song one of his classics for Decca Records.

Author's collection

The prosperity of *Shuffle Along* helped usher in the Harlem Renaissance. The phenomenon got started when white show business people began spreading the word about the play's excitement. Soon celebrities and politicians were attending and *Shuffle Along* became a society fad. Well-heeled whites began to venture into Harlem. Some called it "slumming." One black newspaper wrote that there seemed to be among whites a "morbid interest" in the nightlife of Harlem. White music critic Carl Van Vechten was representative of the intellectuals and urban wealthy who were getting bored with middle class values and the "Machine Age." Van Vechten chronicled Harlem with sensitive articles and photographs about black artists, musicians, and writers. This was, after all, the post-war period, and there was a persuasive, new-found sense of freedom. Women for example, had just gained the vote. There was also, a new kind of music in the air—jazz. To the socialites and intellectuals the Negro embodied exotic and thrilling qualities. Harlem, and the speakeasies and cabarets to be found therein, was the place to go. Harlem in the twenties and thirties was bustling with energy and excitement.

Frank Driggs Collection

Artist E. Simms Campbell put together his annotated "Night-Club Map of Harlem" in 1932 and commented that the only omission was the location of various speakeasies, "but since there are about 500 of them you won't have much trouble." There was the Radium Club, which was known for breakfast dances every Sunday morning at 4 a.m. and the Club Hot-Cha, for which the map noted, "Nothing happens before 2:00—ask for Clarence." Another late-hour spot was the Clam House, on 133rd Street, where Gladys Bentley cross-dressed and sang double-entendre songs. Others included Small's Paradise, noted for its "cafe au lait girls" and dancing waiters; Barron's Exclusive Club, which featured Willie "The Lion" Smith, Ada "Bricktop" Smith, and Elmer Snowden's Washingtonians; the Nest Club, Pod's and Jerry's, Tillie's Chicken Shack, the Yeah Man, the Hollywood Cabaret; and Connie's Inn, located on the corner of 131st Street and Seventh Avenue, which reached its peak in 1929 when it housed Louis Armstrong and Fats Waller starring in *Hot Chocolates*.

Three Portraits by Carl Van Vechten. *Left*, Cab Calloway, *center*, Ethel Waters, and *right,* Bill Robinson. Van Vechten was a writer-photographer and bon vivant. He and his wife hosted parties that mixed well-known writers, artists, and musicians. Van Vechten introduced many black performers to his afternoon and evening salon gatherings.

The most famous Harlem night spot of all was the Cotton Club, located on the corner of 142nd Street and Lenox Avenue. The Cotton Club was owned by gangster Owney Madden, who wanted to develop an elegant nightclub that would cater to the downtown white crowd. The venue would also serve as an outlet for selling "Madden's No. 1 Beer." Madden seldom showed up at the club, putting, instead, George "Big Frenchy" DeMange in charge. Most of the early help were brought in from the Chicago operations. The venue was completely run by whites to entertain other whites. The performers were all black.

The club, which was upstairs, was enlarged to seat about seven hundred, and the decor was that of a jungle. Service was professional and those in attendance were expected to be quiet during performances. The shows were actually revues. The Cotton Club put on two revues per year and each performance lasted one and a half to two hours. The shows were fast-paced and elaborate. The club's grand opening came in the fall of 1923, with Jimmy McHugh writing most of the music, Lew Leslie producing, and Andy Preer leading the band, which changed its name from the Missourians to the Cotton Club Syncopators. By 1925, Leslie was replaced by Don Healy, who put a high premium on glossy production numbers and miniature stage sets.

December 4, 1927 marked the arrival of a talent that would "make" the Cotton Club, in the words of "The Aristocrat of Harlem", Lady Mountbatten. **Duke Ellington** (1899-1974) was brought in from the Kentucky Club to become the resident bandleader. He would lead his Cotton Club orchestra for five years, performing featured compositions as well as background music for the dancers and singers. This period has been referred to as Ellington's "jungle period" because he featured musical numbers with jungle themes to satisfy the white patron's appetite for exotic fare. Ellington performed so many of these numbers that at first his unit was labeled Duke Ellington's Jungle Band. It played tunes such as "Jungle Blues," "Jungle Jamboree," "Jungle Nights in Harlem," and "Echoes of the Jungle." Mark Tucker in *Ellington: The Early Years* observes that once he left the Cotton Club, Ellington "moved away from the stylized primitivism" of the jungle-oriented compositions, and found ways to work "its surface manner deeper into the substance of his music".

Cotton Club mural with depiction of blacks as exotic, noble savages—the image evoked by the "jungle motifs" in many of the club's numerous dance numbers. This image of African-Americans was the stereotype that the wealthy white clubgoers expected when they went "slumming" up in Harlem. And artists such as Duke Ellington and Cab Calloway, as well as the Cotton Club dancers and singers, were expected to perform songs to enhance that stereotype.

Courtesy Decca Records/MCA

The Jungle Band. "The Brunswick Era" refers to the recordings Ellington's band made for Brunswick Records between 1929 and 1931. Ellington had signed a contract with the Victor Talking Machine Company (later RCA Victor) that specified that his name could not appear on any other label. As a result he listed his unit as "The Jungle Band" when recording for Brunswick. On Banner/Perfect, Ellington recorded as the "Whooppee Makers"; Okeh called them "Harlem Footwarmers"; Diva and Clarian dubbed them "Ten Black Berries."

Ellington did not start out as a jazz performer, and, as the years went on, he felt the term was limiting. As noted earlier, Ellington's was an educated, middle-class upbringing. His father had worked as a butler in the White House and later as a blueprint maker for the navy. Growing up in Washington, D.C., young Ellington knew little of what was going on in the world of New Orleans jazz or blues. When he came to New York in 1923, it was with Elmer Snowden's society band, the Washingtonians. The band played at the Hollywood Inn, located in mid-Manhattan, for four years (after a fire the club was renamed the Kentucky Club). Snowden left in 1925 and Ellington took over as leader. In 1926 Ellington recorded as

Duke Ellington and His Washingtonians. That same year, in the words of John Edward Hasse in *Beyond Category: The Life and Genius of Duke Ellington*, "Ellington began a relationship with Irving Mills. Of all the people Ellington met in the 1920s, Mills and Bubber Miley would become the most significant to the establishment of his sound and career." Mills became Ellington's astute manager.

Bubber Miley: The jazz connection. Miley was one of the greatest "growling" trumpeters of all time. His muted, eerie smears were called "freak" playing by fellow musicians. According to Gunther Schuller, an authority on "Ellingtonia", Miley was not only a distinctive soloist but the best writer in Ellington's band. Two lasting classics (co-authored with Ellington) were "East St. Louis Toodle-oo" and "Black and Tan Fantasy." Ellington acknowledged that Miley shifted the character of his band towards jazz: "He used to growl all night long, playing gut bucket on his horn. That was when we decided to forget all about the sweet music." Miley educated trombonist Charlie Irvis on the use of the plunger for freak effects. When Irvis left the band, Miley showed his replacement, Joe "Tricky Sam" Nanton, the same techniques. Cootie Williams, who subsequently replaced Miley, continued the tradition of the great "Freak Master." Here, Miley (on trumpet) is seen with dancer (and later dance and jazz critic) Roger Pryor Dodge right, in *Sweet and Low* (1930). They also appeared in Billy Rose's *Third Little Show* in 1931 and later that year Ellington's manager, Irving Mills, created a show around Miley titled *Harlem Scandals*. Miley died of tuberculosis, in May 1932 at the age of 29.

A musical revue of Duke Ellington-related songs, *Sophisticated Ladies*, opened on Broadway in 1981, at the Lunt-Fontanne Theatre. The cast included Gregory Hines, Phyllis Hyman, and Judith Jamison.

The jazz elements absorbed by Ellington came from the after-hours clubs that featured stride pianists, and from two important New Orleans players who joined his band: Bubber Miley and Sidney Bechet. **James "Bubber" Miley** (1903-1932) mastered the plunger-muted trumpet style that growled, smeared, and vocalized. His influence on the band was immeasurable. One element of what composer Billy Strayhorn referred to as the "Ellington effect" was Bubber Miley's "freak effects," which would be passed on to trombonist Joe "Tricky Sam" Nanton, and Miley's replacement, Cootie Williams. Miley was the cornerstone of the jungle sounds heard on the 1927 recordings "Flaming Youth," "Creole Love Call" (featuring Adelaide Hall's wordless vocal), and the band's first theme song, "East St. Louis Toodle-oo." Ellington pointed out that when Miley joined the band, the sweet, commercial music they had been playing became a thing of the past. Bechet, who joined around 1926, was considered by Ellington to

149

have been the foundation and very epitome of jazz. Soon a national radio hook-up broadcast via the Columbia Broadcasting System, with Ted Husing announcing, brought the Cotton Club into the living rooms of America. The Cotton Club became nationally famous, and, as a result, white tourists came to Harlem in larger numbers than ever before. By the end of 1930, Duke Ellington was weary of the Cotton Club and would move on to new levels of accomplishment, which will be investigated as part of the swing era.

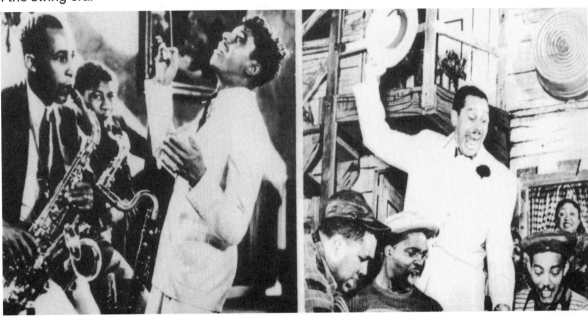

Mr. Hi-De-Ho. *Left,* Cab Calloway in his youth at the Cotton Club. During this period he made a number of films, including *The Big Broadcast of 1932* and *International House,* as well as popular recordings. By the 1940s Calloway fronted a band that had future modernists such as Dizzy Gillespie. *Right,* the master of "Hi-De-Ho" playing the part of Sportin' Life in a 1952 revival of *Porgy and Bess.* George Gershwin allegedly wrote the part for Calloway. Calloway had the longest active career of the Harlem Renaissance performers. In 1967 he played in the all-black version of *Hello, Dolly!* In 1980 he played in the revue *Bubbling Brown Sugar* and in the movie *The Blues Brothers.* In the early 1990s Calloway played in a Janet Jackson music video.

Cab Calloway (1907-1994) fronted a band called the Missourians and appeared in the 1929 musical revue *Hot Chocolates.* That same year he led the Alabamians at the Savoy Ballroom. By 1931 he would become Duke Ellington's replacement at the Cotton Club. Calloway was one of the most stylish and extroverted entertainers in the history of American popular music. He set trends in dress with his zoot suits, and in language with his jive talk. Long before Little Richard upset the popular music scene with wild hair and frantic stage antics, there was Calloway dancing, prancing, and bowing in front of the bandstand. He was known as the "Hi-De-Ho" man, a reference to the choruses to some of his songs, including "Minnie the Moocher," "Kicking the Gong Around," "Reefer Man," "The Scat Song," and "Jumpin' Jive." By 1932, Calloway was featured in Hollywood films and later would star on the Broadway stage. Jimmie Lunceford would replace him as the Cotton Club's bandleader in 1934. In 1944 Calloway authored his *Hepster's Dictionary* ("hep" being the general patois employed by musicians and entertainers in New York's teeming Harlem).

150

Calloway returned in 1936 to headline, with Bill "Bojangles" Robinson, the new Cotton Club, which was located downtown. The stylish entertainer was provided with many songs from the pen of Harold Arlen, most importantly his biggest hit, 1942's "Blues in the Night." In 1976 Calloway published his autobiography, *Of Minnie the Moocher and Me*.

Harold Arlen's Post-Cotton Club Classics

Song Title	Source (Hollywood/Broadway)	Performer	Year
Let's Fall in Love	Let's Fall in Love (H)	Ann Sheridan	1934
Last Night When We Were Young	Metropolitan (H)	Lawrence Tibbett	1935
Over the Rainbow	The Wizard of Oz (H)	Judy Garland	1939
Lydia, the Tattooed Lady	At the Circus (H)	Groucho Marx	1939
Blues in the Night	Blues in the Night (H)	William Gillespie	1941
This Time the Dream's on Me	Blues in the Night (H)	Priscilla Lane	1941
That Old Black Magic	Star Spangled Rhythm (H)	Johnny Johnston	1942
Hit the Road to Dreamland	Star Spangled Rhythm (H)	Mary Martin & Dick Powell	1942
Happiness Is Just a Thing Called Joe	Cabin in the Sky (H)	Ethel Waters	1943
Stormy Weather	Stormy Weather (H)	Lena Horne	1943
My Shining Hour	The Sky's the Limit (H)	Fred Astaire	1943
One for My Baby (And One More for the Road)	The Sky's the Limit (H)	Fred Astaire	1943
Ac-cent-tchu-ate the Positive	Here Come the Waves (H)	Bing Crosby & Sonny Tufts	1945
Out of This World	Out of This World (H)	Bing Crosby	1945
Come Rain or Come Shine	St. Louis Woman (B)	Harold Nicholas & Ruby Hill	1946
Hooray for Love	Casbah (H)	Tony Martin	1947
Last Night When We Were Young	In the Good Old Summertime (H)	Judy Garland	1949
Get Happy	Summer Stock (H)	Judy Garland	1950
A Sleepin' Bee	House of Flowers (B)	Diahann Carroll	1954
Two Ladies in de Shade of de Banana Tree	House of Flowers (B)	Ada Moore & Enid Mosier	1954
The Man That Got Away	A Star Is Born (H)	Judy Garland	1954

Courtesy Smithsonian Collection of Recordings

Buffalo's most famous songwriting son, Harold Arlen.

Harold Arlen (1905-1986) was born in Buffalo, New York, son of a cantor who wanted him to follow his footsteps. Much to his father's chagrin, Harold preferred the jazz and blues music of the Original Memphis Five, Ethel Waters, and Bessie Smith. Working as a singer-pianist with local groups with names like the Snappy Trio, the Southbound Shufflers, the Yankee Six, and, finally, a touring unit called the Buffalodians, Arlen decided to shuffle off to the Big Apple in 1925. Once Arlen realized that his future was as a composer rather than as a singer, he began to find success. Arlen's greatest contributions were made between 1930 and 1957, writing for revues, musical comedies, and films. His three principal collaborators were Ted Koehler, E.Y. Harburg, and Johnny Mercer. Arlen's maxim was, "A good lyric writer is a composer's best friend."

Arlen's first hit was a collaboration with Koehler called "Get Happy," for the 1930 *Nine-fifteen Revue* (the show ran only seven performances). On the strength of "Get Happy" Arlen signed on to write music for the Cotton Club revues. After auditioning Arlen and Koehler material at the Silver Slipper nightclub, owner Owney Madden decided to replace McHugh and Fields (they moved on to Broadway to write for *Blackbirds of 1928*). No hits resulted from the December 1930 show called *Brown Sugar: Sweet but Unrefined Nightclub Revue*. The second Cotton Club revue Arlen wrote for resulted in a hit for Cab Calloway, "Kickin' the Gong Around." The *Cotton Club Parade* revue of April 1932 resulted in a followup to Calloway's "Minnie the Moocher," and "Minnie the Moocher's Wedding Day."

In October 1932 Arlen and Koehler had success for Aida Ward with "I've Got the World on a String" and for Calloway with "The Wail of the Reefer Man" in 1933's *Cotton Club Parade*. That revue would also prompt the songwriting team's greatest accomplishment, providing Ethel Waters with a show-stopping classic, "Stormy Weather." The next year would be the final one for Arlen working at the Cotton Club. "Ill Wind" was sung by Adelaide Hall and "As Long as I Live" featured sixteen-year-old chorine Lena Horne in a duet with Avon Long. Jimmie Lunceford and His Orchestra made their debut as the Cotton Club house band.

Courtesy ASCAP

Harold Arlen .

Arlen's penchant for the blues was underscored when Ethel Waters called him "the Negro-ist white man I've ever known." Inside the musical world, this gentle man was known for his "musical jots," which he would place on a composition to indicate a separate song idea or melodic springboard to develop into future songs. One of Arlen's greatest champions was Alec Wilder, who stated, "Of all the better songwriters, I can think of very few who have any emotional kinship with the jazz musician and his bittersweet, witty, lonely, intense world. This love for the jazz players and their marvelous inventiveness has had a profound effect on Arlen's songs." Among jazz-pop composers, Hoagy Carmichael and George Gershwin are the other two most celebrated. In comparing the music of Arlen and Gershwin, Wilder concluded, "I've examined the music of both composers very carefully and without prejudice. I respect Gershwin, but I envy Arlen."

Ethel Waters (1900-1977) was the consummate black female talent of the first half of the century. She not only performed as a singer of blues, cabaret, and pop, but performed on Broadway and in Hollywood in musicals as well as dramatic roles. Early in her career Waters was tall and thin, thus gaining her nickname "Sweet Mama Stringbean." Between 1921 and 1934, she had some twenty-five hits in the top twenty. Water's signature tune was, "Stormy Weather," from the twenty-second of the Cotton Club shows. This song literally stopped the show. Waters had to sing numerous encores nightly and the singer referred to the song as the turning point in her life. Lena Horne, who was a young chorus girl at that time, was greatly influenced by Waters, and in 1943 starred in the film *Stormy Weather*, featuring Cab Calloway, Bill "Bojangles" Robinson, and the Nicholas Brothers, all one-time members of the Cotton Club.

In 1984 Francis Ford Coppola released *The Cotton Club* starring Richard Gere, Diane Lane, and Gregory Hines. The result was less than hoped for; for historical accuracy read *The Cotton Club* by Jim Haskins.

Ethel Waters. (Cotton Club, Harlem) Museum of the City of New York. The Theater Collection

Ethel Waters: Sweet Mama Stringbean.

Ethel Waters with the Duke Ellington Orchestra and the Cotton Club chorus at the Cotton Club performing "Stormy Weather." Waters was one of the most versatile female entertainers of all time. She sang blues in a smooth style during the twenties ("Georgia Blues," "Memphis Man," and "My Handy Man"). She performed on stage as a dancer and actress (*Hello, 1919!* and *Africana*). She introduced popular music standards such as "Sweet Georgia Brown" (1925), "Dinah" (1926), "Am I Blue?" (1929), "Stormy Weather" (1933), and "Heat Wave" (1933). She was the first prominent black woman to star on Broadway (Irving Berlin's *As Thousands Cheer,* 1933), and was said to be the first black woman to star on network radio (1933), and to appear on television, (1939).

During the forties and fifties Waters was featured in major dramatic Hollywood films such as *Cabin in the Sky* (1943), *Pinky* (1949), *Member of the Wedding* (stage 1950, film 1952), and *Sound and the Fury* (1959). And Waters was an active member of the Billy Graham Crusades and wrote two autobiographies, *His Eye Is on the Sparrow (*1951), and *To Me it's Wonderful* (1972). Henry Pleasants writes in *The Great American Popular Singers,* "Along wtih Bessie Smith and Louis Armstrong, she [Waters] was a fountainhead of all that is finest and most distinctive in American popular singing. Of the three, she may well have been the most widely and the most perceptibly influential."

The original Cotton Club closed its doors on February 16, 1936. By September a new Cotton Club, headlining Cab Calloway and Bill "Bojangles" Robinson, opened on Broadway and 48th Street. The mid-Manhattan club would remain in operation until June 10, 1940. The demise of the original Cotton Club pretty much reflects the end of the Harlem Renaissance. The Depression and the repeal of Prohibition were just two of many reasons for the change. In *The Big Sea* Langston Hughes wrote, "That spring for me (and, I guess, all of us) was the end of the Harlem Renaissance. We were no longer in vogue, anyway, we Negroes. Sophisticated New Yorkers turned to Noel Coward. Colored actors began to go hungry, publishers politely rejected new manuscripts, and patrons found other uses for their money. The cycle that had charlestoned into being on the dancing heels of *Shuffle Along* now ended in *Green Pastures with de Lawd*."

153

Cotton Club Highlights

Fall 1923   The Cotton Club opens its doors
> Andy Preer and the Cotton Club Syncopaters
> Jimmy McHugh, prior to the arrival of Duke Ellington, wrote key songs for the club:
> "I Can't Believe You're in Love With Me," "Freeze and Melt," and "When My Sugar Walks Down the Street"

December 1927   Duke Ellington and His Jungle Orchestra debut:
> Jimmy McHugh & Dorothy Fields write key songs ("Harlem River Quiver", and "Doin' the Frog")
> Dancer Earl "Snakehips" Tucker (called "The Human Boa Constrictor")
> Edith Wilson sings "adult songs"; Mildred and Henri, dance team; Ellington's "Blue Bubbles," Black Beauty," and Jubilee Stomp"

Spring 1928   *Cotton Club Show Boat*
Fall 1928   *Hot Chocolate*
Spring 1929   *Spring Birds*
Fall 1929   *Blackberries*
Spring 1930   *Blackbirds of 1930*
Fall 1931   *Brown Sugar; Sweet, But Unrefined*
> Harold Arlen and Ted Koehler write key songs

Spring 1931   *Rhythmania*
> with Arlen and Koehler songs
> Aida Ward introduces "Between the Devil and the Deep Blue Sea"; Cab Calloway introduces
> "Kickin' the Gong Around," "Trickeration," and "Minnie the Moocher"

Fall 1931   Arlen and Koehler write key songs
> Cora La Red, trick dancing; Swan and Lee, create intricate dance steps
> Aida Ward and Leetha Hal sing torch songs

1932   *Cotton Club Parades*
> Arlen and Koehler songs (on risque songs Arlen uses a pseudonym)
> Cab Calloway performs "The Wail of the Reefer Man" and "Minnie the Moocher's Wedding Day"
> Torch songstress Leitha Hill sings "Pool Room Papa," "My Military Man" and "High Flyin' Man"
> Aida Ward: "I've Got the World on a String," "A New Kind of Rhythm," "That's What I Hate About Love"

Spring 1933   *The Stormy Weather Show*
> Arlen and Koehler write the classic "Stormy Weather"
> Ethel Waters introduces "Stormy Weather" in the eleventh scene of *Cabin in the Cotton Club*
> Dusty Fletcher comedy; "Rubberlegs" Williams specialty dances; songs include "Happy As the
> Day is Long," "Raisin' the Rent"; Sally Gooding sings "I'm Lookin' for Another Handy Man"

Fall 1933   *Cotton Club Parade*; Lena Horne joins cast
Spring 1934   *Cotton Club Parade*
> Jimmie Lunceford Orchestra replaces Cab Calloway Orchestra
> Harold Arlen's last Cotton Club show
> Adelaide Hall sings "I'll Wind" and "Primitive Prima Donna"
> the Cotton Club Boys singing dancing troupe debuts
> Avon Long and Lena Horne sing "As Long As I Live"

Spring 1935   Edition known as *The Truckin' Show*
> Jimmie Lunceford and Cotton Club Boys perform, "Everybody's Truckin' "

February 1936   Cotton Club closes in Harlem
September 1936   The new Cotton Club reopens in mid-Manhattan at Broadway and 48th Street
> Bill Bojangles Robinson and Cab Calloway headline most lavish opening ever
> Bessie Dudley dances to "Rockin' in Rhythm"

Spring 1937   *The Cotton Club Express*
> Fayard and Harold Nicholas: "Tap Is Tops"; they stay five years
> Ivie Anderson, vocalist who had been with Ellington since 1931 joins cast
> Ethel Waters reprises "Stormy Weather" and "Happiness Is Just a Thing Called Joe"
> Finale with Nicholas Brothers in chicken costumes perform; "Peckin'" (a bow to Bert Williams)

Fall 1937   Robinson and Calloway headline again
> Mae Johnson: does Mae West impersonations

Spring 1937   Duke Ellington headlines: "I Let a Song Go out of My Heart"
> Peters Sisters, 300 pounds each, sing "Swingtime in Honolulu" and "Poison"
> Peg Leg Bates, dance specialty "Slappin' 7th Avenue With the Sole of My Shoe"

Fall 1938   Cab Calloway headlines: "A Lesson in Jive"
> W. C. Handy, Nicholas Brothers, Jigsaw Jackson, and Whyte's Lindy Hoppers
> Sisters Rosetta Tharpe sings "Hallelujah Brown," "Rock Me," and "The Preacher"

Spring 1939   *The World's Fair Edition of the Cotton Club*, headlined by Robinson and Calloway
> Dandridge Sisters sing "A-Tisket, A-Tasket"

Summer 1939   Andy Kirk Orchestra with Mary Lou Williams: "Roll' Em" (a rollicking boogie woogie number)
Fall 1939   Louis Armstrong, comedian Stepin Fetchit, and singer Maxine Sullivan
June 1940   Cotton Club closes for good

The 1943 major Hollywood film featuring Cotton Club alumni Lena Horne, Bill "Bojangles" Robinson, Cab Calloway, and the Nicholas Brothers. The story is told in flashback from the point-of-view of Bill Robinson. Along the way are great musical numbers, including a guest visit by Fats Waller, until the "big celebration" at the film's conclusion which includes Lena Horne's rendering of "Stormy Weather" (with a dance sequence from the Katherine Dunham troupe) and Calloway and the Nicholas Brothers raving up the "Jumpin' Jive."

The Flash Dancers. The amazing Nicholas Brothers dance duo at the Cotton Club. Harold (left) and Fayard (right) were known for their great agility. They were outstanding tap dancers, but they gained fame by their amazing leaping splits and flips. This acrobatic style led them to be called "Flash Dancers." The brothers were managed by Herman Starks, one of the producers of the Cotton Club shows.

By the late 1930s and throughout the 1940s and '50s, with the initial push from Starks, the Nicholas Brothers made a bevy of Hollywood films (*Sun Valley Serenade, Orchestra Wives,* and *The Pirate,* among others), and played the classiest night clubs in America. In later years Harold worked solo in America and overseas. During the late 1980s and into the 1990s the brothers have performed on many occasions—Fayard was even able to tap out a number of intricate steps after rehabilitating after two hip replacements.

Lena Horne featured in the black film *The Bronze Venus*. Unlike the major Hollywood films, black films allowed the stars to be featured as characters in leading roles.

The "new Cotton Club" opened on Broadway and 48th Street in 1936. Cab Calloway and Bill "Bojangles" Robinson often headlined and the exciting dance duo, the Nicholas Brothers, were among the new club's stars.

Chapter 7

COUNTRY AND FOLK MUSIC

This family, playing fiddle and guitar and singing, is an example of "parlor music making" in rural communities. String bands derived from this tradition.

Southern Background

In early America the original thirteen states were made up largely of Anglo-Saxon peoples of British and Scottish heritage. Although there were geographical differences between the northern and southern parts of the United States, it wasn't until the slavery issue became paramount that these two areas of America became almost separate. The music of North and South had the same lineage, but by the 1920s, when records and radio spread commercial music throughout the nation, the North and South had different types of music. Why was the South so radically different from the North? The answers lie in the South's agricultural economy and rural way of life. The economy of the South became dependent upon cheap labor, and thus the "peculiar institution" of Negro slavery became integral to it. This slavery issue drew criticism from elements of northern society, and as a result many southerners set up a wall of isolation to defend themselves. This meant holding on to old traditions and rejecting some of the industrial advancements that had been introduced in the North. The South became a distinct "family" unit.

B. A. Botkins states that, "The folk group is one that has been cut off from progress and has retained beliefs, customs, and expressions with limited acceptance. In his book *The Mind of the South*, Wilbur Cash contends that isolation, deficiencies in education, and lack of communication all contributed to the fact that traditions lasted longer in the South than in the North. He notes that this was especially true in music.

Because southerners were dependent upon a more agrarian lifestyle and were cut off from much economic progress, they preserved their old-time ballads and folk songs longer than other areas. The earliest settlers of what would become the United States were British and Scottish, and the folk songs of that heritage were to have a dominant influence on southern rural music. Between 1916 and 1918 folk song scholar Cecil Sharp spent forty-six weeks in the mountain areas of Tennessee, Kentucky, Virginia, West Virginia, and North Carolina, and found that, "Singing was almost as universal a practice as speaking. Country people adapted the folk music of their ancestors so that it became more meaningful to them, changing names and towns to fit their environment. References to the supernatural were often omitted and sexual improprieties were censored. The songs they sang came from three primary sources:

Library of Congress

Music from the backwoods was made by family members to entertain themselves and their neighbors. The Puritan settlers brought with them instruments such as fiddles (as the violin is called in country and folk music). Religious songs and British and Scottish ballads were preserved for longer periods of time in areas that were cut off from industrialization.

1. Native old-time religion, with its emphasis on the fundamentalist concept that life was difficult on earth, but if one was religious, one would be rewarded in the "afterlife."

2. European ballads—the British and Scottish folk songs. The best-known collections are Cecil Sharp's *English Folk Songs From the Southern Appalachians* (1917) and *Nursery Songs From the Appalachian Mountains* (1923), and Francis James Child's *English and Scottish Popular Ballads* (1882), a five-volume study of 305 folk songs with a multitude of variations for each.

3. Show business, including songs derived from an earlier period of blackface minstrelsy together with Civil War ballads and other popular songs of the day. Many of these were first performed by the traveling medicine shows, ubiquitious throughout the South.

Once instruments were introduced, the modal scale was abandoned. Modes were derived from the natural acoustics of the human voice and were predominate in early folk music. Harmony singing was established and church singing became an intregal part of the southern experience. The white song pattern of the South included:

1) Solo voice, usually with nasal tone and rigid pitch;

2) Simple melodies with emphasis upon the telling of a story and the use of refrain; and

3) Eventual introduction of instruments like banjo, fiddle, and guitar for accompainment.

The folk music of the South was based on the Anglo-Saxon traditions of religious song, children's song, play-party song, agrarian song, and the ballad. The most intensively studied folk song was the ballad. The literary analogue of the ballad is the short story. Folklorists recognize three types of English-language ballads: Child, broadside, and native. These types of ballads dominated the nonreligious

Ballad + short story

music preferred by rural singers of the South. The Child ballads were collected by noted Chaucerian scholar Francis James Child.

About one third are still sung in the United States, and those who sing them usually have little notion that they are of English or Scottish origin. Many of the early country artists, especially the solo performers like Bradley Kincaid, Kelly Harrell, Dock Boggs, Clarence Ashley, and Buell Kazee,—performed a repertoire of old-time traditional songs, many of which were Child ballads.

The folk revival of the 1950s and 1960s, led by the Kingston Trio, and later, Joan Baez and Judy Collins, was heavily influenced by the Child ballads. Titles such as "The Cherry Tree" and "Barbara Allen" (Baez) and "Pretty Polly" (Collins) are examples. Perhaps the most celebrated of the rural purists has been Kentucky native **Jean Ritchie** (1922-) who describes the hill country culture of the first wave of immigrants from England, Scotland, Wales, and Ireland in her 1955 book *Singing Family of the Cumberlands*. Ritchie tells of the hard life tending the cornfield, and all family members pitching in to create a working and living environment. Evenings were spent singing and playing banjos, dulcimers, guitars, and fiddles. Songs were passed down orally and

Jean Ritchie with dulcimer, an instrument widely used in the Kentucky region. It is of German origin, very delicate, and with a tinny sound. Solo performers often used the instrument; its weak volume made it unsuitable for ensembles. Women favored the dulcimer and the autoharp and were especially fond of ballad material. During the folk revival of the 1950s and 1960s artists like Joni Mitchell occasionally played the dulcimer.

Jean Ritchie learned the ballad "The Golden Vanity" (Child 286) from her mother. It was a romantic ballad about a defeated hero, a ship named the "The Golden Vanity," a cabin boy offering to sink an enemy ship. The captain of "The Golden Vanity" offers his daughter if the boy succeeds. The boy swims to the other ship and bores holes in the hull, causing it to sink. As he swims back, the captain, from his vantage of power, capriciously rescinds his offer and the cabin boy drowns. In some variants the cabin boy is amply rewarded. In others he takes his revenge by returning to sink the captain's ship. Jean Ritchie's version was titled "The Merry Golden Tree," and it carries neither the sad nor the happy ending. Ritchie's clear, but adorned voice merely reports the lad's successful deed.

ballads such as "Fair Ellender," "Lord Bateman," "The Cuckoo," as well as native songs and play-party tunes were particular favorites that remained in the family's repertoire.

Scholar M. J. C. Hodgart divided the Child ballads into five general categories, of which only the romantic and tragic ballads appeared with any regularity in the New World. Hodgart's contention is that the great majority of the American Child ballads are of two types: morality or romance. In both forms there is a simple dramatic movement from an internal conflict to its resolution. In a morality pattern, like "The Two Sisters," action begins because of a violation of a law, taboo, or common sense; it is ended by the imposition of an appropriate punishment; in the end, the ugly sister who kills her more attractive sibling-rival winds up paying for her crime at the stake. The most popular form of American Child ballad was the romantic song, which begins with the separation of lovers and usually ends in reunification.

The second category of ballads, broadside ballads, emanated from the printing presses of the eighteenth and nineteenth centuries. In Britian and colonial America, publishers widely and cheaply sold song texts printed on single sheets of paper (broadsides). The texts often described newsworthy events and headnotes sometimes suggested commonly known tunes to which the words could be sung. The broadside precipitated the sheet music of Tin Pan Alley.

Some Popular Child Ballads

Ballad #	Song Titles
2	Whittingham Fair; Scarborough Fair
4	False Sir John; Lady Isabel and the Elf-Knight; Pretty Polly
7	Sweet William; Earl Brand
10	The Cruel Sister; The Two Sisters
54	The Cherry Tree Carol; The Cherry Tree
73	Lord Thomas and Fair Eleanor; Fair Ellender
84	Barbry Ellen; Barbara Allen
147	Robin Hood's Golden Prize
200	Gypsy Laddie
247	The House Carpenter
286	The Golden Vanity; The Merry Golden Tree; The Sweet Kumadee

---

Library of Congress

Joan Baez began her folksinging career in the Boston area in the late 1950s, playing coffeehouses such as the Golden Vanity, the Ballad Room, and Club 47. She gained wider recognition by appearing at the 1959 Newport Folk Festival and recording a series of LPs on Vanguard Records beginning in 1960. Baez was hailed as the "Queen of the Folksingers," presenting lovely versions of traditional folk ballads such as "Silkie" (Child 113), "The Cherry Tree Carol" (Child 54), and "Barbara Allen" (Child 84). Like Jean Ritchie, Baez followed the accepted course of singing the older, traditional repertoire. A couple of years later Baez would move into the protest tradition of Bob Dylan and Phil Ochs. During the late 1960s European folk rockers like Pentangle and Steeleye Span would rework the older ballads into their repertoires. A thorough investigation of the Cambridge and Boston folk music scene is covered in Eric Von Schmidt and Jim Rooney's *Baby Let Me Follow You Down.*

The third type of ballads common in the United States were the native ballads, which were often songs about actual events. Songs like "Lilly Schull," "Naomi Wise," and "Tom Dooley" (the latter was a top hit for the Kingston Trio in 1958) recounted real-life murders. With the advent of the commercial period of country music, which began with the release of the first country records in the early 1920s, the native ballads were referred to as event songs. Popular with audiences, they combined the topicality of the broadside with the native recounting of actual events. For example, country artist Vernon Dalhart sang about such contemporary topics as "The John T. Scopes Trial" and "The Death of Floyd Collins."

Early Commercial Music

The emergence of the phonograph record industry and the radio in the 1920s enabled country music to be commercialized. The music was not called country and western until the late forties. Instead, record companies referred to the music as "old time tunes," "hill country melodies" and "hillbilly." Enterprising record company talent scouts began combing the South, announcing their arrivals in local newspapers, explaining that they were seeking talent to record. The talent scouts were much like the folk song collectors who preceded them, except that instead of writing down the songs, they used recording machines. Ralph S. Peer, Frank Walker, Art Satherley, and Eli Oberstein are a few of the outstanding scouts who recorded early country performers.

Ralph S. Peer (1892-1960) had supervised Mamie Smith's successful "Crazy Blues" session in 1920, which led to the popularity of the "race record" market. From 1923 to 1932 Peer made numerous trips into southern cities: Nashville, Memphis, Charlotte, New Orleans, El Paso, Bristol, and others, recording hundreds of blues, gospel, jazz, and country artists. In 1923 Peer was in Atlanta, Georgia, and recorded the state fiddling champion, Fiddlin' John Carson. Peer thought little of the odd-sounding music, but furniture dealer Polk Brockman (even into the 1960s, furniture stores were big sellers of records) bought the entire pressing of the Carson songs, selling it all as well as a number of repressings. At this point Peer realized that there was an audience for what could eventually be called country music.

Okeh Records titled its country music releases "Old Time Tunes." This advertisement features some of that company's stars of the 1920s. Henry Whitter and John Carson are described in the text. Ernest V. Stoneman performed solo but was better known for his group performances with the Cornshuckers, and with his family group, where he often went by the name "Pop." The Jenkins Family of Atlanta, Georgia, was centered on the talent of Andrew Jenkins, who was often billed as the "Blind Radio Poet" and "The Blind Newsboy Evangelist." One of Jenkins best-known made-to-order ballads, "The Death of Floyd Collins" (1925) came directly from the headlines of the daily newspapers. It told the story of a young coal miner from Kentucky who eventually died after being entombed for several days in a cave-in. Years later, in 1951, director-writer Billy Wilder made a film based on the incident. *The Big Carnival*, also titled *Ace in the Hole*, starred Kirk Douglas as a hard-boiled reporter who deliberately delays rescue operations so that his story will make national headlines.

Roba Stanley (1910-1986) is credited with making country music's first solo female record at the age of fourteen. She was the daughter of a Georgia fiddle champion, Roba Stanley, and backed her father at square dances, tours, and WSB radio programs. In 1924 Stanley played guitar and sang on selections such as "Devilish Mary," "All Night Long," and "Little Frankie." The next year she recorded with Henry Whitter ("Old Maid Blues" and "Single Life"). The feminist stance on her song "Single Life" ("I am single and no man's wife and no man shall control me") is strong stuff for its time, especially in the rural South. But the sentiments of that song were not to be realized because shortly after that recording, at age fifteen, Stanley married, never to record again. Stanley's husband disapproved of her playing in public.

Frank Walker (1890-1965), who joined the Columbia Phonograph Company in 1921, helped establish the special 15000 catalogue series, which never used the term "hillbilly." Walker's choice, "Old Familiar Tunes" was later changed to "Songs of the Hills and Plains," and finally just "Country." Country and western music was given a variety of different titles during the early commercial periods. Columbia Records used the designation "Old Familiar Tunes" in this ad of Gid Tanner and the Skillet Lickers with Riley Puckett. Note the iconography of the peaceful homestead situated in an idyllic setting, a warm, friendly reflection of home and hearth. Walker is credited as the first representative of a major record company to record traditional country music. He also recorded blues artists such as Bessie Smith on the Columbia 14000 race series. Walker carried wax disk masters in a Model T Ford or by horse and muleback to remote rural hamlets. Key country artists he recorded for Columbia included Gid Tanner, Riley Puckett, Clarence Ashley, and Charlie Poole. In 1933 Walker joined RCA Victor, where he set up a low-cost line called Bluebird. In 1945 Walker started a new major label, MGM. In 1947 he signed Hank Williams, who went on to become a country legend.

Art Satherley (1889-1986) began producing records in 1923. Later in the 1920s he joined Plaza Music, which became the American Recording Corporation (ARC), which was absorbed into Columbia Records in 1939. Satherley specialized in the underground forms of black blues and hillbilly music. Satherley, affectionately known as "Uncle Art," signed Gene Autry, Roy Acuff, Bob Wills, the Light Crust Doughboys, the Prairie Ramblers, the Hoosier Hot Shots, Hank Penny, Al Dexter, Ted Daffan, and many other country artists. Satherley was inducted into the Country Music Hall of Fame in 1971.

Southern Folklife Collection, University of North Carolina

Ralph S. Peer and country music. Left to right: Jimmie Rodgers, Mrs. Peer, Ralph Peer, Mrs. Carrie Rodgers, and, front, Anita Rodgers. This picture was taken in 1931 at Jimmie Rodgers's home in Kerrville, Texas, which was near a tuberculosis sanitarium. Rodgers's frail health led to his move to Texas. Rodgers called the mansion "Blue Yodeler's Paradise" and much of the success the singer achieved was the direct result of the man who first signed him to a record contract in the summer of 1927, Ralph Sylvester Peer. After Peer helped establish "race records" for Okeh in 1920, he began recording various country artists, most importantly Fiddlin' John Carson, whose early releases Peer thought to be "plu-perfect awful."

By 1927 Peer had worked out a deal with the Victor Recording Company that gave him the right to sign artists to his own publishing company in lieu of a salary. Peer realized he would make his money on original songs by artists he signed when he went to Bristol, Tennessee, to hold auditions in August 1927. He was seeking country performers who wrote their own material. The famous "Bristol Sessions" resulted in his signing the Carter Family and Jimmie Rodgers within a three-day period. Both became members of his Southern Music Publishing Company, associated with ASCAP. Peer would later be affiliated with Broadcast Music Incorporated (BMI). Peer regarded Sara Carter's voice as the outstanding feature of the Carter clan. He also became friendly with Jimmie Rodgers. However, Peer merely tolerated country music. His real love was flowers and horticulture. In *Country: The Music and the Musicians* Nolan Porterfield observes, "Peer was the product of an urban, cultivated background, in an era when the lines between social classes were far more rigidly drawn than they are today. All his life he seems to have resented the fact that his money and reputation derived from the work of crusty old fiddlers, rustic balladeers, and yodeling roustabouts."

The early country entertainers were usually the better-known fiddlers, banjoists, or singers in a given area. The state fiddling conventions were one of the best ways to find some of the more accomplished regional talent. The fiddlers spent much time devising special routines so that they might stand out from the competition. Fiddlin' John Carson, Gid Tanner, G. B. Grayson, and Eck Robertson, all fiddlers who played at these conventions, were among the first to make country records. Most of these early recording "hillbilly" or "folk" artists were not able to sustain themselves as full-time entertainers. This period of the 1920s and 1930s was described by John Edwards of Australia as the "Golden Age of Hillbilly Music." Edwards, called "the most prolific hillbilly-record collector, and possibly the most informed," by Bill Malone, felt that this early period was untouched by a commercial slickness that would, in his opinion, later taint the folklore aspects of the earlier string band traditions.

Eck Robertson (1887-1975), a champion old-time fiddler from Amarillo, Texas, may have been the first country artist to record, as well as the first to perform on the radio. In June 1922, he and Henry Gilliland, a fiddler from Virginia, traveled to New York unannounced and recorded some selections for the Victor Talking Machine Company (renamed RCA Victor in 1929). "Sally Goodin," one of the releases from that first session, became a song associated with Robertson throughout his career. In March 1923 Robertson played "Sally Goodin" and "Arkansas Traveler" over radio station WBAP, making him one of the earliest performers to promote his own records over the air waves. Victor did not market the record (Robertson did not record again until 1930) and it wasn't until Fiddlin' John Carson's record came out that country music gained the attention of the phonograph industry.

Library of Congress

Judges and observers watch as fiddlers compete at a West Virginia contest in 1926.

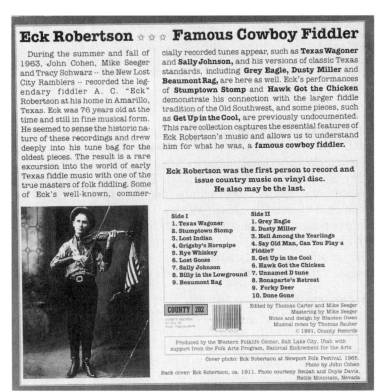

Eck Robertson ☆ ☆ ☆ Famous Cowboy Fiddler

During the summer and fall of 1963, John Cohen, Mike Seeger and Tracy Schwarz -- the New Lost City Ramblers -- recorded the legendary fiddler A. C. "Eck" Robertson at his home in Amarillo, Texas. Eck was 76 years old at the time and still in fine musical form. He seemed to sense the historic nature of these recordings and drew deeply into his tune bag for the oldest pieces. The result is a rare excursion into the world of early Texas fiddle music with one of the true masters of folk fiddling. Some of Eck's well-known, commer-

cially recorded tunes appear, such as **Texas Wagoner** and **Sally Johnson**, and his versions of classic Texas standards, including **Grey Eagle, Dusty Miller** and **Beaumont Rag**, are here as well. Eck's performances of **Stumptown Stomp** and **Hawk Got the Chicken** demonstrate his connection with the larger fiddle tradition of the Old Southwest, and some pieces, such as **Get Up in the Cool**, are previously undocumented. This rare collection captures the essential features of Eck Robertson's music and allows us to understand him for what he was, a **famous cowboy fiddler.**

Eck Robertson was the first person to record and issue country music on vinyl disc.
He also may be the last.

Side I
1. Texas Wagoner
2. Stumptown Stomp
3. Lost Indian
4. Grigsby's Hornpipe
5. Rye Whiskey
6. Lost Goose
7. Sally Johnson
8. Billy in the Lowground
9. Beaumont Rag

Side II
1. Grey Eagle
2. Dusty Miller
3. Hell Among the Yearlings
4. Say Old Man, Can You Play a Fiddle?
5. Get Up in the Cool
6. Hawk Got the Chicken
7. Unnamed D tune
8. Bonaparte's Retreat
9. Forky Deer
10. Done Gone

COUNTY 202

COUNTY RECORDS
PO Box 191
Floyd, Virginia 24091

Edited by Thomas Carter and Mike Seeger
Mastering by Mike Seeger
Notes and design by Blanton Owen
Musical notes by Thomas Sauber
© 1991, County Records

Produced by the Western Folklife Center, Salt Lake City, Utah with support from the Folk Arts Program, National Endowment for the Arts

Cover photo: Eck Robertson at Newport Folk Festival, 1965.
Photo by John Cohen
Back cover: Eck Robertson, ca. 1911. Photo courtesy Beulah and Doyle Davis, Battle Mountain, Nevada.

Courtesy County Records

The record says: "Eck Robertson was the first person to record and issue country music on vinyl disc."

Fiddlin' John Carson (1868-1949) would become the first successful country artist, and his record sales would encourage other companies to seek out country talent and record it. Carson performed rustic, down-home tunes that appealed to rural listeners. Releases like "Little Old Log Cabin in the Lane" (the first commercial country release, in 1923), "The Old Hen Cackled and the Rooster's Going to Crow," "It's a Shame to Whip Your Wife on Sunday," "You Can't Get Milk From a Cow Named Ben," "The Farmer Is the Man That Feeds Them All," "Who Bit the Wart off Grandma's Nose?" and "What You Gonna Do When Your Licker Runs Out?" were some of Carson's more popular ditties. He recorded over 150 sides as a member of the Virginia Reelers.

Carson is significant not because he was "better" than the other fiddler-singers, but because his were the first conscious attempts to program music toward a rural audience with the help of a record company promoting the effort. Carson is a prime example of a local musician who gained added status by placing the words "Recording Artist" above his name on his announcement posters and on his touring car. He often performed with his daughter, who was billed as "Moonshine Kate." Carson stopped touring after 1934, and spent his last years running an elevator at the Georgia State Capitol. He received that job in thanks for campaign songs he wrote and sang for Gov. Herman Talmadge, the most famous being "Georgia's Three Dollar Tag."

Fiddlin' John Carson performed one of the first documented solo performance by a country artist over the radio when he fiddled on Atlanta's WSB in September 1922.

Early country stars: Fiddlin' John Carson and Henry Whitter.

Unlike the musical forms of pop, jazz, and blues, country music has had very little historical writing about its early development. Not until Bill Malone's *Country Music USA* was published in 1968 was there a universally acclaimed history on the music. *Fiddlin' Georgia Crazy: Fiddlin' John Carson, His Real World, and the World of His Songs* by Gene Wiggins (1987) is one of the few biographies of a country music artist of the early period. While researching Carson's life, Wiggins discovered that there was not enough information available for a detailed history and admitted, "It is not possible to give much of an account of John Carson's nineteenth-century life." The book ended up being part biography and part songbook and song study. Of particular interest is Wiggins's analysis of Carson's recorded repertoire of 121 numbers. The author set up seven categories: 1) Pre-twentieth-century folk songs, 2) fiddle tunes, 3) minstrel-show tunes, 4) Nineteenth-century popular songs, 5) Twentieth-century popular songs, 6) Twentieth-century folk songs, and 7) religious songs. The largest grouping was that of twentieth-century folk songs (over a third), while the smallest was that of the religious songs (just eight).

Left, Henry Whitter; right, George Grayson.

Henry Whitter (1892-1941), from Virginia, worked in cotton mills and recorded before Carson. However his records were not issued until after Carson's success. Whitter's first release, in December 1923, was a song he learned from a fellow mill hand in 1914, "The Wreck on the Southern Old 97." This selection was backed with "Lonesome Road Blues." Whitter formed a successful partnership with southern fiddler George Grayson. Whitter is exemplary for his cross-pollination of recorded works, for which he was amply rewarded (even enabling him to buy a Model T Ford in 1924). Whitter's repertoire included among other styles, British ballads such as "George Collins," "The Butcher Boy," and "Rose Conley," native ballads like "Ellen Smith" and "New River Train" and minstrel coon songs such as "Keep My Skillet Good and Greasy" and "Watermelon Hanging on the Vine".

On "The Wreck on the Old Southern 97" Whitter sang and accompanied himself with guitar and harmonica. His use of a wire neck rack for his harmonica was later emulated by a young Bob Dylan, who began singing in Greenwich Village clubs in the early 1960s.

Library of Congress

Buell Kazee with banjo and Bible at the ready. Kazee was a religious man who preached and collected traditional songs, which he performed outside religious settings. He played piano and guitar as well as banjo and sang cowboy songs ("The Roving Cowboy"), roustabout tunes ("Hobo's Last Ride"), ballads ("The Wagoner Lad"), and religious songs ("Amazing Grace" and "The White Pilgrim").

Henry Whitter was just one of many musicians who, for decades, preserved oral renditions of the traditional songs characteristic of rural southern music. Bill Malone (*Country Music USA*), contends that, "The commercial hillbilly recordings of the twenties provide one of the most fertile fields of investigation for folklorists, since the early hillbillies were the first white folk musicians to be commercially recorded in the United States."

A majority of the early hillbilly recordings were folk songs that had been passed down from generation to generation. Clarence Ashley gained notoriety by singing and playing rousing five-string banjo renditions of old British ballads such as "The Coo Coo Bird" and "The House Carpenter." Kelly Herrell was another traditionalist who recorded British-Scottish classics such as "Charles Guiteau" and "Cuckoo, She's a Pretty Bird." And Bascom Lamar Lunsford, the "Minstrel of the Appalachians," preserved folk songs and started the first country music festival (in Asheville, North Carolina).

Buell Kazee (1900-1976) was a Kentucky-born ordained minister who graduated from Georgetown College of Kentucky, where he gave a number of folk music recitals. As an English major he was interested in Elizabethan literature, which fired his curiosity about the ballads he had known as a boy. Kazee became an avid collector of folk songs and, when not tending to his duties as church pastor, he performed in public. Kazee eventually settled down to a twenty-two- year tenure as pastor of the First Baptist Church in Morehead, Kentucky, and he also had a long career as a country music artist.

Certainly one of the most fascinating stories in all of country music is that of Vernon Dalhart. A performer that only the most avid country music history buff has ever heard of, Dalhart would have been crowned the "Father of Country Music," instead of Jimmie Rodgers, if he hadn't been so intent on being recognized as a more respectable artist (in his case, an opera and operetta singer). It is estimated that Dalhart made more recordings (five thousand) than any other country artist. The fact that he was embarrassed by country music led him to use over a hundred pseudonyms, thus resulting in the obscurity of his country music successes.

In his later years Dalhart's resume mentioned his rave reviews in opera and operetta, but not one word was given to his associations with country music. During the 1930s, after his recording career had faded, Dalhart created the radio voice of "Sam, the Barbasol Man." This added to his income but not his prestige. Dalhart's last years were spent in Bridgeport, Connecticut, where he worked part time as a night watchman and hotel clerk at the Barnum Hotel. During this time he also advertised for "Voice placing-professional coaching." Walter Darrell Hayden, Dalhart's biographer, states, "Before Chicago studio broadcast experiments were about to become the WLS National Barn Dance and well before the show could develop a country recording star with any sort of national following, Dalhart had millions of country records sold around the world."

VERNON DALHART

Southern Folklife Collection, University of North Carolina

Library of Congress

Thomas Hart Benton's classic painting of the "Wreck of the Old 97." Henry Whitter's song, "The Wreck on the Southern Old 97," was based on Henry Work's melody for "The Ship That Never Returned." Whitter's adaptation was inspired by a train that was traveling from Lynchburg to Danville, Virginia at ninety miles an hour. It crashed, resulting in the death of the engineer at the throttle. The final words of the song give the moral: "Never speak harsh words to your husband/He may leave you and never return." The Kingston Trio sang an altered version of this in 1959 ("M.T.A."), about a man who rides forever "'Neath the streets of Boston/He's the man who never returns."

Kazee's dry and mournful readings of British ballads such as "The Wagoner Lad," "The Butcher's Boy," and "Lady Gay" proved to be popular with the secular audiences of the South. Charles Seeger, father of folksinger Pete and a noted musicologist, referred to Kazee's "Lady Gay" as "about the finest variant of 'The Wife of Usher's Well' that has ever been sung." In 1941 Kazee wrote a book titled *Faith Is the Victory*, and by 1950 had moved over to Lexington Baptist College as professor of Old Testament studies. During the folk revival of the 1950s Kazee was introduced to a newer audience—the urban folk community. Folkways Records made Kazee's work available to this audience with the LP, *Buell H. Kazee, His Songs and Music* (1959).

Southern Folklife Collection, University of North Carolina

Frank Driggs Collection

One of the earliest "picture discs" in country music history, by Vernon Dalhart (date unkown). Dalhart was the best-selling artist of country records. His vocal style was rather stiff and formal compared to most of the rural singers, but his records were well produced. In addition to the sentimental songs Dalhart released a number of "event" songs that were in the folk tradition of the broadside ballads: "The Death of Floyd Collins" and "The Sinking of the Titanic" stand out. In many ways this light opera singer, who had made New York his home, was an outsider who used country music as a way of keeping his career afloat. Today we would label such attempts "crossover," not unlike the music of Olivia Newton-John, John Denver, and Kenny Rogers during the 1970s.

History shows that Vernon Dalhart was not initially interested in "down home" music. His first record release was in 1916 for the Columbia label entitled "Just a World of Sympathy," a sentimental weeper. In 1917, as a result of a successful audition for Thomas Edison, Dalhart recorded his first hit, "Can't Yo Hea'h Me Calling Caroline," for Edison's Diamond Disc label. For a period of time, until 1924, Dalhart released nothing but sentimental pop ballads and light opera, until his record sales dropped and he decided to turn to "hillbilly" material.

Author's collection

Grandaddy of the Hillbillies. One of the early commercial songwriters in country music, **Carson Robison** (1890-1957), for years provided a series of hits for Vernon Dalhart. Dalhart's "The John T. Scopes Trial" and "The Sinking of the Titanic" were penned by Robison. After leaving Dalhart this composer-singer-whistler formed his own group, the Buckaroos, followed by the Carson Trio, and finally the Pleasant Valley Boys. Robison was affectionately known as the "Granddaddy of the Hillbillies." When he performed in England, Robison was billed as "Radio's Hillbilly King."

The Kansas-born entertainer settled in the Pleasant Valley region of New York, where he helped build a strong following for country music in the East with his pioneering efforts on radio throughout the 1940s and 1950s. Robison's best-known compositions include "My Blue Ridge Mountain Home," "Carry Me Back to the Lone Prairie," "Goin' Back to Texas," "Barnacle Bill the Sailor," and "Life Gets Tee-Jus, Don't It?" During the last year of his life Robison even flirted with rock'n'roll by recording "Rockin' and Rollin' with Grandmaw."

Some of Vernon Dalhart's Pseudonyms

Dalhart recorded as: James Ahern, John Albin, Mack Allen, Wolfe Ballard, James Belmont, Harry Blake, Harry Britt, Billy Burton, Jeff Calhoun, Jess Calhoun, Jimmy Cannon, Jimmy Cantrell, Ed Clifford, Al Cramer, Al Carver, James Cummings, Frank Dalbert, Frank Dalhart, Vernon Dall, Charles Dalton, Vernon Dell, Hugh Donovan, Joseph Elliot, Frank Evans, Clifford Ford, Jeff Fuller, Jep Fuller, Albert Gordon, Leslie Gray, David Harris, Harry Harris, Francis Harold, Lou Hays, Fern Holmes, Howard Hull, Frank Hutchinson, Joe Kincaid, Fred King, Louis Lane, Hugh Latimer, Hugh Lattimore, Tobe Little, The Lone Star Ranger, Bob Massey, Guy Massey, B. McAfee, Bob McAfee, Carlos B. McAfee, Warren Mitchell, George Morbid, Dick Morse, Mr. X, Charles Nelson, Gwyrick O'-Hara, Sam Peters, Joseph Smith, Josephus Smith, Cliff Stewart, Edward Stone, Howard Stone, Billy Stuart, Will Terry, the Texas Tenor, Bob Thomas, Al Turner, Allen Turner, Sid Turner, Bill Vernon, Billy Vernon, Herbert Vernon, Bal Veteral, Bel Veteran, Tom Watson, Bob White, Bobby White, Robert White, Walter Whitlock, and George Woods.

Groups Dalhart recorded with : Allen & Parker, Arkansas Travelers, Arkansas Trio, Ballard & Samuels, Barbary Coast Four, Birmingham Blue Bugles, Broadway Quartet, Calhoun & Andrews, California Ramblers, Cramer Brothers, Dalhart's Big Cypress Boys, Dalhart's Texas Panhandlers, Domino Quartet, Evans & Clark(e), Harmony Four, Jewel Trio, Archie Ruff Singers, Jones Brothers, Kanawha Singers, Ladd's Black Aces, Mitchell & White, Oriole Trio, Fred Ozark's Jug Blowers, Peters & Jones, Regal Rascals, Archie Ruff Singers, Salt & Pepper, Virginians, Windy City Duo, and Windy City Jazzes.

Pseudonym	Song Title
Mack Allen	At Father Power's Grave
Harry Britt	Hide Me Always in the Hills of Virginia
Al Carver	Sentenced to Life Behind These Gray Walls
Fern Holmes (singing as a woman)	There's a New Star in Heaven Tonight - Rudolph Valentino
Walter Hyde	You're in Kentucky, Sure as You're Born
Hugh Latimer	Pick Me Up and Lay Me Down in Dear Old Dixieland
Tobe Little	Picture That Is Turned Towards the Wall
Warren Mitchell	Alabamy Blacksheep
Dick Morse	It Ain't Gonna Rain No More
Mr. X	Just a Girl That Men Forget
Sid Turner	Go 'Long Mule
Tom Watson	Wish That I Was Single

Source: Chet Hagan, Country Music Legends in the Hall of Fame, *and Walter Darrell Haden,* The Journal of Country Music

Vernon Dalhart (1881-1941), born Marion Try Slaughter in Jefferson, Texas, would sell more recordings than any of the early country artists. He probably would have been labeled the father of country music if he hadn't felt embarrassed by his association with "hillbilly songs." Dalhart attended the Dallas Conservatory of Music, then moved to New York, where he performed light opera for numerous organizations, including the Century Opera Company. In 1912 he had a part in Puccini's *Girl of the Golden West*, and in 1913-14 he was included in Gilbert and Sullivan productions. Dalhart recorded numerous operatic arias and patriotic World War I songs as well as popular songs. One day, when his career had begun to take a downward slide, Dalhart decided to record some country songs.

In 1924 Dalhart recorded "The Wreck of the Old 97" (he changed the title slightly) and "The Prisoner's Song" for Victor. The record became a massive hit, becoming the topselling record of that year. It is estimated that it sold over six million copies. This is the first country recording to sell a million records. Walter Darrell Haden states, "Vernon Dalhart failed to use any part of his legal name on any of his more than 5,000 recordings released between 1916 and 1938. Instead, his recordings for every major and minor label (and their subsidiaries) east of the Mississippi River competed with one another under more than 110 different names." Dalhart saw his career in country music as a mere stop on the way back to success in opera and operetta, which he held in higher esteem.

The String Bands

Before the well-known singers like Jimmie Rodgers and the Carter Family became stars, the most prevalent form of rural music was that made by the string bands. The preferred instrument of the early English and Scottish settlers was the fiddle. The banjo, autoharp, mandolin, and guitar were introduced into the homes of the rural settlers later. Collective ensembles performed at house parties and dances, and when record companies came looking for local talent, many of these units auditioned.

These groups performed religious songs, blues, sentimental tunes, dance numbers, and novelty items, and were the forerunners of the bluegrass music of later years. Often these groups used bizarre and colorful names such as Gunboat Billy and the Sparrows, Wilmer Watts and the Lonely Eagles, Birds's Kentucky Crackers, Ephriam Woodie and His Henpecked Husbands, Seven Foot Dilly and His Dill

Pickles, the Fruit Jar Drinkers, Dr. Smith's Champion Hoss Hair Pullers, Doctor Humphrey Bate and His Possum Hunters, and Fisher Hendley and his Aristocratic Pigs, to list a few.

Al Hopkins' Hill Billies. The original Hill Billies, from left, were John Rector, banjo; Al Hopkins, piano; Joe Hopkins, guitar; Tony Alderman, fiddle. This group is considered the source of the name "hillbilly," for early country music. The first "Elvis" in music was not Presley but the talented trick-playing fiddler of the Hill Billies, Tony "Elvis" Alderman. The group recorded as the Hill Billies for Vocalion and as Al Hopkins and His Buckle Busters for Brunswick. Many rural players took umbrage at the term hillbilly, feeling it was a condescending reference to back hills and ignorant rednecks. Out in California, a group led by accordionist Zeke Manners took on the name the Beverly Hillbillies in 1928. The California group was a hit on the West Coast with their strange looking outfits and primitive sounding music. Their act was part music and part comedy. This group, unlike the original group from the East, made a number of motion pictures and gained some national acclaim. In 1963, some former members sued and won a settlement from the television producers of *The Beverly Hillbillies* for name infringement.

One of the earliest groups to record as a working string band was **Al Hopkins' Hill Billies** (1925-1933). In Galax, Virginia, during the spring of 1924, a barber by the name of Alonzo "Elvis" Alderman was cutting a customer's hair when he noticed a man walking down the street with a guitar. The young man was Joe Hopkins, a railway express agent from White Top Gap, Virginia. Alderman, who was called Tony, had played French horn in his father's Dixieland band but had recently been turned on to the fiddle. Business was slow, so Alderman accosted Hopkins and then raced home to get his instrument. Alderman and Hopkins sat down and made music together. Eventually, Hopkins's brother Al joined the twosome. News of the musical sessions reached John Rector, a general shopkeeper who played banjo. The young musicians decided to form a group.

Rector had just returned from New York, where he made three records for Okeh with Henry Whitter's Virginia Breakdowners. A few days later Rector and the newly formed quartet went to the same Okeh recording studio to cut their own record. They had to play into a large horn, which was the recording microphone. For some reason they couldn't hear each other very well, and the other three, being novices in the studio, got nervous. The first session was a bust. The next year, recording in the same studio, things improved. The boys were able to stand next to and hear each other better, because the industry had converted to new electronic recording equipment.

The recording supervisor at the 1925 session was none other than Ralph S. Peer. The as-yet unnamed group cut six sides with Alderman on fiddle, Rector on banjo, Joe Hopkins on guitar, and the leader, Al Hopkins, on piano. When Peer asked the group what their name was, the leader, who was unprepared, blurted out, "We're nothing but a bunch of hillbillies from North Carolina and Virginia. Call us anything." Peer told his secretary to list "Hill Billies" on her ledger slips for the six selections. From that moment on much of the recorded music by string bands from rural regions was referred to as "hillbilly" music.

Southern Folklife Collection, University of North Carolina

The First Country Music Elvis. Tony "Elvis" Alderman, left, with Charlie Bowman in 1927, when they were members of the Hill Billies. The gimmick of trick fiddle playing (in this case, playing each other's instruments) was a big crowd pleaser and survives to this day. The best-known group to include this fun in their stage performance is the southern rock band Alabama.

Southern Folklife Collection, University of North Carolina

An ad for records by Gid Tanner and Riley Puckett declares, "No Southerner can hear them and go away without them. And it will take a pretty hard-shelled yankee to leave them."

Gid Tanner (1885-1960) and **Riley Puckett** (1884-1946) were also early leaders of this newly recorded music. They called themselves the Skillet Lickers. Tanner, a fiddler from Georgia, was one of John Carson's principal rivals at Atlanta fiddling contests. He was a fine entertainer who played traditional folk songs and fiddle tunes of the nineteenth century. Tanner's guitar player was Riley Puckett, who was accidently blinded at birth. Puckett made his radio debut in 1922 with fiddler Clayton McMichen's Hometown Boys on station WSB.

GID TANNER AND HIS SKILLET-LICKERS
WITH RILEY PUCKETT

GID TANNER also has his own dance orchestras, known as "Gid Tanner and His Skillet-Lickers" and "Gid Tanner and His Georgia Boys."

No country dance down in Gid's part of the country is considered complete unless Gid and his pals furnish the music.

BULLY OF THE TOWN
PASS AROUND THE
BOTTLE AND WE'LL
ALL TAKE A DRINK

15074-D
10-inch
75c

GID TANNER AND HIS SKILLET-LICKERS
WITH RILEY PUCKETT

Southern Folklife Collection, University of North Carolina

Riley Puckett gained his greatest claim to fame as a member of the "all star" unit the Skillet Lickers, put together by Frank Walker in 1926. Clayton McMichen's jazzy fiddling and Gid Tanner's old-timey fiddling techniques along with Tanner's natural bent for comedy mixed well with Puckett's advanced guitar runs and lead voice. McMichen claimed that it was Puckett's singing that "put them over." Puckett was the first singer of note to establish the yodel on record (Jimmie Rodgers made it popular). And Puckett was the first guitarist of note to play melodic lines on the bass string of the guitar (Maybelle Carter popularized the technique and over the years it was referred to as the "Mother Maybelle lick").

As a solo artist, Riley Puckett recorded traditional items ("Ragged But Right") and popular songs ("When I Grow Too Old to Dream"), traveled the South with his own tent show, and appeared on numerous radio programs. Unfortunately Puckett never had the kind of success his talent deserved. In *The Illustrated History of Country Music* Charles Wolf asserts, "If one discounts citybilly singers like Vernon Dalhart, Riley Puckett was the first genuine country singing star. He made numerous records with just himself and his guitar, and many approached hit status; he and Vernon Dalhart dominated Columbia's early country music charts. After he left the Skillet Lickers, he began to record for Victor, but, unlike Jimmie Rodgers, he was never really able to attract a national audience."

RILEY PUCKETT

Southern Folklife Collection, University of North Carolina

Puckett teamed with Tanner and McMichen in the Skillet Lickers. All three sang, but it was Puckett's baritone that stood out. Puckett's first record, "Rock All Our Babies to Sleep" (1924), is regarded as having the first influential yodel on record. Puckett's single-note guitar melodies played on the bass string presaged Maybelle Carter's technique, and his use of double- and quadruple-time runs behind the fiddlers was advanced for its time. The Skillet Lickers signed with Columbia Records in 1924 and split up in 1931. During that time they released some eighty sides and were one of the most popular string bands in the nation, recording a variety of styles. "A Corn Likker Still in Georgia" was a playlet—a song story intermixed with comic dialogue-that proved so popular it inspired a series of sequels (some histories say four, others say eighteen). The Skillet Lickers even had minor mainstream popular hits such as "John Henry" and "Turkey in the Straw" in 1926-27. Tanner reformed the Skillet Lickers in 1934 with his son Gordon. Their biggest hit was 1934's "Down Yonder".

Southern Folklife Collection, University of North Carolina

An example of a two-man string band. The emphasis in this group was on the intricate interplay between the two guitars. Most important was Jimmie Tarleton's mastery of Hawaiian-inspired solos on the dobro, or resonator guitar, closely intertwined with steel guitar solos. A small shim that fit over the nut to raise the strings created a sliding, voice-like tone.

The full lineup of the original Skillet Lickers included Gid Tanner, Bert Layne, Lowe Stokes, Clayton McMichen, Riley Puckett, and Fate Norris. This group was the best known of the early string bands. Tanner, Puckett, and McMichen were the most advertised of the group, whose recorded works debuted in 1926 with "Bully of the Town." This unit utilized three fiddles, with Tanner and McMichen playing high fiddle lead. By the fourth session twin leads played the melody in close harmony and the new leader on fiddle was the seldom publicized Lowe Stokes. Stokes was under contract to Columbia Records and was viewed by the original trio as merely "helping out." He won first place at the National Fiddling convention in 1922. Stephen Vincent Benet, the esteemed American poet and Pulitzer Prize winner, read about the event in a newspaper and wrote a poem based on it called "Mountain Whip-poor-will or How Hillbilly Jim Won the Great Fiddlers Prize." The Skillet Lickers worked under a number of off-shoot group titles, including Stokes' North Georgians, McMichen's Melody Men, the Layne String Orchestra, Arthur Tanner's Cornshuckers, and the Georgia Organ Grinders, in which Stokes played organ.

Jimmie Tarleton (1892-1979) teamed up with Tom Darby in a string duo that was very influential primarily because of Tarleton's steel guitar performances. Darby played guitar and both sang. Along with Frank Hutchinson and Cliff Carlisle, Tarleton was one of the pioneers of the steel guitar, an instrument generally placed on the lap and played flat with the performer fretting the strings with a hard substance (it could be a bone or metal bar). The steel guitar had been transported by Portuguese and Spanish seamen to the Hawaiian islands, where it was mastered by the native musicians. During the turn of the century Hawaiian bands played in vaudeville and theater circuits, creating an interest in the unconventional, sliding sounds that the lap guitar, as some called it, produced. The steel guitar became the basis for a special, musically amplified guitar that went by a number of names, the generic one being resonator guitar. Bill Malone notes, "In the days before electrical amplification, the American enthusiast either converted a conventional guitar by elevating the strings, or bought one of the specially constructed amplified guitars which the manufacturers began placing on the market. Among these items two brand names predominated: National, which was probably the first, and Dobro, which was the most popular. Both guitars were equipped with metal vibrating discs, which amplified them without benefit of electrification."

National began making resonator guitars around 1926; in 1929 one of the company's partners split off and began marketing Dobros. Five years later he was persuaded to re-merge his company with National. Resonator guitars were favored by some bluesmen (for example, Son House and Bukka White), who played them in the normal guitar position, fretting strings with fingers or a glass or metal slide on one finger.

In 1927 Tarleton went to Atlanta with Darby in tow to record "Columbus Stockade Blues" and "Birmingham Jail." Both songs were written by Tarleton and when the team was given the option of royalty payments, Darby insisted on settling for seventy-five dollars for both songs. Tarleton continued to travel and record until 1935, when he retired from an active musical career. He worked various jobs outside of music until the mid-1960s, when he was rediscovered by folk music collectors, who helped him return to performing.

After Gid Tanner and the Skillet Lickers, **Charlie Poole** (1892-1931) and the North Carolina Ramblers were one of the most highly regarded groups of the early "hillbilly" era. Many writers have pointed out that they were direct precursors of future bluegrass sounds. Poole was a textile mill worker most of his life. He was a colorful, hard-drinking man who also happened to be a master of the five- string banjo as well as an entertaining vocalist. Poole teamed up with fiddler Posey Rorer in 1917 playing the North Carolina-West Virginia axis. The duo later added a guitarist and made their recording debut in 1925 for Columbia Records. In *The Listener's Guide to Country Music* Robert Oermann and Douglas Green praise the easygoing jazzy-bluesy qualities of the groups' performances, and of Poole they contend, "He was part bluesman, part jokester, part picker, and part sentimental balladeer." The North Carolina Ramblers represent some of the best old-timey string band music on record. Their most successful recording was "Don't Let Your Deal Go Down," but others, such as "It's Movin' Day," "White House Blues," "If the River Was Whiskey," and "Take a Drink on Me", were just as good. The last two songs reflected troubles within the band. Hard drinking eventually took its toll on Poole, who was contacted by Hollywood to provide background music for a film in 1931. But Poole died of a heart attack before he could make his mark in film. He was thirty-nine years old.

Courtesy Rounder Records

By the turn of the century the sound of the Hawaiian guitar and the music of Hawaii had become quite popular in America. In 1914 Tin Pan Alley reflected this fad after two songs imported from Hawaii had become popular, "On the Beach of Waikiki" and "Song of the Islands." In 1915 "Hello, Hawaii, How Are You?" became a hit song. The next year a wave of Hawaiian novelties erupted: "Oh, How She Could Yacki, Hacki, Wicki, Wacki, Woo" (Eddie Cantor wowed the audience with this song in his *Ziegfeld Follies* debut), "They're Wearing 'Em Higher in Hawaii," "Yacka Hula Hickey Dula" (Al Jolson sang this at the Wintergarden), and "The Honolulu Hicky-Boola-Boo," among a number of others. These songs created an awareness of the sounds of the Hawaiian guitar in popular music. In country music, however, the "sound" of the slithering, whining steel guitar became a fixture that went beyond novelty. Touring Hawaiian musicians like Frank Ferara, Pali Lua, and Sol Hoopii, above, became important influences on country players.

CHARLIE POOLE WITH
THE NORTH CAROLINA RAMBLERS

Southern Folklife Collection, University of North Carolina

Left to right, Charlie Poole, banjo; Posey Rorer, fiddle; and Harvey Roy, guitar.

Early String Bands

String Band	State	Representative Song
Dr. Humphrey Bate & the Possum Hunters	Tennessee	Throw the Old Cow Over the Fence
Binkley Brother's Dixie Clodhoppers	Tennessee	Give Me My 15 Cents Back
Crockett's Kentucky Mountaineers	Kentucky	Rabbit Where's Your Mammy
The Crook Brothers	Tennessee	Goin' Across the Sea
The Dixie Mountaineers	Virginia	Kitty Wells
The Fruit Jar Drinkers	Tennessee	Sleepy Lou
The Gully Jumpers (Paul Warmack)	Tennessee	The Little Red Caboose
Theron Hale and His Daughters	Tennessee	Hale's Rag
Earl Johnson and His Clodhoppers	Georgia	Red Hot Breakdown
Kentucky Thorobreds	Kentucky	Shady Grove
The Leake County Revelers	Mississippi	Wednesday Night Waltz
Hoyt Ming and His Pep Steppers	Mississippi	Indian War Whoop
Charlie Poole's North Carolina Ramblers	North Carolina	Don't Let Your Deal Go Down
The Roane County Ramblers	Tennessee	Callahan Rag
Dr. Smith's Hoss Hair Pullers	Arkansas	Where the Irish Potatoes Grow
Arthur Smith Trio (or: Dixieliners)	Tennessee	Beautiful Brown Eyes
Stoneman's Blue Ridge Corn Shuckers	Virginia	The Sinking of the Titanic
The Tennessee Ramblers	Tennessee	The Preacher Got Drunk and Laid His Bible Down
Fields Ward and His Buck Mountain Band	Virginia	Ain't That Trouble in Mind
Wilmer Watts and the Lonely Eagles	North Carolina	Cotton Mill Blues
Whitter's Virginia Breakdowners	Virginia	Last Train Blues
Da Costa Woltz's Southern Broadcasters	North Carolina	Sunny Home in Dixie

Radio and the Barn Dances

Of the great impact radio had on Americans E. B. White wrote that it was "a pervading and somewhat god-like presence which has come into their lives and homes."

During the twenties the radio emerged from being a crystal set for amateurs to becoming a widely popular and relatively inexpensive necessity for millions of Americans. In 1922 the annual sale of radios amounted to $60 million; by 1929 the figure had escalated to over $800 million. The radio was an especially important commodity for country folk because of their isolation. In fact, along with the automobile, the most profound urbanizing influence upon rural areas was the radio. Bill Malone points out in *Country Music USA* that, "The development of southern radio broadcasting was important in the discovery, refinement, modification, and eventual standardization of southern country music. With the coming of radio, southern folk singers had an additional outlet for their entertainment." Pete Welding

Georgia Fiddlers Invade Radio World

Journal's Radio Truck

At the places and hours announced below, The Atlanta Journal's radio truck will receive and amplify programs transmitted by WSB, the radiophone broadcasting station of The Atlanta Journal.

Sunday

10:54 a. m., at Piedmont park.
5 to 6 p. m., at city stockade.
8 to 9 p. m., at Grant park.

Monday

7 to 8 p. m., at Riverside.

Tuesday

7 to 8 p. m., at Battle Hill sanatorium.

Wednesday

7 to 8 p. m., at Rock Springs.

Thursday

5 to 6 p. m., at Oglethorpe university.
7 to 8 p. m., at Chamblee, Ga.

Friday

7 to 8 p. m., at corner of Kennedy and Davis streets.

Fiddlin John Carson, famous champion of Georgia, and some of his cronies, who is now spreading his name and fame far and wide with the aid of The Journal radiophone. The Fannin county mountaineer scored heavily on two of WSB's program last week and will be presented again before he picturesque gathering of old-time fiddlers at the auditorium soon.

wrote in *Roots and Blues: The Retrospective 1925-1950* (a four-CD, 107-track mix of country and blues from Columbia Records) that, "Great, rapid improvements in transportation and mass communications led inevitably to increasing cultural homogeneity as people traveled more widely and easily, and regional differences in musical idioms blurred through the twin influences of radio and phonograph recordings." Radio in the 1920s had a greater impact on white country music than it had on black blues forms because, unlike country, blues had few outlets on radio. The advent of radio, which dispensed free music into American homes on a daily basis, crippled the record industry. The cost of a radio and a phonograph player were about the same, and with radio the listeners had nothing more to purchase. On the other hand, a record usually cost 75 cents to a dollar. The annual sales of records sold fell from over two hundred million disks a year in the late 1920s to just six million in 1932 (of course, the Depression had significant bearing on those figures).

Radio company owners soon realized that they could sell a great deal of advertising time to producers of rural products. Because rural dwellers were physically isolated radio became the best medium in which to "sell" their products. As Clayton McMichen wryly declared, "I've noticed in my thirty-five years of show business that there's five hundred pairs of overalls sold to every one tuxedo suit. That's why I stick to swamp opera." The first high-powered radio station in the South to feature country music as a means of selling advertising was WSB in Atlanta, Georgia, which went on the air on March 16, 1922. Soon the better- known local artists like Fiddlin' John Carson and blind gospel singer Rev. Andrew Jenkins were appearing with regularity over airwaves on WSB. In an article in *Radio Digest* in 1925, Carson claimed, "Radio made me. Until I began to play over WSB more than two years ago, just a few people knew me, but now my wife thinks she's a widow because I stay away from home so much, playing around over this part of the country."

One of the most popular radio show formats was the weekend barn dance shows that began to spring up during the twenties. These programs ran two to four hours on a Friday or Saturday evening (sometimes both evenings). Typically the program featured a friendly announcer-host who would establish a personal rapport with the radio audience by telling stories, pitching products, and, most importantly, introducing a wide variety of entertainers who often were signed up to an exclusive contract to appear on a weekly basis. In this way, the barn dance took on a sense of community or family. Radio stations received letters that informed them of the wishes of their audience. In no time at all the more popular performers began receiving fan mail. The pay was often low or nonexistent, but the barn dance shows allowed performers a chance to publicize their personal appearances. Some of the more popular entertainers were able to make a comfortable living. However, this was not the case for a great majority of the country performers, who worked their regular jobs or tended to their farms the rest of the week. Barn dances were flourishing throughout America by the thirties.

Chicago's WLS station was the first to present the barn dance in what could be considered its native form. The WLS show eventually consisted of a hillbilly variety show with a regular "family" of performers. The station was owned by the Sears Roebuck Agricultural Foundation, which billed itself the "World's Largest Store." Sears stated its dedication to "serve the people on the farms of America." Beginning in April 1924 at the Sherman Hotel, fiddler Tommy Dandurand performed "Leather Breeches" on a small mezzanine referred to by the broadcasters as "the old hayloft." At first the new WLS show was called "The Aladdin Play Party," a reference to its sponsor, the Aladdin Kerosene Lamp Company. Shortly thereafter it was titled "The Old Fiddlers' Hour." By 1926 the show was renamed the "National Barn Dance" and moved to the Eighth Street Theater in response to the demand for tickets.

George Biggar was the director of the show. He was aided by George Dewey Hay, who was known as the "Solemn Old Judge." Hay used the title of "Howdy Judge" for his newspaper column in the *Memphis Commercial-Appeal*. Those early Saturday night frolics featured a varied mixture of backwoods pickers: Chubby Parker ("The Stern Old Bachelor"), operetta vocalist Grace Wilson ("The Girl With a Million Friends"), solemn religious incantations by Karl and Harty, organ recitals by Ralph Waldo Emerson, string bands such as the Cumberland Ridge Runners, vaudeville comedy by the Hoosier Hot Shots, and cowboy and cowgirl groups like Gene Autry, Patsy Montana and the Prairie Ramblers, Louise Massey and the Westerners, and the Girls of the Golden West.

THE W L S NATIONAL BARN DANCE CREW—STAGE OF THE 8TH ST. THEATRE, CHICAGO, ILL.

The National Barn Dance. The most important of the early barn dance shows was the "National Barn Dance" out of Chicago, Illinois. Beginning in April 1924 on station WLS the show was broadcast from "the old hayloft" in the Sherman Hotel.

Bradley Kincaid represented the voice of pure mountain music during the 1920s and 1930s. Among his numerous titles, were "Original Authentic Folksong Singer, " "The Kentucky Mountain Boy," and "The Kentucky Mountain Boy with His Houn' Dog Guitar." Kincaid tried to lend an air of respectability to his music (he disdained the term "hillbilly") by associating it with the good values of Appalachian mountain folk. He brought to WLS a collection of mountain folk songs that were sung each week in a high, mournful voice. By bringing Appalachian folksongs to a national radio audience, he became, in the words of biographer Loyal Jones, "the first artist to become a radio star using almost entirely authentic folk music." In *Radio's Kentucky Mountain Boy' Bradley Kincaid*, Jones points out that Kincaid was the first star of country music north of the Ohio River. His biggest impact was on radio and not records. The book, originally written in 1980 and revised in 1988, includes an annotated checklist of Kincaid's 332-song repertoire, a list of his published songbooks, and transcriptions of fifty songs. Jones's book is especially valuable because there is so little information on the early stars of country music history. And rarer yet are biographies of those early stars.

One of the earliest "stars" of the "National Barn Dance" was a collector of folk songs from the hills of Kentucky who rejected the label "hillbilly." **Bradley Kincaid** (1895-1989) was the first star of the "National Barn Dance," from 1926 to 1931. Billed as "The Kentucky Mountain Boy With His Houn' Dog Guitar," Kincaid sold his songbooks over the air. He made substantial profit from his thirteen songbooks, which were titled *My Favorite Ballads and Old Time Songs*. Kincaid is said to have sold at least one hundred thousand copies. Kincaid said that when he joined the "National Barn Dance" he and his wife were not too well off, but "four years later our worldly possessions consisted of twin daughters, a new Packard and more than $10,000 in the bank."

Kincaid was one of the first to popularize dozens of unpublished mountain ballads with his far-reaching radio exposure. Throughout the twenties and thirties the WLS barn dance was much more influential than the "Grand Ole Opry." Kincaid is a prime example of the early connections between folk and country. During this period folk and country music are considered the same thing. Kincaid was also billed as the "Original Authentic Folksong Singer." His most popular selection was a heart-breaking rendition of the Child ballad "Barbara Allen," which he sang every Saturday night for four years straight. Other Kincaid favorites included "Blue Tail Fly," "Ain't It Crazy," "Some Little Bug Is Goin' to Get You Some Day," "Two Little Orphans," "The Letter Edged in Black," and his theme song, "In the Hills of Old Kentucky."

Country music authority Archie Green contends that, "Our very conception today, that much American folksong is by definition undefiled, a precious elixir for national well-being, stems in part from Bradley Kincaid's achievement."

Author's collection

Bradley Kincaid described his music as "southern mountain" songs. He learned many folk songs through his long association with Berea College, located at the foothills of the Cumberland Mountains in Kentucky. Kincaid entered Berea Academy at nineteen and eventually obtained a high school diploma, underscoring that school's "mission of educating and uplifting the mountain children." Later he went to college in Chicago and eventually joined the "National Barn Dance," after that playing in numerous barn dance shows or various radio stations, including WLW Cincinnati, WMVA Wheeling, WSM Nashville, WHAM Rochester, and WWSO Springfield. Notice in this later picture of Kincaid, he is sporting a cowboy image rather than a hilbilly image.

LuLu Belle (Myrtle Eleanor Cooper) (1913-) and **Scotty Wiseman** (1909-1981) were one of the most beloved duos in country music history. They began working together on the "National Barn Dance" in 1933 and, for more than twenty-five years, were said to be more familiar to midwesterners than governors or movie stars. The married couple had hits in 1934 with "Home Coming Time" (penned by Wiseman) and "Whippoorwill Time" and had their own top-rated morning show on WLS, "Breakfast in the Blue Ridge." Known as "The Sweethearts of Country Music" and "The Hayloft Sweethearts," they were so successful that *Radio Digest* accorded Belle the distinction of being the most popular woman on radio for two consecutive years during the late 1930s. The duo could command $500 a day and transportation expenses for public appearances. Their signature tune was Wiseman's "Have I Told You Lately That I Love You."

Lulu Belle

SHE IS THE BELLE OF THE
BARN DANCE

Every Saturday Nite

The NATIONAL BARN DANCE

Hear It Over

45 NBC STATIONS
COAST-to-COAST

Over 40 Radio Artists including the Cumberland Ridge Runners, Maple City Four, Lulu Belle, Hoosier Hot Shots, Uncle Ezra, Tune Twisters, Arkansas Woodchopper, Joe Kelly, and Verne, Lee and Mary. A rollicking program of old time singing, dancing and homespun fun. Brought to you direct from WLS, Chicago, every Saturday night over

WJZ
9:30 to 10:30 P.M., EST
Sponsored by Alka Seltzer

Frank Driggs Collection

The Sweethearts of Country Music. Lulu Belle and Scotty Wiseman both hailed from North Carolina and became the most popular of the male-female duos in country music. They teamed up in 1933 and had a string of hits including "Home Coming Time," "Whippoorwill Time," "Mountain Dew," "Empty Christmas Stocking," "Time Will Tell," "My Heart Cries For You," "Does the Spearmint Lose Its Flavor on the Bedpost Overnight," "Turn Your Radio On," and their classic, "Have I Told You Lately That I Love You." After leaving the "National Barn Dance" they were members of WLW's "Boone County Jamboree" and guest starred on the "Grand Ole Opry" in 1950 and 1952, and Red Foley's "Ozark Jamboree" in 1957-58. They also made several movies (*Harvest Moon*, 1938; *County Fair*, 1939; *Village Barn Dance*, 1940; S*wing Your Partner*, 1942; *Hi Ya Neighbor* and *National Barn Dance*, 1943).

When the Wisemans retired from professional music in the mid-1950s, Scotty completed bachelors and masters degrees at Northwestern University. He and Lulu Belle moved back to North Carolina, where he taught speech at Spruce Pine College. Lulu Belle became interested in politics in the mid-1970s and was elected to the North Carolina House of Representatives. After Scotty's death in 1981 she remarried and moved to Florida.

Gene Autry (1907-   ) was a star in bloom from 1930 to 1934 on the "National Barn Dance," there he became the first recognizable radio cowboy. Billed as "Oklahoma's Singing Cowboy" he, like Lulu Belle and Scotty, had his own show on WLS. Like Bradley Kincaid, Autry sold his own songbooks over the air. His records were prominently displayed in the Sears catalog, as was his "Roundup" guitar. The Sears Roebuck Catalog was an important marketing vehicle for Autry. After the family Bible and the *Farmer's Almanac* the Sears Catalog was the most important printed page in rural America. Autry's career as a superstar singing cowboy will be highlighted in Chapter 13. The "National Barn Dance" featured many other stars, including one of the zaniest units in country music history, the Hoosier Hot Shots.

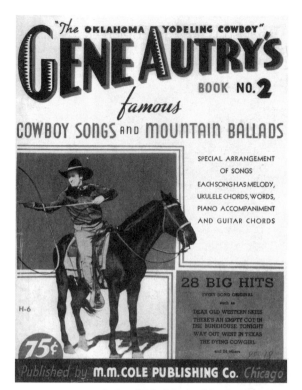

Southern Folklife Collection, University of North Carolina

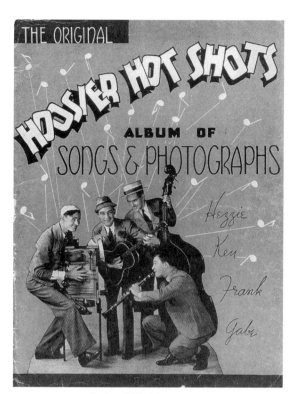

Southern Folklife Collection, University of North Carolina

J. R. Young writes in *The Illustrated History of Country Music,* "Roundup? Ranch? Oklahoma's Yodeling Cowboy? In a master stroke of image building, Gene had taken on the guise of a cowboy (B Western Variety, Very Streamlined), because it was in rural America that the legend of the cowboy loomed largest, and it was in rural America that the Sears Roebuck catalogue was only second in importance to the family Bible. By 1934, Gene's popularity in small-town America was unparalleled, whereas in New York and other sophisticated metropolitan areas (even as late as 1940, by the way), the name Gene Autry meant very little. That in itself might explain why Hollywood was somewhat dubious about a singer who almost invited himself to the big audition."

One of the greatest of the novelty troupes in country music, the Hoosier Hot Shots blended ingenious novelty instrumentation with songs that produced big smiles all around. They opened their shows with their trademark question, "Are you ready, Hezzie?" They were fine musicians, with leader Gabe Ward on clarinet; Hezzie Triesch on song whistle, washboard, drums, alto saxophone; Kenny Triesch on banjo, tenor guitar, and bass horn; and Frank Kettering on banjo, guitar, flute, piccolo, bass, and piano. Gabe Ward claims the group's greatest hit was "Sioux City Sue," but not far behind were such fun songs as "I Like Bananas (Because They Have No Bones)," "The Dummy Song," and "Wah-Hoo." Their predilection for novelty instrumentation predates that of Spike Jones and his popular band.

John Lair, like George D. Hay, would be an important purveyor of barn dance music once he left the "National Barn Dance" in the late thirties. Lair was the leader of the Cumberland Ridge Runners, a group that adhered to old-time music and dance traditions. Lair's group featured Red Foley ("Old Shep," "Chattanoogie Shoeshine Boy"), and Linda Hopkins ("The Sunbonnet Girl"). Lair eventually returned to the Berea, Kentucky, area and formed the "Renfro Valley Barn Dance," which featured true, old-time traditional music of local stars: the Coon Creek Girls, Old Joe Clark, Aunt Idy, Little Clifford and Uncle June, Karl and Harty, comedians Whitey Ford (known as the Duke of Paducah), and Homer and Jethro, along with Parker and Foley.

Southern Folklife Collection, University of North Carolina

179

WSM and the "Grand Ole Opry"

George D. Hay (1895-1968) had been helping direct the course of the "National Barn Dance" for a year and a half, acting as librarian and announcer, when the National Life and Accident Insurance Company of Nashville called on him to direct a similar show in Nashville. Hay joined WSM, "The Air Castle of the South," in the capacity of station director and host of the show, which made its debut on November 28, 1925. That first show had only two entertainers, an eighty-year-old mountain fiddler and his niece. The fiddler, Uncle Jimmy Thompson, boasted that he had just won an eight-day fiddling contest down in Dallas, Texas, and could play all night and would answer requests for old-time tunes. His niece, Mrs. Eva Thompson, provided piano accompaniment for the spirited entertainer.

Some of the people of Nashville were not happy to learn about a hillbilly show originating in the area they so proudly hailed as "the Athens of the South," so there were numerous protests. In this case it wasn't "uppity" northerners who resented the country rubes from the hills. But this became an afterthought once National Life received an overwhelmingly positive response from listeners who wanted to hear more music and requested tickets to see the show.

Courtesy Grand Ole Opry

"The Solemn Old Judge," George D. Hay, *above*, as an elderly man with his train whistle, and *below*, as a young man introducing the first regular performer on the "Grand Ole Opry", Uncle Jimmy Thompson. The emergence of the Opry as one of the significant barn dances in America developed slowly.

Charles Wolf points out four early stages in the Opry's early growth. The first stage was the informal period when no one received any money and just about any picker could come on the show. The second stage was the addition of the live studio audience, first in the studio located on the fifth floor of the National Life and Accident Insurance Company building and then in a theater. The third stage was the conscious attempt to develop "star" personalities. The fourth stage was the inroduction of professionalism—performers were paid and outside advertisers solicited for fifteen-minute segments of the show. The creation of the Artist Service Bureau, which helped book group tours of Opry stars, cemented this professionalism in 1933.

The "Grand Ole Opry" was a direct result of the vision of George D. Hay, who understood the rural audience's preference for "down home" music and humor. Hay insisted that the entertainers "keep it down to earth." Bands like those of Dr. Humphrey Bate, the Crook Brothers, and Paul Warmack had all been photographed in business suits to give them a degree of "professionalism." Many of these performers were merchants, not backwoods farmers. Hay had a different idea. He wrote press releases that trumpeted the rustic values of his charges. Hay's public relations acumen resulted in releases that read, "Every one of the 'talent' is from the back country," and "the unique entertainment that only Tennessee mountaineers can afford." Hay gave the groups colorful, hayseed monikers like the Possum Hunters (Bate's group), the Gully Jumpers (Warmack's group), and the Fruit Jar Drinkers and trumped up such publicity photos as posing these groups in overalls with floppy hats drinking from fruit jars, standing in corn fields with coon dogs, and wallowing in pig pens.

THE FRUIT JAR DRINKERS, WSM GRAND OLE OPRY.

Southern Folklife Collection, University of North Carolina

"Keep it down to earth, boys!"

The Opry also featured the first black artist of note in country music, **Deford Bailey** (1899-1982). Specializing in harmonica pieces like "Fox Chase," "John Henry," and his most notable song, "Pan American Blues," Bailey was treated more like a mascot than an equal professional partner. He referred to his music as "black hillbilly" and his style was in keeping with the Southeast seaboard blues tradition of Peg Leg Howell, Blind Willie McTell, and the numerous jug and jook bands that mixed fiddles with guitars, bass, mandolins, harmonicas, kazoos, and jugs. In 1928 Bailey appeared in forty-nine of fifty-two Opry broadcasts, making five dollars a performance. Bailey was dismissed by Hay in 1941, allegedly for refusing to bring new songs into his repertoire.

Courtesy County Records

Dr. Humphrey Bate playing harmonica (second row, second from the left) with an all-star string band from the Opry that includes Sam McGee and Uncle Dave Macon on banjo (front row, left and right, respectively).

Southern Folklife Collection, University of North Carolina

Before there was a Charley Pride, there was Deford Bailey, the first African-American country music star. Bailey was "discovered" by Dr. Humphrey Bate, who convinced George D. Hay to sign him.

The Opry's first true star was **Uncle Dave Macon** (1870-1952). Macon bridged the gap between nineteenth century show business and early commercial country music. Macon's father had a hotel and Macon met vaudeville and circus entertainers there. One of them taught Macon to play the banjo. As an adult Macon owned a farm in Readyville, Tennessee, and operated the Macon Midway Mule and Wagon Transportation Company. He entertained family and friends until 1918, when he was first paid to perform. By 1923, Macon was in such demand that he toured the Loew's vaudeville circuit. In 1925, now in his mid-fifties, Macon began playing the Opry. He was a stirring entertainer who stomped his feet and played intricate banjo runs on such novelty numbers as "Molly Put the Kettle On," "Rock About My Sara Jane," and "Cumberland Mountain Deer Race."

Macon's motto was, "It ain't what you got, it's what you put out; and, boys, I can deliver." His show-stopping finale was titled, "Uncle Dave Handles a Banjo Like a Monkey Handles a Peanut." The gambit had Macon flailing at the banjo and dancing as he shouted asides and tossed the banjo into the air, catching it and playing some more. Macon swung the banjo between his legs and behind his back, all the while entertaining with song and dance. Macon billed himself "The World's Greatest Banjo Player." He did much to preserve numerous old classics, stayed with the Opry twenty-six years, and was featured in the 1940 Republic film *Grand Ole Opry*.

Courtesy Rounder Records

Dave Macon, a great banjoist and songster, made his first recording for Vocalion Records in 1929, "Hillbilly Blues," which is one of the first uses of that term in song. Macon was one of the most energetic performers of early country music and a real crowd pleaser with his foot-stomping show-cases like "Keep My Skillet Good and Greasy," "Bake That Chicken Pie," "Eleven Cent Cotton," "Chewing Gum," "From Earth to Heaven," and "All In, Down and Out Blues." He was *the* crowd favorite of the early Opry.

Courtesy Grand Ole Opry

The Opry through the years.

Early "Grand Ole Opry" Performers

Performers	Specialty	Year Began
Asher & Little Jimmy	Dad and son (Sizemores); "heart songs"; closed their programs with prayer	1930
Deford Bailey	First black country artist of note; "Harmonica Wizard"; fired by Hay	1925
Dr. Humphrey Bate	Led Possum Hunters; first on WSM; "Dean of the Opry"	1925
Binkley Brothers	Given rustic name Dixie Clod Hoppers by George D. Hay	1925
Zeke Clements	"And His Bronco Busters"; Clements called the "Alabama Cowboy"	1933
Curly Fox and Texas Ruby	Cowboy duo; Ruby billed as "Radio's Original Yodeling Girl"	1930
Crook Brothers	Traditionalist; longest- lasting barn dance group; played into the late 1980s	1925
Delmore Brothers	Alton and Rabon; first Opry vocal harmony duo ("Beautiful Brown Eyes")	1932
Dixieliners	McGees joined by jazzy fiddle virtuoso "Fiddlin" Arthur Smith	1930
Therone Hale	"And His Daughters"; sentimental parlor songs ("Listen to the Mocking Bird')	1926
Jamup and Honey	Best known of the barn dance black-face humorists; ran their own Tent Show	
Robert Lunn	Lefty guitarist called the "Talking Blues Boy"	1930
Uncle Dave Macon	The Opry's first commercial "star" performer; "The Dixie Dew Drop"	1926
Mangrum and Schriver	Two blind musicians held "jam sessions" on fiddle and piano-accordion	1926
McGee Brothers	Sam on guitar and Kirk on fiddle, two stalwarts of Opry tradition	1925
Vito Pellettieri	Led first Opry orchestra; stage manager 1934 to 1974	1930
Pickard Family	Leader Obie (Dad) considered early vocal star; sentimental tunes	1926
Ed Poplin	"And the Old Timers"; fiddler's group had two women and boy pianist	1926
Sarie & Sallie	Sisters presaged gossipy rural humor later popularized by Minnie Pearl	1933
Jack Shook	"And the Missouri Mountaineers," stringband with accordion and xylophone	1930
Uncle Jimmy Thompson	Old-time fiddler on first show; niece Eva contralto and piano accompaniment	1925
Vagabonds	Urbane vocal trio; pop-oriented material; no hillbilly image	1931
Paul Warmack	Led Gully Jumpers; made first Nashville recording by Ralph S. Peer in 1928	
George Wilkerson	Led the Fruit Jar Drinkers, one of the earliest string bands	1925

Early Barn Dance Shows

Station	Show	Area	Performers	Year
WSB	Barn Dance	Atlanta, GA	Fiddlin' John Carson, Rev. Andrew Jenkins, Raymond James, Marth Carson, Cotton Carrier	1922
WBAP	Barn Dance	Fort Worth, TX	M. J. Bonner, Fred Wagner's Hilo 5	1923
WLS	National Barn Dance	Chicago, IL	Tommy Dandurand, Walter Peterson, Claud Moye (Pie Plant Pete, "The Ozark Mountain Boy"), Bradley Kincaid	1924
WSM	Grand Ole Opry	Nashville, TN	Uncle Jimmy Thompson, Dr. Humphrey Bate, Crook Brothers, Gully Jumpers, McGee Brothers	1925
KMPC	L.A. Barn Dance	Los Angeles, CA	Beverly Hillbillies, Charlie Marshall and His Mavericks	1930
KMOX	Old Fashioned Barn Dance	St. Louis, MO	Cousin Emmy, Uncle Henry's Original Kentucky Mountaineers	1930
WHO	Iowa Barn Dance Frolic	Des Moines, IA	The Calico Maids, Texas Ruby	1932
WMVA	Wheeling Jamboree	Wheeling, WV	Cowboy Loye, Just Plain John, Doc Williams and the Border Riders	1933
WBT	Crazy Water Crystals Barn Dance (later Dixie Jamboree)	Charlotte, NC	Claude Casey, Arthur Smith, Mainer's Mountaineers	1934
WHN	Barn Dance	New York, NY	Co-hosts Tex Ritter and Ray Whitley	1935
WLW	Boone County Jamboree (later Midwestern Hayride)	Cincinnati, OH	Red Foley, Cumberland Ridge Runners, Drifting Pioneers (Merle Travis)	1936
WHAS	Renfro Valley Barn Dance	Renfro Valley, KY	John Lair and Cumberland Ridge Runners, Red Foley, Coon Creek Girls, Old Joe Clark, Frankie Moore's Log Cabin Boys and Girls, Bog Trotters	1937
KVOO	Saddle Mountain Roundup	Tulsa, OK	Harold Goodman (ex-Vagabond), Ray Whitley, Georgia Slim & Big Howdy	1937

A plethora of shows went on the air in 1938, including: WRVA's "Old Dominion Barn Dance," Richmond, Virginia; WINS's "The Village Barn Dance," New York, New York; WOWO's "Hoosier's Hop," Fort Wayne, Indiana; KSTP's "Sunset Valley Barn Dance,"
Minneapolis-St. Paul, Minnesota; "Hollywood Barn Dance," Hollywood, California; KWKH's "Roundup," Shreveport, Louisiana.

Certainly a book on the history of radio barn dance shows would be a welcome addition to the literature of country music history. Radio was the ideal music-mediator for rural audiences. Charles Wolf, writing in *Country: The Music and the Musicians,* states, "Through the 1930s the barn dance fad grew, spreading like Kudzu throughout the South and into other parts of the country. At the beginning of the decade, in 1932, there were 137 stations in the South and Southwest, most of them broadcasting at less than 1,000 watts; only nine stations were broadcasting with more than 20,000 watts: Atlanta, Birmingham, Louisville, Charlotte, Cincinnati, Tulsa, Nashville, San Antonio, and Dallas. Only 45 of the 137 stations had made affiliations with the national broadcasting networks, which meant that most were still originating most of their programming live, a good thing for local country music and barn dances. (Even stations that had network affiliations, like Nashville's WSM, worked compromises between canned network feeds and local shows; for years every Saturday night the Grand Ole Opry stopped for thirty minutes so WSM could take the NBC show 'Amos'n'Andy!)

"Station signals, too, carried much further in those days of uncluttered airways; WSM's original signal was heard easily throughout the eastern United States, and even (100-watt stations could be heard for a hundred miles across the flatlands of the deep South or Southwest. Some stations had directional signals that beamed their shows toward a specific area. WWVA in Wheeling, West
Virginia, for instance, tended toward the Northeast creating country fans in Pennsylvania and Maryland; KVOO's signal from Tulsa carried westward well into California, but a motorist driving into town from the east could pick-up the signal only a few miles from the city limits. In 1944, during the high-water mark of live radio, *Billboard* magazine estimated that there were some six hundred regular country radio shows [not all barn dances] in the United States and that they played to a combined audience of around forty million people."

The Friendly WWVA Jamboree Family

Standing, left to right; Sunflower, Paul Miller, Pepper, Lew Childre, Big Slim, Joe Barker, Vivian Miller, Brother Cy, Smilie Sutter, Lew Clawson, Doc Williams, Tommy Sutton, Millie Wayne.
Seated, left to right; Smile Sisters (Rose and Helen), Newcomer Twins (Eileen and Maxine), Little Shirley, Davis Twins (Honey and Sonny).

WWVA Jamboree Theme Song

Now here's the Jamboree to greet you,
In the good old fashioned way.
We'll do our best to please you and hope that you'll feel gay.
We are more than glad to see you and hope you'll be carefree,
So laugh and smile with us awhile
On the Midnight Jamboree.

WWVA publicity photo of the artists and crew of the station's barn dance offering, the "Wheeling Jamboree."

WLW promotional material showing the main attractions of its barn dance show, "Midwestern Hayride."

The First Family of Country

Maybelle Carter, Alvin Pleasant Carter, and Sara Carter. With Sara's strong soprano lead, Maybelle's alto harmony, and A.P.'s baritone, the Carter Family was not only one of country music's most influential groups, but a tremendous link to the music's folk heritage. Many traditional songs that might have been lost were saved thanks to A. P.'s "song hunting" trips into the mountains with black musician Lesley Riddle. Riddle influenced the guitar stylings of Maybelle and had two of his songs recorded by the Carters: "Lonesome for You" and "Cannonball Blues."

The Carter Family's harmony singing was learned in the church singing schools, which emphasized sadness and the wickedness of life on earth, thus the celebration of the joys of heaven and the afterlife. Many Carter Family songs sound maudlin to the point of anachronism to audiences of today, but in this respect their music really differs very little from modern country. Between 1927 and 1941 they recorded over 350 selections which formed a body of work that influenced a pattern for harmony singing in country music. Though they broke up in 1943, their offspring have carried on the Carter legacy to this very day.

The Carter Family was made up of Alvin Pleasant Carter (1891-1960), Sara Carter (1899-1979), and Maybelle Carter (1909-1978). A. P. Carter was a collector of songs who often took trips into the hills with a black musician, Lesley Riddle, who would remember the melodies as Carter jotted down lyrics. Many historians have referred to Carter as a "song pirate" because he took credit and copyrighted many songs that had been part of the uncommercial folk tradition and there upon taken from unwary mountain people. But like numerous folk song collectors, he helped preserve many songs that might otherwise have gone undiscovered.

A. P., who hailed from Maces Spring, Virginia, married Sara Dougherty. Sara's cousin, Maybelle Addington, married A.P.'s brother Ezra. The three, A.P., Sara, and Maybelle, became the best-known family unit of singers in country history. With Peer guiding them they launched a career that would last into the early 1940s. Maybelle continued performing with her daughters into the 1970s. The original trio sang wholesome, family-oriented songs about home and hearth. The fundamentalist belief that life was difficult on earth but being religious and good to one's family brought reward in the afterlife was a Carter Family philosophy stressed in song after song. "Room in Heaven for Me," "Meeting in the Air," "I'm Thinking Tonight of My Blue Eyes," "Bury Me Under the Weeping Willow," and "Will the Circle Be

Unbroken?" are some of the popular Carter songs that dealt with the joys of life ever-after. The unit performed songs that they advertised as "Morally Good," and the Carters did not disappoint. They established a wholesome, warm atmosphere that was appropriate for the entire family. Much of their performing was done in local schoolhouses, churches, and small stages not far from their home state. Admission was between fifteen and twenty-five cents. The Carters cut their final records in 1941 and disbanded two years later. In addition to being called the "First Family of Country Music," they were also labelled the "Patron Saints of Country Music."

Southern Folklife Collection, University of North Carolina

Courtesy Arhoolie Records, 10341 San Pablo Ave., El Cerrito,CA. 94530

The most famous single record sessions in country music were the auditions held by Ralph S. Peer in Bristol, Tennessee in August 1927. Both the Carter Family and Jimmie Rodgers were signed to contracts—the Carters found success with their first release ("Bury Me Under the Weeping Willow Tree"). The editors of *Country: The Music and the Musicians* claim, "Music historians and others fond of dates and places have a special weakness for 'Bristol, August 1927.' As a sort of short-hand notation, it has come to signal the Big Bang of country music evolution, the genesis of every shape and species of Pickin'- and - Singin' down through the years . . . The idea is oversimplified, but it works."

Ralph S. Peer acted as the unofficial manager of the group and established a royalty payment formula for the trio. According to writer John Atkins, they received .45 percent royalty per record (that's right: less than half a percent per record). For every $200,000 worth of record sales made, they would receive $900 split three ways. It wasn't much of a bargain, but it was more than most country artists received in royalties: none. Unlike Jimmie Rodgers, who played the theater circuit, the Carter Family played schoolhouses in backwater communities. For publicity the group nailed announcements to trees and telephone poles, and posted them on church bulletin boards.

A. P. and Sara divorced in 1936, but they continued to perform within the family context until the early 1940s. The Carter Family gained their greatest audience when they performed over the Mexican radio station XERA from 1938 to 1941. Border stations, with their transmitters located just across the Rio Grande River in Mexico, could operate with wattage far in excess of that permitted in the United States. The era began in 1932 when John R. Brinkley, "the goat-gland doctor," who promoted a cure for male sexual impotence, established XER (later XERA), with offices in Del Rio, Texas. Because of the national coverage afforded the Carter Family during their stay in Del Rio, they were able, for the first time, to sustain themselves as full-time professionals.

After the demise of the original trio in 1943, Maybelle (now referred to as Mother Maybelle) began a new version of the Carter Family that included her daughters Helen, June, and Anita. The unit was titled Mother Maybelle and the Carter Sisters. This unit played the "Grand Ole Opry" for seventeen years beginning in 1950. In 1968 June married Johnny Cash and Mother Maybelle and her daughters stayed with his road show until 1973. That year Maybelle was one of a number of "old timers" who took part in recording the historic three-record set entitled *Will the Circle Be Unbroken*, with the Nitty Gritty Dirt Band, for its time a rare connection between rock and country. *The Comprehensive Country Music Encyclopedia* (1994) notes, "For 50 years now, some part of this original Carter Family has been a fixture on the country scene, from the pure folk sound of the original trio to the rock-flavored sound of Maybelle's granddaughter, Carlene."

The Father of Country Music

Courtesy Biograph Records

In *Country Music USA*, Bill Malone claims that before the emergence of the "western" music of the 1930s, country music was dominated by two forms: "mountain" and "country." The "mountain" form is identified with the Appalachians: It was conservative, religious, and relied more on traditional songs and instruments. This form is exemplified by the music of the Carter Family and bluegrass forms of today. The "country" form stressed more individual solo singing, utilized more nontraditional instruments, and was influenced by popular music and African-American blues. Jimmie Rodgers was the main leader of this movement. Jimmie Rodgers, from the time he made his first recordings, never publicized himself as a "hillbilly" character. He viewed himself as a professional entertainer. The fact that he played on vaudeville stages of the South, rather than at schoolhouses and churches, lent an added veneer of showbiz-pizazz to his persona. Also, because he was balding prematurely, his publicity photos never showed him without a hat.

While the Carter family did not make the necessary tours needed to spread their fame, this was not the case for the solo singing star Jimmie Rodgers.

Jimmie Rodgers (1897-1933), in his brief six-year record career, established himself as the "Father of Country Music." Born in Meridian, Mississippi, September 8, 1897, the son of a railroad man, Rodgers learned to play guitar from the railroad workers. He mixed a style of traditional country music, rural blues, and railroad songs and offered it up to his future manager, Ralph S. Peer, at a 1927 talent search. Rodgers recorded "Sleep, Baby, Sleep" and "The Soldier's Sweetheart" for his first release and the Victor company was swamped with orders for it. On "Sleep, Baby, Sleep" Rodgers yodeled and this would become a regular feature of his performances. He was known as "The Blue Yodeler" and "The Singing Brakeman."

Frank Driggs Collection

Country music artists who play guitar invariably have their name inscribed on the necks of their guitars. This was a tradition that Jimmie Rodgers made famous. In 1928 a guitar company out of Philadelphia thought it would be good business to have Rodgers advertise its product. Long before the days of basketball players and coaches providing sneaker endorsements, or stock-car racers wearing product emblems, or golfers teeing off with specialized clubs, Rodgers was presented with a customized guitar, personalized with his name inlaid in mother-of-pearl, by the Waymann Guitar Company. He, in turn, would promote their "Jimmie Rodgers Special" model guitar.

Rodgers released 110 selections (just one of his recordings failed to be commericially distributed) and he was billed as an "exclusive Victor recording star." Rodgers was the rare combination of entertainer and artist. His compositions, often written with his sister-in-law, Elsie McWilliams, have lasted the test of time. Rodgers was the "eclectic genius" of country music, blending traditional values with down and dirty blues, Hawaiian steel guitar sounds, jazz instrumental backing, Swiss yodels, and pop crooning. Rodgers learned the blues first hand, working while a youngster as a water boy in the railroad yards. Rodger's "Blue Yodel No. 8 (Muleskinner Blues)" borrows directly from "Ma" Rainey's 1928 "Southern Blues," and "Train Whistle Blues" borrows from bluesman Peetie Wheatstraw's "C&A Blues," to cite just two specific examples. One of Rodgers's good friends was popular crooner Gene Austin, Rodgers shared time on Austin's boat, the "Blue Heaven."

Two more examples of Rodgers mixing outside musical forms with country are his use of Hawaiian sounds on "Tuck Away My Lonesome Blues" and "Everybody Does It in Hawaii" with Joe Kaipoon on Hawaiian guitar, and the use of the jazz sounds of trumpets and clarinets on selections such as "Any Old Time," and "Blue Yodel No. 9" (with Louis Armstrong). Rodgers adventurous musical combinations placed him in a different constellation from the other country players of his time.

Rodgers was that rare breed who could tug at the heart with sentimental weepers like "Mother, Queen of My Heart," "Daddy and Home," "Why There's a Tear in My Eye," and "The Drunkard's Child," and then turn around with raunchy double-entendre ditties like "Pistol Packin' Papa," or "Let Me Be Your Sidetrack." Not many popular artists could get away with singing raunchy songs, but Rodgers did. He said, "If the people like you when you're nice, they'll accept you when you're naughty." Rodgers's love of the railroad resulted in many songs dedicated to trains and his cowboy songs introduced western imagery for the first time to most of his audience ("Yodeling Cowboy Blues" and "Cowhand's Last Ride"). It was no wonder, then, that farmers across America would go to the general store and order "a loaf of bread, a pound of butter, and the latest Jimmie Rodgers record."

It has been written that Rodgers sold twenty million records during his short lifetime, but this is quite unlikely. Rodgers's career coincided with the Depression and his main audience was the impoverished rural dweller, who was not buying too many records during this time—at seventy-five cents to a dollar a platter, many Americans did without. If a southerner did buy a record, however, it was likely to be one by Rodgers. It was more likely that Rodgers's record sales ended up totaling between five million and six million copies, still very impressive. Names of artists much better known than his during his lifetime (Isham Jones, Ruth Etting, Russ Columbo, Morton Downey, Nick Lucas, to name just some, are unknown to today's audiences, while Rodgers is considered a giant. Paul Ackerman of *Billboard* magazine wrote that Rodgers was America's true native balladeer and that someone "had to fuse and synthesize . . . musical elements (pop, folk, country, blues and jazz) to prepare the way for the Elvis Presleys and Johnny Cashes of today. It was Rodgers who did this."

Frank Driggs Collection

No country artist had created such an eclectic body of recorded work as Jimmie Rodgers. His love of pop-oriented songs, blues, jazz, and Hawaiian numbers was quite amazing for its time. Rodgers was one of the first, if not the very first, "hillbilly" star to record with black artists. In addition to his collaboration with Louis Armstrong, he recorded an unissued "Frankie and Johnny" in 1929, another unissued side with St. Louis bluesman, Clifford Gibson and "My Good Gal's Gone Blues" with the Louisville Jug Band. Take Rodgers's love of Hawaiian sounds, for example. He loved the sliding glissando of the steel guitar, and beginning with "Blue Yodel #2" featured Ellsworth Cozzens playing Hawaiian steel sounds behind him. John Westbrook provided the steel sounds on "Waiting for a Train," and Hawaiian Joe Kaipo backed Rodgers on "My Rough and Rowdy Ways." Bill Carlisle, who teamed with his brother Cliff, and also had a fine solo career, was one of the best known of the steel guitar players in country music and backed Rodgers on "When the Cactus is in Bloom" and "Lookin' For a New Mama." Hawaiian, blues, pop or jazz, Rodgers incorporated them all into his country fusion melting pot.

The influence of Jimmie Rodgers on country music history is almost impossible to describe. Rodgers was a catalyst for his obvious followers, such as Gene Autry and Ernest Tubb, of whom most country fans are aware. But he was also an important influence on such lesser-known disciples as Bill Carlisle and Frankie Marvin, and contemporary artists such as Leon Redbone and Maria Muldaur. It would not be an exaggeration to call Rodgers the greatest influence on early country music.

The Emergence of the West

The Southwest was crucial in the establishment of the "western" look and sound that made an impact on country music during the twenties and thirties. The diverse ethnic groups in the states of Texas, Oklahoma, and Louisiana brought together middle-Europeans (Germans, Poles, and Bohemians), Blacks, French, Mexicans, and Anglo-Celtics. Each of these groups had unique customs to offer and the musical melting pot resulted in a different sound than that of the Southeast. Fiddles were mixed with accordions as the two-step dance proved popular, and with the addition of mariachi brass and jazz solos on sax and trumpet, a louder form of music emerged.

In the thirties western music spread to the Hollywood silver screen with the singing cowboys. Americans have always been fascinated with the independent cowboy and his faithful horse, riding the range unencumbered by modern civilization. More often than not, however, the reality was that cattle drives were boring, lonely, and not at all glamorous.

The real cowboys were not Hollywood stars like Gene Autry or Roy Rogers. The movement west occurred after the Civil War. In 1867, Abilene opened up as the first stockyard to which cattle from all over Texas were driven, then shipped by rail for slaughter in the packing houses of Chicago. After the completion of the transcontinental railroad in 1869, and the western expansion of the telegraph, roving correspondents for eastern papers enthralled their readers with tales of Indian wars, shootouts, and cattle drives. But the cowboy life was filled with drudgery. With the constant dust and large herds, rounding up cattle seldom called for melodious song; that was usually saved for later, around the campfire.

189

Carl T. Sprague (1895-1978) was raised near Houston, Texas, where he helped in roundups and branding on his uncle's ranch. Sprague attended Texas A&M in 1915 and later completed graduate work there. While in college he led a campus band. The success of Vernon Dalhart's "The Prisoner's Song" gave him the idea to audition for RCA. Although Jules Vern Allen used the title "The Original Singing Cowboy" and even wrote a book in 1933, *Cowboy Lore*, Sprague had the biggest hit of the early cowboy singers, "When the Work's All Done This Fall." As a result Sprague was also billed "The Original Singing Cowboy." "When the Work's All Done This Fall" is an example of a song that worked its way into the oral tradition that actually came from Tin Pan Alley. The melody is from Charles K. Harris's classic, "After the Ball."

Between 1925 to 1934 he recorded 32 numbers for RCA Victor, most of them cowboy songs like: "Cowman's Prayer," "Cowboy Love Song," "Cowboy's Dream," "Cowboy's Meditation," "Here's to the Texas Ranger," "If Your Saddle is Good," "Last Great Roundup," and "Oh Bury Me Not on the Lone Prairie." After years of inactivity, Sprague appeared at folk festivals and made a couple of recordings for the Bear Family in 1972 and 1974.

The earliest studies of authentic cowboy songs were Nathan Howard Thorp's 1908 *Songs of the Cowboys* and John A. Lomax's 1910 *Cowboy Songs and Other Frontier Ballads* . The first of the cowboy songs heard on record were often folk songs sung by authentic working cowboys.

Rapid industrialization, and the oil boom, together with ethnic diversity set the musical heritage of the Southwest apart from that of the Southeast. A romantic concept of the West resulted in novels such as Owen Wister's *The Virginian*, and the "dime novels" of Ned Buntline and Bret Harte. Buntline went west in 1869 and found a new hero in William "Buffalo Bill" Cody. His interviews with Cody led to books such as *Buffalo Bill: The King of the Border.* By the mid-1890s Buffalo Bill was making kinetoscopes, hand-cranked peep shows that preceded the movies as an entertainment form.

In 1903, Thomas Edison released a ten-minute film entitled *The Great Train Robbery*, which became a sensation in America. The first full-fledged movie star was a cowboy: G. M. Anderson. Bronco Billy, as he became known, starred in some 375 "one-reelers" and nearly 1,000 "two-reelers". About a thousand feet of 35 mm film fit on an old-fashioned reel, which ran about ten minutes. Thus short films were spoken of as one-reelers, two-reelers and so on. The next important western movie star was "good-bad man" William Hart, who made a series of adult westerns. Then came the clean-cut "Lothario on Horseback," Tom Mix, whose lavish, streamlined westerns found great favor with kids and women. By 1925 it is estimated that Mix was earning $17,000 per week at Fox Pictures. This success led to imitators such as Tim McCoy, Hoot Gibson, Buck Jones, and many others. But by 1929, sound had wiped out many of the careers of the early cowboys. Lodged between the silent film cowboy and the singing cowboys of the mid-1930s are the recorded works of traditional cowboy songs by authentic cowboys. Charles Nabell's 1924 Okeh recording was one of the first releases of a range song. More influential was Carl Sprague, whose 1925 recording of "When the Work's All Done This Fall" caused a stir of interest in songs of the West.

Jules Vern Allen rivaled Nabell and Sprague for title of the "Original Singing Cowboy." He was a cowboy who worked cattle on the range in Texas, and was known as "Longhorn Luke" on radio in San Antonio; neither he nor Sprague were "drugstore cowboys." By contrast, there was Goebel Reeves, known as the "Texas Drifter," who chose, despite a wealthy family background, to be a traveling hobo singing "Hobo Lullabye," "The Hobo and the Cop," "Railroad Boomer," and "The Cowboy's Prayer." Perhaps as important as the "real" cowboys, was the image created by Jimmie Rodgers. Rodgers romanticized the West in a number of cowboy songs, such as "Pistol Packin' Papa," "When the Cactus is in Bloom," "Cowhand's Last Ride," and "Yodeling Cowboy," and he dressed in full cowboy regalia for one of his publicity shots.

Left, **Jimmie Rodgers as a singing cowboy.** Jimmie Rodgers released only nine songs with western themes, but with this small part of his output he created the romantic figure of the singing cowboy on records. Gene Autry idolized and imitated this aspect of Rodgers's image. Building on the less successful vocal efforts of cowboy movie stars like Ken Maynard and John Wayne (Singin' Sandy), Autry united the singing cowboy with the already existing appeal of the action cowboy, and in the process single-handedly created both a film genre and an element of the American mass iminagination.

Right, Harry "Haywire Mac" McClintock sang cowboy songs over West Coast radio beginning in 1925. In the 1930s he led a group called Mac's Haywire Orchestry.

Harry McClintock (1882-1957) was one of the most versatile entertainers in country and western music. Born in Knoxville, Tennessee, he travelled widely, literally "singing for his supper" for many years. He was often referred to as "Mac" and after singing for troops during the Spanish-American War he wrote a song titled "Hallelujah, I'm a Bum" (1908), which became the unofficial theme song of the Industrial Workers of the World. McClintock's association with the I.W.W. resulted in a closer historical affiliation with folk music histories than with country music. However, as has already been pointed out, country and folk music were very much the same thing during the pre-Guthrie-Seeger era. McClintock wrote and sang songs in praise of the working and out-of-work American. By 1925, McClintock was featured on a radio show in San Francisco and he began making records around that time (recording for Victor from 1927 to 1931). McClintock also popularized cowboy songs such as "Texas Rangers," "Sam Bass," and "Jesse James," among many others. In *Country Music USA* Bill Malone contends, "McClintock's Western labor songs of the 1920's make him one of the important progenitors of Western music."

Cowboys and Cowgirls

With the advent of the talking picture it was inevitable that western action would be combined with singing. Among the cowboys who sang, Gene Autry, Roy Rogers, Tex Ritter and the Sons of the Pioneers are rightly remembered as the most famous; however, their greatest accomplishments were all after 1934. The first of the singing cowboys is not known to many. He was **Ken Maynard** (1895-1973). Born in Vevay, Indiana, Maynard became an expert trick rider and roper who worked with the Kit Carson show in 1914 and also appeared with Pawnee Bill in a western rodeo show. The first western talkie to feature a cowboy singing songs was either Maynard's *Songs of the Saddle* in 1930, in which Maynard sang four songs, most of them around a campfire, or *Wagon Master*, listed by many histories as also appearing in 1930 (there is much confusion here, as in many areas of early country history, as already noted).

Maynard played fiddle or guitar in his films. His was not a particularly "tuneful" voice, but Maynard's songs smacked of authentic cowboy spirit. As Fred Hoeptner observes in his liner notes to *Authentic Cowboys and Their Western Songs*, "I never did hear a cowboy with a real good voice. If he ever had one to start with, he lost it bawling at cattle." Ken Maynard's other claims to fame are his use of plots that revolved around the title song, as in *The Strawberry Roan* or *In Old Santa Fe*, and his use of songs as momentary breaks between action scenes such as barroom brawls or chases, a technique that the more famous cowboy singers would later use. Maynard is also important for being the star of the films that introduced Gene Autry to the Hollywood screen. Autry had small parts in Maynard's *In Old Santa Fe* and *Mystery Mountain.*

In 1934 authors George Fenin and William Everson in *The Western: From Silents to Cinerama* rightly credit Maynard as the first singing cowboy working the genre some five years before Autry. "Songs in his Westerns were usually sung around the campfire episodes, introduced logically to provide moments of relaxation between melodramatic action. They remained essentially masculine affairs, quite without dance-hall singers or even a vocally inclined heroine. Maynard was not only the first of the cowboys to sing with regularity on film, he was also the first of the celluoid cowboys to sing on record. In 1930 he released eight songs, including "Home on the Range," "Jesse James," "Roundup's Done," and the only two sides released, "Lone Star Trail" and "Cowboy's Lament". Maynard was an expert horseman, and during the silent era he worked as a stuntman and eventually starred in hundreds of films, beginning with a small role in 1923's *The Man Who Won*. He continued making films until 1944, with *Harmony Trail*. In *The Filming of the West* film historian Jon Tuska praises Maynard's early efforts, claiming that he was a top western star when he filmed *In Old Arizona* in 1929, which "was an experiment in an all-talking outdoor drama, a feat [Universal Pictures head Carl] Laemmle's sound engineers said was impossible. 'My Tonia' was the principal song, and the musical setting was charming." Maynard's voice may have been too much like the real thing; "I had this kinda high, nasal-soundin' Texas voice, but it sounded real enough, I reckon, for me to get into talkies." Audiences of 1934 were more charmed by the melodious tones of Gene Autry than the rough-hewn cowboy rasp of Ken Maynard. "Perhaps due to Maynard's own limitations as a singer, and the fact that he still adhered to the traditional Western, the idea for musical Westerns did not catch on at that time," speculate Fenin and Everson.

As things stand, Maynard is considered only a precursor to the singing cowboy on film. The movement, as such, didn't really take hold until after 1934. However, during the pre-singing cowboy period, roughly 1925 to 1934, the genre of commercialized singing cowboys and cowgirls of the romanticized West began to establish itself. The image of the cowboy began to replace the hillbilly by the end of the 1920s, because, as Bill Malone observes in *SInging Cowboys and Musical Mountaineers,* "The cowboy, unrestrained by the confining regimens of city life, but bound by a code of proper behavior and loyalty to friends, symbolized freedom and independence. The mountaineer had once been identified with such qualities, but by the end of the 1920's comic depictions of hillbillies or accounts of snake handling and other forms of eccentric behavior tarnished much of the romance associated with the mountains. The cowboy remained a figure of unblemished virtue and assertive manhood."

Movie Star News

The first singing cowboy of the movies: Ken Maynard. On film, Maynard had much to do with the early romantic notions about the cowboy. It is too bad, then, that, as Douglas Green concludes, "Maynard's major contribution to the singing cowby genre was, in fact, neither his own singing nor his pioneering role as a singer: it was the introduction of Gene Autry to the world, in a 1934 Maynard feature called *In Old Santa Fe,* as a singer of modern cowboy songs." Maynard's horse, Tarzan, was billed "the Wonder Horse."

A brief sidenote should be given here about, of all people, **John Wayne** (1907-1979). The best known of all dramatic western stars, Wayne was also featured as a singing cowboy before Autry and his followers. By 1933 Wayne had starred in Warner Brothers' first major western, *The Big Trail.* The film did poorly at the box office and Warner released him. Wayne then signed up with Harry Cohn at Columbia Pictures, then, in the summer of 1933, with Monogram Pictures' Lone Star Productions, to do a series of eight westerns at $2,500.00 per picture. Wayne's first film was titled *Riders of Destiny* and Wayne was billed as "Singin' Sandy," the singing secret agent of the U.S. Secret Service. Singin' Sandy was a role created for Wayne by director-author Robert Bradbury. Wayne sometimes sang up to four songs in a picture (his voice was not dubbed by Smith Ballew as previously thought, but by Bradbury's son Bill). Wayne completed the sequence of the Sandy series with *Sagebrush Trail, Blue Steel, Randy Rides Alone, The Star Packer, Rainbow Valley* and *Paradise Canyon.* John "Duke" Wayne gladly left Singin' Sandy behind in 1935 when he starred in the Republic studio's first film, *Westward Ho.* He had been explicit about not singing. There are claims he yelled at Republic's leader, Herbert Yates, "I've had it, I'm a goddamned action star, you son of a bitch. I'm not a singer. Go get yourself another cowboy singer." Yates did just that. He signed Gene Autry.

The romanticized image of the West became a country music obsession by the time the singing cowboys came into vogue in the late 1930s. Anticipating this fascination with the singing cowboys were a number of artists we are investigating: Maynard, Autry, and the "hot string bands," which we deal with a little later in this chapter. This was not only a game for men, however. Women were among the earliest stars to adorn western outfits and sing lovingly about the wide open spaces of Texas and

Oklahoma. Leaders of the "cowgirl" movement in the early 1930s were Louise Massey, Patsy Montana, and the Good Sisters. Historically women in the South were expected to tend to the home. There they kept many ballads alive by singing and playing for family and friends. Women were not encouraged to become professional entertainers during the early period of country music and those who did were usually part of a family unit. Sara and Maybelle of the Carter family, Rosa Lee Carson ("Moonshine Kate"), who played guitar for her father, Fiddlin' John Carson, Hattie Stoneman of the Stoneman Family, Aleyone Bate, who played in her dad's Possum Hunters, Eva Thompson, the niece of Uncle Jimmy Thompson (she played piano), and Mary Lee and Irene Eskew of the Andrew Jenkins Family were the best known of the women who performed as accompanists or background singers in family bands (there were isolated examples of independent females who made their own careers outside the "family" unit such as string band duo of Samantha Bumgarner and Eva Davis, and solo stars Roba Stanley and Billie Maxwell).

Frank Driggs Collection

First of the singing cowgirls. The first of the cowgirls to fully exploit the flashy western image was the beautiful leader of the 1928 group the Musical Massey Family. Billie Maxwell's career began earlier, but she didn't exploit the role like Massey did. Dad Massey soon recognized that the main feature of the group was Louise and so the unit eventually took on the name Louise Massey and the Westerners. Between 1933 and 1943 they cut more than a hundred titles, most of which featured the lead voice of Louise, who sang many of the songs in Spanish. "We were never hillbilly. We were western from the beginning and loved to be called western," she proclaimed. One of the family members, her brother Curt, became musical director for the popular 1960s television series "The Beverly Hillbillies." He wrote the theme song ("Come and listen to my story 'bout a man named Jed") and then wrote and sang the theme of "Petticoat Junction," a television spin-off of "The Beverly Hillbillies."

In *Country: The Music and the Musicians* Robert Oermann affirms, "The morals of any woman who dared to pick up an instrument and climb on a stage were considered questionable at best. Even after it became fairly common for women to be included in professional bands, female performers felt it necessary to at least give the appearance that they were married to, or related to, one of the men in the band." The most liberated of the country operations during the twenties and thirties was the "National Barn Dance" show out of Chicago. Perhaps it was because the show emanated from outside of the "Deep South" that it was more congenial to women. The show provided support to solo singers Grace Wilson and Linda Parker ("The Sunbonnet Girl"), as well as to Lulu Belle Wiseman, Louise Massey, the Good Sisters, and Patsy Montana.

Louise Massey (1908-1983) began her career as part of her father's mid-1920s group, the Musical Massey Family. She can be seen in a 1928 portrait seated at the piano surrounded by four cowboys (her dad, two brothers, and her husband, Milt Mabie). It wasn't long before Massey became the central focus of the unit and the group took on the name Louise Massey and the Westerners. Billie Maxwell may have been the first of the cowgirls to record, but it was Louise Massey who became the first "star" cowgirl in country music to lead her own band. The group became favorites at the WLS "National Barn Dance," as well as recording stars under the direction of producer Art Satherley.

In 1929 the group signed a five-year radio contract with KMBC in Kansas City. From there the troupe joined the "National Barn

Dance" in 1933, just in time for the show's national network connection to NBC radio. Massey established the fancy and glamorous aspect of cowgirl beauty; the *New York Times* once described her's as "the perfect face." In 1976 Massey stated, "We were western from the beginning, we had beautiful costumes. We had a Spanish costume for 'Ramona' as our big number and two or three other Mexican tunes with Spanish words. That was my job in the act, to see that we were dressed right."

When the group left the "National Barn Dance" in 1936, they headed for New York, where they introduced their own NBC Tuesday night program, "The Log Cabin Dude Ranch." The group continued performing until 1948, when Massey retired to New Mexico. Among over a hundred recordings, the group's key successes included "When the White Azaleas Start Blooming," "South of the Border (Down Mexico Way)," "I Only Want a Buddy (Not a Sweetheart)," and the group's biggest hit, "My Adobe Hacienda." In 1982 Massey became the first western singer inducted into the National Cowgirl Hall of Fame in Herzford, Texas.

Southern Folklife Collection, University of North Carolina

The Girls of the Golden West. Millie and Dolly Good's careers really began to take off after the pair received exposure over the powerful Mexican border radio station XER. They then returned to St. Louis and station KMOX, where they were discovered by talent scouts from WLS. Billed as "The Girls of the Golden West," they were well represented on records, recording for Vocalion/Okeh, Columbia, and Bluebird. Their most popular number was "I Want to Be a Real Cowboy Girl," in which they sang that they wanted to pose in the chaps and six-shooter gear of a macho cowboy. They were excellent yodelers and also made vocal imitations of the Hawaiian guitar.

The **Good Sisters**, Millie (1913-1993) and Dolly (1915-1967), became the most popular of all the sister teams in country music during the 1930s and 1940s. Born Millie and Dolly Goad in Mount Carmel, Illinois, they became professional entertainers when they were fifteen and seventeen in St. Louis, changing their names to Good, dressing up in western regalia, and calling themselves the Girls of the Golden West. The cowgirl duo fabricated a western past that boasted of hailing from Muleshoe, Texas, and joined the "National Barn Dance" in 1933 performing in front of a prop campfire on stage. Their close harmony vocalizing on romanticized western numbers like "Bucking Bronco," "Texas Moon," "Lonely Cowgirl," "Two Cowgirls on the Lone Prairie," "Give Me a Straight Shootin' Cowboy," "Bucking Bronco," and their most popular number, "I Want to Be a Real Cowboy Girl" catapulted them to the ranks of the first really popular female country duo.

By 1935 the sisters were in New York working with Rudy Vallee on his radio show. Shortly after that they had their own NBC program and then moved to star slots at WLW to work the "Renfro Valley Barn Dance" and the "Boone County Jamboree" throughout the 1940s. They retired in 1949.

Cowgirl Sister Duos of the Depression

The influence of the Girls of the Golden West, according to Mary Bufwack and Robert Oermann, "was felt at virtually every country barn dance of the 1930s and 1940s. A sister duo was practically an essential part of every show's cast."

Sister Duo	Comments by, Bufwack and Oermann
Judy and Jen	Stars of "The Hoosier Hop," "Midwestern Hayride," "Brush Creek Follies," and "Old Dominion Barn Dance"
Judie and Julie	West Virginia's Jones sisters recorded both western ("There's a Birdie Hanging on the Wall") and sentimental ("A Letter to Mother")songs for Bluebird Records
The Leatherman Sisters	Lucille and Lillian dressed in western garb but stressed old-time tunes such as "Just a Little While" and "Lonesome for You, Darling," recorded for Bluebird in 1936
The Melody Sisters	June and Kaye Buitendorp from rural Michigan, cowgirl-clad midwestern radio stars.
The Rodik Twins	Verna and Verda, elaborately coiffed Minnesota blondes with cowgirl outfits but singing old-time sounds
The Steelman Sisters	Sis and Shang, who sang "The Cowgirl's Prayer" and "I'm Drifting Back to Dreamland" in 1936
The Sweeney Sisters	Toured with Grand Ole Opry troupes of the early and mid-1930s

Patsy Montana (1912-), born Ruby Blevins, became the best known and had the longest-lasting career of all of the singing cowgirls in country music history. After winning a talent contest in 1931 (she sang a Jimmie Rodgers yodeling blues) the college-educated fiddler-singer joined an all-girl trio, the Montana Cowgirls. The trio was part of cowboy star Stuart Hamblen's radio show in Inglewood, California. Hamblen gave Blevins the nickname Patsy and when the group broke up she adopted the name Montana. While working as a solo performer on radio in Louisiana, Montana was heard by Victor recording star Jimmie Davis ("You Are My Sunshine"), who signed her to sing backup on his records. It was at this time, 1932, that Montana made her first recording, "When the Flowers of Montana Were Blooming." The record listed her as "Patsy Montana, Montana's Yodeling Cowgirl." She also recorded "Montana Plains," which was to become her theme song (this was a reworking of "Texas Plains", a song by Montana's old boss, Stuart Hamblen. Hamblen had worked with the Beverly Hillbillies, and eventually played "bad guys" in western movies. He was a very successful songwriter —his biggest success was a non-western pop hit, "This Ole House" (Rosemary Clooney, 1954).

Southern Folklife Collection, University of North Carolina

The best known of the singing cowgirls. Montana's "I Want to Be a Cowboy's Sweetheart" is acknowledged to be country's first million-selling record by a woman. Mary Bufwack and Robert Oermann state, "As the leading cowgirl on the nation's leading barn dance show, Patsy Montana was virtually to define the role."

196

Patsy auditioned for a female spot in the Kentucky Ramblers group and by 1933 the unit had changed its name and image to that of a cowboy band, The Prairie Ramblers. The Ramblers were regarded as one of the most musically innovative hot string bands in the Midwest, and with the addition of a yodeling cowgirl who played fiddle, they soon became regulars on the "National Barn Dance." By this time, 1934, the group was billed Patsy Montana and the Prairie Ramblers. In 1935, under the direction of producer Arthur Satherley, the group recorded "I Want to Be a Cowboy's Sweetheart," reputed to be country music's first million-selling record led by a woman. In song after song Montana yodeled her way through tales of independence ("Ridin' Old Paint," "The She-Buckaroo," "Swing Time Cowgirl," and "A Rip-Snortin' Two Gun Gal").

Montana continued performing into the early 1990s, and as Mary Bufwack and Robert Oermann point out in their exhaustive study *Finding Her Voice: The Saga of Women in Country Music,* "By popularizing the cowgirl image, the strong, good-humored saddle pal, Patsy Montana gave female country performers their first new solo style. The cowgirl was an alternative to the sly country sweetheart, yet it sidestepped the lone-woman sexuality of the cabaret torch singers, jazz chanteuses, and the Broadway stars of the day. Patsy found a respectable way to swing. This independent yet compassionate image was soon adopted by dozens of other Depression-era female entertainers."

Cowboy Hot String Bands

One of the most important features of the music of the Southwest is the fact that much of it was for dancing. The hot string bands played an important community function at ranch parties and outdoor pavilions and picnics by providing exciting dance music. In the Southeast, where many a household believed that the fiddle was "the devil's instrument," dancing was often forbidden. But in the ethnically mixed Southwest dancing (and often drinking) were approved past times. In the Southwest a "barn dance" was not necessarily a sit-down performance like that of the "Grand Ole Opry," but rather a swinging dance that occurred in a barn. Above, square dancers whirl about at an outdoor picnic in Texas.

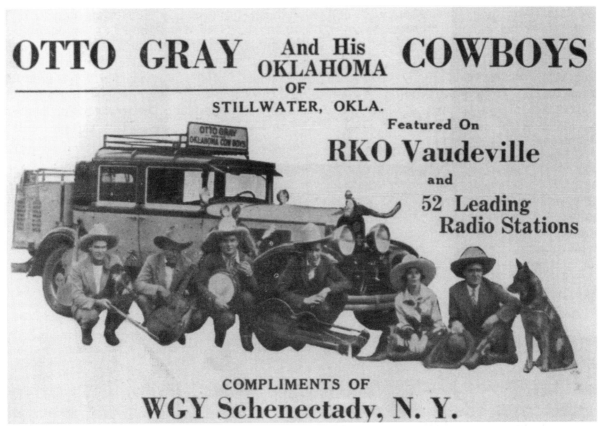

OTTO GRAY And His OKLAHOMA COWBOYS

— OF —

STILLWATER, OKLA.

Featured On

RKO Vaudeville

and

52 Leading
Radio Stations

COMPLIMENTS OF

WGY Schenectady, N. Y.

Frank Driggs Collection

Otto Gray's Oklahoma Cowboys did much to promote a western image in the days before the popularity of the singing cowboys. They appeared on radio and played all the major entertainment circuits, including RKO, Fox, Loew's, and Pulex. They also helped popularize cowboy music in the East with their stay in Schenectady, New York. Their show, of which a ten-minute sequence can be seen on the Shanachie video, *Things Ain't Like They Used to Be,* was a fast-paced, intentionally hokey series of vaudeville routines. One of the group's press releases of the time reads, "Some cowboys are only drugstore cowboys and some cowboy bands are only cowboy bands. But some cowboy bands are both riding, roping, shooting, bronco-busting cowboys and musicians as well. That's the kind of cowboy band that came to town yesterday when Otto Gray and His Oklahoma Cowboys drove in with their custom-built train of autos that are really a sight to see."

The southwestern states of Texas and Oklahoma had a rich heritage of raucous fiddle sounds and square dancing. Unlike the mournful modes that emanated from the Scottish and British heritage of the southeastern states, the middle European mix of aggressive fiddles, accordions, and the beer hall tradition resulted in a more spirited form of song making. Added to this was a more open attitude to the culture of Mexican, French, African-American, and other ethnic groups. It was not unusual for string bands in Texas and Oklahoma to include large doses of blues, jazz, and Mexican mariachi sounds.

Before the commercial recordings and films of the singing cowboys, **Otto Gray** (1890-1967) was performing southwestern music for large audiences and establishing his reputation as one of the first hot string cowboy bands in American show business. In early 1924 Billy McGinty organized the Oklahoma Cowboy Band as "a fiddlin', singin', and dancin' unit for the purpose of bringing back to the present generation the music and songs of the early days in the West." McGinty chose Gray to lead the touring group and provided elaborate publicity, as well as constant advertising in *Billboard* magazine between 1928 and 1932.

Gray and his Oklahoma Cowboys began on Bristow radio station KFRU and soon they were playing vaudeville stages all over America, traveling in three custom-built automobiles and two custom trailers. Their shows featured fast-moving, straight fiddle tunes, comic routines, and even a dog, Rex.

The group mixed sentimental parlor songs with cowboy tunes and novelty items such as "The Song of the Dying Cowboy," "The Cowboy's Lament," "She'll Be Comin' Round the Mountain," "Who Broke the Lock on the Henhouse Door," and "I Had but 50 Cents." Their recordings for Gennett and Vocalion are difficult to find today; Gray's is a rare example of a group that was very popular without having any hit records.

Southern Folklife Collection, University of North Carolina

Prince Albert Hunt is on the right in blackface with the fiddle. The little boy in the front is Prince Albert Hunt, Jr. Hunt was a popular southwestern performer at dances and made a number of recordings for Okeh featuring his bluesy fiddle style and vocals. Hunt's connection with black music was a major facet of his performance style.

Little is known about another influential Texas fiddler-show-man, **Prince Albert Hunt** (died 1931), who led a group called the Texas Rambler. His music was considered a bridge between breakdown fiddle tunes and what would become western swing. Hunt often performed in blackface. He went from playing house parties to performing more in professional venues such as dance halls and taverns. Growing up in the black section of Terrell, Texas, Hunt played informally with black musicians, which resulted in his recording blues selections such as "Blues in a Bottle." Hunt was shot to death by a jealous husband in 1931.

The **East Texas Serenaders** (1927-1936) presaged the western swing movement of the mid-thirties more than any other group. Led by left-handed fiddler D. H. Williams, the group featured, guitar, tenor banjo, and a three-string cello. The Serenaders had an expansive repertoire that covered old mountain tunes like "Old Joe Clark," ragtime selections such as "Combination Rag" and "The Beaumont Rag," waltzes like "Serenaders Waltz" and "Sweetest Flower Waltz," and popular songs such as "Five Foot Two" and "Star Dust." The Serenaders were one of the best early string bands recorded. The group recorded twenty-four sides for Brunswick, Columbia, and Decca from 1927 to 1936. The group created a dynamic rhythm ensemble sound, with the guitar and banjo providing a driving pulse. Henry Bogan's outstanding bowed and pluck-ed cello enhanced the rhythm—sounding like a jug in a jug band.

Courtesy County Records

Although the Serenaders were among the best-known string bands in the Texas area (they recorded for Columbia, Brunswick, and Decca), none of the members ever considered music a full-time occupation. Throughout most of the band's career the individual members worked variously as a truck farmer, postal service employee, florist/undertaker, and gas station owner. In his 1961 *The Disc Collector* Fred Hoeptner says, "They have preserved on phonograph records some of the best examples of the early Western folk instrumental style."

Finally, better known and more directly responsible for western swing were the **Light Crust Doughboys** (1932-1990s). Wilbert Lee O'Daniel, a flour executive for Burrus Mill, thought that having a musical group associated with his flour could be a commercial bonanza. He brought together fiddler Bob Wills, singer Milton Brown, and guitarist Herman Arnspiger after hearing them in 1931 on radio as the Aladdin Laddies, a name the Wills Fiddle Band acquired to placate their sponsor, the Aladdin Lamp Company. By 1932 the Laddies became the Light Crust Doughboys with O'Daniel acting as manager and master of ceremonies. Among their many recordings were "Texas Breakdown," "On to Victory Mr. Roosevelt," "Bluebonnet Waltz," "Saturday Night Rag," "Alamo Waltz," and "Beautiful Texas." When O'Daniel insisted that Brown and Wills not perform independent engagements (the source of additional revenue for the artists) they left to form their own separate organizations. O'Daniel continued leading his hot string bands, even forming his own firm, the Hillbilly Flour Company. He later parlayed his popularity into two terms as governor of Texas. Ken Maynard, the Light Crust Doughboys, and the other early western performers of string band sounds set the stage for more popular forms that would occur after 1934: the singing cowboys, western swing, and honky tonk. These forms will be investigated more thoroughly in Chapter 13.

Southern Folklife Collection, University of North Carolina

The original Light Crust Doughboys. Left to right, Milton Brown, Durwood Brown, Truet Kimzey, Bob Wills, and Herman Arnspiger. The roots of western swing are to be found in this hot string band. Milton Brown and Bob Wills would emerge as the leaders of western swing when they formed their own groups, the Musical Brownies and the Texas Playboys, respectively.

Chapter 8

POPULAR MUSIC: 1935-1950

		Presidents	
Years	**President**	**Theme/Slogan**	**Party**
1933-36	Franklin D. Roosevelt	"A New Deal to Restore This Country to Prosperity"	Democrat
1937-40	Franklin D. Roosevelt	"We Will Carry On"	Democrat
1941-44	Franklin D. Roosevelt	"The Same Franklin Roosevelt You Have Known"	Democrat
1945-48	Franklin D. Roosevelt/ Harry S Truman	"Don't Change Horses in Midstream" (F.D.R. dies of a cerebral hemorrhage April 12, 1945)	Democrat
1949-52	Harry S Truman	"Give 'Em Hell, Harry!"	Democrat

By the mid-1930s, the country had somewhat recovered from the worst of the Depression. Roosevelt's New Deal had created many jobs via the "alphabet soup" programs for the "everyman" in society. Most Republicans and big business felt that the New Deal smacked of socialism and that America's free enterprise system was in danger of going the way of Communism. In 1935, this philosophy was succinctly summarized by *Buffalo Evening News* writer Mark Sullivan: "The New Deal is to America what the early phase of Nazism was to Germany and the early phase of Fascism to Italy." From this point of view, there seemed some relief when Roosevelt's National Industrial Recovery Act was overturned by the Supreme Court. For the rest of the country, there was some solace that same year, when Roosevelt's Works Progress Administration was voted in by Congress. Among other ventures, this program established literary, musical, and artistic projects underwritten by the government.

Library of Congress

President Roosevelt proclaimed, "Yesterday, December 7, 1941, a date which will live in infamy, the United States of America was suddenly and deliberately attacked by naval and air forces of the Empire of Japan."

Courtesy Down Beat

Everyone got into the act during World War II. In this *Down Beat* cover from 1944 musicians strike a pose on a tank. Note the exhortation at bottom: "Buy more war bonds!"

Courtesy Buffalo & Erie County Public Library

War songs proved just as popular during World War II as they had during World War I. A list of hit songs from the second war is found in a chart on page 204. One well-known artist, who, despite her fame never charted well, is British singer Vera Lynn, whose best known song of the period was "We'll Meet Again." Lynn was known as "The Forces' Sweetheart." One song listed in the chart is by country singer Elton Britt, who provided America with one of the most dearly loved war songs of the forties, "There's a Star Spangled Banner Waving Somewhere."

Movie Star News

Even with the political conflicts, there were a few calm years between the economic collapse of the early thirties and the ensuing calamity of World War II. During the period between 1935 and 1941, America was buoyed by the optimistic, bouncy, popular music of the "swing era." At the same time, America was keeping a watchful eye on the drama unfolding in Europe and the Far East. By 1937, Adolph Hitler had thoroughly consolidated power in Germany, Benito Mussolini was in his second decade of fascist rule in Italy, the Spanish Republic was under attack by Francisco Franco, and Japan had begun her methodical aggression in China. In each instance, America remained aloof and isolationist. Roosevelt, who had promised to keep America out of war, was faced with the same situation that had confronted Wilson before World War I.

In 1939, Hitler invaded Poland, causing Great Britain and France to declare war on Germany. By the next year Germany had invaded and conquered France and its Luftwaffe was bombing British cities. British Prime Minister Winston Churchill proclaimed, "I have nothing to offer but blood, toil, tears, and sweat." Congress, unsettled by all of this European aggression, passed the Selective Service and Treasury Acts, the first peacetime draft in U.S. history.

The story of the year in 1941 was the December 7 surprise attack on the U.S. naval base at Pearl Harbor, which destroyed or heavily damaged eighteen ships and killed 2,403 men. Congress declared war on Japan the following day. Germany and Italy then declared war on the United States. World War II was to pit the Axis powers (Germany, Italy, and Japan) against the United States, Britain, France, and the Soviet Union. In America, 1942 to 1945 were known as the "war years," and nearly everyone in the country was committed to the war effort. There were gas rationing, paper drives, victory gardens, women working in the factories (hence the title "Rosie the Riveter"), days of fasting, and entertainers imploring homebound Americans to buy war bonds.

Entertainment for the swing shift. With "around the clock" work for the war effort, all-hours entertainment became necessary. *Above*, swing shift workers attend a dance held at the Main-Utica Ballroom of Buffalo, New York, from midnight to four a.m. These were weekly affairs. *Below*, a line at a late Buffalo movie picture show that started between 1:30 and 2 a.m. once a week for workers on the swing shift. Both of these photographs were taken in the spring of 1943 and distributed by the U.S. Office of War Information.

Johnny Mercer, one of the most talented, all-around lyricists of his time, wrote a delightful ode to the war-weary workers in 1942 — "On the Swing Shift." Mercer wrote a large number of war songs for a bevy of Hollywood films that used military themes throughout the 1940s. In 1942 alone, Mercer provided songs for *The Fleet's In*, *You Were Never Lovelier*, *Captains of the Clouds*, and *Star-Spangled Rhythm* (which included "On the Swing Shift").

In 1944, President Roosevelt was re-elected to a unique fourth term (no other president had served more than two) to finish guiding America through another great crisis. On April 12, 1945, on the eve of military victory, Roosevelt died, to be replaced by Vice President Harry S Truman. As the Allied powers gained victory and the Axis forces fell, Mussolini was executed by his own people, and Hitler committed suicide. By May 8 the war in Europe had come to an end. To bring the war in the Pacific to a rapid conclusion, the United States dropped atomic bombs on the Japanese cities of Hiroshima, on August 6, and Nagasaki, on August 9. Japan signed an unconditional surrender aboard the U.S. battleship *Missouri* on September 2, 1945.

The enthusiasm of the post-war period was not unlike the euphoria felt after World War I. Great expectations bubbled up from a nation that had made major sacrifices to attain victory. With the help of the G.I. Bill, returning servicemen sought education, jobs, and housing. Large tracts of land outside city centers were put aside for new homes, and modern suburbia was inaugurated. One of the major roadblocks to the never-never land of bliss and world peace was the ideological conflict with America's one-time ally, the Soviet Union. In 1946, Churchill warned that the differences between the Western, capitalist world and the Eastern, communist world seemed irreconcilable. He noted that the Soviet Union wanted to extend its power and influence, and that the United States and Great Britain should be wary of the "Iron Curtain" that had descended across Europe, dividing the Western and Soviet spheres of influence. In 1947, Bernard Baruch pointed out that the United States should not be deceived about the realities of this conflict, and that the country was indeed in the midst of a "cold war."

Key Hit Songs of World War II

Artist (lead vocalists)	Song	Year	Peak Pos
Andrews Sisters	Boogie Woogie Bugle Boy	1941	6
J. Dorsey (Eberly & O'Connell)	Yours	1941	2
Kay Kyser (Glee Club)	(There'll Be Bluebirds Over) The White Cliffs of Dover	1941-42	1
Harry James (Helen Forrest)	I Don't Want to Walk Without You	1942	1
Spike Jones (& His City Slickers)	Der Fuehrer's Face	1942	3
Glenn Miller (Modernaires)	Don't Sit Under the Apple Tree (With Anyone Else but Me)	1942	1
Sammy Kaye (Don Cornell)	I Left My Heart at the Stage Door Canteen	1942	3
Kay Kyser (Glee Club)	Praise the Lord and Pass the Ammunition!	1942	1
Kay Kyser (Harry Babbitt)	He Wears a Pair of Silver Wings	1942	1
Bing Crosby	White Christmas	1942	1
Elton Britt	There's a Star-Spangled Banner Waving Somewhere	1942-43	7
Vaughn Monroe	When the Lights Go on Again (All Over the World)	1942-43	1
Harry James (Dick Haymes)	I'll Get By	1944	1
Duke Ellington (Al Hibbler)	Don't Get Around Much Anymore	1943	8
Song Spinners	Comin' in on a Wing and a Prayer	1943	1
Harry James (Helen Forrest)	I Had the Craziest Dream	1942-43	1
Bing Crosby	Sunday, Monday, or Always	1943	1
Bing Crosby	I'll Be Home for Christmas	1943	3
Dick Haymes	You'll Never Know	1943	1
Bing Crosby & Andrews Sisters	Don't Fence Me In	1944	1
Bing Crosby	I'll Be Seeing You	1944	1
Frank Sinatra	I Couldn't Sleep a Wink Last Night	1944	4
Dinah Shore	I'll Walk Alone	1944	1
Jo Stafford	Long Ago and Far Away	1944	6
Johnny Mercer	G.I. Jive	1944	11
Johnny Mercer	Ac-Cent-tchu-ate the Positive	1945	1
Betty Grable	I Can't Begin to Tell You	1945	5
Harry James (Kitty Kallen)	It's Been a Long, Long Time	1945	1
Pied Pipers	Dream	1945	1
Les Brown (Doris Day)	Sentimental Journey	1945	1
Peggy Lee	Waitin' for the Train to Come In	1945	4

Source of chart positions: Joel Whitburn's Pop Memories, 1900-1954

The Swing Bands Swing

To provide some idea of how music was changing by 1935, let's take a look at the most productive leader of the past section, Paul Whiteman. Between 1920 and 1934, Whiteman had a total of 220 charted singles and 32 songs that reached number one on the charts. But between 1935 and 1950, he charted only fifteen selections in the top twenty, none higher than seven, and did not have any number one hits. Whiteman was still a well-known and highly regarded celebrity leader, featured on radio and early television into the early 1950s, but his was no longer the popular music of choice. Perhaps the most interesting thing about the swing or big band era is that the underground spirit of the previous period is so much in evidence. The old adage, "what the soloist plays today, the arranger writes tomorrow," applies.

Picture Collection, The Branch Libraries, The New York Public Library

King of pop no more. Although Paul Whiteman had been "King" of popular music between 1920 and 1934, by the swing era his music made nary a dent on the pop charts. Whiteman's orchestral sounds seemed hopelessly dated to an audience, many of them young, who wanted to dance to the new sounds of "swing." This is the nature of popular music—like cotton candy, styles evaporate quickly.

Another point should be made. Sometimes a performer or group has a big hit or series of hits but makes no real impact, or has no real staying power. For example, the record that stayed number one for the longest time in the history of American commercial music according to Joel Whitburn's charts is "Near You," recorded by Francis Craig and His Orchestra. This record ran an amazing seventeen consecutive weeks as the top hit in 1947 (it later became Milton Berle's theme song). Yet, beyond Craig's role as a Nashville-based piano player and composer, his place in popular music is negligible, much like the one-hit wonder status of Debby Boone's "You Light Up My Life" in 1977.

The jazz bands that had developed during the twenties were somewhat silenced during the early years of the Depression. Loud and brassy didn't seem to fit the mood of America between 1929 and 1934. One key band, the Casa Loma, using the precision arrangements of Gene Gifford, found great success with the college crowd and with radio. This popularity impressed former Ben Pollack clarinet star Benny Goodman so much that Goodman decided to form his own band.

Courtesy Down Beat

Magazines like *Down Beat* went into business during the mid-1930s because of the fanatical interest in swing music. Audiences of this era were not only familiar with the leaders and singers of the well-known orchestras, but also with the sidemen in those or-ganizations. Key players such as Gene Krupa, Teddy Wilson, Lionel Hampton, Harry James (all with Goodman at one time), Bunny Berigan, Buddy Rich, and many others had large followings.

Right, it was big news when a sideman left to join another band or tried to form his own unit. *Left,* some writers and bandleaders were not happy when youthful fans left their seats to dance in the aisles during concert engagements.

Benny Goodman (1909-1986) was a classically trained clarinet player who had performed traditional jazz in Chicago during the twenties and early thirties. Goodman's breakthrough came when NBC signed him to play for a late night radio show, "Let's Dance," in 1934. Goodman's band featured special arrangements by creative black writers Fletcher Henderson, Benny Carter, and Jimmy Mundy. When he toured the country in May 1935, Goodman found that audiences were resistant to the jazzy arrangements. By the time the group reached California in August the leader was ready to disband because of the general disinterest in the midwest. What Goodman didn't realize was that his late-hour East Coast show was a big hit with college listeners on the West Coast, where it was heard much earlier in the evening. They were ready for exciting dance music, not sweet melancholia. When Goodman's unit played the Palomar Ballroom in Los Angeles the dancers crowded the bandstand and were wildly enthusiastic. The swing era was born.

As with most things in history, timing is essential. Goodman's band, and others like it, had been playing an aggressive dance style for several years, but the popular audience wasn't ready for it until 1935. Actually, the underground arrangements of Henderson, Don Redman, Luis Russell, and other black bandleaders reaffirm the concept that the "underground" is usually ahead of the popular music scene. That Goodman was white and more palatable to the dominant white pop audience should be of little surprise to anyone. Even while making a radical shift, (and perhaps especially then), popular culture seizes upon that which is most accommodating and secure.

Goodman, who was an excellent technician and a thoroughly demanding taskmaster, set the tone for the swing leaders. The swing era was dominated by capable, recognizable frontmen (many of whom featured their own solos) who were able to secure national radio shows and major recording contracts. The bands featured soloists and singers who were all part of a large, family-like environment that was very much a feature of the swing movement. Just as there are thousands of rock and soul units today, there were untold numbers of aspiring bands that played dance music in their communities, hoping to establish a "sound" that would become commercially successful. That sound was achieved by the ways in which the arranger wrote the band's musical charts. Some bands eschewed the jazzier aspects of the music and they came to be referred to as "sweet" bands. Some featured novelty tricks and some played for cafe society.

Courtesy of Sony Music

Benny Goodman was the man most identified with the explosion of swing music.

Goodman was viewed as the pied piper of jazz because of his tremendous following among the youth of the day. Known also as the "King of Swing," he featured gutsy jazz soloists such as trumpeters Ziggy Elman and Harry James and drummer Gene Krupa, and he broke the color barrier by bringing into his small groups black soloists such as pianist Teddy Wilson, vibist Lionel Hampton, and electric guitarist Charlie Christian. In 1939, Goodman hired Fletcher Henderson to play piano. All of the popular bandleaders featured vocalists, and Goodman was especially fortunate to have a series of outstanding singers: Helen Ward, Martha Tilton, Peggy Lee, Buddy Clark, and Buddy Greco.

In 1937, Goodman played the Paramount Theater in New York and created pandemonium as "bobby soxers" screamed with delight and danced in the aisles, presaging the outbursts by fans of Frank Sinatra, Elvis Presley, and the Beatles. In 1938, Goodman presented an evening of integrated jazz, with a printed program, at Carnegie Hall (see Chapter 9). From there it was on to Hollywood, where Goodman and his band members, like a host of others, could often be seen playing themselves in cinematic nightclub scenes performing the latest hits of the day. Key films featuring Goodman and his band were *Hollywood Hotel* (1937), *The Powers Girl* (1942), *The Gang's All Here* (1943), *Stage Door*

Canteen (1943), and *Sweet and Lowdown* (1944). In 1955, Hollywood made the *The Benny Goodman Story,* starring Steve Allen as Goodman and featuring Sammy Davis Jr. as Fletcher Henderson.

Courtesy Library of Congress

The "Sentimental Gentleman of Swing." When Tommy Dorsey walked off the stage after an argument with brother Jimmy in 1935 at the Glen Island Casino, the Dorsey Brothers were on the verge of stardom. They had arrangements by Glenn Miller, vocals by Bob Crosby, and a contract with Decca Records. Tommy Dorsey lost no time building his own career. He took over the Joe Haymes organization and brought in arrangers like Alex Stordahl and Paul Weston. Tommy Dorsey placed a premium on the vocal portion of his shows. His first star vocalists were Edythe Wright and Cliff Weston. Wright was featured on the band's first number one hit, the 1935 "On Treasure Island," followed by another number one selection, "The Music Goes 'Round and 'Round." Weston had hits on "Take Me Back to My Boots and Saddle" (1935) and "Alone," a number one hit in 1936.

Jack Leonard replaced Cliff Weston in early 1936 and became one of the top male band vocalists in America until he was released by Dorsey in early 1940. Leonard's big hits were "No Regrets" (1936), "I'm in a Dancing Mood," "Marie," "Josephine," "In the Still of the Night," and "Who?" (1937), "Yearning (Just for You)" and "Now It Can Be Told" (1938), "The Lamp Is Low," "Oh, You Crazy Moon," "Indian Summer" and "All the Things You Are" (1939), and "The Starlit Hour" (1940). Alan DeWitt replaced Leonard for a couple of months until Frank Sinatra joined the crew and recorded his first hit in early 1940, "Polka Dots and Moonbeams." Connie Haines, Jo Stafford, and the Pied Pipers also had numerous hits with the Dorsey orchestra.

George T. Simon's *The Best of the Music Makers* has high praise for Dorsey: "Tommy soon developed probably the greatest all-around dance band of all time. It combined Tommy's penchant for perfection with his flair for romantic ballads."

Competing with Goodman for the title of the "King of Swing" was the trombone-playing bandleader **Tommy Dorsey** (1905-1956). Like Goodman, Dorsey started as a Dixieland player and then became an in-demand studio stalwart with his brother, Jimmy, who played reeds. Together they formed a band. However, after a bitter argument at the Glen Island Casino on Long Island in 1935, Tommy walked off the bandstand and left the organization for good. Jimmy's unit, which featured the vocals of Bob Eberly and Helen O'-Connell ("Green Eyes," "Maria Elena," "Yours," and "Tangerine"), was one of the most popular units of the swing era.

Shortly after the split, Tommy took over Joe Haymes's society band. The band's theme (first recorded in 1932) was "I'm Getting Sentimental Over You," which featured Tommy's warm, smooth trombone style. Tommy was an outstanding ballad player, and he worked diligently at developing breath control that would allow him to play long, fluid lines. Arrangers Alex Stordahl and Paul Weston created dreamy orchestrations that featured the leader's solos. The pair also wrote beautiful arrangements for the band's vocal group, the Pied Pipers, which spotlighted Jo Stafford and, beginning in 1940, Frank Sinatra. Lesser known to today's audiences were vocalists Edythe Wright ("Treasure Island," "Music, Maestro, Please") and Jack Leonard ("Marie").

© 1992 BMG Music

207

Later, Tommy Dorsey's band featured swing luminaries such as trumpeters Bunny Berigan, Yank Lawson, and Pee Wee Erwin, reedmen Buddy DeFranco and Bud Freeman, drummers Dave Tough and Buddy Rich, and arrangers Dean Kincaid and Sy Oliver. Like Goodman, Dorsey featured a specialized jazz combo within the band known as the Clambake Seven. Also, like Goodman, his band was featured in numerous Hollywood films including *Las Vegas Nights* (1941), *Ship Ahoy* (1942), *Girl Crazy* (1943), and *Du Barry Was a Lady* (1944). The 1947 biopic, *The Fabulous Dorseys,* starred Jimmy and Tommy and their parents.

Artie Shaw (1910-   ) made it fashionable to put show tunes of the day in a swing-band setting. Cole Porter's "Begin the Beguine" was resurrected in 1938 and became a number one hit. The Jerry Gray arrangement is one of the greatest in swing history. Handsome and debonair, Shaw was as famous for his Casanova ways (he was married to such Hollywood beauties as Ava Gardner, Lana Turner, and Evelyn Keyes, along with five others), as he was for his wizardry on the jazz clarinet. Shaw was one of the most creative leaders of the entire era. Always trying to break new ground, he introduced a string section that recorded and even toured with his band ("Frenesi"). Another of Shaw's innovations was adding oboes and French horn.

Shaw featured such swing stars as trumpeters Billy Butterfield and Roy Eldridge, reedman Tony Pastor, and pianist Johnny Guarnieri in a small jazz unit called the Gramercy Five. The leader and his band were featured in *Dancing Co-ed* (1939) and *Second Chorus* (1940). Because Shaw was highly critical of the emphasis on the "star system" in popular music, he quit the business at the peak of his popularity (detailed in his bright and witty autobiography, *The Trouble With Cinderella).* Hollywood didn't call on Shaw much because of his early departure from the music scene. And because Hollywood couldn't figure out a safe angle on his highly publicized love life, no biopic was made.

Courtesy of Charly Records   © 1987 BMG Music

Jazz historian Chris Albertson calls May 24, 1936, a jazz milestone because it was "the first real jazz concert." Joe Helbock, the owner of the 52nd Street nightspot the Onyx Club, decided to capitalize on the recent success of "swing" music by staging a concert at the Imperial Theatre. Helbock titled the event a "Swing Music Concert," and it headlined Bob Crosby's band and the Casa Loma Orchestra. Small units led by Tommy Dorsey, Paul Whiteman, and Louis Armstrong filled out the bill. Artie Shaw was unknown at the time and was asked to provide transitional music during a stage setup between the bands.

Shaw was the hit of the evening with his "swing string ensemble." His composition "Interlude in B-Flat" garnered such applause that the group repeated the number; it was the only one they had rehearsed. On the strength of that evening the twenty-six year-old clarinetist decided to form his own swing band. After a couple of false starts Shaw finally found success in 1938 with his classic interpretation of Cole Porter's "Begin the Beguine." Being fawned over as a "star" instead of being treated like a serious musician irked Shaw. In his autobiography, *The Trouble With Cinderella,* he specified, "The mass American public is by and large musically illiterate, and as is the case with any uneducated group when confronted with a highly specialized, technically involved form of activity, there is always this engrossment with surface detail rather than intrinsic merit."

By the late 1930s Glenn Miller's band had emerged as the most popular musical organization in the land. In *Down Beat* polls the Miller band placed second in both the swing and sweet categories. This had never happened before; bands were then considered either jazzy, that is, swing oriented, or non-jazzy, that is, sweet. Miller had the unique ability to appeal to both audiences.

Glenn Miller's "signature" sound, the clarinet-reed effect, doubling the tenor sax lead on clarinet, was unusual. Miller said in an interview, "We're fortunate that our style doesn't limit us to stereotyped intros, modulations, first choruses, endings or even trick rhythms. The fifth sax, playing clarinet most of the time, lets you know whose band you're listening to."

Movie Star News

The Glenn Miller Story. James Stewart and June Allyson as Glenn and Helen Miller in the 1953 Universal Studio biopic.

The last of the "Big Four" swing giants was trombonist-bandleader **Glenn Miller** (1904-1944). After working in Ben Pollack's band (1926-28), Miller freelanced and performed in pit bands on Broadway before finding success with his own unit in 1938. Miller's unique orchestral "voicing" of clarinet lead over the reed section and his ability to incorporate medley arrangements into a melodic and danceable format made his unit the most popular of the bands of the 1940s. His music is considered the least jazz-oriented of the four, and perhaps that is why today's listeners gravitate to his sound more readily than to the other three.

Miller's success began in 1939 with his remote broadcasts from Long Island's Glen Island Casino. Miller ended each broadcast with medleys of "something old, something new," which proved to be a winning formula. The main musical highlights of the Miller pop legacy were outstanding arrangements by Jerry Gray and Bill Finegan, melodic solos by trumpeter Bobby Hackett and saxophonist-singer Tex Beneke, combined with vocals by Marion Hutton, Ray Eberle, and the Modernaires.

The band's first major hit, "Moonlight Serenade" (1939), was to become its theme song. Other classics included "Little Brown Jug," "In the Mood," "Chattanooga Choo Choo," "Elmer's Tune," "A String of Pearls," and "(I've Got a Gal in) Kalamazoo."

In September 1942, at the peak of the band's popularity, Miller enlisted in the Army Air Force and led the war's most famous service band. During a mission to perform for U.S. troops in France, Miller's plane was lost over the English Channel on December 15, 1944. In 1953 Hollywood made *The Glenn Miller Story.*

Other Popular Jazz Bands

Leader	Key Jazz Figures	Singer	Top 20 Hits	#1's	Best Known Song	Year
Charlie Barnet	Billy May (tpt)	Mary Ann McCall	22	1	Cherokee	1939
Count Basie	Lester Young (sax)	Jimmy Rushing	19	1	One O'Clock Jump	
	Buck Clayton (tpt)	Helen Humes				1939
Bunny Berigan	Bunny Berigan (tpt)	Bunny Berigan	13	0	I Can't Get Started	1937
	George Auld (sax)					
Les Brown	Billy Butterfield (tpt)	Doris Day	22	3	Sentimental Journey	1945
	Ted Nash (sax)					
Larry Clinton	Toots Mondello (sax)	Bea Wain	35	4	The Big Dipper	1937
Bob Crosby	Gil Rodin (sax)	Bob Crosby	35	3	Day In Day Out	1939
	Bob Haggart (bs)					
Duke Ellington	Johnny Hodges (sax)	Ivie Anderson	34	1	Take the A Train	1941
	Bily Strayhorn (arr)	Herb Jeffries				
Woody Herman	Stan Getz (sax)	Woody Herman	39	1	Blues in the Night	1941-42
	Ralph Burns (arr)	Frances Wayne				
Harry James	Harry James (tpt)	Helen Forrest	57	8	I'll Get By	1944
		Dick Haymes				
Stan Kenton	Stan Kenton (pno)	Anita O'Day	12	0	Artistry in Rhythm	1944
	Pete Rugolo (arr)	June Christy				
Gene Krupa	Roy Eldridge (tpt)	Anita O'Day	19	0	Let Me Off Uptown	1941
		Irene Daye				
Red Norvo	Red Norvo (vbs)	Mildred Bailey	15	2	Please Be Kind	1938
	Herbie Haymur (sax)					
Tony Pastor	Tony Pastor (sax)	Tony Pastor	13	0	Bell-Bottom Trousers	1945
	George Auld (sax)	Rosie Clooney				
Charlie Spivak	Charlie Spivak (tpt)	Irene Daye	15	0	My Devotion	1942
	Nelson Riddle (arr)	The Stardusters				
Claude Thornhill	Claude Thornhill (pno)	Maxine Sullivan	8	0	Loch Lomand	1937
	Gil Evans (arr)	The Snowflakes				
Teddy Wilson	Teddy Wilson (pno)	Billie Holiday	38	2	Carelessly	1937

Source of chart positions: Joel Whitburn's Pop Memories, 1890-1954

Courtesy Down Beat

Courtesy Down Beat

The Sweet Bands

Most of the bands during the swing era were categorized as "sweet" bands that played conservative, relaxed music with an emphasis on melodious section work rather than hot solos. The sweet bands were especially popular with older audiences, who preferred calmer sounds for their dancing pleasure. These bands were the favorites of middle America. However, the jazz-oriented critics of newly formed magazines such as *Down Beat* and *Metronome* found these units lacking in musical innovations and hard-edged swing. These critics often referred to the less daring outfits as "Mickey Mouse" bands.

Perhaps the model for taste, precision, and smooth-sounding dance music was Britisher **Ray Noble** (1903-1978). By the time he came over to America in late 1934 to front a band assembled for him by a then-unknown Glenn Miller, Noble had already managed four number one hits: "Love Is the Sweetest Thing" "The Old Spinning Wheel" (1933), "The Very Thought of You" and "Isle of Capri" (1934).

"The Very Thought of You," music and words by bandleader Ray Noble, was one of the most popular songs of 1934. This song was used prominently in the 1944 Hollywood film.

Noble's new American band featured future leaders such as Miller, trumpeter Charlie Spivak, pianist Claude Thornhill, and trombonist Will Bradley. The band's star was vocalist Al Bowlly, England's top singing star of the 1930s (he was killed by an air raid bomb in London in 1941). During the second half of the 1930s Noble accompanied Fred Astaire and was a fixture at New York's swanky Rainbow Room (today called the Rainbow and Stars) in Rockefeller Center, New York, "sixty-five stories nearer the stars."

The sweet bands were a diverse group indeed. Most didn't spotlight jazz soloists, preferring instead melodic ensemble work and individual as well as glee-club-like vocals. Many leaders worked hard to find a gimmick that would set them apart. For example, Shep Fields featured an accordion player, the constant tapping of temple blocks, and his own blowing of bubbles through a straw, resulting in his trademark "Rippling Rhythm." Society bandleader Ted FioRita and Gray Gordon both featured the beating of two temple blocks to create a recognizable band sound (Gray was referred to as the leader of "Tic-Toc Music"). The lovely Rita Rio fronted a female band dressed in tuxedos; Spike Jones and His City Slicker Band created barnyard sounds on homemade instruments, whistles, guns, and other items as they broadly satirized pop tunes of the day in such songs as "Cocktails for Two" (1945). Fred Waring was noted for his tightly organized glee club sounds, and his band eventually produced two eminently influential choir directors, Kay Thompson and Robert Shaw. Freddy Martin found success by reworking classical themes into pop hits. The list could go on and on (see chart of sweet bands on page 216). Here is a brief look at three of the most successful sweet bands.

Guy Lombardo: The sweetest music this side of heaven. So read the promos for this all-time great dance band, the only band to be one of the top ten best selling groups during the two major periods covered in this book, 1917-1934 and 1935-1950. During the 1920s and early 1930s the Lombardo band was considered hip. It could play hot, and its muted trumpet sound and vibrato-laden reed section projected a floating, light, swinging bounce. During the swing era, most of the jazz world eschewed Lombardo's approach, but audiences, especially the older set, kept this band at the "top of the pops" well into the 1950s.

Esteemed record producer Milt Gabler is quoted in George T. Simon's *The Big Bands*, "It's the most completely responsible band I've ever known. The men are always punctual, and they're always strictly business. They arrive on each recording date with their complete library, and each man carries in and is responsible for his own book [musical arrangements] . . . Sometimes Guy works with me in the control room, but I've noticed that when he's out there in front of the band, waving his stick, the men play better. As soon as they've finished, each man picks up his own music and his instruments, and out they go. I've never seen a band leave a studio quicker—or cleaner."

Guy Lombardo (1910-1977) led perhaps the most successful dance band of all time. Hailing from London, Ontario, his Royal Canadians began their recording career in 1924. By 1927, the band had moved to Chicago, where they performed instrumental medleys (brief arrangements of popular songs often requested by patrons). By 1929, Lombardo made New York's Hotel Roosevelt Grill his home, appearing there into the early 1960s. Lombardo began as a violinist but did not play with the band—he was strictly a frontman-conductor. Lombardo brothers Carmen, who played lead saxophone and sang, and Lebert, who played lead trumpet, completed the band's ownership and brain trust.

The band's tightly structured arrangements combined sweet, muted trumpets with saxophones awash with vibrato and unobtrusive rhythm. The result was to become one of the most recognizable sounds in the business, regularly referred to as "the sweetest music this side of heaven." Louis Armstrong named the Lombardo band his favorite band and, when leading large units of his own, Armstrong had the reed section emulate Lombardo's. How successful was Lombardo? *Joel Whitburn's Pop Memories* claims that Lombardo's is the only dance band to sell more than 100 million records. The band set numerous all-time attendance records, including that of the Savoy Ballroom in Harlem, and also played for more presidential inaugural balls than any other.

The Lombardo band's first big hit occurred in 1927, with the chart-topping "Charmaine!" Between 1927 and 1934 the band had eleven more top hits. Unlike Paul Whiteman, Lombardo was able to remain a musical force during the swing era (between 1935 and 1950 the band had 102 top-twenty hits and four number ones). Today's audiences are most familiar with Lombardo's theme song, which over the years became the anthem of New Year's Eve, "Auld Lang Syne." Lombardo's easygoing charm is best summed up by a review from big band chronicler George T. Simon: "If you can dance at all, you can dance to Lombardo's music."

After graduating from Ohio University, **Sammy Kaye** (1910-1987) formed a band that became popular in the Midwest from 1935 on through his radio show from Cleveland. The reed-playing leader was a strict disciplinarian whose major contribution was an audience participation routine entitled, "So You Want to Lead a Band." This consisted of inviting members of the audience up on stage to conduct the band. The results were often humorous and winners were awarded a Sammy Kaye baton. Like most of the other sweet bands, Kaye eschewed jazz solos for ensemble passages and vocals (the most famous being Don Cornell's 1950 hit "It Isn't Fair").

Kaye was always thinking up new ways to keep his audience listening, but his band was one of the most scorned by jazz mavens, partly because of the gimmicks, partly because of the band's lack of swing (ironically, the band's slogan was "Swing and Sway with Sammy Kaye"), and, one must presume, partly because of the band's great popularity. Kaye's band had eighty-two top twenty hits during

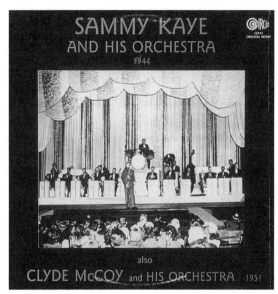

Courtesy Circle Records

Swing and Sway with Sammy Kaye. Like fellow bandleader Kay Kyser, Sammy Kaye used the gimmick of singing song titles. His theme song was the self-penned "Kaye's Melody." Many singers worked with Kaye's organization. Jimmy Brown, Tommy Ryan, Nancy Norman, and Betty Barclay are mostly forgotten or unknown to today's audience. Billy Williams, Don Cornell, and the musical groups the Three Kaydets, and Three Smart Girls are better known.

Jazz writer George T. Simon, reviewing the band's New York debut at the Commodore Hotel in 1938, wrote, "The 'swing' of Sammy Kaye can truthfully be described as follows,   . End of description of Sammy Kaye's swing." Like a majority of the sweet bands, Kaye's organization didn't really swing, but it was a disciplined, well-oiled machine that provided melodic, romantic sounds for the masses.

this period, as well as seven number one hits: "Rosalie" (1937), "Love Walked In" (1938), "Dream Valley" (1940), "Daddy" (1941), "Chickery Chick" (1945), "I'm a Big Girl Now" (1946), and "The Old Lamp Lighter" (1947). By the 1950s and 1960s, Kaye had a series of television shows and minor hits even though his musical style was considered passe.

Kay Kyser (1906-1985) led the most successful novelty band of all time. Kyser began his band at the University of North Carolina and moved it to Chicago with the help of UNC alumnus Hal Kemp, a band leader. Replacing Kemp's band at the Blackhawk Restaurant, Kyser initiated an audience participation music quiz. As Kay Kyser's Kampus Klass, the band, dressed in academic robes, played snatches of well-known songs while contestants, often prompted by Kyser, tried to guess the title. Kyser also read the names of people who sent in title suggestions, further adding to the popularity of the show. The Kampus Klass soon became Kay Kyser's Kollege of Musical Knowledge and featured trumpet player and comedian Ish Kabibble. Another of Kyser's commercial gimmicks was the singing of song titles. In this gimmick a few bars of music would be played near the start of each selection, accompanied by the vocalist, who would sing just the words of the title—Kyser felt this replaced the announcing of the song. Then the band would harmonize a few bars of its theme. Sammy Kaye, among others, adopted this technique.

Kay Kyser gained added fame by playing all over the world at military bases during World War II. He also appeared in numerous films, including this one, *Swing Fever* (1944). This slight film featured Kyser as a musician with an uncanny gift for hypnosis. The film added guest, gag appearances by bandleaders Harry James and Tommy Dorsey.

One of Kyser's arrangers, George Duning, later went on to write film scores (*Picnic,* 1956) and television scores (*Star Trek*). With a mix of novelty songs, comedy routines, and terrific ballads, Kyser was one of the superstars of the big band era.

Novelty band supreme, Kay Kyser's Kollege of Musical Knowledge. Kyser's Kollege in action from the RKO film *You'll Find Out* (1940). Kyser is in the foreground, in the dark suit, leading his mirth-making men. Kyser originally made his name on radio for long-time sponsor, Lucky Strike cigarettes.

One of the main ingredients of Kyser's success was his comedic trumpet star, Merwyn Bogue, better known to popular audiences as Ish Kabibble. In *Ish Kabibble: The Autobiography of Merwyn Bogue*, the underrated trumpeter relates how he modeled his playing style after that of Bix Beiderbecke and Red Nichols. The trumpeter was a member of the Kay Kyser organization longer than any of the other sidemen—from 1931 to 1951. Long periods between playing dates led Kabibble to become the most active of all big band sidemen. "By this time, I had adopted the philosophy of giving your employer more than you get, and so I had volunteered at every opportunity. I was now trumpet player, publicity man, transportation man, bookkeeper and paymaster, public address system installer in some cases, and, last and probably at that time least important, comedian." In time Kabibble became best known for his comedy. The trumpeter played sour notes at the wrong time, offered humorous poems, and played the stooge for the many sight gags that were the band's stock in trade. Kabibble also introduced a nutty haircut that featured bangs not unlike the Beatles thirty years later, and the look sported by actor Jim Carrey in the 1995 hit film *Dumb and Dumber.* Ish Kabibble went solo in the 1950s with a six-piece Dixieland band he called the Shy Guys.

The bespectacled Kyser couldn't play an instrument or read a note, but he was corny and silly, commanding his musical troops with fast-paced entertainment. He contributed to the mayhem on stage and actually seemed to enjoy himself. Singing was the forte of the band and Harry Babbitt, Ginny Simms, Mike Douglas, and Georgia Carroll, the eventual Mrs. Kyser, were the best known of Kyser's smooth- sounding vocalists. Novelty songs, as might be expected, were among his biggest hits: "The Umbrella Man" (1938), "Three Little Fishies," "Chatter Box" (1939), "Jingle, Jangle, Jingle" (1942), and "Woody Woodpecker" (1948). Kyser also presented some of the prettiest love songs of the era: "Thinking of You" (1935), "Stairway to the Stars" (1939), "Who Wouldn't Love You" (1942), "Ole Buttermilk Sky" (1946), and "On a Slow Boat to China" (1948). During the war years, Kyser's band was constantly in the foreground, performing on radio and at live engagements for service personnel.

It has been noted on a number of occasions in this text that many popular music artists who weren't taken seriously by their contemporary writers were, in time, excluded from a prominent place in history. Most of the historians who have written about the big band era over the past fifty years have focused on the jazzier units. Except for biographies of individual bandleaders like Lawrence Welk, Guy Lombardo and a few select others, the leaders of the sweet bands have been treated with scorn and indifference. This is certainly an area that is ripe for further scholarship.

As we have seen, bands were the main staple of popular music during this period. However, during the war years, solo singers would take on added importance. All of the singers who gained prominence during this time worked in one way or another with a band, jazz-oriented or sweet.

Author's collection

Freddy Martin (1906-1983) was a smooth-sounding tenor player who put together one of the greatest of the sweet bands in the early 1930s. He was billed as "Mr. Silvertone." Martin's group featured vibrato-shaking reeds, and a series of classical-cum-pop arrangements: "Piano Concerto in B Flat" (Tchaikovsky), "Greig Piano Concerto," "Bumble Boogie" (Rimsky-Korsakov), "Sabre Dance Boogie" (Khachaturian), and "Warsaw Concerto" (Addinsell). Martin's vocalists included Russ Morgan and Merv Griffin ("I've Got a Lovely Bunch of Coconuts"). Martin's band was often featured at L.A.'s Coconut Grove from 1938 into the 1960s.

Lawrence Welk (1903-1992) was known for his polkas, his "Champagne Music," and his "Polish" accent, which was really the product of ethnic mixing in the long-disputed Alsace-Lorraine era on the German-French border. Welk's theme song was "Bubbles in the Wine" (1939). Emerging from the Midwest during the thirties, where his polka-flavored music was very popular with the heavily Germanic and Scandinavian audiences, Welk shrewdly organized a national television program (1955 to the 1970s) that brought him his greatest fame. At a time when most big band music was a thing of the past because of rock'n'roll, Lawrence Welk's television crew was perhaps the best known band in the land during those years.

The Sweet Bands

Leader	Theme or gimmick	Star vocalists	Key song
Blue Barron	"King of the Mickey Mouse Bands"	Don Brown	Sometimes I'm Happy
Frankie Carle	Leader's energetic piano stylings	Marjorie Hughes	Sunrise Serenade
Casa Loma	Glen Gray's imaginative leadership	Kenny Sargent	Smoke Rings
Xavier Cugat	Top Latin band for polite-society set	Pretty wives (4)	My Shawl
Eddy Duchen	Established piano-lead for society bands	Lew Sherwood	Be My Lovely; Twilight Time
Shep Fields	"And His Rippling Rhythm Orchestra"	Bob Goday/ Hal Derwyn	Rippling Rhythm
Jan Garber	Known as the "Idol of the Air Lanes"	Lee Bennett/ Liz Tilton	My Dear
Gray Gordon	"Tic-Toc Rhythm"	Cliff Grass	One Minute to One
Horace Heidt	"The Pot O' Gold"; telephone quiz	King Sisters	I'll Love You in My Dreams
Hudson-DeLange	Gentle swing featuring female vocalists	Nan Wynn	Sophisticated Swing
Dick Jurgens	Midwest favorite	Eddy Howard	Day Dreams Come True
Art Kassel	"Kassels in the Air"	Various	Hell's Bells
Hal Kemp	Opened with "Got a Date With an Angel"; closed with "How I Miss You"	Skinnay Ennis Smoothies	When Summer Is Gone
Wayne King	Known as the "Waltz King"	Buddy Clark	The Waltz You Saved for Me
Freddie Martin	"Music in the Martin Manner"	Merv Griffin	Bye-Lo-Bye Lullaby
Russ Morgan	His "Wah-Wah" style trombone	Russ Morgan	Does Your Heart Beat for Me?
Ozzie Nelson	Dad of TV classic "Ozzie & Harriet Show"	Harriet Hilliard	Loyal Sons of Rutgers
Jan Savitt	"And His Top Hatters"	Bon Bon	Quaker City Jazz
Phil Spitalny	"And His All-Girl Orchestra"	Various	Just a Little
Orrin Tucker	"With Wee Bonnie Baker"	Wee Bonnie Baker	Oh, Johnny, Oh Johnny, Oh!
Tommy Tucker	"Tommy Tucker Time"	Don Brown	Love You
Ted Weems	Midwest leader from '20s to late '40s	Perry Como/ Elmo Tanner	Out of the Night
Lawrence Welk	And his "Champagne Music"	Jayne Waton	Bubbles in the Wine

The Singers Emerge

When the big band era is reprised in television advertisements and nostalgia backtracks, the singers are usually represented by Frank Sinatra singing his swoon-and-sway songs to the bobby-soxers, and the Andrews Sisters dressed in army outfits, singing novelty songs. What gets lost in the translation is the overwhelming dominance of the popular music scene by **Bing Crosby** (1903-1977). Perhaps this is because Crosby had made such an early impression during the tail end of the Jazz Age, that by the swing era he was considered something of an institution. Whatever the reason, when one looks at the overall numbers of successful hit records, radio shows, and motion pictures, Crosby emerges as this period's most luminous star.

Crosby had been among the first of the vocalists to break away from the hold of the band leader. During the period when popular music was being dominated by Goodman, the Dorseys, Lombardo, and their anointed singers, Crosby was the one singer who didn't need orchestra affiliation. He was the measuring stick for all male singers. They were either high Crosby or low Crosby, meaning the vocalist either sang in a high baritone range or a low baritone range. Perry Como, one of the many who followed Crosby, noted, "In 1940, unless you sang like Bing you didn't eat." Crosby not only influenced the white singers of his day, but also many of the black ballad singers as well. Harlan Lattimore of Don Redman's Orchestra, Roy Felton, Herb Jeffries, Billy Eckstine, and future rhythm and blues great Roy Brown were referred to at various times in their careers as "Black Bings" or "Colored Crosbys."

Remember, Crosby's solo career didn't take off until 1931. Therefore, when the swing era came he was just warming up. While others from the previous era didn't fare too well, Crosby was versatile enough to withstand the new cycle of popular music. His move in 1935 to Decca Records with Jack Kapp as producer meant a break from the jazz tradition. The jazz press abhorred the change. Kapp's motto was any song, no matter how silly, was a good song as long as it sold. Kapp also resisted attempts by singers to take liberties with the melody. As jazz-oriented vocalist Lee Wiley caustically observed, "There was a sign over the Decca recording door that said, 'Sing the melody.'" Under Kapp's influence Crosby often sang inferior material, but this allowed Crosby the widest repertoire of any singer of his time. Crosby introduced new musical genres to the pop audience, including Hawaiian numbers ("Sweet "Leilani" and "Blue Hawaii," 1937), country music ("I'm an Old Cowhand," 1936, "San Antonio Rose," 1940, "Pistol Packin' Mama," 1943, "Don't Fence Me In," 1944), and holiday music ("White Christmas" and "Silent Night," 1942, and "Jingle Bells," 1943).

Crosby's stature as a movie star almost paralleled that of his radio and record careers, as we shall see in the section on Hollywood. From 1935 to 1950, Crosby had an astonishing 203 top hits, 29 of which went to the top of the charts. During this time Crosby was the established star of the industry and the choice of the adult audience. By the early 1940s, young music listeners sought someone closer to them in age and someone they didn't have to share with their parents. His name was Frank Sinatra.

Photographs and Prints Division, Schomburg Center for Research in Black Culture, The New York Public Library, Astor, Lenox and Tilden Foundation

Movie Star News

Singer and record producer Larry Carr might have hit the bull's eye when he proclaimed, "Popular singing can quite literally be divided into two periods: B.C. and A.C., Before Crosby and After Crosby." Crosby was not only a singing star of radio, records, and film, in 1944 he surprised everyone by playing a serious role, that of a young priest in conflict with an elderly priest (played with Irish fervor by Barry Fitzgerald) he'd been sent to eventually replace. The film was *Going My Way.* Crosby hesitated at taking the role at first because he didn't want to mix religion with entertainment, but he was eventually convinced to take the part by the film's writer-director, Leo Mc-Carey. Crosby won an Academy Award for best actor, Fitzgerald won for supporting actor, and the film was accorded the award for best film of the year. "Swingin' on a Star" won best song. A year later Crosby again played a priest, opposite Ingrid Bergman in the sequel, *The Bells of St. Mary.*

Frank Driggs Collection

Frank Sinatra with the Harry James Orchestra at the Panther Room of the Hotel Sherman in Chicago, 1939. Typical of the swing era, the singer (Sinatra is in the front row, third from the left) is seated with the band as it performs. Singers remained seated until the leader of the band called them up to sing a number of songs. Here leader Harry James stands out from the rest of the band with his white tuxedo.

Early Sinatra Swoon Songs

Setting/Group	Song	Top Chart Position	Year
Tommy Dorsey Band	Polka Dots and Moonbeams	18	1940
Tommy Dorsey Band & Pied Pipers	I'll Never Smile Again	1	1940
Tommy Dorsey Band	Fools Rush In	12	1940
Tommy Dorsey Band & Pied Pipers	The One I Love Belongs to Somebody Else	11	1940
Tommy Dorsey Band	Our Love Affair	5	1940
Tommy Dorsey Band	We Three (My Echo, My Shadow, and Me)	3	1940
Tommy Dorsey Band & Pied Pipers	Stardust	7	1941
Tommy Dorsey Band & Connie Haines & Pied Pipers	Oh, Look at Me Now	2	1941
Tommy Dorsey Band & Pied Pipers	Dolores	1	1941
Tommy Dorsey Band	Do I Worry?	4	1941
Tommy Dorsey Band	Everything Happens to Me	9	1941
Tommy Dorsey Band	This Love of Mine	3	1941
Tommy Dorsey Band & Pied Pipers	There Are Such Things	1	1942
Tommy Dorsey Band	In the Blue of the Evening	1	1943
Tommy Dorsey Band	It's Always You	3	1943
Frank Sinatra with Harry James and His Orchestra	All or Nothing at All	1	1943
Frank Sinatra	You'll Never Know	2	1943
Frank Sinatra	Sunday, Monday or Always	9	1943
Frank Sinatra	People Will Say We're In Love	3	1943
Frank Sinatra	I Couldn't Sleep a Wink Last Night	4	1944
Frank Sinatra	Saturday Night (Is the Loneliest Night of the Week)	2	1945
Frank Sinatra	Dream	5	1945
Frank Sinatra	I Should Care	8	1945
Frank Sinatra	If I Loved You	7	1945
Frank Sinatra	Nancy (with the Laughing Face)	10	1945
Frank Sinatra	White Christmas	5	1946
Frank Sinatra	Oh! What It Seemed to Be	1	1946
Frank Sinatra	They Say It's Wonderful	2	1946
Frank Sinatra	Five Minutes More	1	1946

Chart positions: Joel Whitburn's Pop Memories 1890-1954

August 15, 1943

Courtesy Down Beat

Frank Sinatra (1915-) was born in Hoboken, New Jersey, and at the age of sixteen quit school to sing at weddings. In 1933, at the age of eighteen, he saw a Bing Crosby movie at Jersey City's Lowes Journal Square Theatre and decided that he would become the greatest singer in the world. By 1935 Sinatra was singing with a group named the Hoboken Four on the radio broadcast of the Major Bowes Amateur Hour talent show. After that he performed as a solo artist at the Rustic Cabin, a road house near Englewood, New Jersey, where he doubled as a head waiter between 1937 and 1939. After marrying his sweetheart, Nancy, in 1939, Sinatra started singing for free on a radio program, "Dance Party." The aspiring star worked for free because he hoped that someone with influence would hear him. And someone did. Harry James, who had just started his own band after leaving Benny Goodman, heard the youngster and in mid-1939 hired him for $75 a week as the male vocalist. Sinatra was on his way.

Sinatra's first appearance with an established big band came on June 30, 1939, at the Hippodrome Theatre in Baltimore. His first recording was made the next month,"The Bottom of My Heart." It reportedly sold only eight thousand copies. Sinatra had no major hit with James, but "All or Nothing at All" would be re-released in 1943, after he was a star with Dorsey, and it became a number one hit. The young Sinatra was as confident as he was talented. According to James, even after his first recording went nowhere, Sinatra continued to think of himself as the greatest.

Sinatra moved on to join Tommy Dorsey from January 1940 to September 1942, during which time he made eighty-four recordings, most of them following the pattern of band-chorus-vocal-chorus-band-chorus. When a song became a hit, it was listed under the title of the band leader, not the vocal unit or soloist. Sinatra's first film appearances were as a member of the Dorsey band and it was Dorsey who received the billing in those films, not Sinatra. In 1941 the band was featured in *Las Vegas Nights* (Sinatra soloed on "Dolores" and "I'll Never Smile Again") and in 1942 in *Ship Ahoy* (Sinatra sang "On Moonlight Bay," "The Last Call for Love," and "Poor You"). By this time the youngster was eager to have his name as the featured artist on the record label. He finally got his wish on two recordings cut on January 19, 1942. By September of that year, he left Dorsey and bought out his contract (otherwise Dorsey would have made close to a third of Sinatra's earnings over the next ten years).

Sinatra's timing in striking out on his own was perfect. He had heard that Jimmy Dorsey's star vocalist, Bob Eberle, was getting ready to leave the band, and he felt that he had to establish himself as the first since Crosby to make it on his own. Appearing as an "extra added attraction" with the Benny Goodman band at New York's Paramount Theater on December 30, 1942, Sinatra created such a sensation that many swing era enthusiasts feel the event marked the beginning of modern pop hysteria. The young female fans simply went wild, as they would later with Elvis and the Beatles. The bobby-soxers, as they were called, swooned as Sinatra leaned his microphone forward and sang such caressing ballads as "Where or When," "There Are Such Things," and "The Song Is You." Sinatra began to be referred to as the "Sultan of Swoon" and "The Voice." The original four-week engagement at the Paramount was extended another four weeks, this time with Sinatra as the headliner.

From this point on, Sinatra was the most important item in popular music and things happened fast as his career gained momentum. Sinatra signed a solo recording contract with Columbia Records in 1943 and he convinced Alex Stordahl to leave Tommy Dorsey to become his arranger (in the process Stordahl went from making $150 per week to $650 per week). Between 1943 and 1945 Sinatra hosted the weekly radio show "Your Hit Parade." He also signed a movie contract with RKO and starred in his first film, *Higher and Higher,* in 1943. (He was billed behind Michele Morgan and Jack Haley, but played the romantic lead and introduced two future standards, "I Couldn't Sleep a Wink Last Night" and "A Lovely Way to Spend an Evening"). There were other films, radio shows, hit records, and night club and concert appearances throughout the 1940s. On October 12, 1944, Sinatra returned to the Paramount and the bobby-soxers created such mayhem that the press called it "The Columbus Day Riot." The press criticized Sinatra for not being in the service, however he had signed up for the service twice only to be classified 4-F because of a punctured eardrum. With so many young men drafted into the military, Sinatra represented (he said) the boyfriend at the corner drug store.

Courtesy Stash Records

To contemporary audiences Sinatra is known as "Ol' Blue Eyes," "The Chairman of the Board," and "Mr. Show Business." But during the 1940s, when "Sinatrauma" was at its peak, he was called, in addition to "The Sultan of Swoon" and "The Voice," "Swoonlight Sinatra," "The Voice That Is Thrilling Millions," "The Lean Lark," "Croon Prince of Swing," "The Bony Baritone," "Shoulders," and "Prince Charming of the Juke Boxes."

On the surface it would appear that Sinatra simply copied Crosby's easy manner with a microphone, and was more youthful than his model. Not quite. Crosby had come up with Louis Armstrong and

Dixieland's two-beat form in his veins. He was a terrific scat singer and whistler and loved to have jazz solos accompany his singing, at least until Kapp's anti-jazz stand after 1935. Sinatra, on the other hand, had no feel for the two-beat sound; he was reared on the big band sound with the rhythm section laying down four regular beats. Whereas Crosby was somewhat cool and detached, almost playful at times, Sinatra was deadly serious. He consciously sought out ways of differentiating his style from Crosby's. Sinatra's hybrid style was much more heartfelt and involved, much like the Italian "bel canto" ("beautiful singing") style. Sinatra replaced the syncopated (rhythmically choppy) approach for a technique that was more legato (an unbroken connection of notes). Tommy Dorsey's trombone solos, which featured long, fluid lines, fascinated Sinatra. He learned from Dorsey how to master breath control so that he could sustain lyrics over bar lines and he followed some of his boss's regimented exercises. Sinatra spent hours listening to violin recordings of Jascha Heifetz, who, like Dorsey, mastered the technique of seamless soloing. This phrasing was an important element of Sinatra's achingly romantic swoon songs, which provided the ideal foreground music for loved ones separated by the war.

Movie Star News

Sinatra in his first starring role for RKO, *Higher and Higher,* 1943. The early films for RKO and MGM featured Sinatra as a song and dance man. The *Los Angeles Times*, reviewing Sinatra's debut as a leading man proclaimed, "He plays himself in *Higher and Higher*, appears more at ease than we expected, and should find his place as a film personality with careful choice of subjects. Crosby did it, didn't he?"

Movie Star News

Picture Collection, The Branch Libraries, The New York Public Library

The Swooner vs. The Crooner. There was more than a contrast in singing styles that set Frank Sinatra and Bing Crosby apart. While both men were reared Catholic, Crosby assimilated into the American culture more easily than Sinatra. Crosby was German-American, sometimes called "Der Bingle" (Tyrolian hat, pipe, and golf clubs). Crosby represented family values (a widower who remarried and had a number of sons). Frankie "boy," on the other hand, was an Italian "swinger" who represented loose living (he was vilified by the press for his divorce from childhood sweetheart Nancy). Sinatra's much-ballyhooed relationship with Hollywood star Ava Gardner convinced many that success had "gone to his head." Years later, Crosby would be seen to have clay feet (illicit affairs, being a cold father, and the like), but at the time Sinatra was the one viewed as an outsider in terms of lifestyle.

Although Crosby and Sinatra found success as solo performers, most of the other vocalists still worked with the band leaders. Dick Haymes, Helen Forrest, and Kitty Kallen had their biggest hits with the Harry James band. Perry Como's first hits were recorded with the Ted Weems band. Others, like Helen Ward, Dick Todd, and Buddy Clark, moved from band to band. Dinah Shore and the Andrews Sisters were among the few who were able to sustain their careers throughout the war years without a regular band connection. By the time the war ended, audiences had grown accustomed to vocals dominating popular music, and the swinging, jumping instrumental songs that had been the forte of the 1935-41 period became a thing of yesterday. In January 1947, a total of eight major bands folded, among them Benny Goodman's and Tommy Dorsey's.

What we might refer to as the Post-Swing Era was dominated by the singers. The film that best shows this post-war turnaround is Martin Scorcese's *New York, New York* (1977), in which a Tommy Dorsey-like band leader has to play second fiddle to emerging vocal star (and soon-to-be film star) played by Liza Minnelli. Her love interest, played by Robert DeNiro, is a saxophone player bored with big band arrangements. He is drawn to the modern sounds of bebop. The film failed at the box office, but its thematic details accurately reflect the time period.

One of the great vocalists of the forties, Dick Haymes possessed a pleasing baritone that he put to good advantage on classic hits such as "I'll Get By," "Little White Lies," "Mam'selle," "It Can't Be Wrong," "A Slow Boat to China," and his biggest hit, "You'll Never Know." He was featured in a series of films for 20th Century-Fox throughout the forties.

Dick Haymes (1916-1980) was the closest rival to Frank Sinatra during the forties. He was known for his mellow, velvet baritone voice and his matinee-idol good looks. Haymes was raised by his mother, a concert singer and singing instructor, in Buenos Aires, Argentina (where he was born), France, Britain, Switzerland, and America. After working as a radio announcer in the mid-thirties, he shifted career gears and became a vocalist and songwriter for Freddie Martin and Orrin Tucker. Haymes' big break came in 1939, while trying to sell some songs to bandleader Harry James, who had just left Benny Goodman and was in need of new material. After Haymes had auditioned his material, James said to him, "Your song, no, but you, yes." Haymes replaced Sinatra, who had been with the James band for six months before moving on to Tommy Dorsey's orchestra.

Audiophile Records

Dick Haymes may not have had any hit recordings after the 1940s, but he did make a number of fine albums throughout the fifties and into the seventies, as this fine Audiophile release attests.

Haymes stayed with the James band for two years, polishing his style and learning to phrase ballads (his forte) to suit arrangements designed to keep dancers on the floor. Haymes's effortless vocal approach was closer to Crosby than Sinatra. His earliest recordings on the small Varsity label included "How High the Moon" and "Fools Rush In" (1940) and "I'll Get By" (1941). The last was a huge hit and from there Haymes joined Benny Goodman in 1942 and Tommy Dorsey in 1943, after which he worked solo for Decca Records. "You'll Never Know," introduced by Alice Faye in the film *Hello, Frisco, Hello* (1943), was a number one hit for Haymes. From there it was on to Hollywood and wine, women, and song. "My swinging days got so involved with my own ego that I blew it," he said. "When you live at the rate I lived, fast cars, luxury homes, and women who want money spent on them, you soon get rid of your dollars."

All that aside, Haymes endured throughout the forties as one of the finest singers of that era. Will Friedwald in *Jazz Singing* summarizes, "When we talk about Dick Haymes, now, we're talking about a genuinely superior artist and easily the best of the post-Bing generation (outside of Billy Eckstine, anyway). He developed a voice which was fine and pure, and had a gift for interpreting love songs so convincingly and meaningfully that the blase arrangements Decca gave him never mattered, and his personality even rendered his accompaniments a nonconsideration."

Courtesy Down Beat

Two of the top female singers of the forties were **Dinah Shore** (1917-1994) and **Doris Day** (1922-   ). Shore began her career on radio in Nashville and became one of the few singers who was not affiliated with a big band. Her star began to get brighter when she was featured on the Eddie Cantor radio show in 1941. Shore was seen in a series of films beginning in 1943 and gained even greater fame during the 1950s and 1960s with her successful television variety shows. Doris Day made her mark initially as a member of the Les Brown Orchestra in 1940, where she waxed her signature song, "Sentimental Journey." Day became the most successful Hollywood star of the female band singers, beginning in 1948 with her debut in *Romance on the High Seas*. Throughout the 1950s and 1960s she was such a big movie box office attraction that audiences hardly knew she had begun as a band vocalist.

The Andrews Sisters, Laverne (1915-1967), Patti (1920-   ), and Maxene (1918-   ), a close harmony vocal trio modeled on the Boswell Sisters, mixed ballads with jump tunes and novelty songs in such a perky and listenable manner that they became the biggest-selling and most popular female group of the first half century. Led by Patti, who handled most of the vocal leads and served as the personable spokeswoman, the trio appeared in many motion pictures (most for Universal Studios), and their unmistakable sound helped define the wartime era. Daughters of Greek and Norwegian parents, the Andrews Sisters began their careers on the RKO theater circuit around 1931. Their first major orchestra work was the little-known Jack Belasco unit in New York. The singers got their big break when they were signed to a contract by Jack Kapp of Brunswick Records.

The Andrews Sisters began their phenomenal string of hit recordings in 1937 with their second release on Brunswick, an adaptation of a 1933 song, "I Would If I Could," called "Bei Mir Bist Du Schoen," from the Yiddish musical of the same name. From that point the hits continued unabated until the early fifties. By the forties the Andrews Sisters had become major stars of both radio and film. They made nearly twenty movies, in which they always played themselves. They recorded with Judy Garland, Carmen Miranda, Danny Kaye, Les Paul, Russ Morgan, and, most significantly, Bing Crosby, with whom they had some classic hits: "Pistol Packin' Mama" (1943), "A Hot Time in the Town of Berlin" and "Don't Fence Me In" (1945), all number one hits, "Victory Polka" (1943), "Is You Is or Is You Ain't (Ma' Baby)" (1944), "Ac-Cent-Tchu-Ate the Positive," and "Along the Navajo Trail" (1945), and "South America, Take It Away" (1946).

The Andrews Sisters were the first of the vocal groups to cash in on the boogie woogie phenomenon, which was introduced to "pop America" at the "From Spirituals to Swing" concerts at Carnegie Hall in December 1938 and 1939. "Rhumboogie" and "Beat Me, Daddy, Eight to the Bar" (1940), "Scrub Me, Mama, With a Boogie Beat" and "Boogie Woogie Bugle Boy" (1941), and "Boogie Woogie Piggy" (1942) created a national awareness and appetite for boogie woogie. In 1973 Bette Midler covered "Boogie Woogie Bugle Boy" and helped launch a revival of older music. This also resulted in a revival of the careers of the two remaining sisters, Maxene and Patti, who were cast in a Broadway musical in 1974, *Over Here*.

Author's collection

The Andrews Sisters were the most successful female vocal group of the first half of the twentieth century. Vic Schoen, their longtime arranger and director, is quoted in *The Best of the Music Makers* as saying he "never could understand their phenomenal success. And I don't think they did either. Certainly they didn't handle it too well. They had led a very sheltered life and they always wanted to break loose."

Library of Congress

Unlike a majority of band singers during the forties, the Andrews Sisters starred in a good number of films. These included *Argentine Nights* (1940), *Buck Privates*, *In the Navy*, and *Hold That Ghost* (1941), *What's Cookin'*, *Private Buckaroo*, and *Give Out Sisters* (1942), *How's About It?*, *Always a Bridesmaid*, and *Swingtime Johnny* (1943), *Follow the Boys*, *Hollywood Canteen*, *Moonlight and Cactus*, and *Her Lucky Night* (1945), *Road to Rio* (1947), and *Melody Time* (1948).

Swingtime Johnny featured the Andrews Sisters as a trio who served their country during the war by donning overalls in a munitions fac- tory and making shell casings. This 61 minute B-film musical reprised "Boogie Woogie Bugle Boy," (first sung in 1941's *Buck Privates*), and included "Boogie Woogie Choo Choo," "Sweet and Low," "Poor Nell," and "I May Be Wrong But I Think You're Wonderful," among others.

The Broadway Musical

George Gershwin.

As noted earlier, most of the great tunesmiths provided songs for various shows performed on Broadway: the operetta, the revue, and the musical comedy. But despite their talented authorship, few Broadway songs ever became big hits during the swing era. There are a number of reasons for this. First, the main hits between 1935 and 1941 were products of the big bands, and many of them were original, uptempo, instrumental dance numbers written by group members. Second, by 1935 many of the best songwriters had moved to Hollywood, where the pay was better. Third, when the war began, love songs about separated couples were in favor, and this was not the characteristic subject of musical comedy (lack of topicality we might call it). And finally, Broadway shows were becoming more serious in tone and vision. The Depression and its aftermath struck an artistic nerve that would be reflected on the stage. New York City, after all, didn't have to worry as much about how controversial subjects played, while movies, which were shown in every hamlet in America, needed to be more sensitive.

The 1935 Broadway season opened with the music of **George Gershwin** (1898-1937) and Ira Gershwin set to a 1925 novel written by black author DuBose Heyward. *Porgy and Bess* dramatized the story of a crippled beggar named Porgy, his love interest, the seductive Bess; the brutish Crown, Porgy's rival for Bess's affection; and Sportin' Life, the dealer of "happy dust" (cocaine), who would take Bess away from South Carolina's Catfish Row to "a boat leaving soon for New York." George Gershwin considered this to be a "folk opera." Today the musical's score is considered one of the high points of Broadway's past, with classic standards like "It Ain't Necessarily So," "I Got Plenty o' Nuttin'," "I Loves You Porgy," and "Summertime." Fifty years after its initial run, *Porgy and Bess* entered the repertory of the New York Metropolitan Opera.

Bess, 1935. Museum of the City of New York. The Theater Collection
from the original New York stage production of
s played by Todd Duncan, is seen waving from a win-
aginative set was designed by Sergei Soudeikine.

The all-black cast was headed by Todd Duncan as Porgy, Anne Brown as Bess, and John Bubbles as Sportin' Life. With an all-black cast, Gershwin couldn't convince the legitimate classical music establishment to stage the production, so the collaborators had to adapt the project for the musical stage. The play opened at the Alvin Theatre on October 10 to less than sterling reviews—only one major critic, Brooks Atkinson, realized its greatness, and the show closed after only 124 performances. However, starting in 1942, the classic was revised repeatedly. In 1959 Sidney Poitier, Dorothy Dandridge, and Sammy Davis Jr. starred in the Hollywood adaptation. George Gershwin's life was portrayed in film by Robert Alda, father of actor Alan in the 1945 biopic *Rhapsody in Blue*. In 1992, a musical loosely based on Gershwin's *Girl Crazy* opened on Broadway to sparkling reviews. The show, *Crazy for You*, incorporated some of Gershwin's most memorable tunes. Theater critic Clive Barnes noted in the *New York Post*, "What is most important of all is that those George and Ira Gershwin songs keep on going and going and going. You have to be crazy for Gershwin so you have to be *Crazy for You*."

Broadway's diminished rule of the pop charts wasn't the result of Cole Porter and Rodgers and Hart failing to do their part. **Cole Porter** (1893-1964), who jetted between palatial homes in New York, Paris, Venice, and Hollywood, was the busiest of all the composers. In 1935 his libretto, a story designed to be set to music to Moss Hart's *Jubilee*, a satire of upper-crust life, produced future standards "Why Shouldn't I?" "Just One of Those Things," and a song that went nowhere until three years later, when Artie Shaw resurrected it as a swing instrumental, "Begin the Beguine." In 1936 Jimmy Durante, Ethel Merman, and Bob Hope were all billed equally in *Red, Hot and Blue!* "It's De-lovely," "Ridin' High," and cabaret favorite "Down in the Depths (On the Ninetieth Floor)" were Porter classics from this production, which, despite its star-studded cast, ran only 183 performances at the Alvin Theatre. Porter's more fruitful 1938 musical at the Imperial Theatre, *Leave It to Me!*, ran for 291 performances and is best remembered today for Mary Martin's riveting debut, coyly singing "My Heart Belongs to Daddy." Porter forged on with others: *Dubarry Was a Lady* (1939, Bert Lahr and Ethel Merman, "Do I Love You?" "Friendship," 408 performances), *Panama Hattie* (1940, Ethel Merman and Arthur Treacher, "Make it Another Old-Fashioned, Please," 501 performances), *Let's Face It!* (1941, Danny Kaye and Eve Arden, "Ev'rything I Love" and "Ace in the Hole," 547 performances), and *Mexican Hayride* (1944, Bobby Clark and June Havoc, "I Love You," 481 performances).

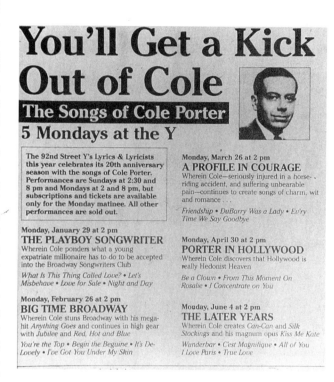

Courtesy 92nd Street YMCA, New York City

The biographical essay by Brendan Gill in Robert Kimball's book *Cole* begins with a rumination about Cole Porter as a child: "In any casual snapshot of an outing held who knows when in Paris, Cairo, Venice or Hollywood, it is Cole that one instantly singles out and gives a name to. The face of the little boy on ponyback . . . is the face of the debonair undergraduate at Yale, already an accomplished charmer . . . All his life he will be accused of being a snob and all his life he will deny the charge, but his snobbery, real or imaginary, is beside the point, which is that at every turn, unfailingly, he furnished the world with far more joy than he got back. In the unspoken bargain struck between genius and the rest of us, it is the rest of us who come home with full hands and, in this instance, dancing feet."

Porter's greatest musical came together in 1948, when he was reunited with the husband-and-wife team of Samuel and Bella Spewack (ten years earlier they collaborated on *Leave It to Me!*) to adapt Shakespeare's *Taming of the Shrew* into a musical. *Kiss Me, Kate*, presented as a play within a play, was based, theoretically, on the backstage quarrels of real-life theatrical duo Alfred Lunt and Lynn Fontanne. Alfred Drake and Patricia Morison led an exuberant cast through such songs as "Another Op'nin', Another Show," "Wunderbar," "So in Love," "Too Darn Hot," and "Always True to You in My Fashion." The use of Shakespearean dialogue and song was witty, and the result was the most fully realized of all of Porter's attempts to combine music and words with a book. *Kiss Me, Kate* played at the New Century Theatre for 1,070 performances, making it the fourth-longest-running musical of the forties.

Cole Porter was the quintessential pop music sophisticate. In 1946 Cary Grant played the songwriter (with no hint of Porter's homosexuality) in *Night and Day*. Porter's laundry-list lyrics and bon mots captivated followers of theater as well as the jazz crowd. Apparently, contemporary rock and rap musicians appreciate Porter as well. In the early nineties, nearly two dozen of them combined to interpret Porter classics on a video and CD release titled *Red, Hot and Blue*. Among the interpretations were U2's version of "Night & Day," Neneh Cherry's "I've Got You Under My Skin," k.d. lang's "So in Love," and Aaron Neville's "In the Still of the Night."

Even more prolific than Porter was the team of **Richard Rodgers** (1902-1979) and **Lorenz Hart** (1895-1943), who began their partnership in 1920. Hart was a lyricist who needed to hear the music before he could write the words to a tune, and that was how this team collaborated. Between 1935 and 1942, they produced music for nine musical plays, all of which contained some certifiable standards. In 1935 they wrote the music for producer/showman Billy Rose's circus spectacular, *Jumbo*, starring comedian Jimmy Durante. "Little Girl Blue," "The Most Beautiful Girl in the World," and "My Romance" all ballads from that show, became standard tunes. The next year the duo again collaborated with director George Abbott (though he received no credit) on a dance-oriented musical, *On Your Toes*. Rodgers and Hart wrote the book as a movie script for Fred Astaire, who turned it down because he thought it too far off the beaten path of his typical top-hat, white-tie-and-tails image. This is the musical that introduced master dance choreographer George Balanchine to the musical (he utilized ballet as an intregal part of the story in the celebrated "Slaughter on Tenth Avenue" number) and helped make a star out of loose-limbed Ray Bolger, who went on to play the Scarecrow in 1939's *The Wizard of Oz*. "Glad to Be Unhappy" and "There's a Small Hotel" were ballads that became perennial favorites. The show ran 315 performances at the Imperial Theatre and also featured Monty Woolley and Tamara Geva.

Courtesy ASCAP

Left, a brilliant, cosmopolitan lyricist, Lorenz Hart placed the music of Richard Rodgers into an urbane world of wit and grace. *Right*, Oscar Hammerstein II, whose lyric-writing style was more akin to European operetta, viewed his work as made up more of sentimentality than witty understatement. Hammerstein's main concern was that the audience keep the "story" in mind first and foremost. Rodgers began a long collaboration with Hammerstein starting with *Oklahoma!* in 1943.

In *The Poets of Tin Pan Alley: A History of America's Great Lyricists* ,Philip Furia writes, "When *Oklahoma!* opened in 1943, a new songwriting team was established, the Broadway musical became an 'integrated' blend of songs and story, and an age of elegance, sophistication, and urbanity in popular song was over. It seems only fitting that an era that began with the cosmopolitan sparkle of Manhattan should close with the homespun yawp of Oklahoma."

Author Benny Green's comparison of the Rodgers of Hart with the Rodgers of Hammerstein is insightful. Writing in *Let's Face the Music: The Golden Age of Popular Song*, Green contends, "Of the thousands of working musicians and singers who still approach Rodgers-and-Hart with the eagerness of kindred spirits, there is hardly a one who warms to the popular appeal of Rodgers-and-Hammerstein. As for the vast theatre-going armies who continue to march on the great Rodgers-and-Hammerstein set pieces, their knowledge of or interest in or affection for Rodger-and-Hart is vague, to the brink of indifference.

"It would be only a slight over-simplification to say that while Rodgers-and-Hart has triumphantly outlived the incident of production to become part of the standard repertoire of modern popular music, Rodgers-and-Hammerstein has failed to move out of the theatre, chained forever to the context of the theatrical event for which it was conceived. No doubt Rodgers, who all his life pursued the chimera of something called the integrated score, that is, a score which arises directly out of the dramatic process and carries that process forward, would claim that this very failure of the Hammerstein songs to venture out into the nightclubs and on to the bandstands and the recital stages is the ultimate proof of their superiority as dramatic pieces. That may or may not be so, but the world does not arrrange its affairs in that way. Affection for a song arises not out of its dramatic context, but from its intrinsic merit as a performable piece of music."

In 1937 Rodgers and Hart had two shows running. One was a political satire written by George Kaufman and Moss Hart that cast George M. Cohan as Franklin D. Roosevelt. *I'd Rather Be Right* met with some critical indifference but still ran for 290 performances at the Alvin Theatre ("Have You Met Miss Jones?" was its musical hit). *Babes in Arms* is a Rodgers and Hart story about teenagers whose vaudeville parents are out of work. The kids decide to put on a revue to save themselves from being sent to a work farm (a "hip" variation on the future Busby Berkeley "Let's put on a show" formula). No less than five tunes became hits ("Where or When," "I Wish I Were in Love Again," "My Funny Valentine," "Johnny One Note," and "The Lady Is a Tramp"). The show ran for 289 performances at the Shubert Theatre but was an even greater success as a movie two years later with Mickey Rooney and Judy Garland leading the youthful charges ("Hey, kids, let's put on a show!").

I Married an Angel ("Spring Is Here") and *The Boys From Syracuse* ("Falling in Love With Love," "This Can't Be Love"), both 1938, and *Too Many Girls* ("I Didn't Know What Time It Was"), 1939, followed in quick succession. More importantly, *Pal Joey* opened for an eventual 374 performances on Christmas Eve 1940 at the Ethel Barrymore Theatre. Based on John O'Hara's tale about a small-time nightclub entertainer played by Gene Kelly, the play broke new ground by featuring a protagonist who was a heel. Producer-director George Abbott used a firm hand sending Kelly through his paces in his only starring role on Broadway. "I Could Write a Book" and "Bewitched (Bothered and Bewildered)" were the musical hits. *By Jupiter*, 1942, starring Ray Bolger, was the team's last project together. Rodgers and Hart provided the music and the book, which was somewhat like *The Boys From Syracuse* in that it was set in ancient Greece (and was based on Shakespeare's first play, *Comedy of Errors*). "Wait Till You See Her" (dropped shortly after the opening), "Nobody's Heart," and "Ev'rything I've Got" became standard tunes.

Oklahoma! Museum of the City of New York, 48.210.1838. The Theater Collection

Oklahoma! "No Legs, No Jokes, No Chance." Legend has it that super producer Mike Todd walked out on the first act of the show's New Haven, Connecticut, tryout, then returned to New York to utter these now-famous words. However, recent information, most notably Max Wilk's 1993 *O.K.! The Story of Oklahoma!,* contends that the secretary of newspaper columnist Walter Winchell saw the New Haven show, and she who wired him the pithy but famously wrong critique. Above, Agnes de Mille's choreography for the dancing cowboys.

By this time Lorenz Hart had become a very sick man. Alcoholism and insecurities about his closet existence as a homosexual left Hart with little desire to undertake the next project, which had a rural setting, "empty spaces" that urbanite Hart despised. He died on November 22, 1943. Of the lyricists of this era, only Cole Porter and Ira Gershwin matched Hart's sophisticated, often wicked wit. Today's audiences are more familiar with the collaborative team of Rodgers and Hammerstein, but jazz singers and instrumentalists are much fonder of the Rodgers of Hart rather than of Hammerstein, probably because Hart brought a love of urbane refinement and bittersweet humor to Rodgers. Mickey Rooney starred as Hart and Tom Drake played Rodgers in MGM's 1948 biopic *Words and Music*.

The first original cast album of a Broadway musical. Originally, an album meant a bound collection of four to eight 78 rpm records placed in a series of sleeves bound with a hard, protective cover.

Carousel, sheet music cover. *Museum of the City of New York, 63.43.7. The Theater Collection*

Oscar Hammerstein II (1895-1960) introduced an aura of nostalgic sweetness and sentimentality that smacked of Old World charm. Before joining forces with Rodgers he had worked with many others, most importantly Jerome Kern (*Show Boat*, 1927). He was asked by Rodgers if he would be interested in writing the lyrics and book for a Theatre Guild project based on a Lillian Riggs play about a turn-of-the-century love story set in Indian territory, *Green Grow the Lilacs*. What resulted from this collaboration changed the face of the musical comedy forever. Originally titled *Away We Go!* (when it opened as an out-of-town tryout in New Haven, Connecticut), *Oklahoma!* opened at New York's St. James Theatre on March 31, 1943, and was hailed as the most important musical in the history of theater.

Under the direction of Rouben Mamoulin, *Oklahoma!* brought to the musical stage a sense of realism and coherence that *Show Boat* had only suggested. This was a musical play, also referred to as lyric theater, that fused elements of the storyline with songs and dances flowing logically from the dramatic action. Critics eventually called this the "integrated musical"—the music was an integral part of the plot development. Agnes de Mille choreographed a cowboy ballet and dream sequences that revealed the hidden yearnings of the characters with poetic brilliance.

This frontier story portrays the rivalry of Curly (Alfred Drake) and Jud (Howard Da Silva) for the affections of Laurey (Joan Roberts). Other subplots include a romantic triangle and even the coming statehood of the territory. With a murder and a burial scene, *Oklahoma!* was certainly not the stuff of earlier, revue-like comedies. Every song advanced the plot. There is rumor-romance in "People Will Say We're in Love," conflict in "The Farmer and the Cowman," death in "Pore Jud (Is Dead)" and riding off into the sunset to start a new life in, "Surrey With the Fringe on Top." *Oklahoma!* would become Broadway's longest-running musical, with 2,212 performances, until it was overtaken by *My Fair Lady* fifteen years later.

In 1945, the same collaborators (Theatre Guild, Rouben Mamoulin, and Agnes DeMille) joined Rodgers and Hammerstein in an adaptation of another period-piece story. This time it was Ferenc Molnar's tale about a Budapest carnival barker, Billy Budd (John Raitt), and his love of a factory worker, Julie Jordan (Jan Clayton). In *Carousel*, set in 1873, Hammerstein changed the locale to a New England fishing village. The tale takes the twosome from early infatuation ("If I Loved You") to marriage and Billy's impending fatherhood ("Soliloquy") The young father, desperate for money, is murdered in an attempted robbery. The fantasy allows the father to return to earth to complete a good deed. At her high school graduation, the lonely daughter is given courage by her unseen dad, who exhorts her to have confidence in herself ("You'll Never Walk Alone"). The musical was a big hit, playing at the Majestic Theatre for 890 performances.

The next project, while not as successful as the first two, was no less ambitious. *Allegro* was the account of a young, idealistic doctor faced with the corrupting influence of big institutions, and, unusual for a musical, an unfaithful wife. The Majestic Theatre housed the play, which opened in October 1947 and ran 315 performances. No hit songs resulted from the innovative effort, which used multiple non-representational sets and a Greek chorus commenting on the action to the actors as well as to the audience.

South Pacific (1949), was the brainchild of director Joshua Logan, who suggested to the songwriting team that they adapt a short story, "Fo' Dolla," from James Michener's collection of wartime *Tales of the South Pacific*. A second short story, "Our Heroine," was added to build up a secondary storyline. The musical dealt with racial prejudice, multicultural and cross-generational love, and the death of one of the main characters. Mary Martin and Ezio Pinza played the main roles and the musical was filled with great songs such as "Some Enchanted Evening," "There Is Nothing Like a Dame," "Younger Than Springtime," and "This Nearly Was Mine." The play won a Pulitzer Prize for drama and was the second-longest-running Broadway play of the 1940s, running 1,925 performances at the Majestic Theatre.

Other Serious Broadway Musicals

Musical (Music/Lyrics)	Year	Theme	Stars	Notable Song(s)
I'd Rather Be Right (Rodgers-Hart)	1937	FDR-related satire	George M. Cohan	Have You Met Miss Jones?
Pins and Needles (Harold Rome, et al.)	1937	Liberal, pro-union, anti-war, and bigotry	Garment workers & union members	Sing Me a Song of Social Significance
Hooray for What! (Harold Arlen-E.Y. Harburg)	1937	International espionage, diplomatic duplicity	Ed Wynn	Down With Love
The Cradle Will Rock (Marc Blitzstein)	1938	Struggle for unionization in a steel town	Howard DaSilva Will Geer	The Cradle Will Rock
Knickerbocker Holiday (Kurt Weill-Maxwell Anderson)	1938	Totalitarianism vs. democracy; Peter Stuyvesant	Walter Huston Ray Middleton	September Song
Cabin in the Sky (Vernon Duke-John Latouche)	1940	Fantasy-parable of black soul in conflict	Ethel Waters	Taking a Chance on Love
Lady in the Dark (Kurt Weill-Ira Gershwin)	1941	Psychiatry, dream analysis, the publishing world	Gertrude Lawrence Danny Kaye	Jenny; My Ship
St. Louis Woman (Harold Arlen-Johnny Mercer)	1946	Like Porgy and Bess	Nicholas Bros. Pearl Bailey	Come Rain or Come Shine
Street Scene (Kurt Weill-Langston Hughes)	1947	New York tenement with tragic affair and dead-end relationships	Anne Jeffreys	Moon-Faced, Starry-Eyed
Lost in the Stars (Kurt Weill-Maxwell Anderson)	1949	Race problems in South Africa	Todd Duncan Leslie Banks	Lost in the Stars; Cry the Beloved Country

Rodgers and Hammerstein completed their musical teamwork with *The King and I* (1955), *Me and Juliet* (1953), *Pipe Dream* (1955), *Flower Drum Song* (1958), and *The Sound of Music* (1959). They enlarged the form of the big-time musical so that it included serious themes, and integrated the music in such a way that each song advanced the plot and expressed the motivations of the characters. Many songs were almost operatic in their delivery and intent. There was also a tendency to preach about issues and focus on the sentimental. Hammerstein often took umbrage at critics who thought his works were too sentimental, arguing that beauty and richness of love and affection were needed at all times in history. Rodgers and Hammerstein were not the first to bring serious themes to the American musical (see chart on previous page), but they were masters of the form.

Courtesy ASCAP, Carnegie Hall Archives

Irving Berlin: Dean of American songwriters. Irving Berlin kept rolling longer than any of the early leaders of Tin Pan Alley; he lived to be 101. *Left*, Berlin on stage in *This is the Army*, his salute to the men in the armed forces. The musical raised nearly $2 million for the Army Emergency relief, an astronomical sum for the time. In 1943 the stage hit was made into a film. In both the stage and film productions Berlin appeared in his old World War I uniform (which he had also worn in the musical play *Yip-Yip-Yaphank* in 1918) and sang "Oh, How I Hate to Get up in the Morning." The film was faithful to the original, and featured the 350 soldiers who had appeared in the Broadway production. Ronald Reagan, Joan Leslie, George Murphy and Charles Butterworth were the main Hollywood stars added to the film, and popular mainstream singers Frances Langford ("What Does He Look Like") and Kate Smith ("God Bless America") made guest appearances. Other Berlin songs included "This is the Army Mr. Jones," "The Army's Made a Man Out of Me," "I'm Getting Tired So I Can Sleep," "What the Well-Dressed Man in Harlem Will Wear," "I Left My Heart at the Stagedoor Canteen," "How About a Cheer for the Navy," "Poor Little Me I'm on K.P.," "With My Head in the Clouds," "Your Country and My Country," and "Mandy," along with six others.

Right, a Carnegie Hall celebration reprised many of Berlin's classic songs. Many veterans of "the Alley" couldn't compete in the world of the new integrated musicals. This wasn't the case for Berlin. He created a sensational score for *Annie Get Your Gun*, starring Ethel Merman and Ray Middleton, in 1946. Gerald Mast claimed *Annie* "contained more individual hit songs than any musical ever, before or since." The popular song hits included "Anything You Can Do," "Doin' What Comes Naturally," "They Say It's Wonderful," "I Got the Sun in the Morning," "I Got Lost in His Arms," and what would become an all-time classic of the theater, "There's No Business Like Show Business." Berlin's last Broadway success was 1950's *Call Me Madam,* a vehicle for his favorite female performer, Ethel Merman ("She makes sure you can hear my lyrics in the back row of the balcony."). In *They're Playing Our Song*, Max Wilk cites a letter sent by Jerome Kern to writer Alexander Woollcott in 1925 that summed up Berlin's stature: "The average United States citizen was perfectly epitomized in Irving Berlin's music. He doesn't attempt to stuff the public's ears with pseudo-original ultra-modernism, but he honestly absorbs the vibrations emanating from the people—what I really want to say, my dear Woollcott, is that Irving Berlin has no place in American music. *He is American Music.*"

The Hollywood Musical

In the mid-1930s Hollywood movies entered their Golden Era. By 1930, sound film had become the medium for all major film releases. Since studios had lots of money to throw around, and were suddenly in need of actors who could talk and sing, it became the normal course for major talents from Broadway (actors, directors, choreographers, scenic designers, and songwriters) to go to Hollywood to try making movies. Between 1935 and 1941 Hollywood produced an average of forty-eight musicals per year, not counting the singing cowboy movies. In 1942 and 1943 the number jumped to seventy-four and seventy-five because of the war—America needed to be entertained more than ever, and the studios made one film after another featuring well-known stars playing the parts of either servicemen or entertainers performing for servicemen. Perhaps the easiest way to look at the musical is to consider the studios. During this time, the studio system controlled not only the actors, but also when and where films would be booked to play. (When this control was declared an illegal monopoly by the courts, the "studio system" disappeared.) Musicals were the most expensive of the film genres, since they required the most collaboration. They were the domain of the bigger studios. Those studios developed a particular look and attitude that had emerged, as noted earlier, during the period of the early talkies.

Warner Brothers continued its stories of gritty, hard-working chorus boys and girls in their backstage musicals. The most notable was *Gold Diggers of 1935,* which featured the music of Harry Warren and Al Dubin, and the direction of Busby Berkeley, and starred Dick Powell and Ruby Keeler. The Academy-Award-winning song of the year, "Lullabye of Broadway," was performed by a large crew of dancers and shot in a dizzying series of tilted angles that ranks as one of the greatest ensemble numbers ever filmed (it was Berkeley's own favorite, and, for once, the dancers actually danced). Dick Powell was a busy entertainer for Warner in 1935, churning out five films that year.

Although the studio repeated its backstager show formula over and over, nothing would top *Gold Diggers of 1935*, although *Gold Diggers of 1937, Hollywood Hotel, Gold Diggers in Paris* (1938) did provide a couple of musical highlights. James Cagney's memorable 1942 portrayal of George M. Cohan in *Yankee Doodle Dandy* won him an Academy Award for best actor, and Irving Berlin's spirited 1943 homage to the armed services, *This is the Army*, were highlights from a studio that had lost its touch.

Movie Star News

Backstage musicals continued until the end of the thirties for Warners. In addition to the above titles, the "Berkeley girls" could be seen in the *Gold Diggers of 1937*, where two large-scale numbers stood out: "Let's Put Our Heads Together," featuring couples on huge rocking chairs, and a military-type finale in which Joan Blondell led seventy high-stepping girls across a glossy black floor to the tune of "All's Fair in Love and War." Dubin and Warren still provided the hits, but by 1939 Berkeley would move on to the Mickey Rooney and Judy Garland films at MGM.

Like Warner Brothers, Radio Keith Orpheum, or RKO, continued a formula that had brought them prosperity, in this case the Astaire-Rogers package. *Top Hat* (1935) and *Follow the Fleet* (1936) united the couple with composer Irving Berlin. Jerome Kern and Dorothy Fields wrote the Academy-Award-winning "The Way You Look Tonight" for Astaire to sing to Rogers in *Swing Time* (1936), and the music of the Gershwins was featured in *Shall We Dance* (1937). By 1939 the most famous dancing couple in film history would dissolve their partnership at the studio. Astaire and Rogers made a total of nine films together, but they eventually exhausted the formula, and it was time for both of them to move on to other projects (they would be reunited ten years later in their only Technicolor outing for MGM, *The Barkleys of Broadway*). In 1938 the studio collaborated with Walt Disney and distributed the first full-length animated film, *Snow White and the Seven Dwarfs*. The film established animation as a new and vital art form and marked the beginning of the amazing Disney empire, of which *Pinocchio* and *Fantasia* (1940), *Dumbo* (1941), and *Bambi* (1942), were standouts.

Movie Star News

Movie Star News, Library of Congress

Studio RKO producer Pandro Berman, art director Van Nest Polglase, and stars Fred Astaire and Ginger Rogers sailed through a series of frothy, Art Deco dreamlands that kept tickets selling throughout the thirties. *Halliwell's Filmgoer's Companion* gives Ginger Rogers a coveted rosette for "being everybody's favorite working girl of the thirties; and for being so unarguably right for Fred Astaire." The Astaire-Rogers pairing was most notably commented on by actress Katharine Hepburn: "He gives her class and she gives him sex."

Howard Mandelbaum and Eric Myers note in *Screen Deco*: "For millions of people, RKO's Astaire-Rogers series epitomizes the ideal Art Deco dreamscape, a Manhattan of the mind where nights are danced away on the gleaming floors of penthouse nightclubs, in an aura of luxury and elegance. The films feature the major motifs and materials of the Streamline Moderne period, complementing the smooth sophistication of Fred and Ginger. The sets take one's breath away, but are not allowed to distract from the dances."

Many great pop songs came from the Walt Disney studio. During the early days of animation, Disney's Mickey Mouse cartoons were so musical that they even generated a term, "Mickey Mousing," shorthand for tightly animated cartoon movements coordinated with music. The early cartoons dating from the 1920s, were among the very first true musical films. Later, music historians used a similar term to describe various sweet and novelty bands: Mickey Mouse bands. The Disney studios were among the most concerned with tying music together with storylines. If songs didn't advance the plots, they were taken out. For example, in *Snow White and the Seven Dwarfs*, only eight of twenty songs composed for the film were used.

Columbia Pictures was most noteworthy for its talented and glamorous Rita Hayworth vehicles, such as *You'll Never Get Rich* (1942), *You Were Never Lovelier* (1942), both costarring Fred Astaire, and *Cover Girl* (1944), which teamed Hayworth with Gene Kelly. Universal Studio was the home of comedians Bud Abbott and Lou Costello, and they managed to include musical visits from Martha Raye, Ella Fitzgerald, and the most successful vocal unit of the war years, the Andrews Sisters. But it took a fifteen-year-old girl to keep Universal's fortunes afloat in 1936. Deanna Durbin, a classically trained vocalist, won hearts with her first film, *Three Smart Girls*, and followed with *100 Men and a Girl* (1937), which featured classical conductor Leopold Stokowski. After that, Durbin starred in a series of teenage musicals as "Miss Fixit", until her retirement in 1948.

Author's collection

Rita Hayworth was one of the pin-up queens of World War II, but she was also a solid screen personality and talented dancer who could hold her own with dance greats Fred Astaire and Gene Kelly. In addition to comedic and musical ability, Hayworth was a success as a femme fatale in the dark, psychological drama of film noir classics like *Gilda* (1946) and *The Lady from Shanghai* (1948). Hayworth oozed glamour but she was amiable and funny, too.

Over at Paramount, Bing Crosby was the main box office attraction. By 1940 the studio brought Crosby together with Bob Hope, and the freewheeling twosome wreaked havoc with film convention (they improvised on camera, made comments to the film audience, and the like) as they merrily chased Dorothy Lamour across the world in a series of *Road* films. Beginning with *Road to Singapore* and ending with *Road to Hong Kong* in 1962, the boys made a total of seven films. **Bob Hope** (1903-) was more than just a second banana to Crosby. He was a fine song and dance man who starred in the *Ziegfeld Follies* (he introduced "I Can't Get Started" in the 1936 *Follies*) as well as Broadway musicals, among them *Roberta* (1933) and *Red, Hot and Blue!* (1936). Before joining Crosby, Hope introduced three classic standard songs with the vastly underrated actress-vocalist Shirley Ross: "Thanks for the Memory" (*The Big Broadcast of 1938*), "Two Sleepy People" (*Thanks for the Memory*, 1938), and "The Lady's in Love With You" (*Some Like It Hot*, 1939). The last would be retitled *Rhythm Romance* for TV release to prevent it from being confused with the later film of the same title starring Marilyn Monroe, Jack Lemon, and Tony Curtis.

Just as Warner and RKO dominated the early period of the musicals, Twentieth Century-Fox and MGM would dominate the period from 1935 to 1950.

Courtesy Buffalo & Erie County Public Library   *Courtesy Stash Records*

Bing Crosby was one of many entertainers who donned battle fatigues in films as well as in real life to provide songs and easygoing merriment during the war years. Crosby's activity on radio and at the battlefront as an entertainer was a welcome reminder of home and normalcy to the members of the armed forces. *Holiday Inn*, which introduced Irving Berlin's "White Christmas," was remade as *White Christmas* for Paramount in 1945 and became the top grossing film of that year.

On the Road with Crosby, Hope, and Lamour. The comedy musical at its best was the series of *Road* films, which contained big Bing Crosby vocal numbers, patter comedy and musical duet by Crosby and Bob Hope, and native specialties for Dorothy Lamour. Ethan Mordden, whose opinionated *The Hollywood Musical* is the cheekiest and most delightfully written history of the musicals, says that the *Road* films baffle some, but they do stand as a rare case of Hollywood's admitting that personality is the art. The *Road* pictures depend on Hope as Hope—cowardly but devious—and Crosby as Crosby—disloyal but lovable—and a dangerous exotic place with Lamour as local beauty. Constant ad libs and asides to the audience shatter any sense of story."

Darryl F. Zanuck had saved Twentieth Century-Fox with the little curly-top, **Shirley Temple** (1928-　) in 1934. In Andrew Bergman's *We're in the Money: Depression America and Its Films*, we get the picture of Shirley Temple as the embodiment of "America's search for some vanished innocence. Shirley Temple's stardom and longings for the country were part of the same process; 'back to earth' was less a coherent plan for the future than a musing over things, imagined and real, that had been lost." In 1935 she starred in *The Little Colonel* with Lionel Barrymore as her grandfather and danced with the legendary Bill "Bojangles" Robinson. Temple sang "Animal Crackers in My Soup" and "When I Grow Up" in *Curly Top,* and again danced with Robinson in *The Littlest Rebel.*
While delighted that he had Hollywood's top box office, Zanuck was smart enough to realize that soon young Shirley would grow up, so he showcased other potential stars with her.

I have such fun curling my dolly's hair. Now I can always keep her looking nice.
Shirley Temple

234

The most successful child star in film history, Temple began her career at the age of three in a series of short film spoofs. At first her movie shorts were called *Baby Burlesks*, which satirized hit movies. Later she was featured in shorts titled *Frolics of Youth*. After small parts in three 1932-33 movies, she played in nine films in 1934. Her best loved musical numbers include "On the Good Ship Lollipop," "At the Codfish Ball," and "Animal Crackers in My Soup." Her star vehicles began in 1934 with *Little Miss Marker* and ended in 1949 with *A Kiss for Corliss*. A genuine prodigy, Temple usually played little waifs who overcame obstacles to bring sunshine and optimism to Depression-riddled America. She received a "Special Award" Oscar (a miniature statuette): "In grateful recognition of her outstanding contribution to screen entertainment during the year 1934."

In 1936 Temple was matched up with Alice Faye in *Poor Little Rich Girl* ("Military Man" and "You've Gotta Eat Your Spinach, Baby"). Thus began the succession of the "Cuddly Blondes" or the "Daisy Chain" at Fox. This chain begins with Temple, is carried on through the early 1940s by Faye and Betty Grable, is handed over to June Haver in the late 1940s, and continues into the 1950s with Marilyn Monroe. For some reason film historians haven't included Sonja Henie in the mix (perhaps because she didn't perform with any of the others in the "link"), but we will add her, as well.

Movie Star News

Alice Faye: The Queen of Fox, 1938-43.

Alice Faye (1915-) was a sleepy-eyed blonde songstress who made her mark originally as a Jean Harlow lookalike. Between 1938 and 1943 she was Fox's reigning singing star, appearing in such lavish period productions as *In Old Chicago* and *Alexander's Ragtime Band* (1938), *Rose of Washington Square, Lillian Russell,* and *Tin Pan Alley* (1939), and *Hello, Frisco, Hello* ("You'll Never Know," 1943) . Faye was also featured in contemporary settings, but it would be the stories from the past that would be her forte. In the opinion of Ethan Mordden in *The Hollywood Musical,* "One might date the Second Era [of Hollywood musicals] from the emergence of Alice Faye as a top draw in 1937, for Faye, who remained one of the biggest stars till she retired in 1945, set a style that held right up to the collapse of the studio musical in the 1950s. She is the nice woman who tries to look tough, a superb singer, a good dancer, and so rich a personality that her success depends not on playing a role but on letting a role play itself while she entertains. The Faye palette dabs anger, panting, tears; it paints sweet frocks and bad sequins and favors period (usually the wrong one for the film) costumes."

The two reigning superstars (blondes, of course) of 20th Century-Fox during the thirties and forties, Alice Faye, *left*, and Betty Grable, *right*. With her husky voice, pouting face, and hourglass figure, Faye was more of a singer than a dancer, while Grable, with her great legs and buoyant personality, was more of a dancer than a singer. Both were featured in costume musicals as well as the resort musicals that proved so popular for Fox. Neither of these stars became top recording artists like Dinah Shore or Doris Day. Of the two, Faye was considered a superior vocalist. *Left*, Faye in a typical, formulaic Fox nostalgia film, *Hello, Frisco, Hello*. This better-than-average tale featured a main love interest between Faye and John Payne, as well as the pairing of a comedic secondary couple played by Jack Oakie (Fox's king-pin character-clown specialist) and Lynn Bari. *Right*, Grable showcased in *Sweet Rosie O'Grady* (1943), a nostalgic showbiz tale set in the 1880s.

Author's collection

Lyrics by MACK GORDON • Music by HARRY WARREN

DOWN ARGENTINA WAY

Spanish Lyrics by
CARLOS ALBERT

DOWN ARGENTINE WAY

A 20th-Century-Fox Picture with
DON AMECHE • BETTY GRABLE • CARMEN MIRANDA
CHARLOTTE GREENWOOD • J. CARROL NAISH • HENRY STEPHENSON
Produced by Darryl F. Zanuck
Photographed in Technicolor

MILLER MUSIC, INC.
BROADWAY • NEW YORK

Author's collection

Betty Grable had appeared in nineteen films (usually as a chorus girl or secondary singer or dancer) before replacing Alice Faye in her first leading role opposite Don Ameche in *Down Argentine Way* in 1940. Ethan Mordden checks in again: "Betty Grable was . . . the happy Judy Garland [that Garland herself] seldom projected. Like Hayworth a pin-up and no great singer, Grable . . . was essentially the nation's wartime mascot, and Grable knew it. 'I'm strictly an enlisted man's girl,' she explained, 'just like this has to be an enlisted man's war.' Like Faye, Grable was a working-class Cinderella."

Betty Grable (1916-1973), who got her big break when she replaced Faye in a south-of-the-border opus, *Down Argentine Way* (1940), was the pinup queen of World War II. While, like Faye, she was often cast in period pieces (*Sweet Rosie O'Grady*, 1943, *The Dolly Sisters*, 1945, and *The Shocking Miss Pilgrim* and *Mother Wore Tights*, 1947), Grable was seen to best advantage in films where she could show off her main asset—her famous legs. Grable's "gams" were the focal point of the U.S. soldiers' most famous pinup during the war years.

Sonja Henie (1912-1969) was the blonde godess of the ice. The Norwegian-born ice skater was the only woman figure skater to ever win gold medals in three consecutive Olympics (1928, 1932, and 1936). "She was the greatest sports personality that Norway's ever had," declared Norwegian filmmaker Edward Hambro, producer of the documentary *Sonja Henie: The Queen of the Ice*. She starred in her first Fox film, *One in a Million* (1936), opposite Don Ameche. In 1937 Henie's love interest was Tyrone Power in *Thin Ice*. Cesar Romero was her costar the next year in *Happy Landing*. Henie's was one of the biggest box office attractions in Hollywood between 1936 and 1942, and she was one of the highest-paid women in the world during that time. Like most musicals, her pretty-ice-skater-meets-handsome-boy role was formulaic, but no one has ever matched her ice-skating grace on screen.

The European war effectively had begun by the late 1930s, so Zanuck sought another avenue for film distribution: South America. Hollywood's version of the federal government's "Good Neighbor Policy" led to a series of foreign locales south of the border. All of the adult blonde leading ladies of the forties (though not Henie, who needed cold climates for her ice capades) played opposite **Carmen Miranda** (1909-1955). Fox led the way with movies that took place in sunny, palm-tree-laden ports. This was the perfect setting to introduce Miranda, the fiery queen of exotica. A camp delight, she stood barely five feet high in her six-inch wedgies, bedecked with flashy outfits and crowned with a tutti-frutti hat. The collision of brilliant colors that Fox became known for exploded in splashy, crimson reds, deep-sea blues, and vibrant greens in such tropical delights as *Down Argentine Way*, *That Night in Rio*, *Weekend in Havana* (1941), *Springtime in the Rockies* (1942), and the penultimate Miranda experience, *The Gang's All Here* (1943). MGM might have been the "Tiffany of the studios," but at Fox they certainly knew how to have fun. Zanuck prided himself on being a leader in the industry by making films with a strong social message,(such as *Pinky*, *Gentleman's Agreement* and *The Grapes of Wrath*). Zanuck understood how the "Daisy chain" formula worked—after all, he created it—but his real passion was creating a product that would be taken seriously. Serious fillms usually assured producers and their studios a badge of prestige in the industry. But, as one observer noted about the success of the pretty women who populated the Fox musicals, "'Twasn't Zanuck, but beauty that paid for *The Grapes of Wrath*."

From 1940 to 1946, Carmen Miranda played comic roles at Fox. These films introduced both Grable and Miranda as well as the "south of the border" resort film.

Hollywood and the War Musicals Sampler

Film	Studio	Stars/Musical Performers	Song(s)	Year
Buck Privates	Universal	Abbott & Costello/Andrews Sisters	Boogie Woogie Bugle Boy	1941
Keep 'Em Flying	Universal	Abbott & Costello/Martha Raye	You Don't Know What Love Is	1941
Swing It Soldier	Universal	Ken Murray/Francis Langford	My Melancholy Baby	1941
Four Jacks and a Jill	RKO	Anne Shirley, Desi Arnaz	Boogie Woogie Conga 1941	
You'll Never Get Rich	Columbia	Fred Astaire, Rita Hayworth/ Delta Rhythm Boys	So Near & Yet So Far	1941 1941
Holiday Inn	Paramount	Bing Crosby, Fred Astaire	White Christmas	1942
Private Buckaroo	Universal	Andrews Sisters/Harry James	Don't Sit Under the Apple Tree	1942
For Me and My Gal	MGM	Judy Garland, Gene Kelly	For Me & My Gal	1942
Star-Spangled Rhythm	Paramount	Betty Hutton, Eddie Bracken Victor Moore	That Old Black Magic	1942
When Johnny Comes Marching Home	Universal	Allan Jones/Phil Spitalny & His All Girl Orchestra	This Is It	1943
Reveille With Beverly	Columbia	Ann Miller/Bob Crosby, Duke Ellington, Count Basie	Big Noise From Winnetka	1943
Stage Door Canteen	United Artists	Benny Goodman, Kay Kyser, Freddy Martin, Guy Lombardo	Why Don't You Do Right?	1943
The Sky's the Limit	RKO	Fred Astaire, Joan Leslie/ Freddie Slack Orchestra	One for My Baby (And One More for the Road)	1943
Thousands Cheer	MGM	Gene Kelly/Lena Horne	Honeysuckle Rose	1943
This Is the Army	Warner Brothers	George Murphy, Ronald Reagan, Joan Leslie/Kate Smith	God Bless America; Mandy	1943
The Gang's All Here	20th Century-Fox	Alice Faye/Benny Goodman, Carmen Miranda	Brazil; No Love, No Nothin'	1943
Two Girls and a Sailor	MGM	June Allyson, Van Johnson/ Lena Horne, Jimmy Durante	Paper Doll; Inka Dinka Doo	1944
Four Jills in a Jeep	20th Century-Fox	Carole Landis, Kay Francis, Martha Raye, Mitzi Mayfair	Cuddle Up a Little Closer	1944
Follow the Boys	Universal	George Raft/Dinah Shore, Dick Haymes, Andrews Sisters	I'll Walk Alone; I'll Get By	1944
Pin Up Girl	20th Century-Fox	Betty Grable/Charlie Spivak	Once Too Often	1944
Up in Arms	RKO	Danny Kaye, Dinah Shore	Tess's Torch Song	1944
Something for the Boys	20th Century-Fox	Carmen Miranda, Perry Como	Samba Boogie	1944
Here Come the Waves	Paramount	Bing Crosby, Betty Hutton	Ac-Cent-Tchu-Ate the Positive	1944
Anchors Aweigh	MGM	Gene Kelly, Frank Sinatra/Kathryn Grayson/ Jose Iturbi	I Fall in Love Too Easily	1945 1945
Bring on the Girls	Paramount	Eddie Bracken/Spike Jones	Chloe	1945
Thrill of a Romance	MGM	Esther Williams, Van Johnson	I Should Care	1945

The acknowledged leader of the musical film was MGM. The studio was responsible for rekindling the operetta craze in 1935 when it paired Jeanette MacDonald with Nelson Eddy in *Naughty Marietta*. The duo became the most famous singing couple in film history, making a total of eight films together. The studio apparently thought it had a duty to elevate the cultural appetite of movie audiences, and opera-like films were considered wholesome and refined. Producer Joe Pasternak was brought aboard by the company's leader, Louis B. Mayer, in 1942, the date of the final MacDonald-Eddy film. Pasternak had produced ten of the Deanna Durbin films at Universal. At MGM he either worked opera numbers into a contemporary film or concocted full-blown operettas. Pasternak was a high-profile producer, and gave the studio a regal bearing. He helped launch the careers of Jane Powell (eight films), Kathryn Grayson (six), and Mario Lanza (five).

Of all the producers of Hollywood musicals, none is as highly esteemed as **Arthur Freed** (1894-1973). He started as a songwriter but wanted to get more involved in the moviemaking process, so he campaigned within the studio for a spot to prove himself as a producer (producers made far more money and had greater prestige in Hollywood than songwriters). Freed was an assistant to Mervyn Leroy on *The Wizard of Oz* (1939) and had been instrumental in bringing Harold Arlen and Judy Garland to that project. He was rewarded by being named sole producer of another 1939 film, *Babes in Arms,* which starred Judy Garland and Mickey Rooney and began the "Hey kids, let's put on a show!" formula. *Strike Up the Band* (1940), *Babes on Broadway* (1942), and *Girl Crazy* (1943) completed the cycle.

Top, the Arthur Freed unit began in 1939 with the one-time songwriter working as an assistant producer on *The Wizard of Oz*. The film was Judy Garland's most beloved role in terms of audience response (she originally resented playing the role of Dorothy because of the young age the part called for). Today the film is considered a classic, but in 1939 MGM did not make a profit, and *Oz* was not considered a blockbuster hit. Garland's simple, heart-tugging version of "Somewhere Over the Rainbow" became her lifetime theme song. *The Making of the Wizard of Oz* by Aljean Harmatz gives a fascinating account of this classic.

Bottom, Freed's *Babes on Broadway* (1942) was not as successful as *Babes in Arms,* but it did showcase the all-around abilities of this talented twosome. Garland and Rooney did a series of impersonations of famous people in a dream sequence and Rooney's Carmen Miranda number from *Down Argentine Way* was right on the mark. The film ended with a spectacular minstrel show featuring its two young stars in blackface. Songs relating to the minstrel era, such as "Old Folks at Home (Swanee River)" and "Waiting for the Robert E. Lee," were performed.

Part of Freed's success came because he knew that if he wanted complete control of his projects, he would have to sign up talent that was beholden only to him. As a result, Freed sought out Broadway talent such as dancer/singer/choreographer Gene Kelly (twelve films), director Vincente Minnelli (eleven), and scriptwriters Betty Comden and Adolph Green (eight), among others. Freed's closest associate was Roger Edens, who wrote songs, composed, and eventually worked as an associate producer with Freed on nineteen pictures.

The master of musicals was **Vincente Minnelli** (1909-1986) seen here with Garland. Celebrated for his imaginative use of colors and his artistic use of design and decor, Minnelli's midas touch graced such films as *Cabin in the Sky* (1943), *Meet Me in St. Louis* (1944), *Yolanda and the Thief* (1945), *The Pirate* (1948), *An American in Paris* (1951), *The Band Wagon* (1953), *Brigadoon* (1954), and *Gigi* (1958), among others. If there is a reigning auteur (director with a powerful vision) of American musical films, it is Minnelli. All of his work (including such excellent dramatic releases as *Two Weeks in Another Town* and *The Four Horsemen of the Apocalypse*) reflect a touch of visual brilliance.

Film critic Molly Haskell in a tribute to Minnelli in *Nostalgia* magazine summarizes, "The key to the director's style is his intense, expressionistic approach to all genres. His films are never earthbound. Sometimes in flights of fancy, he, like Daedalus, came crashing down, but in championing risk over realism, Minnelli never played it safe."

Meet Me in St. Louis: Margaret O'Brien (who won a miniature Oscar for her performance) and Judy Garland doing the Cake Walk in the song "Under the Bamboo Tree." *Meet Me in St. Louis* tells the tale of the Smith family, which goes into crisis when the father decides to move the family to New York after Christmas,1902. Of course this sad state of affairs doesn't occur, and by the end of the film the family is seen attending the opening of the St. Louis Exposition of 1903. As in *The Wizard of Oz*, MGM promoted the values of family, and the theory that "there's no place like home." The little girl with the big heart, Judy Garland, would go on to become the single greatest female star of Hollywood musicals. This dance, with the charming, scene-stealing O'Brien, is one of the happiest musical numbers in musical film history.

Judy Garland (1922 -1969) made fourteen pictures under Freed's leadership and he allowed her natural talent to develop. First and foremost, Garland was a great singer. When she auditioned for Freed in 1935 he was so impressed that he brought her around for all of the studio heads to hear (she sang "Zing Went the Strings of My Heart"). Under his guidance Garland finally moved away from little girl roles into mature female leads, something that Shirley Temple didn't achieve. Freed paired Garland with newly arrived Gene Kelly in a wartime film called *For Me and My Gal* (1942). In this story Garland was caught in the middle of a love triangle with Kelly and George Murphy. She rebelled at being cast as a teenager in *Meet Me in St. Louis* (1944), and at first was openly hostile to the director, Vincente Minnelli. But Minnelli gained Garland's confidence (they eventually married) and the film resulted in one of the classic evocations of Americana with hit songs such as "The Boy Next Door," "The Trolley Song," and "Have Yourself a Merry Little Christmas." Garland became the major female star of MGM, appearing in *The Harvey Girls* (singing the Academy-Award-winning song by Harry Warren and Johnny Mercer, "On the Atchison, Topeka and the Santa Fe") in 1946. Garland was also in *The Pirate* with Gene Kelly in 1948, and in that same year, *Easter Parade* with Fred Astaire. The great dancer came out of retirement to replace Gene Kelly, who had broken his ankle. Garland had been hooked on pills for years and the eventual emotional toll began to interfere with her moviemaking at MGM. Garland was taken off of *Annie Get Your Gun* and replaced by Betty Hutton. She barely got through *Summer Stock* (which included "Get Happy," an ironically titled Harold Arlen composition considering the circumstances) in 1950. Garland was released by the company in 1950 but had a major comeback in 1954 in *A Star Is Born* for Warner Brothers.

Gene Kelly and Jerry Mouse in *Anchors Aweigh*.

Betty Comden and Adolph Green were a songwriting and playwriting team that came from the New York stage. The duo began their professional careers as part of an experimental comedy troupe known as the Revuers, a satiricial unit that included singer-comedienne Judy Holliday. The group was given a chance to hone their craft at Max Gordon's Greenwich Village jazz club, the Village Vanguard. The Revuers were precursors to comedy groups like Second City, Canada's "SCTV" troupe, and New York's "Saturday Night Live" crews. On Broadway, Comden and Green had a hit with *On the Town* (1944) and came to the Freed unit in 1947, where they helped put together such musicals as *Good News*, *Take Me Out to the Ball Game*, *The Barkleys of Broadway*, *On the Town*, *Singin' in the Rain*, *The Band Wagon*, *It's Always Fair Weather* and *Bells Are Ringing*.

Gene Kelly (1912-) ranks with Fred Astaire as the ultimate film dancer. Whereas Astaire projects a lithe, aristocratic figure adorned in top hat, white tie and tails, Kelly conjures up the image of a regular guy who might be a service man, or even a house painter. Kelly brought a brash, cocky, and sometimes even mean-spirited persona to his roles that could only be tamed by the sensitivity of song and dance. He had established that image in his Broadway roles in *Pal Joey* and *For Me and My Gal*. In the latter he brashly tries to steal Judy Garland away from George Murphy. Like Astaire, Kelly understood what kinds of dance best suited his strengths and so he choreographed with that in mind. Kelly was not content to only play in front of the camera; he wanted to direct. His chance came at the end of the forties, when he and Stanley Donan co-directed *On the Town* (1949). This was one of the most successful adaptations of a Broadway musical. Originally conceived for the stage by Betty Comden and Adolph Green with the music of Leonard Bernstein, it told a story of three servicemen on a twenty-four-hour leave in New York City. This was the first major musical to shoot segments on location and was the beginning of Kelly's preeminence as a director and star.

Kelly would continue as a superstar of the 1950s with classics such as *Summer Stock* (1950), *An American in Paris* (1951), *Singin' in the Rain* (1952), *Brigadoon* (1954), *It's Always Fair Weather* (1955), *Invitation to the Dance* (1956), and *Les Girls* (1957). Leslie Halliwell's *Filmgoer's Companion* gives Kelly that book's highest award, "for terpsichorean delights performed with cheerful proletarian grace."

You Came Along was a wartime film that featured Helen Forrest singing the title song.

Herman Hupfeld's classic song "As Time Goes By" was given a second life in the film drama *Casablanca*. Originally introduced by Oscar Shaw and Frances Williams in the stage musical *Everybody's Welcome* in 1931, the song was only moderately successful once Rudy Vallee recorded it. The song was by no means a standard when it was interpreted by Dooley Wilson in *Casablanca* a decade later, however. In the film the song is a connecting memory for Ingrid Bergman and Humphrey Bogart. At different times the protaganists both ask Wilson, playing the part of Sam, the piano player-singer and confidante to Bogart, to sing it for them. Wilson, a contract player at Warner Brothers, did not play piano, but the cameramen cleverly disguised this fact.

Because "As Time Goes By" was practically forgotten, *Casablanca* is usually thought of as the original source of the song. "As Time Goes By" has since reached the status of an all-time classic. There's hardly a piano-player-singer alive who hasn't been asked to perform the song. The song, the film and Bogart's tough-guy persona, were all playfully lampooned by Woody Allen in his 1972 comedy *Play It Again, Sam*.

Author's collection

Great Songs From Nonmusicals

Song	Film	Star/vocals/instrumentals	Recording Artist	Year
Again	Road House	Ida Lupino, (Richard Widmark, Cornel Wilde	Vic Damone	1948
As Time Goes By	Casablanca	Humphrey Bogart, Ingrid Bergman, Dooley Wilson	Dooley Wilson	1942
Black Market	A Forgotten Affair	Marlene Dietrich	Marlene Dietrich	1948
Golden Earrings	Golden Earrings	Marlene Dietrich	Peggy Lee	1947
Hong Kong Blues	To Have and Have Not	Humphrey Bogart, Lauren Bacall, Hoagy Carmichael	Hoagy Carmichael	1944
Hooray for Love	Casbah	Yvonne DeCarlo, Tony Martin	Tony Martin	1948
How Little We Know	To Have And Have Not	Lauren Bacall (legend has it a young Andy Williams dubbed her vocal)	Hoagy Carmichael	1944
It Can't Be Wrong	Now Voyager	Bette Davis, Paul Henreid (the film had a haunting instrumental theme)	Dick Haymes	1942
Laura	Laura	Gene Tierney, Dana Andrews, Clifton Webb (the instrumental theme later had lyrics by Johnny Mercer)	Johnny Johnston, Woody Herman, Dick Haymes	1945
Love Letters	Love Letters	Joseph Cotton, Jennifer Jones	Dick Haymes	1945
Love for Love	Escape Me Never	Ida Lupino, Errol Flynn	Claudia Thornhill w/ Fran Warren	1947
Mam'selle	The Razor's Edge	Tyrone Power, Gene Tierney	Art Lund, Dick Haymes, Frankie Laine	1947
Mona Lisa	Captain Carey	Alan Ladd, Wanda Hendrix	Nat King Cole	1950
Moon Over Manakoora	The Hurricane	Dorothy Lamour, Jon Hall	Dorothy Lamour	1937
Memphis in June	Johnny Angel	George Raft, Hoagy Carmichael	Hoagy Carmichael	1945
My Foolish Heart	My Foolish Heart	Dana Andrews, Susan Hayward	Billy Eckstine	1949
My Own True Love	Gone With the Wind	Clark Gable, Vivien Leigh ("Tara's Theme" with lyrics)	Margaret Whiting	1939
Ole Buttermilk Sky	Canyon Passage	Dana Andrews, Susan Hayward, Hoagy Carmichael	Hoagy Carmichael, Kay Kyser	1946
A Portrait of Jenny	A Portrait of Jenny	Jennifer Jones, Joseph Cotton	Nat King Cole	1948
Put the Blame on Mame	Gilda	Rita Hayworth, Glenn Ford	Anita Ellis	1946
Stella by Starlight	The Uninvited	Ray Milland, Ruth Hussey	Victor Young, Nat King Cole	1944
To Each His Own	To Each His Own	Olivia deHavilland, John Lund	Eddy Howard, Ink Spots, Tony Martin	1946
You Came Along (From Out of Nowhere)	You Came Along	Robert Cummings, Liz Scott, Helen Forrest	Helen Forrest	1945

PRISONER OF LOVE

Words and Music By
LEO ROBIN, CLARENCE GASKILL and RUSS COLUMBO

Recorded by
PERRY COMO

Courtesy Buffalo & Erie County Public Library

Perry Como (1912-) was an ex-barber from Pennsylvania who joined the Freddy Carlone band in 1933 as a vocalist and by 1936 was making records with the Ted Weems orchestra. In 1943 Como signed with RCA Victor and between 1944 and 1955 was second only to Bing Crosby among male singers in the total number of records he landed on the bestseller charts. Como was a star on radio and by the 1950s he was the most successful of the singers to adapt to the variety television show.

Roy Hemming and David Hajdu, in *Discovering Great Singers of Classic Pop,* point out: "For every new song he sent on its way to 'Your Hit Parade,' including 'Long Ago and Far Away,' 'Hubba, Hubba, Hubba (Dig You Later),' 'Don't Let the Stars Get in Your Eyes,' 'It's Impossible,' and 'Papa Loves Mambo,' Como revived an older song and put it back on the charts with a new, straightforward arrangement, including 1918's 'I'm Always Chasing Rainbows,' 1931's 'Prisoner of Love,' 1933's 'Temptation,' 1902's 'Because,' and 1898's 'If You Were the Only Girl in the World.' This mixture of old and new helped Como's popularity to cut across the generations more solidly and successfully than that of most other singers of the 1940s and 1950s."

The Post-War Baritone Belters

After the war years, songs that projected wistful longings, such as Sinatra's "Saturday Night Is the Loneliest Night of the Week" and "I'll Never Smile Again," seemed a bit out of place for a nation that was whooping it up in a spirit of celebration. As Arnold Shaw notes in *The Rockin '50s*, "A new postwar generation of youngsters did not react to soft, tender, reflective, moonlke singing. Bedroom idol during the war to girls without men, he [Sinatra] was no longer communicating to the former bobby soxers, now young marrieds and bedeviled by the tensions of a postwar economy." Baritone singers who belted romantic ballads and sang powerhouse uptempo tunes gained favor during the postwar years and set the stage for younger singers who would eventually introduce rock'n'roll during the fifties. Some of the pre-rock "exciters" (as Shaw calls them) of the early fifties were Vic Damone, Al Martino, Don Cornell, Johnny Desmond, Dean Martin, Tony Bennett, Jerry Vale, Tony Martin, and Frankie Laine. They were all Italian. Shaw wondered, "Considering the preponderance of 'paisanos,' is it any wonder that mainstream pop, until the advent of rock'n'roll, was a 'pasta' of Neapolitan, 'bel canto,' pseudo-operatic singing?"

The two leading exponents of the forties "belting style" were Vaughn Monroe and Frankie Laine. So let us complete this umbrella view of the popular music scene of 1935 to 1950 by briefly examining their careers. Keep in mind that the shift from the crooning and swooning of Crosby and Sinatra to the dramatic belting of Monroe and Laine reflected social changes that created a demand for faster-paced music. The result, rising in the late forties, was the beginning of rock'n'roll. The underground forms of jump and jive, honkers and shouters, and the country western movement known as honky tonk were strong barometric indicators of the coming of rock, as we shall see in Chapters 12 and 13.

Vaughn Monroe (1911-1973) began as a trumpet player in a variety of dance bands and then studied opera. Working in the Boston area (he was attending the New England Conservatory) he fronted a society band during the mid-thirties. According to George T. Simon, Monroe was "a large, handsome man with a great smile, one of the most romantic-looking leaders of the big band era." The most successful aspect of Monroe's band was his big, chesty vocals on early hits such as "Racing With the Moon" (1940), "There! I've Said It Again" and "Let It Snow! Let It Snow! Let It Snow!" (1945), "I Wish I Didn't Love You So" and "Ballerina" (1947). From that point on, Monroe's band became merely a support system for his singing, and because Monroe moved away from instrumental jazz soloing, he lost many of his better players. Not to worry, though. Monroe responded by placing an even greater emphasis on singing, as he featured the Murphy Sisters and, later, the Moonmaids (named after his first big hit and theme song). By the end of the forties Monroe was making hits out of his interpretations of hit

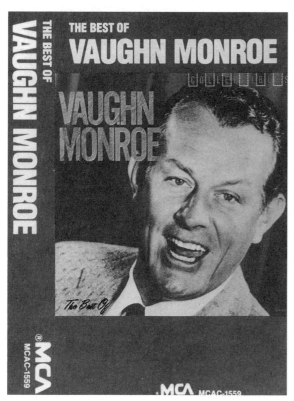

Courtesy MCA Records

Known for his stentorian baritone belting, Vaughn Monroe was an early influence on Frankie Laine. Monroe began his recording career in 1940 on Bluebird Records, where he had a hit with "There I Go." From there Monroe transferred to the parent label, RCA Victor, and began a string of top ten hits. Although today's audiences are not familiar with Monroe, they might recognize his inimitable vocal stylings from his rendering of the song "Let It Snow! Let It Snow! Let It Snow!" which was used for the closing credits of the first two of Bruce Willis's hit *Die Hard* films (1988 and 1990).

Frank Driggs Collection

Frankie Laine calling the wild goose.

country western songs like, "Cool Water" (1948), and "Riders in the Sky," "That Lucky Old Sun," and "Mule Train" (1949).

Frankie Laine (1913-   ), born Frank Paul Lo-Vecchio, hailed from Chicago, where he set records during the Depression, winning dance marathons. Laine's early singing was influenced by Al Jolson and Midred Bailey, and his later style borrowed from Cab Calloway and Billie Holiday. After Hoagy Carmichael heard him sing "Rockin' Chair" in 1946, Laine was booked into Billy Berg's club in Hollywood at the same time Charlie Parker and Slim Gaillard were introducing bop to California. Occasionally Laine was called on to sing a couple of songs. Laine's career took off when he recorded "That's My Desire" (Laine shouted out the lyrics with such assertiveness that the 1946 Mercury release was noticed by all who heard it because it was so different). "Everybody thought I was colored. They didn't use the word 'black' in those days. My manager, Sam Lutz, kept getting into arguments with disc jockeys who argued that 'no white man sang like that,'" Laine claimed in an interview with Arnold Shaw in *The Rockin' '50s*.

Monroe began a long association with arranger Carl Fisher in 1947 and together they created a string of powerful songs belted out with a gusto that was matched only by black shouters in the rhythm and blues field such as Big Joe Turner, Roy Brown, and Wynonie Harris. Laine's late-1940s hits included "That Lucky Old Sun," "Mule Train" (the same song done by Monroe), and "The Cry of the Wild Goose." Laine had landed in the upper echelon of the popular music business. As Laine described his entry into the big time,"In September, 1947, I went into the Million Dollar Theatre in downtown Los Angeles. The week before that at the Morocco I was getting $750. At the end of the first week at the theatre, my percentage of the box office brought $11,700. When Carl and I saw the check, we were so overwhelmed we both started to cry." Laine's love of black music and his friendship with rhythm and bluesman Charles Brown led him down the path of rhythmically charged music that was highly upbeat and headed in the direction of rock'n'roll. By early 1950, when crowds chanted "Frankie!" they were referring to Laine, not Sinatra.

Left, Frankie Laine continued having hits in the 1950s. "I Believe" was a chart-topper in 1953, as were his rousing renditions of "Jezabel" and "Jealousy" in 1951. In 1952 Laine covered Tex Ritter's movie soundtrack hit "High Noon (Do Not Forsake Me)." *Right,* **Tony Martin** (1912-) began, like Rudy Vallee, as a saxophone-player-turned-singer during the mid-1930s. A handsome, big-chested belter, Martin made his radio debut as a singer on "The Lucky Strike Hour" and went to Hollywood in 1936. After being featured in the film *Sing, Baby, Sing* (1936), Martin married the star, Alice Faye. He starred in a spate of films throughout the 1940s and 1950s, where he spotlighted his baritone on hit songs like "Begin the Beguine" (which he claims sold over eight million copies, but no other source seems to confirm anything close to that number), "You Stepped Out of a Dream," "Tonight We Love," "There's No Tomorrow," "I Get Ideas," and "Kiss of Fire." After his divorce from Faye, Martin married dancer Cyd Charisse, who became a film star for MGM (*Singin' in the Rain,* 1952; *The Bandwagon,* 1953; *Brigadoon,* 1954; *It's Always Fair Weather,* 1955; and *Silk Stockings,* 1957).

Top-Selling Big Bands: 1935-1950

Band	Chart Hits	No. 1 Hits	Top #1 Hit	Year	Weeks at #1
Tommy Dorsey	185	17	I'll Never Smile Again	1941	12
Benny Goodman	150	15	Goody Goody	1936	6
Glenn Miller	129	23	In the Mood	1939	12
Guy Lombardo	124	15	Third Man Theme	1950	11
Jimmy Dorsey	100	11	Amapola	1941	10
Sammy Kaye	98	8	Daddy	1941	8
Freddie Martin	79	5	Piano Concerto in B Flat	1941	8
Kay Kyser	78	11	Jingle, Jangle, Jingle	1942	8
Eddy Duncan	75	8	Lovely To Look At	1935	4
Harry James	69	8	I've Heard That Song Before	1943	13
Russ Morgan	53	4	Cruising Down th River	1949	7
Horace Heidt	52	3	Ti-Pi-Tin	1938	6
Woody Herman	52	1	Blues in the Night	1941	4
Artie Shaw	50	3	Frenesi	1940	13
Hal Kemp	45	4	This Year's Kisses	1937	4

Source: Joel Whitburn's Pop Memories,1890-1954

Courtesy Michael's Pub

Vic Damone (1928-   ) began as a Sinatra follower in the mid-1940s. After winning a place on "Arthur Godfrey Talent Scouts," in 1947, Damone started singing regularly on radio and in nightclubs. Recording for Mercury Records, he had his first hit in 1947 with "I Have But One Heart," and followed with the great ballad from the film *Roadhouse*, "Again" (1948). In this film, Ida Lupino played the part of pianist-singer who seems to sing only one song each set! Her pouty reading of "Again" was one of the highlights of her career—although she was not normally cast as a musical performer.

In 1951 it was on to motion pictures where Damone's matinee-idol good looks had him featured in a number of undistinguished films (1955's *Kismet* was the most memorable). Damone's dramatic readings of "Just Say I Love Her," "Why Was I Born," and "On the Street Where You Live" led Frank Sinatra to rave that Damone had "the best pipes in the business." Damone's short-lived marriage to Diahann Carroll in 1987 and duets they performed sparked a minor comeback for the singer in Las Vegas.

Roy Hemming and David Hajdu describe Damone's career in *Discovering Great Singers of Classic Pop* thusly: "Neither a band singer nor a Broadway star nor an established night club attraction, Vic Damone was one of the first singers to become a success through the star-production machinery of the record business, which fully came into its own after the Second World War. For the next forty years (until the rise of music videos, which changed the system again), the Damone model would serve as the standard formula for alchemizing green kids into gold-record makers."

Like most singers of the 1940s Damone was very much under the influence of Frank Sinatra. He admitted in a 1958 interview that, "Sure I copied Sinatra. Who didn't? I used to save my money for those 25 cent 'Record Your Voice' machines and practice singing just like Frank." Ken Barnes, writing in *Sinatra and the Great Song Stylists*, claims, "Fine technique and his inherent knowledge of the popular music idiom ensured that Damone's upper register was at all times under complete control, and he remains (except perhaps for Gordon MacRae) the finest example of a singer who could handle popular songs and more legitimate material with no sense of anachronism. He could problably be called the latter-day counterpart of Tony Martin and almost certainly he's probably the sole survivor of the school of great romantic ballad singers."

Top Selling Vocalists: 1935-50

Vocalist	Chart Hits	#1 Hits	Top #1 Hit	Year	Weeks at #1
Bing Crosby	227	27	White Christmas	1942	10
Andrews Sisters	89	6	Rum and Coca Cola	1945	11
Frank Sinatra	80	4	Oh! What It Seemed To Be	1946	8
Perry Como	66	7	Till the End of Time	1945	10
Fats Waller	63	6	It's a Sin to Tell a Lie	1936	4
Dinah Shore	63	4	Buttons & Bows	1948	10
Vaughn Monroe	57	9	Riders in the Sky	1949	12
Jo Stafford	50	1	Candy	1945	1
Ink Spots	45	6	The Gypsy	1946	13
Ella Fitzgerald	43	3	A-Tisket, A-Tasket	1938	10
Dick Haymes	43	2	You'll Never Know	1943	7
Billie Holiday	39	1	Carelessly	1937	3
Margaret Whiting	35	1	A Tree in the Meadow	1948	5
Mills Brothers	30	2	Paper Doll	1943	10
Eddy Howard	30	1	To Each His Own	1946	8

Source: Joel Whitburn's Pop Memories, 1890-1954

Songs in the Grammy Hall of Fame: 1935-1950

Song	Year	Performer	Label	Inducted
I Can't Get Started	1937	Bunny Berigan and His Orchestra	Victor	1975
One O'Clock Jump	1937	Count Basie and His Orchestra	Decca	1979
Sing, Sing, Sing	1937	Benny Goodman	Victor	1982
Carnegie Hall Concert	1938	Benny Goodman and His Orchestra	Columbia	1975
September Song	1938	Walter Houston	Brunswick	1984
A-Tisket, A-Tasket	1938	Chick Webb Orchestra (Ella Fitzgerald)	Decca	1986
Body and Soul	1939	Coleman Hawkins and His Orchestra	Bluebird	1974
Strange Fruit	1939	Billie Holiday	Commodore	1978
Over the Rainbow	1939	Judy Garland	Decca	1981
God Bless America	1939	Kate Smith	Victor	1982
In the Mood	1939	Glenn Miller and His Orchestra	Bluebird	1984
Tea for Two	1939	Art Tatum (piano solo)	Decca	1986
And the Angels Sing	1939	Benny Goodman (M. Tilton, Z. Elman)	Victor	1987
If I Didn't Care	1939	Ink Spots	Decca	1987
Moonlight Serenade	1939	Glenn Miller and His Orchestra	Bluebird	1991
Ballad for Americans	1940	Paul Robeson	Victor	1980
I'll Never Smile Again	1940	Tommy Dorsey	Victor	1982
Star Dust	1940	Artie Shaw and His Orchestra	Victor	1988
Gershwin: Porgy and Bess Highlights	1940	Broadway revival cast	Decca	1990
God Bless the Child	1941	Billie Holiday	Okeh	1976
Take the "A" Train	1941	Duke Ellington and His Orchestra	Victor	1976
Cool Water	1941	Sons of the Pioneers	Decca	1981
White Christmas	1942	Bing Crosby	Decca	1974
Oklahoma!	1943	Original Broadway cast (Alfred Drake)	Decca	1976
Begin the Beguine	1944	Artie Shaw and His Orchestra	Bluebird	1977
Black, Brown and Beige	1944	Duke Ellington & His Famous Orchestra	Victor	1990
Artistry in Rhythm	1945	Stan Kenton and His Orchestra	Capitol	1985
Lover Man	1945	Billie Holiday	Decca	1989
The Christmas Song	1946	Nat King Cole	Capitol	1974
Ornithology	1946	Charlie Parker Sextet	Dial	1989
This Land Is Your Land	1947	Woody Guthrie	Asch	1989
Four Brothers	1948	Woody Herman	Columbia	1984
Call it Stormy Monday	1948	T-Bone Walker	Black & White	1991
Birth of the Cool	1949	Miles Davis	Capitol	1982
Rudolph the Red-Nosed Reindeer	1949	Gene Autry	Columbia	1985
South Pacific	1949	Original Broadway cast (Mary Martin and Ezio Pinza)	Columbia	1987
The Song of Mr. Jelly Lord	1949	Jelly Roll Morton	12LPs/Circle	1980
Charlie Parker with Strings	1950	Charlie Parker	Mercury	1988

Source: National Academy of Recording Arts and Sciences

Chapter 9

BIG BANDS AND SMALL BANDS

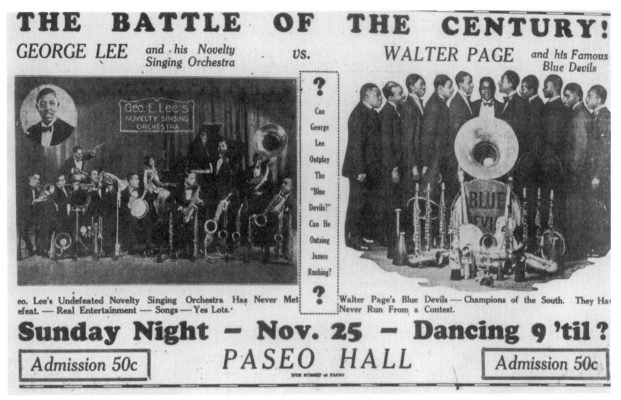

Frank Driggs Collection

We have seen how the pre-swing units of organizations such as Fletcher Henderson and the McKinney Cotton Pickers introduced the concepts of riffs, section playing, and solos to the popular big bands of the swing era. Unmentioned so far is the impact of swing-era Southwest "territory" bands on big band jazz. Ross Russell in *Jazz Style in Kansas City and the Southwest* outlines: "In overview, the territorial bands of the Southwest could be divided into three main groups—Kansas City bands, Texas bands, and bands associated with various cities like Denver or Omaha. Most of these bands traveled frequently and widely. Jumps of 800 or 1,000 miles between engagements were not uncommon, and, among the less affluent orchestras, these trips were made by passenger car, with perhaps a truck carrying the instruments and arrangements, if any." According to Nathan W. Pearson, Jr. in *Goin' to Kansas City,* "During the Depression, Kansas City became the focal point for scores of out-of-work musicians and bands, but during the twenties Kansas City was only one lively town among many. All of the states of the Territories jumped with the sweet thunder of jazz."

Kansas City Jazz

The Kansas City of musical history is Kansas City, Missouri, which is across the Kaw River from Kansas City, Kansas. During Prohibition, Kansas City, Missouri, was called an "open city." In musician-speak, that meant it ignored the laws against drinking. Kansas City in this period literally operated twenty-four hours a day. Because it was an "open town," there were more demands for live music than in closed, or dry towns. Accordingly, musicians flourished there.

Kansas City ignored the law of the land because of its mayor, Tom Pendergast. "Boss Tom" ran Kansas City from the 1920s until 1938, when he was indicted for income tax fraud. During Pendergast's tenure, the police allowed the illegal operation of liquor-dispensing establishments. Even after Prohibition had been repealed, Kansas City continued what has been termed "Pendergast prosperity." It was estimated that the city had hundreds of nightclubs of all descriptions during the prime years of the Pendergast regime featuring live music. Many included floor shows. The combination of the Pendergast reign and the fact that Kansas City had been a crossroads for the livestock business, giving it a large population of transient workers, meant that there was a large market for entertainment at the many clubs, dance halls, and brothels.

The Late Bennie Moten's 1931 Victor Recording Orchestra

He Made Kaycee a Musicians' Paradise

Here it is, one of the best of the colored jazz bands of a decade ago. The late Bennie Moten, patron saint of Kansas City style jazz, fronted this group at Fairyland Park in Kansas City the summer of 1931. In the photo are (left to right, staggered) Booker Washington, trumpet; Eddie Durham, trombone; Ed Lewis, trumpet; Bennie Moten, piano; Thamon Hayes, trombone; Oran (Hot Lips) Page, trumpet; Jimmy Rushing, vocals; the late Willie McWashington, drums; Buster Moten, front; Le-Roy Berry, banjo; Harlan Leonard, alto; Vernon Page, bass horn; Jim Webster, alto; Woodie Walder, tenor, and Bill (Count) Basie, piano. The band was recording stuff like *South, Lafayette, Moten Swing* and *Toby* for Victor at this period.

Kaycee Strictly A Colored Town

Although Kansas City rates as second only to New Orleans as a spawning ground of great jazz musicians, it is a peculiar fact that its sons are all colored. Except for Joe Sanders, Leith Stevens and Paul Tremaine, Kaycee has produced no unusually talented white musicians.

The city's population is 401,-000. It is located in Jackson County, Missouri, on a tall bluff overlooking the muddy Missouri and Kansas (Kaw) Rivers. It is one of America's greatest railroad, livestock and milling centers and attracts huge numbers of visitors annually. Although the Chamber of Commerce doesn't publicize it, Kaycee is also famous for its many Negro jazzmen.

Courtesy Down Beat

Kansas City's Reno Club and Sunset Cafe are best remembered today because they hired Count Basie, Big Joe Turner, and Pete Johnson. Other popular spots were the Hey-Hey Club, the Deluxe Night Club, and Dante's Inferno. Dante's was notorious for its status as the city's key "drag" club, where cross-dressers and transvestites like "Mr. Half-and-Half" held sway. Another element of the underground was the direct connection between musicians and gangsters. Eddie Durham, the guitarist-trombonist with Bennie Moten and Count Basie, observed, "Those gangsters would always treat everybody right. If you touched a musician, or one of the girls, you'd go out on your head. Nobody ever harassed musicians." And saxophone great "Professor" Buster Smith added, "In Kansas City all them big clubs were [run by] them big gangsters, and they were the musician's best friend. They gave you a job, and something to eat, and work regular. We didn't know nothing about their business, they didn't know nothing about ours, all they want us to do is play music, and keep the crowd happy." A white, society-type jazz dance band, the Coon-Saunders Nighthawks, played host at the most exclusive hotel in town, the Muehlebach. Other white bands, such as those led by Hal Kemp, Glen Gray, and Ben Pollack, visited Kansas City to play in hotels and large ballrooms. In general during this era, white bands played for white audiences. The black bands played different venues, including large dance

Kansas City Jazz was nurtured at this spot, the now-famous old Reno Club on Kaycee's brightly-lighted 12th street. This photo, made in 1936, shows Oran (Hot Lips) Page up front with trumpet. Ira (Bus) Moten is the pianist. Bassist is Bill Hadnott, now with Harland Leonard; Jess Price beats his tubs and Dee (Prince) Stewart is visible on one trumpet. The joint wasn't fancy, but it always jumped. It was here that Count Basie was "discovered" by John Hammond. Note how convenient the men's room is for the musicians. *Down Beat Photo.*

Courtesy Down Beat

Courtesy Route 66 Records

This compilation LP contains good examples of a variety of "territory" bands and their recordings between 1936 and 1939. Trumpeter-bandleader Don Albert featured pianist-arranger Lloyd Glenn, who would go on to be one of the leading club combo stars of the California scene during the 1940s. "True Blue Lou" and "Rockin' and Swingin'" are two representative selections. The Ernie Fields Orchestra weighs in with "Blues at Midnight" and "High Jivin'." The Carolina Cotton Pickers Orchestra under the direction of Wesley Jones stomps on "Marie" and "Western Swing," while Boots and His Buddies, led by drummer Clifford "Boots" Douglas, is featured on "San Antonio Tamales" and "Lonesome Road Stomp."

halls and ballrooms like the Paseo Hall (which could handle three thousand dancers). However, it was the smaller cabarets that made the major impact on jazz history, most significantly in Kansas City, the Sunset Cafe and the Reno Club.

The three key musical elements of the black Kansas City style were the blues riffs, head arrangements, and boogie woogie piano.

Blues riffs were short musical phrases repeated again and again. Head arrangements were riffs created spontaneously, learned by ear, and kept in the heads of the players. Head arrangements were the basis of the Kansas City riff band styles. Boogie woogie was the pre-modern piano style characterized by a repetitive left hand bass figure that hit almost every beat by dividing it into dotted-eighth and sixteenth-note patterns. Walter Page and His Blue Devils, the George E. Lee Orchestra, Jesse Stone's Blue Serenaders, Harlan Leonard and His Rockets, and, most importantly, Bennie Moten and His Kansas City Orchestra, were leaders in this tradition.

Andy Kirk and His Twelve Clouds of Joy became one of the best-known alumni to feature the Kansas City sound during the swing era. The band spotlighted one of the great pianists of this period, Mary Lou Williams. The group reached international stardom by 1936 with the smooth vocals of Pha Terrell, and a big hit, "Until the Real Thing Comes Along." Jay McShann was an outstanding pianist-bandleader whose late-thirties/early-forties unit would spotlight saxophonist Charlie Parker, the future leader of the new jazz known as bop. McShann was touring well into the 1990s, playing his boogie woogie piano in trio and solo settings at leading jazz clubs and festivals.

Key Territory Bands

Band	Home	Sidemen	Representative Songs
Don Albert Orchestra	San Antonio	Herb Hall, Lloyd Glenn, Ernestine Allen	Rockin' and Swingin'
Phil Banks Orchestra	Kansas City	Ed Lewis, Jap Allen, Charlie Parker	Mississippi Mud; Sweet Sue
Phil Baxter & His Texas Tommies		Al Jennings	I Ain't Got No Gal Now; Down Where the Blue Bonnets Grow
Tommy Douglas Orchestra	Kansas City	Curtyse Foster, Bill Scarcy, Charlie Parker, Jo Jones	[recording not found]
Troy Floyd Orchestra	San Antonio	Don Albert, Hershal Evans, Buddy Tate	Shadowland Blues
Thamon Hayes's K.C. Skyrockets	Kansas City	Jesse Stone, Vic Dickenson	South
Lloyd Hunter's Serenaders	Omaha	Deb Mills, Sir Charles Thompson	Sensational Mood
Jeter-Pillars Club Plantation Orchestra	St. Louis	Harry Edison, Sy Oliver, Floyd Smith	Lazy Rhythm
Andy Kirk and His 12 Clouds of Joy	Kansas City	Mary Lou Williams, Claude Williams, Dick Wilson, Don Byas, Pha Terrell	Until the Real Thing Comes Along
Milt Larkin's Orchestra	Houston	Eddie "Cleanhead" Vinson, Arnett Cobb, Cedric Haywood	Chicken Blues
George E. Lee & His Singing Novelty Orchestra	Kansas City	Budd Johnson, Jesse Stone, Baby Lovett, Herman Walder, Julie Lee	St. James Infirmary
Harlan Leonard's K.C. Rockets	Kansas City	Eddie Durham, Buster Smith, Jesse Stone, Baby Lovett, Ed Lewis, Vic Dickenson, Tadd Dameron	I Don't Want to Set the World on Fire
Clarence Love Orchestra	Tulsa	Jim Daddy Walker, Lester Young, Eddie Haywood, Joe Smith	[never recorded]
Jay McShann Orchestra	Kansas City	Charlie Parker, Gene Ramey, Walter Brown, Gus Johnson, John Jackson	Confessin' the Blues; Hootie Blues
George Morrison Orchestra	Denver	Hattie McDaniel ("Female Bert Williams")	After the Ball; Double Eagle
Bennie Moten Orchestra	Kansas City	Count Basie, Jimmy Rushing, Lester Young, Eddie Durham, Hot Lips Page, Ben Webster, Buster Smith, Walter Page	Moten Swing; Toby; South
Walter Page's Blue Devils	Kansas City	Count Basie, Jimmy Rushing, Buster Smith, Hot Lips Page, Eddie Durham, Ernie Williams	Blue Devil Blues; Squabblin'
Jesse Stone's Blue Serenaders	Kansas City	Druie Bess, George Bell	Boot to Boot
Alphonso Trent Orchestra	Dallas	T. Holder, Stuff Smith, Harry Edison, Peanuts Holland	I Found a New Baby
Nat Towles Orchestra	Austin	Buddy Tate, C. Q. Price, Sir Charles Thompson	Smooth Sailing

Jay McShann (1909-   ), pianist-singer-bandleader extraordinaire, is the least known of the Kansas City pantheon (Count Basie, Jimmy Rushing, Big Joe Turner, and Lester Young are arguably the others). Known as "Hootie," McShann emerged out of Kansas City with a hit in 1941, "Confessin' the Blues," which he co-authored with his singing star, Walter Brown. McShann was still playing some of the funkiest piano on the music scene as late as 1995.

Courtesy Rhapsody Films

William "Count" Basie (1904-1984), was born in Red Bank, New Jersey, and began his schooling as a disciple of Fats Waller, from whom Basie developed his great love for the pipe organ. Basie traveled to Kansas City and joined Walter Page's group in 1928. He and Page's singer, Jimmy Rushing, left to join Bennie Moten's band in 1929. By the time Basie joined Moten, the band had already established itself as the leading jazz unit in Kansas City, with successful recordings of "South," "Kansas City Shuffle," and "Moten Stomp." There Basie remained until Moten died in 1935.

Choosing some of the best men from Moten's group, Basie joined up with Moten's saxophonist, Buster Smith, to co-lead the Buster Smith and Count Basie Band of Rhythm. Nicknamed "Professor," Smith had been the outstanding soloist of Moten's group, and he and Basie made $21 a week playing every night at the Reno Club. Work started at nine o'clock at night and didn't finish until four or five in the morning.

Basie, who at that time was called by his first name, Bill, acquired his nickname one evening in 1936 when an announcer, broadcasting from the Reno, noted in his introduction that there was royalty in jazz with an earl (Hines), and a duke (Ellington), so there should also be a count. The band's famous theme song, "One O'Clock Jump," was established at the Reno Club during 1935. The key phrase was a musical figure Basie lifted from his mentor, Fats Waller. The phrase was reworked and recorded by the Chocolate Dandies as "Six or Seven Times" in 1929, then reprised by its arranger, Don Redman, on record by the McKinney Cotton Pickers. Buster Smith remembered the song and suggested the opening musical figure to Basie, who worked out a head arrangement for the rest of the song, which was originally titled "Blue Balls." Playing the song over the air one night an announcer, nervous about using a title he found embarrassing, asked if he might call it something else. Since it was nearing one o'clock in the morning, it was agreed to refer to the song as "One O'Clock Jump."

The band got its big break when record producer John Hammond heard them on the radio. He convinced Basie, but not Smith, to sign a management contract. Smith was suspicious about vague promises of stardom from an unknown white New Yorker. The group, now under the sole direction of Basie, made its first recordings as a five-man instrumental group for Vocalion in October 1936. "Shoe Shine Boy" and "Oh, Lady Be Good" were recorded by Count Basie on piano, Carl Smith on trumpet, Lester Young on tenor saxophone, Walter Page on bass, and Jo Jones on drums. There were two other recordings from that session, which featured vocalist Jimmy Rushing: "Evenin'" and "Boogie Woogie."

Author's collection

Count Basie's "One O'Clock Jump" is one of the most famous of all big band theme songs.

Courtesy Stash Records

Count Basie with his most famous saxophone star, Lester Young (with hat).

The Count Basie Band: 1937-39

Brass	Buck Clayton, Joe Keyes, Carl Smith, Ed Lewis, Shad Collins, Harry "Sweets" Edison (trumpets), George Hunt, Dan Minor, Eddie Durham, Bennie Morton, Dickie Wells (trombones)
Reeds	Hershal Evans, Lester Young, Jack Washington, Earle Warren (saxophones)
Rhythm	Count Basie (piano), Walter Page (bass), Jo Jones (drums), Claude Williams, Freddie Green (rhythm guitar), Eddie Durham (electric guitar)
Vocals	Jimmy Rushing, Helen Humes
Key recordings	Shoe Shine Boy; Boogie Woogie; Lady Be Good; Swingin' at the Daisy Chain; One O'Clock Jump; Topsy; Sent for You Yesterday; Every Tub; Swingin' the Blues; Blue and Sentimental; Doggin' Around; Texas Shuffle; Jumpin' at the Woodside; Shorty George; Jive at Five; Taxi War Dance; Clap Hands Here Comes Charlie; Dickie's Dream; Lester Leaps In

A fuller, newly reinforced band (brass and reed players were added so the band could compete in the bigger ballrooms) recorded for Decca in January 1937. "Roseland Shuffle" and "Honeysuckle Rose" received good notices from the jazz press. "One O'Clock Jump" was recorded in July, and in early 1938 the band laid down twenty-four sides, including a number of classics-to-be: "Every Tub," "The Swinging Blues," "Shorty George," "Texas Shuffle," "Doggin' Around," "Blue and Sentimental," and "Jumpin' at the Woodside." These recordings continue to sound fresh today.

The greatest contribution to jazz by Count Basie's new band was to be found in the rhythm section. Basie, Page, Jones, and guitarist Freddie Green laid down what Basie liked to call "four honest beats with no cheating." It was this section that became the first in jazz history to swing in a smooth and relaxed way. In *Jazz Styles* Mark Gridley praises the group for "achieving a balance among the sounds of its members. The four parts were so smoothly integrated that one listener was inspired to compare the effect to riding on ball bearings. If you listen carefully to recordings of the band, you will notice that it is unusual for one member to dominate. Guitar, bass and drums are all carefully controlled to avoid disturbing the evenness and balance of sound."

Another significant aspect of the Kansas City legacy is that of the blues shouters. Many of the small clubs in the twenties didn't have microphones, so these singers had to sing loudly above the riffing horn sections and rambunctious boogie woogie piano to be heard. Some used megaphones (a la Rudy Vallee) to be heard above the roar of the band. The first singer of note in this style was **Jimmy Rushing** (1902-1972). He was a short, heavy man nicknamed "Mr. Five By Five" for his stoutness. Rushing established his easygoing blues style at the Reno Club with Basie. In addition to his early Basie releases, Rushing coauthored with Eddie Durham "Good Morning Blues" and "Sent for You Yesterday (And Here You Come Today)." "Every Day I Have the Blues" became Rushing's unofficial theme song. Popular blues guitarist B.B. King was a fan of Rushing's and eventually would use "Every Day I Have the Blues" as his theme song. The closest Rushing ever got to having a hit song came later in his career with the humorous "Berkeley Blues," which lamented "Ronnie Reagan" as the then-governor of California.

Mr. Five By Five: Jimmy Rushing.

Author's collection

After leaving Basie, Rushing recorded under a number of different instrumental backings, but he never lost touch with the riffing, call-and-response elements that characterized the Kansas City atmosphere. Rushing was a much-beloved figure in the blues and jazz community and especially popular in England, where he was treated like royalty. Rushing often noted, rather sadly, the relative lack of appreciation for his music in America. Rushing once claimed that the difference between black religious music and the blues was that sacred songs sang about God, while the blues sang about a woman. Black novelist Ralph Ellison has a fine essay about Rushing in his collection *Shadow and Act*.

Bruce Ricker's film *The Last of the Blue Devils* played only a few selected art houses when it was originally released in the 1980s. Thankfully the world of video tape has allowed a larger audience to view the warm tribute to known Kansas City veterans (Big Joe Turner, Jay McShann, and Count Basie) who returned to the local colored musicians' union hall. Lesser-known Kansas City legends like drummer Baby Lovett, saxman "Professor" Buster Smith, and Claude Williams are also given screen time in this loving look at a long-gone era. Rare pictures of Kansas City nightclubs, interviews with participants, and a wide variety of musical selections give audiences of today a sample of the exciting Kansas City "jump blues." Classic Kansas City numbers such as "Moten Swing," "One O'Clock Jump," "Piney Brown Blues," and "Roll 'Em Pete" are featured. Ricker worked on the major Hollywood film *Kansas City* (1996), directed by Robert Altman, and planned to produce a documentary history of the colorful city in tandem with the filming of the motion picture.

Big Joe Turner (1911-1985) was the other giant of the Kansas City vocal tradition. Born in Kansas City, this big youngster was a bartender by the age of fourteen, so he soaked up musical tradition early on. Turner began his musical career as a no-nonsense blues shouter and eventually combined forces with boogie woogie pianist Pete Johnson to write and sing the blues at the Sunset Cafe. One of their early songs, "Piney Brown Blues," was a salute to the manager of the Sunset, Piney Brown, a favorite of the musicians because he was a kindred soul.

Boss of the Blues: Big Joe Turner. Seen here leaning on top of the piano at the Cafe Society in New York in 1939, Turner usually performed with his buddy Pete Johnson (in the background to the left). Boogie woogie star Albert Ammons is at the keyboard. The three were on the bill with trumpeter Frankie Newton and vocalist Billie Holiday.

The back and forth interplay between Turner and Johnson was infectious on such originals as "Roll 'Em Pete," where the singer exhorts his piano partner to roll the boogie (ostinato pattern); "Cherry Red," the singer is going to eagle-rock his baby, in his Hollywood bed, until his face turns cherry red; and "Wee, Baby Blues," in which the singer laments not listening to his mother, who warned him not to fall in love with a woman until he at least learned her name. Big Joe didn't cry the blues. His was a he-man growl that insisted that a woman be good to him. Turner would be associated with rhythm and blues during the later 1940s, and in the early 1950s he became one of the founding fathers of rock'n'roll with his rambunctious, raunchy version of "Shake, Rattle, and Roll." This song was cleaned up and made into a top hit by Bill Haley in 1954.

Rushing and Turner were masters of the jazz-blues style that mixed blues lyrics and format with improvised solos from trumpet, trombone, saxophone, and piano. These two giants established the opposite poles of the jazz-blues tradition: the sweet-smooth jazz-blues tenor of Rushing and the gruff-growling rhythm and blues baritone of Turner. The blues shouting form was part and parcel of the big band custom that Kansas City veterans like Basie, McShann, and Kirk brought to New York at the beginning of the swing era. At first, the indelicate sounds caught northerners off guard, but it was hard to deny the pulsating rhythm and joyous sounds that the Southwest tradition brought to the world of jazz.

Carnegie Hall and Jazz

Franklin M. Heller, Carnegie Hall Archives

Carnegie Hall, the best known concert hall in America, is located in New York City on 57th Street and Seventh Avenue. The hallowed hall opened its doors on May 5, 1891, with the Symphony Society conducted by composer Peter Illich Tchaikovsky. Steel magnate Andrew Carnegie donated $2 million to build the hall. Architects William Burnet Tuthill and Dankmar Adler were responsible for the design and acoustics, respectively. Carnegie Hall soon became associated with classical music of the highest level. An old joke describes a man seeking directions to Carnegie Hall. He asks a passerby, "How do I get to Carnegie Hall?" The reply: "Practice, man, practice."

We have noted many times so far how jazz and blues were considered a lower-class musical form. Accordingly, the legitimate (classical) music community was concerned when the announcement was made that, on January 16, 1938, Benny Goodman and his orchestra would perform the first purely jazz concert ever held in Carnegie Hall. "We were young. We were like the Beatles when they came over here. We knew we were important, and I guess we thought we were worthy of it," claimed Goodman trumpeter Chris Griffin, some fifty years after the historic concert.

Benny Goodman raised the ire of many classical music snobs when he brought an evening of swing to the Carnegie Hall stage. Goodman and his band were in the midst of a hugely successful fourteen-week engagement at New York's Pennsylvania Hotel and a three-week engagement at the Paramount Theater, where the young fans had been dancing in the aisles. Goodman was nervous about the reaction of skeptics to a jazz band playing on the stage accustomed to Beethoven and Rachmaninoff. Goodman's trumpet star, Harry James, underscoring everyone's uneasiness, was quoted as saying, "Tonight I feel like a whore in church." The billboard at the front of the hall read "S. Hurok Presents the First Swing Concert in the History of Carnegie Hall: Benny Goodman and His Swing Orchestra." According to swing historian George T. Simon, after a jittery opening on "Don't Be That Way," the band settled into a groove that had the audience swaying and bouncing in their seats. The highlight of the evening was an explosive, twelve-minute version of "Sing, Sing, Sing," which featured a soaring, impromptu piano solo by Jess Stacy, and maniacal, driving drumming by Gene Krupa. One of the significant aspects of the concert was the fact that Goodman included African-Americans such as Teddy Wilson and Lionel Hampton, as well as members of the Count Basie and Duke Ellington bands.

Carnegie Hall Archives

Swingin' with Benny at Carnegie Hall. *Top,* Benny Goodman jamming with a racially mixed crew of Cootie Williams on trumpet, Vernon Brown on trombone, and Johnny Hodges on clarinet. George T. Simon's *The Big Bands* claims that just prior to the Carnegie Hall concert, "The band's fame had been spreading, thanks to its recordings, its numerous air shots from the Pennsylvania and its new half-hour, prime-time radio commercial, 'The Camel Caravan,' on which it was allowed to play all its best numbers with practically no sponsor interference."

Bottom, The Benny Goodman Quartet in action: Lionel Hampton on vibes, Goodman on clarinet, Gene Krupa on drums, and Teddy Wilson, behind Hampton and Goodman, is on piano.

Benny Goodman and Racial Integration

Carnegie Hall Archives

Top, Benny Goodman on clarinet with dancer Paul Dresser mixing it up after the concert. Teddy Wilson is at the piano. When Wilson became part of Benny Goodman's trio in 1935, it served notice that popular music was going to be integrated. There had been isolated examples of blacks and whites performing together in clubs and on recordings, including white fiddler Dennis McGhee and black accordionist Amede Ardoin in Cajun music, Jelly Roll Morton with the New Orleans Rhythm Kings in 1923, and Eddie Lang recording with Lonnie Johnson and King Oliver. But these were essentially ad hoc sessions. Wilson joining Goodman was important because Goodman's was the top band in the country in 1935, and Wilson became part of the featured trio segment of the show—the rest of the band took a break during the trio's performance.

Bottom, the most famous small group combo in swing history: the Benny Goodman Quartet. Left to right, Lionel Hampton, Gene Krupa, Teddy Wilson, and Benny Goodman.

The jazz press celebrated the event. George T. Simon wrote, "Benny Goodman and his veritable, virile vipers had, in the opinion of a record gate, cut to the core John Barbirolli and the Philharmonic Cats (the house band)." The established music critics, most of whom had never written about jazz before, were unimpressed. Robert Bagar, of the *World-Telegram* wrote that the orchestra was "a frenetic-faced crew of rhythmaniacs, one of whom, the drummer, did everything but skate on the ceiling. There was no refining or dressing up the commodity for the sake of the hallowed surroundings." Olin Downes of the *New York Times* complained, "There is hardly an attempt at beauty of tone and certainly not at construction of melody." And *New York Post* critic Samuel Chotzinoff bemoaned the fact that Goodman "didn't conduct with his hand, but with his left trouser leg instead." Critical slings and arrows from the establishment aside, the concert was hailed by most as the highest achievement yet for swing music. Fifty years later, Carnegie Hall hosted a re-creation of the event led by archivist Bob Wilber and his orchestra. Wilber's concert was a big event (tickets were sold out six weeks in advance) and he pointed out that, "Benny's music was the music of joy. It was so optimistic and so full of hope and good feeling. It was just what the country needed then."

Something else was needed then, and Benny Goodman, as the "King of Swing," helped provide it, too: racial integration in the music business. In the summer of 1935 the leader, with encouragement of producer John Hammond, hired Teddy Wilson, a black pianist from Chicago, for two recording sessions, and then made him a regular part of his small groups (first the trio and then the quartet). Other African-Americans following Wilson into the band in the ensuing years were Lionel Hampton and Charlie Christian, as well as arrangers Fletcher Henderson, who also played piano in later sextet settings, Edgar Sampson, and Jimmy Munday. Until Benny Goodman came along, there were no widely popular, racially mixed bands in popular music. "There was a lot of integration in the Goodman band and Benny was the guy responsible for it," claimed John Hammond. Not quite. Actually, it was Hammond, Goodman's manager, who provided the push for Goodman's heroic stance. As Milt Hinton, a black bassist and photographer observed, "Everyone was going along with the rules of the day. The average person didn't have any idea of changing this thing. So the rebel was John Hammond. That Teddy Wilson thing, that was a daring, daring thing, both on John's part and on Benny Goodman's part."

Courtesy Sony Music

John Hammond was one of the most important nonmusicians in the history of American popular music. In addition to his uncanny ear for musical genius, Hammond was steadfast in his belief that music should be open to all races, that segregation on the bandstand and in the audience was wrong. He felt that his greatest contribution was getting black and white artists together in the recording studio and on stage.

John Hammond (1910-1987) was one of the most important nonmusicians in the history of American music. He was an heir of the Vanderbilts and Sloanes. He grew up in a six-story mansion on East 91st Street in New York, where there were sixteen ready servants and a second-floor ballroom that could accommodate more than two hundred people. As a youngster Hammond absorbed classical music from the family's phonograph and took violin lessons. By the time he was twelve he had heard race recordings and began collecting blues and jazz. Hammond spent much time traveling up to Harlem to buy records and to go to the clubs and theaters to view the black bands and singers. He dropped out of Yale because he knew a college degree would be of little use to him in the quest to make his hobby a vocation. Hammond was in love with jazz and blues music but perplexed by the racial inequality. Hammond said, "New York City was just about as segregated as Birmingham, Alabama. I mean a black person couldn't even eat at Child's," a chain of cheap restaurants. Hammond decided that bringing "recognition to the Negro's supremacy in Jazz" was the most effective and constructive form of social protest he could think of. Hammond's autobiography, *John Hammond on Record*, details with much humility his career as a record producer and social activist.

First as a record collector and then as a record producer, Hammond tried to secure recognition for those he thought the most talented. He produced sessions by Fletcher Henderson and supervised Bessie Smith's last session in 1933 and Billie Holiday's first session that same year. Hammond was an early advocate of Benny Goodman and produced Count Basie's classic sessions. In later years Hammond would sign such artists as Pete Seeger, Aretha Franklin, Bob Dylan, George Benson, Leonard Cohen, Bruce Springsteen, and Stevie Ray Vaughn to Columbia Records.

On December 23, 1938, Hammond put together a concert at Carnegie Hall entitled "From Spirituals to Swing." It was an attempt to put the evolutionary process of the African-American musical convergence into perspective. As the program title suggests, the music ranged from representative spirituals to various blues styles to traditional jazz, right up to the most modern of jazz forms at that time, swing. What made Hammond's experiment so noble was his attempt to showcase what he felt was the most complete representation of America's top black talent.

Frank Driggs Collection

The original cover of the first "From Spirituals to Swing" program featured the image of the late Bessie Smith. Just above her head are the words "Dedicated to Bessie Smith."

Frank Driggs Collection

The seldom-seen program cover of the second "From Spirituals to Swing" concert, held on December 24, 1939.

The concert was chaotic. The tickets were sold out but extras were somehow released so that over three hundred patrons had to be seated on the stage. The master of ceremonies failed to appear and it was decided that Hammond, as producer, had to assume the duties. He was terrified, having never before appeared in front of a large crowd. According to Hammond's "Random Notes on the Spirituals to Swing Recordings," the annotation to the Vanguard Records release of the concert recording, "It is doubtful where the concert could have happened less auspiciously. The plan had been to have me make some opening remarks, and then play an excerpt from the recordings of the Turner expedition in Africa. I was so nervous that my voice couldn't be heard, and I remember Carl Van Vechten yelling 'louder' from his front row perch, where upon I gave a signal to the sound man to increase the amplification. He misread the cue and instead put on the record of wild African chanting, while I was still talking to the audience. Everybody broke up, of course, but from then on it was a continuous ball."

The New Masses Presents

AN EVENING OF AMERICAN NEGRO MUSIC

"From Spirituals to Swing"

FRIDAY EVENING, DECEMBER 23, 1938

Carnegie Hall

Conceived and Produced by John Hammond; Directed by Charles Friedman

---

Note: The following program is not in chronological order

Introduction

AFRICAN TRIBAL MUSIC: From scientific recordings made by the H. E. Tracy Expedition to the West Coast of Africa. THEME: Count Basie and His Orchestra.

I. Spirituals and Holy Roller Hymns

MITCHELL'S CHRISTIAN SINGERS, *North Carolina.* William Brown, Julius Davis, Louis David, Sam Bryant.
SISTER THARPE, *Florida.* (Courtesy Cotton Club) with guitar accompaniment.

II. Soft Swing

THE KANSAS CITY SIX, *New York City.* Eddie Durham (electric guitar), Freddie Green (guitar), Buck Clayton (trumpet), Lester Young (clarinet and tenor saxophone), Jo Jones (drums), Walter Page (bass).

III. Harmonica Playing

SANFORD TERRY, *Durham, North Carolina.* Washboard playing by artists to be announced at the concert.

IV. Blues

RUBY SMITH, *Norfolk, Virginia.* Accompanied on the piano by JAMES P. JOHNSON, *New York City.*
JOE TURNER, *Kansas City, Missouri.* Accompanied by PETE JOHNSON, *New York City.*
BIG BILL, *Chicago, Illinois.* Accompanied by himself on the guitar.
JAMES RUSHING, *Kansas City, Missouri.* Accompanied by the KANSAS CITY FIVE. Freddie Green (guitar), Buck Clayton (trumpet), Lester Young (clarinet and tenor saxophone), Jo Jones (drums), Walter Page (bass).
HELEN HUMES, *Louisville, Kentucky.* Accompanied by the KANSAS CITY FIVE.

V. Boogie-Woogie Piano Playing

ALBERT AMMONS, *Chicago.* MEADE "LUX" LEWIS, *Chicago.* PETE JOHNSON, *Kansas City.* "A Cutting' Session."

INTERMISSION

VI. Early New Orleans Jazz

SIDNEY BECHET and his NEW ORLEANS FEET WARMERS. Sidney Bechet (clarinet and soprano saxophone), Tommy Ladnier (trumpet), James P. Johnson (piano), Dan Minor (trombone), Jo Jones (drums).

VII. Swing

COUNT BASIE AND HIS ORCHESTRA. Count Basie (piano), Walter Page (bass), Freddie Green (guitar), Jo Jones (drums), Ed Lewis (first trumpet), Buck Clayton (second trumpet), Shad Collins (third trumpet), Harry Edison (fourth trumpet), Benny Morton (first trombone), Dickie Wells (second trombone), Dan Minor (third trombone), Earl Warren (first alto saxophone), Jack Washington (second alto sax and baritone), Lester Young (third tenor sax and clarinet), James Rushing and Helen Humes (vocalists). Arrangers: Eddie Durham, Count Basie, Albert Gibson, Buck Clayton, etc.
BASIE'S BLUE FIVE. Count Basie, Shad Collins, Walter Page, Jo Jones, Herschel Evans.
THE KANSAS CITY SIX. Eddie Durham, Freddie Green, Buck Clayton, Lester Young, Jo Jones, Walter Page.

Frank Driggs Collection

259

From Spirituals to Swing: 1938. In this rare shot taken by Dunc Butler from the loge we get a bird's-eye view of the stage (crammed with members of the audience much like the Goodman concert earlier in the year). Performing is the Kansas City Six, left to right, Buck Clayton, trumpet, Jo Jones (behind and above Clayton), drums, Lester Young, tenor sax, Freddie Green, rhythm guitar, Walter Page, (behind and above Green), bass, and Eddie Durham, electric guitar. At the right, seated in front of the upright piano, are composer Goddard Lieberson, left, and John Hammond, right. Earlier in the year these Basie sidemen cut eight sides without piano for Milt Gabler's new Commodore label. The first three, without Lester Young, were labeled the Kansas City Five, and the remaining numbers, with Young, were called the Kansas City Six—outstanding among them were "I Want a Little Girl," and "Pagin' the Devil."

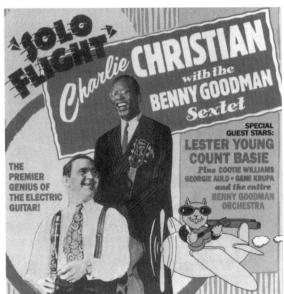

Charlie Christian, the first important electric guitar player in jazz.

Hammond and a struggling young composer named Goddard Lieberson (he eventually became president of Columbia Records) had traveled to North Carolina to sign up much of the folk-blues and gospel talent that appeared that evening. The Golden Gate Quartet sang selections such as "Gospel Train" and "I'm on My Way," and Mitchell's Christian Singers offered up "What More Can My Jesus Do?" and "My Mother Died A Shoutin'." Sonny Terry blew harmonica and sang. Big Bill Broonzy was brought in as a replacement for Robert Johnson (while trying to locate him they were told Johnson had been murdered). Count Basie's band played, as did a New Orleans traditional group led by Sidney Bechet and trumpeter Tommy Ladnier.

The racial integration that Hammond was so keen on was not much in evidence at this first concert. However, the following year, on Christmas Eve, Hammond mounted a second "From Spirituals to

Swing" (Hammond and others often referred to the concerts as simply "Spirituals to Swing"). That second concert spotlighted integration of black and white performers. Benny Goodman was the top bill and he performed with Charlie Christian on his electric guitar, Fletcher Henderson on piano, and Lionel Hampton on vibes, as well as with members of the Basie band.

Charlie Christian (1916-1942) was the pioneer electric jazz guitarist. He joined Goodman in September 1939. He was not the first to play electric jazz guitar. That distinction belongs to Eddie Durham, who played electric guitar on the 1935 recording of "Hittin' the Bottle" with the Jimmie Lunceford Orchestra. In 1937, Christian bought a Gibson ES-150, which was the best amplified guitar on the market at that time. Christian's sustained, single-note lines elevated the electric guitar to a front-line position. Whenever a new voice has emerged in jazz on the electric guitar, it has always connected, historically, with the advances introduced by Christian with Benny Goodman, and at jam sessions with the modernists (the pioneers of bebop).

Frank Driggs Collection

Rosalie and Theodore Cron Collection, Carnegie Hall Archives

Cavalcade of boogie woogie. Albert Ammons, left, and Meade Lux Lewis, right, at John Hammond's first "From Spirituals to Swing" concert. Pete Johnson was the third pianist, seated at the same battered upright that appears in the photo of the Kansas City Six. The "cutting session" (musical battle between players) was supposed to feature each boogie woogie specialist playing on a grand piano. However, due to cost and a mix-up, there was only one grand piano on stage. The day of the concert Hammond reportedly bought a battered upright piano for ten dollars and had it placed on the stage. When the boogie woogie trio came on stage to perform, Ammons and Lewis shared the grand piano and Johnson played the upright. The three hammering keyboardists created pandemonium that night, resulting in a national boogie woogie craze. The trio was immediately booked into Barney Josephson's Cafe Society to play boogie woogie nightly.

Perhaps the highlight of the first concert was the three-piano player explosion of boogie woogie at the first "From Spirituals to Swing" concert by **Pete Johnson** (1904-1967), **Albert Ammons** (1907-1949), and **Meade Lux Lewis** (1905-1964). Lewis had earlier made an impression on Hammond when the producer first heard his 1929 recording of "Honky Tonk Train," a rambunctious boogie woogie number that conjured up a roaring train. After a couple years of searching, Hammond finally located Lewis in 1935. Albert Ammons, like Lewis, had played piano around Chicago. He made his first records for Decca in 1936 as "Albert Ammons' Rhythm Kings." The trio opened the three-and-a-half-hour concert with an electrifying selection entitled "Cavalcade of Boogie." For many in the audience it was the first time they had heard, or at least seen, a performance of boogie woogie piano.

Boogie woogie goes to cafe society. *Above,* left to right, Meade Lux Lewis, Big Joe Turner, Albert Ammons, and Pete Johnson. Ex-shoe salesman Barney Josephson opened Cafe Society Downtown on 2 Sheridan Square in Greenwich Village around 1939. After visiting clubs in Harlem during the Harlem Renaissance, he couldn't understand why clubs uptown and downtown refused to seat people of different races together. Josephson was determined to start his own club, one that would champion the cause of racial equality both on the bandstand and in the audience. To this end Josephson connected with John Hammond, who lined up the talent. Frankie Newton, a black swing-style trumpeter ("Rootin' Tootin' Frankie Newton") was the first artist to open Josephson's Cafe Society. He was followed by vocalist Billie Holiday and then "The Famous Boogie Woogie Boys," Big Joe Turner, and elegant pianist-singer Hazel Scott.

Radio City Boogie Bash

New York—Two noted boogie pianists, Pete Johnson and Albert Ammons, display their 8-to-a-bar talents to the critical ears of arrangers Bob Mersey, left, and Roger Segure in New York's Radio City. Mersey recently was hired by Abe Lyman; Segure is turning out scores for the Lunceford, Kirk and Armstrong crews. *Down Beat Photo by Mickey Goldsen.*

Let us page back into the early blues history we covered in Chapter 4. Boogie woogie was first introduced in the Deep South by itinerant pianists who played at lumber camps and roadside juke joints. Sometimes these little cafes were called barrelhouses because barrels were turned upside down and used as tables, and the bar might even have been a slab of lumber placed over two barrels. The piano players would often use repeated figures in the left hand (ostinato), often eight notes to the bar. Such players were often said to be playing barrelhouse piano. Of the earliest practitioners of boogie woogie, Clarence "Pine Top" Smith was probably first to coin the phrase on record, with his 1928 "Pine Top's Boogie Woogie." The legendary Jimmy "Papa" Yancy, who quit playing in 1925 and worked as a groundskeeper for the Chicago White Sox baseball team at Comisky Park, was rediscovered because of the new attention given boogie woogie.

"From Spirituals to Swing" sparked a boogie woogie craze. The "Cavalcade" trio was immediately brought into New York's Cafe Society, one of the first clubs to openly institute an integrated policy for both patrons and bandstand, and stayed for a couple of years (the individuals worked there both singly and in pairs). Tommy Dorsey recorded his own rendition of "Pine Top's Boogie," which became a top hit for the leader in late 1938 and again in 1943. Bandleader Will Bradley followed with "Beat Me Daddy, Eight to the Bar" in 1940, and the Andrews Sisters recorded a rash of boogie numbers, including "Rhumboogie" (1940), "Beat Me Daddy to the Bar" (1940), "Scrub Me, Mama, With a Boogie Beat," and "Boogie Woogie Bugle Boy" (1941). By the mid-1940s, boogie woogie had been killed by kindness, and while it didn't disappear, it was no longer a pop music fad.

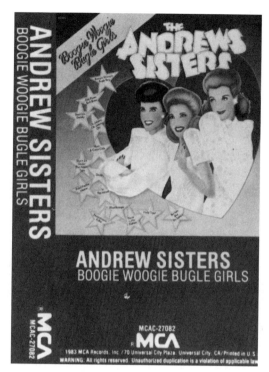

Courtesy MCA Records

Boogie goes pop. The most popular female singing group of the first half of the twentieth century was the Andrews Sisters. More than any other popular entertainers this female trio helped bring boogie woogie to the masses with a bevy of songs using that rhythm.

The Black Jazz Bands

The success of the Count Basie band in New York in 1937 whetted appetites for a more rhythmic and driving band sound than had been heard previously. Basie's band created a style known as "jump blues." The boogie woogie bass lines and constant riffing between sections, mixed with red-hot solos, made listeners want to jump up and dance. For the most part, the black bands instilled the jump feel more than the white bands (Goodman, Charlie Barnet, and Gene Krupa's eventual band were among the exceptions). Aside from Duke Ellington and Fats Waller, most of the black bands did not achieve widespread acceptance on the popular music charts. This is not to say, however, that many black bands weren't successful. Black bands did have records that made the pop music charts, but these bands never attained the dominant position in the popular music world held by Benny Goodman, Kay Kyser, and the others noted in chapter 8. The problem was that America remained segregated. The attitudes of Benny Goodman and John Hammond were the exception, not the rule, and popular music reflected that fact.

Like the white bands, the black swing bands played clubs and ballrooms throughout the country. In New York City, after the Cotton Club moved to mid-Manhattan (1936-40), the "big three" venues in Harlem were the Apollo Theater, the Savoy Ballroom, and the Golden Gate Ballroom. Many great black bands played during the swing years; some of them are listed in the chart "Other Black Swing Bands." Here is a brief look at three representative black bands.

Chick Webb (1909-1939), a diminutive black hunchback, was one of the most dynamic drummers in jazz history. Webb's band was associated with the Savoy Ballroom, where they shared the bandstand with the house band, the Savoy Sultans. Between 1932 and 1934 the band had gained a solid following in Harlem based on the trumpet and vocal stylings of Taft Jordan. Composer-arranger Edgar Sampson provided the band with many of its hits. Sampson wrote and arranged "Blue Lou," "Don't Be That Way" (also a big hit for Goodman), "Let's Get Together" (the band's theme), and the unit's most famous number, "Stompin' at the Savoy" (another big hit for Goodman).

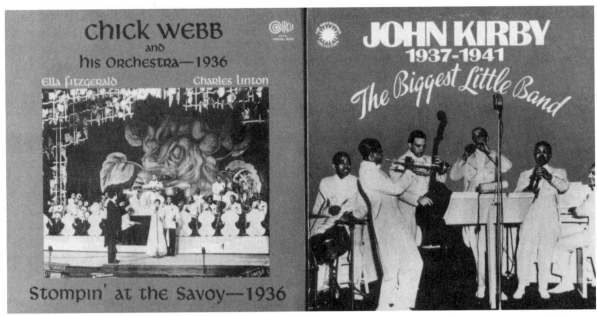

Courtesy Circle Records   Courtesy Smithsonian Collection

Big band and small band. The swing era offered a dazzling array of band makeups. The Chick Webb Orchestra created a full-throttle blast of exciting dance music for the large throngs of dancers at the Savoy Ballroom in Harlem. Bassist **John Kirby** (1908-1952), led a smaller contingent that played the small club scene rather than the large ballroom event. Beginning in 1937, nestled first at the Brittwood Club on Harlem's Lenox Avenue right next door to the Savoy Ballroom, Kirby's unit played swinging arrangements in an intimate setting for customers seated at tables. By 1939 Kirby's group, with some new personnel, became one of the key small groups in all of jazz. Bouncing between the Onyx Club and the Famous Door, the Kirby sextet became popularly known as "The Biggest Little Band in the Land." An eclectic group, Kirby's men played zany novelty numbers like "Jumpin' in the Pump Room," "Zooming at the Zombie," "Cuttin' the Campus," and "Dizzy Debutante," as well as smooth ballad material such as "Pastel Blue" and "Can't We Be Friends." The band was also known for swinging the classics: "Anitra's Dance" (from Grieg), "Minute Waltz" and "Impromptu" (from Chopin), "One Alone" (from Romberg), "Humoresque" (from Dvorak), and their most popular classical items, "Beethoven Riffs On," "I Love You Truly," "Opus 5," "Serenade," and "Chloe." Kirby's wife, Maxine Sullivan, had a popular hit, [with Claude Thornhill in 1937, "Loch Lomand,"] and she often appeared with the group. At its peak the sextet was featured on the popular radio shows "Duffy's Tavern" and the "Chamber Music Society of Lower Basin Street." Kirby even had his own radio show, "Flow Gently, Sweet Rhythm." The group, seen above in their Pump Room outfits, left to right: O'Neill Spencer, drums; Charlie Shavers, trumpet; John Kirby, bass; Buster Bailey, clarinet; Russell Procope, alto sax; and Billy Kyle, piano.

Courtesy Smithsonian Collection

After winning a "Harlem Amateur Hour" contest, Ella Fitzgerald joined Chick Webb's band and began recording in 1935. In addition to the hits listed in the text, she also recorded the following key releases with the Webb organization: "Sing Me a Swing Song," "Vote for Mr. Rhythm," "When I Get Low, I Get High" and "Wacky Dust" (both were overt drug songs), "Rock It for Me," "The Dipsy Doodle," "F.D.R. Jones," "Little White Lies," and "Sugar Pie."

In 1935 the band was joined by Ella Fitzgerald, a seventeen-year-old girl for whom Webb would serve as legal guardian. Young Fitzgerald's singing brought new prosperity to a band that might otherwise have been only a "musician's band." Most of the Webb band's hits after 1935 featured Fitzgerald ("I'll Chase the Blues Away," her first, and "A-Tisket, A-Tasket, I Lost My Yellow Basket," a number one hit in 1938).

Along with the Savoy and Fitzgerald, the band is best remembered for its ability to perform in contests known as "Battles of the Bands." Audience response determined the winners. Webb was recognized as the master of driving a big band from behind his drum set. When Benny Goodman came to the Savoy in 1937 to battle Webb, more than twenty thousand fans tried to get in. Webb was declared the winner, after which Goodman's Gene Krupa, the world's best-known drummer by this time, said that he had been bested by a better man.

The next year the great Basie band was also defeated by Webb at the Savoy. The band was then at its peak of popularity. Webb's health began to fail as the band toured, and he died of a liver ailment in 1939. Fitzgerald took over the band, putting saxophonist Louis Jordan in charge of running the rehearsals, but things were not the same without the spirit of Chick Webb. The organization disbanded by 1941, with Fitzgerald working solo and Jordan fronting a group that would make history in the world of rhythm and blues.

"The Home of Happy Feet": The Savoy Ballroom. One of the most famous dance ballrooms in the world, and certainly the jumpingist, was the Savoy Ballroom, located at 596 Lenox Avenue in Harlem. Established in 1926, it was the largest dance hall in Harlem, occupying the second floor of a building that ran a full block, from 140th to 141st Streets. Owner Moe Gale booked the Fletcher Henderson Orchestra for the opening, which drew a crowd of five thousand. Businessman Charles Buchanan managed the ballroom and it was he who established the popular feature known as "The Battle of the Bands," which pitted bands against each other, the winners being decided by audience response.

Arnold Shaw notes film star Lana Turner, remarking about the spirited dancing at the Savoy, gave the ballroom its nickname, "The Home of Happy Feet." The resident dancers referred to the ballroom simply as "The Track," and it became the spot where many famous dance steps were invented, like the Lindy Hop, the Suzy Q, Peckin', and Truckin'. The area of the club where the professionals demonstrated and tried out new steps was called "Cat's Corner."

Although Chick Webb was the Savoy's most famous leader, it was reedman Al Cooper who led the house band between 1937 and 1946. Known as the Savoy Sultans, the band was capable of keeping the dancers on the floor at all times. This was no easy task, because the Savoy crowd was experienced and demanding. Many bandleaders credited the Sultans as one hot band. The Sultans were billed as the "Originators of Jump Rhythm," and album titles such as *Jump Steady* and *Jumpin' at the Savoy* attest to that. During the 1980s, veteran drummer Panama Francis formed a new Sultans unit and released a couple of albums on Stash Records (*Grooving*, 1980, and *Everything Swings*, 1983). Also on that same label was the Widespread Depression Orchestra, an excellent, enthusiastic revivalist organization that successfully rekindled some of the excitement of the bygone days of black swing. Their releases were also on Stash Records.

Jimmie Lunceford Band at Buffalo Shea's Theatre, 1935. The Lunceford band was the showiest of the swing bands. Willie Smith would sing nursery rhymes with a bonnet on his head, the trumpeters would throw their horns to the ceiling and catch them in regimented unison, and band members would do dance routines as well as comedy drumming such as playing sticks on chairs, body parts, and the like. Some observers called the band "trained seals," but in fact the players made up one of the sharpest and most disciplined bands in the world. Lunceford made a great deal of money, buying (and flying) airplanes and driving a Lincoln Continental. But Lunceford paid his sidemen meagerly and eventually lost his most talented players, who left for better paying jobs.

Jimmie Lunceford (1902-1947) had studied music with Paul Whiteman's father and went on to get a music degree at Fisk University. After teaching high school in Memphis in 1927, Lunceford entered the big band field full-time in 1929. At first his band featured two-beat rhythms and a lightly swinging style. Lunceford gained recognition in 1934 as the new house band at the Cotton Club. His hot numbers began to attract a wider audience. "White Heat" and "Jazznocracy" (one of the band's themes; the other was "Rhythm Is Our Business") were both arranged by Will Hudson. Lunceford's band was one of the slickest and most precise in America. The group played with a clean ensemble attack and was noted for its outstanding showmanship.

Lunceford was a sophisticated bandleader, proficient on all the reed instruments. However, he preferred to front the band strictly as a conductor. From 1933 to 1939, Sy Oliver was the band's arranger, responsible for the band's oddly loping, medium dance tempos, which were fast enough for the Lindy, yet relaxed enough for couples to promenade all night ("'Tain't Whatcha Do," "Organ Grinder's Swing," and "For Dancers Only"). Oliver was lured away in 1939 by a better financial offer from Tommy Dorsey and replaced by trumpeter-arranger Gerald Wilson. Willie Smith (alto sax and vocals), Eddie Tompkins (trumpet), Trummy Young (trombone and vocals), Eddie Durham (trombone and guitar), and Jimmy Crawford (drums) were some of the band's better-known sidemen. Smith, in particular, was a standout soloist who ranked with Johnny Hodges and Benny Carter as a top altoist of the swing era.

Two master arrangers of swing. Sy Oliver, left, and Billy Strayhorn, right, with Duke Ellington. **Sy Oliver** (1910-1988) created the swinging sounds for Jimmie Lunceford ("My Blue Heaven," "Stomp It Off," " Dream of You," "Four or Five Times," "Margie," "Le Jazz Hot," "'Tain't Whatcha Do," "For Dancers Only," and "Organ Grinder's Swing") and then moved on to inject new-found rhythm into Tommy Dorsey's band in the early 1940s ("Easy Does It," "Swing High," "Well, Git It!," and "Opus No. 1").

In his *The Swing Era: The Development of Jazz, 1930-1945*, Gunther Schuller praises Oliver's impact on the Lunceford band: "There is for me no question that Sy Oliver was its major catalyst and chief stylistic architect. From early 1934 on, for almost two years, Oliver produced a series of arrangements that really set the Lunceford band apart, and give it a sound and performance style that at its best could compete even with Ellington's . . . Under Oliver's coaching the band played with a behind-the-beat feeling that at first no one else could imitate or master (except Louis Armstrong, who was, of course, the pioneer in this kind of 'open-beat' playing)." In addition to his arranging skills, Oliver was the band's outstanding trumpet soloist and a vocalist of exceptional charm, both as a solo voice and as part of a vocal trio with Henry Wells and Willie Smith.

Billy Strayhorn (1915-1967), nicknamed "Swee' Pea," debuted with Ellington with his own composition and arrangement of "Something to Live For" in 1939. *The Penguin Encyclopedia of Popular Music*, edited by Donald Clarke, summarizes, "He became Duke's amanuensis and collaborator until, often, neither of them could remember which had done this or that, and nobody else could tell either. He arranged many of the pop songs Duke occasionally included in LPs in the 1950s-1960s, and also helped with more ambitious works, from *The Perfume Suite*, mid-'40s, through *Suite Thursday, A Drum Is a Woman, Such Sweet Thunder*, adaptations of Tchaikovsky's *Nutcracker*, and Grieg's *Peer Gynt* in the '50s; some critics think Strays may have been entirely responsible for some of the suites which carried both names."

Although he is best known for "Take the A Train" and "Lush Life," a number of Strayhorn's other efforts, including "Chelsea Bridge," "Day Dream," "Passion Flower," and "A Flower Is a Lovesome Thing" are also works of high artistic merit. Strayhorn's last composition "Blood Count," was perhaps the most chilling premonition of death ever recorded in jazz. The song was sent to the band from the hospital where he soon died of cancer. In 1988 jazz vocalist Mark Murphy rendered a moving tribute to Strayhorn by singing the first vocal version of "Blood Count."

Duke Ellington (1899-1974) headed what most historians have regarded as the most important jazz band in the history of the music. Ellington's vision was to lead a group that reflected the peerless talents of his sidemen, who became, in a sense, his main instrument. Ellington's career is generally broken down into three major sections. The first can be referred to as the "jungle music" period, when he was part of the Cotton Club. Ellington's second period began around 1934, and is characterized by his concentration on the thirty-two-bar popular song format. Ellington's third period, which began with the world premier of the fifty-minute *Black, Brown and Beige* suite in 1943, can be called his "extended forms" era. These last two forms dominated the band's basic repertoire until Ellington's death in 1974.

The years 1940-43 are often considered Ellington's greatest. Bassist Jimmie Blanton and tenor saxophonist Ben Webster had been added to a band that was already top-notch. Blanton, who died of tuberculosis in 1942, revolutionized the bass by playing melody lines separate from his required walking bass lines ("Jack the Bear" was his best-known solo feature). Webster became the first great tenor soloist for the band; his big, lush, breathy sound can be heard on his uptempo spotlight, "Cotton Tail," and on ballads such as "All Too Soon." Ivie Anderson ("I Got It Bad") was Ellington's principal vocalist until 1942. Al Hibbler joined the band in 1943 and was best known for his vocalizing on "Do Nothin' Till You Hear From Me") and "Don't Get Around Much Anymore." Hibbler left the band in 1951 to go solo (1955's "Unchained Melody" was his biggest solo hit). Other Ellington pop songs included "Solitude," "In a Sentimental Mood," "Things Ain't What They Used to Be," and "I'm Beginning to See the Light."

In 1939 arranger-writer Billy Strayhorn joined Ellington and became his alter-ego. Strayhorn provided the band with its new theme song in 1940, "Take the A Train," and assisted not only on the pop songs but also on the more adventurous suites that dominated the third period of Ellington's career. In addition to Strayhorn (whose best-known work away from Ellington was the haunting "Lush Life"), Ellington had the services of a virtual army of dedicated instrumentalists.

Five selections from this period, "Harlem Air Shaft," "Ko-Ko," "Jack the Bear," "Concerto for Cootie (Do Nothin' Till You Hear from Me)," and "Cotton Tail" are considered by many authorities to be the master-pieces of Ellington's career. None of these gained great popularity with the pop audience, but they featured more themes, internal conflict, timbral variety, and dancing harmonics per chorus than any other jazz recordings before or since.

Courtesy Stash Records

In his *Beyond Category: The Life and Genius of Duke Ellington,* John Edward Hasse states, "The Ellington Orchestra was recorded often on location, but rarely as memorably as in Fargo, North Dakota, November 7, 1940. Two and one half hours of music have been reissued as a two-CD set, documenting a typical night's dance, pieces that were twice as long as the versions he recorded commercially thus allowing the soloists to stretch out and a num-ber of fine solos, including Jimmie Blanton's on 'Sepia Panorama' and Ben Webster's on 'Stardust.'"

Library of Congress

Duke Ellington in action during the early 1940s.

The Duke Ellington Band: 1940-42

Brass	Wallace Jones, Rex Stewart, Cootie Williams, Ray Nance (trumpets), Joe "Tricky Sam" Nanton, Juan Tizol, Lawrence Brown (trombones)
Reeds	Barney Bigard, Johnny Hodges, Harry Carney, Otto Hardwick, Ben Webster (saxophones)
Rhythm	Duke Ellington, Billy Strayhorn (piano), Jimmie Blanton (bass), Sonny Greer (drums), Fred Guy (guitar)
Vocals	Herb Jeffries, Ivie Anderson
Key recordings	Jack the Bear; Ko-Ko; Concerto for Cootie (Do Nothin' Till You Hear From Me); Cotton Tail; Never No Lament (Don't Get Around Much Anymore); Bojangles (A Portrait of Bill Robinson); A Portrait of Bert Williams; Harlem Air Shaft; All Too Soon; Sepia Panorama (Night House); In a Mellotone; Warm Valley; Flamingo; Take the A Train; Blue Serge; Just A-Sittin' and A-Rockin'; I Got It Bad and That Ain't Good; Jump for Joy; Rocks in My Bed; Chelsea Bridge; I Don't Know What Kind of Blues I Got; Perdido; The "C" Jam Blues; What Am I Here For?; My Little Brown Book; Main Stem

While Ellington continued to front his band throughout the forties and thereafter, swing-oriented music began to take on a different look during the war years. Much of that look and sound was reflected in an area known as "Swing Street." These players were given individual salaries which were financed primarily by Ellington's royalty checks from his compositions. Even though Ellington had the most prominent black band, club dates, concerts, and recordings did not generate enough money to meet the weekly payroll.

Other Black Swing Bands

Bandleader	Key Sidemen	Key Recording
Willie Bryant	Joe Thomas (tpt), Roger Ramirez (pno)	It's Over Because We're Through
Cab Calloway	Chu Berry (sax), Jonah Jones (tpt)	I Don't Stand a Ghost of a Chance
Benny Carter	Doc Cheatham (tpt), Eddie Heywood (pno)	Poinciana
Chris Columbus	Ray Copeland (tpt), Rudy Williams (sax)	The Mad Men
Billy Eckstine	Dizzy Gillespie (tpt), Gene Ammons (sax)	A Cottage for Sale
Mercer Ellington	Ray Copeland (tpt), Clark Terry (tpt)	Things Ain't What They Used to Be
Lionel Hampton	Illinois Jacquet (sax), Arnett Cobb (sax)	Flying Home
Erskine Hawkins	Haywood Henry (sax), Avery Parrish (pno)	Tuxedo Junction
Earl "Fatha" Hines	Freddie Webster (tpt), Budd Johnson (sax)	Deep Forest
Claude Hopkins	Vic Dickenson (tbn), Jabbo Smith (tpt)	I Would Do Anything for You
John Kirby	Charlie Shavers (tpt), Buster Bailey (clt)	Undecided
Andy Kirk	Mary Lou Williams (pno), Dick Wilson (sax)	Until the Real Thing Comes Along
Jay McShann	John Jackson (sax), Charlie Parker (sax)	Confessin' the Blues
Don Redman	Tyree Glenn (tbn), Don Byas (sax)	Chant of the Weed
Luis Russell	Red Allen (tpt), Louis Armstrong (tpt)	Saratoga Shout
Noble Sissle	Buster Bailey (sax), Eddie Cole (bs)	Viper Mad
Sweethearts of Rhythm	Anna Mae Winborn (leader)	Man With the Horn

Swing Street: 52nd Street

Much of the best jazz playing during the swing years occurred in the smaller, combo settings rather than in the larger, more formal big band environment. Big bands were restricted by their arrangements, while the smaller groups could be more informal, which allowed for expanded improvising. Many of the better jazz soloists sought more opportunities to experiment and "stretch out" in settings that placed more of an emphasis on freedom and innovation by the individual player. Often these players would seek out after-hours jam sessions held in smaller clubs, or would "sit in" as unpaid guests after the nightly shows with their big band. Big cities all had places known to musicians for this kind of extracurricular activity, but no city could match New York for the variety and number of opportunities for musical "jamming."

By 1935, the general area between 5th and 6th Avenues around 52nd Street was known as "Speakeasy Street," an area marked out during the Prohibition era. The little clubs along these streets became, in the words of *Variety* magazine editor Abel Green, "the nocturnal heart of America." What had started in Harlem during the Harlem Renaissance would be picked up and transferred to "The Street" by the mid 1930s. And what had started as informal, after-hours noodling became standard small group jazz performance. This fit 52nd Street clubs perfectly because most were small and could not adequately house big bands. These clubs played host to three types of small group jazz: traditional jazz units, instrumental swing combos (piano trios, quartets, quintets, sextets), and featured vocalists with a swing combo.

In his book *52nd St.: The Street of Jazz*, Arnold Shaw says that pianist Art Tatum and Leo Watson started what he called "The Street," on its historic jazz journey in 1934. With his Spirits of Rhythm group, Watson laid down most of the rules for future swing-cum-bop scat singers on tunes such as "Junk Man," "Scattin' the Blues," "Dr. Jekyll and Mr. Jive," and "Tutti Frutti." In 1935, two musical cut-ups, brass men Mike Riley and Ed Farley, gained fame with their smash novelty hit, "The Music Goes 'Round and Around." At first it was musicians performing the novelty numbers and the jazz and jive fun that drew attention to 52nd Street. Jazz and jive mixed jazz with novelty street lingo of hot musicians (hep cats, eventually known as hipsters). Nonjazz audiences (some journalists called them "thrill seekers") were drawn to the antics of Watson, Stuff Smith, Louis Prima, Slim Gaillard, and Harry "The Hipster" Gibson.

Frank Driggs Collection

Courtesy Buffalo & Erie County Public Library

Night and day on Swing Street. The score of clubs that dotted 52nd Street were swinging. Located between 5th and 6th Avenues, "The Street" mixed all styles of jazz. Arnold Shaw's introduction to *52nd St.: The Street of Jazz* pronounces, "In 1948, when *Metronome* magazine ran an historical, if premature obituary on 52nd St., it noted: 'Even today, when you leave a musician and say, 'See you on The Street tonight,' he doesn't have to ask you which street you mean.' For that matter, 1948 and for a score of years before then, neither did the average cabdriver. If you flagged a taxi in NYC and asked to be taken to *The Street* you would be driven, without giving a number or avenue, to 52nd between Fifth and Sixth Avenues.

"Not only musicians but to people generally—to the spenders, to Ivy League collegians, to the sophisticates of any age, to people of the theatre, and to jazz fans the world over—The Street was known as a swinging place between 1934 and 1950." Called "the nocturnal heart of America," "America's Montmartre," and "The street that never sleeps," its kind will likely not be seen again.

The song that launched "The Street." If there is one song that ignited the flames of excitement on 52nd Street it was "The Music Goes 'Round and Around" by Mike Riley and Ed Farley. The novelty tune was the first hit for the newly formed Decca Records in 1935 and it was introduced at the Onyx Club. The song became so popular at the Onyx that the audience used to join in and sing along with Riley and Farley.

In his *History of Jazz in America,* Barry Ulanov claims that this selection is responsible for "inaugurating modern jazz in general" and helping launch the swing period. "The Music Goes 'Round" (as it is usually referred to), drew attention to "The Street." Arnold Shaw writes in *52nd Street: The Street of Jazz*: "As its popularity grew and word of its origin was circulated by the columnists, people began flocking to 52nd Street. For a period during 1935-1936 the Onyx, like the Peppermint Lounge during the twist craze, could not accommodate the hordes that descended on it. So great was the popularity of the song that Riley and Farley were quickly booked into the New York Paramount, rushed out to the Coast, and by February 29, 1936, *The New Yorker* was carrying a review of a new film hastily titled *The Music Goes 'Round.*"

Violinist/entertainer **Stuff Smith** (1909-1967), with trumpeter Jonah Jones and drummer Cozy Cole, helped make the Onyx Club The "Cradle of Swing," with antics similar to that of Watson. Smith, born Hezekiah Leroy Gordon Smith, was the most influential violinist in jazz history. A member of Alphonse Trent's territory band in Dallas, Smith worked with Trent at Dan Montgomery's in Buffalo for a while, then moved on to New York. Smith and his swinging, amplified violin produced equal doses of good music and humor with selections such as "I'se a Muggin'," "You'se a Viper," and "Here Comes the Man With the Jive." At the height of his popularity Smith played to overflow crowds. Other jazz violinists of this era associated with the swing era included Eddie South ("Dark Angel of the Violin") and Duke Ellington's Ray Nance, a trumpeter who doubled on violin.

Traditional jazz received a boost when New Orleans trumpeter/singer **Louis Prima** (1911-1978) and His New Orleans Gang opened on 52nd Street at the Famous Door in 1935. An extroverted showman, Prima followed in the footsteps of his hero Louis Armstrong, except he was completely manic on stage, exhorting one and all to "Swing it" and "Let's have a jubilee!" Prima called the Famous Door a little fun joint for musicians, but he made fun for the audience as well. Prima would lead his band off the stage and parade around the room, playing all the while. Prima was not only an extroverted performer, but also a fine trumpeter and composer ("Sing, Sing, Sing" and "Sunday Kind of Love"). He was featured in a number of movies during the thirties and forties. In 1938 he renamed his group the Gleeby Rhythm Orchestra.

Nick Tosches rightly places Prima on a pedestal as one of the key precursors of rock'n'roll. In his book *Unsung Heroes of Rock'n'Roll: The Birth of Rock'n'Roll in the Dark and Wild Years Before Elvis*, Tosches declares: "Prima presaged Rock'n'Roll of the Ridiculous. He perceived and embraced, in all its tutti-frutti glory, the spirit of post-literate, made-for-television America. His was a brave new world of chrome, not gold; of Armstrong linoleum, not Carrara marble; of hep talk, not meaningful dialogue (what did words matter to Louis, when noise could be made instead?). It was a world in which everything came down to broads, booze, and money, with plenty of linguini on the side." In 1952 Prima married his fourth wife, Keely Smith, who played poker-faced wooden Indian to his jive Italian craziness. Years later Sonny & Cher would recast the Prima-Smith theatrics for the rock audience. Prima and Smith were joined by frenetic sax man Sam Butera (and the Witnesses) and they became huge favorites with the Las Vegas and Lake Tahoe crowd. Theirs was a white rhythm and blues/rock'n'roll entertainment for adults who wouldn't think of listening to either of those forms of music in the later 1950s and even up into the 1970s. Butera's "Gleeby Rhythm" was a precursor to rock'n'roll, and he rocked the house every night he played. (Listen to rendition of "I Ain't Got Nobody" and then match it with the direct copy by David Lee Roth in 1985.) Prima became the highest paid entertainer on 52nd Street.

Frank Driggs Collection

"Let's have a jubilee!" Two of the key "jazz & jive" kingpins of 52nd Street. *Above*, trumpeter Louis Prima; *below*, violinist Stuff Smith. Along with the underappreciated Spirits of Rhythm of Leo Watson, Prima and Smith created the initial interest for "outsiders" to venture to mid-Manhattan to visit "The Street."

Courtesy Arhoolie Records, 10341 San Pablo Ave., El Cerrito, CA 94530

Whether he was "vouting oreenie or oroonie," Slim Gaillard was one of the inventors of jive language and a precursor to rap and hip-hop lingo.

Slim Gaillard (1916-) was another of the jump and jive comic performers who combined hep-cat language and swing with some of the newer sounds known as bop. Gaillard sang and played guitar and piano to his outrageously titled concoctions like "Vout Oreenie," "A-Reet-a-Voutee," "Tutti-Frutti," and "Cement Mixer (Put-ti Put-ti)." Gaillard's best-known work was with bassist Slam Stewart, who was noted for his technique of bowing his bass and humming in unison. As Slim and Slam, in 1939, the duo recorded Gaillard's most popular creation, "Flat Foot Floogie," novelty hit. Gaillard was also part of the Los Angeles scene recording with Charlie Parker and Dizzy Gillespie on the modern jazz front. Both he and saxophonist Jack McVea shifted from the jazz approach to the rhythm and blues style in the late 1940s. Gaillard spent his later career in England.

Handsome Harry The Hipster Illustrates His Song Of That Title

Courtesy Down Beat

Handsome Harry "The Hipster" Gibson. The *Down Beat* caption from this mid-1940s entry reads: "They call him 'Handsome Harry the Hipster' is the first line of the song by Harry Gibson, one of the more frantic pianists, who poses as the hero of his own saga here. 'He's the boy with all the chicks,' the lyric continues, so here's Handsome Harry with his chicks, Pearl Howard, Gertrude Cohen, and Jeanne Brody (left to right). Nice work, if you can get it, 'He plays piano like mad, his singing is sad,' says the song. And here's Harry playing so madly, and singing so sadly. Where'd those chicks go? 'And he digs those mellow kicks,' is the next line. So Mr. Gibson gets on a mellow kick by way of illustration. A drink's a drink, of course, but personally we'd rather get back to the chicks. 'They call him Handsome Harry the *Clipster,* 'cause he'll take you for your gold,' and he'll leave the clip. There is much more to the song but the photographer just ran out of flash bulbs!"

The jazz and jive antics of Slim Gaillard and Harry "The Hipster" Gibson created excitement as well as curiosity for visitors to Swing Street, but the drug references created problems. Arnold Shaw writes in *52nd Street: The Street of Jazz*, "Although bop created in-group controversy shortly after it began to be heard on 52nd St., it did not become a public issue until 1946. In March of that year station KUPC of Los Angeles banned bebop on the grounds that it 'tends to make degenerates out of our young listeners.' Singled out for censure were the records of Slim Gaillard and Harry 'The Hipster' Gibson, neither of whom had anything to do with the new jazz. But both were then appearing in a Hollywood club which, of course, immediately began doing SRO business. *Time* joined the fray with an article in which it described bebop as 'hot jazz overheated, with overdone lyrics, full of bawdiness, references to narcotics and double-talk.' Following the station's lead, *Time* managed to see Gibson as the Mr. Big of the evil movement with Bulee 'Slim' Gaillard as its No. 2 man."

Courtesy Rhapsody Films

Harry "The Hipster" Gibson (1915-1991) was known as the "Unofficial Mayor of the Street." This blond-haired piano dynamo was one of the most exciting and notorious entertainers in jazz history. Because of his outlandish stage behavior (he jumped on the piano, playing it with his elbows, head, and feet) and drug-oriented lyrics, Gibson had been held at a long arm's length by most jazz historians. That's a shame, because Gibson was an excellent musician who was pals with Art Tatum, Charlie Parker, Billie Holiday, and a gang of other greats. Gibson was a graduate of the Juilliard School of Music and made his New York jazz debut at an Eddie Condon Town Hall concert, where he received critical kudos for his Bix Beiderbecke piano interpretations of "In a Mist" and "Candlelights."

But it wasn't the sensitive side of Gibson's well-rounded talent that caught the eye and ear of audiences of the Street. Gibson became a cult favorite on the basis of his unorthodox stylings on stomping tunes like "Barrelhouse Boogie," "Stop That Dancing Up There," "Boogie-Woogie in Blue," and his signature tune, "Who Put the Benzedrine in Mrs. Murphy's Ovaltine?" Harry was often noted in *Down Beat*, but is rarely found in jazz histories because his histrionics linked him more to Jerry Lee Lewis (who was influenced by Gibson without even knowing it!) than to Art Tatum. *Down Beat* featured him on its cover in 1947, calling him "a wild boogie-woogie key boarder with a froglike, frantic voice."

Courtesy Down Beat

The 52nd Street scene hosted an admixture of musical styles. As noted, in 1935 Louis Prima created a renewed appreciation for Dixieland. Traditional jazz was also hosted at Jimmy Ryan's, which featured Milt Gabler's jam sessions, and Eddie Condon's. Both places were a haven for players like Bobby Hackett (trumpet), Pee Wee Russell (clarinet), Joe Sullivan (piano), and Bud Freeman (saxophone), among many others. While the Hickory House was better known for its keyboard artists and broiled steaks, it got started originally as a place for traditionalists such as trumpeter Wingy Manone and clarinetist Joe Marsala, as well as Condon, who eventually moved the music over to his own club. These players were not creating slavish imitations of 1920s New

Orleans jazz. Many of them imbued a swing feel to a music that was being touted as Dixieland. It should be noted that Benny Goodman and the Dorseys started as Dixieland players but evolved into swing players by the mid-1930s. The regulars at Ryan's and Condon's mixed these styles. Some of the players considered themselves Dixie exponents. However, a number of these artists, especially Bobby Hackett and Bud Freeman, were equally versed in the swing style.

Art Tatum (1909-1956) was partially blind and attended special schools in Columbus and Toledo, where he showed piano abilities. He made his first recordings in 1933 after touring with vocalist Adelaide Hall. Tatum developed an amazing pianistic touch and technique that astounded fellow musicians. Fats Waller once announced in a club, "Ladies and gentlemen, I play piano, but tonight God is in the house." Tatum was a master of harmonic invention and technical virtuosity, preferring to reconstitute and embellish standard songs rather than compose. His use of substitute chords and sixteenth-note runs, and his ability to master the mannerisms of all piano styles and then personalize them, led Tatum to be considered the master of jazz piano.

High Salaried Combination

New York—Highest paid trio on 52nd Street (or on any other street for that matter) is this Art Tatum Trio at the Three Deuces. Art snags a round thousand every payday, proving that he's no square.

Frank Driggs Collection

Art Tatum in his favorite environment, an intimate club on 52nd Street. Duke Ellington, one of Tatum's many admirers, called the piano virtuoso one of the "preeminent soloists" of our time. James Lincoln Collier points out that Tatum's double runs and complex arpeggios were played at blinding speeds. In 1949 his super-fast playing of "I Know That You Know" was clocked at a metronome speed of 450, meaning that there were moments when Tatum was playing at a rate of a thousand notes a minute.

In *Too Marvelous for Words: The Life and Genius of Art Tatum*, James Lester wrote: "The complexity of things going on when Tatum played, and the speed at which they went on, could have been more baffling than dazzling to listeners, but Tatum's material, basically, the American popular song, was so familiar that it provided listeners with a road map, and gave him a free hand to tantalize the ear with new combinations and challenge the perceptions of his listeners. Tatum never lost sight of the melodies of the songs he played no matter how much he varied their surroundings, so listeners seldom felt lost."

When Leonard Feather asked a hundred musicians to name the greatest jazz players on various instruments, sixty-eight voted for Tatum on piano. No other instrumentalist came anywhere near that consensus of praise. While he usually played solo, Tatum enjoyed the trio setting he established in 1943 with guitarist Tiny Grimes and bassist Slam Stewart. During the fifties, Norman Granz presented Tatum in concerts and recorded him extensively in a variety of independent dates with other instrumentalists, such as clarinetist Buddy DeFranco, trumpeter Roy Eldridge, saxophonists Benny Carter and Ben Webster, and vibist Lionel Hampton.

In *Jazz Styles* Mark Gridley summarizes, "Art Tatum's impact on jazz history was enormous. His astounding mastery of the keyboard became a pinnacle for which other pianists aspired. His practice of changing keys within a single phrase and adding chords were absorbed by tenor saxophonist Don Byas and modern saxophonist Charlie Parker. Tatum also influenced two highly innovative pianists who played pivotal roles during the early days of modern jazz: Bud Powell and Lennie Tristano. Bud Powell and Tristano, in turn, went on to influence numerous pianists of the 1950s who further extended Tatum's impact."

The heirs apparent of Tatum are Billy Taylor and Oscar Peterson. Both were performing during the forties and continued as outstanding artists into the early nineties. Adam Makowitz is one of the better contemporary pianists who works in the Tatum style.

Courtesy Delmark Records

Courtesy Stash Records

Roy Eldridge and Coleman Hawkins were two of the most representative small group stars of the swing era. Lewis Porter and Michael Ullman note in *Jazz: From Its Origins to the Present*: "Even more important to him [Eldridge] were what musician and scholar John Chilton has called 'the fast running intricacies of Coleman Hawkins.' Eldridge told Chilton that he learned Hawkins's solo on the Fletcher Henderson record 'Stampede' note for note, and that his early style, especially his long, legato phrases, was an attempt to play Hawkins on the trumpet. Hawkins and Eldridge eventually became best friends."

Coleman Hawkins (1901-1969) is a prime example of a swing artist who initially gained fame in the big bands but found a nest on the Street as a featured soloist. Hawkins was one of the earliest innovators of the jazz saxophone. When he began as a section player in Fletcher Henderson's band, the saxophone was considered a novelty instrument. The reed section helped give "body" to the sound of the band, but it wasn't until Hawkins began to solo that the instrument was taken seriously in jazz. Hawkins's early attempts at jazz solos embarrassed him years later because they featured an overly choppy "slap-tongue" technique that sounded corny. He eventually developed an expressive, vibrato-laden approach that was often referred to as "virile."

After spending five years in Europe, in 1939 Hawkins returned to New York and went directly into the recording studio with a makeshift band. One of the recordings, "Body and Soul," written by composer Johnny Green in 1930, would become one of the most famous jazz instrumentals of all time. It was so popular that eight versions were recorded in the fall of that year, three by the torchiest singers of that era, Libby Holman, Helen Morgan, and Ruth Etting. Hawkins's version is masterful in that he doesn't start off with the melody, but rather plays around it. Hawkins used flatted fifths and augmented harmonies (soon to be common techniques in bop), causing many of his contemporaries to complain that he was playing the "wrong notes." In spite of the technical advances of Hawkins's playing, it was not so far out that the general audience couldn't appreciate it. To Hawkins's amazement, "Body and Soul" became a million-selling record and allowed him unprecedented freedom to work as a soloist.

Roy Eldridge (1911-1989) was known as "Little Jazz." Just as Louis Armstrong was the premier trumpeter of the 1920s, Eldridge was the leading trumpeter of the swing era. He was one of the early black stars to be featured with white bands. He worked with Gene Krupa's vastly underappreciated organization between 1941 and 1943 (his biggest hit was a 1941 duet with Krupa's featured songstress, Anita O'Day, "Let Me Off Uptown") and with Artie Shaw between 1944 and 1945, where he was a featured soloist with the leader's jazz unit, the Gramercy Five. Eldridge has been called the midpoint between Louis Armstrong's traditional style and Dizzy Gillespie's modernist approach. The trumpet was replaced by the saxophone as the most important horn in jazz by the 1940s, and it is somewhat ironic that swing's premier trumpet man often improvised in the manner of saxophonists by using scale-like lines. Gridley notes, "Roy Eldridge demonstrated that long, sinewy lines were possible on the trumpet.

These, though easy to execute on saxophone, do not lend themselves to the mechanics of the trumpet. Eldridge's influence caused modern trumpeters to cultivate greater instrumental facility and to improvise in more intricate and unpredictable ways than their early jazz counterparts. His conception also extended the average phrase length used by improvising trumpeters. Eldridge's influence extended into the 1950s because trumpeter Dizzy Gillespie built his own influential modern style upon the foundation of Eldridge's bristling high-register work, unorthodox choice of notes, and saxophone style of phrasing."

Courtesy Polygram Records

Lester Young (1909-1959) was raised in New Orleans and played drums and alto saxophone in a carnival band led by his father. His sister played tenor. Young joined Walter Page's Blue Devils in 1932, then Benny Moten before he joined Fletcher Henderson's band, where he replaced Coleman Hawkins in 1934. Young's main influences were the lyrical stylings of Frankie Trumbauer's C-melody sax on Bix Beiderbecke's records, and Jimmy Dorsey's fluid alto stylings. Young made his first recordings with Count Basie, where he was the star soloist from 1937 to 1940. With those first recordings, Young brought a new conception to the tenor saxophone, using a lush, smooth, style without any perceptible interruption between notes. His approach was cool (airy, detached) without losing power. Despite this innovation, Young played (and gained fame from) a number of uptempo tunes, "Shoe Shine Boy," "Every Tub," "Doggin' Around," "Texas Shuffle," "Taxi War Dance," and his best-known recording, "Lady Be Good."

Frank Driggs Collection

Lester Young at Kelly's Stables on 52nd Street in 1941. Young's group (left to right): Doc West, drums; Nick Fenton, bass; Shad Collins, trumpet; Clyde Hart, piano; Young, tenor; John Collins, electric guitar. Writer Ralph J. Gleason called Young, "Kansas City jazz incarnate." Young could play romp 'em, stomp'em jump numbers with one of the swingiest bands in the world, Count Basie's, and then create the lushest, most feathery ballads ever performed.

Young thought it imperative to think of the words of the song when creating his improvisations. Thus in Young's soloing there is a "singing" quality to his legato-oriented playing. Young performed at Benny Goodman's 1938 Carnegie Hall concert, recorded with Teddy Wilson, and was featured on small group recordings for Billie Holiday. He also cut classic records for Commodore in 1938. Some authorities feel that after the war the quality of Young's work declined. However, the Keynote recordings of the 1940s and the Verve releases of the 1950s still offer some glimmers of greatness. Young was a pivotal influence on modern jazz stylists, both the "hot" bop saxophonists such as Charlie Parker and Dexter Gordon, and the "cool" players like Stan Getz and Lee Konitz.

The Singers on the Street

The intimacy of the smaller clubs was ideal for singers. Instead of sitting on the bandstand and waiting to be called upon by a paternalistic bandleader to sing a couple of songs, the club setting allowed featured singers to take full command of the spotlight. According to Will Friedwald in *Jazz Singers,* "The real harbinger of the species of female jazz-and-band singers was the virtually simultaneous appearance of three women, the Three White Goddesses, who invented and defined the canary tradition of the early thirties: Mildred Bailey, Connee Boswell, and Lee Wiley." Of these three, Bailey and Wiley made their main contributions with swing combos during the mid-1930s and throughout the 1940s. **Mildred Bailey** (1907-1951) had her start with the Paul Whiteman Orchestra, but she really made her mark at the Famous Door in 1938 with her husband, vibraphonist Red Norvo. Her high, lilting voice and gently swinging manner was perfectly suited to the smaller club setting. She was considered a "musician's singer," that is, she was musically accomplished and inspirational without having gained great popularity. Bailey's rendition of Hoagy Carmichael's "Rocking Chair" caused her to be called the "Rocking Chair Lady." She and Norvo were called "Mr. and Mrs. Swing."

Courtesy Sony Music

Mildred Bailey was born in Tekoa, Washington and was one-eighth American Indian. She became the first female big band singer with Paul Whiteman in 1929, but unlike the maestro, Bailey forged a path as a leader in the next popular music style—swing. Unfortunately for her, she never gained the popularity her great talent deserved. Bing Crosby, her old bandmate from the Whiteman days called her, "a genuine artist with a heart as big as Yankee Stadium."

Ken Barnes writes in *Sinatra and the Great Song Stylists,* "Mildred Bailey belonged to that select band of singers who are equally at home in jazz or popular music. She was a big, fat woman and it was always something of a surprise to hear emerging from that large body a small and rather high-pitched voice with a sweet, pure and very distinctive tone. Her phrasing owed much to Ethel Waters, Louis Armstrong and Bessie Smith, as did her use of vibrato, and she could swing with the best of them."

After her divorce from Norvo in 1940, Bailey made New York her home base and focused on radio and small clubs like the Cafe Society, the Famous Door, the Onyx, and the Blue Angel. John Hammond called Bailey "one of the three or four greatest singers in jazz," but she never achieved the recognition that she deserved and it made her unhappy. George T. Simon, one of the most knowledgeable historians of the swing era, wrote that Bailey "seemed incapable of controlling her emotions, which alternated between towering rages (she felt special bitterness toward less musical but more successful, and, especially, better-looking, girl singers) and tender displays of deep affection that she showered on close friends, constant companions, and her two dachshunds." For such a large woman, Bailey had a bright, paper-thin voice that weaved in and around jazz instrumentalists on interpetations such as "These Foolish Things" and "Can't Help Lovin' Dat Man." Of Bailey's inability to transform her jazz vocalizations into mainstream pop success, writer Bucklin Moon summarizes, "She chose to be neither the one thing nor the other, but a combination of all that was good in both. She was too deeply rooted in jazz to have a large popular following . . . Songs she introduced, records that she made, had an alarming habit of turning up as somebody else's hits."

Courtesy Stash Records

Another important singer from the street was the traditionalist's favorite, **Lee Wiley** (1915-1975). Wiley began singing with the Condon gang around 1939, and at the same time she began to make a series of historically significant recordings for Milt Gabler's Commodore Records. Wiley was the first to sing a body of songs by one composer and have them issued as an album. At that time, an album was a series of four or six separate 78-recordings released in a hardbound protective cover. An album of songs that focused on the works of one composer, or lyricist, was eventually referred to as a "song-book." Wiley's breathy vibrato was tastefully backed by Condon's men and pianist Jess Stacy, whom she later married. Subsequent albums were released by Gabler on his Liberty Music Shop label and included *Lee Wiley Sings Ira & George Gershwin and Cole Porter* (1939-40), and *Lee Wiley Sings Richard Rodgers & Lorenz Hart and Harold Arlen* (1940-43). So the songbook tradition that Frank Sinatra, Ella Fitzgerald, and Bobby Short would later make famous was originally the domain of a smoky-voiced talent who, like Bailey, was to become a musician's and jazz aficionado's treasure, an underground figure not appreciated by the masses.

Courtesy Audiophile Records

Lee Wiley: Inventor of the Songbook. Like Mildred Bailey, Lee Wiley was partly of American Indian extraction and shared a similar, cult audience. Max Kaminsky, who often played trumpet behind Wiley, wrote in his autobiography, *My Life in Jazz,* "The Lee Wiley albums were years ahead of their time. Lee set a style for years to come, and later everyone else copied her." Roy Hemming and David Hajdu, writing one of the few noteworthy books on jazz and pop vocalists, *Discovering Great Singers of Classic Pop,* say about Wiley, "Hers was a sweet, sultry-toned alto that critics delighted in referring to as sexy or erotic. There was a softly intimate, one-to-one manner in which Lee sang most songs. It was usually straightforward, mellow, and unforced." They point out that her diction was once described as "an intriguing amalgam of Oklahoma, Park Avenue, and Fifty-second Street."

John Wilson, writing in the *New York Times*, correctly assessed Wiley's most significant contribution to the jazz world: "The first association in depth of a jazz singer, jazz musicians and show tunes came in 1939 and 1940 when Lee Wiley made albums of songs by George and Ira Gershwin, Cole Porter and Rodgers and Hart, backed by small groups of jazz musicians that included Max Kaminsky, Joe Bushkin, Pee Wee Russell, Fats Waller, Bud Freeman, Bunny Berigan, Billy Butterfield, Bobby Hackett and George Wettling." Wiley had a loyal following among the musicians with whom she performed, which was uncommon because, for the most part, jazz instrumentalists thought little of female singers. Will Friedwald contends in *Jazz Singers*, "Wiley became virtually the only artist in history to be equally admired by devotees of both Louis Armstrong and Bobby Short; the combination of jazz and cabaret patronage made one of her albums, the 1950 *Night in Manhattan*, go legitimately gold after thirty-five years in record-shop racks."

Courtesy Audiophile Records

Jazz writer-producer Frank Driggs, a one-time friend of Wiley, points out that she was demanding and somewhat independent, which, for a woman, in a business dominated by men, was not always appreciated. Driggs is quoted in *Discovering Great Singers of Classic Pop*: "The world of show business demands one be in certain places with certain people at certain times. Lee Wiley did this up to a point and then said unprintable things. There were rules to be followed, and Lee Wiley, a free spirit if there ever was one, was not that particular about living by any set of rules." In the 1970s Piper Laurie starred in *Something About Lee Wiley*, a television drama with many factual and chronological inaccuracies.

Courtesy Sony Music

Roy Hemming and David Hajdu in *Discovering Great Singers of Classic Pop* maintain: "The first psychological singer, Billie Holiday introduced the emotional interior to American song. When she sang, the words and the music were suddenly subordinated to the internal emotions her singing seemed to suggest."

Billie Holiday (1915-1959) was one of the few vocalists loved by fellow jazz musicians and also popular with the record-buying public. Originally inspired by Bessie Smith and Louis Armstrong, Holiday developed a swing vocal method that was more akin instrumentally to the laconic, lag-behind-the-beat approach of Lester Young. Lyrically she owed something to Mabel Mercer's precision and articulation. Holiday found a soulmate in Lester Young, who nicknamed Holiday "Lady Day." She, in turn, nicknamed him "Prez" (sometimes spelled "Pres") for being the president of the saxophonists. Musically, Holiday and Young shaded and intoned musical phrases in a similar manner. Together they made forty-nine sides, beginning in 1937 with "This Year's Kisses" and "I Must Have That Man." Rudi Blesh, in *Combo: U.S.A.*, counts "Foolin' Myself,"

"Me, Myself and I," "When a Woman Loves a Man," and "A Sailboat in the Moonlight" (Young's favorite), as recordings in which "voice and sax sing together." Friedwald says of the musical connection, "The ninety minutes or so of recorded sound they produced together stands as a milestone in Western music, from Bach to Mozart to Ornette. Holiday's round, chubby voice (which matches the zaftig young Billie captured in contemporary snapshots) and her off-center way of attacking the beat so perfectly matches Young's feathery alto-tenor (his own term) tone, strikingly original melodic concept, alternately languorous legato and ferociously up-tempo use of time. You can sense they had an understanding of each other far beyond what musical terminology or metaphoric imagery can describe."

Holiday made approximately one hundred sides between 1935 and 1942 with Teddy Wilson's orchestra. Many of the songs chosen for her to sing have been labelled inane and the work of hacks. However, she could take those inane songs and make works of art out of them, as she did with the opening lines of the now classic "What a Little Moonlight Can Do." Although Holiday sang intermittently with the big bands, like Hawkins's, hers was a free spirit and she was at her best on her own. Holiday sang many sad songs. "God Bless the Child" and "Strange Fruit" were two notable classic recordings that focused on downcast themes. Because she often sang sad songs, the uninformed categorized her as a blues singer, but Holiday seldom sang blues material, preferring instead the standard song repertoire. Nat Hentoff observed in *Listen to the Stories*, "She didn't sing many blues, but Billie Holiday often had them. Backstage, in her autumnal years, she'd sometimes growl, 'The only reason they're out there is to see me fall into the damn orchestra pit.'... So, as in the final years of Charlie Parker, there were those who paid money in hope of seeing a legend fall apart before their very eyes."

Frank Driggs Collection

In April 1935 Billie Holiday made a highly acclaimed debut at Harlem's Apollo Theatre. Master of ceremonies Ralph Cooper rehearsed Holiday and bought her gown and slippers for her first show. Holiday was so frightened, she said that her knees were shaking until comedian Pigmeat Markham pushed her on stage, where she sang "Them There Eyes," "If the Moon Turns Green," and, for an encore, "The Man I Love." At that time she had been calling herself Halliday because she didn't want to use her father's name (Clarence Holiday, an absentee father, who was a banjoist in the Fletcher Henderson orchestra). A couple of months later she began to use her given name, Holiday. From that point on she was always a headliner at the Apollo. Ralph Cooper could only say of Holiday's singing, "It ain't blues, I don't know what it is, but you got to hear her."

Courtesy Polygram Records

Holiday's was a unique voice of jazz. Her ability to infuse any lyric she sang with depth and heart-felt conviction raised the level of the listening experience to new heights. Holiday's celebrated involvement with drugs was ongoing and added to the drama that unfolded on stage and in the recording studio. As Holiday noted in her autobiography, *Lady Sings the Blues* (as told to William Dufty), each night they brought her the white gardenia, white gloves, and her white powdered drugs (heroin).

Billie Holiday had one of the unique voices in American popular music. It has been described as hoarse, coarse, smoky, weary, grating, horn-like, and gravelly.

Henry Pleasants, in *The Great American Popular Singers,* points out that Holiday worked around her limited vocal range; she had a meager voice that was small and hoarse at the bottom and thinly shrill at the top, with an octave and a third limit. "Given these physical limitations," Pleasants writes, "what she achieved in terms of color, shading, nuances and articulation, and in terms of the variety of sound and inflection she could summon from such slender resources, may be counted among the wonders of vocal history. She did it by moving, with somnambulistic security, along or back and forth across the thin, never precisely definable line separating, or joining, speech and song.

Carl Van Vecthen Library of Congress

Singer Peggy Lee called Holiday "the angel of darkness." Carmen McRae, who would become the keeper of the flame of all things Holiday from the 1950s on, observes, "I'll say this about her, she sings the way she is. That's really Lady when you listen to her on a record. Singing is the only place she can express herself the way she'd like to be all the time. Only way she's happy is through a song."

NEW YORK—An idea hatched eight years ago in the minds of Leonard Feather and Arnold Shaw has finally reached fruition. As of June 26, 1979, New York City's 52nd St. between Fifth Avenue and the Avenue of the Americas has been officially recognized as "Swing Street," so proclaimed by two gleaming new street signs. The former home of such clubs as the Famous Door, the Three Deuces, the Onyx and Jimmy Ryan's, 52nd St. now sports massive office buildings, one of which belongs to CBS, who was mainly responsible for the implantation into the sidewalk of the first five "Prez Awards."

At a ceremony on the street last year, 12 musicians were honored with the awards and stars naming the first six of these—Dizzy Gillespie, Charlie Parker, Lester Young, Billie Holiday and Coleman Hawkins—are now embedded into the sidewalk, to be followed in the near future with the rest of last year's honorees: Thelonious Monk, Roy Eldridge, Sarah Vaughan, Stuff Smith, Art Tatum, Kenny Clarke and Miles Davis and the six who were honored this year: Erroll Garner, Slam Stewart, Red Norvo, Fats Waller, Oscar Pettiford and Ben Webster.

This year's awards were presented in a ceremony hosted by Max Roach, jazz fan Kareem Abdul-Jabbar and New York's Mayor Ed Koch. Norvo and Stewart were on hand to accept their awards and many other musicians, including Jo Jones, Count Basie, Ted Curson, Buck Clayton, John Lewis and Milt Jackson, were present for the ceremony, which included a short concert given by Ernie Wilkins and the CETA Ensemble.

As Roach put it to the assemblage, "You folks are standing on hallowed ground." —*lee jeske*

Courtesy Down Beat

"This accomplishment, or ambiguity, has always been characteristic of the greatest blues singers. In this respect, Holiday was a child of Bessie Smith, although she rarely sang a traditional blues. Holiday's 1936 recording of 'Billie's Blues' gives us a glimpse of what a blues singer she might have been had she chosen to be one." As Whitney Balliet writes, jazz is "the sound of surprise." That is, jazz is a music that can tolerate surface irregularities for the sake of overarching musical virtuosity.

Critics have called Holiday the first lady of jazz singing. She gained this title without ever scat singing. More than any other jazz vocalist, she lived her last painful years through her songs of torment. What sounds all too tragic was given a lift by her wonderful ability to mesh sensual interpretations with jazz instrumental solos. One year before her death Frank Sinatra called her the most important influence on popular singing in the previous twenty years. Today's audiences are probably aware of Billie Holiday through the 1972 movie *Lady Sings the Blues*, which starred Diana Ross. While the intentions were noble, the film focuses primarily on Billie's torment and drug problems, and not enough on the joyous music that she made.

Key 52nd Street Clubs

Club	Noted Performers
Onyx Club	Mike Riley and Eddie Farley, John Kirby, Leo Watson and the Spirits of Rhythm, Maxine Sullivan, Art Tatum, Joe Sullivan, Red McKenzie, Billie Holiday, Stuff Smith and His Onyx Club Boys, Thelma Carpenter, Dizzy Gillespie, Oscar Pettiford, Sarah Vaughan
Leon & Eddie's	Eddie Davis (the "Saloon Caruso"), Fran Warren, Lennie Hayton, The Revuers, Slim Gaillard, Harry Gibson (cocktail pianist three years prior to becoming headliner, "The Hipster"), Sherry Britton (stripper)
Adrian's Tap Room	Adrian Rollini, Eddie Condon's All Stars, Wild Bill Davison
Hickory House	Wingy Manone, Joe Marsala, Hazel Scott, Marian McPartland, Joe Buskin, Billy Taylor, Eddie South, Lee Wiley
Downbeat Club	Art Tatum, Phil Moore, Mildred Bailey, Mary Lou Williams, Coleman Hawkins, Billie Holiday, Tiny Grimes, Lester Young, Eddie Heywood
The Famous Door	Louis Prima and His New Orleans Gang, Red Norvo's Swing Sextet, Count Basie Orchestra, Benny Berigan Orchestra, Charlie Barnet Orchestra, Woody Herman Orchestra, Teddy Powell Orchestra
Kelly's Stable	Coleman Hawkins, Benny Carter, Roy Eldridge, Billie Holiday, Lee Wiley
Yacht Club	Fats Waller, Frances Faye, Billy Daniels
Three Deuces	Art Tatum, Charlie Parker, George Shearing, Erroll Garner, Slim Gaillard, Harry "The Hipster" Gibson, Fats Navarro, Dizzy Gillespie, Miles Davis
Jimmy Ryan's	Eddie Condon Gang, Red Allen, Milt Gabler's Commodore Jam Sessions, Sidney Bechet (a haven for traditional jazz)
Tony's	Tony Soma (owner who was known to occasionally sing standing on his head), Mabel Mercer, Bricktop, Jimmy Lyon, Cy Walter
Jack & Charlie's 21	The only 52nd Street club that remains today, a legendary, ritzy hangout that was, however, never a music club.
Spotlite	Dizzy Gillespie, Harry "The Hipster" Gibson, Charlie Parker, J.J. Johnson, Billy Daniels
Dixon's	Joe Mooney Quartet

The Mainstream Awakening

Just as there was renaissance for the blues (via the "Archivists in Action" discussed in chapter 5) and for traditional jazz music, there was also a reawakening for the swing-oriented music beginning in the 1970s and into the 1990s. Norman Granz's 1940s touring jam sessions, which he labelled "Jazz at the Philharmonic" was the start of an ongoing revival of swing music that, by the 1970s, was referred to as "mainstream"; a melodic, swing-oriented performance style that places an emphasis on reinterpreting older jazz originals or standard tunes from classic songwriters such as Irving Berlin, Cole Porter, George Gershwin, and other Tin Pan Alley greats. According to Nat Hentoff in *The Jazz Life*, "The term, 'mainstream,' as first coined by critic Stanley Dance, was meant to apply to the kinds of jazz that developed out of the late 1920s and through the 1930s and early 1940s." But by 1974, Hentoff thought Dance's conception needed to be expanded. "It seems time to me to extend the meaning of 'mainstream jazz' to apply as well to such of the creators of post-swing-era-jazz as Charlie Parker, Dizzy Gillespie, and in this book, Charles Mingus and Thelonious Monk."

More than twenty years later, "mainstream" has, indeed, included those modern jazz greats. In the "trad revival" section of chapter 5, we saw how various artists have replicated the classic jazz of the ragtime to traditional jazz period. Some writers have used the term "classic jazz" to define all jazz before the advent of fusion, a form of jazz blended with electric instrumentation and rock and soul roots in the late 1960s. Trad styles, swing, and the modern jazz of bop, cool, and the post-1950s movements of those forms all fall under that heading. Our focus, however, will remain on those contemporary performers and programs of the past thirty years or so who have reworded and celebrated swing-oriented material.

In much the way that the Western European music of Brahms, Beethoven, Bach, and Mozart is still a major part of the chamber music and philharmonic repertoires, colleges and universities have embraced jazz music and incorporated it into curricula beginning in the 1960s. Although jazz may be defined more by improvisation than any of its other musical characteristics, the academic elevation of classic recordings of Louis Armstrong's Hot Five and Seven bands, Jelly Roll Morton's Red Hot Peppers, and Fletcher Henderson's ground-breaking orchestrations has helped establish a tradition for playing classic jazz in two basic ways: note-for-note, the specific works, or by the recreation of the works' structure's (usually by playing the introductions, or musical "heads," as well as the closing statements, or recaps/codas), and then allowing the soloists freedom to improvise solos in the middle of the tune. Sometimes writers refer to this replication of older music as "classic jazz." For our purposes the "mainstream" revival will refer to the revival of swing-oriented music of the thirties and forties that began in the seventies and extends to the present day.

Courtesy Down Beat

Left to right, Norman Granz, Coleman Hawkins, Flip Phillips, and Ella Fitzgerald. The Jazz at the Philharmonic logo is seen in the background. The design was by David Stone Martin, whose work was among the most artistic visions of jazz performers during the 1940s and 1950s, adorning not only scores of Granz's Verve record covers and JATP advertisements, but also many *Down Beat* covers.

Norman Granz (1918 -   ) started producing jazz concerts at the Los Angeles Philharmonic in 1944 when he was a student at University of California at Los Angeles. According to Leonard Feather in *The Encyclopedia of Jazz*, "From the mid-1940s his concerts, in the U.S. and also later overseas, set a pattern for informal jazz stage shows and tremendous international popularity. Granz also pioneered the concept of recording 'live' at actual performances instead of in recording studios. In 1960 Granz sold his Verve Record company to MGM for $2,800,000 which was sold to a company that eventually, became known as Polygram." Granz's first concert was a fundraiser for twenty-one Chicanos who had been arrested in Los Angeles and convicted for murder in what was dubbed the "Zoot Suit Riots." The concert included saxophonist Illinois Jacquet, guitarist Les Paul, and pianist-singer Nat King Cole. The future touring concerts came to be known as "Jazz at the Philharmonic" ("JATP" to the hip set) and featured outstanding soloists like sax men Jacquet, Ben Webster, Flip Phillips, Big Jay McNeely, and Coleman Hawkins, pianists Oscar Peterson and Nat King Cole, and singer Ella Fitzgerald, among many others. By recording his concerts "live" from the stage, Granz instituted a tradition that today is commonplace. Granz's first record release, in 1944, was by Illinois Jacquet, whose "Blues, Part 2," became a hit.

Granz's concerts were often assailed by the critics. According to one *Down Beat* reviewer, in the summer of 1944, "The kids went wild over the screaming harmonics produced by Jacquet, who registered 'hot' facial expressions for the benefit of the galleries." Years later, Granz defended himself by saying, "They said Illinois Jacquet and Flip Phillips played differently in the jam sessions than they did with Hampton and Woody Herman. That was nonsense. Critics would ignore a set by Lennie Tristano, hardly a panderer to public tastes; a set by Ella Fitzgerald, who did mostly ballads; or a set by Oscar Peterson or the Modern Jazz Quartet." In all instances Granz refused to perform before segregated audiences, or register in a hotel that didn't allow blacks, or eat in restaurants that wouldn't serve blacks. Granz's performers usually traveled first class and were well paid. Granz became a millionaire and his artists were treated with respect and made excellent wages.

Up to this time, Granz had three labels going—Clef, Norgran, and a distribution deal with Mercury Records. In 1956, he formed Verve Records, which was born out of a dispute with Decca Record company. Ella Fitzgerald, who had been the star of JATP, had had an exclusive contract with Decca since the 1930s and Decca would not let her record for Granz's companies, nor let Granz supervise any of her recording sessions (he officially became her manager in 1954). But Decca needed to record several of Granz's artists for the soundtrack of *The Benny Goodman Story*. Granz completes the story: "Now I had Decca over a barrel. They asked me what I wanted. I said I wanted to buy Ella's contract, and they said okay. I immediately formed Verve because I felt I needed a broader label for her. Call it a pop label, I guess. Pretty soon I decided it was silly to have four labels, so in 1957 I consolidated them all under Verve." Granz placed Fitzgerald in front of a big band and featured her singing songbooks, the first of which, a Cole Porter song book set, became a best seller. This allowed Granz to insert his jazz

Oscar Peterson (1925-   ) is the best known Canadian to make a major impression on the jazz world. Peterson began playing piano at the age of six in Montreal and was a superstar throughout the 1940s before coming to America to play with Norman Granz's Jazz at the Philharmonic in 1949. Peterson's great power and dazzling technique have caused many to compare him to Art Tatum. Peterson's piano trios of the 1950s were exhaustively recorded by Verve Records. He later signed with Granz's Pablo label.

Len Lyons, evaluating Peterson in *The Great Jazz Pianists: Speaking of Their Lives and Music*, contends, "There are critics who downgrade the effect of his glorious technical command of the keyboard, accusing him of an overly mechanized style and of indulging in virtuosity for its own sake. True, Peterson can be showy and rococo; but more often than not, his technique operates in service of his art. I have heard him solo using a stride technique or a walking-bass line in the left hand. The music gathers momentum until the piano itself seems to be strutting across the stage." The album was one of many "tributes" Peterson recorded. Throughout the second half of the twentieth century, Oscar Peterson maintained the closest link to Art Tatum's virtuoso keyboard style.

artists into a more pop-oriented setting, as well as to allow others, for example, Art Tatum, to record the material they wanted the way they wanted. In 1975, after being out of the recording business since 1960, Granz joined RCA records and crafted a deal granting him his own company, which he named Pablo, after his favorite artist, Pablo Picasso. Granz's Verve and Pablo releases have been important testimonies to the popularity of mainstream jazz. On April 6, 1994, Verve Records celebrated its fiftieth anniversary with a Carnegie Hall concert filmed by the Public Broadcasting Service. Writing in *The New York Times*, Peter Watrous declared that Verve had "profoundly influenced music in this century. Ella Fitzgerald, the Velvet Underground, Louis Armstrong, Frank Zappa, Lester Young, the Righteous Brothers, Charlie Parker, Janis Ian, Dizzy Gillespie, and Stan Getz all recorded for Verve. Subtract just Ms. Fitzgerald's series of American standards, the early encounters between Afro-Cuban and jazz musicians, Getz's Bossa Nova albums, Parker's sessions, and Billie Holiday's lavish recordings and the twentieth century already sounds different. Mr. Granz knew about jazz as show business, but his particular genius was to make show business subservient to jazz."

Concord Jazz. *Left*, Ruby Braff, for years one of the underrated disciples of Louis Armstrong and a contemporary of Bobby Hackett, with the late George Barnes on guitar. This release features non-Dixie performances of lightly swinging yet intricate interpretations of the music of Gershwin. *Center*, led by young devotees of swing-oriented jazz in the 1980s and 1990s, saxist Scott Hamilton and cornetist Warren Vache, with the Concord All-Stars, keep what writer Chip Deffaa calls the "swing legacy" alive. *Right*, One of the longest and most fruitful careers in jazz belongs to venerable multi-instrumentalist composer Benny Carter, who formed his own band in 1933 and has been active and innovative ever since, as this 1985 showcase affirms.

Another important label to champion the cause of mainstream jazz is Concord Records, the brainchild of car dealer and jazz enthusiast Carl Jefferson in the early 1970s. Dick Gibson, a businessman who made a fortune producing his teeth-cleaning invention, the Water-Pik, had begun hosting jazz parties in 1963 in Aspen, Colorado. Gibson chose players to perform together and charged friends a minimal fee for a weekend jazz party. The yearly event combined many of the best traditional and swing players and soon Gibson underwrote the World's Greatest Jazz Band (a combination of trad and swing players). This was one of the beginnings of the mainstream revival.

Carl Jefferson took the movement to the next step. Concord continued the musical aesthetic established by Norman Granz, primarily acoustic, anti-multi-tracking technology, melodic jazz, often recorded in live concert settings. Concord Records was established around 1973. By 1975 the Concord Pavilion opened and housed the annual Concord Jazz Festival (in Concord, California), and the label had an all-star super band and a well-rounded roster that included venerable old-time masters such as the late violin great Joe Venuti, the redoubtable Benny Carter, and modernists George Shearing, Barney Kessel, and Gene Harris. Concord also provides a home for younger mainstream players like Scott Hamilton and Warren Vache, and vocalists like Rosemary Clooney, Ernstine Anderson, and Mel Torme.

Pianist **Dave McKenna** (1930-   ) continued on the path set by the late Dickie Wellstood of playing in the solo, stride-oriented keyboard tradition. McKenna's powerful piano excursions and cleverly woven medleys makes one wonder why the solo stride tradition was heard so infrequently in the 1990s. "The Master of the Medleys," Dave McKenna is not only a one-man band, but also a reservoir of Tin Pan Alley songs. McKenna is quoted in Whitney Balliett's *American Musicians: Fifty-six Portraits in Jazz:* I don't know if I'm a bona-fide jazz guy. I play barroom piano. I like to stay close to the melody. When I play, I just tool along, and the only thing I think about is what I'm going to play next. Very few jazz musicians are complete improvisers. The greatest have little patterns they follow. I have my own patterns, my own licks. Sometimes I play in runs, because people like to hear those things."

New York nightclubs such as The Ballroom, Fat Tuesdays, Condons, and, especially, Michael's Pub, have been supportive of mainstream music throughout the 1980s and 1990s. Michael's Pub is the premier club for concept engagements. Mention should also be made of the 1990s concert retrospective at the Lincoln Center, whose musical director, trumpeter Wynton Marsalis, put together programs recreating the classic works of Duke Ellington, Thelonious Monk, Sidney Bechet, Louis Armstrong, and other greats. The same can be said for trumpet star Jon Faddis, who heads the Carnegie Hall concert series of retrospectives. Finally, a special accommodation should be given to the 92nd Street YMCA, which has been in the forefront of keeping the music of the past alive. The institution's tributes to the composers of the standard song forms and its retrospectives of jazz masters has been going on since the 1970s.

Pianist **Dick Hyman** (1927-   ) has been musical director of the 92nd Street YMCA since 1985. Over the years he recorded albums and dedicated concerts that featured, in some cases, literal transcriptions of the music of Jelly Roll Morton, Louis Armstrong, Fats Waller, James P. Johnson, Willie "The Lion" Smith, and Cy Coleman.

Courtesy 92nd Street YMCA, New York City

Hyman has performed as pianist, organist, arranger, composer, and conductor on over one hundred albums released under his own name and, even more so, in support of others. Hyman is so knowledgeable and in demand as a performer, it's hard to imagine how he decides on the projects he agrees to. As a studio musician, for instance, Hyman has won six Most Valuable Player Awards from the National Academy of Recording Arts and Sciences. He has worked as music director for numerous broadcast programs, including Benny Goodman's last television appearance. Hyman received Emmys for his scoring of *Sunshine on the Way* and for a PBS special on Eubie Blake. He also composed the scores for PBS's "Tales from the Hollywood Hills," and "Ask Me Again," and served as music director for the 1989-90 series "In Performance at the White House." Filmgoers might recognize Hyman's name from his many musical collaborations with actor-writer-director Woody Allen. Hyman worked as composer-arranger-conductor-pianist for Allen's *Broadway Danny Rose, Stardust Memories, Zelig, Hannah and Her Sisters*, and *Radio Days*.

Courtesy 92nd Street YMCA, New York City
Dick Hyman on piano with trumpeter Joe Wilder rehearsing at the 92nd Street Y.

Down Beat magazine, reviewing Hyman's *From the Age of Swing* album in April 1995, praises, "If the same criteria that define great actors also applied to great musicians, Hyman would be the Olivier, the Streep, of his trade. But the versatility so prized in actors becomes an encumbrance in jazz, and has left Hyman undervalued in an art that honors those who speak in a single voice and distrusts those endlessly fluent in so many." The album featured numerous mainstream players, including Joe Wilder, seen at the left.

Chapter 10

REVIVAL OF 1930s AND 1940s

Courtesy Manhattan Rhythm Kings

The Manhattan Rhythm Kings as a human key-board, played by Tony-Award-winning choreographer-director-entertainer Tommy Tune. One of the key ingredients of revival of 1930s and 1940s music is not only an awareness of the songs and dances of the past by performers of today, but also a bow to the sophisticated "After Six" formal attire that was often favored. These stylistic dress elements offered an alternative to the pop outfits of the rockin' fifties, the hippie sixties, the disco seventies, the alternative eighties, and the grunge and rap nineties.

This chapter focuses on contemporary artists linked by choice to the songs and styles of the 1930s and 1940s. Of all of the commercial music prior to the "Age of Rock" (post 1950s) none has been as re-worked and kept alive as that of "The Golden Age of Pop" (those classic standards from the 1920s to 1950). The majority of the music in this chapter, and the reigning visual style, reflected or eminated from the 1930s and 1940s—thus the choice of title. This chapter will reprise much of the music that has been covered in the previous two chapters. In some cases, such as those of Frank Sinatra and Ella Fitzgerald, it will update and put into perspective how entertainers from one era adapted to changes in the music industry. In other instances it will try to show how new talent, from the fifties to the nineties, was drawn to the sights and sounds of past eras. The performers fall into four general headings. The intent here is to give a broad overview of artists, primarily vocalists, who for various reasons have chosen to work within a past musical form. The first three categories, "jazz-pop," "creme de la creme cabaret," and "jazz-cabaret cult," are composed of singers whose careers have been inextricably bound to the standard song form. The fourth category, "camp nostalgia," presents contemporary, rock-oriented singers who used the music and fashion of an earlier time as a platform for their various projects.

The singers of all four categories focused their attention on the popular standards: songs composed between 1900 and 1950 by Irving Berlin, Jerome Kern, Cole Porter, George Gershwin, Richard Rodgers, Harold Arlen, and Harry Warren, among others. The dates and composers reflect the milestone analysis of composer-historian **Alec Wilder** (1907-1980) in his book *American Popular Song: The Great Innovators, 1900-1950*. Alec Wilder was held in high esteem in the musical community for his adventurous classical compositions as well as popular songwriting from the 1930s through the 1980s. Wilder was also viewed as intellectually demanding, scholarly, and an indefatigable champion of high standards for music, be it classical or popular. Wilder's book examines with great insight and wit some eight hundred of the three hundred thousand American songs submitted for copyright in the first half of the century. Wilder's one oversight was that he did not include his own songs, which are highly valued and are included in the musical repertoires of many of the better cabaret and jazz vocalists.

American Popular Song was published in 1974 and no book has done as much to elevate the status of American songwriters of the Broadway theater and Hollywood film axis. Wilder's suggestion that the better works of Berlin, Gershwin, and some others could stand up to Bach and Mozart was revolutionary and eye-opening for many. Wilder's principles are both demanding and lofty: "I should make clear that my criteria are limited to the singing (melodic) line and include the elements of intensity, unexpectedness, originality, sinuosity of phrase, clarity, naturalness, control, unclutteredness, sophistication, and honest sentiment. Melodrama, cleverness, contrivance, imitativeness, pretentiousness, aggressiveness, calculatedness, and shallowness may be elements which result in a hit song but never in a great song."

The revival of Broadway musicals of the past was especially apparent during the 1990s. *Show Boat, Carousel, Damn Yankees, The Most Happy Fella, Guys and Dolls* and *Girl Crazy* (retitled and given a face lift in *Crazy for You*) were some of the early '90s revivals on Broadway. The wonderful Gershwin catalogue was combined to give *Crazy for You,* starring Harry Groener (right) and Karen Ziemba a sprightly presentation. With Mike Ockrent's crafty direction, creative dance sequences choreographed by Susan Stroman, and snappy performances by the Manhattan Rhythm Kings, *Crazy for You* projected a radiant air of loftiness that more bombastic musicals of the '90s could not match.

To recap Alec Wilder's dictum: "Melodrama, cleverness, contrivance, imitativeness, pretentiousness, aggressiveness, calculated-ness, and shallowness may be elements which result in a hit song but never in a great song." *Crazy for You* is filled with "great" songs by the Gershwins, and is a testimony to the connection of human emotions that great art achieves despite the ever-quickening changes in contemporary lifestyles. Great art transcends style and fashion. Author Gene Lees, commenting on the durability of yesterday's songs, declares, "Popular music was good and good music was popular."

Author Whitney Balliett has been a champion of many of the singers who have adhered to the high demands set forth by Wilder. In his book, *Alec Wilder and Friends,* Balliett prescribes some of the tenets that many such singers subscribe to: "They hold a vision of life that has lately fallen low. They are highly moral people who have refused to compromise. They have gone without jobs, when fashion has turned against them, rather than demean themselves in shoddy ones. They have kept their spirits intact despite neglect, near-privation, and even semi-oblivion. Pre-eminence, no matter how tardy or circumscribed, has been their reward."

A couple of points should be made about these singers. First is the low status that many jazz-oriented writers have given singers. Seldom will the names of singers such as Sinatra ("Is he a singer of jazz, or merely a jazz-oriented singer?"), Bobby Short ("He and his kind only sing for the rich folks"), or Mark Murphy ("A fringe jazz singer, not in the same league as Sarah or Ella or Louis") be found in books on the history of jazz. Perhaps because most people cannot play an instrument but can sing, (we all sing in the shower, for better or for worse), music historians assume that the ability to play an instrument is the more elevated talent. Indeed, during the big band era many relatively untalented singers became stars, perhaps to the detriment of some of those bands' many talented instrumentalists, who often gained little attention and very little money. That is part of the nature of pop. Certainly there were many vocal technicians more talented than Madonna or Janet Jackson in the 1980s and 1990s who failed to gain enormous fame and money.

The issue with Sinatra, Short, Murphy and their colleagues is more one of respect than money. All are singers in the jazz tradition. Their music is formed by songwriters, arrangers, and instrumentalists who wrote in the 1933 tradition. So what is the problem? Perhaps another point will explain.

As will be detailed in the next chapter, when the "new jazz" (bebop, often referred to simply as bop) came on the scene during the early 1940s, it brought a new mind-set. Jazz became a serious art form. There is nothing wrong with that; musical forms should develop and expand. What happened over the years, however, was a kind of disregard for some of the older forms. Except for their historical educational shows, the programs of most jazz radio stations today would lead even the most casual listener to conclude that the music goes no further back in history than the music of 1960s great John Coltrane. Singers have been given especially short shrift. Of the older-style vocalists, Louis Armstrong and Billie Holiday are usually given proper respect, though seldom will Crosby, the Boswells, or Lee Wiley be given their due. It gets worse for the singers of the forties. A few, including Ella Fitzgerald, Sarah Vaughan, and Billy Eckstine, are praised not just because they are tremendous talents, but because, in one way or another, they adapted to bebop. The great ballads and swing tunes that all three performed when they were part of the swing era are just as much a part of their jazz heritage as their later development in the modern mode but they are given far, far less attention. What then, became of the singers from the swing era who didn't move on to the next jazz form? Those singers and their followers will be the main concern of this chapter.

Another point should be made before we move on to some of the representative pop-oriented vocalists—the place of the popular singers in the eyes of "serious" historians and academics. Henry Pleasants is a music critic who at one time wrote only about classical music. He contends in *The Great American Popular Singers* that the artistry and musical achievements of the better popular singers has been largely ignored because they have mined the music of language, and of American English, in contrast to the more elevated form of foreign tongue in opera.

Speaking of the pop singer, Pleasants declared, "His place in the hierarchy of his own musical society is certainly closer to that of the seventeenth- or eighteenth-century vocal virtuoso than is that of the latter's twentieth-century counterpart. The popular singer is the center of attention. The song, the arrangement, the recording, the setting, the lighting are built around him. He has interpretive privileges denied the classical singer, who is inhibited by the priorities accorded the composer and the conductor, and by the vigilance of critics safeguarding those priorities. He also bears commensurate responsibilities."

The Jazz-Pop Singers

The jazz-pop singers are those vocalists who were a part of the big band era of swing and, through the years of popular music fads, have continued to use the standard song form. The audience base they established during the big band era grew up with them, getting them through the musical changes of fifties rock 'n' roll, sixties new rock, seventies disco, and the MTV era of the eighties and nineties. These are singers who usually have a high recognition factor with audiences who don't even listen to their music: heavy metal or rap listeners are likely to have heard of, if not listened to, Sinatra or Fitzgerald (although that might not be the case for a lower-profile artist in this category, like Joe Williams or Rosemary Clooney). These artists play the more prestigious nightclubs and perform in the bigger rooms in hotels, usually accompanied by their own pianist/arranger, and a large band or small combo playing from sheet music. Most of them made guest appearances on television talk shows (especially Johnny Carson's "The Tonight Show") and have been seen in motion pictures. As a result, these performers often engage in "personality patter" (such conversation between certain songs comments on their celebrity). And, for the most part, they have, or had, recording contracts with major labels that often allowed them to record with full orchestras.

Frank Sinatra (1915-) exemplifies all of this; he is, without a doubt, the leader of this category. Sinatra, as noted in an earlier chapter, was the rage of the early and mid-forties. After 1947, things did not go so well for him. He began a five-year decline that left him at a career crisis by 1952. From 1948 to 1951, Sinatra had no hits on the *Billboard* chart higher than number ten. Sinatra seemed caught up in

America's star-making machinery. He was constantly on the go, making recordings, movies, and various radio shows, and his voice seemed worn. Public disenchantment developed as a result of controversy over his politics (the right-wing press labeled him a Communist supporter because of his liberal views), and allegations of Mafia connections. Sinatra's highly publicized divorce from wife Nancy, and subsequent marriage (albeit stormy and brief) to film star Ava Gardner in 1951, added to his problems.

In 1953, Sinatra was granted the coveted role of Maggio in the film *From Here to Eternity,* for which he won an Academy Award for supporting actor. The role later put Sinatra into the world of larger-than-life myth-making when Francis Ford Coppola slyly referenced it in the 1972 motion picture *The Godfather*.

Observing Sinatra's overall career, it is plain to see that he found almost everything he could ask for in the big band-swing idiom. Between 1940 and 1949 he all but invented the standard. As Will Friedwald confirms in *Jazz Singing,* before Sinatra, the basic repertoire for popular singers consisted of the latest plug tunes. Singers rarely recorded anything written more than six months before because such songs were thought to be out of fashion. Sinatra rejected this practice. Friedwald contends that in picking songs for his recording sessions, and ultimately shaping and controlling the results, "Sinatra codified the basic repertoire of adult popular music."

After one too many conflicts with Columbia record producer Mitch Miller (the low point in Sinatra's career was the making of "Mama Will Bark," in May 1951, with blonde bombshell Dagmar), Sinatra signed a new contract with Capitol Records in 1953. At Capitol, Sinatra developed what author Arnold Shaw has termed the "swinging ballad," thanks to the arrival of arranger Nelson Riddle.

Frank Sinatra made the transition from a "singles" artist during the 1940s, to that of an "album" artist in the 1950s. In a sense, when performers "mature" with their art in contemporary pop, they often make a transition to making artistic statements on albums. Between 1957 and 1965, Sinatra released no singles. He realized he couldn't compete with the new music, rock'n'roll, so he created long-play records based on themes. Sinatra's brooding, down-in-the dumps *In the Wee Small Hours* (1955), has been cited by a number of authorities as the first true "concept" album; i.e., all the songs on the album are connected thematically. In the case of *In the Wee Small Hours*, the theme is lost love. Bob Dylan did this in the 1960s and the Beatles followed, beginning with *Rubber Soul* in 1965 (it is usually the Beatles who are credited with creating the first concept album in 1967 with *Sgt. Pepper's Lonely Hearts Club Band*). Sinatra continued recording scores of records into the 1990s. Writer Benny Green places the legend in proper perspective: "What few people, apart from musicians, have ever seemed to grasp is that he is not simply the best popular singer of his generation, a latter-day Jolson or Crosby, but the culminating point in an evolutionary process which has refined the art of interpreting words set to music. Nor is there even the remotest possibility that he will have a successor. Sinatra was the result of a fusing of a set of historical circumstances which can never be repeated."

Sinatra eschewed rock'n'roll throughout the 1950s and 1960s. However, in the September of his years he did come up with projects that brought him together with rock and soul-oriented artists. The result was his two *Duets* releases, 1993 and 1994. Literally the stars came to the mountain to pay their respects and sing alongside the master. From Bono of U2 to Aretha Franklin, Neil Diamond, and Jon Secada, they came forth with reverence and humility. *New York Times* critic Stephen Holden concluded, "In his masterpieces of the 1950's and 1960's, Frank Sinatra made the pop album a place for exploring the psychology of middle age. On the *Duets* albums he has proven that old age has its place in pop, too."

Nelson Riddle (1921-1985) had been a trombonist and arranger for bands during the swing era and by 1950 he had signed on as a staff arranger with Capitol Records. Riddle developed an unobtrusive big band sound that featured swinging brass sections, a pulsating rhythm section, and intelligent use of strings. Riddle orchestrated lush and swinging backdrops for Judy Garland, Dean Martin, Peggy Lee, Margaret Whiting, and Nat King Cole, who had big hits with Riddle's arrangements on "Mona Lisa" and "Too Young" (1950-51). Later Riddle would join forces with Ella Fitzgerald and Linda Ronstadt.

Beginning in 1953, Riddle and Sinatra established a rapport that helped the veteran singer reach new levels of artistic achievement. Shaw's "swinging ballad" appeared on Sinatra's first album release for Capitol, *Swing Easy.* Sinatra praised the arranger: "Nelson had a fresh approach to orchestration and I made myself fit into what he was doing."

Mel Torme (1925-   ) is the jazziest of the male pop singers, and the most versatile. A multi-talented youngster in Chicago vaudeville and radio (he got his start at the age of four), Torme began writing his own songs by age fourteen. Torme joined the Chico Marx Orchestra as a drummer and singer when he was sixteen. By the time he was twenty, Torme had a singing group, the Mel-Tones, and was recording with Artie Shaw. By this time Torme had sold some of his songs ("Lament to Love" was a jukebox hit for Harry James), and performed as a pianist. Soon he would move on to Hollywood to be featured in a series of musicals, most importantly *Good News,* for MGM in 1947.

Courtesy Polygram Records

Mel Torme with one of his classic albums, featuring the arrangements of Marty Paich. Along with his *California Suite* (which was the first successful attempt by a popular vocalist to create an audio Hollywood soundtrack via songs), *Mel Torme Swings Shubert Alley* is one of the most important orchestrated vocal albums in jazz-pop history.

Will Friedwald praises the album in *Jazz Singing*: "Its virtues could be extolled ad infinitum, but the point is that the strength of the album does not lie in any of the individual elements, nor do certain tracks stand out above the others. Instead, from start to finish, *Mel Torme Swings Shubert Alley* is a masterpiece. Neither the vo-cool specifically nor vocalizing in general got any better than this."

By 1946, Torme was being touted as "the "Velvet Fog," a nickname he hated. From the fifties into the nineties, Torme has been a resourceful and dynamic interpreter of the standard song. On stage he would often play drums, piano, and vibes, and he would vocalize ballads and scat with a high degree of artistry. Torme cleverly conceived and arranged tribute medleys: two standouts are "The Gershwin Medley" and "The Fred Astaire Medley." Some of his own compositions include "A Stranger in Town," "Whisper Not," "Born to Be Blue," and the perennial holiday favorite, "The Christmas Song." Torme's autobiography, *It Wasn't All Velvet,* was published in 1988. During the 1980s Torme recorded a vocal with the electric rock band Was Not Was ("Jazz Turned Blue") and joined pop music star Barry Manilow on the concept album *2:00 A.M. Paradise Cafe.* Throughout the 1990s Torme continued touring and recording. Chip Deffaa writes in his 1989 *Swing Legacy*, "Torme maintains a frenetic pace of productivity. He is now working on his fourth book, a biography of Buddy Rich. Torme writes entire shows for himself. If you see a concert at which Torme is the host or chief participant, whether it's saluting Gershwin, big bands, or sixty years of singing in America, chances are he's put the whole thing together."

One of the few areas where females were allowed to shine in the world of jazz was as a vocalist. If career mobility was difficult for females in jazz, it was doubly so for the African American. Donald Bogle in *Brown Sugar: Eighty Years of America's Black Female Stars*, appraised the situation thusly: "In the eyes of the white world, the black woman was never thought of as pretty, soft, or sweet. If anything, she was an awkward hag or nag. At best, she was considered little more than a lusty sexual object, to be used, dumped, and forgotten. Or if she were older, then she became a sexless motherly figure,

be used, dumped, and forgotten. Or if she were older, then she became a sexless motherly figure, miraculously endowed with certain spiritual powers and the ability to heal all wounds. To paraphrase black writer Zora Neale Hurston, 'the black woman was the mule of the world!' Often, too, she represented Mystery, the Other Dark Side of Experience. But she was never accepted simply as herself."

The two most successful of the black divas to blend pop and jazz were Sarah Vaughan and Ella Fitzgerald. Both struggled throughout their careers trying to break down the stereotype described by Bogle in *Brown Sugar*. Both are so incandescent that over the years they have come to be known by just their first names. **Sarah Vaughan** (1924-1990) sang as a child at the Mount Zion Baptist church in Newark and studied piano for over ten years. After winning an amateur contest at the Apollo Theatre in 1942, she joined Earl Hines's band as a vocalist and duo pianist. The next year Vaughan was featured with Billy Eckstine and his orchestra. Her first recordings, in 1944, were duets with the handsome baritone ("I'll Wait and Pray" and "I Love You").

With Fitzgerald, Vaughan was the first of the major female band vocalists to fully embrace the harmonic complexities of bebop. She had a wide vocal range, used vibrato and distortion effectively, was a supreme scat singer, and developed a warm, luscious vocal color that became the envy of many jazz singers. Over the years Vaughan became known as "Sassy" and the "Divine One." Like Torme, Vaughan's first recordings were released on Musicraft, after which she moved on to Columbia, Mercury, Roulette (where she dabbled in pop—1959's "Broken Hearted Melody" was her biggest success), Mainstream, and Pablo.

Courtesy Polygram Records

Some of Sarah Vaughan's best jazz recordings are found on this re-release. "Sassy," as she was sometimes called, is given firm support from pianist Jimmy Jones and trumpeter Clifford Brown on scintillating interpretations of "Lullabye of Birdland," "Embraceable You," and "Cherokee," among others. Dan Morgenstern's notes to the release above points out, "Her range, a full two octaves, enabled her to execute dazzling swoops from high to low or vice versa, and her command of dynamics was exceptional, making it possible for the voice to move from a whisper to a shout in the course of a few measures without any sign of strain. Most significantly from a jazz point of view, she had impeccable pitch and an ear for harmonic 'changes' that was the equal of any great instrumental improviser's."

Courtesy Big Nickel Publications

Sarah Vaughan possessed one of the most marvelous voices in jazz and popular music. Vaughan had the vocal range of an opera singer and she knew how to use it for dramatic results. She and Billy Eckstine were among the first pop-oriented vocalists to incorporate modern bebop sounds into their repertoire ("I thought Bird and Diz were the end"). Vaughan was as much a musician as a singer. She had her first crossover hit in 1947 with "It's Magic." Throughout the 1950s and 1960s Vaughan had occasional pop hits, including "Misty" (1958), "Broken Hearted Melody" (1959), and "A Lover's Concerto" (1966). Over the years she recorded for numerous record companies and had a variety of different management teams, which resulted in a wide disparity in the quality of her recorded work. In most cases, her great vocal talent overcame all obstacles.

Courtesy Polygram Records

Courtesy Polygram Records

The *Cole Porter Songbook* was the first of Ella Fitzgerald's Verve Records songbooks. This marked the beginning of her recording career with manager Norman Granz, in 1956. Fitzgerald had been with Decca Records for twenty years with results that were less than ideal. The Decca braintrust liked to mix labelmates in recording sessions. Some of the collaborations, as well as some of the orchestrations, steered Fitzgerald away from jazz and material suitable to her talents. However, in her last year with Decca, Fitzgerald recorded a songbook album with pianist Ellis Larkins, *Ella Sings Gershwin*. This was an eight-song tribute on a ten-inch LP; thereafter all LPs would be twelve inches and allow for more music. This is not to say that Fitzgerald's Decca career was not worthwhile; she sold millions of records and was a well-known commodity, making the cover of *Life* magazine in 1955. But it is with Verve Records that Fitzgerald's ascendence into her mature artistry really took hold. *The Cole Porter Songbook* became one of the biggest-selling jazz records of all time and introduced the public at large to the concept of the songbook. This album, a two-volume set, included thirty-two Porter compositions orchestrated by Buddy Bergman. The release set in motion a pattern that Fitzgerald, and many other singers, would follow from that point onward.

Paul Weston, an ex-Tommy Dorsey arranger, orchestrated the 1958 songbook dedicated to the work of Irving Berlin. Fitzgerald glides effortlessly through the great variety of Berlin's Americana. Fitzgerald's Verve catalog (later releases were on Norman Granz's Pablo label) is staggering. Along with Frank Sinatra, Fitzgerald has one of the largest recorded body of works in the annals of post-swing popular music. And like Sinatra and the rest of the jazz-pop singers, Fitzgerald, during the past thirty years, had no significant pop singles on the *Billboard* chart.

Fitzgerald had the versatility to sing ballads beautifully and up-tempo numbers with force. She remarked in an interview, "Despite the differrent kinds of songs I sing, I still consider myself a ballad singer." She also said, "These bop musicians have stimulated me more than I can say. I've been inspired by them and I want the world to know it." Fitzgerald combined both: ballads and bop, sensitivity and power. She sat on Mount Rushmore looking down at the rest of the female singers. As Rosemary Clooney said, "That's the goal we tried to reach for—to be as good as Ella or at least approximate that, because there's Ella right there and then there's a big, big blank space and there's the rest of us down there who are doing it, too, but not like Ella."

Ella Fitzgerald (1918-   ), whose parents died when she was young, was adopted by bandleader Chick Webb and his wife in 1934, when she was a sixteen-year-old singer in his band. Fitzgerald's big hit with the band was "A-Tisket A-Tasket" in 1938. She assumed leadership of the band after Webb's death in mid-1939, moving on to solo work in 1942. Fitzgerald's earliest influences were Connee Boswell (for her swing and ballads) and frenetic bop vocalizer Leo Watson (for scat and harmonic liberties). Aptly titled "The First Lady of Song," Fitzgerald was comfortable in lush ballad settings, as well as in driving bop excursions featuring her scat singing. After twenty years with Decca (1936-55), Fitzgerald signed on with Norman Granz and Verve Records. Granz had started the Jazz at the Philharmonic series in the mid-forties and used Fitzgerald as his featured vocalist. Granz became Fitzgerald's manager and transformed her. At Verve, Fitzgerald sang in the most elegant settings, devised by arrangers like Nelson Riddle and Quincy Jones. Most significantly, Granz established Fitzgerald's songbook series, dedicated to the works of the outstanding songwriters of Tin Pan Alley. Lee Wiley may have initiated the concept of the "songbook" with her Commodore releases in 1939 and the early 1940s, but it was Fitzgerald who made the songbook an integral part of the standard song tradition among vocalists.

Ella Fitzgerald and the Songbook Tradition on Verve/Pablo		
Album	**Orchestra Arranger**	**Released**
The Cole Porter Songbook (2 CDs)	Buddy Bergman	1956
The Rodgers & Hart Songbook (2 CDs)	Buddy Bergman	1956
The Duke Ellington Songbook (3 CDs)	Duke Ellington	1956
The Irving Berlin Songbook (2 CDs)	Paul Weston	1958
The George & Ira Gershwin Songbook (3 CDs)	Nelson Riddle	1959
The Harold Arlen Songbook (2 CDs)	Billy May	1960
The Jerome Kern Songbook	Nelson Riddle	1963
The Johnny Mercer Songbook	Nelson Riddle	1964
Dream Dancing	Nelson Riddle	1978
Ella Abraca Jobim	Erich Buling	1981
Nice Work If You Can Get It (Gershwin songs)	Andre Previn	1991

There are many other post-swing band vocalists who continued singing the popular standard repertoire throughout the years, such as Peggy Lee, Carmen McRae, Rosemary Clooney, Anita O'Day, and Joe Williams. Concord Records has been a champion for the continuation of what jazz authorities have labelled "mainstream jazz"—jazz that rests between the early New Orleans traditional forms and the modern bop styles. The singers below have reached wide audiences over the past fifty years and mix swing standards with cherished Broadway and Hollywood chestnuts of the past.

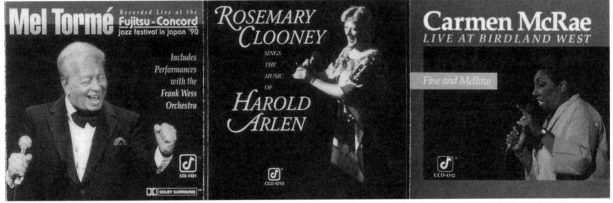

Courtesy of Concord Jazz, Inc.

Three from Concord Records. Three celebrated singers from the 1940s who continued performing into the 1990s. All three carried on the tradition of interpreting the standard song form of the masters of Tin Pan Alley: Irving Berlin, Jerome Kern, the Gershwins, and others. Mel Torme and Carmen McRae were both inspired by modern jazz, while Rosemary Clooney stayed closer to the roots of swing. All three are consummate artists of the highest order.

Tony Bennett (1926-   ) was born Anthony Dominick Benedetto in Queens, New York. He was the son of Italian immigrants. He was drafted into the military in 1944, and became a professional singer upon his discharge. Bennett sang in small clubs and learned from artists who were performing along 52nd Street in the late 1940s. Art Tatum, Charlie Parker, Billie Holiday, and Mabel Mercer were Bennett's main models. In 1950 Bennett signed a record contract with Columbia and worked under the supervision of artist and repertoire man Mitch Miller. Bennett became an immediate hit, bellowing chesty-voiced songs like "Because of You" and "Cold, Cold Heart" (1951) and "Stranger in Paradise" and "Rags to Riches" (1953). Like fellow contract-mate Rosemary Clooney, Bennett viewed himself as a jazz-oriented singer. But both Bennett and Clooney (she had novelty pop hits like "Come-On-A-My-House," "Botch-A-Me" and "Mambo Italiano") got locked into a formulaic success orchestrated by Mitch Miller. In time, both would reestablish themselves with the world of jazz.

Tony Bennett Croons to the MTV Generation

Courtesy DRG Records

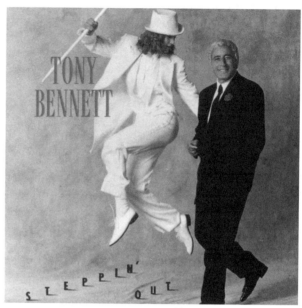

Courtesy Sony Music

The success of Tony Bennett is a lesson in fortitude, patience, good fortune, and good taste. Unlike the majority of jazz-pop vocalists, Bennett just missed out on the big band world of swing as a professional singer. By the late 1940s, when he was beginning his career, many of the bands were breaking up or cutting back. Bennett's inspiration, however, came from that era: "I got my education by playing hooky and listening to Sinatra at the Paramount. He opened up a whole new bag with the microphone, the artful use of intimate singing to show psychology, real thinking."

Bennett has made a career out of steadfastly sticking with the tried and true standards. Through very hard times during the late 1960s and 1970s he believed in singing standard songs with a jazz backing, usually a trio of piano, bass, and drums. Bennett's present musical director and confidant, Ralph Sharon, has been with him for years.

In *Steppin' Out,* Bennett sings songs associated with Fred Astaire. Astaire is fondly remembered, of course, as the pentultimate dancer, but he was also a fine singer, and, after Bing Crosby, introduced more future standard songs in film than any other Hollywood star. Bennett's interpretations are respectful and swinging, as usual.

Alec Wilder called Bennett the ultimate "believer," that is, one who sets his sights high and doesn't make concessions or follow mere trends. Wilder's description of Bennett's singing style helps explain his 1990s acceptance by the "slacker set" of MTV: "There is a quality that lets you in. Frank Sinatra's singing mesmerizes you. In fact, it gets so symbolic sometimes that you can't make the relationship with him as a man, even though you may know him. Bennett's professionalism doesn't block you off. It even suggests that maybe you'll see him later at the beer parlor."

Bennett introduced his signature song, "I Left My Heart in San Francisco," in 1962. By the time the Beatles and the British Invasion had established a second wave of rock'n'roll in the mid-1960s, Columbia pushed Bennett to record contemporary material. By 1972 Bennett was without a recording contract and at a low point in his career. Nonetheless, he refused to compromise. "It's beautiful not to compromise in what you sing, and yet I've done business since I had my first record hit for Columbia in 1951. I've always tried to do the cream of the popular repertoire and yet remain commercial. Hanging out with good songs is the secret. Songs like 'All the Things You Are' and 'East of the Sun' are just the opposite of singing down." After many years of not recording, Bennett re-signed with Columbia in 1986, and, under the management of his son Danny, recorded *The Art of Excellence.* Thus began one of the most stunning comebacks in popular music history. Bennett won back-to-back Grammys for 1992's *Perfectly Frank*, a collection of Sinatra's saloon songs, and 1993's *Steppin' Out,* an eighteen song salute to Fred Astaire.

But Danny had even bolder ideas. He was intrigued with the idea of presenting his father to the younger rock audience after he read an essay by *Spin* magazine publisher Bob Guccione, Jr., who claimed that

Bennett and James Brown were the greatest influences on rock. Bennett zoomed into the 1990s like a rebuilt Jaguar. He was the first star to do a cameo on the television show "The Simpsons". He had a surprise hit video on MTV, the stylish Fred Astaire salute, *Steppin' Out With My Baby*. At the 1993 MTV music video awards Bennett rubbed elbows on stage with rock admirers Flea and Anthony Kiedis of the Red Hot Chili Peppers. He drew standing ovations at six rock concerts hosted by alternative radio stations; he performed between sets by the Lemonheads and Bad Religion. And he was joined by guests k.d. lang and Elvis Costello on "MTV Unplugged" (for years Bennett performed with no accompaniment or microphone, making him, in effect, "The Father of Unplugged"). Although Bennett never even flirted with rock'n'roll, he projected a soul and commitment that young audiences could pick up on. John Marchese wrote in the *New York Times* ("When He Croons, Slackers Listen," May 1, 1994): "By successfully navigating the shifting currents of hipness, the gray-haired and dapper Mr. Bennett has made the transition from one eon of Johnny Carson's 'Tonight Show' to David Letterman regular. He is now a known quantity at alternative rock stations, where his songs are played among a roster that includes bands like the Meat Puppets, whose names still make the singer chuckle with grandfatherly indulgence."

Bennett seemed pleased that younger audiences were enjoying his music: "Young people are the most enthusiastic audience I've ever had, and I'm just doing what I've always done, singing Gershwin or Cole Porter. I never sing songs I don't like. Frank Sinatra is the one who told me, 'Just stay with the good songs.' That philosophy sustained me no matter what the fashion was, whether it was rock or disco or rap. If there's not a sense of timelessness, I don't go near it."

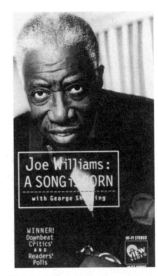

Courtesy of V.I.E.W. Video, 34 E. 23rd St., New York, NY 10010 800-843-9843

Joe Williams, singer of blues and standards. Williams was a late bloomer. He had been singing with bands in the late 1930s and early 1940s (with Jimmy Noone, Coleman Hawkins, Lionel Hampton, Andy Kirk, among others) but his career didn't get very far. That changed when Williams joined the Count Basie band in 1954 on a regular basis. The period established Williams as a solid blues singer who could also sing the standard song repertoire. Williams stayed with Basie until 1961, when he left to seek fame and fortune as a solo singer. Since that time, Williams has been one of the most popular jazz vocalists on the music scene—his big, friendly baritone voice is distinctive and warm.

Jazz-Pop Vocalists' Band Associations

Singer	Pop Associations
Tony Bennett	1st to break on TV in 1950 without big band connections (Arthur Godfrey & Jan Murray); Mitch Miller productions for Columbia
June Christy	Boyd Raeburn (1940-43); Stan Kenton (1945-48)
Rosemary Clooney	Tony Pastor (1945-49) and Mitch Miller orchestrations for Columbia in 1950s
Chris Connor	Claude Thornhill (1949-51); Stan Kenton (1952-53); small groups thereafter
Bing Crosby	Throughout the '30s and '40s *the* main solo vocalist in pop music
Billy Eckstine	Earl Hines (1939-43); formed his own band for the rest of 1940s
Ella Fitzgerald	Chick Webb (1934-41); then led her own bands
Buddy Greco	Benny Goodman (1949-52); lively singer-pianist from 1950s onward
Cleo Laine	Post 1940s UK queen of jazz-pop with hubby-bandleader Johnny Dankworth
Peggy Lee	Benny Goodman (1941-43); Capitol Records solo star thereafter
Carmen MacRae	Benny Carter (1944); Mercer Ellington (1946-47); close bebop connections
Anita O'Day	Gene Krupa (1941-43); (1945); Stan Kenton (1944-45); spirited bop stylist
Frank Sinatra	Harry James (1939-40); Tommy Dorsey (1940-42); solo superstar
Jo Stafford	Tommy Dorsey's Pied Pipers (1941-42); Pipers (1942-44)
Mel Torme	Chico Marx (1942-43); Artie Shaw (1945-46)
Margaret Whiting	1940s with Freddie Slack, Billy Butterfield, & Paul Weston
Joe Williams	Andy Kirk (1948-49), Count Basie (1954-61)
Nancy Wilson	Post-1940s recordings with George Shearing & Cannonball Adderley
Sarah Vaughan	Earl Hines (1942-43); Billy Eckstine (1944-45)

Creme de la Creme Cabaret

Creme de la creme cabaret: "Cafe Society" at Bricktop's in Paris, 1933. Bricktop is in the center with her arms around the men. Mabel Mercer is at the far right. The cabaret tradition of well-dressed men and women smoking cigarettes, drinking champagne, and socializing while jazz bands and singers perform in the background was epitomized at nightclubs owned and operated by an American singer and hostess supreme, Bricktop.

The creme de la creme cabaret style of entertainment is an intimate style of theatrical singing with little or no melodic deviation and an emphasis on clearly enunciated lyrics that tell a story. Whereas the jazz singer concentrates on improvisation or variations on the melody, the cabaret performer focuses on its narrative potential. Both cabaret and jazz singers characteristically enhance their interpretations of the lyrics with instrumental backing. The jazz pop performer often allows for improvised piano, saxophone, trumpet, or trombone solos from the backup band.

In big cities, especially New York, after a dinner party or the theater, couples often topped off the evening by visiting a club to hear a favorite performer. Robert Connolly, writing in *Stereo Review,* observed about the New York club scene of the 1950s: "There was an entertainer, an ambiance, and a price tag to fit every taste. In Greenwich Village at Cafe Society, Bon Soir, and the Village Vanguard, you could hear Mae Barnes, Josh White, Susan Reed, and a very young Harry Belafonte; at jazz joints on 52nd Street, Maxine Sullivan and Sarah Vaughan; at the big hotels, Hildegarde and Sophie Tucker; and at the Versailles, Le Ruban Bleu, or Le Vie en Rose there were the French artists Mistinguett, Jean Sablon, and Edith Piaf. During that golden era of American night life, going to a club could provide a unique and wonderful musical experience that cannot be duplicated elsewhere."

The styles of certain jazz pop vocalists, like Mel Torme, Carmen McRae, Ella Fitzgerald, and Sarah Vaughan, have been informed by modern jazz, and occasionally feature scat singing. But in the cabaret interpretation there is little emphasis on the instrumental solo and rarely bebop scatting. Another distinction is that cabaret is more closely associated with the upper-class socioeconomic tradition of elegant theater parties and exclusive dining establishments, often located in expensive midtown hotels. Jazz, on the other hand, has been tied to lower economic traditions and is historically heard in less opulent settings. The period of the 1930s through the mid-1950s was the peak period of the nightclub tradition. Television and rock'n'roll would change all this.

The jazz connection to cabaret occurred when **Bricktop** (Ada Smith, 1894-1984) left America during the Harlem Renaissance and established her own club in Paris in 1926. Cole Porter became her patron saint and brought into her classy club the rich and famous (like Ernest Hemingway, and the Prince of Wales). Bricktop was a black woman who found in Paris a social freedom that wasn't possible in America at that time (she also shepherded the stardom of Josephine Baker). Bricktop brought jazz and cabaret together on a regular basis in Europe. She also introduced many of Cole Porter's songs in her club, and one in particular, "Miss Otis Regrets," was written especially for her.

Bricktop in front of her club in Paris during the mid-1930s. Although she was a singer, Bricktop's chief attribute was her ability as an overseer, a conduit in the mixing of the underground world of musicians, hustlers, and hangers-on with that of wealthy, high-society figures. Cole Porter had the most to do with Bricktop's success by introducing his world to hers. Porter said, "I've told everyone that Bricktop is Bricktop. Without Bricktop, this place wouldn't make sense. She has the genius of an Elsa Maxwell. She can feel a place slipping, walk across the room and say something to someone, and pick it up again." Bricktop's life, from the Prohibition days of the Harlem Renaissance to the Cafe Society times in Paris and after is recounted in James Haskins' biography, *Bricktop* (1983).

Bricktop was christened Ada Beatrice Queen Victoria Louise Virginia Smith; she had freckles and flaming red hair, which resulted in her nickname (her hair looked like bricks piled upon her head). Bricktop grew up in Chicago and became stage-struck by the time she was in her early teens. The Peking Theatre, established in 1902 and owned by Bob Motts and his nephews, was the first theater of any consequence devoted to African-American drama. The Peking was the site of this awakening. Young Bricktop hung around the stage door, and asked Motts if she could audition for the chorus. By the time she was sixteen Bricktop joined Flournoy Miller and Aubrey Lyles in a travelling blackface act full of humor, songs, and dances. (As we saw in chapter 6, Miller and Lyles would later fashion *Shuffle Along* with Noble Sissle and Eubie Blake.) The youthful entertainer then joined the Oma Crosby Trio, in what reviewers called a "nice, clean act." Bricktop also performed as a saloon singer at the Cafe Champ, owned by Jack Johnson, boxing's black heavyweight champion. She also worked with the Panama Trio, which included Florence Mills. Bricktop eventually headlined at a Harlem hotspot, Barron's Exclusive Club (where she got her nickname), and Connie's Inn. She was then summoned to Paris to work at Le Grand Luc.

The year was 1924 and in time Bricktop would own the place. By 1925 the Montparnasse crowd of writers and artists, led by F. Scott Fitzgerald, became regulars. In *Babylon Revisited*, Fitzgerald called Bricktop's the place where he had spent "so much time and so much money." He often said, "My greatest claim to fame is that I discovered Bricktop before Cole Porter." In time she would teach the "Charleston" and "Black Bottom" dances to the wealthy set, wear expensive gowns by Schiaparelli, and rub elbows with the Duke of Windsor and other Europeans of power and influence. Bricktop established other clubs in Mexico City, Rome, and New York, and gave the cabaret world a sense of style and sophistication.

From 1931 to 1938 Bricktop nurtured a young soprano singer who eventually left for America (the Germans were beginning their march through Europe), establishing the connection of cabaret within the jazz community of New York's 52nd Street. The singer's name was Mabel Mercer.

Author Whitney Balliet, in *American Singers* (his book of profiles, mostly reprints from his perch as a columnist for the *New Yorker*) contends that there have been five consummate cabaret singers in this country: "Their bearing, style, voice, and attack are totally dissimilar, but their repertoires overlap, and they are in the same line of work, singing superior songs, some of them largely unknown, to small audiences in intimate rooms in such a way that song, singer, listener, and room become one." The five singers: Hugh Shannon, Bobby Short, Blossom Dearie, Julie Wilson, and the doyenne of American cabaret, Mabel Mercer.

Mabel Mercer (1900-1984) was born at Burton-on-Trent, Staffordshire, England, into a bohemian household of painters and show business people. Mercer's father was a black entertainer and her mother a white Englishwoman. As a singer at Bricktop's, Mercer learned how to put a song over in the intimate and expressive way enjoyed by the wealthy of the time. Reminiscing about Bricktop, Mercer recalled, "She was a great hostess, as well as a great entertainer, and she made everything like a big party. I learned a lot from Brick. Not how to sing, but everything about night clubs, how to meet and talk to people. When you went to a party you never knew who would be there, and we were constantly being invited to parties. Brick was very strict about that: you can go to a party, but you don't sing; if you go to a party and sing, you get paid for it. We had a lot of fun. I wouldn't exchange those years I worked with Brick for anything." Upon her arrival in the States in 1938, Mercer worked at the elegant Ruban Bleu with accompanist Cy Walter.

By 1941 Mercer was a regular at Tony's on 52nd Street. As highlighted in the last chapter, 52nd Street was America's jazz street. Mercer comingled with this jazz world but infused her own peerless vision of the art of vocalizing. As her soprano voice lowered, she established a talk-sing style with an elaborate rolling of her r's. Alec Wilder defined Mercer's vocalizing as a "graceful parlando," a way of melodiously talking her songs. Mercer became perhaps the most famous teacher of singing (though she never gave a formal lesson). Artists such as Billie Holiday and Frank Sinatra worshiped her during the 1940s (Sinatra even stated, "Mabel Mercer taught me everything I know"). Later Johnny Mathis, Tony Bennett, and Bobby Short became her disciples.

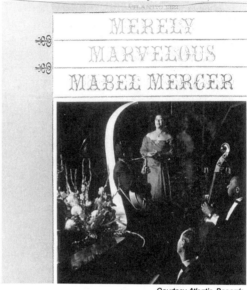

Courtesy Atlantic Records

Here's a voice that seldom has been heard on American radio and certainly never had a record closely resembling a hit, but she was one of the most influential singers in popular music history. Mabel Mercer's vocal delivery is too formal and precise for the mass audience, and she doesn't swing, but the way that she tells a story is poetry to the more demanding listener. Professionally the last years of her career were spent at the St. Regis Room in the St. Regis Hotel at 5th Ave. and 55th St. in New York. Mercer, accompanied by a piano player, would sit in chair (a "Louis Quinze throne") and quietly weave her spell over an attentive audience.

The cabaret tradition of emphasis on lyric story-telling reached its heights with Mabel Mercer. Johnny Mathis, one of her many disciples, observed, "Mabel Mercer has an uncanny ability to interpret lyrics with a realism that is seemingly absolute. You feel she is telling you, a close and much-loved friend, a very personal story rather than just singing. And she sees it all with regal bearing uncommon in today's casual society." Harold Arlen praised Mercer as "the keeper of the show songs that were never heard before. Singing intimately into your ear, she 'reads a song beautifully.'"

Between 1941 and 1957 Mercer sang in only two nightclubs, Tony's and the Byline Room. Mercer noted, "I prefer to stay in one place. It's the only way for people to know where to find you." Mercer's last years were spent at the St. Regis Hotel and she even appeared at the 1982 Kool Jazz Festival. Bobby Short, who headlined concerts with her, observed, "It has been often said that the night club is the bottom level of show business. This is partly true, but a great artist can surmount with what seems like an uncanny ease the din and smoke of such places, transforming their confines into places of magic. Mabel's refined manner, her elegance, and her sweetness have done so over the years both here and abroad. Her enthusiasm, dedication, and devotion to her art cannot but be felt by anyone who has ever known her."

William Livingston, writing in the February 1975 *Stereo Review* about the influence of the woman who was referred to at various times as "the doyenne of American popular singing," the "queen of the supper clubs," and "the high priestess," offered, "Her repertoire, which encompasses about a thousand very carefully selected songs, is said to 'rub a patina on our lives and loves, enriching, beautifying, and spiritualizing our experience.' The writers carry on about her influence on our greatest pop singing stars and America's finest songwriters. They wax eloquent about Mercer's impeccable taste, her flawless diction, her musical phrasing, her penetrating insight, her incomparable projection of lyrics, and her real dignity. And it's all true."

For years people have been complaining about the lack of civility in our society, how standards have broken down and that things aren't the way they used to be (when usually they never were that way to begin with). Mercer's art does recall a time of civility, a touch of class. Rex Reed echoes the feelings of many who subscribe to Mercer's world: "Mabel Mercer is all things to all people. She has kept us all young. In a world slowly going mad with apathy and ugliness, she has pruned away the troubles the way she prunes away the clutter in her country garden, gracing our lives with her unerring beauty and elegance in music. No popular composer of any merit, no singer with any class, has failed to be influenced by her way with a lyric or her weaving of a melody. Her achievement is a legend. I think she is the eighth wonder of the world." Mercer was able to elevate the popular song by her phrasing and her ability to transmit the deepest meaning of a lyric. As Alec Wilder, the brilliant composer-historian and friend of Mercer noted, "When she sings a song it is instantly ageless." He called her "the guardian of the tenuous dreams created by writers of songs."

One of the final highlights of Mercer's distinguished career occurred on February 23, 1983, when she, along with Billy Graham, Jacob Javits, George Balanchine, and Bear Bryant each were awarded the prestigious Medal of Freedom by President Ronald Reagan.

Courtesy of V.I.E.W. Video, 34 E. 23rd St., New York, NY 10010 800-843-9843

The doyenne of cabaret. Mercer's focus on lyrics and story telling are at the heart of her artistry. Too often singers feel compelled to "oversell" a sentiment. Mercer's view of this matter is enlightening: "The first time I heard 'The Way We Were,' I thought that was a beautiful song, and nobody knows what they're singing about. The melody's nice, but when they get to the second part, they screech it out, especially Barbra [Streisand], with that beautiful voice of hers. She has absolutely no perception of what this song is about. Most of them think you have to sing loud or soft. Loud and soft are the only nuances they seem to understand, and they don't get the meaning of certain phrases."

The two videos pictured here capture Mercer being neither just loud or just soft, but rather singing in a warm, controlled style that insinuates a deep understanding of the character of each song. Mercer's vocal delivery is described by author Whitney Balliett, "Above all was her easy, alabaster technique, the ingenious phrasing, the almost elocutionary diction, the dynamics (she never shouted and she never relied on the staginess of the near-whisper), the graceful melodic push, the quick rhythmic sense, and always, the utter authority."

Mabel Mercer Classics

Song	Author	Comment
Just One of Those Things	Cole Porter	Featured at Bricktop's; definitive interpretation
Little Girl Blue	Richard Rodgers-Lorenz Hart	Revived by Mercer, then popularized by others
Thank You for the Flowers	Austin C. Johnson-Clarence Moore	Made famous in Paris by Mercer
While We're Young	Bill Engvick-Alec Wilder	Standard introduced by Mercer
The First Warm Day in May	Bart Howard	Introduced by Mercer
Some Fine Day	Cy Walter	Introduced by Mercer
You Will Wear Velvet	Douglas Cross-George Cory	Written for Mercer
Did You Ever Cross Over to Sneeden's	Alec Wilder	Written for Mercer
The Riviera	Josephy McCarthy Jr.-Cy Coleman	Introduced by Mercer
You Fascinate Me So	Carolyn Leigh-Cy Coleman	Championed by Mercer; others followed
The End of a Love Affair	Edward G. Redding	Introduced by Mercer; a cabaret favorite
By Myself	Arthur Schwartz-Howard Dietz	1938 song Astaire revived in the 1954 MGM film *The Bandwagon*
Remind Me	Jerome Kern-Dorothy Fields	Salvaged from an Abbott & Costello film
Fly Me to the Moon	Bart Howard	Introduced by Mercer
Wait Till You See Her	Rodgers-Hart	Not used in *By Jupiter*; revived by Mercer
Where Do You Go (When It Starts To Rain)	Alec Wilder	Introduced by Mercer and later by Frank Sinatra on *No One Cares* LP

Hugh Shannon (1922-1983), the next important cabaret artist, is the least known of the group of four Whitney Balliett called the "consummate cabaret singers in this country." Bricktop first heard Shannon singing and playing piano on 52nd Street in the late 1940s, doing a song associated with her, "Ballin' the Jack." She was impressed with his good looks and manners, as well as his musical talent, and brought him to Paris in 1950. Shannon also worked under her tutelage in Rome and New York. The first time Billie Holiday heard Shannon sing, at a party during the 1940s, she told him that since he didn't sound like anybody else, he should keep on singing.

Courtesy Audiophile Records

The least-known of the leaders of American cabaret, Hugh Shannon was an effervescent personality who viewed himself simply as a "saloon singer." Shannon's career got a boost when the legendary Bricktop closed her club in Mexico and returned to Paris shortly after World War II with the young, blond piano player-singer in tow. Under Bricktop's tutelage, Shannon learned to engage the wealthy patrons who descended upon Bricktop's cabaret. Over the years he established a loyal following among the rich and famous.

Courtesy Audiophile Records

Shannon met and married the beautiful, wealthy Betty Dodero, best friend of Argentina's Eva Peron. They traveled the world and he played in Capri, New York, and the Hamptons until Dodero's premature death in 1959 from cancer. Throughout the 1960s, until his death, Shannon was unknown outside the jet-set audience that kept him busy playing on cruise ships, the islands during the winter seasons, and New York's chic clubs during the off season. Shannon recorded rarely. The Audiophile recordings pictured here comprise the majority of the Shannon repertoire. Shannon's singing is robust and, unlike Mabel Mercer's style, is accessible to the uninitiated.

The Hugh Shannon Song Sampler

Song	Songwriters	Source	Year
Let's Do It	Cole Porter (special lyrics Noel Coward)	Paris (Broadway)	1928
True Blue Lou	Whiting-Coslow-Robin	The Dance of Life (Hollywood)	1929
The Great Indoors	Cole Porter	The New Yorkers (Broadway)	1930
As Time Goes By	Herman Hupfeld	Everybody's Welcome (Broadway)	1931
Fun to Be Fooled	I. Gershwin-Harburg-Arlen	Life Begins at 8:40 (Broadway)	1934
Down in the Depths (On the 90th Floor)	Cole Porter	Red, Hot and Blue! (Broadway)	1936
Make It Another Old Fashioned Please	Cole Porter	Panama Hattie (Broadway)	1940
Ace in the Hole	Cole Porter	Let's Face It (Broadway)	1941
Disgustingly Rich	R. Rodgers-L. Hart	Higher and Higher (Broadway)	1941
Everything Happens to Me	Tommy Adair-Matt Dennis	Independent release	1941
As Time Goes By	Herman Hupfeld	Casablanca (Hollywood)	1943
I'll Be Around	Alec Wilder	Independent release	1943
Good Morning Heartache	S. Shaw-I. Higginbotham	Independent release	1945
A Bar on the Piccolo Marina	Noel Coward	Independent release	1954
The Other Side of the Tracks	Carolyn Leigh-Cy Coleman	Little Me (Broadway)	1962
Razzle Dazzle	Fred Ebb-John Kander	Chicago (Broadway)	1975
I Never Do Anything Twice	Steven Sondheim	The Seven Percent Solution (Hollywood)	1976
Drinking Again	Johnny Mercer	Independent release	1977
Too Old to Die Young	Murray Grand	Independent release	1977

Source: Audiophile Records, True Blue Lou: Hugh Shannon, *1977;* Saloon Singer, *1982*

In a November 1979 *New York Times* article titled "They Still Call It National Saloon Singing", John S. Wilson acknowledged that Bobby Short was the best known of the "saloon singers" but that "the basic prototype for the entire school is Hugh Shannon, who started building his following more than 30 years ago at the Atlantic House in Provincetown and at Le Perroquet in New York. Julius Monk, the nightclub impressario who guided Mr. Shannon and played dual pianos with him in those early days, considers him a throwback to such singers of the late 1920s and early 1930s as Tommy Lyman, who kept New Yorkers up until daylight listening to 'My Melancholy Baby.'"

Bricktop took Shannon to Europe in the late 1940s and introduced him to her crowd. Bricktop noted, "Hugh was not disillusioned with Paris. He loved it and thrived on the new adventure. I can still see the Duke of Windsor seated on the floor, enjoying his request 'When the Red-Red-Robin Comes Bob-Bob-Bobbing Along,' Porfiro Rubiroso leaning against the piano leg at 10 a.m., listening to Hugh (who must have been playing and singing continuously since the previous evening), Hugh's reluctance to learn to perform for Schiaparelli, 'If I Knew You Were Comin', I'd 'Ave Baked a Cake,' and his stints in Capri where King Farouk and everyone came to listen. And the parties, what parties!"

In the last years of his life, Shannon made David K's at Third Avenue and 55th Street his New York headquarters. By that time, in the early 1980s, Shannon had received the bad news that he was suffering from throat cancer, so he called Audiophile Records and told them they would have to set up a recording session as quickly as possible. Two days after that call, Shannon cut a double album, *Hugh Shannon, Saloon Singer*. It was his last recording (Shannon's voice was hoarse, but the self-defined night person ("I was destined to have a night sound," he said) sounded, if not in top form, at least spirited and comfortable in his milieu). Rogers Whitaker of the *New Yorker* called Shannon an original: "Just a natural-born, wide-eyed giddy boy with a bent for amusing people." And *Esquire's* George Frazier perfectly characterized the spirit of Shannon's bonhomie: "Hugh Shannon has the soul of a young boy who walks along the beach with the bottom of his trousers rolled up, barefoot, sipping a glass of champagne and eating a peach."

Shannon's hoarse, rangy baritone sounded like sandpaper, but he had a warm friendliness that welcomed the listener into his vast collection of familiar and obscure songs. And, although he had a following of very wealthy fans, he projected an endearing, approachable persona. Shannon was the scion of the cabaret singer-pianists.

Bobby Short (1924-) became Shannon's heir apparent. Born of middle class parents in middle America he became a pre-teen star in vaudeville houses and clubs as he dressed in a satin tuxedo, played the piano and sang cosmopolitan songs like "Sophisticated Lady." Short's first autobiography (he's said to be working on a second), *Black and White Baby*, details his early years. Like Shannon, Short has a husky, raspy voice that bursts with great gusto, whether he's singing a Cole Porter ballad like "I Love You" or raucous blues like "New Orleans Hop-Scotch Blues."

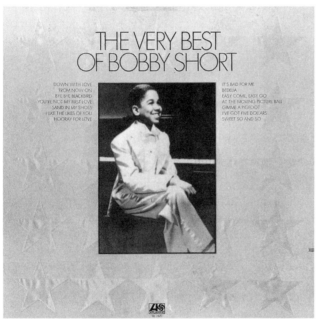

Courtesy Atlantic Reocrds

Unlike Shannon, Short had the good fortune to be amply recorded on Atlantic Records, and, after Ella Fitzgerald, he is the most prodigious singer of the songbook tradition. Short also boasts the longest residency at a club in American popular music: over thirty years at the classy Hotel Carlyle at 76th Street and Madison Avenue in New York. He is known to the uninitiated for his elegant posing at the piano for Charly perfume commercials and for the "I Love New York" campaign.

Courtesy Atlantic Records

Bobby Short's fascination with the standard song fare began at an early age—he toured the country singing and playing piano, decked out in white tie and tails, when he was twelve years old. Short notes in his biography, "The New York thing came to an abrupt end in 1938. I suddenly realized that there I was, a kid with two years of show biz and all the mannerisms of an adult, and I didn't like it, so I went back to Danville and stayed there four years, until I finished high school." After high school, boogie woogie was the rage, but Short sought something else. That's when the great Hildegarde, of "Darling, Je Vous Aime Beaucoup" fame, cast her spell on him. "She had the slickest night-club act of all time. It was produced down to the last sigh and through her I became aware of the Broadway kind of score, of the mystique of the Broadway musical."

By 1954 Short met up with arranger-composer Phil Moore, who, until his death in the early 1990s, was one of the most sought-out vocal trainers in Los Angeles. Moore became Short's manager, enlarged Short's act, and gave the cabaret artist a polished and controlled presentation. In 1954 Short made a tape that was sold to Nesuhi and Ahmet Ertegun of Atlantic Records. Short has recorded for Atlantic ever since that taped audition.

Bobby Short in action at the Cafe Carlyle, located on the second level of the Hotel Carlyle, hidden in its southwest corner. By the 1990s the cost of a show was around $40, with a two-drink minimum. Nesuhi Ertegun, the jazz specialist of Atlantic Records who signed Short to a record contract in 1954, wrote that Short "has emerged as the definitive authentic original genuine interpreter of the American song. Don't miss the chance to see him if you can. You'll see the greatest cabaret singer of our time. You'll also see a great and significant American artist who has no peer in his chosen field."

Bobby Short and the Cafe Carlyle are one and the same to many followers of the cabaret world. The landmark Carlyle opened its doors for business in 1930, and since that time has played host to the rich and famous. Three times a night, five nights a week, eight months of the year Bobby Short sits down at the piano and plays and sings to adoring customers in an elegant setting of Victorian sofas and banquettes and lovely murals by Vertes.

The broad revival of the older songs and styles occurred during the early 1970s, as we shall see in the coming section,"Nostalgia Camp." However, at a sold out concert featuring Short and Mabel Mercer at the Town Hall on May 19, 1968, the comeback of the "swank and sway" of elegant dress, courtly manners, and time-tested songs was given a jump start. Rex Reed, writing liner notes to *Mabel Mercer and Bobby Short at Town Hall* (Atlantic Records, 1968), encapsulated Short's aura as "the last remaining member of that almost-defunct ornithological species of Great Stay-Up-Late Black-Tied Manhattan Nightbirds, sassy and full of the old paprika. He knows just about every song ever written that is still worth hearing and if time had permitted he would have sung them all. There was an old Ivor Novcello song about Maxim's, old Cole Porter songs about Elsie De Wolfe, Monty Woolley, and a girl named Samantha, and the old Bessie Smith song 'Gimmie a Pig Foot and a Bottle of Beer.' There were old Billy Strayhorn songs and old Cy Coleman songs, and one particular crowd pleaser called 'On the Amazon,' a curious bit of musical jabber wacky about a weird oasis where 'prophylactics prowl' and 'hypodermics howl' which was so mutated through the years even Bobby couldn't remember where it came from. Time stood still and the universal language with which Bobby communicates what he knows about us all (he knows a lot!) seemed so sublime that by the time he got around to 'Bojangles of Harlem,' a bit of vintage Jerome Kern introduced by Fred Astaire in *Swing Time*, the rapture was so complete even the kids in the audience who never heard of Bill Robinson knew exactly what the song (and the evening) was all about. See what I mean about 'universal'?"

Blossom Dearie (1926-   ) is a pianist-singer who was befriended by the boppers in the early 1950s (hers is the female voice on the classic King Pleasure vocalese, "Moody's Mood for Love"). During the mid 1950s Dearie moved to Paris and formed the Blue Stars of Paris. From the 1960s to the 1990s she has been an acquired taste for aficionados who like their jazz light and saucy. Blossom Dearie (her real name) came to New York after graduating from high school and hung out with jazzmen like Miles Davis, Gil Evans, and singer Dave Lambert, later of the Lambert Hendricks Ross group. She worked at the Show Spot, underneath the Byline Room, where Mabel Mercer was singing at the time. In 1952 Dearie worked the Mars Club in Paris, at which time she recorded "Lullabye of Birdland," sung in French with the Blue Stars (Bob Dorough, another jazz cult artist, was also a member of the group). Back in America, Dearie began recording for Norman Granz's Verve Records. Most of Dearie's releases have been hard to get.

Film critic and cabaret aficionado Rex Reed says he was offered $1,000 for his collection of Blossom Dearie records on the Verve label. Dearie said, "Verve wouldn't tell me how many they sold. They wanted me to think I wasn't a money-making proposition. But I've been shaking hands with people that have my records for more than 25 years." Today, with the advent of the CD, many of Dearie's Verve classics can be found in record stores that have a section wide enough to include cabaret entertainers. In the mid-1970s Dearie started her own company, appropriately titled Daffodil Records.

Blossom Dearie's "Friend" Writers

Songs	Songwriter(s)/Friends	Year
Discover Who I Am	John Wallowitch	1972
Long Daddy Green (The Almighty Dollar)	Blossom Dearie-Dave Frishberg	1976
My New Celebrity Is You	Johnny Mercer	1976
Peel Me a Grape	Dave Frishberg	1976
Spring in Manhattan	Tony Scibetta-Alicia Reash	1976
The Wheelers and the Dealers	Dave Frishberg	1977
Winchester in Apple Blossom Time	Blossom Dearie-Walter Birchett	1977
You Are There	Johnny Mandel-Dave Frishberg	1977
You're for Loving	Tony Scibetta-John Wallowitch	1977
I'm Hip	Bob Dorough-Dave Frishberg	1979
I'm Shadowing You	Blossom Dearie-Johnny Mercer	1979
I Know My Lines	Blossom Dearie-Jack Segal	1983
Sweet Kentucky Ham	Dave Frishberg	1983
Bruce	John Wallowitch	1984
Hey John	Blossom Dearie-Jim Council	1984
Someone's Been Sending Me Flowers	David Backer-Sheldon Harack	1984
Are You Still in Love With Emily?	John Wallowitch	1985
Good Morning Darling (What's Your Name?)	Jacques Wilson-Jack Segal	1985
The Quiet Time	Duncan Lamont	1985
My Love Went to London	Tony Scibetta-John Wallowitch	1991
Liz and Ralph and Calvin	John Wallowitch	1992

Today Dearie lives in a small Greenwich Village apartment; she also spends time in the family house in East Durham, New York, where she was born. Like Mabel Mercer, who couldn't seem to find enough time to spend in her beloved, wooded retreat in Chatham, New York, Dearie enjoys the quiet country living. Musically there are few artists performing whose name so closely resembles the sound of their voice as Blossom Dearie's does. Hers is a bright wisp, a gently zephyr, what *New Yorker* critic Rogers Whitaker described as a voice going from "the meticulous to the sublime."

Whitney Balliett defined Dearie as "absolutely pure," writing, "Everything about Blossom Dearie is just right. Consider her singing. She is the youngest of the five consummate supperclub singers who rule the upper regions of American song. She has a tiny voice, smaller than Mildred Bailey's. Without a microphone, it would not reach the second floor of a doll house. But it is a perfect voice, light, clear, pure, resilient, and, buttressed by amplification, surprisingly commanding."

Like the other cabaret performers, Dearie often struggled to find the stable and comfortable club setting for her delicate song stylings. In the early 1980s she found such a place at the Ballroom on 28th Street in New York. There, Dearie established her 6:30 to 8:00 sets ("My audience has to go to bed early," she purred). Dearie's early LPs on Verve are collector's items, but her recent releases (CDs or cassettes— "kay-sets," as she calls them), can be purchased at her performances or through mail order from her company, Daffodil Records.

Elegance and sophistication for the nineties. Julie Wilson and John Wallowitch, both on DRG Records, are the epitome of New York's "after theatre" nightclub set.

Julie Wilson (1924-   ) is the heir-apparent to Mabel Mercer. Trim and fit, this beautiful lady with a gardenia in her hair started in theater in Omaha, Nebraska, when she was fourteen (as a chorus girl in Kurt Weill's *Knickerbocker Holiday*). Eventually she went to Hollywood, worked with Phil Moore, came back to New York, where she played the Maisonette in 1948, and then got back into theater. Wilson played in the national touring company of *Kiss Me, Kate,* played in *South Pacific* in London for a year, and performed in the films *Pajama Game, Company, A Little Night Music, Follies,* and several lesser-known movies before retiring to raise her teenage sons.

Today's "Grande Dame of Cabaret" returned to the scene in 1984 to answer the call at Gil Wiest's Michael's Pub for a lead singer for a Cole Porter show. Wilson became a fixture at key cabaret haunts such as the Russian Tea Room and the Algonquin Oak Room and made a series of critically acclaimed releases for the DRG label. When she was with the Johnny Long band in 1940s Wilson fell under the spell of Billie Holiday and today wears a gardenia in her hair as a tribute to the late Lady Day. She has made a number of songbook albums and her cabaret shows are usually conceptually focused on a songwriter such as Cole Porter, Noel Coward, Kurt Weill, or Harold Arlen, among others.

The world of **John Wallowitch** (1930-) is that of a slight, bald-headed (not many male vocalists are willing to admit to baldness) pianist-singer-composer whose songs are the most biting and sophisticated since the days of Cole Porter and Noel Coward. In fact, Wallowitch was dubbed by the *New York Times* "America's Noel Coward." Wallowitch graduated from the Juilliard School of Music and gave a Carnegie Hall piano recital in 1962. After that he made a career out of playing piano in cabarets and took on voice students (including Cass Elliot and Dixie Carter). Wallowitch also composed his own songs, which he sang in his nightclub act. Wallowitch's songs can be hilarious or touching, but in either case, they are highly literate. In 1984 Wallowitch teamed up with Bertram Ross, the legendary partner and choreographer of Martha Graham's dance company for twenty-five years. The Wallowitch-Ross duo made their debut in January 1984 at the Ballroom, where they focused on old but rarely heard pop songs such as Irving Berlin's "Cohen Owes Me Ninety-Seven Dollars" (done in high Yiddish dialect by Ross), Rodgers and Hart's seldom-heard "Moon of My Delight," the Depression ditty "A Cup of Coffee, A Sandwich and You," "When Yuba Plays the Rhumba on the Tuba," and an Eskimo's lament, "Turn on the Heat," among many others. Wallowitch has also written some of the funniest songs in cabaret: "Bruce" (about a cross dresser; it was first recorded by Blossom Dearie on an album entitled *Et Tu, Bruce*), "I'm Twenty-Seven," "Cheap Decadent Drivel," "Cosmetic Surgery," and a topical 1990s New York number, "Don't Do to Me What Woody Did to Mia." The shows Wallowitch and Ross present are tightly choreographed duets with themes that connect all of the music, with titles like *One Night in Manhattan* and *Back on the Town: A Cabaret for the Theater*. John S. Wilson, writing in the *New York Times*, praised the duo as "a singing team with a repertory and style that are primarily funny, often hilarious but balanced with just enough straightforwardness and sincerity to give their program substance." In 1992 Wallowitch's songs were given a lively and theatrical rendering by his good friend and student Dixie Carter in DRG Record's *Dixie Carter Sings John Wallowitch Live at the Carlyle*.

Courtesy Julie Wilson   *Courtesy John Wallowitch and Bertram Ross*

Julie, John, and Bert. Julie Wilson is better known to cabaret audiences outside New York than John Wallowitch and Bertram Ross. The Wallowitch songwriting touch, however, is one of the joys of urbane existence, in or out of New York. The New York scene is the preferred spot for this South Philadelphia-born deadpan raconteur. In "Beekman Place Elegy," Wallowitch salutes "Manhattan the way that we knew it." He laments how time has changed the former elegance of the city, but concludes, "Three cheers for the years, pop the cork/For Garbo, Berlin . . . and New York."

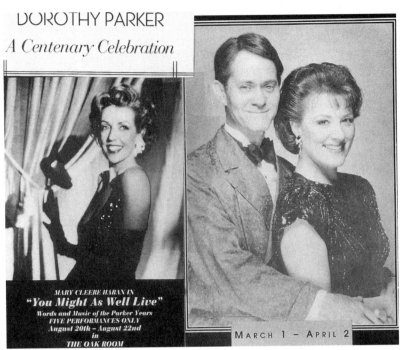

DOROTHY PARKER
A Centenary Celebration

MARY CLEERE HARAN IN
"You Might As Well Live"
Words and Music of the Parker Years
FIVE PERFORMANCES ONLY
August 20th – August 22nd
in
THE OAK ROOM

MARCH 1 – APRIL 2

Courtesy Algonquin Hotel

Courtesy Algonquin Hotel

Mary Cleere Haran emerged as one of the bright, new stars of cabaret during the 1990s. She has proved herself to be one of the most fascinating and informative cabaret practitioners of "dialogue segues" (introductions to songs acting as bridges between them). This is an important component of Haran's performances because, like a historian, she researches her songs and often puts together conceptual shows centered on a theme. One such performance was an Algonquin tribute to Dorothy Parker, the female writer and wit whose barbs and broadsides peppered the daily meetings that were conducted for nearly ten years at the Round Table in the Algonquin Hotel's Rose Room (with fellow colleagues Robert Benchley, Alexander Woollcott, Robert Sherwood, Marc Connelly, among others.).

The Algonquin Round Table celebrated its seventy-fifth anniversary in June 1994. An Academy Award-winning documentary by Aviva Slesin, *Ten Year Lunch* (1987), and a major-release Hollywood film starring Jennifer Jasen Leigh, *Mrs. Parker and the Vicious Circle* (1994), detail the Algonquin Round Table scene.

Steve Ross is another of the pianist-singers who has been playing the clubs for many years. Like Mary Cleere Haran, he has specialized in conceptual tributes to songwriters and themes on movies, individual stars, and the like. The salute Ross performed at the Algonquin Hotel, shown above, was titled *Noel Coward and His Ladies* (the object of Ross's affection in the picture is special guest star Jeanne Lehman).

Noel Coward was one of the most influential artists of the British theater as an actor, playwright, composer, and vocalist. Coward's wry observations on the human condition (usually of the bored upper class) found favor in America via his own droll performances, as well as the sophisticated cabaret artists who were drawn to his work. "Mad About the Boy," "Poor Little Rich Girl," "A Room With a View," "Let's Fly Away," "The Younger Generation," and "Mad Dogs and Englishmen" are some of Coward's notable compositions. Noel Coward was viewed by many theatrical observers to be the British equivalent of America's Cole Porter. They both wrote music lyrics and are foremost on the list of Cabaret performers. Ross, along with Julie Wilson and Bobby Short, has been one of the most successful cabaret interpreters of Noel Coward's works.

Since the 1980s there has been a renewed interest in the elegant cabaret tradition, no doubt a reflection of the revival movement of the 1970s. Some cabaret performers, like Steve Ross and Dardanella, are veterans who would have made their livelihood with or without the revival, while others, like Jeff Harnar and Mary Cleere Haran, were given opportunities they otherwise might not have had. Donald Smith, president of the National Cabaret Association, points out that cabaret artists have been getting more jobs recently and business has been healthy in the 1990s. Smith also feels that the title "cabaret" is "too precious and recherche. Cabaret is just a new word for saloon singing."

In 1988, Smith organized the Mabel Mercer Foundation, dedicated to the preservation and continuation of the art of cabaret. Each fall the foundation holds a week-long celebration of cabaret. In October 1993 a total of 120 artists, including Julie Wilson, Richard Rodney Bennett, John Wallowitch, and Ann Hampton Callaway, performed at Town Hall in New York. Erv Raible, the owner of the cabaret Eighty Eight's, cofounded the Manhattan Association of Cabarets. As president of MAC he created the MAC

Awards, which is a version of the Emmys. There are also the annual Bistro Awards for cabaret. Cabaret may have a small audience, but its following is an intense and devoted one.

Of all of the celebrated newcomers to cabaret, Harry Connick, Jr., and Michael Feinstein have made the greatest impression on audiences outside the intimate world of the nightclub set. Connick, from New Orleans, is really an eclectic jazzman who happened to find cabaret favor when he performed at the historic Algonquin Hotel's Oak Room and then found even greater success singing on the soundtrack of the romantic comedy *When Harry Met Sally* (1988). Feinstein, on the other hand, is a non-jazz player who is closer to the cabaret spirit of Mercer and Short.

Michael Feinstein (1957-   ) is a native of Columbus, Ohio. Unlike the youth of his generation, Feinstein did not get turned on by rock music. "When I was a kid and other kids were listening to pop music, I was listening to my parents' records of Al Jolson and Beatrice Kay. My father was a member of SPEBQSA [Society for the Preservation and Encouragement of Barbershop Quartet Singing in America]. He would take me to meetings and I would harmonize with the guys. I never listened to the radio. I completely missed the Beatles. Gershwin music spoke to me at a very early age." In 1977 Ira Gershwin hired the twenty-year-old Feinstein to organize the legendary catalogue of the Gershwin library. Feinstein stayed with Gershwin as his librarian until the lyricist's death six years later. Feinstein played the clubs of New York, gaining an avid follower in Liza Minnelli, who even threw a party at New York's Le Mondrian so she could introduce the tuxedoed pianist-singer to her friends and family. A critically acclaimed stay at the Oak Room of the Algonquin Hotel, and successful recordings, beginning in 1985, created a buzz in the industry that there was a new star on the scene in the world of cabaret. Feinstein became the most conscientious and historically accurate of the newer generation of cabaret performers. Some detractors feel he is too consumed and precious with his renderings of the classic standards. The majority opinion, however, is that Feinstein is a peerless conservationist who sings beautifully and accompanies himself with fluid grace.

Courtesy Elektra Records & Morra, Brezner, Steinberg & Tenenbaum

The top young cabaret star to emerge since the mid-1980s is Michael Feinstein. Like most performers in cabaret, Feinstein was well aware of history of Tin Pan Alley, the Alleymen, and the nature of the world of cabaret. He wrote of his big break at the Algonquin Hotel: "What a thrill it has been to sing in the Oak Room of the Algonquin Hotel! I never dreamed that I would one day have the opportunity to follow in the footsteps of Greta Keller, Julie Wilson and Steve Ross."

Creme de la Creme Singers

Vocalist	Specialty
Karen Akers	Ermine and pearls elegance singing the classics from Richard Rodgers to Cole Porter
Laurie Beechman	New star rising in classy settings such as New York's Rainbow and Stars Room
Richard Rodney Bennett	Singer-pianist jazzier than most, but British veneer lends touch of Noel Coward class
Betty	Sassy trio from Washington, D.C.; look at '90s romance with humorous song "First Date"
Ann Hampton Callaway	One of the brightest and best of the new breed of cabaret piano player-singers
Barbara Carroll	Evolved from bop pianist to elegant singer-pianist at Bemelman's Bar in New York's Hotel Carlyle
Dixie Carter	"Designing Women" with cabaret panache; *Dixie Carter Sings John Wallowitch Live at the Carlyle*
Charles Cochran	The gentlest of the pianist-singer-balladers; retired to West Palm, Florida.
Harry Connick, Jr.	Jazzier than Feinstein, together they've been a contemporary force for young audiences; Connick no longer a true creme de la creme performer, but his star began to rise after he left New Orleans and gained recognition in New York's Oak Room at the Algonquin Hotel
Barbara Cook	The librarian from Broadway's *Music Man* is a dramatic, high-voltage star; she plays classiest rooms
Dardanella	Veteran pianist-vocalist still blending her unique sound that utilizes vibes with a jazzy touch
Michael Feinstein	Archivist, proselytizer for faithfully rendered incarnations of the standard song form
Mary Cleere Haran	Girl-next-door demeanor who knowingly interlaces great singing with wry commentary and a breezy touch of jazz inflection
Jeff Harner	New star pianist-singer with penchant for theme evenings such as "The 1959 Broadway Songbook," "Dancing in the Dark," and "Vincente Minnelli's Hollywood"
Hildegarde	White gloves & roses; "First Lady of the Supper Clubs"; "Darling, Je Vous Aime Beaucoup"
Robert Kraft	New kid on the block; original '80s slant on form; his contemporary classic is "Cafe Society"
Barbara Lea	The closest we have to the radiance of Lee Wiley today; finds forgotten gems and sings with jazzmen
Andrea Marcovicci	Actress with humor & pathos acclaimed as both Ophelia and St. Joan by New York scribes
Amanda McBroom	Singer-songwriter of "The Rose"; an emotionally charged original talent
Susannah McCorkle	Carrying the cabaret and jazz torch for lovers of husky-voiced standard interpretations; very versatile —she is also covered in the section of the Jazz Cabaret Cult Singers
Maureen McGovern	From "Disaster Theme Queen" to dramatic cabaret princess who plays classier venues
Steve Ross	Singer-pianist of quiet, composed elegance; concept programs of Noel Coward & Fred Astaire
K. T. Sullivan	Like Mary Cleere Haran, presents conceptual shows such as "Ladies of the Silver Screen"
Marlene Ver Planck	Veteran studio & jingles performer with warmth and taste; longtime favorite of the *New Yorker*
Weslia Whitfield	Smoky alto from San Francisco ably assisted by pianist-husband Mike Greensill; mesmerizing ballads
Ronny Whyte	Singer-pianist-interperter of "smart" songs like "Madeira M' Dear?" and "Mary Tyler Moore"
Cassandra Wilson	Mixes far-out Brooklyn jazz connections with Sarah Vaughanish vocalizing; jazzier than most

Also singing in the cabarets: Tom Anderson, Betty Buckley, Baby Jane Dexter, Nancy Dussault, Bernard Fowler, Nancy Harrow, Arnie Hughes, Roslyn Kind, Nancy LaMott, Phillip Officer, Jill O'Hara, Lee Roy Reams, Daryl Sherman, Billy Strich, Wiseguys, and Sara Zahn.

Every cosmopolitan city has a cabaret piano player-singer who entertains by mesmerizing the audience with a command of the "old songs"—in a sense, upon any request they can "play it again, Sam." For example, Buffalo, New York's "King of Cabaret" since the 1950s has been the supremely talented **Jackie Jocko,** who mixes cabaret ballads with boppish piano lines, and campy humor reminiscent of the late-great Francis Faye.

Courtesy Atlantic Records

Ahmet Ertegun brought in his brother Neshui to shore up the jazz end of the company during the 1950s, when rhythm and blues was the money-making style. In spite of all the shifts of styles, Atlantic always had a soft spot for sophisticated cabaret singers. Ahmet was brought up surrounded by affuence. He and Neshui were raised in Washington, D.C., where their father was the Turkish ambassador to the United States. They went to debutante balls and high society affairs. Cabaret was in their background and they specialized in it when they ran Atlantic Records.

This compiliation covers the broad spectrum of New York cabaret. Highlights include broad, raucous barrelhouse blues from Mae Barnes ("Rinka Tinka Man"); elegant and lyrical piano from Joe Bushkin ("I Can't Get Started"), Cy Walter ("Who Cares"), Jimmy Lyon ("Just One of Those Things"), and Billy Taylor ("Thou Swell"); sophisticated, non jazzy cabaret singing from Greta Keller ("My Ship") and Ted Straeter ("What's New"); jazzy cabaret from Joe Mooney ("Nina Never Knew"), Chris Connor ("I Miss You So"), Mel Torme ("Manhattan"), and Carmen McRae ("I'm Always Drunk in San Francisco"); and numerous samplings of Atlantic cabaret regulars Mabel Mercer, Hugh Shannon, and Bobby Short.

The Jazz Cabaret Cult Singers

Mark Murphy, seen above, during his Charles Boyer period (Boyer was an international film star during the 1930s and 1940s). Murphy has been one of the most underrated of all jazz singers, inexplicably immune to interest on the part of the powerful jazz critics. Murphy's performance history, his creative recorded works since 1957, and the high regard in which he is held by other singers make him a "singer's singer." Many jazz artists found their careers in a tailspin when the bottom fell out of jazz in the 1960s, due mostly to the rise in popularity of the Beatles and the other artists of the British Invasion in 1964. Murphy anticipated the hard times by moving to Europe from 1962 to 1972. Even though he made a career of recording with orchestras in England and Holland, Murphy still had the problem of meshing his cabaret and jazz work. "In a way, I guess I was still trying to be a cabaret singer in a tuxedo, but singing the things I liked. It just didn't work."

A majority of the "jazz cabaret cult singers" have been in the music profession for thirty years, and record for the smaller, independent record labels (though many of them may have recorded for major labels at one time). Most of these vocalists entered the business just after the swing era, when jazz and cabaret styles were being eclipsed by rock'n'roll. They all emerged from the cabaret setting of small, intimate clubs and sing a repertoire of sophisticated standard songs as well as modern jazz compositions. These lesser-known singers often travel from city to city without a regular group, unlike the jazz-pop celebrities.

Mark Murphy and the duo of Jackie Cain and Roy Kral are two leaders of this movement. Their versatility allows them to be embraced by the followers of both the jazz and cabaret traditions. Joe Williams, the eminent jazz pop vocalist, stated in a May 1995 *Down Beat* listening test, "Kids in schools who want to learn to scat proficiently should listen to one or two soloists. And by all means, Jackie and Roy, and Mark Murphy, too." More often than not, however, these audiences are split. Many jazz fans and critics claim that the cabaret tradition's careful approach to a clearly enunciated verse and chorus is not rhythmic enough and that these singers fail to take enough liberties with the lyrics. Instead they often will sing the song exactly as the author intended, especially ballads. Yet these same singers have been labeled too jazzy by many of the followers of the "creme de la creme cabaret" tradition because they

311

experiment with complex harmonies, are noted scat singers, and are historically associated with vocalese (placing words to previously recorded jazz instrumentals). The cabaret audience of Mabel Mercer and Bobby Short gets a bit nervous when singers like Mark Murphy create long, "difficult" scat selections—the style being too jumpy, exotic, and far-out for their sensibilities. The fact that the jazz aspect places an emphasis on instrumental and rhythmic elements, while cabaret is more concerned with mood and lyrics puts the jazz carbaret cult singer in a bind. These singers straddle two worlds.

Jazz historian Joachim Berendt has called this problem the "jazz-vocal dilemma." Jazz derives from instrumental music, but jazz singers must sing words. A good example of how a jazz cabaret cult singer combines these two styles can be seen in Mark Murphy's program at a 1979 Carnegie Hall recital concert. In the first half of the concert he sang the cabaret set that he called his "New York songs": compositions by Cy Coleman, Alec Wilder, and Harold Arlen, plus thematic medleys about New York ("Autumn in New York"/"Manhattan"/"Give It Back to the Indians"), sugar ("When I Take My Sugar to Tea"/"Sugar"/"My Sugar Is So Refined"/"Never Leave Your Sugar Standing in the Rain"), and clowns ("Laugh, Clown, Laugh"/"Send in the Clowns"). The second half of the concert featured his modern jazz roots: Horace Silver's "Senor Blues," Gigi Gryce's "Farmer's Market," Benny Golson's "I Remember Clifford," a long medley of Miles Davis songs, and three jazz compositions that Murphy set to lyrics: Herbie Hancock's "Cantaloupe Island," Freddie Hubbard's "Red Clay," and Oliver Nelson's "Stolen Moments."

Jazz Cabaret Cult Singers

Singer	Comments
Lorez Alexandria	Distinctive voice and a warm, husky jazz delivery
David Allyn	Ex-Boyd Raeburn singer who excels on slow ballads; full, rich baritone of great warmth
Ernestine Anderson	Texas gospel roots make for compelling blues interpretations; amply recorded on Concord
Andy Bey	Versatile singer-pianist with range on all types of songs; very eclectic
Oscar Brown, Jr.	At his best with his own songs in cabaret-theater settings; creative blues and jazz stylist
Freddie Cole	Brother of Nat, uncle of Natalie; plays great piano and sounds like his brother (who else?)
Chris Connor	Smoky-voiced jazz stylist who has been a major talent since the 1950s; "All About Ronnie"
Joe Derise	Long-time favorite pianist-singer whose records can be found on the Audiophile label
Matt Dennis	Composer-singer-pianist; wrote "Witchcraft" and "Violet for Your Furs," among many others
Frank D'Rone	Chicago baritone whose guitar accompaniment is as tasteful as ever; another underrated talent
Georgia Fame	Hip British pianist-singer; "Sweet Georgia Fame" by Blossom Dearie; underrated jazz talent
Nancy Harrow	Began as blues chanteuse; now includes standard cabaret fare
Bill Henderson	Full-throated interpreter finding success as film character actor; City Slickers
Jon Hendricks	The "James Joyce of Jive" still keeps the flame burning as solo & with regular group
Etta Jones	Noted for her ballad classics like "Don't Give to Strangers," and "Don't Misunderstand"
Shelia Jordan	Pure bop roots, one of most challenging and inventive vocalists; duets with bassist Harv Schwartz
Bev Kelly	Underrated talent last heard on soundtrack of film The Late Show; early Riverside records rewarding
Morgana King	More sophisticated balladeer than bopper, but exquisite ballads
Nancy King	'90s recordings with bassist Glen Moore wildly eclectic
Janet Lawson	Competent experimentalist of bop and "new thing" (free jazz) sources
Barbara Lea	Lee Wiley-like voice more at home with Dixieland classics
Tom Lellis	Mark Murphy-influenced singer-pianist who investigates post-'60s jazz standards
Abby Lincoln	Dramatic vocalist with dark, burnished, glowing jazz interpretations
Tania Maria	Brazilian, plays mean piano and scats up a storm
Helen Merrill	Singer-producer of demanding material; challenging interpretations
Ann Marie Moss	Bop-pop interpreter once worked with Jon Hendricks and ex-husband Jackie Paris
Jackie Paris	This bopper of "Skylark" fame has a big voice; he is still playing and still vastly underrated
Judy Roberts	Creative singer-pianist mixes rock, bop, and ballads tastefully
Annie Ross	An original girl bop hipster seen in films of Robert Altman (Short Cuts)
Carole Sloane	Continues to get better and better; a luminous sound; recorded in the '90s on Concord
Bobby Troupe	Laconic West Coast pianist-singer-composer; wrote "Route 66" classic
Marano and Monteiro	Duo blending ballads and bebop scat songs to multidimensional-sounding accordion

Also significant (deceased): Earl Coleman, Johnny Hartman, Eddie Jefferson, Teddi King, Irene Kral, Dave Lambert, Jimmy Rowles, Bobby Scott, Maxine Sullivan, Sylvia Syms

VOL. 16—NO. 6

(Copyright, 1949, Down Beat Publishing Co.)

CHICAGO, APRIL 8, 19

Conte, Boots Join Ventura's Bop-Styled Band

Courtesy Down Beat

Jackie and Roy as scatting beboppers in 1949 with Charlie Ventura's Bop for the People unit. The *Down Beat* caption reads, "New York—Two new men were in the Charlie Ventura band when this photo was taken at the Royal Roost. Both ex-Stan Kentonites, trumpeter Conte Condoli and altoist Boots Mussulli (here playing baritone) replaced Norman Faye and Ben Ventura respectively. Also in the photo above are singer Jackie Cain, tenorist Ventura, bassist Ken O'Brien, and trombonist Benny Green. Out of sight are drummer Ed Shaughnessy and pianist Roy Kral. The group left the Roost after 10 weeks."

A December 28, 1955, *Down Beat* article declared, "Jackie and Roy have been called 'Peter Lind Hayes and Mary Healy of Jazz,' and that's not inappropriate at all. For Jackie and Roy have the same sophisticated yet broadbased wit and they have style and flair and class. They have versatility, too, as evidenced by the way they fit easily into clubs ranging from Cafe Society to Birdland."

Jackie Cain (1928-) and **Roy Kral** (1921-) came together as members of the highly visible and popular Charlie Ventura unit in 1948; "Bop for the People." Kral, a pianist-composer-arranger-singer, did radio work in Detroit after World War II and joined Ventura's band as a pianist. Cain was discovered by radio personality Dave Garroway, who later found fame as the original *Today Show* host. The two singers were teamed by Ventura to sing novelty bop arrangements that blended their voices in a unison scat not unlike the earlier experiments of Buddy Stewart and Dave Lambert with the Gene Krupa band (1946's "What's This?"). Jazz authority Leonard Feather referred to this distinct harmonized scatting to boppish numbers as "vocalese," but a better term is probably "unison scat" because most jazz authorities view vocalese as putting words to existing instrumental jazz recordings.

Cain and Kral's unison scat songs included a Ventura-Kral selection, "Euphoria" and a song called "I'm Forever Blowing Bubbles," which made them one of the hippest duos on the music scene. Cain and Kral were married in 1949 and throughout the 1950s and 1960s worked most of the major American jazz clubs.

An example of the split between straight-ahead jazz vocalizing and cabaret—that "jazz-vocal dilemma"—occurred for the first time for the duo in the 1950s. Kral recalls that through a friend they met Alec Wilder, who loved their sound. Wilder got them an audition with Max Gordon at the Blue Angel in New York. According to Cain, "Because jazz clubs were closing and there were more chances to work supper clubs, we had to soft-pedal the jazz elements. We maintained the jazz backgrounds and harmonics, but cut down on the vocalese and toned down some of the blowing choruses. The Blue Angel audiences didn't exactly welcome us with open arms. We had a lot of fans coming in, but there was a certain element of the audience that really didn't understand what we were trying to do."

When the British Invasion and the new rock of the '60s came along, Jackie and Roy, as they were known professionally, didn't stop working like many jazz artists did. Instead, they recorded versions of what they considered to be some of the "best" of the newer songs—those of the Beatles, Paul Simon, and John Sebastian. They made commercial jingles and played the lounges of Las Vegas until the 1970s and the revival of interest in "older songs."

Reunited with their old friend Creed Taylor on his CTI label (they had recorded for him in the 1950s on ABC Paramount Records), Jackie and Roy recorded two exquisitely arranged LPs: *Time and Love* (1972) and *A Wilder Alias* (1973). Cain, who has one of the most beautiful voices in all of jazz, was always given solo songs to do in concert and on record. But it was as a duo that this unit made their mark. Jackie and Roy's rhythmically driving arrangements on selections such as "Mountain Greenery" (on *Sweet and Low Down*, Columbia, 1960), "Daahoud" (*Concert by the Sea*, Concord, 1980), and "Anthropology" (*East of Suez*, Concord Jazz, 1981), assured their title as the "Lovebirds of Jazz." They courted the cabaret crowd with chic evocations of theatrical projects such as *The Stephen Sondheim Collection* (Finesse, 1982), *We've Got It: The Music of Cy Coleman* (Discovery, 1984), and *One More Rose: A Tribute to Alan Jay Lerner* (Audiophile, 1987).

As the 1990s began, more and more of the jazz clubs and cabarets of yesteryear began to close up or shorten their bookings (instead of six day stays, most niteries brought artists in for weekends or just one night). As a result, Jackie and Roy, while not forgotten, do less night club work than they once did. Most jazz and cabaret vocalists have had to deal with this reality.

Courtesy Audiophile Records

Jazz duo Jackie and Roy with the late Alec Wilder (left). Throughout their career they have been supporters of Wilder's compositions. In concert and cabaret settings they regularly sing Wilder's "It's So Peaceful in the Country," "While We're Young," and "Mimosa and Me." Wilder referred to himself as president of the "derriere garde," a reference to his low profile in the popular music world caused by his preference for older material. The scholarly gentleman had low tolerance for what he considered inferior music, bad taste, and phoniness. Wilder split his living accommodations between Rochester, New York and the Algonquin Hotel. Wilder was revered by many top musicians and celebrated in Whitney Balliett's book *Alec Wilder and His Friends*.

Courtesy Finesse Records

Jackie and Roy with Stephen Sondheim (right). Sondheim's compositions are not part of the jazz repertoire. His songs are not the typical 32-bar pop formula. As a result, very few Sondheim songs have been chosen by jazz performers as part of their vocal and instrumental repertoire. Jackie Cain mused, "I was afraid that the music didn't lend itself to jazz treatment, that it wasn't really in our realm." But after repeatedly hearing Kral's musical arrangements, she became intrigued because the music and the lyrics were complex but satisfying. The duo debuted the music at Michael's Pub in 1979.

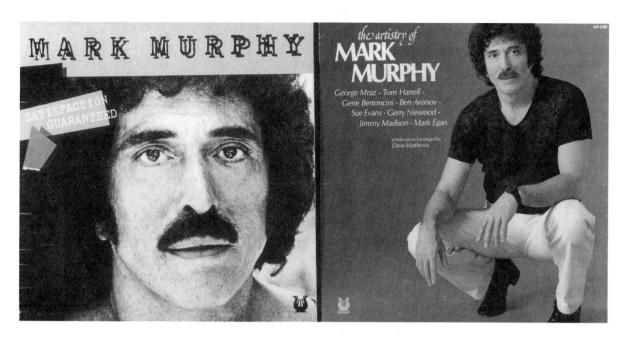

The artistry of Mark Murphy. Mark Murphy's abilities as a jazz artist can be attributed to his understanding of the harmony components of the music, which he learned as a piano player and arranger. This is particularly apparent when Murphy scats - he has a rare ability to scat like an instrumentalist because of his harmonic scope. Jazz pianist-singer Richard Rodney Bennett, quoted in Kitty Grime's book *Jazz Voices,* underscores this: "I think the people I admire most, like Sarah Vaughan, Carmen McRae, Mark Murphy, Shirley Horn, come out of being piano players."

The ability to mix the best of the cabaret world with that of bebop and beyond has always presented a problem for vocalists. Like Jackie and Roy, Murphy has the ability to choose the best of cabaret and relishes singing all the verses (including introductory verses that partly act as dialog, half-spoken and half-sung as a transition into the song) begin the songs with the main melody as well as mixing into his program jazz originals by composers such as Gil Evans, Miles Davis, Sonny Rollins, and Herbie Hancock.

Like the best instrumental improvisers, Murphy's career has always hovered on the exploratory edge. Whether he chooses to record Nat King Cole songs, where he has picked the "B" sides, like forgotten gems such as "I Keep Going Back to Joe's," "Calypso Blues," and "Don't Let Your Eyes Go Shopping," or intermingles bop and the prose of Jack Kerouac and the beat movement (the *Bop for Kerouac* releases), or navigates the British "acid jazz" scene in the mid 1980s. There has always been a sense of exploration in Murphy's work. Neil Tesser writes, "Audaciousness is nothing new to Mark Murphy, singer, erstwhile actor, sometime screenwriter, teller of tales. It has been there since one of his earliest recordings, a 1961 album titled *Rah*, and has steadily grown in the years after. As the singer has matured, the songs have been steeped in still more bravura; from the broadest overview to the slightest quirks in phrasing, everything has come to reflect this bold sense of adventure."

Mark Murphy (1932-   ) was born in Fulton, New York, and raised in a musical family. Sometime during his youth, Murphy's uncle played an Art Tatum record, "Humoresque," and then his older brother, Doc, brought home the sounds of Woody Herman and Stan Kenton. Doc formed a six-piece swing band in high school. Mark, who had learned to play piano by that time, began to go to rehearsals, and when Doc graduated, Mark took over as pianist and singer.

After high school Murphy attended Syracuse University, where he became involved in theater, playing Shakespeare, Gilbert and Sullivan, and even experimental one act plays. After college Murphy moved to New York, where he had a chorus part in *Casey at the Bat.* With money made from summer stock roles, Murphy made a demonstration record of four of his versions of standard tunes. These suggested Murphy's ability to write arrangements for his recordings and for his club back-up groups. With the help of Sammy Davis, Jr., Murphy signed a recording contract with Milt Gabler of Decca Records in 1956. *Meet Mark Murphy*, released in 1957, combined Murphy with the arrangements of Ralph Burns on a series of standard selections.

After Decca, Murphy joined Capitol for three LPs, beginning with *This Could Be the Start of Something* (1959). The follow-up, *Hip Parade* (1960), was one of the first attempts to place a jazz singer in the context of top 40 rock material. The problem for a newcomer on a major label was that he had to stand in line to be heard and pushed by the label's record distributors. The Kingston Trio was doing one quarter of Capitol's business, and then there was Sinatra, Nat Cole, Dean Martin, Peggy Lee, and George Shearing—an embarrassment of riches.

Courtesy Irene Haupt & Buffalo Philharmonic

The Harold Arlen tribute. Mark Murphy and Ernestine Anderson in 1980, singing straight ballads and boppish jazz tunes with the Buffalo Philharmonic Orchestra at a sellout house for a "Harold Arlen Tribute." This was Buffalo's deep bow of gratitude to Arlen, its most famous songwriting son, but it was initiated by out-of-towner Murphy, who had tried for five years to get the project produced.

At this point Murphy moved to the smaller, independent companies, beginning with Riverside in 1963 (*Rah*) and eventually, in 1972, to Muse (*Bridging the Gap*). Murphy created an unusual alliance with Joe Fields at Muse. Instead of royalties and advertisement advances Murphy received a flat fee in exchange for creative freedom to put together conceptual releases that struck his fancy. The result has been one of the most imaginative vocal histories on record. Because of abilities as an arranger and pianist, Murphy has an acute harmonic sense, and he often sings the harmony of the song rather than the melody. As a result he has been referred to as "a singer's singer," "a musician's singer," and "ahead of his time." Jazz critic Leonard Feather has called Murphy "a vocal musician," and Ella Fitzgerald declared, "He's my equal." Alec Wilder admitted, "I honestly consider him one of the very few great singers I have ever heard."

Commenting on Murphy's experimenting from album to album, Will Friedwald says in *Jazz Singers,* "Murphy has devoted his career to exploring all genres known to jazz long before terms like 'eclecticism' and 'neoclassical' became hundred-dollar secret words in the jazz press. He's the Woody Herman of vocalists, being too intrigued by whatever worthwhile movement comes along to limit himself to a single 'house' sound. The streets are still littered with deep thinkers scratching their heads over whether or not Murphy is a 'jazz singer,' but while they ponder the 'jazz' half of the term, he's unconcernedly experimenting with the 'singing' half: letting his spiels and intersong patter seamlessly meander into the music, combining singing with recitations of text and poetry. Murphy switches techniques like other singers do songs, often sequencing directly from one to another like numbers in a medley. No singer, in fact, has ever valued jazz as highly as Mark Murphy."

As might be expected, there are many other worthy vocalists who can be placed in the rather narrowly defined category of the jazz-cabaret cult singer. Brief note must be made of two of the most successful singers of recent times, Betty Carter and Shirley Horn. **Betty Carter** (1929-   ), who had her start with Lionel Hampton in the late 1940s and was known as "Bebop Betty," has gained universal acclaim for her adventurous renderings of the standard song form. Like Murphy, Carter is an experimentalist supreme. She has claimed that the greatest influences on her career were jazz saxophonists Charlie Parker and Sonny Rollins, and her ingenious scatting abilities place her in their company—she is the most capable and inventive vocal improviser on the scene. There are a number of "post-Betty Carter" singers, like Carmen Lundy and Cassandra Wilson, but no female during the 1980s and 1990s has matched Carter's expansiveness and artistry. According to Will Friedwald, Carter is "the best thing happening to jazz singing today."

During the 1980s and 1990s the most celebrated jazz vocalist has been Betty Carter. Jackie and Roy, Mark Murphy, Shirley Horn, and Carter are all part of a mutual admiration society. They visit each others' nightclub performances and praise one another. Carter has been a strong, independent voice throughout her career. She is an extension of Ella Fitzgerald and Sarah Vaughan but adds a soaring, asymmetrical use of musical structure. Bassist Buster Williams said about working with Carter, "Betty is a real musician, and you can play with her just like you would play with any other strong musician. You don't have to hold back or add flowers to the changes. Whatever you know and hear you can use."

Linda Dahl's study of women in jazz, *Stormy Weather: The Music and Lives of a Century of Jazzwomen*, states that, "Betty Carter's sound is so hornlike as to crumble the distinction between vocal and nonvocal jazz. As much as any gifted instrumentalist, Carter has expanded the possibilities of the art of improvisation. In concert she carefully builds her delivery of superfast up-tempo tunes, medium-tempo standards and ballads, pouring herself out on stage like a fine actress or athlete. By the end of the set Betty Carter usually has her audience on its feet. The performance over, the intense body still, she stands at rest, spent like a runner after the race."

Courtesy Polygram Records

After leaving the Lionel Hampton band, Betty Carter didn't have any hit songs to sustain her in the business; she only had a moniker, "Bebop Betty." It wouldn't be until the mid-1970s that Carter started receiving due recognition, which resulted in better club dates. The *Village Voice*, an influential alternative newspaper in New York City, began writing her up. Critic-musician Stanley Crouch was her biggest supporter, and that resulted in a major career boost. Leslie Gourse writes in *Louis' Children: American Jazz Singers*, "At the same time as vintage swing and bebop jazz were coming back into vogue, Betty Carter was getting high cover charges in the best jazz clubs, zooming upward toward concert-artist status for singing Free Jazz—out-and out jazz. If you say that phrase aloud, you will get an inkling of Miss Betty Carter's style if you have never heard of her. She is the only jazz singer who can swing while giving you intimations of Honegger and a flying saucer accident."

In *American Singers*, Whitney Balliett gives an apt description of this surrealist interpreter of song. "Betty Carter is a shock at first hearing, she abstracts her song. She converts her melodies into srangely shaped fragments made up of long-held notes, many of them bent; clusters of eighth notes; quick, driving arpeggios; and a variety of hums and moans. Capacious silences often separate her phrases. The melody, viewed through the heavy scrim of her style, is sometimes there, sometimes not. She stretches time even farther than Billie Holiday. She will sing a song like 'Spring Can Really Hang You Up the Most' in a very slow tempo. This allows her to rocket in and out of double, and even triple, time, to wallow luxuriously along in the chosen tempo, and to engage in a kind of staccato parlando."

Courtesy Calumet Arts Cafe

Nancy Marano and Eddie Monteiro emerged as one of the newest jazz-cabaret cult performance units during the late 1980s. They blend their voices in a unique manner that flows as easily with bebop as it does with the standard song form and Brazilian bossa nova. Monteiro's accordion is a specially produced instrument that can create sounds not only of an accordion but also of vibes, piano, harmonica, and flute. There has never been, in jazz, an accordion sound quite like this.

317

Shirley Horn (1934-), a gently swinging pianist-singer, returned to the music scene in the late 1980s after a long break to raise her child. Essentially her comeback began in 1987 with a series of releases featuring her smooth and pristine vocal renderings of standard tunes. Eschewing the boppish daring of Carter, Horn chose instead to deliberately slow things down. Only Ray Charles can match her brilliance in creating a mesmerizing and spellbinding hold on the listener with "slow-motion swing" interpretations. *Close Enough for Love* (1988), *You Won't Forget Me* (1990), *Here's to Life* (1992), *Light Out of Darkness* (a tribute to Ray Charles, 1993), and *I Love Paris* (1994) offer perfect examples of Horn's incandescent artistry.

Courtesy Jazz Times

Courtesy Calumet Arts Cafe

Horn is another example of a cult performer who finally received much-deserved recognition late in life. When she signed a record contract with Polygram (Verve) and released *Live at Vine Street* (*I Thought About You*) in 1987, Horn put to rest the fears that she would never be heard outside of the Washington, D.C., area, where she resides. On the strength of that album (it made the top 25 on *Billboard's* jazz chart), Horn began touring the country playing the bigger jazz rooms. Later albums did even better (*Here's to Life* topped the *Billboard* jazz chart for many weeks) and a music video of one of Horn's recording sessions was eventually generated. Arranger-composer Johnny Mandel (writer of "The Shadow of Your Smile" and arranger for everyone from Tony Bennett to Peggy Lee and Mel Torme) praised Horn in a 1992 article in *Jazz Times:* "She's the one to whom they pay deference. But she also gives the best lyric reading."

Mandel, who won a 1991 Grammy for his arrangements of Natalie Cole's tremendously successful, career-turning album *Unforgettable*, tried to put Horn's belated success into perspective: "There's an audience for Shirley that has emerged from a lot of people in their 40s, 50s, and earlier that are burned out on metal rap. And, you know, the old rockers, they listen to the Golden Oldie rock stations, they're kind of sick of a lot of the stuff, and they're beginning to realize that their parents' music isn't as bad as they thought. They're hearing those songs for the first time."

Susannah McCorkle reflects the "jazz cabaret cult" tradition. Although younger than the majority of the practioners of this style (her recording career began in the late 1970s), McCorkle melds the cabaret tradition with that of bebop. Her earliest releases focus on the songbook traditions of Harry Warren, E.Y. Harburg, and Johnny Mercer. Audiences and writers began to praise her husky, jazz-infused vocal stylings and soon she was signed by Concord Records. Of all her Concord recordings, the 1994 *From Broadway to Bebop* is probably the most representative of the total scope that a true "jazz cabaret cult" artist embodies. On the album, McCorkle belts out a Broadway classic, "Guys and Dolls" (with Frank Loesser's rediscovered "female" lyric dropped from the original show), and lesser known ballads from the stage. From Hollywood, McCorkle energizes Carmen Miranda's campy "Chica Chica Boom Chic," and a Roy Rogers classic from the 1944 film *Hollywood Canteen*, "Don't Fence Me In." She completes the cycle by singing the vocalese bebop classic "Moody's Mood," as well as self-composes lyrics to the Chet Baker trumpet solo on "My Buddy."

Rex Reed wrote in New York's *Daily News,* "When asking who the great singers of the future will be to carry on the work of Billie Holiday or Mabel Mercer, put this girl on the top of the list. She's become the most accomplished new artist on the girl singer trail . . . The talent's awesome!" McCorkle is also one of the most articulate and winning in-person performers on the circut. Along with Mary Cleere Haran, McCorkle's song introductions are like mini-history lessons on popular culture.

Bob Dorough (1923-   ) is a pianist-singer-composer who co-authored, with fellow pianist-singer-composer Dave Frishberg, one of the most popular underground songs of the 1980s and 1990s, "I'm Hip." Introduced to the cabaret audience by Blossom Dearie, with whom both have performed, "I'm Hip" is a hilarious, boastful claim about being a very with-it character. Dorough is a twangy-voiced singer whose sound is as distinctive as his jagged, irregular, bebop-inspired piano playing. Both he and Frishberg share the legacy of Hoagy Carmichael and songwriter Frank Loesser. Dorough emerged on the music scene during the early 1950s, when he went to Paris as the musical director for ex-middleweight boxing champion Sugar Ray Robinson, who had put a song and dance act together after he hung up his gloves. When Robinson decided to return to the ring, Dorough stayed on at the Mars Club, where he refined his vocal skills. Dorough eventually recorded with Blossom Dearie (singing in French) before heading back to the States.

In 1962, Dorough was contacted by trumpeter Miles Davis, who had been a fan of Dorough's first album, *Devil May Care* (1957), to write a Christmas song. When they recorded Dorough's "Blue Christmas," Frishberg and the singer gained wider recognition in jazz circles. The mid-1960s were tough on jazz performers (as noted, due to the British Invasion). Dorough, like Mark Murphy and Jon Hendricks, another bop-inspired singer, became an expatriate and is quoted in Bill Moody's *The Jazz Exiles* as saying, "Yes, there were even years I couldn't work in the U.S. Jazz was sort of buried by rock'n'roll, except for guys like Dizzy. My stuff just wasn't in vogue, so I got into producing." What Dorough produced was a Saturday cartoon educational tool titled "Schoolhouse Rock." Dorough lives in Pennsylvania's Pocono Mountains. Since the mid 1980s, Dorough has been touring Europe and the United States singing his compositions ("Better Than Anything," "But for Now," "Small Day Tomorrow," pretty ballads all, and tribute songs to jazz heroes like Hoagy Carmichael and Charlie Parker) and knocking out his beloved bebop piano lines. Dorough hasn't had the public acclaim of his friend Dave Frishberg, but he keeps the faith.

Another one of "Hoagy's children," **Dave Frishberg** (1933-   ) now lives on the West Coast after being raised in St. Paul, Minnesota, where as a child he loved listening to records and reading. Frishberg was inspired by the boogie woogie records of Pete Johnson, Albert Ammons, and Jay McShann, and later by the progressive sounds that enemated from Woody Herman's small band sides. Stylistically, Frishberg is a stride piano and mainstreamist who began his jazz career as an accompanist for the Eddie Condon gang, saxmen Al Cohn and Zoot Sims, and singer Carmen McRae, among many others. Frishberg's claim to fame in the jazz world has come from his portrait compositions ("Dear Bix," "Van Lingle Mungo," "Marilyn Monroe," "Zoot Walked In") and his witty observations of life ("My Attorney Bernie," "Blizzard of Lies," "Peel Me a Grape," "Another Song About Paris," and "Slappin' the Cakes on Me"). Cabaret singer Susannah McCorkle calls Frishberg "the Woody Allen of jazz," and Rex Reed observed, "His lyrics are jazzy and snazzy, his sound is a cross between Hoagy Carmichael and Mose Allison. If there is such a thing as a down-home preppie, it's Dave Frishberg. If an alligator could sing, it would probably sound like Dave Frishberg. His music is wrinkle free." Frishberg told Whitney Balliett in *American Singers*, "I don't have any regular work pattern. I'm not a workaholic, although I wish I were. It's easier to write songs to order than for myself. 'My Attorney, Bernie' was written for a friend who was celebrating twenty-five years as a lawyer. 'Listen Here' was done for Mary Tyler Moore. 'Dodger Blue' was written for the Dodgers, and tears came down Walt Alston's cheeks when he heard it. I set 'Van Lingle Mungo' to a romantic, Brazilian-type tune, and I think the contrast is what makes the song funny. When I sing, I want the audience to understand every syllable. Hoagy Carmichael heard me do some of his songs once, and told me, 'you don't have a real good voice, but I understood every word.'"

Dorough and Frishberg, voices of jazz. They share philosophical and music tastes born of the songwriting traditions of Frank Loesser, Johnny Mercer, and, of course, old Hoagy Carmichael. They both write and sing with a sense of nostalgia for simpler times, not coerced by technology or the rat race, but rather informed by a humanist good will touched by the free spirit of hip.

319

Cabaret's 25 Greatest Hits

Song	Composer-Lyricist	Singers
As Time Goes By	Herman Hupfeld	Lee Wiley
Ballad of the Sad Young Men	Tommy Wolf-Fran Landesman	Mark Murphy
Blame It on My Youth	Oscar Levant-Edward Heyman	Carmen McRae
Body and Soul	John Green-Edward Heyman-Robert Sour-Frank Eyton	Libby Holman
But Not for Me	George and Ira Gershwin	Rosemary Clooney
Come a Little Closer	John Wallowitch	Dixie Carter
Down in the Depths (On the Ninetieth Floor)	Cole Porter	Mabel Mercer
Fly Me to the Moon	Bart Howard	Felicia Sanders
Guess Who I Saw Today?	Murray Grand-Elisse Boyd	Carmen McRae
Here's That Rainy Day	Johnny Burke-James Van Heusen	Chris Connor
If Love Were All	Noel Coward	Julie Wilson
It Amazes Me	Cy Coleman-Carolyn Leigh	Blossom Dearie
It Never Entered My Mind	Richard Rodgers-Lorenz Hart	Jeri Southern
Just One of Those Things	Cole Porter	Bobby Short
Lush Life	Billy Strayhorn	Johnny Hartman
More Than You Know	Vincent Youmans-Edward Eliscu-Billy Rose	Sylvia Syms
My Ship	Kurt Weill-Ira Gershwin	Joanne Beretta
Old Friend	Gretchen Cryer-Nancy Ford	Ann Hampton Callaway
Once Upon a Time	Charles Strouse-Lee Adams	Steve Ross
One for My Baby (And One More for the Road)	Harold Arlen-Johnny Mercer	Frank Sinatra
Send In The Clowns	Stephen Sondheim	Sarah Vaughan
A Sleepin' Bee	Harold Arlen-Truman Capote	Barbara Streisand
This Moment	John Wallowitch	John Wallowitch
When the World Was Young	M. Philippe-Gerard-Johnny Mercer	Peggy Lee
While We're Young	Alec Wilder-Morty Palitz-William Engvick	Jackie Cain and Roy Kral

Source: March 1992, James Gavin, Town & Country; *Gavin wrote* Intimate Nights: The Golden Age of New York Cabaret, *1991.*

Camp Nostalgia

By the end of the halcyon 1960s and the denim dullness of Woodstock, a series of movements began in rock that suggested a reaction, a growing taste for glamour. The Beatles had just broken up and the new decade had a sense of self-discovery and new definition. No wonder then, that one of the biggest rock movements was that of the "Glitter Glam" tradition of Marc Bolan, Slade, Sweet, Gary Glitter, David Bowie, and Elton John. The roots of disco appeared during this time, as well as a confounding trip down memory lane called "camp nostalgia."

The camp nostalgia movement began when a camp-oriented performer named Tiny Tim made a record that featured his falsetto reading of Nick Lucas's 1929 hit, "Tip Toe Through the Tulips." Lucas was billed as the "Singing Troubador." Tiny Tim's 1969 rendition of the song not only brought him fame (Tim became a regular guest on Johnny Carson's "Tonight Show"), but it also ignited a fascination for "the old songs." Among other things, this resulted in an unorganized, disparate group of rock-oriented performers that chose to dig into the musical past of older standard songs. In some cases the result was a single conceptual album highlighting songs of the 1930s and 1940s (for example, Ringo Starr's 1970 *Sentimental Journey*). In others, it was a total environmental wrap of songs, clothing, and surroundings of the time period, such as Linda Ronstadt's 1983 *What's New?*

This final section will investigate this movement of primarily younger performers. In some cases the artist might be more closely tied to country music, e.g., Willie Nelson; in other cases the artist might include selections from the 1920s, e.g., Leon Redbone's penchant for pre-1930s ditties by Jelly Roll Morton, Jimmie Rodgers, and Bing Crosby. However, the great majority of selections rest firmly in the 1930s and 1940s.

Nostalgia is a longing for the best elements of something far away or long ago. The songs resurrected by the camp nostalgia movement are, for the most part, the best of the uptempo numbers, ballads, and novelties of the 1930s and 1940s. Another element of this movement is a sense of theatrics—that of camp. Camp is a tongue-in-cheek exaggeration of style that intentionally or unintentionally parodies itself. Often it is expressed by behaving or dressing in a theatrical or bizarre way in order to get attention. Camp can be banal, vulgar, flamboyant, and/or artificial. In his 1984 book *The Lie That Tells the Truth* (the title is drawn from an oft-quoted 1922 description of camp by artist-filmmaker Jean Cocteau), Philip Core points out that camp, originally a creation of gay culture, has two essential characteristics: 1) a secret within the personality that one ironically wishes to both conceal and exploit, and 2) a peculiar way of seeing things, caused by spiritual isolation, that is strong enough to impose itself on others through acts or creations. Core lists four basic features of camp: 1) irony, 2) aesthetics, 3) theatricality, and 4) humor.

With these definitions in mind, one can better understand the emergence of Bette Midler as the leader of the camp nostalgia movement of of early 1970s. Her dress, her chosen surrondings, and her material were in opposition to the youth scene of the late 1960s. Midler's use of Art Deco trappings, and old songs featuring her backup group, the Harlettes, trotting out in top hat and tails, was anathema to the rock audiences of the Woodstock era. Midler used camp humor and a dynamic stage persona to make this all work. The camp sensibility of her Continental Baths audience gave Midler the confidence to take her act further, to the "straight" mainstream crowd.

Courtesy Atlantic Records

Bette and the Baths. In a February 1973 feature article on Midler for *Rolling Stone* magazine, at the height of Midler's early celebrity, Ed McCormack wrote, "It is as if some high priestess at *Vogue* or *Bazaar* suddenly stood up and declared, 'This season we shall all go back to that wonderful period—Berlin, avant la guerre! Bette Midler has been celebrated and hailed everywhere as the bitching, dishing spin of camp, this wicked homosexual wit, so rich in its insights, finally surfacing in the mainstream in respectably feminine form."

The Divine Miss M on Atlantic Records. Camp nostalgia's early album art evoked the stylized art nouveau image that helped create the "look" of the movement. The Manhattan Transfer, also signed to Atlantic, used similar graphics on their early releases. The support of Atlantic Records executive Ahmet Ertegun and talk-show host Johnny Carson did much to transport Midler's brash talent to a more mainstream audience.

Bette Midler (1945-   ) was born in Paterson, New Jersey, but raised in Hawaii. Her high school aspiration was to become a dramatic actress. After high school, Midler took off for New York City with a thousand dollars she had saved from a role as an extra in the film *Hawaii!* (1965). While working as a typist at Columbia University, Midler toiled off-Broadway until she landed a three-year job with the successful Broadway hit *Fiddler on the Roof,* playing Tzeitel, the eldest daughter of the protagonist, Tevye. After the show's nightly performance she worked at local clubs, trying out material as a singer. At first Midler imitated Helen Morgan and Ruth Etting's torch approach, with songs like "Ten Cents a Dance," "My Forgotten Man," and "Am I Blue."

Midler spent her days at the library, digging up information about the singers and songs of the past. Her boyfriend at the time had a record collection of Morgan, Etting, the Boswell Sisters, and Billie Holiday, and Midler absorbed those sounds. She even dressed the part, finding Morgan-like outfits at the Salvation Army.

Midler's big break came when Stephen Ostrow caught her act at the Improv and signed her for fifty dollars a weekend—for one show a night on Friday and Saturday at 1 a.m—beginning in July 1970. Ostrow's club was no ordinary New York venue. It was a gay bathhouse called the Continental Baths, a luxurious, clean environment with a swimming pool, a dance floor, theater lights, palm trees, and neon all near the raised stage. Ostrow wanted to create "a full living cycle, a total environment."

In time Midler transformed herself from a sophisticated, torchy, Helen Morgan wannabe into a '40s-to '60s "trash with flash" belter in a black-lace corset and gold lame pedal pushers. With a "Shangri-las Fan Club" button affixed to her corset, Midler mixed old songs of the past with hot 1950s and early '60s girl-group classics by the Crystals, the Ronettes, the Dixie Cups, and her beloved Shangri-las. Add to this mix scoopfuls of broad double-entendre humor culled from Sophie Tucker, and a large swatch of gay-bitch, cult raillery, and a new persona was born: "The Divine Miss M."

LULLABY·OF·BROADWAY

FIRST NATIONAL PRESENTS

Gold Diggers
of
1935

FEATURING

DICK POWELL
GLORIA STUART
ADOLPHE MENJOU
GLENDA FARRELL
FRANK MᶜHUGH
HUGH HERBERT

DANCES BY
BUSBY BERKELEY

DIRECTED BY
ROBERT LORD

M.WITMARK & SONS
NEW YORK
MADE IN U.S.A.

LYRICS BY
AL DUBIN
MUSIC BY
HARRY WARREN

I'M GOIN' SHOPPIN'
WITH YOU
THE WORDS ARE
IN MY HEART
LULLABY OF
BROADWAY

Courtesy Buffalo & Erie County Public Library

Bette Midler's position as leader of the "camp nostalgia" movement of the 1970s is due as much to her choice of material as to her outrageous outfits and tongue-in-cheek stage vamping. Midler often shared her awareness of America's popular music of the past with her audiences. When playing the New York Palace for the first time, Midler educated her young followers about the *George White Scandals* revues housed by the Palace during the 1920s and 1930s. Midler sang difficult torch songs of the past like Johnny Mercer and Hoagy Carmichael's "Skylark," Kurt Weill's "Surbaya Johnny," and Johnny Mercer's "Drinking Again." Uptempo numbers like "In the Mood" (the Glenn Miller hit of 1939) and Midler's early claim to fame, the Andrews Sisters' "Boogie Woogie Bugle Boy," among others, were the real crowd pleasers.

A word about "Lullaby of Broadway." In 1935 Harry Warren and Al Dubin provided an uptempo dance number to choreographer Busby Berkeley for the film *Gold Diggers of 1935.* As conceived by Berkeley, the number was a surrealistic interpretation of dream-like consequences. Wini Shaw is seen rising from bed very late after spending a night on the town with paramour Dick Powell. At the nightclub, chorus boys and girls tap dance (one of the few numbers in which Berkeley's crew actually dances) and weave about Shaw until she jumps off a balcony to her death. Very strange. The song almost didn't make it into the film because Jack Warner, who was running the studio at the time, didn't like the song. When Al Jolson heard the number, he told Warner he wanted the song for his next picture. Berkeley heard about this and demanded that it be used in the *Gold Diggers of 1935.* Not only did Midler record this number, she used it to open the second act, while descending from a giant highheeled shoe of her 1973 Palace Theater Broadway debut. This number was a spectacular success, and it evoked for Midler memories of her early love of old-time Broadway images. In a 1977 *Crawdaddy* magazine article by Timothy White, Midler recollected her past: "I will never forget that flash of happiness. It came when I sang 'Lullaby of Broadway' as the sixth grade's entry in the school talent show. All the classes voted and I got the $2 first prize."

Midler's frequent visits to Johnny Carson's "Tonight Show" introduced her to the entire nation and allowed Midler to play better-known "straight" clubs such as Mr. Kelly's in Chicago and The Downstairs at the Upstairs in New York. Midler was now making $1,500 per week at the Baths and even took her group on the road. The Bette Midler Traveling Troupe included a backup female trio, which she called her Bang Bangs, a tongue-in-cheek, cheesy unit officially labeled the Harlettes (Melissa Manchester was an original member). The troupe's rhythm section was headed by pianist and musical director Barry Manilow.

By the end of 1972, without benefit of a released recording, Midler filled Carnegie Hall and jammed thousands into New York's Central Park as part of the Shaefer Music Park concert series. The musical amalgamation presented during the "Divine Miss M" shows included Bessie Smith's "Empty Bed Blues," Helen Morgan and Libby Holman's "Something to Remember You By," Dorothy Lamour's "Moon Over Manakoora," the Chords and Crew Cuts' "Sh-Boom," and the Shangri-las' "Leader of the Pack"—the 1920s to the 1960s.

Ahmet Ertegun signed Midler to a record contract for Atlantic and her debut release, *The Divine Miss M* (1972) certified gold and produced two hit singles, "Do You Wanna Dance" and "Boogie Woogie Bugle Boy." Midler's reworking of "Bugle Boy" led to a return to music by the two remaining Andrews Sisters in a Broadway musical, *Over Here.* By the end of 1972 Midler had won *After Dark* magazine's "Ruby Award" as entertainer of the year, a Grammy Award as "Best New Artist," and a special Tony Award for "Superior Entertainment on the Broadway Stage" for her spectacular Palace Theatre presentation. The floodgates had opened for a full assault on the music of the 1930s and 1940s. Since then Midler has become an internationally celebrated star, writing books in addition to making motion pictures and appearing worldwide in concert.

Barry Manilow (1946-) studied at the New York College of Music and the Juilliard School of Music. In 1967 he was conductor-arranger for the "Ed Sullivan Show." He arranged and produced the first two Bette Midler albums before moving on in his own quest for stardom. Manilow would eventually gain great success as one of the biggest middle-of-the-road pop stars of the 1970s and 1980s. Between 1974 and 1983, Manilow had twenty-five top 40 hits, and his feat of having five LPs on the charts at once has been equalled only by Johnny Mathis and Frank Sinatra.

Because of this great success as a middle of the road artist (MOR), and perhaps because many of his songs seemed to pander to what critics sensed to be the lower depths of "wimp rock," Manilow has been variously described as the "peroxide puppet," or a "stuffed dummy." Seldom has such and all-around talent been taken to task so mercilessly by critics.

Manilow actually functioned on two levels within the revival movement. First, he provided '30s-'40s-like ballads and up tunes in newer material ("Mandy," "I Write the Songs," and "Looks Like We Made It") and revived chestnuts like "I Don't Want to Walk Without You," "Avenue C," and "Cloudburst, that didn't utilize the typical trappings of rock. On stage Manilow introduced to his widely based pop audience to the trappings of a glamorous, Hollywood-like studio set that smacked of the opulent MGM and 20th Century-Fox musicals of yesteryear.

Courtesy Arista Records

Musical arbiter of the '30s-'40s revival. While Bette Midler vamped her way into the hearts of her avid followers at the Continental Baths, it was the behind-the-scenes musical adaptations, arrangements, and orchestrations of musician Barry Manilow that gave substance to the flamboyant proceedings. Manilow thought like a musician. He was already aware of the big band sounds of Count Basie, the advanced vocals of the Boswell Sisters and the vocalese bebop experiments of Lambert, Hendricks, and Ross. This musical sophistication brought a glow to much of Midler's material and gave musical shape to her inquisitive yearnings for the older songs.

Even when Manilow was a middle of the road pop star, he brought to his audiences a high level of musicianship. In some ways Manilow's career was similar to that of 1920s superstar Paul Whiteman. Both were schooled musicians who found favor with the popular audiences of the day but were stung by critical disdain. However, both artists, within the context of popular music, presented jazz elements that few of their peers (in pop) were even attempting. Whiteman even allowed his jazz stars (Eddie Lang, Bix Beiderbecke, Henry Busse, Mildred Bailey, the Rhythm Boys/Bing Crosby) brief moments in the limelight. Manilow incorporated big band sounds and boppish harmonics ("Avenue C," "Cloudburst," and the like.)

The two albums pictured here were artistically rewarding attempts to blend jazz, both sultry and swinging, into a new, more subtle way than had been attempted before. While the record sales in no way matched those of his earlier pop releases, Manilow seemed fullfilled as an artist. Kate Meyers, reporting in *Entertainment Weekly* in December 1993, quoted Manilow, "The British press has ripped me to shreds over the years. They've insulted my music, and they've insulted the people who like my music. But all of a sudden I began to feel something flip over. The audiences were louder and younger, and radio stations started to pick up on my music again."

By the mid-1980s, Manilow made an escape from the hit-conscious format he had been caught up in to create a series of conceptual releases directed at combining the forces of cabaret, jazz, and theater. With his *2:00 A.M. Paradise Cafe* (1984) Manilow's streak as a singles hitmaker was broken but the project enhanced his reputation as a composer-arranger with ties to the world of jazz. Manilow surrounded himself with an exemplary rhythm section of Shelly Manne on drums, Bill Mays on second keyboards, George Duviver on bass, on Mundell Lowe on guitar, and even added baritone sax institution Gerry Mulligan. Manilow sang duets with Mel Torme ("Big City Blues") and Sarah Vaughan ("Blue"). He called the album "a milestone in my life." The recording was forty-five minutes of straight playing and singing with no interruptions. There were no second takes or breaks, something unheard of in the record industry. Manilow confessed in his autobiography that, "I was wiped out. It was as if all the years in the hotels and the planes and the struggling frustrations and the going broke and the headaches were all washed away. And it had only needed one take. For me, making the album *2:00 A.M. Paradise Cafe* was much more than just making another album. It represented taking control of a career in which the light of success had been so bright that it had blinded me." On *Swing Street* (1987) Manilow included jazz artists Stan Getz, Dianne Schuur, Tom Scott, Phyllis Hyman, Carmen McRae, Stanley Clarke, and Gerry Mulligan, in addition to pop rockers Kid Creole and the Coconuts. Selections included all-time favorites such as "Stardust," "Stompin' at the Savoy," and "Summertime," along with Manilow originals. The video was produced using a stylized Hollywood musical soundstage of the 1930s. In 1991 Manilow released *Showstoppers*, a collection of Broadway classics and in 1994 Manilow released yet another tribute to the past—*Singin' with the Big Bands*.

Movie Star News

Peter Allen: Bi-coastal camp star. By Allen's teenage years, rock'n'roller Jerry Lee Lewis was a big influence (young Peter liked to rock out on the piano). When Allen became a young professional, Francis Faye, a wild cabaret performer, began to mold him. She was a hot singer-pianist of the 1940s and 1950s who would rant and rave risque numbers with banjos banging ("Gotta go, go, go. Gotta gay, gay, gay, gay, gay, gay with Frances Faye"). Allen's future, manic stage style was a direct result of Faye's influence: "She is truly one of the free people of the world, one of the wildest women I've ever met. She was also the first person I ever met who didn't care what other people thought about her. I think that was the most important thing. The act I do today is more like hers than anyone else. Whatever comic timing I have comes from Frances Faye." Faye would join Allen for a version of "Just a Gigolo" on his 1974 A&M record *Continental American.*

Of course Allen's mother-in-law, Judy Garland, had a strong influence on his later work as well, as did Kay Thompson. Thompson was Liza Minnelli's godmother and had been an important cog in the Arthur Freed unit at MGM during the 1940s and 1950s (she did choral work). Thompson worked on Allen's image and made connections for him between his own persona and those of Hollywood stars he idolized (Thompson's one great screen role was in *Funny Face,* with Fred Astaire and Audry Hepburn.) It was Thompson who used to take Allen to see revival musicals at New York's repertory film houses (before the days of videos) so he could experience the songs and dances of the 1930s and 1940s.

Peter Allen's Judy Garland tribute song "Quiet, Please, There's a Lady on Stage," was based on a scene in the theater district in 1974 with another of the historically connected performers of the past, cabaret artist Julie Wilson. Allen caught Wilson in a tiny cabaret during the height of disco. A table of rude, loud people, infuriated Allen and he sent a note to the table that read, "Quiet, please, there's a lady on stage!" Years later Allen wrote a role for Julie Wilson to play in his Broadway musical *Legs Diamond* (the show folded after mixed reviews but garnered raves, as well as a Tony nomination, for Wilson).

Peter Allen (1944-1992) probably drew the worlds of Hollywood elan and pop performer closer together than any of the other revivalists. Born Peter Woolnough and raised in Australia, Allen had only three records as youngster and he played them all the time, according to his mother, Marion. All three records were by pianist-singer Fats Waller. Songs like "I'm Going to Sit Right Down and Write Myself a Letter" were ingrained in Allen. Al Jolson was the other early influence. From *Peter Allen* by David Smith and Neil Peters: "Those early Fats Waller records are still in my mind. The humor and sophistication of his songs were, along with movie musicals, my first glimpse of the world that I wanted to be a part of. Realize that there was no black music of any kind in Australia, so those early Fats Waller songs and the image of Al Jolson in black face in the movies represented to me the glamour and fun of entertaining. It was very exotic to this pre-teen country boy."

Allen became part of a duo, with Chris Ball, known as the Allen Brothers. He was discovered at the Hong Kong Hilton in 1964 by none other than Judy Garland. She thought he was a reincarnation of the MGM days of the 1940s. Like her dear friend Mickey Rooney, Allen was multi-talented in that he wrote songs, played piano, and was a terrific dancer. Garland introduced Allen to her daughter, Liza Minnelli, and the two were married on March 3, 1967. Allen was an unknown, struggling piano player-singer and Minnelli's star was rising. By 1969 they separated (he composed a lament about their breakup entitled "Harbour").

Allen began to establish himself as a cult performer at places such as New York's Bitter End, the Continental Baths, and the Troubadour in Los Angeles. Allen's big break came when he was the featured performer at New York's Reno Sweeny, called by many the club of the 1970s. The venue was something out of a 1930s movie, with deep, red leather banquettes, black-and-white checkerboard floors, palm trees, big bowls of lilies, and clever neon for impact. Allen worked out a classy camp act as he projected a pansexual gigolo at the piano singing swoon tunes as well as Caribbean jump numbers.

Courtesy Arista Records

Peter Allen at Carnegie Hall. One of the observers who captured the essence of Peter Allen's deft blend of camp entertainment was Stephen Holden. In the October 18, 1976, issue of the *Village Voice,* in an article titled *The Underground, Overground, Singing, Songwriting, Performing Thunderstorm called Peter Allen*, he wrote, "Allen wafts the devil-may-care amusement of the society jester embodied by everyone from Noel Coward to Truman Capote. What makes Peter Allen different is that he has figured out how to work this shtick, better known as 'camp,' into a class act, one that would have scandalized any decade but the 1970s. The naughty pansexual gigolo camping it on stage and loving every minute of it.

"On stage he flashes a glittering fan-magazine smile, then begins to play. Mid-song, he straddles the piano bench and humps, slides, grinds and writhes. The song is 'Love Crazy,' an antic stylization of '40s and '50s glamour poses that sends up Hollywood's stock depiction of Caribbean Swank. One second he looks like Errol Flynn, swashbuckling for the ladies aboard some mythical cruise ship, the next he's the gay camp, twirling orchids and evoking Carmen Miranda. Only Peter Allen has dared to suggest massive sexual ambivalance without qualificaton."

Allen wasn't a big seller of records, though the records do justice to his songwriting talents. More than anything else, it was Allen's dynamic club and theater performances that made him an underground star—today most of his recordings are no longer in print. Besides the songs listed elsewhere in this book, Allen also composed and recorded "Arthur's Theme" (for which he won an Oscar in 1981 as co-composer), "Everything Old Is New Again" (used in a clever dance number in the film *All That Jazz* , 1979), "I Still Call Australia My Home" (a number one hit in that country in 1980), "I Could Have Been a Sailor" (1978), "Continental American" (1976), "I Honestly Love You" (a number one hit for fellow Australian Olivia Newton John in 1974), "Six-Thirty Sunday Morning" (1971), "Don't Cry Out Loud" (a top hit for Melissa Manchester in 1979), and "You and Me" (sung by Frank Sinatra in 1979).

In time, Allen was recording for A&M Records and playing larger halls all over the globe. His performances were madcap and touching. One moment he was singing a poignant ballad about his departed mother-in-law, Judy Garland, "Quiet Please," and the next minute he was straddling the piano, humping and bumping, a la Carmen Miranda, "I Go to Rio." The most lasting of Allen's creations might be the 1988 video of his high-energy song and dance act at Radio City Music Hall, where he became the only male to dance the kick line with the famed Rockettes.

Groups such as the Manhattan Rhythm Kings and the Manhattan Transfer have also provided a captivating mix of stylish vocal harmonizing of the "old songs." The **Manhattan Transfer** (1969-   ) consists of Tim Hauser (the only original member), Janis Siegel, Alan Paul, and Cheryl Bentyne. One of the most versatile vocal harmony groups on the music scene, the Transfer has recorded entire albums of doo wop, vocalese, and Brazilian music, as well as contemporary mixes of styles. The group, named after a novel by John Dos Passos, was formed by Hauser and Gene Pistilli, who coauthored Spanky and Our Gang's 1967 hit "Sunday Will Never Be the Same." The group's first album, *Jukin',* focused on jump and jive numbers from the 1940s like "Java Jive" and "You'se a Viper." The album flopped and Pisilli and Hauser went their separate ways.

Eventually Hauser reformed the Transfer and played up nostalgia elements with campy outfits from the 1930s and 1940s. Singing and vamping in New York clubs like Max's Kansas City, Trude Heller's, The Club 82, and Reno Sweeny, the group caught the attention of Atlantic Records owner Ahmet Ertegun. Their first release on Atlantic in 1975 featured a cover with

Manhattan Transfer

Tim Hauser, the driving force behind the Manhattan Transfer, has a strong love for vocal groups. He says that recordings of the Mills Brothers, the Ink Spots, and the Boswell Sisters inspired him. Hauser is also a fan of the rock'n'roll/rhythm and blues style of vocalizing known as doo wop (the Ravens, Clovers and Drifters are representative examples; the Transfer recorded a doo wop album titled *Bop Doo Wop* in 1985). The longest-lasting of the camp nostalgia leaders from the early 1970s, over the years the group has left its nostalgic elements behind and has at times consciously projected a modernist look and sound ("Twilight Zone," Spyro Gyra's "Shaker Song," and Weather Report's "Birdland").

Another strong influence on the group was modern jazz of the 1940s and 1950s. In 1985 the group recorded an album titled *Vocalese* (words put to instrumental jazz recordings) featuring bop vocalist Jon Hendricks. The Transfer mined the jazz vocalese trunk even further in 1986 with their *Manhattan Transfer—Live* release. Lyrics were provided by Jon Hendricks to jazz classics such as progressive bandleader Woody Herman's "Four Brothers," saxophone collesus Sonny Rollins's "Airegin," trumpeter-bandleader Thad Jones's "To You," Quincy Jones's "(You Should) Meet Benny Bailey," trumpeter Clifford Brown's "(Sing) Joy Spring," and Denzil Best's classic from the pivotal Miles Davis album titled *Birth of the Cool,* "Move." Another bop singer, the late Eddie Jefferson, had a strong influence on the group once they left the camp arena during the late 1970s (the 1979 album, *Extensions*, was "dedicated to Eddie Jefferson (1919-1979)—the world's greatest jazz singer").

the quartet in a drawing that evoked a black- and-white setting straight out of the RKO-Van Nest Polglase Art Deco handbook. Their songs, like Bette Midler's, ranged from the 1930s to the 1960s. "Java Jive" (introduced to popular audiences by the Ink Spots in 1940), "Tuxedo Junction," and "Blue Champagne" were included in the set. Over the years the group performed at a high level of excellence.

The **Manhattan Rhythm Kings** (1979-   ) have remained steadfast in their vision of themselves as purveyors of music and dance from the 1920s to the 1940s. Brian Nalepka, the only original member, fell under the spell of Joe Tarto, an old-time jazz tuba player who had worked with the Dorseys, Vincent Lopez, and Red Nichols. Nalepka and company took to the New York streets, starting out in Sheridan Square in the late 1970s. They wore pleated pants, big, snap-brim felt hats, and two-toned shoes, and sang old songs. Nalepka notes, "We'd open a guitar case and set it out in front of us, and then tune up." They tap danced to attract attention. "We did little shows, ten minute shows. It helped a lot, really taught us to work with a crowd. Let's face it, if you're playing on the street and you can't hold a crowd, they walk away." Hal Shane and Tripp Hanson round out the present-day trio. In 1984, dancer-choreographer Tommy Tune heard the group and asked them to help him assemble an act based on songs written by Fred Astaire. The Rhythm Kings ended up performing in a number of creations with Tune, most recently in *Crazy for You,* a Gershwin musical roughly based on *Girl Crazy.* The Rhythm Kings mix the sounds of the Boswell Sisters with Paul Whiteman's Rhythm Boys. Selections from the past are the bulk of their material ("Smoke Rings," "Heebie Jeebies," "Happy Feet," "Glow Worm," "Shall We Dance," "Soon," and the like.) With boundless energy the kings "tap dance up a storm" and "sing like angels," to paraphrase raves from newspaper reviews. Tune said the Manhattan Rhythm Kings "tap dance like escapees from a Fred Astaire film." In December 1989, John S. Wilson raved in the *New York Times,* "The Manhattan Rhythm Kings are essentially a versatile, whiz-bang vaudeville act. They all sing, separately and in trio. Mr. Hanson, a compact bundle of cheerful energy, and Mr. Shane, tall and solemn, are tap dancers who show the influence of Mr. [Tommy] Tune, particularly when they are working as a duo seemingly blended into a single body. Mr. Hanson plays piano and melodica, Mr. Shane plays guitar and Mr. Nalepka is all-encompassing support on bass. Everything they do pulses with lively rhythms. They stay on top of the tongue-twisting shifts and slides in the Boswell Sisters' 'Heebie Jeebies,' including the ending that the Boswells borrowed from Louis Armstrong, and they sing and dance their way through two songs written by Fred Astaire as well as through a pair of songs from Astaire films."

Courtesy Manhattan Rhythm Kings

Doin' the heebie jeebies with happy feet. *Left,* left to right, Hal Shane, Brian Nalepka, and Tripp Hanson. *Right,* Tommy Tune in front with the Manhattan Rhythm Kings. The group has stayed true to the spirit of recorded productions. More attendant to the 1920s and early 1930s than the late 1930s and 1940s, the group's spirit is more Paul Whiteman-Bing Crosby (of the Rhythm Boys period) than Tommy Dorsey-Frank Sinatra, more Boswell Sisters than Andrews Sisters. The Manhattan Rhythm Kings are today's premier exponent of group singing and dancing on stage and in the clubs. They still outfit themselves in 1930s natty outfits or tuxedos and have been successful in joining Philharmonic orchestras around the country for special performances. Unlike the other major contributors to the revival of the music of the interwar period, the Rhythm Kings have had success on the Broadway stage because their music originates in the time when Broadway and popular music were synonymous. Tommy Tune, a winner of nine Tony Awards for his work on Broadway as a performer, choreographer, and director, wrote in the liner notes to the Kings's 1991 Cabaret Records release, *We Three*: "I first heard the Kings perform at a party Lucie Arnaz was having at Sardi's. They sang like angels. Then one day they dropped off one of their albums at the St. James Theatre, where I was doing *My One and Only* [a musical revue centered on Gershwin music]. A few weeks later I had a party at my house and I put on the album. Before I knew it, everyone was dancing around the room and so was I. And I never dance on my day off! Around that time a friend of mine approached me about doing a show based on music written by Fred Astaire. I told him, 'Get me the Manhattan Rhythm Kings and I'll do it.' That was the beginning of our long-term working relationship."

Only Willie Nelson makes albums that people never seem to get tired of listening to.

And only Willie could have recorded "Stardust."

"Stardust" is an album full of songs you've heard all through your life..."Georgia on My Mind"..."Unchained Melody"..."Blue Skies"..."September Song"... "All of Me"...songs you've heard, but perhaps never really listened to until now.

"Stardust" is an album that will make you perk up your ears and react with pleasure.

And only a man who puts so much love into his music could have pulled it off.

Only Willie.

Courtesy Sony Music

Who else but Willie Nelson could have come out on stage at his annual picnics in Dripping Springs, Texas, singing songs like Hoagy Carmichael's "Georgia on My Mind" and "Stardust" and other Tin Pan Alley standards, and not gotten pelted with bottles of Lone Star beer? Nelson carved a niche for the classic pop standards in contemporary country music. In addition, he tops the list of modern, out-of-context performers, regardless of genre, who have made albums—five at last count—centered on the American popular songs of Tin Pan Alley from the "Golden Age of Pop."

By the 1980s, artists as varied as Linda Ronstadt, Rickie Lee Jones, Harry Connick, Jr., Dr. John, Ben Sidran, and The Ritz had produced albums that were dedicated to the music of the 1930s and 1940s. Rock-oriented females such as Toni Tennille and Carly Simon transformed themselves into chanteuse vamps, vocalizing great standards of yesterday in front of big bands. Two successful films written by Nora Ephron, *When Harry Met Sally* (1988) and *Sleepless in Seattle* (1993), used older songs that gave films an added touch of history and romance. Ephron used the older songs to comment lyrically on the action taking place in the lives of the protagonists set in contemporary times.

Courtesy Arista Records

One of the superstars of the 1970s, Carly Simon, fit into the mold of what was described as middle of the road rock, or MOR, bright, melodic rock. Along with Joni Mitchell and Carole King, Simon was the leading female singer-songwriter of the period. In 1981 Simon made her first foray into the arena of Tin Pan Alley standard songs with *Torch*, which featured Hoagy Carmichael's "I Get Along Without You Very Well." *My Romance*, released in 1991, featured, in addition to the title song by the Gershwins, "In the Wee Small Hours," which was later used effectively in the film *Sleepless in Seattle*.

More than any other established rock artist of the 1970s, **Linda Ronstadt** (1946-) raised the consciousness of the swoon tunes of the 1930s and 1940s. Bette Midler, Barry Manilow, Peter Allen, the Manhattan Transfer, and the Manhattan Rhythm Kings were all unknowns who made careers out of camp and nostalgia efforts. However, Ronstadt (like country music's Willie Nelson) was already a superstar when she decided to turn her attentions toward the older songs in 1983 with the tremendously successful *What's New?* Ronstadt told a New York newspaper columnist about an incident that sparked the interest for her eventual involvement with the popular music standards of "The Golden Age of Pop." Rondstadt was having lunch one afternoon in New York's tony Russian Tea Room on 57th Street and became intrigued by the background music wafting over the sound system. She asked her waiter who was singing the music and was told that one of the workers had put together a tape of Ella Fitzgerald singing with Nelson Riddle arrangements. Ronstadt filed the information away and began thinking about the possibility of interpreting the older songs.

Ronstadt had her producer, Peter Asher, contact bandleader Nelson Riddle about putting together arrangements and orchestrations for a collection of older standards. The result, *What's New?* became a surprise bestseller, and introduced Ronstadt to an entirely new audience of older listeners, while at the same time introducing Ronstadt's younger audience to older songs. The album's success also resurrected Nelson Riddle's career. He dusted-off some of his arrangements from the 1950s for Nat King Cole, Ella Fitzgerald, and Frank Sinatra, and recast them for the youthful Ronstadt. Three of the selections, "I Guess I'll Hang My Tears Out to Dry," "Good-Bye," and the title song, were from Sinatra's down-in-the-dumps classic *Only the Lonely* (1958).

Ronstadt followed up with *Lush Life* in 1984 and *For Sentimental Reasons* in 1986 (the latter was released after Riddle's death in 1985). Ronstadt was brought up on the older songs of the 1930s and 1940s, but like many young people of the 1960s, she rebelled against her parents' music and preferred rock. Speaking of her albums of standard songs, Ronstadt told *Down Beat* in July 1985, "I wanted the first one to have a mood, a very introspective, concentrating mood. *Only the Lonely* was like that too. The second one [*Lush Life*], even though it had songs which are basically about sad things on it, like 'It Never Entered My Mind' had a perkier approach." Ronstadt gives credit to veteran producer Jerry Wexler for encouraging her to take a chance on the older songs. Ronstadt added, "Jerry Wexler invited me out to his house one day. So there we were sitting on the lawn listening to this Mildred Bailey record and I said, 'gee, it would be fun to learn some of these songs.' And then I thought: it would be fun to record them. Once we started talking about recording them, Jerry kept saying, 'You can do these songs.' I kept saying, 'No, my phrasing isn't good enough. I don't have enough technique to do this. I'm too sloppy.' But Jerry kept saying, 'you got the chops, you can do it.' We went into the studio and made a demo. We did 'Someone to Watch Over Me,' 'Lover Man,' and my favorite one, 'I Don't Stand a Ghost of a Chance With You!' We did them in a hurry, in about an hour and a half. They weren't very good. I did it before the evening performances of *Pirates of Penzance*, and was dead tired; I had no voice and my phrasing was terrible. But it was intriguing enough. I remember feeling seduced by the music; in fact, I was completely gone. It was like falling in love and never being able to look at anyone else. I was totally captivated." The early experiment with Wexler didn't pan out, but it set the stage for the singer to conect with Nelson Riddle.

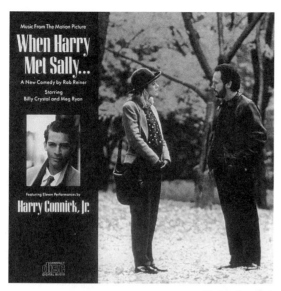
Courtesy Sony Music

Nora Ephron goes to the movies. *When Harry Met Sally* was the key motion picture of the 1980s to cast the older songs ("Where or When," "Let's Call the Whole Thing Off," "Stompin' at the Savoy," "Autumn in New York," "But Not for Me," and others) as costar in a contemporary love story. The songs mirrored the emotions of a likeable/loveable couple (Billy Crystal and Meg Ryan) as they try to reconcile being best friends and lovers. In the movie Louis Armstrong and Ella Fitzgerald, among others, are heard singing in the background. When the soundtrack album was released, however, only vocals by young New Orleans pianist-turned-singer Harry Connick, Jr., appeared. Whatever the contract conflicts may have been for the use of other record companies' artists (if there was any conflict at all) the end result was that it catapulted Connick into the major leagues.

Nora Ephron, who wrote the film script, expertly directed by Rob Reiner, followed up in 1993 with a love story about a young father (Tom Hanks) whose storybook marriage ends abruptly with the sudden death of his wife. Seeking a new start away from the memories of her and the town they shared, he and his young son move to Seattle. One night the boy phones a radio call-in show and recounts the loss of the mother. Meg Ryan hears the show, is touched by the situation, and a long-distance love quest begins. Ephron decided to direct *Sleepless in Seattle* herself and the fuzzy-warm feelings of *When Harry Met Sally* continued in the new film. The songs again played costar to the protagonists. Gene Autry sings "Back in the Saddle Again" and the late vaudeville-comedian Jimmy Durante's sly, off-beat interpretations of "As Time Goes By" and "Make Someone Happy," provide atmosphere as Hanks gets back into the 1990s dating game. Most effective was the underscoring of "In the Wee Small Hours" during a late-night revelation experienced by Meg Ryan. Instead of using Frank Sinatra's version of the song (after all, his was the pentultimate cry of lost, lonely love on the first pop concept album back in 1955); the author-director chose instead to use Carly Simon's version. Some music critics chastised Ephron for choosing a "wannabe's" version over that of the master, but they missed the point. Ephron's choice of a female's yearning cry in the night was most appropriate for the situation. The soundtrack album for *Sleepless in Seattle*, unlike *When Harry Met Sally*, included the same versions of the songs that appeared in the film.

The long-standing musical war that began in the 1950s between post-swing pop and rock'n'roll was in some small way broken down by the artists in the camp nostalgia category, although during the democratic '60s (pre-1968), top 40 radio made room for everybody. Rock, Motown, and R&B might have dominated the charts and the airwaves but there was always room for Sinatra to hit with "Strangers in the Night" or "Something Stupid" and Dean Martin to score with "Memories Are Made of This" or "Julie Do You Love Me." And these records were not only on the same charts as The Beatles, Stones, and Supremes, but they were often played on the same stations. Also, a few performers such as Petula Clark, made a career out of selling big band swing (with a 1960s sensibility) to both teens and their parents. There was really nothing retro or nostalgic about any of this. By the late eighties and early nineties there were numerous examples of modern rock and soul performers delving into the vast repertoire of the "older standards." A couple of good examples of this are the concept albums *Stay Awake* (1988) and *Red, Hot and Blue* (1991).

Stay Awake, subtitled "Various Interpretations of Music From Vintage Disney Films," includes a number of extremely hip modern performers of classic songs from the films of Walt Disney: Sinead O'Connor ("Someday My Prince Will Come"), Bonnie Raitt and Was Not Was ("Baby Mine"), Tom Waits ("Heigh Ho"), Los Lobos ("I Wan'na Be Like You",) James Taylor ("Second Star to the Right"), the Replacements ("Cruella DeVille"), and Betty Carter ("I'm Wishing"), among others.

Red, Hot and Blue brought together an eclectic mix of rock, soul and hip hop dance versions of Cole Porter's music, uniting such diverse artists as U2 ("Night and Day"), Deborah Harry and Iggy Pop ("Well, Did You Evah!"), Erasure ("Too Darn Hot"), Neneh Cherry ("I've Got You Under My Skin"), David Byrne ("Don't Fence Me In"), Lisa Stansfield ("Down in the Depths"), k.d. lang ("So in Love"), Aaron Neville ("In the Still of the Night") and Annie Lennox ("Everytime We Say Goodbye"), among others. Considering the mix of musical styles that occurred during the late 1980s and 1990s—rock'n'rollers doing tributes to bop pianist Thelonious Monk and composer Kurt Weill, the mix of rock stars on *The Glory of Gershwin*, and genre-breaking duet recordings like Frank Sinatra's—it's a wonder that young audiences haven't been attracted to more older artists than just Tony Bennett.

331

One of the best examples of nostalgia for the old songs and images of the past was found in the touching and humorous musical comedy *The 1940's Radio Hour*. The story was written by Walton Jones and conceived as an intimate cabaret theater piece at Yale University. A medium-scale production was mounted at the Yale Repertory Theatre with an eleven-piece band, and then went on to Washington, D.C.'s Arena Theatre. The show opened on Broadway on October 7, 1979 at the St. James Theatre. The musical cleverly mixed prototype characters from the world of 1940s entertainment during a one-hour radio show mounted on Christmas Eve. Future stars of note included jazz vocalist Dee Dee Bridgewater, cabaret star Mary Cleere Haran and character actor-supreme Joe Grifasi *(Deer Hunter, 52 Pick Up,* and *Benny and Joon)*.

The program promo read, in part: "The time is December, 1942—a time when Frank Sinatra, the King of Swoon, made his first appearance at the Paramount Theatre, when Audie Murphy became one of America's most decorated war heroes and when Betty Grable posed for her famous bathing suit pin-up. Ladies' shoulders were padded, their hair upswept and their stockings seamed. The music was Swing, big band and brassy. . . in *The 1940's Radio Hour,* you'll hear 'Chattanooga Choo Choo,' 'You, You're Driving Me Crazy,' 'All the Things You Are,' 'Ain't She Sweet,' 'Blue Moon,' 'I'll Never Smile Again,' 'Blues in the Night,' and many, many more performed against the sounds of our own 16-piece swing band. You'll meet the voices that the listeners knew so well. Johnny Cantone, the featured vocalist with the Sinatra sound, look and attraction. Ginger Brooks, a blond bombshell of a waitress by day, a radio star by night. Connie Miller, the seventeen year-old bobbysoxer from Ogden, Utah, who taps and jitterbugs on the air. Geneva Lee Brown, the beautiful black female singer from the Cotton Club, who can scat like Ella and vamp like Lena, and the rest of the gang from WOV radio in Manhattan. 'The 1940's Radio Hour'—If You Don't Remember it—Discover it!" In 1995, a similarly based musical, *Swingtime Canteen,* a re-creation of a 1944 U. S. O. concert, performed in a night club, played at New York's Blue Angel on 44th Street.

MATINEE TODAY AT 3

BROADWAY'S SWINGING 40's MUSICAL COMEDY HIT!

"THE MUSIC IS SPLENDIDLY MEMORABLE! A GLOWING MIXTURE OF GOLDEN TUNES AND AFFECTION!"
— Clive Barnes, N.Y. Post

The 1940's RADIO HOUR
A New Musical

TICKETS AVAILABLE THROUGH CHARGIT: (212) 239-7177, and TICKETRON (212) 977-9020 AND AT BOX OFFICE
Group Sales Box Office (212) 398-8383 Toll Free (800) 223-7565
ST. JAMES THEATRE 246 West 44th Street 398-0280
SEE ABC'S FOR DETAILS.

Courtesy Paul DePoss

Courtesy Charly Records, Sunnyside Records, Elektra Records

A trio of Cole. Nat King Cole (left) became the best-selling black artist in the history of popular music until the rise of Michael Jackson. His daughter, Natalie, revived her career by reworking her dad's hits on the top-selling *Unforgettable* (1991). Through the miracle of the recording studio, she even sang a duet with her dad, "Unforgettable." Nat and daughter make a bookend portrait above. What about the man in the middle? **Freddie Cole** (1931-) is the least-known of the Cole family. The brother of Nat and uncle of Natalie, Cole has quietly carved a cult following over the years as a touring cabaret pianist-singer. Unlike his brother and niece, Cole had to bolster himself by playing whatever jobs were available during the 1960s and 1970s (cruise ships, international club dates, and lesser-known jazz clubs in and out of the United States). However, Freddie's forebearance, plugging away under the giant shadow cast by his more popular relatives, began to pay off in the 1990s. Cole is a performer of quiet dignity. His shows are very low-key and controlled, yet feature intense interpretations of standard songs and some lesser-known favorites he has made part of his own repertoire. Secondly, Cole incorporates his brother's legacy into his act by singing a tribute song "He Was the King," a hit medley of Nat's songs, and a tongue-in-cheek "I'm Not My Brother, I'm Me." And, finally, Cole has captured the attention of television advertisers in the 1990s. His voice has been heard over the commercials for Hanes undergarments, Hilton Hotels and its tie-in with a major airline, Welch's Grape Juice, and Dodge automobiles ("It Had to Be You").

Nostalgia/Camp Revival Releases

Performer	Release	Year	Standard Song Examples/Comments
Ian Whitcomb	Mad Mod Music Hall	1966	British rocker 1st to move from rock'n'roll to old songs
Tiny Tim	God Bless Tiny Tim	1968	"Tip Toe Through the Tulips" 1st hit of movement
Ringo Starr	Sentimental Journey	1970	Early Beatle solo LP; croons swing songs of '30s & '40s
Ian Whitcomb	Under the Ragtime Moon	1972	Pre-'30s & '40s nuggets from curator-master of early pop
Bette Midler	The Divine Miss M	1972	"Boogie Woogie Bugle Boy" to "Leader of the Pack"
Harry Nilsson	A Touch of Schmilsson in the Night	1973	Best of the early serious interpretations with arrangements by Sinatra veteran orchestrator Gordon Jenkins
Pointer Sisters	The Pointer Sisters	1973	Salvation Army dress and camped-up songs on 1st album
Bette Midler	Bette Midler	1973	Kurt Weill, Hoagy Carmichael, and *Gold Diggers* songs on Midler's second album
Peter Allen	Continental American	1974	He's just a gigolo at Reno Sweeny's Paradise Room
Leon Redbone	On the Track	1975	Dedicated to Jelly Roll Morton & Jimmie Rodgers
Manhattan Transfer	Manhattan Transfer	1975	Black & white '30s movies images and old songs
Bette Midler	Broken Blossom	1977	Bette sings "Make Yourself Comfortable," "A Dream is a Wish Your Heart Makes," and "La Vie En Rose"
Manhattan Transfer	Coming Out	1977	Slick contemporary pop mixed with older standards
Leon Redbone	Double Time	1977	Bing Crosby & Jelly Roll Morton live on with jazz backing
Tuxedo Junction	Tuxedo Junction	1977	'30s-'40s swing clan, meets disco thump
Leon Redbone	Champagne Charlie	1978	Tin Pan Alley mixed with some country western classics
Willie Nelson	Stardust	1978	Lone-Star Beer goes to the "Sunny Side of the Street"
Manhattan Transfer	Pastiche	1978	Another mix of A side standards, B side contemporary pop
Willie Nelson	On the Road	1979	Nelson & Leon Russell double LP; standards and '50s rock
Bug Alley	Bug Alley	1980	Manhattan Transfer wannabes; neat "Boswell Medley"
Manhattan Rhythm Kings	Manhattan Rhythm Kings	1981	Bing Crosby and Boswell Sisters plus tap dance antics
Richard Perry's Swing	Swing	1981	Appealing '80s gloss to swing-oriented tunes
Carly Simon	Torch	1981	1st foray into the world of standard songs of the past
Manhattan Transfer	Mecca for Moderns	1981	A mature group covering all sides of vocal harmonizing
Ben Sidran	Old Songs for the New Depression	1982	Sidran reworks Bette Midler's 1976 LP title via bebop; "Let's Get Away From It All" and "Easy Street"
Linda Ronstadt	What's New?	1983	1st of 3 Nelson Riddle-orchestrated albums; most successful
Rickie Lee Jones	Girl at Her Volcano	1983	Beatnik woman sings the standard song fare
Barry Manilow	2:00 A.M. Paradise Cafe	1984	Jazzy after-hours originals with visits from Sarah Vaughan and Mel Torme; excellent jazz instrumentalists
Linda Ronstadt	Lush Life	1984	Second stop on the road to classic standards with Riddle
Willie Nelson	Somewhere Over the Rainbow	1985	Nelson croons oldies like *The Wizard of Oz* classic; "Mona Lisa," "Exactly Like You," and "Who's Sorry Now?"
Linda Ronstadt	For Sentimental Reasons	1986	Final pairing of Ronstadt with Nelson Riddle
Barry Manilow	Swing Street	1989	Fast side/slow side versions of swing originals and oldies
The Ritz	The Ritz	1987	Combines jump blues, bop, & swinging standards
Harry Connick, Jr.	20	1988	Pre-Sinatra-style duets with Carmen McRae & Dr. John
Steve Miller	Born 2 B Blue	1988	Blends T-Bone Walker blues with Chet Baker & cool jazz
Willie Nelson	What a Wonderful World	1988	Nelson's 4th visit to Tin Pan Alley standards
Ben Sidran	Too Hot to Touch	1988	Song "Critics" should be required listening for all reviewers
Dr. John	In a Sentimental Mood	1989	Sings & swings standards and blues with big band backing
Harry Connick, Jr.	When Harry Met Sally	1989	New Orleans boogie-bopper goes pop a la Sinatra
Barry Manilow	Showstoppers	1991	Broadway classics; took this show on tour
Carly Simon	My Romance	1991	"In the Wee Small Hours" used in *Sleepless in Seattle*
Natalie Cole	Unforgettable	1991	Grammy smash of dad's classic hits; revived her career
Manhattan Rhythm Kings	We Three	1991	Ink Spots classic; cult songs of '20s & '30s
Diane Schurr	In Tribute	1992	Tribute to 13 divas including Ella Fitzgerald and Billie Holiday
Natalie Cole	Take a Look	1993	Double disc encore of oldies from '30s & '40s
Sheena Easton	No Strings	1993	Scotish rock star purrs "Body and Soul," "Moody's Mood," "Someone to Watch Over Me," and other classics
Willie Nelson	Moonlight Becomes You	1993	Nelson returns to the standard songs one more time
Various artists	Sleepless in Seattle	1993	Soundtrack; Nora Ephron strikes again!
Barry Manilow	Singin' with the Big Bands	1994	Swing classics from "Moonlight Serenede" and "Chattanooga Choo Choo" to "I'll Never Smile Again"
Various artists	Forget Paris	1995	Soundtrack; Billy Crystal pulls a Nora Ephron—Billie Holiday Ella Fitzgerald, & others swing and sway

Also important:
Toni Tennille, *More Than You Know, Never Let Me Go,* and *All of Me* (albums of standards); *Stay Awake,* various interpretations of music from vintage Disney films, 1988; Diana Ross, *Stolen Moments; Jazz and Blues of Billie Holiday,* a 1991 video; *Red, Hot and Blue,* various artists, a 1991 Cole Porter tribute, on CD and video; *The Glory of Gershwin,* various artists, 1994.

Chapter 11

BEBOP AND THE DEVELOPMENT OF MODERN JAZZ

Frank Driggs Collection

Charlie Parker (alto sax) with Miles Davis (trumpet) at the 52nd Street club Three Deuces in 1947. The serious look on the faces of the performers (such as Tommy Potter on bass) is representative of the concentration required and the lofty aspirations of the creators of the new jazz music of 1940s bebop. The music has often been referred to as rebellious, and was seen by many fans and critics of the time as revolutionary. The simple, hummable melodies and dancing rhythms featured by the swing bands during the 1930s and 1940s were not part of the musical vocabulary of most boppers. A number of jazz historians view the modern jazz movement not as a revolutionary development, but one that emerged smoothly from the swing styles. While this may be true stylistically, modern jazz clearly broke with the past culturally. The emphasis moved from audience entertainment to the creative act. This was not dance music. It was much more performance art. Even stylistically, however, for many listeners of the time the music was avant garde ("in the advanced guard"). What can now be seen as evolutionary appeared, to those not privy to the less visible, intermediate musical steps, as a radical departure from past technique and style. Most jazz styles that have emerged since the early 1940s (except for revivals of older forms) are classified as modern jazz and are based on many of the musical advances that were initiated by the leaders of the bop movement.

A major new direction in the world of jazz music began to emerge during the early 1940s, and it soon changed the face of jazz. Historians and critics disagree as to whether this was a rebellious, revolutionary rejection of the then-popular swing, or rather a gradual transition by swing-era players into a new musical language. A majority of historians has seen the new sound as a fairly volatile musical form that did not sit well with most of the established players of Dixieland or swing. The majority of the mass jazz audience was not prepared for the explosive new music, and rejected it. In fact, in terms of popularity, jazz-oriented music would never again reach the heights of mass acceptance it had achieved with swing. The modern jazz movement, with bop as its core, took jazz into the realm of art music, a serious, almost formalized, concert music. None of the major bop modernists had hit "songs" on the *Billboard* charts like those of the Goodmans and Dorseys of swing. Also, because of a series of recording bans during the war years, much of the early bebop music experiments were not recorded until 1945. This was, indeed, an underground music.

Bebop was primarily an innovation of key black musicians who had worked in the big bands (outstanding white players such as Red Rodney, Al Haig, and George Wallington played supporting roles). It has been suggested that some of the younger black players were distressed that so much of their heritage (traditional jazz and swing) had been stripped from them by white bandleaders and players, and as a result, they consciously conspired to create an unconventional and intellectual form that could not be "ripped off." The fact that so many of the modernists did not conform to the stereotype of the black entertainer as a smiling, song-and-dance minstrel is one support for this theory. Remember, during this time most black musicians couldn't work with white bands, were paid less, and were segregated in most clubs, dining establishments, and hotels.

Dizzy Gillespie, one of the main architects of the new music, was asked some thirty years after the fact if he had been a conscious revolutionary when bop began. He said the new jazz was not necessarily revolutionary, but "evolutionary." Gillespie noted that the participants didn't have a blueprint for what they were doing. They knew it was different, a new concept, but at the time, most of the creators felt that the new music arose from inner needs rather than from external factors. The swing band was *the* way of making it as a star during the 1940s and Dizzy, like most of his contemporaries, was working from that stratagem. As soon as Gillespie gained some leverage in the industry, he formed his own orchestra and featured the new, modern sounds of bop.

Frank Driggs Collection

Left to right: Coleman Hawkins (tenor sax), Benny Harris (trumpet), Don Byas (tenor sax), Thelonious Monk (piano), Denzil Best (drums), and Eddie Robinson (bass) at the Spotlite Club on 52nd Street in 1944. Here is a perfect example of veteran swing players mixing in with modernists to create a flow of music. Monk would emerge as one of the leaders of bebop. Jazz historian Leonard Feather notes in his 1987 book, *The Jazz Years: Earwitness to an Era*, that during the 1940s the new fraternity of jazz writers (working for publications such as *Down Beat, Record Exchanger, Esquire, Metronome, Melody Maker,* and others) started a war of words over preferred styles of jazz, often pitting players and styles against each other. Modernists who championed the new sounds of bop called the followers of older, Dixieland forms the "moldy old figs," and many of the supporters of the older styles put down the boppers as "anti-jazz."

For veteran musicians like Coleman Hawkins and Don Byas, the controversy was irrelevant. They saw the movement as part of the big picture of jazz music being improvised by individual talents. Hawkins is quoted in Nat Shapiro and Nat Hentoff's 1955 *Hear Me Talkin' to Ya* as saying, "They say what Monk and Dizzy and Bird were doing was so different. Well, whatever they were doing they did great, and whatever they did I liked, and I had no trouble sitting in with them. The reason is that I had studied music so long and completely, not just the horn but composition, arranging, and all that."

Bop was viewed by the jazz establishment as heretical. Louis Armstrong referred to bop as that "modern malice;" he felt that the players of the music were more interested in pleasing themselves than in entertaining their audiences. Tommy Dorsey thought bop had set the music business back twenty-five years, and Cab Calloway used to exhort his young trumpeter at the time, Dizzy Gillespie, to "stop playing those Chinese notes!" One of the reactions against this new movement was the rise of the New Orleans revival (see Chapter 5). It is hard for contemporary audiences to appreciate the musical wars waged during the halcyon days of the forties, when Dixieland, swing, and bop were at odds. The revolutionary/evolutionary spirit of yesteryear is the mainstream of today. Dizzy Gillespie was as much a part of the classic mainstream jazz tradition of the 1980s and 1990s as Armstrong was in previous decades.

Incubators of Bop: Monroe's and Minton's

The new music evolved from the big bands on the bandstand, but its individual innovations took place in after-hours jam sessions all over the country. The new sounds probably first began to crystallize in a couple of little Harlem dives—Monroe's and Minton's. In a sense, these two spots became the incubators of the new music. These were the places that certain jazzmen who were working in the big bands would go after their shows, to jam and experiment. All of the future leaders of the bop movement—Charlie Parker, Dizzy Gillespie, Thelonious Monk, Bud Powell, Kenny Clarke, Max Roach, Tadd Dameron, Dexter Gordon, and Fats Navarro—at one time or another experimented in one of these two spots between 1940 and 1945. In the early 1940s most of them were not well known. These future boppers often shared the bandstand with the well-known swing stars of the day, such as Charlie Christian, Roy Eldridge, Ben Webster, Don Byas, and, occasionally, superstars such as Benny Goodman and Artie Shaw.

Frank Driggs Collection

Al Tinney and Charlie Parker. Tinney at the piano with Parker on alto saxophone (center of three seated saxmen in front) at a jam session in 1943. Parker was quoted in Leonard Feather's *Inside Bebop* as saying, "At Monroe's I heard sessions with a pianist named Allan [sic] Tinney. That was the kind of music that caused me to quit McShann and stay in New York." It was at after-hours Harlem night spots like Monroe's Uptown House that musicians experimented with musical ideas that would eventually develop into a style known as bebop. Al Tinney is representative of the many unheralded artists who took part in these musical jam sessions.

For his part Tinney was quoted in Ira Gitler's book, *Swing to Bop: An Oral History of the Transition in Jazz in the 1940s*, "The first meeting with Bird? Well, he was playing with Jay McShann. He came down, and he sat in with us. And he dug what we were doing. He said, 'Man, what are you guys playing?' So he sat in, and we played 'Cherokee' and things like that, and we had already developed a 'Tea For Two' thing in the middle, the 2-5-1 thing, he dug this, and right away he started fitting into what we were doing. And before you knew it, when I came out of the army he was famous, just like that."

The story is often told that Minton's was the center of the incipient bop enterprise, but in fact, both Minton's and Monroe's were sisters of early bop experimentation, and Monroe's could easily be given the edge in terms of significance. Clark Monroe's Uptown House preceded Minton's. Monroe was an ex-dancer who opened his now-legendary club at 198 West 138th Street on the site of the old Theatrical Grill, with shows, hot bands, and incendiary after-hours jam sessions. In 1943 he moved to 52nd Street and started the Spotlight Club, a night spot that favored bop. Pianist **Al (Allen) Tinney** (1921-) who had performed in a number of Broadway shows (including *Porgy and Bess* and *Sing Out the News*) as a song-and-dance man, was hired by Monroe sometime around 1939 for three dollars a night. Tinney led a group that was truly an *after-hours* unit—they played from "three o'clock in the morning to seven."

The unheralded bop pianist. Al Tinney at the keyboard in Buffalo, New York, during the 1990s. Before Tinney became the leader of Monroe's jazz-jam session in 1939, he had been involved with theatrical productions. During the rehearsals for George Gershwin's *Porgy and Bess* in 1935, young Tinney played rehearsal piano for the chorus and had a part in the play. He walked on stage pulling a cart that had a goat on it. Tinney felt that Gershwin's Innovations had an undeniable impact on jazz. "I did bring it [the 'Tea for Two' pattern] to Monroe's, with the flatted fifths and augmented ninths that I learned from Gershwin," Tinney told James Patrick, director of the Jazz Studies Program at the University of Buffalo. In a 1982 article in the *Annual Review of Jazz Studies* by Patrick, titled *Al Tinney, Monroe's Uptown House, and the Emergence of Modern Jazz in Harlem*, Tinney expressed the opinion that he thought Gershwin's musical ideas had been undervalued by jazz historians. He called the music, "Beautiful. No better music has really ever been written. How much better orchestration can you get than the music of *Porgy and Bess*? And even his older thing he did, 'Rhapsody in Blue,' which was all the way before bop." James Patrick's contention is that the album titled *The Harlem Jazz Scene*, on the Esoteric label from a session in 1941, has a proclamation that reads "After hours. Monroe's/Harlem/Minton's." Patrick claims, "In fact most of the stuff was recorded at Monroe's. And the stuff with Monk and Dizzy and Kenny Clarke was mostly Nick Fenton and various other guys and was done at Monroe's and people always thought it was done at Minton's."

Dizzy Gillespie indicated in his autobiography, *To Be or Not to Bop* that Monroe's sessions were the real key to bop, more so than Minton's: "Though the tale is told that somehow we all wound up in Minton's, gigging, that isn't really true. I never worked at Minton's. Only Monk and Kenny Clarke, who had the house band, actually worked at Minton's and I couldn't go to Minton's when I was playing on Fifty-second Street because we worked at the same time. After hours, I'd go to Monroe's Uptown House to jam. There was as much creativity going on at Monroe's Uptown House as they did at Minton's. That's where we all used to go after hours, until daylight, to play."

Tinney was the leader of these sessions until 1943, when he entered the Army. He was replaced as leader by trumpet player Victor Coulson, who is said to have had a style similar to the eventual sound of Fats Navarro. Tinney hung around with two other future greats of bop piano, Gerald Wiggins and Bud Powell (the trio went from spot to spot challenging other keyboard players and calling themselves "The Three Hoods"). Tinney is a good example of what happens in popular music history to creative artists who don't record. When Tinney was doing his best work, a recording ban was on, and by the time he returned from the army his sideman, Charlie Parker, was a fairly big name.

Dizzy Gillespie wrote one of the most authoritative books about the emergence of bebop. He was there and his recollections in *To Be or Not to Bop: Memoirs*, written with Al Fraser (1979), are prized because not many modern jazzmen from this movement put their thoughts down in book form. Gillespie reminisced: "I first met Max Roach at the Uptown House where he played. He was just a kid from Brooklyn, playing with Ebenezer Paul, Allan [sic] Tinney, Ray Abrams, Victor Coulson, and George Treadwell. Those cats were getting it. Boy! And then Charlie Parker joined their group. It was a non-union gig, a 'scab' place they called it. We used to play there after hours, damn the union!"

Legendary drummer Max Roach recollected in Gillispie's autobiography, "There was a group of us around New York at that particular time, Bud Powell, Allan [sic] Tinney, and people like that.

And I think Dizzy had heard me play, either at Minton's or Monroe's Uptown House, and he said when he left Cab Calloway he was gonna start a band and he'd like for me to play with him." A good number of the bop players were into drugs and Tinney wanted to avoid that scene, so he moved on. From 1968 to the 1990s, Tinney has taught jazz workshops at the University of Buffalo and Buffalo State College and regularly played in the local jazz scene.

Minton's Playhouse was housed in the ground-floor of a grubby stone apartment building at 210 West 118th Street. Ex-band leader Teddy Hill became the manager of the club in January 1940 and immediately instituted Monday night "down home" dinners and jam sessions. The house band featured Thelonious Monk on piano and drummer Kenny Clarke. The group wrote new songs and worked and refined their concepts of rhythm, time, and chord progressions before moving on to 52nd Street around 1943.

© William P. Gottlieb

Left to right: Thelonious Monk, Howard McGhee, Roy Eldridge, and Teddy Hill at Minton's Playhouse. The following musicians are quoted in Nat Shapiro and Nat Hentoff's *Here Me Talkin' to Ya* in regard to the Minton's Playhouse scene:

Mary Lou Williams: "Minton's Playhouse was not a large place, but it was nice and intimate. The bar was in front, and the cabaret was in the back. The bandstand was situated at the rear of the back room, where the wall was covered with strange paintings depicting weird characters sitting on a brass bed, or jamming, or talking to chicks. When Thelonious Monk first played at Minton's there were few musicians who could run changes with him. Charlie Christian, Kenny Clarke, Idress Sulliman, and a couple more were the only ones who could play along with Monk then. Charlie and I used to go to the basement of the hotel where I lived and play and write all night long."

Kenny Clarke: "The first band, around the beginning of 1941, had Joe Guy, Monk, Nick Fenton, and myself. Teddy [Hill] was the one who really hired Monk. It was a funny thing. He hired the musicians and then they made the guy he thought most responsible the leader. Monk and I wrote 'Epistrophy' together, by the way. It was one of the first modern jazz originals."

Tony Scott: "I remember always going to Minton's to play and listen even while I was at Juilliard. There was one night when Ben Webster, Don Byas, and Lester Young were there and the three of them blew together, each with a different style and each blowing."

Teddy Hill: "Monk is definitely a character. He's the type of fellow who thinks an awful lot but doesn't have much to say. Yeah, I've known a lot of musicians who were characters, but none just like him. Monk seemed more like the guy who manufactured the product rather than commercialized it. Dizzy has gotten all the exploitation because Dizzy branched out and got started. Monk stayed right in the same groove."

Dizzy Gillespie: "I was with Cab then, when I first started hanging out with Thelonious Monk, and I don't think Cab could figure out at all what I was trying to blow out of my horn on his stand. It was just the new ideas Monk and I had worked out the night before."

Much of the genesis of the new music is not on record because of the various recording bans instituted during World War II. Also, in August 1942, the American Federation of Musicians went out on strike against the record companies until the end of 1944. Young jazz enthusiast Jerry Newman, taped some of the seminal music produced at Monroe's and Minton's. Newman didn't like the sound of Charlie Parker so he turned the recorder off whenever the altoist played. This unfortunate practice was counterbalanced by the Charlie Parker devotee Dean Benedetti, who in 1947 and early 1948, religiously attended Charlie Parker performances. With a direct-to-acetate-disc home recorder he documented only Parker's playing—turning the recorder off when anyone else played. (The Newman tapes can be found on the Esoteric label, and the Benedetti collection recently saw the light of day on Mosaic Records, increasing the catalog of Parker's improvisations by one quarter.)

By 1943, the focal point for the new music experiments moved from uptown Harlem to downtown-- around 52nd Street. The new music was not given a name as yet, and its main practitioners were mostly working full-time in the big bands. Parker and Gillespie, for example, were members of the Earl Hines orchestra in 1943, and then moved on to what was considered the first orchestra to feature bop-oriented music, the Billy Eckstine Orchestra, in 1944. Just as there are many opinions as to the first rock'n'roll record, there are many diverse theories as to which recording, or series of recordings, constitute the first bebop release.

There isn't even agreement as to when and how the new music got its name. Two of the many speculations are that the word mirrors, onomatopoeically, the scatting sounds murmured by guitarist Charlie Christian when he soloed during jam sessions, and that the resounding aftershock of drummer Kenny Clarke's bass drum attacks created bop-like sounds. One of the first bop units to work before a regular paying audience was Dizzy Gillespie's in early 1944. The band was together for four months playing on 52nd Street. The group consisted of Gillespie on trumpet, Don Byas on tenor sax, George Wallington on piano, Oscar Pettiford on bass, and Max Roach on drums. The music that this group was playing was very different from anything else on the street, and for a while it was called, simply, "Fifty-second Street Jazz."

Musical Elements of Bop

As we have seen, the leaders of the bop movement played in the big bands. The world of big band music is, by necessity, the medium of the arranger, not the soloist. No matter how exciting the band or the arrangements might be, after a while the constant playing of the same charts night after night can become stifling for a player who wants to "stretch out," that is, play extended solos. As a result, the new music primarily became a small group effort. The preferred makeup of the prototypical bop combo was a front line of trumpet and sax and a rhythm section of piano, bass, and drums.

Harmony, melody, tempo, and rhythm were all addressed differently in the new music. Harmonically, bop players used a greater range of notes. The extra notes are called *melodic extensions,* because they are not among the primary notes of a song's chords. The use of the flatted fifth note of the scale gave the music a dissonant feeling, which sounded "weird" to many of the older players as well as to the majority of the Dixie and swing audience. Eddie Condon, one of the leaders of the Dixieland movement, scowled, "We don't flatten our fifths, we drink 'em."

Melodically, the bop players frequently played tunes that were based on the chord structures of popular standards. The popular songs that had interesting harmonic components, such as "I Got Rhythm," "All the Things You Are," "How High the Moon," and "Cherokee" were perfect vehicles for players to use as springboards in jam sessions, because all the players knew these classics. This had been done by some swing players, but most of them stayed close to the melody and simply added ornamentation. Taking a cue from forward-looking, established players like Coleman Hawkins and Lester Young, the bop players often used the chord structure as a guide and created new melodies on the harmonics of the existing melody. Hawkins had done this on his classic reading of "Body and Soul" and Young, an even greater influence on the bop players, used the technique on a regular basis.

339

Tempo was another area of bop innovation. Swing music as played by the big bands was created primarily for dancing. Tempos had to be consistent. Whether a brisk number or a ballad, the arrangement had to maintain the tempo fairly consistently, or perhaps slowly and regularly increase it throughout the piece. In bop, there are often abrupt shifts in tempo in any given piece, which made it impossible to dance to. Where the swing player preferred medium tempos in the range of one hundred to two hundred beats per minute, the bop players often pushed at either a frenetic pace, up to three hundred beats per minute, or at an agonizingly slow tempo substantially below a hundred beats per minute. On both the fast and slow tempos, the bop soloist would cram in batches of sixteenth, thirty-second, and sometimes even sixty-fourth notes.

Finally, the area of rhythm. One of the most astute studies on the subject of jazz can be found in James Lincoln Collier's book *The Making of Jazz: A Comprehensive History*. Collier feels that the most significant difference between swing and bop styles is in rhythm. Let's begin with the drums. In swing, the bass drum was usually hit with the foot pedal on every beat. This reinforced the beat for the dancers, sort of like a regular heart beat—always there. **Kenny Clarke** (1914-1985) found that by placing that ground beat onto the top cymbal he could not only keep up with the super-fast tempos but also create cross rhythms and use the bass drum for propulsive effects. His use of the bass drum for sudden, unexpected thrusts was called "dropping bombs" and created a jolting effect. There was a shift in phrasing from the first and third beats in the measure to the second and fourth—a transfer from phrasing the "on" beat to the "off" beat. According to Clarke, "In 1937 I'd got tired of playing like Jo Jones. It was time for jazz drummers to move ahead. I took the main beat away from the bass drum and up to the top cymbal. I

Drummer

Frank Driggs Collection

Bird and Diz: The leading horn innovators in bop. The two horn leaders of the bebop movement, Charlie Parker on alto saxophone and Dizzy Gillespie on trumpet, May 1945 at Town Hall, New York. Most of the players of bebop created new songs based on the harmonic chord structures of well-known standard songs. In his autobiography, Gillespie explained, "We'd take the chord structures of various standard and pop tunes and create new chords, melodies, and songs from them. We found out what the composers were doing by analyzing these tunes, and then added substitute chords to songs like 'Night and Day,' 'How High the Moon,' 'Lover,' ' What Is This Thing Called Love?' and 'Whispering.' When we borrowed from a standard, we added and substituted so many chords that most people didn't know what song we really were playing. 'How High the Moon' became 'Ornithology' and 'What Is This Thing Called Love?' was 'Hothouse!'"

James Patrick, who won a Grammy for his insightful liner notes to Charlie Parker's boxed record set on Savoy Records, points out the financial considerations for creating new songs based on chord structures of well-known standards: "Under the mechanical right, if a work were duly copyrighted and licensed through a publisher, the record company was obliged to pay two cents per side for each 78 rpm disc sold, one cent each to the composer and the publisher. If, for example, an artist recorded George Gershwin's 'I Got Rhythm,' the record company would have to pay out two cents for every record sold in addition to the musician's session fees and the artist royalties. If, on the other hand, an artist recorded an 'original' composition using only Gershwin's chord progressions to which a new melody had been fit, the record company might save substantial sums or even produce additional income. If the work was uncopyrighted, as was the case for the bulk of Parker's Dial recordings, there is no legal obligation to pay royalties to anyone. The record company, however, might conclude an agreement with the composer of the 'original' whereby, in exchange for a small advance on royalties, the composer agees to license his work through the record-company-as-publisher. Such was the arrangement between Parker and [Herman] Lubinsky, owner of Savoy Records. Thus, for the price of an advance, Savoy could not only save one half of its own mechanical rights obligations (had they recorded copyrighted works), but also could establish its legal claim to one half of any future royalties the work might generate. There were, of course, numerous abuses of this system of rights. But in general, the system provided a legal substructure for a climate that was musically beneficial to both Parker and Lubinsky."

found out I could get pitch and timbre variations up there, according to the way the stick struck the cymbal, and a pretty sound. The beat had a better flow."

Mark Gridley, in *Jazz Styles: History and Analysis* (one of the best sources for explanations of the entire spectrum of jazz styles), adds **Max Roach** (1925-) to the pantheon of bop drummers, saying that the formation of the new techniques "became crystallized" in the playing of Clarke and Roach." Clarke would go on to help establish the Modern Jazz Quartet in 1952 and then leave America for Paris where he played until his death in 1985. According to Gridley, Roach became "the top drummer in bop, known for increasing spontaneous musical communication with the soloists he accompanied. Roach popularized the 'chattering' in bop-style drumming. Having been one of the most-recorded sidemen of the 1940s, Roach became a prominent bandleader in the 1950s and remained active in the 1990s as drummer, bandleader and composer." Roach taught music at Yale and other schools and is professor of music at the University of Massachusetts at Amherst. Another important rhythm change was in the role of the bass player, who in bop became the "heartbeat" of the rhythm section. This allowed the piano player to stop worrying about that function. The pianist could now play chords to "feed" the horn soloists. This "comping" style was a departure from the stride tradition of playing bass-line figures with the left hand. Collier concluded that rhythm most separated the swing player from the bop player because not one established swing player ever succeeded in playing bop (or at the very least became an important player of that idiom).

Courtesy Ed Sabola

Max Roach (left) and Al Tinney reunited in Buffalo in 1990. To the far left is James Patrick, the head of jazz studies at the University of Buffalo, who was responsible for reuniting Roach and Tinney. The two hadn't seen each other since Roach worked in Tinney's group at Monroe's Uptown House. Over the years, Roach was one of the most eloquent spokesmen about the working conditions endured by modern jazzmen. James Patrick produced a video-history titled *The Al Tinney Project: Max Roach*, June 1995. In the video, Roach pointed out that one of the reasons that bop became so adventurous was that during the war years the government imposed a twenty percent "Dance Tax" which most smaller clubs didn't wish to pay—thus the emphasis upon instrumental virtuosity. Roach also attested to the significance of Al Tinney and the fact that in the early 1940s Tinney was further advanced than bebop innovators Charlie Parker and Bud Powell. "When we were working at Monroe's Uptown House, Bud was on the scene, but he wasn't the dominant force on the scene like Allen was. He [Tinney] was the piano [player] of note during that time . . . He was a very important person in there—and even more important than Charlie Parker and Victor Coulson in that band."

Bop vs. Swing

Performance

1. Bop's preferred instrumentation is the small combo rather than big band.
2. Bop's average tempo is faster.
3. Clarinet is rare in bop.
4. Display of instrumental virtuosity is a higher priority for bop players.
5. Rhythm guitar is rare in bop.
6. Bop places less emphasis on arrangements.

Style

1. Bop's melodies are more complex.
2. Bop's harmonies are more complex.
3. Bop's accompaniment rhythms are more varied.
4. In bop, comping is more prevalent than stride style and simple, on-the-beat chording.
5. Bop drummers play their timekeeping rhythms primarily on suspended cymbal, rather than on snare drum, high hat, or bass drum.
6. Bop tunes and chord progressions are more unresolved.
7. Bop's style is more agitated.

Source: Mark C. Gridley, Jazz Styles: History and Analysis, *5th ed. Prentice Hall, 1978-93.*

The Leaders of Bop

Billy Eckstine (1914-1993) was best known to popular audiences for a cavernous baritone voice and sultry style that made him the first black romantic balladeer during the 1940s and 1950s. Between 1945 and 1951 Eckstine had seven million-selling records, including "Everything I Have Is Yours" and his signature song, "I Apologize." The suave, handsome vocalist was a trendsetter in fashion (the roll collars on his shirts were called "Mr. B collars"), and swooning females of all races bought his records and sighed adoringly to his vibrato-laden ballads. Eckstine was a gentleman who seemed miffed at the lack of career options for an African-American ballad singer: "They weren't ready for black singers singing ballads and love songs. It sounds ridiculous, but it's true. We weren't supposed to sing about love, we were supposed to sing about work or blues or some dumb crap," he fumed to jazz writer Lee Jeske.

Eckstine was much more than a smooth balladeer. He was the leader of the first bebop big band. In 1943 Eckstine left Earl "Fatha" Hines's band, where he had been featured as a singer since 1939 (Eckstine's big hit with Hines band was "Jelly, Jelly" in 1940, and he recruited Sarah Vaughan, Dizzy Gillespie, and Charlie Parker into the band). Eckstine formed his own band in 1944. After a short-lived attempt as a solo singer (billed as "Billy X-Tine") he formed the first bop band with Charlie Parker and Dizzy Gillespie, who served as his musical director for a short time before both he and Parker moved on to 52nd Street in early 1945 to play at the Three Deuces.

The Billy Eckstine unit played hot, orchestrated bop of the highest level. Eckstine not only sang but played trumpet and valve trombone. His young hellions included trumpeters Gail Brockman, Kenny Dorham, Shorty McConnell, and Fats Navarro. Navarro replaced Gillespie. According to Eckstine, "As great as Diz is, Fats played his book and you would hardly know that Diz had left the band. 'Fat Girl' played Dizzy's solos, not note for note, but his ideas on Dizzy's parts and the feeling was the same and there was just as much swing." Jerry Valentine wrote most of the arrangements, and tenorist Budd Johnson, who was the chief arranger in the Hines band, along with pianist Tadd Dameron, also contributed written scores.

Mr. B and the first bop big band. Billy Eckstine on valve trombone at the right, with one of his "Unholy Four," Dexter Gordon, on tenor saxophone to the left, at the mike wearing the hat. After Eckstine left the Earl Hines orchestra he formed his own group. Eckstine had developed a following based on his hit with Hines, "Jelly, Jelly" and he pointed out in Gillespie's *To Be or Not to Bop*, "So I got my band together on that pretense [the hit song]. And when I left and started my band, all the guys left with me, Diz and Shadow and Bird all left. Diz was my first musical director with my band. We were working Fifty-second Street, and the offices wanted me to get a band, which at that particular time was about the only way a black person could excel in music, having an orchestra. So Diz was my first musical director, and some of the earlier things that he later became very famous with were written in my band, 'Bebop,' 'Groovin' High,' things like that. Dizzy was with me for about seven months."

When Gillespie left the band, Eckstine brought in tenor saxophonist Budd Johnson as musical director. Most of Eckstine's best-known bop orchestrations were written by Johnson, trombonist-arranger Jerry Valentine, and Tadd Dameron. Unfortunately, the band had to placate an audience that wanted to hear Eckstine's romantic ballads instead of the hard-driving bop figures that his young sidemen preferred. One thing is certain: Billy Eckstine's band was the first large group to make an all-out attempt to play bebop music. Singer Sarah Vaughan, who had been given her big break by Eckstine, said, "I don't think the band was any experiment. They were just playing music that they knew. They weren't experimenting on anything. If it didn't work, it just didn't work. But it worked. They were getting out there and playing what they knew to play. We tried to educate the people. We used to play dances, and there were just a very few who understood who would be in a corner, jitterbugging forever, while the rest just stood staring at us."

Billy Eckstine was the leader of a wild, hot band that was too advanced for its time. Audiences expected orchestras to play easy, flowing melodies and rhythms. In Nat Shapiro and Nat Hentoff's *Hear Me Talkin to Ya*, Eckstine is quoted as saying, "Progressive jazz or bop was a new version of old things, a theory of chords and so on. I said Bird was responsible for the actual playing of it and Dizzy put it down. And that's the point a whole lot of people mess up on. They say, 'Bird was it!' or 'Diz was it!—but there were two distinct things." The main thing that kept Eckstine's band together was not necessarily the dynamic, exciting instrumentals provided by this forward-looking aggregation—but, rather, it was the leader's romantic ballad singing. Eckstine, as a result of his singing was first titled "The Sepia Sinatra," then "The Great Mr. B." He was the first black singer to become a national sex symbol and to make the front cover of *Life* magazine. Leonard Feather has high praise for Eckstine in *The New Edition of The Encyclopedia of Jazz*: "From 1948 on, Eckstine was immersed in the commercial waters of popular ballad singing, but his flirtation with jazz had been a vitally significant one. Even though his band (recording for National) was so poorly recorded and balanced that there is no adequate evidence left of its exceptional musical ability, Eckstine nevertheless, because of his faith in bop and in the stars it produced, gave employment and encouragement to many of them during the transitional era and was, in effect, himself a pivotal figure in jazz history."

The saxophone section of Eckstine's band was a hotbed of frantic bop sounds. It comprised a roster of future bop stars of the 1950s. In an interview in *Jazz Masters of the Forties* with jazz historian Ira Gitler, Gordon said, "I personally thought that the reed section was the best section in the band—the most cohesive, most together. Sonny Stitt was on the band and sounding like a whirlwind then. Part of the sax section was called the Unholy Four—Stitt, myself, John Jackson and Leo Parker. We liked to rehearse so we'd get our parts first from Jerry Valentine. We'd room together, hang out together. We were so full of tempestuous youth that things didn't always go too smoothly." Also part of the Eckstine sax section were star tenorist Gene Ammons, Budd Johnson, Cecil Payne, and Wardell Gray (who would later team up with Gordon on the West Coast). Add to the names mentioned above drummer Art Blakey, who would go on to become one of the primal forces of the East Coast "hot" hard bop sound of the 1950s with his Jazz Messengers group, and you have quite a group.

This band roared with bop fervor on wailing numbers like "I Love the Rhythm in a Riff," "Second Balcony Jump," "Oo Bop Sh' Bam" and "Blues for Sale." As exciting as the band was, a majority of the audience that came to see and hear the band, came to see and hear Eckstine sing lovely ballads such as "A Cottage for Sale," "Love Is the Thing," "Prisoner of Love," "In the Still of the Night," along with those previously mentioned classics. Will Freidwald in *Jazz Singing* has high praise for Eckstine's vocalizing, claiming that he helped merge the baritone trend with the modern jazz movement: "He uses the advanced harmonic ideas brought to jazz by Parker and Gillespie in singing, thinking in terms of bop-oriented intervals as the basis of everything he sings . . . During the three years he led his orchestra, Eckstine perfected the richest, ripest, and perhaps most beautiful voice of any male singer." "Mr. B" left a rich legacy for other black baritone singers who originally modeled themselves after Bing Crosby, but now could point to Eckstine as a colleague and mentor. Among those others were Al Hibbler ("After the Lights Go Down Low"), Johnny Hartman (*John Coltrane and Johnny Hartman*), Earl Coleman, Melvin Moore, Austin Cromer and Arthur Prysock.

Charlie "Yardbird" Parker was the stuff legends are made of. He was the saxophone voice of the new music and his exploits as a musician were often obscured by the tales of his womanizing and drug taking. Parker was a serious musician who was constantly probing and seeking new insights that would take his music into new directions.

Charlie Parker (1920-1955) has been hailed as one of the few true geniuses in American popular music. Although Parker never had any "hits" on the *Billboard* charts, his import is monumental and far outscales the great majority of pop artists of his time. Here again, we see the significance of the underground. Parker's intuitive absorption of scales, advanced harmony, and dexterity on his instrument, the alto saxophone, remain breathtaking to this very day. As jazz pianist Lennie Tristano once put it, Parker was like a man who at one time had a normal vocabulary and overnight swallowed whole a giant Webster's dictionary and could now recite the entire tome at will.

Parker grew up in Kansas City and was immersed in its blues traditions. Local reedman Buster Smith ("the Professor") was probably his first important idol. After that came Lester Young and then Art Tatum. From Lester Young, Parker learned to create new melodies based on the harmonic framework of standard tunes. He also employed the lyrical, singing quality of Young's legato phrasing. Parker learned from Young by memorizing his recorded solos note for note but, because Parker played alto saxophone rather than Young's tenor, he heard Young's solos at higher intervals and at faster speeds. From Tatum, whom he heard nightly while working in a New York club washing dishes, Parker learned how to embellish standard songs and the importance of prodigious technique, something he had already been in the process of mastering.

Parker's first recordings were with the Jay McShann Orchestra. Parker's brief solo on "Hootie Blues" in 1941 was the first time that musicians unfamiliar with his Monroe's/Minton's explorations took notice. Parker also played in the orchestras of Noble Sissle, Earl Hines, Cootie Williams, Andy Kirk, and Billy Eckstine before establishing the prototype bop quintet format of sax, trumpet, piano, bass, and drums.

It was under his own leadership, as Charlie Parker's Ree-Boppers, that Parker recorded the first of his early classic compositions for Savoy Records. On November 26, 1945, Parker recorded "Now's the Time," "Ko Ko," and "Billie's Bounce." The session was crucial in the development (and exposure to the cult followers) of this new music. It is probably not an overstatement when James Lincoln Collier claims that these sides were "the most influential jazz records to be cut since the Hot Fives and Hot Sevens Armstrong had made nearly two decades earlier."

Courtesy MCA Records

Charlie Parker, like all of the leaders of the bebop movement, had his start in the big bands. He played in a variety of units in Kansas City before joining the Jay McShann Orchestra. In the album above, McShann is standing at the far left, Walter Brown is the vocalist at the microphone, and Parker is the second saxophonist on the left. McShann's specialty was stomping blues tunes and Parker was a good fit because he was an exceptional blues player. The basic elements of the Kansas City territory band tradition gave rise to the sweeping jump saxophone style that Parker injected into his advanced playing.

Courtesy Stash Records

Charlie Parker music has been released on a variety of albums over the years. During his lifetime, Parker had three main recording affiliations: Savoy Records (thirty master takes and seventy false and alternate takes); Dial Records (thirty-five master takes, forty-eight alternate takes, and a variety of leftovers); and Verve Records (eigthy-seven master takes, seventeen alternate takes, some jam sessions and the Jazz at the Philharmonic All-star releases). Shown above are a mix of Charlie Parker compilations. *Left,* early examples of Parker in Kansas City that provide a rare glimpse of the artist in his earliest recording sessions, between 1940 and 1942. The album includes examples of Parker on tenor sax, which he played when he was in the Earl Hines band in 1943, and, rarer yet, a collection of Bob Redcross recordings made informally in a hotel room in Chicago. Most revealing are two examples on the album of Parker practicing over actual 78 rpm releases by Benny Goodman ("China Boy" and "Avalon").

Tony Scott, one of the few clarinetists that made a name of himself playing bebop, was greatly impressed by the arrival of Parker and his associates. Scott notes in *Hear Me Talkin' to Ya*, "The first time the Street heard Bird, I think was around 1942. There was a place that later turned out to be the Spotlite Club, next to the Famous Door. And Bird came in one night and sat in with Don Byas. He blew 'Cherokee' and everybody just flipped. That was probably about his first time on the Street.

52nd Street Invades Toronto Studio

Courtesy Down Beat

When Bird and Diz hit the Street regularly a couple of years later, everybody was astounded and nobody could get near their way of playing music. Finally, Bird and Diz made records, and then guys could imitate it." Dizzy Gillespie was one of Parker's closest friends. In his autobiography Gillespie said of Parker: "Yard and I were like two peas. Charlie Parker and I were closer musically than Monk and I. Our music was like putting whipped cream on jello. His contribution and mine just happened to go together, like putting salt in rice. Before I met Charlie Parker my style had already developed, but he was a great influence on my whole musical life. The same goes for him too because there was never anybody who played any closer than we did on those early sides like 'Groovin' High,' and 'Shaw 'Nuff,' and 'Hot House.' Sometimes I couldn't tell whether I was playing or not because the notes were so close together. Charlie Parker definitely set the standard for phrasing our music, the enunciation of notes."

Courtesy Delmark Records

This album is an example of Charlie Parker recording in an all-star setting in 1945 in California, under the direction of pianist Sir Charles Thompson.

Parker recorded his main body of work for three record labels: Savoy, Dial and Verve. In his early works Parker created new compositions based on the chord sequences of established standards. Parker realized that as the composer of a song he could make a couple of extra pennies for every record sold. Thus when Parker recorded "Ko Ko" he realized that the horns were duplicating the source tune, "Cherokee." Because the sounds were so close to the original melody of "Cherokee" the producer, Teddy Reig, whistled the players to stop performing. Such miscues are called false takes. On *The Complete Savoy Studio Sessions*, miscues such as this are included. Recording sessions frequently produce two or more versions of most of the songs, one of which the "master take," is eventually selected for public release. The other versions are called "alternate takes." The master take of "Ko Ko" is a brilliant musical flight away from the source of "Cherokee." Parker compositions "Ah-Leu-Cha," "Chasin' the Bird," "Constellation," "Merry Go Round," "Steeple Chase," "Thriving on a Riff," and "Red Cross" are all examples of "originals" based on the Gershwin standard "I Got Rhythm."

Courtesy Sony Music

In 1988 executive producer and actor-director Clint Eastwood completed a project that had been close to his heart for many years: releasing a movie biography about Charlie Parker. The movie was called simply *Bird* and starred Forest Whitaker as the modern jazz great. The movie featured Parker's solos on classic selections such as "Ko Ko," "Ornithology," "Now's the Time," and "Parker's Mood," among others, with new accompaniment provided by contemporary jazz greats.

Charlie Parker's nickname was "Yardbird" (for his love of chicken, which were kept in the yard by rural people). This was eventually abbreviated to "Bird" (as in bird in flight). Parker's love of all music, from classical to country, kept his imagination open. He simplified the complexity of his playing with the basic attitude that it was all just music. Unfortunately, Parker's personal life was cluttered with drugs and alcohol. When he died prematurely in 1955, at the age of thirty-four, the coroner observed that he had the body of a man of fifty-five.

In *Celebrating Bird: The Triumph of Charlie Parker*, author Gary Giddins writes, "It is no surprise to learn that Parker was embarrassed by the insipid onomatopoeia 'bebop,' which got tarred to modern jazz and which survives his scorn. He never proselytized for modernism in any guise. Impatient with those who attempted to stampede him into aesthetic cubby holes, he jousted with critics, celebrating the traditions in another (*Down Beat*, 1949). Asked to distinguish between his music and that of his predecessors, however, he invariably demurred: 'It's just music. It's trying to play clean and looking for the pretty notes' (1949). His willingness to let people draw their own conclusions is suggested in his one surviving television appearance, when he disdainfully tells the dotty emcee, 'They say music speaks louder than words, so we'd rather voice our opinion that way.' Everyone agrees that he knew his own worth and had neither the need nor the desire to politic on behalf of the new movement. On the contrary, he kept himself humble with an attentive enthusiasm for those modernists, Stravinsky, Hindemith, Schonberg, Bartok, who were skilled in the compositional techniques he coveted. Yet at twenty-five, he was the acknowledged leader of a new music; at thirty, his brilliance was recognized by musicians around the world; at thirty-four, when he died, he was regarded as an elder statesman who had yet to be superseded by his descendants. No sooner was he buried, in Easter season, then the graffiti appeared: 'Bird Lives.'"

Recording Highlights of Charlie "Yardbird" Parker

Charlie Parker made numerous recordings with three principal record companies: Savoy, Dial, and Verve. Norman Granz's company, Verve, had a variety of earlier incarnations. According to Leonard Feather's *Encyclopedia of Jazz*, "Granz produced his own records, but in 1944-45 he released them on the Philo and Asch labels, and from 1948 to 1951 on Mercury. In 1951, having recalled the rights to all his recordings, Granz transferred the entire catalogue to his own Clef label, supplementing this with the Norgran label in 1954." In 1956 and thereafter, all previous releases were repackaged and distributed on Granz's new label, Verve.

Leader	Selections	Label	Date
Jay McShann Orchestra	Hootie Blues/The Jumpin' Blues	Decca	1941-42
Charlie Parker (probably at Monroe's)	Cherokee	Onyx	1942
Tiny Grimes Quintet	Tiny's Tempo/Red Cross	Savoy	1944
Dizzy Gillespie Sextet	Groovin' High/Dizzy Atmosphere	Guild	1945
Dizzy Gillespie All Star	Salt Peanuts/Shaw 'Nuff/ Lover Man/Hot House	Musicraft Guild	1945
Sir Charles Thompson All Stars	Takin' Off/The Street Beat	Apollo	1945
Charlie Parker Ree-Boppers	Now's the Time/Ko Ko/Billie's Bounce/ Meandering	Savoy	1945
Slim Gaillard	Flat Foot Floogie/Poppity Pop	Halo	1945
Charlie Parker Septet	Moose the Mooche/Ornithology/ Yardbird Suite/Night in Tunisia	Dial	1946
Charlie Parker All Stars	Relaxing at Camarillo/Carvin' the Bird	Dial	1947
Charlie Parker All Stars	Donna Lee/Chasin' the Bird/Cheryl	Savoy	1947
Charlie Parker Quintet	Dexterity/Dewey Square/ Embraceable You/Bird of Paradise	Dial	1947
Charlie Parker Quintet	Scrapple From the Apple/My Old Flame/ Klact-oveeseds-tene/Bird Feathers	Dial	1947
The Dean Benedetti recordings	278 tracks and 465 recordings	Mosaic	1947-48
Charlie Parker All Stars	Ah-Leu-Cha/Parker's Mood/ Constellation/Steeple Chase	Savoy	1948
Charlie Parker with Machito Orchestra	Afro-Cuban Jazz Suite	Clef (Verve)	1948
Charlie Parker with Strings	Just Friends/April in Paris	Mercury/Clef (Verve)	1949
Charlie Parker Quartet	Star Eyes	Norgran (Verve)	1950
Charlie Parker Orchestra	Bloomdido/Leap Frog	Mercury/Clef (Verve)	1950
Charlie Parker (at Birdland)	Blue 'n Boogie/Jumpin With Symphony Sid	Temple (Columbia)	1951
Charlie Parker Quartet	Confirmation	Clef (Verve)	1953
Charlie Parker Big Band	Night and Day/I Can't Get Started	Mercury/Clef (Verve)	1952
Jazz at Massey Hall (The Greatest Jazz Concert Ever)	All the Things You Are/Salt Peanuts	Debut (Prestige)	1953
Charlie Parker Quintet	Love for Sale/I Love Paris	Verve	1954

Charlie Parker's last recording session was held on December 10, 1954.

Dizzy Gillespie: Experimenter and teacher. The most outgoing entertainer of the modernists was Dizzy Gillespie. He played advanced, serious music but his demeanor, his persona, was upbeat and lively. In this respect, Gillespie was quite different from his good friend and coleader of bebop, Charlie Parker, who projected the stage manner of a respectful and nonverbal player. Gillespie loved to mug, clap his hands, and create dance steps on stage. He was lively and ebullient.

Gillespie's engaging stage antics and technical virtuosity as a trumpeter, were accompanied by a deep, theoretical understanding of bebop and a willingness to share his knowledge with other players. Gillespie was the most significant "teacher" of the new music. He was a fine pianist and composer who was always showing his contemporaries musical figures on the piano so they could better understand the musical components and strategies of bebop. In his autobiography Gillespie states, "Progressions actually were one of my main contributions to our music. I showed Bird, Al Haig, George Wallington and scores of piano players who voiced the chords like I did how to play comp." Numerous musicians are quoted in *Hear Me Talkin' to Ya* about Gillespie's teaching. Billy Eckstine noted that, "Now Diz is dizzy like a fox, you know. He's one of the smartest guys around. Musically, he knows what he is doing backwards and forwards. So what he hears that you think maybe is going through goes in and stays. Later, he'll go home and figure it all out just what it is. So the arranging, the chord progressions and things in progressive music, Dizzy is responsible for."

Danny Barker, one of the few star Dixieland players who successfully performed bebop, on a regular basis, was in the Cab Calloway band with Gillespie and bassist Milt Hinton in 1941. He claimed, "Dizzy would blow his new idea in progressions and he and Hinton would experiment on different ideas and melodic patterns. Both Hinton and Dizzy were very studious and energetic and they continued those woodshed sessions."

In his book, *Jazz Styles,* Mark Gridley sums up Gillespie's contributions:

1) A model of unparalleled trumpet mastery: speed, agility, and a high register that set the upper limit for almost all jazz trumpeters who followed;

2) A body of original compositions including several that remain jazz standards;

3) A string of high-quality combos and big bands featuring numerous jazz stars-to-be (such as John Coltrane and Milt Jackson);

4) The use of Afro-Cuban music in jazz;

5) A new musical vocabulary of phrases and new ways of matching solo notes to accompanying chords, both of which became second nature to most modern jazz musicians.

349

Dizzy Gillespie (1917-1993) established the look and sound of the archetypal bopper of the forties. Born John Birks, Gillespie was a disciple of high-note swing stylist Roy Eldridge and followed his model into the Teddy Hill orchestra in 1937. Hill gave Gillespie his sobriquet, remarking that the free-spirited Gillespie was "dizzy as a fox." Gillespie enjoyed short stints with bandleaders Lionel Hampton in 1939, Cab Calloway in 1939-40 ("Pickin' the Cabbage," pre-bop), Benny Carter ("A Night in Tunisia," 1942), Lucky Millinder ("Little John Special," 1942, which includes a trumpet riff that is the genesis of "Salt Peanuts"), Earl Hines in 1943, and four weeks with Duke Ellington, also in 1943. After seven months as musical director and soloist for Billy Eckstine in 1944, Gillespie formed his own bands.

Gillespie was in the forefront of the bop movement as a phenomenally gifted prototechnician on trumpet, as well as an early composer who showed many of the early pianists how to navigate through the advanced harmonics of altered and substitute chord progressions. Unlike most of the bop leaders, Gillespie was outgoing and ebullient. He epitomized, to many, the bop musician with his zoot suit, bop bow ties, horn-rimmed glasses, beret, and jive vocals. When *Life* magazine did a study of the new music, it was Gillespie who was the focus, not the sullen Charlie Parker. Gillespie made better copy. Gillespie and Parker went into the recording studios in February and May, 1945 and cut some of the first enduring bop records, such as "Hot House," "Groovin' High," "Shaw 'Nuff," and "Salt Peanuts."

When Gillespie put together a big band to play concert dates in August 1945, the show was dubbed "The Hepsations of 1945." Under the management wing of Billy Shaw, Gillespie put together dancers and some singers only to find hostile audiences, particularly in the South, where they wanted blues and dance music. This enterprise was quickly disbanded. After another disastrous trip, this time out to California at Billy Berg's club with Charlie Parker, Gillespie returned to the safe haven of New York and entered the recording studio of Victor Records in February 1946 for a jazz album called *New 52nd Street Jazz,* which included "52nd Street Theme," "Anthropology," and "Salt Peanuts." The success of this venture allowed the fiery leader to return to his first love, the big band.

The Dizzy Gillespie big band at Carnegie Hall. Gillespie's great success with the album *New 52nd Street Jazz* on RCA Victor led him to take another stab at forming a big band. On June 10, 1946, with his close up sixteen-piece band featuring arrangements by pianist John Lewis, Gillespie cut "Our Delight" and "Good Dues Blues" for Musicraft Records. The next fall, September 29, 1947, the band appeared at Carnegie Hall (right, with Ella Fitzgerald at the microphone). Most of the reviews of the concert were mixed (like Benny Goodman's 1938 concert in Carnegie Hall, staff reviewers on newspapers and magazines were not that knowledgeable about jazz, and bebop was more difficult to understand than swing).

The *New York Times* wrote, "The style is based on Mr. Gillespie's own trumpet playing and that of Charlie Parker, alto sax, which uses ornamental figuration and big skips in unexpected rhythmic patterns. The four-man trumpet section is capable not only of playing the virtuoso passages, but of playing them at deafening pitch. Every player in the band can support a difficult solo line of counterpoint. The band handles rhythmic irregularities, dissonance, and humorous glissandos with apparent ease. Mr. Gillespie's technical deficiencies are many, however, and the lack of shape in his work pervades the whole impression. For all the frenzied virtuosity listening soon became dull, although that has not discouraged his imitators."

Not all the reviews were as uninformed as those of the *Times*. Bill Gottlieb, who worked as a writer and photographer, and in the 1990s showed his premier jazz collection in major galleries, wrote of the Carnegie Hall concert in the New York *Herald Tribune:* "No doubt about it, 'bebop' is replacing swing. The music in spite of its name is not nonsense. Bebop is modern, progressive music, harmonically suited to the times. Like other jazz forms before it, bebop, in diluted form, will eventually alter even the most commercial forms of popular music. It's begun to do so already."

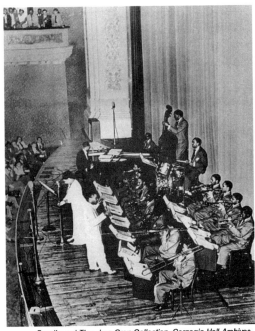

Rosalie and Theodore Cron Collection, Carnegie Hall Archives

From 1946 to 1950 Gillespie kept the large ensemble afloat at a time when most of the big bands were in the process of folding. The band reflected its leader. It was brash and pulsating. At times it seemed disorganized, but it was always challenging. One of the key innovations of Gillespie's big band was the inclusion of the Afro-Cuban habanera rhythm. By adding the multitalented Cuban-born bongo and conga percussionist Chano Pozo to the lineup, a new sound, "Cubop," was born. Selections such as "Cubana Be, Cubana Bop," "Tin Tin Deo," "Afro Cuban Suite," and the best known classic of this ilk, "Manteca," were recorded between 1946 and 1948.

In 1954 Gillespie's trumpet was damaged when a dancer, performing in a club for his birthday celebration, bent it out of shape. The trumpet was fixed at an odd angle and when the trumpeter blew into it the sound radiated upward. From that point on, Gillespie worked with trumpets he designed to point up at a 45-degree angle. That unique trumpet and the sight of Gillespie's cheeks blown out, instead of sucked in like conventional brass players, became part of the jazz legacy.

Gillespie became one of the only well-known bop innovators (Max Roach is another) who did not fall prey to the debilitating drug scourge that thwarted so many others. His healthy and consistently high level of musical output throughout his career placed Gillespie at a somewhat anachronistic plateau when compared to co-conspirator Charlie Parker.

Latin Jazz and Cubop

According to writer Max Salazar writing in *Latin Beat* magazine (April 1993), "Afro-Cuban jazz or Cubop (as it was called by popular New York City DJ Symphony Sid Torin during the late '40s before 'Latin jazz' stuck) was a valuable and probably inevitable synthesis of two musics with a common historical root. It was invented by the Machito orchestra in 1943 when its musical director, Dr. Mario Bauza, wrote 'Tanga.'" In attempting to connect the many dots that make up the Latin and jazz synthesis, we could go all the way back to the early years of the slave trade and draw a line to the "Latin tinge" that Jelly Roll Morton absorbed and then insinuated into many of his own compositions.

The modern phase of the Latin jazz connection, however begins with Xavier Cugat. To most Americans, Latin American dance music was the sole province of this bandleader-violinist-composer, who formed his first American band in 1929. Cugat's was a polite society unit and the band of choice whenever a Latin band was needed for a musical sequence in a Hollywood film (he was featured in scores of them, from his first in 1929, *In Gay Madrid*, to his last in 1969, *The Phynx*). It was Cugat, more than anyone else, who popularized the Latin American dances, music, and costumes during the 1930s and 1940s. According to *Pop Memories,* Cugat had twenty-one hit songs. The most popular were "The Lady in Red," 1935, "Perfidia," 1941, "Brazil," 1943, and "South America, Take It Away," 1946.

Desi Arnaz introduced conga drums to American audiences at Miami's La Conga Club in the late 1930s. In 1936 he helped create a fad in conga sounds when he appeared with the Xavier Cugat band. In 1939 he played the conga, sang, and starred in Rodgers and Hart's Broadway hit *Too Many Girls*. The next year he starred in the film of the same name with Lucille Ball, whom he married that year. Arnaz was best known to American audiences for his portrayal of Ball's husband, Rickie Ricardo, on the classic television situation comedy "I Love Lucy" (1951-59).

In Ole Olsen and Chic Johnson's 1941 Hollywood adaptation of their zany Broadway hit *Hellzapoppin,* Cee Pee Johnson manned three congas, backed by fellow jazzmen guitarist Slim Gaillard, bassist Slam Stewart, and trumpeter Rex Stewart. The Universal Studios publicity promo reads, "It's rhythm time when these gates swing out." Selections such as "Congeroo" and "Congo Beso" got the Lindy Hoppers jumping. The use of congas in this film (and in the 20th Century-Fox Carmen Miranda musicals) anticipated Chano Pozo's entry into the Dizzy Gillespie orchestra by five years. Still, it would be Chano Pozo, and bandleader Machito, who would establish the strongest Latin connection to the "new jazz" of the 1940s.

Machito (1912-1984), born Frank Raul Grillo, was born in Tampa, Florida, and raised in Cuba. He worked as a singer and maracas player for a wide assortment of Latin bands between 1928 and 1937, when he came back to the United States. After recording with bandleader Xavier Cugat, Machito formed his own Afro-Cuban band in 1940. He named it the Afro-Cubans, thus laying down the framework for the term "Afro-Cuban." Machito's first recordings were made for Decca Records in 1941 with trumpeter Mario Bauza as musical director. By the mid-1940s, the Afro-Cubans had performed at concerts with bandleader Stan Kenton and had played, and in some cases recorded, with key bop musicians. In 1948-49 bop stars such as Charlie Parker, Dizzy Gillespie, Flip Phillips, Howard McGhee, Brew Moore, and Armando Peraza recorded with the Machito band. Throughout the 1950s, during the mambo craze and into the 1980s, Machito was the master facilitator between Latin roots and modern jazz, whether it was referred to as Afro-Cuban, Cubop, Latin jazz or salsa. In 1987 Carlos Ortiz released a documentary film, *Machito: A Latin Jazz Legacy*, which includes newsreel material and photographs of this master musician from the 1930s right up to his last years.

Mario Bauza (1911-1993) had played with Machito in a teenage orchestra in Havana, Cuba, called Jovenes de Redencion, before coming to America, where he became bandleader Chick Webb's lead trumpeter and musical director from 1933 to 1938. Bauza

Frank Driggs Collection

Machito's Afro-Cuban Orchestra at the Club Brazil, 1946. Machito, bottom right, Mario Bauza, next to him, Bing Crosby, center, and vocalist Graciela, standing fourth from right. Machito's band is credited as the first significant Latin band to employ black musicians, and the first to feature bop-oriented jazz. Latin record producer Al Santiago wrote in *Latin Beat* magazine (April 1993) "Machito's Afro-Cubans were the greatest Latin band ever, no ifs, ands or buts."

The main force in Machito's band was musical director Mario Bauza, who attempted to raise the standard of Latin music up to that of the American dance bands of the time. Bauza and Cab Calloway arranger John Bartee prepared for the Machito group's 1940 debut at the Park Plaza, on 110th Street and Fifth Avenue, opposite Pagani's Happy Boys. Bauza blended Cuban rhythm and repertoire with trumpets and the saxophone section featured in the jazz bands. Up until Machito's Cuban and jazz fusions, New York Latin music had been all white and society-club-oriented.

According to John Storm Roberts in his book *The Latin Tinge: The Impact of Latin American Music on the United States:* "The early Afro-Cubans consisted of three saxes, two trumpets, piano, bass, bongo, and timbales. From the start, Bauza included non-Latins in his wind sections, partly because he wanted jazz-oriented players, and also because there were relatively few top rank Latin hornmen in New York. Bauza hired musicians rather than 'names,' and few of his sidemen, American or Latin, became particularly well known, with the exception of the young Tito Puente, who spent a while with the band in the early 1940s, and pianist Joe Loco." Roberts states flatly: "Cubop had three creative leaders: Stan Kenton, Dizzy Gillespie, and Machito."

worked briefly with bandleaders Don Redman, Fletcher Henderson, and Cab Calloway (where he became fast friends with fellow sideman Dizzy Gillespie) before joining Machito's Afro-Cubans in 1940. It was Bauza, who also played reeds, and married Machito's sister, Graciela, who is generally regarded as the mastermind behind the idea of combining brass, writing in a jazz context with a Cuban rhythm section, which includes the use of congas, bongos, timbales, and maracas.

In 1946 Bauza telephoned Gillespie, who had been seeking something that could provide the Latin component he felt his big band was lacking. Bauza claimed prophetically to Gillespie, "I have what you've been looking for just arrived from Cuba." That something was **Chano Pozo** (1915-1948), who hailed from Havana, Cuba, and was one of the most colorful and exciting percussionists to gain recognition in the world of jazz. He was a powerful congaist who also sang and danced with such flair that in Cuba during the late 1930s and early 1940s he was a celebrity among the people of the poor district of Pueblo Nuevo. When he joined Amado Trinidad's Cadena Azul orchestra, Pozo's fame increased due to radio broadcasts. In 1943 Pozo was informed that a number of his compositions were hits for New York bands. His song "Paraparampampin" was a hit for Xavier Cugat, Miguelito Valdes, Augusto Coen, Noro Morales, Casino De La Playa, and Machito. "Nague" was also a huge hit for Machito and became his band's theme song. By 1946, after meeting with Mario Bauza, Pozo was convinced that New York City, with its large Latin community, was ready for him.

DOWN BEAT

VOL. 16—NO. 3   CHICAGO, FEBRUARY 25, 1949

(Copyright, 1949, Down Beat Publishing Co.)

Bopper Granz Raises Mercury's Temperature

New York—Danceable bop at last, is what JATP guardian Norman Granz calls the recordings made recently with tenorist Flip Phillips and altoist Charlie Parker, backed by Machito's Afro-Cuban band. Discs were first in Mercury's new Afro-Cuban jazz series. Shown above are Phillips, Granz (on bongos), and part of Machito's unit. Granz will supervise Mercury's bop jazz hereafter.

Courtesy Down Beat

Gillespie said, "I've always been interested in Latin music, so when I formed my big band, I told Mario I wanted a tom tom player—I didn't know it was called a conga drum. Mario had first recommended a bongo player named Chicitco, who was good, but it wasn't the sound I wanted. I needed a conga drummer for a Town Hall concert. Mario took me to Chano's apartment and we hit it off well even though he didn't speak English. When we shook hands it felt like I was being crushed by cinder blocks. Chano played the Town Hall concert and that was the first time the conga was used in a jazz band. Ella Fitzgerald, who was on the same bill, remarked that a new sound of jazz was born that evening."

Pozo's first recordings in the United States occurred in July 1946, when he performed with Gillespie's band on the Musicraft label. In February 1947, Pozo recorded with Tito Rodriguez and the Machito orchestra and Marcelino Guerrs's Conjunto Batamu organization. At that time Pozo was viewed by the general music public as merely an unknown percussionist in a modern jazz band. However, in the Latin community he was accorded star status. At various ballrooms Pozo would perform the first half of his show dressed in a white tuxedo with top hat. But at intermission he would strip to the waist and with his rippling muscles gleaming with oil he would drum and chant until the crowd cheered deliriously, "Chano Pozo, Chano Pozo!"

Gillespie noted, "All of my Afro-Cuban numbers except 'Cubana-Be' [written by George Russell] were composed by Chano and me. It was Chano's ideas and I always added something. Pozo would always sing the instrument parts and then ask if anything was

Frank Driggs Collection

Left to right, James Moody, Chano Pozo, and Dizzy Gillespie in 1948. Pozo on conga was a main connection of Cuban rhythm to the Gillespie orchestra's Cubop sounds between 1946 and 1948.

missing. Man, there was always something missing. Chano and I had different versions of 'Tin Tin Deo.' Mine had chords and Chano's was strictly rhythm and melody. He hummed his idea and all it served for was an introduction. I expanded the introduction and the music." The most important selection that the two collaborated on was "Mantaeca," which became the most important and influential of all of the numbers regarded as Afro-Cuban.

In December 1948, Pozo was gunned down at the El Rio Bar and Grill on the corner of 111th Street and Lenox Avenue in Harlem by a man who felt wronged by the tempestuous percussionist. The connection between Latin music and modern jazz that Pozo, Bauza, Machito, and Gillespie created during the 1940s would live on in the music called "salsa" during the 1980s and 1990s. Bandleader Tito Puente, a master timbales player and multi-instrumentalist known as "El Rey" ("The King") along with Celia Cruz (the "Queen of Salsa"), and the advanced piano explorations of exciting bandleader Eddie Palmieri, have been the most influential of the Latin-jazz performers over the past twenty years.

Chano Pozo and Cubop Recordings

Gillespie Cubop releases	Date
One Bass Hit (part 2) Things to Come He Beeped When He Shoulda Bopped	July 9, 1946
Owl Oo-Pop-A-Da Two Bass Hit	August 22, 1947
Algo Bueno (Woody'n You) Cool Breeze Cubana Be Cubana Bop	December 22, 1947
Manteca Good Bait Ool-Ya-Koo Minor Walk	December 30, 1947
Good Bait Ool Ya Koo Round Midnight I Can't Get Started Oop-A-Da Algo Bueno (Woody'n You) Two Bass Hit Things to Come Afro Cuban Suite	February 28, 1948

After the blazing roar of Afro-Cuban jazz led by Machito, Dizzy Gillespie, and Stan Kenton during the 1940s, came a popular style that occasionally made the top forty charts in the 1950s: the mambo, a true hybrid mix of American and Latin dance music. Perez Prado became the major popularizer of the form during this time.

In *The Latin Tinge,* John Storm Roberts points out that Prado presented mambo in diluted form to meet the needs of the mass audiences. "If Prado symbolized the mambo's impact on the American public at large, Tito Puente and Tito Rodriguez symbolized its creative achievement. The great era of the New York mambo can be said to date from 1952, when the Palladium Dance Hall switched to an all-mambo policy featuring the big bands of Puente, Rodriguez, and Machito. Puente's sound was always busier and more nervous than Rodriguez's, based on heavier brass writing. His arranging, like his timbales playing, was fast, tight, jumpy, bravura."

By the 1970s Puente became the best-known Latin player of Latin jazz. Puente's title of "King of the Mambo," which had started as a public relations gimmick in the 1950s, became a reality by the 1970s. By the 1970s, however, "salsa" was the contemporary word for hot, up-tempo, creative Latin music. Roughly translated, it means hot sauce, and Puente was easily its best-known player.

Courtesy of Concord Jazz, Inc.

354

The two leaders of bop piano were Bud Powell and Thelonious Monk. **Bud Powell** (1924-1966) was the most influential and copied of the bop pianists. Combining the styles of Earl Hines and Art Tatum, Powell created a percussive, linear approach that became the model for most modernists, according to Mark Gridley, in place of the bass-line striding figures employed by Teddy Wilson. "Powell's left hand inserted brief, sporadically placed two-and three-note chords that reduced his statement of harmony to the barest minimum. He mastered the erratically syncopated rhythms of bop and Dizzy Gillespie charged through his solos with terrific force." "Un Poco Loco," "Parisian Thoroughfare," and "Glass Enclosure" are three of Powell's best-known performances. Unfortunately Powell's career was hindered by mental instability as well as drug and alcohol problems.

Courtesy Delmark Records

Bud Powell was viewed as the most influential of the bop pianists. He was an early contributor to the bop scene at Minton's and he played in Cootie Williams' band from 1942 to 1944. Powell played numerous club engagements during the late 1940s and 1950s before moving to Paris in 1959, where he led a trio that featured fellow expatriate Kenny Clarke on drums (1959-62). Powell's strength was his imaginative improvisations as well as his technical prowess, which allowed him to play rapid lines with his right hand while his left hand comped irregularly spaced dissonant clusters.

J. Bradford Robinson's entry on Bud Powell in *The New Grove Dictionary of Jazz* states, "At fast and medium tempos . . . he preferred the spare manner he devised in the early 1940s; rapid melodic lines in the right hand punctuated by irregularly spaced, dissonant chords in the left. This almost antipianistic style (which was adopted by most bop pianists of the time) left him free to pursue linear melody in the manner of bop wind players, and it was as a melodist that Powell stood apart from his many imitators. At its best, Powell's playing was sustained by a free unfolding of rapid and unpredictable melodic invention, to which he brought a brittle, precise touch and creative intensity." Today, Tommy Flanagan, Horace Silver, and Barry Harris are good representatives of the post-Powell heritage. Part of Powell's story of his last years in Paris and his friendship with a young Frenchman named Francis Paudras—was fictionalized in the film *'Round Midnight* (1986).

Thelonious Monk's musical roots go back to Minton's Playhouse during the fall of 1940. One of the regulars at those sessions was an enthusiastic jazz fan, Jerry Newman, who set up a portable recording unit for which Monk first recorded (those early recordings had Monk comping behind others). Monk made four sides commercially in 1944 with Coleman Hawkins ("Drifting on a Reed," "Flying Hawk," "On the Bean," and "Recollections"), but was given little solo space. Barry Ulanov points out in his *History of Jazz*, "The piano was used in bop chiefly as an accompanying instrument; it had little place in a music that was essentially a one-line expression, played by a single-line solo instrument or several in unison."

Monk made his first records of importance in a sextet format for Blue Note Records in 1947. These recordings were released under his own name. Seldom would Monk work strictly as a sideman, and the session resulted in two originals, "Humph," and "Thelonious." Other Blue Note releases included masterpieces "Evidence" and "Criss Cross."

A drug bust in 1951 deprived Monk of New York employment for six years, which helped delay audience recognition of this creative force. Although Monk continued to record during that time, he seldom left his beloved New York. In 1957, Monk created a critical stir that remained unabated throughout his lifetime.

Thelonious Sphere Monk (1911-1982) was the most unconventional of all the keyboard players up to this point in history. His approach is unusual in that it was based on the stride style of James P. Johnson and Fats Waller, but mixed in the discordant, jagged contours of bop. Monk's use of irregular tone clusters and application of space and economy was misunderstood as erratic, unpianistic awkwardness by many listeners and critics. Monk's earliest recordings, made in 1941, reflect the influence of the stride masters as well as swing stylist Teddy Wilson. In time Monk deliberately chose a brusque, percussive attack that was quite the opposite of Wilson's smooth, sophisticated approach. Coleman Hawkins employed Monk for two years, but he wasn't very popular with many of the players, who thought his piano playing primitive. Although Monk gained grudging respect as a composer of future classics such as "Epistrophy," "'Round Midnight," "52nd Street Theme," and "Well You Needn't," he didn't receive much work as a keyboardist after leaving Hawkins. He was fired from Dizzy Gillespie's orchestra for persistent lateness in 1946.

Monk's first sessions as a leader occurred for the fledging independent label Blue Note (1947-52) and became important documents showcasing the pianist in trio, quintet, and sextet settings. Barry Kernfeld's *Blackwell Guide to Recorded Jazz* summarizes Monk's place in the jazz hierachy at the time: "Monk was handicapped by his reputation as an eccentric pianist, an image he did nothing to alter by his bizarre behaviour, and his direct influence on keyboard styles was marginal." Monk was so iconoclastic that there were very few followers of his style. The vastly underappreciated Herbie Nichols was perhaps the most original of his proteges. Others include Randy Weston and Stan Tracey.

Courtesy Rhapsody Films

The High Priest of Jazz: Thelonious Monk. The Thelonious Monk group filmed in concert in 1966. Monk often worked with tenor saxophonist Charlie Rouse, who played with the pianist from 1959 to 1970. This concert featured Monk at the height of his powers. *Time* magazine had featured the unorthodox pianist on its cover in 1964 and Monk began to travel to other countries to perform in concert settings.

Recognition of Monk's stature as leader of the modern jazz movement came late. During the genesis of bebop Monk was overlooked by all but cult followers and fellow boppers. He was unknown to the general public. In a *Down Beat* interview in 1947 Monk was bewildered by all the attention that Charlie Parker and Dizzy Gillespie had received. Monk said, "Bebop wasn't developed in any deliberate way. For my part I'll say it was just the style of music I happened to play. I think all styles are built around the piano developments. The piano lays the chord and rhythm foundations."

Today Monk is viewed by many as a musical genius. His ascension into the ranks of the jazz greats began in the mid-1950s. The reappraisal of his work first began with acknowledgement of his importance as a composer. Later, Monk also came to be appreciated as a masterful and brilliant keyboard original. An indication of Monk's current status is the establishment of the multimillion-dollar Thelonious Monk Institute of Jazz, located in Washington, D.C., with an education arm at the New England Conservatory of Music in Boston, Massachusetts. Since 1987, the institute has held prestigious international jazz competitions that have unearthed a number of young jazz lions, including pianists Marcus Roberts (winner of 1987 competition), Jacky Terrasson (winner in 1993), saxophonist Joshua Redman (winner in 1991), and keyboard star Joey DeFrancesco (a runner-up in 1987), among others.

Left to right, Allan Eager, tenor sax, Fats Navarro, muted trumpet, and Kenny Clarke, drums. This picture shows a portion of the 1941 Tadd Dameron unit in action at the Royal Roost (Dameron, piano and leader, and Curly Russell, bass, were two other members). **Tadd Dameron** (1917-1965) was among the first to write memorable arrangements for small bop aggregations. Dameron's compositions were usually the main feature of his tightly knit, arranged bebop performance. Dameron's "The Squirrel," "Our Delight," "Tadd Walk," "Lady Bird," "If You Could See Me Now," "Good Bait," and "Dameronia" are modern jazz classics that are still played. During the early 1980s, drummer Philly Joe Jones led a group called Dameronia, which played many of Tadd Dameron's compositions.

Fats Navarro (1923-1950), who played in some of Tadd Dameron's ensembles, was the warmest of the bop trumpeters, and was closest to Dizzy Gillespie in creating ingenious solos—his nickname was "Fat Girl." Modern jazz authority Ira Gitler, writing liner notes to the album *Good Bait,* summarized Navarro's technique: "Fats' style was precise, symmetrical, soaring and lyrical. It was also well-nigh impeccable; and this was not because he played it safe, although his playing was less intricate than Gillespie's. His surging power even made itself felt in his muted work." Dizzy Gillespie said that Navarro's musical execution on trumpet consisted of having great force—"Fats probably had the best attack of all of us, and attack is the nub, the essence of the trumpet." Navarro unfortunately fell prey to drugs and tuberculosis, and his career was much too brief. He is often mentioned as the most direct link to Clifford Brown, the brightest trumpet voice of the 1950s, who also had a short career—he died in an automobile mishap in 1956.

Stanley Crouch wrote liner notes for a reissue of Tadd Dameron and Fats Navarro air-check acetates taken from the summer and fall of 1948 at the Royal Roost—*Fats Navarro: Featured with the Tadd Dameron Band*, Milestone Records. Crouch offers: "No one else could make 'Good Bait,' 'Tadd Walk,' 'Dameronia,' or any of the other lines sound precisely as they do here. That broad brassy sound—part public declaration, part introspective examination and riddled as well with a pensive funk and confident urbanity—was perfect for what these compositions and arrangements demanded. Navarro could swallow changes and rhythms with a melodic force, as on 'Anthropology,' or float his lines as he does on 'Our Delight.' His sound was beautiful, muted or open and Dameron almost never had him take the first solo, seeming to use him as a threat for the first soloist or a standard for the third (which had a very good effect on [alto saxophonist] Rudy Williams most of the time)." Crouch concluded that Navarro was therefore, "a perfect collaborator for Dameron."

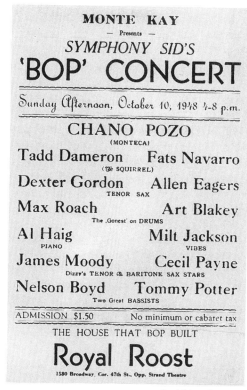

Billed as "The Metropolitan Bopera House" and "The House That Bop Built," the Royal Roost was the most sympathetic club for modern jazz sounds during the late 1940s. Located at 1647 Broadway at West 47th Street in New York, the Royal Roost, which earlier was operated as a chicken restaurant, opened around 1945 and was active into the 1950s. Modernists like Charlie Paker, Tadd Dameron, Miles Davis, and Lennie Tristano played there on many occasions.

The billing at the Royal Roost, shown above, is interesting because it combines stars of modern jazz (Charlie Ventura and Charlie Parker) with those of rhythm and blues (the Ravens and Dinah Washington).

There are far too many worthy modernist players to mention, some of whom are still playing, without overextending this tract (see "Other Bebop Contributors" chart on the next page.) But there are a couple of noteworthy contributors who fall just below the pantheon of the greatest. Tenor tandem **Wardell Gray** (1921-1955) and **Dexter Gordon** (1927-1990), who staged "battles" on selections like "The Chase" and "Steeple Chase," carved out a model for future modernists to approximate. Wardell Gray was one of the most melodically interesting saxophone players among the bop stylists. His catchy, hook-laden solos literally sang to the listener, as evidenced by Annie Ross's expertly crafted vocalese lyrics to three of his best-known recordings—"Twisted," "Jackie," and "Farmer's Market." Gray died mysteriously in 1949, but Gordon was bestowed elder-statesman status when he returned from a long stay overseas in the 1970s. He even won an Academy Award nomination (the first and only for a jazzman) for his portrayal of an expatriate jazzman (based on a combination of Bud Powell and Lester Young, and, in no small measure, himself) in the Bertrand Tavernier film *'Round Midnight* (1986). The movie did win jazz's first Academy Award for best original score for Herbie Hancock.

While New York was the focal point for the modern movement, cities like Philadelphia, Chicago, Detroit, and Los Angeles also had their bebop cliques. Los Angeles had the most impressive group of players. Spurred by the seminal visit to Billy Berg's by Gillespie and Parker in 1945 and spearheaded by those terrors of tenor sax, Dexter Gordon and Wardell Gray, L.A. was a hotbed of activity for young, adventurous converts to the new music. Add to this the large number of clubs along Central Avenue, the numerous disc jockeys who played the new jazz over the airwaves, a couple of promoters who put on sold-out concerts in large halls (Gene Norman's "Just Jazz" and Norman Granz's "Jazz at the Philharmonic"), and you had a full-blown movement.

Frank Driggs Collection

Charlie Parker: Jam session at the Heatwave Club, 1944. Parker is seated second from the right with an unidentified group of musicians. During the 1930s and 1940s jazz jamming was a regular part of a musician's life. Charlie Parker not only jammed a great deal, but also inspired other musicians to "open up" to other forms of music—including country and classical. Nat Hentoff reports on Parker's electicism in *Listen to the Stories*: "Once he was telling me with great enthusiasm about listening again to Bartok's second Piano Concerto: 'I heard things in it I never heard before. You never know what's going to happen when you listen to music. All kinds of things can suddenly open up. But when I hear my own records, I hear all kinds of things I should have done. There's always so much to be done in music. It's so vast.'"

Vocalese: Bop Goes Vocal

Part of the new jazz movement was jazz vocal style inspired by the instrumental lines of artists such as Coleman Hawkins, Lester Young, and Charlie Parker. This style, vocalese, places words and a storyline to previously recorded jazz instrumentals. Jazz historian Leonard Feather introduced the term and lists Buddy Stewart and Dave Lambert as the first to sing what he called vocalese in 1945 with the Gene Krupa band. Their wordless unison scatting on the boppish "What's This" created an interest in vocalized bop that fellow band member Leo Watson had already been navigating. Watson's amazing vocal agility was appreciated by many musicians, but personal problems derailed his career and there is little of his bop scatting to be found on record. One of the earliest reviews of a bop vocal group working as a unit for an entire show (not just one or two numbers with a band) was Babs Gonzales's unit, Three Bips and a Bop. A news feature from *Down Beat* dated May 21, 1947, shows the headline "Fred Robbins' Town Hall Bash Kills the Kids." It describes a concert thought to be aimed at the younger, wilder jazz followers thusly: "An added attraction was Babs and His Three Bips and a Bop, a mildly

Some Bebop Babblers

Performer	Representative Bebop Song	Year
3 Bips and a Bop	Oop-Pop-a-Da	1947
Joe "Bebop" Carroll	School Days	1948
Betty Carter	Thou Swell	1955
Bob Dorough	Yardbird Suite	1956
Double Six of Paris	Scrapple From the Apple	1962
Ella Fitzgerald	How High the Moon	1947
Slim Gaillard	Flat Foot Floogie (with Charlie Parker)	1946
Harry "The Hipster" Gibson	It Ain't Hip to Say Hep	1945
Babs Gonzales	In the Land of Ooh Bla Dee (with Dizzy Gillespie)	1947
Kenny "Pancho" Hagood	I Should Care (with Thelonious Monk)	1948
Jon Hendricks	Four Brothers (with Dave Lambert)	1954
Jackie and Roy	East of Suez	1947
Eddie Jefferson	Bless My Soul (based on Parker's Mood)	1950
King Pleasure	I'm in the Mood for Love	1952
Lambert Hendricks Ross	Everybody's Boppin'	1959
Dave Lambert Singers	Beban Cubop	1949
Manhattan Transfer	Contemplation	1981
Metronomes	A Night in Tunisia	1962
Mark Murphy	Be Bop Lives (Boplicity)	1981
Jimmy Rainey & Terry Swope	Talk a Little Bop	1949
Annie Ross	Twisted; Farmer's Market; Jackie	1952
Buddy Stewart & Dave Lambert	What's This?	1945
Buddy Stewart, Dave Lambert & Blossom Dearie	In the Merry Land of Bop	1948
Clark Terry	Mumbles	1965
Sarah Vaughan	Lover Man	1945
Leo Watson	Ja Da	1939

frantic combination of vocal and instrumental presentation. A 'real cool' outfit, as Robbins tabbed the unit, Bop and His Bips gave a special version of 'Savoy,' tabbed 'Town Hall' with much 'ee-re-dee' and 'oo-ah-oh-uh-uh,' a new brand of jive vocalization sprouting from the be-bop trend. Bippers are Babs Gonzales, vocals and leader, Tadd Dameron, piano, Pee Wee Tinney [Al Tinney's brother], guitar, and Art Phipps, bass." *Time* magazine was not so neutral, calling bop "over-to narcotics and doubletalk." The Tinney brothers later would go on to lead a rhythm and blues group, the Jive Bombers during the 1950s.

Dizzy Gillespie and Joe "Bebop" Carroll made a number of recordings featuring unison scat lines in the mid-1940s ("O-Sho-Be-Do-Be" and "School Days") and Jackie Cain and Roy Kral established their careers singing bop lines in unison (see Chapter 10). Vocalese as we know it today was preceded by something known

360

King Pleasure's key record album, which featured many of bop's bright lights of 1952. Amari Baraka, writing under his original name Leroi Jones, recalled in the 1962 liner notes to James Moody's *Moody Workshop,* "It must be around ten years ago that Moody became so popular with his brilliant solo on 'Moody's Mood for Love,' which I suppose everyone must remember now the way King Pleasure sang it later, 'There I go, there I go, I done gone' (sic). People used to walk through the halls of my high school whistling that solo at almost any hour of the day and the prerequisite for a really hip chick in the school was to be able to sing all the added lyrics of the solo." King Pleasure had a penchant for choosing saxophone lines for his vocalese interpretations. A few of his outstanding saxophone—based vocalese story lines are "Red Top," based on Gene Ammons's late 1940s record; "Parker's Mood," based on Charlie Parker's 1948 disc; "Sometimes I'm Happy," based on Lester Young's original; "It Might As Well Be Spring," based on James Moody's release, and Stan Getz's "Don't Get Scared." Vocalese master Jon Hendricks has noted that it was after he heard King Pleasure's version of "Moody's Mood for Love," that he decided that he, too, was destined to write and sing in that vernacular. Hendricks penned the liner notes to a retrospective of Pleasure's works titiled *The Source* in 1972: "When he [Pleasure] asked me to do 'Don't Get Scared' with him [in 1954] all he gave me was the Stan Getz record and a copy of his words to Stan's solo. 'Where are my words?' I asked. 'Write your own,' he said. 'I wrote mine now you write yours,' and exited laughing, striding cooly away with a combination of the Hastings street strut and the L.A. Getaway. Pleasure definitely had style, to the core. Nobody walks away like *that* anymore."

The song that started vocalese. "I'm in the Mood for Love" was composed by Jimmy McHugh and had lyrics by Dorothy Fields. It was introduced in the film *Every Night at Eight* (1936) by Frances Langford, who sang it with Alice Faye and Patsy Kelly, singing as "The Three Radio Rogues." The song became even more associated with Langford when she became a regular with the Bob Hope overseas tours of military bases throughout World War II. Langford's romantic reading of this song seldom failed to elicit a thunderous ovation from the lonely, lovesick servicemen.

There was nothing unusual about ex-Dizzy Gillespie reedman James Moody's recording of this standard tune for Prestige Records in 1948. Innumerable sax men had done this on many recordings. However, when King Pleasure put Eddie Jefferson's lyrics to the solo in 1952 an avalanche of acceptance was accorded the vocal release. Many, probably most, who bought the record had no idea that it was based on Moody's instrumental effort. They simply enjoyed it as a very "hip" piece of music. *Down Beat* listed the King Pleasure record as the top rhythm and blues record of 1952. The record was selling very well until Jimmy McHugh, the original author of the song, heard the altered lyrics. Hal Holly, writing in his regular column in the September 24, 1952, *Down Beat* titled his feature: "McHugh in No Mood for Love with Moody Discs." Holly first played the instrumental recording of James Moody's interpretation of McHugh's classic. McHugh responded, "I like other jazz treatments of that song much better, Louis' for instance. But it's interesting to know how this fellow Moody, I don't know his work, has used ideas that stem from Armstrong's recording."

Then Holly followed up with King Pleasure's vocal interpretation of Moody's instrumental lines. The composer was not happy. He sat back, according to Holly, and "listened in shocked amazement." McHugh then declared, "Wait until Dorothy [Fields] hears this. Don't these fellows know you can't re-write lyrics without permission of the author?" True to his word, McHugh contacted Fields. Together they lodged a complaint with ASCAP and then went to court. The record was taken out of circulation for about 15 years as a result. To this day "I'm in the Mood for Love" (or "Moody's Mood for Love," or simply "Moody's Mood") is the best-known vocalese piece. Genya Ravan of Ten Wheel Drive was the first rock artist to record the song. In addition to King Pleasure, and Eddie Jefferson, others such as Aretha Franklin, Mark Murphy, George Benson, Sheena Easton, Susannah McCorkle, and Rachelle Ferrell with Take 6, have also recorded this pop-bop vocalese classic.

as vocalese at the time but best referred to today as unison vocalese: arranged or harmonized bop vocals *not* based on previously recorded instrumentals.

The true vocalese recordings did not arrive until 1952, when Clarence Beeks, known professionally as **King Pleasure** (1922-1981) made a successful release for Prestige with "I'm in the Mood for Love." His vocal was based on the 1949 instrumental by saxophonist James Moody. The vocal by Pleasure was considered very hip and was a big hit in jazz circles and on the R&B chart. Soon it was referred to as "Moody's Mood for Love" or simply "Moody's Mood." The following year Pleasure recorded a version of Charlie Parker's "Parker's Mood," but thereafter recorded only a couple more albums before receding into obscurity in California.

Others followed the new tradition of putting words and storyline to instrumental jazz recordings. Outstanding among them was Annie Ross, Bob Dorough, Jon Hendricks, and **Eddie Jefferson** (1918-1979). Jefferson, an ex-dancer, gave Pleasure the words for Moody's version of "I'm in the Mood for Love" to record in 1952. It is Jefferson who should be given the credit for initiating the concept of true vocalese. In the late 1930s or early 1940s (past interviews with the artist vary on the date) Jefferson began to play certain recorded instrumentals on his portable record player and sing lines over the on-going solos. Thanks to the notoriety accorded Pleasure, Jefferson began to record on his own, and he was eventually recognized by the jazz community as the original source of the movement. According to Jefferson, one of his dance partners, Irv Taylor, first came up with the idea of putting words to instrumental recordings. At first Jefferson and Taylor set their solos to the music of swing players like Lester Young ("Lester Leaps In"), Tommy Dorsey ("T. D.'s Boogie" and "Strictly Instrumental"), and Count Basie ("Taxi War Dance"). When Parker and Gillespie began to dominate 52nd Street, Jefferson and Taylor immersed themselves in bebop.

Author's collection

Eddie Jefferson: Father of vocalese. Jefferson helped create the concept of putting words and storylines to previously recorded jazz instrumentals. This is not scat singing, although scatting can occur in a vocalese performance. The picture above shows Jefferson singing with the record playing, which is how he developed the idea. King Pleasure popularized this concept in 1952 by taking Jefferson's words to James Moody's instrumental recording of "I'm in the Mood for Love" and making a successful vocalese record of it.

King Pleasure, writing liner notes for his 1966 album *Golden Days* pointed out, "I have always loved music. In 1946, when modern jazz was new, Eddie Jefferson, now the vocalist and manager with James Moody, created the embryo of a vocal innovation in jazz. Eddie developed the ability to express his own ideas, whatever he wanted to say to anyone about anything, in both time and tune with an instrumental solo. In this form 'cookin', that's what I call this style singin' ('Puttin' the Pots On'), was good only for private, personal sessions and was not developed for public consumption until the 'conversation' of the instrumental solo was applied to the instrumentalist and an interpretation made in relation to the song, mood and the phrases that he was blowing. I made this interpretation and developed Eddie's baby and delivered it to the public."

Jefferson made his first recordings in 1952, due to the popularity of the King Pleasure recording of his lyrics. Jefferson's early recording output was sketchy, but by the late 1960s he finally found an audience and began recording regularly until his untimely death in 1979. Ira Gitler, writing in *Down Beat* about Jefferson's longtime boss and friend, James Moody, said about the vocalese giant, "Jefferson is more than good at his chosen specialty. He doesn't cheat by stretching a word over several notes when it would be easier to sing that way; instead, he fits a word to each note with a rapid-fire delivery that not only swings but can be highly amusing. Above all, he is a fine entertainer with a large sense of humor. The way he duets with himself by singing a falsetto for the girl's part of 'Moody's Mood for Love' never fails to break it up."

By the end of the 1950s, **Jon Hendricks** (1921-) joined forces with Dave Lambert and Annie Ross to record albums based on Count Basie originals (*Sing a Song of Basie,* 1958, and *Sing Along With Basie*, 1959) that created a renewed interest in vocalese. By 1960 the trio was on the cover of *Down Beat* and called "the hottest group in jazz."

Lambert, Hendricks, and Ross continued to preach the word of vocalese throughout the world. Today Hendricks is the leading proponent of vocalese and he has toured, with his wife and daughter in tow, as the Jon Hendricks Singers. They sing everything from the Basie band material to bebop and beyond with a high level of execution and are always entertaining.

A group of French singers led by Mimi Perrin made a series of well-received vocalese recordings in the early to mid-1960s as well. The unit was called the Double Six of Paris. In the 1970s there was a group named Super Sax (five saxophones plus a trumpet

Frank Driggs Collection

The August 1971 *Coda* reported, "Eddie Jefferson has lived through a period as remote from actual lives of jazz fans as the recording session which produced 'Now's the Time' or 'Body and Soul.' He, like us, is a listener, but with a gift to say what jazz means to him in the language of jazz. He is a biographer, if you like. An impressionist artist who uses the speech rhythms of jazz to sing episodes from the lives of the people he's known and obviously loved."

Some critics and historians have been intolerant of the practice of vocalese, many feeling that to add or alter anything to original instrumentals is to disfigure them, or, at best, that the placing of words to originals can only result in something imitative and, therefore, inferior. However, after a time some of the critics have been won over, especially by the happy, infectious readings Jefferson was known for. Harvey Pekar, writing for *Down Beat* in 1963, dismissed Jefferson's work on the album *Letter From Home*: "The practice of putting lyrics to improvised solos and singing them has enjoyed great popularity recently. In my opinion, it is nothing more than a clever novelty." But in 1969, reviewing Jefferson's *Body & Soul,* Pekar conceded that vocalese "is a tricky thing to do and you often wonder how the lyricist and singer are going to be able to bring off a selection. It's a little like watching a high-wire act. Beyond this, a man like Jefferson can make you look at a famous solo from a different point of view and you sometimes notice things about it that hadn't impressed you earlier."

and rhythm section) that played Charlie Parker solos note for note, a kind of sax-along to Bird. They won critical plaudits and a couple of Grammies. In the 1970s Manhattan Transfer and the Pointer Sisters also reworked vocalese, as part of the revival movement covered in Chapter 10.

Vocalese and bop also have connections to a popular form of music that began in the underground in the 1980s—rap. Recall that vocalists Jefferson and later Jon Hendricks got their main ideas for vocalese by singing over jazz instrumental solos on record. Rap, which began as vocal improvisations over instrumental rhythm and blues riffs, has the same origin. Many of the solo lines of bop vocalizing are staccato spurts of rhythmic lines much like the nonmelodic passages found in rap. All of this was not lost on master producer Quincy Jones, who in 1989 created the first major connection between bop, rap, and hip-hop with his groundbreaking release *Back on the Block*. Two of the most adventurous jazzmen, Herbie Hancock and Quincy Jones, were in the foreground of mixing jazz elements with pop in the 1970s, as well as with rap and hip-hop in the 1980s and 1990s. Both worked with many of the jazz greats and were held in high esteem by the jazz community, so when they mixed the seemingly disparate elements of electric rock, soul, and pop as well as rap and hip-hop, eyebrows were raised but not many questioned their taste, motives, or stature.

Hancock played piano in several of Miles Davis's mid-1960s groups and formed his own groups later in the decade. During that time he often played keyboards on Quincy Jones's musical projects, which incorporated jazz and pop (*Walking in Space,* 1969, *Gular Matari,*1970 and *Smackwater Jack,* 1971). Hancock's 1973 *Headhunters* was a best-selling album that blended jazz and funk. It became one of the first jazz LPs to eventually sell a million copies. In 1983, Hancock became the first jazz artist to win a video award for his electro-techno-scratch hit "Rocket."

Courtesy Sony Music

Lambert, Hendricks and Ross became audience favorites in the late 1950s with their ensemble and solo interpretations of Count Basie originals like "Little Pony," "One O'Clock Jump," "Goin' to Chicago" (with Joe Williams), and "Jumpin' at the Woodside." *Time* was so enthralled with the rapid-fire lyric writing and singing of Jon Hendricks that they labelled him "the James Joyce of Jive" (a title that had been bestowed on bop scat singer Leo Watson fifteen years earlier). In addition to the Basie material the trio later did an entire album of Duke Ellington compositions, and bop as well as post-bop (post-1950s) interpretations.

Ralph Gleason, a jazz writer who focused on the positive aspects of the music and constantly sought to point out jazz roots to younger audiences (he became the "roots consciousness" for the fledgling *Rolling Stone* magazine during the late 1960s and early 1970s) referred to LHR as the Gilbert and Sullivan of jazz. Gleason, who also wrote for the *Boston Globe* and the *San Francisco Chronicle,* was a strong proponent of the educational possibilities of vocalese, especially for audiences unaccustomed to instrumental jazz. In the liner notes for LHR's 1959 *The Swingers,* Gleason declared, "What they have worked up, i.e., lyrics to jazz instrumentals with words for all the parts, is of more help to the understanding of what jazz is and how it works than all the radio and TV shows put together. You can never hear the numbers they do again in the original version without mentally (or verbally) singing the lyrics."

Nat Hentoff writes about the album shown here in *Listen to the Stories*: "There is a particularly jubilant scat-singing duet between Lambert and Hendricks on the title track. But exultant scat singing abounds on most of the other cuts as well." The author titled the chapter on LHR, "A Jazz Band Composed Only of Singers."

Jones's 1989 *Back on the Block* brought the world of rap and hip-hop and bebop together as one. Taking Josef Zawinul's original composition "Birdland" as a metaphor for connecting the spirit of bop and Charlie Parker and his followers with those of the new street music of young blacks, Jones made a fusion that hadn't yet existed. In interviews Jones noted great similarities between the street-smart hip sounds of Parker and Gillespie and their disciples of the 1940s with those of the rappers and hip-hoppers of contemporary times. So Jones brought in jazz greats to mingle with rappers Kool Moe Dee and Big Daddy Kane, and a movement was started.

Courtesy Down Beat

Quincy Jones: Bop-rap-hip-hop "Birdland." Birdland was a jazz nightclub named after Charlie Parker. It was located at 1678 Broadway, a few blocks from Times Square. The club was originally named the Club Ebony, then the Clique, which folded in 1948. On December 15, 1949, Birdland opened with a mix of jazzmen: Hot Lips Page and Max Kaminsky's Dixielanders (which had the distinction of being the first and last Dixie group to play the club), Lester Young, Stan Getz, the Charlie Parker group, the Lennie Tristano sextet, and singer Harry Belafonte. From that point until it closed in 1965, Birdland was regarded as "the Jazz Capital of the World."

On Quincy Jones's album *Back on the Block* (1989), the tune "Birdland" begins with an interpolation of master of ceremonies Pee Wee Marquette's introduction to the Birdland club (taken from a 1954 Blue Note album, *A Night at Birdland*, with the Art Blakey Quintet) and then segues into rap introductions by Kool Moe Dee and Big Daddy Kane. They introduce the following soloists: 1. James Moody (sax); 2. Miles Davis (trumpet); 3. George Benson (guitar); 4. Sarah Vaughan (vocals); 5. Dizzy Gillespie (trumpet); 6. Ella Fitzgerald (vocals); and 7. Josef Zawinul (keyboards).

A number of rap groups have followed up on these experiments by rapping over bop-oriented recordings. Digable Planets in the early 1990s led the way, followed by Guru, The Jazz Warriors, Paris-based McSolar, Tokyo's UFO (United Future Organization), and US3. English dance clubs developed a musical style known as acid jazz, which set live and sampled jazz of various eras to a hip-hop beat. In his book *Jazz*, John Fordham adds, "At clubs such as New York's Giant Steps, deejays mixed modal jazz with hot latin, rap, and live shows that revived artists like Roy Ayers and Mark Murphy, and fed new talent." When Miles Davis released his hip-hop jazz conflation, *Doo Wop*, no one in the younger hip-hop audience paid much attention to it. But when US3's "Cataloop" caught the ears of the young in 1994, more and more listeners began to pay attention to the genre-bending of jazz, rap, and hip-hop.

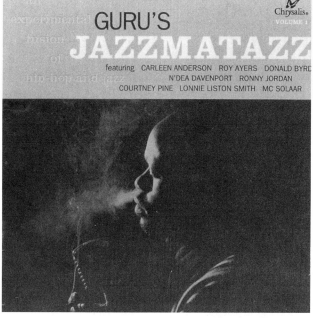

Courtesy of EMI Records

The cover of this 1993 release, *Jazz Matazz,* is a bow to the Blue Note album covers of the 1960s and 1970s. Guru (Keith Elam) was raised on jazz, and one of his first rap connections was a reworking of Dizzy Gillespie's "A Night in Tunisia" into "Words I Manifest" on his first single in 1988. Guru collaborated with Branford Marsalis on "Jazz Thing," which was recorded by Gang Starr (a group composed of DJ Premier and Guru) and heard on the soundtrack of director Spike Lee's '*Mo Better Blues* (1989).

Veteran jazz artists like trumpeters Donald Byrd and vibist Roy Ayres are united with young jazzmen like guitarist Sonny Jordan and saxman Courtney Pine in a mix of rap and hip-hop that resulted in a successful fusion of forms.

Key Vocalese Interpretations by the Big Four

The "Big Four" vocalese performers are the four who centered their careers around vocalese interpretations, and have the biggest body of work on record (not all still in print, unfortunately). The four are Eddie Jefferson, King Pleasure, Lambert, Hendricks and Ross (later Lambert, Hendricks and Bavan), and Double Six of Paris. When the Double Six of Paris broke up, one of the members, Ward Swingle, started another group, the Swingle Singers, who found success singing, scatting, and humming on classical music interpretations. Although they are not formally boppers, Lester Young and Coleman Hawkins compositions are among the sources of vocalese efforts because the two men were forward thinkers who provided models for the modernists. Most often the title of the vocalese interpretation followed that of the original, but sometimes the musical story required a new title.

Instrumental Source	Original Instrumentalist	Artist (revised title)
Body and Soul	Coleman Hawkins	Eddie Jefferson
These Foolish Things	Lester Young	Eddie Jefferson (Baby Girl)
It's Only a Paper Moon	Lester Young	Eddie Jefferson (Come Along With Me)
Now's the Time	Charlie Parker	Eddie Jefferson
Billie's Bounce	Charlie Parker	Eddie Jefferson
Lady Be Good	Charlie Parker	Eddie Jefferson
Parker's Mood	Charlie Parker	Eddie Jefferson (Bless My Soul)
I Cover the Waterfront	James Moody	Eddie Jefferson (Back in Town)
Lester Leaps In	James Moody	Eddie Jefferson (I Got the Blues)
I'm in the Mood for Love	James Moody	Eddie Jefferson
Old Black Magic	James Moody	King Pleasure
Jumpin' with Symphony Sid	Lester Young	King Pleasure
Up and at 'Em	Lester Young	King Pleasure (Jazz Jump)
Sometimes I'm Happy	Lester Young	King Pleasure
Don't Get Scared	Stan Getz	King Pleasure
Don't Worry 'Bout Me	Stan Getz	King Pleasure
Dear Old Stockholm	Stan Getz	King Pleasure (Tomorrow Is Another Day)
Red Top	Gene Ammons	King Pleasure
All of Me	Illinois Jacquet	King Pleasure
Parker's Mood	Charlie Parker	Lambert, Hendricks and Ross
Now's the Time	Charlie Parker	LHR
Twisted	Wardell Gray	LHR
Jackie	Wardell Gray	LHR
Farmer's Market	Wardell Gray	LHR
Four	Miles Davis	LHR
Bijou	Woody Herman	LHR
Cloud Burst	Sam "the Man" Taylor	LHR
Doodlin'	Horace Silver	LHR
Cookin' at the Continental	Horace Silver	LHR
Little Niles	Randy Weston	LHR
Moanin'	Art Blakey	LHR
Summertime	Miles Davis and Gil Evans	LHR
Boplicity	Miles Davis and Gil Evans	Double Six of Paris
Scrapple From the Apple	Charlie Parker and Miles Davis	Double Six of Paris
Ballad	Gerry Mulligan	Double Six of Paris
Artistry Rhythm	Stan Kenton	Double Six of Paris
Early Autumn	Woody Herman	Double Six of Paris
A Night in Tunisia	Dizzy Gillespie	Double Six of Paris
The Champ	Dizzy Gillespie	Double Six of Paris
Anthropology	Dizzy Gillespie	Double Six of Paris
Emanon	Dizzy Gillespie	Double Six of Paris
One-Bass Hit	Dizzy Gillespie	Double Six of Paris
Groovin' High	Dizzy Gillespie	Double Six of Paris

The Cool Movement

What became known as the cool movement in modern jazz was simply a toning down of some of the harsher aspects of bop. Most of the acknowledged leaders of cool, such as Lennie Tristano, George Shearing, Miles Davis, and Stan Getz, were bop players who brought in new concepts to the form.

A majority of the so-called cool school were white and had conservatory training. These musicians were experts in the three B's: Bach, Beethoven, and Brahms. Music education in America during the 1930s and 1940s, when these players were learning, taught classical music; there were no programs that taught history courses on jazz, nor were there jazz laboratory bands. Jazz, blues, and country music were considered inferior forms of music, for the lower classes, and not something to be taught, or even taken seriously, in the rarified air of academe.

Lennie Tristano (1919-1978) was a blind pianist, composer, and teacher who created a following of student players, such as Lee Konitz and Warne Marsh, and performed under the rubric of the "Intuitive School of Music." Tristano was a dazzling technician who absorbed the best elements of two of his models, Art Tatum and Charlie Parker. He was influenced by the harmonic advances of bop but didn't appreciate the loud drumming, which he categorized as "cheap." Tristano insisted that his bass and drums play like a metronome, with no accenting, so that the performances would focus on pure melody played with shifting meters. Tristano's music, while demanding and advanced, was too distant and "cold" for most listeners. However, his ability to blend classical music and jazz and to create a body of technically advanced works ("Wow," "Crosscurrent," and the free jazz explorations "Intuition" and "Digression") put him in the front rank of underappreciated "genius" types in jazz. Bill Evans was the most successful of the post-Tristano-school pianists.

Tristano's recordings of March and April 1949 were considered by altoist Lee Konitz to be the real birth of the cool. Tristano's penchant for "pure improvisation" made him particularly fond of Bach. In fact, when Tristano played Birdland in the early 1950s he sent out Warne

Frank Driggs Collection

Lennie Tristano and the Intuitive School of Music. Tristano did not specifically teach piano in his studios in Chicago and New York. Rather, he taught an approach to improvising that incorporated new ideas about musical phrasing, harmony, and time. In *Jazz Portraits: The Lives and Music of the Jazz Masters,* Len Lyons and Don Perlo explain Tristano's demanding methods: "For example, Tristano would change meters (from 5/4 to 6/4 to 4/4) from one measure to the next, accelerate and decelerate tempo, group notes in fives, nines, and elevens in his highly original improvised lines, and he would have his bassist and drummer play without accents in order to break down the feeling of bar lines. For these innovations, Tristano has often been viewed as one of the prime movers of 'cool' jazz, but in fact he was sui generis in the history of jazz, one of the rare musicians to offer a modern alternative to bebop."

That Tristano never attained the popularity of, say, George Shearing, is understandable because Tristano's music was not as melodic. However, Tristano was an eloquent spokesman for jazz and believed the conflicts between Dixieland and bebop were harming jazz as a whole. Interviewed in *Down Beat* in October 1950 about the cliques in jazz, Tristano mentioned the opening of Birdland, when boppers and Dixieland players shared the bill: "That was a wonderful show. I was afraid that some of the Dixie fans might boo Parker or the boppers might put down Max [Kaminsky], but everybody was very happy."

In that same feature Tristano dismissed the theory that the popularity of pianist George Shearing had helped jazz because his bop was a filling inside a sandwich of familiar melody. Obviously not, Tristano reasoned, because there are "fewer places where jazz can be played today than there were when George and his quintet started out."

Marsh and Lee Konitz to warm up the audience with Bach "Inventions" so the audience would be prepared for the group's intricate interplay. He also gave his musical students instrumental recordings of Lester Young and insisted that they put words to his solos (vocalese), so that they would become more attuned to the lyricism of instrumental music.

Mark Gridley claims that the saxophone style of **Lee Konitz** (1927-   ) was new to jazz. "Konitz's command of the alto saxophone astonished fellow musicians. In fact, players often argued about whether it was Konitz or Parker who had the most speed and agility. These two saxophonists were in a class by themselves, outplaying all others. In addition, it is historically important to remember that Konitz developed and maintained his own Tristano-inspired style at a time when most other young alto saxophonists were imitating Charlie Parker." Konitz, throughout his career, placed an emphasis on playing beautiful melodies with clean precision--he has stated that he attempted to play the way Fred Astaire sang.

Keynote Records Tristano

New York—The piano wizardry of Lennie Tristano, who first attracted attention around Chicago before coming east, has finally been waxed by Keynote. Backing Lennie on his first platters were Billy Bauer, guitarist, and Clyde Lombardi, bass.

Courtesy Down Beat

Lennie Tristano "Originals" Based on Standard Tunes

Of all the jazzmen to use standard songs for their own "original" compositions, Lennie Tristano was undoubtably the champion. More than 90 percent of his compositions were based on the chord progressions of standard tunes. Tristano sidemen from his Intuitive School of Music made similar use of standard tunes. Lee Konitz, especially, borrowed musical figures from standard selections to create originals such as "Fishin' Around," "Midway," "Pennies in Minor," "Palo Alto," and one of his funniest satiric titles, "Hugo's Head," based on "You Go to My Head," among others.

Standard Song	Tristano's "Original"
All of Me	Line Up
All the Things You Are	Ablution
Don't Blame Me	Judy; On a Planet
Fine and Dandy	Blue Boy
Foolin' Myself	Love Lines
Honeysuckle Rose	Out on a Limb
I Can't Believe That You're in Love With Me	Two, Not One
I'll Remember April	April
I'll See You in My Dreams	Dreams
Indiana	Back Home; Deliberation
Just You, Just Me	Just Judy
Lullaby in Rhythm	Progression
My Melancholy Baby	Baby; Scene and Variations
Out of Nowhere	317 East 32nd
Pennies From Heaven	C Minor Complex; East Thirty-Second; Lennie's Pennies
S'Wonderful	Victory Ball
September in the Rain	Marionette (Billy Bauer composition associated with Tristano)
These Foolish Things	Celestia; Retrospection; Speculation
What Is This Thing Called Love?	Becoming; Supersonic
You Can Depend on Me	Wow
You Go to My Head	Pastime
You'd Be So Nice to Come Home To	G Minor Complex

Source: Reece Markewich, The New Expanded Bibliography of Jazz Compositions Based on the Chord Progressions of Standard Tunes, *1974.*

Lullaby of Birdland: George Shearing. Left to right, John Levy, bass, George Shearing, piano and Margie Hyams, vibes. Englishman Shearing made his first visit to the United States in 1947 with the assistance of his fellow countryman, critic Leonard Feather. The next year he moved to the States for good and worked at the Clique Club (which, one year later, was to become Birdland). Shearing developed the locked-hands style of playing (the thumb of the left hand duplicates the melody played with the little finger of the right hand) as a result of listening to Lionel Hampton's star pianist, Milt Buckner. The unique sound of Shearing's tightly harmonized block chords voiced with Margie Hyams's vibes in tandem with Chuck Wayne's gentle guitar proved immensely popular. In addition, the quintet eventually would incorporate exciting Latin rhythms on many selections. Contrary to Lennie Tristano's opinion of Shearing's "watered down" bop stylings, Dizzy Gillespie in an October 1947 *Down Beat* interview said, "I want to make bop bigger, get it a wider audience. I think George Shearing is the greatest thing that's happened to bop in the past year. He's the only one who has helped it along. He plays bop so that the average person can understand it. Anybody can dance to Shearing music. By doing that, he has made it easier for me and anyone else who plays bop."

George Shearing (1913-   ) was the other blind pianist to incorporate bop figures into his style. Unlike Tristano, Shearing was willing to make certain compromises, such as frequent use of pretty melodies and varied and exciting uses of Latin rhythms, to reach a wider audience. Born in England, Shearing absorbed the American jazz sounds from recordings until he mastered the music. He developed a locked-hand or block-chord technique, first introduced by Milt Buckner of the Lionel Hampton band, that featured both hands playing melody and rhythm. He also voiced his piano with the vibes or guitar to create an unusual "doubling" of the melody that can be heard on his best-known pieces, such as "September in the Rain," "Conception," and "Lullaby of Birdland." During the 1950s and 1960s Shearing created a number of best-selling jazz LPs that were listed as "easy listening." Into the early 1990s he remained one of the most successful jazz artists, with Grammy Award-winning and nominated releases and concert tours around the globe.

Three white bandleaders fit, more or less, into this category of cool: Woody Herman, Stan Kenton, and Claude Thornhill. While the three had different outlooks, and evolved through varied aspects of the music business, they and many of their sidemen and arrangers, had a telling impact on the world of cool. By the mid-1950s, the alumni of this trio of bands made up a good portion of the key participants who were among the first to be heard writing and playing television and Hollywood jingles and soundtracks.

Woody Herman and His Herds. Woody Herman on clarinet with Red Norvo on vibes at Carnegie Hall, 1946. This was Woody's famous First Herd, which would break up at the end of the year. Herman put veteran Norvo in charge of a small group within the band called the Woodchoppers. The Woodchoppers recorded ten sides that were progressive attempts to blend bop and classical music on selections such as "Norvo's Conception," "Steps," and "Igor" (for Igor Stravinsky). The arrangements for this band-within-a-band were by Norvo and trumpeter Shorty Rogers. Rogers, and another key sideman of this period, Gerry Mulligan, would soon be leaders of a school of playing during the 1950s called the "West Coast Cool."

Herman's connections to bop were strong, especially by the time arranger Ralph Burns joined his band. Gunther Schuller's magnum opus on the swing period, *The Swing Era: The Development of Jazz, 1930-1945,* places Herman's band at the top of the innovative bands during the mid-1940s. Schuller claims that Herman's work and the magnitude of his group's output, especially with the first and second Herds, has been given too little praise by most historians: "What is so remarkable about the Herman band's stylistic transformation, from an eclectic all-purpose ensemble to the best 'bop' or 'modern jazz' orchestra in the land, is that this metamorphosis resulted from a thorough fusion of several specific early-1940's style ingredients: The feel and swing of Basie's rhythm section; the fresh streamlined and linear virtuoso conception of brass-writing already articulated by Dizzy Gillespie; and the new harmonic language previously explored by Ellington, Eddie Sauter, Sy Oliver, Buster Harding, and Ray Conniff. The primary synergistic agent in all this was the new post-swing-era technical skills possessed by the best young players, relentlessly energetic and virtuosic."

Woody Herman's desire to incorporate the modern sounds into his big band "dance" unit led to difficulties in terms of the business of economics. In his autobiography, *The Woodchopper's Ball: The Autobiography of Woody Herman* (co-written with Stuart Troup), he points out, "The band's downfall was caused by a combination of things. But changing the sound was certainly a big factor. The audience that could understand 'Apple Honey,' however couldn't relate to 'Lemon Drop' or 'Four Brothers.' Musically, the bebop route was magnificent. But business-wise, it was the dumbest thing I ever did. These pieces didn't really succeed, except with a small percentage of our listeners, until the mid-1950s. If we had just continued playing 'Apple Honey' and 'Caldonia,' we'd probably have had a fighting chance."

Throughout his long career, Herman had the ability to choose young, creative talent and he allowed that talent to grow. As a leader he always looked to the future, as his band's rock-oriented numbers throughout the 1970s and 1980s attest.

Woody Herman (1913-1987) began his career as a six-year-old imitator of Ted Lewis performing on the vaudeville stage (with top hat and clarinet, reworking items like "When My Baby Smiles at Me"). He took over Isham Jones's band in 1936 and eventually moved the group from Dixieland to blues ("The Band That Plays the Blues"). The band's big break came when they played the Roseland Ballroom in New York in late 1936—they stayed for seven months playing dance music featuring a heavy two- and four-beat style that was easier for the dancers of the time to relate to. For a period during that

Record Woodchoppers Album

Chicago—The Woodchoppers, the popular small combo within the Woody Herman Herd, recorded eight sides at the WBBM-CBS studios here recently for a new Columbia album. In the group, shown, are left to right: Red Norvo, Chubby Jackson (barely visible, background), Sonny Berman, Bill Harris, Woody and Flip Phillips. Not shown are Don Lamond, drums; Jimmy Rowles, piano; and Billy Bauer, guitar.

Courtesy Down Beat

Author's collection

engagement, the Count Basie Band played opposite Herman, and featured an even, four-beat swing style that the dancers seemed to have trouble relating to. In fact, the dance hostesses held meetings with the management of the Roseland because they felt the Basie music was inhibiting the male patrons from buying dance tickets—thus cutting into hostesses' earnings. This was the very heartbeat of the big band business at that time—keeping the dancers on the floor.

George T. Simon, the big band's most famous chronicler, recalls in Herman's autobiography, "I first heard the band in December 1936 after they moved into Roseland in Manhattan. My review in *Metronome* appeared the following month. What was very interesting was that the Basie band was on the opposite stand. And I gave the Herman band a higher rating than the Basie band, for which John Hammond never forgave me. But Bill Basie, and Buck Clayton especially, said that I was absolutely right. The Basie band played out of tune."

The Herman band's first hits were "Woodchopper's Ball," originally listed as "At the Woodchopper's Ball," in 1939, "Blue Flame," the band's theme song, and "Blues in the Night," the band's only number one hit (both recorded in 1941). Herman's band is a good example of how some dance-oriented units were swayed toward the new, modern sounds of the bop generation. The group's connections to the new music began in 1944 with the creation of the first of Herman's many "Herds." Herman's young sidemen over the next couple of years would reflect the musical changes that were going on in classical music and modern jazz.

"Early Autumn" was the popular fourth section of Ralph Burns's "Summer Sequence," recorded in 1948. Because of the great popularity of the fourth section of this impressionistic piece, due largely to Stan Getz's warm, luscious solo, the piece was released separately with lyrics provided by Johnny Mercer.

Stan Getz, interviewed in *Down Beat* for a forty-year celebration of Woody Herman's reign as a band leader, said, "That band could play anything. They were the best bunch of readers I have ever seen. You could place anything before them and they would play it right off. I mean, you had writers for that organization that knew that, and they would lay some heavy stuff on us. Take Ralph Burns. His arrangements, while not terribly complex, were alive with color. Every phrase had to be properly in its place or the chords would not flow. Ralph and I hit it off well. I admired his writing and he admired my playing. That makes for an excellent relationship. He wrote 'Early Autumn' for me. It was my feature but the chords behind me became as important after awhile."

In the *New Grove Dictionary of Jazz*, J. Bradford Robinson offers this analysis: "Drawing his light, vibrato-less tone and basic approach from Lester Young, Getz developed a highly personal manner which, for its elegance and easy virtuosity, stood apart from the aggressive bop style of the late 1940s and 1950s. His justly celebrated performance on 'Early Autumn' (1948), with its characteristically languorous melody and delayed rhythm, captured the imagination of many young white jazz musicians of the time and helped to precipitate the 'cool' reaction to bop in the years that followed."

The "First Herd" (a name coined by George T. Simon) was inspired by bebop. Young soloists like trumpeters Pete Condol and Sonny Berman, saxophonist Flip Phillips, trombonist Bill Harris, and one of the greatest rhythm sections in big band history (Chubby Jackson on bass, Dave Tough on drums, and Ralph Burns on piano) made Herman's a significant unit. Arrangements by Burns and Neal Hefti resulted in classics such as "Northwest Passage," "Caldonia," "Goosey Gander," "The Good Earth," and "Bijou." The Second Herd was formed in 1947, and was centered on the unique saxophone alignment of three tenors and one baritone. The saxophone unit was known as the "Four Brothers," which was the title of a Jimmy Giuffre composition and arrangement that remains to this day one of the most played jazz charts. The Four Brothers consisted of tenor men Stan Getz, Herbie Stewart, and Zoot Sims and baritonist Serge Chaloff.

Burns wrote a four-part, symphonic-like, impressionistic piece entitled "Summer Sequence." The final part of the work, "Early Autumn," featured a brief but beautiful liquid tenor solo by **Stan Getz** (1927-1991) that started him on his way to stardom. As noted, Getz was the star saxophone soloist in the Woody Herman band, and on the strength of "Early Autumn" and "Four Brothers" he became the best-known instrumentalist of the Woody Herman-Stan Kenton axis of the 1940s. At sixteen Getz joined Dixieland trombonist Jack Teagarden's big band and always considered him his main mentor. By 1944 Getz was a member of the Stan Kenton big band and in 1948, at the age of twenty-one, he was a star in Woody Herman's Second Herd. As a stylist, Getz was a disciple of Lester Young's smooth, laconic approach, although he had the ability to play with driving force. Getz developed a breathy, languid sound that was greatly admired. Getz's nickname was "The Sound." Jazz places a great emphasis on uniqueness, and Getz had it. After just a couple of notes played on his tenor sax, most listeners with some jazz knowledge could instantly identify Getz's playing. John Coltrane, who would become the leading saxophone voice of the 1960s (the "Jazz Messiah") noted on several occasions how he and many others marveled at and envied Getz's "sound."

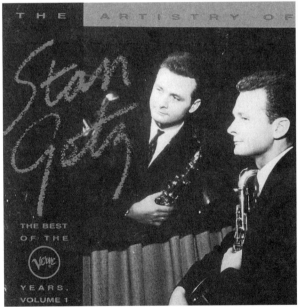

Courtesy Polygram Records

After Stan Getz left Woody Herman and performed as a solo star during the 1950s, drug problems curtailed his career until he made an astounding comeback first in Sweden and then back in America. By the 1960s, Getz would initiate the Bossa Nova boom with recordings that made the pop charts ("Desafinado" in 1962 and "The Girl From Ipanema" in 1964). Getz recorded with modernist players as well as mainstreamers until his death in 1991. He always received an appreciative applause when he requested in large concert halls that the microphones be turned off so that his "pure sound" could be heard in its natural state.

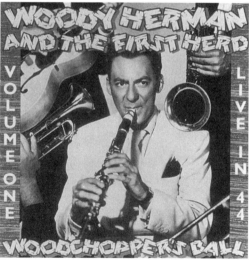

Courtesy Stash Records

Of the Stravinsky-composed "Ebony Concerto" Herman notes in The Woodchopper's Ball that, "The [first] rehearsal was difficult. Most of us had never received any classical training. We had to learn from each other. Our nerves were completely wrenched and some of us were ready to give up. Stravinsky, sensing our collective anxiety, walked over and put his arm around me. 'Woody,' he said, 'you have a lovely family.'" The "Ebony Concerto" received mixed reviews and the band booked college dates to play it in the hope that there would be an interest in culture at the university level.

Stan Kenton and "progressive jazz." The Kenton orchestra at the Rendezvous Ballroom, Balboa Beach, California, 1944. Kenton is directing to the right and a young Stan Getz is the second saxophonist on the right. Kenton became one of the most controversial figures in jazz history. Primarily, there was his bombastic style. Kenton's early bands were dominated by the saxophone section, Latin fusion, and modernist-fluorescent sounds, while his later bands (during the 1940s) emphasized "progressive" experiments that stressed atonality, dissonance, changing tempos, and extravagant orchestration in place of improvisation. There was no ambivalence about Kenton's music—it was either loved or hated.

Stan Kenton (1912-1979) debuted his own band in 1941 at Balboa Beach in his adopted home state of California. He recorded his theme song, "Artistry in Rhythm," the first of many "Artistry"-titled compositions, in 1943. "Artistry in Rhythm" is a good example of Kenton's penchant for symphonic jazz numbers that would lead him to deride the tradition of the bands playing for dancers. This stance led him to call his music "progressive jazz." "Artistry in Rhythm" includes a concerto-like piano section and a number of dramatic shifts of tempo. The composition was based on the classical piece "Daphnis and Chloe" by Maurice Ravel. Future composer/arrangers such as Pete Rugelo and Bob Graettinger continued experiments in the areas of Latin-jazz and semi-classical abstractions, respectively. Kenton's bands created powerful sonic blasts of excitement but were often criticized for being overblown and pretentious. Kenton was much like future 1960s rock popmeister Phil Spector (producer of the "wall of sound" for the Crystals, the Ronettes, and many other groups), as an heir to classical composer Richard Wagner. Stan Kenton's early career can be broken down into four main stages:

1. The period 1940 to 1944, which featured the leader playing exciting dance music in the established swing style dependent upon staccato phrasing of the saxophones. Compositions and arrangements were primarily by Kenton, and in addition to the popular "Artistry in Rhythm" the band's best-known songs from this period include "Etude for Saxophones," "Two Moods," "Lamento Gitano," "Taboo," "Adies," and "El Choclo." The last four selections were early examples of Kenton's direct connections to Latin jazz years before the other modern jazz experimenters. As John Storm Roberts, author of *The Latin Tinge* noted, "Cubop had three creative leaders: Stan Kenton, Dizzy Gillespie, and Machito."

2. The period 1945 to 1949, during which arose the "Artistry" motifs ("Artistry in Bolero," "Artistry Jumps," "Artistry in Brass") and the popularity of vocalist June Christy. This was also the period of what Kenton called "progressive jazz," with new arrangements and compositions by the adventurous Pete Rugolo. The band was now among the most important in jazz, surpassing the once popular Benny Goodman, Tommy Dorsey, and other great orchestras. Kenton's band, featuring bright and brassy trumpets, won the 1947 *Down Beat* poll as best band.

3. The period 1949 to 1954, which saw Kenton's experiments with large string sections, dissonance, broken rhythms, and abrupt tempo changes. Billed as "Innovations in Modern Music," this tangential jazz was closer to the classical music experiments of Bela Bartok than to the swinging dance sounds of Count Basie. Weighty classical works like Bob Graettinger's "City of Glass" was representative of the controversial sounds that emanated from Kenton during this time. This music definitely wasn't for dancing.

4. From 1954 to the 1960s, during which Kenton returned to jazz-oriented dance arrangements and Afro-Cuban experiments that were popular with listening audiences. Arrangements by Shorty Rogers, Bill Holman, and Gerry Mulligan brought the controversial leader back into the mainstream.

Frank Driggs Collection

Stan Kenton and the "Misty Miss Christy." Singer June Christy with the Stan Kenton orchestra, 1945. Kenton had a very solid history with his vocalists. Starting with Anita O'Day and then June Christy, Chris Connor, and the Four Freshmen, the Kenton band was a platform for some of the outstanding bop-oriented (in the case of O'Day) as well as cool-pop (the others) singers of the 1940s and 1950s. The Four Freshmen started with Kenton in the late 1940s and performed with him into the 1950s, and became one of the top jazz vocal groups with hits such as "It's a Blue World," "Holiday," and "Day by Day." They were pioneers in progressive jazz harmonies and played instruments as part of their stage performance. A very underrated vocal group.

June Christy gained more critical attention than the Four Freshmen. Viewed as a follower of Anita O'Day, she developed her own style after replacing O'Day with the band in 1945. Christy had an immediate hit in 1945 with a novelty top-seller, "Tampico." She married bandmate Bob Cooper, a saxophone player, and eventually left the band to start a successful solo career. Christy's recordings with Kenton arranger-supreme Pete Rugolo, and her husband Bob Cooper during the 1950s, were highlights of her career. Called the "Misty Miss Christy" because of her soft, cool vocals, Christy will be best known for her Kenton releases and a 1953 vo-cool song (and album) that most epitomizes her approach, "Something Cool."

The Visionary of the Cool

Claude Thornhill (1909-1965) was not nearly as commercially successful as either Herman or Kenton, nor is he well known to most jazz followers, but his ideas had the strongest impact on the direction of the cool movement. Thornhill was trained at the Cincinnati Conservatory of Music and the Curtis Institute of Music. He worked as a pianist and arranger for various bandleaders during the 1930s, most importantly Ray Noble and Andre Kostelanetz. In 1937, during his stay at the Onyx Club in New York, where he was musical director of an orchestra, Thornhill arranged "Loch Lomand" for vocalist Maxine Sullivan, which became her biggest hit and subsequent signature tune. By 1940 Thornhill was ready to head his own big band. Thornhill's first recordings with his new group, in 1941, established what many consider to be the lushest, most dreamlike sounds produced during the entire big band era. Thornhill's theme song, "Snowfall," showcased the slow-moving harmonies, unison clarinets, and delicate piano that would become typical of the "Thornhill sound." Bill Borden and Thornhill wrote all the arrangements until 1942, when Gil Evans joined the group. Sometimes six clarinets were used to create an unusual lightness in the upper register. At other times trombones were scored with clarinets. More often the band settled for four saxes and two clarinets. Most unusual, however, was the use of two French horns, which added a warm, rounded resonance to the mid-tones. Thornhill emphasized-horns played without vibrato.

Inclusion of classical music was another Thornhill technique sources included: Greig's "Piano Concerto" and "Le Papillon," Brahms's "The Hungarian Dance No. 5," Schumann's "Traumerai," the "Arab Dance" from Tchaikovsky's "The Nutcracker Suite," and "The Troubadour" from "The Old Castle," one of Mussorgsky's "Pictures at an Exhibition"—the last two arranged by Evans. Experimental pieces such as "Portrait of a Guinea Farm," arranged by Thornhill, and "Buster's Last Stand," arranged by Evans, were so advanced that it might be understandable why the band was more popular with the musicians than the audiences of the time.

Thornhill Opens With New Band

New York—Claude Thornhill, whose band opened at the Boston Post Lodge, in Larchmont, N. Y., May 29, rehearsed his new band for a long period before his first dance band job since his navy service. That was just to make certain the outfit would be as smooth as his much talked about pre-war outfit. Claude is hoping to start where he left off then—which was just a short way off from top success.

Courtesy Down Beat

On hiatus during the war, the band reunited in 1946, but the music industry had changed. First, the singer had taken precedence over the bandleader as the most important element in popular music, and second, bop had arrived. Thornhill, ever the visionary, tried to accommodate both. Fran Warren's vocalizing on "A Sunday Kind of Love" gave the band a minor hit in 1946. Most significant, though, was the inclusion of bop into this smoothest of the cool-sounding bands. By this time, Thornhill's unprecendented use of a tuba to play long, low melodic lines adding yet another layer to the overall sound. Evans's arrangements of Charlie Parker's "Yardbird Suite" and "Anthropology" and Miles Davis's "Donna Lee" made the band's connection to the new music. By this time key modernists such as alto saxophonist Lee Konitz and baritone saxist-arranger Gerry Mulligan were making contributions.

The overall "sound," the unusual instrumentation and its voicing, and the temerity with which the leader executed his vision, provided a valuable model for the Miles Davis experiments between 1948 and 1950 that resulted in the industry's acknowledgement of a new movement—"The Cool."

The Claude Thornhill orchestra with the reed section (Lee Konitz is in the top row, second from the right) and two French horns (first row, at left). Gil Evans, who had worked with Thornhill in Skinnay Ennis's orchestra in 1938 on the Bob Hope radio show, joined the band as an arranger in 1941. Thornhill's unique style of voicing unison clarinets (sometimes five at once playing in a high range, imitating violins) voiced over brass could be heard on numbers such as "Liebestraum," "My Heart and Thy Sweet Voice," and "Pizzicato Polka." It was unlike anything else being played by most swing bands at that time.

In Raymond Harvick's biography of Gil Evans, Evans said the Thornhill band was essentially a French horn band. "Trumpets and trombones would play in derby-hats to avoid vibrato. A characteristic voicing for the Thornhill band was a French horn lead, or two French horns playing in unison or as a duet while the clarinet doubled the melody . . . were two altos, a tenor and a baritone, or two altos and two tenors. The reed section sometimes went very low with the saxes, being forced to play in a sub-tone and very soft."

Evans's scoring for the Thornhill band would lay the groundwork for his later associations with Miles Davis. Evans matched the somber, dreamlike qualities of Thornhill's theme, "Snowfall," with delicate ensembles for "Polka Dots and Moonbeams," "There's a Small Hotel," and "Loverman." Later, after the war, Evans became fascinated by the musical experiments of bebop. "I did more or less match up with the sounds of people like Lester Young, Charlie Parker and Dizzy Gillespie. It was their rhythmic and harmonic revolution which was influencing me," he told Harrick. These advanced sounds can be heard in 1946 on the Thornhill orchestra's renditions of "Anthropology," "Sorta Kinda," "Donna Lee," and "Yardbird Suite," bebop pieces that emanated from an orchestra noted for dreamy, sombre dance music.

Thornhill's band remains one of the most underrated organizations in jazz history. The connection to Miles Davis's *Birth of the Cool* experiment is noteworthy. Assessing it in a pithy overview, Gunther Schuller writes in *The Swing Era,* "The relationship of the Davis Nonet to the 1948 Thornhill band is manifold but resides essentially: 1) in the primary role played by Gil Evans in the very formation of the Nonet and providing many of its most characteristic arrangements; 2) the similarity of instrumentation and to some extent of personnel (Lee Konitz on alto, Joe Schulman, bass, Bill Barber, tuba, Sandy Siegelstein, [French] horn). In effect, with the emphasis on [French] horn and tuba colorations and generally middle-to-low register instruments (trombone, baritone saxophone), even Davis's flugelhorn-like sound corresponded to the trumpet sonority Thornhill featured in the lead trumpet work of players like Louis Mucci. The Miles Davis group was the Thornhill big band reduced to a nonet."

Miles Davis and the "Birth of the Cool"

Miles Davis (1926-1991) was born in Alton, Illinois, and reared in an upper-middle-class environment in East St. Louis. His father was a prominent dentist, and when Davis graduated from high school, after playing trumpet in the school band, he was convinced, half coerced into going to college. The compromise was not altogether distasteful for Davis. The school was the Juilliard School of Music and it was located in New York City. Davis had wanted to go there anyway. In St. Louis, Davis had sat in with the visiting Billy Eckstine band, and Charlie Parker had told Davis to look him up if he ever got to New York. Instead of going to classes, Miles found his education in the nightclubs of New York, absorbing the music of the jazz modernists.

Young Miles Davis lacked the technical virtuosity of most of the bop trumpeters like Dizzy Gillespie and Fats Navarro, but he did have a compelling, mid-range "sound." One of the earliest influences on Davis was that of Clark Terry, who had a puckish middle-register approach laced with warmth and wit. Once Davis began working in the bop arena, however, it seems that a very underrated and underrecorded trumpet stylist, Freddie Webster, would have the greatest inspiration on Davis. Webster was highly regarded by musicians who worked with the bands of Lucky Millinder, Earl Hines, Billy Eckstine, Gillespie, Cab Calloway, Carter, and Lance Ford. Webster was known for his "fat, warm" melodic approach, which can be heard to good advantage backing Sarah Vaughan ("If You Could See Me Now"). In *Black Beauty, White*

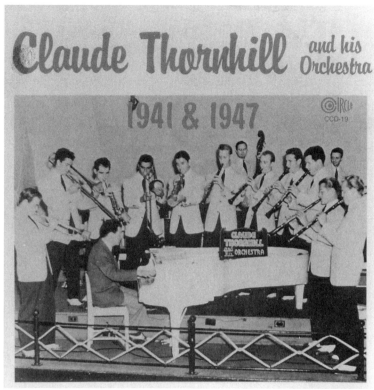

Courtesy Circle Records

The Claude Thornhill Orchestra with clarinets raised to the max. Thornhill liked to weave his delicate, classically tinged piano solos into the clarinet and French horn mix of slow sounds, creating "moody, ethereal and musical aphrodisiacs." While some critics questioned the jazz credentials of Thornhill's bands, especially his 1941-43 units, his slow-tempo numbers were given just enough musical muscle by arrangers Bill Borden ("Isn't It Wonderful?" and "O Solo Mio") and Gil Evans ("Buster's Last Stand") to keep the band out of the "sweet" category.

After 1946 the band not only featured Evans's bop-inspired arrangements, but captured the attention of a number of younger, serious, forward-looking musicians and arrangers like Johnny Carisi, Lee Konitz, Brew Moore, and **Gerry Mulligan** (1927-), a young baritone saxophonist who had hung around 52nd Street while writing arrangements for Tommy Tucker, Gene Krupa ("Disc Jockey Jump" and "Sometimes I'm Happy"), and Elliot Lawrence ("Between the Devil and the Deep Blue Sea" and "How High the Moon"). The fact that Thornhill was drawn to young, bop-oriented players like Mulligan and trumpeter Red Rodney was a testimony to his desire to create a higher musical form that went beyond simple dance music.

Jerome Klinowitz points out in his biography of Gerry Mulligan, *Listen—Gerry Mulligan: An Aural Narrative in Jazz,* "By 1948 Mulligan had joined the band to write arrangements and play baritone in a sax section including Lee Konitz on alto and Brew Moore and Phil Urso as heirs to the Lester Young tradition of wispy, breathy tenor. With Mulligan's affinity for the bari's top notes and Konitz's singularly brittle sound, Thornhill's 1948 sax section proved the perfect vehicle to be matched with his orchestra's soprano and bass clarinets and surrounded by the ethereal French horns, muted trumpets, and high-straining yet delicate trombones. In addition, his ear for the new phraseology of bop and feel for its intellectually impertinent rhythms and complex melodies made Mulligan the ideal new talent for what Thornhill had proposed in 1940 and Evans had begun perfecting a year later, before the wartime service put the band on hold until 1946."

Heat Frank Driggs praised Webster's contributions saying, "Everybody wanted Freddy Webster as a first trumpeter because he had one of the greatest sounds of all time. He was noted for his solo on

William P. Gottlieb Collection

Charlie Parker with Miles Davis. Miles Davis worked under the spell of the great leader of bop, Charlie Parker, but his stay with Parker was not always an ideal working situation. In *Miles: The Autobiography,* written with Quincy Troupe, Davis's earthy and direct language explains: "So I looked up to Bird for being a great musician more than I liked him as a person. But he treated me like his son, and he and Dizzy were like father figures to me. Bird used to build up my confidence by saying he had gone through the same bullshit when he was younger back in Kansas City. I was nineteen years old and playing with the baddest alto saxophone player in the history of music. But Bird didn't teach me much as far as music goes. I loved playing with him, but you couldn't copy the shit he did because it was so original. Everything I learned about jazz back then I learned from Dizzy and Monk, maybe a little from Bean [Coleman Hawkins], but not from Bird. See, Bird was a soloist. He had his own thing. He was, like, isolated. And there was nothing you could learn from him unless you copied him."

Parker was proving to be unreliable because of his personal demons of drugs and alcohol, and as a result Davis more and more had to assume the leadership role on the bandstand. When Parker began completely missing club dates and not paying his sidemen, Davis eventually decided to move on. During this time, 1948, Davis had started visiting Gil Evans at his apartment on 55th Street. In his autobiography Miles detailed the seeds of the *Birth of the Cool* sessions: "Gerry Mulligan, Gil, and I started talking about forming this group. We thought nine pieces would be the right amount of musicians to be in the band. Gil and Gerry had decided what the instruments in the band would be before I really came into the discussions. But the theory, the musical interpretation and what the band would play, was my idea. The *Birth of the Cool* album came from some of the sessions we did trying to sound like Claude Thornhill's band. We wanted that sound, but the difference was that we wanted it as small as possible. *Birth of the Cool* became a collector's item, I think, out of a reaction to Bird and Dizzy's music. Bird and Dizzy played this hip, real fast thing, and if you weren't a fast listener, you couldn't catch the humor or the feeling in their music. Their musical sound wasn't sweet, and it didn't have harmonic lines you could easily hum out on the street with your girlfriend trying to get over with a kiss. Bebop didn't have the humanity of Duke Ellington. It didn't have that recognizable thing. Bird and Diz were great, fantastic, even challenging, but they weren't sweet. But *Birth of the Cool* was different because you could hear everything and hum it also."

'Stardust' with Millinder and Lunceford, though his best work rarely got recorded." Writers James Lincoln Collier and Gene Lees add the influence of trumpeter Bobby Hackett, whose advanced harmonic approach on such classics as "Embraceable You," impressed Davis. Lees notes in *Cats of Any Color*, "I told Miles it seemed as if there were a link and asked whether he had listened a lot to Bix [Beiderbecke]. He said 'No, but I listened a lot to Bobby Hackett and *he* listened to Bix.'"

Davis recorded seminal bop with Charlie Parker on the Savoy and Dial record labels. While not a powerful voice, nor steady on the fast passages, Davis acquits himself very well on selections such as

378

The big, warm sound of Freddie Webster. In jazz as in all fields of endeavor, models are important. While there were many who influenced Miles Davis on a variety of levels, Freddie Webster was the strongest trumpet inspiration for Davis's style. In his autobiography Davis praised Webster, "But my real main music during those first days in New York was Freddie Webster. I really liked what Freddie was doing on the horn then. I loved the way he played, that he didn't waste notes and had a big, warm, mellow sound. I used to try to play like him, but without the vibrato and 'shaking about the notes.' He was about nine years older than me, but I used to show him everything they taught me at Juilliard about technique and composition, technical things, which Juilliard 'was' good for. Freddie was from Cleveland and grew up playing with Tadd Dameron. We were as close as real brothers and a lot alike. We were about the same size and used to wear each other's clothes."

The middle-register style that Davis preferred was similar to that of Webster. In *Swing to Bop*, Ira Gitler quotes a number of musicians who praised Webster's trumpet mastery. Saxophonist Art Pepper, who roomed with Webster, said, "He had . . . the most huge sound, and down low it was just gigantic. I never heard anybody who had a sound that big down low." Charlie Rouse, who played with Thelonious Monk, offered, "Freddie was a big influence, man, [on] Dizzy and all of them, from Fats on down. 'Cause he had a trumpet sound, and he would hit a note and expand it." Trumpeter Benny Bailey said, "I happen to know for instance that on the recording of 'Billie's Bounce,' which Miles made with Charlie Parker, [Davis's] solo is exactly the one Freddie played for this particular blues. Evidently Miles said he was nervous on the date and couldn't think of anything to play, so he did Freddie's solo note for note." Whether or not this tale is true, the fact of Webster's incalculable influence on Davis remains indisputable.

"Billie's Bounce," "Now's the Time" and "Scrapple From the Apple," among others. It is apparent when listening to Miles playing on these recordings that he lacked the assuredness of a Gillespie, Navarro, or even Howard McGhee, who had recorded with Parker on the West Coast for Dial. By the end of 1947, Davis was looking in a new direction for inspiration.

The impact of the Claude Thornhill Orchestra, circa 1946-48, is undeniable. In 1950 Davis told an interviewer from *Down Beat* that, with the exception of the Billy Eckstine band with Parker, "Thornhill had the greatest band, the one with Lee Konitz, during these modern times." And echoing Gil Evans's observation about Thornhill's horn voicing and the use of legato phrasing, Davis claimed, "That's how I tried to play, fast and light—and no vibrato."

If Thornhill was the overall cause of Davis's move to a cooler approach to bop, then **Gil Evans** (1912-1988) was the means to getting there. Evans had a one-bedroom basement apartment on 55th Street that became the hangout and focal point for musicians such as Gerry Mulligan, Lee Konitz, Dave Lambert, Parker, and Davis. Modern classical composer/performer David Amram, in his autobiography *Vibrations*, notes that he, and others regularly experimented with the new sounds at the apartment and that Evans was the guru of these activities.

A group that could distill the overall conception and tone coloring of Thornhill's large dance band into an experimental nonet that played bop-oriented music was the overall goal of Evans, Mulligan, and Davis. In *Jazz Styles,* Mark Gridley places a greater emphasis on the contribution of Lee Konitz than Gerry Mulligan on these recordings. "The influence of Konitz and Davis was evident in their saxophone and trumpet styles, respectively, some performances felt more like the Count Basie-Lester Young combo recordings of the 1930s than the Charlie Parker-Dizzy Gillespie collaborations of the 1940s. Some of the music was especially subdued and understated, precisely those qualities that journalists associated with Lester Young and the term 'cool jazz.'" At that time Evans and Mulligan were pretty much unknown commodities in the music industry. Davis was known because of his recordings and club dates with Parker. The musical ensemble, under Davis's leadership, played the biggest jazz spot on Times Square, the Royal Roost (tabbed the "Metropolitan Bopera House") in early September 1948. The two-week stand was met with disdain by audiences accustomed to the hard-driving excitement created by Roost favorites such as Eckstine and Dameron.

Undeterred by audience indifference, Davis was able to sign a contract with Capitol Records to record the nonet. Three recording sessions between 1949 and 1950 resulted in the prophetically titled album *Birth of the Cool*. The use of French horn and tuba, along with two saxophones, trombone, rhythm section, and Davis's trumpet was Thornhill in miniature. The various arrangers achieved the required layered sounds by voicing mid-toned instruments such as the trombone, trumpet, and French horn in the middle, with the baritone sax and tuba playing low, deep melodic lines and the alto sax and trumpet play the higher scales. Classic selections such as "Boplicity" and "Moon Dreams" (both Evans arrangements) underscored what Evans had sought to accomplish with the smallest number of instruments, "to get the sound and still express all the harmonies that Thornhill used."

Davis moved on to much greater fame soon after these sessions, while Evans worked in relative obscurity until the two would collaborate again in the late 1950s for a series of exquisitely conceived projects that revived the nonet ideas into large-scale orchestrations (*Miles Ahead*, *Porgy and Bess*, and *Sketches of Spain*). In 1959 Davis and Evans debuted three songs from *Miles Ahead* on the "Robert Herridge Theater Show," a local New York television program on the arts. "The Duke," "Blues for Pablo," and "New Rhumba" are the only filmed evidence so far of Davis and Evans in action with the Thornhill-styled orchestra.

After years of refusing to "look backward" at his past accomplishments, Davis was prodded by Quincy Jones to recreate his collaborations with Evans. The event, and this was rightly viewed as an "event," occured at the 1991 Montreux Jazz Festival, three months before Davis's death. Recreations from *Birth of the Cool*, *Miles Ahead*, *Porgy and Bess,* and *Sketches of Spain* were all expertly conducted by Jones. A weakened Davis couldn't perform the high notes (which were ably handled by Wallace Roney) but did manage to create some haunting and lyrical solos. Lee Konitz rekindled the nonet ensemble on a number of occasions throughout his career (such as 1977's *Lee Konitz Nonet*), and Gerry Mulligan formed a tentette in 1953 that recaptured the Thornhill-Evans-Davis conceptions. In 1992 he rerecorded the selections on the *Birth of the Cool* as *Re-Birth of the Cool* with Wallace Roney playing Davis's solos.

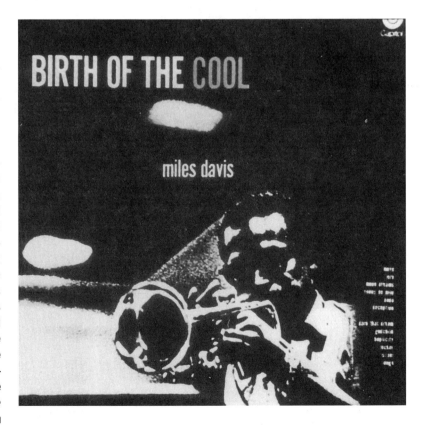

© 1989 Capitol Records, Inc.

Miles Davis and Gil Evans on Columbia Records. Davis on trumpet with Evans conducting at a Columbia Records date in 1960. The series of recordings that Davis and Evans made between 1957 and the early 1960s was not only an extension of cool jazz, but even had an impact on future jazz-rock fusions that each artist would explore in the late 1960s and after. Davis's *In a Silent Way* (1968) was the most direct echo of Evans-Davis. Evans continued his experiments with multitextured-experimental-orchestral jazz and rock, releasing albums that showcased everything from originals (the sublime *Out of the Cool,* 1961), to compositions by Jimi Hendrix (*The Gil Evans Orchestra Plays the Music of Jimi Hendrix,* with guitar solos by Ryo Kawasaki,1974).

Let us conclude this portion of the cool-modernist section by noting the accomplishments of band leader Boyd Raeburn, an artist who eschewed commercial dance music for an intoxicating mixture of bop and European concert music that was much influenced by Igor Stravinsky. Raeburn commissioned arrangements from leading modernists of the 1940s—Dizzy Gillespie ("A Night in Tunisia"), Johnny Mandel, and George Handy ("Tonsillectomy" and "Dalvatore Sally"). *The New Grove Dictionary of Jazz*, under the entry "progressive jazz," notes, "Boyd Raeburn's output during the same period [as Stan Kenton in the 1940s] was also self-consciously modernistic, as is suggested by titles such as 'Boyd Meets Stravinsky.' Yet the scores, by George Handy (a pupil of Aaron Copeland), Ed Finkel and others, retain their interest; their characteristically complex texture and dissonant harmony were qualified by the exhilaratingly full-throated power of the band's performance." By the 1950s the term "progressive jazz" was used as a synonym for "modern jazz."

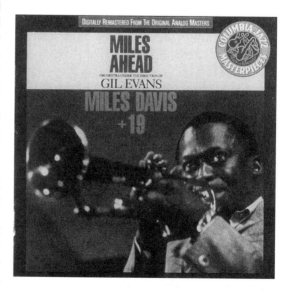

Courtesy Polygram Records

Pianist **John Lewis** (1920-) studied music and anthropology at the University of New Mexico. Upon graduating, Lewis served in the army (1942-45), where he met bebop drummer Kenny Clarke. Lewis was a fine pianist, and Clarke opened the door for him to join the Dizzy Gillespie big band of 1946. While in Gillespie's band, Lewis studied at the Manhattan School of Music. He was fond of classical music, particularly Bach, and in 1946 Gillespie premiered the pianist's first major work, "Toccata for Trumpet and Orchestra." Eventually Lewis, vibist Milt Jackson, bassist Ray Brown, and drummer Clarke (all members of Gillespie's band) would form a quartet that played together during concerts and became the beginnings of one of the most famous chamber groups in jazz history, the Modern Jazz Quartet (the group officially formed 1952).

Lewis played piano on segments of Miles Davis's *Birth of the Cool* sessions (he arranged "Budo" and "Move"). Lewis's long association with formal classical music and counterpoint began when he heard a radio performance by the Philadelphia Orchestra of the "D Minor Toccata and Fugue," arranged and conducted by Leopold Stokowski. Lewis enjoyed playing Bach's two-and three-part inventions and he eventually worked these techniques into the Modern Jazz Quartet's repertoire, beginning with "Vendom" in 1952.

During the 1950s the Modern Jazz Quartet, Miles Davis, (who did not reside in California) Gerry Mulligan, Chet Baker and Chico Hamiliton were leaders of the laid-back "Cool School" of jazz, which manifested itself in California as the "West Coast Cool" movement. After a break from the Modern Jazz Quartet, Lewis reformed the unit in 1982 and, in addition to recording with the band, made a series of Bach recordings, such as the release pictured above.

Courtesy Carnegie Hall Archives

By the 1950s, the musical experiments of the 1940s (bebop and cool) had become the norm in jazz. Carnegie Hall had begun hosting jazz-oriented music back in 1912 with James Reese Europe's Clef Club Orchestra playing what was called ragtime. On April 27, 1928, Carnegie Hall presented "The Father of the Blues," W. C. Handy. Theodore Cron and Burt Boldblatt note the significance of this event in *Portrait of Carnegie Hall:* "The arrival of W. C. Handy, his wife, three daughters, and son in Carniegie Hall for their historic program was a peak in jazz music's long uphill battle for acceptance by the white majority." The program was titled, "W. C. Handy's Orchestra and Jubilee Singers," and included headings such as "Prologue," "Spirituals," "Blues," "Plantation Songs," "Work Songs," "Piano Solo," and "Negro Rhapsody." At the very end of the program was the listing "Jazz Finale," which included performances by Clarence Williams and Fats Waller (in 1944 there would be a special Carnegie Hall "Tribute to Fats"). Greater emphasis has been placed on the 1938 as the date for jazz coming to the stage at Carnegie Hall because it was the main focus of the concert, rather than an addendum to other forms.

We have seen how jazz created controversy when it was first introduced at Carnegie Hall in 1938, via the Benny Goodman concert and John Hammond's *From Spirituals to Swing* concert. By the late 1940s, the music introduced at those concerts (swing and boogie among other, older jazz and blues and gospel forms) had become the standard sound accepted, if not embraced, by most listeners in and out of jazz. In 1947, bebop was brought to Carnegie Hall stage in a concert arranged by Monte Kay, Symphony Sid, and Leonard Feather. Modernist stars Sarah Vaughan, Dizzy Gillespie, and Charlie Parker were featured. Critical appraisal was mixed, not unlike that for the 1938 concerts, but the fact that Carnegie Hall offered modern jazz sounds did much to lend credibility to the form. In the 1952 concert, advertised here, swing-oriented artists Duke Ellington and Billie Holiday share the stage with modernists Dizzy Gillespie, Charlie Parker, and Stan Getz. This is an example of experimental music that had once been shunned by a majority of the jazz audience (making it a kind of underground within the underground) eventually becoming part of the status quo.

382

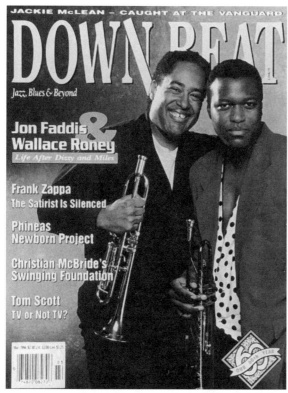

Courtesy Down Beat   *Courtesy Down Beat*

The young lions of jazz. During the 1980s, there was a renaissance of sorts—many writers referred to as neo-bop. This resurgence was generated by a number of younger musicians who emulated the sounds, compositions, dress, and professional comportment of earlier modernist players like Charlie Parker, Dizzy Gillespie, Thelonious Monk, and Miles Davis. Many of the younger breed, like Wynton Marsalis, Terrance Blanchard, Jon Faddis, and Wallace Roney eschewed the electronic fusion of jazz-rock and pop sounds of the day, choosing instead to play acoustic, boppish material that echoed the 1940s, 1950s, and 1960s.

Jon Faddis (1954-   ) and **Wallace Roney** (1960-   ), in particular, had specific links to trumpet greats associated with the emergence of the modern jazz movement in the 1940s. Faddis, a close friend and disciple of Dizzy Gillespie, became musical director of the Carnegie Hall Jazz Orchestra (which presents evenings of classic jazz) in 1992. He was also a featured soloist with the Lincoln Center jazz projects organized by Wynton Marsalis. In the March 1994 *Down Beat* interview from the issue pictured here, Faddis notes, "People refer to me as 'Dizzy Gillespie's protege.' And, of course, I still 'sound like Dizzy.' But I think they do it for convenience's sake, Y'know, the need to label everything."

In the case of Wallace Roney, K. Leander Williams writes, "In the public mind, 34-year old Roney seems inextricably linked to the late Miles Davis. He's been gigging with Tony Williams for seven years now, and when the remaining members of Davis' last earthshaking quintet of the 1960s went on tour in 1992 as the Miles Davis Tribute Band, Roney got to see the world in the presence of giants. That same year, when Gerry Mulligan recreated Davis' classic *Birth of the Cool* sessions from 1949-50, Roney made that date also. And, as last year's recording and video *Miles and Quincy Live at Montreux* illustrate, the ailing Prince of Darkness also considered Roney a rather capable deputy. Their moving pas de deux on 'Solea' was lyrical as it was haunting."

Wynton Marsalis (1961-   ) is part of the musical New Orleans family led by father Ellis, pianist and teacher, and brothers Branford (saxophone) and Delfeayo (trombone). At the age of eight Wynton was part of Danny Barker's children's marching band. He studied both jazz and classical music and has won numerous Grammys in both categories. In 1980, while he was a student at the Juilliard School of Music, Marsalis joined Art Blakey's Jazz Messengers, the primary hard-bop training school for young players from the 1950s through the 1980s. A 1982 Elektra release that put seventeen younger musicians, including Marsalis, in various combinations at the Kool Jazz Festival, was titled *The Young Lions,* a label that writers have used to describe these neo-boppers of the 1980s and 1990s.

In 1991 Wynton Marsalis was appointed artistic director of New York's Jazz at Lincoln Center program which assigns commissions of new compositions and performs concerts of classic jazz, both under the rubric called the Lincoln Center Jazz Series. Today Marsalis is among the most powerful and influential jazz musicians on the scene. There have been controversies about his choice of commissions and celebrations of which classic jazz artists to honor. However, the fact remains that, like Jon Faddis and a number of others, classic jazz of the 1920s to the 1950s is being presented. And so again we have significant contemporary artists who are keeping yesterday's music alive. As the late music writer and historian Ralph Gleason always reminded his reading public, "It's all right there in the roots."

Chapter 12

RHYTHM AND BLUES

The movement of rural blues to the city centers during the 1930s and 1940s, resulted in a musical changeover. Record companies often described the "race" records of country blues artists as "blues singer and guitar." When blues singers added piano, bass, and drums or washboard to their performances, the description on the record would occasionally read "blues singer and his rhythm." Washboard Sam and Bill Broonzy were among the first to have such record designations. The added instruments allowed the creation of a heavier dance beat. The new emphasis on larger ensembles and more upbeat tempos reflected the faster-paced lifestyles of city living; thus "rhythm and blues" became a reasonable substitute for terms such as "blues" and "race music."

By the 1940s, the use of the term "race" to designate recordings made by black artists for black listeners was becoming embarrassing to the record companies. *Billboard* magazine began charting the top black recordings on October 24, 1942. The first designation it gave the music was "Harlem Hit Parade." On February 8, 1945, the magazine listed the top entries under the title "Juke box race records." Finally, on June 25, 1949, the magazine began referring to the music as "rhythm & blues." Jerry Wexler, one of the gurus of rhythm and blues, was working for *Billboard* at the time, and in his autobiography, *Rhythm and the Blues: A Life in American Music*, he asserts, "Maybe 'race' was too close to 'racist.' In 1949, my suggestion for change was adopted by *Billboard*; I came up with a handle I thought suited the music as well, 'rhythm and blues.' 'Rhythm and blues,' I wrote in a turn-of-the-decade essay for the *Saturday Review of Literature*, 'is a label more appropriate to enlightened times.' I liked the sound of 'rhythm and blues.' It sung and swung like the music itself, and I was happy when it stuck; it defined a whole new genre of music. The handle worked its way into our language and it managed to survive four decades." We will hereafter refer to the urbanized blues forms of the period from 1935 to 1950 as rhythm and blues.

The bifurcation of jazz. Many of the rhythm and blues stars of the 1930s and 1940s, such as Lionel Hampton, Louis Jordan, Nat King Cole, Big Jay McNeely, and others, were really jazz players in the earlier tradition of artists like Louis Armstrong and Fats Waller, who emphasized "happy jazz" and saw themselves as entertainers first and foremost. They joked around, did dance steps, and generally tried to keep their audiences entertained. When modern jazz performers such as Charlie Parker, Thelonious Monk, Miles Davis, and Lennie Tristano came along, the concept of performer as "entertainer" was discarded. This breakdown between jazz-oriented artists can be viewed as a generational split between the "old guard," which viewed music as pure entertainment, and the younger players—the "avant-garde," who sought dignified stature, much like that accorded to classical music artists.

Top, Lionel Hampton on top of a drum, with one of his saxophone players cavorting with him as the band plays riffs in the background. Rhythm and blues groups like Hampton's were playing jazz, but it was a kind of jazz that featured repeated riffs, honking sax solos, singing, dancing, and humorous, exhibitionist theatrics. Performers of this type were considered jazzmen before the emergence of bebop and cool in the early to mid-1940s; after, they were suddenly labeled "Harlem Hit Parade" performers—a euphemism created by *Billboard* magazine to replace the term "race music." By the end of the 1940s, these terms would be changed to "rhythm and blues."

Bottom, a picture just as telling. Charlie Parker on alto sax, and Miles Davis on trumpet, performing modern jazz with the seriousness of classical chamber groups. The jazz-oriented rhythm and blues artists, and the more serious-minded chamber artists of bebop and cool, both born of swing, took jazz in completely opposite directions.

A number of factors besides the black migration to city centers were responsible for the rise of rhythm and blues during the 1940s. First was the development of independent record companies, many of which went into business after the war because shellac, a component in record manufacturing needed to make bullets and bombs, was once again plentiful.

The major record companies dominated the music industry, selling approximately 80 percent of the records sold in America. Very few blacks recorded for the major record companies, and those who did were signed on because they were recognized as having "crossover" possibilities—the potential appeal to the mass white audience. The Mills Brothers, the Ink Spots, Nat King Cole, Louis Armstrong, Duke Ellington, Count Basie, and Louis Jordan were among the few black stars to regularly record on the major labels.

Although the majors had subsidiary labels or specially numbered series of releases intended specifically for the "specialty" markets such as "race," "hillbilly," and "gospel," the independent companies went into business because there was a vacuum in the industry. Regional talent was not being fully tapped by the majors because it didn't seem to make economic sense. The majors wanted artists for their specialty lines only if they could generate national sales.

This made it possible for independent companies such as Aladdin, King, Savoy, DeLuxe, and Atlantic to sign lesser-known talent for little money and distribute their records in the artist's region, where the talent was recognized and could make a profit if overhead could be kept down. The "indies" didn't have national distribution outlets like the majors, but, in time, some of the more successful companies were able to market their records throughout the country, and in some cases, even work out deals to distribute overseas. One of

Courtesy Big Nickel Publications (Galen Gart)

One of the most important independent record companies was Syd Nathan's King Records. Nathan set up his company in an old ice house in Cincinnati, Ohio, and tried to serve the needs of Midwest audiences with separate companies for specialized musical forms. Established in 1945, King originally issued country and western music for the rural white audience interested in the radio barn dances. Nathan established Queen Records as a rhythm and blues company for the black audience. By the late 1940s, both styles were released on King. King Records was the first independent company to regularly have its specialized artists "cover" each other's works. Later, in the early 1950s, Sam Phillips would oversee Sun Records (Elvis Presley's first company) in Memphis, Tennessee, and attempt to cover the same bases that King Records had initiated during the 1940s. *Above*, a King ad attempting to appeal to three markets: "hillbilly" (rural white), "pop" (rural and urban white), and "sepia" (urban black).

Atlantic Records was founded by Ahmet Ertegun and Herb Abramson in New York in 1947. By 1953, Abramson had been bought out and Jerry Wexler had bought in. Atlantic began as a jazz label with recordings of Dixielanders like Eddie Condon, modernists such as Eddie Safranski's Poll Winners (mostly Stan Kentonites), and swing stars like Tiny Grimes and Rex Stewart.

Ahmet Ertegun felt that songwriter and arranger Jesse Stone provided the essence of Southern blues previously missing from the Atlantic fold. Ertegun told author Charlie Gillett in *Making Tracks: Atlantic Records and the Growth of a Multi-Billion-Dollar Industry*, "Jesse Stone did more to develop the basic rock'n'roll sound than anybody else, although you hear a lot about Bill Haley and Elvis Presley. He was a great, reliable, loose arranger, who could update a five-year-old arrangement with a couple of chord changes. Those arrangements were very important." Stone wrote one of Atlantic's earliest hits, Frank Culley's "Cole Slaw" (1949), and worked with the Cardinals, Clovers, Ruth Brown, and Big Joe Turner (it was Stone, under the pseudonym Charles Calhoun, who composed "Shake Rattle and Roll" for Turner in 1954).

Atlantic would also specialize in creme de la creme cabaret artists such as Mabel Mercer and Bobby Short. Later on, in the 1960s, Ahmet Ertegun would sign such important rock acts as the Buffalo Springfield, Led Zeppelin, Yes, and Crosby, Stills, Nash and Young (and worked out a distribution deal with the Rolling Stones), among others, before eventually selling the company to Warner in 1968. But it was as a rhythm and blues label that Atlantic would make its greatest contribution. *Right*, an ad showing some of Atlantic's early rhythm and blues stars. By the 1950s, the roster would boast of doo wop groups like the Clovers, the Drifters, and the Coasters, and individual stars such as Ruth Brown, LaVern Baker, Ray Charles, Big Joe Turner, and Bobby Darin. During the 1960s, Wexler made connections with the Memphis-based Stax label and recorded such "soul" stars as Sam and Dave, Wilson Pickett, Joe Tex, Solomon Burke, Booker T. and the MGs, and, his biggest coup of all, Aretha Franklin.

Courtesy Big Nickel Publications

386

these was Chess Records, which, with its roster of electric bar blues greats such as Muddy Waters, Howlin' Wolf, and Sonny Boy Williamson, was a valuable source of inspiration for the British Invasion.

In addition to the rise of independent record companies, another factor in the growth of rhythm and blues was the establishment of Broadcast Music Incorporated (BMI). When ASCAP threatened to raise fees for broadcasting rights in 1939, the broadcasters fought back by forming BMI, a licensing agency that stated in its 1939 charter that it would seek out minority music forms such as blues and hillbilly. The indies recorded a major portion of such music, and BMI protected much of it. When rock 'n' roll emerged in the mid-1950s, most of it was released on independent record labels and licensed by BMI.

The jukebox was a third important element in the growth of rhythm and blues. By the late 1930s, most restaurants, diners, and taverns had jukeboxes. Communities with large black populations were not all that interested in the latest Kay Kyser, Sammy Kaye, or Frank Sinatra releases, but in hearing black artists whom they could relate to. The ability of the jukebox to cater to specific regional tastes and demands greatly enhanced the importance of the independent record companies, bringing stature, and, in some cases, stardom to black artists who would not have been given a chance by the bigger companies.

Library of Congress

By the late 1930s, jukeboxes were installed everywhere from soda shops to cafes. A jukebox was likely to be found wherever people congregated during leisure hours to relax with food and drink. Local "stars" who were not nationally known, were often able to get exposure through independent record companies and the jukebox. If an "indie" was fortunate, a local star might have a national breakout record, and that disc might be placed in jukeboxes throughout the country. Trade magazines like *Variety* and especially *Cash Box* and *Billboard* kept close track of rhythm and blues records, listing the best-selling and most-played songs on jukeboxes as the "Harlem Hit Parade."

By 1942, the tremendous popularity of the jukebox prompted the president of the American Federation of Musicians, James Petrillo, to call the record "the No. 1 scab" of the music industry. He established a ban on recording by union musicians. This ban, along with a lack of shellac during the war (shellac was a main ingredient in the making of records, and Japan, which was at war with the United States, controlled the Far East market which was the main source of shellac), drastically curtailed record production. With the end of the war, a number of independent record companies went into business, and jukebox placements became a major source of their sales.

The Panoram: A video jukebox. Actor Cary Grant (left) and popular vocalist Dick Todd (baritone star of radio and records; his biggest hit was "The Gaucho Serenade" in 1940) shaking hands in front of a Mills Panoram. Television—and the Panoram's high maintenance costs—would lead to the Panoram's demise.

The Mills Panorams were usually found in the better hotels, restaurants, and taverns across the United States. The Panoram looked like a big television set and held a 16 mm projector inside. For a dime it would play a three-minute short called a "soundie."

To most people, the Mills Panoram was known as the Soundies Machine. In an era when racial discrimination was very much in effect, the Soundies Machine allowed black entertainers a chance to be seen and heard. As noted a number of times, black entertainers were seldom given substantial parts in major Hollywood films , and in many cases were eliminated from films when they were shown in the South.

In 1941 a video juke box, the Mills Panoram, made its debut. The Panoram featured a roll of eight videos per reel that could only be played in successive order (if you were interested in one particular video and wanted to play it again you had to play the other seven to get to it). All kinds of music could be seen on video juke boxes—novelty acts, hillbilly, popular bands, and rhythm and blues. The resultant videos were known as "soundies," and today they can be purchased in some video stores. The soundies provide a rare glimpse of some of the greatest black talent of the 1941-48 period. Soundies were the MTV videos of their day.

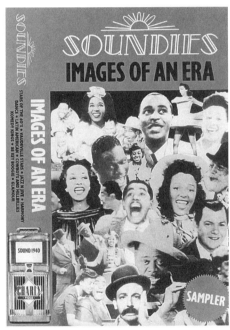

This Charly Records release provides a good sampling of the medium's diversity: "Stars of the 40's, Vaudeville Stars, Jazz'n'Jive, Harmony, Dance, Latin American, Cowboys and Hillbillies, Komedy Kings, 88 Key Boogie, Glamour."

Radio was a final agent in the popularization of rhythm and blues. For many years, national radio broadcasts could not legally replay records. If it wanted to broadcast music, a network had to feature it live, performed by union musicians. For all but the biggest networks, like NBC and CBS, this proved prohibitively expensive. But in 1940, Judge Learned Hand of the Second U.S. Circuit Court of Appeals reversed an earlier decision that forbade station WNEW from playing Paul Whiteman records. The door was opened for all radio stations to spin records. Hand ruled that, "The common-law Property of orchestra leader and corporation manufacturing phonograph records ended with the sale of the record, so that the radio broadcasting company could not be restrained from using records in broadcasts." Licensing fees still had to be paid, of course, but now smaller stations that couldn't afford union musicians every time they wanted to broadcast some music could instead hire a disc jockey to play records. By the mid-1940s, black disc jockeys were spinning independent record company releases in most black communities.

Key Major Labels

Label (founded)	Popular Recording Artists	Black Artists
Columbia (1885)	Frank Sinatra, Les Brown, Buddy Clark, Doris Day, Benny Goodman, Horace Heidt, Woody Herman, Harry James, Gene Krupa, Kay Kyser, Ray Noble, Tony Pastor, Kate Smith, Claude Thornhill, Orrin Tucker	Sarah Vaughan Billie Holiday
RCA Victor (1901)	Perry Como, Larry Clinton, Tommy Dorsey, Shep Fields, Benny Goodman, Sammy Kaye, Hal Kemp, Guy Lombardo, Freddy Martin, Tony Martin, Glenn Miller, Vaughn Monroe, Ozzie Nelson, Ray Noble, Tony Pastor, Artie Shaw, Dinah Shore, Charlie Spivak, Three Suns, Dick Todd, Fran Warren, Paul Whiteman	Duke Ellington Lionel Hampton Erskine Hawkins Fats Waller Arthur "Big Boy" Crudup
Decca (1934)	Andrews Sisters, Bing Crosby, Bob Crosby, Jimmy Dorsey, Helen Forrest, Jan Garber, Glen Gray, Dick Haymes, Woody Herman, Frances Langford, Johnny Long, Russ Morgan, Ted Weems, Lawrence Welk, Victor Young	Ella Fitzgerald Lionel Hampton Ink Spots Louis Jordan Andy Kirk Mills Brothers Chick Webb
Capitol (1942)	Peggy Lee, Gordon MacRae, Dean Martin, Johnny Mercer, Ella Mae Morse, Les Paul, Pied Pipers, Tex Ritter, Andy Russell, Freddie Slack, Jo Stafford, Kay Starr, Mel Torme, Jimmy Wakely, Paul Weston, Margaret Whiting	Nat King Cole Julia Lee Nellie Lutcher
Mercury (1946)	Eddy Howard, Frankie Laine, Vic Damone, Patti Page	Sarah Vaughan

Key Independent Labels

Label (founded)	Owners	Artists
East Coast		
Apollo (1942)	Ike and Bess Berman	Dixie Hummingbirds, Wynonie Harris, Mahalia Jackson
Savoy (1942)	Herman Lubinsky	Nappy Brown, Big Jay McNeely, Johnny Otis, Paul Williams
National (1942)	A.B. Green	Billy Eckstine, Dusty Fletcher, Ravens
Jubilee (1948)	Jerry Blaine	Four Tunes, Edna McGriff, Orioles,
Atlantic (1948)	Herb Abramson and Ahmet Ertegun	Ruth Brown, Frank Culley, Tiny Grimes, Ivory Joe Hunter, Stick McGhee
Midwest		
King (1945)	Syd Nathan	Tiny Bradshaw, Roy Brown, Lucky Millinder, Todd Rhodes Wynonie Harris, Bullmoose Jackson
Chess (1947)	Phil and Leonard Chess	Gene Ammons, Willie Dixon, Muddy Waters, Sonny Boy Williamson II
West		
Aladdin (1945)	Eddie and Leo Mesner	Charles Brown, Big Jay McNeely, Amos Milburn
Modern (1945)	Jules and Saul Bihari	Floyd Dixon, John Lee Hooker, Lightnin' Hopkins Johnny Moore's Three Blazers, B.B. King, Jimmy Witherspoon
Specialty (1945)	Art Rupe	Jimmy Liggins, Joe Liggins, Roy Milton, Soul Stirrers, Pilgrim Travelers
Imperial (1947)	Lew Chudd	Dave Bartholomew, Fats Domino, Smokey Hogg, T-Bone Walker

Country Blues Comes to the Cities

Before we move on to the urbanized sounds of this era, let's investigate the migratory patterns to key city centers that led to them. The changing economic and social conditions just prior to and during World War II were directly responsible for a great expansion and evolution of black music. Black migration followed the highway and railroad networks of America. Three general patterns can be noted:

1. Departure from the Delta area of Mississippi, Arkansas, and Louisiana, using Highway 61 or 51 or the Illinois Central Railroad, to get to Memphis and Chicago.

2. Blacks from the southern Atlantic states utilized a variety of highways and railroads to get to Memphis, Cincinnati, Baltimore, Washington, Philadelphia, and New York.

3. Departure from the southwest territories (Texas, Oklahoma, and Missouri), traveling west on the Santa Fe or Southern Pacific Railroads, or along Highway 80 or 66, to California.

Many of the southern blues performers who had recorded in the 1920s and early 1930s had already moved to the city centers by 1935. These rural songsters, who patterned themselves on the traditions of Blind Lemon Jefferson and Charlie Patton, plied their trade in city centers such as Memphis, Chicago, St. Louis, Detroit, and Los Angeles. The one-man band heritage sounded archaic to many blacks, some of whom wanted to leave the "plantation songs" behind, but for others it was a welcome island of hospitality in the big, faceless city (Lightnin' Hopkins will represent this group). There were others who came to the city centers to record but chose to continue living in the country (Arthur "Big Boy" Crudup will exemplify this group).

Sam "Lightnin" Hopkins (1912-1982) hailed from Texas, where he sang on the streets, in buses, at barbecues, and in the jook joints until he began recording in 1946. Balancing a career that jumped back and forth between Houston and Los Angeles (and literally hundreds of other spots), Hopkins was one of the most recorded bluesmen in the history of the music, a songster in the truest sense, improvising on the spot and at home in any kind of setting. Hopkins's delicate, single-note guitar lines were drawn from his earliest inspiration, fellow Texan Blind Lemon Jefferson, and he could play boogie woogie on guitar with great assurance. Hopkins recorded so many outstanding selections over the years that it is nearly impossible to pick out a signature tune. His works were imbued with great humor, and a sly awareness that he was an anachronism. Hopkins was a towering presence from the 1940s until his death.

Arthur "Big Boy" Crudup (1905-1974) was a guitarist, singer, and composer born in Forest, Mississippi. He traveled the state playing at parties, jook joints, and lumber and levee camps until he recorded for Bluebird (a subsidiary race and hillbilly designation of RCA Victor) in the 1940s. Crudup had a big, gruff vocal delivery, booted along by his chunky electric guitar scraping. On some recordings, Crudup was assisted by acoustic rhythm guitar, bass, and drums, and his blending of country and city on hard-driving selections. "Mean Old 'Frisco Blues" and "Cool Disposition" are forerunners of the rockabilly of the 1950s.

To listen today to Crudup's "That's All Right," "My Baby Left Me," "Cool Disposition," "Hey Mama, Everything's All Right," and "So Glad You're Mine" is to hear the genesis of Elvis Presley's classic Sun recordings of 1954 and 1955. Presley's first record release in 1954 was a perfect mix of underground influences from this section. The A side of Sun #209 is a reworking of Bill Monroe's bluegrass classic, "Blue Moon of Kentucky." The B side—the one that created the real excitement—is a cover of Crudup's "That's All Right." Presley, who later sent a plaque to Crudup acknowledging his debt to "That's All Right," recorded Crudup's "My Baby Left Me" and "So Glad You're Mine" in 1955.

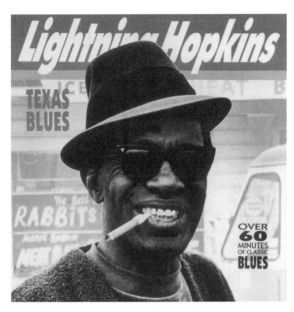

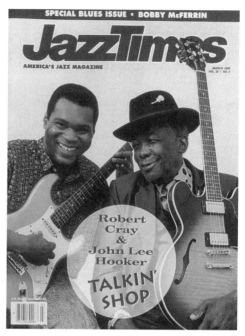

Lightnin' Hopkins often recorded for cash, rather than settling for long-term record contracts. His songs were composed for every type of occasion: "Short Haired Woman," "Automobile Blues," "Sad News From Korea," "Slavery Time," "Penitentiary Blues," "Love Like a Hydrant," "Meet You at the Chicken Shack," and hundreds of others. Hopkins also had the ability to improvise on the spot. Even though he traveled a great deal, Hopkins was most at home in the African-American communities of Texas and Louisiana. He was especially fond of the cafes along Dowling Street in Houston.

The Blackwell Guide to Blues Records, edited by Paul Oliver, notes that Hopkins captured the changes in boomtown Houston, in the days before the oil slump. "As capable as anyone of feeling back to his roots, he nonetheless sensed the modernity about him with the likes of 'Airplane Blues,' and 'Automobile Blues.'"

Record company owner and archivist extraordinare Chris Stachwitz had been a fan of Lightnin' Hopkins for a number of years when fellow blues collector and historian Sam Charters located the singer in Houston in 1959. Charters sent a card to Strachwitz, who was living in California, and informed him that he had found Hopkins. Strachwitz took a bus to Houston to meet Hopkins. Strachwitz continues the story in the liner notes to the album above: "During that visit I heard him at neighborhood beer joints and taverns singing his heart out and I decided to start a record label primarily to document this extradinary folk poet. That was the beginning of Arhoolie Records."

Robert Cray (at left) created a renewed interest in blues with his succession of hit recordings and music videos in the 1980s. In *The History of the Blues* by Francis Davis, the author contends that Robert Cray is the leading "Great Black Hope" of the blues. "A case could also be made for Cray as a Soulster, and not just because he travels and records with horns and occasionally lets loose with a convincing shriek. As classic soul was, Cray's songs are driven by a perception of sex as sin—and by an acceptance of sin as the only thing in this world that affords pleasure, whatever the ultimate cost." Next to Cray is John Lee Hooker, one of the last remaining older country-to-city bluesmen on the music scene during the 1990s. In 1943, Hooker moved from the Mississippi Delta region to Detroit, where he played at house parties and in the clubs along Hasting Street. In 1948, Hooker's recording of "Boogie Chillen" for Modern Records became a hit on the rhythm and blues charts, and he quit his factory job for good.

Hooker eventually met a smooth operator, Bernie Bessman, who paid him well while leasing the bluesman's records to numerous companies including many small labels, for whom the singer used pseudonyms such as Delta John, Texas Slim, Birmingham Sam and his Magic Guitar, John Lee, the Boogie Man, Johnny Williams, John Lee Cooker, and John Lee Booker.

Hooker's dark, brooding vocals were demonstrative and muscular, and selections such as "Crawling Snake Blues," "Boom Boom," and "I'm in the Mood" are considered classics. He recorded with modern artists like Canned Heat (*Hooker 'n' Heat* in 1970), and Bonnie Raitt, among others. Hooker more than lived up to the title of "King of Boogie."

The Chicago Blues Scene

While some rural-oriented artists like Hopkins remained steadfast in their compliance with the songster custom, most adapted to the fast-paced city lifestyle by incorporating rhythm sections and occasionally adding a trumpet or saxophone to the mix. Performing before more sophisticated audiences in larger club settings required rehearsals to achieve ensembles with precise timing. One man playing guitar and singing could continue a phrase or verse until another one was thought up or remembered without ruining an interpretation. However, when a group performed in public it was necessary to have in place some kind of arrangement, so that all of the players were in "synch."

A Trio From the Bluebird Beat

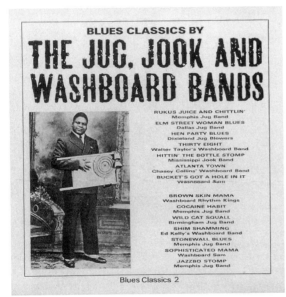

BLUES CLASSICS BY
THE JUG, JOOK AND WASHBOARD BANDS

RUKUS JUICE AND CHITTLIN'
Memphis Jug Band
ELM STREET WOMAN BLUES
Dallas Jug Band
HEN PARTY BLUES
Dixieland Jug Blowers
THIRTY EIGHT
Walter Taylor's Washboard Band
HITTIN' THE BOTTLE STOMP
Mississippi Jook Band
ATLANTA TOWN
Chasey Collins' Washboard Band
BUCKET'S GOT A HOLE IN IT
Washboard Sam

BROWN SKIN MAMA
Washboard Rhythm Kings
COCAINE HABIT
Memphis Jug Band
WILD CAT SQUALL
Birmingham Jug Band
SHIM SHAMMING
Ed Kelly's Washboard Band
STONEWALL BLUES
Memphis Jug Band
SOPHISTICATED MAMA
Washboard Sam
JAZZBO STOMP
Memphis Jug Band

Blues Classics 2

Courtesy Arhoolie Records, 10341 San Pablo Ave., El Cerrito, CA 94530

Born Robert Brown in Arkansas, Washboard Sam was representative of the bluesmen who brought downhome blues to downtown. He scrapped away on his washboard, which had a turntable and a couple of cowbells attached to it, creating a jangly, rhythmic backdrop for his hokum-inspired vocals. Washboard Sam was the longest-lasting "name" player to feature the washboard, and one of the few players of the washboard to record as lead vocalist. Jumping tunes like "Mama Don't Allow," "Diggin' My Potatoes," "Jumpin' Rooster Blues," and "Washboard Swing" are representative examples of his artistry.

Of these assemblages, the most significant was the combination of acoustic guitar and voice with a rhythm section of piano, bass and drums. There were many outstanding country players who took this new approach, and they recorded for a number of different record companies. Performers such as Washboard Sam, influential pianist Big Maceo Merriweather, and Big Bill Broonzy were the leaders of a sound known as the "Bluebird beat," a name given because it appeared so prominently on a series of recordings that began in 1932 with RCA Victor's subsidiary company, Bluebird Records. Record producer Lester Melrose had connections with RCA Victor as well as Columbia, and he put together a clique that included Big Bill Broonzy, Arthur "Big Boy" Crudup, Washboard Sam, John Lee "Sonny Boy" Williamson, Tampa Red, and Memphis Minnie. Melrose claimed that from March 1934 to February 1951 he recorded at least 90 percent of all rhythm and blues talent for Columbia and RCA Victor. Scholar Samuel Charters labelled the country-blues-to-city sound, with piano accompaniment as the unifying force behind the "Bluebird Beat."

Big Bill Broonzy (1893-1958) was the most important of the transitional blues artists who mined the Bluebird beat. Born in Mississippi and raised in Arkansas, he began his recording career in 1926. Like a great majority of the male blues performers noted so far, he worked at many different jobs while cutting records. Very few black male blues artists could sustain themselves without a regular day job. Broonzy worked as a redcap, a janitor, and a barkeeper. He even ran a farm at one point in the late 1930s. Broonzy was the best known of the rural-oriented recording artists of the 1930s to 1950s, and if he had trouble making a career out of the blues, imagine what kind of a struggle most of the other bluesmen faced throughout their careers.

What set Broonzy apart was his technical proficiency on guitar, his storehouse of material, his chameleon-like versatility, and, above all else, his effortless and easy manner before crowds of both colors. Recording in Chicago with pianists such as Black Bob, Memphis Slim, Joshua Altheimer, and Washboard Sam, Broonzy created stomp-like blues releases such as "Bullcow Blues," "Baby I Done Got Wise," and "Night Time Is the Right Time" that were big favorites with black audiences. Broonzy recorded in a multitude of settings, sometimes with a string or jug band, other times with trumpet players. Toward the end of his career he returned to the one-man songster tradition, recording for Moses Asch's company Folkways and being referred to as a "folk singer."

BLUES CLASSICS BY
MEMPHIS MINNIE

IN MY GIRLISH DAYS
BLACK RAT SWING
LONESOME SHACK BLUES
IT'S HARD TO PLEASE MY MAN
I'M SO GLAD
NOTHING IN RAMBLING
ME AND MY CHAUFFEUR BLUES
JOE LOUIS STRUT

IT'S HARD TO BE MISTREATED
MAN YOU WON'T GIVE ME NO MONEY
BOY FRIEND BLUES
MOONSHINE
MY BABY DON'T WANT ME NO MORE
WHEN THE LEVEE BREAKS
YOU GOT TO MOVE - Pt. 1

Blues Classics 1

Courtesy Arhoolie Records, 10341 San Pablo Ave., El Cerrito, CA 94530

Living Blues magazine simply stated, "Memphis Minnie was one of the greatest blues singers of all time." Memphis Minnie's biographers, Paul and Beth Garon, assess her career thusly: "Many people who have heard of Big Bill Broonzy or Tampa Red still don't know much about Minnie. But her songs have been recorded by performers as diverse as Bob Wills and His Texas Playboys, Mance Lipscomb, Muddy Waters, Clifton Chenier, and dozens of others, both obscure and well known. It would be no exaggeration to say that Memphis Minnie was one of the most influential blues singers ever to record. Few today realize how extremely popular she was, with a string of hits and nearly 100 records to her credit." Memphis Minnie was tough and demanding. She had to be—she traveled in a world dominated by men. The majority of Minnie's performances were given in country juke joints and city taverns. Early in her career, Minnie was known to chew tobacco, gamble, and cuss. She bossed sidemen around with abrupt directions on how tunes were to be played. And she wrote some of the roughest, raunchiest songs being performed on record in Chicago. In addition to those previously noted there were "New Dirty Dozen" (Minnie added some new lyrics to Speckled Red's classic) and "What's the Matter with the Mill?" (1930), "My Butcher Man" (1933), "Dirty Mother for You" (1934), "Selling My Pork Chops" (1935), "Ice Man (Come on Up)" and "If You See My Rooster (Please Run Him Home)" (1936), "Wants Cake When I'm Hungry" (1937), "Good Biscuits" (1938), and "It's Hard to Please My Man" (1940).

Not all of these songs (and many others) were directly copywrited to Minnie, but her biographers make a case for these and other songs being written in whole or part by her. Also, not all of Minnie's appearances featured blues material. Like many blues artists Minnie was expected to record blues songs exclusively (Lester Melrose directed her in the studio that way). But a photograph of one of Minnie's "request" lists shown in the Garons' biography shows her hand-printed scrawl of twenty-two songs, most of them popular standards, including: "Prisoner of Love," "Marie," "Summertime," and "Lady Be Good."

Memphis Minnie (1897-1973) was the one female who stood out as a superb guitarist, as well as a composer and singer. She began recording in 1929, and much of her career included sessions with her husbands, Joe McCoy and Little Son Joe (Ernest Lawlars).

After recording classics such as "Bumble Bee," "I'm Talkin' About You," and "Fishin' Blues," McCoy and Minnie went their separate ways in 1935. McCoy teamed up with his brother Charlie to form the successful Harlem Hamfats. Minnie made recordings with various rhythm sections in Chicago under Melrose's supervision. In 1929 she married Little Son Joe, working with him in a twin-guitar setting; their most successful releases included "Me and My Chauffeur" and "Black Rat Swing" in 1941, with Minnie on electric guitar. Minnie was once referred to as the "female Big Bill [Broonzy]" because not only did she tailor her music to the new city style but she was also a technically advanced guitarist. Minnie defeated Broonzy in a number of cutting contests in Chicago. Her life story is thoroughly documented by Paul and Beth Garon in their book *Woman With Guitar: Memphis Minnie's Blues.*

Also known as the "Lester Melrose Sound," the style wasn't the only Chicago blues sound of the 1940s. Although it was the dominant early style, by the late 1940s a rougher and less jazzy blues form would be housed in the stables of another record company: Chess Records. Chess, called Aristocrat until 1950, was formed by two Polish-Jewish immigrants, Leonard and Phil Chess, who ran a liquor store business and, later, in 1947, a nightclub called the Macomba, where jazz stars like Billy Eckstine appeared. Realizing they couldn't record the big names like Eckstine and Sarah Vaughan, the company's talent scout, Sammy Goldstein, suggested recording pianist Sunnyland Slim, who in turn brought in guitarist-singer Muddy Waters. Eventually Waters became Chess's first blues star.

Muddy Waters (1915-1983) was born Mc-Kinley Morganfield in Rolling Fork, Mississippi. He was brought up on a plantation where his father raised hogs and chickens and grew watermelons. Waters learned harmonica and then guitar, and made extra money playing at fish frys and picnics. Son House was his greatest inspiration. By 1940, Waters was touring with the Silas Green Tent Show, and by 1942 he had recorded a couple of country blues sides for the Library of Congress. In 1943, Waters left the Delta for Chicago. By 1946, he had a job driving a delivery truck that manufactured venetian blinds (he called it "the best job I ever had in my life"), and at night he played and sang in the clubs.

Waters's big break came when he recorded "I Can't Be Satisfied" and "I Feel Like Going Home" in 1948 for Aristocrat. The song featured Waters singing in his gruff and authoritative style about missing the Deep South but unwilling to return. The cold Midwest might be anonymous, but jobs were better paying and blacks had more freedom. The songs, which featured only Waters's electric slide guitar and an acoustic bass, struck a sensitive nerve with the displaced southerners in Chicago and the record sold in large numbers. Waters confided to Robert Palmer in *Deep Blues* that, "I had a hot blues out, man. I'd be driving my truck, and whenever I'd see a neon beer sign, I'd stop, go in, look at the jukebox, and see if my record is on there. I might buy me a beer and play the record and then leave. Don't tell nobody nothing. Before long, every blues joint there was, that record was on the jukebox. And if you come in and sat there for a little while, if anybody was in there, they gonna punch it. Pretty soon I'd hear it walking along the street. I'd hear it driving along the street. About June

Courtesy Living Blues

Muddy Waters reclaimed the harsh, Mississippi Delta sound of primal, Charlie Patton-Son House-Robert Johnson roots and plugged it into an amplifier in Chicago. Before Waters left for Chicago in 1943, his sister warned him that they didn't listen to the old blues anymore. She was right. Lester Melrose's Bluebird beat had mixed southern roots with jazz hornmen. Melrose mixed instruments like washboard, saxophone, clarinet, trumpet, piano, guitar, drums, and string bass on blues tunes as well as pop novelties and jazz. Muddy Waters would change all this by the late 1940s.

When Waters arrived in Chicago, Maxwell Street was the main thoroughfare on the South Side, an open-air bazaar of musicians, snake oil salesmen, hustlers and pimps. Ira Berkow's memoir *Maxwell Street* cites bluesman Hound Dog Taylor: "You used to get out on Maxwell Street on Sunday morning and pick you out a good spot, babe. Dammit, we'd make more money than I ever looked at. Sometimes a hundred dollars, a hundred twenty dollars. Put you out a tub, you know, and put a pasteboard in there, like a newspaper? When somebody throw a quarter or a nickel in there, can't nobody hear it. Otherwise, somebody come by, take the tub and cut out. I'm telling you, Jewtown was jumpin' like a champ, jumpin' like mad on Sunday morning."

For the most part Muddy Waters avoided outside venues like Maxwell Street. He had a higher goal in mind—serious recognition as a professional musician. After trying to play in a jazzy way on his first Aristocrat recording with pianist Sunnyland Slim ("Johnson Machine Gun" and "Fly Right, Little Girl" in 1947) and on his first solo venture that same year ("Gypsy Woman" and "Little Anna"), Waters returned to his original rough-and-tumble Delta approach in 1948. That "rough and tumble" style, forceful, full-throated vocals with electric slide guitar, reminiscent of the aggressive, down-home tradition of Walters's mentors, Charlie Patton, Son House, and Robert Johnson, proved successful. Waters's blend of the past with the future (amplification) won over audiences.

or July that record was getting really hot. I would be driving home from playing, two or three o'clock in the morning, and I had a convertible, with the top back 'cause it was warm. I could hear people all upstairs playing that record. It would be rolling up there, man. I heard it all over. One time I heard it coming from way upstairs somewhere, and it scared me. I thought I had died."

Courtesy Arhoolie Records, 10341 San Pablo Ave., El Cerrito, CA 94530   *Courtesy Charly Records*

Along with Little Walter Jacobs, Sonny Boy Williamson was the pantheon player of the harmonica (sometimes simply called "harp") in Chicago on Chess Records.

The role he played in pioneering blues on radio and amplifying the harmonica is significant. *The Blackwell Guide to Blues Records* compares the two leaders of Chicago harmonica: "It has been said that Williamson was not the technical virtuoso that Little Walter was, but this isn't entirely evident, as *Down and Out Blues* reveals. Certainly what Little Walter achieved with energetic virtuosity, Williamson sought with more subtlety and a genius of his own, though he did not seem to have Walter's reach or breadth. His tone harkened back to Memphis and Noah Lewis instead of forward to the harsh new inflections of industrial modernism.

Much confusion exists about Sonny Boy because there was an earlier Sonny Boy Williamson (John Lee Williamson), a popular harmonica player who sang and played primarily about male-female relationships ("Sugar Mama Blues"). He was murdered in 1948.

Sonny Boy Williamson No. 2 (Rice Miller), above, claimed he was "the" Sonny Boy, and that John Lee Williamson, who was at least fifteen years younger, had appropriated the "Sonny Boy" tag in 1937.

Sonny Boy No. 2 (this is the confusion, of course, because he always claimed to be the original, but most reports list him as No. 2) achieved popularity in Helena, Arkansas, with guitarist Robert Junior Lockwood broadcasting on KFFA's "King Biscuit Time." Eventually Williamson recorded for Chess Records and toured England, recording with Eric Burdon and the Animals as well as with British studio musicians, including former Led Zeppelin guitarist Jimmy Page. Williamson died in 1965, but lived on in the impact he had on the British and American blues-rockers of the 1960s and 1970s. Some of Williamson's best-known songs were "Fattening Frogs for Snakes," "Sad to Be Alone," "Eyesight to the Blind," "One Way Out," and "Nine Below Zero."

Muddy Waters is a perfect example of an underground figure whose name became well-known to audiences after the 1960s, but throughout his earlier career had been familiar only to the followers of black blues. There was no established rock press when rock'n'roll surfaced in the mid-1950s, and few jazz writers paid any attention to this form of music, especially the loud electric blues.

It wasn't until the second major rock'n'roll wave, the British Invasion (1964-65) that rock fans even heard Waters's name uttered. British rockers like members of the Rolling Stones, the Beatles, the Animals, the Yardbirds, and others, revered Waters and told interviewers about him, B.B. King, Howlin' Wolf, and the late Robert Johnson.

The first serious rock journals, *Crawdaddy* (out of Boston) and *Rolling Stone* (out of Berkeley, California), began publishing in 1967 and started spreading the word. While Waters never became a pop star, he and some of the other blues innovators became recognizable names and their innovations were at least noted as being influential in the development of rock. British groups should also be credited with insisting that blues veterans like Waters, King, Wolf, and others be allowed to open their shows while they were touring, thus opening the doors for these black originators to larger clubs and concert appearances closed to them in the past.

Blues artists like Muddy Waters and B.B. King did much to establish blues as a music of integrity to today's audiences. Waters told James Rooney in *Bossmen: Bill Monroe and Muddy Waters*, "I'm a gentleman with my blues singing. If I tell you I'm going to do something, I'm going to do it. I ain't gonna lie to you. This is my business. And I'm intelligent with it. You don't have to have a white face to be a gentleman and up to date with what you're doing. You can be black, brown, or any color, but you've got to carry yourself in a way that people know you're it. I don't think you should be down on the blues or any other kind of music as long as it's done right . . . no music should be criticized."

In the late 1940s, Waters formed an electric blues band that played the South Side clubs, with Little Walter Jacobs on harmonica, Jimmy Rogers on guitar, and Baby Face Leroy doubling on guitar and drums (later he was replaced by Elgin Evers). Waters didn't record with this band until 1950. By then Waters had established his sound, essentially plugged-in and rocked-out Mississippi Delta blues, played with volume and attitude. Waters's next hit, 1950's "Rolling Stone," became the source of the name for the British group. By the mid-1950s (with Otis Spann on piano) Waters was recording such classics as "Hoochie Coochie Man," "I'm Ready," "Got My Mojo Working," and "I Just Want to Make Love to You."

Waters's style, called the "electric blues band," "electric bar-band blues," or "Chicago rhythm and blues" by a variety of writers, was the basic electric blues style imitated by Britishers Alexis Korner and Cyril Davis in 1962, the Rolling Stones in 1964, and the Paul Butterfield Blues Band and Canned Heat in the United States in 1965. In the last half of the 1960s and the first half of the 1970s there were literally hundreds of blues bands both in the United States and abroad that played in the 1950s Chicago style.

The style introduced by Waters was used by others as early as the mid-1950s. Electric slide guitarist Elmore James blasted sliding, tremolo figures with his Broomdusters groups. He also added a saxophone beginning in 1952. Howlin' Wolf (Chester Burnett) featured his cement-mixer rasp over a rocking, electric guitar support on "Moanin' at Midnight" (1951), "How Many More Years" (1952), "No Place to Go" (1954), and "Smokestack Lightning" (1956), among many others. Little Walters's solo endeavors with his Jukers group ("Juke" and "My Babe" both Willie Dixon songs), Sonny Boy Williamson No. 2 (Rice Miller), and Hound Dog Taylor were an important influence on other preeminent Chicago blues bands of the 1950s.

Peter Guralnick writes in *Feel Like Going Home: Portraits in Blues and Rock'n'Roll*, "Just about everyone who plays modern Chicago-styled blues has passed through Muddy's band at one time or another. Walter Horton, Junior Wells, Willie Dixon, James Cotton, Hubert Sumlin, Earl Hooker, and Buddy Guy have all played and recorded with Muddy. Like Bill Monroe in bluegrass [see Chapter 13] and Miles Davis in jazz, his band has been a kind of proving ground for young musicians, and if he has never assembled a group which is the equal of the first it is more because there is no one to replace Little Walter—it would be impossible to duplicate a musical partnership like Muddy's and Jimmy Rogers', like Muddy's and Otis Spann's—than through any lack of trying."

Big Band Rhythm and Blues

The original success of the swing bands had an overriding impact on rhythm and blues. Musicians were thought to have commercially "made it" if they fronted a band, which became a primary concern for many musicians. A *Billboard* headline from April 1938 proclaimed, "Colored Band Biz Becoming Big Biz." Most of the big-selling records on the *Billboard* charts, which began in 1942, emanated from the big bands. Most of the singers and combo leaders came directly from the traditions of the jazz bands. The "pantheon" (Lionel Hampton, Dinah Washington, Louis Jordan, Nat King Cole, T-Bone Walker, the Mills Brothers and Ink Spots) all came from the jazz world.

The difference between a jazz artist and a rhythm and blues artist was often negligible. For instance, when Lionel Hampton left Benny Goodman to form his own band in 1940, he was very much a part of the jazz community. Some observers feel his was always a jazz band. Others cite his flamboyant stage presence, his overly repetitive, riff-based charts, and predilection for screaming, honking saxophone players as a reason to place him in the category of rhythm and blues, not jazz.

Both points of view have validity. A comparison of Hampton's 1940s aggregations to those of his former boss, Benny Goodman, shows that both used arrangements, had similar instrumentation, allowed for individual solos, and featured vocalists. The main difference was in the way Hampton's bands responded to the black audience, which favored a "hotter" and "looser" performance style. Many jazz critics decried Hampton's jumping up and down in front of the band, and his constant exhortations to his sidemen to play with frenzied abandon. Most of these critics, by the way, were white. Whatever one might have thought about Hampton's wild performances (reminiscent of Cab Calloway), one thing was certain: he had the most popular and entertaining black big band of the 1940s. If ever there was a band that provided "Saturday night revelry" for its audience, it was the Lionel Hampton band. Rhythm and blues's premier honking sax man, Illinois Jacquet, and its foremost singer, Dinah Washington, both got their start with Hampton.

The Lionel Hampton Orchestra at the Savoy Ballroom in 1942. Hampton is standing fourth from the left and Illinois Jacquet is at the microphone playing tenor saxophone. The Hampton band became the premier box-office attraction of the black big bands of the 1940s, although a number of jazz observers and writers frowned at his histrionics.

One of the most astute jazz writers was Leonard Feather, a strong supporter of bebop and the author of the first popular music encyclopedia—*The Encyclopedia of Jazz* (1955). Feather's entry on Lionel Hampton was strongly opposed to the bandleader's wild performance style. In *The New Edition of the Encyclopedia of Jazz*, Feather is more tempered, but he still has misgivings about Hampton's emphasis on rhythm and blues. "The Hampton band, operating on the premise that excitement was the main objective of jazz, gradually reduced the accent on musicianship, and by the early '50s had become as much a rhythm-and-blues as a jazz attraction, with circus overtones; nevertheless, the band remains the medium for the introduction of many great jazz talents."

Lionel Hampton (1913-) went to a Catholic boys school in Wisconsin, where a nun taught him to play the snare drum. Hampton later mastered drums and the marimba in a variety of bands beginning in 1929. Hampton's 1930 recording of "Memories of You" with the Louis Armstrong Orchestra spotlighted him on vibraharp (an amplified xylophone), the instrument that he would be most identified with. After fronting his own band in Los Angeles, Hampton joined Benny Goodman in 1936, becoming a crucial part of the integrated quartet.

After heading numerous all-star recording sessions from 1937 on, all while still a member of the Goodman band, Hampton decided to start up his own big band in 1940. The bands he led throughout the 1940s featured some of the best swing and bop players of the time. Milt Buckner, a pianist who is often credited with formulating the lock-hand chordal style later popularized by George Shearing, was a leading soloist as well as arranger; Arnett Cobb was a passionate and hard-blowing tenor man; and Dexter Gordon's full-bodied tenor was equally at home in swing and bop setting.

Musically, Hampton was always trying to win the approval of his audiences, not the critics. He could play his vibraharp with great tenderness on ballads, and led his charges through mid-tempo swing numbers with faultless assurance. But it was the uptempo numbers for which Hampton's band is most remembered, jump and jive selections like "Jack the Bellboy," "Central Avenue Breakdown," "Chasin' with Chase," "Air Mail Special," and the flag-waver of all time, "Flying Home." Not only was Hampton's band supercharged, it was "electrified." Hampton's vibraharp was plugged in and had speakers to expand its sound. Irving Ashby's guitar was electric and also had special speakers. Vernon Alley played on one of the first electric basses ever made and Ray Perry was occasionally featured on electric violin.

Like his ex-boss, Benny Goodman, who put up some of the financing for his band, Hampton liked to feature some of his better soloists in a small group setting, often a septet (two saxes, trumpet, piano, bass, drums, and vibes). It was the septet that introduced Hampton's most famous number, "Flying Home." This was recorded in 1942 and was the big solo feature for tenor- man Illinois Jacquet, who would set the standard for all of the other rhythm and blues blowers (they would eventually be tabbed "honkers").

On "Flying Home," Jacquet created a series of repetitive note clusters, played over and over while the rest of the group vamped riffs in support. The tenorman forced high, squealing notes in the upper register. These falsetto screeches and the subsequent playing of extremely low notes that sounded like gurgles and burps created tremendous excitement. Audiences went wild. It is difficult to envision the revivalist spirit engendered when listening to a three-minute recorded version of what was widely acknowledged as an awesome

Courtesy MCA Records

Readers may find it difficult to imagine the excitement that many of the Hampton songs created with audiences of the 1940s because the 78 rpm recorded versions of them last only about three minutes. On a record like "Flying Home" the band plays an introduction (the "head") and a conclusion (the "recapitulation"). In between there is a saxophone tenor solo by Illinois Jacquet. When the band played in front of audiences this song might last twenty or thirty minutes, with Jacquet (and those who replaced him, like Arnette Cobb) playing a solo for fifteen or twenty minutes. Also, there were occasions when the band would parade around the concert hall during the number, or the sax soloist might appear at the beginning of the solo entering from the wings of the stage or from the balcony. This excitement is impossible to replicate on record.

The band had a number of other uptempo features, including "Hey! Ba-Ba-Re-Bop," "Loose Wig," and "Hamp's Boogie," which featured the boogie woogie piano playing of Milt Buckner, and, as an added attraction, Hampton's dynamic two-finger piano technique played in the upper register.

When Alan Freed began the early "Moondog Rock'n'Roll" concerts in the early 1950s in Cleveland, and later when he moved his radio show and rock'n'roll caravan to New York, he always had a featured big band. Freed's theme song was "Blues for the Red Boy," a jump band blues number recorded by King Records' Todd Rhodes. Early rock'n'roll featured screaming trumpets and honking saxophones. Lionel Hampton was a precursor of that style. Hampton wrote in his autobiography, "I tried a new direction in the middle 1940s. In January 1946 I recorded a rock and roll album for Decca called *Rock and Roll Rhythm*. But they never released it; they said it was 'too cacophonous.' I was ahead of my time on that. Rock and roll wouldn't be big for another ten years. In the forties it was still a black thing, which is why I was into it."

live performance. Imagine being surrounded by a huge audience swaying and stomping to a fifteen-to-twenty-minute solo by Jacquet while Hampton jumps up and down, running from the vibes to the piano to the drums, culminating it all by leaping up on a drum pedestal at the climax of the sax solo!

Just one example of the disinclination of the jazz historians to praise Hampton's exciting aggregation can be noticed in Gene Fernett's *Swing Out: Great Negro Dance Bands*: "By the late 1940s, he came to rely more and more upon excitement, upon noisy displays of kicking at the drums (in a fashion more befitting a boilermaker than the fine musician he was) in order to appeal to the audience. But in the light of the increasing popularity, by then, of rock'n'roll, his actions in retrospect seem, in part at least, excusable because of economic necessity."

Hampton performed in a rhythm and blues style not just at the tail end of the 1940s, but right at the beginning of the 1940s. And rock'n'roll didn't emerge until the mid-1950s, although Hampton's band established many of the precedents that came to characterize early rock'n'roll—shouting vocalists, wild antics by band members (or, at the very least, one manic performer), and screeching, honking saxophone solos.

For a good example of how point of view determines attitude, let's read what Leroi Jones (Amiri Baraka) wrote about the same type of performance described by Fernett. In liner notes to saxman Willis "Gatortail" Jackson's album *Thunderbird,* and quoted in Charlie Gillette's *The Sound of the City*, Jones says, "Lloyd's Manor in Newark, N.J., was a place where they'd have groups like Illinois Jacquet's, Erskine Hawkins, Earl Bostic's, Tab Smith's, Big Jay McNeely's and all the other wild swingers of the day. There were absolutely no holds barred, musically or socially, and a band was considered successful if it succeeded in blowing the dancers off their feet. There was also a place called 'Teen Canteens' but a lot of the people must have been teenagers for 20 or so years. It was a loud blues, climaxed by those shattering saxophone 'battles' which featured heavy horns like Jacquet, McNeely and Ammons-Stitt groups and big throated singers like Wynonie Harris, Larry Darnell and Little Esther."

Although Jones doesn't mention Hampton, all of these performers were inspired, and their performance styles established, by Hampton; these were his disciples. Hampton hired young stars-to-be like Jacquet, and fellow saxmen Dexter Gordon, Jack McVea, and Arnette Cobb, as well as high-note trumpeters. Hampton's main goal was to entertain the crowd. The leader used to remind his sidemen that they were in the business of entertaining a paying audience.

When the Hampton band played the Apollo Theater, crowds lined up around the block for tickets, even when the leader played nine or ten shows in a day. In his autobiography *Hamp* (written with James Haskins), the leader recalled the long, exciting sets he established at the Apollo: "We had that audience in a frenzy, and that brought out every bit of my showmanship. I used to do a bit where I jumped up and down on my drums, and I made an arrangement with Bob Hall, the Apollo electrician, to let loose with his smudge pot so that it would look like the stage was blowing up. The first time he did that, everybody ran out of the theater. But word got around that it was just a special effect, so the next time everybody stayed in the seats. "Some funny things happened at the old Apollo. There was a time when a guy in the second balcony was high on too much reefer. When we were playing 'Flying Home,' he got inspired. He climbed up on the rail and started shouting, 'I'm flying, I'm flying.' And then he jumped. It was a miracle that no one was hurt. They say that Jerry Valentine wrote 'Second Balcony Jump' for Earl Hines on the inspiration of that incident."

Courtesy Big Nickel Publications (Galen Gart)

Lucky Millinder fronted one of the most exciting rhythm-and-blues-oriented big bands of the 1940s. Millinder was not an active musician. He strictly operated and fronted the band. He was at his peak during the 1940s, when he featured gospel guitarist and singer Rosetta Tharpe and flamboyant blues shouter Wynonie Harris. Millinder's biggest hits were "Apollo Jump" (1943), "Who Threw the Whiskey in the Well?" (1945), "Shorty's Got to Go" (1946), "D Natural Blues" (1949), and "I'm Waiting Just for You" (1951).

Significant R&B Bands

Leader	Label	Big R&B Hit	Peak R&B Position	Year
Tiny Bradshaw	King	Well, Oh Well	2	1950
Paul Gayton	DeLuxe	Since I Fell for You	3	1947
Griffin Brothers	Dot	Street Walkin' Daddy	7	1950
Tiny Grimes	Atlantic	Midnight Special	1	1945
Lionel Hampton	Decca	Hey! Ba-Ba-Re-Bop	1	1946
Erskine Hawkins	RCA	Tippin' In	1	1945
Edgar Hayes	Exclusive	Fat Meat and Greens	11	1949
Buddy Johnson	Decca	When My Man Comes Home	1	1944
Jimmy Liggins	Specialty	Tear Drop Blues	7	1948
Joe Liggins	Exclusive	The Honeydripper	1	1945
Lucky Millinder	Decca	Who Threw the Whiskey in the Well?	1	1945
Roy Milton	Juke Box (Specialty)	R. M. Blues	2	1946
Johnny Otis	Savoy	Double Crossing Blues	1	1950
Todd Rhodes	King	Blues for the Red Boy	4	1948
Sonny Thompson	Miracle	Long Gone, Parts. 1&2	1	1948
Cootie Williams	Hit	Somebody's Got to Go	1	1945

Chart positions: Joel Whitburn's Top R&B singles, 1942-1988

Courtesy Delmark Records

No less than four well-known people claim to have changed Ruth Jones's name to Dinah Washington. Trumpeter Red Allen told writer Whitney Balliett that when she worked with him on occasion at Chicago's Down Beat Room, he would announce her to the stage, with a big fanfare, as "Dynamite Washington." Lionel Hampton's manager, Joe Glaser, often claimed to have given Jones the name Dinah Washington. Lionel Hampton wrote in his biography that when Jones sang with his band for the first time at a matinee at the Regal Theater in Chicago, he told her he didn't like the name Ruth Jones and asked if he could change it. According to Hampton, she replied, "I don't care what you call me as long as you give me the job." Hampton continues the story: "So I said, 'Well from now on your name is Dinah Washington.' It came to me right out of the clear blue sky." According to historian Chris Albertson, in the liner notes to the 1993 Mercury/Polygram Compilation, *The Dinah Washington Story,* "Most people who moved in Dinah Washington's circles during that time give the credit to Joe Sherman, the proprietor of Garrick's Show Bar, a popular Chicago hangout where Dinah occasionally appeared before joining Hampton."

R&B Big Band Vocalists

Lionel Hampton's band provided the forum for rhythm and blues's most influential vocalist of the 1940s, **Dinah Washington** (1924-1963). Born Ruth Lee Jones in Tuscaloosa, Alabama, Washington was drawn to piano studies and gospel music as a youngster. By 1940, she was touring with gospel pioneer Sallie Martin as a piano accompanist and singer. Washington's break from gospel into the secular world of blues and pop came in 1943, when Louis Armstrong's manager, Joe Glaser, heard her sing at the Garrick Bar in Chicago. Glaser passed on a glowing report to Lionel Hampton, who signed her to a contract after hearing her belt out a rousing rendition of "Evil Gal Blues." Washington's debut recordings were made with Hampton's small group in 1943 ("Evil Gal Blues" and "Salty Papa Blues," both authored by composer and historian Leonard Feather). Washington would be a mainstay, though not the primary focus, of the band until late 1945, making $75 per week. Washington was in the workshop stage of her career with Hampton's band, but even then one could notice the compelling gospel power of her honey-toned, slightly strident vocals.

Dinah Washington
«If You Don't Believe I'm Leaving»

Courtesy Jukebox Lil, a division of Mr. R&B Record Sales

When Dinah Washington first appeared with the Lionel Hampton band, she was an immediate hit. Jazz writer Barry Ulanov, writing for *Metronome* magazine in 1943, was greatly impressed, but at the time Washington was so unknown that Ulanov got her name wrong: "This was one of the greatest stage shows ever. From beginning to end Lionel and his inspired band at the Apollo put on a driving, jumping performance that eclipsed all but the greatest jazz shows. Foremost among the surprises was a new girl singer, one Diana [sic] Washington. Diana sings much like Billie Holiday, in a langorous style, in a relaxed voice and with an authority that is amazing in a girl of nineteen. She did 'The Man I Love' and a series of blues choruses that properly brought the house down."

Washington became one of the most versatile singers in popular music history, equally at home with blues, gospel, jazz, and pop. Linda Dahl wrote about her in *Stormy Weather: The Music and Lives of a Century of Jazzwomen*, "With her gospel approach to secular song, Washington remained a top soul singer on the scene throughout her life, though she cut plenty of jazz sides as well as r&b and commercial numbers; two of her big hits were 'What a Difference a Day Makes' and 'Unforgettable.'

"A riveting personality came through on all of Washington's material, and her phrasing remained confident, intimate and conversational in the best Afro-American manner. Her personal life rivaled Bessie Smith's and Billie Holiday's for tumultuousness: like them, she had a famous temper. She married seven times, got into various legal scrapes and finally died at age thirty-nine, probably from an overdose of pills and alcohol. Her sensuous, easy delivery, salty declamatory phrasing and innate mastery of rhythm inspired many singers who followed."

Washington's successor as queen of rhythm and blues during the 1960s and 1970s was Aretha Franklin. In 1961 Franklin recorded an entire album of songs associated with rhythm and blues's first female superstar—it was titled *Unforgettable*.

Upon leaving Hampton's band, Washington began to work solo, and in 1947 she opened at the Ritz Lounge in Chicago at $250 per week. After two months of standing-room-only crowds, Washington's salary was raised to $750 per week. Between 1948 and 1961 Washington had a string of some thirty hits for Mercury Records, beginning with "Baby, Get Lost." Washington was known as the "Queen of Rhythm and Blues" long before Aretha Franklin. She had the rare ability to sing straight blues, rhythm and blues, jazz, and popular music with equal distinction. Washington's legion of followers included Esther Phillips and Nancy Wilson.

Many women worked in Washington's shadow during the 1940s. Some, like Sister Rosetta Tharpe, shared Washington's gospel connections ("Shout, Sister, Shout"). Others, like Savannah Churchill, "Little" Esther Phillips (as she was known early in her career), Ella Johnson, Ella Mae Morse, and Annie Laurie, also mixed blues and jazz. They all made recordings as singers with big bands.

Another group of female singers was tied to the general cabaret-jazz heritage of piano player singers. Julia Lee and Her Boy Friends, for example, recorded a series of double entendre ditties such as "Snatch and Grab It" (1947) and "I Didn't Like It the First Time," while others, such as Hazel Scott, played classical pieces to a boogie beat for the cafe society audiences of New York.

Then there was **Lil Green** (1919-1954). Here's a name you won't find in most of the music encyclopedias and there is very little information to be found anywhere about her career. Green was born in Chicago and achieved notice as a singer in her mid-teens. She was eighteen when she made her first recordings for Bluebird. Part of the Bluebird beat, she was often accompanied by Big Bill Broonzy and was a popular midwest nightclub attraction during the 1940s. Music critic Leonard Feather once described Green's voice as having a high-pitched "salt-and-vinegar sound." Indeed, Green's distinctive voice is all highs.

In *Stormy Weather,* Linda Dahl writes that Green "was another popular singer who had a gospel background. Jailed for killing a man in a roadhouse brawl, she sang at the prison church services and later popularized a blues-cum-gospel style with a hit record, 'Romance in the Dark.'" That record was

Frank Driggs Collection

Lil Green: "Why Don't You Do Right?"

Courtesy Artpark-at-the Church, Lewiston

The Incredible Dorothy Donegan.

Green's first hit and it had upfront sex in the lyrics. It was later recorded by Billie Holiday, Woody Herman vocalist Mary Ann McColl, and one of the great singer-pianists of the 1950s, Jerri Southern. "Give Your Mama One Smile," "Country Boy Blues," and "My Mellow Man," all recorded in 1940 and 1941 and all recorded by Bill Broonzy, followed.

"Knockin' Myself Out" was written by Green and is about pot smoking (using terms like "tea," "mezz," "reefers," and "gauge"). Green's lines included, "I started blowin' my gauge and I was havin' my fun/I saw the police and I started to run." Green's best-known song was "Why Don't You Do Right?" a hit for her, but an even bigger hit for Peggy Lee, who sang it with Benny Goodman's band on record and in the 1943 film *Stage Door Canteen*. The song was written by Bluebird stablemate Joe McCoy, who was Memphis Minnie's first husband, but he never received royalties for the song.

"Why Don't You Do Right" was first recorded by McCoy with his group, the Harlem Hamfats, as "Weed Smoker's Dream" in 1936, then reissued as "Why Don't You Do Now?" Green's 1941 version excised the exhortation to the woman to "put her stuff on the market." Needless to say, that refrain was also dropped from Peggy Lee's pop version, which was based strictly on the Green interpretation. Memphis Minnie is quoted in Paul and Beth Garon's biography, *Woman With Guitar: Memphis Minnie's Blues*: "Joe wrote this song, 'Why Don't You Do Right?' and Irving Berlin presented this song at the Chicago Theater, with Peggy Lee and all that thing. And at this particular time, Joe McCoy was lying in state at the Metropolitan Funeral Home, and we had to beg for money to bury him. Boy, I'll never forget that. I thought that was a damn shame. They had the headlines of the Chicago Theater, 'Peggy Lee and Irving Berlin.' And here's the man who wrote it, and he told me he never got no money. That Lester Melrose. The 'great' Lester Melrose. He stole all our money."

The dynamic **Dorothy Donegan** (1924-) is another example of an underground performer who fell between the cracks because of her great versatility. The jazz circle has always thought her style too flashy, and she never charted any rhythm and blues or pop hits, so Donegan wasn't written about or even given an entry in the music encyclopedia books. In Arnold Shaw's otherwise thorough study, *Black Popular Music in America: The Singers, Songwriters and Musicians Who*

Pioneered the Sounds of American Music, there is a two-page entry on white skiffle artist Lonnie Donegan ("Rock Island Line," 1956), but nothing on Dorothy Donegan.

Donegan was a popular item in the supper clubs and cabarets during the 1940s and 1950s. A brilliant technician as a pianist, her main inspiration was Art Tatum. She was a regular at The Embers in New York during the 1950s and even made an album there. Donegan toured and recorded during the late 1980s and 1990s and was always a crowd pleaser. Her specialty was boogie woogie numbers like "Piano Boogie" and "Bumble Bee Boogie." Like Hazel Scott, Donegan also continued the tradition of "jazzing up the classics," and was partial to medleys. She was a much more manic and driving performer than Scott, who was considered "lady-like." Donegan was closer to Harry "The Hipster" Gibson than jazzman Teddy Wilson in her conception of how the piano ought to be played.

One testimony to Donegan's continued dynamism comes from Arthur Elgort, a noted high-fashion photographer and television commercial cinematographer, who in 1990 was filming a documentary on saxophonist Illinois Jacquet, the first in a series titled *American Heroes.* Jacquet was performing on the S.S. *Norway* during the Floating Jazz Festival in October 1990. It just so happened that Dorothy was also performing. Elgort had been forewarned by Donegan's drummer, Sal Mosca, that, "She's better than ever, maybe the greatest piano player in the world. Don't forget to check it." Elgort recounts his impressions in the liner notes to the 1992 Chiaroscuro release, *The Incredible Dorothy Donegan Trio:* "I hadn't ever seen so many people at that end of the ship except when they put out the food for the midnight buffet. People were spilling out the doorway of this, the most elegant room on the ship. Those lucky enough to be inside were shouting, and cheering, I tried to hear every note she played that week and I learned pretty quick she's a special performer." This grand lady of the piano was romping and stomping at the piano well into her seventies, with an energy level of youngsters much, much younger. She hums along as she solos, stands up and tosses her elbows at the keyboard, manages to get her feet involved, and also sings. But most of all, Donegan gave audiences of the 1990s a healthy dose of something they used to call 'entertainment.'

The male vocalists of the r&b big band tradition tended to be powerhouse shouters. The leaders of this style were Big Joe Turner, Wynonie Harris, and Roy Brown.

The Ladies of Rhythm and Blues

Name (singer or singer-pianist)	Label	Biggest R&B Hit	Peak Position	Year
Hadda Brooks (s-p)	Modern	That's My Desire	4	1947
Cleo Brown (s-p)	Capitol	Cook That Stuff	13	1949
Savannah Churchill (s)	Manor	I Want to Be Loved (But Only by You)	1	1947
Martha Davis (s-p)	Decca	Don't Burn the Candle at Both Ends	6	1948
Dorothy Donegan (s-p)		Jumpin' Jack Boogie	did not chart	1947
Lil Green (s)	Bluebird	Let's Be Friends	8	1942
Camille Howard (s-p)	Specialty	X-Temperaneous Boogie	7	1948
Helen Humes (s)	Philo	Be Baba Leba	3	1945
Annie Laurie (s)	Regal	Cuttin' Out	6	1949
Julia Lee (s-p)	Capitol	King Size Papa	1	1948
Nellie Lutcher (s-p)	Capitol	He's a Real Gone Guy	2	1947
Ella Mae Morse (s)	Capitol	Shoe-Shoe Baby	1	1943
Little Esther Phillips (s)	Savoy	Double Crossing Blues	1	1950
Paula Satson (s-p)	Supreme	A Little Bird Told Me	2	1948
Mabel Scott (s-p)	Exclusive	Elevator Boogie	6	1948
Sister Rosetta Tharpe (s)	Decca	Strange Things Are Happening Every Day	2	1945
Dinah Washington (s)	Mercury	Baby, Get Lost	1	1949
Georgia White (s-p)	Decca	Hot Nuts	did not chart	1936

Source: Joel Whitburn's Top R&B Singles, 1942-1988

Courtesy Jukebox Lil, a division of Mr. R&B Record Sales   Courtesy Arhoolie Records, 10341 San Pablo Ave., El Cerrito, CA 94530

The Boss of the Blues goes R&B. Vocalist Big Joe Turner made his entrance into the national spotlight with his buddy-pianist Pete Johnson in 1938 at the "From Spirituals to Swing" concert. From there, the duo moved into the Cafe Society nightclub for a couple of years. *Left*, an album featuring one selection with Joe Sullivan and his Cafe Society Orchestra ("I Can't Give You Anything but Love," 1940), and fourteen songs from Turner's stay in Los Angeles, including songs with Freddie Slack's Trio ("Goin' to Chicago Blues," 1941), the Dootsie Williams Orchestra ("Born to Gamble," 1948), the Lorenzo Flenny Trio ("I Don't Dig It," 1949), and Joe Houston's Orchestra ("Fuzzy Wuzzy Honey," 1949).

During this period, Turner was to be outshone by the new shouters who entered the rhythm and blues scene: Wynonie Harris and Roy Brown, as well as the "King of the Jukeboxes," Louis Jordan. This is not to suggest that Turner had lost any of his talent, only that he didn't score many hits. In fact, Turner's only real hits during this time were "My Gal's a Jockey," (1946), with Bill Moore's Lucky Seven on National Records, and "Still in the Dark" (1950) on Freedom. Turner recorded for a series of indies during this period: National, Stag, Swingtime, RPM, Freedom, Excelsior, Aladdin, Imperial, MGM, and Bayou, before returning to New York and finding the biggest success of his career with Ahmet Ertegun's Atlantic Records. At Atlantic, urner had some of the earliest rock'n'roll hits, including "Chains of Love," "Honey Hush," "Flip, Flop and Fly," "Corinne Corinna," and his biggest hit, 1954's "Shake Rattle and Roll," which was famously covered by Bill Haley and the Comets soon after.

Right, Turner and Pete Johnson reunited in Los Angeles in 1948 and 1949. Turner originally went out to California with Meade Lux Lewis in 1941 because Duke Ellington was putting on his musical *Jump for Joy* at the Mayan Theater in Los Angeles, and had signed Turner on. After recording with a variety of groups and traveling back and forth from his home base in Chicago to Los Angeles and Texas, Turner made these recordings with Johnson, which included Kansas City blues like "Wine-O-Baby Boogie" and "Old Piney Brown Is Gone."

Wynonie Harris (1915-1969) presaged rock'n'roll of the 1950s with his dynamic blues shouting. He began his professional career as a "buck dancer" in the late 1930s (he was referred to as "Sugar Cane"), moving on to vocalizing by the early 1940s. Harris made his first records ("Who Threw the Whiskey in the Well" and "Hurry, Hurry," 1944) with bandleader Lucky Millinder on Decca Records. Millinder led a tremendous band during this time. Sister Rosetta Tharpe, vocalist-saxman Bull Moose Jackson, pianist-arranger Bill Doggett, and tenorist Eddie "Lockjaw" Davis were some of the stars during this period. Only Hampton's band topped the Millinder unit's excitement in the r&b arena.

On his very first recording with Millinder, Harris is listed on the label as "Mr. Blues." Few vocalists have ever measured up to Harris's frantic intensity. He was said to have had lungs of steel as he boomed out lusty evocations of carnal desire ("All She Wants to Do Is Rock," "Sittin' On It All the Time," "I Like My Baby's Pudding," and "Lovin' Machine") and bad boy mischief ("Young and Wild," "Drinkin' By Myself," "Blow Your Brains Out," "Good Morning Judge," and "Bloodshot Eyes"). Harris's biggest hit was a cover of Roy Brown's "Good Rockin' Tonight," in 1949. Harris was the man who loved to "rock the blues." During the mid-1940s he appeared as guest artist with some of the biggest names of the time: Lionel Hampton, Charlie Barnet, Duke Ellington, Tommy Dorsey, and Cab Calloway. Harris appeared as a headliner at jazz palaces like Birdland and Bop City and was in the movie *Hit Parade of 1944.* After recording with a variety of indies under his own name, he switched to Syd Nathan's King Records in

December 1947. Harris's time with King proved to be the highlight of his record career. At King, Nathan had his country and blues artists "cover" each other's material. Key country hits that Harris covered included Louie Innis's "Good Morning Judge," Hank Penny's "Bloodshot Eyes," and Moon Mullican's "Triflin' Woman Blues."

Mr. Blues, Mr. Bascomb, Go South

Wilmington, N. C.—A big night for this North Carolina town was the appearance of Wynonie (Mr. Blues) Harris and Dud Bascomb's combo at a one-niter at The Barn. That's ex-Erskine Hawkins trumpeter Bascomb on the left and blues shouter Wynonie at the mike. Photo by Bill Deppe.

Courtesy Down Beat

Harris's frantic stage movements and thunderous blues shouting anticipate rock'n'roll. In fact, when Harris sang of rockin' and rollin' there was no doubt that he was using the term in its earliest meaning—making love. Songs like "Good Rockin' Tonight," "All She Wants to Do Is Rock," and "Rock Mr. Blues" are good examples of "rock" being used as a lovemaking term. And Harris's 1945 release of "Around the Clock Blues" on Philo with Johnny Otis's All Stars anticipates Bill Haley's "Rock Around the Clock" by nearly ten years (although it's not the same song). There aren't too many interviews with Harris to be found, but an extensive article in the October 1954 edition of *Tan* magazine is priceless for its insights into Harris's awareness of his appeal: "Several years ago, when I was headlined at Joe Louis' Old Club Rhum-Boogie in Chicago, I was on the floor one

Courtesy Route 66, a division of Mr. R&B Record Sales

Elvis Presley covered Wynonie Harris's hit "Good Rockin' Tonight" (which itself was a cover of Roy Brown's original) in 1954. King Records super-star producer and songwriter Henry Glover said on a number of occasions that Presley was a "mild version of Wynonie Harris." Presley saw Harris perform in Memphis and in addition to having a regional hit on Sun Records with "Good Rockin' Tonight," Presley also shook his hips and sang another Harris song, "That's the Stuff You Gotta Watch," on the stage of the "Louisiana Hayride."

night singing 'Here Comes the Blues' to a standing-room-only crowd. I was in the mood that night and I suppose the people felt it too. I hollered as loud as I could, 'Here comes the blues, baby, please open up your door.' When I hit the second stanza, "When I leave you this time, baby, I won't be back no more," a woman sitting on the rail in the balcony threw one shapely leg over it and the next thing I knew, she had jumped to the dance floor. She broke her leg as a result of the fall. Strange as it may seem, I don't have any trouble at all with bobby-soxers. I leave all that breed to Billy Eckstine and Billy Kenny of the Ink Spots. My female fans are good-doing landladies and Thursday night girls with good, steady jobs. Some of them own restaurants and beauty parlors. Others are nice-looking preachers' and deacons' wives who still like to listen to 'sinful' music, especially the way I sing it. These women along with others are the ones who keep me alive.

"As a statement of fact, clean of any attempt to brag about it, I'm the highest paid blues singer in the business. I'm a $1,500 a week man. Most of the other fellows sing for $50 to $75 a night. I don't. That's why I'm no Broadway star. The crooners star on the Great White Way and get swamped with Coca-Cola-drinking bobby-soxers and other jail bait. I star in Georgia, Texas, Alabama, Tennessee and Missouri and get those who have money to buy stronger stuff and my records to play while they drink it."

Of course, that became part of Harris's problem. He couldn't adapt to the changing times. Those "bobby-soxers" became the gateway to popular music adulation and the coming changes in the music industry at the very time he was theorizing on his success. In 1995, Tony Collins wrote a biography about this dynamic forefather of rock'n'roll, *Rock Mr. Blues: The Life and Music of Wynonie Harris.*

Roy Brown (1925-1981) was born in New Orleans, where he began singing with local bands. In 1945, he won an amateur singing contest by duplicating two of Bing Crosby's hits, "I Got Spurs That Jingle Jangle Jingle" and "San Antonio Rose." Brown had heard very little blues during his youth, and Crosby was his hero. This phenomenon—white artists having a great influence on black leaders of jazz and blues—has been widely ignored by music writers. New Orleans vocalist Aaron Neville has recounted being an avid fan of the singing cowboys, Roy Rogers and his yodeling style in particular, and bluesman Howlin' Wolf attempted to yodel like country star Jimmie Rodgers early in his career.

Brown's first jobs as a stand-up singer featured him singing popular ballads such as "Stardust," "Blue Hawaii," and his theme song at that time, Bing Crosby's "There's No You." Like a number of black Crosby imitators who sang with bands during the 1930s and 1940s, Brown was something of a novelty, being a black man singing in a crooning style a la Crosby to a black audience. As previously noted, some billed themselves as "Black Bings" and "Colored Crosbys"; others simply emulated Crosby's smooth ballad sonorities. Prior to Brown, there were Billy Eckstine ("I Surrender Dear," "I've Got to Pass Your House," and "I Apologize"), Harlan Lattimore (with the Don Redman band), Roy Felton (with Benny Carter), and Herb Jeffries (with Duke Ellington).

Brown broke away from the crooning of his idol when he belted out a blues song he had written entitled "Good Rockin' Tonight." He recorded the song for independent label, DeLuxe, in 1947 and it became one of the biggest r&b hits of that year. From that moment on, Brown established himself as the leader of New Orleans rhythm and blues and as one of the big-time blues shouters. A series of top-charting hits such as "Long About Midnight" (1948), "Rockin' at Midnight" (1949), "Boogie at Midnight" (1949), "Hard Luck Blues" (1950), and "Big Town" (1951) made Brown one of the biggest names in r&b. Brown often listed his backup band as "His Mighty Men." One of Elvis Presley's earliest recordings was a cover of "Good Rockin' Tonight" (Sun 210, 1955) and in 1984, former Led Zeppelin singer Robert Plant reprised a Brown classic, "Rockin' at Midnight" with a studio unit billed as The Honeydrippers.

John Broven's excellent history, *Rhythm and Blues in New Orleans,* places Brown as the first star of New Orleans rhythm and blues: "Roy Brown, with his crying, pleading, swooping gospel-based style, always had a story to tell his expectant audience, whether in an exuberant fast boogie or a slow sad blues. He was the first singer of soul, and B. B. King and Bobby Bland have headed this popular urban blues style through to this day."

Both Brown and Harris were overlooked when rock'n'roll surfaced in the 1950s. They were both good-looking, appealing vocalists who never caught on with the new music. They blended blues with jazz orchestrations under the title of rhythm and blues. Like any classic art, their recordings still have great appeal and excitement, and both are fittingly given tribute in Nick Tosches' scintillating study of underground greats, *Unsung Heroes of Rock 'n' Roll*. As neglected as Roy Brown's story is, the fact remains that "Good Rockin' Tonight" launched the golden age of rhythm and blues in New Orleans.

New Orleans could boast of many outstanding musicians, but it was a record engineer, Cosimo Matassa, and a college professor who doubled as a disc jockey, Vernon Winslow, who did the most to establish the rhythm and blues tradition in the Crescent City once Roy Brown's hit record started to create interest. Most of the recordings of the late 1940s and 1950s were made at Matassa's small studio located behind his record shop and leased to record companies. Winslow, who couldn't be on the air waves because he was black, wrote scripts in street lingo for a white disc jockey (Poppa Stoppa) for a show called "Jam, Jive and Gumbo." A short time later Winslow was hosting his own show and calling himself Dr. Daddy-O, broadcasting from Matassa's studio, featuring Dave Bartholomew's band. Recordings were the mainstay of this show, however, and "Good Rockin' Tonight" was the song that created all the excitement. This was the beginning of New Orleans becoming a

Frank Driggs Collection

Roy Brown was born and raised in New Orleans in a very religious setting. At the age of twelve, he led a gospel group called the Rookie Four. After a stint as a boxer in 1942, Brown embarked on a career in music as a singer. He used to go to Bing Crosby films and write out the lyrics to the songs Crosby sang. After winning an amateur contest at the Million Dollar Theater in Los Angeles, Brown moved to Galveston, Texas, forming a combo, the Melodeers. During this time he expermented with the shouting blues style instead of crooning.

In 1947, at Foster's Rainbow Room in New Orleans, Brown visited Wynonie Harris, whom he greatly admired, to show him a tune he had written. Harris paid no attention to the unknown singer-songwriter. Brown then went to visit singer-pianist Cecil Gant at the Dew Drop Inn. Gant was sympathetic and made a late night call to De-Luxe Records owner Jules Braun in New Jersey. Brown sang the song over the phone and Braun told Gant to give Brown a $50 advance. A couple of days later Braun recorded Brown at Cosimo Matassa's J&M Studio. Because of a recording ban, the record didn't come out until June 1948. "Good Rockin' Tonight" charted for the week on the "Harlem Hit Parade" (Wynonie Harris's cover version made number one and charted for twenty-five weeks for King Records in 1948).

Brown may not have had the big hit of "Good Rockin' Tonight," but it started him on the road to stardom. Between June 1948 and June 1957, Brown cut thirteen hit records on the r&b charts. However, his career did not reach the financial heights that some others would achieve. In fact, Brown's "Hard Luck Blues" song is really the professional reality of Brown's snake-bitten career. Brown's personal manager, Jack Pearl, did not give him BMI artist rights forms to sign. As a result, BMI didn't pay Brown performance or writer's royalties.

The Male Shouters and Balladeers

Shouter or Balladeer	Band Affiliation	Biggest R&B Hit	Peak Position	Year
Trevor Bacon (s)	Lucky Millinder	Big Fat Mama	did not chart	1940s
Roy Brown (s)	Griffin Brothers	Hard Luck Blues	1	1950
Walter Brown (s)	Jay McShann	Confession' the Blues	did not chart	1942
Larry Darnell (b)	Paul Gayton	For You, My Love	1	1949
Billy Eckstine (b)	Earl Hines	Stormy Monday Blues	1	1942
Billy Farrell (s)	Solo	You've Changed	12	1949
Wynonie Harris (s)	Solo	Good Rockin' Tonight	1	1948
Al Hibbler (b)	Solo	Trees	3	1948
Herb Jeffries (b)	Duke Ellington	My Little Brown Book	4	1944
Bullmoose Jackson (b)	The Bearcats	I Love You, Yes I Do	1	1947
Percy Mayfield (b)	Solo	Please Send Me Someone to Love	1	1950
Stick McGhee (s)	And His Buddies	Drinkin' Wine, Spo-Dee-O-Dee	2	1949
Arthur Prysock (b)	Buddy Johnson	They All Say I'm the Biggest Fool	5	1946
Big Joe Turne (s)	Pete Johnson	S.K. Blues, Pts. 1&2	3	1945
Eddie "Cleanhead" Vinson (s)	Solo	Ole Maid Boogie	1	1947
Jimmy Witherspoon (b)	Solo	Ain't Nobody's Business, pts. 1&2	1	1949

Chart positions: Joel Whitburn's Top R&B Singles, 1942-1988

hotbed of rhythm and blues activity. It wasn't long before out-of-town labels like Imperial and Specialty out of Los Angeles, and Atlantic out of New York, came seeking talent. Grace Lichtenstein and Laura Dankner's *Musical Gumbo: The Music of New Orleans* pinpoints the importance of "Good Rockin' Tonight": "Since it got far more response than the smoother records of the national stars like Nat Cole, and since white stations ignored such records, listeners of both races tuned in to his [Dr. Daddy-O's] show to hear that racy black music. Under the sponsorship of Jax Beer, his Jivin' with Jax show soon captivated New Orleans' budding audience of r&b fans. By the early fifties, Dr. Daddy-O was such a fixture on WMRY, a station that could be heard throughout South Louisiana and East Texas, that Jax appointed additional Dr. Daddy-O's on stations in Houston, Baton Rouge, and elsewhere to pattern themselves after the original. Winslow spawned imitators on other stations with names like Jack the Cat and Okey Dokey." Of all the instruments that gained importance in New Orleans rhythm and blues, none was more important than the piano. The authors continue: "Honking saxes and blues shouters never drowned out the piano, the instrument that, along with the cornet, had underlaid New Orleans music from the turn of the century onward. Tuts Washington and other players, such as barrelhouse pianists Sullivan Rock and Archibald, kept the boogie woogie flame alive. As the forties closed, two dynamic keyboard performers were creating tunes that hammered home the thumping foundation for Crescent City's distinctive R&B style. One was to become a legend after his death, the other the biggest star the city had given music since Louis Armstrong. Their names were Professor Longhair and Fats Domino."

Professor Longhair (1918-1980) was born Henry Roseland "Rosy" Byrd in Bogalusa, a rural town north of New Orleans. As a young man he made money as a street dancer (he was called "Whirlwind") and picked up piano techniques watching the boogie woogie masters playing in the jook joints in New Orleans. Tuts Washington taught Byrd boogie woogie by showing him how to play the 1928 Pinetop Smith classic, "Pinetop's Boogie Woogie." Like Jelly Roll Morton before him, young Byrd learned the "Latin Tinge," and he gained a professional fondness for Perez Prado's mambo recordings. Byrd got his moniker in 1947 while he was playing at the Caldonia Inn. He had very long hair, for that time period, and the proprietor called the group Professor Longhair and the Four Hairs Combo. During this time Professor Longhair made most of his money playing cards (a game called coon-can was his specialty). The Caldonia was a black nightclub, like the Dew Drop Inn, known for floor shows featuring female impersonators. The *Louisiana Weekly* announced on April 3, 1948, "Biggest female impersonator show in town at the Caldonia, with music by the Three Hair Combo, featuring Professors Longhair, Shorthair, and No Hair!" Professor Longhair's mixture of "rhumba, mambo and calypso" was heard to good advantage in his first song of note, written about one of New Orleans's biggest celebrations. It was called "Mardi Gras in New Orleans," and has been the official Mardi Gras song for years. The song was recorded at what appears to have been the Professor's first recording session, in October 1949 for Dallas-based Star Talent Records. Four songs were recorded but had to be taken off the retail shelves because of union regulations. The group was listed as "Professor Longhair and his Shuffling Hungarians."

Courtesy Big Nickel Publications (Galen Gart)

Right from the beginning of Professor Longhair's recorded career there were problems. This ad by Star Talent Records was placed in the trade magazines to call attention to Professor Longhair's releases on Mercury and Atlantic.

Courtesy Alligator Records

The album *Crawfish Fiesta* was recorded at Seasaint Studio, owned by businessman Marshall Sehorn and performer Allen Toussaint. The Studio became the hub of New Orleans recording sessions from the 1970s on. It was a modern, state-of-the-art studio compared to Cosimo Matassa's modest J&M Studio, which had so ably served the earlier performers of New Orleans. This November 1979 session proved to be Professor Longhair's last, but it was one of his best. Dr. John played guitar on the session and acted as a middleman throughout the proceedings, which was seen by participants on the project as his gift to the elderly man. "It's My Own Fault," "Bald Head," "Whole Lotta Lovin'," and a jaunty Carribbean instrumental teased along with a second-line tuba, "Crawfish Fiesta," stand out.

Andy Kaslow, who played sax and helped produce the session, is quoted in *Up From the Cradle of Jazz:* "His poverty had to do with the structure of the music industry, music consumed by the white public after it's watered down from black origins. Look at the fame of Elvis Presley compared to the obscurity of Professor Longhair, the notoriety of [popular West Coast jazz pianist] Dave Brubeck compared to the lesser fame of Thelonious Monk. Fess [an abbreviation for Professor] was a bridge between all the different forms that led to rock-and-roll, jazz, blues, calypso, rhythm-and-blues. He was the purest expression of what rock-and-roll is all about, and he deserved one hell of a lot better."

For outsiders, one of the most difficult things about artists like Professor Longhair is trying to understand what it is they are singing. The New Orleans patois is often impossible to comprehend. Dr. John writes in his autobiography, *Under a Hoodoo Moon,* that Longhair, "was a charter member of a little clique of characters, all of them cats had their own oola-ma-walla-malla language, which Fess incorporated into his song lyrics. It was wholly worked-out street Pig Latin patter, his 'shalawalla oola mallawalla make me wanna holla' jive that shows up in 'Tipitina' and a lot of his other recordings. This language was based on the tricks of street characters, who wanted to disguise what they were talking about when they were around squares. For instance, if you were discussing jail, you might not necessarily want to give yourself away, so you might say 'jaoolla-mallwallaila.' He could stretch one little word into a freight train. That's how he would talk among the cats so the narcs and the vice and people he didn't trust would never know what the hell was going down."

Reverting to his real name to avoid possible legal problems with Star Talent, Roy Byrd and his Blue Jumpers released "Baldhead" for Mercury (a remake of "She Ain't Got No Hair") and the record reached number 5 on the r&b hit parade during August of 1950. To further complicate an already bizarre series of recording events, Atlantic Records brought Longhair into Cosimo Mattasa's J&M Studio and cut ten sides in early 1950. These sides included "Mardi Gras in New Orleans," "Professor Longhair Blues," and "Hey Little Girl." The first was released under the credit "Roy 'Baldhead' Byrd. The second credited "Professor Longhair and his Blues Scholars," and the third listed "Roy Byrd." None of this helped create a stable national vision of the new artist, not to mention the potential legal problems. In 1953 Atlantic released the now classic "Tipitina." Professor Longhair continued to record and play local clubs throughout the 1960s ("Big Chief," a song about the black Mardi Gras Indian celebrations, was an important selection during this time) but no one outside New Orleans really knew who he was. It wasn't until the 1970s, with the help of Quint Davis and Allison Minor Kaslow, two young music enthusiasts, that Professor Longhair began to receive proper management and to achieve national recognition.

Professor Longhair was called the "Bach of Rock" by one of his disciples, New Orleans pianist, songwriter, and producer Allen Toussaint. According to Jason Berry, Jonathan Foose, and Tad Jones, in their *Up From the Cradle of Jazz*, another of Profesor Longhair's disciples, Dr. John (Mac Rebenback), said, "I think Fess put funk into music. I don't think an Allen Toussaint or a Huey Lewis or a lot of other piano players here would have the basics of style without Fess. All those cats have absorbed a lot of other piano players, but Longhair's thing had a direct bearing I'd say on a large portion of the funk music that evolved in New Orleans."

Antoine Fats Domino (1928-) was born in New Orleans and drawn to the piano at an early age. As a youngster he used to hang around the Club Desire and ask Tuts Washington to play a song popularized by Roosevelt Sykes, "The Honeydripper." Just after the

Courtesy Ahmet Ertegun and Atlantic Records

Ahmet Ertegun and the Professor. Ahmet Ertegun emerged as the single most important owner of independent records. His taste for "roots music" and his vision of what chould be made commercially viable were unprecedented. It also helped that Ertegun had a real passion for the music he recorded. In 1968, Ertegun sold Atlantic Records to what eventually became Warner Communications, although he remained co-chairman of the board and co-chief executive officer of Atlantic Records. He became a principal founder and chairman of the Rock and Roll Hall of Fame Foundation, and in January 1987 he was inducted into the Hall of Fame, an acknowledgement of his pioneering role in the history of contemporary music.

Ertegun's description of his and Atlantic co-founder Herb Abramson's trek into the Louisiana hinterlands to find Professor Longhair is retold in *Up From the Cradle of Jazz:* "He was sitting there with a microphone between his legs. He used to play an upright piano, and he had a drumhead, you know, attached to the piano. He would hit it with his right foot while he was playing. He made a percussive sound. It was very loud. And he was playing the piano and singing full-blast, and it really was the most incredible sounding thing I ever heard. And he was doing it all by himself. It was one of the most primitive dance halls I had ever been in, people jammed in there dancing and this wild thing going on, and they hid us in the corner there and we were listening to the music.

"I thought, my god, we've really found an original. And I said, 'No white person has ever heard this man.' So as soon as he finished, Herb and I, very excited, said, 'Look, we have to tell you, we're just astounded by your playing, you know, and shaking his hand." We want very much to record you.' He said, 'Oh, what a shame. I just signed with Mercury!'"

war, the teenage Domino played piano at the Hideaway Club as a member of Billy Dramond's Band. During the daytime, Domino worked at a bedspring factory. In 1949 Domino met up with a bandleader, Dave Bartholomew, and a record executive, Imperial Records owner Lew Chudd, who would change his life. Unlike Professor Longhair, Domino was fortunate to have excellent guidance. Prior to that fateful meeting, Domino had been given direction by an elderly brother-in-law, Harrison Verrett, who had played banjo and guitar with Kid Ory and Papa Celestine and taught Domino piano at an early age. He also instructed Domino about dressing neatly and acting professionally as a musician.

Bartholomew had played trumpet with Fats Pichon's band between 1939 and 1941 on the S.S. *Capitol*, a Mississippi River steamboat. The trumpeter also toured with Duke Ellington, and in 1947 he started his own band, which played local venues such as the Rocket Club, the Starlight, the Greystone, the Robin Hood, Al's Starlight, and the Dew Drop.

Bartholomew also worked with disc jockey Dr. Daddy-O and recorded for the DeLuxe label. When Lew Chudd came down to New Orleans seeking talent for his Los Angeles-based Imperial Records company, he signed on Bartholomew as an artist and talent scout. Bartholomew told Jeff Hannusch in his detailed study of New Orleans rhythm and blues, *I Hear You Knocking: The Sound of New Orleans Rhythm and Blues*: "I'd heard about this guy who was supposed to play pretty good boogie woogie piano down at the Hideaway Club. It was Friday night, and I wasn't working, so Lew and I went down there. This was the first time we heard Fats Domino. He was singing this tune 'The Junker's Blues,' and Lew really liked it. So at intermission I introduced Fats to Lew Chudd and that's how everything got started."

For his recording session on Imperial Records, Domino changed the drug lyrics of "Junker's Blues" to those of "The Fat Man" ("They call me the Fat Man/'Cause I weigh 200 pounds"). Domino's jump blues version, which placed the piano in front and featured his nonsense "wa-wa," trumpet-like scatting, proved intoxicating. Throughout the 1950s and early 1960s Domino and his musical director became one of the top-selling teams in popular music.

"We were actually searching for a sound in those days. I never wanted to get things too complicated," Bartholomew recounted in *I Hear You Knocking*. "It had to be simple so people could understand it right away. It had to be the kind of thing that a seven-year-old kid could start whistling. I just kept it simple. I always felt Fats was a country and western singer because he didn't sing from the bottom. Fats played triplets at the piano; he got it from a guy called Little Willie Littlefield out in California. That was Fats' style; so once he started, he couldn't leave it, 'cause that's what the people wanted to hear."

In his book *Jazz Rock Foundations*, William Tallmadge points out that, "New Orleans dance-beat rhythm and blues began to develop at the time California rhythm and blues was achieving maturity (1949-1950). Furthermore, both the [Amos] Milburn Texas-California instrumental format and, to a certain extent, the musical style was appropriated by the Cosimo Matassa studio musicians in New Orleans that backed various singers and pianist-singers who recorded in that city from 1949 through the 1960s. Virtually all New Orleans rhythm and blues was recorded at the Cosimo Studios, and most of it was backed by the same coterie of musicians under the musical guidance of trumpeter-songwriter-producer-band director Dave Bartholomew." Charles Gillett's appraisal in *Sound of the City* is that, "Domino's complete transformation into a rock 'n' roll singer was possible because he sang with a plaintive tone which did not seem so adult and alien . . . He seemed to be singing about experiences equivalent to those his white listeners knew about, and he was able to take established pop songs like 'My Blue Heaven' and 'Blueberry Hill' and not sound incongruous while singing them, as, say, Amos Milburn or Roy Brown would have done."

The 1950s and early 1960s exploded with rock and soul hits by followers of Professor Longhair and Fats Domino: Huey "Piano" Smith, James Booker, Allen Toussaint, Mr. Google Eyes, Earl King, Guitar Slim, Smiley Lewis, Shirley and Lee, Irma Thomas, Chris Kenner, Frankie Ford, Bobby Marchan, Jesse Hill, Lee Dorsey, and Ernie K-Doe, among others. With today's newfound awareness and appreciation of Cajun and zydeco and the overwhelming success of the annual New Orleans Jazz and Heritage Festival, the Crescent City sound of the Neville Brothers and their contemporaries is not nearly as insular and isolated as it once was. Dr. John (Mac Rebennack) is an example of an outstanding musician who is also a fine historian. The guitarist-piano player is especially knowledgeable and informative about the many great keyboard stylists who came from New Orleans. His young friend, Harry Connick, Jr., grew up in the rich musical terrain of New Orleans and was playing with Dixieland stars by the time he was ten years old. Connick studied with the late blues great James Booker. In 1989, Connick and Dr. John recorded and made a video of the classic "Do You Know What It Means to Miss New Orleans?"

Early New Orleans R&B Artists

Artist	Specialty	Key Recording	Label	Year
Archibald	Pianist	Stack-A'Lee	Imperial	1950
Dave Bartholomew	Trumpeter-bandleader	Country Boy	DeLuxe	1949
Roy Brown	Shouter	Good Rockin' Tonight	DeLuxe	1948
Cousin Joe	Singer-pianist	Saw Man Mill Blues	Unknown	1945
Larry Darnell	Romantic balladeer	For You My Love	Regal	1949
Fats Domino	Singer-pianist	The Fat Man	Imperial	1950
Champion Jack Dupree	Singer-pianist	Junker's Blues	Unknown	1940s
Paul Gayton	Bandleader	True	DeLuxe	1947
Jewel King	Singer	3x7=21	Imperial	1950
Annie Laurie	Singer	Cuttin' Out	Regal	1949
Smiley Lewis	Singer	Tee-Nah-Nah	Imperial	1950
Little Richard	Singer-pianist	Every Hour	RCA	1951
Mr. Google Eyes	Singer	Poppa Stoppa's Be Bop Blues	Coleman	1948
Chubby Newsome	Bandleader	I'm Still in Love With You	Regal	1950
Professor Longhair	Singer-pianist	Baldhead	Mercury	1950
Tommy Ridgely	Bandleader	Shrewsbury Blues	Imperial	1950

Louis Jordan and the Jump and Jive Combos

While Lionel Hampton may have been a key figure in the transition from big band to small combo rhythm and blues, it was **Louis Jordan** (1908-1975) who showed that the small group could compete with the bigger bands and would, in fact, become the dominant form throughout the 1940s and early 1950s. Jordan started his career as a saxophonist in the Chick Webb big band in 1936. He stayed with the band until 1938, when he formed his own nine-piece group, Louis Jordan and the Tympani Five, and debuted at the Elks Rendezvous on Lenox Avenue in Harlem. Eventually Jordan scaled the combo down to six to eight pieces, though he continued to bill the group as the Tympani Five. The group did pretty much everything that a big band did and featured Jordan's vocals and alto sax solos as well as trumpet and piano solos (his small units didn't feature trombone). As Jordan aptly put it, "I made the blues jump." Jordan's success at the Capitol Lounge in Chicago in 1942 coincided with his first recorded hits on Decca Records, "I'm Gonna Move to the Outskirts of Town," backed with "Knock Me a Kiss" and "What's the Use of Getting Sober?" From that point until the early 1950s Jordan was the most consistent hit maker in black music. Unlike today's artists, who work on an album and then tour to introduce the new songs, Jordan tried the new songs out first before recording them. The songs that received little positive response were discarded and those that the audience liked were immediately put to wax at the next recording session.

Excellent musicianship and masterful, uplifting entertainment with a big smile were the keys to Jordan's prosperity. Also, he had an instinctive feel for blending self-effacing humor and hep/hip (the term was in the process of change) street jargon of the black jive cats with clearly enunciated, non-threatening entertainment for the white audiences. "I made just as much money off white people as I did off colored,"

Inimitable Louis Jordan Pantomimes His Own Song Titles

Louis Jordan, song writer as well as leader of a popular small combo, illustrates one of his hits, *Knock Me A Kiss.*

This one was Louie's first big success, *I'm Gonna Move to the Outskirts of Town.* Remember his recording of the tune?

What's the Use of Getting Sober?, asks Maestro Jordan in this number. Louie and the boys open at Club Bali in Washington, D. C., March 7.

Louie revived *Deacon Jones* to a successful platter sale. The Jordan band is due at the Regal in Chicago on April 7.

This is a timely topical to *Ration Blues,* shows Lou talent as comedian. *(All pho by Warren Rothschild.)*

Courtesy Down Beat

Jordan proclaimed. He was aware of marketing his music to achieve the maximum audience, and with the help of manager Berle Adams and recording supervisor Milt Gabler, Jordan became one of the few blacks to "cross over" into pop music. An example of Jordan's awareness of "straddling" (as he called it) black and white tastes was his decision to play only white clubs, not black. He appeared in front of blacks only in the big auditoriums, such as Harlem's Apollo Theater, for a percentage of the gate. He also recorded with big names such as Bing Crosby, the Mills Brothers, and his ex-bandmate from the Chick Webb days, Ella Fitzgerald.

Jordan's combo was featured in numerous movies, including *Follow the Boys* (1944), *Meet Miss Bobby Socks* (1944), *Beware* (1946), and *Swing Parade of 1946,* as well as musical shorts made for black movie theaters like *Caldonia* (1946) and an infinite number of soundies. Jordan's recorded works spotlighted his shuffling, boogie-oriented rhythms with a variety of entertaining topics such as having a good time ("Let the Good Times Roll" and "At the Swing Cats Ball"), jump and jive ("Jumpin' at the Jamboree" and "Reet Petite and

HOT Rhythm & Blues

LOUIS JORDAN
Vocals and Alto Sax
Decca Records
The ebullient, bubbling musical dynamo has been one of R&B's hottest attractions for many years. A former member of Chick Webb's orchestra, he organized his own unit, The Tympany Five, in 1938. Their many Decca hits include "Choo Choo Ch' Boogie," "Outskirts of Town," "Saturday Night Fish Fry" and dozens of others.

Courtesy Big Nickel Publications (Galen Gart)

413

Gone"), dating ("The Chicks I Pick Are Slender, Tender and Tall," and "Safe, Sane and Single"), ethnic humor ("Saturday Night Fish Fry" and "Ain't Nobody Here but Us Chickens"), calypso ("Bahama Joe" and "Run Joe"), and straight blues ballads like "Don't Let the Sun Catch You Cryin'."

By the mid-1940s, Jordan was known as the undisputed "King of the Juke Boxes," and his combo makeup of sax(es), trumpet, and rhythm section became the model for a majority of players who had started in the big bands. Jordan's best year, 1946, coincided with the growth of the indies and the emergence of the combo as the preferred group makeup. Jordan's two biggest sellers were made that year, "Caldonia" and "Choo Choo Ch' Boogie." Jordan's trumpeter, Aaron Izenhall, notes in John Chilton's *Let the Good Times Roll* that the group was a Technicolor movie on stage. "We were the first ones to wear those bright colors and that became an automatic part of rock, and even now you can go back to our version of 'Beware' and realize that it's the earliest sort of rap." Like most of the r&b stars of the 1940s, Jordan would be pushed aside by rock and roll. His legacy lives on in some of the work of Ray Charles (who declared, "I loved Louie Jordan. Everything worked.") Chuck Berry, and Jon Hendricks. In 1981, British new wave artist Joe Jackson rekindled the Louis Jordan-Cab Calloway flame with his album, *Joe Jackson's Jumpin' Jive*. In 1990, Clarke Peters, an American actor working in London, put together a musical revue based on twenty Louis Jordan songs, calling it a "revusical." *Five Guys Named Moe* captured the attention of producer Cameron Mackintosh, who took it to the West End Theatre in London in December 1990, where it became an overwhelming success. The show opened in New York at the Eugene O'Neill Theater in April 1992 and began touring America in the spring of 1993.

Courtesy Jukebox Lil, a division of Mr. R&B Record Sales

Louis Jordan is an example of a jazzman who was labelled a rhythm and blues performer. When he joined the Chick Webb big band at the Savoy Ballroom, he replaced Edgar Sampson, who left the reed section because he was too busy writing arrangements. Jordan was a fine saxophonist who also wanted to sing, but Webb already had three other vocalists. Taft Jordan, the trumpeter sang some; Charlie Linton was featured on most of the ballads; and Ella Fitzgerald was singing rhythm songs (including novelties) and some ballads. Jordan was featured on "I've Got You Under My Skin," sang and played soprano on "Mayor of Alabam," and he did a selection called "Rusty Hinge," which was the only number he got to sing with the band on record.

The Harlem Hamfats, led by trumpeter Herb Morand and featuring brothers Joe and Charlie McCoy, formed in 1936 under the guidance of black musical entrepreneur J. Mayo Williams, was most likely the strongest influence on Louis Jordan's brand of jump and jive. The Hamfats, strictly a recording unit, released close to one hundred records between 1936 and 1939. Their biggest hit was "Let's Get Drunk and Truck," in which the initial consonant of "Truck" became increasingly indistinct. This, however, is a kind of risque song that Jordan would *never* do. However Jordan did pick up on the jivey, shuffle rhythms of Hamfatmania. Producer Jerry Wexler is quoted in Arnold Shaw's *Honkers and Shouters* as saying, "Shuffle was a crucial rhythm—Texas Shuffle, Kansas City Shuffle. Back in 1934-35 [1936-39] you had the Harlem Hamfats on Decca. They were essentially a New Orleans transplant and the antecedents of Louis Jordan with their shuffle style." James Lincoln Collier, writing in *Jazz: The American Theme Song*, feels that the creation of the Harlem Hamfats is the real beginning of rock 'n' roll, and the main unit to sway Louis Jordan toward their style of jump and jive. "It was the Hamfats who had the great success with black audiences, and as a consequence the group became the primary model for similar groups coming along after. The most important, by far, of the Hamfats' followers was a group led by an alto saxophone player named Louis Jordan . . . This group used the Hamfats' formula of jazz-based blues with erotic content and a good dollop of hokum, all melodically simple and rhythmically hard-driving. The shuffle beat was a staple, as on 'Reet, Petite, and Gone' and 'Salt Pork, West Virginia.'"

414

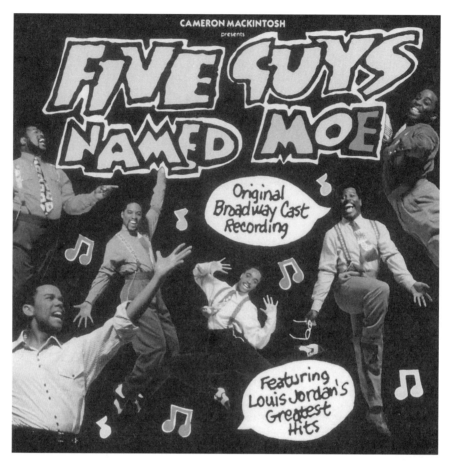

CAMERON MACKINTOSH presents

FIVE GUYS NAMED MOE

Original Broadway Cast Recording

Featuring Louis Jordan's Greatest Hits

Courtesy Sony Music

Louis Jordan goes to Broadway. *Five Guys Named Moe* was one of the breeziest musical revues to play the Broadway stage during the early 1990s. The source of the title of the play was a song about an incident involving a white singer-songwriter, Larry Wynn, who used to play Harlem night spots during the 1940s. One night, he sang one of his jivey numbers, "Ol' Man Mose," which always resulted in cries for an encore. In the song, the title character, Ol' Man Mose, is dead, but Wynn's delivery kept him very much alive. On this particular night, Louis Jordan came up, introduced himself, and said with a smile, "You sure you're white?" Wynn had captured the jump and jive spirit as well as the hip street lingo of the era.

Wynn came up with the song "Five Guys Named Moe" by accident. He had just gone into the recording studio with Billie Holiday, who recorded his song, "I'm All for You," with a nine-piece jazz group. The next day he was asked who the musicians were and as he named them his memory faltered, so he blurted out, "and five guys named Moe." Wynn thought it would make a great song title. He wrote the song and sang it for Jordan, who loved it and recorded it. The humorous tale lists the Moes as Big Moe, Little Bitty Moe, Four-Eyed Moe, No Moe, and Eat Moe. It was a perfect song for Jordan, one of the happiest and hippest entertainers of the 1940s.

In the musical production of *Five Guys Named Moe*, an announcer introduces the quintet thusly, "Ladies and gentlemen, the Funky Butt Club is proud to present that Sepia Symphonette, those Crooning Cavaliers, those Soulful Seraphs of song, those . . . No Moe, Little Moe, Four-Eyed Moe, Big Moe, Eat Moe, and No Max" (the protagonist who learns his lessons about life from the songs of Louis Jordan, presented by the Moe-Men, is called "No Max").

415

Louis Jordan: King of the Jukeboxes

Song	Year	R&B Position	Weeks Charted	Pop Position
I'm Gonna Leave You at the Outskirts of Town	1942	3	3	
What's the Use of Getting Sober/	1942	1	14	
The Chicks I Pick Are Slender, Tender and Tall	1942	10	1	
Five Guys Named Moe/	1943	3	10	
That'll Just About Knock Me Out	1943	8	1	
Ration Blues	1943	1	21	11
G.I. Jive/	1944	1	26	1
Is You Is or Is You Ain't (Ma' Baby)	1944	3	16	2
Mop Mop/	1945	1	17	
You Can't Get That No More	1945	2	13	11
Caldonia/	1945	1	26	6
Somebody Done Changed the Lock on My Door	1945	3	10	
Buzz Me/	1946	1	13	9
Don't Worry 'Bout That Mule	1946	1	11	
Salt Pork, West Virginia/	1946	2	15	
Reconversion Blues	1946	2	7	
Beware/	1946	2	9	20
Don't Let the Sun Catch You Cryin'	1946	3	8	
Stone Cold Dead in the Market (He Had It Coming)/	1946	1	20	7
Petootie Pie (both)	1946	3	2	
Choo Choo Ch' Boogie/	1946	1	26	7
That Chick's Too Young to Fry	1946	3	11	
Ain't That Just Like a Woman	1946	1	17	17
Ain't Nobody Here But Us Chickens/	1946	1	27	6
Let the Good Times Roll	1946	2	23	
Texas and Pacific	1947	1	15	20
Open the Door Richard	1947	2	6	6
Jack, You're Dead	1947	1	20	21
I Like 'Em Fat Like That	1947	5	1	
I Know What You're Putting Down	1947	3	4	
Boogie Woogie Blue Plate	1947	1	24	21
Look Out/	1947	5	6	
Early in the Morning	1947	3	10	
Barnyard Boogie/	1948	2	13	
How Long Must I Wait for You	1948	9	1	
Reet, Petite, and Gone	1948	4	6	
Run Joe/	1948	1	15	
All for the Love of Lil	1948	13	1	
Pinetop's Boogie Woogie	1948	14	1	
Don't Burn the Candle at Both Ends/	1948	4	7	
Pettin' and Pokin'	1948	5	6	
Roamin' Blues	1949	10	2	
You Broke Your Promise	1949	3	2	
Coleslaw	1949	7	10	
Every Man to His Own Profession	1949	10	2	
Baby, It's Cold Outside (with Ella Fitzgerald)	1949	6	4	
Beans and Cornbread	1949	6	4	9
Saturday Night Fishfry (part 1)	1949	1	11	
School Days	1950	5	7	
Blue Light Boogie-pts. 1 & 2	1950	1	16	
I'll Never Be Free (with Ella Fitzgerald)	1950	7	2	
Tamburitza Boogie	1950	10	1	

Note: Jordan's last three chart hits ("Lemonade," "Tear Drops From My Eyes," and "Weak Minded Blues") were released in 1951; he never had a hit during the rock'n'roll era.
Source: Joel Whitburn's Top R&B singles, 1942-1988

The Honkers

Left to right, Maxwell Davis, Hal "Cornbread" Singer, and Clifford Scott with bandleader Lionel Hampton. All three of these tenor saxophonists dabbled in jazz, but were associated with rhythm and blues saxophone playing. Maxwell Davis was best known for leading house bands in Los Angeles at various recording sessions and rhythm and blues shows. He also provided the audio for one of the only films to feature a manic "honker" in action. This scene was recorded during the filming of *D.O.A.*, an excellent black- and-white film noir that starred Edmond O'Brien as a poisoned man desperately trying to find whoever tried to murder him—the perpetrator poured a radioactive element into his drink while he was distracted by a cacophonous black band at a nightclub. Saxman James Von Streeter, fronting for his Wig Poppers, dipped, rocked, and sweated up a storm as the cameras rolled. For whatever reason, Maxwell Davis ended up "ghosting" the sound for Von Streeter. Years later, Dennis Quaid starred in a color remake of this classic film.

Hal "Cornbread" Singer hailed from Tulsa, Oklahoma, and had played in the big bands of Jay McShann and Lucky Millinder before recording a romping original titled "Cornbread" for Savoy Records in 1948 under his own name. "Cornbread" was based on a series of riffs that big bands used with regularity. The popularity of the song resulted in Singer's nickname. The saxman later worked overseas, and recorded with Alexis Korner's British bluesmen.

Clifford Scott was immortalized in rock'n'roll history by having one of his sax solos, recorded in 1956 on Bill Doggett's "Honky Tonk." This song became the best-selling rock'n'roll instrumental of the 1950s and one of the only ones to feature the saxophone. By 1956 the guitar had replaced the saxophone as the most important instrument in rock, so that Scott's driving, spirited romp was one last hurrah for rock sax . During this period of the 1950s, the honking sax was relegated to brief spurts of joy behind doo wop groups such as the Teenagers ("Why Do Fools Fall in Love?" with Jimmy Wright's solo) and the Coasters (first Gil Bernel, then King Curtis), among many others. The only other big hit of the 1950s to highlight an extended, hot sax solo was the Champs' "Te-quila" (with Danny Flores, aka Chuck Rio, performing).

An entire "school" of wild, honking saxmen became a fixture shortly following the great success of tenorman Illinois Jacquet's incendiary solo on Lionel Hampton's "Flying Home." By the end of the 1940s, many of the so-called honkers, such as Big Jay McNeely, Hal "Cornbread" Singer, Paul Williams, and Wild Bill Moore were leading small combos of their own. No doubt the two pantheon band leaders of rhythm and blues, Lionel Hampton and Louis Jordan, had illuminated the importance of aggressive showmanship as a cardinal rule for prosperity. Remember that at the very same time Hampton and Jordan were topping the r&b *Billboard* charts, Charlie Parker and Miles Davis were moving jazz music from dance and entertainment toward self-conscious, cerebral art music.

It was the saxophone, not the guitar, that was the r&b power instrument in the 1940s. The stars of the honking, wailing style of sax had studied the masters of swing-oriented reed jazz: Coleman Hawkins, Lester Young, Ben Webster, Johnny Hodges, Don Byas, Chu Berry, and Benny Carter. These younger players had played in the swing bands but now saw a different way to express themselves, often at the expense of great ridicule by the master players and jazz critics, who viewed the demonstrativeness of r&b honking as grandstanding. Arnold Shaw, in his groundbreaking study of rhythm and blues,

Honkers and Shouters: The Golden Years of Rhythm and Blues, cites Amiri Baraka's view that the evolution of r&b out of the world of swing-oriented jazz was a three-part break from the past: from the sound of Western music, from white popular song, and from the Negro middle class. Modern jazz would break from the same roots even more radically, but in much different ways.

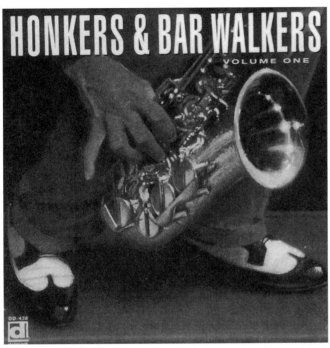

Courtesy Delmark Records

Paul Williams, who had a big instrumental hit with "The Hucklebuck" (1948-49), featured a midget who jumped up on the bar and danced the hucklebuck as the saxman walked alongside, blowing furiously while patrons stuffed dollar bills in the bell of his horn. Other hornmen developed the technique of jumping up on the bar, crouching down, and "walking" the entire bar while blowing the saxophone. Meanwhile, the rhythm section kept the music going on the bandstand. This was known as "walking the bar."

In his 1967 book of short stories, *Tales*, Leroi Jones (who later changed his name to Amiri Baraka) relates the true-life saxophone antics of Lynn Hope, a devout black Muslim who wore a bejeweled turban. Jones describes an evening in a Newark club where Hope, blowing furious tenor, ascends the bar, walking and kneeling his way across the timber, while patrons scream with delight. Not to be limited by bar-walking, the turban-topped exciter leaves the club, and with his saxophone honking and bleeting, leads the happy revelers down the street like a pied piper. Jones called this communal connection a "Black Dada Nihilismus" with the honkers as "ethnic historians, actors, priests of the [black] unconsciousness."

The rhythm and blues players were working in the critical arena of jazz and popular music. The critics of the day had defined an aesthetic for performance style and stage behavior, and the rhythm and blues artists were adhering to it. Magazines such as *Down Beat, Metronome, Orchestra World, Tempo,* and *Music and Rhythm*, among others, covered the jazz and pop scene, but there were no magazines at that time writing positively about rhythm and blues. There were no r&b histories of consequence until Charlie Keil's sympathetic *Urban Blues* was published in 1966. The main area of support for these players came from the black audiences that wanted entertainment with a party atmosphere.

At some auditoriums, Lionel Hampton was known to parade the entire band around the auditorium during one of his "flag waving numbers." Critics carped about Hampton's "circus atmosphere." While the majority of jazz critics were condemning the antics of Hampton and the "honkers," the audiences were standing and screaming with joy. Fortunately, for many of the honking saxmen and bandleaders, the rousing audience response was a stronger influence than that of the aforementioned critics.

Illinois Jacquet (1922-) was the "Father of the Honkers." He was just one of many Texas saxophone players who played with a robust, soulful sound. While he was taken to task by many critics and jazz purists for his extroverted solos, Jacquet was able to court that crowd successfully with his warm ballad playing. At one point during the 1960s, Jacquet played bassoon. Over the years, he toured the world with an assortment of supporting players who were more in the jazz than the rhythm and blues tradition. In fact, if one views Jacquet's career as a whole, one would discover he was more closely associated with jazz than rhythm and blues. The same could not be said for most of his followers. Arnett Cobb, for example, who took over the "Flying Home" spotlight with Hampton when Jacquet left to join Cab Calloway, remained a dedicated "honker."

There can be no doubt that the main inspiration in "honker history" is Illinois Jacquet's sax solo on Lionel Hampton's 1942 "Flying Home." Jim Dawson's historic study of the honking saxophone, *Nervous, Man, Nervous: Big Jay McNeely and the Rise of the Honking Tenor Sax*, underscores the impact of this record on the truest believer of saxophone-as-incendiary-rocking-instrument, Big Jay McNeely: "At the age of 19, Jacquet blew a 64-bar solo on Hampton's hit version of 'Flying Home' that struck McNeely as well as many other young hornmen as being a seminal moment in recording history. 'Every saxophone player back then was trying to redo that solo on "Flying Home." Every time we picked up our horns we were just elaborating on that, trying to make it bigger, wilder, give it more swing, more kick. If you want to know where rhythm and blues began, that's it, brother. That put blues in a whole new bag, 24-bar blues, 32-bar blues, and we all worked on it. Some of us slipped over to jazz, but me, I was always a rhythm and blues man at heart.'

"'Flying Home' would pop up later in McNeely's own work, and the tune became a staple of his shows, although his recording of it would not be released until 1984. 'Flying Home' was the quintessential saxophone workout number, as basic to the tenor as 'Lady of Spain' was to the accordion."

Dawson points out that two other Texans, Big Jim Wynn and Wild Bill Moore, elaborated on what Jacquet had started. Jacquet was not just a one-hit wonder. He became a featured star of Norman Granz's "Jazz at the Philharmonic" concerts, where his proto-tenor was featured on solos and in battles with fellow saxmen like Jack McVea and Flip Phillips. After the honking fever died down during the late 1950s, Jacquet found acceptance in the jazz community as an energetic jazzman who played rousing uptempo numbers as well as warm ballads. Wynn and Moore, however, were full-fledged precursors of rock'n'roll saxophone, and like Big Jay McNeely, never entered the anointed inner sanctum of the jazz circle.

Courtesy Rhapsody Films

Illinois Jacquet is the saxophonist who started the honking furor. By the 1980s and 1990s, the "Mighty-Mite of the Tenor" was recognized as an established jazzman who could play stomp tunes as well as breathy ballads. In 1944, Jacquet followed his seminal "Flying Home" with the first live-concert recording released commercially, "Blues, Part 2," recorded at the Los Angeles Philharmonic Hall. Norman Granz staged the show to raise money for a defense fund for Chicanos imprisoned after the "Zoot Suit" riots of June 1944 (see Chapter 9).

Jim Dawson and Steve Propes, in their book *What Was the First Rock 'n' Roll Record*, describe the number as a blues introduced by saxophonist Jack McVea, whose solo is followed by a trombone solo and then Jacquet's entry: "As the tune heats up, Illinois Jacquet steps forward and launches a two-and-a-half-minute, rabble-rousing solo. He slips way down into his horn and brings up a throaty growl that rises from the bell like a tornado. He begins to shriek, squeal, pinch off the ends of his phrases somewhere in the stratosphere. Each new assault on the melody drives the crowd into a frenzy. This is clearly something new, a mixture of stage antics and musical prototechnics that, in only a few magic choruses, blew open the boundaries of jazz and rhythm and blues. On that July day at the Philharmonic, Jacquet introduced the phenomenon of the honking saxophonist, and black music, hell, American music, would never be the same again."

Big Jim Wynn provided a model for McNeely. Wynn was one of the first saxmen to walk around the room blowing sax. He was known for getting down on his knees and rolling around on stage as he blew. In 1948, Wynn released "Blow, Wynn, Blow," but after 1951, Wynn's career as a honker was surpassed by McNeely. Wild Bill Moore first gained notoriety for his hot sax solo behind Helen Humes's classic 1945 rave number, "Be-Baba-Leba" (which, according to Dawson, was Big Jim Wynn's composition "Ec-Boba-Leba," but never credited to him). In 1947 Moore recorded "We're Gonna Rock," which utilized a chanting call and response, "We're gonna rock, we're gonna roll." "We're Gonna Rock," with Moore's pounding, mirthful tenor, is surely one of the top candidates for the first rock'n'roll record. Jacquet, Wynn, and Moore then, were the main influences on the man who would reign supreme as the saxophonist who never tried to apologize for his antics as a madman of histrionic, demented showmanship saxology—Cecil "Big Jay" McNeely.

Courtesy Jim Dawson and Collectibles Records

Big Jay McNeely: Back and note-bending in all his glory!

Big Jay McNeely (1926-   ) can rightfully lay claim to the title the "King of the Honkers." He was the most outrageous and enduring of these outgoing stompers of sax. Unlike Jacquet, McNeely didn't seek jazz acceptance after his early involvement in bebop. He began his career in the mid-1940s in California, gigging with jazzmen such as Howard McGhee, Sonny Criss, and Teddy Edwards. He was at Billy Berg's when Charlie Parker brought bop saxophone to the West Coast. He played on stage with Parker and Harry "The Hipster" Gibson and seemed to have incorporated elements of both into his playing.

Harry "The Hipster" Gibson, the wildest of the white jazz and jivers noted in chapter 9, is quoted in Dawson's *Nervous, Man, Nervous*: "Just before Bird came in, Big Jay McNeely played there [San Francisco's Say When club] and Big Jay used to lay on the floor and kick his feet and stomp and romp while he blew his tenor sax. Well, I got a tenor and I started down with him, takin' off our shirts and layin' down on the floor and jumpin'. I'd go stompin' onto the bar, jumpin' on tables goin' Honk onk, onk-onk-a-donk! Playin' riffs, you know. Well, Charlie Parker came in and he saw what was goin' on and he starts joinin' us. He's blowin' Honk onk-onk. So we're walkin' all around the place, before his set is going to start. We walk out onto the street with no shirts on, just our horns on, and we walk out of the front while the band is still playin' on the bandstand. We get out on the steet and the bus comes by and the driver and the people know us 'cause we've been in town for a while. The driver's yellin' to us and the people are wavin' at us and the bus stops on the corner and I walk into the bus. Bird decides to follow me. Bam, we get on the bus and just as we get to the back of the bus, the bus takes off. We walk up to the front of the bus and say, 'Hey, we gotta get off at the next corner,' and the driver says, 'I'm sorry, there's no stop till we get to Market Street.' And here we are with our horns on us, no shirts, I'm tryin' to get a cab but the cabs won't stop and pick us up! So we had nothin' else to do, we marched right back into the joint and we came in right on the beat! Bonk ba-donk bah! Ba-ba-bahdah'n doo-ba-dah! They're still blowin', waitin' for us to come back! That's a wild story and it's a true story too."

BIG JAY McNEELY & HIS BAND

Courtesy Jim Dawson

Big Jay McNeely on his back with brother Bob on baritone lending riff support. *Down Beat* published a feature article about McNeely in January, 1953 entitled, "Big Jay McNeely Big Noise in R&B: McNeely, McSquealy, Either Way You Pronounce It, Means Box Office." The article notes the spellbinding effect McNeely's sax playing had on unsuspecting teenagers, who were sometimes as fevered as teenagers had once been at Frank Sinatra and Benny Goodman concerts. The article pointed out that McNeely, or "Mr. Honk," or "The Go-Go-Go Boy," upstaged everyone he shared a bill with, so no one wanted to follow his act because the audience got so frenzied. McNeely's act apparently created the kind of response normally associated with Bill Haley or Elvis Presley, who would both soon replace the honker as the envy of teenage adultation: "Big Jay's act consists mainly of blasting away on some relatively simple theme (the variations are chiefly in tonal inflections described by his detractors as 'honks' and 'snorts') while the rhythm section beats out a steadily driving background consisting of a bopped-up form of the blues idom. As he blows, Big Jay marches back and forth across the stage, closely shadowed by his brother Bob (baritone sax), who comes in for an occasional solo chorus himself when Jay runs out of wind.

"As a finale Jay, followed by Bob, marches down off the stage into the aisles, or through the crowd if it's in a dancehall. Or they may disappear behind the curtain at one side of the stage and then, some minutes later (the amount of time seems to add to the suspense), appear from the other side to be welcomed by a resounding roar from his fans.

"But the real 'climax' comes when Jay, while blowing away mightily, takes off his coat, lies down on his back and kicks his feet in the air while someone holds the mike over him to catch the full blast of whatever it is that is coming from his horn."

By the mid-1990s Jim Dawson, McNeely's manager, claimed that McNeely was making more money and in greater demand than ever before. The veteran saxman was amazingly strong at a summer 1993 booking at the New York City blues club Tramps. McNeely, who had a special mike hook-up that allowed him to leave the stage to walk the bar as well as tour the streets outside while sound continued to emanate from the stage monitors, played forty-five-minute solos and created such excitement that each show resulted in standing ovations.

McNeely would play a solo on "Decon's Hop" for forty-five minutes to an hour while walking throughout the crowd, sitting on the laps of people in the audience, playing on his knees, playing on his back with his feet up in the air, doing splits, and having the lights in the room turned off while his sax lit up! Upon its release in 1988, *Az Bootin'* was Big Jay McNeely's first domestic studio album in thirty years. The powerful tenor man found large crowds responding to his manic, driving sounds in places like Vienna, Morocco, England, Australia, and Germany (the German press dubbed him "the rock'n'roll Joshua"). Jim Dawson notes in *Nervous, Man, Nervous* that, "While he had hits such as 'Decon's Hop' (1949), '3-D' (1953), and 'There Is Something on Your Mind' (1959), the rambunctious saxman was always better in person. Tales abound in regard to McNeely's show-stopping escapades. Of all of them, this description of how he topped super bandleader Lionel Hampton at the 5th Annual Cavalcade of Jazz at Los Angeles' Wrigley Field, July 30, 1949, gives a good indication as to why he was billed as the 'Go Go Go Man,' 'the Deacon of the Tenor Sax,' 'The Pied Piper,' 'Big Jay McSquealy' and, finally, the most appropriate title, the 'King of the Honkers.' The *Sentinel*, the local African-American newspaper that would eventually call McNeely the unofficial 'Mayor of Watts' titled their review 'Local Sax Star Steals Jazz Cavalcade Show.' Hunter Hancock introduced Big Jay and his boys, and they blew some of the weirdest, wildest, rockingest and swingingest music heard around this neck of the woods since the full-sized Basie band first popped in port many years ago.

"'This guy McNeely is a showman. He went through the stands blowing his horn. He walked around the field, sweating, swearing and swinging! It was a hot day at Wrigley Field, but Big Jay blew. It was a pleasure to watch him. Wotta horn-tooter!'"

Jim Dawson, interviewing McNeely about the incident, reveals that after the first part of the show, Hampton's wife and manager Gladys, tried to get the wild tenor man off the bill lest he upstage the headliner. But Hampton made the mistake of bringing McNeely back to solo on "Flying Home." McNeely recalled, "I started marching into the stands, and naturally Hamp and his boys had to follow me. Then I laid down at home plate and started crawling on my back to first base and on over to the dugout. Hampton couldn't follow that. The crowd was going nuts. Hamp and his wife never forgave me for stealing the show like that."

The controversy over categorizing bands like those of Lionel Hampton or Big Jay McNeely as jazz or rhythm and blues really misses the point. Hampton and McNeely and their followers were jazz-oriented performers who placed a strong emphasis on dance and entertainment. Benny Goodman did pretty much the same thing; the difference is in degree and the preferences of the respective audiences. The Hampton/McNeely audience was largely black; Goodman's was white. Both played with a strong "swing" feel. Actually, the major break with the jazz tradition came with the emergence of bop and cool as the "new" jazz direction into the 1950s. Most of the stage mannerisms, playing styles, and emphases of bop and cool, and rhythm and blues, respectively, are at odds with each other. Each form sought a different musical aesthetic.

Courtesy Big J Records (Jim Dawson)

King of the Honkers: Big Jay McNeely. Big Jay McNeely lived long enough to see a renewed interest in his powerful saxophone playing and wild and woolly stage manner. One of the highlights of his performance were gloves and saxophone that lit up when the lights were turned off in the venues he played. But, like the rest of the r&b honkers, he was never able to connect with the rock'n'roll audiences of the 1950s. Jim Dawson in *Nervous Man, Nervous* avers, "Perhaps southern California, where the honking phenomenon had its greatest popularity, was too isolated. Perhaps the movement had what advertisers call bad demographics: poor blacks, Chicanos and working-class whites. Perhaps the ephemeral quality of the music—the hysteria and mania of the live shows rarely made the transfer to wax—limited its appeal. Or maybe the honking musical style lacked the romance, sentimentality and melodic hooks required to attract a core audience of young girls—the heart of any mass music phenomenon. In any event, the era of the honking tenor saxophonist ended just as rock'n'roll music had absorbed its anarchic energy, its exhibitionism, its mannerisms and many of its practitioners."

The Honkers

Saxophonist	Key Chart Recording	Label	R&B Position	Year
Frank Culley	Cole Slaw	Atlantic	11	1949
Big Joe Houston	Worry Worry Worry	Mercury	10	1952
Bull Moose Jackson	Sneaky Pete	King	10	1948
Illinois Jacquet	Flying Home (for Lionel Hampton)	Decca	3	1943
Big Jay McNeely	Decon's Hop	Savoy	1	1949
Jack McVae	Open the Door, Richard!	Black & White	2	1947
Wild Bill Moore	We're Gonna Rock, We're Gonna Roll	Savoy	14	1948
Paul Williams	The Hucklebuck	Savoy	1	1949
Eddie "Cleanhead" Vinson	Ole Maid Boogie	Mercury	1	1947

Source: Joel Whitburn's Top R&B Singles, 1942-1988

Other Solo and Backup Honkers

Jim Dawson, authority on all things that go honk-in-the-night, notes that the "Fifth Voice" of the 1950s doo wop groups was the saxophone solo in the background. Dawson cites Frank Culley's forceful sixteen-bar solo on the Clovers' hit "Don't You Know I Love You So," on Atlantic Records in 1951 as the first use of the "Fifth Voice." The following is a description of honkers in solos and backup roles.

Saxman	Description
Lee Allen	New Orleans backup star of 1950s and 1960s; had solo hits like "Walkin' With Mr. Lee"
Gene Ammons	Jazz great who made sax battle records with Johnny Griffin; honked on "Rockin' Rocker"
Gil Austin	Series of sax hits in 1950s; "Slow Walk" charted #3 in 1956
Gil Bernard	Backup sax on the Robins' hit "Smokey Joe's Cafe" and early Coasters hit "Youngblood"
Rusty Bryant	Ex-Hampton player whose "All Night Long" was a hit on Dot Records in 1954
Sam Butera	Raving tenorist who jumped and rocked with Louis Prima; Butera's unit called the Witnesses
Jimmy Cavallo	His House Rockers were the mainstay of Alan Freed's Rock'n'Roll Caravans; "The Big Beat" played in the first rock'n'roll film with Freed's *Rock Rock Rock*, 1956
Arnett Cobb	Ex-Hampton tenorist who replaced Jacquet; 1950s and 1960s bouncy "party time" LPs
King Curtis	Atlantic's "Fifth Voice" (with Sam "The Man" Taylor); solo "soul" hits in the 1960s
Joey D'Ambrosia	Bill Haley's saxman on "Rock Around the Clock"; 1990s performing as Joey Ambros
Maxwell Davis	Led many backup bands including Amos Milburn's; released "Rockin with Maxie"
Donny Flores	Played sax lead on hit by the Champs ("Tequila"), aka Chuck Rio
Jimmy Forrest	Ex-Basie tenor star soloed on biggest sax solo dance number of 1952, "Night Train"
Herb Hardesty	Like Lee Allen, key saxman associated with Little Richard and other New Orleans stars
Chuck Higgins	Follower of Big Jay McNeely; "Pachuko Hop" (1952) hit with barrio population of East Los Angeles
Raymond Hill	Immortalized by hot 32-bar solo on Jackie Brenston's "Rocket 88" in 1951
Lynn Hope	Wore a turban and walked the bars and neighborhoods; "Blow, Lynn, Blow," 1951
Willis "Gatortail" Jackson	Funky tenorist with soul LPs in 1960s and 1970s; "Chuck's Chuckles," 1950
Morris Lane	One of many honkers with a minor hit release; "Luke the Spook" for Savoy, 1947
Bob McNeely	Baritone "bottom" (low-notes) for younger brother Big Jay; shadowed Big Jay during his walks
Leo Parker	Another jazz baritonist; blues and bop with Billy Eckstine; "Leo's Boogie," a rocker (1940s)
Cecil Payne	Primarily jazz baritone player; honked occasionally; "Ham Hocks," 1950
Rudy Pompilli	Bill Haley's extroverted tenorist after D'Ambrosia; Dawson says 1956's "Rudy Rock" may be "the greatest white honking record ever made"
Red Prysock	Big tenor sound with Tiny Grimes; 1960s with funk organist "Brother" Jack McDuff
Clifford Scott	Classic tenor solo on biggest instrumental r&b and pop hit of 1950s, Bill Doggett's "Honky Tonk"
"Big" Al Sears	Played booting tenor solos behind countless 1950s doo wop groups
Johnny Sparrow	Billed as "The Mad Sax Man" in 1950s; best known release "Sparrow's Flight," 1950
Sam "The Man" Taylor	"Fifth Voice" for many Atlantic hits; "Red Top" and "Cloudburst" were vocalese sources
Nino Tempo	Stan Getz-like tenorman; mid-1950s honker in first color rock film *The Girl Can't Help It* (1957) where he did wild parody of honkers on "Tempo's Tempo"
Ted Tuchstone	Billed as "Mr. Rhythm" on 1950s release "Chicken Coop Blues"
Alvin "Red" Tyler	Another Crescent City saxman who backed many New Orleans stars
James Von Streeter	Played saxman in film *D. O. A.* (1949); audio dubbed by saxman Maxwell Davis
Jimmy Wright	The "Fifth Voice" on Frankie Lymon and the Teenagers's "Why Do Fools Fall in Love?" (1956)
"Big" Jim Wynn	Started idea of rolling on floor and walking the bar Los Angeles; claims Big Jay McNeely copied his act; best known recording "Blow, Wynn, Blow" (1948)

California R&B

"Get hip to this kindly tip, when you make that California trip, get your kicks on Route 66." So concludes the Bobby Troupe song "Route 66," which detailed the road that brought so many people of the Southwest out to California. Ever since Jimmie Rodgers sang about the glories of the idyllic land where the water tasted like wine and you could sleep out every night, in his song "Blue Yodel #4 (California Blues)," the Golden State had possessed a mythic hold on many inhabitants of the Texas-Oklahoma-Missouri axis. During World War II, jobs in war-related industries were plentiful and paid excellent wages. The black population especially was drawn to California. There were slightly more than 80,000 blacks in California in 1930. By 1940, there were 120,000, and by 1950, over 450,000.

In his political and musical investigation of California rhythm and blues, *Upside Your Head! Rhythm and Blues on Central Avenue*, Johnny Otis reports, "When Duke Ellington's great ballader, Herb Jeffries, looks back and says 'Central Avenue was our Harlem Renaissance,' he echoes the sentiments of all who lived through that fertile and creative time before, during, and after World War II. The history of

rhythm and blues music in Los Angeles is inseparably tied to the development of the African-American culture that formed and flourished in the Central Avenue area, that area that was fondly referred to by the people of the thirties, forties, and fifties as 'The Avenue.' . . . Central Avenue itself, first at 11th Street and Central Avenue, and later and more importantly at 42nd and Central, was the heartland and the main focus of the activity.

"Almost without exception, the old-timers of the period display a sadness when comparing the early days to the present time. 'We had so much then,' Jimmy Witherspoon laments, 'We had so many nice night spots, places like the Last Word and the Down Beat, and full-scale cabarets too like The Club Alabam and Shepp's Playhouse, big ballrooms such as Joe Morris's Plantation, blues incubators like the Barrelhouse in Watts and after-hours spots all over the place. Johnny Cornish's Double Vee, Alex Lovejoy's Big-Legged Chicken, Brother's, Staff Crouch's Backstage, Black Dot McGee's, The Jungle Room, and Jack's Basket Room. And sharp restaurants like Ivie's Chicken Shack, WOW! No wonder so much great music came out of Central Avenue. But it's all gone now, nothing left but crack and hardship.'"

All of the influential bluesmen from the Southwest made frequent trips to California to perform and record. Charles Brown, Ivory Joe Hunter, Lloyd Glenn, Lightnin' Hopkins, Smokey Hogg, Amos Milburn, Roy Milton, T-Bone Walker, Lowell Fulson, Oscar and Johnny Moore, and Joe and Jimmy Liggins were among the many southwestern territory bluesmen who helped shape the new rhythm and blues styles in California. Bandleader, disc jockey, and historian Johnny Otis contends that rhythm and blues started in Los Angeles because of the migration of the performers noted above and the growth of the independent record companies there.

Otis formed a big band in Los Angeles in 1945. On his first recording session for independent label Excelsior he had a hit with "Harlem Nocturne." By 1947, Otis realized he could no longer afford to keep a full band employed, so he began working with smaller combos. The burgeoning independent labels signed all of the Southwest talent, including Otis and a few other unknowns, and by the late 1940s "it was set—we had an art form, though we didn't know it then." Otis would lead a "Rhythm and Blues Caravan" throughout the 1970s.

Johnny Otis (1921-) was born in California of Greek parents. He grew up in an integrated neighborhood that was soon to be dominated by the black culture to which he was drawn. Otis has always considered himself a member of the African-American community, according to his autobiographies *Listen to the Lambs* and *Upside Your Head!* During the late 1930s and early 1940s, Otis worked professionally as a drummer-vibist for a variety of bands, most importantly Harlan Leonard and His Kansas City Rockets in 1943. Otis met and became lifelong best friends with saxophonist-arranger Preston Love, who wrote in the forward to Otis's *Listen to the Lambs*, "I first saw Johnny playing the drums in a Denver night spot in June 1941. My first impression was that he was just another white kid down in the ghetto trying to learn to play like the negro jazz musicians. I reasoned that the pretty brown-skinned girl with him was some little chick he had picked up in an extension of his effort to 'get that colored feeling.' I was very mistaken on both counts. The girl was his wife, Phyllis, and he was as 'Black' as I."

After playing with the Rockets on Central Avenue at the Club Alabam, Otis formed his own groups throughout the 1940s. The groups featured jazz-oriented arrangements and introduced future r&b stars like Little Esther and Mel Walker ("Double Crossing Blues," 1950), the Robins, and a score of others who toured with his cross-country All Star units.

The Club Combos

One of the most intriguing rhythm and blues styles to emanate from the West Coast was that of the club combo. The club combo consisted of a piano player/singer augmented by guitar and bass (occasionally a percussionist was added) rendering soft ballads, blues, and medium-tempo jive selections in well-appointed lounges. The clubs were more upscale than a typical bar or tavern, usually featuring curtain backdrops on the stage, rugs, and low, indirect lighting. These venues often had a cover charge, and placed an emphasis on proper dress and hushed conversation. Cocktails, rather than beers and a shot, were the beverage of choice.

The success of a whining piano player-singer from Nashville, **Cecil Gant** (1913-1951), is said to have set the stage for the fast-growing independent labels ot the West Coast. Gant, who was equally adept with growling boogie woogie ("Cecil's Boogie," "Rockin' the Boogie," and "We're Gonna Rock") as he was with blues ballads ("I Wonder," "Another Day, Another Dollar", and "I'm a Good Man, But a Poor Man"), created a furor at tiny independent label Gilt-Edge. Billing Gant as "The G.I. Sing-Station," and releasing full-record picture discs, Gilt-Edge proved that an unheralded record company, with the right artist, was capable of having hit records. Gant's first release in 1945, "I Wonder," proved the case. "I Wonder" reached the top of the "Harlem Hit Parade" charts, leading a number of enterprising businessmen to enter the hit-and-miss landscape of independent record production. Gant can be viewed as a trailblazer as far as early achievements in the growing independent records story, but as an artist his career was beset by drinking problems. Next to the three giants of the club combo tradition, Nat King Cole, Ivory Joe Hunter, and Charles Brown, Cecil Gant is only a colorful footnote.

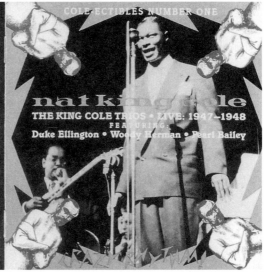

Courtesy MCA Records   *Courtesy Stash Records*

The Nat King Cole Trio provided the model for the club combo in California during the 1940s. Legend has it that Cole was first prodded to sing by a drunk who insisted that he sing the lyrics to "Sweet Lorraine" (the incident was even depicted in *The Nat King Cole Story*). Cole was probably given his name, "King" Cole by Bob Lewis, the manager of the Swanee Inn on Hollywood's La Brea Boulevard. Before that, Cole had been known by his real last name, Coles. Before Nat Cole became a star for Capitol Records, he recorded for a number of small, independent companies, then signed with Decca Records in 1940. *Left,* many of the arrangements and future hits with Capitol were recorded earlier on Decca.

Right, recordings taken from the radio show Cole did on NBC. Cole had been a hit attraction in 1945 on the "Kraft Music Hall" and, as a result, he shared a half-hour weekly show with Woody Herman. Broadcast nationally on Saturdays from 5:30 to 6:00 p.m. the "Wildroot Cream Oil Show" opened with Woody Herman and His Orchestra for the first fifteen minutes and wound up with the Nat King Cole Trio for the second fifteen. Herman created his hit, "Wildroot" for the occasion, and radio devotees fondly remember the commercial jingle that went, "You better get Wildroot Cream Oil, Choaarr-ly, it keeps your hair in trim." During the 1956-57 period, Cole broke the color barrier in television by being the first black artist to host a regular, nationally syndicated television show, which, like the radio show, featured famous guest artists each week.

Nat King Cole's career is one that saw him move from being a highly regarded instrumentalist known only to the jazz cognoscenti, to that of a "race" hitmaker on the first *Billboard* "Harlem Hit Parade" during the 1940s, to that of an out-and-out mainstream popular artist during the 1950s and 60s.

Nat King Cole (1917-1965) was to become a towering figure in black music history. He formed his own jazz piano trio in the mid 1930s and began playing in the Los Angeles night clubs. At this early juncture Cole was strictly an instrumentalist, playing piano in a post-Hines style. As a pianist, he had a beautiful "touch" and was a fluent and inventive soloist. Contemporary jazz pianists Oscar Peterson and Ramsey Lewis, to name just two, were strongly influenced by Cole's savory stylings. Cole established the club combo's piano-guitar-bass configuration by accident. In 1940, on his first evening at the Swanee Inn on LeBrea Boulevard in Hollywood, Cole's drummer, Lee Young, brother of tenorist Lester, received an offer to go on the road with a big band and didn't show up at the club. The remaining players, pianist Cole, guitarist Oscar Moore, and bassist Wesley Prince, performed as a trio, and the unusual sound was captivating. The King Cole Trio was born.

The early trio featured unison singing, instrumentals, and an occasional solo vocal by Cole. Ballads with a bounce ("Sweet Lorraine") and light jump tunes ("Hit the Jive, Jack") made up most of the group's first recordings on Decca Records. The unit was billed at that time as the "King Cole Trio." It didn't take long to realize that the most important aspect of the trio was the smooth and articulated vocals of Nat Cole. When Cole signed with the newly formed Capitol Records in 1943 (Stan Kenton had just been moved to the label by his manager, Carlos Gastel, who also managed Cole), the group was billed "Nat Cole and His Trio."

"Straighten Up and Fly Right" was Cole's first big hit in 1944, followed by "Gee, Baby Ain't I Good to You," "It's Only a Paper Moon," and "I'm a Shy Guy" (1945), "Route 66," "The Christmas Song," and "(I Love You) For Sentimental Reasons" (1946). During the years 1944 through 1946, Cole won jazz polls both as a singer and as a pianist. He made numerous "soundies," headlined his own radio shows (1948 and 1949), and began singing with large orchestras ("Nature Boy," 1948). By the time "Mona Lisa" hit number one on the pop charts in 1950, Nat Cole was a featured "stand up" singer. Cole had left the jazz and r&b underground behind him; he was now a full-fledged popular entertainer, and his financial success and high profile (Cole became the first black artist to host a nationally syndicated television show in 1956) caused many black singers to imitate his smooth, pop style.

When Cole left California in 1945, his guitarist, Oscar Moore, stayed behind. He and his brother Johnny Moore, on bass, put together a series of groups, called The Three Blazers, which carried on the quiet, sophisticated jazz approach suitable for the supper club trade. Johnny Moore and The Three Blazers featured two singer/pianists who, after Cole, became the most important figures in the club combo constellation: Ivory Joe Hunter and Charles Brown.

Courtesy Route 66, a division of Mr. R&B Record Sales

Pianist-singer Ivory Joe Hunter was the first r&b star to consistently "cross over" to country and western music. After recording a number of country-tinged hits, he scored with "Empty Arms" in 1958, then left Atlantic Records for a country-based company, Randy Woods's Dot Records. Hunter's last charted hit was for Dot, a country cover titled "City Lights." In December 1973 Hunter was taken to a Memphis hospital to begin treatment for lung cancer. A benefit concert was held for him in Nashville in October 1974, to help him with the mounting medical costs. Headlining the benefit were country and western stars Sonny James, Tammy Wynette, and George Jones, along with Memphis soul great Isaac Hayes.

Ivory Joe Hunter (1914-1974) first recorded in his home state of Texas for the Library of Congress in 1933. He had his own radio show in Beaumont, Texas (where he was billed as "Rambling Fingers"), and for five years he played the Uptown Tavern in Houston, Texas, before coming to Los Angeles in 1942. Emulating his hero Fats Waller, Hunter worked the clubs in Oakland, San Francisco, and Los Angeles as a solo pianist-singer. In 1945 he used members of Johnny Moore's Three Blazers and recorded the Leroy Carr classic "Blues at Sunrise" on Exclusive Records. The song hit number three on the r&b charts. Before 1945 was over, Hunter had moved on his own as a solo performer again, booking himself as the "Baron of the Boogie."

Hunter had twice tried his hand at record company ownership (Ivory in 1945 and Pacific shortly after; both failed). He signed with 4 Star ("Did You Mean it?") and King ("Landlord Blues") before finding greater success with MGM in 1949. "I Need You So" and "I Almost Lost My Mind" were both number one hits on the r&b charts in 1950. During the mid-1950s,

Hunter had big hits on Atlantic ("Since I Met You Baby" was number one on the r&b charts in 1956-57) and in the 1960s, he found a home in country music as a regular on the "Grand Ole Opry." Hunter was the first of the r&b stars to "connect" with the white country audience. This anticipates the foray of another club combo artist, Ray Charles, on Atlantic and ABC-Paramount in the late 1950s and early 1960s. Early in his career, Hunter reworked a country song that had been introduced by c&w star Jimmie Davis ("Lord, Please Don't Let Me Down"), and one of his biggest hits for King was a cover of Jennie Lou Carson's country weeper, "Jealous Heart," which soared to number two on the r&b charts in 1949.

Courtesy Route 66 and Jukebox Lil, a division of Mr. R&B Record Sales

After Charles Brown had tried teaching and working as a chemist, he decided to travel to California to seek employment as an entertainer. He won an amateur contest at the Lincoln Theater performing a boogie woogie classical piece, "The Warsaw Concerto." Brown worked a day job as an elevator operator and eventually auditioned with guitarist Johnny Moore for a job at L.A.'s Talk of the Town in September 1944. The trio consisted of Johnny Moore on electric guitar, Eddie Williams on bass, and Charles Brown on piano and vocals. *Left,* from left to right, Brown, Moore, Williams. *Right,* Moore, Brown, Williams. The group beat out twenty other trios. The Three Blazers's first record was cut for Bob Sherman's Atlas Records.

Charles Brown retold the background story of that first release in an interview in the Winter/March 1984 *Blue Suede News:* "He [Sherman] wanted to record the Three Blazers with Oscar Moore and he wanted me to sing. He gave us some songs to learn like 'Melancholy Madeline.' I didn't think the number would fit me too well. Frankie Laine used to come over all the time, and we were good friends. I said, 'Why not get Frankie Laine to do this number because he's very popular in California.' So he did one side called 'Melancholy Madeline,' and he was able to take that side to Mercury Records, they listened to his style, and his career started. I did the other side, called 'Tell Me You'll Wait for Me.' That was the first record we ever made."

The trio's big break came later in 1945, while they were playing the Copa in Los Angeles and a producer from Philo Records heard "Driftin' Blues." In September 1945, the Three Blazers, with Johnny Otis added on drums, recorded "Driftin' Blues" for Eddie Mesner's company. Between 1945 and 1947 the trio recorded for Modern, Exclusive, and Swing Time and were represented by the prestigious William Morris Agency. They played the best venues available to black artists during that time.

The glory days and harmonious times of the Three Blazers ended around 1947. Charles Brown continues, "Everything always happens about money. We decided that we were gonna split things down the middle and become like a corporation, but when Oscar Moore left Nat Cole we had a four-way split. They (Oscar and Johnny) were greedy for money. The deposits that were there were used up by Johnny. He was the leader so he could get any money he wanted. My money was $11,000 of the deposits. He took up my money, he took Eddie Williams' money. My grandfather told me, 'You don't need to be with them 'cause you're the major influence of the trio anyway. Get on your own.'" Brown did just that.

Charles Brown (1920-) would become the most pure club combo practitioner in terms of longevity and adherence to the form; he is the "Uncrowned King of Club Combo." As a singer/pianist, Brown was an original member of Johnny Moore's Three Blazers (Moore played guitar and Eddie Williams was on bass). Brown, who hailed from Texas City, Texas, where he had studied classical piano, was not a professional singer when he joined Moore's trio. However, the owner of the Talk of the Town in Beverly Hills insisted that the group sing if they wanted to keep their jobs. The model for the trio, of course, was the King Cole Trio, which was working at that time at the 331 Club in Los Angeles (that trio, too, had been forced to sing by nightclub management; audiences wanted to hear songs with words).

Charles Brown: "Uncrowned King of Club Combo."
After Nat King Cole, Pha Terrell was the greatest influence on Brown's early vocal stylings. As Brown would, Terrell sang unusually slow ballads, such as his signature "Until the Real Thing Comes Along" with the Andy Kirk Orchestra. Brown, in turn, heavily influenced Ray Charles. In his biography, *Brother Ray*, Charles is quoted, "Charles Brown was a powerful influence on me in the early part of my career, especially when I was struggling down in Florida. I made many a dollar doing my imitation of his 'Drifting Blues.' That was a hell of a number."

The group found success with a despondent blues written by Brown entitled "Driftin' Blues." *Billboard* listed this song as number two and it stayed on the charts for twenty-three weeks. *Cash Box* awarded the song "The Best R&B Record of 1946." Johnny Moore's Three Blazers, with Charles Brown as the main attraction, had a string of hits on Philo/Aladdin, Modern, and Exclusive ("Sunny Road," "So Long," "New Orleans Blues," "Changeable Woman Blues," and "More than You Know"). One hit, "Merry Christmas Baby," written by Brown and recorded for Exclusive in 1947, became the first certifiable r&b Christmas classic. Brown left the group in 1948 to begin his career as a solo act (he was replaced by Billy Valentine).

Brown recorded most of his remaining hits for Aladdin Records. Most were far more blues oriented than either Nat Cole's or Ivory Joe Hunter's output. Brown seemed to bask in the gloom and doom of lost love on classics such as "Get Yourself Another Fool," "Trouble Blues," "Homesick Blues," and "I Miss You" (1949), "My Baby's Gone" (1950), "Black Night" and "Seven Long Days" (1951), and "Hard Times" (1952). Brown never considered himself a blues singer—his idea of blues singers were songsters like Lightnin' Hopkins or John Lee Hooker. Brown called himself a "blues balladeer." Brown's impact on Ray Charles during the late 1940s is unmistakable, and the fact that Brown continued to tour and record throughout the 1970s and 1980s is a testimony to both his talent and his tenacity. In the early 1990s, Brown made new recordings, toured with Bonnie Raitt, and was finally recognized as one of the great innovative "stars" of rhythm and blues.

Club Combo Piano-Player Singers

Artist	Biggest R&B Hit	Label	R&B Position	Year
Charles Brown	Trouble Blues	Aladdin	1	1949
Ray Charles	Confession Blues	Downbeat	2	1949
Nat King Cole	Straighten Up and Fly Right	Capitol	1	1944
Floyd Dixon	Sad Journey Blues	Peacock	8	1950
Cecil Gant	I Wonder	Gilt-Edge	1	1944
Lloyd Glenn	Old Time Shuffle Blues	Swing Time	3	1950
Ivory Joe Hunter	I Almost Lost My Mind	MGM	1	1950
Little Willie Littlefield	It's Midnight	Modern	3	1949
Percy Mayfield	Please Send Me Someone to Love	Specialty	1	1950
Memphis Slim	Messin' Around	Miracle	1	1948
Piano Red (Dr. Feelgood)	Rockin' With Red	RCA	5	1950
Sugar Chile Robinson	Numbers Boogie	Capitol	4	1949
Roosevelt Sykes	The Honeydripper	Bluebird	3	1945
Billy Wright	Blues for My Baby	Savoy	3	1949

Source: Joel Whitburn's Top R&B Singles, 1942-1988

Jump Blues Combos of California

Roy Milton and Joe Liggins were California stars who used major elements of big band jazz (riffs, section work, and solos) within a small-group setting. Milton hailed from Tulsa, Oklahoma, and after working as a crooner in the Ernie Fields Orchestra in 1933, he moved to California. During the war years in Los Angeles, Milton, who now added drumming to his repertoire, formed his Solid Senders, which played sweet and sentimental songs for white audiences on the Sunset Strip and then played late hours gigs in the black section of town blasting away boogie-blues numbers. Liggins will always be remembered for his signature tune, "The Honeydripper." Liggins told Charlie Lange in liner notes to the album above, "We recorded 'The Honeydripper' April 20, 1945. Leon Rene, the owner of Exclusive Records, took it to Silver's Drug Store at 54th and Central and put it on the jukebox around 8:00 in the morning. He went back that night around 7:00 to see if it had been played. It had been played 135 times! So he knew he had a hit." "The Honeydripper" was a huge success. It held the number one position on the *Billboard* race chart for twenty-five weeks, and its estimated sales was over two million copies by the end of 1946.

To illustrate the importance of royalty payments for songwriters, and how so many artists got ripped off, Liggins told Lange: "Well, when you have a hit everyone else is jumping on it trying to cash in on it also. On Exclusive I was getting 1 cent per record but 'The Honeydripper' was a two-sided record so I was only getting a half a cent a side. One day at the Exclusive offices, which incidentally I helped furnish and prosper, Otis Rene asked me how much Leon was giving me for 'The Honeydripper.' I told him 1 cent per disc and he told me to tell Leon that if I didn't get 3 cents per disc, I would leave him. So when I told Leon this, I also threw in that Otis said to make it retroactive, whatever that meant. So Leon says OK, it would show up in my next royalty check. Well, my next check was almost ten thousand dollars! I could hardly believe it!"

Following the lead of Louis Jordan and His Tympani Five, Big Joe Turner, and Pete Johnson, many West Coast leaders realized that they couldn't afford the luxury of performing with a full orchestra. As a result, they pared down their units to include a rhythm section with a couple horns. In the small clubs, leaders of such colorfully named organizations as Roy Milton and His Solid Senders, Joe Liggins and His Honeydrippers, Jimmy Liggins and His Drops of Joy, and Amos Milburn and His Chickenshackers rocked and swayed black audiences night after night. Most of these units continued the swing-oriented technique of riff-laden horn parts, shouting blues, boogie woogie piano and bass lines, and shuffle rhythms. Drummer vocalist Roy Milton had tremendous success on Specialty Records with his 1945 hit "R.M. Blues" and his vocal rendition of "Hucklebuck" in 1949; pianist-vocalist Joe Liggins had number one hits with "The Honeydripper" in 1945 for Exclusive, and "Pink Champagne" in 1949 for Specialty. Guitarist singer Jimmy Liggins (Joe's younger brother) had more modest success with "Tear Drop Blues" in 1948 and "Don't Put Me Down" in 1949, both on Specialty.

Amos Milburn (1927-1980) deserves special attention because he established the Texas-California instrumental format for the sax-dominated combo, as well as the stylistic character for one of the basic rock'n'roll sounds of the 1950s. Milburn was a Texas boogie pianist-singer who came to California in 1946. He greatly admired Charles Brown, and as labelmates on Aladdin they recorded a number of duets together. But it is Milburn's break with the jazz-riff-cum-solo technique that gives him a special place in rhythm and blues. William Tallmadge in his *Jazz Rock Foundations* points out, "Unlike Johnny Otis, Roy Milton, and the Liggins brothers, Milburn came to the rhythm and blues scene without a lot of stylistic ballast inherited from jazz and swing." What Milburn did in essence was create a consistent use of 1) the back-beat by the drummer (putting heavy accents on the second and fourth beats) and 2) piano triplets (pattern of three to the beat) with the right hand. He broke away from the trumpet-sax riffs that were so much a part of swing jazz, thereby transmuting those jazz elements into an unalloyed, definitive rhythm and blues sound.

Courtesy Big Nickel Productions (Galen Gart)

Courtesy Route 66, a division of Mr. R&B Record Sales

Amos Milburn and his good friend Charles Brown recorded a number of duets and toured together. Milburn practiced what he preached during the wild days of his rhythm and blues hits. He told author Nick Tosches in *Unsung Heroes of Rock 'n' Roll*: "'I was a heavy drinker, I loved that scotch and the devil kept tellin' me: "Go on, Amos, drink all you want to, it'll never hurt you none." 'I drank myself into two strokes.' It was a low, faint voice that spoke. It bore little resemblence to that cool, tough Amos Milburn voice of 25, 30 years ago, that voice that bespoke the ceaseless saxophones of salvation, the crossing and uncrossing of terrible nylon knees, the eightfold path of the unfiltered cool, and the miracle of our Lady of the After-Hours Joint. But the party has been over for years now."

The source of the name of Milburn's backup group, the Chickenshackers, was his first hit, "Chicken Shack Boogie," a rollicking, dance-party number that made number one on the r&b charts in 1948. Milburn's group featured the tenor saxophone of Maxwell Davis with a rhythm section made up of piano, bass, drums, and electric guitar. The tenor often doubled the bass part for extra rhythmic emphasis. The use of boogie woogie bass lines, which Milburn had learned from listening to Meade Lux Lewis and Pete Johnson records, also added strong, repetitive underpinnings in the rhythm section and perpetual piano triplets in the right hand. Milburn had created a repetitious format that differed from the jazz-based techniques followed by so many of the r&b jump combos of California.

Milburn was a consistent hitmaker until 1954, ironically the year that rock'n'roll began to emerge and overtake many of the pioneers, including the "Chicken Shack" master. Milburn's biggest hits included "Bewildered" (1948), "Hold Me Baby," "Roomin' House Boogie," "Empty Arms Blues," and "Let's Make Christmas Merry, Baby" (1949), "Bad, Bad Whiskey" (1950), "Let's Rock Awhile" (1951), "Thinking and Drinking" (1952), "Let Me Go Home Whiskey" and "One Scotch, One Bourbon, One Beer" (1953), and "Good, Good Whiskey" (1954).

Frank Driggs Collection

T-Bone Walker: Father of r&b electric guitar. Walker, of Cherokee Indian descent, began his career early. After "leading" Blind Lemon Jefferson around for a time, he made the rounds of the traveling minstrel and medicine shows, blacking his face to sing numbers such as "She'll Be Coming 'Round the Mountain" for the Breeden Medicine Show. Walker tap-danced, mastered all of the string instruments, and played banjo in "Ma" Rainey's Carnival shows, as well as with Ida Cox's traveling troupe, all while still a teenager. After playing guitar in the Texas big bands of Count Beloski and Milt Larkin, Walker joined bandleader Les Hite on the West Coast.

Jim O'Neal, writing in *Living Blues* magazine in 1972, quotes saxophonist Big Jim Wynn, who played with Walker as saying, "I began to play the blues in the Harlem Club in Watts in 1936. A fellow came to town, name of T-Bone Walker. He was dancing and picking up tables with his mouth. He'd dance on a table and then grip it with his teeth and whirl it around. He started singing with the first small band I had. The people went mad about him." No doubt, Walker's acrobatic whirls of duck walking, playing the guitar behind his head, and doing splits encouraged Wynn to do the same thing with his saxophone.

The influence of the Kansas City tradition of Count Basie and his band was very much in evidence in Walker's work, as demonstrated in Walker's reworking of Jimmy Rushing's vocal with Basie, "Evening," in 1945. Walker's recordings of "Mean Old World Blues," "T-Bone Boogie," "I'm Still in Love With You," and "Sail on Boogie," released in 1945 with the Marl Young Orchestra in Chicago, all show a strong Basie influence.

Walker moved to Chicago for a couple of years (1942-45) at the Rhumboogie Nightclub, owned by heavyweight boxing champion Joe Louis. It was here that the master guitar showman was finally showcased properly. Helen Oakley Dance described the professional floor show at the Rhumboogie in her biography, *The T-Bone Walker Story: Stormy Monday:* "The upcoming show caused so much talk on the street that the dress rehearsal was like a preview. Ringside tables were crowded with entertainers from other locations and with local big names. The opening number featured the chorus in elaborate headdresses and sequined tights. As the coda faded, the sound of T-Bone's guitar vibrated in the wings. He moved out on the floor singing 'T-Bone Boogie,' and the audience of pros let him know they had been waiting for this. 'Too Lazy to Work,' which followed, was the kind of show number he knew how to present, and the crowd laughed as he kidded and mimed. To wind up the production, [producer] Ziggy Joe had devised an impressive finale built around 'Evenin',' the hit song of the show. In the wings a fringe of moonlit palms suggested a tropical setting. The company, in carnival attire, dimly seen behind a scrim, swayed to faint music. Down front on the darkened stage a bright spotlight focused on T-Bone in top hat, white tie, and tails. Very softly he intoned the opening stanzas of a song meant to evoke nostalgia and grief. Weaving through verse after verse was a leitmotif inspired by the mystery and music of night. The number seldom failed to evoke a standing ovation."

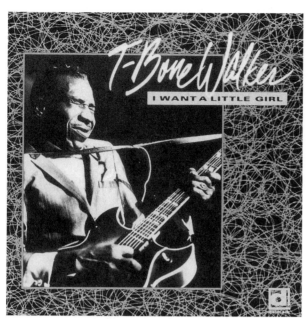

Courtesy Delmark Records

T-Bone Walker with his classic pose, holding his guitar away from his body with the strap over just one shoulder. This allowed Walker to swing the guitar around his body, among other tricks. Duke Robillard, who attained national recognition with the Roomful of Blues group during the 1980s and sustained solo stardom thereafter as a "burning" guitarist, wrote an introduction to Helen Oakley Dance's biography in which he said, "T-Bone was really the first to use 'sustain,' which all guitarists use today, but electronically that is, by feedback. Also, something different about T-Bone, something original, was the way he held the guitar. It takes some getting used to at first, but it's a comfortable way of playing. When you hold the guitar out from yourself, like he did, against your chest, your hand just rests on the strings, and it seems good. You get a loose feeling.

"T-Bone was a great influence on other guys, especially the way he worked the guitar in with the lyrics he sang. That had a definite influence on B.B. King, I feel. He says so, and it's real easy to hear that playing obligato to your own vocal lines. Another thing: What other guitarist was equally at home playing *either* jazz or blues? If you don't count George Benson, that goes for today as well. This gives T-Bone an eminence all his own."

T-Bone Walker (1910-1975) is the final entry in our history of the California jump combo tradition. Walker was born and raised in Linden, Texas, and later moved to the more cosmopolitan Dallas. As a youngster he acted as leadboy for family friend Blind Lemon Jefferson. Jefferson and Leroy Carr were the two major influences on Walker's career, the former for his large song repertoire and single-note guitar solos, the latter for his jazzy vocal technique. Lonnie Johnson, the most jazz-oriented of the rural guitarists, also made an impression on the young Walker.

By the end of the 1920s Walker had recorded as "Oak Cliff T-Bone," toured with medicine shows, and played on street corners and at house parties, picnics, barbecues, drive-in soda drink stands, country golf clubs, and country dances. Before he was twenty years old, Walker was a full-time musician making a good living in Dallas. By the time he was ready to leave for the greener pastures of Los Angeles in 1934, Walker was working in a big band led by Lawson Brooks. Walker chose Charlie Christian, who was Walker's good friend and street corner companion (they danced and played guitar; Walker called this "busting music") as his replacement. Christian, as we have seen, went on to be the most important electric guitarist in jazz history. Walker, for his part, would become the leader of rhythm and blues electric guitar.

Without recounting the controversy and confusion about who the very first electric guitarist was, let us note that Walker claims to have been playing pure electric guitar in 1935 (not an acoustic resonator guitar, which Eddie Durham used with Jimmie Lunceford in 1935). For our purposes, let us note the three most influential electric guitarists in the underground: Charlie Christian (jazz), Bob Dunn (country), and T-Bone Walker (rhythm and blues). Other important electric guitarists prior to the 1940s included jazzmen Hurley Ramsey with the Earl Hines band, Floyd Smith with Andy Kirk, Al Norris with Jimmie Lunceford, and, in country music, Leon McAuliffe with Bob Wills.

In Los Angeles, Walker led his own small groups in a variety of clubs, most importantly the Little Harlem, between 1934 and 1939. This was the period in which he experimented with electric guitar. When Walker joined Les Hite's Cotton Club Orchestra in Los Angeles in 1939, he began to receive some recognition for his jazz-infused, "horn-like" guitar solos. Walker's electric guitar solo on "T-Bone Blues" with the Hite band in 1939 was his first nationally successful recording. By 1940, Walker was recording with white boogie woogie specialist Freddie Slack. "Mean Old World" in 1940 and "Riffette" in 1943, both on Capitol, were the most successful recordings Walker made with Slack.

By 1945, Walker was on his own, leading the most successful electric guitar-based jump group in rhythm and blues. Walker's ability to create long, sustained notes and to use echo feedback were revolutionary during this period. The distortion and echo sounds were not recorded during this era because recording engineers sought "purity of sound," a problem that Beatle Paul McCartney would run into in 1965 when Capitol Records didn't want to release *Rubber Soul*'s "Think for Yourself" for the same reason. (The executives feared audiences would think the distorted bass sounds were due to sloppy engineering. Beatles producer George Martin solved the "problem" by having the company place a disclaimer on the record jacket: "Paul on fuzz bass.") Given this attitude toward the most successful musician of the 1960s, imagine the attitude of record companies toward a black r&b performer during the 1940s.

Walker's classic tune was "Call It Stormy Monday" (usually called "Stormy Monday"), which was recorded on the Black & White label in 1947. The song was a big hit in 1948, and over the years has proven to be one of the absolute classics of modern blues, and a particular favorite for rock'n'roll jam sessions. B.B. King and the majority of the other great rhythm and blues electric guitarists made their most important recordings after 1950, so they won't be reviewed here—just another indication of how far ahead of everybody T-Bone Walker was.

A final note about Walker's stage presentation. The guitarist placed the guitar strap over just one shoulder—in front of, rather than behind, his neck—so that he could have freedom to swing the instrument above or behind his head. Like that of Big Jay McNeely, Walker's stage show was electrifying. He played the guitar behind his head, with his teeth, and while cavorting across the stage. He did deep knee bends and even splits while playing. All of these techniques were looked upon with horror by those in the more "respectable" forms of music—classical, pop, and jazz. Future rockers, who would become a part of the mainstream popular music scene, such as Bill Haley, Elvis Presley, the Rolling Stones, and Jimi Hendrix, followed the patterns established by great r&b revolutionaries like Lionel Hampton, Louis Jordan, Amos Milburn, Big Jay McNeely, and T-Bone Walker. These underground rhythm and blues greats forged their own direction without the support of music critics. They responded to the wishes of their audience. Remember that during 1935-1950, there were no history books written about the blues forms, rural or urban. The early music histories were dedicated to jazz only. There were hardly any books about mainstream popular music. Unlike today, curiosity about popular culture and mainstream popular music was confined to a couple of monthly magazines such as *Song Hits*, and the weekly business trades, such as *Variety*, *Cash Box*, and *Billboard*. There were no blues magazines like *Living Blues* and *Blues Revue* to keep audiences abreast of the latest events. There were only jazz magazines, and most jazz writers condemned most rhythm and blues music as simplistic, musical, or both.

The Electric Guitar Combo Leaders

Guitar Leader	Biggest R&B Hit	Label	Peak Position	Year
Gatamouth Brown	Mary Is Fine	Peacock	8	1949
Pee Wee Crayton	Blues After Hours	Modern	1	1948
Arthur "Big Boy" Crudup	Rock Me, Mama	Bluebird	3	1945
Lowell Fulson	Blue Shadows	Swing Time	1	1950
Slim Gaillard	Cement Mixer (Put-Ti, Put-Ti)	Cadet	5	1946
Tiny Grimes	Midnight Special	Atlantic	12	1948
Elmore James	Dust My Broom	Trumpet	9	1952
Lonnie Johnson	Tomorrow Night	King	1	1948
B.B. King	Three O'Clock Blues	RPM	1	1951
Saunders King	Empty Bedroom Blues	Modern	9	1949
Johnny Moore	Drifting Blues	Philo	2	1948
Robert Nighthawk	New Orleans Blues	Exclusive	2	1947
Tampa Red	Let Me Play With Your Poodle	Bluebird	4	1942
T-Bone Walker	Bobby Sox Blues	Black & White	3	1947
Muddy Waters	(I Feel Like) Going Home	Aristocrat	11	1948

Source: Joel Whitburn's Top R&B Singles, 1942-1988

Photographs and Prints Division, Schomburg Center for Research in Black Culture, The New York Public Library, Astor, Lenox and Tilden Foundation

The Ink Spots in action. Both the Ink Spots and the Mills Brothers set the standards that would be emulated by all the other vocal groups that followed: tight vocal harmonies, professionalism on stage, sharp, matching suits, and a variety of material that included romantic ballads and finger-snapping, uptempo tunes.

The Vocal Groups: Pre-Doo Wop History

The final section of rhythm and blues styles is that of the vocal groups (known as doo wop, a term given to the movement sometime in the 1970s). Doo wop was close harmony singing by primarily male groups of four to six members that were popular in the 1950s and 1960s. Examples are the Clovers, the Dominoes, the Drifters, and the Four Tops. The sounds created by the backup singers for the groups, such as "bim bam boom," "sha na na na," "dip dip dip boom" and the like, were primary sources of the term doo wop. Today there are multitudes of revival groups touring the nostalgic, memory-lane circuit.

The roots of doo wop go back to the 1930s. The history of the vocal group is long and convoluted, but it can be reduced to a focus on two pop-oriented units that got their start in the mid-1930s: the Mills Brothers and the Ink Spots. These groups had a prevailing influence on the more rhythmically charged assemblages of the 1940s.

The **Mills Brothers** (1931-1968) of Piqua, Ohio, brought into their style not only barbershop harmonies but also jazzy arrangements inspired by Louis Armstrong and Duke Ellington. They had appeal for both white and black audiences. Their cleanly articulated vocals and smooth, unruffled harmonies resulted in their becoming the most successful male vocal group of all time, with 71 chart singles (the Andrews Sisters beat them for the all-time record with 112) spanning four decades.

The early works of the brothers had them imitating big band horn sounds and scat singing. Their first hit, in 1931, was "Tiger Rag." The brothers also sang close-harmony ballads such as "Paper Doll," their biggest hit, in 1943. The Mills Brothers became important models for many blacks because they were seen in numerous major motion picture releases, often impeccably dressed and treated as professional entertainers--this during an era when most blacks were portrayed as shuffling comic figures (the history of blacks in film can be traced by the superior account provided by Donald Bogel in *Toms, Coons, Mulattoes, Mamies and Bucks: An Interpretive History of Blacks in American Films*, 1973).

The Mills Brothers were also the first black group to have a major network radio show, on CBS in 1931. The group included brothers Herbert, Harry, Donald, and John, Jr. (when John died in 1935, he was replaced by the father, John, Sr., who sang with the group until he died in 1967).

Courtesy MCA Records

The Mills Brothers performed in the late 1920s on WLW radio variety shows out of Cincinnati. Their versatility shone through when a variety of sponsors gave the group new names in order to make it appear there was more than one group—the Steamboat Four, Will, Willie, Wilbur and William, and the East Jesters, among others. Tommy Rockwell, who managed Louis Armstrong for a while, brought the brothers east, where they signed a contract with CBS radio. During 1931, the brothers began imitating instrumental sounds, which led their record company, Brunswick, to boast on the label: "No musical instruments or mechanical devices used on this recording other than one guitar." The group was also seen in a number of Hollywood films including *The Big Broadcast*, (1932); *Operator*, (1933), and *Twenty Million Sweethearts*, (1934). During these formative years, the group recorded "Rockin' Chair" (1932), a song listed by a number of historians as the first talking-bass part in vocal group history.

By the 1950s the Mills Brothers had done away with imitating musical instrument sounds and expanded their own sound by recording with large orchestras. The Mills Brothers' last big hits were "Glow Worm" (1952) and "Cab Driver" (1968), although they still headlined shows into the 1990s with Donald and his son John III continuing as a duo. Jay Warner summarized the group's importance in *The Billboard Book of American Singing Groups: A History, 1940-1990*: "The Mills Brothers' influence was pervasive: they made black music acceptable to a wide audience and encouraged other black vocalists to carry on what they had started. And lest we forget, they did it with dignity and grace in difficult racial times, carried forward by their warmth of character and mellow sound."

The Ink Spots rose in the shadow of the great Mills Brothers. They didn't find their niche until songwriter Jack Lawrence brought his composition "If I Didn't Care" to a January, 1939 recording session set up to record the jivey, nonsense song, "Knock-Kneed Sal." The group, impressed with Lawrence's ballad, placed Bill Kenny's high tenor lead and Orville " Hoppy" Jones's talking-bass to work, and the result was the song that made the group's career. Jack Lawrence later wrote a song for his lawyer's daughter, "Linda," which became a big hit. The Linda of the song was Linda Eastman, who later married Paul McCartney, who in turn bought the rights to Lawrence's catalog of songs. Like many doo wop groups of the 1950s and 1960s, the Ink Spots had many members perform with them over the years, and by the 1990s, it was estimated that some forty groups had claimed to be the Ink Spots at one time or another. During the 1940s, Deek Watson sold the rights to the group name to Bill Kenny for $20,000. Later, fill-in Johnny Smith supposedly had exclusive rights to the name by authority from Bill Kenny's widow.

While the Ink Spots can't be considered a rock'n'roll group, their impact on the form was surprisingly strong. The group set down the model high tenor lead: Bill Kenny paved the way for Sonny Til of the Orioles, Maith Marshall of the Ravens, Frankie Lymon of the Teenagers, Curtis Mayfield of the Impressions, and numerous others. The group also established the talking-bass format that Jimmy Ricks of the Ravens and all others in their wake have emulated, often in parody, but emulated just the same. The Platters, the most successful doo wop group of the 1950s and early 1960s, was a direct copy of the Ink Spots, covering many of their songs ("My Prayer," "Smoke Gets in Your Eyes," "If I Didn't Care"), except that on record Herb Reed seldom got to replicate the talking bass. Another rock'n'roll connection to the Ink Spots, who themselves were not at all rock-oriented, is the fact that the band's songs were among those that a young Elvis Presley chose to record on the personal audition discs he made at Sam Phillips's Memphis recording service—at the then steep price of $3.98 apiece.

Of the many vocal groups that followed the trail set by the Mills Brothers, **The Ink Spots** (1931-1990s) had the most influence on the future of doo wop. The group originally formed in Indianapolis in 1931 with Deek Watson as leader. After a series of names (the Swingin' Gate Brothers; King, Jack and Jester; and King's Jesters) the group settled on one, the Ink Spots, given them by the owner of the Savoy Ballroom, Moe Gale, who was also their manager. It just so happened that King's Jesters was the name of Paul Whiteman's vocal group at the time, so a name change was necessary.

The significance of the Ink Spots can be found in two individuals: **Orville "Hoppy" Jones** (1905-1944), who joined the group in late 1931, and **Bill Kenny** (1915-1978), who joined in 1936 to sing lead. These two key individuals put a stamp of originality on a band that will be forever noted in vocal group history. Jones's talking bass and Kenny's high tenor on ballads became the most-copied individual elements of vocal group singing, beginning with their signature tune "If I Didn't Care" (1939). Number one hits "Address Unknown" (1939), "We Three (My Echo, My Shadow, and Me)" (1940), "I'm Making Believe," and "Into Each Life Some Rain Must Fall" (1944), and "The Gypsy" and "To Each His Own" (1946) catapulted the Ink Spots into the best rooms in the country.

Like the Mills Brothers, the Ink Spots also became known to the wider public via radio and movies. Both groups recorded a majority of their classics for Decca Records, a company that didn't support the jazz and jive elements of their repertoire (Bing Crosby's jazz had been quieted by the same company). While the imposition of company dictates may have limited the total artistic variety of the post-1935 work of these groups, by focusing on the melodic elements, both groups were able to "cross over" to the popular audience.

While the Mills Brothers and the Ink Spots were the grandfathers of future doo wop groups, there were a number of other black groups that were performing successfully at the same time, such as the Cats and the Fiddle ("I Miss You So," 1940), the Charioteers ("Swing Low, Sweet Chariot," 1939), the Deep River Boys ("Recess in Heaven," 1948), and the Delta Rhythm Boys (Just A-Sittin' and A-Rockin'," 1945), as well as a spate of gospel units led by the Dixie Hummingbirds, the Golden Gate Quartet, and the Five Blind Boys of Mississippi.

But it wasn't until the Ravens and the Orioles emerged in the mid-1940s, that a rhythm and blues direction was firmly established for vocal groups. If the Mills Brothers and Ink Spots are the "grandfathers" of doo wop, then the Ravens and the Orioles are its "Founding Fathers."

Notes from the R.&B. Beat

RAVENS REORGANIZED: The Ravens, one of the groups responsible for the current r.&b. vocal group trend, have reorganized. Three of the group were replaced, with singer Jimmy Ricks still the key factor with the unit. The new Ravens will debut on October 12 on a one-niter in Yonkers, and will work a series of promotions in a package with Joe Thomas' ork for the remainder of October. Group already is booked for the week of Nov. 2 at the Paradise Theater, Detroit, and for the week of Nov. 23 at the Apollo Theater, New York. Latter engagement will also headline Ruth Brown and the Willis Jackson band.... Lee Magid has signed Maithe Marshall, former lead singer of the Ravens, to an exclusive contract and will form a new group called the Marshall Brothers. Group will wax for Savoy. Marshall at this moment is working as a single at the Apollo Bar, Harlem.

MAITHE MARSHALL

Courtesy Big Nickel Publications (Galen Gart)

According to Jay Warner in *The Billboard Book of American Singing Groups: A History, 1940-1990,* **The Ravens** (1945-1959) "have stood the test of time as one of the best of all pioneering rhythm and blues groups. They were the first to make continuous use of a brass vocalist (Jimmy Ricks) and a falsetto tenor (Maithe Marshall) on lead. They were also the first to incorporate dance steps into an R&B act." The Ravens were initiated when Jimmy Ricks and Warren "Birdland" Suttles, two waiters in Harlem who harmonized together to jukebox records of their favorite group, the Delta Rhythm Boys, decided to form a unit of their own. With Howard Biggs as their musical arranger they began performing in 1946 at the Club Baron in Harlem.

The early recordings of the group on the Hub label ("Honey" and "My Sugar is So Refined") got them an opening spot at the Apollo Theatre with Nat King Cole and Stan Kenton. When Ricks began to sing with his deep, booming bass, he brought the house down, and from that point on, his bass leads became a main focus of the group. The group's recordings on National Records, beginning in 1947 with "Write Me" and then "Old Man River," established the Ravens internationally. The records usually featured Ricks singing lead on the A side of the record, and Marshall singing lead on the B side. This led Marshall to label himself a "B-side singer."

A majority of the Ravens' releases were older standards such as "Again," "White Christmas," "Begin the Beguine," and "September Song," not unlike the repertoire of the Ink Spots and the Mills Brothers. However, the group added a more rhythmic background sound than these established units. For example, the Ink Spots and the Mills Brothers often used long, sustained vowel sounds ("ohoos" and "ahaaas") behind the lead singer, whereas the Ravens used bouncy nonsense sounds ("doo-do-do-wop" or "bum-buh-buh-bum-bum").

Jack Sbarbori, who spent ten years researching the Ravens, is of the opinion that they were the greatest vocal quartet in the history of rhythm and blues. After listening to some of their swing-styled performances recorded for Mercury during the period 1952-54, many listeners would agree, particularly those who are white, in their fifties or sixties, and partial to music of the big band swing era. But judging from their paucity of hits after 1950, apparently the Ravens' beautiful, technically perfect, sophisticated, swing-styled, adult-oriented recordings were mostly ignored by the greater part of the black rhythm and blues audience, listeners whose preferences at that time were for the rougher, less polished sounds of the Robins, the Cardinals, the Dominoes, and the Midnighters. Also, as younger black listeners began to make their influence felt during the 1950s, they did not find the adult-oriented lyrics of the Ravens appropriate to their emotional needs.

Let us not, however, forget that during the mid-to-late 1940s and the pre-rock 1950s, the Ravens offered a distinct option to the Mills Brothers and the Ink Spots. The Ravens may have shared much of the same material of those older groups, but they were younger and injected more forcefulness into their music. Also, the Ravens projected a hip attitude that was influenced by modern jazzmen like Dizzy Gillespie and Charlie Parker, with whom they often shared the bill in jazz clubs like

Frank Driggs Collection

The Ravens, with Jimmy Ricks, top. The Ravens followed in the path cut by the Mills Brothers and the Ink Spots, the first of the great secular rhythm and blues groups. Like their predecessors, the Ravens recorded Tin Pan Alley pop-music standards such as "Summertime," "Deep Purple," "September Song," "White Christmas," and their biggest hit, "Ol' Man River." "Ol' Man River," of course, goes back to 1927, with Jimmy Ricks intoning the Jerome Kern-Oscar Hammerstein II perennial made famous by the great African-American bass singer Paul Robeson in the musical play *Show Boat*.

In *Jazz Rock Foundations* William Tallmadge points out, "On 'Ol' Man River,' the listener is always aware that the voices of the Ravens proceed from black singers, a fact that was not always so evident in the singing of the Mills Brothers or the Ink Spots. The voices, however, are the blackest element in the song. The rest of the arrangement follows a late 1930s swing style with unison vocals and close harmonies backed by a string bass and a guitar playing evenly accented beats. The voices are also backed by a swing-styled piano."

In *The Billboard Book of American Singing Groups* Jay Warner notes that the Ravens' road manager, Nat Margo, bought the group's name from Ricks, and a variety of Ravens toured the doo wop revival circuit during the 1960s and 1970s. Warner also notes the significance of the Ravens' dance routines, which eventually filtered into the stage acts of later groups like the Coasters (who delivered playful comedic skits to act out Jerry Leiber and Mike Stoller's humorous compositions like "Yakety-Yak") and the Spinners. "Leonard Puzey had introduced the 'applejack'[a simple dance step] to group choreography. Ironically, the Ravens themselves didn't like the dance step ideas, but the audiences loved them, so Ricks and company kept them and Puzey's moves became part of vocal group performances from the Orioles and the Cadillacs to the Temptations and the Miracles for decades to come."

438

the Royal Roost and Birdland. These young lions also projected a "black and proud" image. The Mills Brothers were often listed on their label as "Four Boys with Rhythm Accompaniment," while the Jones-Kenny vocal unit was, after all, billed as the Ink Spots (as in spots of black ink).

Like a majority of the vocal groups, the Ravens endured numerous personnel changes, and after 1957 (Warner claims that "Dear One," recorded in 1957, was the unit's last great effort), Ricks sold the group's name to road manager Nat Margo. Ricks then worked solo with minor successes for numerous labels (he never charted) and even performed with Count Basie.

The Orioles (1946-1981) hailed from Baltimore, where they began harmonizing on street corners. The group's professional name was the Vibranaires when they were heard performing in a local bar by songwriter Deborah Chessler. She became their manager and provided them with the song that became their entree into the bigtime in 1948, "It's Too Soon to Know."

Courtesy Big Nickel Publications (Galen Gart)

Sonny Til (Earlington Tilghman) was the main draw of the Orioles, plain and simple. A former Orioles road manager, Chester Smith, quoted on the liner notes of the album above, noted: "Sonny reached the young ladies with intelligent lyrics that shot straight to the heart. With him the song was the thing. He was Frank Sinatra all over again, young ladies followed him everywhere. Sonny didn't have a drug habit, he didn't smoke or drink; essentially he was a religious man, a philosophical man, so when the group broke up, he continued to work because he had the need and desire to sing. He'd go anywhere for this opportunity." By the mid-1960s the charismatic singer discovered he had diabetes and his battle against it continued until his death at the age of fifty-one in 1981.

Jack Schiffman writes in *Uptown: The Story of Harlem's Apollo Theatre*: "Sonny affected the girls like an aphrodisiac. When he bent over the mike and leaned to one side, sensuously grating his shoulders and caressing the air with his hands, the girls would shriek, 'Ride my alley, Sonny! Ride my alley!' . . . it was the oral as well as the visual aspects of their routine that had captured the teenagers' fancy. The Orioles had produced what we now think of as the 'group' sound, a combination of gospel and jazz, the vocals punctuated with glottal stops in the middle of a strain, and high-flying tenor solos. They caught the sensitive ears of a generation looking for its own symbols of identification, and when you added the Orioles' dance routines, actually choreographed and stylized down to the last stride, you had an irresistible new play thing for a restless young audience. A decade and a half after the Orioles constructed this new sound and style, their reverberations could be heard in the Temptations, the Supremes and every other singing group worthy of the name."

Courtesy Dr. Horse, a division of Mr. R&B Record Sales

By this time, the group had changed its name to that of the Baltimore Bird, no doubt influenced by the success of the first of all the bird groups, the Ravens (by the fifties there would be an amazing number of vocal groups named after birds). Chessler had arranged an appearance on "Arthur Godfrey's Talent Scouts" television show in New York. The group came in second to future jazz great George Shearing, but Godfrey was so taken with the group that they became semiregulars on his morning radio show. The key component of the Orioles' success was the high-flying tenor lead of Sonny Til (Earlington Tilghman), who followed the pattern established by Bill Kenny of the Ink Spots. The Orioles did not use a deep bass singer augmenting the high tenor lead; they simply used a thrilling high tenor lead with four-part harmony. The five-man group was moving up the r&b ladder of success when guitarist Tommy Gaither fell asleep at the wheel of their station wagon in 1950. The ensuing accident killed Gaither and seriously injured members George Nelson and Johnny Reed. The group had its biggest hit in 1953, crossover smash "Crying in the Chapel." From that time until 1981, Til regularly recreated new versions of the Orioles. Aside from Til's significance as the most important tenor lead in doo wop history, the Orioles stand out as the first black group to gain national popularity by recording black songs (the Ravens recast white swing material). The Orioles were inducted into the Rock'n'Roll Hall of Fame as "Early Influences" in 1994.

Unlike the Ravens, the Orioles made their mark by focusing on black songs rather than white-oriented swing material. Phil Groia wrote in the first history of doo wop, *They All Sang on the Corner*, that the Orioles had "a mellow, soft second tenor lead, a blending baritone featured as a [gravelly] second lead, a floating high first tenor and a dominant bass." The Orioles also are viewed by a number of historians as being the innovators of what would later be defined as pure, r&b four-part harmony. When songwriter Deborah Chessler took the group under her songwriting and management wing, she helped them get on national television (Arthur Godfrey's show) and signed to National Records. By picking a bird name, the group started an ornithological trend among vocal groups. After the Ravens and Orioles, there suddenly emerged a swarm of "bird groups." Here is a list, with the date of the group's first recording, just up to 1954: Bluebirds and Robins, Cardinals, Larks, Skylarks, and Swallows (1951), Blue Jays, Crows, Flamingos, Parrots, Sparrows, Swans and Whipoorwills (1953), Buzzards, Eagles, Hawks, Parakeets, Peacocks, Pelicans and Penguins and Quails, Starlings and Wrens (1954).

The great success of the Orioles came to a screeching halt in 1950, when an automobile accident killed the group's guitarist-singer, Tommy Gaither and seriously injured Johnny Reed and George Nelson. In 1951 the group sang a tribute song to Gaither entitled "Pal of Mine." While the group recorded many fine songs, they will be remembered for two genuine classics: "It's Too Soon to Know" and "Crying in the Chapel." Both highlighted by Sonny Til's careening high tenor lead. "It's Too Soon to Know" (1948) established the group as a top-fight draw in the clubs and on the theater circuit for years to come. "Crying in the Chapel" (1953) became an early crossover hit in the pop market. A reviewer for *Billboard* wrote, "The Orioles have here what is undoubtedly the strongest record in the past two years, and one of the strongest R&B discs released in the past few months. The tune is seriously now getting action in the country and pop markets and the boys hand it a powerful rendition, full of feeling and spark by the fine lead singer. This could be a big, big hit!" The Orioles, like the Ravens, would soon be displaced by the newer groups who had used the two trailblazers as models. Til put together new Orioles units in 1945, 1952, and 1971, but never with the success of the earlier groups.

The Pre-Doo Wop Vocal Groups

Group Name	Comments	Key Recording	Label	Year
Baslin Street Boys	Lead Singer Ormond Wilson	I Sold My Heart to the Junkman	Exclusive	1946
Beavers	Also recorded as Hamptones of Lionel Hampton's band	That Lucky Old Sun	Sittin' In	1949
Blenders	Leader Ollie Jones, original tenor lead of Ravens in 1946	I'm So Crazy for Love	Decca	1950
Brown Data	Deek Watson, original Ink Spots tenor	For Sentimental Reasons	Manor	1945
Four Tunes	Forced to change name from Sentimentalists by Tommy Dorsey; chose new name because they had only 4 tunes in repertoire	Do I Worry	RCA	1950
Charioteers	Lead singer Billy Williams	A Kiss and a Rose	Columbia	1949
Deep River Boys	Theater & radio success	A Recess in Heaven	RCA	1948
Delta Rhythm Boys	Appeared in 15 motion pictures	Just A-Sittin' and A-Rockin'	Decca	1945
Dixie Hummingbirds	Best-known gospel group (Ira Tucker)	Joshua Journied to Jericho	Decca	1939
Five Blind Boys of Mississippi	Archie Bromley (ear-piercing shreiks)	Our Father	Peacock	1950
Five Red Caps	Multi-talented instrumentalists-dance-comics led by Steve Gibson	I've Learned a Lesson I'll Never Forget	Beacon	1944
Four Knights	Genie Afford (lead & whistler)	Just in Case You Change	Decca	1946
Four Vagabonds	Midwest radio regulars mid-1930s and 1940s	It Can't Be Wrong	Bluebird	1943
Golden Gate Quartet	Most popular of the Jubilee quartets (secularized form of church music)	Shadrack	Columbia	1947
Mariners	Racially integrated; 7 years on Arthur Godfrey's radio show	Sometime	Columbia	1950
Pilgrim Travelers	Gospel group; Lou Rawls a member	Standing on the Highway	Big Town	1948
Soul Stirrers	R.H. Harris; later Sam Cooke	By and By	Specialty	1950
Swan Silvertones	Paul Simon's songs: Bridge Over Troubled Water and Loves Me Like a Rock (both drew inspiration from Mary, Don't You Weep)	Mary Don't You Weep	Specialty	1955

Courtesy Jazziz

During the 1990s, a number of vocal rhythm and blues groups have harkened back to the doo wop days of yore. James Jones, writing in *USA Today* on June 27, 1994, claimed that doo wop and male group vocalizing really hadn't changed that much in forty years. He cites the group Take 6 as the leading force in a movement of group singing that doesn't simply replicate older doo wop hits, but, rather, continues the legacy with original material. Jones writes, "Just as hordes of doo woppers dominated the 1950s, a stampede of male groups has emerged today: Silk, Shai, Hi-Five, Intro, Funky Poets, Jodeci, Portrait, H-Town, Color Me Badd and the popular Boyz II Men. The trend shows no signs of abating as All-4-One's 'I Swear' tops the pop singles list a third week. "People have 'a natural attraction to male groups,' says Take 6's Mark Kibble. 'We jumped into it when no one else did. Now the record companies realize it and are signing groups right and left.' However, such groups differ from Take 6, borrowing more from rap. Boyz and Color have even called themselves doo-wop hip-hoppers. 'The thing now is to be hard,' Kibble says, 'but it's still a male vocal thing.' In the same way, 1950s male groups 'rode the crest of the rock'n'roll wave throughout the mid- to late 1950s,' scholar Bob Hyde writes in *The Doo Wop Box's* liner notes."

Chapter 13

COUNTRY AND WESTERN

Library of Congress

Musical star Jimmie Davis (fourth from the left) was also two-time governor of Louisiana. Here he stands with Adolph Hofner (fourth from the right) and his group, the Pearl Beer Wranglers.

Country music became much more popular between 1935 and 1950 than it had been in the period 1917-34. The music also broke into more specific geographic styles and factions—bluegrass, the singing cowboys, western swing, honky tonk, and the urban folk movement. The roots of these styles and factions were all evident in the early period of the "old timey" or "hillbilly" movement, but they blossomed after 1935. In the 1940s, a jigsaw puzzle of activity throughout the states resulted in a staggering burst of creativity in country music. *Billboard* began charting the hits of country music for the first time in January 1944. The first chart title used was "Most Played Juke Box Records." From September to November 1947, the title was changed to "Most Played Juke Box Hillbilly Records." The magazine then returned to the initial title until June 25, 1949, when for the first time "country and western" was used—"Most Played Juke Box (Country & Western) Records."

Country music's *retail* sales were tracked separately. *Billboard*'s first such chart, inaugurated in May 1948, was called "Best Selling Retail Folk Records," which changed on June 25, 1949, to "Best Selling Retail Folk (Country & Western) Records." The reference to "Folk" is notable, as is the use of "Western" in these charts. Country, hillbilly and folk were all synonymous during this time. As we shall see, folk will begin to take on a new meaning by the late 1940s and will be viewed as a separate form by the 1950s and 1960s because of the urbanization and politicization of the form initiated by Leadbelly, Woody Guthrie, Pete Seeger, and their followers. The impact of the West, as in "Western," reflects the break from the earlier dominance of the Southeastern forms of hillbilly. These developing music forms can be put into a more cohesive perspective by beginning with the evolution of the Southeastern forms, then highlighting the emergence of the westernization process, and concluding with the birth of the urban folk movement.

The Southeastern Continuum: Mountaineers

Perhaps Douglas Green was right when he theorized that by the early thirties, country music was made up of four basic styles: 1) the fiddle or string bands, 2) the solo singers, 3) followers of the Carter Family, and 4) followers of Jimmie Rodgers.

Musical Mountaineers of the Southeast

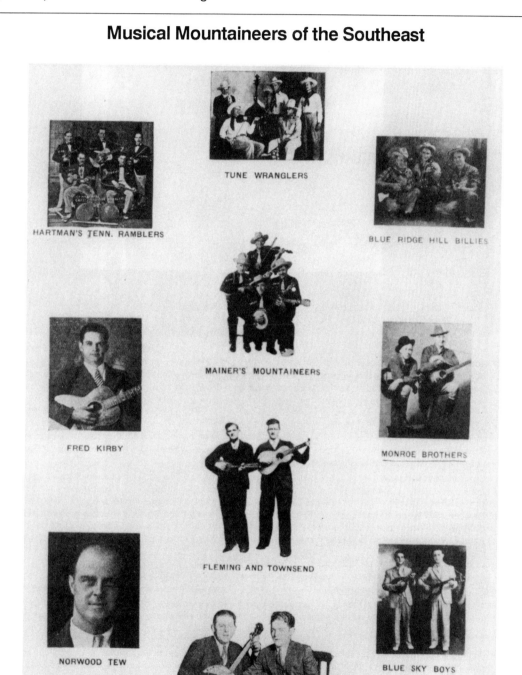

Southern Folklife Collection, University of North Carolina

A bevy of string bands, duos, and solo artists from a 1930s record company advertisement. In the mix are a few of the greatest brother groups in country history: Mainer's Mountaineers, the Allen Brothers, the Monroe Brothers, and the Blue Sky Boys.

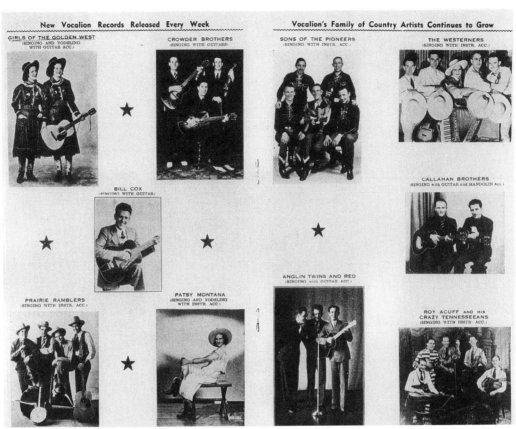

Southern Folklife Collection, University of North Carolina

The musical mountaineers and the singing cowboys and cowgirls. The 1930s was a period rife with brother groups that sang high harmony sounds. Of the Crowder Brothers and Anglin Twins there is little information. The Callahan Brothers hailed from North Carolina, and both Homer and Walter played guitar in the early 1920s. By the late 1930s, they changed their first names to Bill and Joe, and Bill switched to mandolin. Like many of the units of their time they performed for a multitude of radio stations throughout the South: WHAS in Louisville, Kentucky; WWVA in Wheeling, West Virginia; WLW in Cincinnati, Ohio; KVOO in Tulsa, Oklahoma; KRLD in Dallas, Texas; KWFT in Wichita Falls, Texas. Although they were tremendously popular in the western states (they sold great numbers of their own songbooks), the Callahan Brothers were essentially a southeastern mountaineer duo that sang music rooted in the past. Selections included novelty rhythm numbers, as well as older standards such as "Banks of the Ohio" and "House of the Rising Sun," which they called "Rounder's Luck."

Bill Cox was a solo star who sang a variety of tunes inspired by Jimmie Rodgers. He was also a songwriter of note: "Sparkling Brown Eyes" and "Filipino Baby" became country standards. Billed the "Dixie Songbird," Cox was known for his political songs, such as " Franklin Roosevelt's Back Again," "NRA Blues," and "The Democratic Donkey Is in His Stall Again." The final southeastern representative group of note is an early Roy Acuff assemblage called the Crazy Tennesseeans. The Hawaiian sounds of the dobro were always an important part of Acuff's music. At the bottom right we can see Acuff's first dobro player, James Clell Summey, who later went on to greater fame as a cornball comedian known as Cousin Jody. Summey was replaced by Beecher Kirby ("Oswald") in 1938.

The Southwest is amply represented in this advertisement, first with a group of western stars from the "National Barn Dance": the Prairie Ramblers, Patsy Montana, the Girls of the Golden West, and the Westerners. All of these artists are covered in Chapter 7 to show the existence of western influences before the explosion in the popularity of the singing cowboy after 1934. The careers of Patsy Montana, her backup group, the Prairie Ramblers, the Girls of the Golden West, and Louise Massey and the Westerners gained even greater momentum with the advent of the singing cowboys on the silver screen. The Prairie Ramblers progressed from a group that played southeastern mountain music, featuring string band classics such as "Shady Grove," to that of a western swing operation. The group was originally named the Kentucky Ramblers, but when they joined the "National Barn Dance" and backed cowgirl singer Patsy Montana, they took on the more western-sounding name of the Prairie Ramblers. The Ramblers remained with the "National Barn Dance" from 1932 to 1955, and the group was considered one of the most accomplished western bands of its time. The Ramblers recorded a number of risque songs under the name of the Sweet Violet Boys. Patsy Montana recorded with the Prairie Ramblers between 1934 and 1952. Her classic "I Want to Be a Cowboy's Sweetheart" was released in 1935 and Montana went on to become, along with Dale Evans, the best-known cowgirl in the world. Both the Girls of the Golden West and Louise Massey and the Westerners had long careers as western stars. Massey and her family unit had bigger hits, and "The Honey Song" and "My Adobe Hacienda" became classics. No western group produced more classics than the Sons of the Pioneers (more on them later). One of the founding members of this group, Leonard Sly, is seen seated to the left. Sly formed the Pioneers with Bob Nolan and Tim Spencer, singing with them in a couple of singing cowboy films. Sly later changed his name to Dick Weston, and then to Roy Rogers.

444

As detailed in Chapter 7, Bill Malone theorizes that the early country music entertainment axis partnered willingly with northern recording agents, publicists, and Tin Pan Alley tunesmiths in establishing a misty-eyed, nostalgic image of the mythic South. In *Singing Cowboys and Musical Mountaineers: Southern Culture and the Roots of Country Music*, Malone presents a tidy similarity between the musicians of the Southeast and the West. In each area, he contends, the artists dressed and performed in a manner that allowed themselves to represent a mythical land.

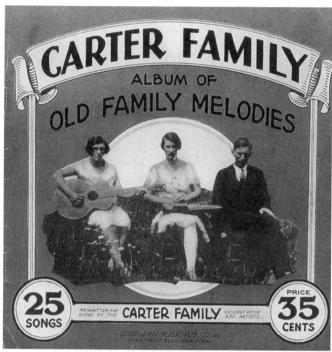

Southern Folklife Collection, University of North Carolina

Another example of a group covered in Chapter 7's discussion of early country whose career extended into the late 1930s and beyond. According to John Atkins, writing in his *Stars of Country Music,* "The Carter Family's most popular period with today's musicologists [were] their sessions with Decca, from June, 1936 to June, 1938. Maybelle's guitar picking was now at its very sharpest, and Sara and Maybelle had perfected their duet singing, with Maybelle's sympathetic harmony providing the perfect foil for Sara's rich lead. The songs the Carter Family sang during this period were also more interesting, again covering all possibilities, from spirituals ('Honey in the Rock') through blues ('Coal Miner's Blues') to railroading songs ('Jim Bloake's Message' and 'Reckless Motorman'). Lyrically, too, the Decca recordings were more ambitious, and certainly A.P. had matured as a composer."

During the late 1930s the Carters moved west, where they performed on the powerful border stations (XEG, XENT, XERA), but by 1943, then working together on WBT in Charlotte, North Carolina, they disbanded.

Maybelle formed a group with her three daughters, appearing as Mother Maybelle and the Carter Sisters, eventually landing a coveted spot on the "Grand Ole Opry." By 1952 A. P. Carter brought together his son Joe, daughter Janette, and ex-wife Sara to form a reconstituted Carter Family, sometimes billed as the A. P. Carter Family.

Atkins concludes: "Today the Carter Family's music enjoys a wider audience than ever before. Their music and style have survived analysis; their lives, both public and private, have been laid bare for all to see. But even before these words and many other similar treatises were written, it has always been there for inspiration and analysis, because *everything* the Carter Family ever did, *everything* they ever were, is captured on the wonderful legacy of recordings they have willed to the world at large, and to country music for all time."

"Until the neutral and relatively respectable term 'country' won general usage in the mid-1940s, the musicians and their promoters resorted most often to the exploitation of images surrounding two of America's most romantic groups: moutaineers and cowboys. Mountaineers and cowboys were not simply colorful and exotic: they were vivid reminders of frontier America and of the allegedly individualistic traits that had once characterized American life. Unlike most of the other local characters, mountaineers and cowboys had the additional advantage of being 'Anglo-Saxon,' a deeply satisfying attribute to many people who viewed with regret the inundation of the nation by 'new' and perhaps unassimilable immigrants. Furthermore, mountaineers and cowboys valued, and presumably embodied, freedom and independence; both were heroic and fearless; both preserved those traits that had ensured survival on the frontier and that were distinctive and defining ingredients of American life. Cowboys and mountaineers, in short, were profoundly American."

The Depression deeply hindered the record industry, as we have seen, but for most country performers, radio and public appearances were more important ways of making money. Very few country artists were able to make much money from record sales because they were paid a flat fee for each side (much as the "race" artists were), and, unlike the Carter Family and Jimmie Rodgers, most didn't receive royalties. Regional radio shows not only allowed the country performer a chance to be heard on a regular basis, but also provided an opportunity to advertise where and when they would be playing in the coming weeks.

Southern Folklife Collection, University of North Carolina

Barn dance stars. Independent country music radio shows as well as the more formalized weekend barn dance shows dispensed mountaineer music throughout America's rural areas. Fiddler J. E. Mainer fronted one of the most influential string bands in country music history with his brother Wade on banjo. In 1932 they formed Mainer's Crazy Mountaineers (the name was inspired by their first sponsor, the Crazy Water Crystals Company).

Arkie the Arkansas Woodchopper was one of the stars of the "National Barn Dance." Born Luther Ossenbrink, Arkie wore a cowboy hat, a lumberjack shirt, riding breeches, and hightopped boots. Ossenbrink was a member of a number of various shows on station WLS from 1929 to 1960.

The bottom photos represent stars from WSM's "Grand Ole Opry" in Nashville, Tennessee. The early history of the Opry is covered in chapter 7. Throughout the 1930s and 1940s, the Opry gained greater and greater success by touring during the weekdays with a tent show. During the war years the show expanded its tours to include military bases and national radio hookups. In 1943 the Opry moved into the Ryman Auditorium, which had been the Union Gospel Tabernacle, built by a reformed riverboat captain, Thomas Ryman, in 1892. Seating three thousand people, the Ryman served as the Opry's home base until 1972, when the multimillion-dollar Opryland opened for business. Asher Sizemore and his son, Little Jimmie, sang sentimental songs that tugged at the heart. The Delmore Brothers, Alton and Rabon, seen here on the cover of one of their song folios, mixed blues numbers with novelties and sentimental songs.

Weekend barn dance shows were the most important showcase for the most established country stars. The "Grand Ole Opry," today's most famous barn dance show, reflected the popularity of most of the Southeast's biggest names during the 1930s and 1940s.

Robert Oermann and Douglas Green write in *The Listener's Guide to Country Music,* "There is no question that radio was the major force in country music in the 1930s. The Depression made the purchase of record players and, indeed, records themselves at 75 cents, a luxury far out of reach of much of country music's audience, but radio (once the set was purchased) was free. And the airwaves were jammed with country music, particularly around dawn and at noon. On Saturday nights, barn dance shows were broadcast from Nashville to Hollywood, from Shreveport to Minneapolis, from Atlanta to Chicago, and in St. Louis, Des Moines, Cincinnati, New York, and Wheeling [see the barn dance chart in chapter 7]. It was not long before transcribed shows, like today's taped broadcasts, made their appearance, presenting a live-sounding show on a mammoth sixteen-inch disc. Several such programs, most notably Charlie Monroe and his Kentucky Pardners on County [Records] and the Sons of the Pioneers, (who probably made more transcribed shows than anyone else, on [label] JEMF) are a particular joy, for they provide the otherwise unobtainable feel of live radio as it was in its heyday."

By 1944, *Billboard* estimated that there were nearly six hundred regular country radio shows in the United States (not all of these were barn dances, of course). The shows were paid for by ads for flour, overalls, farm machinery, candy bars, soap, cola, and, most lucratively, "medicines." The medicine show tradition of touring brokers selling patented elixirs was maintained in contemporary times by radio programs, sponsored by companies peddling similar substances. The most popular patent medicine of the time was a laxative called Crazy Water Crystals. The manufacturer sponsored Bill and Charlie Monroe, Lew Childre, the Tennessee Ramblers, and the Callahan Brothers, among many others. The company claimed to deliver boxcar loads of the product to stations that advertised it and described it as "minerals which are taken from Natural Crazy Mineral Water from our wells at Thorndale, Texas, by simply evaporating the water away. Nothing is added. You simply dissolve them in ordinary drinking water, and make your drinking water contribute to your physical well-being. At home, at work, wherever you are, you can drink Crazy Water, at just a few cents a gallon. From the beginning of the practice of medicine, doctors have recognized the importance of cleansing the bowels as the first step in treating almost every ailment. If you suffer from rheumatism, neuritis, arthritis, biliousness, constipation, acid and upset stomach, extreme nervousness, kidney trouble, or any other disorder brought on or made worse by sluggish, clogged up bowels, drink Crazy Water frequently, made from Crazy Water Crystals." The ads must have worked, because the company was the top sponsor of hillbilly programs throughout the 1930s.

Single-artist radio shows supported by a sponsor like Crazy Water Crystals were slotted as fifteen-minute or half-hour programs each day or once a week on local stations. A different kind of support for country music programs is described in *Country: The Music and the Musicians*: "Another arrangement, one that worked especially well on smaller or mid-sized stations, was the 'P. I.,' or 'per inquiry,' system. P. I. advertisers paid a station not a flat rate, but by a commission for each unit of product sold by the station. The more bottles of Hamlin's Wizard Oil sold, the more the station made. It was a good system in the Depression, when sponsors were nervous about committing good flat-rate money to an unproven act or singer or product. The Monroe Brothers, Buddy Starcher, Lew Childre, Clayton McMichen, the Bailes Brothers, the Blue Grass Boys, and Little Jimmy Dickens are only a few stars who at one point worked with this system; indeed, it still exists today in different forms at independent television stations and cable systems like the Nashville Network, and has helped singers like Slim Whitman [and Boxcar Willie] sell thousands of their own records. It was a system that forced entertainers and announcers to become personalities and pitchmen, and it helped define country performing style."

The string bands and solo singers that emerged from the hills of Virginia, Tennessee, and Kentucky reflected the pastoral rural connections that embodied George D. Hay's trademark conclusion for the "Grand Ole Opry":

That's all for now friends
Because the tall pines pine
And the paw paws pause
And the bumble bees bumble all around
The grasshoppers hop
And the eaves droppers drop
While, gently, the old cow slips away
George D. Hay saying, so long for now!

The "National Barn Dance" out of Chicago was the most influential country music show until the late 1940s, when Nashville's "Grand Ole Opry," with new stars like Pee Wee King, Bill Monroe, Red Foley, Eddy Arnold, Roy Acuff, and Hank Williams surpassed the midwestern champion in popularity. Of these new stars, Acuff combined three of the four basic styles set forth by Douglas Green: the string band format, the Carter family respect for "morally good" material, and solo singer status.

Southern Folklife Collection, University of North Carolina

Cowboy singers from the Southwest dominated the country music charts throughout the 1930s and 1940s. Ted Daffan and His Texans and Al Dexter and His Texas Troupers, top, represented the honky tonk music style. Daffan and Dexter, along with another Texan, Ernest Tubb, were the main innovators of honky tonk music.

Shelly Lee Alley, bottom left, fronted a western swing group called—what else?—the Alley Cats. Alley, posing with guitar, was actually a fiddler. He was the featured vocalist in his group, which played bluesy jazz selections like "Try It Once Again" and "Women, Women, Women." Alley hailed from the Houston, Texas, area and was known to spotlight saxophone, clarinet, and piano solos just like the small groups on New York's 52nd Street. The only difference was that these jazz numbers featured steel guitar and fiddles, and were played by cowboys. In fact, before it was named western swing, many observers referred to the music as "cowboy jazz." Roy Hall and His Blue Ridge Entertainers are at bottom right.

Roy Acuff (1903-1989) was the first solo star to achieve national acclaim within the comfortable confines of the traditional string band format. Mainer's Mountaineers, a successful North Carolina unit led by fiddler J. E. Mainer and his younger brother, banjoist Wade, had some major hit records in the 1930s, but otherwise Acuff was the major representative of old timey southeastern music in terms of widespread popularity. At a time when the western styles dominated, Acuff, eschewing drums, electric instruments, and cowboys, stood tall and righteous for the older, time-worn values of hearth and home. Acuff maintained that his group was "a country band, and did country music, and thus dressed like country people not cowboys!"

But Acuff was one of a dwindling few. In *Country Roots: The Origins of Country Music*, Green lists the top five recordings of 1935. All were by western stars.

1. "Tumbling Tumbleweeds"—Gene Autry
2. "I Want to Be a Cowboy's Sweetheart"—Patsy Montana
3. "Nobody's Darlin' but Mine"—Gene Autry/Jimmie Davis
4. "Under the Double Eagle"—Bill Boyd's Cowboy Ramblers
5. "Cattle Call"—Tex Owens

Acuff was raised on a tenant farm in the Smoky Mountains of Tennessee. He was on his way to a major league baseball career when he suffered a sunstroke severe enough to end his professional athletic aspirations. While recuperating, Acuff sharpened his skills at singing and fiddle playing. Soon he was touring with Doc Hower's Medicine Show. Acuff's stay with the good doctor no doubt enhanced his stage presence (throughout his long career Acuff would regale his audiences with yo-yo tricks and his trademark, balancing his fiddle bow on his nose). By 1933 Acuff was leading his own group, the Crazy Tennesseans. The group signed a record contract in 1936, and by 1938 the Smokey Mountain Boys, as they were then called, joined the "Grand Ole Opry."

Two of Acuff's cherished standards, "The Great Speckled Bird" and "The Precious Jewel," underscore his strong commitment to wholesome and morally correct material. The first is set to the Carter Family melody of "I'm Thinking Tonight of My Blue Eyes" and envisions the church and Bible as being persecuted by hostile sinners. Salvation will be found in the afterlife: "Mine heritage is unto me as a speckled bird, the birds round about are against her" (this line is based on Jeremiah 12:9) The second song was laced with heartfelt sincerity about the loss of a loved one ("God bless her in heaven").

Other important classics included "It Won't Be Long (Til I'll Be Leaving,") which preaches that loved ones up in heaven will be met when the singer joins that "heavenly band," and "Wreck on the Highway," where Acuff proclaims, "I didn't hear nobody pray" after seeing a car crash that killed people. "The Prodigal Son," "This World Can't Stand Long," and "A Sinner's Death (I'm Dying)" are representative of this strand of Acuff's music. Uplifting songs about trains, like "Wabash Cannonball," "Fireball Mail," "Night Train to Memphis" (shouts of jubilee and hallelujah abound), and "Freight Train Blues" assured audiences that they would receive a strong dose of toe-tapping numbers to shake

Courtesy Sony Music

The song that helped establish Acuff was "The Great Speckled Bird." In 1936, the song had been a featured number of a young Bible college student named Charly Swain, who had been working part-time as a radio singer. Acuff paid Swain 50 cents to write down the words. In 1938, Acuff received thousands of letters supporting his audition at the "Grand Ole Opry," and this song was the main reason. Above, one of the best collections of classic Acuff material. The best-known Acuff perennials are all here: "Great Speckle Bird" (later "The Great Speckled Bird"), "Steel Guitar Blues," "The Precious Jewel," "Wreck on the Highway," "Fireball Mail," "Night Train to Memphis," "The Prodigal Son," "Freight Train Blues," and "Wabash Cannon Ball." Many of his songs were provided by Acuff's music publishing partner, Fred Rose, who often used the pseudonym Floyd Jenkins.

During the early era of music, it was not uncommon for popular artists, who were always on the lookout for new material, to purchase songs outright and then claim authorship. Three songs that stand out in Acuff's repertoire that were listed as his own compositions but were, in fact, bought from composer Jim Anglin, brother of Jack Anglin of Johnny & Jack fame: "Searching for a Soldier's Grave," "As Long as I Live" and "(Beneath That) Lonely Mound of Clay." During the 1940s, Acuff was the best-known singer of traditional music, hillbilly or mountaineer, in the world. He went to Hollywood to make films, eight in all, beginning with *The Grand Ole Opry.* Others included *Night Train to Memphis, Cowboy Canteen,* and *Home in San Antone.*

off the sad tales of woe. By the war years Acuff's income was averaging $200,000 per year, far beyond that of most country performers. He helped initiate Nashville as a future center of country music in 1942 when he joined forces with songwriter Fred Rose ("Blue Eyes Crying in the Rain") to form Acuff-Rose, which would eventually become the most successful publishing company in country music history. Acuff attained near-mythical stature when the Japanese attacked the Marines at Okinawa in 1945; banzai battalions yelled, "To hell with President Roosevelt, to hell with Babe Ruth, and to hell with Roy Acuff!"

Roy Acuff and His Smokey Mountain Boys. Acuff wore the title "King of Country Music" with great pride. It all started during World War II, with retired Hall of Fame baseball pitcher Dizzy Dean. A national television baseball announcer who often launched into a spirited rendition of the "Wabash Cannonball" in the middle of games, Dean labelled Acuff "King of the Hillbillies." Shortly after, the title was amended to "King of Country Music."

Acuff realized early on that the men in the audience enjoyed seeing women on stage, so he added them to his act. In the picture above, there are two women in the group, which at that time was called the "Smokey Mountain Boys and Girls," later altered to "Smokey Mountain Boys." The most successful "Smokey Mountain Girl" was Rachel Veach, who joined the band as a banjoist in 1939. Some members of the audience wrote in complaining about a women traveling with a group of men, so Veach was made part of a brother and sister act, with dobro player Beecher "Pete" Kirby (who later became known as Bashful Brother Oswald) becoming the brother. The two of them were dressed as country bumpkins with their front teeth blackened out, and they immediately became comic stars. Acuff was the main reason for the beginning of the ascendency of the "Grand Ole Opry" to national fame. His emergence as the star of the Opry led R. J. Reynolds Tobacco Company to sponsor the broadcast of a half-hour national hookup on the NBC network in 1939. It was billed as "The Prince Albert Show," Roy hosted, and the fortunes of the local barn dance show improved with each passing year.

Eddy Arnold (1918-) was a different kind of musician. During his early years, Arnold projected the rustic image of the Tennessee mountaineer spirit. He was nicknamed "The Tennessee Plowboy," and his singing featured a high, plaintive vocal style. By late 1943 Arnold was ready to quit as a sideman with Pee Wee King's Golden West Cowboys. As we have seen before, once certain sidemen received a big audience response and built up their confidence, that often meant it was time to begin a solo career, or start a band of their own. Arnold began recording as an independent artist for RCA, and he was managed by Colonel Tom Parker, who would later manage Hank Snow and Elvis Presley for the same record company. Arnold's recordings for RCA between 1945 and 1955 were the best-selling discs in all of country music. Though the label inscribed "The Tennessee Plowboy" moniker on all of his records up to 1954, the singer by that time had ceased to represent the rough-hewn mountaineer spirit. In fact, Arnold's success was wholly dependent on his break with the mountaineer image and sound. The vocalist developed a smooth, pop, crooning delivery that was closer to Perry Como than it was to Jimmie Rodgers. Arnold's vocals became the hallmark of the "Nashville Pop Sound" that

450

emerged during the 1950s and 1960s. Bob Millard, writing in *Country Music: 70 Years of America's Favorite Music*, notes that by 1948, Arnold decided to leave the "Grand Ole Opry" because of the rule that all contractees must perform at the Opry on Saturday night (which in most areas of the music business is the biggest financial "take" evening of the week). Millard concludes, "Arnold had his own daily syndicated radio program sponsored by Purina Mills (proving his continued popularity with rural audiences despite his emerging crooner style). Alone among country singers, he made appearances on nearly every big-time radio variety show of the day. By the mid-1950s he had, in the minds of trade chart analysts, outgrown country music entirely, though his many fans never thought so. Television in the 1950s spread his cosmopolitan country sound ever further into urban enclaves. He may not have pleased the haystack traditionalists, but his undeniable impact on country music beyond his own impressive success was evidenced by Jim Reeves and the whole Nashville sound movement of Chet Atkins and company." Arnold was inducted into the Country Music Hall of Fame in 1966. (See Eddy Arnold Chart, page 453.)

Library of Congress

Eddy Arnold: The Tennessee Plowboy, shown here during his early "mountaineering" days. By the mid-1940s, Arnold's vocal sounds were closer to those of Bing Crosby and Perry Como than to those of Fiddlin' John Carson and Roy Acuff. While it may seem a contradiction of his original nickname, Arnold's country crooning found a willing country audience, a fact that says much about his appeal. Not every country fan was drawn to the high-pitched emotionalism of Roy Acuff, for instance. Eddy Arnold sang with a warm, quiet confidence that was reassuring to many listeners. In fact, during the late 1930s and throughout the entire 1940s and early 1950s, no country artist outsold Arnold. In *Country Music USA,* Bill Malone writes, "Eddy Arnold's popularity, in terms of hit records, began to level off by 1950, but he had had a long string of record successes in the late forties. With the recording of such songs as 'That's How Much I Love You' and 'Don't Rob Another Man's Castle,' Arnold became the best-selling Victor recording artist. In one of the rare statements about record sales, Victor announced that, in 1947, over 2,700,000 Eddy Arnold records had been sold. Even without his recording success, Arnold had enough additional interests to ensure a very substantial income. In addition to his regular 'Grand Ole Opry' appearances, he had his own daily show for Purina Mills, carried on at least three hundred Mutual stations. He also achieved a distinction seldom attained by country singers, a series of guest appearances on big-time radio shows. A half-page ad in *Billboard* [on May 22, 1948] announced the following Arnold appearances: 'RCA Victor Show,' 'We the People,' 'Spike Jones Show,' 'Hayloft Hoedown,' 'Luncheon at Sardi's,' 'Paul Whiteman Club,' 'The Breakfast Club,' 'Sunday Down South,' and 'Western Theatre.'"

One main ingredient in Eddy Arnold's success was the smooth steel accompaniment of Roy Wiggins, whose modified western approach behind Arnold's vocals lent, according to Wiggins, a "sweet and smooth" sound meant to complement the singer's style. Arnold enabled a number of "sweet and smooth" country artists to succeed in much the same way that earlier "crooners" followed Bing Crosby's lead in popular music during the 1930s. Counted among Arnold's followers were George Morgan, of "Candy Kisses" fame, Pete Cassell, Wesley Tuttle, Wally Fowler, Leon Payne, and, later, in the 1950s, Jim Reeves, Don Gibson, and Bill Anderson. The last three were leaders of a style which Arnold fathered: Nashville Pop.

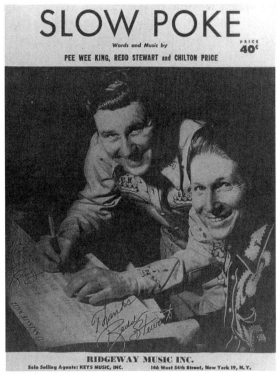

SLOW POKE

Words and Music by
PEE WEE KING, REDD STEWART and CHILTON PRICE

PRICE 40¢

RIDGEWAY MUSIC INC.
Sole Selling Agents: KEYS MUSIC, INC.   146 West 54th Street, New York 19, N. Y.

Author's collection

The songwriting team of Pee Wee King, left, and Redd Stewart, right, was responsible for a number of enduring classics, including "Bonaparte's Retreat," (which gave rise to the career of Kay Starr in 1946,) "Tennessee Waltz," and, pictured above, "Slow Poke."
Pee Wee King (1914-   ) was born Frank Anthony Kinczynski and grew up in Milwaukee, Wisconsin, where his musical family encouraged him to play a number of instruments. By 1933 ,the fiddler-accordionist joined the cast of the WRJN "Badger State Barn Dance." Gene Autry asked King to bring his band to Louisville, Kentucky, in 1934. About his transformation to a western look and sound, no doubt influenced by his stay on the "Gene Autry Show," King stated in the *CMA Country Music Close Up* of May 1976, "So I got into the Western end of the business. But I cut my eyeteeth on what they call country music by listening to a band led by Clayton McMichen [the Georgia Wildcats]." King was to become one of the new superstars of the "Grand Ole Opry" beginning in 1936, when he made a guest appearance on the show. He became a regular cast member in 1937. By the time Autry left for Hollywood, Pee Wee King had named his musical organization the Golden West Cowboys, and, more than any other group, introduced the "western" look and sound to the stage of the "Grand Ole Opry." Both Ernest Tubb and Eddy Arnold were one-time members of the Golden West Cowboys. Redd Stewart joined King's group in the early 1940s as a multitalented sideman (fiddle, guitar, and piano) as well as songwriter.

The songwriting team of King and Stewart had their biggest success with "Tennessee Waltz." In 1946 the two heard Bill Monroe's "Kentucky Waltz" over the radio. Stewart remarked that it was odd that nobody had written a waltz in praise of Tennessee. They took the melody of their theme song, which was called the "No Name Waltz," added words to it, and the "Tennessee Waltz" was born. It didn't become a hit for the Golden West Cowboys until 1948. In 1951 Patti Page, a popular mainstream singer who recorded for Mercury Records, released her version of "Tennessee Waltz" and it became the top hit of that year. King was elected to the Country Music Hall of Fame in 1947. "Tennessee Waltz" eventually became Tennessee's official state song.

Hank Williams (1923-1953) was the most influential and famous of the southeastern mountaineer solo singers. Born in rural Alabama, some sixty miles south of Montgomery, Williams is a perfect example of what Bill Malone calls the "universal tendency in country music to mask the performer's true identity under a romantic western stage name in an ersatz cowboy costume." Williams was influenced by the church music that his mother used to play for him, and by a black street singer named Tee-Tot (Rufus Payne), who showed young Hank guitar chord progressions and blues rudiments. At twelve, Williams made his stage debut singing his own composition, "The WPA Blues," in an amateur contest in Montgomery. By fifteen, Williams was working steadily as a professional musician; his mother, Lilly, acted as manager, collecting the receipts, disbursing salaries, and providing a place for the musicians to stay in her rooming house in Montgomery. Williams was reed-thin and had a back injury that made him unfit for military service and dependent on painkillers. After some years playing the juke joints and taverns of Alabama with his group, which he called the Drifting Cowboys, Williams was ready for a record deal. In 1944, he married Audrey Sheppard, who took over some of the responsibilities performed by Williams's mother. The couple separated in 1952. In 1946, Williams made a decision that would change the direction of his career: he sought out Acuff-Rose publishers. Roger Williams, writing in *Stars of Country Music: Uncle Dave Macon to Johnny Rodriguez*, relates this story: "As Wesley Rose [Fred's son] remembers it, Hank and his first wife, Audrey, interrupted the Roses' lunchtime ping-pong game at Nashville's WSM radio studio. At a busier moment, the Roses might have turned the young couple away. But they put down their paddles and listened to the lanky, sad-looking young man sing a half-dozen of his songs. Among them were 'When God Comes and Gathers His Jewels' and 'Six More Miles to the Graveyard,' both destined to become standards in the Williams songbook. A widely told story has it that Fred Rose, unsure of the stranger's real talent, sent him off by himself to compose a song, and that Williams came back a short while later with the famous 'Mansion on the Hill.' The Roses needed no such test. Fred Rose made critical contributions to Williams's songwriting career. Nashville people often talk about how Rose 'polished' Williams's material, but his influence went far beyond polishing. Rose was a master craftsman, a veritable sculptor with raw materials of music, words and music. The Rose contributions to Williams' material varied widely, because the material reached Rose in many different stages: as complete songs, as a couple of verses and a few lines of melody, as a chorus, or even less. In each case, Rose did whatever had to be done to make the song successful." Rose acted as Williams's manager. He secured record contracts from the Sterling label in 1946, and from the MGM label in 1947. Williams's first hit was for MGM in 1947, "Move It on Over."

Nick Tosches, writing in *Country: The Music and the Musicians,* writes, "Hank's music, Hank himself, really was a mixture of whiskey, lamb's blood, and grave dirt. It was for him quite natural to drift, as he did in the studio on April 21, 1947, from 'Move It on Over' to 'I Saw the Light' to 'Six More Miles (To the Graveyard).' Hank Williams was a consummate songwriter. This is a statement so obvious that it would

Eddy Arnold's Top Singles: 1944-1950

Song	Peak Position	Weeks Charted	Year
Each Minute Seems a Million Years	5	2	1945
All Alone in This World Without You	7	1	1946
That's How Much I Love You	2	17	1946
Chained to a Memory	3	2	1946
What Is Life Without Love?	1	22	1947
It's a Sin	1	38	1947
I Couldn't Believe It Was True	4	2	1947
I'll Hold You in My Heart (Till I Can Hold You in My Arms)	1	46	1947
To My Sorrow	2	15	1947
Molly Darling	10	2	1948
Anytime	1	39	1948
What a Fool I Was	2	21	1948
Bouquet of Roses	1	54	1948
Texarkana Baby	1	26	1948
Just a Little Lovin' (Will Go a Long, Long Way)	1	32	1948
My Daddy Is Only a Picture	5	19	1948
A Heart Full of Love (For a Handful of Kisses)	1	21	1948
Then I Turned and Walked Slowly Away	2	17	1948
Many Tears Ago	10	1	1949
Don't Rob Another Man's Castle	1	31	1949
There's Not a Thing (I Wouldn't Do for You)	3	10	1949
One Kiss Too Many	1	22	1949
The Echo of Your Footsteps	2	19	1949
I'm Throwing Rice (At the Girl I Love)	1	22	1949
Show Me the Way Back to Your Heart	7	4	1949
C-H-R-I-S-T-M-A-S	7	8	1949
Will Santy Come to Shanty Town?	5	4	1949
There's No Wings on My Angel	6	2	1949
Take Me in Your Arms and Hold Me	1	17	1949
Mama and Daddy Broke My Heart	6	7	1950
Little Angel With the Dirty Face	3	12	1950
Why Should I Cry?	3	13	1950
Cuddle Buggin' Daddy	2	17	1950
Enclosed, One Broken Heart	6	12	1950
Lovebug Itch	2	16	1950
Prison Without Walls	10	1	1950

Between 1944 and 1983 Arnold charted a total of seventy-six top one hundred country hits. His other number one hits after 1950 were "There's Been a Change in Me" and "Kentucky Waltz" (1951), "Easy on the Eyes" and "A Full Time Job" (1952), "Eddy's Song" (1953), "I Really Don't Want to Know" (1954), "The Cattle Call" and "That Do Make It Nice" (1955), "What's He Doing in My World" and "Make the World Go Away" (1965), "I Want to Go With You" and "Somebody Like Me" (1966), "Lonely Again" and "Turn the World Around" (1967), and "Then You Can Tell Me Goodbye" (1968).

Source: Joel Whitburn's Top Country Singles: 1944-1988.

453

not even have to be made, were it not for the mundane fact that paragraphs need beginnings. From the perfect simplicity of 'Cold, Cold Heart' and 'You Win Again,' to the accomplished imagery of 'I'm So Lonesome I Could Cry,' to the sublime surliness of 'Mind Your Own Business,' Hank gave country music its most enduring songs. Yet it was a song older than he that brought him two things he could handle no better than liquor: Fame and Fortune, those twin bitches from across the tracks."

Tosches is referring to "Lovesick Blues," which was written by a Tin Pan Alley vaudevillian, Cliff Friend, with words supplied by Irving Mills (Duke Ellington's manager and collaborator on several songs). "Lovesick Blues" was the song that Hank Williams sang for his "Grand Ole Opry" debut on June 11, 1949, and it ranks as one of the most memorable moments in country music history. The audience began cheering so wildly that Williams did six encores. Master of ceremonies Red Foley was almost helpless trying to calm the crowd down to allow the rest of the program to continue. Minnie Pearl said of that evening, and of Williams in general, "He had a real animal magnetism. He destroyed the women in the audience."

Many observers consider Williams the original outlaw and singer-songwriter. As an outlaw, presaging "Waylon, Willie and the boys," he cut a path of individuality by following his own rules. Unfortunately, Williams drank excessively and abused barbiturates, resulting in uneven performances and an early death in the back seat of his Cadillac on January 1, 1953. As an artist, Williams featured primarily his own songs. By the 1951 period, the Roses began to convince northern music performers that Williams' songs could be popular. Mitch Miller, who was the most powerful artist and repertoire man in the business during the pre-rock'n'roll 1950s, decided to have

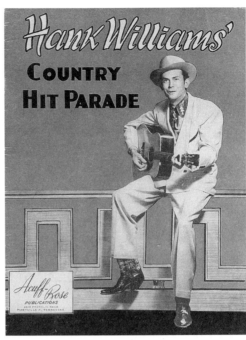

Southern Folklife Collection, University of North Carolina

Hank Williams was the most noteworthy country artist to record under two separate identities, in contrast to artists, like Vernon Dalhart, for instance, who recorded under pseudonyms simply to make more records under a variety of guises. As "Luke the Drifter," Williams was able to record non-honky tonk songs, material focusing on religious-type material. Williams's fans were aware of the transparent pseudonym, which allowed for morbid morality messages on numbers such as "Help me Understand," "The Funeral," "A Picture From Life's Other Side," "Men With Broken Hearts," and "Please Make Up Your Mind." These recitations, often featuring a forelorn, wheezing organ in the background, were a far cry from standard fare, such as "Honky Tonkin'" (1948), "Move It on Over" and "Honky Tonk Blues" (1949), "Ramblin' Man" (1951), and "Settin' the Woods on Fire" (1952).

Hank Williams: The Complete Lyrics, edited by Don Cusie, includes comments by Cusie that attempt to place the artist in historical perspective: "Hank Williams was more than a songwriter, he was a true poet. He has been called 'the Hillbilly Shakespeare,' and the title is more than an empty tribute: Shakespeare reached the masses with his words, his plays and especially his sonnets articulating the emotion of every man and woman. Hank Williams achieved the same thing. At the heart of Hank Williams, though, were loneliness and despair; even in his most purely humorous or devout songs, it can be heard and felt. When he focuses on it, in the songs that are his best and most memorable, the effect is awesome: few writers in any medium have matched his naked sincerity. 'Cold, Cold Heart,' 'I Can't Help It (If I'm Still in Love With You),' 'I'm So Lonesome I Could Cry,' 'There'll Be No More Teardrops Tonight,' 'You Win Again,' and 'Your Cheatin' Heart.' They are his best songs, his best known and his most memorable. In our mind they have etched the image of the tortured man, of the one whose soul has been wrenched, whose world has been taken away. Sadly, it is this collection of songs that probably came closest to the heart and soul of the man behind the genius."

Roger Williams (no relation) wrote in his biograph of Williams, *Sing a Sad Song*, "Why did alcohol get a foothold with Hank when it did? His moonshine rivalries could not have been responsible, not unless one accepts the theory that persons with an innate craving for alcohol are sure to become alcoholics once they taste it. The hectic, free-wheeling life of the honky tonk musician is more to blame, as drinking was a natural by-product of that sort of life. But the main reason has to be Hank's emotional deficiencies." Whatever the reasons behind Williams's drinking, they proved to be debilitating, though often romanticized (see Hank Williams, Jr.'s video "There's a Tear in My Beer").

his pop singers, like Tony Bennett ("Cold, Cold Heart") and Jo Stafford ("Jambalya"), cover Williams's songs.   Others covered his songs, as well. In 1964, MGM made a movie version of Williams's life starring George Hamilton with Hank Jr. providing the vocals (unfortunately, it was a typical Hollywood fluff job). Of special note, too, is Chet Flippo's 1981 biography, *Your Cheatin' Heart,* which faces Hank's sordid life of booze, pills, fights with his mother and his wives, and mysterious death. As a regular contributor to *Rolling Stone* when he wrote the book, Flippo was assailed by the Nashville community, but *Your Cheatin' Heart* is revealing, and its well-supported insights make it a worthwhile read. In 1994, Colin Escott, with George Merritt and William MacEwen, synthesized previous information with important new facts to come up with the prime biography on the subject: *Hank Williams: The Biography.*

Other Southeastern Mountaineer Solo Singers

Name	Born	Hit Song/ Note	Peak Position	Weeks Charted	Year
Arkie the Arkansas Woodchopper	Arkansas	Star of "National Barn Dance," yodels & ballads	no charted hits		
Cecil Campbell	North Carolina	Steel Guitar Ramble	9	1	1949
Judy Canova	Florida	Most popular radio & film hillbilly of 1940s	no charted hits		
Bill Carlisle	Kentucky	Rainbow at Midnight	5	1	1946
Lew Childre	Alabama	Hawaiian guitarist & comedian; "Dr. Lew"	no charted hits		
Cousin Emmy	West Virginia	Ruby (Are You Mad at Your Man)	no charted hits		1940s
Little Jimmy Dickens	West Virginia	Take an Old Cold 'Tater (And Wait)	7	7	1949
Red Foley	Kentucky	Tennessee Saturday Night	1	40	1948+
Tennessee Ernie Ford	Tennessee	The Shot Gun Boogie	1	25	1950+
Hawkshaw Hawkins	West Virginia	Dog House Boogie	6	15	1948
Doc Hopkins	Kentucky	"National Barn Dance" star	no charted hits		
Grandpa Jones	Kentucky	Mountain Dew	no charted hits		
Pee Wee King	Wisconsin	Tennessee Waltz	3	35	1948
Red Kirk	Tennessee	Lose Your Blues	7	7	1950
Lily Mae Ledford	Kentucky	One of the Coon Creek Girls; "Original Banjo Pickin' Girl"	no charted hits		
Hank Locklin	Florida	The Sweet Shame Girl	8	5	1950
Robert Lunn	Tennessee	Called "The Talking Blues Boy"	no charted hits		
Clyde Moody	North Carolina	I Love You Because; "The Hillbilly Waltz King"	8	2	1950
George Morgan	Tennessee	Candy Kisses	1	23	1949
Molly O'Day	Kentucky	Tramp on the Street	no charted hits		1947
Jimmy Osborne	Kentucky	The Death of Little Kitty Fiscus	7	6	1949
Kenny Roberts	Tennessee	I Never See Maggie Alone	4	11	1949
Carson Robison	Kansas	Life Gits Tee-Jus Don't It	3	28	1948
Jimmie Skinner	Ohio	Tennessee Border	15	1	1949
Arthur "Guitar Boogie " Smith	South Carolina	Guitar Boogie	8	7	1948
Hank Snow	Nova Scotia	I'm Moving On	1	44	1950
Buddy Starcher	West Virginia	I Still Write Your Name	8	1	1949
Zeb Turner	Virginia	Tennessee Boogie	11	1	1949
Curly Williams	Georgia	Southern Belle (From Nashville, Tennessee)	no charted hits		

Others soon to have hits after 1950: Patsy Cline, Jimmy Dean, Jimmie Driftwood, Don Gibson, George Hamilton IV, Harlan Howard, Ferlin Husky, Webb Pierce, Ray Price, Jim Reeves, Marty Robbins, Jean Shepard, Carl Smith, Red Sovine, Doc Watson, Kitty Wells, Slim Whitman, Johnny Wright, and Faron Young

Duos and Brother Groups

By its nature, rural music is made in the home by family members. During the 1930s and 1940s, there was a rash of brother groups and duos that featured harmony vocalizing and string instruments. The most typical setup was that of guitar and mandolin, or guitar and banjo. Sentimental songs, religious favorites, and blues made up the typical repertoire. Although the brother groups are our main concern

by family-oriented units in the Southeast. The Carter Family, the Stoneman Family, the Pickard Family of the "Grand Ole Opry" (and later the "National Barn Dance"), and the Lear Family out of West Virginia were just a few of the big family aggregations that provided home-and-hearth songs. Husband-and-wife teams such as Wilma Lee and Stoney Cooper, legendary vocalist Molly O'Day and husband Lynn Davis, and Lulu Belle and Scotty, whose large following in the Midwest on the "National Barn Dance" made them the best-known duo of any kind during the 1930s and 1940s, were three of these outstanding duos.

Unlike popular music, jazz, and, to a lesser extent, blues forms, country music had very little written history until Bill Malone's 1968 treatise, *Country Music USA*. Even more lacking are first-hand accounts from the performers of country music's early period. This makes the partial manuscript of Alton Delmore's autobiography, *Truth Is Stranger Than Publicity* (1977), so significant. The book covers the up-and-down professional career of the Delmore Brothers, ending with outlines of post-1945 chapters such as: "25—Indianapolis and the fine people up there, Friends from WLW, The Bosses, we become dissatisfied, "27—Del Rio, Texas, I learn to love that country, the desert country they call the last frontier, A heart attack in San Antonio, Texas, Leaving Del Rio," and "30—One can do better even if they are handicapped, How people laugh with their silence and attitudes, Politics, Teaching and false teaching." The last chapters were never found, so eminent country historian and academican Charles Wolfe finalized the post-1945 section of the book with an "editor's postscript" of those final years.

Truth Is Stranger Than Publicity is written beautifully and simply by a well-meaning rural musician who, by his own account, was "divinely innocent" of the dog-eat-dog nature of the entertainment world. The book is an excellent window into the world of the "hillbilly entertainer" of the time. The constant moves from place to place seeking stable radio showcases, personal appearances "on the road," recording sessions, royalty payments (and lack thereof), as well as the limited fame and disappointment are all described. As the only book of its kind from this time period it is important; as a document of a country performer who sought artistic goals, not necessarily "fame and fortune," it is both touching and heartbreaking.

The brother groups such as the Callahans, Sheltons, Allens, Dixons, and many, many others will all be represented here by three entries: the Delmore Brothers, who were the first and longest-lasting of the duos; the Bolick Brothers, who had the most direct impact on the 1950s and 1960s groups, and the Monroe Brothers, who would have the most direct impact on "bluegrass" music.

The Delmore Brothers, Alton (1908-1964) and Rabon (1910-1952), hailed from Elkmont, Alabama. They began their recording activities in 1931 and continued until Rabon's death. Like most of the duos, the Delmore Brothers mixed religious and sentimental songs such as "Southern Moon," "Beautiful Brown Eyes" (recorded as the Arthur Smith Trio), "The Wrath of God," and "Weary Day" into their repertoire. Unlike most duos, they both played guitar (the traditional six-string and a larger-bodied guitar called a jenor guitar) and placed a greater reliance on black blues and ragtime numbers. The brothers were heavily influenced by black bluesman Blind Boy Fuller. Their assured picking and singing on "Freight Train Boogie," "Peachtree Boogie," "Blues Stay Away From Me," and their signature tune, "Brown's Ferry Blues," place them in the front rank of the brother duos.

Many passages in Alton Delmore's autobiography, *Truth Is Stranger Than Publicity*, give insight into the rigors and injustice faced by the duo. For example, although they were receiving thousands of letters per week on the "Grand Ole Opry," they were still making only $5 per week each. They were taken advantage of because they were "just two country boys, very young and green and timid and never had coped with the cruel world of reality. We were living on the manna of inspiration."

Here is Alton's description of a hillbilly performer's place in the world of entertainment during the 1930s and 1940s: "In Nashville, Tennessee, in those days, nobody in the country and western field had a manager but there were people in New York, Chicago and Hollywood and I think St. Louis that had managers. The people in the North accepted country and western music much sooner than the people in the South. There are too many 'southern aristocrats' in the South. They would listen to the "Grand

Ole Opry' on the sly and pretend to their friends of the upper bracket that they didn't listen at all. Or they would pretend that the kids had turned the radio on and they didn't have a chance to turn it off. Now I hope you get the idea, because with their attitude, there was no prestige. Rabon and I played just as correctly as any of the large bands on the networks. We read music and made our own arrangements but we were still classified as 'hill-billies' by the long-nosed guys who looked down from a pedestal of superficial knowledge and preference. But nowadays, let Roy Acuff, the Louvin Brothers, Ferlin Husky or any one of the other stars of the Opry come to town and you can't get near them for the big shots who used to take Uncle Dave Macon, Sam and Kirk McGee, the Fruit Jar Drinkers, Arthur Smith and others with contempt and scorn. And I might add, also, the Delmore Brothers. The Kingston Trio are classified as popular singers. The Everly Brothers are, too, but if they had been on the scene when we were, you know what the label would have been? *Hillbilly.*

"I hope I don't sound bitter by these comparisons. It is just a means of clarifying the difference and appreciation in the changes and trends of the times in respect to quality of the performer. Stephen Foster was not appreciated in his time. Neither was Edgar Allan Poe. So I guess we might as well write it off to the strange acts of man and his seeming stupidity of presence of mind. Don't get mad, now, for I am in that class myself. What little I know was hard to come by. I had to struggle like hell to learn to read music. And anything that requires deep and thoughtful concentration has always been difficult for me. And, oh yes, I will add this as a last reminder: What was the man's name who made the long speech at Gettysburg?"

Charles Wolfe's introduction to *Truth Is Stranger Than Publicity* claims that the book "stands as the final contribution to country music by one of its major artists,

THE DELMORE BROTHERS

BROWN'S FERRY BLUES
1933-41 RECORDINGS

Courtesy County Records

In addition to being one of the most important duos in country music history, the Delmore Brothers helped the careers of a number of aspiring country musicians. Alton Delmore noted in his autobiography that he and his brother, Rabon, felt scared and isolated when they went to their first recording session in Atlanta, Georgia, for Columbia Records in 1931. The two youngsters, born of tenant farmers who barely eked out an existence in rural Elkmont, Alabama, thought Atlanta was forbidding and always remembered the kindness of Fiddlin' John Carson and Rev. Andrew Jenkins, who greeted them in the waiting room of the studio and sang along with them informally. They also appreciated the excellent advice of the Allen Brothers: make certain to have "original" material. It was the only reason the record companies would record unknown groups.

After "Pa" Pickard, of the Pickard Family, prepared them as their replacements at the "Grand Ole Opry," the Delmores would do the same for a raw but earnest newcomer from East Tennessee, Roy Acuff. "When we had finished our program, he was ready to go back to East Tennessee. We tried to get him to go on out to the tabernacle with us, but he would not go. He said he was afraid Judge Hay would run him away again. He seemed bewildered with the whole set-up around the station. He thought everybody was as friendly as they sounded, but they were not, as we had learned the hard way."

Eventually the Delmores chose Acuff to open for their show, even though Acuff's group was the weakest of four bands to audition for the slot. "The other bands had played better, but they didn't seem nearly as sincere as Roy did. Maybe that is the reason we picked him. We had known almost nothing but trouble since we had come to the Opry, and we thought we could get along with him better than the rest. And besides, I always thought the band would be better after they got used to the atmosphere of the Opry. And this turned out to be correct also."

The Delmore Brothers were among the few brother units to succeed in the pre-World War II years and then have continued success after the war, when the music changed considerably. The Delmores incorporated boogie woogie into their act and this enhanced their reputation with younger listeners. Today, Alton's son, Lionel, has kept the Delmore tradition alive by writing a number of country classics, including John Anderson's "Swingin'."

abounding

Alton Delmore. For years Alton was known to countless fans as a prolific composer of over 1,000 country songs, and as one half of the famed singing duo known as the Delmore Brothers. Alton and his brother Rabon gained fame in the 1930's as one of a number of brother duets specializing in close-harmony singing. Far more than just another duet act, they were one of the first of these acts, and they retained their popularity longer than any of the rest. They sang original songs, and performed them in such a unique musical style that they influenced generations of country and bluegrass performers. Today they are seen as a vital transitional group in country music's development; they link the blues, ragtime, and shape-note sacred singing of the rural 19th century South with polished, complex, media-oriented styles of the thirties and forties. In the late 1940's, at a time when the other close-harmony duets of the 1930's were retiring or feeling hopelessly out of style, the Delmores were infusing elements of what was then called 'rhythm and blues' into their music and had become more popular than ever. Indeed, the Delmores were among the first country acts to appeal to a wider audience; they had some of the first 'crossover' hits in records like 'Beautiful Brown Eyes,' 'More Pretty Girls Than One,' and 'Blues Stay Away From Me.' As Alton's manuscript makes clear, both brothers were remarkably eclectic in their musical taste; they were interested in all kinds of early popular music, and their broad-minded creativity helped expand the definition of country music for millions of listeners."

Significant Delmore Brothers Recordings

Song	Comments	Label	Year
I've Got the Kansas City Blues	1st record by the brothers	Columbia	1931
I Ain't Got Nowhere to Travel	1st record session for RCA Victor subsidiary	Bluebird	1933
Brown's Ferry Blues	1st hit country song	Bluebird	1933
Blue Railroad Train	Alton's tribute to Jimmie Rodgers	Bluebird	1933
Alabama Lullabye	Like 1933 "I'm Goin' Back to Alabama," a paean to home state	Bluebird	1935
The Nashville Blues	Tribute to new home town	Bluebird	1936
Don't You See That Train?	Featuring Fiddlin' Arthur Smith, who toured with them; one of their many train songs	Bluebird	1936
15 Miles From Birmingham	Original by Alton; backed by string band	Bluebird	1938
Gambler's Yodel	One of a number of yodel tunes	Bluebird	1939
Back to Birmingham	Followup to earlier Birmingham hit	Bluebird	1940
Honey, I'm Rambling Away	From their last session for RCA Victor	Bluebird	1941
Prisoner's Farewell	1st release for Syd Nathan's newly formed independent company	King	1944
Somebody Else's Darling Midnight Train	By Brown's Ferry Four: originally a religious quartet with Merle Travis, Grandpa Jones & sometimes Red Foley	King	1944
Hillbilly Boogie	Rabon's pre-rock'n'roll classic	King	1945
Freight Train Boogie	Another boogie classic written under pseudonyms: Jim Scott (Alton) and Bob Nabor (Rabon)	King	1946
Born to Be Blue	Another blues by Rabon	King	1946
Mobile Boogie	With Wayne Raney	King	1947
Barnyard Boogie	With Wayne Raney	King	1947
Blues Stay Away From Me	Classic blues co-authored by the Delmores and Raney	King	1949
The Atomic Telephone	Alton and Rabon as the Harlan County Four	King	1951
That Old Train	From last session of 4 recordings by Delmores	King	1952

Alton Delmore wrote over a thousand compositions, and Rabon a couple hundred. They were regulars on different radio stations and made personal appearances in nearly forty states. They recorded over two hundred sides under their own name, recorded as members of the Arthur Smith Trio, and backed Uncle Dave Macon on some of his later recordings. In 1971, the Delmore Brothers were elected to the Nashville Songwriter's Hall of Fame.

The 1940s union recording ban and the war ban on making records put the Delmores and many others somewhat out of circulation for a while. Radio broadcasts and personal appearances became more important than ever. It should be noted that even though recordings gave country musicians added stature, it was radio and personal appearances that brought them the greatest revenue.

The Bolick Brothers, Bill (1917-) and Earl (1919-), from Hickory, North Carolina, eschewed the blues material of the Delmores. They placed an emphasis on the somber, other-worldly side of old-time country music. Their beautifully harmonized voices created a haunting evocation of traditional mountain sounds gleaned from the Church of God services they attended as boys. Their mountain district in Hickory was known as the "Land of the Blue Sky," which led them to be called the Blue Sky Boys. Bill played mandolin and sang tenor, while Earl played guitar and sang baritone. Together, their voices produced angelic sounds on selections such as "The Sunny Side of Life," "Down on the Banks of the Ohio," "Turn Your Radio On" (their radio theme), and "Kentucky." The Louvin Brothers and the Everly Brothers of the 1950s were directly influenced by the Bolicks.

Bill, interviewed in 1976 by Barry and Sharon Poss for a record release for County Records, stated, "We were very conscious of our harmony and we strove to sing softly, which very few groups did. Most of them were louder and harsher. And we did strive to smooth our harmony down and make sure that both of us weren't singing the same part. If we have affected any of the later groups, I think it's to make them more conscious of their harmony, because until we started singing together I think there were very few duets that really had the close harmony we had. I felt the vocals were more important than the music. To me the mandolin was an instrument to use with the singing and guitar accompaniment. I felt that some little musical introduction and some little musical interlude would give the singer a break, but it could also cut in a little and take away from the singing. Now if you start taking too long an interlude in between playing, you're going to detract from the song. We never tried to make our playing very forceful."

The Monroe Brothers, Charlie (1903-1975) and Bill (1911-) were the most successful and influential of the vocal groups of this period. Born in Rosine, Kentucky, they came from a culture in which music and religion were one in the same. Holiness, Methodist, and Baptist churches held singing conventions attended by the boys, and the material was later transformed into recordings such as "When Our Lord Shall Come Again," "God Holds the Future in His Hands," "On That Old Gospel Ship," "Sinner, You Better Get Ready," and "What Would You Give in Exchange (For Your Soul)?"

Charlie was tall, handsome and outgoing, while Bill was very introverted—it is said that he was self-conscious about his crossed eyes and poor vision. When performing, Charlie took the lead and he exuded a confident stage appearance that placed an emphasis on entertainment ("I do everything that's in my power to entertain them, to make them laugh, to make them like it"). Bill, while not comfortable as an entertainer, drew from his quiet, intense nature to express himself forcefully.

Although the Monroe Brothers only lasted two years as a recording unit (they made sixty songs for Bluebird between 1936 and 1938), their impact was immense. The instrumental passages of Charlie's guitar and Bill's mandolin were intricate and played with great speed. Charlie was an excellent guitarist, but it was Bill's driving power on the mandolin that created their unique sound. The mandolin is a delicate instrument with a sharp but tinny sound. Bill had observed that in string bands, such as the Skillet Lickers, the mandolin (played by Ted Hawkins) was often obscured by the twin fiddles and guitar. Bill did not allow that to happen. He single-handedly elevated the mandolin to a solo instrument in country music. Vocally the brothers sang harmony with a visceral, high-pitched intensity that complemented their instrumental acumen. Bill's emotive vocalizing in the upper reaches of the tenor range was referred to as the "high, lonesome sound," and would become one of the distinguishing features of his legacy to country music. When the brothers decided to split up in 1938, Charlie led a successful string band called the Kentucky Pardners and Bill formed a group he called the Blue Grass Boys.

Bluegrass

"Bluegrass" is a term recognized by nearly everyone. The term, like "doo wop" and "western swing," would not come into vogue until a number of years after the movement had developed. Between 1939 and 1945, Bill Monroe and his Blue Grass Boys were quite successful. Monroe fronted a couple of different ensembles, which included, at various times, a rhythm banjoist (David "Stringbean" Akeman, who also did comedy routines), an accordionist, and a jug player who also played spoons and

Bill and Charlie Monroe were both influenced by their mother, Melissa, who played both fiddle and the accordion, and by her fiddling brother Pendleton Vandiver (celebrated in "Uncle Pen"). The three youngest of eight offspring, Charlie, Birch, and Bill all became professional musicians. Birch eventually dropped out. Like many rural dwellers of this time period, the trio took jobs in oil refineries. The Monroes did so in Whiting, Indiana, in 1929. Before becoming professional singers, they worked on the "National Barn Dance." The musical groups on the show at that time, Karl and Harty, Mac and Bob, and the under-appreciated progressive string band the Prairie Ramblers, made a deep impression on the brothers.

By 1934, Bill and Charlie became a full-fledged professional singing duo, working for a number of radio stations in Shenandoah, Iowa; Omaha, Nebraska; Columbia, South Carolina; and then Charlotte, North Carolina; where they gained their greatest popularity. Because there was little money to be made from recording during the Depression, the Monroes ignored the initial overtures from Victor superproducer Eli Oberstein. They eventually made their first recordings, ten in each of six recording sessions over a period of about two years. Typical of the recording sessions of the early period of roots, underground musical forms of country and blues, Victor rented rooms in hotels or radio stations to record the Monroes' music and released their records on a subsidiary label, in this case, Bluebird.

In addition to sweet religious songs such as "What Would You Give in Exchange?" and "On That Old Gospel Ship," the Monroes released a number of future bluegrass classics-to-be such as "Roll in My Sweet Baby's Arms," "Nine Pound Hammer Is Too Heavy," "On Some Foggy Mountain Top," and "Roll on Buddy."

Like the Monroe Brothers, the Bolick Brothers played mandolin and guitar, sang a number of sad, religious songs, and first recorded for Eli Oberstein in an impromptu setup on the second floor of the Southern Radio Corporation Building in Charlotte, North Carolina, in June 1936. In the Bluebird recording shown here, the liner notes include this description of that date by Bill Bolick: "When we walked in they were recording the Dixon Brothers, we just sat down and were listening, and Earl picked up something to read. After we had been there a while Eli Oberstein, the A&R man for Victor came back and said something like 'What do you think this is, a reading room?' or something to that effect. Earl was pretty high-tempered along that time, and he told Eli he didn't give a damn what it was! We told him we were supposed to record. Eli wasn't too congenial, and he said, 'You're the boys that copy the Monroe Brothers aren't you?' and I told him, 'No, definitely, we do not copy the Monroe Brothers!' And so he said, 'Well, just stick around a little while. And I said 'Well, if you want us to,' but really, we were just about out of the mood of making records or fooling with anyone. He was just finishing up the Dixon Brothers, so after that we went up on stage and tuned up, and played 'The Sunny Side of Life' for him as an audition number, and I don't think we had finished more than one verse and the chorus 'til he came rushing out of that little booth and said 'That's enough! That's great! I think you've got something there!' He said, 'Whoever said you sounded like the Monroe Brothers sure didn't know what he was talking about!' He said our style was much different, and he believed that we could sell a lot of records, and since then Eli and us got along real well."

performed in blackface. These early groups were much like most other string bands playing sentimental songs, religious numbers, and some blues. What placed Monroe's groups a notch above most of the other string bands of the time was the leader's vocal and instrumental abilities, the groups' extremely fast tempos, and their serious, business-like presence: they wore white shirts, neck ties, jodhpurs, riding boots, and dark Stetson hats—the band leaders looked like southern sheriffs or Kentucky planters. Later the jodhpurs would be replaced with creased dress pants and the Stetsons with ten-gallon cowboy hats. All of Monroe's immediate disciples followed this dress style.

It wasn't until 1945, however, that Monroe's Blue Grass Boys (with Lester Flatt on guitar, Earl Scruggs on banjo, Chubby Wise on fiddle, Cedric Rainwater (Howard Watts) on bass, and, of course, Bill Monroe on mandolin) created the classic format and style that we know today as bluegrass music. Vocally, Monroe's high-pitched, emotional tenor soared over Lester Flatt's lead. The banjo, guitar, mandolin, and fiddle created a unison sound in the front line that was similar to the traditional jazz of Louis Armstrong's Hot Five unit. Like Armstrong, Monroe's front line played polyphonic ensemble passages and spotlighted improvised solos. In fact, it would not necessarily be hyperbole to declare that Monroe's 1945-to-1948 aggregation is for old-time country music what Armstrong's 1920s ensembles are for traditional jazz—the high water marks for their respective forms. The changing roles of the instruments led to a continued interaction that, in the hands of these virtuoso players, was electrifying. Monroe, like Armstrong in traditional jazz, provided the vision and spiritual force for bluegrass.

Frank Driggs Collection

Library of Congress

From left, Bill Monroe (mandolin) and Charlie Monroe (guitar). **Bill Monroe.**

In his *Bluegrass Breakdown: The Making of the Old Southern Sound*, Robert Cantwell makes a case for jazz and bluegrass being connected as improvisatory art forms: "Since the early days of bluegrass, as [Alan] Lomax observed, bluegrass has not only adopted the ground rules of jazz, and absorbed its experimentalist spirit, but actually echoed the music itself. In Chubby Wise's fiddle, Bill Monroe's mandolin and Earl Scrugg's banjo, one can detect the imprint of Johnny Dodds, King Oliver, and Mr. Jelly Roll; one wonders if Armstrong's trumpet does not figure somewhere in the genealogy of the bluegrass singing style. Bluegrass fiddlers very early took the influence not only of country-jazz fiddlers such as Clayton McMichen and Arthur Smith whom Monroe cites as a major influence but of Joe Venuti and Stephane Grappelli, opening avenues of influence which have brought swing and rhythm-and-blues into bluegrass instrumental breaks. Kenny Baker [a fiddler with Monroe] cites Benny Goodman and Tommy Dorsey among his influences. . . . bluegrass, then is bound up with jazz; but *all* serious American music is bound up with jazz. More to the point, perhaps, is that the deposits of jazz in bluegrass have already entered our musical vocabulary and acquired a glow of connotation that colors the bluegrass sound. In the voluptuous glow of Storyville, the hillbilly heart song may cast an ironic shadow, while the rustic mountain breakdown, sizzling with the nervous riffs of atomic-age bohemians and black pariahs, may burn with forbidden thought."

Monroe's simple credo for playing music of high quality was, "Play it good and clean and play good melodies with it, and keep perfect time. It takes really good timing with bluegrass music, and it takes some good high voices to really deliver it right." This quote is similar to Charlie Parker's succinct appraisal of producing good jazz: "It's just a matter of playing the pretty notes."

Bluegrass's ensemble passages, its improvised solos, and its rhythmic, syncopated drive (the result of African-American influences) has frequently placed this rural, "hillbilly" creation on par with jazz. Today one thinks of jazz as Charlie Parker and Miles Davis, as a contemporary form born of the city.

But it is useful to remember that jazz roots took hold early on in the Deep South. And while a few jazz writers might grudgingly concede connections between jazz and the western swing of Bob Wills and company, because of the similar instrumentation—saxophones, trumpets, clarinets, and piano—virtually no jazz writers note the connection of jazz and bluegrass, probably because of the *dissimilar* front line: fiddle, mandolin, banjo, acoustic guitar, and dobro.

Cantwell, more than most historians, has tried to make a case for connections between bluegrass and jazz: "It is simply one of the mysteries of human communication that in aural cultures such as the African a level of synchrony operates which to the European or Europeanized American is imperceptibly profound, and thus becomes a source of considerable misery and misunderstanding between cultures and between people, especially when we are entirely at the mercy of communications made to us which we do not understand or to which we have an irrational response. A quick anticipation of actions and reactions, a close attention to and understanding of minimal cues and other subtleties of communication are essential to the success of improvised ensemble music such as jazz and bluegrass. Many of the recordings of the parent bluegrass bands, such as Monroe's, as well as the Stanley Brothers, Lester Flatt and Earl Scruggs, Jimmy Martin and the Sunny Mountain Boys, Don Reno, Red Smiley and the Tennessee Cut-Ups, and a handful of others less well known, seem to display something of the deep organic unity of the audially bonded jazz ensemble. We hear in the King recordings of the Stanley Brothers, for example, or in Monroe's Columbia recordings, or in the early Mercury recordings of Flatt and Scruggs, a solid mass of integrated sound, sharply discriminated and richly developed in every dimension, rhythmically alive and, perhaps most importantly, interresponsive in every vocal and instrumental part. That was the original bluegrass sound, which contemporary bands of every stamp are very hard put to achieve."

Alan Lomax refers to bluegrass as "folk music in overdrive," and went so far as to describe the music of the Monroes as "the first clear-cut orchestral style to appear in the British-American folk tradition in five hundred years." Mayne Smith's 1964 masters thesis, "Bluegrass Music and Musicians," and an article he distilled from it in 1965, "An Introduction to Bluegrass," presents a succinct definition of bluegrass: "A style of concert hillbilly performed by a highly integrated ensemble of voices and non-electrified stringed instruments, including a banjo played Scruggs-style." The now-famous "Scruggs style" refers to the use of the thumb and first two fingers, also known as the "three-finger" style that Earl Scruggs absorbed from other North Carolina banjoists such as Snuffy Jenkins and Smith Hammet. Examples of classic bluegrass recorded by the 1945-48 Blue Grass Boys can be heard on "Blue Moon of Kentucky," "My Rose of Old Kentucky," "Will You Be Loving Another Man?" "Blue Yodel No. 4," "Mule Skinner Blues," "I Hear a Sweet Voice Calling My Name," and "Why Did You Wander?"

Neil Rosenberg's excellent study, *Bluegrass: A History*, states, "Bluegrass is part of country music; it originated with Bill Monroe and his band, the Blue Grass Boys, during the 1940s. During the fifties it was named and recognized as a unique form, a music in which singers accompany themselves with acoustic rather than electric instruments, using the fiddle, mandolin, guitar, five-string banjo, Dobro, and bass. Its performance demands mastery of virtuoso instrumental techniques (such as Earl Scruggs' banjo style), often executed at rapid tempos. This emphasis on individual virtuosic self-expression led some to call bluegrass the jazz of country music. Bluegrass singing is high-pitched, lonesome sounding; it often involves tightly arranged harmonies. The form and content of its songs and its vocal styles, reminiscent of mountain folksinging traditions, have prompted some observers to define it as modern folk music."

Rosenberg points out that the term "bluegrass" was not being used to define the music during the 1940s or early 1950s. "Bluegrass" at that time was used solely for Bill Monroe's groups. He had recorded four instrumentals using the words "blue grass," titled the band's touring limousine the "Blue Grass Special," named his baseball team the "Blue Grass Club," and called his 1950 songbook *Bill Monroe's Blue Grass Country Songs*. Rosenberg cites the folk music boom in the mid-1950s and two young performers at that time, who also became historians, Mike Seeger and Ralph Rinzler, as defining the term and broadening the legacy. In 1957, Seeger produced and recorded an album for Folkways Records entitled *American Banjo Scruggs Style*, which included fifteen different banjo pickers, including

The obvious Scottish-British influence of string band music has been noted throughout this history of the Southeast "music from the hills." The other main influence, African-American blues and subsequent jazz, has also been noted. For Bill Monroe this second influence came by way of a fiddler-guitarist named Arnold Schultz, an African-American who loaded coal at the Horton Coal Company in Rosina, Kentucky. As a youngster, twelve to fourteen years old, Monroe learned blues licks from the elderly Schultz and played with him at a number of dances. Monroe did his first in-depth interviews with Ralph Rinzler, who was later to become his manager. He confided, "The first time I think I ever seen Arnold Schultz, this square dance was at Rosine, and Arnold and two more colored fellows come up there and played for the dance. People loved Arnold so well all through Kentucky there. If he was playing a guitar they'd go gang up around him till he would get tired. There's things in my music that comes from Arnold Schultz, runs that I use a lot in my music. I tried to keep in mind a little of it, what I could salvage to use in my music. Then he could play blues, and I wanted some blues in my music too, you see."

In an entry on Monroe for *Stars of Country Music,* Rinzler points out that Monroe and his Blue Grass Boys recorded for three major companies: Victor, 1940-41, Columbia, 1945-49, and Decca (now MCA), from 1950 continuously to the present. It was during the period with Columbia that Monroe refined the already established matrix of bluegrass music. "Three major changes were yet to come, and by the time of the second Columbia session, September 16, 1946, two of these were realized. First was the deletion of the accordion, which never was to return, and second was the addition of the driving, three-finger banjo style introduced by Earl Scruggs and never to be deleted. From December 1945 until February 1948, Earl performed with the Blue Grass Boys. Lester Flatt, who had been with Bill prior to Earl's coming, remained with Monroe until March of 1948. It was this group, including Chubby Wise on fiddle and Howard Watts ('Cedric Rainwater') on bass, that defined bluegrass style and instrumental techniques. Flatt was given to songwriting, and both he and Monroe helped produce the first body of original bluegrass repertoire, most of which continues to be performed and recorded by groups in the United States and abroad. The favorites from that period include 'Will You Be Loving Another Man,' 'Sweetheart You Done Me Wrong,' 'The Wicked Path of Sin,' 'I'm Going Back to Ole Kentucky,' 'Blue Moon of Kentucky,' 'Toy Heart,' 'My Rose of Old Kentucky' and 'I Hear a Sweet Voice Calling.' The third change, which was not to come until after Flatt and Scruggs left the group, was the emergence of Monroe as the creator of autobiographical, or, as he calls them, 'true' songs. The first of these, 'Can't You Hear Me Calling,' was recorded at the final Columbia session, October 22, 1949, with Mac Wiseman singing lead; most of them appear on Decca. At the first Decca recording session, February 3, 1950, the Blue Grass Boys had a new and distinctive sound, quite different from that of the Flatt-Scruggs-Wise group. The introduction of Jimmy Martin as lead singer and guitarist accounts for a certain measure of this change." It was during the Decca years that Monroe classics such as "Uncle Pen," "Memories of Mother and Dad," "Memories of You," "When the Golden Leaves Begin to Fall," and "Letter From My Darling" were recorded.

Some other classics recorded by Monroe during the Columbia period must be noted here. First was "Kentucky Waltz." According to Neil Rosenberg in *Bluegrass: A History,* the song was Monroe's first composition, and along with "Mule Skinner Blues," it was also his first hit song, reaching number three on *Billboard*'s "Most-Played Juke Box Folk Records" chart. The "Kentucky Waltz" (1946), was also the inspiration for Pee Wee King and Redd Stewart's writing of a waltz for Tennessee ("The Tennessee Waltz"). Other important Monroe classics include "Orange Blossom Special" (1941), which may be the most-known bluegrass song outside country circles, "Footprints in the Snow" and "Why Did You Wander" (1946), "Blue Grass Breakdown" and "Molly and Tenbrooks" (1948). In 1948 Monroe featured the Blue Grass Quartet (Bill, Lester, Earl, and Bill's brother Birch), which sang religious songs.

Snuffy Jenkins and Earl Scruggs. A brochure inside the album jacket included an introduction by Rinzler pointing out the importance of Monroe, an obscure figure to the folk audience at the time, and containing this description of Scruggs: "Scruggs worked with Monroe for a short time before he and Lester Flatt, then Monroe's guitar picker, organized a band of their own. Before long this type of music was becoming popular in the South. The banjo, along with many of the 'Old-time' songs, had been revived and numerous 'bluegrass' bands, patterned on those of Scruggs and Monroe, were soon doing performances and making recordings for well-known companies."

Rosenberg points out that this was the first definition of bluegrass in terms of instrumentation and repertoire. Rinzler also brought out the fact that Monroe, not the more popular (at that time) Flatt and Scruggs, was the main leader of this music. Rinzler became Monroe's manager in 1958, and from that point on, Monroe's career gained popular momentum. Rosenberg writes, "By 1958, the word bluegrass was being used by fans, disc jockeys, record companies, and critics to describe this musical genre because they were involved in a movement which sought to revitalize a music perceived as either 'country' or 'folk' music. The musicians themselves, particularly the full-time professionals, hesitated about becoming involved in this movement . . . they were wary of being 'tagged.' The emergence of the word bluegrass into the lingua franca of the music business was the beginning of a split between fans and musicians which would widen during the sixties as bluegrass broke away from Nashville and was 'discovered' by the folk music boom."

Monroe is rightly titled the "Father of Bluegrass Music." Monroe not only created the super-speed ensemble approach to string band music and elevated the mandolin to an important solo instrument, he also created the "look" and professionalism that sustained and advanced an archaic Appalachian tradition into a modern country form. Monroe sidemen who left and formed their own groups made up the majority of the first generation of bluegrass leaders: Lester Flatt and Earl Scruggs (Foggy Mountain Boys), Carter Stanley (Clinch Mountain Boys), Don Reno (Reno and Smiley), Jimmy Martin (Sunny Mountain Boys), Sonny Osborne (Osborne Brothers), and Mac Wiseman (Country Boys). Monroe was elected to the Country Hall of Fame in 1970.

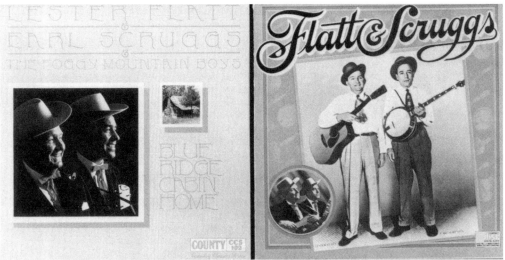

Courtesy County Records   Courtesy Sony Music

Over the years there has been much confusion about the departure of Lester Flatt and Earl Scruggs from Bill Monroe's Blue Grass Boys. Flatt and Scruggs have both said they simply wanted to stop the grueling travel and that there was no plan or conspiracy. Monroe was bitter at the move (the pair took bass player Cedric Rainwater with them) and he refused to patch things up with Flatt and Scruggs for years. Flatt's long-time friend and biographer, Jack Lambert, in his *Biography of Lester Flatt,* "Flatt and Scruggs, as well as the rest of the boys, were making about sixty dollars a week, and that wasn't bad money, with the exception of the long hours. Lester Flatt did the MC work on all the shows, while Earl took care of the money. Earl was the only one in the group that had a high school education. Earl told me that on many Saturdays, when the Blue Grass Boys rolled into Nashville, he would be carrying from five to seven thousand dollars. So, both Flatt and Scruggs could see where the money was. They knew they would never be made as 'sidemen' but as the 'star,' or leader. Monroe was making all the money, yet he was doing less work than the sidemen."

Flatt and Scruggs and their new group, the Foggy Mountain Boys, took with them much of the sound and look that had characterized the Blue Grass Boys. After working in Bristol, Tennessee, they moved on to a variety of medium-sized southeastern stations and recorded for Mercury and Columbia. While in Knoxville, Tennessee, in 1953, they established a relationship with Martha White Flour, a sponsorship that would last until their breakup in 1969. In 1955 Josh Graves joined the band on acoustic steel guitar and by the end of the 1950s the Foggy Mountain Boys had been embraced by the folk movement. By the 1960s, helped by the management acumen of Earl's wife, Louise, Flatt and Scruggs were the best-known bluegrass band in the country.

Lester Flatt (1914-1979) and **Earl Scruggs** (1924-) left Monroe in 1948 and started their own group, the Foggy Mountain Boys, which became the best-known bluegrass group until they broke up in 1969. The instrumental makeup of the group was the same as that of Monroe's, except that instead of a mandolin, they featured a steel dobro guitar (the best known of the steel players in bluegrass was Josh Graves, who came on board in 1955). Signed to Mercury Records in 1948, Flatt and Scruggs recorded their classic version of "Foggy Mountain Breakdown" as well as a Carter Family selection, "Jimmy Brown the Newsboy," and "Roll in My Sweet Baby's Arms," which was highlighted by Flatt's famous high-pitched vocal. The Foggy Mountain Boys were the first bluegrass group to become popular outside of the tight country community. Their appearances at the Newport Folk Festival, their theme for the hit television series "The Beverly Hillbillies" ("The Ballad of Jed Clampett," 1962), and the use of "Foggy Mountain Breakdown" in the film *Bonnie and Clyde* led them to become the best-known bluegrass group in the world. A difference in opinion about the direction of the group led to its breakup. Flatt went on to perform traditional, authentic bluegrass with his Nashville Grass group, while Scruggs brought in electric instruments, keyboards, and drums to play a mixture of standard bluegrass and contemporary rock. Scruggs and his sons, Randy, Gary, and Steve, became the Earl Scruggs Review.

The Stanley Brothers, Carter (1925-1966) and Ralph (1927-), hailed from the Shenandoah Valley region of Virginia. Carter played lead guitar and Ralph played banjo in a group they formed in 1946 called the Clinch Mountain Boys. Their duet vocals are considered among the most beautiful and haunting evocations of church-related mountain music ever recorded. An early member of the Clinch Mountain Boys was Darnell "Pee Wee" Lambert, who with Carter Stanley had played in the Roy Skyes band out of Norton, Virginia, on radio station WNVA. Lambert closely followed the course of Bill Monroe's mandolin and vocal style. In 1947 fiddler Leslie Keith joined the group. Keith composed a classic fiddle tune he called "Black Mountain Blues," which was picked up and recorded by others as "Black Mountain Rag."

As Jesse McReynolds of Jim and Jesse bluegrass fame told Rosenberg in *Bluegrass: A History*: "The Stanley Brothers had a great thing going there, far as playing show dates and everything. On the whole, fact was, they started the thing off wrong, the Stanley Brothers and a couple more went in there and started giving stations 10 or 15 percent of their show dates [receipts] to be on the station. They started paying off that way and the station actually got rich off it. And for a while there it was as hard to get on that station as it would have been the Grand Ole Opry. You just couldn't get on, you know, because it was the hottest thing going. That's where the Stanley Brothers done their biggest, they used to clean up there, everywhere they'd go. They'd play ball parks and things and fill 'em up."

The popularity of the Stanleys led to a record contract in 1946 with Rich-R-Tone Records. The Stanley brothers' first hit, in 1947, was "Little Glass of Wine." In September 1948, the Clinch Mountain Boys released "Molly and Tenbrooks" with a vocal featuring Pee Wee Lambert, who had assembled his version from Bill Monroe's live performances. Monroe got terribly upset that the Stanley brothers were copying his style, and remained hostile to them for years. However, the patterning of the sound and look of the Stanley brothers (and that of Flatt and Scruggs in 1948) on Bill Monroe's Blue Grass Boys, led to the beginning of the formal style that is bluegrass music.

According to Rosenberg, "The Stanley Brothers record of 'Molly and Tenbrooks' is the first direct evidence that the total 'sound' of Monroe's 1946-48 band was being imitated by other bands. It marks the transition from the sound of Monroe's band to the musical genre known as bluegrass, as Monroe himself eventually acknowledged in 1965 at the first bluegrass festival, in Roanoke. At that time Monroe was able to view the Stanley Brothers' copying in a magnanimous way. He and Carter Stanley had just sung a duet in a portion of the show called 'The Story of Bluegrass,' an illustrated history of the music that reunited Monroe with former Blue Grass Boys. Monroe told the narrator, Carlton Haney, 'You might not know this, and a lot of these folks here might not know this, but the Stanley Brothers was the first group I ever heard that was following in my footsteps on the Grand Ole Opry with the banjo, guitar, mandolin, the bass fiddle and the little fiddle. They're the first group that I ever knowed that had a bluegrass string band. I heard 'em at Bristol, and they was really picking and singing mighty good."

Monroe failed to mention that he had originally been so upset at the Stanley brothers for copying his style, that when his own label, Columbia, signed the brothers to a contract in 1949, he left the company in a huff for Decca. Monroe harbored even more serious hurt feelings against Flatt and Scruggs, who took three-fifths of his group to form their own group. He resented the publicity Scruggs received, and helped keep them off the "Grand Ole Opry" until 1955. Later, as with the Stanleys, he would reconcile.

During the 1990s, Ralph Stanley remained one of the last links to the first wave of bluegrass originators. His tight-clenched acappella vocals of religious songs continued to be one of the most moving sounds in country music. After the death of his brother, Carter, Ralph placed a greater emphasis on his solo singing, although duets and four-part harmony remained important. Ralph is captured in a series of unforgettable and highly moving segments of old-time, religious incantations in a video on the Shanachie label, *High Lonesome Sound.*

Today bluegrass is the only southeastern stringband form of country music that even remotely connects to the current *Billboard* "Hot Country." Ricky Skaggs has been one of the few contemporary artists able to achieve chart prosperity with bluegrass. Nevertheless, Bill Monroe and many of the second- and third-generation bluegrass performers have sustained themselves quite nicely due to the plethora of worldwide bluegrass festivals. There are even magazines devoted to the form. One of the reasons for the healthy state of the music is that during the folk revivals of the 1950s and 1960s, younger musicians began adapting bluegrass to their own needs. From the "hyper bluegrass" of the Country Gentlemen to the "newgrass" experiments of artists as diverse as Tony Trishka, David Grisman, and groups like New Grass Revival, Bottle Hill, the Red Clay Ramblers, the Grateful Dead (*Working Man's Dead*), and the Byrds (*Sweetheart of the Rodeo*), the music has endured.

Southern Folklife Collection, University of North Carolina

In the early 1940s, banjoist-tenor vocalist Carter Stanley had been a member of the Roy Skyes group in Norton, Virginia, broadcast by station WNVA. Pee Wee Lambert, a mandolinist and singer who modeled his style on Bill Monroe's, was also part of the Skyes unit. Lambert, Carter Stanley, brother Ralph, and old-time fiddler Leslie Keith signed with WNVA in 1947. Along with bassist-comedian Ray Lambert they had a midday show, "Farm and Fun Time," and advertised their personal appearances throughout the region. They often played six nights a week at school houses, tent shows, and other rural venues.

James Hobart Stanton, who had just started an independent record company, Rich-R-Tone, noticed the attention the Stanleys had created and signed them to a record contract. In September 1947, they recorded four songs: "The Girl Behind the Bar," "Mother No Longer Awaits Me at Home," "Death Is Only a Dream," and "I Can Tell You the Time." The latter two were quartet vocals sung in the church tradition. The Stanleys dressed and sang and played in the style of Bill Monroe's Blue Grass Boys. Ralph had begun using the two-finger banjo-picking style, but changed over to the three-finger style by the time the group recorded "Little Maggie" in the spring of 1948. Ralph claims he learned the style from Snuffy Jenkins, who also had an influence on Earl Scruggs. When the Stanleys, who called their group the Clinch Mountain Boys, recorded Bill Monroe's "Molly and Tenbrooks" before even Monroe himself, it was apparent that they were very much under Monroe's spell.

After Carter's death, Ralph carried on with various versions of the Clinch Mountain Boys, with the emphasis on his own haunting, clenched, tenor vocals. Important sidemen with Ralph's groups included guitarist-lead vocalist Larry Sparks, Melvin Goins, Keith Whitley and Ricky Skaggs (both of whom performed as teenagers), and longtime fiddler Curley Ray Cline. In 1992, Ralph released a highly praised double album on Freeland Records, *Saturday Night and Sunday Morning,* which featured the elderly master with well-known contemporary stars such as Vince Gill, Emmylou Harris, Dwight Yoakam, Tom T. Hall, George Jones, Charlie Waller, Patty Loveless, Alison Krauss, and Jimmy Martin. Larry Sparks and Bill Monroe also appeared on the release.

Left, **John Lair** (1894-1985) at his beloved "Renfro Valley Barn Dance" show in 1978. Lair, who died in 1985, was considered a "Renaissance Man." He had headed the music library at the WLS "National Barn Dance" in Chicago from 1928 to 1937, and fronted an old-time unit known as the Cumberland Ridge Runners. While in Chicago, Lair fostered the dream of "coming back to the Valley, restocking the streams, taking off the weatherboard, and reconstructing a pioneer village that would feature a radio barn dance and ultimately become a tourist attraction." The "Valley" in question was the Renfro Valley region of Kentucky. Lair's dream was realized on November 5, 1939, when he and a troupe he had assembled left Cincinnati's "Boone County Jamboree" and opened the "Renfro Valley Barn Dance." Beginning in 1942, Lair held the "Renfro Valley Gatherings," a Sunday morning radio performance of religious music. Stars such as Red Foley, the Coon Creek Girls, Karl and Hardy, Linda Parker, Whitney Ford (the Duke of Paducah), and Old Joe Clark maintained folksy, rural traditions that reflected Lair's vision. The Kentucky Historical Highway Marker Program's Renfro Valley tribute to Lair's preservationist spirit reads, "From Renfro Valley in November of 1939 originated the first series of radio broadcasts aimed at preserving the customs, culture and music of pioneer America. The Renfro Valley Barn Dance and Sunday Morning Gatherin', carried by network radio, consisted of local people and unknowns who later became prominent in country music."

Right, the McLain Family Band with Buck White on piano, at the first "McLain Family Band Family Festival," August 18-20, 1978, in Renfro Valley, Kentucky. This bluegrass festival featured family bands from all over the world, and included Jim and Jesse and the Virginia Boys, the Lewis Family, Don Reno and Sons with the Tennessee Cut-Ups, the Goins Brothers, Janette and Joe Carter of the Carter Family, and Buck White and the Down Home Folks. Bluegrass festivals are a common occurrence today. The concept of bluegrass festivals was born in 1961, when Bill Clifton produced an "All Day Bluegrass Festival" at Luray, Virginia, with Clifton, Bill Monroe, Jim and Jesse, Mac Wiseman, the Country Gentlemen, and the Stanley Brothers. From this early seedling of a one-day gathering of bluegrass groups was born the all-out, three-day bluegrass festival, established by Carlton Haney on the weekend of September 3, 1965, at Cantrell's Horse Farm in Fincastle, Virginia. The affair was advertised as "The nation's first All Blue Grass Music Festival" and officially titled the "Roanoke Bluegrass Festival."

A number of younger artists emerged during the 1980s seeking refuge in the musical past. Some of these performers linked with the traditions of the Southeast, while others honed in on the Southwest styles of western swing and honky tonk. Emmylou Harris and Ricky Skaggs represented the former, while John Anderson, Reba McEntire, and George Strait were the early leaders of the latter. Just as the neo-bop movement of the 1980s and 1990s had its "Young Lions," country music had its "New Traditionalists." Rich Kienzle, writing in *The Comprehensive Country Music Encyclopedia,* notes that, "The feeling that Skaggs, McEntire, Strait and the others were on to something grew. Warner Bros.' sister label, Reprise, signed Dwight Yoakam, a college-educated Kentucky native who made his name playing hard country in punk-rock clubs and who idolized Buck Owens. Epic signed Ricky Van Shelton, another hard country vocalist. The success of Travis, Yoakam, and Shelton, followed by the acoustic duo, The O'Kanes, and the Sister-act, Sweethearts of the Rodeo, and other back-to-basics singers like Patty Loveless made it clear that the sound had a following. Critics dubbed the music's exponents 'New Traditionalists.' Though Anderson's career flagged (later to be revived), Strait, Yoakam, [Randy] Travis and McEntire eventually emerged as major lights. Strait's cowboy hats were copied by other male vocalists, who were dubbed 'hat acts.' The success of Garth Brooks, himself a Strait devotee, and the infusion of more rock and pop music attitudes into country in the early '90s effectively ended the New Traditionalist era, while some of its leading practitioners like McEntire have moved toward a more middle-of-the-road sound. Yet Travis, Strait, Anderson, and Yoakam continue to be major stars, faithful to their New Traditionalist origins."

467

Courtesy Sony Music

Courtesy Shanachie Music

Along with Bob Dylan, the Byrds are the seminal group in synthesizing folk music and rock'n'roll as well as country and rock'n'roll. In 1965, the band electrified Bob Dylan's "Mr. Tambourine Man," which, in a sense, gave Dylan the impetus to move from acoustic to electric backing to create a form that would be called "folk rock." Author Bud Scoppa in his *The Byrds* quotes the band's Roger McGuinn, "It became just electrified folk music to me. And the Beatles, whether they knew it or not, were doing what I'd always dug in music, but with electric instruments. They were into modal music, like mountain music and banjo picking, bluegrass harmonies, and things like that."

In 1968, the Byrds came to Nashville to record *Sweetheart of the Rodeo*. Chris Hillman, who had started as a bluegrass player on mandolin (the Scottsville Squirrel Barkers, and the Hillmen) and Gram Parsons, who was also a country music devotee, were the main instigators in shifting the Byrds toward country sounds. Dylan had first experimented with elements of country music in 1966, but he featured only a song or two, and hired Nashville sidemen. The Byrds, while they did bring in a guest or two (Johnny Hartford and Clarence White), played their own instruments, including fiddle and mandolin.

Under the supervision of producer Jim Dickson, the Byrds opened up a whole new world of opportunities for folk musicians and rock performers. *Sweetheart of the Rodeo* was an historic event in the bridging of country and rock music. Selections such as Woody Guthrie's "Pretty Boy Floyd," the Louvin Brothers' "The Christian Life," Merle Haggard's "Life in Prison," and Gram Parsons' "Hickory Wind" were a blending of rock'n'roll with the high harmony vocals and twang of rustic bluegrass. Hillman and Parsons left the Byrds after this epochal album to form an even more overtly country-rock band, the Flying Burrito Brothers, in late 1968. The future "Cosmic Cowboy" sound of the Eagles and Riders of the Purple Sage, among many others, was essentially sparked by *Sweetheart of the Rodeo* and the later projects led by Hillman and Parsons, the true founding fathers of "country rock."

On the strength of *Sweetheart of the Rodeo*, the Byrds played the "Grand Ole Opry" in 1968, but they faced a conservative and hostile audience. In 1986 a sister duet team, Janis Gill and Kristine Arnold, made their duet album *Sweethearts of the Rodeo*. The album title, like the title name of the duet, was inspired by the classic 1968 Byrds album.

High Lonesome Sound: The Story of Bluegrass Music was the brainchild of writer-director-documentary filmmaker Rachel Liebling. The film was conceived in 1987, when Liebling saw Bill Monroe and the Blue Grass Boys at New York's Lone Star Cafe. She was so impressed by the show that she felt driven to make a documentary film about the history of bluegrass. In 1994 Liebling told Ann Hornaday of the *New York Times*, "I realized who Bill Monroe was, that he left home in 1929 and went on the road and that he had been doing that for 50 years. Bill's story was really the story of all these rural people who were completely uprooted from the South during the Depression and in World War II. He was the center of the wheel of musicians who founded bluegrass music and are still doing it." Along with footage of Monroe, the documentary contains brief interviews and musical clips of Jim and Jesse, Ralph Stanley, Jimmy Martin, and Mac Wiseman, early founders of the music. The film also deals with the coming of rock'n'roll and the newer performers of bluegrass, some of whom incorporated electric instrumentation, drums, and contemporary songs into the old-time fabric of bluegrass: the Osborne Brothers, the Seldom Scene, the Newgrass Revival, the Nashville Bluegrass Band, and the first major female superstar of the music, Alison Krauss, and her band Union Station.

For most people outside of the axis of bluegrass, the music is accessible only through television and film: "The Beverly Hillbillies" ("The Ballad of Jed Clampett" by Lester Flatt and Earl Scruggs), *Bonnie and Clyde* ("Foggy Mountain Breakdown" by Flatt and Scruggs) and *Deliverance* ("Dueling Banjos" by Eric Weisberg and Steve Mandell).

Female Southeast Mountaineer-Style Groups

Group	Comments
Ashley Sisters	Billed as "The Three Prairie Daisies" on the WLS "National Barn Dance"
Calico Maids	Featured on WHO's "Iowa Barn Dance" during the 1930s
Carter Family Trio	Mother Maybelle's daughters, Helen, Anita, and June (Aunt Polly)
Coon Creek Girls	First all-female string band; "National Barn Dance," 1936, then on to John Lair's "Renfro County Barn Dance" show (later called "Renfro Valley") over Cincinnati's WLW
DeZurick Sisters	Mary Jane and Carolyn, "Queens of the Yodel" on "National Barn Dance"; in 1945 simultaniously working "Grand Ole Opry" as the "Cackle Sisters";1947 Mary Jane replaced by fourth sister Lorraine; Bufwack and Oermann state that the "yodels became more complicated than ever. They developed 'triple-tongue,' 'machine-gun' yodels, gaining a measure of fame that carried them into the early 1950s."
Dinning Sisters	"National Barn Dance" stars, 1941; "The Sweethearts of Sunbonnet Swing"; numerous "soundies"; hits included "My Adobe Hacienda" and "Buttons and Bows"
Flannery Sisters	"National Barn Dance" duo from Michigan who sang home-and-hearth tales
Hickory Sisters	Pat and Lindy, stars of New England radio; "The Most Beautiful Hillbillies in the East"
Jenson Sisters	"National Barn Dance" changed their names to Winnie, Lou, and Sally to match WLS call letters
Judie & Julie	Jones sisters on variety of radio shows; hailed from West Virginia; "A Letter to Mother"
Judy & Jen	Starred on "The Hoosier Hop," "Midwestern Hayride," "Brush Creek Follies " and "Old Dominion Barn Dance"
Kendall Sisters	Dolly and Polly; most popular country radio act in Cleveland, Ohio
Kentucky Girls	Taylor Sisters, Jo and Alma, used this moniker on "National Barn Dance"
Maids of the Prairie	Faye and Cleo, a duo on WHO's "Iowa Barn Dance Frolic"
Moore Sisters	Viola, Bella, and Yvonne on New York's WOR; regional hit "Boogie Woogie Cowboy"
Ozark Sisters	"National Barn Dance" unit specializing in old folk songs
Owens Sisters	Regulars on KMBC's "Brush Creek Follies" out of Kansas City
Poe Sisters	Nellie and Ruth; joined the "Grand Ole Opry" in 1944
Sunbonnet Girls	Bonnie and Connie Linder of "National Barn Dance"; during WWII the Sunbonnets promoted the planting of "Victory gardens"
Sunshine Sisters	Kentucky's Amburgey Sisters; Bertha (fiddle), Irene (guitar), and Opal (banjo/mandolin); also billed the Hoot Owl Holler Girls, Mattie, Martha and Minnie, and the Amber Sisters
Three Little Maids	Eva, Evelyn, and Lucille Overstake; most popular of the "National Barn Dance" non-western girl groups; group broke up when Eva married Red Foley; Lucille went on as a solo star, first singing raunchy songs in 1939 ("Chiselin' Daddy," "I Married a Mouse," and "I Love My Fruit"; changed her image and name in the 1940s and was reborn as cowgirl Jenny Lou Carson ("Let Me Go Lover" and "Jealous Heart," among many famous compositions)
Three Wisconsin Honeybees	Farm-girl sisters Vern and Lee Hassel, with friend Mary Bygger; this "National Barn Dance" trio was sometimes billed as Vern, Lee, and Mary

Source: *Mary Bufwack and Robert Oermann*, Finding Her Voice: The Saga of Women in Country Music

Other Southeast Mountaineer Duos and Brother Groups

Group	Comments
Allen Brothers	Austin (banjo) and Lee (guitar, kazoo); bluesy duo famous for classic "New Salty Dog"
Asher & Little Jimmie	Father and son duo on "Grand Ole Opry"; sang rustic home-and-hearth songs and closed their section of the show each week with a prayer
Bailes Brothers	Four brothers on Opry, 1942-48, then "Louisiana Hayride"; classic song "Dust on the Bible"
Bailey Brothers	Formed the Happy Valley Boys, similar to Blue Grass Boys, in 1947
Callahan Brothers	Bill (mandolin) and Joe (guitar); started in Log Cabin Boys performing yodels, blues, and comedy
The Carsons	Husband-wife team of Martha and James; WSB's "Barn Dance Sweethearts"
Crook Brothers	Herman (harmonica) and Lewis (banjo); Opry regulars from 1926 to the 1960s
Dixon Brothers	Dorsey (guitar) and Howard (steel); "Weave Room Blues," "Intoxicated Rat," "I Didn't Hear Anybody Pray" (better known as "Wreck on the Highway") (all 1936)
Goins Brothers	Melvin (guitar) and Ray (banjo); formerly of Kentucky-West Virginia Lonesome Pine Fiddlers
Homer & Jethro	Henry Haynes (guitar) and Ken Burns (mandolin); premier comedy team, 1940s to 1960s; specialty: parodies of best-selling pop and country songs; "Baby It's Cold Outside" (1949)
Jim & Jessie	Jim (guitar) and Jessie (mandolin) McReynolds; debuted 1947; high-powered bluegrass with Virginia Boys on train songs like "Diesel on My Trail" and "Freight Train"
Johnny & Jack	Johnny Wright and Jack Anglin (guitars) formed in 1938 with The Tennessee Mountain Boys
Karl & Hardy	Karl Davis (mandolin) and Hartford Taylor (guitar); "National Barn Dance" and "Renfro Valley"
Lilly Brothers	Everett (mandolin) and Bea (guitar); West Virginia bluegrass group
Lonzo & Oscar	John and Rollin Sullivan cornball comedy, 1945-67; "I'm My Own Grandpa," novelty hit
Louvin Brothers	Ira (mandolin) and Charlie (guitar); gained early success on Knoxville's WNOX "Mid-Day Merry-Go-Round" in the 1940s; joined Opry in 1955; influence on rock'n'roll Everly Brothers
Mac & Bob	Lester McFarland (mandolin) and Robert Gardner (guitar); influenced bluegrass stars
Mainer's Mountaineers	J. E. (fiddle) and Wade (banjo); legendary precursors of bluegrass; "Maple on the Hill"
Joe Maphis and Rosa Lee	Husband-wife duo began in 1948 in Richmond, Virginia ("The Old Dominion Barn Dance"); "Twin Banjo Special" and "Katy Warren Breakdown"
McGee Brothers	Multi-instrumentalists Sam and Kirk performed on Opry from 1926 to 1960s; mixed blues, gospel, and pop with country and influenced scores of future brother duos
Morris Brothers	Zeke (guitar) and Wiley (mandolin) of North Carolina; influential pre-bluegrass sounds
Murphy Brothers	Dewey (mandolin), Fred (guitar), and John (bass); late 1940s southeastern string band modeled after the Blue Grass Boys
Reno & Smiley	Don Reno (banjo) and Red Smiley (guitar); early bluegrass unit Tennessee Cutups formed 1951
Sauceman Brothers	Another brother group that emulated the Blue Grass Boys; "Please Don't Make Me Cry" (1948)
Turner Brothers	William and James Grishaw; William had hit in 1938 "Zeb Turner's Stomp," which provided his stage name—his brother became Zeke; 1945 "Mountain Boogie," "It's a Sin," and "Texas in My Soul," 1947
Wilburn Brothers	Teddy and Doyle (guitar); as pre-teens were members of Opry in 1940
Wilma Lee and Stony Cooper	West Virginia traditionalists married in 1941; worked as duet The Musical Pals; late 1940s stars of WWVA's "Wheeling Jamboree"

BLUEGRASS CHRONOLOGY

[W.H. TALLMADGE – "JAZZ ROCK FOUNDATIONS" – DEC. '76 – 1st ED.]

CHARLIE POOLE [banjo] & N.C. Ramblers – 1925-31

GID TANNER & the Skillet Lickers w/ RILEY PUCKETT [gtr, banjo] (Ga.) 1926-'31

J.E MAINER'S MOUNTAINEERS
Wade Mainer [banjo] – Claude "Zeke" Morris (N.C.) 1934

UNCLE PEN
ARNOLD SCHULTZ (black)

[banjo players:]
SMITH HAMMET (N.C.)
SNUFFY JENKINS (N.C.)
↳ EARL SCRUGGS (N.C)
DON RENO

BILL & CHARLIE MONROE
1936 -38

The BLUEGRASS BOYS
• BILL MONROE [mandolin]
 – 1938 - 44 –
• CLEO DAVIS [gtr]
• ART WOOTEN [fdl]
• AMOS GAREN [bs]
 – 1944 –
• LESTER FLATT [gtr]
• DAVID AKEMAN [banjo]
1945-48 "The Classic Group" –
• LESTER FLATT
• EARL SCRUGGS
• CHUBBY WISE [fdl]
• CEDRIC RAINWATER [bs]

MORRIS BROS. '42
Wiley [mand], Zeke,
E. Scruggs ('44)
D. Reno ('47)

JIM & JESSE McREYNOLDS (1946 -)

ROY HALL & BlueRidge Entertainers w/ Carter Stanley (1943)

RALPH & CARTER STANLEY & Clinch Mt. Boys 1946 -

FLATT & SCRUGGS & the Foggy Mt. Boys (1948-69) Buck Graves [dobro] '55

• DON RENO [banjo] '48
• JIMMY MARTIN [gtr] '49
• MAC WISEMAN [gtr]
• VASSAR CLEMENTS [fdl] 1960-64

RENO & SMILEY Tenn. Cutups (1949)

~~~~ 2nd GENERATION ~~~~

EARL TAYLOR & Stony Mt. Boys (hyper bluegrass)

The COUNTRY GENTLEMEN (hyper bluegrass) John Duffey [dobro], Frank Wakeman [mand]

~~~~ 3rd GENERATION ~~~~
Progressive, NewGrass, Jazzgrass, Country Rock, etc.

OSBORNE BROS. Bob [mand], Sonny [banjo]

KENTUCKY COLONELS Clarence White [gtr]

GREENBRIAR BOYS w/ F. Wakeman

The DILLARDS Doug [banjo] Byron Berline [fdl]

The BYRDS w/ C. White 1969-72 Gram Parsons 1968

The SELDOM SCENE w/ J. Duffey

COUNTRY GAZETTE w/ B. Berline

also mid-late '70's:

Earl Scruggs Review
Grateful Dead
NewGrass Revival
Bottle Hill
Country Cooking

Tony Trishka
David Grisman
JazzGrass (V. Clements, David Bromberg, etc.)

The Westernization of Country

Courtesy Arhoolie Records, 10341 San Pablo Ave., El Cerrito, CA 94530

The Patek Family Orchestra in the late 1940s. This band's history dates back to 1895, when John Patek arrived from Czechoslovakia and formed his orchestra, which eventually was populated by his numerous sons. The first recordings by Joe Patek and His Bohemian Orchestra were made in San Antonio for Decca Records in the mid-1930s. By the second half of the twentieth century Shiner, Texas, would be known for two things: Shiner Beer and the home of the Joe Patek Orchestra.

The Czechs and Bohemians came to America in large numbers during the mid-1800s, in the same wave of immigration that brought most of America's Germans. Texas and Oklahoma were key areas where these Central Europeans settled and established their "Leiderhosen Oompah" bands—groups using accordions, tubas, and other horns. The music of the Central European population was often played in beer halls—places with large tables in a hall or garden setting. Festive music for drink and dancing was part of the middle-European lifestyle. The old-time polkas and waltzes were still popular in south and central Texas into the 1990s. The Czech language can still be heard in small towns like Moulton, Halletsville, LaGrange, and Fayetteville.

Bob Pinson and Douglas B. Green writing in *The Illustrated History of Country Music*, note that, "the Tex-Mex music of late is really nothing new to native Texans, and while the coming of Johnny Rodriguez and Freddy Fender may seem to many country fans as the opening of new doors and the breaking of old taboos, it is old hat to the creators of Texas' music, who assimilated long ago this Norteno music as well as Mariachi, German, Appalachian, Slavic, the blues, and many other strains to form the many thriving, energetic forms of the music of the Lone Star State."

By the mid-1930s, the popularity of music forms originating in the West was the most obvious break from the older traditions that had dominated popular music from the early 1920s. Many country and folk music purists cited the breakdown of regional styles and the popularity of commercialized country by 1941 as the end of the "Golden Age" of country music. In *Country Music USA* Bill Malone tenders the argument that this period actually signaled the rise of country's golden era. He points out that the financial health of country music was stronger than ever, due to the emergence of BMI, the jukebox, the intermingling of servicemen during the war, touring barn dance shows, the growth of folk and country music parks, and the popularity of solo stars. Within the solo star axis came the many individuals who brought the "western" style of dress and music into popularity.

The flourishing mixture of Tex-Mex music, Cajun and zydeco (covered in Chapter 4), the singing cowboys, western swing, and honky tonk were major reasons for the newfound growth and popularity of country music. Texas and Oklahoma were the primary states of the Southwest that fed into this multicultural hodgepodge. By the war years, many people from this area were drawn to California (Route 66 didn't exist just for the r&b audience). By the mid-1940s, California was much more a country music center than Nashville was. Record companies, most importantly Capitol and MGM, signed a host of country artists. Radio shows and large dance pavilions entertained thousands of fans. And, of course, there were the movie studios, which churned out cowboy films. Herewith is a brief overview of the expanding forms of "western" music between 1935 and 1950.

Tex-Mex Music

Tex-Mex, which began to surface around the turn of the century, is the music produced along the border between Texas and Mexico. It reflects the cultural influences of both regions. Unlike Cajun and zydeco, the various forms of Tex-Mex never reached beyond regional isolation, notwithstanding Ritchie Valens' 1958 "La Bamba," Carlos Santana's cross-cultural rock of the 1960s and 1970s, Freddie Fender's hits of the 1970s, and the late 1980s and early 1990s emergence of the rock fusion band Los Lobos, country fusion band the Texas Tornados, and Selena Quintanilla-Perez, the late leader of a Tex-Mex music known as Tejano. The natural border of the Rio Grande River that separates Texas from Mexico is both a barrier and a bond between the two countries. The music tradition among Chicanos—Americans of Mexican descent—is a mixture of German and Bohemian waltzes and polkas played on accordions (established

descent—is a mixture of German and Bohemian waltzes and polkas played on accordions (established in Texas), combined with backing by cowboy ranchera (established in Mexico, *bajo sexto* (a Mexican twelve-string guitar), and the brass sections of *mariachi* bands, (original Mexican ensembles, more popular with wealthier ranch or estate owners, that included bass guitarron, violins, trumpets, trombone, and flute).

Texan-Mexicans, sometimes called Tejanos, played a form of dance music that to the ears of an outsider seems similar to *nortena* (U.S.-Mexican border music), *conjunto* (carnival street bands used to support political songs referred to as *corridos* or *rancheros*), or *mariachi.* This wide variety of music, when performed by anyone of Mexican descent, used to be called "musica Chicana." Independent record companies and subsidiary labels of some major companies began recording these musical forms around 1928, but it wasn't until the mid-1930s that the first two Tex-Mex stars were brought to the attention of Americans in the Southwest.

Narciso Martinez (1911-1984) grew up in Texas after leaving Mexico and mastered the accordion in 1927. By 1935 he and bajo sexto player Santiago Almeida had a hit record on Bluebird, "La Chicarronera," backed by "El Tronconal." Martinez traveled throughout Texas and California making hundreds of records. He was a "house musician" for Ideal Records, a label formed after World War II to fill a void when major labels stopped producing regional Tex-Mex records, and he and Almeida backed many vocal groups on record, including Carmen and Laura. Nicknamed the "Hurricane of the Valley," Martinez was the master of dance-oriented numbers as well as his beloved conjuntos. Martinez had a strong influence on fellow accordionist **Santiago Jimenez** (died 1984) with whom he shares the title of the "Father of Conjunto." Known as "El Flaco" (The Skinny One), Jimenez introduced the *tololoche* (double bass) into the conjunto ensemble. Jimenez had many regional hits, including "La Piedrera" and "Viva Seguin." Santiago Jimenez is now best known to modern audiences as the father of Flaco Jimenez, who gained a reputation from his work with Ry Cooder (*Chicken Skin Music*, 1976, and *Showtime*, 1977) and the all-star group known as the Texas Tornados, which included Doug Sahm, Augie Meyers, and Freddy Fender.

Courtesy Arhoolie Records, 10341 San Pablo Ave., El Cerrito, CA 94530

Adolph Hofner has been referred to as the "Sultan of Swing," the "Prince of Polka," and a "Country Crosby." Born in Moulton, Texas, a small town between Houston and San Antonio, of German and Czech ancestry, Hofner grew up listening to polka music; but it was Hawaiian sounds that got Hofner playing string instruments. While Adolph played guitar, his younger brother, Emil, played steel.

An aspiring musician who wanted to sing like Bing Crosby, Hofner was sold on western music the moment he heard Milton Brown and His Brownies. Hofner once declared, "I even changed my style of singing to try to sound like Milton." Hofner's first recordings were made with Jimmie Revard's Oklahoma Playboys in 1936. Hofner had a taste of success when his vocal of "It Makes No Difference Now," with Tom Dickey's Showboys, was a regional jukebox hit. By 1939, Hofner decided to make a full commitment to the music business. Up until this point, he had continued to work as a mechanic. During the war years, Hofner recorded and toured as the leader of his own group. He was living in San Antonio, so he called the group Dolph Hofner and the San Antonians, or Dub Hofner and His Texans (or San Antonians). He made the change to Dolph and Dub because of American hostility to Adolph Hitler.

After the war years, Hofner put more of an emphasis on the polkas and waltzes of his youth: "Happy Go Lucky," "Jessie Polka," and "Shiner Song" (an adaptation of an old tune, "Farewell to Prague"). By 1948, Hofner's group had established a relationship with sponsor Pearl Beer, and for more than thirty years Hofner called his hoedown hipsters Adolph Hofner and His Pearl Beer Wranglers. The Wranglers produced some of the best examples of German-Czech-western swing music ever recorded. Fiddler J. R. Chatwell (second from the left) was an especially talented soloist. Hofner (direct center) was an engaging vocalist who often sang in Czech. Michael Goodwin, writing a review of a spate of western swing releases for the *Village Voice* in 1981, had high praise for Hofner's unit. "This excellent collection includes a number of classic 78s, plus a radio transcription from the '50s that's easily the best late western swing I've heard. Hofner proves to be a warm, charming performer, even on the pop stuff, and his Pearl Beer Wranglers (with J. R. on fiddlle!) swing like crazy. I wouldn't be surprised if Hofner ends up rated with Bob Wills and Milton Brown as a first-line band."

473

Courtesy Rounder Records   Courtesy Arhoolie Records, 10341 San Pablo Ave., El Cerrito, CA 94530

Lydia Mendoza (1916-) is considered the greatest and most influential female artist in Tex-Mex history. Mendoza's career began in 1928, when she played mandolin on the first records made by her parents, Francisco and Leonor Mendoza, playing under the name Cuarteto Carta Blanca. Right up to the 1990s, Mendoza has been an amazingly versatile and resourceful legend who has long been a major force keeping Mexican roots music in circulation. Preferring to play the full-bodied twelve-string guitar, Mendoza recorded solo as well as with mariachi bands, orchestras, and accordion conjuntos. Mendoza referred to herself as a "singer of the people" and was as comfortable singing to the poorest farm workers as she was singing to the wealthy. Throughout most of her career, Mendoza was billed "La Alondra de la Frontera" ("The Lark of the Border"). Today she is known as "La Gloria de Texas" ("The Glory of Texas"). Linda Ronstadt tried to raise awareness of Mexican music with a series of albums released in the late 1980s, such as *Canciones de Mi Padre*, 1988, which included a number of songs associated with Lola Beltran, "The Queen of Mariachi."

The Singing Cowboys

While the artists noted above do not figure large in public popular music consciousness, Mexican tradition has had an enormous influence in the area of cowboy tradition. The roots of this tradition were outlined in Chapter 7, where we saw the early history of the folk cowboys and the introduction of the singing cowboy on film via Ken Maynard, John "Singin' Sandy" Wayne, and Gene Autry. Beginning in 1935, the movie industry attempted to duplicate the surprise success of Gene Autry's 1934 film, *Tumbling Tumbleweeds*. It wasn't long before there was an avalanche of singing cowboys, occasionally referred to as "Lotharios on Horseback." Small film studios realized that they could make substantial profits grinding out western films without spending large amounts of money or time. These films were perfect for children who sought roughneck action and adventure at Saturday matinees, though the fact that they were willing to sit through a sixty-minute action western that stopped every twenty minutes or so for a song is probably hard for today's audience to understand. The small film companies such as Republic (the most successful of the lot), Monogram, Grand National, Beacon, Majestic, Puritan, PCR (Producer's Releasing Corporation), among others, were situated together in an area called "Poverty Row." These small companies produced the westerns for the bottom half of a double film bill—"B" films. Usually under seventy minutes in length, these films were often called "six-day wonders" because of the speed with which they were produced. Production values, scripts, and acting were often laughable, but fans didn't seem to notice.

There were formulaic patterns in the singing cowboy films that were strictly adhered to by a vast majority of filmmakers. These patterns included clean, wholesome heroes with a strong code of ethics (see Gene Autry's "10 Commandments" on page 480), fast-paced action and adventure, clearly defined villians (black hats or outfits, smoking, drinking, hanging around dance halls with tainted women, mustached), three to six musical numbers per film, stars using their own names from film to film, featured comic sidekicks, a named trusty horse the cowboy likes better than the heroine (kids wouldn't put up with mushy stuff from their cowboy stars), and always victorious heroes. With the exception of an occasional Gene Autry song, the singing cowboys and western groups such as the Sons of the Pioneers had no pop hits. But around this time, Tin Pan Alley and a number of popular singers, most notably Bing Crosby, began to "cover" numerous songs of the West. This is yet another example of how "underground" music can impact prevailing popular music.

Ken Maynard established the early tradition of western films with cowboys who sang songs and had a trusty horse (his was called Tarzan), but when Gene Autry literally "stole" the film *In Old Santa Fe* from him in 1934, Maynard's days as a premier cowboy singer were over. One of the factors that helped Autry emerge as the new leader of the singing cowboys was a merger in 1935 of film companies Mascot, Liberty, Monogram, Majestic, Imperial, and Chesterfield, all under the new corporate logo of Republic Pictures. Republic owner Herbert Yates thus took over Mascot Pictures' and its most valuable cowboy property, Gene Autry. Yates did not squander Autry's potential.

Autry starred in a total of ninety-three singing cowboy films, most of them (fifty-eight) for Republic. In 1947, Autry worked out a distribution contract with Columbia Pictures, which released Autry's films for the rest of his career, beginning with *The Last Roundup*. In his autobiography, *Back in the Saddle Again* (written with Mickey Hersakowitz), Autry writes, "By the time *Robin Hood of Texas* had reached the movie houses, I had parted ways with Republic. The courts had upheld my suit and I was now free to make my own deals, and pick my own friends. We had offers from several studios. But I wanted to form my own company, frankly, because of the tax angles. If you earned over $100,000 in those days, 85 percent of it was taxable. The only way to hang on to your money was to form a corporation. So I became the president and executive producer of Gene Autry Productions, and we signed a contract with Columbia to release our pictures. It was as good a deal as anyone in Hollywood had at that time. I had complete say over my films and I could take home half the profits."

Songwriters who were not cowboys, some of them sitting in office buildings in New York City, wrote the great majority of the western cowboy "hits" of the day. In *For a Cowboy Has to Sing,* Jim Bob Tinsley notes, "A number of eastern composers moved to California in the late 1920s and early 1930s and began writing songs and musical scores for western movies in Hollywood. Their efforts then took on added sophistication and reflected a better knowledge of the subject. Even with expanding radio programming and recordings by big bands and influential singing stars like Bing Crosby and Rudy Vallee, the nationwide introduction of cowboy songs through movie westerns, more than through any other medium, probably accounts for their prodigious growth in popularity during the thirties."

Tinsley is correct about the great popularity of the singing cowboys and the newfound acceptance of all things western by the end of the 1930s. However, just as Jimmie Rodgers had created a mythological, romantic image of the cowboy in the late 1920s for rural audiences, Bing Crosby did the same for the popular audiences of the 1930s and 1940s. He had a series of western hits beginning in 1933, with "The Last Roundup." Crosby also made an important cowboy film in 1936, Paramount's *Rhythm on the*

Range, in which he sang a number of cowboy songs, most importantly Billy Hill's "Empty Saddles" and Johnny Mercer's "I'm an Old Cowhand." The Sons of the Pioneers (with Leonard Slye, aka Roy Rogers) provided backup singing in this film. Crosby, then, must take his rightful place alongside Gene Autry, Roy Rogers, Tex Ritter, and the Sons of the Pioneers as an important factor in the popularizing of cowboy songs (see Crosby's country and western song chart on page 492).

Gene Autry (1907-) had proven himself the nation's top cowboy attraction between 1930 and 1934. Texas born, he started out as a saxophone player but preferred singing so he switched over to guitar. While working as a telegraph operator in Oklahoma, Autry was encouraged by Will Rogers to get professional experience as an entertainer. After hosting his own radio show on station KVOO in Tulsa, Oklahoma, Autry became a regular member of the WLS "National Barn Dance" from 1930 to 1934. He was greatly influenced by Jimmie Rodgers, and during his stay at WLS billed himself as "Oklahoma's Yodeling Cowboy—Gene Autry." Autry had hit recordings with "That Silver Haired Daddy of Mine" and "Moonlight and Skies" (1932), "Yellow Rose of Texas" and "There's an Empty Cot in the Bunkhouse Tonight" (1933), and "The Last Roundup" (1934).

Courtesy Sony Music

Autry had consciously marketed himself as a singer of cowboy songs before he was to find success as a film star. With the weekly promotional muscle of America's most influential barn dance show, he was able to sell his songbooks, guitar instruction manuals, and "Roundup" guitar. After making guest appearances in two Ken Maynard films, Herbert Yates, owner of Republic Studio, and his key producer, Nat Levine, thought it was time to place Autry in a starring role. The film, *Phantom Empire* (1934), was a twelve-part science fiction western. Autry plays himself, a radio personality who sings cowboy songs. His Radio Ranch sits above a subterranean civilization called Murania; Autry is hounded by both the Muranians, who think they're going to be destroyed, and bad guys above ground. Each week Autry manages to get out of seemingly impossible predicaments just in time to make his radio show. In eight of the chapters he sings "That Silver Haired Daddy of Mine."

In his *The Filming of the West,* Jon Tuska declares, "I sincerely feel that Autry's massive appeal as a modest cowboy troubadour leading a uniquely charmed life, a musical magician who could turn darkness into light, sorrow into happiness, tarnish into splendor, a Pied Piper able to control men and alter the course of world events by means of a song, is the most tremendous single occurrence in the history of the American Western cinema. Gene Autry in his magnificent outfits, yodeling a pop tune, is an image so remote from the actual man of the frontier as to rival any fairy tale. Critics of the film mock Autry or dismiss him; they try to ignore him, term him an anomaly, discredit him as a temporary lapse into lunacy, reject him bitterly, sneer at him, or are silent; but Gene Autry made more money and was more consistently popular during his time in the movies than any of his Western peers. His career was without the rise and fall of nearly every other cowboy player. The Autry Fantasy like the [Tom] Mix Legend only reinforces the fact that the Western is basically an imaginative myth."

Douglas Green agrees in part. He notes that the Gene Autry Fantasy is more than just image, engaging singing, or Depression-era escapism. In the liner notes to the album pictured here, Green concludes, "Some were bewildered by his sudden overwhelming popularity; in retrospect it seems clearer that his voice and his presence had that special quality of warmth and utter believability that makes for great recording and screen artists. In times of financial peril, threatening and hostile presences in Europe and Asia, of agonizing social upheaval, of separation from loved ones, Gene Autry's voice on record and on radio, and his image on the screen, was warm and comforting, unassuming and unpretentious, open and honest and caring. It is a magic quality which transcends technique and pierces straight to the heart."

The shift from the hillbilly outfits of overalls, checkered shirts, and straw hats to the western garb of stylish Stetsons and glittery cowboy ensembles was a distinctive change of fashion. Autry opened up the idea of the West to the rest of the nation, which had slowly been turned off by what it came to think was the hayseed nonsense of the hillbilly image. Autry's films may have been nonsensical, but they were stylish and they did introduce some fine songs.

Aided by his companion steed, Champion, "The Wonder Horse," and his faithful sidekick, Smiley Burnette (who made $75 per week compared to the star's $100 per week), Autry began 1935 by starring in *Tumbling Tumbleweeds*, followed with *The Singing Troubadour* and *Singing Vagabond*. By 1936, Autry had been featured in eight films. All had similar plots—bad guys trying to rip off hard-working citizens. Autry, Champion, and Burnette, all had a hand or hoof in dispensing with the evil-doers before sixty minutes was up. Along the way, Autry and Burnette managed to sing a few songs. For six years, from 1937 until the beginning of World War II (for the United States) in 1942, Autry was voted the top western star in Hollywood, and finished in the box office top ten. In 1942, he made $600,000, far surpassing any other country artist in combined salary for a given year. Between 1934 and 1953, Autry starred in films for Republic, Monogram, and Columbia Studios. Most of Autry's films featured Burnette as his sidekick; several films toward the end of Autry's movie career featured Pat Buttram.

Let us pause here to briefly investigate the comic sidekicks. Smiley Burnette, like many of the other partners of the cowboy movies, was able to get co-star billing and even had his own featured horse (ring-eyed Nellie). Burnette toured the country music circuit as a full-fledged star throughout his career and played the comic companion to numerous other cowboys, not all of them singers. One important source of information on the cowboy sidekicks is David Rothel's *Those Great Cowboy Sidekicks*, which focuses on the cowboy "series" (films that featured the same star character from film to film, for example, the Gene Autry singing cowboy series, the Hopalong Cassidy action cowboy series, and so on).

Sidekicks such as George "Gabby" Hayes, Fuzzy Knight, Emmett Lynn, Andy Devine, and Pat Buttram, among others, provided not only a comic relief "lift" to the cowboy films, but also managed to convey a sense of trusting friendship. In addition to the comic relief and friendship, a number of sidekicks, such as Slim Andrews, Art Davis, and in particular Ray Whitley and Smiley Burnette, provided musical numbers. (See sidekick chart, next page.)

Smiley Burnette was the "King of the Sidekicks." He made about two hundred films as a sidekick. Burnette began with Gene Autry in 1934, and made eighty-one features with him and seven with Roy Rogers. In addition to making appearances in independent films (those not associated with a series) Burnette also was featured as a sidekick in the Eddie Drew series (two films in 1943), the Robert Livingston series (three films in 1944), the Sunset Carson series (three in 1944), and the Charles "Durango Kid" Starrett series (fifty-seven films between 1946 and 1952). Only George "Gabby" Hayes comes close to Burnette in the number of films made as a sidekick.

Autry states in his autobiography that, "It was through Smiley that we established the sidekick as a permanent feature of the B movie. At least, I seem to get the credit for that. Some referred to such characters as stooges, but I reject the term. Theirs were inventive roles, relying not so much on slapstick as on timing and diversion. Sure, some of it was broad as a washtub. But it borrowed from the subtle art of the rodeo clown, drawing the angry or confused bronc away from the fallen rider. We used them in that sense to break the mood, change the pace, divert the audience."

Burnette's character of Frog Millhouse was indeed diverting, but it was also musically entertaining. Burnette's singing and playing of a variety of instruments were highlights of Autry's films. Burnette toured the South as a star in his own right, providing comic antics and playing music on an assortment of instruments he had mastered. In 1945 he had a minor hit with his bluesy composition "Hominy Grits." He recorded for a number of labels, including ARA, Bullet, Abbott, Columbia, Decca, and Capitol. In addition to performing songs, Burnette also wrote over three hundred compositions. Television audiences may recognize Burnette as Charlie Pratt from the "Petticoat Junction" show, but fans of the singing cowboy films know him as the Frog.

Southern Folklife Collection, University of North Carolina

Sidekicks of the Singing Cowboy

Name	Comments
Slim Andrews	Known as "Arkansas Slim" in a number of Tex Ritter films; his mule was Josephine; also in nonsinging series of Tom Keene and Don "Red" Barry; comic expression "Great gobs of goose grease!"
Roscoe Ates	Best known for his role as Eddie Dean's pal Soapy; facial contortions and stuttering
Pat Brady	Latter-day member of Sons of the Pioneers; Roy Rogers's TV sidekick with his jeep Nellybelle; known as the "sage" of Winston County"
Pat Buttram	Teamed with Gene Autry on radio for 15 years, most of Autry's Columbia movies, and the "Gene Autry Show" on television; on tour with Autry, Buttram billed as the "Romeo of the Huskin' Bees—Billy of the Hills", played Mr. Haney in TV's "Green Acres"
Smiley Burnette	The "King of the Sidekicks" made close to 200 films with Gene Autry (81 films), Charles Starrett (64), Roy Rogers (7), and many others; Burnette's Frog Millhouse role became best-known sidekick; first sidekick with regular horse, ring-eyed Nellie
Andy "Jingles" Devine	High-pitched voice and good-natured personality made him one of the most popular of the latter-day comics; nicknamed "Jingles"; a member of Roy Rogers's troupe 1947-48; in Wild Bill Hickok series (later on TV)
Jimmie Dodd	Part of the three Mesquiteers; later became the head mouseketeer on Disney's TV "Mickey Mouse Club"
Cliff Edwards	Popular singer of the 1920s known as "Ukulele Ike"; provided music and comic relief for Charles Starrett (1941-43), nicknamed "Harmony"; voice of Jimminy Cricket in *Pinocchio* (1940)
George "Gabby" Hayes	Along with Smiley Burnette the best-known and best-loved sidekick; bearded, toothless, irascible character actor of "Yur durned tootin'" fame; sidekick to Singin' Sandy, then Hopalong Cassidy (as Windy Halladay), Bill Elliott, and Roy Rogers (1939-42 and 1944-46)
Raymond Hatton	Part of the Three Mesquiteers; sidekick to Roy Rogers, Rough Rider, and Johnny Mack Brown
Sterling Holloway	Frail and funny redhead comedian, had a short run as Gene Autry's sidekick Po Key (1946-47)
Paul Hurst	Sidekick to Monte Hale (1946-50)
Fuzzy Knight	Called "King of the Cowboy Comedians"; musical character; backed Bob Baker (1937-38), Johnny Mack Brown (1939-43), and Tex Ritter (1942-44)
Emmett Lynn	Frail, bearded character actor with droopy eyes; worked with Eddie Dean (1945-46) and in Red Ryder series with young Bobby Blake as Little Beaver
Horace Murphy	Comic in Tex Ritter films after 1936; long, handlebar mustache and sad, droopy face
Snub Pollard	Tex Ritter comic sidekick, usually called Pee Wee (1936-39)
Al "Fuzzy" St. John	Began in Fred Scott films in 1936; called Fuzzy and Fuzzy Q. Jones; comic relief for many nonsinging cowboy series including Billy the Kid, Don "Red" Barry, Lone Rider, Billy Carson, and Lash LaRue
Max "Lullaby" Terhune	Part of the Three Mesquiteers series in 1939 and after; very talented as a comic star who did magic tricks, impersonations, and ventriloquism; dummy was Elmer Sneezewood
Lee "Lasses" White	Comic relief in Jimmy Wakely series (1944-47)
Ray Whitley	Musical shorts for RKO (1937-40) with his Six Bar Cowboys led to a couple of films as lead, but he was soon relegated to a noncomedic musical sidekick; best known for his "Back in the Saddle Again"

Also: Art Davis (musical backing for early Gene Autry films, then with Bill "Cowboy Rambler" Boyd, 1941-42); Rube Davis (Three Mesquiteers); Buddy Ebsen (Rex Allen, Davy Crockett); Gordon Jones (Rex Allen, Roy Rogers); Pinky Lee (Roy Rogers); Slim Pickens (Rex Allen); Dub "Cannonball" Taylor (Wild Bill Hickok, Russell Hayden, Charles Starrett, Durango Kid, and Jimmy Wakely)

When Autry insisted on being given a significant raise in 1938, Republic Pictures owner Herbert Yates refused and let his star walk. Yates found a replacement in Roy Rogers. Autry continued making films until World War II, when he joined the service. After the war, he continued making films, recordings, and radio programs (his "Melody Ranch" series). Autry had hit recordings that became seasonal classics, such as "Here Comes Santa Claus," "Rudolph the Red Nose Reindeer," "Frosty the Snowman," and "Here Comes Peter Cottontail." Autry invested wisely (his portfolio was staggering) and became the wealthiest country artist ever. He entered the Country Music Hall of Fame in 1969. By all measures, Gene Autry was the most successful country entertainer of the first half of the twentieth century.

Within months of Autry's first films, an onslaught of actors and singers adopted cowboy roles. In the same manner that record studios sought out crooning male vocalists to duplicate the style of Bing Crosby, and in the same way that record companies attempted to emulate Mamie Smith's success as a blues singer and later Bill Monroe's bluegrass sound, so did film companies scour the hinterlands for their versions of Gene Autry. Two months after *Tumbling Tumbleweeds* was released in 1935, Warner Brothers introduced their hope, Dick Foran, billed as "The Singing Cowboy," in *Moonlight on the Prairie*. Foran made twelve singing cowboy films, none of them famous, in a film career that boasted over eighty films.

After Foran came Fred Scott, who was billed "The Silvery Voiced Baritone." Like George Houston and Jack Newell, Scott was an ex-opera singer who braved the jingle-jangle of spurs, holster, and horse to become a singing cowboy. There were ex-big band singers (Smith Ballew, Ken Curtis), country singers (Bob Baker, Red Foley, Ernest Tubb, Jimmy Wakely), real cowboys (Tex Ritter), as well as a singing cowgirl (Dorothy Page) and a black cowboy (Herb Jeffries) among the many attempts at stardom in the singing cowboy genre. There were regular cowboys who did not sing that had their own running series—Charles Starrett, Hoot Gibson, Sunset Carson, Wild Bill Elliott, Tim Holt, and Johnnie Mack Brown, to name a few. These movies had an occasional song or two sung by a sidekick or a vocal group, but the stars themselves were action-only cowboys. One of the first of these action series cowboys who used his name from film to film was William Boyd, who was known as Hopalong Cassidy.

Fred Scott was the first of the opera-trained singing cowboys and was billed the "Silver Voiced Buckaroo." Don Miller's *Hollywood Corral* features a segment on the singing cowboys who immediately followed the success of Gene Autry. He notes that a good singing voice and a handsome face were the first things on the minds of producers trying to find their own Gene Autry-like stars: "[Dick] Foran and his later compatriots Fred Scott and Jack Randall, if they could be likened to anybody, could be said to follow the trail of MGM's blonde thrush, Nelson Eddy. Like Eddy, Foran, Scott and Randall possessed vocal equipment within the operatic sphere. Indeed, they would be entirely at ease with a robust rendition of 'Stout-Hearted Men,' but the simple, bucolic pleasures of 'Ridin' Down the Canyon' would be beyond them. However, the booming baritones didn't last much beyond 1940, while Autry, and Tex Ritter, two of the more comfortable and idiomatic vocalizers, pursued lengthy careers in the field."

Robert W. Phillips, in *Singing Cowboy Stars*, counters that Fred Scott, who made nearly two dozen films with his horse White Dust, was a "Cowboy star who combined it all: horsemanship, charisma, comedy, and one of the best-trained voices ever heard as a Hollywood buckaroo."

Southern Folklife Collection, University of North Carolina

BACK IN THE SADDLE AGAIN
From the Republic Picture "ROVING TUMBLE WEEDS"
Words and Music by RAY WHITLEY and GENE AUTRY

Courtesy Buffalo & Erie County Public Library

Gene Autry's 10 Commandments

of the Singing Cowboy

1. He must not take unfair advantage of an enemy.

2. He must never go back on his word.

3. He must always tell the truth.

4. He must be gentle with children, elderly people, and animals.

5. He must not possess racially or religiously intolerant ideas.

6. He must help people in distress.

7. He must be a good worker.

8. He must respect women, parents, and his nation's laws.

9. He must neither drink nor smoke.

10. He must be a patriot.

Source: Arthur McClure and Ken Jones, Heroes, Heavies and Sagebrush

Roy Rogers (1912-) was born Leonard Slye and raised in Ohio, where he worked in his father's shoe factory. By the thirties he was in California working as a singer in a variety of different groups: the Slye Brothers, Uncle Tom Murray's Hollywood Hillbillies, the Rocky Mountaineers, the International Cowboys, the O-Bar-O Cowboys, the Texas Outlaws, and the Pioneer Trio. The Pioneer Trio, formed in 1934 and including Tim Spencer and Bob Nolan, appeared in Gene Autry's bizarre western serial *The Phantom Empire*. By this time Slye had taken on the name Dick Weston. With the addition of the Farr brothers, fiddler Hugh and guitarist Karl, the group's name was changed to the Sons of the Pioneers. By 1935 they had signed a record contract with Decca and the next year they added tenor vocalist Lloyd Perryman.

By 1938, as Roy Rogers, Slye replaced the disgruntled Gene Autry in a film titled *Under Western Skies*. The **Sons of the Pioneers** (1934-) lost their lead singer but moved on to become the best-known cowboy singing group in country music history. Tim Spencer was a solid harmony singer and underappreciated songwriter. The Farr brothers added excellent musicianship (John Morthland refers to them as "the Joe Venuti and Eddie Lang of western music"). Lloyd stayed with the group for forty-one years, becoming the leader when Spencer and Nolan retired, separately, in 1949). Nolan was the main inspiration of the group. A devotee of romantic poets such as Byron, Shelly, and Keats, Nolan wrote beautiful odes to the West like "Tumbling Tumbleweeds" (in college he published a weekly column titled "Tumbleweed Trails"), "Cool Water," "Song of the Prairie," and "Way Out There." There were many followers, Foy Willing and the Riders of the Purple Sage the best known, but none came close to matching the movie or recording accomplishments of the Sons of the Pioneers. The group was elected to the Country Music Hall of Fame in 1980.

Rogers, the original force behind the early Pioneers, never sounded as good as when he sang with the group. Unlike Autry, Rogers had very few hits as a recording artist. But as a movie star Rogers was splendid. He was a more forceful and athletic action hero than Autry. And while Autry was away flying planes during the war, Rogers was making good on his claim to being "King of the Cowboys." With his palomino horse, Trigger, the "Smartest Horse in the Movies," and his colorful outfits (no cowboy could match Rogers's taste in clothing—what shirts!), Rogers blazed the trail in nearly a hundred films. In 1947 he married Dale Evans, "Queen of the West." After his final series film in 1951, *Pals of the Golden West*, he, like Autry, moved on to television.

The Sons
Of The Pioneers

Courtesy JEMF/Arhoolie Records, 10341 San Pablo Ave., El Cerrito, CA 94530

The greatest of the western singing groups was the Sons of the Pioneers. After an assortment of names, the group, originally established by Leonard Slye (Roy Rogers), Bob Nolan, and Tim Spencer, settled on Sons of the Pioneers in early 1934 after a radio broadcaster on KFWB announced them that way. They had been calling themselves the Pioneer Trio (even though fiddler Hugh Farr had just joined their ranks, swelling them to a quartet) and demanded to know why they were given the unusual introduction. The announcer, nonplussed, reasoned that they were not actual pioneers, but perhaps the sons of pioneers. That made sense, and the name took hold.

The Sons of the Pioneers helped formalize the art of trio singing and yodeling, and brought that sound and the dreamy beauty and poetry of the West to a wide audience. More often than not, their songs were remade by popular singers of the day (the group never made the pop charts). However, they were seen in numerous cowboy films beginning with *The Old Homestead* in 1935, and as a result helped create the tradition of backup singing groups in these kinds of films. These singing groups did not star in singing cowboy films, but they were very much a part of the sagebrush musicals. On the heels of the Sons of the Pioneers came the Jimmy Wakely Trio, Foy Willing and the Riders of the Purple Sage, the Cass County Boys, Andy Parker and the Plainsmen, the Saddle Pals, and a number of lesser-known groups.

Before Slye left in 1938, he made twelve films with the group. There were numerous personnel changes, but the overall sound and repertoire remained constant through the years. Douglas Green, the great singing cowboy historian, turns into a post-Sons of the Pioneers singer when he dons his cowboy outfit and becomes Ranger Doug of the group Riders in the Sky. Speaking to Michael Bane in *Country Music* about the impact of the Sons of the Pioneers, Green/Ranger Doug observed, "'Little Joe the Wrangler,' 'Strawberry Roan,' 'When the Work's All Done This Fall.' They were all about the ranch. All about work. Some of them were kind of tragic, or some deed of heroism. I think that what Bob Nolan and Tim Spencer, the two great writers of the genre, essentially did was to give the West a vision that America believed in. Suddenly, it wasn't just a work song, only about horses. It was a song about being free, like the Cowboy National Anthem says, 'Lonely but free I'll be found, drifting along with the tumbling tumbleweeds.' That song encapsulates everything. It's the Cowboy Way. It's a code of honor. It's a love and appreciation of nature and of the West. If that sounds serious, by golly, it is!"

Movie Star News

The "King of the Cowboys," the "Queen of the West," and "The Smartest Horse in the Movies" were the recognized titles that Roy Rogers, Dale Evans, and horse Trigger went by. Right from the beginning, Rogers was destined for greatness in film. First of all, he inherited a fine story tailored for Gene Autry about a cowboy getting elected to Congress on a free-water platform. Rogers shows the congressmen a film that displays his constituents' fight with Dust Bowl conditions as he puts forth his plan for public ownership of utilities. The film was originally set to be titled *Washington Cowboy*, but when Autry went on strike and Rogers was brought in as his replacement the title was changed to *Under Western Skies*. Bosley Crowther wrote in the *New York Times* that the film company had found "a new Playboy of the Western World in the sombrero'd person of Roy Rogers, who has a drawl like Gary Cooper, a smile like Shirley Temple, and a voice like Tito Guizar."

In the early 1940s, Rogers's films became more elaborate, featuring big musical numbers that were often minor-league versions of MGM and 20th Century-Fox efforts. It was around this time that an ex-band singer by the name of Dale Evans entered the scene. She was cast opposite Rogers in the 1944 opus *The Cowboy and the Senorita*, where she played Senorita Ysobel Martinez to good notices. That same year she received an opportunity to sing and dance in *The Yellow Rose of Texas*. Rogers and Evans made eighteen more films together, and were married in 1947 (Dale co-authored what would become Rogers's theme song, "Happy Trails to You").

The Roy Rogers and Dale Evans Museum, in Victorville, California, documents Rogers's career (and later that of Evans) and is run by Rogers and their son Rusty. In addition to the films, pictures, and cowboy paraphernalia, the museum houses the stuffed and mounted body of the most famous palomino horse in the West, Trigger.

481

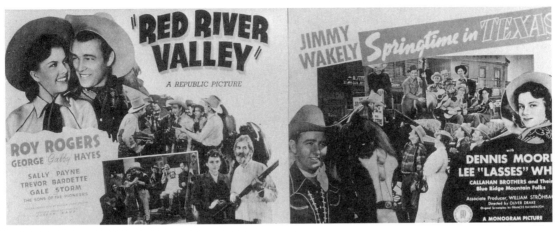

Left, Roy Rogers opposite Gale Storm, who would go on to popular music success in the 1950s as well as TV sitcom fame on her show "My Little Margie." *Red River Valley* was the same title that Republic had used earlier for a 1936 Gene Autry film. Rogers didn't officially change his name until 1942, because shortly after the release of his first film he and Republic Studios were sued by a small-time vaudevillian by the name of Roy Rogers. After Republic settled the suit, the *Variety* headline read, "Rep Pays Off Rogers, Keeps Tag for Oat Star."

Right, singing cowboy Jimmy Wakely. In 1937, Wakely played piano for Merle Salathiel and His Barnyard Boys and worked in Little Doc Roberts' Medicine Show in Oklahoma City, before forming the Jimmy Wakely Trio (with Johnny Bond and Scotty Harrell). Gene Autry heard them and signed them to his CBS radio show, "Melody Ranch." After backing Autry and others on screen for a while, Wakely went on to star in twenty-eight of his own films and recorded a number of top hits, including "One Has My Name (The Other Has My Heart)" and "I Love You So Much It Hurts" in 1948 and "Slipping Around" in 1949, all number one hits on the country and western charts. Wakely once said, "Through the grace of God and Gene Autry, I got a career."

Tex Ritter and his horse White Flash send a hardy greeting to saddle pals of all ages. One of the top-ranked cowboys, Tex Ritter made fifty-eight films between 1936 and 1945, more than any other singing cowboy after Gene Autry (ninety-three) and Roy Rogers (between eighty-six and eighty-eight). Ritter appeared seven out of nine years in the exhibitors' poll of top money-making western stars, although never higher than sixth, and tenth twice, according to David Rothel. This advertisement for Screencraft may give some indication as to the level of film studios he toiled for: "Screencraft Presents: Tex Ritter With His Horse 'White Flash' and Little Tommy Bupp and His Police Dog 'Smokey' [starring in] 'Hittin' the Trail.'"

Tex Ritter (1906-1974) was born Maurice Woodward Ritter on a farm and ranch in Nederland, Panola County, Texas, where he learned to rope and ride. Upon graduating from high school with honors, he enrolled as a law major at the University of Texas. His love for cowboy folklore led Ritter to work up a combined lecture-singing program he titled "The Texas Cowboy and His Songs." Ritter even toured with the one-man show, ending up in Chicago, where he enrolled at Northwestern University. In 1930 Ritter gave up the idea of becoming a lawyer and decided to seek theatrical fame and fortune in New York City.

Ritter joined the New York Theatre Guild, and in 1931 he appeared in the Broadway play *Green Grow the Lilacs*, a homespun tale by Lynn Riggs about a ranch community. Later that play would provide the basis for the Rodgers and Hammerstein musical blockbuster *Oklahoma!* A number of observers have noted that this 1943 smash musical, along with Bing Crosby's many cowboy recordings, helped popularize the music of the West.

Next, Ritter created radio roles that reflected cowboy imagery. He performed on major shows like "Death Valley Days" and hosted "Tex Ritter's Camp Fire" and "Cowboy Tom's Round-Up." Ritter helped bring cowboy folklore to New York radio, and in 1933 he signed a record contract with Columbia. In 1936, Edward Finney of Grand National Pictures put Ritter under personal contract to him rather than the studio. The Grand National film series were budgeted for $12,000 to $18,000, with Tex receiving $2,400 per picture.

Ritter's first film for Grand National was *Song of the Gringo* in 1936. Like most of the films Ritter would make, it was plagued by poor production values. As the films wore on, Ritter's his sidekicks, such as Horace Murphy, Snub Pollard, and "Arkansas Slim" Andrews, received only fair-to-middling ratings by fans and critics. Ritter moved on to Monogram, where films such as *Roll, Wagon, Roll* (1939) *Rhythm of the Rio Grande*, and *Rainbow Over the Range* (1940) also received mixed reviews. By the time Ritter joined Columbia Pictures, he had been reduced to sharing the spotlight with Bill Elliott. Writing about their first picture together, *King of Dodge City* (1941), a critic for *Variety* summed up the problem: "Interest suffers from attempt to split hero functions equally between the two westerners, and indications are that studio will have to revise formula for teaming Elliott and Ritter whereby either one or the other will have to take secondary importance." This didn't happen, and after eight pictures Ritter was teamed with Johnny Mac Brown at Universal Studios. They made seven films together. After three solo turns at Universal Ritter moved on to PRC, where he made his last films in the Texas Ranger series.

David Rothel wrote in the most comprehensive tome about western vocalists in continuous series, *The Singing Cowboys*, "In examining the Tex Ritter film career one is always tempted to consider 'What might have been' had Tex been hired early in his career by, say, Herbert Yates at Republic Pictures. With the slick Republic production values, plus better direction, scripting, and promotion, who knows? As it was, Tex had another career well underway when the cameras ran out of film." That career was as a recording artist for the new Capitol Records, formed in 1942. Ritter became the first cowboy singer on Capitol's roster, and remained there for the rest of his life.

Some of Ritter's song hits for Capitol included "Jingle, Jangle, Jingle" (1942), "I'm Wastin' My Tears on You," "There's a New Moon Over My Shoulder," and "Jealous Heart" (1944), "You Two-Timed Me One Time Too Often," "You Will Have to Pay," and "Christmas Carols by the Old Corral" (1945), "Have I Told You Lately That I Love You?" (1946), "Rye Whiskey," "Deck of Cards," and "Rock and Rye Polka" (1948), and "Daddy's Last Letter" (1950). In 1952 Ritter provided the off-camera vocal for the film *High Noon*. The song, the score, the editing, and the film's star, Gary Cooper, all received Academy Awards. In 1964, Ritter was elected to the Country Music Hall of Fame, and in 1965 he was made a member of the "Grand Ole Opry." Ritter's son John starred in the TV series "Three's Company" and "Hooperman" and in numerous films. Many other singing cowboys had film series modeled after those of Autry and Rogers, but none came close to matching the consistency or longevity of the leaders. Johnny Bond and Jimmy Wakely both got their start with Gene Autry and made a number of passable westerns. David Rothel contends in *The Singing Cowboys* that the closest thing to Autry and Rogers was Rex Allen. Allen had the looks and charisma but his career began when the formula had run its course. He would become "The Last of the Singing Cowboys."

Unlike bluegrass, western swing, and honky tonk, the singing cowboy tradition has not had a major revival. Contemporary country artists will sing a classic cowboy song every so often, but that does not make a movement. Michael Martin Murphy and ex-rodeo circuit star Chris LeDoux are two premier solo revivalists of singing cowboy music today. The cult trio Riders in the Sky has also attended to the charming saddle-pal custom. The group, formed in 1978, is made up of fiddler "Woody" Paul Chrisman, guitarist "Ranger" Doug Green (the eminent music historian Douglas Green), and bassist Fred "Too Slim" LaBour. The group has projected a genuine love of the tradition, which they perform with an off-center, loopy sense of fun. The Riders in the Sky give modern audiences a touch of a past-tense tradition that is tuneful, gentle, and wistful.

Singing Cowboys (Chronologically)

Name	Comments
Ken Maynard	First singing cowboy beginning with a series of films in 1930; first to use a western song as a title, in *Strawberry Roan* (1933); introduced Gene Autry to films (*In Old Santa Fe*); horse named Tarzan
John Wayne	Second singing cowboy as Singin' Sandy, an undercover G-man in *Riders of Destiny*, 1933; made a total of 16 releases for Lone Star Productions; singing not done by Wayne
Gene Autry	Along with Roy Rogers and Tex Ritter the best known; 93 starring films where he established: the 10 Commandments of the singing cowboy; regular sidekicks; featured and "billed" horse-companion; use of actual name film to film; songs part of the plot development
Dick Foran	Only Warner Brothers singing cowboy; 12 features, first was *Moonlight on the Prairie* (1935), last *Prairie Thunder* (1937); companion Palomino Smoke
Fred Scott	Spectrum Production Films featured this ex-opera vocalist in nearly two dozen films, first *Romance Rides the Range* (1936), last *Two Gun Troubadour* (1937); called the "Silvery Voiced Baritone"; horse White Dust, sidekick was usually Al "Fuzzy" St. John
Bob "Tex " Allen	Developed the Ranger series for Columbia; lost out to Roy Rogers for Republic's replacement for Autry because he didn't play guitar; first film *Unknown Ranger* (1936); out of singing cowboy business by 1938
Ray Whitley	Starred in successful musical shorts in 1936; no series of own; played musical sidekicks to George O'Brian and Tim Holt for RKO; wrote "Back in the Saddle"
Tex Ritter	Dedicated student of the cowboy; first film *Song of the Gringo* (1936), last *Flaming Bullets* (1945); after Autry and Rogers, he made the most singing cowboy films; horse White Flash
Smith Ballew	Ex-big band leader and singer; 20th Century-Fox's only singing cowboy; made 5 films, 1st *Western Gold* (1937), last *Penamint's Bad Man* (1938); horse named Sheik
Bob Baker	Known as "Tumble Weed" on "National Barn Dance"; first film *Courage of the West* (1937), last *Bad Man Red Butte* (1940); horse named Apache
Jack Randall	Made 5 films for Monogram; first *Riders of the Dawn*, last *Land of the Fighting Men* (1938); horse named Rusty; carried triggerless guns fired by fanning the hammer
Herb Jeffries	Ex-Earl Hines baritone vocalist who later gained fame with Duke Ellington; first and most famous black singing cowboy; 4 musicals: *Harlem on the Prairie* (1937), *Bronze Buckaroo*, *Harlem Rides the Range*, and *Two-Gun Man From Harlem* (1938)
Roy Rogers	Leonard Slye and Dick Weston were his names with Sons of the Pioneers before becoming "King of the Cowboys"; first film *Under Western Skies* (1938); last *Pals of the Golden West* (1951); horse Trigger
George Houston	Ex-opera and Broadway performer; made 11 Lone Rider films for PRC beginning in 1941; first film *Frontier Scout* (1938), last *Outlaws of Boulder Pass* (1942); Bob Livingston took his place and he returned to opera
Gene Austin	Popular singing star of "My Blue Heaven" fame; a native Texan; made only one singing cowboy film, *Songs and Bullets* (1938)
Tex Fletcher	New York's "Lonesome Cowboy" on radio; only film *Six Gun Rhythm* (1939) for Grand National
Dorothy Page	First cowgirl in a series; Grand National's final fling in 1939 produced *Ride 'Em Cowgirl*, *The Singing Cowgirl*, and *Water Rustlers*
John "Dusty" King	Ex band member Ben Bernie; Range Busters series (a trio with Max Terhune and Ray "Crash" Corrigan) for Monogram; first film *Trailing Double Trouble* (1940), last *Texas to Bataan* (1942)
James Newill	Ex-opera singer; made 14 Texas Ranger films (trio with Dave O'Brian and Guy Wilkerson) for PRC; first film *The Rangers Take Over* (1942), last *Pinto Bandit* (1944); replaced as Ranger by Tex Ritter
Bill Boyd	The western swing "Cowboy Rambler," not Hopalong Cassidy's Bill Boyd; Frontier Marshall trio (with Art Davis and Lee Powell) made 6 films for PRC; first film *Texas Manhunt* (1942), last *Along the Sundown Trail* (1942); horse named Texas
Eddie Dean	From "National Barn Dance" to Judy Canova's radio show; made over 100 films as backup sideman with Lone Ranger, Hopalong Cassidy, Roy Rogers, Gene Autry; his horses called White Cloud, Flash, Copper; 21 films of his own for PRC's Cinecolor series; first film *Song of Old Wyoming* (1945), last *The Tioga Kid* (1948); biggest hits "Wagon Wheels" and "I Dreamed of Hillbilly Heaven"
Ken Curtis	Replaced Sinatra in Tommy Dorsey's band; made 12 films for Columbia in two years beginning with *Song of the Prairie* (1945); joined Sons of the Pioneers (1949-53); played Festus on TV's "Gunsmoke"
Monte Hale	Supporting role in Sunset Carson series in 1946, then own series for Republic, where he made 19 features; horse Partner; first film *Home on the Range* (1946), last *The Missourians* (1950)
Jimmy Wakely	Led popular vocal trio featured on Gene Autry's "Melody Ranch" CBS radio show; 28 features for Monogram; first film *Ridin' Down the Trail* (1947), last *Lawless Code* (1949); pop hits in late 1940s
Dave McEnery	As Red River Dave, made brief entry for Universal in 1948; *Swing in the Saddle*, *Hidden Valley Days*, and *Echo Ranch*; later known for his saga songs
Elton Britt	Successful cowboy yodeler and hitmaker; made 3 films, including *Laramine* (1948)
Tex Williams	Ex-Spade Cooley vocal star replaced Dave McEnery in Red River Dave series in 1949; made 4 musical films extracted from a series of 15 musical shorts known as *Tales of the West*
Spade Cooley	Billed himself the "King of Western Swing"; made 2 musicals, *The Silver Bandit* (1949) and *Border Outlaws* (1950)
Rex Allen	"The Last of the Singing Cowboys" with his faithful horse Ko Ko (the "Miracle Horse of the Movies"); made 19 films for Republic, first *The Arizona Cowboy* (1950), last *The Phantom Stallion* (1954)

Three disciples of the Sons of the Pioneers (who borrowed a portion of Foy Willing's Riders of the Purple Sage title), Riders in the Sky have done more than any other group to keep the songs of the cowboys alive and kicking from the late 1970s into the 1990s. The colorfully decked-out cowboy trio effectively mix classic western standards like "Tumbling Tumbleweeds," "Ghost Riders in the Sky," and "Don't Fence Me In" with originals like "Three on the Trail," "That's How the Yodel Was Born," "Blue Montana Skies," and "So Long, Saddle Pals."

Riders in the Sky have been seen on television and regularly take part in any major tribute to singing cowboys. Bob Nolan wrote of Riders in the Sky for the liner notes to this album, "As I was listening to this album I was keenly aware that they were tracking down special harmonies for special passages in the songs just to get that special sound for the listener. And the determination it takes to master the complexities of three-part yodeling I wonder how many of you could guess the amount of work and constant practicing it takes to perfect that! For Riders in the Sky to have put that much effort and devotion into what they are doing, there is but one conclusion: they're going to keep getting better and better."

Courtesy Rounder Records

Western Swing

Courtesy Arhoolie Records, 10341 San Pablo Ave., El Cerrito, CA 94530

A compilation of groups playing western swing, the little-remarked musical style of the West that mixed hoedown fiddles with blues and jazz, reflecting the dance-conscious mood of America during the 1930s and 1940s. Benny Goodman and Count Basie, to use two representative organizations of the swing era, weren't the only bands mixing blues and jazz into the popular music consciousness. In the West the groups added fiddles and did the same thing for their regional followers. That fact that a great majority of jazz writers were indifferent to the movement doesn't negate the fact that a good number of these groups were playing as much jazz as many of the units that have long been written about and lauded as leaders of the form.

During the early years of the western swing movement, most of the groups dressed very much like their northern swing band counterparts. Perhaps the Southwest swing units were trying to emulate the dress of Benny Goodman, Tommy Dorsey, Duke Ellington, and the rest. By the early 1940s, groups like those of Bob Wills, Bill Boyd, Adolph Hofner, and Spade Cooley, among others, cast aside their business suits and ties and dressed like cowboys.

While the singing cowboys established a national awareness of all things western, the movement did little that was musically innovative. Clip-clop rhythms, starry-eyed visions of "little doggies gittin' along," and heroic, lonely cowboys on the range was really nothing new. But western swing and its small-group offshoot, honky tonk, charted new musical ground. Like the singing cowboys, western swing had roots in the music of lesser-known artists from an earlier time. Milton Brown and Bob Wills broke away from W. Lee O'Daniel's Light Crust Doughboys and synthesized those roots—blues, pop, jazz, hoedown fiddle tunes, Eastern European two-steps and waltzes, and Tex-Mex music—into western swing. The great majority of the western swing units were not large like the swing big bands of sixteen to twenty-two pieces (although there were some of this size, such as those led by Bob Wills and Spade Cooley), but rather units of six to eight pieces. And, as noted in Chapter 7, during the thirties and forties these groups were seldom referred to as western swing groups. Instead, they were listed as "hot string bands," "hot fiddle music," "Southwestern swing," "hot Texas rhythms," or "Okie jazz."

However, like the groups led by Benny Goodman, Tommy Dorsey, and Count Basie, these gatherings played for audiences that came to dance. At the beginning of the western swing movement, many of the groups drew inspiration from the heritage of Dixieland two-step. Eventually the groups fell in line with the even four beats to the measure of the standard swing form. Most of these assemblages hailed from Texas or Oklahoma, although by the early 1940s, once Bob Wills was the reigning king, swing-oriented units with a western bent could be found in most states outside the North.

Milton Brown (1903-1936), who broke with W. Lee O'Daniel's Light Crust Doughboys before Bob Wills did, established the first important western swing band. Had he not died prematurely in an auto accident just when the movement was gaining momentum, Brown very well might have come to hold the crown of "King of Western

Frank Driggs Collection

Top, Bob Wills (foreground) and the Texas Playboys. *Bottom,* Milton Brown (far left)and His Musical Brownies. Notice the early dress outfits of the two leading groups of western swing—both proudly display business suits, not cowboy outfits.

Swing." As it is, Brown certainly deserves the sobriquet, "Father of Western Swing." Brown wanted to run the Doughboys but when he realized he couldn't, he took his brother Durwood and left to form Milton Brown and His Musical Brownies in September 1932. The fledging band played on radio station KTAT, Fort Worth, Texas, with a lineup that, by 1933, included the leader on vocals, his brother on guitar, Ocie Stockard on tenor banjo, Jesse Ashlock and Cecil Brewer on fiddles, Wanna Coffman on bass, and the first jazz pianist of western swing, Fred "Papa" Calhoun. This was a string-dominated group with the blues orientation of the leader. In addition to playing blues numbers the band was fond of reworking jazz standards and popular songs of the day such as "The Object of My Affection." In April 1934, the group made its first recordings for Bluebird. Three months later, the Brownies were joined by a valuable addition on steel guitar, **Bob Dunn** (1908-1971). Along with Milton Brown, Dunn is one of the unsung heroes of American music. Before joining Brown, Dunn had been fascinated by the sound of the Hawaiian guitar. He studied the instrument via correspondence with Walter Kolomoku. After playing steel guitar with an Oklahoma band, the Panhandle Cowboys and Indians, from 1927 to 1934, he joined up with the Musical Brownies. Dunn bought a standard flattop guitar, raised and magnetized the strings, attached an electrical pickup, and plugged the unit into an amplifier. According to David Rothel's *The Singing Cowboys*, in January 1935, at a Chicago recording session with Brown, Dunn made probably the very first electrical guitar recordings (most historians have credited Jimmie Lunceford's Eddie Durham as the first to record guitar electrically, in September 1935 on "Hittin' the Bottle"). Dunn was an excellent technician with a real flair for jazz picking; his swinging guitar solos often ring out with a sound reminiscent of a hot clarinet, trumpet, or trombone (which he also played). Dunn later made valuable contributions to Cliff Bruner's Texas Wanderers and with his own group, Bob Dunn's Vagabonds. Dunn's guitar stature ranks with the best of the early electric pioneers, Eddie Durham, Charlie Christian, and T-Bone Walker. Brown's passion for blues and jazz is very much in evidence on selections such as "Corrine Corrina," "Baby Keeps Stealin'," "Brownie Special," "Texas Hambone Blues," and his most successful recording, "St. Louis Blues." In his short time as a leader, Brown left a legacy of close to a hundred sides, most of them of extremely high quality. Cary Ginell's

Milton Brown and the Founding of Western Swing, makes a compelling case for the leader of the Musical Brownies being the first leader of the form. Ginell notes that Brown established the music's basic instrumentation, style, and early repertoire—his group introduced the slapped bass, jazz piano, and amplified steel guitar, and popularized the use of twin fiddles in the ensembles.

Milton Brown and His Musical Brownies. Left to right, Ocie Stockard (banjo), Fred "Pappa" Calhoun (piano), Wanna Coffman (bass), Milton Brown (vocal and leader), Cecil Brower (violin), Bob Dunn (steel guitar), and Durwood Brown (guitar). Brown's groups played string band blues and jazz. Like Bob Wills, Brown promoted musical experimentation by his players. Brown's steel guitarist, Bob Dunn, and his pianist, Fred Calhoun, were the most noticeable jazz improvisers. Later Jesse Ashlock and Cliff Bruner brought their jazz band fiddles to the group and "Take-off" solos (as westerners called jazz improvising) abounded. Brown's choice of blues and popular songs of the day made him a leader in the Southwest dance halls such as the Crystal Springs Dance Pavilion. He was the first true western swing bandleader in country music, and it would not be far-fetched to agree with biographer Cary Ginell, that Brown was the "Father of Western Swing."

Bob Wills (1905-1975), a fiddle player par excellence, was also a lover of blues and jazz. His dynamic leadership qualities and ability to adapt and change his bands throughout the years placed him in the forefront of a movement that eventually crowned him "King." His first versions of the Texas Playboys operated out of Waco, Texas (they were simply called the Playboys at this time), then, in 1934, out of Tulsa, Oklahoma. Between 1934 and 1941, the band found tremendous success broadcasting over radio station KVOO and playing big dance halls like Cain's Academy. After 1941, the band literally followed its Southwest audience out to California, via Route 66.

Arthur Satherley of American Recording Corporation signed the popular local group to a record contract. At the first recording session, September 23, 1935, the Wills band opened with a version of "Osage Stomp," with the band roaring at full steam. Wills yelled his typical jivey asides to individual band members as he had always done when they performed. Satherley was mortified—he stopped the number and admonished the leader, "Bob, you're covering up the musicians when you talk and holler." Without blinking an eye, Wills reportedly shot back, "Is that right?" Wills then turned to his band and ordered, "Pack up, we're going home!" Fortunately, Satherley backed down and the session continued. Before long, Satherley, who had also signed Gene Autry and Roy Acuff, among numerous others, became the band's biggest supporter and acquired family-like status with Wills. Wills stayed with Satherley and Columbia (ARC became part of Columbia in 1938) until 1947, in the meantime laying down the bulk of his classics, such as "Steel Guitar Rag" and "New San Antonio Rose" (1940), "Twin Guitar Special" and "Take Me Back to Tulsa" (1941), "Stay a Little Longer" and "Roly Poly" (1945), and "Fat Boy Rag" and "Bob Wills Boogie" (1946).

The Texas Playboys were a formidable array of individual musical stars. Aside from Milton Brown, Tommy Duncan was the premier vocalist of the western swing movement. Aside from Bob Dunn, Leon McAuliffe was its most influential steel guitarist. Al Stricklin was a fine jazz pianist; Zeb McNally provided rock-solid saxophone accompaniment; Eldon Shamblin hailed from the swing bands and was one of

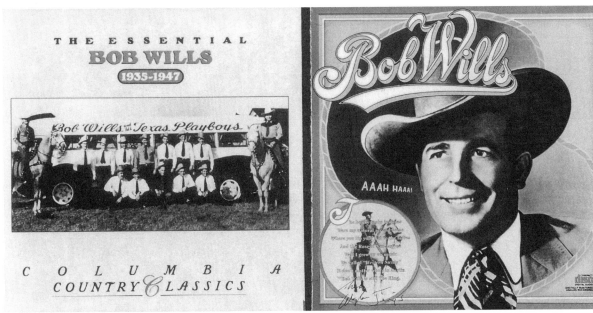

Courtesy Sony Music

The King of Western Swing: Bob Wills. "We're hep. We're the most versatile band in America," pronounced a proud Bob Wills. When the Music Corporation of America booking agency took on Wills as a client in 1944, it advertised his group as "America's most versatile dance band." On February 11, 1946, *Time* wrote: "Bob Wills' music is called 'folk' in the trade for want of a better name; there's a lot of fig in the fold. Wills is more a backwoods Guy Lombardo than a balladeer like Burl Ives. His trick is to bring ranch-house music nearer to the city. He is tired of being patronized by the swing kings. Says Bob: 'They say, "That guy made $340,000 last year and don't know what he's doin'." Hell. I know what I'm doin' all right, I'm just playin' the kind of music my kind of folks like to hear.'"

The music that Wills liked to play was a wide mixture of styles—at least some of the music played by any band that had ever existed during the 1930s and 1940s. The band was reputed to have had a repertoire of thirty-six *hundred* selections by 1938, according to Ruth Sheldon's biography, *Hubbin' It: The Life of Bob Wills.* The Texas Playboys played blues ("St. Louis Blues"), fiddle tunes ("Beaumont Rag"), Dixieland ("Wang Wang Blues"), swing ("In the Mood"), cowboy songs ("Little Joe the Wrangler"), boogie woogie ("Bottle Baby Boogie"), Spanish novelties ("La Cucaracha"), guitar music ("Steel Guitar Rag"), folk dance music ("Bob Wills Schottische"), standard tunes ("Star Dust"), classical selections (Liszt's "Liebestraum"), Hawaiian music ("Hawaiian War Chant"), Jimmie Rodgers tunes ("I'm in the Jailhouse Now"), original selections ("Maiden's Prayer"), waltzes, rhumbas, holiday classics, and on and on. Most importantly, Wills and his mates played in these styles without a condescending attitude. They played them all with a spirited fervor that is captured on record. As Wills once boasted, "Sure we give 'em western music like 'Mama Don't Allow No Lowdown Fiddlin' 'Round Here,' and 'Little Liza Jane,' but we give 'em rhumbas, too. And when there are jitterbugs in the joint we get 'em so happy they can't stay off the floor. We lay it on like they want it." All one has to do is listen to 1941's "A Maiden's Prayer" to get a sampling of Bob Wills's big band jazz sound. The tune sounds like a chart of Tommy Dorsey or Benny Goodman—a listener can't tell that this arrangement is by a country band except for Bob Wills's occasional exhortations. Saxophones and trumpets play in unison to an accented rhythm of four even beats. Tommy Duncan's smooth, pop-like vocal lightly cascades for a couple of choruses, and then the reed and brass sections take the tune out without any fiddles added. Pure jazz.

Wills and his Texas Playboys performed into the 1960s. By that time the band was more fiddle oriented rather than horn dominated. The demise of the "good old days" for Wills occurred in the fall of 1948, when vocalist Tommy Duncan, who had been with Wills since 1932, was fired. Duncan had grown weary of covering for the leader, who often missed performances at that time because of a drinking problem. Duncan formed his Western All Stars, which lasted only a couple of years, and Wills continued on with his troupe of Playboys, even charting one of the group's biggest hits, "Faded Love," in 1950.

the more harmonically advanced electric guitarists in country music; and Smokey Dacus was the first drummer of consequence in country music.

Like Jimmie Rodgers, Wills was a master at synthesizing the better elements of various styles and sources. He not only added trumpets and saxophones to his groups, but he encouraged the musicians playing them to play jazz solos. Wills had the rare ability to fuse modern with old-time traditions, as exemplified by his passion for twin fiddle ensembles and hoedown stomps. Like most great leaders, Wills had a sense not only of what the audience wanted, but how far he could stretch their listening sensibilities.

Courtesy Kaleidoscope Records

Frank Driggs Collection

The Tiffany transcriptions were cut from 1945 to 1947 in San Francisco for Cliff Sundin's Tiffany Transcription Service. Songs were pressed onto large, sixteen-inch disks (allowing for longer play), which were then sent to radio stations around the country, where announcers would read a prepared script, simulating a live radio show with the band, while playing the records. Bob Wills and the Texas Playboys cut more than 370 songs for the company, but it folded after fewer than half of the discs were released. After Sundin's death in 1981, the masters began to be re-released.

Some of the later members of the Texas Playboys can be heard on these transcriptions. For instance, Leon McAuliffe wasn't the only steel player to work with the group. Noel Boggs and Herb Remington, both heard on this album, were formidable players. Millard Kelso was an excellent jazz pianist, and Louis Tierney was a versatile multi-instrumentalist featured on fiddle and saxophone. Joe Holley was one of the best fiddlers to work with Wills, and Tiny Moore's electric mandolin playing was outstanding. These are just a few of the many talented musicians who went through the ranks of the Texas Playboys over the years. In his *San Antonio Rose*, Charles Townsend appropriately summed up Wills's career: "Bob Wills played a variety of jazz called western swing. It was a new American music. Like so many other pioneers, such as George Gershwin, Paul Whiteman, Fletcher Henderson, and Count Basie, his music and much of theirs was still jazz and greatly indebted to that musical form. Like these men, and Louis Armstrong, and his favorite, Bessie Smith, Wills was fortunate enough to have lived in the greatest and most creative period in American music."

Bill Boyd (fourth from the right) with his Cowboy Ramblers in 1946. The group stands proud before the enlarged advertisement of an RCA Victor record. Boyd was not the Bill Boyd of Hopalong Cassidy fame. This Boyd was a true cowboy raised on a ranch in Fanin County, Texas. Together with his brother Jim, Boyd formed a musical group in the late 1920s called Alexander's Daybreakers, which led to the Cowboy Ramblers and a 1934 record contract with RCA. Boyd became leader and played guitar and sang lead on traditional cowboy songs like "Strawberry Roan" and fiddle tunes like "Under the Double Eagle."

By 1938, Boyd's Cowboy Ramblers had grown from a four-man string band to a ten-man western swing operation. The band's best-selling records were "New Spanish Two Step" and "Spanish Fandango" in 1939 and "Lone Star Rag" in 1949. Like many Texans, Boyd was proud of his home state and as a result recorded a number of songs praising it, such as "The Eyes of Texas." In addition to releasing over three hundred sides for RCA, Boyd was featured in a number of films. He retired shortly after his last recording session, in 1950. Brother Jim continued the Boyd musical tradition after his brother's death in 1977 by playing with the modern-day Light Crust Doughboys in the Dallas-Forth Worth area.

489

There were many figures of note in western swing, such as the early ensemble led by Bill Boyd. He was a singer and a bandleader of a group called the Cowboy Ramblers, who were especially effective playing blends of German and Spanish roots music—"Under the Double Eagle" and "Spanish Two-Step" are respective examples. Adolph Hofner led his Pearl Beer Wranglers through some of the most swinging and jazz-oriented music of the later western swing period. Eastern European German and Czech roots are in evidence on many of the numbers, particularly in polkas occasionally sung in Czech. Some groups, such as the Tune Wranglers, produced wild, jivey numbers; others, like the band led by Smokey Wood, invoked incantations of boogie woogie; and some, such as Roy Newman and His Boys, went straight ahead to the jazz without the fiddles. Out in California there was a fiddle player, Spade Cooley, who probably gave the music its name when he billed himself the "King of Western Swing." Cooley led a huge orchestra of over twenty members, including a harp player. By the late 1940s western swing, like its more popular jazz cousin (the jazz writers seldom, if ever, acknowledged western swing's

Frank Driggs Collection

Spade Cooley (1910-1969) was born in Oklahoma and raised in Oregon ("I was born poor and raised poor"). As a youngster he learned classical violin and later played violin and cello in his school orchestra. Determined to get away from farm work, Cooley began playing fiddle in a variety of local clubs until he got his first break as a stand-in for Roy Rogers at Republic Pictures. In 1939, Cooley got a small role in the first of several Rogers movies, and by 1945 had made many films. During this period Cooley sang with Foy Willing's Riders of the Purple Sage. By the early 1940s, Cooley's excellence as a sideman had resulted in his acquiring quite a reputation among musicians with whom he played at the Venice Pier Ballroom in Venice, California. At the suggestion of the ballroom's management, Cooley started his own band in 1942. In 1945 Spade Cooley and His Orchestra, *left*, recorded "Shame on You," which became a number one hit on the country music charts. Cooley began billing himself the "King of Western Swing" and drew thousands of dancers to the Venice Pier and the Riverside Rancho. From there Cooley moved on to the Santa Monica Ballroom. Cooley's "orchestra" (he never called it a band or made references to its hillbilly roots) featured horns, violins, and a harp. Cooley's best-known sidemen were Joaquin Murphy, a highly regarded steel player, and bassist-vocalist Tex Willams. In addition to films like *Chatterbox, The Singing Bandit, The Singing Sheriff, Outlaws of the Rockies*, and *Texas Panhandle*, Cooley recorded a number of big-selling records, including "A Pair of Broken Hearts" and "I've Taken All I'm Gonna Take From You" (1945), "Detour" and "You Can't Break My Heart" (1946), and "Crazy Cause I Love You" (1947). No one packed the dancers in the way Cooley did on the California coast. One of the reasons for Cooley's big success was his singing star, Tex Willams. *Right*, Tex Williams's Western Caravan (1948). Williams is third from right. Like Cooley, his former boss, Williams had a harp player (Spike Featherstone), second from left, and brought over Joaquin Murphy on steel (first on left). Murphy was regarded as the top steel player in California.

Tex Williams (1917-1985) moved to California from Decatur, Illinois, where he had worked on WJBL radio and appeared with his band, the Reno Rocketeers. Williams played a variety of instruments and when he arrived in California he met Tex Ritter and worked with him in the film *Rollin' Home to Texas*. Eventually Williams would appear in over twenty-five films, some of which included headliners like Judy Canova and Charles Starrett. As the featured vocalist in Spade Cooley's orchestra, Williams sang "Shame on You," which became Cooley's theme song. In 1946, Williams formed the Western Caravan, a twelve-piece band, and signed a contract with Capitol Records. The band's first release was "The Rose of the Alamo." Williams then recorded "Smoke! Smoke! Smoke! (That Cigarette)," a Merle Travis song that became Capitol's first million seller and thrust Williams into the national spotlight. Capitol teamed Williams with labelmates like Jo Stafford, Dinah Shore, and Tennessee Ernie Ford, which increased his popularity. He starred at the Riverside Rancho in southern California and his own club, the Tex Williams Village, in Newhall. Williams had other hits, like "California Polka," "Texas in My Soul," "Leaf of Love," and "Deck of Cards," but he'll always be remembered for "Smoke! Smoke! Smoke!"

very existence: see how many of the hundreds of jazz histories give it even one note of mention) was on its way out of popular favor.

Western swing was pretty much forgotten about until the early 1970s, a time when contemporary audiences seemed to experience a general reawakening to the riches of the past. In earlier chapters, we saw how groups such as the Manhattan Transfer, the Manhattan Rhythm Kings, and individuals such as Bette Midler, Barry Manilow, and Peter Allen revived earlier pop forms. In western swing the revival leaders were Commander Cody and His Lost Planet Airmen, Austin Crowe and the Pleasant Valley Boys, and Ray Benson and his group **Asleep at the Wheel** (1978-   ). Of the three, Asleep at the Wheel has had the longest-lasting popularity.

From its first album, the band has mixed blues, jazz, western swing, and honky tonk styles into one of the most eclectic oeuvres in contemporary music. The band's exuberant early covers—Nat Cole's "Route 66," Count Basie's "Jumpin' at the Woodside" and "One O'Clock Jump," Louis Jordan's "Choo Choo Ch'Boogie" and "Ain't Nobody Here but Us Chickens," Billie Holiday's "God Bless the Child," Moon Mullican's "Cherokee Boogie," and Bob Wills's "Take Me Back to Tulsa"—all swing and sway and show a deep respect for the past. Benson, who stands six foot six, doesn't feature only archival selections. The old songs are mixed in with originals like "Miles and Miles of Texas" and "The Letter That Johnny Walker Read." In 1993, Asleep at the Wheel released a double CD, *Asleep at the Wheel Tribute to the Music of Bob Wills and The Texas Playboys,* which won a Grammy. The release featured well-known country artists joining the Wheel on Wills classics as well as a number of his lesser-known songs: "Big Balls in Cowtown" (George Strait), "Yearning (Just for You)" (Vince Gill), "Deep Water" (Garth Brooks), "Blues for Dixie" (Lyle Lovett), "Billy Dale" (Dolly Parton), "Ida Red" (Willie Nelson and Huey Lewis), "Dusty Skies" (Riders in the Sky), and "I Wonder If You Feel the Way I Do" (Merle Haggard).

Cool Cooley

Hollywood—That's the King of Western Swing, Spade Cooley, and his vocalist, Betty Barfield, above. Spade dressed his whole band in white tie and tails for a recent KTLA telecast. Show was from the Santa Monica ballroom, and many of the dancers swung to Spade's rhumba and tango rhythms.

Courtesy Down Beat

Individual country greats like Willie Nelson and Merle Haggard throughout the years have instructed and cajoled their audiences with deep bows of gratitude to western swing and Texas-Oklahoma music in general. Both of them feature a good deal of jazz playing in their music. Listen closely when Nelson takes an extended guitar solo—Django Reinhardt is evident. And when Merle Haggard gets swinging with his phenomenally talented Strangers, Bob Wills easily comes to mind. One of Haggard's most esteemed albums is his 1970 Bob Wills outing with the Strangers and former Texas Playboys, *A Tribute to the Best Damned Fiddle Player in the World.* Haggard then assembled a number of Texas Playboys (Wills was there in a wheelchair and managed to talk on one number for the 1974 release that was titled *For the Last Time).* Both Haggard and Nelson over the years chose to work in groups that were much smaller than the bigger western swing organizations. This was in keeping with a movement that came out of the western swing axis during the 1930s—honky tonk.

Courtesy Buffalo & Erie County Public Library

During the 1930s and 1940s, Bing Crosby did more to popularize country and western music than any other artist of the first half of the twentieth century. Crosby focused the majority of his country songs on cowboy imagery and western swing and honky tonk styles.

Courtesy Arista Records

Big Ray Benson and his Asleep at the Wheel group first came together when he and high school mates and steel guitarist Lucky Oceans played Hank Williams and Jerry Lee Lewis songs together. They formed a group in West Virginia and moved on to the Washington, D.C., area, where they developed a yearning for western swing.

Bing Crosby's Western Songs

Song	Year
Just an Echo in the Valley	1932
There's a Cabin in the Pines	1933
The Last Roundup	1933
Home on the Range	1933
Take Back My Boots and Saddle	1935
I'm an Old Cowhand	1936
Empty Saddles	1936
Yodelin' Jive	1936
We'll Rest at the End of the Trail	1936
Twilight on the Trail	1936
Roundup Lullabye	1936
My Little Buckaroo	1937
There's a Goldmine in the Sky	1937-38
Home on the Range	1938
It's a Lonely Trail	1938
When the Bloom Is on the Sage	1938
The Funny Old Hills	1938
Mexicali Rose	1938
Silver on the Sage	1938
El Rancho Grande	1939
Whistling in the Wildwood	1939
Sunbonnet Sue	1939
Missouri Waltz	1939
Home on the Range	1939
Tumbling Tumbleweeds	1940
Marchita	1940
The Singing Hills	1940
Rhythm on the River	1940
Sierra Sue	1940
Prairie Land Lullabye	1940
Lone Star Trail	1940
Chapel in the Valley	1940
New San Antonio Rose	1940-41
It Makes No Difference Now	1940-41
Clementine	1941
Along the Santa Fe Trail	1941
You Are My Sunshine	1941
Ridin' Down the Canyon	1941
Deep in the Heart of Texas	1942
Nobody's Darlin' but Mine	1942
Pistol Packin' Mama	1943
San Fernando Valley	1943
On the Atcheson, Topeka & the Santa Fe	1944
Don't Fence Me In	1944
The Three Caballeros	1944
Along the Navajo Trail	1945
Sioux City Sue	1945
A Gal in Calico	1946
Country Style	1946
Rose of Santa Rose	1946
Go West Young Man	1947
Tallahassee	1947
Feudin' and Fightin'	1947
Kentucky Babe	1947
Pass That Peace Pipe	1947
Blue Shadows on the Trail	1947
The Story of Sorrento	1947
Riders in the Sky	1949
Mud Trail	1949
The Yodel Blues	1949

Hangin' out in the taverns and honky tonks of the Southwest. Full bands like those of Bob Wills and Spade Cooley were not the province of these smaller taverns. Instead they hosted groups of four to six musicians who usually featured drums with electric guitars that could be heard over the barroom atmosphere. Add a dash of cheating and lost love songs and uptempo Texas two-step prance sounds, and voila!—honky tonk.

Honky Tonk

Like western swing, honky tonk developed in the Texas-Oklahoma territories. A small combo music that was popular in the region's roadhouses and jook joints, honky tonk, like western swing, is dance-oriented, but the emphasis is on electric lead guitar over a rhythm section of drums, amplified steel guitar, bass, and sometimes piano. There are no brass or reed sections in honky tonk music, although sometimes one can detect a single trumpet in the background of records by Al Dexter or Merle Travis, two of honky tonk's important exponents. Another distinguishing factor is honky tonk's thematic consistency—the style's songs deal mostly with drinking, broken hearts, and illicit love affairs. As more and more rural dwellers moved away from their homes and took jobs in the oil refineries and other industrial plants, the images of mother, home, and religion began to lose their appeal. Home and hearth of the older traditions seemed far away and out of place. Honky tonk was a music for jukeboxes—it jumped like Louie Jordan's music, but it catered to the white, southwestern audience.

Bob Pinson and Douglas Green, in *The Illustrated History of Country Music,* have pointed out that with the exception of Ernest Tubb and Al Dexter, every major early figure in the evolution of honky tonk came out of one band—the Blue Ridge Playboys. This group started as a western swing operation led by ex-Crystal Springs Ramblers fiddler Leon Selph in 1935. Selph's lead singer was Floyd Tillman, a man of unusual voice and heart-tugging song ("Slippin' Around," "I'll Keep on Lovin' You," "Each Night at Nine," and "I Love You So Much It Hurts"). Tillman possessed one of the eeriest voices in country music (Lyle Lovett is the modern contender for that distinction). Writer John Morthland in *The Best of Country Music* goes so far as to crown Selph the "Father of Honky Tonk." The pianist for the Blue Ridge Playboys was Moon Mullican. Mullican became the principal honky tonk keyboard player, with solo hits such as "I'll Sail My Ship Alone," "New Pretty Blonde (Jole Blon)," and "Cherokee Boogie."

A third key member of the Blue Ridge Playboys, **Ted Daffan** (1912-), easily stands alongside Al Dexter and Ernest Tubb as the main influence on the honky tonk movement. Daffan was a steel-guitarist-songwriter-singer who joined Blue Ridge Playboys in 1934. Between 1936 and 1940 he was a member of the Bar X Cowboys in Houston, Texas. In 1939, Daffan wrote what is probably the first truck driver song, "Truck Driver's Blues." By 1940, he was signed to a record contract by Arthur Satherley. Fronting his own group, the Texans, Daffan featured his own "tear in the beer" classics, "Worried Mind" (1940), "Always Alone" (1941), "Born to Lose" (1943), "No Letter Today" (1944), "Heading Down the Wrong Highway" (1945), and "I've Got Five Dollars and It's Saturday Night" (1950).

Ted Daffan and His Texans in California, 1945. The leader is seventh from the left, with cowboy hat. Commenting on his turn to country music, Daffan told writer Kevin Reed Coffey in *The Journal of Country Music*, (no. 16:2, 1994),"I didn't like country music. When it would come on the radio, I would turn it off. But when I started playing with them [the Blue Ridge Playboys] we played a lot of pop stuff . . . and I discovered that good country music is jazz. It's up there. So I learned to like country music." Daffan was the first songwriter to help define the honky tonk image spirit, but he did not usually sing the words he wrote on his hits. That task fell to the prolific and underrated Chuck Keeshan, who sang most of Daffan's hits with the Texans. With the 1943 release of "Born to Lose," backed with "No Letter Today," Daffan became a star. During this period, when most country artists were trying to secure a radio spot, Daffan felt that radio was not significant. He thought that it was more important to make recordings because of the tremendous popularity of the jukebox. On September 4, 1943, *Billboard* reported in a column titled "American Folk Tunes and Tunesters," "'Born to Lose' ranks very high in most of the bierstubes, along with 'No Letter Today.' In fact, the taverns consider Daffan their Sinatra."

Daffan left the Southwest for the West Coast in 1944 because of better job offers. Foreman Phillips, who had two large clubs in Los Angeles, wired Daffan to come out to play his Venice Pier Ballroom, which could accommodate five thousand people. Daffan stayed on the coast for two years, holding his own against traditional jazz bands as well as western swing operations like those of Spade Cooley and Bob Wills. In 1946, the popular leader moved to Arlington, Texas, and played the Dallas-Fort Worth area. In the early 1950s Daffan tried his hand at rhythm and blues with no success.

"Born to Lose" is Daffan's best-known number. It has been recorded by over 130 artists, the most successful being Ray Charles's version, which sold over three million copies. One of the most unusual versions is by Elton John and Leonard Cohen, released on John's *Duets* album. Reworkings of "Born to Lose" and a number of his other songs allows Daffan, who is a charter member of the Nashville Songwriters Hall of Fame, a comfortable retirement in his Houston home, which is lined with BMI citations.

"Born to Lose" is an especially important song. Like Cecil Gant's "I Wonder" in rhythm and blues, and Bing Crosby's "White Christmas" in pop, it is a song that gained popularity during the war years, when loved ones were separated and the song's words took on special meaning. Daffan's song had significance for displaced country folk who had been uprooted from home and safety. If there was a honky tonk theme song during the war years, a song that conjured up guilt and loneliness ("Every dream has only brought me pain"), "Born to Lose" is it.

Al Dexter (1905-1984) helped give honky tonk its name. The term had been around for years, but Dexter began writing a series of songs that described the honky tonk lifestyle, beginning in 1936 with "Honky Tonk Blues." Dexter followed up this first of the honky tonk songs with "Honky Tonk Baby" (1937) and "When We Go A-Honky Tonkin'" and "Poor Little Honky Tonk Girl" (1940). Dexter's group was named The Texas Troopers and they had other hits, including "Too Late to Worry, Too Blue to Cry" and "Rose of Mexico." However, the song for which Dexter will always be best remembered is "Pistol Packin' Mama" (1943), a humorous tale about a gun-toting woman somewhere in the oil fields of Texas who enters a tavern looking to shoot her boyfriend (she's told to "lay that pistol down, babe"). "Pistol Packin' Mama" became one of the biggest hits of the 1930s and 1940s. It was covered by Bing Crosby and the Andrews Sisters and went to the top of the pop music charts. The song engendered some controversy, however. Dexter had owned and operated a roadside tavern, the Round-Up Club in Turnertown, Texas, and remembered some of the male-female conflicts he saw in his club. "Pistol Packin' Mama" originally opened with the line "Drinkin' beer in a cabaret, " which led to the song being banned on the "Hit Parade" radio show. It has also been suggested that the show's host and star, Frank Sinatra, couldn't, or wouldn't, sing it. Whatever, when the author changed the opening line to "Singin' songs in a cabaret" the song promptly went to number one on the pop charts. There were still problems. *Newsweek* wrote that the song was "obnoxious," and claimed that it was "naive, folksy, and almost completely devoid of meaning." *Life* criticized it for giving citizens "a national earache."

Ted Daffan   Al Dexter

Southern Folklife Collection, University of North Carolina

Nick Tosches has written a great deal in several places on the source and development of the term "honky tonk," as well as on the style's musical form. Tosches found a newspaper item from Ardmore Oklahoma's *The Daily Ardmorite* of February 24, 1894, that reported on page one that "the honk-a-tonk last night was well attended by ball-heads, bachelors and leading citizens." Tosches also details the rich etymology of "honky tonk" in pre-1936 songs. But the fact remains that it was not until Al Dexter's November 28, 1936, Vocalion release of "Honky Tonk Blues" that musical style, lyric content, and tavern tradition all came together. In 1975, Dexter told Tosches in *Country: The Biggest Music in America*, about the genesis of his biggest hit: "I used to go sit around these honky-tonks, beer joints. At one time I owned a tavern, the Round-up Club, in Turnertown, Texas. I had a bunch of girls workin', and there was this little cross-eyed feller who brought a girl in one night by the name of Jo Ann, and he asked me if I'd give her a job, and I said yeah. I had a pretty good-sized business. This was over in the East Texas oil field. I gave her a job. The next day, three or four women came up in the same V-8 Ford that little cross-eyed feller drove up in the day before, and they're lookin' for Jo Ann. This woman said she's gonna kill her and wanted me to fire her and all that. So I told all this to Jo Ann. That guy, his name was Webb Jay, he's as cross-eyed as he can be. Jo Ann, she always said, 'I love that little cross-eyed man.' She didn't know he's a married man.

So, I sold that place. Later on, about two or three years later, I was sittin' in this joint over close to Longview, tryin' to get ideas for a song, and the jukebox is playin' that song of Bob Wills's, 'Take Me Back to Tulsa,' and in came this gal Jo Ann. She's scratched up and looks like she's been fightin' wildcats. I said, 'Well, god sakes, Jo Ann, what happened?' And she said, 'Jay's old lady's came after me with a gun.' I said, 'I told you to leave that married man alone, that woman gonna kill you 'bout that man.' She said, 'Yeah, but Dex,' she always called me Dex, 'but Dex, I love that little cross-eyed man.' Woman had chased her about two miles through wire fences, through briars, and everything else. She was a pretty girl, 'bout eighteen, twenty years old. So I got the idea, 'Lay that pistol down, babe, lay that pistol down.'" The popularity of the song even led to the release of a Republic Studio film that is not listed in most film anthologies or film guides.

B-film from about 1944 based on Al Dexter's classic song.

Frank Driggs Collection   Southern Folklife Collection, University of North Carolina

Left, Al Dexter. When he was inducted into the Nashville Songwriters Hall of Fame in 1971, Dexter recalled trying to find the right kind of royalty arrangement. "It was 1935 and times were not so good. The record company said they could not pay much royalty on records [that] sold for sixteen cents wholesale then, but I said I would take it as 'I'm not doing much anyway now.'" Things improved for the honky tonk songwriter. After his major success with "Pistol Packin' Mama" in 1943, he was named the leading artist of 1946 by the Juke Box Operators Association. Like most honky tonk players, Dexter played taverns, nightclubs, county fairs, and rodeos throughout the 1940s and 1950s. Professionally he slowed down in the mid-1950s, opened another nightspot, the Bridgeport Club in Dallas, and diversified financially into real estate and federal savings and loan operations.

Right, the troupe known as Lew Childre and His Act featured on a WWVA radio show out of Wheeling, West Virginia. Leader Childre is far left, and **Floyd Tillman** (1914-   ) is seated at right. Tillman would eventually join the Blue Ridge Playboys, where he worked with future honky tonk greats Ted Daffan and Moon Mullican. During this time Tillman, in need of money, sold the rights to a song he had written to Jimmie Davis, who recorded it a couple of months after Cliff Bruner did in 1938. "It Makes No Difference Now" became a country hit. When Bing Crosby recorded it in 1941, it became a national pop hit. Tillman, of course, received no royalties because he had already sold the rights for a few hundred dollars. The author retrieved partial rights in 1966, when his copyright was revived (Jimmie Davis held co-authorship). Tillman's exaggerated, long-drawl vocal delivery was one of the most distinctive in all of country music. His rendering of his composition "I Love You So Much It Hurts" (1948) is one of the most haunting and distinctive recordings in music history. This song, and most of Tillman's vocals, are worth investigating for anyone wishing to hear how an individual can put a unique stylistic stamp on material. Tillman's reign in Austin, Texas, during the 1960s led him to be referred to as the "Original Cosmic Cowboy."

Ernest Tubb (1914-1980s) began his recording career in the mid-1930s, and, like Gene Autry, started as a Jimmie Rodgers imitator. Tubb's early career was given a boost when Rodgers's widow, Carrie, personally endorsed his talent. She placed her pictures in promos for him, praising his abilities and underscoring her commitment to the youngster by stating that she had given him Jimmie's guitar. Rodgers even arranged Tubb's first recording session, with Victor, her late husband's company, at the Texas Hotel in San Antonio, October 27, 1936. Tubb recorded six selections, two of them heart-felt pledges of tribute to the dear-departed Blue Yodler: "The Passing of Jimmie Rodgers" and "The Last Thought of Jimmie Rodgers." But despite Carrie Rodgers's strong efforts, Tubb's career didn't take off. First as the Gold Chain Troubadour (he was promoting flour), later as the Texas Troubadour, Tubb's career simply stood still. Imitation may be the sincerest form of flattery, but it doesn't necessarily make for success.

But in April 1940, Tubb finally stopped being a mere imitator. The change began in 1939, when Tubb had his tonsils taken out, only to find that he could no longer yodel like his hero. This forced Tubb to develop his own identity and establish a new sound. Also in 1940, Tubb shifted from RCA Victor to Decca and recorded "Blue-Eyed Elaine" and "I'll Get Along Somehow," a song that brought him immediate success. Casting aside the image of the Singing Brakeman, and developing, for the first time, his own image as a honky tonker, did the trick. Tubb went on to add electric guitars and drums, and became the best-known honky tonk artist in the world.

Tubb opened his own bar, the E&E Tavern in San Angelo, Texas, in 1940, and played to the barroom audiences with a new-found understanding of what this new music was all about. In the summer of 1941, Tubb recorded one of the all-time honky tonk classics, "I'm Walking the Floor Over You," which was followed by "I Ain't Goin' Honky Tonkin' Anymore." By 1943, Tubb had signed on with the "Grand Ole Opry," making him the first honky tonk performer to join that barn dance show. Cowboy outfits had been introduced in 1937 to the Opry by Pee Wee King, but it was Tubb who brought in the drinking and infidelity songs. Tubb may not have been one of the innovators of the honky tonk style, because he

was struggling with the ghost of Jimmie Rodgers during the 1930s, but he did bring it to a much wider audience. Tubb would also be the longest-lasting regular performer in honky tonk in terms of national acclaim. As recently as 1994, you could find a large selection of Tubb recordings in major music stores outside of the South, but you would be hard pressed to find even one release of Floyd Tillman, Ted Daffan, or Al Dexter.

By the end of the 1940s and into the 1950s and 1960s, honky tonk music, along with Nashville pop, was the primary style of choice for most listeners of country music. Hank Williams became one of the most recognized figures in the history of country music singing heart-break songs and honky tonk swingers such as "Move It on Over" (1947), "Lovesick Blues" (1949), and "Why Don't You Love Me?" (1950). His popularity grew nationally after 1950 when Mitch Miller of Columbia Records had his northern pop singers, like Tony Bennett ("Cold, Cold Heart") and Jo Stafford ("Jambalaya"), create crossover hits of Williams's songs. Hank Thompson and His Brazos Valley Boys blended western swing with honky tonk with great success, but the greater majority of Thompson's hits came after 1950. Ditto for future post-honky tonk stars such as Ray Price, Lefty Frizzell, Hank Snow, and Webb Pierce.

Southern Folklife Collection, University of North Carolina

Like most artists, Ernest Tubb began by emulating others. His world changed when he heard Jimmie Rodgers's recording of "In the Jailhouse Now." In 1935, while working for the Works Progress Administration and hosting a fifteen-minute, early morning radio show for San Antonio's KONO, Tubb called Jimmie Rodgers's widow, Carrie, who lived in San Antonio. Tubb told her how much Rodgers meant to him. Tubb visited her, and Rodgers eventually listened to his show; she ended up liking his work so much that she sponsored him and lent him Jimmie's tuxedo and his $2,000 guitar (as pictured above). Rodgers later presented the instruments to him as an outright gift.

Tubb's 1941 songbook, *Ernest Tubb's Folio of Sensational Success*, has a picture of a demurely dressed Carrie Rodgers with the following inscription: "A Personal Forward By Mrs. Jimmie Rodgers. Of all the artists I've auditioned since the passing of my husband, Ernest Tubb is my choice. I think America's Blue Yodeler would have been proud of my having selected Ernest Tubb to sponsor as he has proven worthy in every respect. He has the voice, personality and ability to put the feeling into his songs that have won him many admirers among Jimmie's fans and Ernest is very grateful, as Jimmie Rodgers has been his inspiration since his youth. For radio work and personal appearances, as well as recordings, I am proud to extend to Ernest the privilege of using Jimmie's famous guitar, for which privilege he has expressed his gratitude. MRS. JIMMIE RODGERS."

Frank Driggs Collection

Ernest Tubb is a perfect example of a vocalist whose voice is rough-hewn and less than ideal—not what most observers would regard as "a good voice." However, Tubb was a superb *stylist.* He created an identifiable sound that was imbued with deep feeling and conviction. Tubb once said, "I'm not saying I'm a good singer, but I sing like I feel, I think you can tell the feeling is there."

Peter Guralnick's *Lost Highway: Journeys and Arrivals of American Musicians,* summarizes Tubb's place in American music: "A member of the Country Music Hall of Fame, an Opry star since 1943, he is the father of honky tonk music and patriarch to a whole Texas clan which extends in a direct line to Waylon Jennings and Willie Nelson. ('A lot of people reacted to me as a rebel when I first started out, because I did what I felt like doing. I think Willie Nelson and Waylon Jennings are doing exactly the same thing.') Ernest Tubb is the man credited with having removed the 'hillbilly' label and 'hillbilly' stigma from country music; he was among the first to bring the electric guitar to the Opry stage; along with Red Foley and A&R man Paul Cohen, he helped to establish Nashville as a recording center just after World War II." Tubb also led the first honky tonk recital at Carnegie Hall, in 1947, and along with Hank Snow he helped establish Meridan, Mississippi's annual Jimmie Rodgers Day in 1953.

Southern Folklife Collection, University of North Carolina

Frank Driggs Collection

King of the Hillbilly Piano Players. Texas-born **Aubrey "Moon" Mullican** (1907-1967), who learned to play the pump organ at eight years old, mastered the piano and as a young man worked Houston's houses of ill repute. Mullican's nickname, Moon, may have been a shortened version of "Moonshine," or referred to his late-hours work. Mullican signed up with King Records in Cincinnati in 1946. There he had his first hit under his own name, 1947's "New Pretty Blonde (Jole Blon)." Henry Glover, King's renowned rhythm and blues producer, noted that Mullican's awareness of jazz was apparent in his composition "I'll Sail My Ship Alone," which was similar to bandleader Jimmie Lunceford's "I'm Like a Ship at Sea." Mullican was a regular visitor at Cincinnati's top black night spot, the Cotton Club, where he was extremely popular for his hard-driving boogie woogie playing. Between 1947 and 1951, Mullican was the nation's hottest hillbilly boogie artist.

The line between western swing and honky tonk is blurred when it comes to **Hank Thompson** (1925-). Thompson grew up in Waco, Texas, where he absorbed the music of Jimmie Rodgers, Gene Autry, and Bob Wills. After his parents bought him a four-dollar guitar and he mastered it, Thompson got a job performing on station WACC as a youth. Eventually he had his own show, "Hank the Hired Hand." In 1943, Thompson enlisted in the navy and after the war he put together his own band, the Brazos Valley Boys.

In 1946, Thompson recorded "Whoa Sailor" and "Swing Wide Your Gates of Love," which garnered him local star status in Waco. Tex Ritter enjoyed the band, which was like many of the western swing units around Texas and Oklahoma. With the help of Ritter, Thompson signed a record contract with Capitol in 1948 (he stayed with the company until 1966). "Humpty-Dumpty Heart" and "Today" were hits the next year. Thompson remade "Whoa Sailor" and released a new song, "Green Light." Thompson would have his greatest success after 1950, most significantly with the 1952 honky tonk classic, "The Wild Side of Life."

Other Singers of Cowboy Songs

Name	Comments	Hit	Year
Rosalie Allen	Nicknamed "Queen of the Yodelers" and "The Prairie Star"	Guitar Polka	1946
Charlie Arthur	One of earliest honky tonk women; first to wear slacks on stage in the 1940s	I've Got the Boogie Blues	1949
Johnny Bond	Ex-member of Jimmy Wakely and Gene Autry units; supported vocalists in many westerns	Cimarron	1945
Elton Britt	Cowboy singer billed the "Highest Yodeler in the World"	Someday	1946
Cactus Cowboys	Movie and touring singing group in Sons of the Pioneers mold; backed Roy Rogers on occasion	—no hits—	
Jenny Lou Carson	"National Barn Dances"' Lucille Overstake of the popular Three Little Maids becomes a cowgirl	Jealous Heart	1944
Wilf Carter	"Montana Slim," an authentic Nova Scotia cowboy; a member of the Horseman's Hall of Fame	Sittin' on the Doorstep	1949
Zeke Clements	The "Alabama Cowboy," an early cowboy on the "Grand Ole Opry"; voice of Bashful in *Snow White and the Seven Dwarfs*	Smoke on the Water	1944
Carolina Cotton	Yodeling beauty in string of cowboy films and the most prolific country music female soundies star; various titles such as the "Yodeling Kid," the "Four Way Treat," "Rodeo Queen," the "Yodeling Blonde Bombshell," and "Queen of the Range"	I Love to Yodel	1949
Jimmie Davis	Jimmie Rodgers disciple; twice governor of Louisiana	You Are My Sunshine	1940
Good Sisters	Sisters Milly and Dolly of the Girls of the Golden West; most popular of all cowgirl groups	Lonely Cowgirl	1935
Ken Hackley	Led the Oklahoma Cowboys, unit similar to Otto Gray's	—no hits—	
Stuart Hamblen	Ex-Beverly Hillbilly; appeared in many cowboy films	(Remember Me) I'm the One Who Loves You	1950
Hawkshaw Hawkins	Cowboy star of WWVA's "Wheeling Jamboree"	Dog House Boogie	1948
Herrington Sisters	Winnie, Ida Nell, and Olga, dressed in cowgirl gear; out of Wichita Falls	—no hits—	
Jerry Irby	Led Texas Ranchers; wrote "Crying in My Beer"	Great Long Pistol	1948
Maddox Brothers and Rose	California unit billed "Most Colorful Hillbilly Band in the Land"; pre-rockabilly sounds	Philadelphia Lawyer	1944
Zeke Manners	Founder of Beverly Hillbillies; played piano and accordion	Sioux City Sue	1946
Frankie Marvin	Comedian with Duke of Paducah; steel guitar	Rainbow on the Rio Colorado	
Louise Massey	Earliest cowgirl on "National Barn Dance" with Westerners	My Adobe Hacienda	1944
Patsy Montana	"National Barn Dance" with the Prairie Ramblers; best-known cowgirl in country music	I Wanna Be a Cowboy's Sweetheart	1935 1935
Laura Lee Owens	"First Lady of Western Swing" in Wills's Playboys, 1943	Betcha My Heart I Love You	1944
Tex Owens	Authentic cowboy; brother of Texas Ruby and dad of Laura Lee of Bob Wills's Texas Playboys	Cattle Call	1935
Cowboy Slim Rinehart	"King of Border Radio" became a top singing cowboy of 1930s and 1940s without records or films	—no hits—	
Jim Robertson	Led Texas Jim Robertson and the Panhandle Punchers	Filipino Baby	1946
Rodik Twins	Verna and Verda, blonde Minnesota cowgirls	Did You Ever Go Sailing	1944
Jesse Rogers	Billed as "The Western Balladeer"	Wedding Bells	1949
Shelton Brothers	Known as the Lone Star Cowboys; pre-honky tonkers	Just Because	1933
Cliffie Stone	Mid-1940s hosted "Hollywood Barn Dance," "Lucky Stars," and late '40s "Hometown Jamboree"; A&R Capitol Records wrote "Divorce Me C.O.D." and "No Vacancy"	Silver Stars, Purple Sage, Eyes of Blue	1947
Texas Ruby	Teamed with husband Curly Fox; "The Sophie Tucker of the Cowgirl Singers"	Don't Let That Man Get You Down	1946
Wesley Tuttle	West Coast performer in films with Sons of the Pioneers; "Town Hall Party" regular	With Tears in My Eyes	1945
T. Texas Tyler	Cowboy; had TV series "Range Round Up"; billed "The Man With a Million Friends"	Deck of Cards	1948
Cindy Walker	Greatest female country songwriter in the 1st half of the 20th century: "Two Glasses Joe," "Take Me in Your Arms and Love Me," "Oklahoma Waltz," "Lorelei," "Cherokee Maiden," "Bubbles in My Beer"	When My Blue Moon Turns to Gold Again	1944
Foy Willing	Formed Riders of the Purple Sage, 1940; many films; "Hollywood Barn Dance"	Have I Told You Lately That I Love You	1946

Others: Bob Atcher, Denver Darling, Rex Griffin, Jack Guthrie, Tiny Hill, Sherby Long, Red River Dave, Steelman Sisters

Other Western Swing Bands and Honky Tonk Roots

Group	Comments
Shelly Lee Alley and His Alley Cats	Houston-based unit led by fiddler-vocalist Alley included clarinet and piano; 1938 featured Ted Daffan and Cliff Brunner, future honky tonk leaders
Jesse Ashlock Band	One of western swing's greatest fiddlers, an ex-member of the Cowboy Ramblers and later star with Texas Playboys; guested with Asleep at the Wheel and Austin Crow
Bar-X Cowboys	String band led by Leon Selph out of Houston featured Jenny Irby and Ted Daffan
Doug Bine's Orchestra	Out of Waco, Texas; a string band that had electric steel guitarist and pianist in 1937
Blue Ridge Playboys	A seminal and underrated swing band led by Leon Selph that housed future honky tonk greats Floyd Tillman, Moon Mullican, and Ted Daffan
Cliff Bruner's Texas Wanderers	Early honky tonk unit started as swing band behind Bruner's vocal and fiddling; Moon Mullican, Floyd Tillman, Bob Dunn, and guitarist-vocalist Dickie McBride cut early classic "It Makes No Difference Now," 1939
Cowboy Copas	Oklahoma honky tonk hit maker for King Records; "Signed, Sealed & Delivered"
Crystal Springs Ramblers	Named after famous dance hall outside Fort Worth; excellent single record session in 1937 with fiddler Joe Holly and Link Davis on vocals
Art Davis Band	Oklahoma bandleader and ex-Cowboy Rambler
Tommy Duncan and His Western All Stars	Along with Milton Brown considered western swing's greatest vocalist; with Texas Playboys 1933-48; one major hit with own band, "Gamblin' Polka Dot Blues", 1949
Lefty Frizzell	Honky tonk great; Country Music Hall of Fame 1982; "If You've Got the Money"
Hi-Flyers	Fort Worth string group in early 1930s; considered one of first to create "take-off" solos; member Sleepy Johnson later joined Bob Wills group
Buddy Jones	Ex-singing partner of Jimmie Davis; member of Cliff Bruner group; Jones was the "Louisiana Honky Tonk Man"; his songs "Butcher Man Blues" (1937) and "Rockin Rollin' Mama" (1939) are pure honky tonk grit
Pee Wee King and His Golden West Cowboys	Southeast's premier cowboy swing unit of the "Grand Ole Opry," "Tennessee Waltz," 1948 and "Bonaparte's Retreat, 1950
Light Crust Doughboys	Seminal western swing group that housed leaders W. Lee O'Daniel, Bob Wills, and Milton Brown in early 1930s; continued under pianist Knocky Parker and was still touring and playing radio spots for flour company in 1990s
Leon McAuliffe and His Cimarron Boys	Steel guitar great of "Steel Guitar Rag" fame with Bob Wills; Wills' shout "Take it away, Leon" is legendary; "Pan Handle Rag," 1949, his biggest hit
Modern Mountaineers	Late 1930s made swinging sounds with fiddle great J. R. Chatwell and pianist Smoky Wood; "Everybody's Truckin'" and "You Got to Know How to Truck and Swing," jump and jive numbers that must be heard to be believed
Moon Mullican	Ex-Blue Ridge Playboy and Texas Wanderer; "King of the Hillbilly Piano Players"
Roy Newman and His Boys	One of the best jazz groups of western swing; "Everybody's Trying to Be My Baby" later appropriated by rockabilly pioneer Carl Perkins, covered by Beatles
Leon Payne	Blind leader of Lone Star Buddies; Songwriters Hall of Famer whose classics include "I Love You Because" and "Lost Highway"
Hank Penny and His Radio Cowboys	Premier Southeast western swing band based on Milton Brown's style; featured Noel Boggs on steel guitar and fiddler Boudleaux Bryant; an underappreciated star who later performed honky tonk material; theme "Won't You Ride in My Little Red Wagon"
Prairie Ramblers	Best known for backing Patsy Montana; an underrated swing unit that also recorded double entendre items as the "Sweet Violet Boys"
Jimmie Revard and His Oklahoma Playboys	Inspired by Wills's Playboys, the group was closely associated with Adolph Hofner's group; "Tulsa Waltz" a classic of western swing
Bob Skyles' Skyrockets	Western string band; reed player out of Pecos area of Texas
Merle Travis	Great guitarist-composer of "Smoke! Smoke! Smoke (That Cigarette)," Divorce Me C.O.D," "So Round, So Firm, So Fully Packed," "Sixteen Tons"; Country Music Hall of Fame 1977
Johnny Lee Wills and His Boys	Fronted band that covered older brother Bob's songs; started as a minor-league Playboy unit and developed into a long standing western swing perennial (1940-64); top hits "Rag Mop" and "Peter Cottontail" in 1950
Tune Wranglers	Swinging string band with accordionist; excellent vocals of Buster Coward

Others: Slim Harbert and His Boys, Doug Hullum and His Swing Boys, Nite Owls, Hoyle Nix and the West Texas Cowboys, Oklahoma Melody Boys, Pine State Playboys (of Claude Casey), Range Riders, Roadsiders, Ocie Stockard and His Wanderers, Sunshine Boys, Swift Jewel Cowboys, Johnny Tyler and His Riders of the Rio Grande, Village Boys, Washboard Winders, Curly Williams and His Georgia Peach Pickers, Billy Jack Wills Band (Bob's other brother-led unit), and Smokey Wood and His Gang

Chapter 14

THE URBAN FOLK MOVEMENT

Left, Pete Seeger, seated with banjo, and group entertain children in the early 1940s. *Right*, left to right: Lee Hays, Burl Ives, Cisco Houston, and Woody Guthrie, 1944.

Library of Congress

The Ramblers, singers of the United Federal Workers of America Union, entertaining at a Black church in Washington, D.C., November 1942.

Given country music's roots in "hillbilly" forms, the early period of recorded music had placed country and folk music together as one idiom. Record companies listed early country releases in the 1920s as folk and even *Billboard*'s cataloging of country hits in the 1940s called the music folk. George D. Hay, the founding father of the "Grand Ole Opry," noted the wealth of folk music in the hills of Tennessee when he recounted, "Your reporter, who was the first director of WSM, had considerable experience in the field of folk music when the station opened in October 1925."

How, then, did such a break occur between the followers of country and folk music? Politics played an important part. The rural traditions of the South had been conservative. The many references to home and hearth included the love and respect of the church and the American flag. When certain folk-oriented musicians of the 1940s began to perform songs that expressed radical "liberal" theories, a break was bound to occur. This bifurcation of country and folk led to two distinct musical forms by the end of the decade—country and western, and urban folk. It is intriguing to look back and pinpoint just how the original road forked into two separate directions.

Two Southerners, Huddie "Leadbelly" Ledbetter and Woody Guthrie, along with a Northerner, Pete Seeger, were the main architects of the urban folk movement. There were other important players in this transition, such as Aunt Molly Jackson and Sara Ogan Gunning, both paramount in transmitting themes dealing with the terrible treatment of coal miners; Burl Ives, whose early radio show "The Wayfaring Stranger" and recordings of folk songs helped popularize the music for urban audiences; and Sis Cunningham, who sang at union functions and edited *The People's Art* magazine, among many others. These performers sang at rallies that fought for the right of workers to unionize. They sang songs that demanded better treatment for Blacks and other minorities. They sang antiwar songs just before World War II. These artists were labeled "liberal," meaning they favored reform in both politics and religion. Liberalism of the time was an attitude and political outlook that was broad-minded, not intolerant or prejudicial, and characterized by generosity or lavishness in giving. Many of these ideas during the 1930s and 1940s were also shared by the Communist Party.

The Communists and their intellectual followers had united behind President Roosevelt. In New Deal America, Communism was an all-American radical style for a number of years. Pete Seeger confirmed that, "I don't mind telling people I was a member of the Communist Party, and I still consider myself a communist, in the broadest sense of the word." R. Serge Denisoff, in his book *Sing a Song of Social Significance*, points out that over the years, many writers have used euphemistic jargon such as "socialist-oriented," "left-wing," "radical," "anti-fascist," "worker," "workin' folks," "progressive," "one big union," and "trade unionists" in place of communist. Denisoff decries this "selective avoidance." Perhaps when communism was viewed as "anti-American" during the cold war period of the late 1940s and early 1950s, writers supportive of leftist folk involvement simply chose to avoid the term because so many of the accused had been damaged personally and professionally by what they viewed as government witch hunts. "Traditionally, when one spoke of 'the progressive movement' or 'the left' during the 1930s, one meant the Communist Party," Denisoff said.

By the 1950s, due to the advent of the cold war with the Soviet Union (that is, the war of suppression and third-country conflict, rather than outright military confrontation), anyone who had been associated with the Communist Party during the 1930s or 1940s was cast as a traitor. The anti-communist hearings led by U.S. Sen. Joseph McCarthy and the hearings of the House Un-American Activities Committee placed such an emphasis on left-wing collusion that an "us versus them" mentality resulted. "Us" meant all good, God-fearing Americans and "them" meant the one-time communist sympathizers who were likely to do things such as try to overthrow the government.

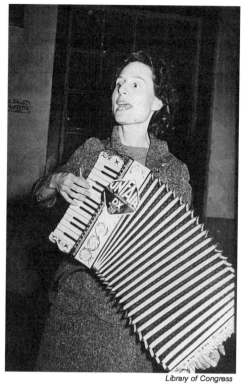

Library of Congress

Agnes "Sis" Cunningham (1909-) was born in Blaine County, Oklahoma, to a father who was a supporter of socialist labor organizer Eugene Debs. Cunningham attended a teacher's college and taught and sang before joining the Southern Tenant Farmers Union. She presented topical skits and songs for sharecroppers and for members of the Oil Workers Union.

Cunningham married activist Gordon Friesen in 1941 and then moved to New York, where she joined the Almanac Singers. During 1941 and 1942, Cunningham and her husband lived in the Almanac House in Greenwich Village.

In *Folk Music: More Than a Song,* by Kristin Baggelaar and Donald Milton, Cunningham recalls her association with the Almanacs: "I was duly chosen as a member of the Almanac Singers at a meeting which also included Bess Lomax. After I was designated a member, I lived with my husband at Almanac House as long as it was in existence. The last of the Almanac Houses—a third or fourth-floor walk-up on Hudson Street in the Village—was occupied by myself, my husband, and Woody Guthrie, who was then writing his book *Bound for Glory*."

Even after the Almanac Singers officially broke up in 1942, Cunningham, along with blues singers Sonny Terry and Brownie McGhee, Guthrie, and Cisco Houston, performed as the Almanacs. In 1962, Cunningham and her husband cofounded a topical folk music publication titled *Broadside*. The first issue had Bob Dylan's first song in print, "Talking John Birch." Throughout the 1960s and 1971, the magazine would continue to champion undiscovered writers of topical folk songs.

Denisoff argues that most writers covering the music scene tended to have liberal leanings and, as a result, avoided the communist issue. Woody Guthrie's association with the Communist party has been deliberately dodged by most scholars outside of the radical right. Denisoff summed up his position by agreeing with historian Archie Green's contention that little objectivity had been accorded "the role of Communists in the unions before and after the World War II. Woody Guthrie, Leadbelly, Pete Seeger (and their fellow People's Artists partisans) were important figures. To date students have shied away from this trio's politics in favor of accounts of charisma and conquest." So what does all this political clamor mean? A lot, given the conservative attitude of the country music establishment. Woody Guthrie, a songwriter and performer with a status to rival that of Jimmie Rodgers, Gene Autry, and Hank Williams, as we will see shortly, has yet to be placed in the Country Hall of Fame. (He already is a member of the Rock and Roll Hall of Fame.) No songwriter ever captured the shattered hopes and dreams of the displaced rural people of the Southwest like Guthrie did in his "Dust Bowl Ballads," yet there has been nary a word of praise for him from the country establishment. That situation is symbolic of the schism that developed between country and urban folk movements.

Leadbelly (1885-1949), Huddie Ledbetter, was the first of the key Southerners to come to New York City (in 1934) and intermingle with the urban folk crowd. He was born in Louisiana and traveled that state and Texas playing in brothels, at picnics and work camps, and on street corners to make a living. Leadbelly worked with Blind Lemon Jefferson, and eventually mastered the twelve-string guitar, becoming known as the "King of the Twelve String Guitar." Leadbelly led a turbulent life and twice served time in prison. His first sentence was for killing a man in Texas, for which he was incarcerated from 1918 to 1925. In the second incident, Leadbelly nearly murdered a man in Louisiana. For this he was imprisoned from 1930 to 1934. On both occasions, Leadbelly was eventually granted a reprieve, the first time by Texas Gov. Pat Neff, the second by Louisiana Gov. O. K. Allen. On a song-collecting trip for the Library of Congress Archive in 1932, John Lomax sought out Leadbelly and was amazed at his song repertoire. Lomax helped the imprisoned songster prepare a plea for freedom. Upon his release, Lomax brought Leadbelly to New York City, where the singer performed at concerts set up by his mentor. (He also worked as a chauffeur for Lomax.) Leadbelly was viewed as "the real thing" by local audiences, who were riveted by his powerhouse blues performances. Songs like "Pick a Bale of Cotton," "Midnight Special," "Gray Goose," "Easy Rider," "Fannin Street," "Bourgeois Blues," "Rock Island Line," and "Good Night, Irene" were just some of the numbers that became classics as a result of Leadbelly's exposure to urban audiences.

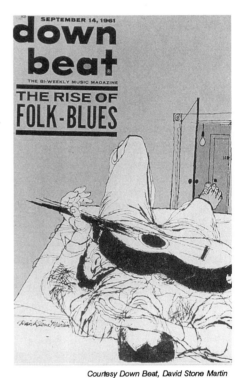

Courtesy Down Beat, David Stone Martin

"Folk Blues" here refers to the African-American singers from the South who became part of the urban folk movement during the 1940s and 1950s. At labor functions and in Greenwich Village nightclubs, black artists played to primarily white audiences who supported left-wing causes.

Leadbelly represented an example of a poor, Black, rural performer who came to the big city and shared his vision of oppression and racism with an audience that had only vague notions of such living conditions. Leadbelly and his wife Martha lived in Greenwich Village, a small artists' community in lower Manhattan. At a time when most black artists in America did not openly protest their lowly status, Leadbelly and the other folk bluesmen, with the encouragement of liberal white followers, sang forcefully about prejudice. Leadbelly made a plethora of recordings and sang with Woody Guthrie in a unit called the Headline Singers. He died of amyotrophic lateral sclerosis (more commonly known as Lou Gerhig's disease), a spinal chord illness that causes muscle wasting.

Huddie "Leadbelly" Ledbetter and his wife Martha Primrose Ledbetter. At some point in the 1930s, Leadbetter's nickname, Lead belly, was fused into one word, Leadbelly. In the autumn of 1990, a news quarterly titled the *Lead Belly Letter* began publication using the original spelling of the legendary singer's name.

Like Woody Guthrie, Leadbelly hailed from the Deep South and had aspirations of becoming a cowboy performer. Leadbelly grew up near Shreveport, Louisiana, on a sixty-eight-acre farm. As a youngster he had his own horse and gun. Black cowboys made up one third of the men working the cattle trails of the Southwest between 1875 and the early 1890s. Unlike Gene Autry, Roy Rogers, and Tex Ritter, black singing cowboys like Oklahoma's John Henry Harris did not make it to Hollywood.

This did not deter Leadbelly, who could ride, shoot, play guitar, and sing like the real or fictionalized cowboys with which mainstream America was familiar. The Spring 1991 *Lead Belly Letter,* in an article titled "Out on the Western Plain," describes Leadbelly's optimistic Hollywood trip in 1944: "He acquired a handsome white Stetson hat which he was quite proud to wear. In one of his favorite publicity photos, shot by Berenice Abbot, Lead Belly is wearing a western shirt and bandana, supposedly given to him by Gene Autry. In his 1948 *Last Sessions* recording, Lead Belly tells us that he met Autry on New York City's Sullivan Street in December, 1934, and taught him how to play the twelve-string guitar, an instrument which Autry had never seen before. Lead Belly also croons, in what he believed to be the fashion of the day, the title song of Autry's popular 1937 film *Springtime in the Rockies.*

"When Lead Belly sings, 'When I was a cowboy out on the western plains, the bullets were falling just like a shower of rain,' he meant those words and knew their meaning from his own experience. He also knew that he was aware of the reality of that lyric much more so than many of the stars making it big in Hollywood. He knew about the West, and he knew about being a cowboy. In 'Western Plains' [also titled 'Cow Cow Yicky Yicky Yea'], he tells us that he is 'the best cowboy that ever herded cattle' and that he 'made a half a million, pulling the bridle reins.' He tried in Hollywood to bring that realization before the producers, directors and money men, but no one would take the chance. Had someone given sufficient attention and believed him, we may have had yet another dimension of Lead Belly to appreciate."

As it stands, Leadbelly is best known for bringing his vast musical repertoire to New York and the urban folk movement. Much of the history about Leadbelly has been gleaned from John Lomax and his son Alan. The first third of John Lomax's book *Negro Folk Songs* is titled 'The Worldly Nigger,' and the evidence of Lomax's superior, paternalistic attitude toward the singer is hard to deny. Leadbelly disliked the 1936 book and hired legal help to block its publication. The book depicts Leadbelly as enormously talented but childlike and dim-witted. There have been some other attempts to tell the story of Leadbelly's great impact on the music scene, but we will have to wait until the publication of *Lead Belly Letter* editor Sean Killeen's *Lead Belly*: The Music, The Man, The Myth to get the entire picture.

Left, **Josh White** (1908-1969) was one of the smoothest-sounding singers associated with the blues. His clean, articulate vocals, combined with tasteful guitar playing, made White a natural for nightclub entertaining. Early in his career White worked as a lead-boy for a number of blind Southern singers such as Blind John Henry Arnold, Blind Lemon Jefferson, and Blind Jo Taggart. He made recordings in the early 1930s as Joshua White, "The Singing Christian" (religious songs), and as Pinewood Tom and His Blues Hounds (secular songs). White's success as a singer led him to New York, where he billed himself "The Sensation of the South" and made his debut on the theatrical stage in *Harlem Fantasy* (1933) and *John Henry* (1940). White's success on the WBS radio programs "Back Where I Come From" and "The School of the Air" introduced the singer to a national audience. Studs Terkel, the Chicago author and radioman, wrote, "During the early 1940s Josh was one of the first voices that brought folk music to big cities on records and radio stations. He made people aware that there was another music for people in large cities aside from that of Tin Pan Alley."

White and Leadbelly played Max Gordon's Greenwich Village club the Village Vanguard for six months, playing to racially mixed crowds. White then moved on to Barney Josephson's Cafe Society Downtown, where he established himself as a top-flight solo attraction for five years (1940-45). Billed as "Josh White and his guitar," the bluesman introduced his on-stage trademarks (copied years later by Harry Belafonte): a long-sleeved sportshirt with one of two buttons open at the neck and dark slacks. A black man making his way in a white man's world, White oozed sex appeal, according to folksinger Lee Hays. In 1940, he released an album of songs, *Chain Gang,* and in 1941 another album, *Southern Exposure: An Album of Jim Crow Blues Sung by Joshua White.*

In 1941, White sang off and on with the first important protest singing group, the Almanac Singers. It was as a social protest singer and sophisticated nightclub entertainer that White made his mark—a black man singing about bad housing, sickness, and race prejudice in the defense industries and in the army. These were "social documents," wrote a left-wing magazine, the *New Masses.* In 1942, White and Libby Holman, a white torch singer, put together a nightclub program—a black man and a white woman singing as a duet that raised many an eyebrow. They recorded and sang at the upscale clubs such as La Vie Parisienne, the Cafe Society Uptown, the Cafe Society Downtown, and the Blue Angel.

Right, Leadbelly playing his guitar as a lap-steel with his wife, Martha, watching. Like Josh White, Leadbelly offered up a multitude of blues songs to urban audiences, including protest songs about the plight of black people. His best-known protest songs include "Bourgeois Blues," "Jim Crow Blues," "Scottsboro Boys," and "We Shall Be Free."

Greenwich Village became the center of the folksinging movement in the 1940s, because the key clubs, The Village Vanguard and Cafe Society Downtown, were located there; and the rent was cheap. Many of the forces of the folk movement could be found at Leadbelly's apartment. Lee Hays recalled, with fondness, the charity that the great Leadbelly showed him. Doris Willens writes in her biography of Hays, "Those were good times, the busy days at People's Songs sometimes running into song-filled nights at the Lower East Side apartment of Martha and Huddie Ledbetter, the black ex-convcict folk singer known as Leadbelly, a man all of them, Pete, Lee, Woody, Cisco Houston, Alan Lomax, and every folk singer and folk song maven, worshiped and learned from.

"Lee wished Leadbelly could break the habit of calling them 'Mr. Pete' and 'Mr. Alan' and 'Mr. Lee,' but Leadbelly couldn't, or wouldn't. On the other hand, Lee chuckled over the irony (which he pointed out to Pete) that Leadbelly dressed in a dignified shirt-and-tie fashion while Pete, the New England aristocrat, turned up everywhere in farmer's overalls. Pete didn't see the humor at all." A 1975 movie, *Leadbelly,* directed by Gordon Parks and starring Roger E. Mosley, includes songs such as "Fannin' Street," "The Midnight Special," "Rock Island Line," "Cotton Fields," "Bring Me a Lil' Water, Silvy," and "Goodnight, Irene." Brownie McGhee and Sonny Terry also appear in the film.

People's Songs Give Pre-concert Party For Josh White

Courtesy Down Beat

Left, Josh White; *center,* Woody Guthrie and Janice Kingslow; *right,* Leadbelly.

Protest Songs by the Big Three

Leadbelly

Bourgeois Blues
Hangman Jury
I Don't Want No More Army Life
Jim Crow Blues
Mister Tom Highes Town
National Defense Blues
Scottsboro Boys
We Shall Be Free

Josh White

Bad Housing Blues
Defense Factory Blues
Free and Equal Blues
One Meatball
Southern Exposure
Strange Fruit
Uncle Sam Says

Big Bill Broonzy

All By Myself
Black, White and Brown
Just a Dream
Looking Up at Down
When Will I Be Called a Man?

Woody Guthrie (1912-1967) was born in Okemah, Oklahoma, to a pioneer family. He quit high school and hoboed around the country playing harmonica and guitar while working odd jobs. He played "in barber shops, at shine stands, in front of shows, around the pool halls, and rattled the bones, done the jig dances, sang and played with Negroes, Indians, whites, farmers, town folks, truck drivers and with every kind of a singer you can think of." After playing stand-up bass in a cowboy band, he headed out for California, where he joined Maxine "Lefty Lou" Crissman on a popular radio show that aired 2:15 to 2:45 p.m. on KFVD. Guthrie talked and sang of the terrible plight of the "Okies," who had been devastated by the droughts and dust storms that had forced them off their land and out to California. "Oklahoma Hills" and "Talkin' Dust Bowl Blues" are two examples of songs that Guthrie sang to give hope to the displaced migrants who found themselves unwanted in a hostile state. John Steinbeck wrote of this catastrophe with warmth and insight in his novel *The Grapes of Wrath*. When Guthrie saw the brilliant John Ford-directed film made from the book, he was so moved that he wrote "Tom Joad," a song based on the protagonist of the story. *The Grapes of Wrath* (1940), produced by Darryl Zanuck for Twentieth Century-Fox, is a rare instance of Hollywood masterfully conveying a serious story without mawkish sentimentality.

After developing a friendship with actor-to-be Will Geer, Guthrie traveled with him to New York City, in 1939. There he met up with Pete Seeger and John Lomax's son, Alan. The younger Lomax presented Guthrie on his CBS network show, "Folk School of the Air," and eventually made the first commercial recordings of Guthrie, on April 26, 1940. Twelve sides were released in two volumes in the summer of 1940 under the title *The Dust Bowl Ballads.* Included were "Vigilante Man," "Do Re Mi," "Tom Joad," "Pretty Boy Floyd," "Dust Bowl Blues," and "I Ain't Got No Home."

Woody Guthrie the cowboy. Guthrie began his professional career as a country and western singer. Guthrie joined Matt Jennings, who later became his brother-in-law, and Cluster Baker in a group called the Corncob Trio, which played for Saturday night dances and house parties in Pampa, Oklahoma. In 1936, Guthrie (first on the left, holding the bass) and Jennings (second from the right) were part of the Pampa Jr. Chamber of Commerce Band. Guthrie's Oklahoma and Texas background had introduced him to all kinds of musical styles—Irish, Native American, and Black, among others.

The following colorful description by Guthrie of his home roots in Okemah and later Pampa are taken from *American Folksong, Woody Guthrie*: "Okemah was one of the singingest, square dancingest, drinkingest, yellingest, preachingest, walkingest, talkingest, laughingest, cryingest, shootingest, fist fightingest, bluedingest, gamblingest, gun, club, and razor carryingest of our ranch and farm towns, because it blossomed out into one of our first oil Boom Towns. Here came the Lawyer Man, Doctor Man, Merchant Man, Royalty Man, Lease Man, Tonk Bucker Man, Pipe Liner Man, Greasy Gloves Man, Big Wrench Man, the Cowboy and the Cowman, the spirit and the Hoodoo Man, the ladies for all of these, the girls, and the Mistresses for the Pool Stick and Domino Sharker, the Red Light Pimper and Sidewalk Barker. I sold newspapers, sang all of the songs I picked up. I learned to jig dance along the sidewalks to things called portable phonographs and sung for my first pennies the 'Dream of the Miner's Child,' 'Sinking of the Titanic,' 'Drunkard's Dream,' 'Sailor's Plea,' 'Soldier's Sweetheart,' 'It Was Sad When That Great Ship Went Down,' 'Hindenburg Disaster,' 'Mary Gagin,' 'Barbara Allen.'

"I went into the oil town of Pampa and got a store job, and the boss had an old busted guitar. Jeff [Guthrie's uncle, considered the best fiddler in the area] got a deputy job and taught me how to chord on the guitar. After a while I was rattling around with him playing my way at the ranch and farm house dances. We worked our way up to playing inside of the city limits, and then for a banquet thrown by the Chamber of Commerce. We played for rodeos, centennials, carnivals, parades, fairs, just bust down parties, and played several nights and days a week just to hear our own boards rattle and our strings roar a round in the wind. It was along in these days I commenced singing, I guess it was singing. We done this for several years around at country school houses till the mud on the upper plains clogged in our wheels and caught us with an empty gas tank and a flat pocketbook with a high norther blowing up bringing dust storms down across the oil fields where the big tall derricks waved above the wheat's oceans and where the cattle stood and chewed and tried to figure out how the poor families got stripped of everything and had to hit the old crooked road going west of nowhere."

"The Great Dust Storm" that ravaged the Southwest during the 1930s was so severe that houses were surrounded and half-covered with sand and dirt. Four summers of drought set the conditions for the big storm. During this time, Woody Guthrie married Mary Jennings, and they had two daughters. The dust storms forced Guthrie to move to California, where he worked on radio with Lefty Lou. Guthrie eventually sent for Mary and the kids, but, shortly after that, the marriage dissolved.

The dust storms provided ample material for Guthrie the songwriter. Joe Klein's biography, *Woody Guthrie,* gives an apt description of the catastrophic scene: "On April 14, 1935, a great wall of blackness appeared to the north of town, late on an unseasonably hot Sunday afternoon. It extended as far as the eye could see to the east and west. There were red flecks at the upper edges of the blackness which led some of the faithful in town to believe that it was fire ('the fire next time') and this was Judgement Day, but it was dust. It was thousands of tons of dust from as far away as the Dakotas and Nebraska, dark topsoil and red clay, carried on winds of 45 to 70 miles per hour, and it was chewing up the countryside. Flocks of birds flew ahead of the storm; smaller animals caught in it choked to death. The sky blackened and, for about forty-five minutes, Woody and Mary could barely see their house. The bare light bulb in the parlor glowed like a cigarette in the dark; they covered their faces with wet washcloths and hoped for the best. In three hours the temperature dropped 50 degrees and the humidity plummeted to below 10 percent. After the first hour, the sky lighted somewhat but the winds kept blowing until after nightfall. The next morning, even the rich people who lived in brick houses needed shovels to clean out."

When Guthrie released an album of songs titled *Dust Bowl Ballads* in 1940, he received some favorable notices but negligible record sales. RCA Victor released no more than a thousand copies, according to Klein, a far cry from the popular music releases accorded Benny Goodman, Tommy Dorsey, and the other stars of the time. Howard Taubman, reviewing the album along with other recent folk releases in the *New York Times*, presented the most perceptive observations: "These albums are not a summer sedative. They make you think; they may even make you uncomfortable. The albums show that the phonograph is broadening its perspective, and that life as some of our unfortunates know it can be mirrored on the glistening disks."

Woody wrote articles for the Communist Party newspaper, the *Daily Worker,* and sang at union gatherings with the Almanac Singers, and with his own group, the Headline Singers. He wrote and sang antiwar songs before World War II and prowar songs once the war began. A book of political songs, *Hard Hitting Songs for Hard Hit People*, recorded with Pete Seeger in 1940, wasn't released until his death in 1967. (The publishers were leery of its radical politics.) During the war, Guthrie and his closest friend, fellow folksinger Cisco Houston, joined the merchant marines. After the war, when communism became a political hot potato; Guthrie disguised his past sympathies by saying, "I'm not a Communist, but I've been in the red all my life."

Guthrie recorded dozens of albums for Moe Asch's Folkways Records throughout the late 1940s and 1950s. Guthrie was more than a politicized folk proselytizer. He was a "Singing American." His songs are of and about the people of this country. At a time when popular music was focused on songs of love, Guthrie told stories about the broader struggles and joys of the average person. Along with Irving Berlin's "America the Beautiful," Guthrie's "This Land Is Your Land" ranks as the most beloved anthem to our country ever written. Both are more singable and humane than our official anthem, "The Star Spangled Banner," a war song.

Rosalie and Theodore Cron Collection, Carnegie Hall Archives

After the release of *Dust Bowl Ballads*, Woody Guthrie became a part of the urbanized brand of country music. Along with fellow Southerners Leadbelly and Aunt Molly Jackson, who had first come up North to plead the case of the coal miners in Kentucky, Guthrie helped create a kind of singing spirit that attempted to deal with the realities of the common person.

The first great period of radical propaganda songs was between 1905 and 1915, with the rise of the Industrial Workers of the World. The leading light of that movement was Joe Hill, who wrote songs about the power of community and unionization ("There Is Power in a Union," "Casey Jones, the Union Scab," "The Tramp," "The White Slave," and "The Preacher and the Slave"). The second main period of the protest song, in which Guthrie played a leading role, came between 1935 and 1943, with the left-wing union functions held with the support of the Congress of Industrial Organizations, the umbrella group of unions representing unskilled workers. In the 1950s, the CIO would join the American Federation of Labor, originally a collection of unions of skilled workers, to form today's AFL-CIO. Guthrie was also a big part of the third stage of protest music, 1945-50, dominated by People's Songs Incorporated.

Guthrie's legacy was continued by a young Bob Dylan, who traveled to New York in February, 1961 from the University of Minnesota, just to visit Guthrie in the Greystone Hospital in New Jersey, where he was dying of Huntington's chorea, a disease of the central nervous system that causes involuntary movements and dementia. Guthrie's dry, talking blues style was very much in evidence on Dylan's first album, produced by John Hammond for Columbia Records in 1961. "Talkin' New York" and "Song to Woody" were direct bows to the dying bard. Guthrie's penchant for outfits that mirrored those of the working man—blue work shirt, uncreased pants and boots or plain shoes—became the apparel of choice of Dylan and the contemporary folksingers, in general, and, through them, influenced youth dress style in the 1960s and early 1970s. Musically, from Dylan and his followers of the 1960s right up to the political concerts given in the 1980s and 1990s by the likes of Billy Bragg and U2, the influence of Woody Guthrie remains significant.

Courtesy Sony Music   Courtesy Rounder Records

Bob Dylan's early career echoed the sound, style, sentiments and dress of Woody Guthrie. Born Robert Zimmerman in Hibbing, Minnesota, Dylan was Jewish in a city of mostly other nationalities. Dylan's talent was self-evident, and, out of nowhere, he was rubbing elbows with the important folk leaders of the early 1960s. Guthrie often asked for Dylan: "Is the boy here?" Unlike most people who first heard Dylan perform, Guthrie liked the raspy whine of the youngster's delivery, actually preferring the voice to the songwriting. Like most important artists, Dylan used Guthrie's style as a stepping stone to find his own, unique artistry. Guthrie had a tremendous influence on Dylan's first album, *left*, on which are found: 1) the Guthrie instrumental style 2) the Guthrie vocal style (an unprettified coloring and "talking" delivery) 3) socially observant content and 4) Guthrie's proletarian dress—pictured on a typical Guthrie album cover, *right*.

Courtesy Vanguard Records

Woody Guthrie and Pete Seeger had an extensive musical, political and even fashion influence on the folk movement of the 1960s. The charismatic image of these two men remains to this very day. However, the folk singers of the 1960s were more "star-driven." When Guthrie and Seeger headed the Almanac Singers, their emphasis was on group participation and anonymity of the individual. Like the goal of union membership, the focus of the Almanacs, and later the Weavers, was that of a united front. This was not so much the case during the 1960s. R. Serge Denisoff claims in *Great Day Coming: Folk Music and the American Left* that, "As opposed to the Almanacs' ethic of 'anonymity,' the 'new protesters' asserted their individuality. Phil Ochs, one of the major polemicists of the revival, stated, 'I'm only singing about my feelings, my attitudes, my views.' Tom Paxton in an interview indicated that many of his songs were personal statements of discontent. He wote 'The High Sheriff of Hazard' because a lawman was a 'bastard.' Paxton further commented, 'Every artist's first responsibility is to himself.' Bob Dylan on a number of occasions indicated that his main responsibility was to himself and that protest songs were a means to an end, a way of launching his career. This is a far cry from the collective ethics of the proletarian renaissance, where performers 'sang everywhere for all sorts of causes' in order to change the social structure."

Woody Guthrie Song Sampler

Songs of Workers
The Ballad of Bob Wood
Boomtown Bill
Cowboy's Philosophy
Great Historical Bum
The Jolly Banker
Sharecropper Song
My Uniform's My Dirty Overalls
The Philadelphia Lawyer
Talking Sailor

Dust Bowl Songs
Blowin' Down the Road
Do Re Mi
The Great Dust Storm
I Ain't Got No Home
Dust Bowl Blues
Dust Bowl Refugee
Dust Can't Kill Me
Dusty Old Dust
Dust Pneumonia Blues
Vigilante Man

Children's Songs
Car Car
Don't You Rush Me Down
Howdy Doo
I'll Race You Down the Mountain
Little Sack of Sugar
Mail Myself to You
Make Me a Bubble
Rattle My Rattle
Swimmy Swim
Washy Wash Wash

Tributes
Ballads of Sacco and Vanzetti (album)
Ballad of Isaac Woodward
Belle Starr
Billy the Kid
East Texas Red
Joe Hillstrom
Pretty Boy Floyd
Jesus Christ
Tom Joad
Mr. Tom Mooney Is Free
Here Come Woody and Lefty Lou

Bonneville Power Administration Songs
In one month in 1941, for a salary of $266, Guthrie wrote 26 songs for the U.S. government in praise of the Columbia River electric project, including:
The Grand Coulee Dam
Hard Traveling
It Takes a Married Man to Sing
  a Worried Song
Jack Hammer John
Pastures of Plenty

Labor Songs
Good Old Union Feeling
On My Own
Union's My Religion
The Ludlow Massacre
The Song of the Deportees
You Got to Go Down and
  Join the Union
The Union Burying Ground
Union Maid
We Shall Not Be Moved
Why Do You Stand There in the Rain?

Studs Terkel called **Pete Seeger** (1919-) "America's Tuning Fork," and more than any other artist of the 1990s, Seeger remains the main link to the halcyon days of the birth of the urban folk movement. Alan Lomax observed that the meeting of Woody Guthrie and Pete Seeger constituted "the renaissance of American folk song." Unlike Guthrie, Seeger's background was one of privilege. He had gone to prepatory school and entered Harvard University. Seeger's mother was a violin teacher at the Juilliard School of Music, and his father, Charles Seeger, was a renowned musicologist who had been active in the Worker's Music League and subscribed to the "art as a weapon" ethos. Seeger didn't stay long at Harvard once he realized that he wanted to play and sing "songs of the people."

Seeger's first public appearance was at a folk song benefit for migratory workers in March 1940. Appearing that evening were the prime movers of the folk movement: Aunt Molly Jackson, Burl Ives, Leadbelly, Josh White, the Golden Gate Quartet, Alan and Bess Lomax, and Woody Guthrie. Young Seeger was greatly influenced by Guthrie, who told him, "You ought to see what a big country America is. You can use the rule of thumb. Or, if you can't get a hitch, you can jump a freight train." That summer Seeger saw America for the very first time traveling down famed Route 66. (He wrote his first song on that trip, "Route 66 Blues.") Returning to New York, Seeger started a collective folk group, the Almanac Singers, with Millard Lampell and Lee Hays, who had been an organizer in the 1930s for the Sharecroppers' Union. Hays contended that the farmers often had only two books in their possession—one to get them through this life (the *Farmer's Almanac*) and the other to get them through the next life (the *Bible*). The Almanac Singers were dedicated to "the music of the people," and set up a cooperative apartment on West 10th Street that they called the Almanac House. Guthrie joined the group in June 1941, after returning from a trip to the West, where he had been commissioned to write songs of praise for the Bonneville Dam. The Almanacs sang union songs and held hootenannies (a gathering of folk singers) to raise rent. They formed, with Sis Cunningham, the Almanacs People's Music Library, which collected and preserved union songs. The unit was very loosely structured. Guthrie said it was the only group he knew that rehearsed on stage. The Almanacs often used black singers in their union presentations, making them the only group in commercial music, aside from a few jazz assemblages, to integrate. The Almanac Singers had many members. Guthrie, Pete Hawes, Bess Lomax and Sis Cunningham were the main cast; but, at various times, Burl Ives, Sonny Terry, Brownie McGhee, Josh White, Aunt Molly Jackson, Richard Dyer-Bennett and Arthur Stern played roles.

Left, Pete Seeger (left) and Woody Guthrie in a bookstore performance in Tulsa, Oklahoma, in 1940. Seeger and Guthrie traveled across the Southwest into Mexico and then along the West Coast to Seattle, where they sang for the Commonwealth Federation of Washington, farmers' unions, and office and factory workers' unions, before they drifted back to the Almanac Singers in New York. Pete Seeger wrote in *The Incompleat Folksinger,* "I learned so many different things from Woody that I can hardly count them. His ability to identify with the ordinary man and woman, speak their own language without using fancy words, and never be afraid, no matter where you were: just diving into some situation, trying it out. When he and I used to go around singing together, we hit all kinds of places: CIO unions, churches, saloons, meetings, parties.

"I learned from him how just plain orneriness has a kind of wonderful honesty to it that is unbeatable. He was going to cuss, he was going to speak bad language, he was going to shock people, but he was going to stay the way he was. He wasn't going to let New York make him slick and sleek and contented. He was going to stay a rebel to the end." Guthrie was, indeed, a rebel to the end. He had a slogan scrawled across the front of his guitar that read, "This Machine Kills Fascists." For his part, Seeger had the words, "This machine surrounds hate and forces it to surrender," lettered on his banjo.

Right, **Burl Ives** (1909-1995) pointing at Woody Guthrie during a radio program in the 1940s. Ives came to New York in 1937 to attend New York University and later the Juilliard School of Music. By 1938, he was on the Broadway stage with a small role in Rodgers and Hart's *The Boys From Syracuse.* Ives then moved on to radio, where he had a popular show singing folk songs like "Bluetail Fly" and "Foggy Dew." The show was called "The Wayfaring Stranger," which became his nickname and the title of his 1948 autobiography. Ives was also part of the 1940 CBS radio show "Back Where I Come From" with Guthrie, the Golden Gate Quartet, a comedian, a master of ceremonies, and an orchestra.

During this period, Ives was the best-known folk singer in the nation, not Guthrie, Seeger, or Lee Hays. In time, Ives, a true Renaissance man, (he played string instruments, composed, wrote books, starred on radio, television, and films, and had modest success as a recording artist) became best known for his character roles in motion pictures, particularly as Big Daddy in Tennessee Williams's *Cat on a Hot Tin Roof* (1958).

Ives was very much a part of the folk scene in the 1940s and was a sometime member of the Almanac Singers. He told a reporter in 1978, "I've never defined what a folk song is exactly. But now I think I do know what a folksinger is. It has to do with the country, the soil. Now you take Leadbelly, he was a folksinger, born and raised in the country and he sang like it. I was born in the country, on the Illinois prairies, and moved to the big city at age twenty-four. I sing folk songs, but I'm not a complete folksinger. I have a foot in both camps, don't you know."

The Almanac Singers first album of six songs, released in spring 1941, was titled *Songs for John Doe.* The songs were proclamations for peace, not war. Titles such as "The Strange Death of John Doe," "Washington Breakdown," and "C for Conscription" were pleas for noninvolvement in the European conflicts, much like earlier pacifist songs against participation in World War I (such as "I Didn't Raise My Boy to Be a Soldier"). This stance was consistent with the American Communist Party's 1939 platform, inspired by the Hitler-Stalin pact and shared by the party's left wing supporters, of not directly opposing fascism. American Stalinists parroted this position with slogans like, "The Yanks Are Not

Comin'" and "Keep America Out of War." Dalton Trumbo's antiwar novel *Johnny Got His Gun* was serialized in the *Daily Worker*. (Trumbo would be a member of the "Hollywood Ten" that was blacklisted during the 1950s hearings of the House Un-American Activities Committee.)

The reaction to *Songs for John Doe* was much stronger than the members of the Almanac Singers had bargained for. New York City leftists were pleased, but *Time* magazine, which at the time was ironically also opposed to U.S. involvement in Europe, warned its readers, "Honest U.S. isolationists last week got some help from recorded music that they would rather have not received. Professionally performed with new words to old folk tunes, *John Doe's* singing scrupulously echoed the mendacious Moscow tune." *Time* also called the group an "anonymous Manhattan Communist ensemble." *Atlantic* magazine characterized the songs as "strictly subversive and illegal."

The Almanac Singers' second album, *Talking Union*, featured the songs the group performed in union halls. All of the songs were credited to the group, as a whole, rather than to any individuals, in keeping with the collectivist spirit of their housing arrangement. This wasn't anything new. A circle started in Paris in the early 1930s by a group of poets called the Anonymous Movement; a New York theatrical community of equals, known as Group Theater, had similar arrangements.

In *Woody Guthrie: A Life,* Joe Klein presents a different perspective: "The pseudonyms and militant animosity invested the Almanac Singers with a certain air of romance and drama. The members tended to mythologize themselves and each other shamelessly. They invented proletarian (especially rural) backgrounds for themselves, spoke with a southern lilt, and, as time went on, made quite

Southern Folklife Collection, University of North Carolina

Pete Seeger, looking back on the halcyon days of the Almanacs, tried to put things in perspective in his book *The Incompleat Folksinger*: "We held normal commercial musical endeavors in contempt. We were convinced that the revival of interest in folk music would come through the trade unions. Union educational departments had already put out many fine songbooks. There was the singing tradition of the old I.W.W. to build on. We envisioned a singing labor movement spearheading a nation-wide folk revival, just as the Scottish progressives sparked a song revival at the time of Robert Burns and the Czech progressives sparked another at the time of Dvorak.

"How our theories went astray! Most union leaders could not see any connection between music and pork chops. As the cold war deepened, 'Which Side Are You On?' was known in Greenwich Village but not in a single miner's union local. We worked our way up to a high circulation of 2,000 [of *People's Songs Bulletin*, 1946-49] before the shoestring ran out and we still hadn't learned to tie on another." By the end of 1949, Seeger was getting ready to form a more commercial group (the Weavers) and another magazine (*Sing Out*).

a show of dressing like down-trodden workers. Few were aware that Pete Seeger had gone to Harvard; he seemed more a figment of Erskine Caldwell's imagination. Millard Lampell, formerly of Paterson, New Jersey, now claimed to come from Kentucky, except when he slipped and said West Virginia. Lee Hays' past was a mysterious raveling of dire illnesses and tragedies, which seemed to change slightly with each retelling. Most of it was harmless posturing, the sort of youthful playacting that would seem more embarassing in retrospect than it was serious at the time. Apparently, they brought off their respective acts rather well, though: Mike Gold, the *Daily Worker* columnist, who became a regular at the left on Sunday afternoons, certainly was hornswoggled. 'The boys are Southerners,' he wrote, 'born with a sense for the right rhythm and drawl of these songs. When they get going, they are irresistible. Here, above the huffing trucks and grimy factories of Fourth Avenue, an American folk legend was being made right under one's nose, yet hasn't the revolutionary workers' movement thus stimulated folk-art in every land?'" The union songs released on *Talking Union* included Joe Hill's "Casey Jones," Ralph Chaplin's "Solidarity Forever" (probably the greatest song in American labor history), a 1932 miner's song called "Which Side Are You On," Guthrie's "Union Maid" and "Got to Join the Union," and the Almanacs' "Talking Union" and "Get Thee Behind Me," among others. An example of the group's anticapitalist fervor could be heard in "All I Want," which claimed that the singers didn't want millions, or diamond rings, or Rolls-Royces, or pleasure yachts. No, all they wanted was a right to live with a basic job so they could have simple needs like shelter and food for hungry babies.

After two more albums, *Sod Buster Ballads* and *Deep Sea Shanties*, which gave the group enough money to tour by automobile to Detroit, Chicago, Milwaukee, Denver, and San Francisco, the Almanacs made an album of pro-war songs, *Dear Mr. President*. The Soviet Union had been invaded by Germany and the bombing of Pearl Harbor had just taken place; so, antiwar songs were inappropriate and union songs were not helpful, since strikes would hurt the effort to aid the Allies. The group made up songs against Hitlerism and fascism as well as songs about the Allies. Best known were "Round and Round Hitler's Grave" and the touching, patriotic "The Reuben James" (to the tune of the Carter Family's "Wildwoodflower"), which mourned the tragedy of the U.S.S. *Reuben James*, which was torpedoed by the Nazis off the coast of Iceland in late October 1941, killing eighty-six and wounding forty-four.

To give some idea of the wide gulf between protest and government during this period, let's briefly investigate America's first anticommunist riot at Peekskill, New York, on Septem-

Courtesy Rounder Records

The connections between unionizing and the Communist Party were especially strong in the South. In Harlan County, cries of "Run the Reds out of Kentucky" rang loud and clear. Aunt Molly Jackson fought to improve the conditions of the coal miners. In her song "I Am a Union Woman," she described the effects of the anti-union stance—"And when I joined the union, they called me a Rooshian Red. When my husband asks the boss for a job these is the words he said: Bill Jackson, I can't work you, sir, your wife's a Rooshian Red."

In *Only a Miner: Studies in Recorded Coal-Mining Songs*, Archie Green says flatly, "No industry in the United States produced more disaster songs than coal mining." Green contends that Aunt Molly Jackson's arrival in New York from Kentucky, was intended, "to agitate for her miner friends, she gravitated toward intellectuals, for she was acutely conscious that her lore could be used in the cause."

R. Serge Denisoff in *Great Day Coming: Folk Music and the American Left*, subscribes to the theory that Woody Guthrie, along with three members of the Garland-Kentucky clan—Jim Garland, Sarah Ogan Gunning, and Aunt Molly Jackson, provided a model that fit the American image of the Communist Party. Denisoff contends, "The proletarian renaissance (1939-1942) was a sort of 'folk music revival' in miniature. It represented a subculture and a style of life which fitted into the working-class ethos of the Communitst party. The renaissance was a manifestation of all the elements of folk consciousness—field contacts, ideology, tactics, and personnel. During this time 'folk music' became what one listened to at informal gatherings and social affairs given by radicals. Folk entrepreneurs were featured performers at benefits for migratory workers, refugees of the Spanish conflict, and fund-raising drives for militant unions."

ber 4, 1949. At Peekskill, a summer resort north of New York City, a great wall of 2,500 union men formed a human chain around a bowl-shaped amphitheatre playing host to a concert featuring Paul Robeson and a number of other performers, including the Weavers. The concert organizers had attempted to hold the concert the previous week, but a gang of self-styled patriots, who blamed Jews, Blacks, and city-type intellectuals for their troubles, had smashed and burned chairs, beaten concertgoers with clubs, and put a cross on the stage where Robeson was to have sung. In response, the union promised and delivered a security force of close to three thousand people.

When the Weavers arrived around 9:00 a.m. the roads were clogged with anticommunists who had vowed to stop the concert. The mob was made up of war veterans and local community groups; they held signs that read, "Wake Up America, Peekskill Did," and "Down to the Dump With All Red Junk." Amidst chants of "you'll get in—but you won't get out," the concert for some twenty-five thousand people went smoothly. Paul Robeson raised spirits with "Ol' Man River," and Pete Seeger performed "The Hammer Song" ("If I Had a Hammer"). The danger arose when the Westchester police diverted outgoing traffic up a steep, winding road to the confusion of those leaving. Waiting for the cars, were the locals who had stones and rocks the size of softballs that they hurled at the vehicles. It was a set-up. David Dunaway, writing in the *Village Voice* on January 21, 1980 declared, "It was a battle of two Americas: the country and the city, the native-born and the immigrants. Goaded by red-baiting in the daily press and radio, the attackers blamed radicals for the frustration of wartime dreams. The attackers were true Americans, as patriotic as the know-nothings who tortured Irish and Catholics during the Civil War." Indeed, according to Dunaway, the Weavers would become the first American musicians investigated for sedition.

The Weavers were born in 1948, when Pete Seeger, Lee Hays, and Fred Hellerman decided to create a more formal vocal ensemble. The trio added female singer Ronnie Gilbert and made its debut on fellow-folksinger Oscar Brand's New York radio show billed as "The No-Name Quartet." Hays later said that the group's members chose the eventual name, because they would "weave" through the warp and woof of American life: "I'll take care of the woofing and the others will continue being warped." Actually, Hellerman

Courtesy Buffalo & Erie County Public Library

Pete Seeger was uncomfortable with the Weavers' sudden success, which had them dressing up in suits and ties (tuxedos on one or more occasions) and singing only pop-oriented folk songs like "Kisses Sweeter Than Wine," "On Top of Old Smokey," and "When the Saints Go Marching In." He wrote in *The Incompleat Folksinger*: "Our then manager would not let me sing for the hootenannies and workers' groups. Decca, hungry for more hits, insisted on teaming us with a big band; predictably, the result was almost the opposite of how we wanted to sound."

The other side of this story comes from *Lonesome Traveler*, Doris Willens's biography of Lee Hays, in which the author notes that Hays took issue with Seeger's version. Willens quotes Hays's typed memoirs: "It's true [the group's manager] believed we should concentrate on our commercial work and not sing for any unrespectable things like hootenannies and what Pete calls workers' groups. But it is also true that we had a meeting at which we decided that at that point in our career and at that point in history, we should try to continue to be as commercial and successful as possible in order to beat the blacklist on its own ground and to avoid any controversial appearances that would work against our reputation as commercial singers. That was a joint decision which Pete agreed to. It is also true that having agreed to it he said, 'I'll go along with it, but I will feel like a prisoner.' All during the rest of our time together, he felt and acted like a prisoner. Life became very uncomfortable for all of us."

Courtesy Vanguard Records

Left to right: Pete Seeger, Lee Hays, Ronnie Gilbert, and Fred Hellerman. In 1952, blacklisting put an end to the Weavers' pop aspirations; their bookings went from national television shows and classy nightclubs and concert halls to a single booking at Cleveland's Daffy's Bar before the group broke up. But it wasn't the final curtain for the group. In 1955, Harold Leventhal re-launched the Weavers with a Christmas Eve concert at Carnegie Hall. The response was tremendous. The result was a series of reunion concerts and limited tours over the next couple of years. Vanguard Records, formed in 1948 by Maynard and Seymour Solomon, issued the concert record and two reunion records, *At Carnegie Hall '60* and *Reunion at Carnegie Hall '63*. The group finally disbanded after 1963. In between there were a number of replacements for Pete Seeger, who left in 1958.

In 1981, Leventhal put together one last hurrah for the Weavers with another Carnegie Hall concert. Leventhal knew Lee Hays was in deteriorating health (a diabetic condition had forced amputation of both legs and the implantation of a pacemaker) and thought a reunion would be spiritually uplifting for Hays as well as the rest of the group. The concert was a success, and a documentary filmmaker, Jim Brown, who had known and revered Hays as a youngster, filmed the concert and a subsequent reunion picnic at Hays's land in Creton-on-Hudson, north of New York City. The moving documentary film, *Wasn't That a Time!*, named after one of Hays's songs, also includes individual interviews.

The film stands as a posthumous memoir to Hays, who was never able to write his own story. He died a month after viewing the final cut of the movie. Leventhal's letter to Lee Hays (reprinted in *Lonesome Traveler*) reads, "The reunion was above all a triumph for *you*. You made it possible, otherwise it would not have been The Weavers. I know what you went through, uncertainties, doubts, concern, but with all these problems you stayed with it and *you made it*. It was an experience and an event that 5,400 people will never forget. It was a celebration of Love, Respect and Admiration, and it was a great musical event. Above all, Lee, I am proud of you and love you more for the great joy you gave us all. And now I will officially recognize your 'retirement.'"

How time changes things. When the "Hammer Song" was rerecorded as a top ten hit as "If I Had a Hammer" by Peter, Paul and Mary in 1962, there was no political fallout over the lines "Love between the brothers and sisters," as there had been when the Weavers recorded it.

came up with the name after reading Gerhart Hauptmann's play *The Weavers*, about a nineteenth-century Silesian peasant revolt.

Seeger's wife, Toshi Ohta, through her friendship with club owner Max Gordon, secured a two-week job for the group at the Village Vanguard. Alan Lomax brought famed poet Carl Sandburg to see them, and his praises led newspaper editors to review them. The subsequent rave reviews led to a six-month stay at the night club. In 1950, Decca Records put the Weavers together with ex-Tommy Dorsey arrranger Gordon Jenkins. The subsequent orchestrated release of Leadbelly's "Goodnight, Irene" went on to sell a couple million copies and thrust the group to the top of the popular music charts. By the end of the year the Weavers had other hits, as well. Ohta could no longer keep up with the demands for this new hit group; so, she handed over the reins of management to Harold Leventhal, who booked the group into some of the top rooms in America.

The success story didn't last long. The cold war had given way to the Korean War and the blackballing of Communist sympathizers. America's one-time Russian allies had become the "Red Menace." The blacklist had its roots in 1947, with the start of a red-baiting newsletter called *Counterattack*, and swelled in force by 1950. A 213-page booklet, *Red Channels: Communist Influence on Radio and Television*, published in June 1950, listed the names of 151 writers, actors, singers, dancers, and other entertainment figures reported to have belonged to the "Communist front." Suffice it to say, after 1952 the Weavers were no longer able to work steadily, and the individual members were effectively blacklisted.

The Weavers, and before them the Almanac Singers, established the strong link with left-wing politics that in the late fifties and early sixties would be rekindled by Harry Belafonte, Peter, Paul and Mary, Bob Dylan, the Byrds, and many others. Our musical trip to the year 1950 is now ended. The next half of the century would build on the foundations laid down in the first half. Rock'n'roll, which combined elements of underground country and blues, would replace Tin Pan Alley standards as the popular music of choice from the mid-1950s to 2000. And, just as the underground had provoked and inspired the popular music forms of the period 1900 to 1950, so, too, would it inform and influence the music of the second half of the century.

Postscript: The Kings of Rock'n'Roll

Left, Bill Haley (top left) with his Comets, and *right*, Elvis Presley.

Throughout this history of mainstream and underground forms of music, there has been an attempt to show connections between various artists, musical styles and musical time periods. Rock'n'roll music is a form of underground elements of white country and black blues that came together and surfaced between the years 1954 and 1956, as a new kind of popular music. It is revealing that the first leaders of the form, Bill Haley and Elvis Presley, started out as country-oriented artists, added rhythm and blues elements and created a new form. Of course, as Peter Allen would sing, everything old is new again. To the pop audience of the 1950s, this was revolutionary music.

We have seen how the outrageous stage actions of wild pianists like Harry "The Hipster" Gibson, Dorothy Doregan, jump and jive meister Louis Jordan, and honker Big Jay McNeely were rejected by the jazz mavens. Country music—be it Roy Acuff's archaic cry, Eddy Arnold's country crooning, Bob Wills' western swing versatility, or Ernest Tubb's crying-in-his-beer honky tonk—was viewed as strictly regional hillbilly dreck by most people outside the form.

Bill Haley and Elvis Presley brought the forms of blues and country together in a new context. Consider the post-swing pop state of mind between 1945 and 1955. Artists like Frank Sinatra, Perry Como and Doris Day were in control of their emotions as they sang. They stood in front of the orchestra calm, adult and sane. This was expected of artists hoping to gain popularity. To paraphrase Comden and Green from *Singin' in the Rain*, "Dignity, always Dignity." Haley and Presley broke down this code of dignified stage demeanor. Haley's Comets flung their bodies on the floor. Al Rex, the bassist, would lie on his back and hoist the bass up with his feet, at times throwing his giant bass up into the air. He also would mount the bass like a rider, while still playing it. Rudy Pompilli, the Comets' saxman, executed breathtaking acrobatics, dropping on his knees and laying on his back while blowing the horn (a la Big Jay McNeely). Elvis Presley not only shook his hips and gyrated wildly, but, early in his career, he even lay down and rolled around on the stage. This was not mature adult behavior. No, this was rock'n'roll, a new pop attitude, to be sure, but one that had existed—albeit underground—for years. Suddenly, it raised its demonic head to thrill and horrify the pop audiences of the 1950s and everafter.

Bill Haley started as a yodeling cowboy. In 1944, he joined Shorty Cook's country band, the Downhomers, based out of Fort Wayne, Indiana, where they appeared on WOWO radio and hosted the popular Saturday night barn dance "Hoosier Hop." Haley was brought in to replace Kenny Roberts, who had been drafted. Roberts taught Haley the intricacies of yodeling before he left. Haley eventually moved on to Chester, Pennsylvania, where he hosted a radio show as a disc jockey and formed cowboy groups with names like the Four Aces of Western Swing (1948-49) and the Saddlemen (1949-52). Haley's groups were a unique blend of Louis Jordan's jump and jive and Bob Wills' western swing. Haley, like Wills, billed his group "the most versatile band in the land." He also promoted the Saddlemen as "The CowBoy Jive Band," describing their music in ads as "Jive, Cowboy, Popular and Hillbilly."

The Saddlemen recorded pre-rock songs like "Rocket 88," a cover of Jackie Brenston's rhythm and blues hit, and "Rock the Joint," another r&b cover. Haley always thought that the 1951 "Rock the Joint" marked the beginning of rock'n'roll. This A-side of the record was what Haley called a race record (r&b) and the B-side, "Icy Heart," was country, a play on Hank Williams's hit "Cold, Cold, Heart." There is much more to be said about the innovations of Bill Haley as the father of rock'n'roll (so many firsts)—but that is for another time and place (and book). Nonetheless, Haley has long been critically lambasted, especially by rock writers. Such criticism is totally without merit, given the indisputable facts of his early, ground-breaking accomplishments.

Elvis Presley was discussed at some length in Chapter 4 (under the subheading "Sex, Drugs, and Rock'n'Roll"). Presley grew up in the South listening to the "Grand Ole Opry" as well as to Memphis's black radio station WDIA, which featured DJ-singers like B.B. King, who had his own show in 1949 singing jingles for Peptikon, a patented cure-all, and Rufus Thomas, who had four regular shows— "Sepia Swing Club," "Cool Train," "Hoot'n'Holler," and "Boogie for Breakfast." Presley's mother used to chide him for listening to the station, because church-going folks weren't supposed to indulge in such sinful activities.

When Presley made his first recordings for Sam Phillips's Sun Records in 1954, he blended pop crooning, Southern gospel, country, and rhythm and blues together. The five releases Presley made for Sun between 1954 and 1955, mixed white country and black blues equally: the A-side of each record was country-oriented, the B-side, rhythm and blues. Nonetheless, Presley was viewed as a country singer who "bopped the blues," it wasn't until he signed with a major label, RCA Victor, in 1955 (his recordings for RCA were released in early 1956), that he was called a rock'n'roller.

Colin Escott and Martin Hawkins write in *Sun Records: The Brief History of the Legendary Record Label*: "So much has been written about Presley, especially since his death in August 1977, that it is almost superfluous to comment upon his contribution to popular and rock music. He was also a pivotal figure in the development of country and western music. He was not doing anything radically different, but he took some developments further than their originators intended. White country singers had freely plagiarized and overtly covered r&b material since the war and many country boogie artists used black rhythms and black instrumentation. Wayne Raney and the Delmore Brothers, for example, had mastered the boogie idiom as successfully as any jump blues combo."

Presley's first recording, Sun #209, featured a cover of Bill Monroe's bluegrass anthem, "Blue Moon of Kentucky," and a cover of Arthur "Big Boy" Crudup's blues original, "That's All Right." Presley and his trio were billed as the "Blue Moon Boys," and their first club appearance was at the Bel Air club in Memphis with Doug Poindexter's Starlite Wranglers, a country and western band. Bob Neal, Presley's first professional manager, placed an advertisement in the trade papers, in September 1954, calling Presley "the freshest, newest voice in country music." That same month, Presley was being billed as the "King of the Western Bop." Even in 1955, Presley was being introduced on stage as the "Bopping Hillbilly."

As previously noted, much has been made about the influence of r&b on early rock'n'roll, but too little credit has been given to country music. Presley, Buddy Holly, Jerry Lee Lewis, Johnny Cash, and the Everly Brothers, all seminal rockers, grew up listening to country music. When Presley went into the

Sun studios in 1956 with Jerry Lee Lewis, Johnny Cash, and Carl Perkins and casually sang some spirituals (Sam Phillips put the tape player on and the session was later released as *The Million Dollar Quartet*), four of the selections were Bill Monroe songs: "Little Cabin Home on the Hill," "Summertime Is Past and Gone," "I Hear a Sweet Voice Calling," and "Sweetheart You Done Me Wrong." When Presley sang "Blue Moon of Kentucky" on the "Grand Ole Opry," he came over to Monroe and apologized for the way he changed the tune. Monroe told Presley that if it would help him get his start and give him a different style, then it was all right. Interestingly, Monroe immediately changed his interpretation of his own theme song as a result of Presley's uptempo alterations.

Bill Haley, the underappreciated synthesizer, also had some influence on Presley that has seldom been credited. After Presley had a couple of records out on Sun, Colonel Tom Parker took over Presley's management. Parker's first move was to call Haley's manager, Lord Jim Ferguson, and ask if Presley could go out on tour with Haley to get some experience. Hank Snow opened, followed by Presley, then Haley, who, of course, closed the show. As a result Presley saw first hand the wild antics of the Comets—the riding of the bass, the madcap saxophone squealing, and the generally rocking sounds of the hottest group in popular music. Presley first talked to King Haley in Kansas City and told him he was a fan. Haley related in John Swenson's *Bill Haley: The Daddy of Rock and Roll*, "I remember one night he went out and did a show and asked me what I thought. I had watched the show and I told him, 'Elvis, you're leaning too much on ballads and what have you. You've got a natural rhythm feeling, so do your rhythm tunes.' Now this was a long time before he was a big hit, you know. (I think he was doing a tune called 'That's All Right, Mama,' or something at the time.) So he went out and he had the attitude which most young kids do that he was really going to go out there and stop the show and knock Bill Haley off the stage, which at that time was an impossibility because we were the number one and what have you. And he went out there facing Bill Haley fans."

Rock and Roll Hall of Fame Inductees: Pre-1950 Career Starts

1986	**1990**
John Hammond	Louis Armstrong
Robert Johnson	Charlie Christian
Jimmie Rodgers	"Ma" Rainey
1987	**1991**
Leonard Chess	Dave Bartholomew
Ahmet Ertegun	John Lee Hooker
Bill Haley	Howlin' Wolf
Louis Jordan	
B.B. King	**1992**
Big Joe Turner	Leo Fender
T-Bone Walker	Elmore James
Muddy Waters	Professor Longhair
Hank Williams	Doc Pomus
1988	**1993**
Leadbelly	Ruth Brown
Woody Guthrie	Milt Gabler
Les Paul	Dinah Washington
1989	**1994**
The Ink Spots	The Orioles
Bessie Smith	
The Soul Stirrers	

Haley made the first series of rock'n'roll records beginning in 1951, releases directly aimed at the youth market ("Rocket 88," "Rock the Joint," "Shake, Rattle and Roll," and "Rock Around the Clock," among others). Haley also made the first rock'n'roll films in 1955 (*Rock Around the Clock* and *Rock, Rock, Rock*) and provided the first rock'n'roll record on film ("Rock Around the Clock" from *Blackboard Jungle*). However, the reader will be hard-pressed to find a book on the life of this adventurous pioneer—he simply wasn't "cool" enough. (John Swensen's biography will not likely be found in your local bookstore.) On the other hand, there are more books written about Haley's successor, or co-founder, of rock'n'roll, Elvis Presley, than any musician in the history of American popular music. Presley was a more glamorous and a more versatile performer than Haley, and perhaps that is part and parcel of popular culture pizzazz. The two leaders of rock'n'roll: the "Daddy," Bill Haley, and the eventual "King," Elvis Presley, added equal doses of underground musical forms—white country and black blues—to offer up to the world a new sound that would dominate the second half of the twentieth century's popular music mainstream: rock'n'roll.

Rock'n'Roll's First Recordings: 1944-1950

Recording	Artist/Group	Comments	Year
Blues, Part 2	Jazz at the Philharmonic	1st "live" hit of honking sax (Illinois Jacquet and Jack McVea)	1944
The Honeydripper	Joe Liggins & His Honeydrippers	1st r&b combo hit	1945
Be-Baba-Leba	Helen Humes w/ Bill Doggett	1st bop influence on r&b	1945
House of Blue Lights	Freddie Slack w/ Ella Mae Morse	1st white r&b stars	1946
That's All Right	Arthur "Big Boy" Crudup	1st blues/r&b 45; prototype of rockabilly	1946-49
Open the Door, Richard	Jack McVea & His All Stars	Early r&b novelty; 1st commercial record to fade out at end; inspired spate of successful covers	1947
Tomorrow Night	Lonnie Johnson	1st country blues pop hit	1948
Good Rockin' Tonight	Wynonie Harris & His All Stars	Started trend of records concerned with "rockin"	1948
We're Gonna Rock, We're Gonna Roll	Wild Bill Moore	1st "honking" saxophone hit record	1948
It's Too Soon to Know	The Orioles	Early r&b vocal group hit; defined "doo wop" era	1948
Boogie Chillen'	John Lee Hooker	1st major electrified Delta blues hit	1948
Guitar Boogie	Arthur Smith and the Crackerjacks	Popularized boogie-woogie music on the guitar	1945-48
Drinkin' Wine Spo-Dee-O-Dee	Stick McGhee & His Buddies	Early party-time drinking song to become a hit	1949
Rock the Joint	Jimmy Preston & His Prestonians	Early all-out rocker, ultimately led to Bill Haley's changeover from country music to proto-rockabilly	1949
Saturday Night Fish Fry	Louis Jordan & His Tympany Five	Early unabashed, uninhibited pop hits about black high life	1949
Mardi Gras in New Orleans	Professor Longhair & His Shuffling Hungarians (or His New Orleans Boys)	1st of many New Orleans recordings to capitalize on the city's peculiar rhythms.	1950
The Fat Man	Fats Domino	1st of almost 70 Imperial records and 63 r&b charters for Domino; 1st New Orleans hit that *sounded* New Orleans	1950
Rollin' and Tumblin'	Muddy Waters	One of earliest modern, amplified Chicago blues records	1950
Birmingham Bounce	Hardrock Gunter & the Pebbles	Early white, popular record about rockin "'on the dance floor"	1950
I'm Movin' On	Hank Snow & His Rainbow Ranch Boys	1st major train song set to a boogie rhythm	1950
Teardrops From My Eyes	Ruth Brown w/ Budd Johnson's Orchestra	1st major jump hit for Atlantic's earliest consistent hitmaker, the "First Lady of R&B"	1950
Hot Rod Race	Arkie Shibley & His Mountain Boys	Introduced auto racing into pop music and underscored the car's relevance to youth culture	1950

Source: Jim Dawson and Steve Propes, What Was the First Rock 'n' Roll Record

DISCOGRAPHY AND VIDEOGRAPHY

This is a selective list of music and video releases that will enhance and reinforce the historical information provided in the text. In most cases, the discs listed in the discography are in print. Record albums (LP) and cassettes (cas) are listed only if compact discs are not available at the time of this book's printing (Fall 1995). The *Schwann Spectrum*, Summer 1995 (volume 6, number 3) and the *Billboard/Phonolog Music Reference Library*, 1995, Trade Service Corporation, were the main discography references. (In a couple of instances where there is a dearth of musical releases—minstrelsy, for example—I have included an out of print recording in hopes that the record company listed will see fit to re-release the item. These few items are designated as "out of print" [OP].) The videos selected are a combination of documentaries, concert films, and feature films listed as being commercially available, according to *Videolog*, 1995 Trade Service Corporation. Many of the videos are in black and white—color videos will be noted as such. Video prices, like audio box sets, are included when such a price is listed; all prices are current as of 1995.

The listings begin with Chapter 2, because Chapter 1, *Mainstream Popular Music and the Underground*, is a general overview. Each chapter is broken up into subtitles found therein, and the appropriate listings then follow. In cases where compilation discs or videos cover the entire spectrum, i.e., *Music From the New York Stage, 1890-1929*, or *The Blues: A Smithsonian Collection of Classic Blues Singers*, the chapter that first introduces that style of music or subgenre of a form, will house that collection. *The Music From the New York Stage* is thus covered in Chapter 2 because early vaudeville and commercial ragtime artists are covered in the subtitle *Tin Pan Alley*. In the case of *The Blues* collection, the chapter which introduces the history of the blues, Chapter 4, lists that compilation, even though some artists and styles found within that collection are covered in later chapters. The rule of thumb: if a good portion of the music and artists are discussed in the earlier chapter, that's where the collection is covered.

In the listings under each chapter subheading, the recordings are noted first, followed by the videos (if available). For the most part, I have tried to select for each main artist (bold face entries within each chapter) a minimum of two representative recordings if they exist—and, in some cases, a more extensive boxed set. In the case of compilations, I have tried to let the reader know what artists or songs are featured. The author is personally familiar with, and has copies of, over 90 percent of the recordings and films listed in the Discography and Videography.

Chapter 2: THE BEGINNING 1900-1917

This section is, by far, the least represented on record and video.

Recordings

African Rhythms & Instruments, Vol. 1—Samples of music from Mali, Niger, Ghana, Nigeria, Upper Volta, and Senegal. African percussive patterns, antiphonal call and response, syncopation, polymeter, and the rest are heard in abundance. There are two other volumes as well. LYRCD-7328

Savannah Syncopators—Subtitled: "African Retention in the Blues," this album illustrates many of the important points that Paul Oliver, author of the book *Savannah Syncopators* (1970) makes. The spirituals, gospel songs, work songs, jazz and blues which flourished during the past century, were developed in America, but were *informed* by the African connection.
Columbia 52799 (LP) (OP)

Minstrelsy: Blackface or Ethiopian Music

Recordings

Banjo & Minstrel Days—This out of print record is a "plink-plank-plunk" banjo extravaganza of classic songs of minstrel days by a unit called The Happy Harts—a "singing banjo band" that made a series of recordings during the 1950s. Other collections include *Banjo on My Knee: A Collection of Old Established Minstrel Songs*, and *Hey! Mr. Banjo*. These, and the next release by Bill Cullen, are listed because I've found them useful in class—and because hardly anything else exists. Let's hope there will be a reissue series forthcoming.
Kapp KL-1061 (LP) (OP)

Bill Cullen's Minstrel Spectacular—Television host ("The Price Is Right") and panelist ("I've Got A Secret") of the 1950s and '60s, Cullen plays master of ceremonies to a simulated minstrel show that reflects the era beautifully. Selections such as "Old Dan Tucker," "Beautiful Dreamer," "Rufus Rastus Johnson Brown," "Georgia Camp Meetin'," "Waiting for the Robert E. Lee," "Dixie," "Camptown Races," and "Banjo on My Knee," among others, give a flavor of the musical sounds of that bygone era. ABC-Paramount-264 (LP) (OP)

Minstrels & Tunesmiths—Very early recordings by pioneer country music performers who incorporated minstrel tunes into their repertoire. Not as "representative" of a true minstrel show, but this recording is in print and does reflect the ways in which early country musicians and medicine show men utilized the form.
Arhoolie Records-409 (LP)

American Dreamer: Songs of [Stephen] Foster—Formal interpretations of Stephen Foster's more sentimental "parlor songs," rather than his rambunctious minstrel novelties. "Beautiful Dreamer," "Jeanie with the Light Brown Hair," and "Old Home Medley" comprise his best known numbers. "Linger in Blissful Repose," "Open the Letters, Love," "My Wife is a Most Knowing Woman," and "Gentle Annie" are examples of the softer side of this

important early American composer.
Angel Records CD-C-54621

Williams, Bert–*Nobody & Other Songs*
Folkways RBF-602 (LP)

Videos
There seem to be no commercially available videos of minstrelsy (please inform me if I'm misled). *Harmony Lane* (1935), *Swanee River* (1939), and *I Dream of Jeanie* (1952) are all Hollywood films about Stephen Foster, but are seldom aired on television. *Dixie* (1943), starring Bing Crosby as minstrel man Dan Emmett of the Virginia Minstrels, is occasionally shown on television–but that's about the extent of it.

Ragtime (Classic and Pop)

Recordings
Alexander's Ragtime Band–Motion picture
    soundtrack which features 20 Irving Berlin classics. Berlin was the widely hailed "King of Ragtime," and his punchy, lilting pop songs were the rage of the pre-1920s. Beginning with "Alexander's Ragtime Band" in 1911, America caught the fever, and the soundtrack is filled with commercial ragtime selections such as "Ragtime Violin," "Everybody's Doing It," "Everybody Step," "Blue Skies," and "International Rag."
Stash Records

Easter Parade–Another motion picture soundtrack
    featuring early ragtime numbers from the pen and piano of Irving Berlin. "Everybody's Doing It," "Stepping Out With My Baby," "I Love a Piano," "Shaking the Blues Away," "Ragtime Violin," "Snooky Ookums," and "When the Midnight Choo-Choo Leaves for Alabam," among others.   Sony Music Special Products AK-45392

George M!–Classic songs written by and associated
    with the great George M. Cohan, starring Joel Grey. This 1968 Broadway musical showcased Grey and a lively supporting cast interpreting "Forty-Five Minutes from Broadway," "You're a Grand Old Flag," "All Aboard for Broadway," "Harrigan," "Yankee Doodle Dandy," and others. The play followed Cohan from birth to his final 1937 Broadway triumph, playing President Roosevelt, in George and Ira Gershwin's *I'd Rather Be Right*, the only musical in which he appeared that he did not write himself.   Columbia CK-03200

George M. Cohan: A Tribute To–Speech from Cohan's
    60th birthday celebration, plus vocal selections from Broadway shows.   Folkways RFS-604 (LP)

Joplin, Scott–*Joplin: The Original Rags, 1896-1904*
EPM (Jazz Archives) 15726-2
King of Ragtime Writers (From Classic Piano Rolls)
Biograph BCD-110

Maple Leaf Rag: Ragtime in Rural America–Intriguing
    concept of black and white rural, underground performers playing ragtime tunes. The black stylists include Blind Willie McTell ("Kiss It Kid"), Bunk Johnson

("The Entertainer"), and Blind Rev. Gary Davis ("Maple Leaf Rag"). White artists covered in the book include Jimmie Tarlton ("Mexican Rag"), Gid Tanner and the Skillet Lickers ("Hawkins Rag"), Bill Boyd and His Cowboy Ramblers ("Barn Dance Rag"), and Flatt and Scruggs and the Foggy Mountain Boys ("Randy Lynn Rag").   New World Records NW-235 (LP)

Morath, Max–*The Best of Scott Joplin and Other Rag Classics*
    Includes solo piano as well as a ragtime quartet of piano, bass, guitar, and banjo. In addition to Joplin classics such as "The Entertainer," "The Ragtime Dance," "Elite Syncopations," "The Cascades," and "Original Rags," Morath includes Tom Turpin's "St. Louis Rag," James Scott's "Grace and Beauty," Joseph Lamb's "American Beauty," and Clarence Woods' "Slippery Elm."
Vanguard Twofer VCD-39/40

Rifkin, Joshua–*Joshua Rifkin Plays Rags and Tangos* A
    series of delicate piano interpretations. It appears that the popular Rifkin items that caused a sensation back in the early 1970s on Nonesuch Records (*Scott Joplin Piano Rags*), and orchestrator Gunther Schuller's interpretations of Joplin's *Red Back Book* releases, are no longer in print.   London 425225-2

The Sting–Marvin Hamlisch and his piano and
    orchestrations of ragtime music that underscored the Hollywood hit film.   MCA MCAD-31034

Videos
Alexander's Ragtime Band (1938)–The smash hit film of
    Alexander and his San Francisco unit wowing 'em in a turn-of-the-century tale filled with Irving Berlin's commercial ragtime nuggets. Tyrone Power plays the serious-minded Alexander, and Don Amechie is his piano-playing buddy. Love enters the picture with the ever pouty Alice Faye. Jack Oakie and Ethel Merman provide comedy and musical pizzazz.
109 min. FOX 1121V $19.98

Easter Parade (1948)–Another Irving Berlin name-
    above-the-title compendium of ragtime era selections–this time in New York's theater district with Fred Astaire as a song and dance man whose partner, played by Ann Miller, ups and leaves him for a shot at the bigs in the *Ziegfeld Follies*. Judy Garland plays the sweet-singing novice who, at first, is miscast by Astaire as a dance partner. He finally gets it right and places the emphasis on his new partner's singing abilities. Astaire came out of retirement to replace Gene Kelly, who broke his ankle playing volleyball, and was in his usual great form. A wonderful peek into the hurly-burly days of early vaudeville–and what great musical numbers!
103 min. color MGM/UA 202419 $19.98

Johnny Maddox Plays Ragtime (1985)– Ragtime master
    Maddox, performs at the IL Porto Theatre in Alexandria, Virginia. Concert footage of ragtime numbers include: "Sunflower Slow Drag," "Maple Leaf Rag," "Creole Belles," "Friday Night Stomp," "Whistlin' Rufus Cake Walk," and "The Teasin' Rag."
60 min. color KARTES 762-7V

Little Johnny Jones (1980)–The Goodspeed Opera House presents the George M. Cohan 1904-5 musical comedy hit about a jockey who goes to Britain to race his horse Yankee Doodle Dandy in the Derby. Along the way, he's accused of throwing the race. He's framed by an American gambler, and with the help of a private detective, he clears his name and celebrates by singing and dancing "Give My Regards to Broadway" on the Southampton Pier. "Life's a Funny Proposition After All," and "The Yankee Doodle Boy" are two of many other jaunty Cohan titles that bounce with patriotic fervor.
92 min. color WHV 3405 IV $59.95

The Story of Vernon and Irene Castle (1939)–Fred Astaire and Ginger Rogers' final outing for RKO was a biopic which was enhanced (or detracted) by Irene Castle's presence on the set. She insisted on faithful duplication of all things Castle. An excellent sampling of the dances and music of the pre-jazz period, and the best example we have today of these glorious tunes and dances of the era: "Cuddle up a Little Closer," "The Darktown Strutters' Ball," "Oh You Beautiful Doll," "Way Down Yonder in New Orleans," "Rose Room," "By the Light of the Silvery Moon," "Syncopated Walk," and many more. 93 min. NM NM8029V B $19.98

Yankee Doodle Dandy (1942)–James Cagney's Academy Award winning performance as George M. Cohan of the musical Cohan family. One of the top biopics in film history. Cagney plays the arrogant, energetic Cohan to a "tea" even though certain liberties were taken in telling the tale. From the early days of vaudeville as The Four Cohans, to the heady days of success in 1937 when Cohan is decorated for service to the American Musical Theatre, the film leaves little doubt as to the significance of this "Yankee Doodle Boy." Irene Manning played the legendary Fay Templeton, and acquits herself well on two Cohan classics, "Mary's a Grand Old Name" and "So Long Mary." 126 min. CBS/FOX 4513 V $29.98

Tin Pan Alley

Recordings
American Musical Theater: Shows, Songs and Stars (1898-1964)–A four volume chronological collection of Broadway show songs, recorded from 1906 to 1964. In most cases, this set includes original cast members; the accompanying brochures include composer and lyricist credits, recording dates, and more. Volume One (1898-1933) includes selections by Lillian Russell, George M. Cohan, Al Jolson, Eugene Cowles, Ann Wheaton, Edith Day, John Steel, and Fred and Adele Astaire. The entire package of four volumes is offered via mail by the Smithsonian Institution, Washington D.C. (4CDs/4-Dolby chrome cassette/6-LP boxed set). Each boxed set comes with a 132-page companion booklet. Purchasers of the single CDs at retail, like above, may order the book separately by mail. For further mail order information, individuals may call the Smithsonian Recording's toll-free number, 800-678-2677.
Vol. 1 Smithsonian Collection of Recordings CDRD 036-1

Music From the New York Stage, 1890-1908–Volume One: 1890-1908, includes selections from our earliest record of theatrical performances. Pearl PAST-CD-9050
Volume Two: 1908-1913– Pearl PAST-CD-9053
Volume Three: 1913-1917– Pearl PAST-CD-9056
Volume Four: 1917-1929– Pearl PAST-CD-9059

A Victor Herbert Showcase–Selections by Alfredo Campoli and His Salon Orchestra, Harry Horlick and His Orchestra, Yerkes Jazarimba Orchestra, The Musical Art Quartet, Victor Light Opera Company, The Paramount Theatre Orchestra, Jeanette MacDonald and Nelson Eddy, and others. Stage successes include numbers from *Babes in Toyland* (1903), *Mlle. Modiste* and *The Red Mill* (1906), *Naughty Marietta* (1910), and *Sweetheart* (1913). Pearl (Flapper Series) PAST-CD-9798

Videos
The Best of Burlesque–Listed as a glittering array of singers, dancers, and strippers–ribald baggy-pants comedy sketches. The "Olio" section of the minstrel show had a burlesque of a well-known play of the day (burlesque originally meaning a parody). In time, vaudeville replaced the minstrel show up north, and the rowdier and more risque elements of women stripping found favor among the less high-falutin' common folks (mostly men). An instructive and entertaining movie about this transitional period, captured beautifully by director William Friedkin, is *The Night They Raided Minsky's (1968)*, starring Jason Robards, Britt Ekland, Norman Wisdom, and Bert Lahr, in his last film. Don't miss it if it plays on television! I haven't seen the former production. But this is all there seems to be in print right now, so ... 60 min. AHV 632V $24.95

Tin Pan Alley (1940)–20th Century-Fox's follow-up to their successful 1938 *Alexander's Ragtime Band* was intended for the same stars. Instead, John Payne and Jack Oakie played the male leads as a songwriting team trying to create hits in New York's publishing house district known as Tin Pan Alley. Alice Faye and Betty Grable play the parts of a dancing sister act. Song and dance numbers include "The Sheik of Araby," "I'll Get By," "Goodbye Broadway, Hello France," "Moonlight Bay," "America I Love You," and "K-K-K-Katy."
94 min. FOX V 1818 V $19.98

Musical Stars

A sad situation here. No Billy Murray, Ada Jones, Peerless Quartet, Lillian Russell, Nora Bayes, Harry MacDonough, Blanch Sweet, or Henry Burr to be found on separate discs. At this time, even Sophie Tucker doesn't have a listing for a recording under her own name! The compilation releases are a hit or (mostly) miss situation–here's what appears to be around.

Recordings
Come Josephine in My Flying Machine–A New World recording that's subtitled "Inventions and Topics in Popular Song 1910-1929." Informative notes provided by then (still?) head of the division of Postal History at the Smithsonian Institution, Carl H. Scheele. "Hello, Frisco"

was the 1915 hit used later for a nostalgia film starring Alice Faye (*Hello, Frisco, Hello*); Harry MacDonough sings a then timely song about the emergence of magazines in Irving Berlin's "The Girl on the Magazine Cover"; Blanche Ring vocalizes a ragtime number "Come, Josephine in My Flying Machine"; Bert Williams laments prohibition with "Every One Wants a Key to My Cellar"; Nora Bayes romanticizes about "The Argentines, the Portugueses and the Greeks"; Blossom Seeley (who appeared in seven musical productions as well as regular vaudeville performances between 1911 and 1928) is "Alabamy Bound"; and finally, a song from the king of the early days of recordings, Billy Murray, who sings "Take Your Girlie to the Movies." Between 1920 and 1925 the paragraph that Victor Talking Records plugged Billy Murray's records with was repeated without change in their catalogues. The opening sentence read: "Billy Murray is one of the most successful of all American singers of Humorous songs, and probably entertains, through his Victor records, a larger audience than any other singer who has ever lived." New World Records NW 233 (LP)

Jolson, Al–*The Salesman of Song, Volume 2, 1911-1923*
Pearl (Flapper) PAST-CD-9796
You Made Me Love You; His First Recordings, Volume 1
Stash ST-CD-564

Nipper's Greatest Hits: 1901-1920–Selections by the early recording stars of mainstream popular music of this time period: Enrico Caruso, Blanche Ring, Al Jolson, Billy Murray, Ada Jones, Nora Bayes, John Steel, Alma Gluck, Jack Norworth, John McCormack, George M. Cohan, John Philip Sousa, et al. RCA 98364-2-R

The Sousa and Pryor Bands–Original recordings of the two leading bands of the pre-jazz era, John Philip Sousa's and Arthur Pryor's. Sousa's band was the premier unit of the time, with Pryor as his primary conductor. Sousa would not involve himself with the recording industry. He even wrote a warning of the dangers of the phonograph in 1906, entitled "The Menace of Mechanical Music." Sousa was first impressed by Pat Gilmore's bands and followed the tradition of march band music in 1880, he led the Marine Band, which he greatly improved. By 1892, the Marine Band had become world renowned, and Sousa was hailed as the "March King." From 1892 until his death in 1932, Sousa led his own bands–making world tours and delighting audiences with selections heard in this disc, such as: "Federal March" (1910), "Creole Belles", (1912), "At a Georgia Camp Meeting" (1908), "The Patriot" (1902), "Glory of the Yankee Navy" (1909), et al. Arthur Pryor carried Sousa's tradition with his own fine band (some say better than the master's). He's heard performing "Yankee Shuffle" and "The Teddy Bear's Picnic" (1908); "Falcon March" (1910); and "General Pershing March" (1926).
New World Records NW 282 (LP)

Stepping' on the Gas: Rags to Jazz 1913-1927–The transitional sounds that fit somewhere between ragtime and jazz are heard on this compilation of dance bands.

Lawrence Bushee's liner notes stress the problem of today's audiences and yesterday's jazz critics in fully appreciating the early jazz-oriented bands that played ensemble-oriented dance music for the masses. Included in this recording are James Reese Europe's renderings of "Castle House Rag," "Castle Walk," "Memphis Blues," and "Clarinet Marmalade." Early jazz sounds such as Freddie Keppard's "Stock Yard Strut," Kid Ory's "Society Blues," Sam Morgan's "Stepping' on the Gas," and Clarence Williams' Blue Five interpretation of James P. Johnson's "Old Fashioned Love," are heard to good advantage in this set. New World NW 269

Note:
One of the very best sources for historical music presentations comes from: New World Records, 701 Seventh Ave., New York, NY 10036: Tel. (212) 302-0460

Currators of Early Pop America

Recordings

Morris, Joan and William Bolcom–*After the Ball* Classic old song hits performed by this successful husband and wife duo, include: "Meet Me in St. Louis," "Shine on Harvest Moon," "I've Got Rings on My Fingers," "Wait 'Til the Sun Shines Nellie," "Bird in a Gilded Cage," "Come Down My Evenin' Star," "I Don't Care," "After the Ball," et al. Nonesuch Records CD-79148-2

Whitcomb, Ian–*Treasures of Tin Pan Alley* Whitcomb blends pre and post-1920s songs so that they all have that early Tin Pan Alley innocence. "The Farmyard Cabaret," "Lazy," "T'Aint' No Sin," "On the Pier," "You're in Kentucky Sure as You're Born," and "Down in Honky Tonk Town" are some of the obscure, but highly enjoyable numbers. Audiophile AP 115 (LP)
Crooner Tunes and *At the Ragtime Ball*
Ian Whitcomb, Inc. (LP)
Ragtime Revels and *Ian Whitcomb's Ragtime America*
Ian Whitcomb, Inc.

Videos

Don't Say Goodbye Miss Ragtime–A history of ragtime played as a musical variety show presented on a showboat. An array of singers and dancers, as well as plenty of Irving Berlin songs. IAN WHITCOMB, INC.

Tin Pan Alley–A PBS special shot in Los Angeles, in front of an appreciative audience. The best video history I've seen yet about the roots of Tin Pan Alley. Studio segments and numerous photographs are interspersed with songs and dances from the turn of the century to World War I. Sentimental pop classics ("After the Ball," "Bird in a Gilded Cage"); war songs "I Didn't Raise My Boy to Be a Soldier," "Belgan Rose," "When AlexanderTakes His Ragtime Band to France"); ragtime numbers ("When the Bees Make Honey Down in Sunny Alabam'," "Dance and Grow Thin"); jazz ("Everybody Step," "Masculine Women and Feminine Men") and crooner tunes ("Sleepy Time Gal," "My Blue Heaven"). This all adds, up to wonderful entertainment, plus this is a stirring evocation of period music.

IAN WHITCOMB, INC.

Chapter 3: POPULAR MUSIC: 1917-1934

The Roaring Twenties: The Jazz Age

Recordings

Billboard Pop Memories: The 1920s—Ten number one-hits which include Ben Selvin's "Dardanella," Isham Jones' "Swingin' on Down the Lane," Al Jolson's "April Showers," Paul Whiteman's "Whispering" and "Valencia" and "Charmaine!" by Guy Lombardo. The biggest hit of the first forty-two years of the century—Gene Austin's "My Blue Heaven," is also heard.
RCA/BMG/Rhino R 2-71575-DRCI-1104

Nipper's Greatest Hits-The 1920's—A bigger package than above (there are 20 hits), which covers the entire territory of the decade. Highlights include Irving Aaronson's madcap "Let's Misbehave," George Olsen's "The Varsity Drag," Eddie Cantor singing his classic, "Makin' Whoopee," and dance favorites such as "Charleston," "Black Bottom," and "Lucky Lindy."
RCA 2258-2-R

Yes Sir, That's My Baby (1920-1929)—Some of the same songs as the other two packages (Paul Whiteman's "Whispering," Austin's "My Blue Heaven," Vernon Dalhart's "The Prisoner's Song"), as well as Whispering Jack Smith's "Gimme a Little Kiss, Will Ya Huh?" Fred Waring's "Collegiate," Ted Lewis' "A Good Man is Hard to Find," and Blossom Seeley singing the title tune.
New World Records 279 (LP)

Broadway (and the Composers)

American Musical Theater: Shows, Songs, and Stars—A 40 song set with a lavishly illustrated 130-page booklet annotated by Dwight Bowers. This history goes right up to *Fiddler on the Roof* (1964). Here, are to be found early samples of musicals such as *Oh, Boy!*, *Lady, Be Good!*, *Girl Crazy*, *The Band Wagon*, *Roberta*, and *Anything Goes*, among others.
Smithsonian Collection of Recordings 4 SMI-CD-R 036-P6
20483

American Popular Song: Six Decades of Songwriters and Singers—This 5 CD set, with a 152-page booklet, offers a general history of each popular song, with notes on the selections, and photos and biographies of the songwriters and singers. Over 110 performances are included—although a number of the performances extend beyond 1934. Still, this is a great package, which the *Los Angeles Times* trumpeted as, "The best collection of American Songs and Singers ever assembled."
Smithsonian Collection of Recordings 5-SMI-CD-RD031

American Songbook Series: Irving Berlin—
Smithsonian Collection of Recordings CD-RD-048-1

American Songbook Series: George Gerswin—
Smithsonian Collection of Recordings CD-RD-048-2

American Songbook Series: Cole Porter—
Smithsonian Collection of Recordings CD-RD-048-3

Anything Goes—1987 Revival Cast album
RCA 7769-2-2 RC
1989 Studio Cast—The 1934 Broadway version with original orchestrations by Robert Russell Bennett.
Angel CDC-49848-2

Berlin, Irving—*The Irving Berlin 100th Anniversary Collection*
MCA MCAD-3934

Cantor, Eddie—*A Centennial Celebration: The Best of Eddie Cantor* (4 CDs, bonus tracks). RCA 07863-66033-2
Rare Early Recordings, 1919-1921
Biograph BLP-12054 (LP)

Cole Porter in the '30s, Vol. 1: How's Your Romance? 1930-1934— Koch International Classics KIC-CD-7217

Great Hits From Sigmund Romberg—Operetta favorites by artists from the time period (Jack Hylton Orchestra, Nelson Eddy, etc.), and classic shows-including *The Desert Song*, *Maytime*, *New Moon*, *Blossom Time*, among others. Pearl (Flapper Series) and PAST-CD-9761

The Great Ziegfeld—From the 1936 biopic that featured Fanny Brice and Louise Rainer, as well as William Powell as the great Ziegfeld.
Classic Int'l Filmusicals CIF-3005 (LP)

Legendary Entertainers—Stars like Cliff Edwards ("Singin' in the Rain"), Sophie Tucker ("Some of These Days"), Vaughn DeLeath ("Blues Skies"), Helen Kane ("Button Up Your Overcoat"), Nick Lucas ("Tiptoe Through the Tulips"), Charles King ("Wedding of the Painted Doll"), Kate Smith ("Clementine"), Whispering Jack Smith ("Me and My Shadow"), et al.   ProArte/Fanfare CDD-483

Jerome Kern Showcase—Early works such as *Sunny* and *Sally* are included. Pearl (Flapper Series) PAST-CD-9767

Merman, Ethel—*I Get a Kick Out of You*
Pearl (Flapper Series) PEACD-7056

No, No, Nanette—(1971 Broadway revival cast)
Columbia CK-30563

Stars of the Ziegfeld Follies—Selections by Eddie Cantor, Nora Bayes, Will Rogers, Van and Schenck, Marilyn Miller, Helen Morgan, Bert Williams.
Sandy Hook CSH-2018 (cas)

Show Boat—Music from the 1989 Broadway Show Album— The original 1927 Broadway version with original orchestration by Robert Russell Bennett.
Angel CDC-49847

Music from the 1993 Studio Cast   Pickwick PWK-4161

S'Wonderful: The Music of George Gershwin—Selections by Fred Astaire, Gertude Lawrence, Dorothy Dickson, Cliff Edwards, Fred and Adele Astaire, Al Jolson, Buddy Lee and the Gilt-Edged Four, et al.
Pearl (Flapper Series) Past CD-9777

The Will Rogers Follies: A Life In Revue—The 1991 Broadway Show Album starring Keith Carradine as Will Rogers. Music provided by Cy Coleman, Adolph Green and Betty Comden.   Columbia CK-48606

Ziegfeld Follies of 1919—With members of the original cast. Songs from this reconstruction of the original production include: "I'm Sorry I Ain't Got It (You Could Have It If I Had It)," "Checkers (It's Your Move Now)," "Bring Back Those Wonderful Days," "Somebody," "The Moon Shines on the Moonshine," and "Everybody Wants the Key to My Cellar," all by Bert Williams; "My Baby's Arms" "Tulip Time," and "A Pretty Girl is Like a Melody," by handsome ballad vocalist, John Steel; "Mandy," "Oh! How She Can Sing," and "Sweet Kisses," by the successful comedy duo Van and Schenck; "I've Got My Captain Working for Me Now," "You Don't Need the Wine to Have a Wonderful Time (While They Still Make These Wonderful Girls)," "Oh! The Last Rose of Summer (Was the Sweetest Rose of All)," "When They're Old Enough to Know Better (It's Better to Leave Them Alone)," and "You'd Be Surprised" by comic-singer-superstar Eddie Cantor.
Smithsonian American Musical Theater Series P-14272 R-009 (LP)

Videos
George White's Scandals (1945)—Not the original film version that featured Alice Faye and Rudy Vallce in 1934. This one stars Joan Davis, Jack Davis, Jack Haley, and Gene Krupa. At least the viewer can grasp the feeling of putting on a revue. Musical highlights include Ethel Smith's rendition of Gershwin's "Liza," and Joan Davis and Jack Haley's interpretation of the Scandal's 1931 smash hit "Life is Just a Bowl of Cherries."   95 min. REP 525880748

New Deal Rhythm (1930-1937)—A compilation of five one-reelers (short films about ten minutes in length) made during the Depression. Ruth Etting in "Roseland," bandleader Ina Ray Hutton in "I'm 100% for You," and trumpet star Red Nichols in "The Story of the Dixieland Band," are featured. 55 min. VIDEO IMAGES 372 $9.95

Show Boat (1936)—Black and white adaptation directed by James Whale—a memorable event. Irene Dunne as Magnolia Hawks, Allan Jones as her Ravenal. Charles Winninger as Cap'n Andy, Paul Robeson, outstanding as Joe ("Ol' Man River"), and Helen Morgan as the tortured-soul Julie (the mulatto).
113 min. MGM/UA M301757B $19.98

Show Boat (1951)—The newly refurbished print shows off the Technicolor splendor of this era-remake (this was the third version—there had been a silent release).

Critics were not kind to this Arthur Freed interpretation, but the opening scene of *The Cotton Blossom* docking on shore and putting on a teaser-show for the town folk is spectacular, as well as inviting.
115 min. MGM/UA M202302V $14.95

Show Business (1944)—The girls of vaudeville join up with the boys of burlesque in this romantic musical comedy that stars Eddie Cantor, George Murphy, and Joan Davis. Especially good for the atmosphere it evokes of the early days of show business. Also important are the classic song hits performed, such as "It Had to Be You," "Alabamy Bound," "While Strolling Through the Park One Day," "Making Whooppee," "Dinah," and "The Curse of an Aching Heart."
92 min. NHV N035204H $19.95

That's Singing—The Best of Broadway (1982)—A contemporary melange of songs from the earliest days of Broadway to recent times.
117 min. color WHV 067B $19.98

Ziegfeld Follies (1946)—William Powell as the "Great Ziegfeld" is in heaven as he reminisces about his life and his beloved Follies. Guest spots by Fanny Brice, Fred Astaire, Gene Kelly (Astaire & Kelly dance on film for the first time in "The Babbitt and the Bromide"), Lucille Ball, Judy Garland, and many more. Today's viewers can get a sense of the opulence & the showmanship of Ziegfeld, who did more than just "Beautify the American Girl."
115 min. MGM/UA M600173 $19.98

The Dance Bands

A number of excellent examples of the Coon-Sanders Nighthawks, Nat Shilkrat's Victor Orchestra, Johnny Hamp's Kentucky Serenaders, Ben Selvin's Novelty Orchestra et al. can be found in the subheading, "The Roaring Twenties: The Jazz Age." However, little can be found in print of the many outstanding dance bands of this era with an entire recording under their name. The father of big bands, Art Hickman, can hardly be found for even one song selection, not to mention an entire album of his work. Alas, here is what we have at this time.

Recordings
King, Wayne—Known as "America's Waltz King," or simply "The Waltz King." Wayne King's smooth, dreamy orchestrations on songs such as "The Waltz You Saved for Me," "I Wonder Who's Kissing Her Now," "Let Me Call You Sweetheart," and "Goodnight Sweetheart," are still played by bands today.
The Good Music Record Co. 124826

Legendary Bands of the 20's—Selections by the orchestras of: Paul Whiteman, Ted Weems, Guy Lombardo, the Ipana Troubadors, Ben Pollack, George Olsen, Nat Shilkret, Isham Jones, Ben Bernie, Jean Goldkette, Ben Selvin, Vincent Lopez, and more
ProArte/Fanfare CDD-484

Lewis, Ted—*Ted Lewis' Orchestra, Vol. 1* (1926-33)
Biograph C-7 (LP)
Ted Lewis' Orchestra, Vol. 2 (1928-33) Biograph C-8 (LP)

Waring, Fred—*Fred Waring & His Pennsylvanians*
MCAC2-4008

Whiteman, Paul—*Paper Moon*   ProArte CDD-437
Paul Whiteman & His Orchestra—with Bing Crosby, Bix
Beiderbecke, Henry Busse, Tommy Dorsey, Frankie
Trumbauer, Eddie Lang, and Mildred Bailey.
EPM (Jazz Archives) 15764-2

Videos

The King of Jazz (1930)— An imaginative musical revue
from Universal Studios which stars bandleader Paul
Whiteman. Director John Murray Anderson's concepts
for musical numbers were copied by a number of future
directors. Most notable was Busby Berkeley's use of
Anderson's "A Bench in the Park" for his "Pettin' in the
Park" in *Gold Diggers of 1933*; and his use of New York
skyscrapers (cut-outs) in *42nd Street* from Anderson's
similar design for "Happy Feet." The Rhythm Boys (with
Bing Crosby) sing, and George Gershwin's "Rhapsody
in Blue" is the centerpiece for Whiteman's grandiose
"The Melting Pot of Jazz." 92min. MCA 55119 $19.98

The Singers

Recordings

Art Deco: The Crooners—A CD set with Gene Austin, ("Did
You Ever See a Dream Walking?"), Seeger Ellis, ("There
Was Nothing Else to Do"), Smith Ballew ("Miss You"),
Lew Bray ("We Can't Use Each Other Any More"),
Harlan Lattimore ("How Do You Do It?"), Cliff Edwards
("Everything I Have is Yours," and "Did You Ever See a
Dream Walking?") Pinky Tomlin ("The Object of My
Affection"), Chick Bullock ("Anytime, Any Day,
Anywhere"), and more—and, yes, of course, Crosby and
Columbo. Includes a smart 35 page booklet.
Columbia/Legacy C2K-52942

Art Deco: Sophisticated Ladies—Companion set to
above—35 page booklet with two or more samples from
Ruth Etting ("Ten Cents a Dance"), Helen Morgan
("Sand in My Shoes"), Annette Hanshaw ("Moanin'
Low"), Connie Boswell ("Under a Blanket of Blue"),The
Boswell Sisters ("Mood Indigo," "Sophisticated Lady,"
and "Rock and Roll"), Nan Wynn ("You Go to My
Head"), and others. Columbia/Legacy C2K-52943

Brice, Fanny—*Makin' Whoppee, with Eddie Cantor*
ProArte/Fanfare CDD-460

Columbo, Russ—*Russ Columbo*
Sandy Hook CSH-2006 (cas)

Crosby, Bing—*Bing Crosby 1927-1934* Decca Jazz GRD-603
Bing Crosby, The Crooner; The Columbia Years 1928-1934
Columbia X3T-44229 (cas)
Bing: His Legendary Years, 1931-1957
MCA 4 MCAD4-10887
The Immortal (film songs of 1930s; includes 16-page

booklet).   Empire/Avid AVC-535

Etting, Ruth—*Ruth Etting: America's Radio Sweetheart* (with
Ben Selvin and his orchestra, Victor Young and his
orchestra, Frank Balack and Benny Kruegar and their
orchestras; radio recordings from 1930-1947).
Sandy Hook CSH-2033 (cas)
Ten Cents a Dance—(recordings dating from1926-1930).
ASV Living Eva ASL-CD-5008

The First Torch Singers: Volume One, The Twenties—
Fanny Brice's classic "My Man," along with the "Torch
Trio": Ruth Etting ("The Right Kind of Man," "Love Me or
Leave Me"); Helen Morgan ("Can't Help Lovin' Dat Man,"
"Don't Ever Leave Me"); and Libby Holman ("Why Was I
Born?," "More Than You Know"), among others.
Take Two Records TT407 CD

Flappers, Vamps and Sweet Young Things—Twenty
original recordings from 1924 to 1931, including Marion
Harris ("The Blues Have Got Me"), Lillian Roth ("Why Am
I So Romantic?"), Gretta Keller ("Blues in My Heart"),
Kate Smith ("Maybe, Who Knows"), Libby Holman ("Am I
Blue?"), Jane Green ("I'm Gonna Meet My Sweetie
Now"), Helen Kane ("Dangerous Nan McGrew"),
Gertrude Lawrence ("Do, Do, Do"), Aileen Stanley ("I'll
Get By"), Esther Walker ("Ya Gotta Know How to Love"),
Zelma O'Neil ("Do Something"), and Blossom Seeley ("A
New Kind of Man, With a New Kind of Love for Me").
ASV Living Era CD-AJA-5015

Funny Girl—Music from the 1967 film, based on the life of
Fanny Brice, starring Barbra Streisand.
Columbia CK-03220

The Helen Morgan Story—A 1957 release, featuring Gogi
Grant singing Helen Morgan classics from the Warner
Brothers film of the same name.   RCA-1030-2R

Jolson, Al—*Jolson Sings! You Ain't Heard Nothin' Yet: Jolie's
Finest Columbia Recordings* ("Art Deco" series; includes
telling liner notes, a thorough discography and rare
photos).   Columbia CK-53419
The Best of the Decca Years   MCA MCAD-10505
*You Ain't Heard Nothin' Yet: Jolie's Finest Columbia
Recordings*   Columbia CK-53419

Love Me or Leave Me (Doris Day)—music from the 1955
film, based on the life of Ruth Etting.
Columbia/Legacy CK-47503

Night and Day: Balladeers of the 1930s—Twenty-two
selections from crooners such as Al Bowlly ("Be Still My
Heart"), Dick Powell ("With Plenty of Money and You"),
Sam Coslow ("Please"), Bobby Howes ("Got a Date With
an Angel"), Arthur Tracy ("Stay Awhile"), Bing Crosby
("Moonburn"), Tino Rossi ("Serenade in the Night"), Cliff
Edwards ("The Hunkadola"), Rudy Vallee ("There is a
Tavern in the Town"), Denny Dennis ("You Oughta Be in
Pictures"), Russ Columbo ("Sweet and Lovely"), Fred
Astaire ("A Five Romance") and Hutch ("Night and Day").
Conifer CDHD-187

They Called It Crooning–Bing Crosby ("Where the Blue of the Night [Meets the Gold of the Day]"), Rudy Vallee ("The Thrill is Gone"), Russ Columbo ("Living in Dreams"), and their followers: Seager Ellis ("Cheerful Little Earful"), Val Rosing ("Please"), Whispering Jack Smith ("She's a New Kind of Old Fashioned Girl"), Al Bowlly, et al.   ASV Living Era ASL-CD-5026

Tracy, Arthur–*The Street Singer: Arthur Tracy.* Accordion-playing troubador who would be announced on radio thusly, "Around the corner and down your way comes Arthur Tracy, your street singer." Twenty-two hits of yesteryear include "Pennies from Heaven," used in the 1981 film of the same name starring Steve Martin, and his theme song, "Marta."
The Good Time Music Co. CD-130427

Vallee, Rudy–*Heigh-Ho Everybody, This is Rudy Vallee*
ASLV Living Era CD-AJA-5009

Vallee, Rudy & His Connecticut Yankees–*Vagabond Lover*
ProArte/Fanfare CDD-459

Videos

The Al Jolson Collection–Eight feature films of Al Jolson in a single package. Included are *The Jazz Singer, The Singing Fool, Big Boy, Wonder Bar, Mammy,* and *The Singing Kid.* None of these films at this time are listed as being available as a single item for purchase. So it is a steep investment to view the dynamo singer who was billed, "The World's Greatest Entertainer."
701 min. Fest LV MGM/UA $149.98

Bing Crosby Festival (1930)–Young Bing featured in a series of shorts that include him singing "Billboard Girl," "Blue of the Night," and "I Surrender Dear."
52 min. HHT V $34.95

Funny Girl (1968)–The musical biography of Fanny Brice and her rise to stardom in the *Ziegfeld Follies.* Her heartbreak affair with Nicky Arnstein (Omar Sharif) deflates her happiness ("My Man"). A remarkable screen debut for Barbra Streisand, who positively glows. "People," "I'd Rather Be Blue," "Second Hand Rose," and Herb Ross's choreography for "I'm the Greatest Star," and "Don't Rain on My Parade," make this film one of the greatest of all biopics.
155 min. color COL/TRI 0191 $19.95

Going Hollywood (1933)– Bing Crosby plays the part of a popular radio crooner, who is pursued by an ex-school-teacher, who moves to Hollywood to catch her prey. She works her way on to the film set and into his heart. Bing croons "Temptation," "Beautiful Girl," and "An Echo in the Valley," among others.
77 min. MGM/UA 202829 $19.98

The Al Jolson Story (1946)–Larry Parks stars (but doesn't do the actual singing) in the popular biography of the great Jolson. Cliches abound, but it's an entertaining movie which gives audiences of today a taste of the early vaudeville world, and of Jolson's magnetism.
129 min. COL/TRI 60686 $29.95

Love Me or Leave Me (1955)–The musical biography of the best-selling female recording artist of the first forty years of this century–Ruth Etting ("Queen of Chicago"). Doris Day is terrific as Etting, and James Cagney is powerful as the bully-husband-manager, Mo "the Gimp" Snyder. Great songs throughout.
122 min. MGM/UA M200755 $19.98

The Depression and the Early 1930s/Hollywood

Records
Astaire, Fred–*Fred Astaire Rarities* (with Adele Astaire and Ginger Rogers).   RCA-2337-2-R
Top Hat: Hits From Hollywood– ("Art Deco" series; contains 16 songs originally introduced in the movies Astaire made during the 1930s; includes liner notes, discography, and photos).   Columbia CK-64172

Betty Boop–*Boop-Boop-Be-Doop*. (Helen Kane sings).
ProArte CDD-440

The Big Broadcast of 1932–Music from Bing Crosby's first major leading role. Includes selections by George Burns and Gracie Allen, the Mills Brothers, Cab Calloway, et al. (See list of songs in chart on page 67.)
Sandy Hook CSH-2007 (cas)

Brother, Can You Spare A Dime? American Song During The Great Depression–In-depth notes by historian Charles Hamm, as well as a compendium of releases from all genres of music–pop, jazz, blues and country. Selections include: "Brother Can You Spare a Dime?" (Bing Crosby), "The Boulevard of Broken Dreams" (Hal Kemp), "Life is Just a Bowl of Cherries" (Rudy Vallee), "Love Walked In" (Kenny Baker), "On the Good Ship Lollypop" (Shirley Temple), "Gold Diggers Song (We're in the Money)" (Dick Powell). There are also a number of titles from underground performers like Big Bill Broonzy ("Unemployment Stomp"), Uncle Dave Macon ("All In and Down and Out Blues"), and others.   New World Records NW-270 (LP)

The Busby Berkeley Album– (featuring songs from classic Warner Bros. musicals, including *42nd Street, Gold Diggers of 1933,* and *Dames*). Selections by contemporary artists, singers & orchestration by the London Sinfonietta.   Angel CDQ-55189

42nd Street–The Original Broadway Cast recording (1980).
RCA CBLI-3891 (LP)

The Great Depression–Various artists (a radio sound portrait of hard times in the 1930s; the Depression's start and end; voices, movies, music, etc.).
Radiola CMR-1120 (cas)

Hollywood Sings: Stars of the Silver Screen; Original Recordings from 1923-1931–Selections by Paul Whiteman's Rhythm Boys, Al Jolson, Janet Gaynor, Rudolph Valentino, Charles King, Harry Richman, et al.
ASV Living Era CD AJA-5011

Hooray for Hollywood—Various artists.
RCA2 07863-66099-2

More Musicals, 1927-1936—Selections by Al Jolson, Fred
Astaire, Ginger Rogers, Maurice Chevalier, Gloria
Swanson, Mae West, et al.   ABC Music 836-044-2

Those Fabulous Busby Berkeley Musicals—Various artists
(1930's radio shows with highlights from Berkeley's first
big film hits).   Radiola CDMR-1161

Those Were The Days—Those were the days when stars
such as Ruth Etting, the Boswell Sisters, Guy
Lombardo, Dick Powell, Rudy Vallee, Ozzie Nelson,
Eddy Duchin, and Ukelele Ike helped keep spirits high.
Forty-two hits of the 1929 to early '30s period.
The Good Music Record Co. 2CD-130328

Videos

The Boy Friend (1971)—Director Kurt Russell's wildly
imaginative visuals make this one of the most
underrated musicals in film history. Its connections to
musical stage and film history are constant. A third-
rate British troop is putting on a matinee and the star
breaks her ankle (Glenda Jackson in an unbilled
appearance) and is replaced by a none-too-prepared
backup (Twiggy). The musical numbers are awful, but
a Hollywood director, who happens to be at the
performance, keeps imagining what these numbers
could look like if he created them. His "mind's eye"
conjurs up bizzare notions of Busby Berkeley and Fred
and Ginger numbers that are truly dazzling! Plus, the
movie is kinetic and funny, and has the dancing talent
of Tommy Tune.
137 min. color MGM/UA M200306 $19.98

The Broadway Melody (1929)—Hollywood's first Academy
Award winning talkie picture. A backstage musical
about sisters (Anita Page and Bessie Love) in love with
the same song-and-dance man (Charles King). Arthur
Freed and Nacio Herb Brown composed the score—the
first conceived especially for the screen. "You Were
Meant for Me" became a standard.
111min. MGM/UA M301 1492 $19.98

Dames (1934)—Berkeley set pajamas dancing to Joan
Blondell's serenading; Scores of cut-out Ruby Keeler
faces to Dick Powell's crooning of "I Only Have Eyes for
You"; and kaldeiscopic geometric human figures in the
dizzying number "Dames."
92 min. MGM/UA M301675 $29.95

Flying Down to Rio (1933) Fred Astaire and Ginger
Rogers were billed after the main love-interest couple
(Dolores Del Rio and Gene Raymond). In this film
Astaire and Rogers play the secondary, comic pair.
However, Fred and Ginger stole the picture, and, as the
saying goes, the rest is history. They set America
dancing when they pranced across seven white pianos
showing that two heads were, indeed, better than one,
in "The Carioca." Deco set by set designer Van Nest
Polglase established the tone for the Astaire-Rogers

"Big White Sets" in films to follow.
89 min. FHV 8003 $19.95

Footlight Parade (1933)—Dynamic James Cagney as the
creative director whose ideas for dance numbers are
being stolen. His "prologues" (musical interludes
preceding feature films) eventually get produced, and
we see: "Honeymoon Hotel" (naughty-but-nice Dick
Powell and Ruby Keeler), "By a Waterfall" (15 minutes of
splashing about in a giant aquacade), and the finale
with Cagney looking for his "Shanghai Lil" (Ruby
Keeler).   104 min. MGM/UA M 301676 $29.95

42nd Street (1933)—The film musical that saved Warner
Bros. The backstage musical of tapping chorus boys
and girls trying to please their manic director. Warner
Baxter as Julian Marsh, director extraordinaire, and
Ruby Keeler and Dick Powell as the young couple in
love. Warren and Dubin's songs and Berkeley's visually
stunning choreography make this a classic.
89 min. MGM/UA M 301672 $29.95

The Gay Divorcee (1934)—In their second film, Fred Astaire
and Ginger Rogers were top billed. Astaire pursues
Rogers and wins her heart with his romantic dance
abilities. No kisses needed. Large ensemble numbers
by Dave Gould copied Busby Berkeley, and were not to
Astaire's liking. The seventeen-minute extravaganza
"The Continental" won the Academy Award for original
song in a picture. "Night and Day" (Cole Porter's
classic was not eligible; because it was written a year
earlier for the stage production) was the romantic pas
de deux.   107 min. DVT 1014 $19.98

Gold Diggers of 1933 (1933)—The quintessential
Depression musical. Everyone's broke and the play
needs money to go on—the opening number is halted
as the sheriff's men put a restraining order on the
production ("We're in the Money" ironically was being
performed) In "Shadow Waltz" sixty violins lit up in neon
as Berkeley shot the scene perched high-up on his
beloved monorail, and Joan Blondell lamented as 150
sad-faced, and down-and-out ex-servicemen marched
by in "Remember My Forgotten Man."
99 min. MGM/UA M301673 $29.95

Pennies From Heaven (1981)—Like *The Boy Friend*, I feel
this is a musical of our time—too bad it's the wrong time
at the box office. But for our purpose, and historical
connections, this film covers much of what this past
chapter is all about. A sheet music salesman, working
Depression-ravaged Chicago, visualizes life via "mind's
eye" Hollywood musical numbers. For many, Dennis
Potter''s story was too bleak, but what musical
numbers! A loan rejection from a banker leads to a
Busby Berkeley number with dancing girls and
oversized coins ("My Honey Says Yes"). Also, on a
bleak, rainy night in a Edward Hopper-inspired diner,
Vernel Bagneris dances to "Pennies From Heaven"
(Arthur Tracy, the Street Singer's vocal was used).
Christopher Walken's solo strip dance on the bar ("Let's
Misbehave"), and Steve Martin and Bernadette Peters
dance with Astaire and Rogers from *Follow the Fleet*

("Let's Face the Music and Dance") are mind-bending exercises in media referencing. A wonderful film!
107 min. color MGM/UA ML 100191

Singin' in the Rain (1952)–Considered by most film historians to be one of the top musicals of all-time. A joyous Comden and Green tale of Hollywood's transitional years, reflecting the change from silent film to talkies. The writers interviewed many "old timers" about the problems, and the results are often hilarious. Gene Kelly stars as the silent action star Don Lockwood, whose on-screen love match with Jean Hagen is a typical Hollywood hype. Donald O'Connor plays Chester, Lockwood's best friend and one-time vaudeville partner. Debbie Reynolds is winsome as Cathy, Lockwood's true love. Comden and Green established a storyline centering on producer Arthur Freed's (and Nacio Herb Brown) song catalog.
103 min. color MGM/UA M2025397 $19.98

Till the Clouds Roll By (1946)–Jerome Kern died in the midst of this musical cavalcade's filming, so the studio shut down the operation and performed rewrites. As a result the film begins with Kern's 1927, masterpiece, *Show Boat*, and then flashes back in time to the early days of Kern (Robert Walker) as a struggling composer, receiving counsel from Van Heflin as a kindly mentor. The hits begin to mount, and we see examples of Marilyn Miller (Judy Garland) introducing many of Kern's early hits from shows like 1919's *Sally* ("Look for the Silver Lining") and 1925's *Sunny* ("Sunny" and "Who?"). MGM marched out its many stars to sing such beautiful melodies as: "Make Believe" (Kathryn Grayson and Tony Martin); "Can't Help Lovin' Dat Man" (Lena Horne); "Ol' Man River" (Caleb Peterson and later in the film, Frank Sinatra); "Till the Clouds Roll By" (June Allyson and Ray McDonald) and "They Didn't Believe Me" (Dinah Shore); "All the Things You Are (Tony Martin) et al. 123 min. color MGM/UA M700094 $19.98

Chapter 4: THE BLUES

The first record entries are compilation packages covering the large scope of most blues forms. These musical packages *do not* stop at 1934; however, they are listed here, because they give a big picture of the blues and thus a sense of wholeness.

Recordings
The Blues: A Smithsonian Collection of Classic Blues Singers–The title "Classic Blues Singers" in this package refers to singers of the highest order and lasting significance, and doesn't cater solely to the female singers that some historians, including this one, have given that same label. This handsome, four-CD boxed set includes a beautifully illustrated and annotated 94-page booklet. All the early styles and key singers of Chapter 4 are covered: Female Classic Blues ("Ma" Rainey–"Shave 'Em Dry" and "Countin' the Blues"); (Sippie Wallace–"Special Delivery Blues"); (Sara Martin–"Death Sting Me Blues"); country blues styles of the Southeast, Southwest, and Mississippi Delta; citified

and hokum blues; and the post-war forms of rhythm and blues are also included.
Smithsonian Collection of Recordings CDRD-1-1

Blues Retrospective: 1925-1950–From Columbia's Legacy "Roots N' Blues" series. This is the best mix of black and white blues extant. The more obscure performers of early black rural forms are here: Mississippi John Hurt ("Big Leg Blues"), Bumble Bee Slim ("Hard Rocks in My Bed"), Little Son Joe ("Black Rat Swing"), Peetie Wheatstraw ("Police Station Blues"). Also to be found are examples of the lesser known female classic blues singers: Lucille Bogan ("Skin Game Blues"), Mamie Smith ("My Sportin' Man"), Elizabeth Johnson ("Empty Bed Blues"), Gladys Bentley ("Worried Blues"), Clara Smith ("You Had Too Much"). In addition to the black blues, there are good examples of the black sacred music that was popular with the religious audience– including the fire and brimstone sermons and songs of Reverend J. M. Gates, a gospel superstar of the 1920s and '30s. Examples of the sacred recordings include: Reverend J.M. Gates ("Death's Black Train is Coming"), Reverend Johnny Blakey, assisted by the Sanctified Singers ("Warming by the Devil's Fire"), Tindley Ruaker City Singers ("Hallelujah Side"). There are also examples of barrelhouse pianists, jug bands, and citified singers like Muddy Waters.

The unusual element of this collection is that close to half of the samples are by white performers. Included are selections by Frank Hutchison ("The Last Scene of the Titanic"), Charlie Poole with the North Carolina Ramblers ("Whitehouse Blues"), Dallas String Band with Coley Jones ("Hokum Blues"), Tom Darby and Jimmie Tarlton ("Lonesome Frisco Line"), Sweet Violet Boys ("You Got to See Mama Ev'ry Night [or You Can't See Mama At All"]), Blue Ridge Ramblers ("D Blues") and Breaux Freres ("Blue Eyes Waltz"). This set is packaged with a 60-page booklet that was compiled by blues scholar Lawrence Cohn, assisted by Gary Pacheco.
Columbia/Legacy 4 C4K-47911 $52

Videos
Bluesland: A Portrait in American Music–The best overall video history of the blues. Archival film of field hands working in the hot Southern sun, clips of juke joints, rural jug bands, classic blues singers, pianists, bands of the 1930s swinging the blues, and electrified stylings by urban stars of the 1940s like T-Bone Walker, B. B. King, and Muddy Waters. Historians Robert Palmer and Albert Murray are intermittently interviewed, and their cogent appraisals are enlightening. This is a must-purchase.
90 min. BMG 7233379973 $29.98

Classic Blues Singers

Recordings
Black and Blue–The soundtrack from Claudio and Hector Orezzoli's Broadway musical revue from 1989. Capturing the tone and spirit of the black classic blues divas of yesterday are, Ruth Brown ("St. Louis Blues"), Carrie Smith ("Am I Blue," "I've Got a Right to Sing the Blues"), and Linda Hopkins ("After You're Gone," "Call It

Stormy Monday" "I'm Getting' Long Alright"). The highlight is a show-stopping battle of one-upsmanship between Ruth Brown and Linda Hopkins on Bessie Smith's classic "T' Ain't Nobody's Bizness If I Do."
DRG Records CD 19001

Better Boot That Thing: Great Woman Blues Singers of the 1920s—The only compilation I've been able to find that specifically focuses on the female classic blues singers. Includes versions of blues songs by Alberta Hunter, Bessie Tucker, Victoria Spivey, and Ida May Mack. Bluebird CD 07863-66065-2

Bogan, Lucille (Bessie Jackson)—*Lucille Bogan 1923-1935*
Story of Blues SB-3535

Rainey, "Ma"—*"Ma" Rainey's Black Bottom* Yazoo CD-1071
"Ma" Rainey—The Paramount Chronology 1923-1924 Vol. 1
Black Swan HCD-12001

Saffire—*The Uppity Blues Women*
Alligator Records ALCD-4780

Smith, Bessie—*The Complete Recordings, Vol. 1: Empress of*
the Blues   Columbia/Legacy 2 C2K-47091
Vol. 2   Columbia/Legacy 2 C2K-47471
Vol. 3   Columbia/Legacy 2 C2K-47474
Vol. 4.   Columbia/Legacy 2 C2K-52838
Bessie Smith Sings the Jazz (with Louis Armstrong, Joe Smith, Charlie Green, Fletcher Henderson, Coleman Hawkins, Clarence Wililams, James P. Johnson).
EPM-15790-2

Videos
Alberta Hunter-*My Castle's Rockin'*—The venerable star in action at Barney Josephson's Cookery, singing classics such as "Down Hearted Blues," "Rough and Ready Man," "Handy Man," and the title song. Includes her history with samples of early recordings and great photos, as well as interviews. This is presently the best video available about the history of a classic blues singer.   60 min. Color VIEW VIDEO 1331 $19.98

Jazz at the Smithsonian: Alberta Hunter—Hunter in concert in 1982.   60 min. color KUL 1270 CXV $29.95

Black Jazz and Blues—Three movie shorts. These were called race movies during the 1930s and '40s, and were shown in black theaters throughout America. Often these ten to twenty minute shorts (as they were called) were given top billing on the marquee. Such was the case for Bessie Smith's short, *St. Louis Blues*. The story line consisted of Bessie being treated lousy by her man—he beats her up and laughs at her. She goes to a club, and while drinking a beer at the bar sings "St. Louis Blues." This was her only screen appearance. Duke Ellington and Louis Jordan are seen in the other two shorts.   44 min. V-YES 328 $24.95

Sippie Wallace—The life and wisdom of the elderly singer via old photos, rare recordings, and concert footage. Bonnie Raitt was a staunch supporter of Wallace.
23 min. RHAP B $24.95

The Rural Blues

Recordings
Cannon's Jug Stompers-*The Complete Recordings*
Yazoo 2-CD-1082/3

Jefferson, Blind Lemon-*King of the Country Blues*
Yazoo CD-1069

Johnson, Blind Willie-*Sweeter As the Years Go By* The most popular and influential guitar evangelist of the 1920s and 1930s.   Yazoo CD-1078

Johson, Robert-*The Complete Recordings.* Contains never-before issued alternative takes. Best selling country blues package of all time. Two CDs in a boxed set: contains informative booklet. A necessary purchase.
Columbia/Legacy 2-C2K-46222 $20

House, Son-*Delta Blues: The Original Library of Congress Sessions*   Biograph BCD-118
Father of the Delta Blues: The Complete 1965 Recordings
Columbia/Legacy 2 C2K-48867

Hurt, Mississippi John-*Avalon Blues*   Rounder CD-1081
1928 Sessions   Yazoo 1065

McTell, Blind Willie-*The Definitive Blind Willie McTell*
Columbia 2 CK-53234
1927-33 The Early Years   Yazoo CD-1005

Patton, Charley-*Founder of the Delta Blues* Yazoo CD-1020
King of the Delta Blues   Yazoo 2 CD-2001

Roots of Rhythm and Blues: A Tribute to the Robert Johnson Era—Followers of Robert Johnson, like David "Honeyboy" Edwards, Robert Junior Lockwood, Johnny Shines, Henry Townsend, and others, perform his songs.   Columbia CK-49584

The Roots of Robert Johnson—Selections on this CD are based on recordings that had an influence on Robert Johnson. Among the 14 entries are: Leroy Carr's "When the Sun Goes Down," Johnnie Temple's "Lead Pencil Blues," Hambone Willie Newbern's "Roll and Tumble Blues," Henry Thomas' "Red River Blues," and Kokomo Arnold's "Milk Cow Blues."   Yazoo CD-1073

Shines, Johnny-*Traditional Delta Blues* Biograph BCD-121

The Slide Guitar: Bottles, Knives & Steel—Great examples of sliding guitar sounds by the likes of Blind Boy Fuller ("Homesick and Lonesome Blues"), Tampa Red ("You Can't Get That Stuff No More"), Bukka White ("Special Stream Line," and "Bukka's Jitterbug Swing"), along with Robert Johnson, Son House, Leadbelly, Blind Willie Johnson, Barbeque Bob, and others.
Columbia/Legacy CK-46218

Wild About My Lovin' Beale Street Blues 1928-1930—Selections by key leaders of jugband sounds. A minimum of four selections are heard from: The Memphis Jug Band ("K. C. Moan"); Jim Jackson ("I'm

Wild About My Lovin'"); Cannon's Jug Stompers ("Walk Right In"); and Frank Stokes ("Take Me Back").

RCA 2461-2-R

Videos

American Patchwork: The Land Where Blues Began—
The video captures performances by various artists and traces the development of the blues by showcasing known (Leadbelly), and unknown bluesmen.

60 min. PBS 260V $14.95

Arhoolie's 25th Anniversary Party—Subtitled "It's Got to Be Rough and Sweet." The company's live concert features interviews and commentary with founder and president Chris Strachwitz. One of America's premier companies for underground, roots music, Arhoolie represents Strachwitz's encompassing world view. The music seen on this video includes Tex-Mex, Cajun, zydeco, country, traditional jazz—and more.

120 min. color ARH ARV 402 $19.98

Best of Blank—The Finest Musical Moments from the Films of Les Blank—The best known and most revered of the film documenters of roots music in the world. For years Blank has documented "Truly American Originals." Included are glimpses from his features on Lightnin' Hopkins, Mance Lipscomb (blues singers), Tex-Mex, zydeco and polka.

94 min. color/b&w FF 1144V $49.95

Good Morning Blues—Documentation of country blues, from turn of the century roots in the Mississippi Delta. Includes work songs and field hollers of pre-blues styles right up to Memphis and up Highway 61 to Chicago. The story is narrated by B. B. King and showcases older bluesmen like Furry Lewis, Big Joe Williams, and others.

60 min. SRC 505 $19.95

Legends of Country Blues Guitar—Rural one man band troubadors like Blind Reverand Gary Davis (noted in Chapter 1), Son House, Mississippi John Hurt, Big Bill Broonzy, Mance Lipscomb, and others.

58 min. VESTA 13003

Out of the Black Into the Blues—Part one of a two part series, this volume is subtitled "Along the Old Man River." Insightful documentation of old black bluesmen sometimes performing in the living room of Furry Lewis' home. Personal anecdotes and explanations on the bottleneck guitar technique. Bukka White, Robert Pete Williams, Sonny Terry and Brownie McGhee, and piano great Roosevelt Sykes.

52 min. color YAZOO 506 $19.95

The Search for Robert Johnson (1992)—Bluesman John Hammond takes us along as he travels throughout the Mississippi Delta, visiting haunts of the legendary Robert Johnson. Hammond interviews those who knew him—including an old girlfriend who was the source of the song "Love in Vain" (Willie Mae Powell—"Ooh Willie Mae" moans Johnson in the song). She hears this record for the very first time—talk about weird historic

events!). Hammond also spends time with two of Johnson's musician friends/followers, David "Honeyboy" Edwards and Johnny Shines. The video includes performances of classic Johnson songs, and even an enactment of a muscian's battle, known as "cutting heads." A remarkable documentary.

72 min. color 1992 SONY MUSIC SMV 19V-49113 $19.95

Barrelhouse Piano and Boogie Woogie

Recordings

Barrelhouse Piano 1927-1936—Some of the earliest piano boogie on record by a fleet of lesser known pianists, including Joe Dean, Raymond Barrow, Charley Taylor, Jesse James, and prominent bluesmen like Little Brother Montgomery and Lonnie Johnson (this great guitarist also played fine piano). Yazoo CD-1028

Boogie Woogie Blues—Piano roll solo by Cow Cow Davenport, Clarence Williams, Jimmy Blythe, James P. Johnson, Hersal Thomas, and others.

Biograph BCD-115

Piano Blues—A mix of early piano (Paramount releases from 1928-1932). Includes Charlie Spand, Louise Johnson ("By the Moon and Stars"); Wesley Wallace (Fanny Lee Blues"); James Wiggins ("Evil Woman Blues"); Blind Leroy Garnett ("Louisiana Glide"); Will Ezell ("Pitchin' Boogie"); Charles Avery ("Dearborn St. Breakdown"); Lonnie Clark ("Down in Tennessee"); Skip James ("If You Haven't Any Hay"); and Little Brother Montgomery ("Vicksburg Breakdown").

Black Swan HCD-12011

Piano Red—*Atlanta Bounce*   Arhoolie CD 378

Sunnyland Slim—*Chicago Blues Session*
Southland Records SCD-10

Speckled Red—*Dirty Dozens*   Delmark DE-601 (LP)

Sykes, Roosevelt—*The Honeydripper*
Fantasy/OBC OBCCD-557-2

Yancy, Jimmy—*Chicago Piano, Volume One* Atlantic 82368-2
In the Beginning   Solo Art SACD-1

Citified Blues & Hokum/ Sex, Drugs, & Rock 'n' Roll

Recordings

Bawdy Blues—Hokum raunch by Tampa Red, Victoria Spivey, Pink Anderson, Memphis Willie B., Blind Willie McTell, et al.   Fantasy/OBC OBCCD-544-2

Carter, Bo—*Bananas in Your Fruit Basket: Red Hot Blues 1931-36*   Yazoo 1064
Please Warm My Weiner   Yazoo L-1043

The Copulatin' Blues—A wild mix of down and dirty songs from Lil Johnson ("You Stole My Cherry"), Coot Grant and Kid Wesley Wilson ("Take Your Hands Off My

533

Mojo"), Merlene Johnson–the Yas-Yas Girl ("Don't You Make Me High"), Frankie "Half-Pint" Jaxson ("Wet It!"), Georgia White ("If I Can't Sell It, I'll Keep Sittin' on It [Before I Give It Away]"), Tampa Red's Hokum Jazz Band with Frankie "Half-Pint" Jaxon ("My Daddy Rocks Me with One Steady Roll"), plus 15 more.

Jass Records J-CD-1

Johnson, Lil–*Hottest Gal In Town*
Story of the Blues CD-3513-2

Johnson, Lonnie–*He's a Jelly Roll Baker* Bluebird 07863
Steppin' on the Blues Columbia/ Legacy CK-46221

Raunchy Business: Hot Nuts & Lolly Pops–The liner notes by Paul Oliver are crucial for total understanding of the history of blues metaphors. Excellent analysis and some glorious race record ads underscore all of this. Twenty selections, including Hunter and Jenkins' "Lollypop," Lil Johnson's scandalous "Get 'Em from the Peanut Man (The New Hot Nuts"), "Lonnie Johnson's boastful "The Best Jockey in Town," Lillie Mae Kirkman's up-front "He's Just My Size," and the downright pornographic "Shave 'Em Dry" by Lucille Bogan, are just some of the tunes from this collection.
Columbia/Legacy CK-46782

Reefer Songs–Subtitled "23 Original Jazz & Blues Vocals," these selections yell the praises of drugs that were legal prior to 1934. Selections include Bea Foote's "Weed," Julia Lee's "Lotus Blossom (Sweet Marijuana)," "Reefer Man" by Don Redman and His Orchestra, "If You're a Viper" by Bob Howard and His Boys, The Harlem Hamfats' "The Weed Smoker's Dream," and other scurrilous titles like "Wacky Dust," "Light Up," "Here Comes the Man with the Jive," and "Save the Roach for Me." Jass Records ST-119

Tampa Red–*Don't Jive Me* Yazoo C-1039 (LP)
The Guitar Wizard Columbia CK-53235

Viper Mad Blues–More songs about drugs, including Stuff Smith and His Onyx Club Boys intoning "You'se a Viper," Memphis Jug Band's "Cocaine Habit Blues," "Smoking Reefers" by Larry Adler, Fats Waller's "The Reefer Song," and other obvious titles such as "Cocaine," "Reefer Head Woman," "Dope Head Blues," and "Reefer Hound Blues." Jass Records J-CD-630

Lousiana Blues: Cajun and Zydeco

Recordings
Alligator Stomp: Cajun & Zydeco Classics–A compilation that includes rocking sounds from colorfully named groups like Rocking Dopsie & the Zydeco Twisters, Rockin' Sidney, Beausoleil, Boozoo Chavis and the Magic Sounds, Clifton Chenier & His Red Hot Louisana Band, et al. Rhino R2-70946

Ardoin, Amedee–*His Original Recordings 1928-1938*
Old Timey 124 (LP)

Beausoleil–*Parlez-Nous a Boire & More* Arhoolie CD-322

Buckwheat Zydeco–*On a Night Like This*
Island 422-842739-2

Chenier, Clifton–*Bon Ton Roulet* Arhoolie CD-345
Louisiana Blues & Zydeco Arhoolie CD-329

Choates, Harry–*Fiddle King of Cajun Swing*
Arhoolie CD-396

Falcon, Joseph–*Live at a Cajun Dane* Arhoolie 5005 (LP)

Hackberry Ramblers–*Jolie Blonde* Arhoolie CD-399

J'ai Ete Au Bal (I Went to the Dance), Vol. 1–A combination platter from Arhoolie Records which includes old time Cajun favorites like Amedee Ardoin, Dennis McGee, Nathan Abshire, Joseph Falcon and Cleoma Breaux, Iry LeJeune, Harry Choates, and Leo Soileau & His Four Aces, along with more contemporary artists like Queen Ida & the Bon Ton Zydeco Band, Lionel LeLeux & Michael Doucet, and Marc and Ann Savoy, among others. Arhoolie CD-331

LeGran Mamou: A Cajun Music Anthology–Historic collection of some of the earliest Cajun music on record 1928-1941, culled from Victor Records and its subsidiary Bluebird label. An accompanying booklet provides educational notes and pictures, as well as English and French lyrics to the songs. Representative selections include works by most of the early innovators like Joseph Falcon ("La Valse J'Aime"), Leo Soileau ("Basile"), Amedee Ardoin & Dennis McGee ("Les Blues DeVoyage"), Nathan Abshire & the Rayne-Bo Ramblers ("One Step De Lacassine"), Hackberry Ramblers ("Jolie Blonde"), The Four Aces ("Lake Charles Waltz"), Happy Fats & His Rayne-Bo Ramblers ("La Veuve De La Coulee"), et al.
Country Music Foundation Records CMF-013-D

Videos
American Patchwork–Cajun Country– A roving camera explores Louisiana bayou country and visits the dance hall scene, front porch picnics, large music festivals, and so on. The white Cajun world is examined, as is that of the black Creole.
60 min. color PBS 250 $19.95

Buckwheat Zydeco–Takin' It Home–Today's best known purveyor of zydeco music, Stanley Dural, aka Buckwheat Zydeco, is captured in concert in London, performing selections from his then-recent releases, *On a Night Like This* and *Takin' It Home*.
55 min. color IVA 082369-3

Dry Wood–This is the highly touted documentary from filmmaker Le Blank (1980). Blank captures Louisiana rural life in the black Creole world of musicians Bois Sec Ardoin and Conroy Fontenot.
37 min. FAC S09293 $49.95

J'ai Ete Au Bal (I Went to the Ball): The Cajun and Zydeco Music of Louisiana–Definitive film on the history of the southwest Louisiana French speaking white and blacks. Use of archival photos and film, as well as interviews and music performances, make this an exciting lesson in another culture.

84 min. color BRAZOS 103 $29.98

Zydeco Gumbo—A mix of some of today's stars who have made inroads as internationally known zydeco musicians. Since the advent of Cajun food into the culinary sensibilites of America the last ten years, the music of Louisiana has been gaining favor too. This fast-paced tour of Louisiana's wet lands brings us closer to performers like Clifton Chanier, Boo Zoo Chavis, John Delafose, Terence Simien, and others.

60 min. color XHV RH 009 $24.95

Zydeco Nite' N' Day—This video opens with Ambrose Sam simply playing accordion and explaining about the early history of playing house dances with only washboard and accordion—these dances were called "La La." The performers talk to the camera explaining their lives and art. They are seen playing at outdoor dances, clubs, picnics, and at large concerts. Artists include: Nathan Williams and the Zydeco Cha Chas ("Steady Rock"), Boo Zoo Chavis and the Magic Sounds ("Where the Pretty Women At?"), Rockin' Dopsie and the Zydeco Twisters ("I'm All For You, Baby"), Buckwheat Zydeco, Alphonse Bois Sec Ardoin and Canray Fontenot, and many others. There is even a flashback to Clifton Chenier who functioned as the wellspring of zydeco music during the 1960s and '70s when no one outside of Louisiana even knew this music existed. Black and white film accompanies his "Black Gal" that plays in the background during the sequence that shows past clips of the man they called "The King of Zydeco." C. J. Chenier, Clifton Chenier's son, reminisces about his dad and shows how he's continued his father's tradition. Visits also include a church performance (the Holy Ghost Church choir) and a trail drive. A real instructional video on the lives of the black Creoles.

70 min. color/b&w ISLAND 440 083 259-3 $19.95

Archivists In Action

Recordings

Clapton, Eric—*From the Cradle*   Duck 45735-2

Cooder, Ry—*Chicken Skin Music*   Reprise 2254-2
Paradise and Lunch   Reprise 2179-2

Grossman, Stefan—*Love, Devils and the Blues*
                                                          Shanachie CD-97001
Yazoo Basin Boogie   Shanachie CD-97013

Hammond, John— *John Hammond ("Sixty-Plus Series"*
    compilation).   Rounder CD-11532
Nobody But You   Flying Fish FF-70502

Mahal, Taj—*The Best of Taj Mahal, Vol.1* Columbia CK-36258
Giant Steps/Ole Folks at Home   Columbia CGK-00018

Redbone, Leon—*Champagne Charlie*   Warner Bros. 3165-2
Leon Redbone Live!   Pair PCD-2-1309

Rising Sons—*Rising Sons featuring Taj Mahal and Ry Cooder*
                                                      Columbia/Legacy CK-52828

Rucker, Sparky—*Treasures and Tears* Flying Fish FF-70534

Traum, Happy and Artie—*Hard Times in the Country*
                                                      Rounder 3007 (LP)
The Test of Time   Roaring Steam RS-201

Videos

Eric Clapton—The Cream of Eric Clapton—Not a pure "Archivist in Action" peformer, but his stature as the most widely recognized guitar super hero justifies his presence here, because he has educated his audience for years as to the importance of older blues players. Robert Johnson was a primary inspiration to Clapton's style, and the Britisher was quick to acknowledge it. He often recorded and played Johnson tunes in concert. "Crossroad Blues" is an anthem of Clapton's, and the song is a Johnson classic. Clapton also has recorded the songs of Willie Dixon, Muddy Waters, and Leroy Carr, among many others.

75 min. color POZY 081189-3 $9.95

Maintenance Shop Blues Taj Mahal—The self-taught artist plays over a dozen instruments, and over the years has been an invaluable resource for keeping old blues numbers alive. In this set, he interprets Robert Johnson's "Sweet Home Chicago," as well as minstrel type tunes like "Cakewalk Into Town," and "My Little Sugar Mama." 60 min. color SRC 510 $19.95

Stefan Grossman—Grossman in concert displaying his dazzling fingerstyle techniques, from bottleneck and ragtime to Celtic and jazz. 60 min. SRC 801 $19.95

Chapter 5: ORIGINS OF JAZZ

Recordings

The Smithsonian Collection of Classic Jazz—A five CD set comprised of 95 selections spanning more than seven decades. This collection is generally regarded as the very best overall package of jazz history extant. Jazz historian Martin Williams put together the 120-page booklet, which contains a well documented history of jazz, musical analysis on each selection, and biographies of the musicians. Volume One (Scott Joplin, Bessie Smith, King Oliver, Louis Armstrong, Sidney Bechet, Jelly Roll Morton, Bix Beiderbecke, and Frankie Trumbauer, among others), is particularly apropos for this chapter. Volume Two covers, roughly, material found in Chapter 6 (The Harlem Renaissance) and Chapter 9 (Big Bands and Small Bands). Volumes Three and Four coincide nicely with the emergence of modern jazz and the post-bop and cool extensions into the 1950s—Chapter 11 (Bebop and Modern Jazz). Volume Five goes beyond the timelines of this book, and includes stars and modern styles of the 1960s and '70s.

Smithsonian Collection of Recordings CDRD-033-1 $55

Videos

The Story of Jazz—Making its debut in 1993, this

fascinating video, part of the Masters of American Music series, is a seamless mix of photos, paintings, graphics of all kinds, and generous film clips covering the emergence of jazz from the 1880s to the 1990s. Narrated by Lloyd Richards, the video weaves interviews with dozens of great jazz artists with rare and classic film clips of jazz music's best. Profiles of pivitol jazz figures like Louis Armstrong, Jelly Roll Morton, Duke Ellington, Count Basie, Billie Holiday, Charlie Parker, and Miles Davis, make it possible for the viewer to better comprehend the numerous evolutionary changes that jazz went through over the years. This, like the audio package by the Smithsonian, is the very best jazz video history available.

> 97 min. BMG Video BMG 72333-80088-3 $24.95

New Orleans Scene

Recordings

Louis Armstrong–Portrait of the Artist as a Young Man: **1923-1934.** A four disc collection, beautifully boxed and enhanced by a 78 page- booklet, written by jazz historian Dan Morganstern (with additional notes by Loren Schoenberg). This is a model for what most tributes would like to achieve; it's simply one of the best packages I've ever seen or heard! It's all here–the great music of Armstrong, packaged in chronological order and explained by the annotators. Discs one and two showcase Armstrong in a variety of settings, first as a sideman for others (King Oliver, Clarence Williams's Blue Five, Bessie Smith, Maggie Jones, Fletcher Henderson), and then leader of his own Hot Five and Hot Seven group. However, even as he led his own groups, beginning in 1925, he still played as a sideman for others such as Johnny Dodds' Black Bottom Stompers, Erskine Tate's Vendome Orchestra, Carroll Dickerson's Savoyagers, et al. Discs three and four find Armstrong moving on to popular music, interpreting such classics as "When You're Smiling" (1929), "Song of the Islands" and "Sweethearts on Parade" (1930), "Stardust," (1931), and "On the Sunny Side of the Street" (1934). This is an indespensible collection.

> Columbia/Legacy C4K-57176 $60

The Complete Deeca Studio Recordings of Louis Armstrong and the All Stars (booklet by jazz authority Dan Morgenstern; includes rare photos).

> Mosaic 6 MD6-146 $90

The Essence of Lousis Armstrong
> Columbia/Legacy CK-47916

Great Original Performances 1923-1931
> ABC Music AMB-CD-836184

The Hot Fives, Vol. 1
> Columbia Jazz Masterpieces CK-44253

The Hot Fives and Hot Sevens, Vol. 1
> Columbia Jazz Masters CK-44049

The Hot Fives and Hot Sevens, Vol. 2
> Columbia Jazz Masters CK-44253

Louis Armstrong of New Orleans (1927-50)
> MCA MCAD-42328

16 Most Requested Songs   Columbia/Legacy CK-57900

What a Wonderful World   MCA MCAD-11168

Bechet, Sidney–*The Best of Sidney Bechet*
> Blue Note B21S-28891

The Complete Sidney Bechet, Vol. 1 & 2 (1932-1941)–
(extensive liner notes).   RCA2 07863-66498-2

Great Original Performances 1924-1938
> ABC Music 838-032-2

The Victor Sessions/Master Takes 1932-1934
> Bluebird 2402-2-RB

Eureka Brass Band–   American Music AMCD-70

Hines, Earl "Fatha"–*Earl Hines, 1928-1932*   Classics 545
Earl Hines, 1932-1934   Classics 514

Lewis, George, Ragtime Jazz Band of New Orleans–
> American Music AMCD-29

Morton, Ferdinand "Jelly Roll"–*Vol.1: The Pianist and Composer*
> Smithsonian Collection of Recordings CDRD-0043

Vol. 2: Chicago: The Red Hot Peppers
> Smithsonian Collection of Recordings CDRD-0044

Vol. 3: New York, Washington, and the Rediscovery
> Smithsonian Collection of Recordings CDRD-0045

Great Original Performances (1926-1934)
> ABC Music 836-199-2

Jelly Roll Morton & His Red Hot Peppers
> Bluebird 6588-2-RB

Oliver, King–*King Oliver's Jazz Band 1923-1926* Classics 639
King Oliver 1926-1931   Topaz Jazz PEACD-1009

The Original Dixieland Jazz Band–*Complete USA Recordings 1917-21*   King Jazz KJCD-6155
The Original Dixieland Jazz Band
> ASV Living Era CD-AJA-5023

New Orleans Brass Band: Down Yonder–Part of the "Sixty-Plus Series" CD with many bonus cuts. The rich tradition of marching bands is featured with selections by Dejan's Olympia Brass Band, The Chosen Few, The Rebirth Marching Jazz Band, The Dirty Dozen Brass Band, and others.   Rounder CD-11562

New Orleans Giants–A good number of lesser known figures in the mixed web of colorful jazz groups from the early days of Crescent City jazz. Some of the groups are: Freddie Keppard's Jazz Cardinals, Kid Ory's Sunshine Orchestra, The California Poppies, Hightower's Nighthawks, Original Midnight Ramblers Orchestra, et al.   EPM Musique 15222-2

New Orleans Jazz–Another compilaton of varied members of the early New Orleans jazz community. Kid Thomas Valentine & His Creole Band, the New Orleans Ragtime Orchestra, Kid Howard's LaVida Band, Punch Miller's New Orleans Band, and John Handy's Louisiana Shakers, among others are heard.   Arhoolie CD-346

Preservation Hall Jazz Band–*The Best of* CBS MK-48189

Videos
Always for Pleasure (1979)– New Orleans and Mardi Gras

celebration overview focusing on small celebrations, from the solomn marches to the raucous Dixieland bands and African antiphonal stomps. Rare glimpses of the Olympia Brass Band, and Kid Thomas and the Preservation Hall Jazz Band.

58 min. color NR FFV $49.95

America's Music: Vol. 9, Jazz Then Dixieland—Trumpet King, Al Hirt hosts guests such as vocalist Clara Bryant and pianist Johnny Guarnieri. Selections include "Maple Leaf Rag," "Blue Skies," and "When It's Sleepy Time Down South." 60 min. CENT CV09 V $19.95

America's Music: Vol. 10, Jazz Then Dixieland—This show brings in Dixieland bandleader Bob Crosby and trumpeter Teddy Buckner. Songs performed include "Royal Garden Blues," "Big Noise from Winnetka," and "Please Don't Talk About Me When I'm Gone." 60 min. CENT CV010V $19.95

American Patchwork—Jazz Parade: Feet Don't Fail Me Now—Host Alan Lomax shows us the history of New Orleans. He takes us on tours through the dance halls, and to parades and night clubs where the many jazz groups perform—including the Dirty Dozen Brass Band and more. 60 min. color PBS 26IV $14.95

Kid Punch Miller—'Til the Butcher Cuts Him Down— A profile of one of those venerable musicians of New Orleans, trumpeter Kid Punch Miller. Old timers play New Orleans traditional jazz with fire and great humor and enthusiasm. Miller's roots go all the way back to the first days of recordings. He reflects on the music played in Dejan's Olympia Brass Band ("Oh, Didn't He Ramble"), and the Algiers Stompers ("Algiers Strut"). 53 min. color RHAPV $39.95

Louis Armstrong—Satchmo—A warm and moving tribute to the late, great trumpet superstar. This diverse portrait follows Armstrong from his humble roots in New Orleans to popular music success in the 1960s. Great photos, interviews and musical clips. 87 min. SMVE V49024V $19.98

Trumpet Kings—Hosted by Wynton Marsalis, this history includes the early trumpet stars as well as modern players in the 1990s. The video is placed in this slot because much of the trumpet in jazz is derived from the innovations of Louis Armstrong. Other early stars covered include Armstrong's rival Henry "Red" Allen, Muggsy Spanier, Bix Beiderbecke, and Red Nichols—all associated with traditional/Dixieland jazz. 72 min. color/b&w VAI 69036 $29.95

Chicago and the White Influx

Recordings
Beiderbecke, Bix—*Bix Beiderbecke, Vol. 1: Singin' the Blues*
Columbia Materpieces CK-45450
Bix Beiderbecke, Vol. 2: At the Jazz Band Ball
Columbia Masterpieces CK-46175
Bix Lives! (with the orchestras of Jean Goldkette and Paul Whiteman). Bluebird 6845-2-R

1924-1927 (with the Wolverine Orchestra, Souix City Six, Bix & His Rhythm Jugglers, Broadway Bell-Hops, Willard Robinson & His Orchestra, and the Chicago Loopers). Classics 778-2
Bix 'n' Bing ASL Living Era CDAJA-5005

Boswell Sisters—*Everybody Loves My Baby* ProArte CDD-550
Boswell Sisters 1930-1936 L'Art Vocal LA 13-2

Carmichael, Hoagy—*Hoagy Sings and Plays Carmichael, 1927-1939* King Jazz KJCD-6154
Stardust, and Much More Bluebird 8333-2

Challis, Bill—*And His Orchestra, 1936* Circle CLP-118 (LP)

Chicago Jazz 1927/1928—A compilation of early white Dixielanders like McKenzie and Condo's Chicagoans, Miff Mole's Molers, Eddie Condon and His Footwarmers, Bud Freeman, and the Chicago Rhythm Kings. OSCAR OSC-30

Chicago/New York Dixieland: At the Jazz Band Ball—More of the same with Eddie Condon's Hot Shots, Muggsy Spanier and His Ragitme Band, Bud Freeman and His Summa Cum Laude Orchestra, et al.
Bluebird 6752-2

Condon, Eddie—*The Definitive Eddie Condon and His Jazz Concert All-Stars, Vol. 1* Stash ST-CD-530
Town Hall Concerts, Vol. 1 Jazzology JCD-1001/2

Crosby, Bob —*Bob Crosby & His Orchestra & The Bob Cats 1937-1939* EPM (Jazz Archives) 15766-2
Stomp Off, Let's Go ASV Living Era CD-AJA-5097

Lang, Eddie—*Jazz Guitar Virtuoso* Yazoo CD-1059

New Orleans Rhythm Kings—*Complete Vol. 1*
King Jazz KJCD-6109
New Orleans Rhythm Kings, Vol. 2, 1924
King Jazz KJCD-6110

Nichols, Red—*Red Nichols & His Orchestra* Circle CCD-110

Red Nichols and Miff Mole—*Great Performances 1925-1930*
ABC Music 836-185-2

Reinhardt, Django—*Django & Le Quintet Du Hot Club*
RDC RDCD-40009
Django Reinhardt & Le Quintet Du Hot Club De France
EPM (Jazz Archives) 15752-2

Teagarden, Jack—*Jack Teagarden and His Orchestra 1934-1939* Classic 729

Vennti, Joe—*Violin Jazz 1927-1934* (with Eddie Lang)
Yazoo CD-1062

Videos
Bob Crosby: Golden Anniversary Tribute—Bing's brother fronted one of the greatest Dixieland bands in America durring the 1930s and '40s. Dixieland fans are particularly fond of his band-within-a-band, the Bob

Cats. Outstanding soloists like Yank Lawson on trumpet and the duet of bassist Bob Haggart and drummer Roy Bauduc ("Big Noise for Winnetka") are best remembered today. This program features the group's hits, and brings in guest artists such as Louis Armstrong and comedian Jack Benny.

90 min. CRM V $29.95

Django: A Jazz Tribute (1994)– Features contemporary followers of the Reinhardt legacy–specifically Bireli Lagrene and Django's son Babik.

26 min. VIEW 1347 $19.98

The Dukes of Dixieland & Friends–Over the years, this has been one of the best known and loved (although not by critics) traditional units. The group performs along with the New Orleans Pop Orchestra, presenting versions of "Basin Street Blues," "A Closer Walk with Three," "Midnight in Moscow," and "The Cantina Suite."

75 min. color L-VID MV 1058V $29.98

The Five Pennies (1959)–Danny Kaye plays the popular prohibition jazz trumpeter who became a big success. Much of this biopic deals with the personal problems of raising a daughter who is crippled. A sympathetic portrait but not enough music for our concern. Louis Armstrong, Bob Crosby, and others play fictional muscians–includes some fine musical numbers.

117 min. color PAR 5823 V $19.95

Goodyear Jazz Concerts:

Bobby Hackett	27 min. color VYES $19.95
Eddie Condon	27 min. color VYES $19.95
Louis Armstrong	27 min. color VYES 730V $19.95

Gypsy Guitar: The Legacy of Django Reinhardt–Excellent study of the great guitarist's career. We see old photos of Reinhardt, and are taken to gypsy sites in Holland, as well as to a Parisian guitar shop; the annual music festival held at Samois-Sur-Seine, the French village where Reinhardt spent his last years; and a pub in the back streets of the Liverpool docks. Titles include: "All Love," "Nuages," " Djangology," " Minor Swing," and others. The documentary spotlights the Django tradition via the playing of Babik Reinhardt, Bireli Lagrene, Boulou and Elios Ferre, The Gypsy Kids, Gary Potter, and Serge Krief and the Stochelo Rosenberg Trio. 52 min. color SHANACHIE V6301 $29.95

Stephane Grappelli Live in San Francisco–Master jazz violinist and one-time member of Django Reinhardt's group, this venerable road warrior was still touring during 1995. Songs include: "I Got Rhythm," "Minor Swing," "Tea For Two," "Sweet Georgia Brown," "Honeysuckle Rose," and more.

60 min. color RHAP $29.95

Dixieland Revival & Today's Traditionalists/Revivalists

Recordings

Challis, Bill–*Bill Challis & the Goldkette Project* (led by Vince Giordano). Faithful recreations of master arranger Bill Challis by Giordano, co-conducted by Challis and Giordano. Includes "Ostrich Walk," "On the Alamo," "Riverboat Shuffle," "The Blue Room," "Singin' the Blues (Till My Daddy Comes Home)," "Sometimes I'm Happy," "Clementine (From New Orleans)," "I've Found a New Baby," and 8 others. Circle CD 118

Chicago Jazz Summitt–A George Wein concert extravaganza recorded at New York's Town Hall during the 1986 JVC Jazz Festival. Young (Vince Giordano, and the Nighthawks, Kenny Davern) and old stars (Wild Bill Davison, Max Kaminsky, Art Hodes, Jimmy McPartland) perform individually and in jam session settings. Atlantic Jazz R2-81844

Hoagy's Children–*Vol. 1 and Vol. 2* (Bob Dorough, Barbara Lea and Dick Sushalter).

Audiophile Records ACD-291/2

Jelly's Last Jam–(music from the 1991 Broadway show).

Mercury 314-510846-2

Johnson, Bunk–*Bunk Johnson and His Superior Jazz Band*

Good Time Jazz GTJCD-12048-2

Bunk Johnson 1944/45 American Music AMCD-12

Murphy, Turk–*And His San Francisco Jazz Band*

GHB BCD-91

Rose, Wally–*Ragtime Classics*

Good Time Jazz GTCD-10034-2

Scobey, Bob–*Bob Scobey's Frisco Band, Vol. 1*

Good Time Jazz GTJCD-12032-2

Spanier, Muggsy–*Muggsy Spanier, 1939-1942* Classics 709

Waldo's (Terry) Gotham City Band–*Footlight Vanities*

Stomp Off CD-1201

Watters, Lu, Yerba Buena Jazz Band–

Fantasy 4 4GTJCD-4409-2

Live at Hambone Kelly's: 1950 GHB BCD-93

Wilber, Bob–*And His Famous Jazz Band, with Sidney Bechet*

Jazzology J-044 (LP)

The Bechet Legacy Live at Bechet's, New York City

Jazzology J-141

Soprano Summit in Concert (with Kenny Davern)

Concord Jazz CCD-4029

Videos

Chicago And All That Jazz–A television special on Chicago jazz, shown on "The Dupont Show of the Week," November 2, 1961, hosted by Gary Moore. Tributes to Bix Beiderbecke, the Original Dixieland Jazz Band, and Louis Armstrong. Performers include Eddie Condon, Gene Krupa, Red Allen, Meade Lux Lewis, and more. 60 min. VINTAGE JAZZ VJC-2002

Jazz at the Smithsonian–A Tribute to Sidney Bechet: Bob Wilber–America's premier interpreter of Sidney Bechet, Bob Wilber, leads the Smithsonian Jazz

Repertory Ensemble through a salute to the master of
the soprano sax. Wilber, who studied and played with
Bechet, keeps the flame burning in this set of Bechet
classics such as "Summertime," "Coal Cart Blues," "Lady
Be Good," "China Boy," "Dans Les Rues D'Antibes," and
"Down in a Honky Tonk."

60 min. color KULTUR 1279 $29.95

Chapter 6: THE HARLEM RENAISSANCE

Harlem Stride Piano and Big Band Jazz

Recordings

Armstrong, Louis–*Young Louis Armstrong, 1930-1934* This
is the period that Armstrong was playing popular tunes
of the day. His introduction to pop songs was cemented
during his stay at Connie's Inn in Harlem.

RCA2 07863-66469-2

Black Jazz and Blues–A compilation of artists who made
their mark in New York's Harlem clubs during the late
1920s and early '30s. The great Bessie Smith is heard,
and so are Duke Ellington, Cab Calloway, Billie Holiday,
and others. Sandy Hook CDSH-2068

Black Rhythm Radio–Exerpts from World War II period
focuses on black stars like Lena Horne, Eddie
"Rochester" Anderson, Ernie "Bubbles" Whitman, and
the Fletcher Henderson Orchestra. These African
American artists broadcast uplifting material that was
aired specifically for the black servicemen. All of these
stars were part of the earlier, bustling nightclub scene in
Harlem. Sandy Hook CSH 2991 (LP)

Blake, Eubie–*Memories of You* (from rare piano rolls).

Biograph BCD-112

Chocolate Dandies 1928-1933– Swing CDSW-8448

The Greatest Ragtime of the Century–Not all ragtime
here, as the title suggests. Yes, there are a few ragtime
pieces by Scott Joplin, and one or two others. For the
most part, these are good examples of transitional
piano artistry moving from ragtime to the jazzier style of
stride. Harlem stride greats like James P. Johnson,
Eubie Blake, ("Charleston Rag"), Jelly Roll Morton ("King
Porter Stomp"), Clarence Jones ("Daddy Blues" and
Doggone Blues"), and Fats Waller ("Squeeze Me" and
"I'm Crazy 'Bout My Baby"), are heard on these rare
piano rolls from 1915 to 1931. Biograph BCD-103

Harlemania–A cornucopia of stylish bands from the
exciting period of the 1920s and early '30s. In addition
to the Fletcher Henderson and Duke Ellington bands,
there are selections from Noble Sissle & His Orchestra,
Don Redman & His Orchestra with vocalist Harlan
Lattimore, vocalist Adelaide Hall with The Mills Blue
Rhythm Band, Fats Weller & His Buddies, Lena Horne,
Don Redman's Orchestra with Bill "Bojangles" Robinson
and Ethel Waters, Louis Armstrong & His Orchestra,
Cab Calloway & His Orchestra, and Willie "The Lion"
Smith & His Cubs, among others.

Empire/AVID AVC-532

Henderson, Fletcher–*Fletcher Henderson and the Dixie
Stompers* Swing2 CDSBL-8445/6
The Fletcher Henderson Story: A Study in Frustration
Columbia/Legacy CK-57596

Hyman, Dick–*Dick Hyman Plays Duke Ellington*
Reference RR-50-DCD
Dick Hyman Plays Fats Waller Reference RR-33CD
Jelly and James (Morton and Johnson).
Sony Masterworks MDK-52552

Johnson, James P.–*Carolina Shout* (14 QRS piano rolls,
1917-1925). Biograph BCD-105
James P. Johnson 1921-1928 Classics 658

McKinney's Cotton Pickers (1928-1930)–*The Band Don
Redman Built* Bluebird 2275-2

New York Horns 1924-1928– Examples of many of the
superb, but not widely known, soloists of the period,
like Bubber Miley, Thomas Harris, Louis Metcalf, Rex
Stewart, June Clark, Jimmy Harrison, et al.
EPM Musique 15182-2

New York Jazz, 1928-1933–Exciting New York bands like
Luis Russell & His Gingersnaps, Earl Jackson's Musical
Champions, Adrian Rollin's Orchestra with Bunny
Berigan and Benny Goodman, Hoagy Carmichael's
Collegians, and more Historical HLP-19 (LP)

Russell, Luis–*Luis Russell and His Orchestra 1930-1934*
Classics 606
Smith, Willie "The Lion"–*Echoes of Spring*
Milan 73138-35623-2
Pork and Beans Black Lion BLCD-760144

Waller, Fats–*The Definitive Fats Waller: His Piano, His
Rhythm* Stash SJ-CD-528
Fats and His Buddies Bluebird 07863-61005-2
The Indispensible Fats Waller, Vols. 9 & 10
RCA 2 07863-66466
The Joint is Jumpin' (1929-1943) Bluebird 6288
The Last Years: Fats Waller & His Rhythm 1940-1943
Bluebird 9883-2-RB
You Rascal You ASV Living Era Cd-AJA-5040

Videos

Great Jazz Bands of the '30s (1935)– I've never seen this,
but it looks like it has early film clips of key bands from
the Harlem Renaissance period–Duke Ellington, Don
Redman, Cab Calloway, and Eubie Blake. I'm putting
in an order. 50 min. DVT V

History of Jazz–Dr. Billy Taylor takes the viewer on a tour
of jazz styles from past to present. An expensive
package. 49 min. AAI 0193V $200.00

Jazz and Jive (1930)–Period pieces of Duke Ellington and
his band, amateur hour host Major Bowes, and a jazz
cartoon. 60 min. KUL 1276

Jazz Classics: Cab Calloway and His Orchestra–Rare
footage of Cab Calloway cavorting in front of the band

on "Minnie the Moocher," "Virginia, Georgia and Caroline," "The Skunk Song," "Hi-De-Ho," and "Little Old Lady from Baltimore." There are also movie shorts entitled, *Cab Calloway's Jitterbug Party*, and *Manhattan Merry-Go-Round*. Calloway also sings two blues ballads "Blues in the Night" (his biggest hit on the charts), and "St. James Infirmary."

30 min. JAZZ CLASSICS JCVC 103 $19.98

Jazz Classics: Fats Waller and Friends—Fats at his best, entertaining with funny songs like "Your Feet's Too Big," "Ain't Misbehavin'," "Honeysuckle Rose," and "The Joint is Jumpin'." His "friends" include Mabel Lee ("Chicken Shack Shuffle"), The Three Chefs ("Breakfast in Rhythm"), Tiny Grimes ("Tiny Grimes Boogie"), Dorothy Dandridge ("Cow Cow Boogie"), Cook and Brown ("Moo Cow Boogie"), Bob Howard ("She's Too Hot to Handle"), and Dusty Brooks and His Four Tones ("Shout, Brother, Shout").

30 min. JAZZ CLASSICS JCVC 107 $19.98

Piano Legends—Hosted by Chick Corea, the informative history introduces us to 23 piano players—from Willie "The Lion" Smith up to avant gardist Cecil Taylor. This goes beyond our time line and Harlem stride scope—but jazz piano history *begins* here with Smith, James P. Johnson, Duke Ellington, and Fats Waller.

63 min. color/b&w VAI JAZZ VIDEO 69038 $29.95

Black Show Music and Jazz

Recordings

Ain't Misbehavin' (1978) (Broadway sound track with Nell Carter). RCA 2965-2

Arlen, Harold—*(American Songbook series)*—Presently, there is no collection on Arlen that investigates the work he did with Ted Koehler for the Cotton Club shows. This Smithsonian tribute is a collection of disparate singers from various time periods, interpreting the composer. Selections by Judy Garland, Jack Teagarden, Bobby Short, Lena Horne, Pearl Bailey, Tony Bennett, and many more.

Smithsonian Collection of Recordings CDRD-0485

Baker, Josephine—*Josephine Baker* (includes one CD in English and one in French, plus a 28 page booklet).

Sandstone 2 D22Z-33072

The Josephine Baker Story   ProArte/Fanfare CDD-3401

Blake, Eubie & Noble Sissle—*Early Rare Recordings, Vol. 1*

Eubie Blake Music EBM-4

Early Rare Recordings, Vol. 2   Eubie Blake Music EBM-7

Calloway, Cab—*Are You Hep to the Jive?*

Columbia/Legacy CK-57645

Cab and Company (extensive liner notes in French and English).   RCA2 07863-66496-2

Cruisin' with Cab   Forlane UCD-19004

Jumpin' Jive   EPM (Jazz Archives) 53732-2

The Cotton Club—Selections by Irving Mills with Duke Ellington and His Orchestra, Duke Ellington and His

Cotton Club Orchestra, Bill "Bojangles" Robinson with the Brunswick Studio Orchestra, Ethel Waters, Adelaide Hall, Harold Arlen, Cab Calloway, and Jimmie Lunceford and his Chickasaw Syncopators, et al.

ASV Living Era CDAIA-5031

Cotton Club Stars—Selections by The Three Peppers, Duke Ellington, The Missourians, Bill "Bojangles" Robinson with Irving Mills & His Hotsy-Totsy Gang, Billy Banks & His Blue Rhythm Boys, Claude Hopkins & His Orchestra, Buck & Bubbles, The Nicholas Brothers, The Dandridge Sisters, Lena Horne, and more.

Milan RNDCD-1302

Ellington, Duke—**Beyond Category: The Musical Genius of Duke Ellington**. A masterful boxed set chronicling Ellington's career—includes a 32-page booklet with an illustrated to the recordings.

RCA2 755174-9000 $30.00

The Brunswick Era, Vol. 1 (1926-1929) MCA MCAD-42325
At the Cotton Club: Band Remotes From Harlem

Sandy Hook CDSH-2029

Jubilee Stomp (1928-1934)   Bluebird 07863-66038-2
The Jungle Band: The Brunswick Era, Vol. 2 (1929-1931)

Decca Jazz MCAD-42348

Jungle Nights in Harlem   Bluebird 2499-2RB

Hall, Adelaide—*The Croonin' Blackbird 1927-1939*

ASV Living Era CD-AIA-5098

Horne, Lena—*Stormy Weather: The Legendary Lena (1941-1958)*.   Bluebird 9985-2-RB

Short, Bobby—*Guess Who's in Town: The Lyrics of Andy Razaf*

Rhino R2-81778

Shuffle Along—Here is the most important black musical show of the 1920s. Noble Sissle and Eubie Blake's music for this 1921 production features members of the original cast: Sissle and Blake, Gertrude Saunders, Flournoy Miller, Aubrey Lyles, the Sizzling Syncopators, Tim Brymm, and His Black Devil Orchestra, Lt. Jim Europe's 369th Infantry ("Hell Fighters") Band, and the Shuffle Along Orchestra—there's even a selection by Paul Whiteman's Orchestra. Unfortunately Florence Mills was never recorded. Excellent pictures and liner notes by Robert Kimball.

New World Records NW 260 (LP)

Sophisticated Ladies—(1981) (Music from the Broadway show). RCA 07863-56208-2

Souvenirs of Hot Chocolates—Highlights from the 1929 Broadway show *Hot Chocolates*. The show had its start up in Harlem at Connie's Inn—and then moved downtown at the Hudson Theater, 44th Street east of Broadway, on June 20, 1929. The show ran 219 performances, placing it seventh from the top in a field of 34 Broadway musicals that opened in 1929. Selections include: Fats Waller (he, Andy Razaf and Harry Brooks wrote the score) playing "Sweet Savannah Sue" and "Ain't Misbehavin'"; Edith Wilson singing "My Man is Good for Nothing But Love" and "(What Did I Do to Be So) Black and Blue"; The Harlem Footwarmers jive up "Jungle Jamboree" and "Snake Hips Dance"; and Louis Armstrong performs "Ain't Misbehavin'," "(What Did I Do to Be So) Black and Blue," and "That Rhythm Man." Smithsonian American Musical Theater Series Smithsonian Collection R012 (LP)

Stormy Weather–(music from the 1943 Hollywood film).
Fox 07822-11007-2

Waters, Ethel–*Ethel Waters, 1931-1934* Classics 735
Ethel Waters ("The Swing Era" series) Best of Jazz 4013-2

Welch, Elisabeth–*Where Have You Been?*
Cabaret DRG SLD-5202

A Tribute to Black Entertainers–A double CD package that investigates the African American contribution to the entertainment world–from Bert Williams to Marvin Gaye. For our needs, this is one terrific package. Of the 50 selections, about 30 can be connected to the Harlem Renaissance. Here are just a few examples: "I'm a Little Blackbird Looking for a Bluebird" (from *Dixie to Broadway*, by Clarence Williams' Blue Five); "I Ain't Scared of You" (Butterbeans and Susie); "Dinah" (Ethel Waters); "Aux Iles Hawaii" (Josephine Baker); "Oh! Lady Be Good" (Buck and Bubbles); "Go Harlem" (Jimmy Johnson and His Orchestra); "How'm I Doin'? (Hey! Hey!)," "The Man from Harlem" "(Cab Calloway); "Doin' the New Low Down" (Bill "Bojangles" Robinson); "Miss Otis Regrets" (The Four Blackbirds); "Margie" (Claude Hopkins and His Orchestra); "Catch On?" (Blanche Calloway and Her Orchestra); "A High Hat, a Piccolo and a Cane" (Putney Dandridge and His Orchestra); "It Was a Sad Night in Harlem" (Duke Ellington); "Keep a Twinkle in Your Eye" (The Nicholas Brothers); "When Lights are Low" (Elisabeth Welch); "Camp Meeting Day" (Noble Sissle and His Orchestra); "Prisoner of Love" (Lena Horne); "The Moon Shines on the Moonshine" (Bert Williams); "You Gave Me Everything but Love" (Adelaide Hall); and Monette Moore's medley "A Shine on Your Shoes"/ "Louisiana Hayride" from Deitz and Schwartz's *The Band Wagon*.
Columbia/Legacy C2K-52454-2

Videos
At the Jazz Band Ball–Vintage videos from the early era of sound films–1925 to 1933. A good portion, not all, represent the Harlem Renaissance period. Some rare, on location clips in taverns, clubs and dance halls. Some of the acts are unintentionally funny– such as the Al Jolson imitation of Charlie Wellman's "Alabamy Snow," and the rigid band styles of Ben Bernie and Tommy Christian. Highlights: Duke Ellington at the Cotton Club ("Old Man Blues"); Louis Armstrong's great version of "Dinah," and his soaring trumpet on "Tiger Rag"; and a wild evening of Lindy Hopping at a dance contest. Bessie Smith sings, in her only film appearance, "St. Louis Blues," and Bill "Bojangles" Robinson dances with his wooden taps. There's even a rare clip of Paul Whiteman with Bix Beiderbecke, and the marvelous Boswell Sisters, scatting up a storm in "Heebie Jeebies." 60 min. SRC 514 $19.95

Baby Laurence–Jazz Hoofer–From Harlem swing to bebop, old time dancers like Baby Laurence led "tap into its last creative phase." This reinforces those connections not seen too often today, between jazz and dance. 28 min. RHAP B $19.95

The Story of Duke Ellington–A tribute to Ellington in three parts: 1) Ellington in concert in 1962; 2) a 1930 Paramount short entitled *Black and Tan*; 3) another, undated, concert clip. 90 min. V-YES 764

Duke Ellington's Sophisticated Ladies–The award-winning Broadway show with the Hines Brothers (Gregory and Maurice) and Phillis Hyman. The Duke Ellington Orchestra plays all the classics.
108 min. color LIFE LS 73793 V $59.95

Jazz Classics: Harlem Harmonies–Includes Duke Ellington's "Hot Chocolate," Bill "Bojangles" Robinson's "Let's Scuffle," a lesson on how to be a hep cat by Cab Calloway in "Jive Talk Dictionary," and Lena Horne singing "Unlucky Woman," among others.
30 min. JAZZ CLASSICS JCVC 111 $19.98

Lena Horne–The Lady–Lena Horne's definitive moment on Broadway with her scintillating one-woman show. She sings and tells stories of the old days–"But Not for Me," "I Want to Be Happy," and "Stormy Weather," along with a host of other classic numbers.
134 min. color RKO 1001 $39.95

Leonard Maltin's Movie Memories: Soundies: Vol. 4, Harlem Highlights–Excellent production values in this trip down memory lane of soundies. Maltin defines and shows what soundies were during 1941-48–we even see a classic Mills Panorama soundie machine as he gives us our lesson about these large TV-like screens that played pre-MTV videos for customers in taverns, hotel lobbies and the classier roadside taverns. Includes Fats Waller, the Delta Rhythm Boys, Mills Brothers, Cab Calloway, Louis Armstrong, Nat King Cole, and others.
50 min. BMG VIDEO VHS 2427-3-R $19.95

Chapter 7: COUNTRY AND FOLK MUSIC

The world of country and folk music of the first half of this century was viewed much differently than it is today. Since the mid-1980s, country music has soared into mainstream popularity. Country music of the early days seldom found favor in popular music–unless someone like Bing Crosby interpreted those songs for the mass audience. Hardly any of the well-known country and folk performers of rural America were known to urbanites. This result has been long lasting. Even today, it is hard to find recordings of most of early country innovators covered in Chapter 7. Thanks to independent record companies like County, Arhoolie, Old Timey, Rounder and a handful of others, it is possible to mail away for catalogs of releases by these artists.

Not only is it difficult to find recordings of these early country and folk performers–it is nigh impossible to locate related film clips from the 1920s and '30s. So, with this admission brought to your attention, I'll march forward with my listings for Chapter 7. Usually commentary is given only on compilations and videos, but in this chapter there will be occasions when other comments are necessary.

Southern Background/Folk Elements

Recordings

Baez, Joan–*Very Early Joan (1961-1963)*. Joan Baez is chosen for a number of reasons. First, she is a wonderful vocalist, and a high-profile artist as well. The main reason she was written about in the text was that during the late 1950s and early '60s, her work was representative of what most folk singers did–reinterpret older folk ballads. This collection on Vanguard represents Baez in her pre-Dylan/pre-protest days. Interpretations of numerous Child ballads highlight this important document.   Vanguard Twofer VCD-79446/47

Folk Song America: A Smithsonian Collection, Vol. 1-4– This boxed set of 4 CDs is one of the only large compilations in print on folk music that covers some of the earlier period of this century. The weakness of this set, for our purposes, is that in volume one and two, it lacks material by early pioneers of the form, covered in this chapter: Charlie Poole, Bradley Kincaid, Eck Robertson, Carson Robison, Al Hopkins, and so on, are not heard. We do get to hear Buell Kazee and Harry McClintock, but that's about it. This is not to say that the interpretations aren't pleasing however.
Smithsonian Collection of Recordings CDRD-046-(1-4)

New Lost City Ramblers- *The Early Years, 1958-1962* The Kingston Trio and Harry Belafonte received national acclaim (and, in the case of the Trio, some critical scorn) during the "Folk Revival," but it was the New Lost City Ramblers who carved out an admiring cult following because of their archivalist zeal. Members wrote insightful liner notes directing their audience to the original recordings from the 1920s and '30s, which they based their interpretations on. The group tried to perform in the style of the artists they were covering; not because they couldn't generate original ideas, but because they wanted to honor musicians like Uncle Dave Macon, Charlie Poole, The Delmore Brothers, and others.   Smithsonian/Folkways CDSF-40036

Old-Time Southern Dance Music: Ballads and Songs–Folk music classics such as "Rose Conley" (Grayson and Whitter), "Pretty Polly" (Coon Creek Girls), "That Fatal Courtship" (Ephraim Woodie), "Black Jack David" (Cliff Carlisle), "Old Ruben" (Wade Mainer), "On the Old Plantation" (Blue Sky Boys), and more. These are old traditional folk songs by early commercial country artists. This record, and most of these types of recordings, are not found in record stores. What to do?
Old Timey 102 (LP)

Note:
Write to: Arhoolie Records: Chris Strachwitz, 10341 San Pablo Ave., El Cerrito, CA 94530

Ritchie, Jean– *Kentucky Songs and Ballads*
Folk-Legacy FSA-3 (LP)

High Hills & Mountains   Greenbays GR-701 (LP)
Jean Ritchie and Doc Watson Live at Folk City
Smithsonian/Folkways CDSF-40005

Smith, Hobart–*Appalachian Songs and Banjo Tunes*
Folk-Legacy FSA-17 (LP)

Watson, Doc–*Songs From the Southern Mountains*
Sugar Hill SHCD-3829

Videos

American Patchwork: Dreams and Songs of the Noble Old–Hosted by folklorist pioneer Alan Lomax, this video celebrates the creative role of the elderly in rural America today. This documentary focuses on non-commercial entertainers of a different stripe. With the exception of Sam Chatmon, who was the sole surivivor of a music-making family from the Mississippi Delta, the elders are commercially unknowns. Lomax also introduces us to a 91-year-old union organizer, an 80-year-old fisher-woman from the Sea Islands, and takes us into the religious services of the Sacred Harp Singers.   60 min. color PBS 301 $14.95

Elizabeth Cotton and Mike Seeger–This video celebrates the music of the "Godmother of the Folk Revival." Cotton has a resevoir of old folk tunes, and Mike Seeger, an ex-member of the New Lost City Ramblers, is a master of finger picking.
60 min. color SRC 804V $19.95

Mike Seeger: Fret 'N' Fiddle–The well-versed Seeger performs a number of rural folk and country tunes showing off his considerable finger-picking talent, as well as fiddling expertise. 55 min. color VESTA 13008V

Early Commercial Music

Recordings

Banjo Pickin' Girl–Rare examples of the earliest females who recorded country music. Fiddlin' John Carson's daughter, Moonshine Kate, is here, as is one of Okeh Records' first star female stars, Roba Stanley. Eva Davis and Smantha Burgamer, and the Coon Creek Girls represent the Southeastern British folk roots, while Billie Maxwell, Patsy Montana, and The Girls of the Golden West reflect the Western heritage of Texas, Oklahoma & Missouri.   Rounder 1029 (LP/cas)

Classic Country Music–Here is an excellent, 4CD set, covering important early, commercial country performers, as well as stars of the 1940s to the 1990s. I'll focus on the artists covered in Chapter 7: Gid Tanner and His Skillet Lickers, Uncle Dave Macon and His Fruit Jar Drinkers, Bradley Kincaid, Vernon Dalhart, The Carter Family, Jimmie Rodgers, Riley Puckett, W. Lee O'Daniel and His Light Crust Doughboys, and Gene Autry. This is the most important package that exists for our early Southern folk music section.
Smithsonian Collection of Recordings 4 CDRD-042

Grayson and Whitter (1928-1930)   County 513

Paramount Old TimeTunes—On the heels of Okeh Records' success with Fiddlin' John Carson, Paramount Records made its first venture into the field of white country music in 1924, recording harmonica player-guitarist Walter C. Peterson. This collection includes recordings by the Kentucky Thorobreds ("Shady Grove"), Wilmer Watts and the Lonely Eagles ("Cotton Mill Blues"), Sid Harkreader and Grady Moore ("Bully of the Town"), The Fruit Jar Guzzlers ("Stack-O-Lee"), and John White ("Little Old Sod Shanty").

Arhoolie Records/JEMF 103 (LP)

Eck Robertson: Famous Cowboy Fiddle—During the summer and fall of 1963, three members of the New Lost City Ramblers, Mike Seeger, John Cohen, and Tracy Schwarz, recorded this legendary Texas fiddler. The 76 year older can be heard reworking his cherished specialties that he perfomed at fiddlers' competitions and early commercial recordings. Selections include: "Texas Wagoner," "Sally Johnson," "Grey Eagle," "Hawk Got the Chicken," "Dusty Miller," "Beaumont Rag," and 13 more.

Country 202 (LP)

Videos

American Patchwork: Appalachian Journey—The hills and flatlands of Kentucky are a rich treasure trove of traditional music. We visit coal miners, mountain tops, moonshiners, banjo pickers, and fiddlers. The original source of the number one hit for the Kingston Trio "The Ballad of Tom Dooley," is presented for our pleasure.

60 min. color PBS 300V $14.95

The String Bands/Barn Dances/Father of Country

Recordings

Blue Hawaii: Vintage Anthology, 1926-1942—Perhaps the most ubiquitious sound of country and western music in the past 70 years has been that of the sliding steel guitar. The Hawaiian influence on country music has been enormous—let this compilation release show you why. Selections include Sol Hoopii and His Novelty Trio, Felix Mendelssohn and His Hawaiin Serenaders, A. P. Sharpe and His Honolulu Hawaiians, Roy Smeck and His Vita Trio, Bing Crosby, et al.

ASV Living Era ASL-CD-5121

The Bristol Sessions—The historic visit to that borderline city between Virginia and Tennessee by Ralph S. Peer led to a 10 day audition seeking local talent. It was Peer's trip for his new company, Victor Talking Machine Company, in the summer of 1927, that resulted in his signing the Carter Family and Jimmie Rodgers. There were others he signed also. Have a listen—some of the performers are: Uncle Eck Dunford ("Skip to Ma Lou, My Darling"), Blind Alfred Reed ("Walking in the Way with Jesus"), the West Virginia Coon Hunters ("Greasy String"), Dad Blackard's Moonshiners ("Sandy River Belle"), Alcoa Quartet ("I'm Redeemed"), El Watson ("Pot Licker Blues"), the Shelor Family ("Billy Grimes, the Rover"), and Jimmie Rodgers' one-time group, the Tenneva Ramblers ("The Longest Train I Ever Saw"), along with a host of others. Besides the Carter Family ("Single Girl, Married Girl") and Jimmie Rodgers ("Sleep,

Baby, Sleep"), only Ernest "Pop" Stoneman and Henry Whitter had any lasting commercial careers.

Country Music Foundation CMF-011-D

The Carter Family—According to the Summer 1995 *Schwann/Spectrum* guide to records in print, the "First Family of Country" has three (3—count 'em) records in print, and none of them is out on CD. I'm reminded again and again that the record industry is only about moving products.

RCA Camden CAK-2473 (cas)
On Border Radio.   Arhoolie/JEMF101 (LP)
The Original and Great Carter Family
RCA Camden CAK-586 (cas)

Darby and Tallton—*Darby and Tarlton Sing the Blues*
Old Timey 112 (LP)

Flatt and Scruggs—*Songs of the Famous Carter Family*
Columbia CK-08464

Hoopii, Sol—*Master of Hawaiian Steel Guistar, Vol. 1*
Rounder CD-1024

Hoosier Hot Shots—*The Essential Hoosier Hot Shots: Rural Rhythm*   Columbia/Legacy CK-52735

Macon, Uncle Dave—*Laugh Your Blues Away*
Rounder Records 1028 (LP)

Note:
Write to: Rounder Records, One Camp Street, Cambridge, MA, 02140

Nashville: The Early String Bands, Vol. 1—A distinguished group of significant "Grand Ole Opry" members who played old time string band music. Dr. Humphrey Bate and His Possum Hunters is represented with "Green Backed Dollar," "My Wife Died Saturday Night," and "Throw the Old Cow Over the Fence," and Uncle Dave Macon flails away on his popular "Railroadin' and Gamblin." Others include, Uncle Bunt Stephens ("Candy Girl"), Paul Warmack and His Gully Jumpers ("Stone Rag"), Binkley Brothers' Dixie Clodhoppers ("Give Me Back My Fifteen Cents"), and Sam McGee ("Chevrolet Car")   County Records 541 (LP)

Note:
Write to: Dave Feeeman, County Records, P.O. Box 191, Floyd, Virginia 24091

Nitty Gritty Dirt Band—*Will the Circle Be Unbroken?* The historic, 3-record set that bridged the gap between long-haired hippies and conservative old time musicians. Great versions of legends' classic songs. Mother Maybelle Carter, Roy Acuff, Merle Travis, Doc Watson, Earl Scruggs.   Liberty 2 C22V-46589

Rodgers, Jimmie—*America's Blue Yodeler 1930-1931*
Rounder CD-1060

The Best of Jimmie Rodgers (features all 18 of his chart hits).   Rhino R2-70942

| *The Best of Jimmie Rodgers* | MCA MCAD-31086 |
| *Last Sessions 1933* | Rounder CD-1063 |

The Skillet Lickers— County 526 (LP)
The Skillet Lickers, Vol. 2 Country 526 (LP)

Stars of Grand Ole Opry (1926-1974)—Early stars include: Uncle Dave Macon ("Railroadin' and Gamblin'") and the Carter Family ("I'm Thinking Tonight of My Blue Eyes") —every other selection comes from artists who joined the ranks of this weekend barn dance after 1935.

RCA CPK2-0466 (cas)

Videos
1992 Merle Watson Memorial Festival—The legendary flat picker, Blind Doc Watson, established this music festival for the memory of his son Merle, who died at the age of 34 in a tractor accident. Merle was an accomplished professional musician who often played with his dad. (Representative recordings of Doc and Merle Watson can be found on Vanguard, Sugar Hill, and Flying Fish Records.) The main focus of this concert is on the traditional southern music of the hill country. Special guests make appearances.

120 min. HOMS VDZWF01 V $24.95

Times Ain't Like They Used to Be: Early Rural & Popular American Music—What a revelation! Here are rare original film clips from 1928 to 1935, most never seen before in movie houses or on television. As the notes to this collection state, "In the early days of sound film, in addition to covering major events, newsreel cameras captured the sights and sounds of everyday life in America, including its music. Musicians were filmed by roving newsreel crews on street corners and front porches, at country dances and summer resorts, in nightclubs, and broadcasting from churches and radio stations."

There are a few examples of popular music artists—but the majority of film space is dominated by the underground forms of blues and country. Highlights of the country music sections include Bascom Lamar Lunceford's string band rehearsing for an upcoming competition by playing, on the steps of someone's rural cottage, "Doggett's Gap"; Uncle John Scruggs, sitting in front of his cabin playing clawhammer banjo and singing "Little Old Log Cabin in the Lane"; the Cumberland Ridge Runners entertaining crippled children at Chicago's Shriners Hospital with the humorous "Goofus"; Bob Wills playing two Texas fiddle breakdowns; a nearly 14-minute filmed short subject, featuring a typical stage show performance of the phenomenally successful vaudeville and radio group, Otto Gray's Oklahoma Cowboys; and the major coup of this amazing documentary, a musical short subject produced by Columbia Pictures in 1929 of Jimmie Rodgers. I had seen stills of this one reel movie house release over the years, but had never seen it—until this video debuted in 1992. Rodgers performs "Waiting for a Train," "Daddy and Home," and "Blue Yodel #1 (T for Texas)." SHANACHIE YAZOO 512 $24.95

Note:
With so little country music available on film, this video stands as the single most important document we have. However, it is not listed in *Videolog*, so you may write to: Yazoo Video/Shanachie Entertainment Corporation, P.O. Box 208, Newton, NJ 07860,

Emergence of the West and Hot String Bands

Recordings
Back in the Saddle Again—Here is the most indispensable collection of cowboy compiled music on record! Charlie Seeman, of the Country Music Foundation compiled music of the last 55 years, which embraces the lore of the cowboy. Our main concern here is finding musical examples that give evidence to the written text in Chapter 7—and this recording answers most of that. Carl T. Sprague, Jules Verne Allen, and Harry "Haywire" McClintock represent early cowboys who recorded and were covered in the chapter. Others of note include the first singing cowboy, Ken Maynard, the Girls of the Golden West, Gene Autry, California's Beverly Hill Billies, and Jimmie Rodgers. Examples of today's cowboy singers are represented by Chris LeDoux and Riders in The Sky.

New World 2 NW-314/315-2

Cowboy Songs on Folkways—A collection of cowboy songs from members of the urban folk movement of the 1940s and 1950s, that were recorded for Folkways records. Most of these interpretations are of authentic, working cowboy selections: "Morning Grub Holler" (Harry Jackson), "Chisholm Trail" (Tex-I-An-Boys), "Whoopie-Ti-Yi-Yo, Get Along Little Dogies" (Woody Guthrie & Cisco Houston), "Trail to Mexico" (Peter LaFarge), "Zebra Dun" (Ray Reed), "Cow Yicky Yicky Yea" (Leadbelly), and "Texan Boys" (John A. Lomax, Jr.), et al. Smithsonian/Folkways SFCD-40043

Montana, Patsy—*The Cowboy's Sweetheart*
Flying Fish FF-459

The East Texas Serenaders 1927-1936— County 410 (LP)

Chapter 8: POPULAR MUSIC: 1935-1950

Of all of the timeline music forms that have been covered in this book, none has the expansiveness and over abundance of material to draw from as this section. After all, this period is the heart and the soul of what has often been referred to as "The Golden Age of Pop." Pages could be filled with just the obtainable records of the popular bands and singers. There is also a treasure trove of material that emanated from the Broadway stage (the last hurrah for that form's direct impact on popular songs), and the Hollywood film.

Up to this point, I had to do a good deal of explaining because of the many gaps that existed in both early pop and country music—underground jazz and blues forms were adequately represented. So, with great trepidation, I will try to briefly describe and list representative music and film samples that coincide with the readings in Chapter 8.

The Swing Bands

Recordings

The Benny Goodman Story (1955) –(music from the film performed by Benny Goodman & his orchestra, trio, quartet, and octet).   MCA MCAD-4055

Berigan, Bunny & His Orchestra–*I Can't Get Started* Along with Harry James, Berigan was the best known of the popular trumpet soloists–I wasn't able to work him into the brief narrative of the text–so here is a belated recognition of his talent.   ProArte CDDD-554

Dorsey, Jimmy–*Plays His Biggest Hits*
Hollywod/MG HCD-335

Dorsey, Tommy–*The Best of Tommy Dorsey*
Intersound 2 CDC-1026
Yes, Indeed!   Bluebird 9987-2RB

Dorsey, Tommy & Frank Sinatra–*All Time Greatest Hits, Vol. 1 (1940-1942)*   Bluebird 8324-2
The Song Is You (includes 100-page booklet, rare photos, previously unreleased material, and a complete sessionography). RCA5 07836-66353-2 $80

Goodman, Benny–*Best of the Big Bands: Benny Goodman (1939-1946)*   Columbia CK-45338
The Birth of Swing (1935-1936)
Bluebird 3 07863-61038-2 4CD $35.98
The Indispensable Benny Goodman, Vol. 3 & 4 (1936-1937)
RCA2 07863-66470-2
16 Most Requested Songs   Columbia/Legacy CK-53774

James, Harry–*The Essence of Harry James*
Columbia/Legacy CK-57151

Miller, Glenn–*Chattanooga Choo Choo: The #1 Hits*
Bluebird 31028-2-RB
The Complete Glenn Miller and His Orchestra (big box set).   Bluebird 13 07863-61015-2 $149.98
Glenn Miller and His Orchestra Go to War
Radiola CDMR-1160

Shaw, Artie–*Begin the Beguine (1938-1941)*
Bluebird 6274-2RB
The Complete Gramercy Five Sessions Bluebird 7637-2-RB

Songs That Got Us Through the War–   Rhino R2-70960

The Words and Music of World War II–
Columbia/Legacy C2K-48516-2

Note:
Both of the two preceding recordings include many songs, and the artists who performed them, that are listed in the chart on page 204.

Swing That Music–(includes a 60-page booklet) A compilation of all types of swing bands–jazz & sweet over ground (mainstream pop) and underground.
Smithsonian Collection of Recordings CDRD-102

Swing Time! The Fabulous Big Band Era (1925-1955)–A bigger package than above.
Columbia/Legacy C3K-52862-3 $39.98

Videos

Benny Goodman: Adventures in the Kingdom of Swing–An excellent biography of Goodman. Historic clips of previous bands and all the excitement that went along with the "King of Swing."
60 min. C0L-MV 19V49186V

Best of the Big Bands–Compilation of video clips of the popular bands in action, including Benny Goodman, Artie Shaw, Harry James, the Dorsey Brothers, Les Brown, Larry Clinton, and more.   80 min. V-YES 762 V

Swing Vols. 1-4–Four independent films that feature between 18 to 20 full numbers each. Each volume spotlights around ten or more bandleaders or singers (usually doing two numbers). Volume one features Tommy Dorsey, Tony Pastor with Rosemary Clooney, Billie Holiday, and Duke Ellington. Volume two: Dorsey Brothers, Nat King Cole, Woody Herman, and Sarah Vaughan. Volume three: Count Basie, Ink Spots, and Harry James. Volume four: Tex Beneke, Mills Brothers, Louis Prima, and Buddy Rich.

Vol. 1	50 min.	MCA 80665V $19.98
Vol. 2	50 min.	MCA 80666V $19.98
Vol. 3	50 min.	MCA 80667V $19.98
Vol. 4	50 min.	MCA 80668V $19.98

The Sweet Bands

Garber, Jan and His Orchestra– *Play 22 Original Big Band Recordings (1939-1941 & 1946-1947)* (Garber was known as "Idol of the Air Lanes").   Hindsight HSCD-403

Jones, Spike–*The Best of Spike Jones and His City Slickers* Jones was leader of the preminent novelty band of the 1940s and 1950s. They wreacked havoc on everything they played, especially ballads, such as "Cocktails for Two."   RCA 07863-53748

Kaye, Sammy and His Orchestra–*Best of the Big Bands: Sammy Kaye*   Columbia CK-45342

Kemp, Hal and His Orchestra–*Got a Date With An Angel*
ProArte CDD-553

King, Wayne–*The Best of Wayne King*   MCA MCAD-4022

Kyser, Kay and His Orchestra–*Best of the Big Bands*
Columbia CK-45343
Kollege of Musical Knowledge (a complete broadcast from October 11, 1944, and a complete band remote from June 12, 1934).   Radiola CMR-1075 (cas)

Legendary Bands of the 30s–Here is a rare package of mostly sweet and society bands–the only jazz units are the Dorseys, Goodman, Bob Crosby and Cab Calloway. The rest are the best-known sweet bands of this era. Orchestras led by: Ozzie Nelson, Clyde McCoy, Paul Whiteman, Ray Noble, Guy Lombardo, Russ Morgan,

Xavier Cugat, Shep Fields, Hudson-DeLange, Larry Clinton, and Hal Kemp. ProArte CDD-485

Lombardo, Guy—*And His Royal Canadians On the Air, 1935-1936* (rare radio recordings from "The Esso Marketer," a Depression broadcast series).
Sandy Hook CSH-2023 (cas)
16 Most Requested Songs Columbia/Legacy CK-44407

Martin, Freddie and His Orchestra—*Freddie Martin and His Orchestra* Ranwood RC-8217

Welk, Lawrence—*The Best of Lawrence Welk*
MCA 2 MCAC2-4044 (cas)

Videos
The Big Bands, V. 109—Five of the top sweet bands in action playing their most loved hits: Frankie Carle, Hal Kemp, Johnny Long, Jan Garber, and Art Mooney.
51 min. KARTES 766-XV $14.95

Lawrence Welk: The Early Years—The early years do not refer to those days in the 1930s, when Welk polkaed about the Southwest and Midwest. The title refers to his television series, which is seen here with Welk's very first broadcast on July 2, 1955, and the debut of the Lennon Sisters, on August 3, 1957.
105 min. WELK W1028 $29.95

Meet the Bandleaders, #107: Guy Lombardo—Guy Lombardo, with his brothers Carmen and Lebert, had the most successful and longest running commercial band in America. Classics such as "Old Gang of Mine," "Seems Like Old Times," and the all-time New Year's Eve favorite, "Auld Lang Syne," are played by Louis Armstrong's very favorite band—the band that played "the sweetest music this side of heaven."
54 min. KARTES 559-4V $14.95

The Singers Emerge

Recordings
Andrews Sisters—*Boogie Woogie Bugle Boy* (with Bing Crosby and Bob Hope). ProArte CDD-506
60th Anniversary, Vol.1 MCA MCAD-42044

Crosby, Bing—*Greatest Hits (1939-1947)* MCA MCAD-1620
The Movie Hits Peal (Flapper Series) CD-9784
Swinging on a Star (classics from movies, including a duet with Bob Hope—"[We're on the] Road to Morocco"). MCA MCAD-31367

Day, Doris—*Doris Day with Les Brown and His Orchestra*
Sandy Hook CDSH-2078

Great Singers, Great Bands—An excellent program that finally highlights the vocalists with the bands. For some readers the names of these singers will be obscure, but they were well-known during the 1930s and 1940s—here is a partial listing of the singers and the band they were featured with: Edythe Wright and Jack Leonard with Tommy Dorsey; the Norton Sisters with Vaughn, Monroe; Bea Wain with Larry Clinton; Martha

Tilton with Benny Goodman; Ray Eberle with Glenn Miller, and one of the most bizarre billings for band and singer(s)— Mitchell Ayres and His Fashions-In-Music with Meredith Blake and the Four Trumpet-Ayres. Pair PDC-21312

Haymes, Dick—*How High the Moon, with Harry James and His Orchestra, Helen Forrest* Memoir CDMOIR-510
Imagination Audiophile ACD-79

Sentimental Journey: Pop Vocal Classics Vol. 1 (1942-1946)—
Rhino R2-71249

Sentmental Journey: Pop Vocal Classics, Vol. 2 (1947-1950)—
Rhino R2-71259

Shore, Dinah—*Blues in the Night: A Tribute to Dinah Shore 1917-1994.* ASV Living Era ASL-CD-5136
16 Most Requested Songs Columbia/Legacy CK-45315

Sinatra, Frank—*Greatest Hits (The Early Years)*
Columbia CK-09274
I Remember Tommy Reprise 45267-2
I'll Be Seeing (with Tommy Dorsey and His Orchestra)
RCA 66427-2
The Song is You (with Tommy Dorsey & His Orchestra; five volume set of recordings dating from 1940-1942).
RCA 5 66353-2 $79.98
The Voice: The Columbia Years (1943-1952)
Columbia C4K 40343 $29.98

With Vocal Refrain, Vol. 1: What a Difference a Day Made!— Of all of the band singer compilations in print, and there are many not noted here, I savor this collection. This was the time when the singers were given a short refrain to sing, usually in the middle of the musical arrangement. In addition to the better-known vocalists such as Sinatra, Haymes, Forrest, and the like, here are some of the others: Anita O'Day with Gene Krupa, Maxine Sullivan with Benny Carter, Helen Humes with Count Basie, Mildred Bailey with Red Norvo, Tony Pastor with Artie Shaw, et al.
Empire/Avid AVC-526
Vol. 2: And the Angels Sing (more of the same).
Empire/Avid AVC-527

Your Hit Parade: The Memorable Radio Years 1938 to 1952 (actual broadcasts from the show "Your Hit Parade" with musical director Mark Warnew).
Radiola CDSH-2032

Videos
Frank Sinatra: Relive the Magic—An historical overview of Sinatra's career from the 1940s to the 1970s.
90 min. color SIMI V $9.95

Juke Box Saturday Night—Top recording artists of the 1930s-1950, with a collection of numbers by the Ink Spots, Frank Sinatra, Fats Waller, Sammy Davis Jr., Buddy Clark, Peggy Lee, and the bands of Benny Goodman, Charlie Barnet, Lionel Hampton, and more.
85 min. V-YES 770 V $29.95

Romance on the High Seas (1948)–Doris Day's movie debut, in a convoluted story of mix up and mayhem aboard a luxury liner. Day plays the part of a singer and is billed fourth in the credits–of course, she steals the movie. Day sings "I'm In Love," "It's You or No One," and the two hits that resulted, "Put 'Em in a Box, Tie 'Em With a Ribbon, and Throw 'Em in the Deep Blue Sea," and "It's Magic" (written by Sammy Cahn and Jule Styne).   99 min. MGM/UA M302313 V $29.95

State Fair (1945)–A gentle story of a rural family making their yearly visit to the Iowa State Fair. The father enters his prize hog in competition, and the mother her pickles. The daughter and son fall in love at the fair–he (Dick Haymes) for a too-worldly singer in a band, and she (Jeanne Crain) for a hardened newspaper reporter. Songs were written by Rodgers and Hammerstein, with "It Might as Well Be Spring" (Crain's vocal was dubbed by Louanne Hogan) winning the Academy Award for Best Song of the Year. Haymes sings a number of songs to good advantage.
100 min. color FOX V1348 $19.98

The Swingin' Singin' Years–Originally telecast on March 8, 1960, and hosted by future President of the United States, Ronald Reagan. Band leaders Woody Herman, Freddie Martin, Freddie Slack, Louis Jordan (R&B), and Charlie Barnet eventually give way to the main feature of this program the singers: Jo Stafford ("The Gentleman is a Dope," and "Temptation"–done as a hillbilly rube number by Cinderella G. Stump, Stafford's alias, titled "Tim-Tay-Shun"); Eddy Howard ("To Each his Own"); Dinah Washington ("What a Difference a Day Makes," and "Makin' Whoopee"); and Vaughn Monroe ("Racing with the "Moon," and "There, I've Said It Again").   51 min. VINTAGE JAZZ CLASSICS V-2003

The Broadway Musical

Recordings
American Musical Theater: Shows, Songs and Stars *Vol. 2 (1934-1947)*. Highlights from Volume 2 include: *Porgy and Bess* (Todd Duncan and Anne Browne, "Bess, You Is My Woman Now"); *Babes in Arms* (Wynn Murray, "Johnny One-Note"); *Kickerbocker Holiday* (Walter Huston, "September Song"); *Leave It to Me* (Mary Martin, "My Heart Belongs to Daddy"); *Dubarry Was a Lady* (Bert Lahr and Ethel Merman, "Friendship"); *Pal Joey* (Vivienne Segal, "Bewitched, Bothered, and Bewildered"); *Oklahoma!* (Alfred Drake, "Oklahoma!"); *Carousel* (John Raitt, "Soliloquy"); *On the Town* (male trio, "New York, New York"); *Annie Get Your Gun* (quartet, "There's No Business Like Show Business"); and *Finian's Rainbow* (Ella Logan, "How Are Things in Glorra Morra?").
Smithsonian Collection of Recordings CDRD-036-2
Vol. 3 (1947-1956) Highlights from Volume 3 include: *Brigadoon (Marion Bell, "Almost Like Being in Love"); Street Scene* (Brian Sullivan, "Lonely House"); *Where's Charley?* (Ray Bolger, "Once in Love with Amy"); *Kiss Me, Kate* (Alfred Drake, "Where Is the Life That Late I Led?"); *Gentlemen Prefer Blondes* (Carol Channing, "Dimonds Are a Girl's Best Friend"); *South Pacific* (Ezio

Pinza, "Some Enchanted Evening"); and in 1950, Frank Loesser's delightful *Guy and Dolls* (quartet, "Runyonland Music/Fugue for Tinhorns/Follow the Fold").
Smithsonian Collection of Recordings CDRD-036-3

Annie Get Your Gun (Irving Berlin) [1946]–
MCA Classics MCAD-10047

Coward, Noel–The Master's Voice: HMV Recordings–
1928-1953   Angel 2DCD-54919

From This Moment On: The Songs of Col Porter–
Selections by pop, cabaret, theater, and jazz singers.
Smithsonian Collection of Recordings CD-RD-047

Irving Berlin: A Hundred Years–Various selections by artists from the 1930s and '40s.   Columbia CGK-40035

Oklahoma! (Rodgers and Hammerstein)[1943]–
MCA Classics MCAD-10046

Pal Joey (Rodgers and Hart [1950 revival cast]–
Columbia CK-04364

Porgy and Bess (George Gershwin) [1940-1942 original cast–   MCA Classics MCAD-10520

Rodgers and Hmmerstein Gift Set–(4CD set of various stage productions–*Oklahoma!, Carousel, The King and I*, and *The Sound of Music*).   RCA 60569-2RG $27.98

Rodgers and Hart ("American Song book" series)–
Selections by Lee Wiley, Bing Crosby, Dick Haymes, Judy Garland, Doris Day, Tony Bennett, Ella Fitzgerald, Bobby Short, Matt Dennis, Peggy Lee, Mel Torme, Maureen McGovern, Carmin McRae, and Margaret Whiting.
Smithsonian Collection of Recordings CDRD-0486

Videos
Carousel (1956)–Rodgers and Hammerstein changed forever the way Hollywood treated products from Broadway. The authors had written into their agreements with the Hollywood producers that no outside songs by the studio's licensed composers could be added to their musicals, nor could any of Rodgers & Hammerstein's songs be deleted (without author's written agreement) from the film.
105 min. color FOXV 1713V $19.98

Girl Crazy (1943)–Busby Berkeley directed Mickey Rooney and Judy Garland in the bubbly Gershwin confection that became the source (though not the exact score) of the 1990s Broadway smash, *Crazy for You.*
100 min. MGM/UA M300567V $19.98

Kiss Me, Kate (1953)–Colorful remake with some great dance numbers of Cole Porter's last successful Broadway musical. Based on Shakespeare's play *The Taming of the Shrew,* Howard Keel and Katheryn Grayson star and sing "So In Love," "Always True to You In My Fashion," and others.
109 min. color MGM/UA M202352 V $19.98

Oklahoma! (1955)—Twelve years after it first debuted on Broadway, this ground-breaking musical play reached the screen in glorious color (the process was known as Todd-AO). Gordon MacRae as Curly, Shirley Jones, radiant as Laurey, and a cast of supporting actors and dancers as well as Robert Russell Bennett's Orchestrations made for an entertaining transformation to the silver screen. 146 min. color FOX V7020 $19.98

Note:
Some of the Broadway musicals on video that were adapted for film will be listed in the next video section ("The Hollywood Musical").

The Hollywood Musical

Recordings
Astaire, Fred—*Fred Astaire, Volume 2: Original Recordings From 1935-1943*   ASV Living Era ASL-CD-51233
Steppin' Out: Fred Astaire at MGM
                                    Sony Special Products AK 47712

Blue Skies (Irving Berlin) [1946]—(starring Fred Astaire and Bing Crosby).   Sandy Hook CDSH-2095

Crosby, Bing—*Bing Crosby and Bob Hope* ("Philco Radio Time," 1947 with Dorothy Lamour, and the "New Swan Show," 1948).   Radiola CMR-1044 (cas)

Faye, Alice—*Alice Faye on the Air, 1932-1934*
                                    Sandy Hook CDSH-2020

Garland, Judy—*The Best of Judy Garland* (features selections from movies *Broadway Melody of 1938, Little Nellie Kelly, Presenting Lily Mars, Babes on Broadway, Girl Crazy, Andy Hardy Meets Debutante, Love Fins Andy Hardy, The Wizard of Oz, Babes in Arms, For Me and My Gal,* and *Every Sunday Afternoon*).
                                    Intersound 2 CDC-1027
Judy at Carnegie Hall (legendary comeback concert).
                                    Capitol 2 C2AY-90013

Hello, Frisco, Hello (1943)— Alice Faye sings in this sentimental musical.
                        Hollywood Soundstage HSC-5005 (cas)

Hoagy Carmichael Songbook—Hoagy wrote for Hollywood, not for the Broadway stage—here are stars of 1930s and '40s, as well as Hoagy Carmichael himself, singing. Pearl (Flapper Series) PAST-CD-7004

Hope, Bob—*The Bob Hope Radio Show* (two complete programs of Hope and his regular troop entertaining at army camps in 1945).   Radiola CDMR-1060

Lullaby of Broadway: The Music of Harry Warren—A master of song-weaving for the Hollywood studio system. 25 Interpretations of his classics by stars of the 1930s and '40s. Like Harold Arlen's music, Warren's songs are better known than he is. This set includes: "Lullaby of Broadway" (Harry Roy & His Orchestra); "I Found a Million Dollar Baby" (Layton & Johnstone); "I Only Have Eyes for You" (Eddie Duchin & His

Orchestra); "Lulu's Back in Town" (Harry Roy & His Orchestra); "September in the Rain: (Hutch); "Jeepers Creepers" (Mills Brothers); "You Must Have Been a Beautiful Baby" (Bing Crosby); "I, Yi, Yi, Yi,Yi, (I Like You Very Much)" (Carmen Miranda); "Chattanooga Choo Choo" (Glen Miller with Tex Beneke & the Modernaires); "You'll Never Know" (Dick Haymes & the Song Spinners).   Pearl (Flapper Series) PAST-CD-9795

MacDonald, Jeanette and Nelson Eddy—Hollywood's most beloved vocal duet sing their classic hits.
                        Pearl (Flapper Series) PAST-CD-7026

Mercer, Johnny—Part of the Smithsonian American Songbook Series.
            Smithsonian Collection of Recordings CDRD-04811

A Party With Betty Comden and Adolph Green [1977 Original Cast]—Features more than 30 songs written by the team and sung by them.   DRG 2 CD2-5177

Snow White (1938)—The Disney film for RKO that started the eventual mania for full-length, animated feature films—Disney's films usually had terrific songs.
                                    RCA 8455-2

Those Sensational Sirens of the Silver Screen—Lena Horne, Alice Faye, Carmen Miranda, Ann Southern, Gracie Allen, Ginger Rogers, and, might you believe, Bette Davis, (singing in the wartime *Thank Your Lucky Stars*, that lament of women of that era, "They're Either Too Young or Too Old").   VJC VJC-1002-2 ACD-291/2

Videos
Broadway Melody of 1940—Fred Astaire became a free agent and during the1940s, and made musical films for MGM, Paramount, and Fox. This film, his first away from Ginger and RKO, teamed him with film's most highly regarded female tap star, Eleanor Powell—they scorch the screen in "Begin the Beguine." Cole Porter wrote the music; other numbers include Astaire-Powell in "I Concentrate on You," and "Juke Box Dance," and Astaire and George Murphy winging it in "Please Don't Monkey with Broadway."
                        103 min. MGM/UA M3 0111 $19.98

Cover Girl (1944)—Columbia Pictures' pinup musical star was Rita Hayworth, and she was given star attention in this lavish musical opposite Gene Kelly. Plenty of flashbacks (Hayworth plays her grandmother) and plenty of music.
                        107 min. color REP C090413V $19.95

Down Argentine Way (1940)— Frothy resort musical that coupled rising star Betty Grable with Don Ameche. No studio did vivid colors and south of the border (studio) locales like 20th Century-Fox. Carmen Miranda camps it up, and the Nicholas Brothers do a specialty number turn.   94 min. FOX V1718 $19.98

Follow the Boys (1940)—Is a typical, wartime parade of talent of the spirits for the boys at the front and audiences back home, as well. Universal Studios used actual footage of celebrities doing wartime entertainment duty. Songs galore! Dinah Shore sings "I'll Get By," "I'll Walk Alone," and "Mad About Him, Sad About Him, How Can I Be Glad Without Him Blues"; Sophie Tucker reprised "Some of These Days," and an obligatory service song "The Bigger the Army and the Navy"; Jeanette MacDonald raised spirits with "Beyond the Blue Horizon," and "I'll See You In My Dreams"; the Andrews Sisters perfomed a medley of hits, including "Bei Mir Bist Du Schoen," "Beer Barrel Polka," and "Shoo Shoo Baby." Also included are appearances and music from Arthur Rubinstein, Louis Jordan, the Delta Rhythm Boys (the last two performed to black-only servicemen), Charlie Spivak, Donald O'Connor, Freddie Slack, and others.

The reason this lesser-known musical is included (besides having some terrific music) is to show that even less than classic films of this era (and this is in no way a classic film) had quality productions. The mass of pop music performed during this era was, and still is, quite amazing. 111 min. MCA 80594 $14.98

Hello, Frisco, Hello (1943)–20th Century-Fox present another of their nostalgic trips to the past, with Alice Faye, John Payne, Jack Oakie, and June Havoc. Includes the Harry Warren's classic "You'll Never Know," and new songs, mixed with over 20 of the old classics from the turn of the century.

98 min. color FOXV 1390 $19.98

Holiday Inn (1942)–Irving Berlin provided the songs, and Bing Crosby and Fred Astaire brought in the talents. "White Christmas was introduced in this film–Bing sang it to Marjorie Reynolds, and, yes, he won her heart. To this very day, "White Christmas" by Bing Crosby is the biggest selling single in the history of popular music.

101 min. MCA 55039 V $14.98

Meet Me in St. Louis (1944)–Beautiful evocation of early Americana through the lens of Vincente Minnelli. A radiant Judy Garland and a scene-stealing Margaret O'Brien stand out. The Smith family is shaken when dad informs them he will be moving up in his company, but, that they will have to move to New York City. Hugh Martin and Ralph Blane created classic songs such as "Have Yourself a Merry Little Christmas, " "The Trolley Song," and ""The Boy Next Door." A true classic. P.S. They don't move to big bad, New York.

114 min. color MGM/UA M201827 V $19.98

Note:
Others not to be missed listed in *Videolog* as being commercially available:

Anchors Aweigh (1945)–Gene Kelly and Frank Sinatra.
Little Miss Broadway (1938)–Shirley Temple and Jimmy Durante.
Moon Over Miami (1941)–Glorious color with Betty Grable in another 20th Century-Fox resort musical.
Naughty Marietta (1935)–Jeanette MacDonald and Nelson Eddy soar.

On the Town (1949)–Comden and Green (and Leonard Bernstein) as interpreted by MGM and the Freed unit with Gene Kelly, Frank Sinatra, and Jules Munchen as three sailors on 24 hour leave in New York.
Pal Joey (1957)–Rodgers and Hart's great score with Frank Sinatra as Pal Joey.
The Pirate (1948) – Cole Porter score with an intentionally campy interpretation by Gene Kelly as actor-pirate out to win the heart and hand of Judy Garland.
Shall We Dance (1937)–Great Gershwin score, and great Astaire-Rogers.
Summer Stock (1950)–Judy Garland's last film for MGM (with Gene Kelly)–he dances with a torn newspaper lying on the stage, and Garland does a knock-out number (added after the film was shot) dressed in a mini tux–"Get Happy."
Sun Valley Serenade (1941) –An example here of a Sonja Henie ice skating film Glenn Miller's Orchestra and the the great dance duo, the Nicholas Brothers join in the fun.
That's Entertainment I (1974)–MGM's first compilation of musical hightlights (and some low points) from past films. No story lines to intrude, just singing and dancing.
That's Entertainment II (1976)–more of the same.
That's Entertainment III (1994)–The difference here is we got to see less famous numbers and some musical segments which were deleted. Most instructional– seeing how they shot an intricate Eleanor Powell number and a breakdown of one of Fred Astaire's classic routines.
Top Hat (1935)–Irving Berlin's music to Astaire and Rodge'rs most famous and loved film.
Weekend in Havana (1943)–Betty Grable, John Payne and Carmen Miranda.
The Wizard of Oz (1939)–Classic for the all ages.
You'll Never Get Rich (1941)–Astaire at Columbia pursuing Rita Hayworth.
You Were Never Lovelier (1942)–Astaire and Hayworth reunited.

The Baritone Belters

Recordings
Como, Perry–*Como's Golden Records*   RCA 07863-58302-2
Yesterday and Today: A Celebration in Song
RCA 3 07863-66098-2 $39.98

Damone, Vic–*Best of Vic Damone Live*   Ranwood RCD-8204
16 Most Requested Songs   Columbia/Legacy CK-48975

Laine, Frankie–*The Essence of Frankie Laine*
Columbia/ Legacy CK-53573
Memories   Columbia CK-08636

Martin, Tony–*This May Be the Night*
ASV Living Era CD-AJA-5099

Monroe, Vaughn–*The Best of Vaughn Monroe*
MCA MCAC-1559 (cas)
Vaughn Monroe and IIis Orchestra: 1943   Circle CLP-45

Videos

The Best of Perry Como, Volume One—Ever since he had his first big hit in 1944 with "Long Ago (And Far Away)," Perry Como has been a major star. Dramatic ballad readings of "Till the End of Time" and "Prisoner of Love" first cast him as a Neopolitan belter, but his low-key, reserved personality eventually won out, and Como became best known for his disarming nonchalance and his easy manner with ballads and novelty songs.

Here is a timeless collection of everything noted in the above paragraph. Songs include "Catch a Falling Star," "Till the End of Time," "If You Were the Only Girl," "Round and Round," "Hot Digggity," "It's Beginning to Look a Lot Like Christmas," and more.
60 min. color A VISION ENTERTAINMENT
50287-3 $19.95

Crooners of the Century—An overview of male singers who followed in the footsteps of Bing Crosby and Frank Sinatra (and, to a lesser degree, Rudy Vallee). Nothing fancy here—just one black and white clip after the other. The 1940s and early '50s belters discussed in Chapter 8 are here, except for Vic Damone and Tony Martin. There is Frankie Laine, Vaughn Monroe—the prototype "Baritone Belters"—Tony Bennett (during his belting days), Dean Martin, and Eddie Fisher, along with others.
52 min. GOOD TIMES HOME VIDEO
VHS 8060 $14.95

Chapter 9: BIG BANDS AND SMALL BANDS

As noted in the previous chapter, the music from 1935 on comes in big numbers. There is now so much music out that even a selective discography is open to major debate. Another problem is the dizzying speed with which recordings are released and withdrawn form circulation. I have, in my collection, a number of outstanding releases purchased in the past two years with 1992-1995 release dates affixed to them, and they are not listed in the present *Schwann/Spectrum* music guide. That's always a main problem with discographies—who knows which of these choices will be deleted in the next five years or more.

Let's begin our jazz journey by visiting the territory bands of the Southwest and Midwest. As this book goes to press, director Robert Altman has been putting together a musical drama entitled *Kansas City*. The Kansas City artists such as Joe Turner, Count Basie, Lester Young, Mary Lou Williams, and others, are set in Kansas City's Hey Hey Club. The roles have been cast and include some of the best contemporary jazz players on the scene: Joshua Redman, Geri Allen, James Carter, Christian McBride, Don Byron, Jesse Davis, David "Fathead" Newman, Mark Whitfield, James Zolar, Nicholas Gayton, and Victor Lewis.

Kansas City

Recordings
Basie, Count—*And the Kansas City 7*
MCA/Impulse MCAD-5656
The Complete Decca Recordings 1937-1939
Decca Jazz 3 GRD-3-611

The First Records He Ever Made
Sandy Hook CDSH-2017

Basie, Count & Joe Williams—*Count Basie and Joe Williams*
Verve 83529-2

Basie, Count/Lambert, Hendricks & Ross—*Sing Along with Basie* Roulette Jazz B21Y-95332

Kirk, Andy, and His Clouds of Joy—Classics 681-2
The 12 Clouds of Joy, with Mary Lou Williams
ASV Living Era CD-5103

McShann, Jay—*Blues from Kansas City*
Decca Jazz GRD-614
Going to Kansas City New World NW-358-2
Jay McShann and His Orchestra, 1941-1943 Classics 740

Moten, Benny—*Benny Moten's Kansas City Orchestra (1929-32): Basic Beggings* Bluebird 9768-2-RB

Rushing, Jimmy— *The Band Singer*
EPM (Jazz Archives) 15725-2
The Essential Jimmy Rushing Vanguard Twofer VCD-65/66

Territory Bands, Vol. 2 1927-1931—Selections by early territory bands that were unknown to the urban North at that time. These bands charted the narrow expanses of Louisiana, Texas, Oklahoma, Missouri, Kansas, Illinois, and into the Dakotas and Montana. George Lee and His Orchestra, with his sister Julia Lee, is heard on this disc, as is the Willie Jones Orchestra, Floyd Mills and His Marylanders, Alex Jackson's Plantation Orchestra, and Walter Page and his Blue Devils which had a young Count Basie on piano and Hot Lips Page on trumpet. Bruce Ricker's film documentary of three returning stars coming back to play with long-time local Kansas City musician was titled in homage to Page's group—*The Last of the Blue Devils.* Historical HLP-26 (LP)

The Territory Bands—Another compilation of obscure but swinging bands that traveled and played the various dance halls and clubs of the territory circuit. These bands and representative song titles are listed in the caption on page 249. Route 66 Records (LP)

Turner, "Big Joe"—*I've Been to Kansas City, Volume 1*
Decca Jazz MCAD-42351
Big Joe Turner 1938-1941 L'Art Vocal 10
Tell Me Pretty Baby, with Pete Johnson's Orchestra
Arhoolie CD-333

Williams, Mary Lou—*Mary Lou Williams 1927-1940*
Classics 630

Witherspoon, Jimmy—*Blowin' in From Kansas City*
Flair V21Y-86299

Videos
Born to Swing (1973)—A retrospective of Count Basie's music as seen from the vantage point of those who worked with him. Count Basie alumni, like trombonist Dickie Wells, trumpeter Buck Clayton, saxophonists

Buddy Tate and Earl Warren, and percussion master Jo Jones are joined by a couple of other swing masters to sizzle on impromptu renderings of Basie classics. The video also inclues recollections by Gene Krupa, band leader Andy Kirk, and Basie's long time friend and producer John Hammond. Jazz historian Nat Hentoff writing in *Video Review*, gives it **** and calls it an "indispensible combination of jazz history, personal epiphanies of jazz experience and the music itself—glowing instrumental conversations and soliloquies by Basie alumni and kindred spirits...The most compelling is Joe Jones, for a long time Basie's drummer, the man who plays like a dancer. The grace and fire of this jazz nonpareil is alone with the price of the cassette."

50 min. color RHAP 8023 $19.95

Buck Clayton All Stars (1961)—Another example of a Basie alumnus carrying on the Kansas City jump blues sounds. Bringing together a small group called from the Basie Orchestra, the trumpet master conjurs up memories of the various small units such as the Kansas City Six. Clayton was one of the warmest and most subtle of the hot swing trumpeters—I like James Lincoln Collier's appraisal of him as a "jazz minimalist." Selections include "Stompin' at the Savoy," "Night Train," and "Ain't Nobody's Bizness If I Do."

54 min. SRC 6303 $19.95

Last of the Blue Devils (1979)—I've always found this Bruce Ricker documentary of Kansas City musicians and their music and memories to be among the most memorable and captivating pieces of film making I've ever experienced. Archival black and white photos and film clips are interspersed with commentary between the artists and to the camera interviewer, along with impromptu and formal concert music. This film has a rhythm that is simpatico with the subject.

A swinging Jay McShann, along with Big Joe Turner's belting blues choruses launches the film into orbit. Lesser-known Kansas City veterans are seen tap dancing, drumming, singing, and playing violin (Claude Williams). The return to the old home town by McShann, Turner, and Basie is touching and the reminiscences are especially that of the cigar chomping manager, who praises the crooked but effective leadership of Boss Tom Pendergast.

And what music—if this jumping, stomping Kansas City music like "hotel Blues," "Moten Swing," "Jumpin' at the Woodside," "One O'Clock Jump." and "Roll 'Em Pete" doesn't move you, them your personal rhythm machine is in big trouble. 91 min. RHAP 8039 $29.95

Swingin' the Blues: Count Basie—Called "A Celebration of Basie's legacy," this Masters of American Music Series production rates thumbs up. The mix of film clips with an informal round table discussion of Basie and the music is very effective. The Basie alumni includes early band members Harry Sweets Edison, Earle Warren Claude Williams and later stars like Illinois Jacquet, Buddy Tate and Joe Williams. Jazz historian Albert Murray moves the reminiscences along, as we see clips

of Kansas City, New York, and a variety of Basie bands (and key sidemen like Jimmy Rushing, Lester Young, and Sweets Edison) stomping through charts like "One O'Clock Jump," "Doggin' Around," "Blues in Hoss Flat," "Jumpin' at the Woodside, " and many more.

60 min. color/b&w BMG VIDEO BMG 80064-3 $29.95

Carnegie Hall Jazz/Black Jazz

Recordings

Ammons, Albert—*Albert Ammons, 1936-1939* Classics 715
Master of Boogie Milan 73138-35628-2

Ammons, Albert and Meade Lux Lewis—*The First Day*
Blue Note B21Y-98450

Anderson, Ivie—*Ivie Anderson with Duke Ellington and His Orchestra, 1932-1940* EPM (Jazz Archives) 15735-2

Berry, Chu—*Berry Story* (profile of a tenor sax great, with a variety of players over the years compiled for this release). EPM (Jazz Archives) 15738-2

Barrelhouse Boogie—Excellent release of original recordings by Pete Johnson & Albert Ammons, Meade Lux Lewis, Jimmy Yancey. Bluebird 8334-2-RB

The Best of Boogie Woogie—A wide mix of boogie woogie styles and interpretations. While the package above concentrates on strictly piano interprations by the one man and sometimes one woman keyboardists, this release combines the aforementioned with bands and singers. Recordings are by Roosevelt Sykes, Monkey Joe Coleman, Little Brother Montgomery, Speckled Red, Benny Goodman, Lionel Hampton, Bob Zurke, Pinetop Smith, Count Basie, and Joe Turner
EPM (Jazz Archives) 15740-2

Carter, Benny—*An Introduction to Benny Carter, His Best Recordings 1929-1940* Best of Jazz 4011
A Gentleman and His Music Few jazz legends have had as productive career as Carter. He was an original force in the 1920s through the 1950s. Since then, he has taken on the aura of a master who lends his knowledge and playing expertise to the entire mainstream movement. Concord Jazz CCD-4285

Christian, Charlie—*The Genius of the Electric Guitar*
Columbia Masterpieces CK-40846
Solo Flight VJC VJC-1021-2

Early Black Swing: The Birth of Big Band Jazz 1927-1934—Here is a good primer for the tradition of swing bands. Some of the bands in this collection are working their way out of a Dixieland style, others are right on course. Included in this collection are seminal organizations like Charlie Johnson's Paradise Ten, McKinney's Cotton Pickers, The Missourians, Bennie Moten's Kansas City Orchestra, and groups led by Louis Armstrong, Henry "Red" Allen, Duke Ellington,

Jimmie Lunceford, Flecher Henderson, and Earl "Fatha" Hines. Bluebird 9583-2-RB

Ellington, Duke— *Beyond Category: The Musical Genius of Duke Ellington* (includes a 32-page illustrated guide to the recordings).   RCA2 755174-9000-2 $29.98
Carnegie Hall Concert: January 1943
                    Prestige 2 2PRCD-34004-2
The Blanton-Webster Band (1939-1942)
                    Bluebird 3 5659-2-RB
Fargo, North Dakota November 7, 1940
                    VJC2 VJC-1019/20-2
The Indispensable Duke Ellington and the Small Groups, Vols. 9/10 (1940-1946)   RCA2 07863-66471-2

The Duke Ellington/Billy Strayhorn Songbook—
                    Verve 314-515391-2

Fitzgerald, Ella— *With the Chick Webb Band (1935-1937)*
                    Pearl (Flapper Series) PAST-CD-9762

From Spirituals to Swing (1938-1939)—John Hammond's noble experiment of bringing the total African-American musical experience to the hallowed concert stage of Carnegie Hall was an overwhelming commercial success—but more important was trhe dismanteling of racial barriers that this concert represented. As we have seen in the text, this was not the first concert of African-American music to be presented at Carnegie Hall. However, this was the first to present African-American music within the context of popular music—and it fosters through the jam sessions and small group mixes, racial integration.

The program for the first of these two concerts is reproduced on page 259. The music on this disc includes concert performances for the second performance which included Benny Goodman and his sextet.   Vanguard Twofer 2 VCD2-47/48

Goodman, Benny, Trio and Quartet—*After You've Gone, Vol. 1*   Bluebird BMG 5631-2-RB
Avalon: The Small Bands, Vol. 2   Bluebird 2273-2-RB

Hodges, Johnny—(Ellington's premier alto saxophonist)
Class Solos 1928-1942   Pearl PEA-CD-1008

Johnson, Pete—*Pete's Blues, House Rent Party*
                    Savoy Jazz SV-0196
Pete Johnson 1938-1939 (with various artists, including Big Joe Turner).   Classics 656

Kirby, John—*John Kirby: The Biggest Little Band 1937-1941*
                    Classics 722 The Smithsonian Collection R013 (LP)
John Kirby and His Orchestra, 1941-1942   Circle CCD-14

Krupa, Gene—*Drum Boogie*   Columbia/Legacy CK-53425
Drummer Man (with Roy Eldridge and Anita O'Day).
                    Verve 827843-2

Lewis, Meade Lux—*Meade Lux Lewis, 1927-1939*
                    Classics 722

Lunceford, Jimmie—*An Introduction to Jimmie Lunceford, His Best Recordings: 1934-1942*   Best of Jazz 4002
Rhythm Is Our Business   ASV Living Era CD-AJA-5091

Webb, Chick—*Spinnin' the Webb* (with Mario Bauza).
                    Decca Jazz GRD-636
Stompin' at the Savoy, 1936 (with vocals by Ella Fitzgerald and Charles Linton).   Circle CLP-81 (LP)

Webster, Ben—*The Horn—1944*   Progressive PCD-7001
Plays Duke Ellington   Storyville STCD-4113

Wilson, Teddy—*Revisits the Goodman Years*
                    Storyville STCD-4046
Teddy Wilson and His Orchestra 1939-1941   Classics 620

The Women: Classic Female Jazz Artists 1939-1952—By the 1940s more women were given the chance to do more in music than just sing—a number of them are found on this release. Mary Lou Williams' Girl Stars, Beryl Booker Trio, Vivien Garry Quintet, Una Mae Carlisle, Alberta Hunter, Mildred Bailey, Helen Ward with Gene Krupa and His Swing Band, Barbara Carroll Trio, Kay Davis with Duke Ellington, Hazel Scott, and the International Sweethearts of Rhythm.
                    Bluebird 6755-2-RB

Videos

All Star Swing Festival (1972)—Hosted by trumpeter Doc Severinson this Award-winning spectacular was filmed at Lincoln Center in New York, and with exception of the Dave Brubeck Quartet, all the featured stars were associated with big band music of the 1930s and 1940s. Ella Fitzgerald, Duke Ellington and Count Basie Orchestras, vocalist Joe Williams, and a last performance by the original Benny Goodman Quartet ("Avalon" and "Moonglow").
                    52 min. color VESTRON MUSIC MA 1048 $19.98

Ben Webster: The Brute and the Beautiful (1992)—One of the best music documentaries about an individual. One gets a sense of the depth of commitment an artist needs to sustain themselves in what is a very lonely business. The evolution of the tenor man from the early days of Kansas City during the Pedergast era to his last professional engagement in Holland in 1973 is captured effectively by the cameras.
                    60 min. color SCR 6302 $19.95

Duke Ellington: Memories of Duke (1968)—The best history presently available— it uses older musical clips and interviews with sidemen who discuss the Duke mystic. Classics include "Take the A Train," "Satin Doll," "Mood Indigo," and Black and Tan Fantasy," and many others.   85 min. RHAP V $17.95

Jazz at the Smithsonian—Benny Carter (1982)—A concert performance by one of the gentlemen of jazz. Carter's long and distinguished career has been marked by versatility (he performs on many instruments—mainly alto) and graciousness.
                    60 min. color KUL 1271 $29.95

That's Black Entertainment—An import video which brings forth a compilation of archival footage, most never before seen by general audiences. Hollywood all but ignored most black talent except for the "Second Tier" underground artists like Duke Ellington, Cab Calloway, the Mills Brothers, Lena Horne, and a couple of others—there are clips of these performers. What is more intriguing are the clips of the lesser-known stars of black cinema (an entire history exists of film releases made for the African American community that most white Americans never saw or ever knew existed).

60 min. UFS 3810V $19.98

Swing Street/Singers on the Street

Recordings
Bailey, Mildred—*Harlem Lullaby*
ASV Living Era CD-AJA-5065
The Rockin' Chair Lady (1931-1950) MCA/GRP GRD-644

The Complete Commodore Jazz Recordings, Vol. 1—A massive undertaking by the produers to collate information and recordings of this important record company run by Milt Gabler. A 48-page booklet with session-by-session notes by Dan Morganstern. The mix of spirited Dixieland (Bobby Hackett, Edmond Hall, the DeParis Brothers, Jack Teagarden, et al.) with that of lightly grooving swing (Billie Holiday, Teddy Wilson, Lester Young, Hot Lips Page, Eddie Heywood, et al.) is what 52nd Street was mostly about. Note: In Nat Hentoff's *Listen to the Voices* there's a chapter on actor Billy Crystal which describes how Crystal grew up surrounded by all these jazz greats because his father worked for Gabler. This is a box set not for the casual listener (see the price)—Vol. 2 continues the story.

Mosaic 23 MR23-128 $230

Eldridge, Roy—*After You've Gone* Decca Jazz GRD-605
Roy Eldridge, 1935-1940 Classics 725
Uptown (with Gene Krupa and Anita O'Day).
Columbia Jazz Masterpieces CK-4548

Eldridge, Roy and Coleman Hawkins—*Just You, Just Me: Live in 1959* Stash ST-CD-531

The Esquire All American Jazz Concert—Recorded January 18,1944 at the Metropolitan Opera House in New York, this brought together the best trad and swing players on stage—Armstrong, Eldridge, Goodman, Hawkins, Red Norvo, singers Mildred Bailey (4 vocals) and Billie Holiday (3 vocals).

EPM Musique 2 FCD-15118-2

Gaillard, Slim—*Laughin' in Rhythm: The Best of the Verve Years* Verve 314-521651
Slim Gaillard, 1937-1938 Classics 705

Gibson, Harry "The Hipster"—*Boogie Woogie in Blue*
Musscraft MVSCD-63
Everybody's Crazy But Me Progressive P-7042

Hawkins, Coleman—*Body and Soul* Bluebird 5717-2-RB
The Complete Coleman Hawkins on Keynote (61 tracks on 4 CDs recorded in New York, 1944).
Mercury 4 830960

Holiday, Billie—*The Complete Billie Holiday on Verve, 1945-*

1959 (220-page book with rare photos and 8 discs).
Verve 10 314-51768-2
The Complete Decca Recordings
Decca Jazz 2 GRD-2-601
The Essence of Billie Holiday
Columbia/Legacy CK-47917
Lady in Satin (Billie with Ray Ellis Orchestra and strings).
Columbia Jazz Masterpieces CK-40247
The Legacy Columbia/Legacy 3 C3K-47724;3 $39.98

The 1930s Small Combos—(The groups include the Gotham Stompers, Jones-Smith Inc., the Chocolate Dandies, the Rhythmakers, as well as units led by Stuff Smith, Coleman Hawkins, Chu Berry, John Kirby, Teddy Wilson, and others).
Columbia/Jazz Masterpieces CK-40833

Norvo, Red—*Red Norvo featuring Mildred Bailey*
Columbia/Legacy CK-53424

Peterson, Oscar—*The History of an Artist*
Pablo 2PACD-2625-702-2 $21.98
A Jazz Portrait of Frank Sinatra Verve 825769-2
The Will to Swing: Oscar Peterson at His Very Best
Verve 2 847203-2

Prima, Louis—*Louis Prima* ("Capitol Collector's" series)
Capitol C2IY-94072
Zoma Zoma: The Best of Louis Prima (1957-1959)
Rhino R2-70225

Smith, Stuff—*Hot Violins* Storyville SJCD-417
Stuff Smith, 1936-1939 (with Jonah Jones, Buster Bailey, Cozy Cole, James Sherman, et al.). Classics 706

South, Eddie—*Black Gypsy: 1927-1941* (jazz violinist).
DRG DRG-8405-2

Sullivan, Maxine—*The Biggest Little Band in the Land, 1940-1941* (with John Kirby). Circle CDD 125

Tatum, Art—*The Complete Pablo Solo Masterpieces* (1953-1956). Pablo 7 7PACD-4402-2 $90
Solos (1940) MCA MCAD-42327
The Tatum Group Masterpieces, Vol. 8, with Ben Webster
Pablo PACD-2405-431-2
Tea For Two Black Lion BLCD-760192

Wiley, Lee—*As Time Goes By* Bluebird 3138-2-RB
Lee Wiley Sings the Songs of Richard Rodgers & Lorenz Hart and Harold Arlen: The Original 1940 Music Box and 1943 Schremer Sessions Audiophile ACD-10
Sings Ira and George Gershwin and Cole Porter: The Original 1939 and 1940 Liberty Shop Sessions
Audiophile ACD-1

Young, Lester—*The Best of Lester Young* Pablo 2405-420-2
The Complete Lester Young on Keynote (16 tracks).
Mercury 830920-2
Complete Small Groups, Vol. 1 1936-1942
Blue Moon BMCD-1001

Videos

After Hours (1985)–Music taken from a 1961 television broadcast which creates a smokey, atmospheric feel of an after hours jazz night club where the "cats are jamming." Highlights include the quintet's interpretations of "Lover Man" and "Sunday." Roy Eldridge and Coleman Hawkins lead the group.

27 min. RHAP $24.95

Boogie in Blue–Hang "The Hipster" Gibson (1991)–If you ever wondered how the musician's term "Hep" (Cab Calloway's progeny) turned into "Hip," this is the video that will tell you. Boogie woogie madman, Harry "The Hipster" Gibson, has been given an loving tribute that may, finally, turn some heads and give him a place in jazz history. Interviews with past sidemen and relatives–as well as with the man himself–illuminate his kinetic and irrepressible stage presence. Soundies reveal a wild, boogie woogie stylist. "Stop That Dancin' Up There," "Who Put the Benzedrine in Mrs. Murphy's Ovaltine," and other amazing selections are heard and seen.

50 min. RHAP 8023 $19.95

Memphis Slim at Ronnie Scotts London–A colorful jazz-jive and blues concert at London's top jazz club. The focus of our attention is cast on the antics of the master of "Vout," a hip language that Slim Gaillard invented and regaled his appreciative audiences with. "Tribute to Gaillard" is just one of the highlights that also includes "Rock the House Tonight," and "Stepping Out."

60 min. color POLY 080225-3

Oscar Peterson: The Life of a Legend–A feature-length documentary that chronicles four decades of music from one of the greatest keyboard artists of our time (he's been called by many "Jazz's Greatest Living Pianist"). Photos from the past and rare film clips–he started as a teenage boogie woogie sensation in Montreal, Canada–are mixed with interviews and recent concert and club performances.

106 min. color/b&w VIEW VIDEO $29.95

Tenor Titans–The major history on video on the study of jazz tenor players. Branford Marsalis hosts and comments on all the major jazz saxmen of the tenor. The show concludes with the host performing.

60 min. PI-A93503 $29.95

Tenor Legends: Coleman Hawkins/Dexter Gordon–Two leaders fo the jazz saxophone are featured in separate programs. Hawkins, the "Father of the Jazz Saxophone," is seen in a concert in Brussels in 1962 performing "South of France Blues" and "Blowing for Adolphe Sax, "among other numbers. Hawkins was a master of swing-mainstream jazz, the style that Dexter Gordon started with. In Gordon's sequences we see how he moved on from swing and embraced bebop as he rocks the club Montmarte in Copenhagen in 1959. Among the numbers played by the bop tenorist, are "Those Were the Days" and "Fried Bananas."

57 min. SRC 6308V $19.95

Mainstream Awakening

Recordings

The American Jazz Orchestra–*The American Jazz Orchestra Performs the Music of Jimmie Lunceford*

Music Masters 0612-65072-2

Ellington Masterpieces

East West Records America 91423-2

Braff, Ruby and George Barnes–*George Barnes Quintet Plays Gershwin*   Concord Jazz CCD-6005

The Concord Sound, Vol. 1–Concord Records is today's home, along with Verve, of mainstream jazz that smacks of the melodic, dancing spirit of 1930s and 1940s pre-bebop jazz. Label mates Rosemary Clooney, The L.A. 4, Dave McKenna, Mel Torme and George Shearing, Scott Hamilton, and others perform.   Concord Jazz CJ-278-C

Francis, Panama and Savoy Sultans–*Everything Swings*

Stash ST-233 (LP)

Get Up and Dance with Panama Francis, and Savoy Sultans–   Stash ST-CD-5

Hamilton, Scott–*In Concert* (young mainstream saxophone giant).   Concord Jazz CCD-4223

Hyman, Dick–*From the Age of Swing*   Reference RR-59CD
The Gershwin Songbook, Jazz Variations

MusicMasters 01612-65094-2
The Kingdom of Swing and the Republic of Ooop Bop Sh' Bam: Jazz in July, Live at the 92nd St. Y

MusicMasters 5016-2C

Lincoln Center Jazz Orchestra–*Portraits By Ellington*

Columbia CK-53145

McKenna, Dave–*Live at Maybeck Hall, Vol. 2*

Concord Jazz CCD-4410
My Friend the Piano   Concord Jazz CCD-4313
Shadows and Dreams   Concord Jazz CCD-4467

The Sound of Jazz–In 1957, "The Robert Heritage Series" produced a nationally syndicated television program which featured jazz greats in an informal setting. This recording includes piano jazz by the Ahmad Jamal Trio and mainstream sounds by artists, as diverse as Thelonious Monk (his "Blue Monk" is equal dashes of stride and bop), Coleman Hawkins, Ben Webster, Henry "Red" Allen, Count Basie, Lester Young, Roy Eldridge, and Billie Holiday. Billie Holiday's languid, slow-drag swing on "Fine and Mellow" is the most celebrated moment of the show.

Columbia Jazz Masterpieces CK-45234

The Verve Story 1944-1994–The fabulous history of Norman Granz's record companies, all under the single heading of Verve, is chronicled here. In 1944 Granz introduced the concept of variety-hall, jazz for the masses with his touring Jazz at the Philharmonic parade of stars. From that first concert is Illinois Jacquet and the Jazz at the Philharmonic (JATP) All Stars. Artists represented are Charlie Parker, Lester

Young, Ben Webster, Oscar Peterson, Ella Fitzgerald, Machito, Billie Holiday, Nat King Cole, Flip Phillips—the list goes on and on. Verve is also represented by Key jazz artists of the past twenty years, such as Betty Carter, Joe Henderson, Charlie Haden, and Shirley Horn. Verve 4 314- 5213272

Widespread Depression Orchestra—*Downtown Uproar/ Boogie in the Barnyard*. A smashing bit of revivalist big band reworks by this sadly underappreciated group produced by Frank Driggs, who says of the WDO, "They are preserving qualities of a classic American music that deserves to be remembered and cherished. What they have done is to rearrange the original Basie, Ellington, Lunceford and Hines music to make it fit their nine-piece instrumentation. In playing Basie's 'Broadway' or 'Jumpin' at the Woodside,' Ellington's 'Main Stem,' or 'Chelsea Bridge' they hew to the spirit of the originals while simultaneously using them as a framework for their own interpretation." Stash ADC-5015

Chapter 10: REVIEW OF 1930s AND 1940s

Before we investigate the key vocalists of the four main sections of Chapter 10 (there are, to be sure, overlaps in some of the categories), I would like to list a *brief* and *selective* number of albums that bring together various vocalists singing the songs of the great composers. After all, the heart and soul of this chapter are the songs of "The Golden Age of Popular Music." Today these songs evoke memories of days long gone, and they have little to do with popular music as we now know it. For the reader who is interested in finding out more about this music and the recordings that are released there is one source I would like to share with you—*Show Music* magazine. It bills itself as "The Musical Theatre Magazine" and two sample covers can be seen on page 288. This magazine is a quarterly and it's beautifully designed.

Articles and reviews of cabaret and pop-oriented entertainers with a theatrical bent are covered—and it's the only magazine that reviews all key reissues and new releases of the music from "The Golden Age of Popular Music." Subscription rates are around $20 a year for four glorious issues—inquiries for subscriptions should be sent to: *Show Music*, Box 466, East Haddam, CT 06423-466

Recordings
Cole Porter Songbook—(assorted artists). RCA 8413-2-R

Crazy for You (George & Ira Gershwin)—(music from the 1992 Broadway original cast). Broadway Angel CDQ-5618

Great American Songwriters, *Volume 1: George & Ira Gershwin*—selections by popular singers such as Tony Bennett, Nancy Wilson, Peggy Lee, Ella Fitzgerald, et al. Rhino R2-71503
Volume 2: Johnny Mercer—Selections by various popular singers. Rhino R2-71504
Volume 3: Rodgers & Hart—Selections by various popular singers. Rhino R2-71505

Volume 4: Irving Berlin—Selections by various popular singers. Rhino R2-71506

The Jazz-Pop Singers

Recordings
Because of the small number of artists in this section, I'm listing a few more records per artist.

Bennett, Tony—*Astoria (Portrait of the Artist)*
Columbia CK-45348
Forty Years: The Artistry of Tony Bennett (contains a 64-page booklet with Bennett's song-by-song commentary). Columbia/Legacy 4 C4K-46843 $59.98
Perfectly Frank Columbia CK-52965
The Rodgers & Hart Songbook DRG CDXP-2102
Steppin' Out Columbia CK-57424

Clooney, Rosmary—*Show Tunes* Concord Jazz CCD-4364
Sings the Lyrics of Johnny Mercer
Concord Jazz CCD-333
Sings Rodgers, Hart & Hammerstein
Concord Jazz CCD-4405

Fitzgerald, Ella—*Cole Porter Songbook, Vol. 1* Verve 821989
The Complete Ella Fitzgerald Songbooks—A monstrous and lovely boxed set of 16 CDs (a small, more affordable Silver Collection is also available).
Verve 16 314-519832-2
First Lady of Song (highlights of best-selling 3 CD set).
Verve 314-523382-2
Mack the Knife: The Complete Ella in Berlin Concert
Verve 314-519564-2

Fitzgerald, Ella and Armstrong, Louis—*Ella & Louis*
Verve 825373-2
Ella and Louis Again Verve 825374-2

Lee, Peggy—*All-Time Greatest Hits, Volume 1*
Curb/CEMA D21K-77379
Close Enough For Love DRG SLCD-5190
Moments Like This Chesky JD-84

Lee, Peggy with George Shearing—*Beauty and the Beat!*
Capitol Jazz C21Y-98454

McRae, Carmen—*Carmen McRae Sings Great American Songwriters* Decca Jazz GRD-631
Fine and Mellow Concord Jazz CCD-4342

Sinatra, Frank—*The Capitol Years*
Capitol 3 C2RD-94317 $49.98
Duets Capitol C212-8961
In the Wee Small Hours Capitol C21Y-96826
Sinatra Sings the Songs of Van Heusen and Cahn
Reprise 26723-2
A Swingin' Affair Capitol C21Y-94518

Sinatra, Frank & Count Basie—*Sinatra at the Sands*
Reprise 1019-2
Torme, Mel—*Back In Town, with Meltones* Verve 833775-2
The Great American Songbook Telarc CD-83328

Sing, Sing, Sing: Live at the Fujitsu Concord Jazz Festival
1992   Concord Jazz CCD-4542
Swings Shubert Alley   Verve 821581-2
A Tribute to Bing Crosby   Concord Jazz CCD-4614

Torme, Mel & George Shearing—*Mel & George "Do" World*
War II   Concord Jazz CCD-4471

Vaughan, Sarah—*At Mister Kelly's*   EmArcy 832791-2
The Complete Sarah Vaughan on Mercury, Vol 1: Great Jazz
Years (1954-1956) (with Clifford Brown, Cannonball
Adderley, Herbie Mann, et al.).   Mercury 6 826320-2
Vol. 2: Sings Great American Songs (1956-1957)
                          Mercury 5 826327-2
The Divine Sarah Vaughan: The Columbia Years: 1949-1953
                          Columbia C2K-44165

Vaughan, Sarah & Billy Eckstine—*Irving Berlin Songbook*
                          EmArcy 822526-2

Williams, Joe—*Ballad and Blues Master* Verve 314-511354-2
Joe Williams Every Day: The Best of the Verve Years
                          Verve 2 314-519813-2
Joe Williams Sings   Savoy Jazz SV-0199

Williams, Joe & The Count Basie Orchestra—
                          Telarc CD-83329

Wilson, Nancy—*Love, Nancy*   Columbia CK-45378
Yesterday's Love Songs, Today's Blues
                          Capitol Jazz B21Y-96265

Wilson, Nancy & Cannonball Adderley—
                          Capitol Jazz B21Y-81204

Videos
Carmen McRae (1986)—The multi-talented McRae is a
perfect example of an artist who is an exception to the
rule, and one who makes taxonimical configurations
(some might rightly term this "pigeon-holing")
maddening. She started in the big time with Benny
Carter's Orchestra in 1944, and then moved on to
Mercer Ellington's big band. She was a regular on
52nd Street during the late 1940s and early '50s, a
commited follower of bebop, and a disciple of Billie
Holiday's. By definition, she's a jazz-pop member, but
she never achieved the popular success of Torme, Ella,
or Sarah Musically, she is their equal, but in reality, her
audience recognition factor was slightly above Mark
Murphy, Jackie and Roy, and Betty Carter during the
1960s to the '90s, placing her closer to the jazz cabaret
cult tradition.

McRae is a true "singer's singer"—that is, appreciated by
other professionals for her excellence, but not widely
known to the general public. This concert tape, filmed
in Tokyo, shows why many regarded her as the closest
(then) living link to Billie Holiday. She could generate
great excitement on rhythm numbers performing
instrumental-like scat lines on one number, and them
follow up with a sensual, and moving slow ballad next.
Plus, it's always good to see McRae sit at the piano and
accompany herself.   82 min. color HOME MCRO

Jazz at the Smithsonian: Joe Williams (1982)—Joe
Willaims is one of the smoothest singers in the
business—he's equally at home with blues or Tin Pan
Alley standards. He sings both forms in this concert
film.   60 min. color KUL $29.95

Meet Singers, Vol. 2—A mix of popular jazz singers—Peggy
Lee, June Christy and Mel Torme. They sing such titles
as Alec Wilder's "While We're Young," the 1934 ditty
"You Oughta Be in Pictures," and Richard Whiting and
Neil Moret's "She's Funny That Way."
                          54 min. SWING 119 V

The Mel Torme Special (1982)—One of America's most
versatile artists. Not only is Torme a dynamic vocalist
and vivid stage personality, but he plays a multitude of
instruments during most shows, writes songs as well as
his intricate arrangements for orchestres to play behind
him, is a screenwriter, novelist, and an historian who
writes profiles of musicians. He sings, among many
other songs, "Lady, Be Good," "When Sunny Gets Blue,"
and "New York State of Mind."
                          53 min. color COL/TRI J0058V

Monterey Jazz Festival—The Monterey Jazz Festival in
California, along with the various Newport Jazz Festival
offshoots and the Montreux Jazz Festival in Switzerland,
is one of the most prestigous gatherings of its kind.
Featured at this concert are Woody Herman and His
Orchestra, and two of the leaders of the jazz pop
tradition, Mel Torme and Joe Williams. Songs include
"New York State of Mind," "Shake, Rattle and Roll," and
"Every Day I Have the Blues."
                          60 min. color COL/TRI J0343 $19.95

Nancy Wilson and Band: A Very Special Concert—Ms.
Wilson stretches her jazz muscles with an outstanding
group of jazz soloists: Chick Corea, piano; Stanley
Clarke, bass; Lenny White, drums; Joe Henderson,
tenor sax. Wilson is in fine form, mixing some
contemporary songs with standards like Vincent
Youman's "I Want to Be Happy," Cole Porter's "I Get a
Kick Out of You," and Gershwin's "But Not for Me."
                          60 min. color COL/TRI 70078V

The Quintessential Peggy Lee (1984)—The legendary ex-
Benny Goodman singer joins the New Jersey
Symphony Orchestra and peforms favorites like "Fever,"
"S'Wonderful," and "As Time Goes By."
                          86 min. color KUL 1397 $19.95

Sarah Vaughan—Live From Monterey (1983)—The original
"Divine One" is heard at the idyllic fall festival on the
California coastline. A guest appearance by her good
friend Joe Williams adds to the festivities. Vaughan
cruises through her set, singing a number of favorites
such as "Time After Time," "Send in the Clowns," and
"Autumn Leaves." 60 min. color COL/TRI J0399 $29.95

Sarah Vaughan: The Divine One (1992)—One of the last
filmed concerts by the great jazz-pop song stylist.
                          60 min. color BMG 80066-3V $29.98

Tony Bennett: MTV Unplugged–The Video (1994)–With his trio led by Ralph Sharon, Bennett sings standards (over 20 of them)–and sings duets with contemporary artists k. d. lang ("Moonglow") and Elvis Costello ("They Can't Take That Away From Me").

74 min. color COL-MV MLV 49193V $19.95

Creme de la Creme Cabaret

Recordings

Ahmet Ertegun's New York Cabaret Music–A
Cross section of jazz and cabaret entertainers that recorded for Ahmet Ertegun's independent record the company, Atlantic Records, during the 1950s and '60s. Ertegun, a major producer and visionary in the world of rhythm and blues, was also music industry's principal supporter of cabaret music. This compilation brings together the jazz and creme de la creme performers in one package (see page 310 for examples songs and artists found in this set, as well as the top notch cover design). Listed among those artists, but not given specific recorded music selections on page 310, are three of cabaret's preeminent masters: Mabel Mercer, Hugh Shannon, and Bobby Short. Mercer sings 11 songs, including "While We're Young," "Little Girl Blue," " Did You Ever Cross Over to Sneeden's?" "Remind Me," and her Cole Porter favorite from the old days at Bricktops, "Just One of Those Things." Hugh Shannon interprets five songs: "True Blue Lou," "Easy Come Easy Go," " You Better Go Now," "Everything Happens to Me," and "Baltimore Oriolle." Bobby Short vocalizes on 11 songs, including "From This Moment On," "At the Moving Picture Ball," "Bye Bye Blackbird," "Flying Downto Rio," and "Slumming on Park Avenue."

Atlantic 4 82308-2 $54.98

Akers, Karen–*Just Imagine*　　　DRG DRG-CD-5231

Bennett, Richard Rodney–*Harold Arlen Tunes*
Audiophile ACD-168

Callaway, Ann Hampton–*Ann Hampton Callaway*
DRG CDSBL-91411

Carroll, Barbara–*Live at the Carlyle*
Cabaret DRG CDSBL-91407

Carter, Dixie–*Sings John Wallowitch: Live a the Carlyle*
Cabaret DRG CDSBL-91409

Cook, Barbara–*Sings: The Walt Disney Songbook*
MCA Classics MCAD-6244

Dearie, Blossom–*Blossom Dearie*　　Verve 837934-2
Et Tu Bruce, Volume III　　Larrikin CDLRF-182
Once Upon a Summertime　　Verve 314-517223-2

Feinstein, Michael–*Live at the Algonquin*　　Elektra 60792-4
The M.G.M. Album　　Elektra 60893-2
Pure Gershwin　　Elektra 60742-2

Flaran, Mary Cleere–*There's a Small Hotel*
Columbia CK-52403

This Heart of Mine: Classic Movie Songs of the Forties
Varese Sarabande VSD-5842

Hartman, Johnny–(the male singer featured on the soundtrack of Clint Eastwood's *The Bridges of Madison County* 1995). *John Coltrane and Johnny Hartman.*
MCA/Impulse MCA-5661

Marcovicci, Andrea–*What Is Love?*
Cabaret DRG-CDSBL-91401

Mercer Mabel–(presently there are only two recordings in print of this influential diva). *At Town Hall, With Bobby Short.*　　Atlantic 2 CS2-604-4 (LP)
Sings Cole Porter　　Rhino R2-71690

Pizzarelli, John, Jr.–*My Blue Heaven*
Chesky JD38 Audiophile

Ross, Steve–*Most of Ev'ry Day*　　Audiophile AP-217 (LP)

Shannon, Hugh–*Saloon Singer*　　Audiophile 2 AP-17Y2
True Blue Hugh　　Audiophile ACD-140

Sherman, Daryl–*I've Got My Fingers Crossed–A Celebration of the Music of Jimmy McHugh*　　Audiophile ACD-264

Short, Bobby–*Bobby, Noel & Cole* (Coward & Porter).
Rhino 2 R2-82062
50 From Bobby Short (50 songs recorded during 20 year with Atlantic Records).　　Rhino 2 R2081715 $29.98
Late Night at the Cafe Carlyle　　Telarc CD-83311
My Personal Property　　Atlantic 82711-2
Short Celebrates Rodgers & Hart　　Rhino2 R4-610 (cas)

Ver Planck, Marlene– *Marlene Ver Planck Sings Alec Wilder*　　Audiophile ACD-218

Wallowitch, John–*Back on the Town*　　DRG CDSBL-91406
My Manhattan, With Dixie Carter and Bertram Ross
DRG DRG-91414

Whyte, Ronny–*All in a Night's Work*　　Audiophile ACD-247

Wilson, Julie–*Sings the Cole Porter Songbook*
Cabaret DRG CDSL-5208
Julie Wilson Sings the Kurt Weill Songbook
Cabaret DRG CDSL-5207
Julie Wilson Sings the Stephen Sondheim Songbook
Cabaret DRG CDSL-5206

Videos

Bobby Short at the Cafe Carlyle–The producers of this package boast that there is no cover and no minimum when you bring this into your home–good, because the Carlyle is expensive ($40 to $45 cover, and sometimes a two drink minimum–New York price minimum). On the other hand the Cafe Carlyle is the premier cabaret room in America, and Bobby Short is the preeminent cabaret performer of our time. Shorty has been there over 25 years–the longest night club stay in the music business. So, enjoy this tape of the master in action. Short barrels through 25 songs, most of them cult favorites like "Cuba," "Pilote-moi (Pilot Me)," " On the Amazon," " (I Love You) Samantha," "Why Shouldn't I ?" and "Losing My Mind."

> 75 min. color VIEW VIDEO NJSC 1307 $29.95

Bobby Short and Friends (1982)–At the Cafe Carlyle, Short shares the stage with actor Jack Lemmon playing piano, and Lucie Arnaz singing.

> 60 min. color MGM/UA M300859 $29.95

Buddy Barnes–Live From Studio B (1984)–Longtime piano accompanist for jazz and cabaret singers, Barnes steps out on his own. In this set he's joined by mainstream trumpet maven, Ruby Braff.

> 30 min. TRI JO 120 $19.95

Hugh Shannon: The Saloon Singer–Raspy voice and all, Shannon was one the greatest of the piano player singers. With his trademark tux, shiny, or battered piano, and the inevitable oversized brandy glass perched upon it, Shannon sang from an endless list of known and not so well known songs of American composers. This set includes his spirited interpetations of such classics as, "I Love a Piano," "I Can't Get Started," " You Fascinate Me So," "It Never Entered My Mind," and "You Better Go Now." (11 in all).

It's an intriguing contrast in opposites that the most elegant and lofty of the musical forms of American popular music–creme de la creme cabaret–would be one of the deepest of the third-tier underground forms. Perhaps some are intimidated by the posh setting that the cabaret artitst performs in, and the cost. I must admit to feeling less than brazen when entering the Cafe Carlyle (with its $40 and up cover charge). When I went to see Hugh Shannon at David K's, where this video was recorded, there were four stretch limos lined up in front of the place. But Hugh Shannon had the ability to make us all (the rich and the rest of us) feel welcome and appreciated. Some writers have used the phrase, "the artist letting us into their world," and that is what a competent cabaret performer (or performer of any style) can do–it has nothing to do with money.

> 30 min. color VIEW VIDEO $29.95

John Pizzarelli (1993)–**Live in Montreal**–A newcomer to the cabaret scene, John is the offspring of much-in-demand jazz guitar great Bucky Pizzarelli. After a number of years touring and recording with his father, John made his move to go solo. The younger Pizzarelli plays guitar and also sings in a very natural jazzy style–he's been written of as a "Crooner of Note."

> 50 min. color BMG 80082-3 V $19.98

Mabel Mercer: A Singer's Singer–called by *Show Music* magazine "the Queen of cabaret and supper club performers," Mercer is captured in the idyllic intimate setting of Cleo's in New York. This video features Mercer singing 17 of her favorites, including "Blame It on My Youth," "Isn't He Adorable," "Remind Me," "Some Fine Day," and "It's All Right With Me."

> 42 min. color VIEW VIDEO $29.95

Mabel Mercer: Cabaret Artist–Joe Altzman (King Features Syndicate) wrote: "Perhaps the greatest cabaret singer of all time was Mabel Mercer, who died (in 1984) at the age of 84. Few singers ever interpreted a lyric better than Mercer, who sang each song with such clarity, precision and freshness that it was as if you were hearing it for the first time." This night club setting is again Cleo's, but all of the songs (20) are different. I'm reminded of Frank Sinatra's many references to Mercer's influence on his lyric reading, and on her impact on him as a maturing artist–"I'm luckiest because I learned the most." I think of that statement, and mention it to my students when I show them a couple of edited clips from this tape ("Lucky to Be Me," and "Down in the Depths [on the Nintieth Floor]"). Many of them may never experience a cabaret, or certainly not a Mabel Mercer performance on radio or MTV–but, they can at least be introduced to her gentle but firm presence on video.

> 58 min. color VIEW VIDEO 1316 $29.95

Note:
For catalog information on *The Great Saloon Singers Series* write to: VIEW VIDEO catalog, 34 East 23rd Street, New York, Ny 10010, or call: (212) 674-5555

The Jazz Cabaret Cult Singers

Recordings

Carter, Betty–*At the Village Vanguard*	Verve 314-519-85-1
Feed the Fire	Verve 314-523600-2
Its Not About the Melody	Verve 314-513870-2
Look What I Got	Verve 835661-2
Ray Charles and Betty Carter	
	DCC Compact Classics DZS-039
Cole, Freddie–*I'm Not My Brother, I'm Me*	
	Sunnyside SSC-1054D
This is the Life	Muse MCD-5503
Connor, Chris–*As Time Goes By*	Enja ENJ-7061-2
A Jazz Date With Chris Connor/Chris Craft	
	Atlantic Jazz Gallery R2-71747
Sings the George Gershwin Almanac of Song	
	Atlantic Jazz 2 601-2
Dorough, Bob–*Devil May Care*	Bloomdido BLCD-9008
Just About Everything	Evidence ECD-22094
Memorial: Charlie Parker	Philology PHCD-4024

Elling, Kurt–*Close Your Eyes* Elling is one of the new jazz cabaret cult stars on the horizon who lists post-bop instrumentalists Tony Williams, Keith Jarrett, and Wayne Shorter as influences who existed "in the right moment of freedom." The handsome vocalist cited Mark Murphy's albums for Muse Records (along with the work of Jon Hendricks and Eddie Jefferson), as having the strongest influence on his singing. He doesn't abide by the historical indifference many critics have shown toward Murphy's work. "I'm not really sure why," he speculates, "except that I think everybody's attention was so focused on people like Ella Fitzgerald and Mel Torme. They just riveted people's attention so much that everybody wanted to sound just like them. Somebody like Mark Murphy, who I think took heavy strides in the direction of freedom, was kind of left out a little bit. Ella's cool–don't get me wrong–but that's sort of like everybody being riveted on Lionel Hampton and missing out on Herbie Hancock." Blue Note 30645

Frishberg, Dave–*Can't Take You Nowhere*
Fantasy FCD-9651-2
Classics Concord Jazz CCD-4462
Live at Vine Street Fantasy F-9638 (LP)
Where You At? Bloomdido BLCD-9010

Jackie (Cain) & Roy (Kral)–*An Alec Wilder Collection*
Audiophile ACD-257
Jackie and Roy (with Charlie Ventura's "Bop for the People"). Savoy Jazz SV-0218
A Stephen Sondheim Collection: Recorded in Performance at Michael's Pub Stet CDS-25102
We've Got It: (The Music of Cy Coleman)
Discovery DSCD-907

Jordan, Sheila–*Heart Strings* Muse MUS CD-5468
Sheila Jordan and Mark Murphy: One for Junior
Muse MCD-5489
Portrait of Sheila Blue Note B21Y-89002

Horn, Shirley–*Close Enough For Love* Verve 837933-2
Here's to Life: Shirley Horn With Strings
Verve 314-51189-2
I Thought About You: Live at Vine Street Verve 833235-2
You Won't Forget Me Verve 847842-2

Lincoln, Abby–*Abbey Is Blue* Fantasy/OJC OJC-069
Abbey Sings Billie: Live at the UJC Enja ENJ-79633-2
Abbey Lincoln and Stan Getz: You Gotta Pay the Band
Verve 314-519697-2

McCorkle, Susannah–*From Bessie to Brazil*
Concord Jazz CCD-4547
From Broadway to Bebop Concord Jazz CCD-4615
Susannah McCorkle: I'll Take Romance
Concord Jazz CCD-4491

Marano (Nancy) & (Eddie) Monteiro–*Double Standards*
Denon CY-78901
A Perfect Match Denon CY-79407

Merill, Helen–*The Complete Helen Merrill on Mercury* (62 performances with jazz greats like Bill Evans and Clifford Brown). EmArcy 314-514074-2
Collaboration, With Gil Evans EmArcy 834205-2

Murphy, Mark–*Bop For Kerouac* Muse MCD-5253
The Complete Nat Cole Songbook Muse MCD-6001
Rah! Fantasy/OJC OJCCD-141-2
Stolen Moments MUSE MCD-5102
That's How I Love the Blues Fantasy/ OJC OJCCD-367-2

Paris, Jackie–*Jackie Paris* (underrated, bop-oriented singer who deserves much wider recognition).
Audiophile AP-158
Sloan, Carol–*Sweet and Slow* Concord Jazz CCD-4564

When I Look In Your Eyes Concord Jazz CCD-4619

Videos
Shirley Horn: Here's to Life (1992)–Hooray for this cult singer who finally is receiving the recognition her considerable talents deserve. Recording sessions for an album of the same name were filmed, and the results are here for all to see (and hear).
55 min. color POLY 084537-3

Camp Nostalgia

Recordings
Allen, Peter–*At His Best* A&M 31454-0090-2
Bi-Coastal A&M SP-4825 (LP) (OP)
Captured Live at Carnegie Hall Arista AL 12-8275 (LP)

Cole, Natalie–*Unforgettable* Elektra 2 61049-4

Connick, Harry, Jr–*20* (with Dr.John and Carmen McRae).
Columbia CK-443-9

Faye, Francis–*Caught in the Act, Vol. 1 & 2* (a prime camp influence on piano player singers, especially Peter Allen). GNP Crescendo GNPD-92

The Glory of Gershwin–Like *Stay Awake* and *Red, Hot and Blue*, this is a compilation album of rock-oriented performers, each interpreting songs of George Gershwin. Some of the songs and perfomers are: "Summertime" (Peter Gabriel), Sting ("Nice Work if You Can Get It"), "Someone to Watch Over Me" and "Our Love is Here to Stay" (Elton John), "How Long Has This Been Going On?" (Jon Bon Jovi), and "Somebody Loves Me" (Meatloaf). Mercury 314-522727-2

Manhattan Rhythm Kings–*We Three*
Cabaret Records CACD-5003

Manhattan Transfer–*The Manhattan Anthology: Down In Birdland* Rhino 2 R2-71053-2 $27.98
Manhattan Transfer Atlantic 18133-2
Mecca For Moderns Atlantic 16036-2
The Very Best of Manhattan Transfer Rhino R2-71560

Manilow, Barry–*Showstoppers* Arista 07822-18687-2
Singin' With the Big Bands Arista 07822-18771-2

Note:
Both *Paradise Cafe* and *Swing Street*, Manilow's jazziest releases, are no longer listed as being in print.

Midler, Bette–*Bette Midler* Atlantic 7270-2
The Divine Miss M Atlantic 7238-2
Mud Will Be Flung Tonight Atlantic 81291-2

Nelson, Willie–*Somewhere Over the Rainbow*
Columbia CK-36883
Stardust Columbia CK-35305
What a Wonderful World Columbia CK-44331
Without a Song Columbia CK-39110

Nilsson, Harry–*A Little Touch of Schmilsson* RCA 3761-2-R

Red, Hot and Blue—The tribute that was made into a video by today's rock stars singing Cole Porter songs. Proceeds go to benefit AIDS research and relief. Among those herard are Neneh Cherry ("I've Got You Under My Skin"), U2 ("Night and Day:), k.d. lang ("So in Love").
Chrysalis F21Z-21799

Ronstadt, Linda—*Lush Life (Nelson Riddle, Conductor/ Arranger).* Elektra 60387-2
'Round Midnight: The Nelson Riddle Sessions Asylum 3 60489-2
What's New Elektra 61545-2

Simon, Carly—*My Romance* Arista ARCD-8582-2
Torch Warner Bros. 3592-2

Sleepless in Seattle—The selections of older songs that comment on contemporary love include "Stardust" by Nat King Cole, "Make Someone Happy" and "As Time Goes By," as sung by Jimmy Durante, "Back in the Saddle Again" by Gene Autry, and "In the Wee Small Hours of the Morning" by Carly Simon.
Epic Soundtrax EK-53764

Stay Awake: Various Interpretations of Music From Vintage Disney Films—Produced by Hal Wilner and co-producer Steve Ralbovsky, this was the first of the "pop songs by rock artists" which started a trend of sorts. Some wonderfully wistful and wacky tunes. On the wistful side are: Bonnie Raitt and Was (Not Was) softly purring "Baby Mine," James Taylor's "Second Star to the Right," and Ringo Starr's "When You Wish Upon a Star." Under the category of wacky are: "Hi Diddle Dee Dee (An Actor's Life for Me)" by Ken Nordine with Bill Frisell and Wayne Horvitz, "I Wan'na Be Like You (The Monkey Song)" by Los Lobos, "Castle in Spain" by Buster Poindexter and the Banshees of Blue, and "Pink Elephants on Parade" by Sun Ra and His Arkestra.
A&M 75021-3918-2

When Harry Met Sally—Harry Connick, Jr. sings 7 vocal and plays 3 instrumental standards with trio and big band. Titles include "They Can't Take That Away From Me," "Let's Call the Whole Thing Off," "It Had to Be You," and "Autumn in New York." Columbia CK-45319

Videos
The Bette Midler Show (1976)—This concert performance is filled with Midler's high camp energy of ribald stories and fast paced musical numbers such as "Boogie Woogie Bugle Boy" and "Friends."
84 min. color NLHV 1251V

Carly Simon: My Romance—A Home Box Office special performed in an elegant night club setting with patrons sitting at circular tables watching Simon perform songs of the 1930s and '40s from the album of the same title. Harry Connick, Jr. makes a guest appearance with his trio and also sings a duet with Simon. Songs include five Rodgers and Hart classics: "My Romance," " Little Girl Blue," "He Was Too Good to Me," "Bewitched" Bothered and Bewildered" and "My Funny Valentine."
80 min. color 6-WEST SW5711 $19.98

Divine Madness (1980)—Bette's back again! With the band and the Harlettes belting out the Bob Crosby big band favorite of the late 1930s, "Big Noise From Winnetka." Midler makes a grand entrance in an outrageous outfi, and rockets forth with her crowd favorites.
86 min. color RCA 13148v $19.98

Harry Connick, Jr. Swinging Out Live (1991)—The glamour-guy, pianist-singer wows a crowd with 15 selections, some his own ("Hudson Bomber"), as well as older standards ("How Deep is the Ocean").
80 min. color IEI ID8265CB $29.95

Judy Garland in Concert (1964)—This is close as we'll get to the riveting, earlier comback, sensational concert at Carnegie Hall. That concert was viewed by many gays as a contemporary landmark event. Philip Core's *Camp: The Lie That Tells the Truth*, contains this appraisal of Garland: "The self-deprecating camp with which she covered all her needs recalls that of another small plain lady with a big voice, Edith Piaf. It also poignantly underscores the cruelty of those fans who wanted an external little girl in place of the big-hearted lonely woman who, alone, could have gone on producing those big-hearted beautiful sounds. Her knowledge of this cruelty and her playing up to an audience which could never love more than the star in her, are tragic acts of camp desperation, which have especially endeared her to all the others who also suffer the insupportable in public." 60 min. RKO 3002 V $14.95

Linda Ronstadt With Nelson Riddle and His Orchestra in Concert—Ronstadt performs a collection of the older standards she recorded with orchestrator Nelson Riddle, on her multiplatinum *What's New* album.
60 min. color IEI VES1012 $29.95

The Making of "2:00 A.M.-Paradise Cafe"—An unusual video. A behind- the-scenes look at the preparation for the studio recording of Manilow's conceptual album. Great jazz session players back Manilow, and he sings one song with Sarah Vaughan, and another with Mel Torme. 55 min. color MUSIC 60417

Manhattan Transfer Live—Hard driving sounds of one of today's most versatile and accomplished vocal groups. The group mixes old and new music—fast and slow with interpretations of "Four Brothers," "Rambo," "Meet Benny Bailey," "How High the Moon," "Java Jive," and "Birdland," among others.
80 min. color WVE 50112-3 $19.98

Michael Feinstein and Friends (1991)—Pianist-singer-archivist supreme, Feinstein joins the Duke Ellington Orchestra and jazz-pop veteran Rosemary Clooney for an evening of standards. Ellington's "It Don't Mean a Thing (If It Ain't Got That Swing)" and Jimmy McHugh and Dorothy Fields' "I Can't Give You Anything But Love" are two of many selections found on this entertaining program. 57 min. color KUL 1322 $24.95

New York, New York (1977)—Martin Scorcese's ode to the studio system's artifical looking studio-set world of the

1940s. A story of a big band singer (Liza Minnelli) who falls in love with a hard-hearted sax player (Robert DeNiro). The opening scene is in a swanky club where a Tommy Dorsey-like band is playing to the celebrants of V-Day. Some spectacular musical numbers were meant to evoke the opulent big studios of yesteryear, and they do, especially the Judy Garland homage from "Born in a Trunk"(Warner Bros. 1954, *A Star Is Born*) in the sinfully cut (thankfully included on video) "Happy Endings" number with Larry Kert. Here's another example (like *Pennies From Heaven* and *The Boy Friend*) of a dynamic musical that makes touching connections to our past but was ignored by the public when it was released. Audiences of the 1960s to 1990s simply won't plug into the musical type films of the past when they are shown. This film, and the other two, will hold up artistically, I predict. Also, this film is especially appropriate for this section of Revival of '30s and '40s—Minnelli plays a big band singer who becomes more important than the band leader who originally hired her. She goes to Hollywood and becomes a big movie star,—sound familiar? DeNiro's character is musically bored by the entire big band scene, so, he goes up to Harlem and experiments with the new music—bebop (jazzman Georgie Auld, taught DeNiro fingerings and played the solos on the sound track). It hurt the movie that DeNiro's character was so mean-spirited. Finally, the ultimate connection of Hollywood musical camp— Minnelli is the daughter of Judy Garland and Vincent Minnelli.
163 min. color MGM/UA M301321B $29.98

Up next, yet another connection to the world of Hollywood musical, singing and dancing, outrageous camp, and the world of Judy Garland—Peter Allen—Liza Minnelli's first husband.

Peter Allen and the Rockettes (1987)—"Everything Old is New Again" sings Peter Allen—and he proves it by coupling old-time images of a song and dance man with new songs he wrote. Dancing and prancing with the Rockettes—to the song noted above, and to "Rio," and "Quiet Please, There's a Lady on Stage" (dedicated to Judy Garland, his one-time mother-in-law)—Allen was the Peter Pan of the entertainment world. He won't be easily replaced. Thrilling entertainment.
87 min. color CBS/FOX 6130 $19.98

Sleepless in Seattle (1993)—I had much to say throughout this book about musical connections of the past.

Here is what *Videology* has to say about *Sleepless in Seattle*: "After hearing a man confess his love for his dearly departed wife on a call-in radio show, a woman falls deeply, inexplicably in love with him. Deciding he is her destiny, she trecks across the country on a wildly romantic impulse to meet him—but will reality be nice, for once?" 105 color COL/TRI 52413 $19.98

When Harry Met Sally (1989)—And this is what *Videology* has to say about this film: "Throughout 12 years of friendship Harry and Sally are convinced they are only friends. But after 12 years there may be no one else

more qualified to be in love in this delightful, anecdotal romantic comedy." 91 min. 01 NLHV 7732 $19.95

Chapter 11: BEBOP AND THE DEVELOPMENT OF MODERN JAZZ

Recordings

The Bebop Era—An anthology of modern players who were experimenting with diifferent harmonies and tempos during the 1940s. Selections from artists such as Cootie Williams, (Duke Ellington's trumpeter) drummer Gene Krupa (he had one of the underrated bop-oriented bands of the 1940s), bandleader Woody Herman, and future bop leaders Charlie Parker, Dizzy Gillespie, and cool pioneer, Miles Davis.
Columbia Jazz Masterpieces CK-40972

The Bebop Revolution—Exceptional recordings in this set, featuring releases that came out between 1946 and 1949. By this time, the conventions of bebop had beeen formulated, and players were beginning to refine the form. Representative examples are offered by the 52nd Street All-Stars and by tenorist Lucky Thompson and His Lucky Street Boys. Bluebird 21772-2RB

Bop Session—Selections by Dizzy Gillespie, Max Roach, Sonny Stitt, et al. Gazell GJCD-1005

Musical Elements/Leadership/Cubop

Recordings
Bauza, Mario—*Anthology* (a leader of the then titled "Afro-Cuban" jazz movement). Messidor CDMSDR-15828

Mario Bauza and the Afro-Cuban Jazz Orchestra: *944 Columbus* Messidor CD-15828-2

Bird Lives—Selections by artists of the 1960s to the 1990s performing compositions associated with the great alto saxophonist, Charlie Parker. Artists heard on this album include today's most revered disciple of Charlie Parker, altoist Frank Morgan. Also heard is another outstanding altoist, Art Pepper, and piano legend of the post-1950s period, Bill Evans. Milestone MCD-9166-2

Dameron, Tadd—*Fontainebleau* Fantasy/OJC OJCCD-055-2
The Magic Touch Fantasy/OJC OJCCD-143-2
Mating Call Fantasy/OJC OJCCD-212-2

Dameronia—*Live at the Theatre Boulogne-Billancourt/Paris* SoulNote 121202-2

Eckstine, Billy—*Everything I Have is Yours: The MGM Years* Verve 2 819442-2
Jazz 'Round Midnight Verve 314-521662-2

Flanagan, Tommy—*The Best of Tommy Flanagan* Pablo PACD-2405-410-2
Confirmation Enja EJA-4014-2

Gillespie, Dizzy—*Big Band in Concert (rec. 1948)* GNP Crescendo GNPD-23
The Dizzy Gilespie Story (with Johnny Richard's

Orchestra, and the Be Bop Boys, Milt Jackson, Ray Brown, James Moody, et al.). Savoy Jazz SV-0177
Groovin' High (with Charlie Parker, Dexter Gordon, et al.) Savoy Jazz SV-0152
Jivin' In Be Bop Bandstand BDCD-1534
Legendary Big Band Live Jazz JV-304
Live, 1946 Bandstand/Sphere BDCD-1534

Gordon, Dexter—*The Best of Dexter Gordon* Blue Note B21Y-91139
Dexter Blows Hot and Cold Boplicity CDBOP-006
Dexter Rides Again (with Bud Powell, Max Roach, et al.) SavoyJazz SV-0120
Dexter's Mood (1945-1947) Cool N' Blue CBCD-9114

Gray, Wardell—*Light Gray* (1948-1950) Cool N' Blue CBCD-9116
Memorial, Vol. 1 (rec. 1949-1953) Fantasy/OJC OJC-050
Memorial, Vol. 2 (rec. 1950-1951) Fantasy/OJC OJC-051

Harris, Barry—*At the Jazz Workshop* (post-bop keyboard leader in club setting). Fantasy/OJC OJCCD-208-2

Machito (Frank Grillo) & His Afro Cuban Orchestra—
Carambola—Live at Birdland 1951 Sky Ranch SRCD-1524
Cubop City (1949-50) Tumbao Cuban classics TCD-1512
Tremendo Cumban—1949-1952 Tumbao Cuban Classics TCD-1504

Machito (Frank Grillo) & His Afro Cuban Salseros—*Mucho Macho* (with Mario Bauza). Pablo PACD-2625-712-2

Monk, Thelonious—*The Best of Thelonious Monk: The Blue Note Years* Blue Note B21Y-95636
The Complete Blue Note Recordings (one of the few examples of Monk as a leader in the 1940s; there are also recordings from the early '50s within). Blue Note 4 B2PP-30363
The Complete Riverside Recordings—It was during the mid-to-late '50s, on Riverside Records, that Monk finally began receiving critical acclaim for his unorthodox genius. This massive boxed set includes everything recorded for Riverside between 1955 and 1961. There's a total of 153 performances—studio sessions, club and concert tapings—presented in chronological order. Riverside 15 RCD-022-2 $225
The Composer—Monk playing 11 of his classic compositions between1962-1968. Columbia Jazz Masterpieces CK-44297
Thelonious Monk: Straight No Chaser—(music from the 1989 documentary). Columbia ZK-45358

Morgan, Frank—*Bebop Lives!* Contemporary CCD-14026
Yardbird Suite Contemporary CCD-14045-2

Navarro, Fats—*Fats Navarro with the Tadd Dameron Band* (recorded 1948). Milestone MCD-47041-2
In the Beginning—Bebop Savoy Jazz SV-0169
Memorial Savoy Jazz SV-0181
Nostalgia Savoy Jazz SV-0123
Royal Roost Sessions (1948 with Tadd Dameron). Fresh Sound FSRCD-171

Nichols, Herbie—*The Art of Herbie Nichols* (a pianist whose style is in the general framework of Monk in terms of uniqueness). Blue Note B215-99176

Parker, Charlie—*The Complete Charlie Parker on Verve* —Here is a huge boxed set with a 35-page booklet (11" by 11") with an introduction by Dizzy Gillespie, and new biographical information by one of the most knowledgeable historians on the jazz scene, Phil Schaap. There are 176 perofmances totaling over 11 hours of music—51 of these have not been issued before. Verve 10 837141-2
Bird on 52nd Street (1948) Fantasy/OJC OJC-114
Charlie Parker Memorial, Vol. 1 Savoy Jazz SV-010
Charlie Parker Memorial, Vol. 2 Savoy Jazz SV-0103
The Complete Birth of Bebop Stash ST-CD-535
The Complete Dial Sessions Stash ST-CD-567-70
Jazz at Massey Hall Fantasy/OJC OJC-044

Powell, Bud—*The Amazing Bud Powell, Vol. 1* (1949) Blue Note B21Y-81503
Vol. 2 (1953) Blue Note B21Y-81504
The Best of Bud Powell on Verve (16-track sampler from the 5-CD box set, *The Complete Bud Powell on Verve*). Verve 314-523392-2
The Complete Bud Powell on Verve—Big box set with 100-page booklet including commentary, essays, interviews & rare photos; recordings include 9 previously unissued complete alternate takes, false starts, incomplete takes & studio dialogue. Verve 5 314-521669-2
Early Years of a Genius, 1944-1948 Mythic Sound MS-6001-1

Puente, Tito—*El Timbal* (rec. 1949-1951) Grey Cliffe ITMGC-900006-2
Master Timbalero Concord Picante CCD-4594

Roach, Max—*Quartet* (1953). Fantasy/OJC OJCCD-202-2

Roach, Max & Clifford Brown—*The Best of Max Roach and Clifford Brown in Concert* GNP Crescendo GNPD-18

Roney, Red—*Bird Lives!* Muse MCD-5371
Modern Music From Chicago (1955). Fantasy/ OJC OJC-048 (LP)

Sphere—*On Tour* (Thelonious Monk's middle name was the source of this group's title. Led by one-time Monk sideman, tenor saxman, Charlie Rouse, the group played Monk tunes). Red Records 123191-2

Stitt, Sonny—*Prestige First Sessions, Vol. 2* (1950-51). (Stitt was a sax player who emerged in the 1940s; he was said to be modeled after Parker, but had his own style and vision). Prestige PCD-24115-2
Stitt Plays Bird Rhino R2-1418

Supersax—*The Joy of Sax!* Former LA session stars harmonized Charlie Parker solos for five saxes and played note-for-note recreations—a kind of instrumental sax-along vocalese. Pair PCD-2-1175
Stone Bird Columbia CK-44436

Supersax Plays Bird   Capitol Jazz B21Y-96264

Videos

The Al Tinney Project–A documentary on one of the early leaders of the bebop movement. James Patrick interviews celebrated bop icons Dizzy Gillespie, Max Roach, and others, as they testify to the seminal contributions of Al Tinney. Additionally, Tinney is interviewed, and he describes the after-hours jam sessions at Monroe's Uptown House during the 1940s–as well as what he has done since that time. Tinney is also captured performing on piano. This video was scheduled to be released during the winter of 1995.

Note:

For more information write to: The Tralfalmadore Jazz Institute Project, 50 Vernon Place, Buffalo NY 14214

Babalu Music–A series of intentionally campy performances of Desi Arnaz's television Ricky Ricardo Orchestra at the Tropicana, as presented on the "I Love Lucy" show. Actually, there are some very hip musical charts of Afro-Cuban jazz–the only example of its kind seen and heard with regularity on national television during the 1950s. Selections include "Cuban Pete," "Straw Hat Song," and "Babalu."
                       51 min. CBS/FOX 9361 $14.98

Barry Harris: Passing It On–Modest bebop inheritor of the Bud Powell piano tradition of bop, who continues to play into the 1990s. He is a teacher, and advocates bebop as the beginning and end of music. This video shows him working with students of piano and popular singing, while he takes lessons from a classical piano teacher. Includes fast-moving clips of his professional playing, as well as his activities at his Jazz Cultural Center, on Eighth Avenue between 28th and 29th Streets in New York.   23 min. color RHAP B $19.95

Celebrating Bird: The Trumph of Charlie Parker (1987)–An excellent mix of old photos, album covers, and Gjon Mili's silent footage to break up and add life to the informative commentary by Parker's wives, Jay McShann, drummers Roy Haynes, and Roy Porter, historian Leonard Feather, and disciple Frank Morgan. Includes the only existing film of Parker with sound: a television clip of Parker, Gillespie and Dick Hyman playing "Hot House." A wonderful portrait. Like many underground musicians, Parker is better known today than during his lifetime. To get a deeper appreciation of him, by all means see this video, which is based on Gary Giddins' excellent book, *Celebrating Bird: The Triumph of Charlie Parker.*
          60 min. color/b&w SONY VIDEO JO509 $29.95

Dexter Gordon Quartet: Jazz at the Maintenance Shop (1978)–Gordon was the most celebrated of the tenor bebop players of the 1940s and '50s. Long, tall Dex is showcased in a public television taping that includes, "On Green Dolphin Street," "The Girl Upstairs," "Tanya," and "Polka Dots and Moonbeams."
                       58 min. color SRC 6304 $19.95

Dizzy Gillespie (1981)–Gillespie performs two numbers ("Be Bop" and "Birks' Works") with his hard-driving combo.   19 min. color COL/TRI 97W00024

Dizzy Gillespie: A Night in Tunisia(1990)–This video features interviews with the bop master as he extols the virtues of the Latin experience. Names like Machito, Mario Bauza, and Chano Pozo are given their due. Sampler of Afro-Cuban rhythms and selections are played in that style.
                28 min. color VIEW VIDEO 1315 $19.98

Max Roach in Concert–Alone on stage, the master drummer performs a series of percussive samples: especially good for those who wonder what function the drums truly accomplish besides making loud noise. "The Smoke That Thunders," "Hi Hat Solo," "Odd Meter Medley," and "Drums Unlimited" will open eyes as well as ears.   60 min. color DCI VH016V $39.95

Thelonious Monk: American Composer (1993)–An overview history of this most unique American composer and pioneer bebop pianist. Includes clips and interviews with other musicians and family members.   60 min. color BMG 80065-3 $29.98

Thelonious Monk: Straight, No Chaser (1989)– This is THE one to see. Amazing documentary footage of Monk on and off stage.   90 min. RHAPV $17.95

Things to Come: The Big Bands of Dizzy Gillespie and Billy Eckstine (1947)–Here is something rare–two bebop film shorts that were shown in black theaters in 1947. Both are constructed with simple story lines about each entertainer trying to advance his respective group up the entertainment ladder of success. Bill Eckstine's short was released with the title *Rhythm in a Riff.* In it he plays himself as an aspiring band leader with luck running out until a club manager gives the band a chance. A subplot where a beautiful assistant, with eyes for Eckstine, is also part of the plot line. Ten musical numbers are presented in rapid succession, and band members include tenorists Gene Ammons and Frank Wess, trumpeters King Kolax and Frank Detson, and drummer Art Blakey. This music is the real-deal big band bebop, and it is a rare thing to see, because there are not many examples of bop in the 1940s on film. Uptempo selections include "Second Balcony Jump," "Rhythm In a Riff" (with Eckstine's scat singing), "Taps Miller," and the Tadd Dameron classic, "Our Delight" (which includes Eckstine soloing on vale trombone). The main attraction of the band, as far as the general public was concerned, was not the hot bebop charts of Gerald Valentine, nor the young soloists, but Eckstine's romantic ballads. He offers up his big, chesty "Mr. B" baritone to two Russ Columbo crooner classics, "You Call it Madness," and "Prisoner of Love," and a selection that would be a favorite of the 1960s saxophone messiah, John Coltrane, "I Want to Talk About You."

The second film short is Dizzy Gillespie's *Jivin' in Be Bop* (that's how it was spelled on the poster advertisements

-in fact, the poster bragged "Top STARS in Sensational VARIETY MUSICAL REVUE," and promised as a dance attraction "The Hubba Hubba Girls"). The structure of this film was that of a basic musical revue. Gillespie's hot big band featured solos by Gillespie on trumpet, Milt Jackson on vibes, bassist Ray Brown, and vocalists Helen Humes and Kenny Hagood. There are 8 musical numbers, including "Salt Peanuts," "Be-Baba-Leba," "He Beeped When He Shoulda Bopped," and the musically advanced "Things to Come."

57 min. VINTAGE JAZZ CLASSICS VIDEO
VJC-2006 $19.95

Vocalese: Bop Goes Vocal

Recordings

Acid Jazz: Collection Two—The mix of jazz recording sampled by rappers and hip-hoppers found favor in underground night clubs in and around London, England in the late 1980s. Scotti Bros. Records has been a major functionary of this music. Selections on the compilation include "I Don't Know" by Colonel Abrams, "Inside Your Mind" by Greg Franks with the Quiet Boys, "Where's the One" by Snowboy and The Latin Section, The Vibrophonics" "I See You," and "Everything is Going to the Beat."

Scotti Bros. Records 72392-75230-2

Acid Jazz: Everything's Going to the Beat—More of the same from artists listed above as well as McTime, Dread Flinstone, Sinfluence, Stone Cold Boners, and Blaq "N" Wyte. Scotti Bros. Records 72392-75428-2

Digable Planets—*Blowout Comb* (one of the top bop-rap-hip-hop units). Pendulum/CEMA E2IZ-30654

Double Six of Paris—*Dizzy Gillespie & the Double Six of Paris*—This is one of two in-print recordings of this swinging vocalese group that sang in French. There are a number of classic recordings in the vaults of Capitol Records that should be re-released—they are superior examples of vocalese. This session added Bud Powell and James Moody into the mix. The Double Six (so named because the six voices were doubled in the studio to create a fuller, big band sound), shared a passion with Gillespie for science fiction, so that his classics like "Salt Peanuts," "The Champ," and "A Night in Tunisia" take on an eerie "Twilight Zone" tone. One of the Double Six members, Ward Swingle, has released number of releases under the title of the Swingle Singers featuring, classical music combined with hummed and scatted sounds.

Double Six With Quincy Jones—*Recontrant* OMD 1518

Gonzales, Babs—*Weird Lullaby*. Gonzalez refused to "copy" solos, so his brand of bebop babbling is different. A real original. Blue Note B21Y-84464

Guru—*Jazzmatazz* (billed "an experimental fusion of hip-hop and jazz"). Chrysalis 09463 2199892

Hancock, Herbie—*Dis Is Da Drum* (jazz and hip-hop).

Mercury

Hendricks, Jon—*Boppin' at the Blue Note*	Telarc CD-83320
Cloudburst	Enja EJA CD-4032
Love	Muse MCD-5258
Recorded in Person	Smash 842141-2

Hendricks, Jon & Friends—*Freddie Freeloader*
Denon CY-76302

Hendricks, Michele—*Carryin' On*	Muse MCD-5336
Keepin' Me Satisfied	Muse MCD-5363

Jefferson, Eddie—*Body and Soul*	
	Fantasy/OJC OJCCD-396-2
Come Along With Me	Fantasy/OJC OJCCD-613-2
Godfather of Vocalese	Muse MCD-6013
The Jazz Singer	Evidence ECD-22062-2
Letter From Home	Fantasy/OJC OJCCD-307-2

Jones, Quincy—*Back on the Block*
Qwest/Warner Bros. 26020-2

Lambert, Hendricks & Bevan—*Swingin' Till the Girls Come Home* Bluebird 6282-2

Lambert, Hendricks & Ross—*Everybody's Boppin'* (1959-1961). Columbia Jazz Masterpieces CK-45020

Sing a Song of Basie	GRP/Impulse GRD-112
Twisted: The Best of Lambert, Hendricks & Ross	
	Rhino R2-70328
Watermelon Man	Jazz Door ITMJD-1247-2

Manhattan Transfer—*Vocalese* (sing bop to Jon Hendricks' lyrics—Hendricks also perfoms with the group).
Atlantic 81266-2

Moody, James—*Hi Fi Party* (1955 with Eddie Jefferson).
Fantasy/OJCCD-1780-2
James Moody's Mood (sax great who created instrumental classic "I'm in the Mood for Love," upon which the most famous vocalese line of all time was written. Today, Moody features his own singing of the tune as a dedication to his late friend and band manager, Eddie Jefferson). Fantasy/OJC OJC-188 (LP)

Pleasure, King—*Golden Classics: Moody's Mood For Love*
Collectables CDL CD-5197

Golden Days	Fantasy/ OJC OJCCD-1772-2
Moody's Mood For Love	Blue Note B21Y-84463
The Source	Prestige 2 P-24017

Pleasure, King & Annie Ross—*King Pleasure Sings/ Annie Ross Sings* Fantasy/OJC OJCCD-217-2

This is Acid Jazz: After Hours—Selections by Kruder & Dorfmeister, DJ Krush, Pal Joe's New Breed, Marden Hill, Dis Jam Brooklyn Funk Essentials, OMU, Coco, Steel & Lovebomb, DJ Food, F. R. I. S. K.
Instinct EX-298-2

Trip Hop & Jazz—Selections by Hedfunk, DJ Food, Up, Bustle & Out, 9 Lazy 9. Instinct EX-298-2

US3—*Hand on the Torch*—A key rap-bop-hip-hop leader that took its name from an album title by Blue Note Records artist, pianist Horace Parlan. All the notes sampled in this collection come from the vaults of this key record label. The selections are primarily from the 1960s post-bop or hard-bop style, produced by Blue Note Records. "Cantaloop (Flip Fantasia)," with its sampled announcement by the midget MC at Birdland (Pee Wee Marquette), became a hit song.

Blue Note 07777 808832 5

Videos
Eddie Jefferson: Live From The Showcase (1979)—Eddie Jefferson, assisted by post-bop firebrand, altoist Richie Cole, sings classics which include "Moody's Mood for Love," "Jeanine," "A Night in Tunisia," " So What," "I Cover the Waterfront," "I Got the Blues," "When Your Smiling," "Body and Soul," "Trane's Blues," "Bennie's From Heaven," "Summertime," and more (see vocalese chart on page 350 for information on what recording Jefferson based some of these interpretations).

50 min. color RHAP $29.95

Jon Hendricks: The Freddie Sessions—Here is the best insiders' look at how a vocalese recording is produced. Jon Hendricks had written a vocalese piece based on Miles Davis' song "Freddie the Freeloader" from the classic album of the late 1950s, *Kind of Blue*. Hendricks, today's "grand *young* man of vocalese" (he never seems to age and his spirit is forever young), gathered up Bobby McFerrin, George Benson, and Al Jearreau—stars all—to sing the solos by John Coltrane, Cannonball Adderley, Bill Evans, and Miles Davis. This video takes us into rehearsals, as we see how the singers try to match up Hendricks' lyrics to the recording of the Davis composition. Hendricks tells about the background of the song and we keep hearing snippets throughout. This is a priceless piece of filmed vocalese history. Not available in stores. 30 min. color A&M RECORDS INC.

Note:
Send for information to: A&M Records Inc.,
1416 N. La Brea Avenue, Hollywood, CA 90028,
Tel: (213) 469-2411

Manhattan Transfer: Vocalese—This is a mix of concert footage and conceptual videos, based on lyrics written by vocalese's "James Joyce of Jive" Jon Hendricks. Selections include "That's Killer Joe," "Blue Bop Blues," "To You," "Another Night in Tunisia," and the Transfer is joined on stage, in night club video, by Hendricks.

28 min. color WVE 50103-3 $12.98

The Cool Movement/Young Lions

Recordings
The Birth of the Cool, Volume II—Selections by late 1940s and 1950s leaders of the cool movement. Included are trumpeters Shorty Rogers, Miles Davis, and Chet Baker; saxophonists Gerry Mulligan, Art Pepper, Jimmy Guiffre, Stan Getz, and Lee Konitz; and pianists George Shearing and Hampton Hawes.

Capitol Jazz C2IY-98935

Blanchard, Terence—*The Billie Holiday Songbook*

Columbia CK-57793

The Malcolm X Jazz Suite Columbia CK-53599

Christy, June—*The Misty Miss Christy* (a "vo-cool" jazz singer). Capitol Jazz B21Y-98452
Something Cool Capitol Jazz B21Y-96329

Davis, Miles—*Birth of the Cool* (1949-1950).

Capitol C21Y-92862
The Blue Note and Capitol Recordings (contains the albums *Birth of the Cool*, *Miles Davis Volumes 1 & 2*, and Cannonball Adderley's *Something Else*, which Miles plays on). Blue Note 4 B2NN-27475

Cool Boppin' at the Royal Roost 1948-1949

Fresh Sound FSRCD-1008
Miles Ahead (with Gil Evans Orchestrations).

Columbia CK-53225
Porgy and Bess (with Gil Evans Orchestrations).

Columbia Jazz Masterpieces CK-40647
The Real Birth of the Cool (Live 1948).

Bandstand BDCD-1512
Sketches of Spain (with Gil Evans orchestrations).

Columbia Jazz Masterpieces CK-40578

Davis, Miles & Quincy Jones—*Live at Montreux* (with the Gil Evans Band). Warner Bros. 45221-2

Evans, Gil—*Gil Evans & Ten* Fantasy/OJC OJCCD-346-2
The Individualism of Gil Evans Verve 833804-2
Out of the Cool MCA/Impulse MCAD-5653

Evans, Gil & Lee Konitz—*Anti-Heroes* Verve 314-511622-2

The Gil Evans Orchestra—*Plays the Music of Jim Hendrix*

Bluebird 8409-2-RB
Tribute to Gil Soul Note 121209-2

Faddis, Jon—*Hornucopia* (with Dizzy Gillespie).

EPIC EK-46958
Into The Faddish Phere EPIC EK-46958

The Four Freshmen—*Greatest Hits* (ex-Stan Kenton cool vocalists). Curb D21K-77612
Live at Butler University (with Stan Kenton Orchestra).

Creative World CD-1059

Getz, Stan—*Prezervation* (1949-1950).

Fantasy/OJC OJCCD-706-2
Quartets (rec. 1949-50). Fantasy/OJC OJCCD-121-2
The Roost Quartets (1950-1951).

Roulette Jazz B21Y-96052

Getz, Stan & Charlie Byrd—*Jazz Samba* (the record that started the Bossa Nova craze in 1962).

Verve 810061-2

Herman, Woody—*Best of the Big Bands; Woody Herman*

Columbia CK-45340
Early Autumn Featuring Stan Getz

Bluebird 07863-61062-2
The Early Woody Herman (1937-1941). Pearl CD-9780

The Thundering Herd, Live in Hi Fi 1944   Jass J-CD-621
The Thundering Herd, 1945-1947
    Columbia Jazz Masterpieces CK-44108

Kenton, Stan—*The Complete Capitol Recordings of the*
    Holman and Russo Charts (includes booklet by Will
    Friedwald with reminiscences by Holman and Russo
    and rare photos).   Mosaic MD4-136 $60
The Kenton Era (recordings 1941-1955, with dialogue by
    Kenton and a 4-page booklet).
    Creative World 4 1030E (cas)

Kenton in Hi Fi (many of the classic hits of the '40s).
    Capitol Jazz B21Y-98451
New Concepts of Artistry in Rhythm (includes four
    selections from the session that produced the original
    album).   Capitol C21Y-92865
Retrospective (with Stan Getz, Kai Winding, Shelly
    Manne, Chris Connor, Shorty Rogers, Maynard
    Ferguson, Art Pepper, Richie Kamuka, Laurendo
    Almeida, Lee Konitz, Frank Rosolino, et al.).
    Capitol Jazz 4 C24Z-97350

Kenton, Stan, June Christy & The Four Freshmen—
Roadshow   Capitol C21Z-96328

Konitz, Lee—*Subconscious Lee* (with Lennie Tristano,
    Warne Marsh, et al.).   Fantasy/OJC OJC-186 (LP)
Yes, Yes Nonet   Steeple Chase SCH-31119

**Lennie Tristano Memorial Concert: Town Hall, New York
    City, January 28, 1979**—Selections by ex-members of
    Tristano's groups, students, and professional musicians
    who admired his work.
    Jazz Records 5 JR-3 (cas) $30.98

Lewis, John—*Bach/Prelude & Fugues, Vol. 2*
    Philips 826698-2
The Chess Game, Vol. 2 (interpretations of the "Goldberg
    Variations").   Philips 832588-2

Marsalis, Wynton—*Black Codes (From the Underground)*
    Columbia CK-40009
Hot House Flowers   Columbia CK-39530
Live at Blues Alley   Columbia 2 G2K-40675
Marsalis Standard Time   Columbia CK-40461

Mulligan, Gerry—*The Best of the Gerry Mulligan Quartet With
    Chet Baker.* This was one of the premier 1950s groups
    that had refined the cool experiments of the 1940s.
    Pacific Jazz B21Y-9548-1
Plays Mulligan (recorded 1951).
    Fantasy/OJC OJCCD-003-2
Re-Birth of the Cool (reconstructions of the classic 1949-
    50 recordings with Wallace Roney playing Miles
    Davis' solos).   GRP GRD-9679
Reunion With Chet Baker (1957) Pacific Jazz B21Y-46857

Raeburn, Boyd & Orchestra—*Boyd Meets Stravinsky*
    Savoy Jazz SV-0185
Experiments in Big Band Jazz 1945   Musicraft MVSCD-65

Roney, Wallace—*Intuition*   Muse MCD-5346

The Standard Bearer   Muse MCD-5372

The Sauter-Finegan Orchestra—*Directions in Music*
    Bluebird 6468-2-RB

Shearing, George—*Live at the Cafe Carlyle*
    Concord Jazz CCD-4246
Lullaby of Birdland (1949-1954)   Verve 827977 (cas)
Mellow Moods   Pair PCD2-1226
The Shearing Touch   Pair PCD2-1302

Shearing, George & the New Quintet—*That Shearing Sound*
    (1994 recreations of Shearing's unique sounds of the
    late 1940s and early '50s).   Telarc CD-83347

Thornhill, Claude—*Best of the Big Bands*
    Columbia CK-46152
1941-1946-1947   Circle CCD-19

Tristano, Lennie—*The Complete Lennie Tristano on Keynote*
    Mercury 830921-2
Lenny Tristano/The New Tristano Atlantic Jazz R2-71595
Live at Birdland 1949   Jazz Records JRI-CD
Live in Toronto 1952   Jazz Records JR-5-CD
Wow (like all above—with Lee Konitz, and Warne Marsh).
    Jazz Records JR-9-CD

Videos
George Shearing—**Lullaby of Birdland** (1991)—The leader
of locked-hand chord style is captured in this
performance film, playing many of his favorites which
include "Freedom Jazz Dance," "Why DId I Choose
You?" "Isn't It Romantic?" and his own, best-known
compositon dedicated to the 1950's New York jazz
capital of the world, "Lullaby of Birdland."
    57 min. color VIEW VIDEO 1332 $19.98

Gerry Mulligan: Jazz in America (1981)—West Coast
baritone saxophonist is filmed during a night club
engagement, playing his cool jazz with a bounce.
Titles include "Walk on the Water," "For an Unfinished
Woman," "K4 Pacific," and "Song from Stayhorn."
    60 min. color NLHV V

Gil Evans and His Orchestra (1987)—Gil Evans held a
Monday ritual at Greenwich Village's Village Vanguard
for his jazz orchestra—sometimes featuring a rehearsal
band in action, other times, performing the straight
business of playing concert-like shows. Selections in
this set include compositions by George Gershwin,
Charles Mingus, Thelonious Monk, and Jimi Hendrix.
    57 min. color VIEW VIDEO 1301 $29.98

Lee Konitz—**Portrait of an Artist as Saxophonist**—
Interspersed with Konitz playing six pieces with pianist
Harold Danko, the film interviews the artist as we see
him in four different settings—at a workshop with music
students, an evening with friends, at rehearsal, and
between breaks during the taping of the music seen
here. Selections are: "Stella by Starlight," "Struttin' With
Some Barbeque," "She's as Wild as Springtime," "Hi
Beck," "Kary's Trance," and the inevitable,
"Subconscious Lee."   83 min. color RHAP $29.95

Live Thunder! Woody Herman and the Thundering Herd!!–Woody Herman leads his contemporary big band Herd through selections culled from his years in the industry 56 min. color FOR 19008V

Miles Ahead: The Music of Miles Davis (1986)–Taken from the superior PBS documentary, which includes the 1959 black and white television kinescopes of Davis with Gil Evans ("Blues for Pablo"), and with John Coltrane ("So What"). The history, intercut with interviews with musicians and star-fan Bill Cosby, follows Miles onto his aggressively hot quintet of the early 1960s with Wayne Shorter, Tony Williams, Ron Carter, and Herbie Hancock ("Footprints"), and finally on to his experiments with fusion ("Time After TIme").
  60 min. color/b&w 800693V $29.98

Miles Davis & Quincy Jones–Live at Montreux (1993)–The filming of Miles Davis' last filmed concert. Behind the scenes intrigue is captured as Miles finally agreed to do a concert of his and Gil Evans' collaborative classics of the late 1940s (*Birth of the Cool*) and the late 1950s (*Miles Ahead, Porgy and Bess,* and *Sketches of Spain*). Miles, who had been ill, was weak, and Wallace Roney helped take some of the solos. Songs include "Boplicity," "Springville," "Miles Ahead" "Summertime," and more.
  77 min. color RHAPV $25.98

Vintage Getz, Vol. 1 & 2–Stan Getz, the saxman the other players referred to as "The Sound," had one of the most distinctive and luscious tones in jazz history. The ex-Woody Herman and Stan Kenton tenorist is filmed in California's lush Napa Valley, and performs such titles as "Spring Can Really Hang You Up the Most," "Desafinado," "The Girl from Ipanema," and "Lush Life."
  108 min. color WVE 50237-3 V $29.98

Wynton Marsalis–Blues and Swing (1988)–Along with excerpts of the steller trumpet star in concert, there are segments of Marsalis directing educational workshops at the Duke Ellington School of Music, in Washington D.C., and at Harvard University. Marsalis' commitment to jazz and education has been, besides his musical contributions, another important facet of this leader of the "Young Lions."
  79 min. color SMVE 19V 49002V $14.98

Chapter 12: DEVELOPMENT OF RHYTHM AND BLUES

The Rise of Rhythm and Blues/Country and City

Recordings
Blues Masters:The Essential Blues Collection, Volume 1: Urban Blues–Here is a package that contains a wide assortment of artists and styles covering the vast urban blues commonwealth. Big band sounds of the swinging Erskine Hawkins and Count Basie are mixed in with electric guitar combos of Albert King, Otis Rush, T-Bone Walker, and Lowell Fulson. The collection has jazz-oriented blues singers as well: Big Joe Turner, Dinah Washington, Joe Williams, Jimmy Witherspoon,

and Charles Brown. Plus there are more–a good overview. Rhino R2-71121

Volume 2: Postwar Chicago–Chicago's South Side along Maxwell Street was a blues paradise for newly-arrived migrants from the deep South. The bars and clubs on the South Side provided paying jobs for entertainers during the mid-1930s and '40s and, in time, most of the better known and highly regarded professionals made recordings. During the late 1940s and after, an electric bar-blues style had been formed. Here are some of those leaders: Muddy Waters, Sonny Boy Williamson, Jimmy Rogers and His Trio, Baby Face Leroy Trio, Eddie Boyd, Earl Hooker, Magic Sam, Little Walter and His Jukes, et al. Rhino R2-71122

Broonzy, Big Bill–*Good Time Tonight*
  Columbia/Legacy CK-46219
1934-1947 Story of the Blues CD-3504-2

Chicago Blues–The urbanized sound of Chicago by the 1950s period had pretty much been set as a style: buzzing, slashing electric guitar leads, backbeat from the drums, electric harmonica closely miked, boogie-oriented piano, and gruff, verile vocals that growled (not groveled) with sexual potency and menace. This was the style that the Britishers of later years would imitate (Rolling Stones, Yardbirds, Animals, and others). Some of the leaders of that Chicago style are: Muddy Waters, Buddy Guy and Junior Wells, Mighty Joe Young, J. B. Hutto, and KoKo Taylor, all heard on this compilation.
  Red Lightnin' REDRL-CD-0080

Chicago: The Living Blues: South Side Blues–Most of the artists in this collection are examples of just-up-from-Mississippi-to-Chicago players during the mid-1930s to early '40s. As a result, the refined stylistics of Muddy Waters and Buddy Guy won't be as apparent. This is a good transitional sampler of "Bluebird Beat" tradition. Bluester's include the Mississippi Sheiks, Mama Yancy, Little Brother Montgomery, and Henry Benson. Fantasy/DBC OBCCD-508-2

Cray, Robert–*Strong Persuader* (a new twist on an old style). Mercury/Hightone 830567-2
Too Many Cooks Tomato R2-70381

Crudup, Arthur "Big Boy"–*Mean Ole Frisco*
  Collectables COLCD-5130
Meets the Master Blues Bassists (originally titled *Crudup's Mood* on LP; includes studio conversation with Crudup, producers/company owners, Bob and Sue Koestler, and master bass player-songwriter-singer Willie Dixon). Delmark DE-621
That's All Right, Mama Bluebird 07863-61043-2

Dixon, Willie–*The Big Three* (Dixon's sophisticated club combo trio of the 1940s). Columbia/Legacy CK-46216
The Chess Box (The Willie Dixon "Songbook" contains 36 songs, written by him, recorded between 1951-1968–a 12-page booklet provides information about the songs and the recordings). Chess CHD2-16500
I Am the Blues Mobile Fidelity MFCD-10-00872

Guy, Buddy—*The Complete Chess Studio Recordings*
Chess 2 CHD2-9337
The Very Best of Buddy Guy (today's heir-apparant to Muddy Waters' throne as "King of Chicago Blues").
Rhino R2-70280

Hooker, John Lee—*Boogie Chillun* Fantasy FCD-24706-2
The Early Years Tomato R2-71659
The Healer (with contemporary blues stars, Robert Cray, George Thorogood, Charlie Musselwhite, Carlos Santana, Los Lobos, members of Canned Heat, and Bonnie Raitt). Chameleon 74808-2
The Ultimate Collection, 1948-1990 Rhino R2-70572

Hooker, John Lee & Canned Heat—*Hooker 'N Heat*
EMI 2 E2AS-97896

Hopkins, Lightnin' (Sam)—*The Complete Aladdin Recordings*
EMI E22V-96843
Mojo Hand: The Lightnin' Hopkins Anthology (boxed set)
Rhino 2 R2-71226 $27.98
The Texas Bluesman Arhoolie CD-302

Howlin' Wolf (Chester Burnett)—*Cadillac Daddy: Memphis Recordings, 1952* Rounder CDSS-28
The Chess Box (his greatest works in anthology set)
Chess CHCD3-9332-3
Howlin' Wolf/Moanin' in the Moonlight Chess CHD-5908
The London Howlin' Wolf Sessions, featuring Eric Clapton, Steve Winwood, Bill Wyman, Charlie Watts
Chess CHD-9297

James, Elmore—*The Sky is Crying: The History of Elmore James* Rhino R2-71190

Memphis Minnie (Lizzie Douglas)—*Early Rhythm and Blues 1949* Biograph BCD-124
Hoodoo Lady Columbia/Legacy CK-46775

Memphis Slim (Peter Chatman)—*The Complete Recordings 1940-1941* EPM (Blues collection) 15803-2
Memphis Slim (rec. 1950-1952). Chess CHD-9250

The R&B Box: 30 Years of Rhythm and Blues (1943-1972)—This is the big one for the entire picture of rhythm and blues. All the styles covered in Chapter 12 are given a couple of examples. Of course this history goes beyond our timelines, but the connections to the more contemporary music will be apparent. Among the artists that are covered in the book are: Louis Jordan & His Tympany Five, Buddy Johnson & His Orchestra, Illinois Jacquet & His All Stars, Joe Liggins & His Honeydrippers, Lionel Hampton & His Orchestra, Johnny Moore's Three Blazers, Roy Milton & His Solid Senders, Paul Williams & His Hucklebuckers, Big Jay McNeeley's Blue Jays, Dinah Washington, The Johnny Otis Orchestra, the Orioles, Jimmy Liggins & His 3-D Music, Big Joe Turner, Professor Longhair, Ivory Joe Hunter, Ray Charles, Ruth Brown, Fats Domino, and the Robins—the rest, about half the package, is post-1950. A 60 page booklet is included.
Rhino 6 R2-71806 $74.98

Sunnyland Slim (Albert Laundrew)—*House Rent Party*
Delmark DD-655
Legacy of the Blues GNP Crescendo GNPS-10021

Washboard Sam—*1935-1947* Story of the Blues CD-3502-2
Rockin' My Blues Away Bluebird 07863-61042-2

Waters, Muddy (McKinley Morganfield)—*The Best of Muddy Waters (1948-1954)* Chess CHD-31268
Can't Get No Grindin' Chess CHD-9319
I'm Ready Blue Sky ZK-34928
One More Mile: Chess Collectibles, Vol.1 (tracks recorded 1948-1972; fully annotated with extensive liner notes, new graphics and photos). Chess 2 CHD2-9348

Williamson, Sonny Boy (Rice Miller)—*The Blues of Sonny Boy Williamson* Storyville STCD-4062
The Essential Sonny Boy Williamson Chess CHD-9343
King Biscuit Time (1951) Arhoolie CD-310
Sonny Boy Williamson, Volume 2 (1940/42)
Blues Collection 15810-2
Vol. 1 1937-1939 EPM 15810-2

Videos
Blues Masters—The Essential History of the Blues, Vol. 1—A wide area of blues is canvassed in this collection. Bessie Smith's one screen appearance in *St. Louis Blues*, Mamie Smith, Leadbelly, and Ethel Waters have been covered in different sections of the blues, but it's always good to see them. More to the point for specific rhythm and blues are the visits made by Big Bill Broonzy (master of the "Bluebird Beat"), Jimmy Rushing (an inspiration to Louis Jordan), and jump blues bandleader Roy Milton, who was one of the most popular jukebox favorites on the West Coast during the 1940s and '50s. 51 min. RNO R32101

Blues Summit—In Chicago—Pre-eminent stars like Muddy Waters, Junior Wells, and today's female queen of Chicago, Ko Ko Taylor, are joined by younger blues followers like Johnny Winter, Buddy Miles, and the late guitar hero, Mike Bloomfield. Together, and separately, they manage to tackle Chicago classics such as "Mannish Boy" and "Hoochie Coochie Man."
60 min. RNO R32081

John Lee Hooker and Charlie Musselwhite: Mark Nafftalin's Blue Monday Party (1981)—The elderly Mississippi blues legend is joined by an all-star band from California led by harmonic virtuoso Charlie Musselwhite. 30 min. color RHAPV $24.95

KoKo Taylor—Queen of the Blues (1991)—A touching visual, biography of today's female blues leader of Chicago. Reunited with fellow windy city bluesmen like guitarist Buddy Guy and bassist Willie Dixon, the all-star congregation performs at Chicago's Legend's Nightclub. Blues such as "Let the Good Times Roll," "Wang Dang Doodle," "Jump for Joy," and "I'm a Woman Now," are given lively readings.
55 min. color/b&w MPI 6243 $19.98

Lightnin' Hopkins—The Blues According to Lightnin' Hopkins—An portrait of this late rural master of blues singing and entertaining. He is seen performing "Hurt Me So Bad," "How Long Has it Been?," "Bring it Home to You," " I'm Walking," and others.

31 min. color FFV $49.95

Maxwell Street Blues (1987)—Maxwell Street in Chicago is where bluesmen applied their trade on weekends. It was literally an open air music market, and nearly every important bluesman in Chicago performed there at one time or another. This is a rare glimpse of the subterranian world of mostly unknowns like Blind Arvella Gray ("John Henry," "There's More Pretty Girls Than One"), Jim Brewer, John Henry Davis, Playboy Venson, Floyd Jones, and the legendary Robert Nighthawk. There is nothing quite like this out on the video market—a real find for its rugged, street-hip reality.

56 min. color RHAP $39.95

Messin' with the Blues (1974)—Recorded at the Montreux Jazz Festival in Switzerland, a Chicago blues trio of Muddy Waters, Buddy Guy, and Junior Wells regale the audience with scorching versions of time-tested perennials such as "Messing With the Kid," "Hoodoo Man Blues," "Ten Years Ago," "Hoochie Coochie Man," "Mannish Boy," "The Same Thing," and "Got My Mojo Working." 54 min. color RHINO RNVD 1991

Chicago Blues: Muddy Waters—Sessions from bluesmen in action documented by Harley Cokless. Some of the performers covered are Muddy Waters, the main focus, ("Hoochie Coochie Man," "Nineteen Years"); Junior Wells ("My Little Girl"); Buddy Guy ("First Time I Met the Blues"); Floyd Jones ("Stockyard Blues"); J.B. Hutto, and Johnnie Lewis. "A fascinating, gritty record of black city life, with all the low-lying smells, sounds, and sights familiar from a thousand blues stories. Some testimonies are droll, others more pointed than the toughest lyric. With comments interpersed by Dick Gregory, the film grows with the existential logic of a plague. The sight of a Miles van der Rohe glass skyscraper suddenly looks like the most obscene sight of all. Few films on American music carry a heavier social and cultural load than this one does."—Kevin Lynch, *Downbeat*. 50 min. color RHAP $39.95

Big Band Rhythm and Blues/Vocalists

Recordings
Brown, Roy—*Good Rockin' Tonight*
Intermedia QS-5027 (LP)
Mighty Mighty Man Ace CDCH-459

Creole Kings of New Orleans—A compilation of New Orleans regulars such as Guitar Slim, Clifton Chenier, Professor Longhair, Jerry Byrne, Li'l Millet and His Creoles, and a gaggle of others.
Specialty SPCD-2168-2

Domino, Fats—*Antoine "Fats" Domino* (boxed package of Domino's hits). Tomato 2 R2-70391 $23.98
My Blue Heaven: The Best of Fats Domino, Volume One

EMI E2IY-92808
They Call Me the Fat Man: The Legendary Imperial Recordings EMI4 E200-96784

Donegan, Dorothy—*The Incredible Dorothy Donegan Trio Live at the 1991 Floating Jazz Festival*
Chiaroscuro CR (D)-318
Live at the 1990 Floating Jazz Festival
Chiaroscuro CR (D)-312
Live at the Widder Bar Timeless CDSJP-247
Sophisticated Lady CMA CM-8011

Dr. John (Mac Rebennack)—*Goin' Back to New Orleans* (player of today with a heart and soul for the music of yesterday—a true New Orleans historian).
Warner Bros. 26940-2
In a Sentimental Mood Warner Bros. 25889-2
Plays Mac Rebennack Clean Cuts CDCC-705

Green, Lil—*Why Don't You Do Right? 1940/1942*
Blues Collections 158212-2

Hampton, Lionel—*Flying Home* Decca Jazz MCAD-42349
Flying Home/Hamp's Blues LRC 2 LRC-CD-9063
Lionel Hampton's Jumpin' Jive (1937-1939), Volume 2
Bluebird 2433-2-RB
Masterpieces (rec. 1937-1940 & 1942).
Jazz Archives 15825-2
Reunion at Newport, 1967 Bluebird 07863-66157-2

Harris, Wynonie—*Bloodshot Eyes: The Best of Wynonie Harris*
Rhino R2-71544
Women, Whiskey and Fish Tales Ace CDCH-457

Harris, Wynonie, & Roy Brown—*Battle of the Blues, Volume 1.* The two shouting bluesmen divide time separately on this album. Harris churns out rockers like "Blood Shot Eyes," "Lovin' Machine," "All She Wants to Do is Rock," "Good Morning Judge," "Shake That Thing," and Roy Brown's "Good Rockin' Tonight." Brown counters with his bump and grind versions of "Big Town," "Boogie at Midnight," "Bar Room Blues," "Miss Fanny Brown," and "Lolly Pop Mama."
King KCD-607

Mardi Gras Indians Super Showdown—If you've never heard New Orleans Mardi Gras Indians, then you are in for a treat—the music is rhythmically seductive, the words are unintelligible, (but it matters not), and the party atmosphere is that of full-tilt boogie. Selections by Bo Dollis, Chief of the Wild Magnolias; Monk Boudreaux, Chief of the Golden Eagles; Rebirth Brass Band; Willie Tee, and others. Rounder CD-2113

Millinder, Lucky and His Orchestra—*Lucky Millinder & His Orchestra* Classic 712
Lucky Millinder: 1942, With Sister Rosetta Tharpe
Hindsight HSC-233 (cas)

Morse, Ella Mae—*Ella Mae Morse* Capitol C21Y-95288

Professor Longhair (Roy Byrd)—*Crawfish Fiesta*
Alligator ALCD-4718

Fess: The Professor Longhair Anthology
Rhino 2 R2-71502 $27.98
Mardi Gras in Baton Rouge   Rhino/Bearsville R2-70736
Mardi Gras in New Orleans: 1949-1957
Nighthawk NHCD-108
Rum and Coke   Tomato R2-71447

Shoutin' Swingin and Making' Love—Energetic blues shouting from Jimmy Rushing, Al Hibbler, Jimmy Witherspoon, and Wynonie Harris, along with others.
Chess CHD-9327

The Specialty Story—Anthology from one of the most productive of the rhythm and blues independents. Owner Art Rupe signed West Coast talent during the mid and late 1940s—some of his stars during that period were: Roy Milton, The Liggins Brothers, Camille Howard, Jim Wynn, Floyd Dixon, and gospel groups, the Soul Stirrers, the Swan Silvertones, the Pilgrim Travelers, and powerhouse preacher, Alex Bradford. When times got tough in the early 1950s, Rupe cast his magic reel into the Crescent City pool of talent and landed Lloyd Price, Guitar Slim, Art Neville, Larry Williams, Don & Dewey, and his biggest catch of all, Little Richard. They are all here in this collection.
Specialty 5 SPCD-4412-2

Spring of New Orleans: The Genius of Dave Bartholomew—Orchestrator supreme, Bartholomew headed Fats Domino's group and did the same for many others. His magic touch is investigated via many lesser known New Orleans performers, as well as some stars, in this collection.   Imperial 2 E22U-80184

Tharpe, Sister Rosetta—*Live in 1960*   Southland SCD-1007

Turner, "Big" Joe—*Big Bad & Blue: The Big Joe Turner*
Anthology   Rhino 4 R2-71550 $44.98
Jumpin' With Joe   EMI E21Z-99293
Memorial Album: The Rhythm & Blues Years
Rhino R2-81663
Tell Me Pretty Baby, With Pete Johnson's Orchestra
Arhoolie CD-333

Washington, Dinah—*The Complete Dinah Washington on*
Mercury, Vol. 1 (1946-1949)   Mercury 3 832444-2
Vol. 2 (1950-1952)   Mercury 3 832448-2
Mellow Mama (1945)   Delmark DL-451
Unforgettable   Mercury 314-510602-2

The Wild Magnolias—*They Call Us Wild*
Polydor 314-519419-2

Videos
Dr. John–New Orleans Swamp (1993)–Dr. John in concert with fellow New Orleans players, guitarist-singer Earl King ("Those Lonely, Lonely Nights"), the Meters ("Look-Ka-Py-Py/Jungle Man"), and Professor Longhair ("Tipitina" and "Whole Lotta Lovin'"). Dr. John includes "Big Chief," "Call a Doctor," "Quitters Never Win," and "Such a Night." This was taken from a PBS special.
60 min. color RNO R32076

Fats Domino and Friends–Immortal Keyboards of Rock & Roll (1988)–A concert filmed at the Storyville Hall in New Orleans in which Fats Domino is the star as he brings out fellow musicians to join him on stage (Ron Wood, Paul Shaffer). Ray Charles and Jerry Lee Lewis also take a turn as the featured keyboardist.
60 min. color HBO 0038V $19.99

Fats Domino (1985)–Fats is the star of this 45 minute concert film shot in Los Angeles. Selections include "Blue Monday," "Ain't That a Shame," "I Want to Walk You Home" and "I'm in Love Again," among many others.   45 min. color MCA 80416V $14.95

Hampton Hawes' LA All-Stars with Big Joe Turner–When Big Joe Turner left Kansas City to play New York in 1938 for the *From Spirituals to Swing Concert*, little did he know his next long stay would be in Los Angeles. In this concert performance, LA jazz luminaries Hampton Hawes (piano), Harry "Sweets" Edison (trumpet), and saxophone mavens Sonny Criss and Teddy Edwards push and cajole Big Joe through a lively set that includes "Feeling Happy" and "Shake Rattle and Roll."
28 min. color RHAP $29.95

Lionel Hampton Live (1983)–A concert film of the roaring big band led by the master of rhythm and blues jazz sounds. Even though Hamp is older, that never dims his enthusiasm, or his manic stage exhuberence. His 20-piece band performs "Air Mail Special," "Smooth Sailing," and "Hamp's Boogie Woogie."
24 min. color COL/TRI 96W00001

Piano Players Rarely Ever Play Together–For New Orleans rhythm and blues, it's the piano player that stands front and center as the leading force–after all, Fats Domino and Little Richard are the Crescent City's best known rock and rollers, and rhythm and blues supplied much of rock's original core. Before Fats and Little Richard emerged, there was a rich continuum that went all the way back to the "Professors" in the houses of ill-repute and the juke joints of New Orleans. In this video three premier pianists from different eras combine to share ideas and play engrossing music. Tuts Washington (the old timer), Professer Longhair (the intermediary), and Allen Toussaint (the contemporary master) are the featured performers.
76 min. color SP PPHV $40.00

Jump Combos/Honkers

Recordings
Atlantic Honkers: A Rhythm & Blues Saxophone Anthology–Atlantic Records successfully utilized the honking sax as an integral part of their musical recipe. In the bands of Joe Morris, Jesse Stone and Tiny Grimes, constant use of repeated, stuttering saxophone solos rang out loud and clear. Saxophonists such as King Curtis, Willis "Gator Tail" Jackson, Frank "Cole Slaw" Culley, and Arnett Cobb got a chance to leave section work behind and lead groups of their own during the 1950s and early 1960s. All of this is detailed in the music in this collection.   Atlantic 2 81666-4 (cas)

Blues Masters The Essential Blues Collection, Volume 5: Jump Blues Classics—This collection brings together masters of mirth and mayhem—you won't be able to sit down while listening to the music—that's why they call it the jump blues! Examples provided by: Red Prysock, Louis Prima, Big Joe Turner, Wynonie Harris, Bullmoose Jackson and His Buffalo Bearcats, Ruth Brown, Big Jay McNeely, and others.   Rhino 2 R2-71125

Cobb, Arnett—*Arnett Blows for 1300*   Delmark DD-471
Arnett Cobb is Back   Progressive PCD-7037
The Wild Man From Texas
          Home Cooking HCS-1144 (LP)

Cobb, Arnett & Eddie "Lockjaw" Davis—*Blow Arnett, Blow*   Fantasy/OJC OJCCD-794-2

Five Guys Named Moe—Music from the Broadway musical revue of Louis Jordan's music).   Columbia CK-52999

Honkers and Bar Walkers—A panoply of wild saxmen who, at times, managed to leave the stage and get up on the bar and honk, honk, honk! Over 40 sax men here and most never got to be known except to those patrons who visited the haunts these players toiled in. Here are a few samples of some of these honkers and their songs: Fats Noel ("Duck Soup"); Doc Sausage ("Sausage Rock"); Cozy Eggleston ("Fish Tail"); Tab Smith ("Because of You"); Jimmy Coe ("After Hours Joint"); and Fred Jackson ("Buck Fever").
          Delmark DD-438
Volume 2   Delmark DD-452

Jackson, Bull Moose—*Bull Moose Jackson Sings His All Time Hits*   Audio Lab ALP-1524 (LP)

Jackson, Joe—*Jumpin' Jive* (Louis Jordan & Cab Calloway jump tunes interpreted by British New Wave rave of the late '70s).   A&M 75021-3271-2

Jacquet, Illinois—*The Black Velvet Band (1947-1950)*
          Bluebird 6571-2-RV
Flying Home   Bluebird 07863-61123-2
Illinois Jacquet All Stars 1945-1947
          Blue Moon BMCD-1011

Jordan, Louis—*The Best of Louis Jordan (1941-1954)*
          MCA MCAD-4079-2
Five Guys Named Moe: Original Decca Recordings, Vol. 2
          MCA MCAD-10503
Five Guys Named Moe (Live 1948-1949)
          Bandstand BDCD-1531
Just Say Moe! Mo' of the Best of Louis Jordan
          Rhino2 R2-71144
No More! Louis Jordan's Greatest Hits Verve 314-51253-2

McNeely, Big Jay—*Big "J" in 3-D*   King KCD-650
Blow the Wall Down   Big J Records CMA 9003
Welcome to California!   JCD-109

Note:
Write to: Big J Records, 6520 Selma Ave. #442, Hollywood, CA 90028

Videos

Louis Jordan–Five Guys Named Moe (1991)—In addition to being called the "King of the Juke Boxes," Louis Jordan could also have been justly titled the "King of Soundies." Surely no performer during the halcyon days of the 1940s made more Mills Panoram soundies than Louis Jordan. This collection contains 21 video "songs" culled mostly from soundies—the non-soundies in this package were excerpted from a couple of his theatrical story-line releases. Included are: "Jumpin' at the Juibilee" (with some of the wildest flash dancing ever seen, by an uncredited male duo); "Beware!" (an early example of rap); "Reet, Petite and Gone"; "That Chick's Too Young to Fry," et al.
          56 min. VINTAGE JAM VJC 2004 $19.95

Louis Jordan and the Tympany Five (1992)—This collection of vintage Louis Jordon clips is more of a documentary. Beginning with the updated connection to Broadway's musical revue, *Five Guys Named Moe*, the program uses narration and old photos and film clips of other influential jazz artists, like Louis Armstrong, Nat King Cole, Cab Calloway, and Fats Waller. Numbers of Jordan's include: "Buzz Me Baby," "Caldonia," "Is You Is or Is You Ain't My Baby," "Honey Chile," and "Five Guys Named Moe," as well as others.
          48 min. BMG 72333-80008-3 $19.95

Texas Tenor: The Illinois Jacquet Story (1993)—Arthur Elgert's artistic framing of Illinois Jacquet and his musical life as an elder statesman is nothing short of riveting. We get to see Jacquet's big band in action, and hear from musicians such as Clark Terry, the versatile trumpeter, and Dizzy Gillespie. Peter Watreous, writing in *The New York Times*, praised that, "The film captures one of jazz's great audience-hounds in action, somebody who dearly loves performing. Mr. Jacquet sings a bit, does a little tap-dancing and plays some extraordinary improvisations, in which his brutal saxophone contrasts with the smooth fabric of the big band. The documentary, in its fixation with abstraction and close-ups, of the big band, reproduces the shiny ecstatic moments of orchestral jazz as well as any film made, its beauty and rounded shapes and sharp punctions, the delerium and sensuality of performance, the congregational ecstacy." 81 min.RHAP 9021 $29.95

Recordings

Brown, Charles—*Driftin' Blues*   DCC Jazz DJZ-603
Driftin' Blues: The Best of Charles Brown
          EMI E21Y-97989
Legend!   Off-Beat OBR-22112-2
One More for the Road   Alligator ALCD-4771

Charles, Ray—*The Early Years* (as club combo style singer).   Tomato2 R2-71656 $27.98
The Early Years (1947-1951) EMI (Jazz Archives) 15707-2
The Great Ray Charles   Atlantic 8131-2

Cole, Nat "King"—*The Best of the Nat King Cole Trio*
          First Choice FCD-4561
The Complete Capitol Recordings of the Nat King Cole Trio (includes a 64-page booklet with session by session

notes, commentary by Will Friedwald, cross-indexed tune list, full discography, and many rare photos).

Mosaic18 MD18-138 $270.00

Early Years of Nat King Cole Trio

Sound Hills SSCD-8002

Hit That Jive, Jack: The Earliest Recordings (1940-1941)

Decca Jazz MCAD-42350

Jumpin' at Capitol; The Best of the Nat King Cole Trio

Rhino R2-71009

Nat "King" Cole 1936-1940 (primarily jazz piano).

Classics 757

Dixie Hummingbirds—*We Love You Like a Rock/Every Day and Every Hour*   Mobile Fidelity MFCD-751

Five Blind Boys of Alabama Featuring Clarence Fountain—*Deep River*   Elektra/Nonesuch 61441-2

The Golden Gate Quartet—*Golden Years, 1939-1952* (these last three groups are important influences on vocal group rhythm and blues).   EMP 15214-2

Hunter, Ivory Joe—*Since I Met You Baby: The Best of Ivory Joe Hunter*   Razor & Tie RAZCD-2052

16 of His Greatest Hits   King KCD-605

Ink Spots—*Greatest Hits, 1939-1946* (original Decca recordings).   MCA MCAD-31347

If I Didn't Care   Pro Arte CDD-555

Ink Spots on the Air (broadcasts from 1935 and 1939).

Sandy Hook CDSH-2084

King, B. B.—*B. B. King's Early '50s Classics*

Flair V21Z-39654

Do the Boogie (early '50s classics)   Ace CDCH-916

(B. B. King's career takes off in the 1950s—there is nothing much in print prior to this time because he was just starting up when our timeline ends.)

Liggins, Jimmy—*Jimmy Liggins and His Drops of Joy*

Specialty SPCD-7005

Rough Weather Blues, Vol. 2   Specialty SPCD-7026-2

Liggins, Joe—*Dripper's Boogie, Vol. 2*

Specialty SPCD-7025-2

Joe Liggins and the Honey Drippers

Specialty SPCD-7006

Milburn, Amos—*Down the Road Apiece*   EMI E21Z-27229

The Mills Brothers—*The Best of the Decca Years* (rec. 1941-1945).   MCA MCAD-31348

Greatest Hits   MCA MCAD-31035

The Mills Brothers, 1931-1938   L'Art vocal 12

Tiger Rag   All Star ALS-23118

Milton, Roy—*Roy Milton and His Solid Senders*

Specialty SPCD-7004

Vol. 2: Groovy Blues   Specialty SPCE-7024-2

Vol. 3: Blowin' with Roy   Specialty SPCD-7060

Otis, Johnny—*Creepin' with the Cats: The Legendary Dig Masters*   Ace CDCHD-325

Spirit of the Black Territory Bands   Arhoolie CD-384

The Ravens (Jimmy Ricks, Maithe Marshall, Leonard Puzey, Warren "Birdland" Suttles, Louis Heyward, Howard Biggs, Bill Sanford)—*Old Man River*

Savoy Jazz SV-0260

Rarities   Savoy Jazz SV-0261

Route 66: Capitol Sings Coast to Coast—

Capitol C21S-80180

Til, Sonny and the Orioles—*Greatest Hits*

Collectables COLCD-5014

Walker, "T-Bone" (Aaron Thibeaux)—*The Complete Recordings of T-Bone Walker 1940-1954* (includes booklet with essay by his biographer, Helen Oakley Dance, complete discography through 1954 and rare photos).

Mosaic 6MD6-130 $90.00

I Want a Little Girl   Delmark DD-633

Rare T-Bone   Off-Beat OBR-220053-2

T-Bone Blues   Rhino R2 R2-8020

Videos

Ernie Andrews: Blues For Central Avenue—Central Avenue was LA's 52nd Street during the 1930s and '40s. Andrews, and others who were there, reminisce about the after-hours clubs, the women, the gambling, and the music. Andrews is a less than household name—but to the blacks of the segregated Central Avenue he was a star—he stood tall as a handsome baritone singer in the mold of Billy Eckstine with hits like "Don't Let the Sun Catch You Cryin'." Andrews discusses his record contract problems and the downside of his career after the war. Clips of him singing sophisticated blues ballads show off his considerable talent.   50 min. color RHAP $39.95

Nat King Cole: Unforgettable—An exceptional documentary on one of the major artists of American popular music. Before Cole became a standup vocal pop star of the 1950s and '60s, he was a jazz pianist and a piano-player singer of note in the underground. This informative video shows rare soundies of Cole during his days as a club combo race star and has interviews with well-known disciples of Cole such as piano great Oscar Peterson. "Route 66," "Sweet Lorraine," "Orange Colored Sky," "Mona Lisa," and "Unforgettable" are but a few of the many hits performed in this profile.

90 min. color/b&w HOME COL 04V

Percy Mayfield—Poet Laureate of the Blues—Father of soul singing super star Curtis Mayfield, Percy Mayfield etched out a solid career for himself as a blues balladeer of note during the 1940s and '50s slotting into what has been defined as club combo style. He was highly regarded for his composing skills as well—his best known creations were "Please Send Me Someone to Love" (his own best selling recording), and "Hit the Road Jack."

Music authority Bob Porter wrote of this portrait that it was "a mixture of performance and reminiscence with pianist Mark Naftalin. It captures his [Mayfield's] lazy Louisiana drawl in the best possible way. There are testimonials from B. B. King and Ray Charles, but the true star is Percy Mayfield. There is no one like him."
30 min. color RHAP $29.95

Chapter 13: COUNTRY AND WESTERN

Today's popularity of contemporary country and western music has been one of the major surprises of popular music trends over the past ten years. However, that hasn't translated to include the earlier forms of country music and its history. There are many significant innovators detailed in Chapter 13 that can't be found in today's record stores—nor can they be ordered from most of the record companies because they are no longer in stock. Let me give you a couple of examples. Going through the most recent music guide— *Schwann/ Spectrum* Summer 1995 (Volume 6, Number 3)—to locate two of the father figures of honky tonk, Ted Daffan and Al Dexter, we find: *no* Daffon, Ted listed between D. A. F. and D. C. 3; and *no* Dexter, Al nestled between Dewan and DeYoung. There are also *no* entries for the "Father of Western Swing," Milton Brown, or for the first commercial electric guitarist in American music, Bob Dunn. Video examples are an even more rare commodity.

Note:
There are a small number of record companies that do have country music of the past which doesn't get listed and I would like to share this information with you—if I have slighted one or two sources, please write me (the P.O. address is listed at end of the Preface/Further Acknowledgements).

Arhoolie Records:10341 San Pablo Ave., El Cerrito, CA 94530: Tel. (510) 525-7471
County Records: Box 191, Floyd, VA 24091
New World Records: 701 Seventh Ave, New York, NY 10036: Tel. (212) 302-0460
Rounder Records: One Camp St., Cambridge, MA 02140: Tel. (617) 354-0700
Shanachie Records: 37 East Church St., Newton, NJ 07860: Tel. (201) 579-7763
And kudos to Rhino Records for the recent packaging of great American music the past couple of years. Rhino Records: 10635 Santa Monica Blvd., Los Angeles, CA 90025: Tel (310) 474-4778

Southeastern Continuum/Brother Groups/Bluegrass

Records

Acuff, Roy—*Best of*   Curb/CEMA D21K-77454
Columbia Historic Edition (1936-1962)
                                    Columbia Historic Edition CK-39998
The Essential Roy Acuff   Columbia/Legacy CK-48956
Wabash Cannonball   Intersound CDA-5098

Acuff, Roy & the Smoky Mountain Boys—*1939-1941; Fly*

Birdie Fly	Rounder SS-24 (LP)
Allen Brothers—*Chattanooga Boys*	Old Timey 115 (LP)
Clara's Boys	Rounder 0154 (LP)
Sweet Rumors	Rounder 0079

Appalachian Stomp: Bluegrass Classics—A new compilation from Rhino that gives a nice overview of the bluegrass history. Selections from early founders such as Billy Monroe, Flatt & Scruggs, Stanley Brothers; as well as the disciples in the 1950s like Jim & Jesse, Osborne Brothers, Jimmy Martin, Country Gentleman; right up to younger practioners of today like J. D. Crowe, Ricky Skaggs, and Alison Krauss, among others.   Rhino R2-71870

Are You From Dixie?: Great Country Brothers Teams of the 1930s—The only in-print collection of its kind. This is a terrific sampling of the best known brothers duos who worked during the Depression period and thereafter. Most of the classics of this subgenre are found herein: Allen Brothers ("New Salty Dog"), Shelton Brothers (also known as the Lone Star Cowboys), Delmore Brothers ("Brown's Ferry Blues"), Dixon Brothers ("Intoxicated Rat"), Blue Sky Boys ("Kentucky"), and the Monroe Brothers ("What Would You Give In Exchange [For Your Soul]?").   RCA 8417-2-R

Arnold, Eddy—*Best of*   RCA 3675-2R
Last of the Love Song Singers: Then & Now (box set).
                              RCA2 07863-66046-2 $23.98
Pure Gold   RCA 07863-58398-2
You Don't Miss a Thing   RCA 3020-2-R

The Best of Bluegrass; Volume One: Standards—Of the historic collections of bluegrass this is one of my favorites—however it doesn't include Bill Monroe's music (probably due to a record company conflict). Key selections include: "I Long to See the Old Folks" (Stanley Brothers & the Clinch Mountain Boys), "Family Reunion" (Carl Story & the Rambling Mountaineers), "Ruby, Are You Mad?" (Osborne Brothers & Red Allen), "Can't You Hear Me Calling" (Country Gentlemen), "Feudin' Banjos" (Arthur Smith with Don Reno), "Blue Moon of Kentucky" (Lonesome Pine Fiddlers), and "Foggy Mountain Breakdown" and "Old Salty Dog Blues" (Lester Flatt, Earl Scruggs & the Foggy Mountain Boys).   Mercury 848979-2

Bluegrass at Newport (1959, 1960 & 1963)-This is an important document of consciousness-raising on the part of the urban folk music crowd that attended the series of Newport Folk Festivals. What was raised during this period known as the "Folk Revival" (a better name would have been the "Folk Arrival"), was the first-hand connection and awareness to Southern country music artists. Flatt and Scruggs became the new-found leaders of bluegrass music as a result of their visits up North—(Bill Monroe was unknown to this audience at the time—Ralph Rinzler would eventually lead a one-man crusade to right this omission.) Also performing at Newport were: the New Lost City Ramblers, Rex Logan with Eric Weissberg, Mac Wiseman and the Country

Boys, Clarence (Tom) Ashley with Doc Watson, the Morris Brothers, and Earl Scruggs with "Hylo" Brown and the Timberliners.   Vanguard Twofer VCD-121/22

Bluegrass Class of 1990—The "new kids on the block" that are carrying the torch: Ricky Skaggs, the Johnson Mountain Boys, Alison Krauss and Union Station, Tony Rice, David Grisman, the Nashville Bluegrass Band, Lynn Morris, Sam Bush, J. D. Crowe, The Dry Branch Fire Squad, the Whitstein Brothers, Bela Fleck, Norman Blake and Tony Rice, the Rice Brothers,Tony Furtado, the Bluegrass Album Band; and "old timers" Jim and Jesse (McReynolds) also are heard.
Rounder CDAN-07

Bluegrass Classics: 1946-1948—This is the key time period for the stylistic formation of bluegrass music. The main leaders are to be found on this release. Selections include music from Bill Monroe and the Bluegrass Boys, Birch Monroe, Lester Flatt, Earl Scruggs, Chubby Wise, and Cedric Rainwater.
Sandy Hook CSH-2113 (cas)

Blue Sky Boys (Bill & Earl Bolick)—*In Concert, 1964*
Rounder CD-11536
Sunny Side of Life   Rounder C 1006 (cas)
The Blue Sky Boys; This is an example of an out of print document that NEEDS to somehow get back in circulation. A beautifully conceived project—double LP (1976); marvelous graphic design for the cover (see page 460); excellent liner notes by Douglas B.Green and masterfully produced by Frank Driggs. Most important, however, is the music—these are classic recordings from 1936 ("I'm Just Here to Get My Baby Out of Jail") to 1950 ("There'll Be No Broken Hearts for Me"). Let's hope RCA/BMG will, in time, find a way to get this document back in circulation.
RCA AXM2-5525 (LP) (OP)
Note:
This is a representative plea to the record companies to release others such as Ted Daffan, Al Dexter, Milton Brown, Tex Williams, Bill Boyd, the Blue Ridge Playboys, Bob Dunn, et al. who presently can not be found with an album listed under their own name.

The Byrds—*Sweetheart of the Rodeo*   Columbia CK-09670

Carter Family—*On Border Radio* (electrical transcriptions 1938-1942).   JEMF-101

Columbia Country Classics, Vol.1—Subtitled "The Golden Age," these are examples of the entire range of country music styles of the 1930s and 1940s. Compilations such as this program can give the listener a broad range of music, and it offers a chance to hear artists that may not be in print under their own name, as is the case for a few in this collection. For example, Ted Daffan's Texans ("Born to Lose"), Al Dexter & His Troopers ("Pistol Packin' Mama"), Texas Ruby ("Don't Let That Man Get You Down"), and Molly O'Day & the Cumberland Mountain Folks ("When God Comes and Gathers His Jewels"), have been out of print for years on albums under their own names. Others that can be

found listed individually in catalogs include: the Carter Family ("Can the Circle Be Unbroken [Bye & Bye]"), Roy Acuff ("Great Speckled Bird"), Chuck Wagon Gang ("After the Sunrise"), Gene Autry ("You Are My Sunshine"), Patsy Montana ("I Want to Be a Cowboy's Sweetheart"), Bob Wills ("Take Me Back to Tulsa"), Spade Cooley ("Shame on You"), Bill Monroe ("Blue Moon of Kentucky"), Flatt & Scruggs ("Don't Get Above Your Raisin'"), and the Stanley Brothers ("The Fields Have Turned to Brown").   Columbia CK-46029

The Delmore Brothers—*Freight Train Boogie*
ACD CDCH-455
Sand Mountain Blues (1944-1949) County CCS-110E (LP)

Flatt, Lester & Earl Scruggs—*Don't Get Above Your Raisin'*
County CCS-CD-102
The Golden Era   Rounder SSCD-05
Lester Flatt and Earl Scruggs
Columbia Historic Edition CK-37469

Flatt, Lester, Earl Scruggs and the Foggy Mountain Boys—*The Complete Mercury Sessions*   Mercury 512644-2

Flying Burrito Brothers—*Farther Along: The Best of the Flying Burrito Brothers*   A&M 75021-5216-2

Foley, Red—*The Country Music Hall of Fame*
MCA MCAD-10084

McLain, Raymond W. (of the McLain Family Band)—*A Place of My Own*   Flying Fish FF-70597

Martin, Jimmy—*You Don't Know My Mind*
Rounder CDSS-21

Monroe, Bill—*Bean Blossom*   MCA MCAD-8002
Bill Monroe at His Best   Hollywood/MG HCD-409
Columbia Historic Edition
Columbia Historic Edition CK-38904
The Essential Bill Monroe and His Bluegrass Boys (1945-1949)
Columbia/Legacy2 C2K-52478
The Music of Bill Monroe 1936-1994 (box set).
MCA4 MCAD 4-11048 $48.98

Monroe, Bill & Charlie—*Feast Here Tonight*
Bluebird 2 AXM2-5510 (LP)

Morgan, George—*American Originals* (1949-1963)
Columbia CK-45076

The Smithsonian Collection of Country Music, Volume 2
—This collection was listed in Chapter 7 for Volume 1 (there are four volumes in all—one and two cover the general area of this book). A good overview of 1935 to 1950—the Mountaineer styles of the Southeast are represented (Blue Sky Boys, Eddy Arnold, Bill Monroe, Jimmy Dickens, Hank Snow, Hank Williams, et al.), and so are the various forms of music from the West (Al Dexter, Merle Travis, Hank Thompson, Moon Mullican, Floyd Tillman, et al.).
Smithsonian Collection of Recordings CDRD-042-2

Snow, Hank—*All-Time Greatest Hits*   RCA-9968-2-R
The Singing Ranger   Pair PCD-2-1314

Stanley Brothers (Carter & Ralph)—*Bluegrass, Vol. 1*
          Rounder SS-09 (LP)
Long Journey Home   Rebel CD-1110
The Stanley Brothers & the Clinch Mountain Boys
          King KCD-615

Stanley, Ralph—*Saturday Night & Sunday Morning*
          Freeland2 CD-9001

Wiseman, Mac—*Grassroots to Bluegrass*   CMH CD-9041
The Mac Wiseman Story   CMH2 CMH-9001 (LP)

Williams, Hank, Sr.—*The First Recordings*
          Country Music Foundation CMF-007
40 Greatest Hits   Polydor 2 821233-2
I Ain't Got Nuthin' But Time (rec. December '46–August '47)
          (first in a series of Williams' complete studio and home
          demo recordings).   Polydor 825548-2
Lovesick Blues (rec. August '47-December'48) (second in
          the series of complete recordings). Polydor 825551-2
Lost Highway (rec. December '48-March '49) (third in the
          series of complete recordings).   Polydor 825554-2
I'm So Lonesome I Could Cry (rec. March-Aug. 1949)
          (fourth in the series of complete recordings).
          Polydor 825557-2
Love Gone Lonesome Blues (rec. August '49-December'50)
          (fifth in the series of complete recordings).
          Polydor 831633-2
Hey, Good Lookin' (rec. December '50-July '51) (sixth and
          the last for our purposes).   Polydor 831634-2

Videos

Hank Williams–In the Hank Williams Tradition (1989)– A
          musical tribute to the late-great "Hillbilly Shakespeare,"
          with luminaries Waylon Jennings, Chet Atkins, Randy
          Travis, Willie Nelson, Kris Kristofferson, Dwight Yoakum,
          Emmylou Harris, Billy Swan, and Hank's son, Hank
          Williams Jr. Interviews with Roy Acuff and Minnie Pearl
          shed insight on the great one. Also, there are rare clips
          of Williams from the 1950s. The above guest stars sing
          and play classics such as "Hey, Good Lookin,'" "You
          Win Again" "Your Cheatin' Heart," et al.
          60 min. color WSV 1659V $19.95

High Lonesome: The Story of Bluegrass Music
          (1994)—Award-winning documentary by Rachel Liebling
          that traces the evolution of bluegrass. Narrated by
          bluegrass star Mac Wiseman, the film manages to
          weave interviews with Bill Monroe, Ralph Stanley,
          Jimmy Martin, and others, with concert footage and
          archival photos and film clips. Performances by Bill
          Monroe, the Stanley Brothers, Mac Wiseman, Jimmy
          Martin, Flatt & Scruggs, the Osborne Brothers, Jim &
          Jessie, the Seldom Scene, Sam Bush, Alison Krauss,
          and the Nashville Bluegrass Band, make this a one of a
          kind video. This is the high measure that other country
          music documentaries can/should look to for guidance.
          95 min. color/b&w SHANACHIE 604

Hank Williams—The Show He Never Gave (1981)–Singer

"Sneezy" Waters portrays the legendary Hank Williams,
Sr.–I've not seen this one. *Videolog* says that Waters
gives "an imaginary impromptu show recounting the
triumphs and sorrows of his life between songs.
Sneezy performs more than 23 of Hank Williams'
immortal classics, including 'Lovesick Blues,' 'Hey
Good Lookin,' 'Your Cheatin' Heart,' 'Jambalaya,' 'Cold
Cold Heart,' and many others."
          86 min. color WSV 1644 $24.95

Western Process/Tex-Mex/Singing Cowboys

Recordings
Autry, Gene—*The Essential Gene Autry (1933-1946)*
          Columbia/Legacy CK-48957
Gene Autry   Columbia Historic Edition CK-37465E

Back In the Saddle Again—Great collection of 55 years of
          recorded cowboy music, compiled by Charlie Seeman
          of the Country Music Foundation. Everything is here.
          The early, pre-singing cowboy fare of the early
          commercial period–Carl T. Sprague, Jules Vern Allen,
          Harry "Haywire Mac" McClintock; the early radio and
          record cowboys and cowgirls–Patsy Montana, the Girls
          of the Golden West, Gibe Rice & His Beverly Hill Billies,
          Arizona Ranglers, Powder River Jack & Kitty Lee; the
          Hollywood singing cowboys–Ken Maynard, Gene Autry,
          Sons of the Pioneers, Rex Allen; and the most recent
          artists who are keeping the cowboy tradition
          alive–Glenn Ohrlin, Chris LeDoux, and Riders in the
          Sky.   New World2 NW-314/315-2

Conjunto! Texas-Mexican Border Music, Vol. 1–Various
          artistry make up this album of Tex-Mex music.
          Reformers include: Flaco Jimenez, Steve Jordan, Los
          Hermanos Barron, Ruben Naranjo y Los Gamblers, and
          Tony De La Rosa.   Rounder 6023 (LP)

The Cowboy Album–Selections by Ken Curtis & the Sons
          of the Pioneers, Gene Autry, Tex Ritter, Roy Rogers,
          Vaughn Monroe, Frankie Laine, Marty Robbins, Fess
          Parker, and Gail Davis.   Kid Rhino R2-70403

Jimenez, Flaco—*Ay Te Dejo en San Antonio*
          Arhoolie CD-318
Partners (with guests Stephen Stills, Dwight Yoakam,
          Linda Ronstadt, John Hiatt, Ry Cooder, Emmylou
          Harris, and Los Lobos).   Reprise 26822-2
San Antonio Soul   Rounder CD-604-2

Jimenez, Santiago, Jr.—*Canciones de Mi Padre*
          Watermelon WM 1019-2

LeDoux, Chris—*Chris LeDoux (1972-1994)*
          Liberty 4 C21Z-28458
Cowboys Ain't Easy to Love   Liberty C21Y-97600
Sing Me a Song, Mr. Radio Man   Liberty C21Y-97601
Songbook of the American West   Liberty C21Y-97603
Watcha Gonna Do With a Cowboy, with Garth Brooks
          Liberty C21Y-97592

Los Lobos—*Just Another Band From East L. A.: A Collection*
          Slash2 45367-2

La Pistola Y El Corazon Slash 25790-2

Martinez, Narciso—*Father of the Texas-Mexican Conjunto*
Arhoolie CD-361

Mendoza, Lydia—*La Gloria de Texas* Arhoolie CD-3012
Mal Hombre Folklyric CD-7002
Mexican-American Border Music, Vol. 1: An Introduction:
The Pioneer Recording Arhoolie CD-7001

Murphy, Michael Martin—*Cowboy Songs*
Warner Bros. 26308-2
Cowboy Songs III—Rhymes of the Renegades
Warner Western 45423-2
Wide Open Country Warner Bros. 26953-2

Riders in the Sky—*Best of the West, Vol. 1*
Rounder CD-11517
The Cowboy Way MCA MCAD-31244
Cowboys in Love Columbia CK-64248
Saddle Pals Rounder CD-8011

Ritter, Tex—*Best of the Cowboys* Richmond NCD-2148
Tex Ritter Capitol C21Y-95036
Greatest Hits Curb/CEMA D21K-77397

Rogers, Roy—*Best of* Curb/CEMA D21K-77392
Roy Rogers Tribute (a tribute with the following artists
performing: Kentucky Headhunters, Randy Travis,
Emmylou Harris, Ricky Van Shelton, Katy Mattea,
Willie Nelson, Dale Rogers, et al.). RCA 3024-2-R

Ronstadt, Linda—*Mas Canciones* Elektra 61239-2
Songs of My Father (Canciones de Mi Padre)
Asylum 60756-2

Silver Screen Cowboys: Hoppy, Gene and Me—The best
of the Hollywood singing cowboy collections presently
available. This is the only package that includes the first
two to regularly vocalize in a Western series: Ken
Maynard and John Wayne. In addition to Gene, Roy,
and Tex, the program includes output from a couple
sidekicks (Gabby Hayes and Smiley Burnette), and
some of the lesser-known cowboys (Eddie Dean, Jimmy
Wakely, and Rex Allen). Now we just need a collection
that would give us examples of Dick Foran, Fred Scott,
George Houston, Ray Whitley, Monte Hale, Herb
Jeffries, et al. Risky Business AK-57475

Songs of the West—This is an appealing large boxed set of
four volumes of cowboy songs—there's a limited
Collector's Edition in a genuine leather-bound box 4-
71451-2 $69.98—with a colorful large booklet. The
volumes, which can be purchased individually are:
Vol. 1: Cowboy Classics Rhino R2-71681
Vol. 2: Silver Screen Cowboys Rhino R2-71682
Vol. 3: Gene Autry & Roy Rogers Rhino R2-71683
Vol. 4: Movies & Television Themes Rhino R2-71684
The entire package Rhino 4 R2-71263-4 $59.98

Sons of the Pioneers—*Cool Water* RCA Nashville 07863
Sons of the Pioneers Columbia Historic Edition CK-37439

Sunset on the Range Pair2 PDC-2-1156
Tumbling Tumbleweeds: The RCA Victor Years, Vol. 1
RCA 9774-2-R

Sons of San Joaquin—*A Cowboy Has to Sing*
Warner Western 26935-2
Songs of the Silver Screen Warner Western 45326-2

Texas Tornados—(Doug Sahm, Freddy Fender, Augie
Meyer, Flaco Jimenez)—*The Best of the Texas Tornados*
Reprise 45511-2

Tex-Mex Fiesta—Includes the historic leaders of the
movement (Narciso Martinez, Santiago Jimenez, Lydia
Mendoza), along with some of the stars of
contemporary Tex-Mex (Steve Jordan, Freddy Fender,
Flaco Jimenez). Arhoolie CDCHD-528

Wakely, Jimmy—*Beautiful Brown Eeys*
Richmond N5-2183 (cas)

Videos

Music of the West: A Tribute to the Singing Cowboys
(1993)—Filmed at the Gene Autry Western Heritage
Museum in Los Angeles, this evening of awards brings
out a presenter who gives historical background about
the recipients while we get a rare chance to see film
clips of the artist in action. Most of those who are given
a plaque, humbly say a word or two and exit; others
perform a song. Some of the presenters are: Clint
Black, who doesn't sing a cowboy song, instead he
interprets Fats Waller's "Aint' Misbehavin'"; Emmylou
Harris, (she sings "Even Cowgirls Get the Blues"),
Richard Farnsworth, Buddy Ebsen, and Dusty Rogers.
Receiving plaques are: Roy Rogers and Dale Evans
(Roy sends a video hello to the audience); Gene Autry
(he is taped in conversation with Farnsworth); Monte
Hale; Patsy Montana; Rex Allen; and Eddie Dean. The
Sons of the Pioneers, and black cowboy, Herb Jeffries,
perform.
70 min. color/b&w WARNER/REPRISE 383603 $29.95

The Singing Cowboys, Vol. 1(1993)—This was a grand
idea—simply show cut-ins of the songs from films of the
singing cowboys. So this is a fast-paced program of
song after song from a variety of films. There are songs
from: Ken Maynard ("Powder and Paint" and "You Are
My Sunshine"); Eddie Dean ("Banks of the Sunny San
Juan"); Bob Wills; the screen's first singing cowgirl,
Dorothy Page; Sons of the Pioneers; Dale Evans and
Smiley Burnette ("Mama Don't Allow").
45 min. PARADE VIDEO 480 $19.95

The Singing Cowboys, Vol. 2 (1993)—The same effective
format as above. In addition to the many different
songs that Autry, Rogers, Evans, and Ritter sing, there
are appearences by the Beverly Hill Billies, the Sons of
the Pioneers (again), and the Light Crust Doughboys.
45 min. PARADE VIDEO 481 $19.95

Tex-Mex: The Music of the Texas-Mexican Borderland
(1990)—The border region between the Rio Grande and
Texas and Mexico runs for over 1,000 miles and is the

meeting ground for these cultures. Music peformed by Lydia Mendoza and Flaco and Santiago Jimenez give a sampling of the rich variety of sounds that make up Tex-Mex music. Add to that the mariachi music, the political music of Little Joe Hernandez, and that of Frank Rodarte, hero of the low riders, and you have a full plate of hot Texas and Mexican sounds.

60 min. color SHANACHIE 1206 $19.95

Western Swing/Honky Tonk

Recordings

Asleep at the Wheel (Ray Benson)—*Asleep at the Wheel*
MCA MCAD-31281
Asleep at the Wheel: Tribute to the Music of Bob Wills and the Texas Playboys—(group is joined by guests: Garth Brooks ("Deep Water"), Suzy Bogguss ("Old Fashion Love"), Merle Haggard ("I Wonder if You Feel the Way I Do"), Willie Nelson ("Still Waters Run the Deepest"), Marty Stuart ("Misery"), Huey Lewis ("Hubbin' It"), Dolly Parton ("Billy Dale"), George Strait ("Big Ball's In Cow Town"), Riders in the Sky ("Dusty Skies"), Brooks & Dunn ("Old Fashioned Love"), plus others—contains previously unreleased tracks).
Liberty CDP-0777-7-81470-2-2
Greatest Hits (Live & Kickin') Artisa 07822
Route 66 Liberty C21-Y-98925
Still Swingin' Liberty 3 C2RD-3084
The Swingin' Best of Asleep at the Wheel Epic EK-53049

Commander Cody & the Lost Planet Airmen—*Country*
Casanova MCA MCAD-661
Live From Deep in the Heart of Texas MCA MCAD-659
Sleazy Roadside Stories Relix RRCD-2028

Cooley Spade—*Spadella! The Essential Spade Cooley (rec. 1944-1946)* Columbia/Legacy CK-57392

Frizzell, Lefty—*American Originals* (rec. 1950-1955).
Columbia CK-45067
The Best of Lefty Frizzell Rhino R2-71005

Hillbilly Boogie—What an addition—just out in 1994. This has got it all! Many of those western swing artists and honky tonkers not found individually are here: Leon McAuliffe & His Western Swing Band ("Take it Away, Leon" and "Blue Guitar Stomp"), Paul Howard & His Cotton Pickers ("Rootie Tootie" and "Drinking All My Troubles Away"), Al Dexter & His Troopers ("Saturday Night Boogie" and "New Broom Boogie"), Johnny Hicks & His Troubadours ("Hamburger Hop"), Curly Williams & His Georgia Peach Pickers ("Georgia Boogie"), Johnny Bond & His Red River Valley Boys ("Mean Mama Boogie"), Andy Reynolds & His 101 Ranch Boys ("Beer Bottle Mama"), and my favorite cowgirl—she's on the cover of this CD and it's the same picture that adorns the front of this book's cover—Louise Massey & the Westerners ("Squeeze Box Polka"). Bob Wills ("Cowboy Stomp"), Spade Cooley ("Three Way Boogie"), Lefty Frizzell, and a couple of others join the fun.
Columbia/Legacy CK-53940

Hillbilly Fever! Vol. 1: Legends of Western Swing—So new (at this time) that *Hillbilly Fever!* (Volumes 1 & 2) isn't even listed in *Schwann*. What a revelation—thank you, Rhino Records. These compliations are done right (good sources compiled by experts Rich Kienzle, James Austin & Patrick Milligan). Too many to list—there are 18 in all—but a few must be mentioned. For example, the nasty "Everybody's Truckin'" by the Modern Mountaineers, Milton Brown's "Taking Off," two examples of Bob Wills' brothers, Johnny Lee Wills ("Milk Cow Blues") and Billy Jack Wills ("Troubles"), and selections of the great steel virtuoso Noel Boggs, Hank Penny, (a glorious rendering of "Won't You Ride in My Little Red Wagon"), and Tex Williams.
Rhino R2-71900/A 26108

Hillbilly Fever! Vol. 2: Legends of Honky Tonk—Again, great choices. The source name of the music is here (Al Dexter's "Honky Tonk Blues"), and classics from Ted Daffan ("Born to Lose"), Rex Griffin ("The Last Letter"), Floyd Tillman ("Drivin' Nails in My Coffin"), Hank Williams ("Honky Tonkin'"), Leon Payne ("I Love You Because"), Cliff Bruner ("It Makes No Difference Now"), and Hank Thompson ("The Wild Side of Life"). The other choices, while not as well known, are still fine examples of honky tonk excitement.
Rhino R2-71901/A26109

Hofner, Adolf—*South Texas Swing* Arhoolie CD-7029

The Maddox Brothers & Rose—*America's Most Colorful Hillbilly Band* Arhoolie CD-391

Mullican, Moon—*Moonshine Jamboree* Ace CDCH-458
Sings His All-Time Hits King KCD-555

Penny, Hank & His Radio Cowboys—*Hank Penny & His Radio Cowboys* Rambler R-103 (LP)

Revard, Jimmie—*Oh Swing It* Rambler R-106 (LP)

Texas Czech-Bohemian Bands—Here are excellent musical examples of the middle European Slavic people who came mainly from the provinces of Bohemia and Moravia. The use of the tuba oompah-sounds, accordions, polka dances, and beer-hall festivities is captured by regional Texas bands led by groups with names such as Bacova's Ceska Kapela, Adolph Pavlas & His Bohemians, Louie & His Old Time Band, and Joe Petek's Orchestra, among others.
Folklyric Records 9031 (LP)

Texas Music, Vol. 2: Western Swing & Honky Tonk—Some hard to get items mingled with some classics. Expecially rewarding is the seminal honky tonk unit, the Blue Ridge Playboys (Leon "Pappy" Selph, Floyd Tillman, Chuck Keeshan, and Moon Mullican), the jazzy Roy Newman & His Boys, and fiddle great J. R. Chatwell with the Saddle Tramps. The well known stars are here as well: Bob Wills, Milton Brown, Ted Daffan, Al Dexter, Floyd Tillman, Cliff Bruner, Harry Choates, and Ernest Tubb. Neo-western swing revivalists Alvin Crow ("Nyquil Blues") and Asleep at

the Wheel ("Roll 'Em Floyd" [Interpolating 'Rebecca and "Roll 'Em Pete"]) round out the program.
Rhino R2-71782

Thompson, Hank–*All Time Greatest Hits*
Curb/CEMA D21K-77329
20 Greatest Hits   Delux DCD-7807

Travis, Merle–*The Best Of*   Rhino R2-70993
Saturday Night Shuffle: A Celebration of Merle Travis, the Man and His Music   Shanachie CD-6006

Tubb, Ernest–*The Country Music Hall of Fame*
MCA MCAD-10086
Honky Tonk Classics   Rounder SS-14 (LP)
Live 1965   Rhino R2-70902

Tubb, Ernest/T. Texas Tyler/Eddy Arnold– (the complete Mutual Network broadcast of November 23, 1946 and January 11, 1950).   Radiola CDMR-1141

Wills, Bob (& His Texas Playboys)–*Anthology (1935-1973)*
Rhino 2 R2-70744 $23.98
Bob Wills   Columbia Historic Edition CK-37468E

Classic Western Swing; with the Texas Playboys
Rhino2-71670
For The Last Time   Liberty 2 C21Y-28331
Encore (with soloing from his sidemen Leon McAuliffe, Al Stricklin, Eldon Shamblin, Johnny Gimble, and Leon Rausch).   Liberty 3 C23U-30275

The Tiffany Transcriptions: Volume 1   Rhino R2-71469
Vol. 2: Best of the Tiffany (out of 9 Volumes).
Rhino R2-71470

Videos
Merle Travis: Rare Performances 1946-1981–Merle Travis was considered one of the greatest of all guitar pickers. Like many of the Depression riddled Southerners, Travis moved out to LA during the war years. It was out in California that Travis developed into one of the most in-demand songwriters and performers in country music. Classics such as "Deliver Me C.O.D.," "So Round, So Firm, So Fully Packed," "Smoke! Smoke! Smoke! (That Cigarette)," and "Sixteen Tons" are his.
60 min. color VESTA 13012V

Still Swingin': The History of Bob Wills & Western Swing Music (1994)–Hosted by Red Steagall (he wrote "Lone Star Beer and Bob Wills Music"), from Cain's Ballroom in Tulsa, Oklahoma, this show gives archival photos and film clips of Bob Wills in action. Ray Benson and Asleep at the Wheel command the stage and feature ex-Playboys such as legend guitarist Eldon Shamblin, singer Leon Rausch, fiddler Johnny Gimble, and a few others, performing past hits of Bob Wills. Wills performs classics such as "Take Me Back to Tulsa," "Sun Bonnet Sue," "Lone Star Rag," "Ida Red," "Bring It On Down to My House," and the "Playboy Theme." Tracy Byrd and his group, Stonehorse, both newcomers to the field of western swing also perform renditions of Wills' classics. This is a welcome addition to the video field of music

documentation–I had looked for years for clips of Bob Wills without any luck, now there is something for us all to view and enjoy.
57 min. color/b&w VCI 7802 $19.95

Chapter 14: THE URBAN FOLK MOVEMENT

Recordings
Broonzy, "Big Bill"–*In Chicago*   EPM ZET-742
Sings Folk Songs   Smithsonian/Folkways SFCD-40023

Dickens, Hazel–*By the Sweat of My Brow*
Rounder 0200 (LP)
Hard Hitting Songs For Hard Hit People
Rounder 0026 (LP)

Dylan, Bob–*Bob Dylan*   Columbia CK-08579
The Freewheelin' Bob Dylan   Columbia CK-08786
John Wesley Harding (this LP, along with *Sweetheart of Rodeo* by the Byrds, both released in 1968, ignited the eventual "Country Rock" movement).
Columbia CK-09604

Elliott, Ramblin' Jack–*The Essential Ramblin' Jack Elliott*
Vanguard Twofer VCD-89/90
Hard Travelin': Songs by Woody Guthrie and Others
Big Beat CDWIK-952

Don't Mourn–Organize!: Songs of Labor Songwriter Joe Hill–An anthology of labor leader Joe Hill's classic songs of, and for, the workers. His political message was simple: "A pamphlet is never read more than once, but a song is learned by heart and updated over and over." Among the contributors are: Billy Bragg singing Phil Ochs' tribute composition "Joe Hill"; "Haywire Mac" McClintock ("The Preacher and the Slave"); Paul Robeson ("Joe Hill"); Pete Seeger and the Song Swappers ("Casey Jones–The Union Scab"); Cisco Houston ("The Tramp"); Alfred Esteban Cortez ("The White Slave"); Hazel Dickens ("The Rebel Girl"); Entertainment Workers IU 630, I. W. W. ("There is Power in a Union") and more.
Smithsonian Folkways SFCD-40026

Folk Classics: Roots of American Folk Music (1935-1966)–Compilation of a variety of folk and country musicians. Selections include recordings by Leon Bibb, Burl Ives, Malvina Reynolds, Pete Seeger, the Beers Family, Mother Maybelle Carter, Orriel Smith, the Clancy Brothers & Tommy Makem.   Columbia CK-45026

Folk Music Radio–This is an essential recording. One of the only commercially available documents of how this music was presented to the general public during the 1940s (notice the similariities to a later radio–Garrison Keillor's "A Prairie Home Companion" and "American Radio Company"). Side A is titled "Hootenanny," and was aired March 10, 1947 on CBS radio. This show was written and produced by Alan Lomax and features Woody Guthrie, Brownie McGhee, Hally Wood, Sidney Bechet, Pops Foster, Eddie Smith, Sonny Terry, Cisco Houston, and the Coleman Brothers, and the show was hosted by John Faulk. Side B is taken from an August

19, 1940 broadcast, program #10 in CBS radio's "Forcast" series. This show was written by eventual filmmaker Nicholas Ray (*Rebel Without a Cause*) and Alan Lomax, and was hosted by Clifton Fadiman. Performances were given by Woody Guthrie, Burl Ives, the Golden Gate Quartet, Len Doyle, Josh White, and Willie Johnson. Radiola CMR-113 (cas)

Folk Song America: A Smithsonian Collection; Vols 3 & 4—Volumes one and two specified the country-oriented performers in Chapter 7. The last two volumes corral folk artists from the 1950s to the 1990s.
Smithsonian Collection of Recordings CDRD-046-4

Folkways: A Vision Shared (A Tribute to Woody Guthrie and Leadbelly)—Here is a touching tribute by contemporary performers. This album and its companion video came out in 1988 which nicely coincided with Leadbelly and Guthrie's induction into the Rock and Roll Hall of Fame. Artists performing the Guthrie compositions are as follows: Bob Dylan, "Pretty, Boy Floyd"; John Mellencamp, "Do Re Mi"; Bruce Springsteen, "I Ain't Got No Home" and "Vigilante Man"; U2, "Jesus Christ"; Arlo Guthrie, "East Texas Red"; Willie Nelson, "Philadelphia Lawyer"; Emmylou Harris, "Hobo's Lullabye"; Pete Seeger with Sweet Honey in the Rock, and Doc Satson & The Little School House Chorus, "This Land is Your Land." The Leadbelly songs and their interpretations are as follows: Sweet Honey in the Rock, "Sylvie" and "Gray Goose"; Brian Wilson, "Goodnight Irene"; Little Richard and Fishbone, "Rock Island Line"; Taj Mahal, "The Bourgeois Blues."
Columbia CK-44034

Guthrie, Arlo—*Alice's Restaurant* Rising Son RSR-CD-002
Hobo's Lullaby Rising Son RSR-CD-2060

Guthrie, Arlo & Pete Seeger—*Precious Friend*
Warner Bros. 2 3644-2
Together in Concert Reprise 2RS-2214 (cas)

Gunning, Sarah Ogan—*The Silver Dagger*
Rounder 0051 (LP)

Guthrie, Woody—*Dust Bowl Ballads* (rec. 1940).
Rounder 1040
The Greatest Songs of Woody Guthrie. A total of 23 Guthrie songs, performed by Joan Baez, Jim Kweskin, Country Joe McDonald, Woody Guthrie & Cisco Houston, Woody Guthrie, Ramblin' Jack Elliott, Odetta, and the Weavers.
Vanguard Twofer VCD-35/3
Library of Congress Recordings (rec. 1940, includes spoken commentary in Guthrie's wry, dry, and witty delivery). Rounder 3 CD-1041/2/3
Long Way to Travel: The Unreleased Folkways Masters 1944-1949 (includes extensive notes and rare photos). Smithsonian/Folkways SFWCD-40046
This Land Is Your Land Folkways 31001E (LP)
Woody Guthrie Sings Folk Songs (with Cisco Houston, Leadbelly, et al.). Smithsonian/Folkways SFCD-40007

Guthrie, Woody & Arlo and the Guthrie Family—*Woody's 20 Grow Big Songs* Warner Bros. 45020-2

Guthrie, Woody & Leadbelly—*Original Vision*
Smisonian/Folkways SFCD-40001

Houston, Cisco—*The Folkways Years, 1944-1961* (includes 8 previously unreleased tracks, 2 of which are duets with Woody Guthrie; extensive biographical and song notes).
Smithsonian/Folkways SFWCD-400059
Sings Woody Guthrie Vanguard VMD-2131

Ives, Burl—*The Best of Burl Ives* MCA2 MCAC2-4034
Sings Little White Duck and Other Children's Favorites
Columbia CK-33183

Jackson, Aunt Molly—*Library of Congress Recordings*
Rounder 1002 (LP)

Leadbelly (Huddie Ledbetter)—*Go Down Old Hannah* (Vol. 6 of The Library of Congress Recordings Series).
Rounder CD-1099
Golden Classics, Part One: Bourgeois Blues
Collectables COLCD-5183
King of the 12-String Guitar Columbia/Legacy CK-46776
Leadbelly Columbia CK-30035E
Midnight Special (The Library of Congress Recordings series) Rounder CD-1044
Sings Folk Songs (with Woody Guthrie, Cisco Houston, Sonny Terry) Smithsonian/Folkways CDSF-40010

Lomax, John A., Jr.—*Sings American Folksongs*
Folkways 3508 (LP)

McGhee, Brownie & Sonny Terry—*Blues Masters, Vol. 5*
Storyville STCD-8005
Brownie McGhee & Sonny Terry
Smithsonian/Folkways CDSF-40011
Jump Little Children EPM (Blues Collection)15785-2

Pastures of Plenty: An Austin Celebration of Woody Guthrie— Dejadisc DJD-3207

The Prestige/Folklore Years, Volumes 1-4:—
Volume One: All Kinds of Folks
Prestige/Folklore PRCD-9001
Volume Two: The New City Blues
Prestige/Folklore PRCD 9002
Volume Three: Roots and Branches
Prestige/Folklore PRCD-9003
Volume Four: Singing Out Loud
Prestige/Folklore PRCD-9904

Seeger, Mike—*Oldtime Country Music* Rounder CD-0278

Seeger, Peggy—*The Folkways Years 1955-1992: Songs of Love and Politics* Smithsonian/Folkways SFCD-40048

Seeger, Peggy & Mike—*American Folksongs for Children*
Rounder 2CD-11543/4

Seeger, Pete—*Abiyoyo and other Story Songs for Children*
Smithsonian/FolkwaysSFCD-45001

American Industrial Ballads
Smithsonian/Folkways SFCD-40058
Darling Corey and Goofing-Off Suite
Smithsonian/Folkways SFCD-40018
The Essential Pete Seeger   Vanguard Twofer VCD-97/98
Live at Newport (1963-1965)   Vanguard VCD-77008
Waist Deep in the Big Muddy and Other Love Songs
Columbia/Legacy CK-57311
*We Shall Overcome: The Complete Carnegie Hall Concert,
June 8, 1963*   Columbia 2 C2K-45312

Seeger, Pete, Jane Sapp & Si Kahn—*Carry It On* (songs of
America's working people).   Flying Fish 2 FF-70104

Talking Union—The pro-union songs by the Almanac
Singers and Pete Seeger and chorus. This album, not
listed as being in print, is accompanied with a booklet
containing introductory notes by Pete Seeger, and
annotation by Philip S. Fouer, as well as lyrics to each
selection. The songs are: "We Shall Not Be Moved,"
"Roll the Union On," "Casey Jones," "Miner's Lifeguard,"
"Solidarity Forever," "Get Thee Behind Me," "The Union
Maid," "All I Want," "Talking Union," "The Union Train,"
and "Which Side Are You On?"
Folkways FH5285 (LP) (OP)
Note:
Send for catalog/record to: Smithsonian/Folkways
Records, Office of Folklife Programs, 955 L'Enfant
Plaza, Suite 2600, Washington, D.C. 20560

A Tribute to Leadbelly—Selections by Pete Seeger, Arlo
Guthrie, Sonny Terry & Brownie McGhee, and the
Lundberg Travelers.   Tomato-70665

A Tribute to Woody Guthrie—A live performance by Arlo
Guthrie, Odetta, Bob Dylan, Judy Collins, Pete Seeger,
Richie Havens, Tom Paxton, Joan Baez, Country Joe
McDonald, Earl Robinson, Jack Elliott, with narration by
Will Geer, Robert Ryan, Peter Fonda, Judy Collins. I
remember the late Phil Ochs, who modeled his topical
protest songwriting on that of Guthrie, saying in a taped
interview that when he wasn't invited to sing at this
concert, he sat in the Carnegie Hall audience with a
heavy heart and much bitterness for being rejected.
Alas, that shouldn't deter any of you from checking this
out, it is very well done.   Warner Bros. 26036-2

**The Weavers (Pete Seeger, Lee Hays, Ronnie Gilbert,
Fred Hellerman)**—*Almanac*   Vanguard VMD-79100
At Carnegie Hall (rec. live, 12/24/55).
Vanguard VMD-73101
Volume 2   Vanguard VMD-79075
Classics   Vanguard VMD-73122
Kisses Sweeter Than Wine (recorded live in 1947;
contains rare, unreleased recordings made during the
blacklist era; includes booklet with notes by Weaver
members and a bonus CD by Leadbelly).
Omega 2 OCD-3021/22
Reunion at Carnegie Hall 1963 (with Vernie Krause,
Frank Hamilton, Eric Darling).
Analogue Productions AAPFLE-005
Wasn't That a Time: The Early Years
Vanguard 4 VCD4-147/50

The Weavers On Tour   VanguardVCD-73116

White, Josh, Jr. & Robin Batteau—*Jazz, Ballads & Blues (A
Tribute to Josh White, Sr.)*   Rykodisc RCD-10033

Videos
Pete Seeger: A Song and a Stone (1972)—A documentary
tour of Pete Seeger traveling from one performance site
to another. We join Seeger on plane flights, during
rehearsals, and pre- and post-concert meetings with
television producers. Most interesting is Johnny Cash
making a plea to his television audience, characterizing
Seeger as a great American and patriot. On the show
Seeger gets the Nashville audience to sing along with
him and Cash—"It Takes a Worried Man to Sing a
Worried Song." Also enlightening is Seeger's radio
pronouncement that "The whole American nation is
going to be judged as criminals after this Viet Nam-
thing is over." Seeger sings children songs, protest
songs, labor songs, and songs of seafaring, love,
ecology, and more. Seeger is also seen on his ship
that's part of The Hudson River Restoration Sloop
Committee to clean up that river.
85 min. color HHT B $14.95

A Vision Shared—A Tribute to Woody Guthrie and
Leadbelly (1988)—Same artists and songs listed in
records section—this time making a video of each song.
70 min. color SMVE 19V49006V $14.98

The Weavers: Wasn't That a Time! (1980)—The film of
the last reunion concert by the Weavers. A touching
documentary that takes into account Lee Hays'
declining health—he's confined to a wheel chair after
losing his legs—and the realization this will be the
original members' last hurrah. Rare footage of the early
days before the McCarthy blacklisting, and interviews
illustrate the different personalities of the four members.
Archival photos and an eerie television clip of the group
from the 1950s are mixed in with concert preparations
and updates on each of the Weavers. The
documentary features more than 20 songs by the
Weavers, including "Wasn't That a Time," "Kisses Sweet
Than Wine," "If I Had a Hammer," "Good Night Irene,"
"Hay Una Mujer Desaparecida," and " How Will I Know."
78 min. color WRV 338304V $19.98

Postscript

At present (Summer 1995) there are only 6 recordings by
Bill Haley on the market—and there are 110 recordings by
Elvis Presley.

TOP 40: BIBLIOGRAPHY

All the quotations and significant appropriated ideas used in *Popular Music and the Underground* are cited by author and title directly in the text. Rather than list all of the many hundreds of books, articles, and liner notes used in this history, I prefer to present here a selected bibliography that will serve as a guide to the best further reading on the subjects discussed in this book.

The following "Top 40" books are what I consider the best general histories of popular mainstream jazz, blues, and country music of the period 1900-1950. This list is not exhaustive. A number of excellent histories did not make the cut. For example, David Ewin's *All the Years of American Popular Music* (Prentice-Hall, 1977) covers the period from 1620 to 1970s in over 800 pages. It includes many important facts; the problem is that a good deal of the book concerns pre-1900 history, and it often only lists facts without giving any analysis. So, let us now move on and examine my choices for the "Top 40" books.

POPULAR MUSIC: TOP 10

1) Clarke, Donald. *The Rise and Fall of Popular Music.* New York: St. Martin's Press, 1995. This is a scintillating read. Author Clarke takes the reader from the "Origins of Popular Music" (Chapter 1), to, what he labels, "The Heat Death of Pop Music" (Chapter 18). In Clarke's downcast view about the music scene of the past twenty years, "The twin problems, fuelling each other, have been overuse of technology and the sound of money shouting." The premise is supported by sound arguments. The book covers minstrelsy, vaudeville and Tin Pan Alley, the Jazz Age and the markets of race and hillbilly, the swing era and its shift to the singers, and the new music of pop of the 1950s to the '90s—rock, soul, and country. Clarke is knowledgeable on all fronts, and everything he writes is of great interest to anyone wishing to expand their knowledge on the *total* music scene. Clarke's *The Penguin Encyclopedia of Popular Music* is the source book that I prefer to all the other "pop" encyclopedias, and his investigation of Billie Holiday, *Wishing on the Moon: The Life and Times of Billie Holiday*, is a warmly written and welcome addition to Holiday-lore.

2) Hamm, Charles. *Yesterdays: Popular Song in America.* New York: W.W. Norton & Co. 1983. Probably the best survey of the entire popular music scene from colonial times up to the rock revolution into the late 1970s. The early sections cover the British concert and stage music in Early America, Irish, Italian, German, and African-American sources not noted in my book (prior to the late 1880s, at least), and consequently can give the reader a stronger foundation in this period. Over half of the Hamm's 475-page book concentrates on pre-1900 music. Of this initial section, the chapter devoted to Stephen Foster's stylistic impact on the songs of the Civil War and the postwar years is particularly enlightening. However, the author's jump from the mid-1930s swing and Broadway hits to the 1950s rock'n'roll is a scant twenty pages. Still, for the early history this book is unsurpassed.

3) Hemming, Roy. *The Melody Lingers On: The Great Songwriters and Their Movie Musicals.* New York: Newmarket Press, 1986. A unique study that concentrates on the essential composers of the "Golden Age of Pop," and examines them in alphabetical order, chapter by chapter, for each. Included are Harold Arlen, Irving Berlin, George Gershwin, Jerome Kern, Jimmy McHugh, Cole Porter, Ralph Rainger, Richard Rodgers, Harry Warren, Richard Whiting. Another section, "And Not To Be Forgotten" treats Nacio Herb Brown, Hoagy Carmichael, Frank Loesser, Arthur Schwartz, Jule Styne, and James Van Heusen. Each chapter begins with a succinct appraisal of the composer, and then goes on to study their major movies and their songs. The book reminds audiences of today that "yesterday's" songs were often written for the stage and film by craftsmen who did not perform the songs themselves and often were constrained by plot line development, character illumination, and the producers' demands, particularly in Hollywood, for a hit song. Each entry concludes with lists of

the composers movies and songs on tape and disc. The book is lavishly adorned with studio stills from representative films, as well as a portrait photo of each composer. The author's collaboration with David Hajdu, *Discovering Great Singers of Classic Pop: A New Listener's Guide to the Sounds and Lives of their Top Performers and Their Recordings, Movies, and Their Videos* (New York: Newmarket Press, 1991), fits nicely as a companion-piece.

4) Kinkle, Roger D. *The Complete Encyclopedia of Popular Music and Jazz 1900-1950.* New Rochelle, New York: Arlington House-Publishers, 1974.
Simply stated, there is absolutely nothing like this work for detailed information about pop music of the first half of this century. It is probably too heavy a burden for most general readers to buy because it is four volumes and, regrettably, out of print. It must be seen (it would take days to read) to be believed. Get thee to a library. Volume One gives a plan to the work and explains the abbreviations, lists the record labels, and gives a cursory overview of "Fifty Years of Popular Music and Jazz," before moving on to a year-by-year listing of Broadway musicals (opening; performances; cast; book and lyrics; music composer; and songs of note) and the most popular songs (and songwriters). Beginning with the year 1909, the popular songs listed are followed by representative recordings--ah, it's so good to finally see list upon list of specific song titles and record labels of neglected though seminal artists such as Billy Murray, Peerless Quartet, Pryor's Band, Selvins Novelty Orchestra, Ted Lewis, Sophie Tucker and many others. Volumes Two and Three are, "Biographies A through K" and "Biographies L through Z," respectively. Each artist is numbered, e.g., Irving Aaronson (1), Fanny Brice (194), Jean Goldkette (679), Vaughn Monroe (1290), Lillian Russell (1585), up to Bob Zurke (2006). Dates and places of birth, and, where applicable, death dates are given, followed by a summation of that artist's achievements and a listing of key recordings (group name recorded under, record company and numerical assignment). Volume Four is a librarian's and discographer's dream: "Indexes & Appendices." Donald Clarke summarizes: "Incredibly accurate, Kinkle's work was computer typeset in the USA twenty years ago, and after many years of using it I finally found one mistake: he got Judy Garland's death date wrong by six months."

5) Mordden, Ethan. *The Hollywood Musical.* London: David & Charles, 1982.
Each year as I prepare for my course on the "Hollywood Musical", I go to the bookstore and make out my order form for this book, knowing full well it won't be available. Hope against hope. This is my favorite book on the history of Hollywood musicals. It's written with acerbic wit, and the ease with which Mordden marches through chapters such as "The Texture of Sound," "What's a Musical?" "The Inertia of Genre," to "The Texture of Rock," is a credit to his enormous knowledge and love for the form. Mordden's concise way of routing through history is readable and truly fascinating. In less than 250 pages, the author presents us with an entire world view of musicals and treats us to the essential stars, studios, composers, and films of note. Again, here is a book that is out of print and I'm recommending it--who else can I tell this to, but to you? Find this in a library--whatta read! His ending is saved for "The Ethan Mordden Hall of Fame and Disrepute," eight pages of scathing, hilarious opinions about such things as: "Best Films/ Worst Films"; "Best Performances/Worst Performances/Most Bizarre Performance/Most Underrated Performances." Some examples: "Most Distinguished & Least Distinguished Cast Assembled for One Film" (*Show Boat*, 1936, most distinguished, and *Show Boat*, 1951, least distinguished); "Most Wonderful Woman" (Rita Hayworth); "Most Wonderful Man" (Fred Astaire); and, my favorite, the "Fernando Lamas Award For Best Male Singer Born in Argentina Who Appeared in *Four Jills And A Jeep*" (Dick Haymes). There is certainly something amiss in the world today, when a book like this is out of print. Almost as valuable is Clive Hirschhorn's *The Hollywood Musical: Every Hollywood Musical From 1927 to the Present Day.* New York: Crown Publishers, Inc. 1981. This is a coffee table book that gives a year by year entry, with a cast listing, summary storyline, list of songs and composers, a still photo, and fine analysis of artistic importance (or lack therof) for every major musical film. Like all other writers on musicals, the author fails to include the singing cowboy series films. Indispensable for a musicals fanatic, and also fun to browse through idly.

6) Pleasants, Henry. *The Great American Popular Singers*. New York: Simon & Schuster, 1985.
Pleasants is one of the most astute writers of popular music. He began as a classical music historian/critic, and as a result, he has some interesting things to say in regard to the different disciplines. This is particularly evident when he compares rehearsal techniques between the two idioms in the chapter entitled "The Art of the American Popular Singer." Pleasants is not interested in whether classical or popular music is better than the other. His premise is that, "The popular singer does things, primary in matters of phrasing, shading, rhythm, enunciation, accentuation and even vocal production, that lie beyond the capabilities and the predilections of most classical singers. It's not a question of superiority or inferiority. It is a question of musical idiom." Pleasants covers the very popular singers such Al Jolson, Bing Crosby, Frank Sinatra, and the less well known such as Mildred Bailey. In each case, he analyzes such musical components as vocal range, timbre, and idiosyncratic deviations that separate the singers from their contemporaries.

7) Simon, George Thomas. *The Big Bands*. New York: Collier Books, 1978.
America's dean of big band history, George T. Simon, began his critical career in the mid-1930s. As a result, he had no models for writing about jazz and pop. (During this era, jazz and pop were made of similar cloth.) The distinction between the two was largely created by magazine reviews. *The Big Bands* gives blanket coverage to all the major, and most minor, big bands of the 1930s and 1940s. In the first part of the book, "The Big Bands--Then," Simon sizes up the scene: the leaders, public, vocalists, arrangers, businessmen, movies, and press, that comprised the context of the rise of the big bands. The second section, "Inside the Big Bands," evaluates band leaders from Charlie Barnet to Paul Whiteman on the basis of their historic position in the pantheon of pop. The third section "Inside More of the Big Bands," covers the horn-playing leaders, arranging leaders, singing leaders, piano-playing leaders, mickey-mouse bands, and so on.

8) Whitburn, Joel. *Joel Whitburn's Pop Memories 1890-1954: The History of American Popular Music*. Menomonee Falls, Wisconsin: Record Research Inc., 1986.
This is just one of many major collections organized by musical genre put out by the "Master of the Charts." The *Billboard* chart references throughout *Popular Music and the Underground* are from this book. The contents include an explanation of the convoluted, yet all-encompassing, manner in which the numbers were arrived at. "Chronology of Milestones in Popular Music/Recording History 1877-1954", is a seven page synopsis of popular music highlights. The book cross-references multiple hit recordings of single songs, and includes a chronological list of the number one hits from 1890 to 1954. The book is organized by artist with a brief description of the artist's career and the charting of every song that placed in the top thirty, its peak position, the date it entered, the record company, and additional tidbits. Many "chart"-oriented books deal with the years after 1930, but for the pre-1930s period this book and Kinkle are *the* prime sources.

9) Whitcomb, Ian. *After the Ball: Pop Music from Rag to Rock*. New York: Limelight Editions, 1986.
Ian Whitcomb brings an insouciant British air to his adopted country, and a mastery of breezy, Tin Pan Alley argot that makes for an enjoyable reading experience. Let me share with you his cheeky writing style: "Women contributed most to the decline of jazz music. Oh, in the beginning they embraced it as a fashion. A new hat, a new drink. Those tomboys, the flappers, leapt on it, joyfully, shimmying, and charlestoning. Observers reported that jazz made some women violent. Girls and matrons jumped on top of tables screaming and tearing their clothes off whenever cornetist Nick La Rocca of the ODJB let fly with some of his hot licks. The illegitimate birth-rate rose dramatically ... solo charlestoning--self-expression--swiftly became smoochy dueting in their hands. They fox-trotted their chosen male to the tune of 'All Alone' down the garden path and into the rose-covered cottage. Thus were boys with genuine interest in the technicalities of music betrayed by their girl partners. 'God! look at that bunch of corny old rackety jazz records' she exclaimed, as she turned out the basement in the late thirties. Scarcely an hour and the trash can was crammed with McKinney's Cotton Pickers, the City Blues Blowers. Poor jazz hadn't got a chance!" Whitcomb has written little that I haven't smiled and nodded a great deal at. Not only is

he a masterful collector of history, Whitcomb is also a performing curator of songs and dances long forgotten--in a more perfect world he would be royalty; instead, he'll have to satisfy himself as one of the many stars, albeit underground, of the popular music world. *The New Yorker* was on target when they praised Whitcomb as, "Brash, learned, funny, and perspicacious ... he goes all the way back to the first pop best-seller (in sheet music, of course), 'After the Ball,' and all the way forward to the nineteen-sixties."

10) Wilder, Alec. *American Popular Song: The Great Innovators, 1900-1950.* New York: Oxford Press, 1990.

A major work in the annals of music criticism, because Wilder had cachet with the classical and scholarly world of academia. When he pronounced, essentially, that the best of popular compositions were equal to those of classical music, he was taken seriously. While some of the author's analysis and musical diagrams (notation) may be foreboding to the general reader, Wilder's explanations quickly land earthbound, bringing the uninitiated back into the fold. Wilder examined about 17,000 compositions, and makes mention of some 800. He discusses the leading composers and their songs with compassion and admiration, but he is quick to dismiss any work that he finds lacking. The only weakness of Wilder's effort is the omission of his own worthy compositions. This book is a good reminder to all of us when making comparisons between the music of today and yesterday. "Yesterday's music" was dependent upon the composer and lyricist to create songs primarily for other performers to sing and dance to in stage and film productions. During the first half of this century Broadway averaged between 20 and 30-some musicals per year--compared to less than five original musicals per year today. Plus, many of those songs became part of the world of pop, unlike original most music from today's Broadway.

JAZZ MUSIC: TOP 10

For some reason, few jazz histories have found universal favor. It can't be for the lack of books on the subject, because there are literally hundreds of works on this very special music. There is such a passion for the music form, and so many styles within the form, that it may be impossible to suit the diversity of readers on the subject. Many of the histories specialize in a particular segment of the music, so that there simply aren't as many overall histories as the massive numbers first imply. Here I have tried to make up a list that reflected the main thrusts of *Popular Music and the Underground.* Most histories shortchange singers because, as noted in the Introduction and Preface, jazz is usually thought of as an instrumental form. My choices include a number of vocal studies.

1) Balliett, Whitney. *American Singers.* New York: Oxford University Press, 1979.
If I could write like Whitney Balliett, I'd never teach another class. Angels sing and Balliett writes. Reading his prose is an experience that all lovers of history should savor. This particular book, like his *Alec Wilder Friends: A Small Aristocracy* (Boston: Houghton Mifflin, 1974), is a series of profiles on vocalists attuned to "The Golden Age of Popular Music." Cult singers with cabaret sensibilities like Teddi King, Barbara Lea, Sylvia Syms (this chapter, titled "Moonbeam Moscowitz," is priceless), Hugh Shannon, Blossom Dearie, Mabel Mercer, and Bobby Short, were given a slight opening into the otherwise restrictive world of jazz because of Balliett's embrace. (This subject is also debated in the text.) A backup choice for the aristocratic creme de la creme tradition of cabaret that Balliett has supported and kept on the jazz front-burner, is James Gavin's *Intimate Nights: The Golden Age of New York Cabaret.* New York: Grove Weidenfeld, 1991. This history admittedly has a more theatrical bent, but as we have seen in the early history of jazz, connections between theater and jazz were not unfamiliar. Gavin is well-versed in jazz history, and for those readers who wish to investigate the chichi fare of the cabaret milieu, this is the best choice.

2) Charters, Samuel B., and Leonard Kunstadt. *Jazz: The History of the New York Scene.* New York: DaCapo Press, Inc., 1981.

Here is a history that really drew me in. The title might suggest, to some, an insulated view of music exclusively east of the Hudson River. That is not the case. By the 1920s, New Orleans and Chicago had been established as the central core of the jazz world (Kansas City was swinging away, but the town was off the main track for any notice at that time). However, all roads would eventually lead to New York, and this history captures it all. The symbiotic relationship between dance halls, the ragtime of James Reece's Europe, the cabarets, the theater, and the influx of out-of-town newcomers made for a fertile and colorful mix. An excellent smattering of visual ephemera gives this book an additional attractiveness—gritty black and white tintypes of yesterday. The collection, and Kunstadt's assiduous research, has been placed in a wonderful history, full of unusually perceptive quotes from those who made the music, and a construct that takes us from ragtime to bebop and cool.

3) Collier, James Lincoln. *The Making of Jazz: A Comprehensive History* London: Papermac, 1981.
And James Lincoln Collier seems to be caught in a vitriolic gun battle of rites and wits with Wynton Marsalis and writer Stanley Crouch over the role of race in the development of jazz. White versus Black (the Lincoln Center showdown—another story...). I feel compelled to bring this matter up because one gets the feeling lately that choosing a book for historic and artistic merit also means choosing sides for Collier (White) and against Marsalis and Crouch (Black). I'll have none of it. I've read most of the books and heard all the arguments. This book, in my opinion, is one of the best written, and most important histories on the music. Collier, to be sure, has opinions, but what historian worth reading doesn't? His is a comprehensive history up to the fusion period, which he does not investigate, although it had occurred by the time of this study. Collier's is one of the few histories that attempt to analyze the music and make the conclusions understandable to the general reader (not as easy as it sounds). This is a book I've enjoyed using for my upper level jazz history classes, and one that is at the top of my list.

4) Driggs, Frank, and Harris Lewine. *Black Beauty, White Heat: A Pictorial History of Classic Jazz, 1920-1950.* New York: W. Morrow, 1982.
No jazz book matches the astounding photos and ephemera (non-photographic pictures like newspaper or magazine ads and club menus) of this delightful study. The book begins with a touching forward by John Hammond, and then moves on to an eleven-page "Jazz Fan Memoir" by Paul Bacon. The memoir is about the joy of collecting jazz records—78 records; the matrix numbers, the label designs, et al. Today's younger readers, bombarded by technology and excess of product, can learn a great deal about past history and may develop a passion for hard-to-get product by reading this entry. Chapters one to six cover jazz in general, chapter seven deals with the relationship of jazz and film, and chapters eight and nine deal with the movement from swing to bop. The book is coffee table size and most pages are filled with between two and eight or more sumptuous graphics. The only problem, and this can be maddening at times, is that there is no separation between caption information to direct the reader. The writing is worthwhile when you can decipher where it goes, picture-wise. However, as I thumb through this book while writing this entry, I'm again stunned by the impact of these images. It is a *must see.*

5) Fordham, John. *Jazz.* New York: Dorling Kindersley, 1993.
The most modern of all the books in the "Top 40," Fordham's smartly sleek white cover and color photography mixed with black-and-white archival reproductions make this a bargain just on its looks. There's more than just good looks here, though. The author and his art and designers have unfurled a project that is unlike any other on the music scene. Historical connections between blues, ragtime, and brass bands are offered up first, and then it's on to Chicago, New York, swing, bop and cool, and the post-1950 movement of hard bop, free jazz, fusion, and jazz of the 1990s. For each ten-year span, until 1970-1990, there is a unique, two-page spread time chart. For each year is listed "Musicians and Bands," "Venues," "Recordings and Show Business," "Musical Developments," and "Historical Factors." Going down the list, the reader gains access to prime nuggets of information along with LP covers, lighted marquees, programs, magazine covers, record

labels, and much more. Kudos to the designers. The next section, "Anatomy of Instruments," demonstrates vocal, instrumental and technical components of jazz. "Jazz Giants" focuses on twenty selected stars with pictures, a boxed highlight chart, and an explanation of each artist's main contributions. "Techniques" is a study of formal elements that combine to formulate the music. Finally, "A Gallery of Classic Recordings" lists representative records according to genre: "Blues & Roots," "Ragtime & Stride," "Early Singers," "Swing," right up to contemporary movements like "Club Jazz" and " World Beat."

6) Friedwald, Will. *Jazz Singing: America's Great Voices From Bessie Smith to Bebop and Beyond.* New York: Charley Scribner's Sons, 1990.
The author declares up front that vocal jazz tastes are very personal, and that one fan's hero or heroine is another's scapegoat. I like Friedwald's wiseguy declarations—you always know where he stands in regard to each individual or group. However, at times, his putdowns are simply too indelicate for my comfort. But Friedwald knows his history and he knows how to share it. There so many sections that I've reread simply because they are not only informative, but they're so supercharged with enthusiasm that the reader can't wait to listen to the artist discussed in the written passages. Friedwald's mentor, Gary Giddins (author of *Celebrating Bird* and *Rhythm-a-Ning*), sums up beautifully: "Will Friedwald has written the most entertaining, capacious, and in the best sense of the word, idiosyncratic book on jazz singing to date. Always a learned fan, he never lets his sound scholarship get in the way of his enthusiasms, which more often than not are contagious (you should see my Al Bowlly collection). In addition to tracking a Byzantine tradition from Armstrong to Cassandra Wilson, he gives Crosby his due, trembles not at the thought of Jolson, and resurrects countless forgotten band singers. *Jazz Singing* will provoke many arguments and resolve many more—to paraphrase Mildred Bailey, it never is a bore."

7) Gillespie, Dizzy, with Al Fraser. *To Be, or Not To Bop: Memoirs.* Garden City, New York: Doubleday & Company, Inc., 1979.
A rarity here, an autobiography by a leading architect of the bebop movement. Surely no major movement in jazz, or any other form of music, lost so many of its main innovators to drugs before they could tell their story. Dizzy Gillespie was able to emerge from the underground of bebop to gain recognition, financial stability, and have a long, productive career. His story is very involving and fascinating. The transition from a sideman in the swing bands, to premier spokesman for an entire musical movement is told from the musician's point of view for once. Gillespie's co-author has done a masterful job getting so many musicians to give engrossing reminiscences and opinions about the music scene. And the reader gets a full measure for their buck—a jam-packed 552 pages. Almost as good is Nat Shapiro and Nat Hentoff's *Hear Me Talkin' to Ya: The Story of Jazz as Told by the Men Who Made It.* New York: Dover Publications, Inc., 1955. Like *To Be or Not to Bop,* the musicians get to tell the story. The book is framed by its authors around a number of themes—the New Orleans story, the trip to Chicago, the New York scene, and modern development of beop and cool.

8) Gridley, Mark. *Jazz Styles: History & Analysis. 5th Edition.* Englewood Cliffs, New Jersey: Prentice Hall, 1994.
This book, is one of only two textbooks chosen for the musical "Top 40." Textbooks usually have an irritating habit of summarizing chapters and giving lead questions to the students at the conclusions of sections so that they can "bone up" for their upcoming test. Over the years, I have used this book as a text for my upper level Modern Jazz class. My friends outside of the college community often ask me to recommend a book for them on the history of jazz, and this one always receives positive comments. Gridley writes more than just history, and does what his book title promises—he analyzes the music in such a way that those readers who are not technically versed in the written score can understand. He does an excellent job describing musical sounds, which is not easy. As a technical guide to the understanding of the music, Gridley's study is a major contribution. An alternative selection for a textbook on jazz comes from Prentice-Hall Publishers

again. This second book offers up the entire scope of jazz history, from the origins up to fusion and the avant-garde. Porter, Lewis, Michael Villman, and Ed Hazell. *Jazz: From Its Origins to the Present.* Englewood Cliffs, New Jersey, 1993. You don't have to be a college student to read either of these books.

9) Kernfeld, Barry, editor. *The New Grove Dictionary of Jazz.* New York: St. Martin's Press, 1994. Of all of the encyclopedias and dictionaries of jazz, this is tops. The one-time two-volume set can now be purchased in bookstores in one complete package. Editor Kenfeld had, at his command, a number of specialists who wrote particular entries suited to their strengths. Each artist is given an entry of historical documentation, and depending on the information available, a bibliography and a discography. The dictionary doesn't just cover musicians or producers who were or are part of the jazz world. The book is filled with intriguing entries. In just the section on blues can be found: Blues (broken down into subheadings such as: "Origins," "Blues and New Orleans Jazz," "Blues Accompanists," "Blues And White Jazz," "Arranged and Big Band Jazz," "Territory And Kansas City Bands," "White Swing Bands," "The New Orleans Revival," "Blues Shouters," "Rhythm-and-Blues," "Blues In Bop And Derivative Styles," "Blues In Free Jazz," and "Blues in Jazz-Rock And Fusions of Jazz With Other Forms". The word "jazz" itself has 27 pages of definition. Other interesting sections include "Mutes" (description, drawings, and methods of muting are presented) and my favorite, "Nightclubs and Other Venues" which lists the hot spots in international as well as U.S. cities. William F. Lee III, President of the International Foundation for Jazz, wrote, "At last the definitive dictionary of America's music, jazz, is completed and available...*The New Grove Dictionary of Jazz* is a major work which will play an important role in the preservation on furthering of world jazz."

10) Schuller, Gunther. *The Swing Era: The Development of Jazz, 1930-1945.* New York: Oxford University Press, 1989. Gunther Schuller's follow-up to his critically praised study, *Early Jazz: Its Roots and Musical Development*, is a major contribution to jazz scholarship. For this book, the author listened to more than 30,000 recordings, and worked for more than twenty years, producing over 900 pages of the most exhaustively inclusive analysis of jazz music I've ever read. Schuller unearthed the most comprehensive study of the white bands, and his findings challenge what he refers to as the "accumulated wisdom" of the majority of other jazz histories. The contents include the main leaders of the form, Goodman, Ellington, Armstrong; what Schuller titles "The Quintessence of Swing"; "The Great Black Bands"; "The Great Soloists"; "The White Bands"; "The Territory Bands"; "Small Groups"; and "Things to Come." The general reader might be put off by the enormity of this book, or, conversely, might be thrilled to delve headlong into the colossal terrain of the world of the big bands.

BLUES MUSIC: TOP 10

1) Cohn, Lawrence. *Nothing But the Blues: The Music and the Musicians.* New York: Abbeville Press, 1993. Cohn presides over this big, beautiful, coffee-table book as editor, leading blues authorities write chapters on their area of expertise: Samuel Charters, "Workin' On The Building: Roots and Influences"; Richard K. Spottswood, "Country Girls, Classic Blues, and Vaudeville Voices" and "Women and the Blues"; John H. Cowley, "Don't Leave Me Here" and "Non-Commercial Blues—The Field Trips, 1924-60"; Mark A. Humphrey, "Holy Blues: The Gospel Tradition," and "Bright Lights, Big City Urban Blues"; Barry Pearson, "Jump Steady: The Roots of R&B"; Bruce Bastin, "Truckin' My Blues Away East Coast Piedmont Styles"; Jim O'Neal, "I Once Was Lost, But Now I'm Found" and "The Blues Revival of The 1960s"; Mary Katherine Aldin, "Standing At The Crossroads: The Blues Today" and finally , Charles Wolfe, "A Lighter Shade Of Blue: White Country Blues." The last entry is an especially welcomed addition, because so many outstanding rural white blues greats like the Allen Brothers, Riley Puckett, Doc Boggs, Frank Hutchison, Darby and Tarlton, Emmett Miller (a jazzy, black face vaudevillian who introduced Hank Williams' first hit "Lovesick Blues" in 1928), the

Delmore Brothers, and, of course, the Blue Yodler himself, Jimmie Rodgers, among many others, are worthy practitioners of the form. The layout and design of the book are exceptional, and really, just about every style, influence, connection, and transformation of blues music is represented in this large, 400-page study. The reader can gain greater insight into the gospel connections via this tome (my book doesn't weigh in as heavily in this area as I would have liked). An indispensable book.

2) Davis, Francis, *The History of the Blues*. New York: Hyperion, 1995.
A welcome new addition into the blues book sphere. This volume is attractively packaged and studies the origins of blues with "Prehistory/The Kind of Music In The South" and emergence of the commercial blues "The Blues As Such/No Such Thing As The Blues" and "Blues Connotation/From Songsters to Soulsters". The book is sprinkled with an assortment of photographs, and is very well written. It covers all of the commercial blues styles and underscores connections to rock and soul of contemporary America. I especially liked the author's "Blues Timeline," which spans thirteen pages. The timeline is broken into three columns: important dates in blues history; related developments in jazz, pop, and literature by or about blacks; and advances in technology, as well as gains or setbacks for African-Americans.

3) Guralnick, Peter. *Feel Like Going Home: Portraits in Blues & Rock-N-Roll.* New York: E.P. Dutton & Co., Inc., 1971.
Peter Guralnick is one of those "gotta read" authors. Anything he decides to write about is worth any reader's time and attention. As the title suggests, this study links the blues with rock-n-roll. The book consists of individual profiles, that underscore historical progressions. The author briefly traces the evolution of blues from traditional country roots up through city centers such as Memphis and Chicago and right into the halcyon days of rock'n'roll. Country-to-city bluesmen like Muddy Waters, and Howlin' Wolf are profiled in separate chapters, as are rural bluesmen like Johnny Shines, Skip James, and Robert Pete Williams. The chapters on producer Sam Phillips, rockabilly pioneers Jerry Lee Lewis and Charlie Rich, and the owners of Chicago's premier blues label, Chess Records, complete the circle of the alliance between blues and rock music.

4) Harris, Sheldon. *Blues Who's Who: A Biographical Dictionary of Blues Singers.* New Rochelle, New York: DaCappo Press, 1991.
Another coffee-table book, this one is not as glossy nor as sophisticated as Cohn's tome, but it is big and heavy (775 pages) and includes 571 biographies of most of the significant commercial blues singers of this century. The project took nearly 18 years of research (it shows). The author notes, "Each entry has been condensed to the bare facts, without embellishment. They have been gathered from personal interviews and correspondence, a variety of books from many fields, magazine articles, old newspapers, current news items, record album liner notes, bibliographies, discographies, filmographies, publicity information, scrap books, library files, private collections, unpublished material and other sources." Most entries include a picture of the artist and a chronological rundown of professional and personal experiences. The citations at the end include awards, key songs associated with the artist, billings (which include nicknames or titles), influences both on the singer and by the singer on others, and references (including suggested sources for further study). Here's a sample of the painstaking inclusion that most of these entries behold. Mamie Smith noted in Chapter 4 in my book, was the first to record a commercially successful blues tune in 1920 ("Crazy Blues" for Okeh Records-4169). Smith was a vaudeville star of the black theaters and made some movies, and that's about it. Harris goes on for a page of dense type, detailing Smith's entire career—all the club dates, musical revues, and movies. The list of Smith's musical reviews and the theater and the cafe and cabarets that she played in, would take half of a page alone. Let me give you an example. Here is a portion of Harris' entry from 1924 to 1926: "City Auditorium, Houston, TX, c. 1924; Chicago Auditorium, 1924; Indiana Theater, Chicago, 1924; app as headliner, *Syncopationland Revue*, Lafayette Theater, NYC, 1924; app in *Dixie Revue*, Lafayette Theater, NYC, 1924; rec Ajax label, NYC, 1924; worked w. own Jazz Hounds, Lafayette Theater,

NYC, 1924; frequently worked Lincoln Theater, NYC, 1924-5; app in own *Syncopated Revue*, Howard Theater, Washington, DC, 1925; frequently worked Entertainers Cabaret, New Orleans, LA, mid-20s; rec Victor label, NYC, 1926; worked Lafayette Theater, NYC, 1926; app in *Frolicking Around Revue*, Lincoln Theater, 1926; worked Delancey Street Theater, NYC, 1926; toured in own Mamie Smith Company working theater dates on Lowes circuit through South, 1926-7..." And we haven't even gotten into her film career yet! You can't find this kind of completeness in any other study. Here again, we have another history that takes on a different scope than some of the others, and becomes a vital research tool for the serious annotator, teacher, and fan, or can be simply another reference for the general reader to complete the story that was touched on in another work.

5) Keil, Charles. *Urban Blues*. Chicago: The University of Chicago Press, 1969.
Keil's study of the urbanized aspects of the blues in 1966, when this book was first published, sent shock waves throughout the academic blues community. At the time, most studies on blues focused on the archaic rural-folk tradition. There had been a complete exclusion of contemporary blues forms in every major study until Keil's additudinal change of direction. Keil had the audacity to propose to all who cared to listen—and this meant the established blues historians such as Mack McCormick, Samuel Charters, Paul Oliver, Harold Courlander, and Alan Lomax (who personified the "moldy fig mentality" of studying only older, "more authentic" folk blues) that, "If we are ever to understand what urban negro culture is all about, we had best view entertainers and hustlers as culture heroes, integral parts of the whole, rather than as deviants and shadow figures." Keil was perceptive enough to realize that Muddy Waters didn't stop becoming important just because he plugged in his guitar. Today, Waters is regarded as one of the pantheon figures in blues history and a direct link to rock-n-roll. But at the time of Keil's book, he was known only to the "black chitlin' event" followers. He had been recorded as a country singer in the 1940s, but once he began wearing shiny suits and catering to denizens of the urban bar circuit, the blues scholars wouldn't study him. Then, along came Keil. *Urban Blues* is a profound book in the history of popular culture. It certainly changed my way of thinking back then, and it still holds true today. Required reading for anyone remotely interested in the world of America's musical heritage.

6) Murray, Albert. *Stomping the Blues*. New York: McGraw-Hill Book Company, 1976.
Murray writes with philosophical concern that many of us miss out on. The reader may find this a welcome relief from the overly taxonomical stance that a majority of historians pursue. The first section of this treatise makes comparison between the black church customs and those of the secular world, assigned with the winsome heading, "The Blue Devils and the Holy Ghosts." One of the author's crucial doctrines is that, "Blues music, regardless of its lyrics, almost always induces dance movement that is the direct opposite of resignation, retreat, or defeat. Moreover, as anyone who has ever shared the fun of any blues-oriented social function should never need to be reminded, the more lowdown, dirty, and mean the music, the more instantaneously and pervasively sensual the dance gestures it engenders." The layout and design of the photographs and graphics, including posters, record labels, commercial announcements, and sheet music, was produced by Harris Lewine, the same compiler who fashioned the Frank Driggs book, detailed in the jazz section. Speaking of jazz, if there is one limitation this book has, and most books have many (mine included), is that Murray is too jazz-oriented. It would have been interesting to read about parallel developments in city blues (rhythm and blues) activities.

7) Oakley, Giles. *The Devil's Music: A History of the Blues*. New York: Harvest Books, 1976.
An excellent blues study. This compact book is broken up into 6 parts: 1 (Early slavery minstrel to ragtime, New Orleans Jazz and Blues, and Formal Blues of W.C. Handy); 2 (Including individual rural innovators like Blind Lemon Jefferson, Charlie Patton, and covering the barrel house piano circuit, and the city migration); 3 (including the Classic Vaudeville blues of Bessie Smith and the rest); 4 (covers early recording history and those field units sent down south to Atlanta and Memphis); 5 (chronicles the emergence of city blues during the Depression and after); 6 (discusses the post-war blues period). The undercurrent is that this music was vilified by upstanding citizenry,

resulting in the title, "The Devil's Music." The author includes many examples of blues lyrics, and interspersed throughout are telling quotations from key blues performers. *The New York Times* wrote, "Numerous quotations from such luminaries as Jelly Roll Morton, Eubie Blake, and Muddy Waters add an impressionistic resonance to the work ... (*The Devil's Music*) is a sound primer on the historical development of the blues. With its fine illustrations and generous sprinkling of authentic lyrics, it is illuminating and altogether in keeping with the spirit of the music."

8) Oliver, Paul. *The Story of the Blues*. Randor, Pa.: Chilton Books, 1982.
Paul Oliver was one of the important chroniclers of blues history in America. This liberally illustrated study begins with the African-American connection in the South. The author is particularly adept at scrutinizing the attitudes of the oppressed and the oppressors, which illuminate the means, chants, work songs and plantation frolics that ensued. Minstrelsy, as well as juke joint revelry, is discussed and, as always in this exploratory work, contextualized by lyrics, posters, and photographs. The author, perhaps stung by Charlie Keil's criticism back in 1966, incorporates the citified blues of shiny suits and electric guitars that he had ignored earlier.

9) Palmer, Robert. *Deep Blues*. New York: Viking Press, 1981.
Deep Blues very well might be a metaphor for Palmer's style—this is a deep, intellectual, probing discourse on the blues. Palmer is insightful, and presents the reader with plenty to think about. There are no pictures or ads. Just Palmer's prose—which, in the skillful hands of a literate writer, conjures up many different kinds of images. Here's a writer I'd love to spend time with. Like Keil, Peter Guralnick, Nick Tosches, and a few others, Palmer stretches the limits of historical writing. Each of these writers fashions history in such a way that it is personal, without losing sight of the music and the practitioners. They each have that rare ability to write in such a way that there is a personal connection, but their personalities do not become the main emphasis. Palmer is one of our "deep" writers worth looking into. Charles Keil agrees: "Palmer's book is full of rich black history, details and dialogue, wonderful memories of recording sessions, parties, performances, and most important, crucial information about the precise points at which deep blues became the highly profitable commodity fetish called 'rock' in the early 1950's."

10) Shaw, Arnold. *Honkers and Shouters: The Golden Years of Rhythm & Blues*. New York: Macmillan Publishing Company, 1978.
I must admit I'm an unabashed fan of Arnold Shaw. Everything he writes is worth reading and thinking about. In many ways, he reminds me of Frank Driggs in that he is interested not *just* in blues, or jazz, or theater music, or popular music, but in the big picture (although, unlike Driggs, I'm not aware of Shaw embracing country & western music in any big way). One of my favorite books is Shaw's study of a swing street in *New York, 52nd St.: The Street of Jazz*, because he made it come alive. Shaw is not a fancy writer, but he gets to the point and knows how to interview his subjects. *Honkers and Shouters* features more than 20 interviews, including some of the last with pioneers such as Louis Jordan and T-Bone Walker. *Honkers and Shouters* was the first full-scale history of rhythm and blues—and it is still the most important. This is the book I use for my upper level "Urban Blues and Rock" class, and each time I use it, I find there are new things yet to investigate.

COUNTRY MUSIC: TOP 10

1) Carr, Patrick, editor. *The Illustrated History of Country Music*. Garden City, New York: Doubleday & Company, Inc., 1980.
This book is officially credited thusly: "by the editors of Country Music magazine, edited by Patrick Carr". I've always associated Patrick Carr with putting this study together since I began using the book as a text for my Country Music USA course. I began the course in 1976 following the tradition established by my mentor, Bill Tallmadge, and, like Tallmadge, I used the bible of country music scholarship, Bill C. Malone's *Country Music U.S.A.* (the source name for our course title). However, when Carr's book came out, I was won over by the variety of writers and their unique take on their

specialized areas. Charles Wolfe authored the two opening chapters about early country music traditions and commercial recordings ("Across the Ocean, "Into the Hills" and "The Birth of an Industry"), as well as Chapter 12 ("Modern Country"). Douglas B. Green wrote Chapters 3, 6, and 8 ("Depression and Boom," "The Road to Nashville", and "The Mountain Sound Revival"); Green collaborated with Bob Pinson on Chapter 4 ("Music From the Lone Star State"), and with William Ivey on Chapters 10 and 11 ("The Nashville Sound" and "The Death of Rock", "The Rise of Country"); J.R. Young wrote Chapter 5 ("The Singing Cowboys"); Roger Williams wrote Chapter 7 ("Hank the Great"); and Nick Tosches was responsible for Chapter 9 ("Rockabilly"). These were among the most important writers in country music at the time of this book's publication. The variety of writing styles, the expertise of their vision, and the thoroughness of the subject matter make this one of the most important history books on the market. This is still my preferred general country music history book.

2) Country Music Foundation. *Country: The Music and the Musicians.* New York: Abbeville Press, 1988. This is the *Big* book of country music. A coffee-table extravaganza and heavy too; make certain your table has fortified legs. Like Carr's book, this colossal tome calls on individual writers to produce various chapters; Wolfe, Green, Tosches and Carr are among the contributors. The book is luxurious—glossy paper, occasional color photos, record labels, posters, advertisements, and multitudinous black and white photos from the extensive treasure trove of the Country Music Foundation's collection. As would be expected, the book covers the early country music traditions of the British ballads and religious songs into the early commercial period into the westernization process, right up through Nashville, pop and rockabilly of the 1950s, into the contemporary country movements of the 1970s to the late 1980s. Besides the already praised format and look of the book, what's so impressive are the writing skills of the participants. The history has been written about since Bill C. Malone's groundbreaking practice in 1968, so that the writers are now liberated to investigate interpretive rifts and solos on the main body of facts. For example, Nolan Porterfield's opening chapter "Hey, Hey, Tell 'Em 'Bout Us: Jimmie Rodgers Visits the Carter Family", is a wonderful essay on the country music ethos—the entire constellation distilled in an essay that is educational, but also thought-provoking. His analysis of the Bristol, Tennessee "Big Bang Theory" and the illusions such a theory produces is exceptional. The other articles are fine, also. A must read.

3) Denisoff, R. Serge. *Sing a Song of Social Significance.* Bowling Green: Bowling Green University Popular Press, 1972.
Ever since two rural Southerners, Leadbelly and Woody Guthrie, made their way to Greenwich Village in the early 1940s, folk and country would never be quite the same again. Although the two arrived separately, but together, they helped establish an urban folk consciousness that created a split between the conservative country philosophy, and that of liberal, Jewish-intellectual inspired theorizing. R. Serge Denisoff recreates the atmosphere in which Ledbelly and Guthrie became the linchpin for liberal city dwellers. Their influence was also embraced by a number of influential performers. These urbanized country performers sang at labor rallies and pushed their commercially viable product into the tiny clubs and coffee houses in the 1940s and, in effect, broke the umbilical cord with country music. Denisoff is a practicing sociology professor, and so his take on the folk and country music beakdown is geared to that discipline. Chapter titles like "Songs of Persuasion and Their Entrepreneurs"; "Christianity, Communism and Commercialism"; "The Song Of Persuasion Revisited"; "Urban Folk Music 'Movement' Research: Value Free?" and "Protest Songs of the Old and New Left" are prime examples of this kind of discipline. This is one of the few books that specifically addresses the split between country and folk. It might be "too heavy" for some not wishing to swim in the stream of   chapter titles like "Protest songs and skits of American Trotskyists." A more basic connection between country and folk is offered as an alternative selection for book number three in the country-folk constellation. Baggelaar, Kristin, and Donald Milton. *Folk Music: More Than A Song.* New York: Thomas Y. Crowell Company, 1976. With the explosion of country and western music's popularity in the past ten

years, no more contemporary studies list country and folk music together. This book is the last of a dying breed. *Popular Music and the Underground* described how country music and folk were literally divorced when politics and race combined to distance the urban folkies from their rural relatives. The vision of country and folk as one in the same is embraced by Baggelaar and Milton. String band stars of the early period (Gid Tanner, Riley Puckett, Buell Kazee, et al.), are mixed in with Cajun, western swing and black rural bluesmen, as well with the urban folkies such as Woody Guthrie, Pete Seeger, Bob Dylan, the Byrds, and others.

4) Green, Douglas B. *Country Roots: The Origins of Country Music*. New York: Hawthorn Books, Inc., 1976.
Douglas B. Green is one of my heroes. This is one prolific guy. During the 1970s and '80s, everytime you'd turn around, he was coming out with yet another article in a magazine, or writing a couple of chapters in somebody else's book when he wasn't writing one of his own, or co-authoring one (oh, yes, I almost forgot–he was also Oral Historian at the Country Music Foundation, a contributing editor of *Bluegrass Unlimited*, an associate editor of both *Country Music World* and *Muleskinner News*, and editor of the *Journal of Country Music*). So you're saying to yourself, "OK, What's the big deal? This guy likes to write." Well, there's just one more thing. In the early 1980s, Green established a singing trio that revived the traditions of the singing cowboys. Now billed as Ranger Doug, "Idol of American Youth" (in addition to his other monikers–"Sgt. Dudley, RCMP" and "Trader Doug"), he leads the colorful and wacky Riders in the Sky. And he writes great cowboy songs to boot. Here is a Renaissance Man for all seasons. This book is a good, solid, easy to read coffee-table history of country history, from the early roots to honky tonk and country pop of that time period (1976). On pages 199 to 213 Green put together a crackerjack "Chronology" of country music history from 1877 to 1975, including the "Top Five Records, 1923-1975." Gerry Woods, reviewing for *Billboard* magazine wrote, "With respect and reverence for the roots, Green paints an historically accurate portrait of what has happened and will happen in country music. A valuable, enlightening chronology ... fascinating photos."

5) Malone, Bill C. *Country Music U.S.A.: A Fifty Year History*. Austin: The University of Texas Press, 1968.
Here is the most important book in the history of country music. Although Robert Shelton's *The Country Music Story* came out first (the book was a combination history and photographic study), Malone's book achieved the scholarly stature required of a serious history. What is so amazing is that this early history still stands up as a valid and significant work. This is the Bible. All other country books owe something to this pre-eminent opus. Malone states in his preface, "The neglect of country music is primarily to two factors: the scarcity of basic source materials and the belief held by many authorities that the music is unworthy of serious attention." The opening chapter, "The Folk Background–Before The Coming of Commercialism", should be read by everyone today to grasp the true roots of this musical heritage. In writing this book, I've probably re-read Malone's work a minimum of 20 times. Malone gave serious attention to country music–and, for that, he deserves a deep bow of gratitude. When *Country Music U.S.A.* came out, it received universal acclaim. *Stereo Review* wrote "It will stand as a basic source of reference for students of country music for many years to come–probably forever. But it is also, I hasten to add, far more than a secure refuge for scholars. It is a fascinating narrative and a model of perceptive and judicious musical and social analysis and criticism." If the reader is looking for something from this author that is not so overwhelming, here is a lighter, more recent alternative. Bill C. Malone. *Singing Cowboys and Musical Mountaineers: Southern Culture and the Roots of Country Music*. Athens, Georgia: The University of Georgia Press, 1993.

6) McCloud, Barry, and contributing writers. *Definitive Country: The Ultimate Encyclopedia of Country Music and Its Performers*. New York: Perigee Books, 1995.
All of the four music forms that make up the "Top 40" need an encyclopedia. For country music, this book is the paramount achievement. McCloud began it ten years ago–what an tour de force!

With over 1,200 entries and over 500 photographs this book weighs in at 1,132 pages—easily the winner of our "Top 40" sweepstakes for the biggest book. Of course, big doesn't mean much if the book isn't good. This book is terrific. Building on all that knowledge gleaned since Malone's book in 1968, it offers new information, and heaps of it. Brother duets and cowboys from the Northeast whom I'd never heard of can be found within these pages. At the end of each entry, the author lists recommended albums. The final 200 pages or so are set aside for awards, addresses, radio stations, movies, and a bibliography. If this book is too expensive, or just too heavy (it ties *Blues Who's Who* in the weight category), then an alternative is the excellent *The Comprehensive Country Music Encyclopedia*. The editors of Country Music Magazine. New York: Random House, 1994. It is a superb choice.

7) Morthland, John. *The Best of Country Music*. New York: Doubleday & Company, 1984.
The Morthland book is billed as "A critical guide to the 750 greatest albums, including: Jimmie Rodgers, the Carter Family, Willie Nelson, Hank Williams, George Jones, Elvis Presley, Johnny Cash, Loretta Lynn, Merle Haggard, Dolly Parton, Bob Wills, and Waylon Jennings." The contents include compilation albums categorized as "Overviews," and a string of informative chapters based on music albums. Chapter titles inclued: "Early String Bands and Balladeers," "The Depression Years," "Singing Cowboys," "Western Swing," "Bluegrass," and "Honky-Tonk and Hillbilly Boogie". The rest is of interest for post-1950s queries. Morthland frames each album with insightful data about the performers, as well pithy analysis. This kind of musical enlargement upon the correlating chapters in *Popular Music and the Underground* can be especially edifying for the reader. The only problem exists when albums written about are deleted from circulation, which, unfortunately happens with great frequency.

8) Oermann, Robert K., and Douglas B. Green. *The Listener's Guide to Country Music*. New York: Facts on File, Inc., 1983.
We make the leap from very large books of the Top 40 to the smallest (137 pages and tiny—4 1/2" by 9"). This compact history is a mini-book survey of the highlights of the form. "Old-Time Music," "Blue Grass," "Depression Era Radio," "Singing Cowboys," "Western Swing," "Country Music 1994," "Honky-Tonk Music," "Southeastern Revival," "Rockabilly," "The Nashville Sound," "Bakersfield," "Cajun Music," "Country-Rock," "The Songwriters," "The Outlaws," "Pop-Country," and out. Each mini history is followed by profiles of five or six leading artists, and a listing of selected recordings by the prime movers of each section. This book is a great addition for someone who is interested in learning more about country music. It can be carried around without causing any distraction, and can be referred to when time allows. Understand, this isn't offered as a "Top 10" country book just because it's small. I have often referred to it in a pinch because the writers are top notch. I haven't mentioned Robert Oermann up to this point. Like Green, Oermann contributed to a vast number of magazines and is music editor at *The Nashville Tennesseean*. He wrote *The Country Catalog*, and in 1993 co-authored with Mary A. Bufwack, the first comprehensive history of women in country music, *Finding Her Voice: The Saga of Women in Country Music*. New York: Crown Publishers, Ind., 1994. If *The Listener's Guide* can't be found, (I haven't seen it lately in the many bookstores I frequent), then a very good, normal-sized substitute is Bob Millard's *Country Music: 70 Years of America's Favorite Music*. New York: Harper Collins Publishers, Inc., 1993.

9) Rothel, David. *The Singing Cowboys*. South Brunswick, New Jersey: A.S. Barnes, 1978.
Hard to find, this is the ultimate book so far on the singing cowboys of the Hollywood series films. Rothel is a fan-turned-historian, and he met and interviewed the well known stars like Roy Rogers, Gene Autry, and Tex Ritter, as well as the more obscure figures like Monte Hale and Herb Jeffries. Rothel's interviews are well organized, and he is able to unearth facts that a less knowledgeable fan would not be aware of. His book includes a listing of films and dates of those films, as well as songs that were sung. Rothel also has a history on the sidekicks, but I'd never seen either of these books in the bookstore. So that necessitates a substitute book or two, because no self-respecting student, fan or afficionado can get through life without a singing cowboy book. The definitive

history has yet to be written on this subject—we'll simply have to wait for Douglas B. Green to take a sabbatical (I think he's the most knowledgeable—I've read his articles on the singing cowboys and his vision includes the best analysis so far). The first alternate book for the singing cowboys includes said article by Green ("The Singing Cowboy: An American Dream", pages 331-374) in Don Miller's *Hollywood Corral: A Comprehensive B-Western Roundup*, Burbank: Riverwood Press, 1993. Edited by Packy Smith and Ed Hulse this is the magnum opus of cowboy books, and it's about all the cowboys, not just the singing ones. If you are crazy for the total cowboy experience, this one's for you. The downside of this back-in-print tome is its expense, though it's worth every penny for the information, pictures, and cowboy rush. A second alternative is Robert W. Phillips' *Singing Cowboy Stars*. Layton, Utah: Peregrin Smith Books, 1994. This is a compact book with colorful reproductions and entries on 25 Western stars who played singing cowboys. Get yourself $20, gallop down to a bookstore and order this nifty book—be a modern day saddle pal.

10) Tosches, Nick. *Country: The Biggest Music in America*. New York: Dell, 1979.
Cover your ears, and put away those 10 Commandments of the singing cowboys; Nick Tosches just rode into town. Nick Tosches is the gonzo writer supreme. What differentiates him from most of the other so-called "gonzo" writers is that he does scrupulous research. Tosches takes the piety out of country music. He's like a guest who comes seeking out the pretentious types who are invited to your proper cocktail party. You just know he'll give them their due (fine, but why at your party?). Tosches writes with relish, and can't wait to share his new research as he makes connections that we mere mortal souls never even consider. He will show you, for example, that for all of the posturing for "God, Flag and Country," patriotic types who for years offered up an image of moral rectitude to their audiences—like Jimmie Davis (two-time Governor of Louisiana), Tennessee Ernie Ford, Johnny Cash and Roy Acuff—at one time, sang out and out dirty songs. He makes his case, and lists those songs in an indelicate chapter titled "Stained Panties and Coarse Metaphors." Other chapter titles include "Thela in the New World"; "Orpheus, Gypsies, and Redneck Rock'n'Roll"; "Loud Covenants"; and "Yodeling Cowboys and Such."

So, there you have the "Top 40" (that is really not 40, but more like 50) of my bibliography. There were many other titles and writers I would like to have shared with you, dear readers, but the books were of a different scope than the specifics of this bibliography called for. Before I take leave, I must suggest to you three final books that pave the way for the second half of the twentieth century. All three of these books make cogent points in regard to historical lineage between *then* and *now*.

1) Griel Marcus, *Mystery Train; Images of America in Rock'n'Roll Music*. New York: Plume Books, 1990.
2) Peter Guralnick, *Lost Highway: Journeys & Arrivals of American Musicians*. New York: Harper Perennial, 1994.
3) Nick Tosches, *Unsung Heroes of Rock'n'Roll: The Birth of Rock'n'Roll in the Dark and Wild Years Before Elvis*. London: Secker & Warburg, 1991.

MUSICAL PERFORMERS AND CONTRIBUTORS
INDEX: 1

Note: Page numbers listed in italics denote the primary entry for each key contributor (including birthdate and where applicable, date of death). This index represents only the text and picture captions on pages 1-521—it does not include: Charts, Bibliography, or Discography and Videography.

Benedetti, Dean, 339
Beneke, Tex, 209
Benet, Stephen Vincent, 171
Bennett, Danny, 295
Bennett, Richard Rodney, 308, 315
Bennett, Tony, 242, *294-296*, 299, 318, 331, 498
Benson, George, 258, 361, 365, 433
Benson, Ray (See Asleep at the Wheel), 16, *491-492*
Bentley, Gladys, 89
Bentyne, Cheryl, 327
Berg, Billy, 350, 358, 420
Bergen, Edgar, 56
Bergman, Buddy, 293
Bergman, Ingrid, 217, 241
Berigan, Bunny, 117, 205, 208, 279
Berkeley, Busby, *63-65*, 227, 231, 323
Berle, Milton, 205
Berlin, Irving, 1, 9, *26-28*, 35-36, 38, 43, 45-47, 49, 52, 54, 59, 60, 67, 153, 230-233, 282, 287, 293-294, 307, 402
Berman, Pandro, 232
Berman, Sonny, 372
Bernel, Gil, 417
Bernstein, Leonard, 240
Berry, Chu, 417
Berry, Chuck, 43, 138, 414
Bessman, Bernie, 391
Best, Denzil, 335
Bestor, Don, 65
Beverly Hillbillies (group), 168, 196
Bigard, Barney, 110
Biggar, George, 175
Biggs, Howard, 437
Bill Moore's Lucky Seven, 404
Biller, John, 24
Birch Brothers, 463
Birds's Kentucky Crackers, 167
Birmingham Jug Band, 76
Blackwell, Scrapper, 85, 85
Blake, Eubie, 26, *142*, 286, 298
Blakey, Art (& His Jazz Messengers), 344, 365, 383
Blanca, Cuarteto Carta, 474
Blanchard, Terrance, 383
Bland, Bobby, 406
Blank, Les, 99
Blanton, Jimmie, 267-268
Blesh, Rudi, 84
Blind Blake, 75
Blind Boy Fuller, 456
Blind Jo Taggart, 506
Blind John Henry Arnold, 506
Blind Lemon Jefferson, 10-11, *78*, 390, 432-433, 504, 506
Blind Reverend Gary Davis, 15, 100-101
Blind Willie Dunn, 120
Blondell, Joan, 65, 231
Blue Flame Syncopators, 70
Blue Friars, 117
Blue Grass Boys (See Bill Monroe), 447, 462-466, 468
Blue Jays, The, 440

Blue Ridge Playboys, 493-494, 497
Blue Sky Boys (See Bolick Brothers), 443
Blue Stars of Paris, 304
Bluebirds, The, 440
Blyth, Ann, 61
Bob, Black, 393
Bobcats, The, 122-123
Bogan, Henry, 199
Bogart, Humphrey, 113, 241
Boggs, Dock, 158
Boggs, Noel, 489
Bogtrotters, 15
Bolan, Marc, 320
Bolcom, William, *35-37*
Bolden, Buddy, 84, 106-107
Bolger, Ray, 226-227
Bolick Brothers, The, 456, *459-460*
Bolton, Guy, 47
Bolton, Michael, 130
Bond, Johnny, 482
Bono, 290
Booker, James, 412
Booker T. and the MG's, 386
Boone, Debby, 205
Boots and His Buddies, 249
Borden, Bill, 375, 377
Bostic, Earl, 399
Boswell, Connie/Connee, 119, 120, 277, 293
Boswell, Hevetia, 119
Boswell, Martha, 119
Boswell Sisters, 117, *119-120*, 289, 322, 324, 327-328
Bottle Hill, 466
Bow, Clara, 63
Bowes, Major, 218
Bowie, David, 320
Bowlly, Al, 212
Bowman, Charlie, 169
Boyd, Bill (& Cowboy Ramblers), 448, 485, 489-490
Boyd, Jim, 489
Boyer, Charles, 311
Boyz II Men, 441
Bradbury, Bill, 193
Bradbury, Robert, 193
Bradford, Perry, 70
Bradley, Will, 212, 263
Braff, Ruby, 285
Bragg, Billy, 510
Brahms, Johannes, 283, 367
Brand, Oscar, 516
Braun, Jules, 407
Breaux, Amidie and Ophy, 95
Breaux, Cleoma, 95
Breeden Medicine Show, 432
Brenston, Jackie, 519
Brewer, Cecil, 486
Brice, Fanny, 46, *59-60*
Bricktop (Ada Smith), 121, 143, 146, *297-299*, 301-302
Bridgewater, Dee Dee, 332
Brinkley, John R., 186

Britt, Elton, 202
Broadcast Music Inc. (B.M.I.), 387
Brock and Harnick, 44
Brockman, Gail, 342
Brockman, Polk, 159
Brooks, Garth, 2, 35, 467, 491
Brooks, Lawson, 433
Brooks, Shelton, 34
Broonzy, Big Bill, 88, 260, 384, *392-393*, 401-402
Brower, Cecil, 487
Brower, Frank, 22
Brown, Anne, 224
Brown, Charles, 243, 424, *426-429*
Brown, Clifford, 292, 327, 357
Brown, Durwood, 200, 486-487
Brown, James, 296
Brown, Jim, 517
Brown, Jimmy, 213
Brown, Joe E., 48
Brown, Johnnie Mack, 479, 483
Brown, Milton (& His Musical Brownies), 200, 473, *485-48.8*
Brown, Nacio Herb, 63
Brown, Piney, 254
Brown, Ray, 382
Brown, Roy, 16, 216, 243, *403-40.'*, 411
Brown, Ruth, 73, 386
Brown, Tom, 113
Brown, Vernon, 256
Brown, Walter, 251, 345
Brubeck, Dave, 409
Bruner, Cliff, 486-487, 497
Brunis, George, 114
Bryant's Minstrels, 22
Bubbles, John, 224
Buck, George Jr., 84, 130
Buck Mountain String Band, 15
Buckner, Milt, 369, 397-398
Buckwheat Zydeco (Stanley Dural), 99
Buffalo Springfield, 386
Buffalodians, The, 151
Bumgarner, Samantha, 194
Burdon, Eric, 395
Burke, Billie, 46
Burke, Johnny, 1
Burke, Solomon, 386
Burnette, Smiley, 477
Burns, (George) & Allen (Gracie), 56
Burns, Ralph, 315, 370-372
Burr, Henry, 14
Bushkin, Joe, 279, 310
Busse, Henry, 53, 324
Butera, Sam, 271
Butterbeans and Susie, 83
Butterfield, Billy, 123, 208, 279
Butterworth, Charles, 230
Buttram, Pat, 477
Buzzards, The, 440
Byas, Don, 274, 335-336, 338-339, 417
Byrds, The, 466, 468, 517
Byrne, David, 331
Cadillacs, The, 438
Caesar, Irving, 47

Goins Brothers, 466-467

Golden Gate Quartet, 260, 437, 512-513

Goldkette, Jean, 50, 115-116, 128, 138

Goldstein, Sammy, 394

Golson, Benny, 312

Gonzales, Babs, 359-360

Good, Millie and Dolly (See Girls of the Golden West), 175, *194-195*, 444

Goodman, Benny, 11, 12, 16, 38, 112, 117, 126, 141, *205-207*, 218-219, 221-222, 255-257, 260, 263-264, 274, 277, 286, 336, 350, 374, 382, 396-398, 402, 421-422, 461, 485-486, 488, 509

Gordon, Dexter, 240, 277, 313, 336, 343-344, *358*, 397, 399

Gordon, Gray, 212

Gordon, Max, 240, 313, 506, 517

Gottlieb, Bill, 350

Grable, Betty, *235-237*, 332

Graettinger, Bob, 373-374

Graham, Martha, 307

Gramercy Five, 208, 275

Grant, Cary, 226, 388

Grant, Gogi, 61

Granz, Norman, 274, *282-283*, 293, 304, 358, 419

Grappelli, Stephane, 121-122, 461

Grateful Dead, The, 77, 466

Graves, Josh, 464

Gray, Glen, 248

Gray, Jerry, 209

Gray, Otto (& the Oklahoma Cowboys), *198-199*

Gray, Wardell, 344, *358*

Gray, "Whispering" Bobby, 55

Grayson County Railsplitters, 15

Grayson, George, 161, 163-164

Grayson, Kathryn, 48, 238

Greco, Buddy, 206

Green, Benny, 313

Green, Charlie, 73

Green, Freddie, 253, 260

Green, Johnny, 275

Green, Juanita, 72

Green, Lil, *401-402*

Green, Silas, 394

Greene, Bob, 128

Greig, Edward, 133

Grifasi, Joe, 332

Griffin, Merv, 215

Grimes, Tiny, 274, 386

Grisman, David, 466

Groener, Harry, 288

Grofe, Ferde, 139

Grossman, Stefan, 101

Guarnieri, Johnny, 208

Guccione, Bob Jr., 295

Guerrs, Marcelino, 353

Guizar, Tito, 481

Gully Jumpers, 180

Gunboat Billy and the Sparrows, 167

Gunning, Sara Ogan, 503

Guru, 365

Guthrie, Jeff, 508

Guthrie, Woody, 442, 468, *502-510*, 512-515

Guy, Buddy, 396

Guy, Joe, 338

Gypsy Kids, 122

Hackberry Ramblers, 96

Hackett, Bobby, 117, 209, 27- 274, 279, 285, 378

Haggard, Bob, 123

Haggard, Merle, 16, 468, 491

Haig, Al, 335, 349

Haines, Connie, 207

Haley, Bill (& the Comets), 38-39, 255, 386, 404-405, 420, 434, *518-520*

Haley, Jack, 21

Hall, Adelaide, 146, 149, 152, 274

Hall, Tom T., 466

Hamblen, Stuart, 196

Hamilton, Chico, 382

Hamilton, George, 455

Hamilton, Scott, 285

Hamlisch, Marvin, 25

Hammer, M. C., 87

Hammerstein, Oscar II, 47-48, 226, *228-230*, 438

Hammet, Smith, 462

Hammond, John (Henry Jr.), 74, 82-83, 101, 123, 142, 252, *257*, 260-263, 371, 382, 510

Hammond, John Paul, 101

Hampton, Lionel, 15, 205-206, 256-257, 261, 274, 284, 296, 316-317, 350, 369, 385, *396-401*, 412, 417-418, 434

Hancock, Herbie, 312, 315, 358, 364

Hand, Judge Learned, 388

Handy, George, 381

Handy, W. C., 1, *30*, 107, 382

Hanson, Tripp, 328

Haran, Mary Cleere, 308, 318, 332

Harbach, Otto, 49

Harburg, E. Y., 151, 318

Hardin, Lil, 11, 108-109

Harding, Buster, 370

Harlan Leonard and His Kansas City Rockets, 249, 425

Harlan, Byron, 14, 32

Harlem Footwarmers, 148

Harlem Hamfats, 87, 89, 393, 402, 414

Harlettes, The, 321, 323

Harlow, Jean, 235

Harnar, Jeff, 308

Harney, Ben, *24*, 26

Harrell, Kelly, 158

Harrell, Scotty, 482

Harrington, George N., 22, 31

Harris, Barry, 118, 355

Harris, Benny, 335

Harris, Charles K., 22, *31-32*, 36, 190

Harris, Dave, 372

Harris, Emmylou, 466-467

Harris, Gene, 285

Harris, John Henry, 505

Harris, Marion, 59, 60

Harris, Wynonie, 16, 91, 243, 399, *403-407*

Harrison, George, 100

Harry, Deborah, 331

Harry Warren and Al Dubin, 231

Harry Warren and Johnny Mercer, 239

Hart, Clyde, 276

Hart, Lorenz (Larry), 1, 46, *226*, 228

Hart, Moss, 225

Hartman, Johnny, 344

Harum Scarums, 88

Hauptmann, Gerhart, 517

Hauser, Tim, 327

Havoc, June, 225

Hawes, Pete, 512

Hawking, Ron, 113

Hawkins, Coleman, 137-138, 175, *275-276*, 283, 296, 335, 339, 355-356, 359, 417

Hawkins, Erskine, 399

Hawkins Family, 87

Hawkins, Ted, 459

Hawks, The, 440

Hay, George D., 175, *179-181*, 447, 457, 502

Haydn Quartet, 5, 15, 32, 34

Hayes, George "Gabby", 477

Hayes, Issac, 427

Haymes, Dick, *220-222*

Hays, Lee, 502, 506, 512, 516-517

Haymes, Joe, 20

Hayworth, Rita, 232-233, 236

Head, Johnny, 78

Headline Singers, 504, 509

Hegamin, Lucille, 70

Heifetz, Jascha, 220

Helbock, Joe, 208

Held, John Jr., 42

Hellerman, Fred, 516-517

Hemingway, Ernest, 298

Henderson, Fletcher, 11, 73, 116, 133, *137-139*, 205-207, 247, 257, 261, 265, 275-276, 283, 352, 489

Henderson, Horace, 137

Hendricks, Jon, 319, 327, *361-364*, 414

Hendrix, Jimi, 381, 434

Henie, Sonja, *235-236*

Henry, Buck, 36

Hepburn, Audrey, 325

Hepburn, Katharine, 232

Herbert, Victor, 31, 44, 63

Herman, Woody, 64, 284, 315-316, 319, 327, *369-372*, 375, 402, 426

Heyward, DuBose, 224

Hi-Five, 441

Hibbler, Al, 267, 344

Hickman, Art, 44, *51-53*, 139

Hildegarde, 297, 303

Hill, Billy, 476

Hill, Jesse, 412

Hill, Joe, 515

Hill, Roy G., 25

Hill, Teddy, 338, 350

606

Williams, Buster, 317
Williams, Clarence, 382
Williams, Claude, 254
Williams, Cootie, 149, 256, 345, 355
Williams, D. H., 199
Williams, Dootsie, 404
Williams, Eddie, 427
Williams, Frances, 241
Williams, Hank, Jr., 448, 454-455
Williams, Hank, Sr., 16, 160, 448, *452-454*, 492, 498, 504, 519
Williams, J. Mayo, 414
Williams, Joe, 289, 294, 296, 311, 364
Williams, Mary Lou, 249, 338
Williams, Mayo, 87
Williams, Paul, 417-418
Williams, Rudy, 357
Williams, Tennessee, 513
Williams, Tex, 490
Williamson, John Lee "Sonny Boy", 392, 395-396
Williamson, Sonny Boy, 387
Willie, Boxcar, 447
Willis, Bruce, 243
Wills, Bob (See Texas Playboys), 10, 15-16, 160, 200, 393, 433, 461, 473, *485-489*, 491, 493-494, 499, 518-519
Wilmer Watts and the Lonely Eagles, 167
Wilson, Al "Blind Owl", 79
Wilson, August, 71
Wilson, Dooley, 241
Wilson, Edith, 144
Wilson, Julie, 2, 299, *306-309*, 316, 325
Wilson, Gerald, 266
Wilson, Grace, 175, 194
Wilson, Nancy, 401
Wilson, Shadow, 343
Wilson, Teddy, 205-206, 254, 257, 277, 355-356, 403
Winan Family, 87
Winchell, Walter, 227
Winniger, Charles, 48
Winslow, Vernon Dr. Daddy-O, 407-408, 411
Wise, Chubby, 460-461, 463
Wiseman, Mac, 464, 467-468
Wiseman, Scotty, 177
Witherspoon, Jimmy, 424
Wodehouse, P. G., 47
Wolfe, George C., 128
Wolverine Orchestra, 114-115
Wood, Harry, 36
Wood, Randy, 427
Wooding, Sam, 121, 133
Woollcott, Alexander, 230
Woolley, Monty, 226, 304
World's Greatest Jazz Band, The, 123, 127, 285
Wright, Edythe, 207
Wright, Herbert, 29
Wright, Jimmy, 417
Wynette, Tammy, 427
Wynn, Big Jim, 420, 432

Wynn, Ed, 46
Wynn, Larry, 415, 419
Yancy, Jimmy "Papa", *83-84*, 262
Yankee Six, The, 151
Yates, Herbert, 476, 478
Yellen, Jack, 34
Yerba Buena Jazz Band, 125
Yes, 386
Yoakam, Dwight, 466-467
Youmans, Vincent, 47
Young, Lee, 426
Young, Lester, 11, 114-115, 138, 251-252, 260, *276-277*, 279, 284, 338-339, 344, 358-359, 361-362, 365, 368, 371-372, 376-377, 417
Young Rascals, 130
Young, Trummy, 110, 227, 266
Zannuck, Darryl F., 64, 234, 236, 507
Zappa, Frank, 284
Zawinul, Josef, 364-365
Ziegfeld, Florenz, 45-46, 59-60, 142
Ziemba, Karen, 288
Zodico Ramblers, 99
Zurke, Bob, 123

MUSIC TITLES
INDEX: 2

These listings reflect songs and albums, unless otherwise noted. Index Key: radio and television shows, quotation marks; Broadway shows, Hollywood films and videos, italics. Like the Musical Performers and Contributors Index, this index represents only the text and picture captions on pages 1-521—it does not include: Charts, Bibliography, or Discography and Videography.

614

617

621